An Introduction to Literature

AN INTRODUCTION
TO *LITERATURE*

EDITED BY

Ralph H. Singleton, OBERLIN COLLEGE

&

Stanton Millet, UNIVERSITY OF ILLINOIS

THE WORLD PUBLISHING COMPANY

Cleveland and New York

ACKNOWLEDGMENTS

The editors wish to acknowledge the assistance of Mary Catherine Burpee, who
prepared the Biographies in this volume.

Poetry

Page 198. "Lucifer in Starlight," by George Meredith. Published by Charles Scribner's
Sons.

Page 199. "After Great Pain a Formal Feeling Comes," by Emily Dickinson. Copyright 1929, © 1957 by Mary L. Hampson. From *The Complete Poems of Emily
Dickinson*, by Emily Dickinson, by permission of Little, Brown and Co.

Page 208. "You Bid Me Try," by Henry Austin Dobson. From *Poetical Works of
Austin Dobson*, by permission of the Executors of the Estate of Henry Austin Dobson
and Oxford University Press, John Brown, Publisher.

Pages 209, 211. "An Ancient to Ancients" and "In Tenebris," by Thomas Hardy.
Reprinted with permission of The Macmillan Company from *The Collected Poems
of Thomas Hardy*, by Thomas Hardy. Also by permission of the Hardy Estate, Macmillan & Co., Ltd., London, and The Macmillan Company of Canada Limited.

Pages 212, 213, 214. "God's Grandeur," "The Windhover," "Felix Randal," "Spring
and Fall: To a Young Child," "Carrion Comfort," by Gerard Manley Hopkins. From
Poems of Gerard Manley Hopkins, Third Edition, edited by W. H. Gardner. Copyright 1948 by Oxford University Press, Inc. Reprinted by permission.

Pages 215, 216. "When First We Met," "London Snow," "Low Barometer," by
Robert Bridges. By permission of the Clarendon Press, Oxford.

Page 217. "Ballade of Dead Actors," by William Ernest Henley. Published by Charles
Scribner's Sons.

Page 218. "Bright Is the Ring of Words," by Robert Louis Stevenson. Published by
Charles Scribner's Sons.

Pages 219, 221. "Terence, This Is Stupid Stuff," "With Rue My Heart Is Laden," "On Moonlit Heath and Lonesome Bank," by A. E. Housman. From "A Shropshire Lad," Authorised Edition, from *The Collected Poems of A. E. Housman.* Copyright 1939, 1940, © 1959 by Holt, Rinehart and Winston, Inc. Reprinted by permission of Holt, Rinehart and Winston, Inc. Permission is also granted by The Society of Authors as the Literary Representatives of the Estate of the late A. E. Housman, and Messrs. Jonathan Cape, Ltd., publishers of *A. E. Housman's Collected Poems.*

Page 222. "Sestina of the Tramp-Royal," by Rudyard Kipling. From *Rudyard Kipling's Verse,* Definitive Edition. Reprinted by permission of Mrs. George Bambridge and Doubleday & Company, Inc. Also from *The Seven Seas.* Reprinted by permission of The Macmillan Company of Canada.

Page 223. "The Second Coming," by William Butler Yeats. Reprinted with permission of the publisher from *The Collected Poems of W. B. Yeats.* Copyright 1924 by The Macmillan Company, renewed 1953 by Georgie Yeats. Also by permission of Mrs. W. B. Yeats and The Macmillan Company of Canada.

Pages 224, 227. "Sailing to Byzantium" and "Among School Children," by William Butler Yeats. Reprinted by permission of the publisher from *The Collected Poems of W. B. Yeats,* by William Butler Yeats. Copyright 1928 by The Macmillan Company, renewed 1956 by Georgie Yeats. Also by permission of Mrs. W. B. Yeats and The Macmillan Company of Canada.

Page 225. "Lapis Lazuli," by William Butler Yeats. Reprinted with permission of The Macmillan Company from *The Collected Poems of W. B. Yeats.* Copyright 1940 by Georgie Yeats. Also by permission of Mrs. W. B. Yeats and The Macmillan Company of Canada.

Page 227. "Crazy Jane Talks with the Bishop," by William Butler Yeats. Reprinted with permission of the publisher from *The Collected Poems of W. B. Yeats,* by William Butler Yeats. Copyright 1933 by The Macmillan Company, renewed 1961 by Bertha Georgie Yeats. Also by permission of Mrs. W. B. Yeats and The Macmillan Company of Canada.

Page 230. "Mr. Flood's Party," by Edwin Arlington Robinson. Reprinted with permission of The Macmillan Company from *Collected Poems of Edwin Arlington Robinson,* by Edwin Arlington Robinson. Copyright 1921 by Edwin Arlington Robinson, renewed 1949 by Ruth Nivison.

Page 232. "Eros Turannos," by Edwin Arlington Robinson. Reprinted with permission of The Macmillan Company from *Collected Poems of Edwin Arlington Robinson,* by Edwin Arlington Robinson. Copyright 1916 by Edwin Arlington Robinson, renewed 1944 by Ruth Nivison.

Page 233. "The Listeners," by Walter de la Mare. Permission has been granted by The Literary Trustees of Walter de la Mare and The Society of Authors as their representative.

Pages 234, 235, 236, 237. "Stopping by Woods on a Snowy Evening," "Desert Places," "Design," "The Tuft of Flowers," "The Road Not Taken," by Robert Frost. From *Complete Poems of Robert Frost.* Copyright 1916, 1921, 1923, 1934 by Holt, Rinehart and Winston, Inc. Copyright 1936 by Robert Frost. Copyright 1944, 1951, © 1962 by Robert Frost. Copyright © 1964 by Lesley Frost Ballantine. Reprinted by permission of Holt, Rinehart and Winston, Inc.

Page 238. "Peter Quince at the Clavier," by Wallace Stevens. Copyright 1923 and renewed 1951 by Wallace Stevens. Reprinted from *The Collected Poems of Wallace Stevens,* by permission of Alfred A. Knopf, Inc.

Page 240. "Tragic Detail," by William Carlos Williams. From *The Collected Later Poems of William Carlos Williams.* Copyright 1944, 1963 by William Carlos Williams. Reprinted by permission of the publisher, New Directions Publishing Corporation.

Page 241. "Piano" and "Snake," by D. H. Lawrence. "Piano" from *Collected Poems of D. H. Lawrence*, edited by Vivian De Sola Pinto and F. Warren Roberts. Copyright 1920 by B. W. Huebsch, Inc., 1947 by Frieda Lawrence. Reprinted by permission of The Viking Press, Inc. "Snake" from *The Collected Poems of D. H. Lawrence*, edited by Vivian De Sola Pinto and F. Warren Roberts. Copyright 1923, 1950 by Frieda Lawrence. Reprinted by permission of The Viking Press, Inc.

Page 243. "Portrait d'une Femme," by Ezra Pound. From *Personae: The Collected Poems of Ezra Pound*. Copyright 1926, 1954 by Ezra Pound. Reprinted by permission of the publisher, New Directions Publishing Corporation.

Page 244. "They," by Siegfried Sassoon. Published by Faber and Faber, Ltd., Publishers. Reprinted by permission of the author.

Pages 245, 246. "Poetry" and "To a Snail," by Marianne Moore. Reprinted with permission of The Macmillan Company from *Collected Poems* by Marianne Moore. Copyright 1935 by Marianne Moore.

Pages 246, 247. "Troy" and "The Gate," by Edwin Muir. From *Collected Poems*, by Edwin Muir. Copyright © 1960 by Willa Muir. Reprinted by permission of Oxford University Press, Inc. Published also by Faber and Faber, Ltd., Publishers.

Page 248. "Hurt Hawks," by Robinson Jeffers. Copyright 1928 and renewed 1956 by Robinson Jeffers. Reprinted from *The Selected Poetry of Robinson Jeffers*, by permission of Random House, Inc.

Page 249. "The Love Song of J. Alfred Prufrock," by T. S. Eliot. From *Collected Poems, 1909–1962*, by T. S. Eliot, copyright 1936 by Harcourt, Brace & World, Inc.; copyright © 1963, 1964 by T. S. Eliot. Reprinted by permission of the publishers. Published in Great Britain and Canada by Faber and Faber, Ltd., Publishers.

Page 253. "Janet Waking," by John Crowe Ransom. Copyright 1927 by Alfred A. Knopf, Inc., and renewed 1955 by John Crowe Ransom. Reprinted from *Selected Poems* by John Crowe Ransom, by permission of the publisher.

Page 254. "Watch Long Enough, And You Will See," by Conrad Aiken. From *Collected Poems*, by Conrad Aiken. Copyright 1953 by Conrad Aiken. Reprinted by permission of Oxford University Press, Inc.

Pages 254, 255. "Ars Poetica" and "The End of the World," by Archibald MacLeish. From *Collected Poems, 1917–1952*, by Archibald MacLeish. Copyright 1952 by Archibald MacLeish.

Page 256. "Speaking of Poetry," by John Peale Bishop. "Speaking of Poetry" from *Now with His Love* (Copyright 1933 Charles Scribner's Sons; renewal copyright © 1961 Margaret G. H. Bronson) by John Peale Bishop is reprinted with the permission of Charles Scribner's Sons.

Page 257. "Dulce et Decorum Est," by Wilfred Owen. From *The Collected Poems of Wilfred Owen*. By permission of Mr. Harold Owen and Chatto and Windus, Ltd., Publishers. And from *The Poems of Wilfred Owen*. All rights reserved. Reprinted by permission of the publisher, New Directions Publishing Corporation.

Page 258. "in Just-spring," by E. E. Cummings. Copyright 1923, 1951 by E. E. Cummings. Reprinted from his volume *Poems, 1923–1951*, by permission of Harcourt, Brace & World, Inc.

Page 259. "The Cool Web," by Robert Graves. From *The Collected Poems, 1956–1965*, by Robert Graves, published by Cassell and Co., Ltd., and Doubleday & Co., Inc. By permission of International Authors N.V.

Page 259. "No Credit," by Kenneth Fearing. From *New and Selected Poems*, by Kenneth Fearing, published by Indiana University Press.

Page 260. "Let Us Now Praise Famous Men," by C. Day Lewis. © Copyright 1954 by C. Day Lewis. Reprinted by permission of Harold Matson Company, Inc.

Page 261. "The Groundhog," by Richard Eberhart. From *Collected Poems, 1930–1960*, by Richard Eberhart. Reprinted by permission of Oxford University Press, Inc.

And from *Collected Poems, 1961*. Reprinted by permission of Chatto and Windus, Ltd., Publishers, and Richard Eberhart.

Page 263. "Nature Morte," by Louis MacNeice. From *Eighty-Five Poems*, by Louis MacNeice. © Louis MacNeice 1959. Reprinted by permission of Oxford University Press, Inc. Published as *Collected Poems* by Faber and Faber, Ltd., Publishers.

Page 263. "The Quarry" ("O What Is That Sound Which So Thrills"), by W. H. Auden. Copyright 1937 by Wystan Hugh Auden. Reprinted from *Selected Poetry of W. H. Auden*, by permission of Random House, Inc. Also published as *Collected Shorter Poems*, by Faber and Faber, Ltd., Publishers.

Page 264. "Musée des Beaux Arts," by W. H. Auden. Copyright 1940 by W. H. Auden. Reprinted from *The Collected Poetry of W. H. Auden*, by permission of Random House, Inc. Also published as *Collected Shorter Poems*, by Faber and Faber, Ltd., Publishers.

Page 265. "The Shield of Achilles," by W. H. Auden. Copyright 1952 by W. H. Auden. Reprinted from *The Selected Poetry of W. H. Auden*, by permission of Random House, Inc.

Page 267. "Elegy for Jane," by Theodore Roethke. Copyright 1950 by Theodore Roethke, from *Words for the Wind*, by Theodore Roethke. Reprinted by permission of Doubleday & Company, Inc.

Page 268. "My Parents Kept Me from Children Who Were Rough" and "The Express," by Stephen Spender. Copyright 1934 and renewed 1961 by Stephen Spender. Reprinted from *Collected poems, 1928–1953*, by Stephen Spender, by permission of Random House, Inc. Also published by Faber and Faber, Ltd., Publishers.

Page 269. "The Death of the Ball Turret Gunner" and "Losses," by Randall Jarrell. Reprinted from *Little Friend, Little Friend*, by Randall Jarrell, with the permission of Mrs. Randall Jarrell.

Pages 270, 271. "In My Craft or Sullen Art" and "Fern Hill," by Dylan Thomas. From *The Collected Poems of Dylan Thomas*. © 1957 by New Directions. Reprinted by permission of the publishers, New Directions Publishing Corporation. And by permission of J. M. Dent & Sons, Ltd., Publishers, and the Literary Executors of the Dylan Thomas Estate.

Page 272. "False Security," by John Betjeman. Reprinted from *Collected Poems*, published by Houghton-Mifflin Company and by John Murray (Publishers), Ltd.

Pages 273, 274. "Children of Light" and "Mr. Edwards and the Spider," by Robert Lowell. From *Lord Weary's Castle*, copyright 1944, 1946 by Robert Lowell. Reprinted by permission of Harcourt, Brace & World, Inc.

Page 275. "Death and the Maiden," by Howard Nemerov. From *New and Selected Poems*, by Howard Nemerov, copyright 1960 The University of Chicago. By permission of the author.

Page 277. "The Death of a Toad," by Richard Wilbur. From *Ceremony and Other Poems*, copyright 1948, 1949, 1950 by Richard Wilbur. Reprinted by permission of Harcourt, Brace & World, Inc.

Page 277. "Mind," by Richard Wilbur. From *Things of This World*, © 1956 by Richard Wilbur. Reprinted by permission of Harcourt, Brace & World, Inc.

Short Stories

Page 345. "La Mère Sauvage," from *The Odd Number*, by Guy de Maupassant, translated by Jonathan Sturges. Reprinted with the permission of Harper & Row, Publishers, Incorporated.

Page 350. "The Lagoon," by Joseph Conrad. Reprinted with the permission of J. M. Dent & Sons, Ltd., Publishers.

Page 360. "The Lady with the Dog," by Anton Chekhov. Reprinted with permission of The Macmillan Co. from *The Lady with the Dog and Other Stories*, by Anton Chekhov, translated by Constance Garnett. Copyright 1917 by The Macmillan Co., copyright renewed 1945 by Constance Garnett. Reprinted also with permission of Chatto & Windus, Ltd.

Page 373. "I'm a Fool," by Sherwood Anderson. Copyright © 1924 by Eleanor Anderson. Reprinted by permission of Harold Ober Associates, Incorporated.

Page 381. "Paul's Case," by Willa Cather. Copyright 1905, 1920, 1933 by Willa Cather. Reprinted from *Youth and the Bright Medusa*, by Willa Cather, by permission of Alfred A. Knopf, Inc.

Page 396. "The Boarding House," by James Joyce, from *The Dubliners*, by James Joyce. Originally published by B. W. Huebsch in 1916. Reprinted by permission of The Viking Press, Inc.

Page 401. "The Rocking-Horse Winner," by D. H. Lawrence, from *The Complete Short Stories of D. H. Lawrence*, Volume III, Compass Edition. Copyright 1933 by the Estate of D. H. Lawrence; © 1962 by Angelo Ravagli and Montague C. Weekly, Executors of the Estate of Frieda Lawrence Ravagli. Reprinted by permission of The Viking Press, Inc.

Page 413. "How Beautiful with Shoes," by Wilbur Daniel Steele. Copyright 1932 and 1959 by Wilbur Daniel Steele. Reprinted by permission of The Harold Matson Co., Inc.

Page 429. "The Doll's House," by Katherine Mansfield. Copyright 1923 by Alfred A. Knopf, Inc., and renewed 1951 by J. Middleton Murray. Reprinted from *The Short Stories of Katherine Mansfield*, by permission of the publisher. Also by permission of the Society of Authors as the literary representative of the Estate of the late Katherine Mansfield.

Page 434. "The Circus," by Katherine Anne Porter. Copyright 1935, 1963 by Katherine Anne Porter. Reprinted from her volume *The Leaning Tower and Other Stories*, by permission of Harcourt, Brace & World, Inc.

Page 438. "The Ice Palace," by F. Scott Fitzgerald. "The Ice Palace" (Copyright 1920 The Curtis Publishing Company; renewal copyright 1948 Zelda Fitzgerald) is reprinted with the permission of Charles Scribner's Sons from *Flappers and Philosophers*, by F. Scott Fitzgerald.

Page 457. "A Rose for Emily," by William Faulkner. Copyright 1930 and renewed 1957 by William Faulkner. Reprinted from *Collected Short Stories of William Faulkner*, by permission of Random House, Inc.

Page 465. "The Killers," by Ernest Hemingway. "The Killers" (Copyright 1927 Ernest Hemingway; renewal copyright 1945) is reprinted with the permission of Charles Scribner's Sons from *Men Without Women*, by Ernest Hemingway.

Page 472. "The Great Mountains," by John Steinbeck, from *The Long Valley*, by John Steinbeck. Copyright © 1933, 1961 by John Steinbeck. Reprinted by permission of The Viking Press, Inc.

Page 482. "The Guest," by Albert Camus. © Copyright 1957, 1958 by Alfred A. Knopf, Inc. Reprinted from *Exile and the Kingdom*, by Albert Camus, translated by Justin O'Brien, by permission.

Page 492. "Zeal," by J. F. Powers. "Zeal," copyright © by J. F. Powers from the book, *The Presence of Grace*, by J. F. Powers. Reprinted by permission of Doubleday & Company, Inc.

Page 503. "A Tree of Night," by Truman Capote. Copyright 1945 by Truman Capote. Reprinted from *A Tree of Night and Other Stories*, by Truman Capote, by permission of Random House, Inc. Originally appeared in *Harper's Bazaar*.

Page 512. "A Late Encounter with the Enemy," by Flannery O'Connor. Copyright

1953 by Flannery O'Connor. Reprinted from her volume *A Good Man Is Hard to Find*, by permission of Harcourt, Brace & World, Inc.

Page 519. "Pigeon Feathers," by John Updike. © Copyright 1961, 1962 by John Updike. Reprinted from *Pigeon Feathers and Other Stories*, by John Updike, by permission of Alfred A. Knopf, Inc. Originally appeared in *The New Yorker*.

Essays

Page 545. "On Tragedy," by Aristotle, by permission of the Clarendon Press, Oxford.

Page 631. "The Ultimate Power in Shakespeare's Tragic World," by A. C. Bradley, from *Shakespearean Tragedy*. Reprinted by permission of Macmillan & Company, Ltd., and St. Martin's Press, Inc.

Page 640. "Preface to *The Nigger of the Narcissus*," by Joseph Conrad. Reprinted with the permission of J. M. Dent & Sons, Ltd., Publishers.

Page 643. "The Idea of Tragedy," by Edith Hamilton. Reprinted from *The Greek Way*, by Edith Hamilton. By permission of W. W. Norton & Company, Inc. Copyright 1930, 1943 by W. W. Norton & Company, Inc. Renewed 1958 by Edith Hamilton.

Page 649. "The Poetry of Amy Lowell," by Robert Frost. Reprinted by permission of *The Christian Science Monitor*.

Page 650. "Flat and Round Characters," by E. M. Forster, from *Aspects of the Novel*, by E. M. Forster, copyright 1927 by Harcourt, Brace & World, Inc.; copyright 1955 by E. M. Forster. Reprinted by permission of the publishers, and by Edward Arnold (Publishers), Ltd.

Page 655. "The Metaphysical Poets," by T. S. Eliot, from *Selected Essays of T. S. Eliot*, New Edition, copyright 1932, 1936, 1950 by Harcourt, Brace & World, Inc.; copyright 1960, 1964 by T. S. Eliot. Reprinted by permission of the publishers, and by Faber and Faber, Ltd., Publishers.

Page 663. "The Case for Comedy," by James Thurber. Copyright © 1960 James Thurber. From *Lanterns and Lances*, published by Harper & Row.

Page 667. "How to Criticize a Poem," by Theodore Spencer. Reprinted by permission of *The New Republic*.

Page 670. "The Four Forms of Fiction," by Northrop Frye. Reprinted from *Anatomy of Criticism*, by Northrop Frye, by permission of Princeton University Press. Copyright © 1957, by Princeton University Press.

Page 680. "Sophocles' *Oedipus*," by Bernard Knox. Reprinted from *Tragic Themes in Western Literature*, by Bernard Knox, published by Yale University Press, by permission of the author.

Page 693. "The Structure of *Measure for Measure*," by Stanton Millet. Reprinted from *Boston University Studies in English* II (1956), 207–225, by permission of the author.

Drama

Page 731. *Oedipus Rex*, by Sophocles. *The Oedipus Rex of Sophocles*: An English Version by Dudley Fitts and Robert Fitzgerald, copyright 1949 by Harcourt, Brace & World, Inc., and reprinted with their permission.

Page 777. *Antigone*, by Sophocles. *The Antigone of Sophocles*: An English Version by Dudley Fitts and Robert Fitzgerald, copyright 1939 by Harcourt, Brace & World, Inc., and reprinted with their permission.

Page 811. *Othello*, by William Shakespeare. Reprinted by permission of Penguin Books, Inc.

Page 919.   *Measure for Measure,* by William Shakespeare. Reprinted by permission of
    Penguin Books, Inc.
Page 1003.   *Hedda Gabler,* by Henrik Ibsen. Translated by Una Ellis-Fermor, published
    by Penguin Books, Ltd.
Page 1089.   *Pygmalion,* by George Bernard Shaw. Used by permission of The Public
    Trustee, The Society of Authors, and Dodd, Mead & Company, Inc. Copyright 1913,
    1914, 1916, 1930, 1941, 1944 George Bernard Shaw. Copyright 1957 The Public
    Trustee as Executor of the Estate of George Bernard Shaw.

Contents

POETRY

Contents

Contents

SHORT STORIES

Contents

CRITICAL ESSAYS

DRAMA

Thematic Table of Contents

MAN—SOME DESCRIPTIONS AND DEFINITIONS

❦ Poetry

LOVE—AND SOME OTHER EMOTIONS

❧ *Poetry*

❧ *Short Stories*

GROWTH, CHANGE—AND DEATH

❧ *Poetry*

❦ Short Stories

RELIGION, MORALITY—AND THE PROBLEM OF EVIL

❧ Short Stories

❧ Drama

LANGUAGE AND ART

❧ Poetry

❧ Essays

STUDIES IN FICTION AND DRAMA

❧ Essays

THE STUDY OF
Poetry

THE STUDENT enrolled in his first college course in literature is often prepared to find the study of poetry difficult and unpleasant. No amount of exhortation from an instructor or from the editors of an anthology can change that or instantly transform such a reader into a literary critic who reads with pleasure and understanding. Something more than a simple shift in attitude is required, for, in fact, poetry *is* difficult. Nor is the difficulty caused simply by the unfamiliarity of the vocabulary used in criticism. Any unfamiliar subject, whether chemistry, psychology, or literature, requires new techniques and new terms in order to isolate and discuss the unique problems that the subject presents. The terms are easily provided and assimilated; it is simply a matter of memorization. The difficulty that poetry presents, however, is more than an encounter with a new vocabulary. It is a difficulty not easily overcome, but, paradoxically, it is the true basis for much of the pleasure of reading.

A poem is not a puzzle or a problem to be solved for a single, correct answer. The curious fact about a good poem is that the process by which the meaning is conveyed is inseparable from the meaning itself: *what* is said cannot be severed from the *way* it is said. Furthermore, even if the process and the meaning could be separated, most readers would insist that the process is more vital to their enjoyment than the meaning. Even in the nursery rhymes we enjoyed as children, we did not really care to know much about the "facts" of the rhymes—the precise moment between twelve and one when the mouse ran up the clock or the texture and taste of pease porridge. What we were interested in was the method of the rhyme—the sounds of the words themselves and the rhythms of their arrangement. For the adult, of course, a great deal more than sound and rhythm is involved. We feel now that we must know precisely what pease porridge or its equivalent really is and how it is related to other elements of meaning in the poem. But the approach to understanding remains essentially the same. In order to comprehend the meaning, we must first comprehend and even participate in the poet's method, his use of particular words, figures of speech, rhymes, and rhythms. It is not enough to understand the general theory of poetry or to take notes on the meanings the poem has conveyed to someone else. We must ourselves come to grips with its particular mode of expression.

This need to deal with a slightly different method in every new poem probably explains why some readers find poetry endlessly interesting, while others find it endlessly frustrating. Those who look for easy answers are not pleased, either, when they discover that it is almost impossible to exhaust the possibilities of meaning in a single good poem, no matter how thorough the analysis. Other interpretations and other shades of meaning are continually suggesting themselves, even when there is general agreement about the superficial, summary meaning of the poem. This is not to say that every interpretation is correct or that criticism is a matter of personal opinion. What it suggests is that poetry is an art, not a science. The poetic "problems" of which we speak are not mathematical; there is no single answer. Instead, they involve judgments, opinions, and statements of feeling. Naturally, then, each statement of this kind—the literal as well as the figurative—suggests a wide range of meanings or shades of meaning. And the complex relationships set up when there are many such statements and images in a single poem still further expand the possibilities of meaning.

It is not lack of precision that is involved here. A different kind of precision distinguishes an artistic statement from a scientific one. The artist strives toward an expanded, total meaning, directs his appeal to the emotions, and, since his is essentially a personal judgment rather than a statement of fact, his meaning cannot factually be "proved." The scientist's statement, on the other hand, works toward strict limitation of the meaning rather than expansion, makes its appeal to the reason rather than to the emotions, and can usually be tested by reference to facts. Each type of communication possesses its own kind of difficulty as well as its own potential for pleasure and understanding. Those who confuse the two, searching for emotion in science or scientific fact in poetry, only confuse themselves.

Because of the special problems of finding the poem's precise, total meaning and the exact relationships among the various elements of the poem, poetry is "difficult." But it does not follow that it is therefore distasteful. Every student discovers for himself that this is a mistaken view at the moment he begins to discover meaning in a particular poem. But since few people are willing to commit themselves to the careful analysis necessary to understand a poem—and hence to enjoy it—if they believe the task will be hopeless or unpleasant, it might be well to clear our minds of a few crippling misconceptions.

Sentimentality

Whether or not it is identified by name, sentimentality is the most common charge against poetry—particularly among men. Sentimentality is any attempt to make us react with strong emotions to a situation that does not warrant our interest. Readers recognize it, however, not by intellectual identification of the strategy, but by their own feelings of embarrassment and disgust. Students who have been exposed to what one commentator has called the "ooh-and-ah" school for appreciating poetry will perhaps be surprised to find that their distaste is perfectly sound criticism. Sentimentality is, indeed, indefensible. It corrupts literature; it corrupts language; and, worst of all, it corrupts the capacity for true feeling, which is one of the marks of a civilized human being.

By definition, sentimentality does not exist in good poetry: if a poem is sentimental—in the literary sense of the word—it is not a good poem. But it does exist, luxuriantly, in the second-rate popular verse that appears in newspapers, slick magazines for women, inspirational publications, and young schoolgirls' scrapbooks. And it may spring up almost anywhere in times of war or other stress when people experience strong feelings of fear, pity, hope, or enthusiasm. At such times, the critical sense is dulled on a national level. It becomes somehow unpatriotic or mean-spirited to examine an author's work too closely if he is expressing the feelings that everyone currently feels—or "ought" to feel.

The task of the critical reader is not to convince himself that he ought to accept these shallow emotional displays. His task is to discriminate between the shallow and the deeply felt, the false and the true. Let us begin, then, with "The Boy Soldier," a minor Civil War poem written by an anonymous "Lady of Savannah." The first stanza is as follows:

> He is acting o'er the battle,
> With his cap and feather gay,
> Singing out his soldier-prattle
> In a mockish, manly way—
> With the boldest, bravest footstep,
> Treading firmly up and down,
> And his banner waving softly
> O'er his boyish locks of brown.

This description of a two-year-old child playing soldier continues for another stanza in much the same vein. Then, in the next, the narrator states the central conflict of the poem:

> There's a struggle in my bosom,
> For I love my darling boy—
> He's the gladness of my spirit,
> He's the sunlight of my joy!
> Yet I think upon my country,
> And my spirit groweth bold—
> Oh! I wish my blue-eyed soldier
> Were but twenty summers old!

The conflict is easily resolved, however. In the two remaining stanzas, largely a repetition of what has already been said, the narrator states that if the boy were indeed twenty years old, she "would give him to his country/For his country's wrong and right."

A mother's conflict between her natural desire to protect her child and her patriotic belief in her country's cause is potentially a powerful theme. If this poem fails to move us, the fault is not in the theme but in the treatment of it. The author *tells* us there is a struggle in her bosom, but she does not *show* us that there is one. Thus, while we may believe her story, we do not care about it. There has been no opportunity to participate in the struggle she says rages within her. That is the fatal weakness of the poem. Nothing the narrator says or thinks, and certainly nothing she does, shows the kind of intensity that ought to be associated with such a struggle in a mother's mind. Even the description is vague and abstract rather than precise and concrete. Friendly readers may do some of the poet's work for her and build up an imaginative picture of the child, but very little can be done for "the gladness of my spirit" or "the sunlight of my joy" or "my spirit groweth bold." What does it *mean,* we ask ourselves, when a spirit grows bold? How does one feel when this happens to him? No answers are supplied. Instead, we are presented with a colorless, stereotyped situation—a vague mother, a vague little boy, a vague war somewhere, and a vague problem of deciding between a son and a patriotic ideal. The sentimentality of the poem comes from the poet's seeming insistence that we be moved and impressed by these shadowy suggestions, and the reader's embarrassment follows close on the heels of this implicit demand— embarrassment partly for the author who has revealed such shallow emotions, partly for ourselves because of the awkward emotional situation into which we have been betrayed. No one likes to ridicule home, country, and a mother's love for her child—even though ridicule might be thoroughly justified, as in this instance.

Now compare Randall Jarrell's "The Death of the Ball Turret Gunner," a very short but justly popular poem about the death of an airman in the Second World War:

> From my mother's sleep I fell into the State
> And I hunched in its belly till my wet fur froze.

> Six miles from earth, loosed from its dream of life,
> I woke to black flak and the nightmare fighters.
> When I died they washed me out of the turret with a hose.

Here, Jarrell accomplishes everything that "The Boy Soldier" tries and fails to say in eight times as many lines. Of course, "The Death of the Ball Turret Gunner" requires closer attention. Time, for example, has been compressed. The gunner is said to have moved directly from his mother's womb to the belly of the aircraft symbolizing "the State." The fur of his flying suit suggests an ironic description of an insignificant, newborn animal. Further, he is caught in a paradoxical situation in which the realities of life on earth have become unreal, dreamlike, and the nightmare battle at thirty thousand feet becomes the only reality he knows. The last line, effectively breaking down into a prose rhythm, is not only a literal—if horrible—description of his body after death, it is also a comment on the significance of the individual man in modern warfare. But the careful study this poem requires is fully justified, whereas the Civil War poem is scarcely worth reading except as a curiosity.

What differentiates Jarrell's poem from the others? Partly, it is the range and intensity of his theme. Like the Lady of Savannah, Jarrell is concerned with the demands of war and the pathos of a young man's death. But he also goes further than that. Jarrell suggests ideas about man's relationship to his society, about the realities of warfare and the meaning of death in war that the Savannah Lady never approaches, even remotely. Second, Jarrell's description is powerfully compressed, whereas the other is vague and diffused. We see the gunner "hunched" in his plexiglass turret, the "nightmare fighters," and the body "washed out of the turret with a hose." Compared to these images, the blurred figures of the little boy and his patriotic mother are no more than shadows in a darkened room. Finally, Jarrell explores his theme thoroughly, without flinching from its bitter implications. In contrast, the imaginary mother's wish that her boy could fight is so facile that the reader doubts whether she has even thought about what she is saying.

But above all, the Civil War poem lacks control, whereas Jarrell's poem is rigorously trimmed of all extraneous elements. It is not that Jarrell's view is brutal or unfeeling; on the contrary, most readers will agree that the gunner's death is infinitely more pathetic—and thought-provoking—than the pseudo-dilemma of "The Boy Soldier." But Jarrell has been content to let a few powerful, *specific*, images generate whatever emotion they are capable of generating. He understates his theme; he refrains from pushing us farther than we are willing to go of our own accord. The Lady of Savannah, on the other hand, fails to provide the means of sharing her emotion, yet insists that we ought to share it. No reputable poet and no competent critic or teacher ever makes such a demand. Those who argue that they do not like poetry because it is sentimental are speaking of second-rate verse, not the poetry worth an intelligent reader's attention.

Morality

The average reader is just as firmly opposed to having his morals improved as he is to having his emotions tampered with. Indeed, the moral-uplift theory of poetry, suggesting as it does that verse will somehow make us better, has done almost as much damage to the attitudes of generations of readers as the notion that poetry is sentimental.

This widespread misconception seems to be rooted in our failure to distinguish between superficial "messages" and worthwhile themes. All good poetry has something to say. The Romantic poets insist, for example, that the power of the poetic imagination can lead to the discovery of truth. The Victorian poets concern themselves with "The Condition of England," "The Condition of the Mind," or "The Condition of the Soul." The so-called Decadents of the 1890's and the poets of our own century, rebelling as they often are against established codes and conventional views, suggest alternative sets of values and new perspectives. But to regard these poems as moral propaganda is a serious mistake. Good poetry is no more concerned with superficial messages and perfectly conventional morality than it is with sentimental appeals to our emotions. Andrew Marvell's "To His Coy Mistress" (p. 80) is anything but a conventional moral comment on the relations between the sexes, yet it is one of the great poems of our literature. Dozens of fine poems in this anthology bitterly attack the established political, social, moral, and religious beliefs of the poet's own time and of our own. They can scarcely be described as conventionally "uplifting." Randall Jarrell's "Death of the Ball Turret Gunner," for that matter, is not the kind of patriotic appeal that sends readers flocking to the recruiting station, yet it is a great poem about war and about man's place in society.

The point is, of course, that good poetry is by definition somewhat unorthodox, somewhat apart from the usual idea of how we ought to live or how we ought to "improve ourselves." Good poetry *is* good poetry because it presents an incident, a scene, an attitude, or an insight that is sometimes daring, often tough-minded, always fresh, original, and even unique in content and/or form. Readers led to believe that poetry is sermonizing meant to improve them while boring them to death will discover that great poetry and perfectly conventional views of life seldom coincide and that the only way poetry "improves" its readers is by offering them an exciting re-examination of man in his relationships with himself, his friends, his society, and his God.

Ornament

The third objection to the study of poetry, fully as common as the views concerning its sentimentality or its moral content, rests on the belief that poetry is a needlessly complicated, needlessly decorated statement. Those who hold this mistaken view see poetic analysis as a process of cutting through difficult words and puzzling grammar that the poet has arbitrarily invented to decorate or to hide his *real* meaning. This real meaning, they suspect, could have been stated in simple prose; since the author has refused to make his statement perfectly intelligible, they must "translate" the poem into comprehensible terms. For them, reading a poem is a sterile occupation, as meaningless as trying to solve a Chinese puzzle.

One cause of this "decorated statement" fallacy is taking the capital letter at the beginning of each line of a poem to mean a new sentence, rather than a printing convention. If a reader fails to see that perfectly comprehensible sentence patterns do exist in a poem even though they may extend over several lines, a syntactical nightmare results. The sense totally breaks down, and the reader accuses the poet of intentionally obscuring his meaning rather than stating it in plain English. If the second stanza of Shelley's "Ode to the West Wind" (p. 145) is read line by line, it makes little sense. But if the reader disregards the capital letters and the line divisions, notes the conventional meanings of the punctuation (the colon to introduce direct address and pairs of commas to enclose parenthetical elements, for instance), and reads the nine poetic lines properly, as a single sentence, he finds that he is able to cope with it after all. It would read as follows:

> Thou [the West Wind] on whose stream, mid the steep sky's commotion, loose clouds like earth's decaying leaves are shed, shook from the tangled boughs of Heaven and Ocean, angels of rain and lightning: there are spread on the blue surface of thine aery surge, like the bright hair uplifted from the head of some fierce Maenad, even from the dim verge of the horizon to the zenith's height, the locks of the approaching storm.

The sentence is still difficult, but it is after all an understandable construction. The same is true of other passages and other poems. If the reader looks at them—or hears them when they are read aloud—as groups of complete sentences rather than as collections of separate phrases or lines, he often discovers that the meaning is less obscure than he had thought.

Understanding of this kind removes some obstacles, but of course not all of them. Another foundation for the "decorated statement" fallacy involves the misunderstanding, mentioned earlier, of the differences between scientific language and figurative language. Occasionally, it is true, confusion of the two modes of meaning produces an amusing reading. In Sonnet 106 Shakespeare compares love to the star a ship steers by ("It is the star to every wandering bark/Whose worth's unknown although its height be taken"). One reader paraphrased this as, "Love is a wandering tree that is of priceless value even though it is cut down." But this kind of fun is a little unkind to the reader who was, after all, struggling to find some kind of meaning. Indeed, the difference between literal and figurative statement is so confusing to so many readers, and so basic to an understanding of literature, that we had better examine it in detail.

Figurative Language

Suppose for a moment that you had just won two hundred acres of land in the upper peninsula of Michigan in a national essay contest. You want to make an immediate decision about whether to sell the land for a moderate price or pay the taxes and keep it for a vacation spot. You cannot go there yourself at the moment, but a good friend who is planning a fishing trip in the area offers to visit it for you. Two weeks later, he reports on a postcard: "It's all right. There's not much fishing and the woods are kind of scrubby. One part of the land is a little marshy, but there's a small creek that runs by a pretty good cabin."

Could you make a proper decision on the basis of this account? Probably not. Your friend has sent you a series of judgments rather than a report. "It's *all right,*" "*not much* fishing," "*kind of* scrubby," "*a little* marshy," "*a small* creek," and "*a pretty good* cabin" are phrases that could mean something quite different to him than they do to you. You may be able to catch more fish than he did, for example. It could be a tarpaper shack that will blow away in the next storm or a three-room log cabin in which you could live comfortably in deer season. Your friend's judgments are all comparative, and you cannot be sure that his standard of comparison and yours are identical.

One solution is to call for a *report* rather than a judgment. Demand facts that will mean the same thing to you and to your observer. For this, you would require a map, photographs, a survey of the kinds of trees on the land, their average height and their numbers per acre, a report on how many fish your friend caught there in an hour, an estimate from a contractor on the work necessary to make the cabin livable. That would be the method of the scientist. But there is another alternative. Suppose your friend tried to make you *see* the land in your mind's eye and at the same time make you *understand* what it is like by offering you not only a series of comparative judgments but also a clear basis for the comparison. He could do it by writing: "The land is a combination of Jones's woods (where we went mushroom hunting last spring) and Okefenokee swamp—about half and half. The fishing is no better than we have at the town millpond. There's a creek the size of a cowpath, and almost as muddy, that runs by an old but usable tarpaper shack that looks like something out of *Tobacco Road.*" That, in a very rudimentary form, is the method of the poet and the imaginative writer of prose. The hypothetical friend has used comparisons between unfamiliar objects and familiar ones, connotative words ("shack" rather than "dwelling"), and even a literary allusion (to *Tobacco Road*) in his attempt to make you see and understand for yourself rather than being dependent on his own unsupported value judgments.

Comparison is the fundamental method of imaginative literature, and particularly of poetry. Connotation is a kind of comparison: when we call a small house a "shack," we are drawing an implicit likeness between the mental image this word evokes and the particular building we are describing. An *allusion* is a comparison between what we are trying to describe and some literary or mythological or even actual person or event. A *symbol* is a comparison with an implied rather than stated element: a poet describes a river that begins in a clear spring, gradually becomes broader, slower, and muddier, then merges with the sea, but what he may really be doing is describing human life *as though it were* a river. Even a dramatic encounter between two or more people may often be regarded as a kind of comparison. In "The Bishop Orders His Tomb at St. Praxed's Church" (p. 163), a sixteenth-century churchman, on his deathbed, tells his sons what sort of tomb he wants—and why—but the attentive reader quickly discovers that the scene conveys something more than a simple incident or even the qualities of one man's character. As John Ruskin put it, "I know of no other piece of modern English, prose or poetry, in which there is so much told, as in these lines, of the Renaissance spirit—its worldliness, inconsistency, pride, hypocrisy, ignorance of itself, love of art, of luxury, of good Latin. . . ." Among other accomplishments in the poem, as Ruskin saw, the author has made his reader understand an abstract idea, "the Renaissance spirit," by embodying it in a particular man and action and by speaking of it in particular, concrete terms. On a much lower level, our hypothetical postcard writer was doing the same when he compared the cabin in Michigan with a shack in *Tobacco Road*.

The uses of comparison are remarkably varied. Connotation, simile, metaphor, symbol, allusion, dramatization, and other forms of figurative speech can convey everything from the simplest visual image to the most complicated abstract ideas. This may be illustrated clearly by three examples from prose. In the first, from Dickens' *Great Expectations*, an extended simile makes us understand how a hungry escaped convict looks when he is eating:

> I had often watched a large dog of ours eating his food; and now noticed a decided similarity between the dog's way of eating and the man's. The man took strong sharp sudden bites, just like the dog. He swallowed, or rather snapped up, every mouthful, too soon and too fast; and he looked sideways here and there while he ate, as if he thought there was danger in every direction of somebody's coming to take the pie away. He was altogether too unsettled in his mind over it, to appreciate it comfortably, I thought, or to have anybody to dine with him, without making a chop with his jaws at the visitor. In all of which particulars he was very like the dog.

Edmund Burke, in his *Reflections on the Revolution in France,* uses a simile to suggest not only how the French Revolutionary Assembly looked to an observer, but also how they seemed to *feel* about two important abstractions, justice and human dignity. His comparison provides both a visual image and an intellectual commentary:

> The Assembly, their organ, acts before them the farce of deliberation, with as little decency as liberty. They act like the comedians of a fair before a riotous audience; they act amidst the tumultuous cries of a mixed mob of ferocious men, and of women lost to shame, who, according to their insolent fancies, direct, control, applaud, explode them, and sometimes mix and take their seats amongst them, domineering over them with a strange mixture of servile petulance and proud, presumptuous authority.

The third example is from the "Prelude" to George Eliot's *Middlemarch,* one of the most subtly complicated, and finest, novels in English. Eliot begins with the following paragraph:

> Who that cares much to know the history of man, and how the mysterious mixture behaves under the varying experiments of Time, has not dwelt, at least briefly, on the life of Saint Theresa, has not smiled with some gentleness at the thought of the little girl walking forth one morning hand-in-hand with her still smaller brother, to go and seek martyrdom in the country of the Moors? Out they toddled from rugged Avila, wide-eyed and helpless-looking as two fawns, but with human hearts, already beating to a national idea; until domestic reality met them in the shape of uncles, and turned them back from their great resolve. That child-pilgrimage was a fit beginning. Theresa's passionate, ideal nature demanded an epic life: what were many-volumed romances of chivalry and the social conquests of a brilliant girl to her? Her flame quickly burned up that light fuel; and, fed from within, soared after some illimitable satisfaction, some object which would never justify weariness, which would reconcile self-despair with the rapturous consciousness of life beyond self. She found her epos in the reform of a religious order.

In the two paragraphs that follow this one, Eliot develops the simile, pointing out that there have since been many women like Theresa whose lives ended not in success but in failure, and whose effort "seemed mere inconsistency and formlessness; for these later-born Theresas were helped by no coherent social faith and order which could perform the function of knowledge for the ardently willing soul."

When one reads *Middlemarch* carefully, he discovers that this extended reference to St. Theresa is a great deal more than decoration or a casual parallel with the experience of the main characters in the novel. It is a clear, fully developed statement of the novel's theme. *Middlemarch* is concerned, above everything else, with "how the mysterious mixture," man, "behaves under the varying experiments of Time." It is concerned with the difficult relationship between high ideals and great resolves on the one hand and "domestic reality" on the other, that is, with the conflicts between a man's hopes and the circumstances of his environment. Further, the novel attempts to show that in place of the "coherent social faith and order" by which Theresa guided her life, men have been forced to substitute any number of philosophies or sets of beliefs that will, they hope, "perform the function of knowledge [give direction] for the ardently willing soul." And finally, Eliot believes that her function as novelist is to examine the apparent "inconsistency and formlessness" of these more modern human struggles, to show their essential similarities with each other, and to suggest some kind of significant law or order that is central to all of them.

As the reader will readily see, this summary statement of the novel's theme is a series of generalizations about abstract ideas. In abstract form, it is difficult to follow, but that is precisely the point. *Eliot's* statement of the theme, presented in terms of a little girl named Theresa who sets out to achieve martyrdom and is brought back home by her uncles, says the same thing—and more—but it says it in concrete, specific terms that we can understand immediately and fully if we think a little. We can see the little girl in our mind's eye. We can *not* see "the relationship between high ideals and the actual circumstances in which an individual may find himself placed." Much the same is true of Burke's comparison of the French Assembly and a group of rude comedians at a country fair, or of Dickens' comparison of the convict's eating with a dog's. In each instance, an abstraction has been made concrete, and a generalization—"the man eats badly," "the group lacks dignity," "a conflict exists between ideals and circumstances"—has been stated in specific terms that we can both visualize and understand.

This, of course, is the answer that must be given to those who think poetry or other imaginative literature is decorated statement and that the reader's or the critic's job is its translation into simpler terms. When we do away with the rustic comedians or the dog or St. Theresa, we also do away with some of the most precise elements of the meaning. When we "translate," we are forced to translate into more general terms, and much is lost, including our interest in what is being said. The job of the reader or critic of figurative language is not to dissolve one part of the comparison into the other, or to "solve" a metaphorical statement to produce only a simplified expository meaning. It is, instead, to make himself aware of both elements in the figurative comparison. To understand imaginative literature, and certainly to enjoy it, the reader must first see and in some sense experience the episodes of the dog eating, the rustic comedians acting, and Theresa toddling out of the city. Then he must try to explain to himself, and perhaps to an audience, the actions, ideas, or emotions that these experiences convey. He will quickly discover that his prose explanation is always less precise and less powerful than the figurative statement—that is, creative art is richer than criticism—but he will also discover that his attempt to experience what is dramatized, and to explain it to his own satisfaction, is the beginning of genuine pleasure in reading.

Poetry and Communication

Poetry is, after all, a kind of communication meant to be understood and enjoyed by a wide audience. The techniques of poetry are not vastly different from the techniques of a short story, a good novel, or an imaginative essay. Read the following example carefully, paying particular attention to the series of pictures, visual objects, images—call them what you wish—that Wordsworth presents:

THE SOLITARY REAPER

Behold her, single in the field,
Yon solitary Highland Lass!
Reaping and singing by herself;
Stop here, or gently pass!
Alone she cuts and binds the grain,
And sings a melancholy strain;
O listen! for the Vale profound
Is overflowing with the sound.

No Nightingale did ever chaunt
More welcome notes to weary bands
Of travellers in some shady haunt
Among Arabian sands;
A voice so thrilling ne'er was heard
In spring-time from the Cuckoo-bird,
Breaking the silence of the seas
Among the farthest Hebrides.

Will no one tell me what she sings?—
Perhaps the plaintive numbers flow
For old, unhappy, far-off things,
And battles long ago;
Or is it some more humble lay,
Familiar matter of to-day?
Some natural sorrow, loss, or pain,
That has been, and may be again?

Whate'er the theme, the Maiden sang
As if her song could have no ending;
I saw her singing at her work,
And o'er the sickle bending—
I listened, motionless and still;

> And, as I mounted up the hill,
> The music in my heart I bore,
> Long after it was heard no more.

In the first stanza, Wordsworth speaks directly to us in a series of commands: Look at her! Stop here or else pass quietly by! Listen! These imperatives are, of course, a means of drawing us into more direct and immediate participation in the poem. Although we do not stop to think about it on a conscious level, we are likely to feel that we are actually with the narrator, observing the scene with him. And what is the scene? A Scottish girl in a valley—perhaps not very far from us—is cutting grain with a sickle, binding it in sheaves, and singing something that we do not immediately identify except in general terms: it is a "melancholy strain," and it seems to fill the entire valley.

The second stanza offers two distinct scenes suggested by the girl's song—a nightingale singing to weary travelers at an Arabian oasis and a cuckoo uttering its two-note call in springtime among the rather barren Hebrides, islands in the North Atlantic, off the west coast of Scotland. Now, setting aside for a moment the relationship between the quality of the girl's song and the songs to which it is compared, we ought to ask ourselves precisely what is conveyed in these two scenes. Wordsworth's original audience would react more immediately, perhaps, since they would have heard both the nightingale and the cuckoo— as we probably have not—and would know instantly both where the Hebrides were and what they were like. But the scenes suggest something to us, even so; for one thing, the contrast between the full, rich, virtuoso performance of the nightingale and the monotonous two-note call of the cuckoo; between all the suggestions of warmth, and perhaps luxury and romance, of "Arabian sands" and "shady haunt" and the cooler, plainer, rockier, less bustling scene suggested by "the farthest Hebrides" and "the silence of the seas." At the same time, the two scenes are similar. Both bird songs are "welcome" and, in different senses, "thrilling." To the Arabian travelers, the nightingale's elaborate performance means that a long day's journey is over; to the inhabitants of the Hebrides, the cuckoo's two-note call marks the end of a long winter. At a later point in our analysis, we will have to ask ourselves why Wordsworth used two analogies to the girl's song rather than one and why he chose these two in particular. Apparently, the contrast and comparison of the two scenes has something to do with the meaning of the poem.

This contrast and comparison is carried on in the third stanza, too. Here, we are concerned less with visual and auditory images than we are with intellectual ones. As in the previous stanza, we are again presented with a minor problem that Wordsworth's original audience would have solved without hesitation: the girl is of course singing in Erse or Scottish Gaelic, the language of the Highlands. That is the reason the poet cannot tell what she is singing. A little reflection on our part (or a footnote from an editor) will enable us to hurdle this obstacle, however, and we can go on to examine the two songs contrasted in the stanza. The first seems to suggest much the same kind of romance and distance, in time, that the shady Arabian haunt of the previous stanza suggests, although the distance there was distance in space. The song in this third stanza is not "a sad ditty" or "a melancholy rhythm" but the more elevated "plaintive numbers." The girl's song may be concerned, the poet thinks, with "old, unhappy, far-off things, / And battles long ago," suggesting perhaps some kind of medieval romance about kings and knights—the sort of thing that troubadours sang. Or perhaps it is not concerned with battles and far-off things at all. It may deal with "humble" rather than noble subjects, with "*Familiar* matter of *to-day*," with some "natural" rather than nobly artificial emotion, with something that has really happened and may happen again. The reader who is familiar with the subject of medieval romance and who knows that such romances are divided into "the *matter* of England" and "the *matter* of Rome," for example, will recognize an element of irony, heightening the contrast with the preceding song, in the line, "Familiar *matter of to-day*." But such special knowledge is by no means necessary. Every reader who takes time to participate in the experience described—who tries to hear in his imagination the two kinds of song described—will recognize the contrast between the old and the new, the "unhappy, far-off things" and the "humble," "familiar," "natural" subjects, between the elevated song suggested by "plaintive numbers" and the more ordinary folksong suggested by "humble lay." And he may also recognize that whereas the first song of this pair corresponds in some ways with the suggestions of the Arabian haunt in the previous stanza, the second, more ordinary song corresponds very closely with the plainer, less lushly romantic scene brought to mind by the phrase, "the farthest Hebrides."

The fourth and last stanza completes the poem by directing our attention once again to the entire scene. Now, however, the statements are all in the past tense rather than the present, as they were in the first stanza. This shift in tense is effective, for it focuses our attention on what is really important in the poem— the poet's own unique reaction to the experience. As we have seen, the use of the present tense in the first stanza was a means of drawing us into a more immediate relationship to the experience, helping us imagine that we were with the poet, actually looking at the girl and hearing her singing. But after all, the poem is not primarily descriptive. At the end, we know very few specific details of the scene. We do not know how the valley looked, how large the field was, how the girl was dressed, how old she was, or even whether or not the sun was shining. But we do know a great deal about *the meaning* of the girl and her song *to the poet*. And it is this personal meaning that is reinforced in the last stanza in the series of statements, "I saw," "I listened," "I mounted up the hill," and, in effect, "I have carried the music in my heart from that day to this."

The reader will now recognize that the central statement made by the poem is much more specific than "I was moved by the song and have remembered it." The statement, "I was moved," has been modified by all the connotations of the nightingale singing to weary travelers at an Arabian oasis, of a cuckoo announcing spring to the dwellers in the Hebrides, of romantic ballads about "old, unhappy, far-off things," and of humble folksongs about ordinary realities. Here, then, Wordsworth has done what every writer of imaginative literature attempts to do. He has presented an abstract emotion or an idea in specific terms, dramatizing it as a series of concrete experiences in which the reader may participate. In fact, he has been so precise about the quality of his reaction that a general statement such as "He was impressed and moved by the song" becomes totally inadequate.

A critical reading of "The Solitary Reaper" could stop at this point and be adequate. But Wordsworth has done something more than simply specify his emotions, and some readers may wish to follow the poem as far as it will take them. The key lies in the structure, in the contrasts that have already been noted between Arabia and the Hebrides, romantic songs of long ago and humble songs about everyday realities. What is going on in these stanzas? Why has Wordsworth so carefully arranged comparisons and contrasts not only within each of the two central stanzas in the poem, but also between them? In looking for the principle that lies behind the selection and arrangement of images in these two stanzas, the reader may notice that the one about the nightingale and the cuckoo involves a spread in space (from Arabia to the Hebrides), while the next involves a spread in time (from "battles long ago" to "familiar matter of to-day"). And each stanza includes a contrast between suggestions of luxurious romance and everyday realities. We have already seen that the poet compares the girl's song to each of these images in turn. It is more welcome than the nightingale in Arabia, more thrilling than the cuckoo in the Hebrides; it might be about ancient battles or it might be an ordinary folksong about modern hardships. Now, however, we may recognize that the girl's song is also compared to the entire *group* of images taken all together. The song is universal in its meaning and importance: it has links with everything from Arabia to the Hebrides, from ancient times to the present and future, from highly colored romance to humble realities.

This realization, in turn, leads to a new understanding of the last two lines of the first stanza, "O listen! for the Vale profound / Is overflowing with the sound." On one level of meaning, Wordsworth is of course asking us to listen because the girl's singing is loud enough to fill and come out of the deep valley in which she is working. But "profound" means something more than physically deep. Ordinarily, the word is used to suggest intellectual depth and significance, something that has deep and perhaps unfathomable *meaning*. And the sense in which the valley "Is overflowing with the sound" seems to involve more than mere loudness. In fact, the song's significance not only overflows the valley, but extends everywhere in space and time. The second and third stanzas, which we have discussed, establish this universality, and the last stanza clinches the point. Surely the poet's comment about the girl singing "As if her song could have no ending" does not mean that he found it interminable or "endless" in the derogatory sense. Wordsworth's obvious pleasure in the song makes that interpretation impossible. Yet the song *is* endless in the sense of being universal, extending endlessly in space and time, having some relationship with everything that exists or has existed. Then, too, the significance that the poet has discovered in the song explains the meaning of the last two lines, "The music in my heart I bore, / Long after it was heard no more." In light of the entire poem, this can scarcely be reduced to "I remembered the tune for a long time." The experience means more than that.

This discussion of a relatively short, though not simple, lyric ought to suggest a number of points about intelligently reading poetry. In the first place, notice the relative lengths of Wordsworth's poetic statement and this critical discussion of it. Even when we make allowances for editorial long-windedness, the fact remains that Wordsworth has tremendously compressed his meaning. It cannot be explained in prose in anything like the same amount of space. And even with all the qualifications and parenthetical asides to which we are driven in our attempt to explain precisely what Wordsworth has said, we have still not exhausted all the possibilities of meaning. Clearly, then, the poem is not a "decorated statement" to be translated into the simpler, clearer language of prose. Second, notice the quality of the central idea: the universality of the song and perhaps the interrelationship of all things in nature. Some readers may wish to describe this theme as a "truth," but it is a truth so much more interesting and original than the trite moral reflections many readers believe to be the substance of poetry that the "message" theory of criticism becomes ridiculously inadequate. Finally, notice the control over emotion exercised by the poet, and the important relationship between emotion and theme. If the girl's song were merely a pretty little tune heard in passing, the poet's reaction to it, with his exclamations, his extended similes, his enraptured concentration as he listens "motionless and still," and his bearing the song in his heart would all seem hopelessly extravagant and sentimental. But as Wordsworth has made clear, the song really has a profound significance for him. It is almost overwhelmingly important, and he gives us enough information and description that we may also experience its meaning. In light of this *demonstrated* importance, his statements about how he feels seem restrained, understated, not sentimental at all. The quality of sentimentality does not depend, then, on the mere intensity of the emotion suggested in a poem, but on the relationship between the strength of the emotion and the situation that causes it. A competent poet does not permit the two to fall out of balance with one another.

A Method of Critical Analysis

The preceding discussion illustrates one kind of approach to a poem. There are other types of criticism, however, and it will be useful to clarify them. Even if we do not choose to adopt elements of every theory, understanding them will help us to see more clearly what we are trying to accomplish when we read and discuss a poem.

The best place to begin is with the four co-ordinates of art criticism outlined by Mr. M. H. Abrams in an extremely interesting technical study titled *The Mirror and the Lamp: Romantic Theory and the Critical Tradition* (New York, 1958). The first of these co-ordinates is *content*, that is, the material with which the author concerns himself, including people and events, nature, human values, the society, ideas and feelings, and everything else about which it is possible to write a poem; second, the *work* that contains this content, or some part of it; third, the *artist* who created the work; and, finally, the *audience* to whom the work is addressed.

Critical approaches to poetry that focus on the content, the "reality" or "real life" with which the work deals, and that try to evaluate the quality of the imitation, are called *mimetic* theories. In this kind of criticism, poetry is imitation of life, and the best kind of poetry is that which most accurately, or powerfully, or elegantly, pictures that reality. Plato's and Aristotle's comments on literature are essentially mimetic theories, and so is Alexander Pope's famous prescription that poetry should present "What oft was thought, but ne'er so well expressed." A second kind of criticism, the *pragmatic* theory, discusses the poem from the point of view of its effect on the audience. Poetry is regarded as rhetorical strategy that aims at achieving certain results in the reader's mind. Parts of the poem are described by reference to the results they usually achieve, and the quality of the poem is evaluated according to a moral standard: is the response worthwhile? Still another approach, the *expressive* theory, is primarily concerned not with the degree to which the poem imitates external objects, not with the poem's effects on the audience, and not even with the poem's own particular structure or meaning. The expressive theory is concerned instead with the poet, with his state of mind while he was creating the poem, with his intentions, and with the unique ways in which his particular genius is reflected in the work. Wordsworth's definition of poetry as "the spontaneous overflow of powerful feelings" is oriented toward the expressive theory, and so is Shelley's *Defense of Poetry,* in which poetry is defined as "the record of the best and happiest moments of the happiest and best minds." In this view of poetry as the expression of an artistic personality, the audience and even the content of the poem may fade into insignificance. According to Shelley, "A poet is a nightingale, who sits in darkness and sings to cheer *its own* solitude with *sweet sounds* [my italics]."

All three of these critical theories finally do say something about the poem as a work of art, of course, but for each of them, evaluation is the primary concern. They try to show how effective the poem is as an imitation, as a piece of rhetoric, or as an exprssion of the poet's mind. Inevitably, close analysis of the text becomes secondary. Analysis is not a secondary consideration, however, for the adherents of the fourth main type of criticism, the *objective* approach.

Objective criticism regards the poem as an artistic structure independent of all the other co-ordinates that have been mentioned—independent of the content, independent of the poet's personality and the facts of his life, independent of the poem's effects on the audience. For the objective critic, both the analysis and the evaluation of the poem are based solely on criteria found within the poem itself, on such elements as the relationship of one figure or structural part of the poem to another. T. S. Eliot's statement, "When we are considering poetry we must consider it primarily as poetry and not another thing," expresses this particular ideal. So does Archibald MacLeish's line, "A poem should not mean / But be," and so do the pronouncements of most major modern critics.

None of these four critical theories ever appears in quite so perfect a form as we have been describing. In actual practice, the reader who seeks a full understanding of a poem like "The Solitary Reaper" will take into account Wordsworth's imitation of the Highland scene, the effect of the poem on the audience, and the degree to which the poem reflects Wordsworth's own personality and his beliefs about poetry and life. It will be useful as well as interesting to discover that the poem was based on an incident in Wordsworth's walking tour of Scotland in 1803 and to attempt to relate the poem to other poems by Wordsworth and to Romantic poetry in general.

In the first encounter with any unfamiliar poem, however, the first goal ought to be discovery of the unique, concrete, special statement the poem contains and of the unique way it presents that statement. This, of course, means careful, orderly analysis of the individual parts and the relationships among them. In the sections that follow, then, let us examine such individual elements as structure, diction, imagery, and metrical devices, defining necessary terms as we go and at the same time outlining a step-by-step method of analysis that can be applied to any poem we read.

STRUCTURE

When we look for a place to begin our analysis, our first intuition is to ask what the poem "really says," to search for some kind of simple prose statement of the facts conveyed. But we have already seen that the poem's more significant meanings and its subtler suggestions are lost in such a prose reduction. Rather than beginning with such a blunt, inevitably misleading paraphrase, we would do better to consider the poem's structure, the way its contents are organized. Even here, of course, there are distinct problems. In "The Solitary Reaper," it is difficult to speak of the general structure without reference to the individual images that compose this structure, and it is difficult to speak of individual images without referring to the way they are organized. Or consider how weak and gushy it would be for a man to say, without any preamble, "Oh, lift me as a wave, a leaf, a cloud! / I fall upon the thorns of life! I bleed!" Taken out of the total context of Shelley's "Ode to the West Wind," the line is weak and silly. But in context, it is as powerful as it is sensible. No question either of its tone or its meaning arises when we realize (from a consideration of the poem's structure) that Shelley has been speaking for three stanzas of the effects of the west wind on leaves and clouds and waves, that he is now identifying himself with these natural objects, and that he is invoking the west wind to act on him and on his poetry with the same mystical power for destruction and preservation that it had exercised on other elements of nature. In this instance, structure and individual figures of speech are so closely related that it is next to impossible to separate them, even for purposes of discussion.

We must begin somewhere, however, and a consideration of structure is both the easiest and the most immediately rewarding. On the basis of one or two rapid readings of a poem, it is possible to make a pretty good judgment about its general effects. We can determine, for example, that the poem is primarily narrative, descriptive, or expository—that it gives an account of an action, describes something, or explains something. A descriptive poem such as Stephen Spender's "The Express" (p. 268) may be discussed in terms of spatial organization: the train leaves the station, passes through the town, by the gasworks, the cemetery, into the open country where it picks up speed, and at last "reaches night / Where only a low streamline brightness / Of phosphorous on the tossing hills is white." Narrative poems are organized chronologically in much the same way that a short story, a novel, or a play is constructed. An expository poem may involve techniques of argument and persuasion, or, what is more common, it may be an explanation of anything from a passing mood to a complicated technical process. In ordering his material, the poet may use any number of structural devices—definition, classification and division, comparison and contrast, or enumeration. "The Solitary Reaper," for instance, could be described as an expository poem that introduces the subject, divides it into two categories of extension in space and extension in time, and draws a conclusion based on the two categories.

Poetic form is not quite the same as rhetorical structure. The term poetic form refers to the entire range of classifying labels—epic, elegy, sonnet, ode, ballad, etc.—that have been assigned to various kinds of poems throughout the history of literature. (Definitions are to be found in the Glossary.) Because of the authority these terms derive from tradition, and, indeed, from their use in modern criticism, they should not be ignored. For the most part, however, they are incomplete descriptions that refer in haphazard fashion to various elements in the poems. As a result, their value as starting points for critical analysis is doubtful. Some terms refer simply to the rhyme scheme and the specific number of lines, without regard to content or organization. Others refer only to the poem's material, to its tone, or to the arrangement of its contents.

Particularly in certain types of lyric, the stringent requirements of poetic form may take over the function of rhetorical structure—or at least appear to do so. The poet who would write a *villanelle*, for example, must produce six stanzas totaling nineteen lines. The first five stanzas must each be three lines long and the last, four. Line 1 of the poem must reappear as a refrain (in exactly the same form) in lines 6, 12, and 18. Line 2 must reappear as lines 9, 15, and 19. Only two rhymes are permitted. Obviously, the poet must fight so hard to fulfill these requirements, while saying something intelligible, that the subtle development of theme becomes secondary. Yet rhetorical structure and poetic form are, in fact, distinctly separate entities. It is as though a master potter were asked to produce a pitcher. The requirements that it hold liquid, that it have an opening at the top and a lip to pour from, that it have a handle, and that there be a flat place on the bottom so that it might be set down on a table all correspond to the requirements of poetic form. But how the potter works within these requirements to produce a pitcher that is distinctly his own work, reflecting his own ideas of beauty and efficient design, corresponds to the rhetorical structure. He may make the neck of the pitcher long and thin or so short as to be practically nonexistent. The lip may be wide or narrow; it may extend from the rim of the pitcher or be reduced to little more than a nick in the edge. In the handle, the size, and even the shape innumerable variations are possible.

The poet is like this imaginary potter. Our understanding and evaluation of his performance will depend both on our knowing the requirements set for him by his choice of a particular poetic form, and on our perceiving his originality at work within these requirements. Every Shakespearean sonnet, for instance, must consist of fourteen iambic pentameter lines in a fixed rhyme scheme. There are three four-line divisions, or quatrains, followed by a couplet, and the whole poem rhymes *abab cdcd efef gg*. Yet the organization of the material may or may not correspond to these rhyme divisions. The poet may choose to treat it in the manner of the Italian sonnet writers, using the first two quatrains to pose a single question, which is then answered in the final quatrain and the couplet. Or he may treat each quatrain as a separate unit of meaning and use the couplet as a means of summing up what he has said. Numerous other variations are possible even though the general form of the poem remains fixed. Similar possibilities also exist in other kinds of poetry, as a comparison of Milton's "Lycidas" (p. 73) and Matthew Arnold's "Thyrsis" (p. 189) will make clear. Both are pastoral elegies meeting all the traditional requirements, yet in Milton's hands the poem becomes a commentary on the value of poetry and a violent protest against religious betrayal; in Arnold's it becomes a means of showing the loss of his own youthful idealism and his recovery of hope. If, in our reading of these and other poems, we can perceive both the traditional poetic form and the unique rhetorical structure, we possess an indispensable foundation for further analysis.

LANGUAGE

We now move to a careful examination of the language within the structural framework. Some of the simpler problems have already been solved, for in outlining the arrangement of the poem's contents, we have had to deal with matters of grammatical construction and define some unfamiliar words. But more is involved. We must also focus sharp attention on qualities of the diction, the imagery, and the figures of speech the poet uses to convey his precise meaning.

First, we must be sure that we understand the *denotation,* or literal meaning, of every word in the poem. Beyond looking up unfamiliar words, we may be faced with more subtle problems presented by archaic and ambiguous words or phrases. Often the whole meaning of a poem turns on such definitions. For example, Gerard Manley Hopkins' "The Windhover" (p. 213) begins with the following lines:

> I caught this morning morning's minion, king-
> dom of daylight's dauphin, dapple-dawn-drawn Falcon, in his riding
> Of the rolling level underneath him steady air, and striding
> High there, how he rung upon the rein of a wimpling wing
> In his ecstasy!

If we take the word "caught" to mean simply "trapped," we will be hopelessly misled in our understanding of everything that follows. In fact, *Webster's New World Dictionary* lists more than twenty definitions of "catch," and we must decide which ones are appropriate in this context. Since the falcon has not been physically clutched by the poet, "to come upon suddenly, surprise, discover" seems appropriate; so does "to take in, understand, apprehend"; and so does the colloquial "to grasp the meaning, understand," as in "Do you catch on?" We must do the same for "minion," "dauphin," "rung," and "wimpling." Only then are we able to see that the meaning (in rough paraphrase) is something like this: "This morning I perceived morning's favorite, the heir apparent to the kingdom of daylight, as he rode the air. At one point, when he was beating his wings as though he were taking great strides, he flew upwards in spirals ["to ring" is a term from falconry] as though he were reined in by a wing that both rippled, like water, and at the same time suggested the folds of a nun's veil."

In the denotative meaning of these few lines there are at least five instances of *ambiguity,* the quality of suggesting, simultaneously, more than one possible meaning for a word or phrase. The phrase "dapple-dawn-drawn Falcon," for example, can mean both a falcon that is *attracted* by a dappled dawn sky and a falcon that is outlined, sketched, or *silhouetted* by the dappled dawn. The phrase "striding high there" is both an explanation of where the bird was and an excited exclamation, "Hi there!" As we have seen, "caught" and "wimpling" each suggest more than one meaning; and "the rolling level underneath him steady air" suggests at least three subtly different possibilities, all equally correct. In all instances like these, we must assume that the poet knows what he is doing, and we must hold all of the possible meanings in mind rather than arbitrarily settling on one of them that happens to please us.

The *connotation* of words in poetry is even more important than the denotation. "Connotation" refers to the full range of suggestions that adhere to a word and that are not part of the denotative meaning. They have become attached to the word either as a result of our personal experience or because an entire group, nation, or culture has tacitly agreed that the word has certain overtones of meaning and that these overtones should be regarded as part of the definition. Denotatively, "minion," in our example from "The Windhover," means only "a favorite, usually of a prince or patron." Connotatively, however, the word suggests a medieval courtier acting zealously on the orders of his patron, as in our cliché, "a minion of the law." Similarly, "dauphin" is the title given to the eldest son of the king of France between 1349 and 1830, but it suggests to most readers a pampered member of the royal family—in this instance, the individual who will inherit the "kingdom of daylight." The reader who reacts fully to the connotations of the words in these few lines will see that Hopkins has powerfully suggested an atmosphere of medieval chivalry and has suggested, too, a great deal both about the character of the falcon and its specific relationship to the "kingdom of daylight." Unfortunately, no dictionary can give much more than a hint of connotative meanings—if that. But the reader who asks himself not only "What does the word mean?" but also "What does it mean *to me*; what does it suggest?" will discover that he knows more about connotation than he thought he did.

"Imagery" is sometimes used—very loosely—to refer to anything in a poem that helps us imaginatively to see, feel, taste, hear, smell, or to experience the sensation of physical movement. Every element of language may be bent to this purpose, and examples could be multiplied to show how, in various poems, authors make appeals to our senses through their use of denotative and connotative meanings, figures of speech, rhythms, and sound patterns. Perhaps it will be sufficient, however, to point out that in Hopkins' lines, the imagery is predominantly kinesthetic—it suggests the physical sensations of various kinds of movement. Note how "caught," "riding," "rolling," "striding," "rung upon the rein," and even "wimpling wing" all suggest powerful motion or the exercise of muscular control. These lines offer little or no appeal to the other senses. Other poems and other passages, however, will suggest every kind of human sensation.

In most modern criticism, "imagery" is used to refer to the entire range of *figurative language,* or *figures of speech,* of the poem. This figurative language must, of course, be examined in detail, always with an eye to the relationship between the individual figure of speech and the total structure within which it operates. But rather than repeat what has already been said about the function of figurative language, let us simply define and summarize the specific kinds of figure that we will encounter. Obviously, not all problems of meaning can be solved on an abstract level, and we will do better to learn the terms and concepts, and then, in reading and class discussion, see how they actually work to convey pleasure and meaning.

Comparison, we have seen, is the essential tool of imaginative literature, and the *simile, metaphor,* and *symbol* are the fundamental kinds of comparison, differing from one another only in the degree to which they are explicit analogies. A *simile* is a direct comparison that may be expressed A *is like* B. The simile may extend throughout an entire poem, as it does in Spenser's "Lyke as a Huntsman" (p. 47), or it may be a very brief analogy establishing a single point of resemblance. In either case, however, we must do two things as we read it: comprehend A, the action, object, or person actually being described by the analogy, and at the same time realize and participate imaginatively in B, the other half of the comparison. It is not enough to say that the woman pursued in Spenser's sonnet is as shy as a deer, as graceful, as difficult to capture, that she gave herself to the poet only when he ceased to pursue her, or even that Spenser is pondering her strange conduct. All of this is true, of course, but we must also "see" the huntsman, the hounds, and the deer. We must experience the fully developed concrete action that conveys the more abstract meaning.

The *metaphor,* expressed A *is* B, differs from the simile only in that the comparison is implied rather than explicit. It is to be read in the same way as a simile, but it is often more difficult to recognize since the comparison may be reduced to a phrase or a single word. If we refer once more to the lines from "The Windhover," we will recognize that they are heavily metaphorical. The falcon is compared to a minion of the morning and to the dauphin of the kingdom of daylight. His flight is described in terms of actions not usually associated with a bird—"riding" and "striding." When he spirals upward, the action is compared to that of a horse, at the end of a long rein, galloping for exercise around and around its trainer. Finally, in the word "wimpling," the falcon's wing is compared to the rippling of water and to a nun's headdress. In this series of metaphors, then, we are presented simultaneously with two kinds of experience, just as in the simile. On the one hand, we perceive the coherent, precisely described flight of the falcon; and on the other, we become aware of a collection of different things—a minion and a dauphin, something riding, something striding on its legs, a galloping horse, and a nun's wimple.

The *symbol* is the next logical degree of comparison. Whereas the simile says A *is like* B; and the metaphor, A *is* B; the symbol speaks only of B, yet implies a further meaning. The symbol may be any concrete thing—an object, a person, an action—that is described for its own sake and also because it contains within itself some further suggestion of meaning. William Blake's "The Sunflower" is a good example:

> Ah, Sun-flower! weary of time,
> Who countest the steps of the Sun,
> Seeking after that sweet golden clime
> Where the traveller's journey is done:

Where the Youth pined away with desire,
And the pale Virgin shrouded in snow
Arise from their graves, and aspire
Where my Sun-flower wishes to go.

Absolutely nothing is said in this poem, at least explicitly, about the poet's own soul or aspirations. The poem describes a sunflower that daily turns from east to west following the course of the sun. Certain intellectual qualities are assigned to the flower—the ability to count and hope, for instance—but it remains a sunflower, engaged in an action perfectly appropriate to it. At the same time, however, the reader who is a little bothered by the curiously heavy load of significance that the poet seems to assign to this simple action will perhaps recognize that the object and the action described parallel a similar experience going on in the poet's mind or in the minds of all of us. The sun-flower's weariness and longing implicitly describe another kind of weariness and longing that is not even mentioned in the poem. That, in briefest illustration, is symbolism. *Allegory* is different, however, and not to be confused with it. In allegory, each concrete element in the poem represents a particular abstraction. To take an example from prose, John Bunyan's *The Pilgrim's Progress from This World to That Which Is to Come* describes characters, a journey, and certain adventures, but none of these is self-contained and interesting in and for itself—as a symbol always is. The names of characters—Christian, Mrs. Timorous, Giant Despair—and the names of places—the Slough of Despond, the Valley of Humiliation, Vanity Fair, the Celestial City—all make it abundantly clear that everything in the work directly corresponds to some abstraction that it is intended to dramatize. The allegory is, in fact, an extended metaphor rather than a symbol.

   Irony, one of the most important and difficult kinds of figurative language, involves a relationship between the reality described and the terms used to describe it. Irony is not exactly "saying the opposite of what we mean," although that may be one form of it. In fact, we can distinguish three main types: verbal, structural, and dramatic irony. *Understatement,* for example, is a kind of verbal irony in which the speaker means infinitely more than he actually says, as when a man sentenced to the firing squad remarks that the experience will be "unpleasant" for him. *Hyperbole* goes to the other extreme, speaking of something in such extravagantly exaggerated terms that it could not be meant literally, as when someone who fails a ten-minute quiz speaks of the experience as his "death warrant" in the course. Between these two extremes lies a range of verbal irony in which the apparent meaning of the statement and the real meaning are somehow slightly out of adjustment. The last line of "The Death of the Ball Turret Gunner" furnishes a good illustration. The statement "When I died they washed me out of the turret with a hose" certainly does not say the opposite of what is meant, yet it is powerfully ironic, for the coolly unemotional tone of the statement contrasts with the strong emotions of sympathy and pity that the poem generates. *Structural irony,* as the term suggests, is a principle of organization rather than a particular kind of statement. In its simplest form, this kind of irony involves two contrasting events or situations, as when Wordsworth, in "A Slumber Did My Spirit Seal" (p. 126), devotes one stanza to his calm assurance that Lucy would remain untouched by the passage of time and the next to his realization that she is now dead, "Rolled 'round in earth's diurnal course; / With rocks, and stones, and trees." "The Death of the Ball Turret Gunner" illustrates a more complicated form of the same device when it collapses the gunner's life into two events—his birth and his entrance into the bomber—and when it contrasts the dreamlike quality of life on earth with the nightmarish realities of the air battle. *Dramatic irony,* on the other hand, refers to a situation in which the audience fully understands the significance of words or actions that the character does not perceive.

Finally, there are several other forms of comparison and rhetorical arrangement with which the reader should familiarize himself. Definitions and brief examples of *allusion, antithesis, apostrophe, epithet, inversion, metonymy, oxymoron, paradox, personification,* and *synechdoche* should be consulted in the Glossary. Obviously, no single poem uses all these less common devices, and we can understand and explain the language of a poem without making any reference to them at all. The terms are worth knowing, however. First, familiarity with them directs our study of the language itself, alerting us to possibilities of meaning that we might otherwise overlook. Second, they furnish a mental shorthand enabling us, for instance, to refer to a statement as antithesis rather than trying to explain that the author has grammatically balanced his statement and that he has set off one part of the meaning against another. We do not need the terms to get at the meaning of the language, but without them, we are forced to go the long way around in our explanations.

RHYME, METER, RHYTHM, AND SOUND

The process of critical analysis we have been outlining has begun with an examination of structure and has moved to an investigation of the language used within this structure. Now, we must turn our attention to the uses of rhyme, meter, rhythm, and sound effects that support the meaning of the poem, and indeed, make it "poetic," differentiating the poem from the imaginative communication of the short story, novel, or play.

Rhyme, the first of these supporting elements, is the correspondence of sound in two or more words, usually the last words in poetic lines. Four types can be distinguished. *Masculine rhyme* is an identity in the last accented syllables of the rhyming words, as in "The Solitary Reaper," where the rhymes of the second stanza are "chaunt," "haunt"; "bands," "sands"; "heard," "bird"; "seas," "Hebrides." *Feminine rhyme* involves identity in the last two syllables of the rhyming words, as when Tennyson, in "The Splendor Falls," rhymes "going," "blowing"; "river," "ever"; and "replying," "dying," "flying."

Slant rhyme, illustrated in the previous example in the words "river," "ever," is an approximation rather than an identity of sounds. Finally, *triple rhyme,* a form used more for ingeniously humorous effects than for serious poetry, is a correspondence of the last *three* syllables of the rhyming words, as in Byron's famous couplet:

> But—Oh! ye lords of ladies intellectual,
> Inform us truly, have they not hen-pecked you all?

Identifying the rhyme scheme of a poem is a simple process. The first line and every succeeding line that rhymes with it is designated *a*. The first new rhyme in the poem is noted as *b*, the next, *c*, and so on, to the end. Thus, a quatrain in which the first two lines rhyme and the next two form a different rhyme would be noted as *aabb*. If the first and third lines and the second and fourth lines rhyme, the scheme would be *abab*.

We have already seen how rhyme patterns may determine poetic form, as in the Shakespearean sonnet. It has been suggested, too, that rhyme patterns may either correspond to the rhetorical structure of the poem or work in a counterpoint to it. That is, a quatrain rhyming *aabb* will naturally suggest two separate units of sense, each two lines long, whereas a quatrain rhyming *abab* or *abba* will suggest a four-line unit of sense. The poet writing a Shakespearean sonnet may make each quatrain (*abab cdcd efef*) correspond to a separate element of the poem's rhetorical structure, or he may treat the first two quatrains as a single unit of sense. If he chooses to do the latter, a tension will be set up between the rhyme scheme, with its suggestion of two separate elements of sense, and the grammatical structure and the idea that insist the two quatrains form a single unit of sense. It will be helpful to give some attention, in our analyses, to this relationship between the rhyme structure and the structure of the ideas in the poem. Frequently, this is one of the best keys to understanding.

Meter, or the pattern of stressed and unstressed syllables in a poetic line, always causes trouble until we learn the traditional terms for describing it and develop an ear for the various beats. This is simply a matter of practice. When normally pronounced, English words of more than one syllable usually possess at least one heavily stressed syllable (marked ´) and at least one unstressed syllable (marked -). We use these stresses in our normal speech to clarify meaning. Consider the difference between a líght hoúsekéepér and a líghthoúse keépér. Notice, too, that in a sentence we may accentuate the stress on words of one syllable or we may remove it entirely, depending on the total context of meaning we wish to convey. If we were casually asked, "What just went by the window?" we might reply, "Thát wās ā hořse, Ī think." But if we were asked, "What do you think of Dan Patch?" we might answer, "Thát wás ā hořse!"

In poetry, words of more than one syllable retain their normal patterns of stress, as in the following examples: púrpōse, bēyónd, súnsēt, wéstērn. Words of one syllable, on the other hand, are either stressed or unstressed according to the context and the particular grammatical construction in which they are used. Words like mý, hólds, tó, sáil, the, ánd, óf, and áll, when pronounced individually, receive stress. But notice that when they are used as part of a larger construction, many of them lose their stresses: "mȳ púrpōse hólds tō sáil bēyónd the súnsēt, and the báths ōf áll the wéstērn stárs, ūntíl Ī díe."

It will be necessary to refer to five patterns of stressed and unstressed syllables in poetry: the *iambic* (-′), as in bēyónd, ūntíl, and tō sáil; the *trochaic* (′-), as in púrpōse, súnsēt, and wéstērn; the *anapestic* (--′), as in "The Assýrīan cáme down líke the wolf ōn the fóld"; *dactylic* (′--), as in stráwbērrīes, póttēry, métricāl, and áll of thēm; and the *spondaic* (′′), as in góld ōre, cōld stónes, stróng fóot, and high nóon.

Each of these individual patterns of stressed and unstressed syllables is called a *foot*, and it is possible to describe a line of poetry by referring to the type and number of feet in the line. Here again, certain traditional terms are used. A line of one foot is *monometer*; two feet, *dimeter*; three feet, *trimeter*; four feet, *tetrameter*; five feet, *pentameter*; six feet, *hexameter* or *alexandrine*; seven feet, *heptameter*; eight feet, *octameter*. Thus we get terms like "iambic pentameter," "anapestic tetrameter," or "dactylic hexameter." The lines from Tennyson's "Ulysses" used above are, for instance, iambic pentameter. The basic pattern is iambic and there are five feet in each line:

> Tō sáil| bēyónd| the sún| sēt, ánd| the báths|
> Ōf áll| the wést| ern stárs,| ūntíl| Ī díe.|

Three points ought to be noted in marking and describing the metrical pattern of a line. First, the foot corresponds to the pattern of stressed and unstressed *syllables*, not words, so that it is possible for the foot division to correspond, as it does in the example above, to a single word, to two words, or to any number of parts of words. Second, the counting of the line is not changed if there is an extra *unstressed* syllable at the end. Third, the basic metrical pattern is not changed if there is *substitution* of a different kind of foot for one of the feet in the line, of a spondee, for instance, in place of one of the iambic feet. In one of the "Holy Sonnets," for example, Donne substitutes trochees, spondees, and one anapestic foot, yet the basic meter of the poem remains iambic pentameter:

> Báttēr| mȳ heárt,| thrée pér| sōned Gód;| fōr yóu|
> Ās yét| but knóck,| bréathe, shíne,| and séek| tō ménd;|
> Thát Ī| māy ríse| and stánd,| o'erthrów| me, and bénd|
> Yōur fórce| tō bréak,| blów, búrn,| and máke| me néw.|

Rhythm, which is not the same thing as meter, is extremely difficult to discuss simply because there is no adequate notation for analyzing and describing it. Yet we must say something about it in our analysis of a poem, for it represents the one absolutely indispensable element of poetry. Good poems can exist without rhyme, regular meter, or significant sound patterns. Figures of speech may be few and rudimentary. Organization may be so simple that the poem exists as little more than a single statement. But if the rhythm is crude—or nonexistent—the poem ceases to be a poem.

To begin with, then, notice that when we reach the end of a sentence, spoken aloud, we come to a full stop for a fraction of a second before going on with the next sentence. Similarly, when we reach the end of a grammatical subdivision within the sentence, like the parenthetical element you are reading now, we pause even more briefly in order to differentiate the unit from the rest of the sentence. If we mark the full stop with three slashes (///) and the pause with two (//), we have something like this:

> Every poem // without exception // possesses rhythm /// Rhythmical language is the fundamental element of poetry ///

"Rhythm" refers to the pattern formed by these units of various length, whether they be counted by syllables, by the number of accentuated beats between pauses and stops, or merely by the length of time it takes to utter each unit. Notice, for instance, how the lines we have already quoted from Tennyson have both a regular iambic *meter* and a separate *rhythm*:

> for my purpose holds
> To sail beyond the sunset // and the baths
> Of all the western stars // until I die ///
> It may be that the gulfs will wash us down ///
> It may be we shall touch the Happy Isles //
> And see the great Achilles // whom we knew ///

The passage from Donne would look like this:

> Batter my heart // three-personed God // for you
> As yet but knock // breathe // shine // and seek to mend ///
> That I may rise // and stand // o'erthrow me // and bend
> Your force to break // blow // burn // and make me new ///

The terms used to refer to rhythm are few and simple. The pause within a line is a *caesura*. When the lines of a poem end in full stops, marking the completion of a unit of sense, they are said to be *end-stopped*. When there is no pause at the end of the line, that is, when the sense must be completed by the line or lines that immediately follow, it is said to be a *run-on line* or to show *enjambment*. These terms say little, however, of the really important matter, the uses to which rhythm is put in emphasizing meaning. In both examples used above, rhythmical patterns and metrical substitutions (particularly the strong spondees in the Donne poem) combine to reinforce the sense of each passage—Ulysses' calm determination to sail on until death, Donne's violent prayer that he be battered and broken by God so that he may be spiritually renewed. Of course, we cannot argue that the rhythms establish the meanings all by themselves, but they do support it appropriately and they do offer pleasing variations to our ear. Something should be said, too, about the occasional virtuoso performance in which rhythm comes very close to establishing the meaning by itself. In "The Solitary Reaper," the first excited stanza consists of short phrases: "Behold her // single in the field // Yon solitary Highland Lass /// Reaping and singing by herself /// Stop here // or gently pass ///." But in the second stanza, when it is necessary to suggest the nightingale's song, the rhythm suddenly lengthens out to include four lines with only a single light pause within them: "No Nightingale did ever chaunt more welcome notes to weary bands of travellers in some shady haunt // among Arabian sands ///." In one section of "Dover Beach" Matthew Arnold brilliantly duplicates the irregular rhythms of the very surf he is talking about: "Come to the window // sweet is the night air /// Only // from the long line of spray Where the ebb meets the moon-blanched land // Listen // you hear the grating roar Of pebbles which the waves draw back // and fling // At their return // up the high strand // Begin // and cease // and then again begin // With tremulous cadence slow // and bring The eternal note of sadness in ///." Obviously, with passages like these, we must do more than simply mark the meter and the rhythm. We must make ourselves aware of the function of these elements in the poem, and we must at least try to describe that function in our analysis.

Sound patterns, like other technical elements, may be more important in some poems than in others, and when they are used, they are a means of subtly supporting the sense rather than establishing it. In understanding how this is so, practical experience will be infinitely better than any theoretical discussion, so we will limit ourselves here to a definition of terms and a few short examples.

Alliteration, the most obvious device for manipulating the sound patterns of a poem, is the repetition of initial consonant sounds, as in the opening lines of "The Windhover": "I caught this morning morning's minion, king/dom of daylight's dauphin, dapple-dawn-drawn Falcon." *Assonance* is identity of vowel sounds within words; *consonance,* identity of consonantal sounds. *Onomatopoeia* is the use of words that suggest their meaning by their own sound, as in "rumble," "mumble," "bleat," "whinny," or "sizzle." In four lines from Keats' poem "To Autumn," all of these devices are effectively used:

> Then in a wailful choir the small gnats mourn
> Among the river sallows, borne aloft
> Or sinking as the light wind lives or dies;
> And full-grown lambs loud bleat from hilly bourn;

The mere existence of alliteration or assonance does not guarantee that the musical effects of the poem will be particularly effective, of course. Much depends on the relative pitch of the vowels, ranging from the high *ee* to low *oh*, and on the inherent sounds of the consonants that are chosen for the pattern. Aside from the difference in denotative meaning, "a mumbling bunch of buzzing bumblebees" *sounds* vastly different from "let little lambs lie in the light." Whether the poet is consciously aware of his musical effects or not is beside the point. What is important is that the poem may contain patterns of sound that reinforce the meaning. In fact, these patterns may exist in more poems than one would think. As Pope put it, in a passage worth careful study:

> 'Tis not enough no harshness gives offence,
> The sound must seem an echo to the sense:
> Soft is the strain when Zephyr gently blows,
> And the smooth stream in smoother numbers flows;
> But when loud surges lash the sounding shore,
> The hoarse, rough verse should like the torrent roar:
> When Ajax strives some rock's vast weight to throw,
> The line too labours, and the words move slow;
> Not so, when swift Camilla scours the plain,
> Flies o'er th'unbending corn, and skims along the main.

In a critical analysis, we should treat sound effects as we do rhythm: investigate them, decide on their relative importance to the poem, and comment on them if comment seems necessary.

CONCLUSION

To summarize the process of analysis we have been discussing, let us examine another very brief poem by Wordsworth and make a set of notes such as we might jot down if we were preparing a full essay:

> A slumber did my spirit seal;
> I had no human fears;
> She seemed a thing that could not feel
> The touch of earthly years.
>
> No motion has she now, no force;
> She neither hears nor sees;
> Rolled round in earth's diurnal course,
> With rocks, and stones, and trees.

I. Structure

    a. The poem is primarily expository rather than narrative or descriptive. It presents an account of the poet's feelings rather than a description of a scene or an account of events.

b. The poetic form of the poem is lyrical, in two quatrains, rhyming *abab*.

c. Its rhetorical structure is built on a sharply ironic contrast between the poet's feelings before the girl died and his feelings now that she is dead.

II. Language

a. The inversion in the first line is a more emphatic way of saying "A slumber sealed my spirit."

b. "Slumber" and "seal" both connote the quality of the poet's assurance that the girl will remain untouched by time. Both words suggest a tinge of lethargic daydreaming. Why "slumber" instead of "sleep"? Why "seal"? Seal off from *what? Reality?*

c. The first reference to the girl as a "thing" takes on ironic significance in the second stanza, where we realize that she has actually become an inanimate object rather than a person. Here, however, the word is carefully qualified: she is a thing that cannot be changed by time.

d. "*Human* fears" and "*earthly* years" seem to be significant phrases, reinforcing the point that the poet was worried about the wrong things—if he was even worried at all.

e. In the second stanza, the poet carefully strips away the girl's human qualities—her "force," her ability to move, hear, and see—and points out that she has become nothing more than a rock, stone, or other inanimate part of the earth. She is "rolled around" in the "diurnal" (daily) course of the planet.

f. The tone of the poem is characterized by strong irony, verbal as well as structural, and by careful understatement of the emotion.

III. Technical details

a. The rhyme scheme *abab* suggests a complete unit of sense. This is borne out by the grammar: each quatrain is, in fact, a single sentence.

b. The meter is iambic, alternately tetrameter (four feet) and trimeter (three feet) lines. This is a typical ballad stanza.

c. The perfect regularity of the meter in the first stanza reinforces the sense of the poet's assurance. In the second stanza, however, spondees have been substituted for iambs at the beginning of the first and third lines. These effectively reinforce the sense that she is now being moved by vast natural forces.

d. The change in rhythm from the long phrases of the first stanza to the short, choppy phrases of the second—particularly evident in the last line—also reinforces the ironic contrast between the two states of the poet's mind, that is, his calm assurance and his present, grief-stricken realization of her death.

e. The poem makes use of alliteration, assonance, and consonance: slumber, spirit, seal; had, human; no motion . . . no force . . . course; rolled round . . . rocks . . . trees. Then too, the high-pitched vowels of the first stanza (sh*e*, s*ee*med, f*ee*l, y*ea*rs) contrast with the very low-pitched vowels of stanza two (n*o* m*o*ti*o*n, n*ow*, n*o* f*o*rce, r*o*lled, c*ou*rse). This, too, is a way of reinforcing the contrast between the two states of the poet's mind, which is, after all, what the poem *is* about.

f. In summary, then, five elements of the poem—its rhetorical structure, its language, its meter, its rhythm, and its sound patterns—all contribute in different ways to the total meaning.

Our analysis might go on from here to an investigation of the poet himself, of the relationship between this poem and his other work, and even to a consideration of the Romantic movement in general. We might wish to comment on these matters, and we should, certainly, try to *evaluate* the poem. Having understood it, do we like it? Why, or why not? This last section of a critical essay would be concerned with pulling the poem together again, with seeing it as a *poem* rather than a collection of individual parts. An evaluative comment is often the best way to do just that.

The division of analysis into separate steps is a convenience, and perhaps even a necessity, but the total meaning of the poem depends not on any one element but on the interrelationships among all of them. Our initial judgment about a poem's meaning is only an hypothesis, a first insight. It is usually necessary to modify our views, and sometimes throw them out and start all over, on the basis of a close study of individual elements of the poem. But really, critical analysis is not so hopeless and endless a process as it may seem. In actual practice, most readers discover that they can frame an adequate working hypothesis on the basis of a single rapid reading or two, that their close study of individual elements in the poem leads to one or more modifications in this hypothesis, and that the poem, as Gerard Manley Hopkins put it, will often "explode into meaning" at about that point when all the elements in it have been carefully examined in the light of a tentative theory, guess, or insight into its meaning.

What helps us here, of course, is that the human brain is a remarkable instrument capable of understanding several levels of meaning at the same time and capable, too, of bringing to bear a tremendous range of experiences with life and language when we focus our attention, in an orderly way, on a particular problem of meaning. After all, poetry *is* meant to be read with pleasure by a wide audience of ordinary people with little or no special training in the intricacies of language. It is well to bear that in mind even if we do speak of the mysteries and complexities of literary analysis.

GEOFFREY CHAUCER

❧ *Prologue to the Canterbury Tales*

WHAN that Aprille with his shoures soote
The droghte of March hath perced to the roote,
And bathed every veyne in swich licour
Of which vertu engendred is the flour;
Whan Zephirus eek with his sweete breeth
Inspired hath in every holt and heeth
The tendre croppes, and the yonge sonne
Hath in the Ram his halve cours yronne,
And smale foweles maken melodye
That slepen al the nyght with open ye   10
(So priketh hem nature in hir corages),
Than longen folk to goon on pilgrimages,
And palmeres for to seken straunge strondes,
To ferne halwes, kouthe in sondry londes;
And specially from every shires ende
Of Engelond to Caunterbury they wende,
The hooly blisful martir for to seke,
That hem hath holpen whan that they were seeke.

Bifel that, in that seson on a day,
In Southwerk at the Tabard as I lay   20
Redy to wenden on my pilgrymage
To Caunterbury with ful devout corage,
At nyght was come into that hostelrye
Wel nyne and twenty in a compaignye,
Of sondry folk, by aventure yfalle
In felaweshipe, and pilgrimes were they alle,
That toward Caunterbury wolden ryde.
The chambres and the stables weren wyde,
And wel we weren esed atte beste.
And shortly, whan the sonne was to reste,   30
So hadde I spoken with hem everichon,
That I was of hir felaweshipe anon,

6. **holt and heeth:** grove and field. [All footnotes to poems are the editors'.]
8. **Ram:** astrologically, the end of March and first of April.
13. **palmeres:** pilgrims.
14. **ferne halwes:** foreign shrines.
17. **martir:** Saint Thomas à Becket.

And made forward erly for to ryse,
To take oure wey ther as I yow devyse.

But nathelees, whil I have tyme and space,
Er that I ferther in this tale pace,
Me thynketh it acordaunt to resoun
To telle yow al the condicioun
Of ech of hem, so as it semed me,
And whiche they weren, and of what degree,   40
And eek in what array that they were inne.

[Chaucer here describes the Knight, the Squire, and the Yeoman.]

Ther was also a Nonne, a Prioresse,
That of hir smylyng was ful symple and coy;
Hire gretteste ooth was but by Seinte Loy;   120
And she was cleped Madame Eglentyne.
Ful weel she soong the service dyvyne,
Entuned in hir nose ful semely,
And Frenssh she spak ful faire and fetisly,
After the scole of Stratford atte Bowe,
For Frenssh of Parys was to hire unknowe.
At mete wel ytaught was she with alle:
She leet no morsel from hir lippes falle,
Ne wette hir fyngres in hir sauce depe;
Wel koude she carie a morsel and wel kepe   130
That no drope ne fille upon hir brest.
In curteisie was set ful muchel hir lest.
Hir over-lippe wyped she so clene
That in hir coppe ther was no ferthyng sene
Of grece, whan she dronken hadde hir draughte.
Ful semely after hir mete she raughte.
And sikerly she was of greet desport,
And ful plesaunt, and amyable of port,
And peyned hire to countrefete cheere
Of court, and to been estatlich of manere,   140
And to ben holden digne of reverence.
But, for to speken of hire conscience,
She was so charitable and so pitous
She wolde wepe, if that she saugh a mous

132. **lest:** pleasure.
136. **raughte:** reached.
137. **sikerly:** certainly.
137. **desport:** merriment.
139. **cheere:** behavior.
141. **digne:** worthy.

Kaught in a trappe, if it were deed or bledde.
Of smale houndes hadde she that she fedde
With rosted flessh, or milk and wastel-breed.
But soore wepte she if oon of hem were deed,
Or if men smoot it with a yerde smerte;
And al was conscience and tendre herte.   150
Ful semyly hir wympul pynched was,
Hir nose tretys, hir eyen greye as glas,
Hir mouth ful smal, and therto softe and reed;
But sikerly she hadde a fair forheed;
It was almoost a spanne brood, I trowe,
For, hardily, she was nat undergrowe.
Ful fetys was hir cloke, as I was war.
Of smal coral aboute hire arm she bar
A peire of bedes, gauded al with grene,
And theron heng a brooch of gold ful sheene,   160
On which ther was first write a crowned "A,"
And after *"Amor vincit omnia."*

Another Nonne with hire hadde she,
That was hir chapeleyne, and preeetes thre.

A Monk ther was, a fair for the maistrie,
An outridere, that lovede venerie,
A manly man, to been an abbot able.
Ful many a deyntee hors hadde he in stable,
And whan he rood, men myghte his brydel heere
Gynglen in a whistlynge wynd as cleere,   170
And eek as loude, as dooth the chapel belle,
Ther as this lord was kepere of the celle.
The reule of Seint Maure or of Seint Beneit,
By cause that it was old and somdel streit,
This ilke Monk leet olde thynges pace,
And heeld after the newe world the space.

---

147. **wastel-breed:** white bread.
149. **yerde:** a stick.
152. **tretys:** well-shaped.
155. **spanne:** handsbreadth with fingers spread.
157. **fetys:** well-made.
162. **"Amor . . . omnia":** "Love conquers all."
164. **preestes thre:** Chaucer later reduced the number to one.
165. **a . . . maistrie:** an excellent choice for the outstanding monk of all.
166. **outridere:** inspector of church property.
166. **venerie:** field sports.
173. **Seint Maure . . . Beneit:** Saints Maurus and Benedict.
175. **ilke:** same.
175. **pace:** pass away.
176. **the space:** in the meantime.

He yaf nat of that text a pulled hen,
That seith that hunters ben nat hooly men,
Ne that a monk, whan he is recchelees,
Is likned til a fissh that is waterlees—   18˹
This is to seyn, a monk out of his closytre,
But thilke text heeld he nat worth an oystre—
And I seyde his opinion was good.
What sholde he studie and make hymselven wood,
Upon a book in cloystre alwey to poure,
Or swynken with his handes, and laboure,
As Austyn bit? How shal the world be served?
Lat Austyn have his swynk to hym reserved!
Therfore he was a prikasour aright:
Grehoundes he hadde, as swift as fowel in flight;   190
Of prikyng and of huntyng for the hare
Was al his lust, for no cost wolde he spare.
I seigh his sleves purfiled at the hond
With grys, and that the fyneste of a lond;
And, for to festne his hood under his chyn,
He hadde of gold ywroght a ful curious pyn:
A love-knotte in the gretter ende ther was.
His heed was balled, that shoon as any glas,
And eek his face, as he hadde been enoynt.
He was a lord ful fat and in good poynt,   200
His eyen stepe, and rollynge in his heed,
That stemed as a forneys of a leed,
His bootes souple, his hors in greet estaat.
Now certeinly he was a fair prelaat;
He was nat pale as a forpyned goost.
A fat swan loved he best of any roost.
His palfrey was as broun as is a berye.

A Frere ther was, a wantowne and a merye,
A lymytour, a ful solempne man.
In alle the ordres foure is noon that kan   210
So muchel of daliaunce and fair langage.

179. **recchelees:** forgetful of discipline.
186. **swyken:** toil.
187. **Austyn:** St. Augustine.
189. **prikasour:** huntsman who rides to hounds.
193. **purfiled:** bordered.
194. **grys:** fine gray fur.
200. **poynt:** condition.
201. **stepe:** bulging.
202. **stemed . . . leed:** glowed (red) like the coals under a cauldron.
205. **forpyned:** suffering.
209. **lymytour:** one who holds the exclusive begging franchise in a district.
210. **kan:** knew.

He hadde maad ful many a mariage
Of yonge wommen at his owene cost.
Unto his ordre he was a noble post.
Ful wel biloved and famulier was he
With frankeleyns over al in his contree,
And eek with worthy wommen of the toun,
For he hadde power of confessioun,
As seyde hymself, moore than a curat,
For of his ordre he was licenciat.   220
Ful swetely herde he confessioun,
And pleasaunt was his absolucioun:
He was an esy man to yeve penaunce,
Ther as he wiste to have a good pitaunce.
For unto a povre ordre for to yive
Is signe that a man is wel yshryve;
For if he yaf, he dorste make avaunt,
He wiste that a man was repentaunt;
For many a man so hard is of his herte,
He may nat wepe, althogh hym soore smerte.   230
Therfore in stede of wepynge and preyeres
Men moote yeve silver to the povre freres.
His typet was ay farsed ful of knyves
And pynnes, for to yeven faire wyves.
And certeinly he hadde a murye note:
Wel koude he synge and pleyen on a rote;
Of yeddynges he baar outrely the pris.
His nekke whit was as the flour-de-lys;
Therto he strong was as a champioun.
He knew the tavernes wel in every toun   240
And everich hostiler and tappestere
Bet than a lazar or a beggestere;
For unto swich a worthy man as he
Acorded nat, as by his facultee,
To have with sike lazars acqueyntaunce.
It is nat honest, it may nat avaunce,
For to deelen with no swich poraille,

216. **frankeleyns:** well-to-do landowners.
220. **licenciat:** licensed to hear confession.
224. **Ther as:** wherever.
227. **make avaunt:** boast.
228. **wiste:** knew.
233. **typet:** cape.
233. **farsed:** packed.
236. **rote:** a stringed instrument.
237. **yeddynges:** songs, ballads.
237. **bar outrely:** utterly took.
242. **lazar . . . beggestere:** leper or female beggar.
247. **poraille:** rabble.

But al with riche and selleres of vitaille.
And over al, ther as profit sholde arise,
Curteis he was and lowely of servyse.   250
Ther nas no man nowher so vertuous.
He was the beste beggere in his hous;
For thogh a wydwe hadde noght a sho,
So plesaunt was his "*In principio*,"
Yet wolde he have a ferthyng, er he wente.
His purchas was wel bettre than his rente.
And rage he koude, as it were right a whelp.
In love-dayes ther koude he muchel help:
For ther he was nat lyk a cloysterer
With a thredbare cope, as is a povre scoler,   260
But he was lyk a maister or a pope.
Of double worstede was his semycope,
That rounded as a belle out of the presse.
Somwhat he lipsed, for his wantownesse,
To make his Englissh sweete upon his tonge;
And in his harpyng, whan that he hadde songe,
His eyen twynkled in his heed aryght,
As doon the sterres in the frosty nyght.
This worthy lymytour was cleped Huberd.

[Chaucer continues with a description of the Merchant.]

A Clerk ther was of Oxenford also,
That unto logyk hadde longe ygo.
As leene was his hors as is a rake,
And he nas nat right fat, I undertake,
But looked holwe, and therto sobrely.
Ful thredbare was his overeste courtepy;   290
For he hadde geten hym yet no benefice,
Ne was so worldly for to have office.
For hym was levere have at his beddes heed
Twenty bookes, clad in blak or reed,
Of Aristotle and his philosophie,

248. **vitaille:** victuals.
253. **sho:** shoe
256. **purchas . . . rente:** the proceeds of his begging were more than his regular income.
257. **rage . . . whelp:** he could dally with the women as if he were a puppy.
258. **love-dayes:** days for settling disputes out of court.
262. **semycope:** short cloak.
290. **courtepy:** short coat.
292. **office:** a job outside the church.
293. **hym was levere:** he would rather.

Than robes riche, or fithele, or gay sautrie.
But al be that he was a philosophre,
Yet hadde he but litel gold in cofre;
But al that he myghte of his frendes hente,
On bookes and on lernynge he it spente,   300
And bisily gan for the soules preye
Of hem that yaf hym wherwith to scoleye.

Of studie took he moost cure and moost heede.
Noght o word spak he more than was neede,
And that was seyd in forme and reverence,
And short and quyk and ful of hy sentence.
Sowninge in moral vertu was his speche,
And gladly wolde he lerne and gladly teche.

[Omitted here are descriptions of the Sergeant of the Law; the Franklin; the group of tradesmen that includes a Haberdasher, a Carpenter, a Weaver, a Dyer, and a Tapestry Maker; the Cook; the Shipman; and the Doctor.]

A good Wif was ther of biside Bathe,
But she was somdel deef, and that was scathe.
Of clooth-makyng she hadde swich an haunt,
She passed hem of Ypres and of Gaunt.
In al the parisshe wif ne was ther noon
That to the offrynge bifore hire sholde goon;   450
And if ther dide, certeyn so wrooth was she,
That she was out of alle charitee.
Hir coverchiefs ful fyne weren of ground;
I dorste swere they weyeden ten pound
That on a Sonday weren upon hir heed.
Hir hosen weren of fyn scarlet reed,
Ful streite yteyd, and shoes ful moyste and newe.
Boold was hir face, and fair, and reed of hewe.
She was a worthy womman al hir lyve;
Housbondes at chirche dore she hadde fyve,   460

296. **fithele:** fiddle.
296. **sautrie:** psaltery (a kind of zither).
297. **philosophre:** the joke of this turns on the double sense of philosopher as al-chemist.
299. **hente:** take.
446. **scathe:** a pity.
447. **haunt:** skill.
448. **Gaunt:** Ghent.
453. **fyne . . . ground:** delicate texture, light; but Alice wears a great many to show her skill.

Withouten oother compaignye in youthe—
But therof nedeth nat to speke as nowthe.
And thries hadde she been at Jerusalem;
She hadde passed many a straunge strem;
At Rome she hadde been, and at Boloigne,
In Galice at Seint Jame, and at Coloigne.
She koude muchel of wandrynge by the weye.
Gat-tothed was she, soothly for to seye.
Upon an amblere esily she sat,
Ywympled wel, and on hir heed an hat   470
As brood as is a bokeler or a targe;
A foot-mantel aboute hir hipes large,
And on hir feet a paire of spores sharpe.
In felaweshipe wel koude she laughe and carpe.
Of remedies of love she knew per chaunce,
For she koude of that art the olde daunce.

A good man was ther of religioun,
And was a povre Persoun of a toun,
But riche he was of hooly thoght and werk.
He was also a lerned man, a clerk,   480
That Cristes gospel trewely wolde preche;
His parisshens devoutly wolde he teche.
Benygne he was, and wonder diligent,
And in adversitee ful pacient,
And swich he was ypreved ofte sithes.
Ful looth were hym to cursen for his tithes,
But rather wolde he yeven, out of doute,
Unto his povre parisshens aboute
Of his offrynge and eek of his substaunce.
He koude in litel thyng have suffisaunce.   490
Wyd was his parisshe, and houses fer asonder,
But he ne lefte nat, for reyn ne thonder,
In siknesse nor in meschief, to visite
The ferreste in his parisshe, muche and lite,
Upon his feet, and in his hond a staf.
This noble ensample to his sheep he yaf,
That first he wroghte, and afterward he taughte.
Out of the gospel he tho wordes caughte,
And this figure he added eek therto,

466. **Galice . . . Jame:** St. James of Campostello, in Spain.
474. **carpe:** chat or joke.
485. **ofte sithes:** often enough.
486. **cursen:** excommunicate.
494. **ferreste:** farthest.
494. **muche and lite:** great and humble.

That if gold ruste, what shal iren do?   500
For if a preest be foul, on whom we truste,
No wonder is a lewed man to ruste;
And shame it is, if a preest take keep,
A shiten shepherde and a clene sheep.
Wel oghte a preest ensample for to yive,
By his clennesse, how that his sheep sholde lyve.
He sette nat his benefice to hyre,
And leet his sheep encombred in the myre,
And ran to Londoun, unto Seinte Poules,
To seken hym a chaunterie for soules,   510
Or with a bretherhed to been withholde;
But dwelte at hoom, and kepte wel his folde,
So that the wolf ne made it nat myscarie;
He was a shepherde and noght a mercenarie.
And though he hooly were and vertuous,
He was to synful men nat despitous,
Ne of his speche daungerous ne digne,
But in his techyng discreet and benygne.
To drawen folk to hevene by fairnesse,
By good ensample, this was his bisynesse,   520
But it were any persone obstinat,
What so he were, of heigh or lough estaat,
Hym wolde he snybben sharply for the nonys.
A bettre preest I trowe that nowher noon ys.
He waited after no pompe and reverence,
Ne maked him a spiced conscience,
But Cristes loore, and his apostles twelve,
He taughte, but first he folwed it hymselve.

[The list of pilgrims is completed by sketches of the Plowman, Miller, Manciple, Reeve, Summoner, and Pardoner.]

Now have I toold you soothly, in a clause,   715
Th' estaat, th' array, the nombre, and eek the cause
Why that assembled was this compaignye
In Southwerk, at this gentil hostelrye
That highte the Tabard, faste by the Belle.

502. **lewed:** uneducated.
503. **keep:** heed.
507. **sette . . . hyre:** did not hire a deputy to perform his duties.
509. **Seinte Poules:** Saint Paul's, where priests were employed to pray for the dead.
511. **bretherhed . . . withholde:** or be retained as chaplain to a guild.
523. **snybben . . . nonys:** scold sharply on such an occasion.
526. **spiced:** overly scrupulous.

[In the evening, the keeper of the tabard offers to accompany the group, and suggests a contest: each of the pilgrims will tell two tales on the way to Canterbury and two on the return journey. Whoever tells the best stories will be banquetted by the others, and anyone who ventures to dispute the judgment of the host will pay for everything spent along the way.]

Amorwe, whan that day bigan to sprynge,
Up roos oure Hoost, and was oure aller cok,
And gadrede us togidre in a flok,
And forth we riden, a litel moore than paas,
Unto the wateryng of Seint Thomas;
And there oure Hoost bigan his hors areste,
And seyde, "Lordynges, herkneth, if yow leste:
Ye woot youre foreward, and I it yow recorde.
If evensong and morwesong accorde,   830
Lat se now who shal telle the firste tale.
As evere mot I drynke wyn or ale,
Whoso be rebel to my juggement
Shal paye for al that by the wey is spent.
Now draweth cut, er that we ferrer twynne;
He which that hath the shorteste shal bigynne.
"Sire Knyght," quod he, "my mayster and my lord,
Now draweth cut, for that is myn accord.
Cometh neer," quod he, "my lady Prioresse,
And ye, sire Clerk, lat be youre shamefastnesse,   840
Ne studieth noght; ley hond to, every man!"
Anon to drawen every wight bigan,
And shortly for to tellen as it was,
Were it by aventure, or sort, or cas,
The sothe is this, the cut fil to the Knyght,
Of which ful blithe and glad was every wyght,
And telle he moste his tale, as was resoun,
By foreward and by composicioun,
As ye han herd; what nedeth wordes mo?
And whan this goode man saugh that it was so,   850
As he that wys was and obedient
To kepe his foreward by his free assent,
He seyde, "Syn I shal bigynne the game,
What, welcome be the cut, a Goddes name!
Now lat us ryde, and herkneth what I seye."
And with that word we ryden forth oure weye,
And he bigan with right a myrie cheere
His tale anon, and seyde as ye may heere.

823. **oure aller cok:** the awakening rooster to all of us.
826. **Seint Thomas:** a watering spot near Southwark.
835. **twynne:** set out.

❦ A *Renouncing of Love*

FAREWELL, love, and all thy laws for ever,
Thy baited hooks shall tangle me no more;
Senec and Plato call me from thy lore
To perfect wealth, my wit for to endeavour;
In blinde error when I did perséver,
Thy sharp repulse that pricketh aye so sore
Taught me in trifles that I set no store,
But scape forth thence, since liberty is lever.
Therefore, farewell! Go trouble younger hearts,
And in me claim no more authority;
With idle youth go use thy property,
And thereon spend thy many brittle darts.
For hitherto though I have lost my time,
Me list no longer rotten boughs to climb.

❦ *The Lover Showeth How He Is Forsaken of Such as He Sometime Enjoyed*

THEY flee from me, that sometime did me seek,
With naked foot stalking within my chamber.
Once have I seen them gentle, tame, and meek,
That now are wild, and do not once remember
That sometime they have put themselves in danger
To take bread at my hand; and now they range,
Busily seeking in continual change.
Thanked be fortune it hath been otherwise,
Twenty times better; but once especial,
In thin array, after a pleasant guise,
When her loose gown did from her shoulders fall,
And she me caught in her arms long and small,
And therewithal so sweetly did me kiss
And softly said, "Dear heart, how like you this?"
It was no dream, for I lay broad awaking.
But all is turned now, through my gentleness,

Into a bitter fashion of forsaking;
And I have leave to go, of her goodness,
And she also to use newfangleness.
But since that I unkindly so am served,
How like you this? What hath she now deserved?

GEORGE GASCOIGNE

❧ *The Lullaby of a Lover*

SING lullaby, as women do,
Wherewith they bring their babes to rest;
And lullaby can I sing too,
As womanly as can the best.
With lullaby they still the child;
And, if I be not much beguiled,
Full many wanton babes have I,
Which must be stilled with lullaby.

First, lullaby my youthful years,
It is now time to go to bed;
For crooked age and hoary hairs
Have won the haven within my head.
With lullaby, then, youth be still!
With lullaby content thy will!
Since courage quails and comes behind,
Go sleep, and so beguile thy mind!

Next, lullaby my gazing eyes,
Which wonted were to glance apace;
For every glass may now suffice
To show the furrows in my face.
With lullaby, then, wink awhile!
With lullaby your looks beguile!
Let no fair face, nor beauty bright,
Entice you eft with vain delight.

And lullaby my wanton will;
Let reason's rule now reign thy thought,
Since all too late I find by skill
How dear I have thy fancies bought.
With lullaby now take thine ease!

With lullaby thy doubts appease!
For trust to this, if thou be still,
My body shall obey thy will.

Eke lullaby my loving boy;
My little Robin, take thy rest!
Since age is cold and nothing coy,
Keep close thy coin, for so is best.
With lullaby be thou content!
With lullaby thy lusts relent!
Let others pay which have mo pence,
Thou art too poor for such expense.

Thus, lullaby my youth, mine eyes,
My will, my ware, and all that was:
I can no mo delays devise;
But welcome pain, let pleasure pass.
With lullaby now take your leave!
With lullaby your dreams deceive!
And when you rise with waking eye,
Remember Gascoigne's lullaby!

EDMUND SPENSER

❧ *Lyke as a Huntsman After Weary Chace*

LYKE as a huntsman after weary chace,
Seeing the game from him escapt away,
Sits downe to rest him in some shady place,
With panting hounds beguiled of their pray:
So after long pursuit and vaine assay,
When I all weary had the chace forsooke,
The gentle deare returnd the selfe-same way,
Thinking to quench her thirst at the next brooke.
There she beholding me with mylder looke,
Sought not to fly, but fearlesse still did bide,
Till I in hand her yet halfe trembling tooke,
And with her owne goodwill hir fyrmely tyde.
Strange thing me seemed to see a beast so wyld,
So goodly wonne with her owne will beguyld.

❧ One Day I Wrote Her Name upon the Strand

ONE day I wrote her name upon the strand,
But came the waves and washed it away:
Agayne I wrote it with a second hand,
But came the tyde, and made my paynes his pray.
Vayne man, sayde she, that doest in vaine assay
A mortal thing so to immortalize,
For I my selve shall lyke to this decay,
And eek my name bee wyped out lykewize.
Not so (quod I), let baser things devize
To dy in dust, but you shall live by fame:
My verse your vertues rare shall eternize,
And in the hevens wryte your glorious name.
Where whenas death shall al the world subdew,
Our love shall live, and later life renew.

SIR WALTER RALEGH

❧ On the Life of Man

WHAT is our life? a play of passion,
Our mirth the music of division;
Our mothers' wombs the tiring houses be,
Where we are dressed for this short comedy;
Heaven the judicious sharp spectator is,
That sits and marks still who doth act amiss;
Our graves that hide us from the searching sun,
Are like drawn curtains when the play is done.
Thus march we playing to our latest rest,
Only we die in earnest, that's no jest.

❧ The Author's Epitaph, Made by Himself

EVEN such is time, which takes in trust
Our youth, our joys, and all we have,
And pays us but with age and dust;
Who in the dark and silent grave,

When we have wandered all our ways,
Shuts up the story of our days;
And from which earth, and grave, and dust,
The Lord shall raise me up I trust.

JOHN LYLY

❧ *Cupid and Campaspe*

CUPID and my Campaspe played
At cards for kisses; Cupid paid.
He stakes his quiver, bow, and arrows,
His mother's doves and team of sparrows;
Loses them too; then down he throws
The coral of his lip, the rose
Growing on's cheek (but none knows how);
With these the crystal of his brow,
And then the dimple of his chin;
All these did my Campaspe win.
At last he set her both his eyes;
She won, and Cupid blind did rise.
O Love, has she done this to thee?
What shall, alas! become of me?

SIR PHILIP SIDNEY

❧ *Loving in Truth*

LOVING in truth, and fain my love in verse to show,
That the dear she might take some pleasure of my pain—
Pleasure might cause her read, reading might make her know,
Knowledge might pity win, and pity grace obtain—
I sought fit words, to paint the blackest face of woe,
Studying inventions fine, her wits to entertain,
Oft turning others' leaves, to see if thence would flow
Some fresh and fruitful shower, upon my sun-burnt brain.
But words came halting out, wanting invention's stay;
Invention, nature's child, fled stepdame study's blows,
And others' feet still seemed but strangers in my way.
Thus great with child to speak, and helpless in my throes,
Biting my tongue and pen, beating myself for spite:
"Fool" said my muse to me, "look in thy heart and write."

❧ *With How Sad Steps, O Moon*

WITH how sad steps, O moon, thou climb'st the skies,
How silently, and with how mean a face.
What! may it be that even in heavenly place
That busy archer his sharp arrows tries?
Sure, if that long with love acquainted eyes
Can judge of love, thou feel'st a lover's case;
I read within thy looks thy languished grace.
To me that feel the like, my state descries.
Then even of fellowship, O moon, tell me,
Is constant love deemed there but want of wit?
Are beauties there as proud as here there be?
Do they above love to be lov'd, and yet
Those lovers scorn whom that love doth possess?
Do they call virtue there ungratefulness?

❧ *Dear, Why Make You More of a Dog Than Me?*

DEAR, why make you more of a dog than me?
If he do love, alas, I burn in love;
If he wait well, I never thence would move;
If he be fair, yet but a dog can be;
Little he is, so little worth is he;
He barks, my songs in one voice oft doth prove;
Bidden (perhaps), he fetcheth thee a glove;
But I unbid, fetch even my soul to thee.
Yet while I languish, him that bosom clips,
That lap doth lap, nay lets in spite of spite
This fawning mate taste of those sugared lips;
Alas, if you grant only such delight
To witless things, then love, I hope (since wit
Becomes a clog), will soon ease me of it.

❧ *Since Nature's Works Be Good*

SINCE nature's works be good, and death doth serve
As nature's work, why should we fear to die?
Since fear is vain, but when it may preserve,
Why should we fear that which we cannot fly?
Fear is more pain than is the pain it fears,
Disarming human minds of native might:
While each conceit an ugly figure bears,
Which were not evil, well viewed in reason's light.
Our owly eyes, which dimmed with passions be,
And scarce discern the dawn of coming day,
Let them be cleared, and now begin to see,
Our life is but a step, in dusty way.
Then let us hold the bliss of peaceful mind;
Since this we feel, great loss we cannot find.

MICHAEL DRAYTON

❧ *The Parting*

SINCE there's no help, come, let us kiss and part;
Nay, I have done, you get no more of me;
And I am glad, yea glad with all my heart,
That thus so cleanly I myself can free.
Shake hands for ever, cancel all our vows,
And, when we meet at any time again,
Be it not seen in either of our brows
That we one jot of former love retain.
Now at the last gasp of Love's latest breath,
When, his pulse failing, Passion speechless lies,
When Faith is kneeling by his bed of death,
And Innocence is closing up his eyes,
Now if thou wouldst, when all have given him over,
From death to life thou might'st him yet recover.

WILLIAM SHAKESPEARE

❧ *Sonnets*

XVIII

Shall I compare thee to a Summer's day?
Thou art more lovely and more temperate:
Rough winds do shake the darling buds of May,
And Summer's lease hath all too short a date:
Sometime too hot the eye of heaven shines,
And often is his gold complexion dimmed;
And every fair from fair sometime declines,
By chance or nature's changing course untrimmed:
But thy eternal Summer shall not fade,
Nor lose possession of that fair thou ow'st;   10
Nor shall Death brag thou wanderest in his shade,
When in eternal lines to time thou grow'st:
So long as men can breathe, or eyes can see,
So long lives this, and this gives life to thee.

XXXIII

Full many a glorious morning have I seen
Flatter the mountain-tops with sovereign eye,
Kissing with golden face the meadows green,
Gilding pale streams with heavenly alchemy,
Anon permit the basest clouds to ride
With ugly rack on his celestial face,
And from the forlorn world his visage hide,
Stealing unseen to west with this disgrace.
Even so my sun one early morn did shine
With all-triumphant splendour on my brow;   10
But out, alack! he was but one hour mine;
The region cloud hath masked him from me now.
Yet him for this my love no whit disdaineth;
Suns of the world may stain when heaven's sun staineth.

8. **untrimmed:** to trim, or adjust, a vessel's sails after tacking.

6. **rack:** broken clouds.
12. **region:** at one level of the sky.

LXIV

WHEN I have seen by Time's fell hand defaced
The rich proud cost of outworn buried age;
When sometime lofty towers I see down-razed
And brass eternal slave to mortal rage;
When I have seen the hungry ocean gain
Advantage on the kingdom of the shore,
And the firm soil win of the watery main,
Increasing store with loss and loss with store;
When I have seen such interchange of state,
Or state itself confounded to decay,   10
Ruin hath taught me thus to ruminate,
That Time will come and take my love away.
This thought is as a death, which cannot choose
But weep to have that which it fears to lose.

LXXIII

THAT time of year thou mayst in me behold
When yellow leaves, or none, or few, do hang
Upon those boughs which shake against the cold,
Bare ruined choirs, where late the sweet birds sang.
In me thou seest the twilight of such day
As after sunset fadeth in the west,
Which by and by black night doth take away,
Death's second self, that seals up all in rest.
In me thou seest the glowing of such fire
That on the ashes of his youth doth lie,   10
As the death-bed whereon it must expire,
Consumed with that which it was nourished by.
This thou perceivest, which makes thy love more strong,
To love that well which thou must leave ere long.

CXVI

LET me not to the marriage of true minds
Admit impediments. Love is not love
Which alters when it alteration finds,
Or bends with the remover to remove;
O no! it is an ever-fixèd mark,
That looks on tempests and is never shaken;

1. **fell:** cruel, deadly.
10. **confounded:** heedlessly mixed together, damned.
11. **ruminate:** ponder.

4. **choirs:** note the double comparison—the speaker is like the bare boughs that are like the places in a ruined church once occupied by the choir.

It is the star to every wandering bark,
Whose worth's unknown, although his height be taken.
Love's not Time's fool, though rosy lips and cheeks
Within his bending sickle's compass come;   10
Love alters not with his brief hours and weeks,
But bears it out even to the edge of doom.
If this be error and upon me proved,
I never writ, nor no man ever loved.

CXXIX

THE expense of spirit in a waste of shame
Is lust in action; and till action, lust
Is perjured, murderous, bloody, full of blame,
Savage, extreme, rude, cruel, not to trust;
Enjoyed no sooner but despised straight;
Past reason hunted, and no sooner had,
Past reason hated, as a swallowed bait
On purpose laid to make the taker mad,
Mad in pursuit and in possession so;
Had, having, and in quest to have, extreme;   10
A bliss in proof, and proved, a very woe;
Before, a joy proposed; behind, a dream.
All this the world well knows; yet none knows well
To shun the heaven that leads men to this hell.

CXLVI

POOR soul, the center of my sinful earth,
Thrall to these rebel powers that thee array,
Why dost thou pine within and suffer dearth,
Painting thy outward walls so costly gay?
Why so large cost, having so short a lease,
Dost thou upon thy fading mansion spend?
Shall worms, inheritors of this excess,
Eat up thy charge? Is this thy body's end?
Then, soul, live thou upon thy servant's loss,

---

7. **bark:** sailing vessel.
8. **height be taken:** as with a sextant, in navigation.
10. **compass:** area enclosed by the sickle-stroke.

11. **in proof:** while being tested.

8. **charge:** responsibility, what you cared about most.

And let that pine to aggravate thy store;   10
Buy terms divine in selling hours of dross;
Within be fed, without be rich no more:
So shalt thou feed on Death, that feeds on men,
And Death once dead, there's no more dying then.

❦ *Fear No More the Heat o' the Sun*

[From *Cymbeline*]

FEAR no more the heat o' the sun,
Nor the furious winter's rages;
Thou thy worldly task hast done,
Home art gone, and taken thy wages:
Golden lads and girls all must,
As chimney-sweepers, come to dust.

Fear no more the frown o' the great;
Thou art past the tyrant's stroke;
Care no more to clothe and eat;
To thee the reed is as the oak: 10
The Sceptre, Learning, Physic, must
All follow this, and come to dust.

Fear no more the lightning-flash,
Nor the all-dreaded thunder-stone;
Fear not slander, censure rash;
Thou hast finished joy and moan:
All lovers young, all lovers must
Consign to thee, and come to dust.

No exorciser harm thee!
Nor no witchcraft charm thee!   20
Ghost unlaid forbear thee!
Nothing ill come near thee!
Quiet consummation have;
And renownèd be thy grave!

10. **aggravate:** increase.

14. **thunder-stone:** the thunderbolt itself.
19. **exorciser:** one who drives away ghosts and evil spirits.

❧ *When Icicles Hang by the Wall*

[From *Love's Labour's Lost*]

WHEN icicles hang by the wall,
And Dick the shepherd blows his nail,
And Tom bears logs into the hall,
And milk comes frozen home in pail,

When blood is nipp'd, and ways be foul,
Then nightly sings the staring owl,
      To-whit!
To-who!—a merry note,
While greasy Joan doth keel the pot.

When all aloud the wind doth blow,   10
And coughing drowns the parson's saw,
And birds sit brooding in the snow,
And Marian's nose looks red and raw,
When roasted crabs hiss in the bowl,
Then nightly sings the staring owl,
      To-whit!
To-who!—a merry note,
While greasy Joan doth keel the pot.

THOMAS CAMPION

❧ *I Care Not for These Ladies*

I CARE not for these ladies,
That must be wooed and prayed,
Give me kind Amaryllis
The wanton country maid;
Nature art disdaineth,
Her beauty is her own;
Her when we court and kiss,
She cries, "Forsooth," let go.
But when we come where comfort is,
She never will say no.

9. **keel**: skim or stir.
11. **saw**: maxim.

If I love Amaryllis,
She gives me fruit and flowers,
But if we love these ladies,
We must give golden showers;
Give them gold that sell love,
Give me the nutbrown lass,
Who when we court and kiss,
She cries, "Forsooth," let go.
But when we come where comfort is,
She never will say no.

These ladies must have pillows,
And beds by strangers wrought,
Give me a bower of willows,
Of moss and leaves unbought,
And fresh Amaryllis,
With milk and honey fed,
Who, when we court and kiss,
She cries, "Forsooth," let go.
But when we come where comfort is,
She never will say no.

❧ *The Man of Life Upright*

THE man of life upright,
Whose guiltless heart is free
From all dishonest deeds,
Or thought of vanity;

The man whose silent days
In harmless joys are spent,
Whom hopes cannot delude,
Nor sorrow discontent;

That man needs neither towers
Nor armour for defence,
Nor secret vaults to fly
From thunder's violence.

He only can behold
With unaffrighted eyes
The horrors of the deep
And terrors of the skies.

Thus, scorning all the cares
That fate or fortune brings,
He makes the heaven his book,
His wisdom heavenly things,

Good thoughts his only friends,
His wealth a well-spent age,
The earth his sober inn
And quiet pilgrimage.

❧ *There Is a Garden in Her Face*

THERE is a garden in her face,
Where roses and white lilies grow;
A heavenly paradise is that place,
Wherein all pleasant fruits do flow.
There cherries grow, which none may buy
Till "Cherry-ripe" themselves do cry.

Those cherries fairly do enclose
Of orient pearl a double row;
Which when her lovely laughter shows,
They look like rose-buds filled with snow.   10
Yet them nor peer nor prince can buy,
Till "Cherry-ripe" themselves do cry.

Her eyes like angels watch them still;
Her brows like bended bows do stand,
Threatening with piercing frowns to kill
All that attempt with eye or hand
Those sacred cherries to come nigh,
Till "Cherry-ripe" themselves do cry.

❧ *The Writer to His Book*

"WHITHER thus hastes my little book so fast?"
"To Paul's Churchyard." "What! in those cells to stand,
With one leaf like a rider's cloak put up
To catch a termer or lie musty there

11. **peer:** one of the nobility.
 4. **termer:** one studying for a term.

With rimes a term set out, or two, before?"
"Some will redeem me." "Few." "Yes, read me too."
"Fewer." "Nay, love me." "Now thou dotest, I see."
"Will not our English Athens art defend?"
"Perhaps." "Will lofty courtly wits not aim
Still at perfection?" "If I grant?" "I fly."   10
"Whither?" "To Paul's." "Alas, poor book, I rue
Thy rash self-love; go, spread thy papery wings:
Thy lightness can not help or hurt my fame."

JOHN DONNE

❧ *The Sun Rising*

Busy old fool, unruly Sun,
Why dost thou thus,
Through windows, and through curtains, call on us?
Must to thy motions lovers' seasons run?
Saucy pedantic wretch, go chide
Late school-boys and sour prentices,
Go tell court-huntsmen that the King will ride,
Call country ants to harvest offices;
Love, all alike, no season knows nor clime,
Nor hours, days, months, which are the rags of time.   10

Thy beams so reverend and strong
Why shouldst thou think?
I could eclipse and cloud them with a wink,
But that I would not lose her sight so long.
If her eyes have not blinded thine,
Look, and to-morrow late tell me,
Whether both th' Indias of spice and mine
Be where thou left'st them, or lie here with me.
Ask for those Kings whom thou saw'st yesterday,
And thou shalt hear, all here in one bed lay.   20

She's all States, and all Princes I;
Nothing else is;
Princes do but play us; compared to this,
All honour's mimic, all wealth alchemy.
Thou, Sun, art half as happy as we,
In that the world's contracted thus;

17. **Indias:** the East and West Indies.

Thine age asks ease, and since thy duties be
To warm the world, that's done in warming us.
Shine here to us, and thou art everywhere;
This bed thy center is, these walls thy sphere.   30

❧ *The Canonization*

For God's sake hold your tongue and let me love,
Or chide my palsy or my gout,
My five gray hairs or ruined fortune flout,
With wealth your state, your mind with arts improve,
Take you a course, get you a place,
Observe His Honour, or His Grace,
Or the King's real, or his stamped face
Contemplate, what you will, approve,
So you will let me love.

Alas, alas, who's injured by my love?   10
What merchant's ships have my sighs drowned?
Who says my tears have overflowed his ground?
When did my colds a forward spring remove?
When did the heats which my veins fill
Add one more to the plaguey bill?
Soldiers find wars, and lawyers find out still
Litigious men, which quarrels move,
Though she and I do love.

Call us what you will, we are made such by love;
Call her one, me another fly,   20
We are tapers too, and at our own cost die,
And we in us find th' Eagle and the Dove.
The Phoenix riddle hath more wit
By us; we two being one, are it.
So to one neutral thing both sexes fit,
We die and rise the same, and prove
Mysterious by this love.

We can die by it, if not live by love,
And if unfit for tombs and hearse

7. **stamped face:** on coins.
13. **forward:** early.
15. **plaguey bill:** list of deaths by the plague.
21. **tapers:** candles.
23. **Phoenix riddle:** the Phoenix was a bird said to die and to be reborn in flame.

Our legend be, it will be fit for verse;   30
And if no piece of chronicle we prove,
We'll build in sonnets pretty rooms;
As well a well-wrought urn becomes
The greatest ashes, as half-acre tombs,
And by these hymns, all shall approve
Us *Canonized* for Love,

And thus invoke us: You whom reverend love
Made one another's hermitage;
You, to whom love was peace, that now is rage;
Who did the whole world's soul contract, and drove   40
Into the glasses of your eyes
(So made such mirrors and such spies
That they did all to you epitomize),
Countries, Towns, Courts: Beg from above
A pattern of your love!

❧ *The Relic*

WHEN my grave is broken up again
Some second guest to entertain
(For graves have learned that womanhead
To be to more than one a bed)
And he that digs it, spies
A bracelet of bright hair about the bone,
Will he not let us alone,
And think that there a loving couple lies,
Who thought that this device might be some way
To make their souls, at the last busy day,   10
Meet at this grave, and make a little stay?

If this fall in a time, or land,
Where mis-devotion doth command,
Then he that digs us up will bring
Us to the Bishop and the King,
To make us relics; then
Thou shalt be a Mary Magdalen, and I
A something else thereby;
All women shall adore us, and some men;

43. **epitomize:** summarize.

16. **relics:** objects of religious veneration.
17. **Mary Magdalen:** a reformed sinner.
18. **a something else:** in Luke 7:37, Jesus forgave her sins.

And since at such time, miracles are sought,   20
I would have that age by this paper taught
What miracles we harmless lovers wrought.

First, we loved well and faithfully,
Yet knew not what we loved, nor why;
Difference of sex no more we knew
Than our guardian angels do;
Coming and going, we
Perchance might kiss, but not between those meals;
Our hands ne'er touched the seals
Which nature, injured by late law, sets free: 30
These miracles we did; but now alas,
All measure, and all language, I should pass
Should I tell what a miracle she was.

❦ *A Valediction Forbidding Mourning*

As virtuous men pass mildly away,
And whisper to their souls to go,
Whilst some of their sad friends do say,
The breath goes now, and some say, No;

So let us melt, and make no noise,
No tear-floods, nor sigh-tempests move;
'Twere profanation of our joys
To tell the laity our love.

Moving of the earth brings harms and fears,
Men reckon what it did, and meant;   10
But trepidation of the spheres,
Though greater far, is innocent.

Dull sublunary lovers' love
(Whose soul is sense) cannot admit
Absence, because it doth remove
Those things which elemented it.

22. **miracles:** to prove their saintliness.
30. **by late law:** the Commandments (?).

8. **laity:** those who know little of love.
11. **trepidation:** a tremor in the crystal spheres on which planets and stars were once thought to be arranged.
12. **innocent:** harmless.
13. **sublunary:** in one sense, ordinary, but note other possibilities.

But we by a love so much refined
That ourselves know not what it is,
Inter-assurèd of the mind,
Care less eyes, lips and hands to miss.   20

Our two souls therefore, which are one,
Though I must go, endure not yet
A breach, but an expansion,
Like gold to airy thinness beat.

If they be two, they are two so
As stiff twin compasses are two;
Thy soul, the fixed foot, makes no show
To move, but doth, if the other do.

And though it in the centre sit,
Yet, when the other far doth roam,   30
It leans, and hearkens after it,
And grows erect, as that comes home.

Such wilt thou be to me, who must,
Like the other foot, obliquely run;
Thy firmness makes my circle just,
And makes me end where I begun.

❦ *Holy Sonnets*

VII

At the round earth's imagined corners, blow
Your trumpets, angels, and arise, arise
From death, you numberless infinities
Of souls, and to your scattered bodies go;
All whom the flood did, and fire shall o'erthrow;
All whom war, dearth, age, agues, tyrannies,
Despair, law, chance, hath slain, and you whose eyes
Shall behold God, and never taste death's woe.
But let them sleep, Lord, and me mourn a space,
For, if above all these, my sins abound,
'Tis late to ask abundance of Thy grace,
When we are there; here on this lowly ground,
Teach me how to repent; for that's as good
As if Thou hadst sealed my pardon, with Thy blood.

X

DEATH, be not proud, though some have callèd thee
Mighty and dreadful, for thou art not so;
For those whom thou think'st thou dost overthrow
Die not, poor Death; nor yet canst thou kill me.
From rest and sleep, which but thy pictures be,
Much pleasure; then from thee much more must flow;
And soonest our best men with thee do go—
Rest of their bones and souls' delivery!
Thou'rt slave to fate, chance, kings, and desperate men,
And dost with poison, war, and sickness dwell;
And poppy or charms can make us sleep as well
And better than thy stroke. Why swell'st thou then?
One short sleep past, we wake eternally,
And Death shall be no more: Death, thou shalt die.

XIV

BATTER my heart, three personed God; for you
As yet but knock, breathe, shine, and seek to mend;
That I may rise and stand, o'erthrow me and bend
Your force to break, blow, burn and make me new.
I, like an usurped town, to another due,
Labour to admit you, but Oh, to no end;
Reason, your viceroy in me, me should defend,
But is captived and proves weak or untrue.
Yet dearly I love you and would be loved fain,
But am betrothed unto your enemy: 10
Divorce me, untie or break that knot again,
Take me to you, imprison me, for I,
Except you enthrall me, never shall be free,
Nor ever chaste, except you ravish me.

ROBERT HERRICK

❧ *To the Sour Reader*

IF thou dislik'st the piece thou light'st on first,
Think that of all, that I have writ, the worst;
But if thou read'st my book unto the end,
And still do'st this, and that verse, reprehend,
O perverse man! If all disgustful be,
The extreme scab take thee, and thine, for me.

7. **viceroy:** reason is God's governing representative in the body.
9. **fain:** an inversion—I would *gladly* be loved.
13. **enthrall:** hold captive.

❧ *Delight in Disorder*

A SWEET disorder in the dress
Kindles in clothes a wantonness:
A lawn about the shoulders thrown
Into a fine distraction,
An erring lace, which here and there
Enthralls the crimson stomacher,
A cuff neglectful, and thereby
Ribbands to flow confusedly,
A winning wave (deserving note)
In the tempestuous petticoat,   10
A careless shoe-string, in whose tie
I see a wild civility,
Do more bewitch me, than when art
Is too precise in every part.

❧ *Upon Prue His Maid*

IN this little urne is laid
Prewdence Baldwin (once my maid)
From whose happy spark here let
Spring the purple violet.

❧ *To the Virgins, To Make Much of Time*

GATHER ye rose-buds while ye may,
Old Time is still a-flying:
And this same flower that smiles today,
Tomorrow will be dying.

The glorious lamp of heaven, the Sun,
The higher he's a-getting

3. **lawn:** sheer linen or cotten fabric.
6. **stomacher:** ornamental covering for the bosom.
8. **Ribbands:** ribbons.

The sooner will his race be run,
And nearer he's to setting.

That age is best which is the first,
When youth and blood are warmer;
But being spent, the worse, and worst
Times, still succeed the former.

Then be not coy, but use your time;
And while ye may, go marry:
For having lost but once your prime,
You may for ever tarry.

❧ *Corinna's Going A-Maying*

GET up, get up for shame! The blooming morn
Upon her wings presents the god unshorn.
See how Aurora throws her fair,
Fresh-quilted colors through the air.
Get up, sweet slug-a-bed, and see
The dew bespangling herb and tree!
Each flower has wept and bowed toward the east
Above an hour since, yet you not drest;
Nay! not so much as out of bed?
When all the birds have matins said   10
And sung their thankful hymns, 'tis sin,
Nay, profanation, to keep in,
Whenas a thousand virgins on this day
Spring sooner than the lark, to fetch in May.

Rise and put on your foliage, and be seen
To come forth, like the springtime, fresh and green,
And sweet as Flora. Take no care
For jewels for your gown or hair.
Fear not; the leaves will strew
Gems in abundance upon you.   20
Besides, the childhood of the day has kept

2. **god unshorn:** Apollo, the sun god.
3. **Aurora:** goddess of dawn.
10. **matins:** morning prayers.
17. **Flora:** goddess of flowers and plants.

Against you come, some orient pearls unwept.
Come, and receive them while the light
Hangs on the dew-locks of the night;
And Titan on the eastern hill
Retires himself, or else stands still
Till you come forth! Wash, dress, be brief in praying;
Few beads are best when once we go a-Maying.

Come, my Corinna, come; and coming, mark
How each field turns a street, each street a park,   30
Made green and trimmed with trees! see how
Devotion gives each house a bough
Or branch! each porch, each door, ere this,
An ark, a tabernacle is,
Made up of white-thorn neatly interwove,
As if here were those cooler shades of love.
Can such delights be in the street
And open fields, and we not see't?
Come, we'll abroad; and let's obey
The proclamation made for May,   40
And sin no more, as we have done, by staying;
But, my Corinna, come, let's go a-Maying.

There's not a budding boy or girl this day
But is got up and gone to bring in May.
A deal of youth ere this is come
Back, and with white-thorn laden home.
Some have dispatched their cakes and cream,
Before that we have left to dream;
And some have wept and wooed, and plighted troth,
And chose their priest, ere we can cast off sloth.   50
Many a green-gown has been given,
Many a kiss, both odd and even;
Many a glance, too, has been sent
From out the eye, love's firmament;
Many a jest told of the keys betraying
This night, and locks picked; yet we're not a-Maying!

Come, let us go, while we are in our prime,
And take the harmless folly of the time!

22. **unwept:** not yet shed, as tears.
32. **Devotion . . . bough:** refers to custom of decorating on May Day.
51. **green-gown:** grass stains.
52. **odd and even:** either stolen (by one) or enjoyed by two.

We shall grow old apace, and die
Before we know our liberty.   60
Our life is short, and our days run
As fast away as does the sun.
And, as a vapor or a drop of rain,
Once lost, can ne'er be found again,
So when or you or I are made
A fable, song, or fleeting shade,
All love, all liking, all delight
Lies drowned with us in endless night.
Then, while time serves, and we are but decaying,
Come, my Corinna, come, let's go a-Maying.   70

❧ His Desire

Give me a man that is not dull,
When all the world with rifts is full;
But unamazed dares clearly sing,
Whenas the roof's a-tottering;
And, though it falls, continues still
Tickling the cittern with his quill.

❧ To Daffodils

Fair daffodils, we weep to see
You haste away so soon;
As yet the early-rising sun
Has not attained his noon.
Stay, stay,
Until the hasting day
Has run
But to the even-song;
And, having prayed together, we
Will go with you along.

We have short time to stay, as you;
We have as short a spring;

6. **cittern:** a stringed instrument resembling a mandolin.

As quick a growth to meet decay,
As you, or any thing.
We die,
As your hours do, and dry
Away,
Like to the summer's rain,
Or as the pearls of morning dew,
Ne'r to be found again.

GEORGE HERBERT

❧ *Easter Wings*

LORD, who createdst man in wealth and store,
    Though foolishly he lost the same,
        Decaying more and more,
           Till he became
           Most poor;

           With thee
           O let me rise,
        As larks, harmoniously,
    And sing this day thy victories;
Then shall the fall further the flight in me.   10

    My tender age in sorrow did begin;
  And still with sicknesses and shame
      Thou didst so punish sin,
          That I became
          Most thin.

         With thee
        Let me combine,
     And feel this day thy victory;
  For, if I imp my wing on thine,
Affliction shall advance the flight in me.   20

---

10. **the fall:** in two senses, as the fall of man redeemed by Christ and the gliding fall of the lark from the height it has reached.
19. **imp:** to graft on, as when new feathers are attached to a falcon's wing.

❧ *The Collar*

I STRUCK the board, and cried, No more;
I will abroad!
What? shall I ever sigh and pine?
My lines and life are free; free as the road,
Loose as the wind, as large as store;
Shall I be still in suit?
Have I no harvest but a thorn
To let me blood, and not restore
What I have lost with cordial fruit?
Sure there was wine   10
Before my sighs did dry it; there was corn
Before my tears did drown it.
Is the year only lost to me?
Have I no bays to crown it?
No flowers, no garlands gay? all blasted?
All wasted?
Not so, my heart: but there is fruit,
And thou hast hands.
Recover all thy sigh-blown age
On double pleasures: leave thy cold dispute   20
Of what is fit, and not; forsake thy cage,
Thy rope of sands,
Which petty thoughts have made, and made to thee
Good cable, to enforce and draw,
And be thy law,
While thou didst wink and wouldst not see.
Away; take heed:
I will abroad.
Call in thy death's head there; tie up thy fears.
He that forbears   30
To suit and serve his need,
Deserves his load.
But as I raved and grew more fierce and wild
At every word,
Methought I heard one calling, *Child;*
And I replied, *My Lord.*

"The Collar": since Herbert was a country parson, the collar here may be clerical, or
a pun on "choler" (anger), or both.

❧ *The Pulley*

WHEN God at first made man,
Having a glass of blessings standing by,
Let us (said he) pour on him all we can;
Let the world's riches, which dispersed lie,
Contract into a span.

So strength first made a way,
Then beauty flowed, then wisdom, honour, pleasure;
When almost all was out, God made a stay,
Perceiving that, alone of all His treasure,
Rest in the bottom lay.

For if I should (said he)
Bestow this jewel also on My creature,
He would adore My gifts instead of Me,
And rest in Nature, not the God of Nature;
So both should losers be.

Yet let him keep the rest,
But keep them with repining restlessness;
Let him be rich and weary, that at least,
If goodness lead him not, yet weariness
May toss him to My breast.

EDMUND WALLER

❧ *Go, Lovely Rose*

Go, lovely rose—
Tell her that wastes her time and me
That now she knows,
When I resemble her to thee,
How sweet and fair she seems to be.

Tell her that's young,
And shuns to have her graces spied,
That hadst thou sprung
In deserts where no men abide,
Thou must have uncommended died.

Small is the worth
Of beauty from the light retired:
Bid her come forth,
Suffer herself to be desired,
And not blush so to be admired.

Then die—that she
The common fate of all things rare
May read in thee:
How small a part of time they share
That are so wondrous sweet and fair.

JOHN MILTON

❧ How Soon Hath Time

How soon hath Time, the subtle thief of youth,
Stol'n on his wing my three-and-twentieth year!
My hasting days fly on with full career,
But my late spring no bud or blossom shew'th.
Perhaps my semblance might deceive the truth,
That I to manhood am arrived so near,
And inward ripeness doth much less appear,
That some more timely-happy spirits indu'th.
Yet be it less or more, or soon or slow,
It shall be still in strictest measure even,
To that same lot, however mean or high,
Toward which Time leads me, and the will of Heaven;
All is, if I have grace to use it so,
As ever in my great Taskmaster's eye.

❧ When I Consider How My Light Is Spent

WHEN I consider how my light is spent
Ere half my days in this dark world and wide,
And that one talent which is death to hide
Lodged with me useless, though my soul more bent

1. **my light:** Milton became totally blind in 1651.
3. **talent:** poetic talent, of course, but also refers to the parable of the talents of silver (Matthew 25:14–30).

To serve therewith my Maker, and present
My true account, lest he returning chide,
Doth God exact day-labor, light denied?
I fondly ask. But Patience, to prevent
That murmur, soon replies, "God does not need
Either man's work or his own gifts. Who best   10
Bear his mild yoke, they serve him best. His state
Is kingly: thousands at His bidding speed,
And post o'er land and ocean without rest;
They also serve who only stand and wait."

❧ *Lycidas*

YET once more, O ye laurels, and once more,
Ye myrtles brown, with ivy never sere,
I come to pluck your berries harsh and crude,
And with forced fingers rude
Shatter your leaves before the mellowing year.
Bitter constraint and sad occasion dear
Compels me to disturb your season due:
For Lycidas is dead, dead ere his prime,
Young Lycidas, and hath not left his peer.
Who would not sing for Lycidas? he knew   10
Himself to sing, and build the lofty rhyme.
He must not float upon his watery bier
Unwept, and welter to the parching wind,
Without the meed of some melodious tear.
    Begin then, Sisters of the sacred well
That from beneath the seat of Jove doth spring;
Begin, and somewhat loudly sweep the string;
Hence with denial vain and coy excuse:
So may some gentle Muse
With lucky words favor *my* destined urn;   20
And as he passes, turn
And bid fair peace be to my sable shroud.
For we were nursed upon the self-same hill,
Fed the same flock by fountain, shade, and rill.
Together both, ere the high lawns appeared

"Lycidas": This poem is a pastoral elegy (see Glossary) on the death of Edward King,
Milton's fellow student at Cambridge. King was drowned in 1637 while on a voyage
to Ireland where he was to assume his duties as a pastor.
1–2. **Laurels, myrtles, ivy:** symbols of poetic excellence, which Milton doubted his
readiness to gather.
15. **Sisters . . . well:** the muses, born in a fountain under Mt. Olympus.

Under the opening eye-lids of the Morn,
We drove a-field, and both together heard
What time the gray-fly winds her sultry horn,
Battening our flocks with the fresh dews of night,
Oft till the star, that rose at evening bright,   30
Toward heaven's descent had sloped his westering wheel.
Meanwhile the rural ditties were not mute;
Tempered to the oaten flute,
Rough Satyrs danced, and Fauns with cloven heel
From the glad sound would not be absent long;
And old Damoetas loved to hear our song.

　　But, O! the heavy change, now thou art gone,
Now thou art gone, and never must return!
Thee, Shepherd, thee the woods and desert caves,
With wild thyme and the gadding vine o'ergrown,   40
And all their echoes, mourn:
The willows and the hazel copses green
Shall now no more be seen
Fanning their joyous leaves to thy soft lays.
As killing as the canker to the rose,
Or taint-worm to the weanling herds that graze,
Or frost to flowers, that their gay wardrobe wear
When first the white-thorn blows,
Such, Lycidas, thy loss to shepherd's ear.

　　Where were ye, Nymphs, when the remorseless deep   50
Closed o'er the head of your loved Lycidas?
For neither were ye playing on the steep
Where your old bards, the famous Druids, lie,
Nor on the shaggy top of Mona high,
Nor yet where Deva spreads her wizard stream.
Ay me! I fondly dream
"Had ye been there"—for what could that have done?
What could the Muse herself that Orpheus bore,
The Muse herself, for her enchanting son,
Whom universal nature did lament,   60
When by the rout that made the hideous roar

28. **What time:** noon.
29. **Battening:** fattening.
34. **Satyrs, Fauns:** Pagan demigods, inhabitants of woods and rural areas, noted for lascivious merriment.
36. **Damoetas:** unknown, probably a friend or tutor at Cambridge.
40. **gadding:** wandering.
54. **Mona:** an island off Wales.
55. **Deva:** the River Dee.
58–59. **What . . . herself:** Calliope, Orpheus' mother, was unable to prevent a mob from cutting off his head and throwing it into the Hebrus.

His gory visage down the stream was sent,
Down the swift Hebrus to the Lesbian shore?
   Alas! what boots it with uncessant care
To tend the homely, slighted, shepherd's trade
And strictly meditate the thankless Muse?
Were it not better done, as others use,
To sport with Amaryllis in the shade,
Or with the tangles of Neaera's hair?
Fame is the spur that the clear spirit doth raise   70
(That last infirmity of noble mind)
To scorn delights, and live laborious days;
But the fair guerdon when we hope to find,
And think to burst out into sudden blaze,
Comes the blind Fury with the abhorred shears
And slits the thin-spun life. "But not the praise,"
Phoebus replied, and touched my trembling ears:
"Fame is no plant that grows on mortal soil,
Nor in the glistering foil
Set off to the world, nor in broad rumor lies,   80
But lives and spreads aloft by those pure eyes
And perfect witness of all-judging Jove;
As he pronounces lastly on each deed,
Of so much fame in heaven expect thy meed."
   O fountain Arethuse, and thou honored flood,
Smooth-sliding Mincius, crowned with vocal reeds,
That strain I heard was of a higher mood.
But now my oat proceeds,
And listens to the herald of the sea
That came in Neptune's plea;   90
He asked the waves, and asked the felon winds,
What hard mishap hath doomed this gentle swain?
And questioned every gust of rugged wings
That blows from off each beaked promontory:
They knew not of his story;
And sage Hippotades their answer brings,
That not a blast was from his dungeon strayed;

64. **boots it:** what good is it?
64. **uncessant:** unceasing.
68. **Amaryllis, Neaera's:** shepherdesses.
73. **guerdon:** reward.
75. **Fury:** one of the three Fates.
77. **Phoebus:** Apollo, god of poetry and music.
85. **Arethuse:** a spring at Syracuse representing pastoral poetry.
86. **Mincius:** a river in Lombardy, also suggesting the pastoral mode.
89. **herald of the sea:** Triton.
90. **Neptune's plea:** Neptune has sent Triton as his representative.
96. **Hippotades:** God of winds.

The air was calm, and on the level brine
Sleek Panope with all her sisters played.
It was that fatal and perfidious bark,   100
Built in the eclipse, and rigged with curses dark,
That sunk so low that sacred head of thine.
    Next Camus, reverend sire, went footing slow,
His mantle hairy, and his bonnet sedge,
Inwrought with figures dim, and on the edge
Like to that sanguine flower inscribed with woe.
"Ah! who hath reft," quoth he, "my dearest pledge?"
Last came, and last did go
The Pilot of the Galilean lake;
Two massy keys he bore of metals twain   110
(The golden opes, the iron shuts amain);
He shook his mitred locks, and stern bespake:
"How well could I have spared for thee, young swain,
Enow of such, as for their bellies' sake
Creep and intrude and climb into the fold!
Of other care they little reckoning make
Than how to scramble at the shearers' feast,
And shove away the worthy bidden guest.
Blind mouths! that scarce themselves know how to hold
A sheep-hook, or have learned aught else the least   120
That to the faithful herdsman's art belongs!
What recks it them? What need they? They are sped;
And when they list, their lean and flashy songs
Grate on their scrannel pipes of wretched straw;
The hungry sheep look up, and are not fed,
But, swol'n with wind and the rank mist they draw,
Rot inwardly, and foul contagion spread:
Besides what the grim wolf with privy paw
Daily devours apace, and nothing said:
—But that two-handed engine at the door   130
Stands ready to smite once, and smite no more."

99. **Panope:** a nereid, or sea-nymph, to whom mariners prayed.
103. **Camus:** the river Cam, associated, of course, with Cambridge University.
106. **sanguine flower:** the Greek hyacinth, which appears to have Greek letters denoting woe within it.
109. **Pilot . . . lake:** St. Peter.
112. **mitred:** as first bishop, he wears a mitre.
120. **sheep-hook:** the shepherd's crook.
122. **recks it:** what do they know of it?
123. **list:** when they wish.
124. **scrannel:** harsh, thin.
128. **grim wolf:** probably the Roman Catholic Church.
130. **two-handed engine:** the two houses of Parliament is one of many possibilities.

Return, Alpheus; the dread voice is past
That shrunk thy streams; return, Sicilian Muse,
And call the vales, and bid them hither cast
Their bells and flowerets of a thousand hues.
Ye valleys low, where the mild whispers use
Of shades, and wanton winds, and gushing brooks
On whose fresh lap the swart star sparely looks;
Throw hither all your quaint enameled eyes
That on the green turf suck the honeyed showers,   140
And purple all the ground with vernal flowers.
Bring the rathe primrose that forsaken dies,
The tufted crow-toe, and pale jessamine,
The white pink, and the pansy freaked with jet,
The glowing violet,
The musk-rose, and the well-attired woodbine,
With cowslips wan that hang the pensive head,
And every flower that sad embroidery wears;
Bid amaranthus all his beauty shed,
And daffadillies fill their cups with tears   150
To strew the laureate hearse where Lycid lies.
For so to interpose a little ease,
Let our frail thoughts dally with false surmise,
Ay me! whilst thee the shores and sounding seas
Wash far away, where'er thy bones are hurled;
Whether beyond the stormy Hebrides
Where thou, perhaps, under the whelming tide,
Visit'st the bottom of the monstrous world;
Or whether thou, to our moist vows denied,
Sleep'st by the fable of Bellerus old,   160
Where the great Vision of the guarded mount
Looks toward Namancos and Bayona's hold.
Look homeward, Angel, now, and melt with ruth:
And, O ye dolphins, waft the hapless youth!
Weep no more, woeful shepherds, weep no more,

132. **Alpheus:** personification of an Arcadian river; hence, pastoral poetry.
138. **swart:** swarthy, dark.
142. **rathe:** early.
143. **crow-toe:** probably the buttercup, but anemones, clematis, and peonies belong
to the family.
144. **freaked:** streaked.
149. **amaranthus:** a purple flower supposed never to fade.
151. **laureate:** decked with laurel.
156. **Hebrides:** islands off the coast of Scotland.
160. **Bellerus:** a giant said to be buried in Cornwall.
162. **Namancos, Bayona's:** Spanish strongholds.
163. **ruth:** pity. The angel is asked to forget the Spanish threat to England for a
moment and protect Lycidas' body.
164. **dolphins:** popularly supposed to assist drowning sailors.

For Lycidas, your sorrow, is not dead,
Sunk though he be beneath the watery floor;
So sinks the day-star in the ocean bed,
And yet anon repairs his drooping head,
And tricks his beams, and with new-spangled ore   170
Flames in the forehead of the morning sky:
So Lycidas sunk low, but mounted high
Through the dear might of Him that walked the waves,
Where, other groves and other streams along,
With nectar pure his oozy locks he laves,
And hears the unexpressive nuptial song
In the blest kingdoms meek of joy and love.
There entertain him all the saints above
In solemn troops, and sweet societies,
That sing, and singing in their glory move,   180
And wipe the tears for ever from his eyes.
Now, Lycidas, the shepherds weep no more;
Henceforth thou art the Genius of the shore
In thy large recompense, and shalt be good
To all that wander in that perilous flood.
     Thus sang the uncouth swain to the oaks and rills,
While the still morn went out with sandals gray;
He touched the tender stops of various quills,
With eager thought warbling his Doric lay:
And now the sun had stretched out all the hills,   190
And now was dropt into the western bay.
At last he rose, and twitched his mantle blue:
Tomorrow to fresh woods, and pastures new.

RICHARD CRASHAW

❦ *I Am the Door*

AND now th'art set wide ope, the spear's sad art,
Lo! hath unlocked thee at the very heart;
He to himself (I fear the worst)
And his own hope,
Hath shut these doors of heaven that durst
Thus set them ope.

183. **Genius:** the god of the shore.
189. **Doric:** rustic or pastoral.

RICHARD LOVELACE

❧ *To Lucasta, Going to the Wars*

TELL me not (Sweet) I am unkind,
That from the nunnery
Of thy chaste breast and quiet mind,
To war and arms I fly.

True: a new mistress now I chase,
The first foe in the field;
And with a stronger faith embrace
A sword, a horse, a shield.

Yet this inconstancy is such
As you too shall adore;
I could not love thee (Dear) so much,
Loved I not honour more.

❧ *Strive Not, Vain Lover, to Be Fine*

STRIVE not, vain lover, to be fine,
Thy silk's the silk-worm's, and not thine;
You lessen to a fly your mistress thought,
To think it may be in a cobweb caught.
What though her thin transparent lawn
Thy heart in a strong net hath drawn?
Not all the arms the god of fire ere made,
Can the soft bulwarks of naked love invade.

Be truly fine then, and your self dress
In her fair soul's immaculate glass: 10
Then by reflection you may have the bliss,
Perhaps, to see what a true fineness is;
When all your gauderies will fit
Those only that are poor in wit:
She that a *clinquant* outside doth adore,
Dotes on a gilded statue, and no more.

15. **clinquant:** cheaply glittering.

ANDREW MARVELL

❧ *To His Coy Mistress*

HAD we but world enough, and time,
This coyness, lady, were no crime.
We would sit down, and think which way
To walk, and pass our long love's day.
Thou by the Indian Ganges' side
Should'st rubies find; I by the tide
Of Humber would complain. I would
Love you ten years before the Flood,
And you should, if you please, refuse
Till the conversion of the Jews.   10
My vegetable love should grow
Vaster than empires, and more slow.
An hundred years should go to praise
Thine eyes, and on thy forehead gaze;
Two hundred to adore each breast;
But thirty thousand to the rest;
An age at least to every part,
And the last age should show your heart.
For, lady, you deserve this state,
Nor would I love at lower rate.   20
But at my back I always hear
Time's wingèd chariot hurrying near;
And yonder all before us lie
Deserts of vast eternity.
Thy beauty shall no more be found,
Nor, in thy marble vault, shall sound
My echoing song: then worms shall try
That long-preserved virginity,
And your quaint honor turn to dust,
And into ashes all my lust.   30
The grave's a fine and private place,
But none, I think, do there embrace.
Now, therefore, while the youthful hue
Sits on thy skin like morning dew,
And while thy willing soul transpires
At every pore with instant fires,
Now let us sport us while we may;
And now, like amorous birds of prey,
Rather at once our time devour,

35. **soul transpires:** exhales through the skin (she is blushing).

Than languish in his slow-chapt power.   40
Let us roll all our strength and all
Our sweetness up into one ball,
And tear our pleasures with rough strife
Thorough the iron gates of life.
Thus, though we cannot make our sun
Stand still, yet we will make him run.

❧ *The Garden*

How vainly men themselves amaze
To win the palm, the oak, or bays;
And their incessant labors see
Crowned from some single herb, or tree,
Whose short and narrow-vergèd shade
Does prudently their toils upbraid;
While all flowers and all trees do close
To weave the garlands of repose!

Fair Quiet, have I found thee here,
And Innocence, thy sister dear?   10
Mistaken long, I sought you then
In busy companies of men.
Your sacred plants, if here below,
Only among the plants will grow;
Society is all but rude
To this delicious solitude.

No white nor red was ever seen
So amorous as this lovely green.
Fond lovers, cruel as their flame,
Cut in these trees their mistress' name: 20
Little, alas! they know or heed
How far these beauties hers exceed!
Fair trees! wheres'e'er your barks I wound
No name shall but your own be found.

When we have run our passion's heat,
Love hither makes his best retreat.
The gods, that mortal beauty chase,
Still in a tree did end their race;
Apollo hunted Daphne so,
Only that she might laurel grow;   30

40. **slow-chapt:** slowly chewing.

29–31. **Apollo . . . Pan:** Daphne escaped Apollo by becoming a laurel; Syrinx became a reed to avoid Pan's attentions.

And Pan did after Syrinx speed,
Not as a nymph, but for a reed.

What wondrous life is this I lead!
Ripe apples drop about my head;
The luscious clusters of the vine
Upon my mouth do crush their wine;
The nectarine, and curious peach,
Into my hands themselves do reach;
Stumbling on melons, as I pass,
Ensnared with flowers, I fall on grass.   40

Meanwhile, the mind, from pleasure less,
Withdraws into its happiness:
The mind, that ocean where each kind
Does straight its own resemblance find;
Yet it creates, transcending these,
Far other worlds, and other seas;
Annihilating all that's made
To a green thought in a green shade.

Here at the fountain's sliding foot,
Or at some fruit-tree's mossy root,   50
Casting the body's vest aside,
My soul into the boughs does glide:
There like a bird it sits, and sings,
Then whets and combs its silver wings;
And, till prepared for longer flight,
Waves in its plumes the various light.

Such was that happy garden-state,
While man there walked without a mate:
After a place so pure and sweet,
What other help could yet be meet?   60
But 'twas beyond a mortal's share
To wander solitary there:
Two paradises 'twere in one,
To live in paradise alone.

How well the skillful gardener drew
Of flowers, and herbs, this dial new;
Where, from above, the milder sun
Does through a fragrant zodiac run;
And, as it works, the industrious bee
Computes its time as well as we.   70
How could such sweet and wholesome hours
Be reckoned but with herbs and flowers!

51. **vest:** vestment or clothing.
66. **dial:** timepiece.

❧ *The Retreat*

HAPPY those early days, when I
Shined in my angel-infancy!
Before I understood this place
Appointed for my second race,
Or taught my soul to fancy ought
But a white, celestial thought;
When yet I had not walked above
A mile or two from my first love;
And looking back, at that short space,
Could see a glimpse of His bright face;   10
When on some gilded cloud or flower,
My gazing soul would dwell an hour,
And in those weaker glories spy
Some shadows of eternity;
Before I taught my tongue to wound
My conscience with a sinful sound,
Or had the black art to dispense
A several sin to every sense,
But felt through all this fleshy dress
Bright shoots of everlastingness.   20
O how I long to travel back,
And tread again that ancient track!
That I might once more reach that plain,
Where first I left my glorious train;
From whence the enlightened spirit sees
That shady city of palm trees.
But ah! my soul with too much stay
Is drunk, and staggers in the way!
Some men a forward motion love,
But I by backward steps would move;   30
And, when this dust falls to the urn,
In that state I came, return.

2. **angel-infancy:** this entire poem depends on a doctrine of pre-existence; compare Wordsworth, "Ode: Intimations of Immortality."
18. **several:** different.
24. **train:** retinue.
26. **city of palm trees:** the Heavenly City.

ALEXANDER POPE

❧ *The Rape of the Lock*

CANTO I

WHAT dire offense from am'rous causes springs,
What mighty contests rise from trivial things,
I sing—This verse to CARYL, Muse! is due:
This, even Belinda may vouchsafe to view:
Slight is the subject, but not so the praise,
If she inspire, and he approve my lays.
    Say what strange motive, Goddess! could compel
A well-bred lord t' assault a gentle belle?
O say what stranger cause, yet unexplored,
Could make a gentle belle reject a lord?   10
In tasks so bold, can little men engage,
And in soft bosoms dwells such mighty rage?
    Sol through white curtains shot a tim'rous ray,
And oped those eyes that must eclipse the day:
Now lap-dogs give themselves the rousing shake,
And sleepless lovers, just at twelve, awake:
Thrice rung the bell, the slipper knocked the ground,
And the pressed watch returned a silver sound.
Belinda still her downy pillow prest,
Her guardian sylph prolonged the balmy rest: 20
'Twas he had summoned to her silent bed
The morning-dream that hovered o'er her head;
A youth more glitt'ring than a Birth-night beau,
(That even in slumber caused her cheek to glow)
Seemed to her ear his winning lips to lay,
And thus in whispers said, or seemed to say:
    Fairest of mortals, thou distinguished care
Of thousand bright inhabitants of air!
If e'er one vision touched thy infant thought,
Of all the nurse and all the priest have taught;   30
Of airy elves by moonlight shadows seen,

3. **Caryl:** John Caryl, a friend of Pope's, suggested that he write the poem as a
means of cooling tempers after Miss Arabella Fermor—Belinda—lost a lock of her hair
to Lord Petre in the manner the poem describes.
18. **pressed watch:** a repeater, which rang the hour when the stem was pressed.
23. **Birth-night:** the queen's birthday celebration, an annual affair.

The silver token, and the circled green,
Or virgins visited by angel-powers,
With golden crowns and wreaths of heav'nly flowers;
Hear and believe! thy own importance know,
Nor bound thy narrow views to things below.
Some secret truths, from learnèd pride concealed,
To maids alone and children are revealed:
What though no credit doubting wits may give?
The fair and innocent shall still believe.   40
Know, then, unnumbered spirits round thee fly,
The light militia of the lower sky:
These, though unseen, are ever on the wing,
Hang o'er the box, and hover round the ring.
Think what an equipage thou hast in air,
And view with scorn two pages and a chair.
As now your own, our beings were of old,
And once inclosed in woman's beauteous mould;
Thence, by a soft transition, we repair
From earthly vehicles to these of air.   50
Think not, when woman's transient breath is fled,
That all her vanities at once are dead;
Succeeding vanities she still regards,
And though she plays no more, o'erlooks the cards.
Her joy in gilded chariots, when alive,
And love of ombre, after death survive.
For when the fair in all their pride expire,
To their first elements their souls retire:
The sprites of fiery termagants in flame
Mount up, and take a salamander's name.   60
Soft yielding minds to water glide away,
And sip, with nymphs, their elemental tea.
The graver prude sinks downward to a gnome,
In search of mischief still on earth to roam.
The light coquettes in sylphs aloft repair,
And sport and flutter in the fields of air.
    Know further yet; whoever fair and chaste
Rejects mankind, is by some sylph embraced:

32. **silver token . . . circled green:** evidences of fairies. A coin or token was left when they stole cream; the "fairy-ring" showed where they had danced. The latter has been explained by some as a lawn disease.
44. **box:** at the theater.
44. **ring:** circular drive in Hyde Park, London.
46. **chair:** sedan chair.
56. **ombre:** a complicated card game a little like euchre.
59. **sprites:** spirits.
59. **termagants:** loud, scolding women.
60–65. **salamanders, nymphs, gnomes, sylphs:** types of spirits corresponding respectively to the elements of fire, water, earth, and air. Ariel is a sylph.

For spirits, freed from mortal laws, with ease
Assume what sexes and what shapes they please.   70
What guards the purity of melting maids,
In courtly balls, and midnight masquerades,
Safe from the treach'rous friend, the daring spark,
The glance by day, the whisper in the dark,
When kind occasion prompts their warm desires,
When music softens, and when dancing fires?
'Tis but their sylph, the wise celestials know,
Though honor is the word with men below.
    Some nymphs there are, too conscious of their face,
For life predestined to the gnomes' embrace.   80
These swell their prospects and exalt their pride,
When offers are disdained, and love denied:
Then gay ideas crowd the vacant brain,
While Peers, and Dukes, and all their sweeping train,
And Garters, Stars, and Coronets appear,
And in soft sounds, "Your Grace" salutes their ear.
'Tis these that early taint the female soul,
Instruct the eyes of young coquettes to roll,
Teach infant-cheeks a bidden blush to know,
And little hearts to flutter at a beau.   90
    Oft, when the world imagine women stray,
The sylphs through mystic mazes guide their way,
Through all the giddy circle they pursue,
And old impertinence expel by new.
What tender maid but must a victim fall
To one man's treat, but for another's ball?
When Florio speaks what virgin could withstand,
If gentle Damon did not squeeze her hand?
With varying vanities, from every part,
They shift the moving toyshop of their heart;   100
Where wigs with wigs, with sword-knots sword-knots strive,
Beaux banish beaux, and coaches coaches drive.
This erring mortals levity may call;
Oh blind to truth! the sylphs contrive it all.
    Of these am I, who thy protection claim,
A watchful sprite, and Ariel is my name.
Late, as I ranged the crystal wilds of air,
In the clear mirror of thy ruling star,
I saw, alas! some dread event impend,
Ere to the main this morning sun descend,   110
But heaven reveals not what, or how, or where:
Warned by the sylph, oh pious maid, beware!

97–98. **Florio, Damon:** conventional names for beaux.
103. **levity:** lack of constancy, frivolity.
110. **main:** (western) ocean.

This to disclose is all thy guardian can:
Beware of all, but most beware of man!
    He said; when Shock, who thought she slept too long,
Leaped up, and waked his mistress with his tongue.
'Twas then, Belinda, if report say true,
Thy eyes first opened on a billet-doux;
Wounds, charms, and ardors were no sooner read,
But all the vision vanished from thy head.   120
    And now, unveiled, the toilet stands displayed,
Each silver vase in mystic order laid.
First, robed in white, the nymph intent adores,
With head uncovered, the cosmetic powers.
A heav'nly image in the glass appears,
To that she bends, to that her eyes she rears;
Th' inferior priestess, at her altar's side,
Trembling begins the sacred rites of Pride.
Unnumbered treasures ope at once, and here
The various off'rings of the world appear;   130
From each she nicely culls with curious toil,
And decks the goddess with the glitt'ring spoil.
This casket India's glowing gems unlocks,
And all Arabia breathes from yonder box.
The tortoise here and elephant unite,
Transformed to combs, the speckled, and the white.
Here files of pins extend their shining rows,
Puffs, powders, patches, Bibles, billet-doux.
Now awful Beauty puts on all its arms;
The fair each moment rises in her charms,   140
Repairs her smiles, awakens every grace,
And calls forth all the wonders of her face;
Sees by degrees a purer blush arise,
And keener lightnings quicken in her eyes.
The busy sylphs surround their darling care,
These set the head, and those divide the hair,
Some fold the sleeve, whilst others plait the gown;
And Betty's praised for labors not her own.

CANTO II
    Not with more glories, in th' ethereal plain,
The Sun first rises o'er the purpled main,

115. **Shock:** Belinda's dog.
118. **billet-doux:** love note.
121. **toilet:** vanity table.
127. **inferior priestess:** Belinda's maid.
148. **Betty:** conventional name for a maid.

Than, issuing forth, the rival of his beams
Launched on the bosom of the silver Thames.
Fair nymphs, and well-drest youths around her shone,
But every eye was fixed on her alone.
On her white breast a sparkling cross she wore,
Which Jews might kiss, and infidels adore.
Her lively looks a sprightly mind disclose,
Quick as her eyes, and as unfixed as those: 10
Favors to none, to all she smiles extends;
Oft she rejects, but never once offends.
Bright as the sun, her eyes the gazers strike,
And, like the sun, they shine on all alike.
Yet graceful ease, and sweetness void of pride,
Might hide her faults, if belles had faults to hide:
If to her share some female errors fall,
Look on her face, and you'll forget 'em all.
    This nymph, to the destruction of mankind,
Nourished two locks, which graceful hung behind   20
In equal curls, and well conspired to deck
With shining ringlets the smooth iv'ry neck.
Love in these labyrinths his slaves detains,
And mighty hearts are held in slender chains.
With hairy springes we the birds betray,
Slight lines of hair surprise the finny prey,
Fair tresses man's imperial race ensnare,
And beauty draws us with a single hair.
    Th' advent'rous baron the bright locks admired;
He saw, he wished, and to the prize aspired.   30
Resolved to win, he meditates the way,
By force to ravish, or by fraud betray;
For when success a lover's toil attends,
Few ask, if fraud or force attained his ends.
    For this, ere Phœbus rose, he had implored
Propitious heaven, and every power adored,
But chiefly Love—to Love an altar built,
Of twelve vast French romances, neatly gilt.
There lay three garters, half a pair of gloves;
And all the trophies of his former loves;   40
With tender billet-doux he lights the pyre,
And breathes three am'rous sighs to raise the fire.
Then prostrate falls, and begs with ardent eyes
Soon to obtain, and long possess the prize:
The powers gave ear, and granted half his prayer,
The rest, the winds dispersed in empty air.
    But now secure the painted vessel glides,

25. **springes:** snares.

The sun-beams trembling on the floating tides:
While melting music steals upon the sky,
And softened sounds along the waters die;   50
Smooth flow the waves, the zephyrs gently play,
Belinda smiled, and all the world was gay.
All but the sylph—with careful thoughts opprest,
Th' impending woe sat heavy on his breast.
He summons strait his denizens of air;
The lucid squadrons round the sails repair:
Soft o'er the shrouds aërial whispers breathe,
That seemed but zephyrs to the train beneath.
Some to the sun their insect-wings unfold,
Waft on the breeze, or sink in clouds of gold;   60
Transparent forms, too fine for mortal sight,
Their fluid bodies half dissolved in light,
Loose to the wind their airy garments flew,
Thin glitt'ring textures of the filmy dew,
Dipt in the richest tincture of the skies,
Where light disports in ever-mingling dyes,
While every beam new transient colors flings,
Colors that change whene'er they wave their wings.
Amid the circle, on the gilded mast,
Superior by the head, was Ariel placed;   70
His purple pinions opening to the sun,
He raised his azure wand, and thus begun:
    Ye sylphs and sylphids, to your chief give ear!
Fays, fairies, genii, elves, and dæmons, hear!
Ye know the spheres and various tasks assigned
By laws eternal to th' aërial kind.
Some in the fields of purest æther play,
And bask and whiten in the blaze of day.
Some guide the course of wand'ring orbs on high,
Or roll the planets through the boundless sky.   80
Some less refined, beneath the moon's pale light
Pursue the stars that shoot athwart the night,
Or suck the mists in grosser air below,
Or dip their pinions in the painted bow,
Or brew fierce tempests on the wintry main,
Or o'er the glebe distil the kindly rain.
Others on earth o'er human race preside,
Watch all their ways, and all their actions guide:
Of these the chief the care of nations own,
And guard with arms divine the British throne.   90
    Our humbler province is to tend the fair,

84. **painted bow:** rainbow.
86. **glebe:** cultivated ground.

Not a less pleasing, though less glorious care;
To save the powder from too rude a gale,
Nor let th' imprisoned essences exhale;
To draw fresh colors from the vernal flowers;
To steal from rainbows, e'er they drop in showers,
A brighter wash; to curl their waving hairs,
Assist their blushes, and inspire their airs;
Nay oft, in dreams, invention we bestow,
To change a flounce, or add a furbelow.   100
    This day, black omens threat the brightest fair,
That e'er deserved a watchful spirit's care;
Some dire disaster, or by force, or slight;
But what, or where, the fates have wrapt in night.
Whether the nymph shall break Diana's law,
Or some frail china jar receive a flaw;
Or stain her honor, or her new brocade;
Forget her prayers, or miss a masquerade;
Or lose her heart, or necklace, at a ball;
Or whether heaven has doomed that Shock must fall.   110
Haste, then, ye spirits! to your charge repair:
The flutt'ring fan be Zephyretta's care;
The drops to thee, Brillante, we consign;
And, Momentilla, let the watch be thine;
Do thou, Crispissa, tend her fav'rite lock;
Ariel himself shall be the guard of Shock.
    To fifty chosen sylphs, of special note,
We trust th' important charge, the petticoat:
Oft have we known that seven-fold fence to fail,
Though stiff with hoops, and armed with ribs of whale;   120
Form a strong line about the silver bound,
And guard the wide circumference around.
    Whatever spirit, careless of his charge,
His post neglects, or leaves the fair at large,
Shall feel sharp vengeance soon o'ertake his sins,
Be stopped in vials, or transfixed with pins;
Or plunged in lakes of bitter washes lie,
Or wedged whole ages in a bodkin's eye:
Gums and pomatums shall his flight restrain,
While clogged he beats his silken wings in vain;   130
Or alum styptics with contracting power
Shrink his thin essence like a riveled flower:
Or, as Ixion fixed, the wretch shall feel

97. **wash:** an early equivalent of liquid make-up.
105. **Diana's law:** of chastity.
128. **bodkin:** a very large needle for tape, ribbon, laces, etc.
133. **Ixion:** bound forever on a burning wheel as punishment for his moral lapses.

The giddy motion of the whirling mill,
In fumes of burning chocolate shall glow,
And tremble at the sea that froths below!
   He spoke; the spirits from the sails descend;
Some, orb in orb, around the nymph extend;
Some thrid the mazy ringlets of her hair;
Some hang upon the pendants of her ear: 140
With beating hearts the dire event they wait,
Anxious, and trembling for the birth of fate.

CANTO III

Close by those meads, forever crowned with flowers,
Where Thames with pride surveys his rising towers,
There stands a structure of majestic frame,
Which from the neighb'ring Hampton takes its name.
Here Britain's statesmen oft the fall foredoom
Of foreign tyrants and of nymphs at home;
Here thou, great ANNA! whom three realms obey,
Dost sometimes counsel take—and sometimes tea.
   Hither the heroes and the nymphs resort,
To taste awhile the pleasures of a court;   10
In various talk th' instructive hours they past,
Who gave the ball, or paid the visit last;
One speaks the glory of the British Queen,
And one describes a charming Indian screen;
A third interprets motions, looks, and eyes;
At every word a reputation dies.
Snuff, or the fan, supply each pause of chat,
With singing, laughing, ogling, *and all that.*
   Meanwhile, declining from the noon of day,
The sun obliquely shoots his burning ray;   20
The hungry judges soon the sentence sign,
And wretches hang that jury-men may dine;
The merchant from th' Exchange returns in peace,
And the long labors of the toilet cease.
Belinda now, whom thirst of fame invites,
Burns to encounter two advent'rous knights,
At ombre singly to decide their doom;
And swells her breast with conquests yet to come.
Straight the three bands prepare in arms to join,
Each band the number of the sacred nine.   30
Soon as she spreads her hand, th' aërial guard
Descend, and sit on each important card:

3. **a structure:** Hampton Court, a royal palace several miles upriver from London.
7. **Anna:** Queen Anne.

First Ariel perched upon a Matadore,
Then each, according to the rank they bore;
For sylphs, yet mindful of their ancient race,
Are, as when women, wondrous fond of place.
   Behold, four Kings in majesty revered,
With hoary whiskers and a forky beard;
And four fair Queens whose hands sustain a flower,
Th' expressive emblem of their softer power;   40
Four Knaves in garbs succinct, a trusty band,
Caps on their heads, and halberts in their hand;
And particolored troops, a shining train,
Draw forth to combat on the velvet plain.
   The skilful nymph reviews her force with care:
Let Spades be trumps! she said, and trumps they were.
   Now move to war her sable Matadores,
In show like leaders of the swarthy Moors.
Spadillio first, unconquerable lord!
Led off two captive trumps, and swept the board.   50
As many more Manillio forced to yield,
And marched a victor from the verdant field.
Him Basto followed, but his fate more hard
Gained but one trump and one plebeian card.
With his broad sabre next, a chief in years,
The hoary Majesty of Spades appears,
Puts forth one manly leg, to sight revealed,
The rest, his many-colored robe concealed.
The rebel Knave, who dares his prince engage,
Proves the just victim of his royal rage.   60
Even mighty Pam, that kings and queens o'erthrew
And mowed down armies in the fights of loo,
Sad chance of war! now destitute of aid,
Falls undistinguished by the victor spade!
   Thus far both armies to Belinda yield;
Now to the Baron fate inclines the field.
His warlike Amazon her host invades,
Th' imperial consort of the crown of Spades.
The Club's black tyrant first her victim died,
Spite of his haughty mien, and barb'rous pride: 70
What boots the regal circle on his head,
His giant limbs, in state unwieldy spread;
That long behind he trails his pompous robe,
And, of all monarchs, only grasps the globe?
   The Baron now his Diamonds pours apace;
Th' embroidered King who shows but half his face,

---

33. **Matadore:** the highest cards, when spades are trumps, are called matadores. Included are Spadillio, the ace; Manillio, the deuce; and Basto, the ace of clubs.
59. **rebel Knave:** the jack of spades, played by an opponent.
61. **Pam:** jack of clubs, high card in loo, a different game.

And his refulgent Queen, with powers combined
Of broken troops an easy conquest find.
Clubs, Diamonds, Hearts, in wild disorder seen,
With throngs promiscuous strow the level green.   80
Thus when dispersed a routed army runs,
Of Asia's troops, and Afric's sable sons,
With like confusion different nations fly,
Of various habit, and of various dye,
The pierced battalions dis-united fall,
In heaps on heaps; one fate o'erwhelms them all.
    The Knave of Diamonds tries his wily arts,
And wins (oh shameful chance!) the Queen of Hearts.
At this, the blood the virgin's cheek forsook,
A livid paleness spreads o'er all her look;   90
She sees, and trembles at th' approaching ill,
Just in the jaws of ruin, and codille.
And now (as oft in some distempered State)
On one nice Trick depends the general fate.
An Ace of Hearts steps forth: The King unseen
Lurked in her hand, and mourned his captive Queen:
He springs to vengeance with an eager pace,
And falls like thunder on the prostrate Ace.
The nymph exulting fills with shouts the sky;
The walls, the woods, and long canals reply.   100
    Oh thoughtless mortals! ever blind to fate,
Too soon dejected, and too soon elate.
Sudden, these honors shall be snatched away,
And cursed for ever this victorious day.
    For lo! the board with cups and spoons is crowned,
The berries crackle, and the mill turns round;
On shining altars of Japan they raise
The silver lamp; the fiery spirits blaze:
From silver spouts the grateful liquors glide,
While China's earth receives the smoking tide: 110
At once they gratify their scent and taste,
And frequent cups prolong the rich repast.
Straight hover round the fair her airy band;
Some, as she sipped, the fuming liquor fanned,
Some o'er her lap their careful plumes displayed,
Trembling, and conscious of the rich brocade.
Coffee (which makes the politician wise,
And see through all things with his half-shut eyes)
Sent up in vapors to the Baron's brain

77. **refulgent:** splendid, radiant.
92. **codille:** being set, failing to make the bid.
106. **berries:** coffee beans are ground in a mill at the table.
107. **Japan:** lacquer-work.

New stratagems, the radiant lock to gain.   120
Ah cease, rash youth! desist ere 'tis too late,
Fear the just Gods, and think of Scylla's fate!
Changed to a bird, and sent to flit in air,
She dearly pays for Nisus' injured hair!
  But when to mischief mortals bend their will,
How soon they find fit instruments of ill!
Just then, Clarissa drew with tempting grace
A two-edged weapon from her shining case:
So ladies in romance assist their knight,
Present the spear, and arm him for the fight.   130
He takes the gift with rev'rence, and extends
The little engine on his fingers' ends;
This just behind Belinda's neck he spread,
As o'er the fragrant steams she bends her head.
Swift to the lock a thousand sprites repair,
A thousand wings, by turns, blow back the hair;
And thrice they twitched the diamond in her ear;
Thrice she looked back, and thrice the foe drew near.
Just in that instant, anxious Ariel sought
The close recesses of the virgin's thought;   140
As on the nosegay in her breast reclined,
He watched th' ideas rising in her mind,
Sudden he viewed, in spite of all her art,
An earthly lover lurking at her heart.
Amazed, confused, he found his power expired,
Resigned to fate, and with a sigh retired.
  The Peer now spreads the glitt'ring forfex wide,
T' inclose the lock; now joins it, to divide.
Even then, before the fatal engine closed,
A wretched sylph too fondly interposed;   150
Fate urged the shears, and cut the sylph in twain,
(But airy substance soon unites again)
The meeting points the sacred hair dissever
From the fair head, forever, and forever!
  Then flashed the living lightning from her eyes,
And screams of horror rend th' affrighted skies.
Not louder shrieks to pitying heaven are cast,
When husbands, or when lap-dogs breathe their last;
Or when rich china vessels fall'n from high,
In glitt'ring dust and painted fragments lie!   160
Let wreaths of triumph now my temples twine,
(The victor cried) the glorious prize is mine!

122. **Scylla's fate:** Scylla was changed to a bird when she betrayed her father by cutting
magic hairs from his head.
147. **forfex:** scissors.

While fish in streams, or birds delight in air,
Or in a coach and six the British fair,
As long as *Atalantis* shall be read,
Or the small pillow grace a lady's bed,
While visits shall be paid on solemn days,
When num'rous wax-lights in bright order blaze,
While nymphs take treats, or assignations give,
So long my honor, name, and praise shall live!   170
What Time would spare, from steel receives its date,
And monuments, like men, submit to fate!
Steel could the labor of the Gods destroy,
And strike to dust th' imperial towers of Troy;
Steel could the works of mortal pride confound,
And hew triumphal arches to the ground.
What wonder then, fair nymph! thy hairs should feel,
The conq'ring force of unresisted steel?

CANTO IV

But anxious cares the pensive nymph oppressed,
And secret passions labored in her breast.
Not youthful kings in battle seized alive,
Not scornful virgins who their charms survive,
Not ardent lovers robbed of all their bliss,
Not ancient ladies when refused a kiss,
Not tyrants fierce that unrepenting die,
Not Cynthia when her manteau's pinned awry,
E'er felt such rage, resentment, and despair,
As thou, sad virgin! for thy ravished hair.   10
    For, that sad moment, when the sylphs withdrew
And Ariel weeping from Belinda flew,
Umbriel, a dusky, melancholy sprite,
As ever sullied the fair face of light,
Down to the central earth, his proper scene,
Repaired to search the gloomy Cave of Spleen.
    Swift on his sooty pinions flits the gnome,
And in a vapour reached the dismal dome.
No cheerful breeze this sullen region knows,
The dreaded East is all the wind that blows.   20
Here in a grotto, sheltered close from air,
And screened in shades from day's detested glare,
She sighs forever on her pensive bed,
Pain at her side, and megrim at her head.

165. **Atalantis:** a notorious book-length account of current scandal.

  8. **Cynthia:** Diana, goddess of the hunt and chastity.
24. **megrim:** migraine headache.

Two handmaids wait the throne: alike in place,
But diff'ring far in figure and in face.
Here stood Ill-nature like an ancient maid,
Her wrinkled form in black and white arrayed;
With store of prayers, for mornings, nights, and noons,
Her hand is filled; her bosom with lampoons.   30
   There Affectation, with a sickly mien,
Shows in her cheek the roses of eighteen,
Practised to lisp, and hang the head aside,
Faints into airs, and languishes with pride,
On the rich quilt sinks with becoming woe,
Wrapt in a gown, for sickness, and for show.
The fair ones feel such maladies as these,
When each new night-dress gives a new disease.
   A constant vapor o'er the palace flies;
Strange phantoms rising as the mists arise;   40
Dreadful, as hermit's dreams in haunted shades,
Or bright, as visions of expiring maids.
Now glaring fiends, and snakes on rolling spires,
Pale specters, gaping tombs, and purple fires:
Now lakes of liquid gold, Elysian scenes,
And crystal domes, and angels in machines.
   Unnumbered throngs on every side are seen,
Of bodies changed to various forms by Spleen.
Here living tea-pots stand, one arm held out,
One bent; the handle this, and that the spout: 50
A pipkin there, like Homer's tripod walks;
Here sighs a jar, and there a goose-pie talks;
Men prove with child, as powerful fancy works,
And maids turned bottles, call aloud for corks.
   Safe past the gnome through this fantastic band,
A branch of healing spleenwort in his hand.
Then thus addressed the power: "Hail, wayward Queen!
Who rule the sex to fifty from fifteen:
Parent of vapors and of female wit,
Who give th' hysteric or poetic fit,   60
On various tempers act by various ways,
Make some take physic, others scribble plays;
Who cause the proud their visits to delay,
And send the godly in a pet to pray.

---

51. **pipkin:** earthen pot, which propels itself like the three-legged stools (tripods) provided for the gods by Hephaestus.
52. **goose-pie:** in a note, Pope commented dryly that a lady of the time actually imagined herself to be in this condition.
56. **spleenwort:** a kind of fern supposed to cure hypochondria.
59. **vapors:** hypochondriac depression.
64. **pet:** fit of pique.

A nymph there is, that all thy power disdains,
And thousands more in equal mirth maintains.
But oh! if e'er thy gnome could spoil a grace,
Or raise a pimple on a beauteous face,
Like citron-waters matrons' cheeks inflame,
Or change complexions at a losing game; 70
If e'er with airy horns I planted heads,
Or rumpled petticoats, or tumbled beds,
Or caus'd suspicion when no soul was rude,
Or discomposed the head-dress of a prude,
Or e'er to costive lap-dog gave disease,
Which not the tears of brightest eyes could ease:
Hear me, and touch Belinda with chagrin,
That single act gives half the world the spleen."
   The goddess with a discontented air
Seems to reject him, though she grants his prayer, 80
A wondrous bag with both her hands she binds,
Like that where once Ulysses held the winds;
There she collects the force of female lungs,
Sighs, sobs, and passions, and the war of tongues.
A vial next she fills with fainting fears,
Soft sorrows, melting griefs, and flowing tears.
The gnome rejoicing bears her gifts away,
Spreads his black wings, and slowly mounts to day.
   Sunk in Thalestris' arms the nymph he found,
Her eyes dejected and her hair unbound. 90
Full o'er their heads the swelling bag he rent,
And all the Furies issued at the vent.
Belinda burns with more than mortal ire,
And fierce Thalestris fans the rising fire.
"Oh wretched maid!" she spread her hands, and cried,
(While Hampton's echoes, "Wretched maid!" replied)
"Was it for this you took such constant care
The bodkin, comb, and essence to prepare?
For this your locks in paper durance bound,
For this with torturing irons wreathed around? 100
For this with fillets strained your tender head,
And bravely bore the double loads of lead?
Gods! shall the ravisher display your hair,
While the fops envy, and the ladies stare!
Honor forbid! at whose unrivaled shrine

69. **citron-waters:** flavored brandy.
71. **airy horns:** the imaginary horns denoting a deceived husband.
75. **costive:** constipated.
82. **Ulysses . . . winds:** a bag of ill-winds given Ulysses by Aeolus.
101. **fillets:** a kind of hair net, or heavy snood.
102. **lead:** lead strips were used to hold pin-curls.

Ease, pleasure, virtue, all our sex resign.
Methinks already I your tears survey,
Already hear the horrid things they say,
Already see you a degraded toast,
And all your honor in a whisper lost!   110
How shall I, then, your helpless fame defend?
'Twill then be infamy to seem your friend!
And shall this prize, th' inestimable prize,
Exposed through crystal to the gazing eyes,
And heightened by the diamond's circling rays,
On that rapacious hand forever blaze?
Sooner shall grass in Hyde Park Circus grow,
And wits take lodgings in the sound of Bow;
Sooner let earth, air, sea, to chaos fall,
Men, monkeys, lap-dogs, parrots, perish all!"   120
    She said; then raging to Sir Plume repairs,
And bids her beau demand the precious hairs:
(Sir Plume of amber snuff-box justly vain,
And the nice conduct of a clouded cane)
With earnest eyes, and round unthinking face,
He first the snuff-box opened, then the case,
And thus broke out—"My Lord, why, what the devil?
Z—ds! damn the lock! 'fore Gad, you must be civil!
Plague on't! 'tis past a jest—nay prithee, pox!
Give her the hair"—he spoke, and rapped his box.   130
    "It grieves me much" (replied the Peer again)
"Who speaks so well should ever speak in vain.
But by this lock, this sacred lock I swear,
(Which never more shall join its parted hair;
Which never more its honors shall renew,
Clipped from the lovely head where late it grew)
That while my nostrils draw the vital air,
This hand, which won it, shall for ever wear."
He spoke, and speaking, in proud triumph spread
The long-contended honours of her head.   140
    But Umbriel, hateful gnome! forbears not so;
He breaks the vial whence the sorrows flow.
Then see! the nymph in beauteous grief appears,
Her eyes half-languishing, half-drowned in tears;
On her heaved bosom hung her drooping head,
Which, with a sigh, she raised; and thus she said.
    "Forever cursed be this detested day,
Which snatched my best, my fav'rite curl away!
Happy! ah ten times happy had I been,

118. **Bow:** the bells of St.-Mary-le-Bow were heard in Cheapside, a poor area.
128. **Z—ds:** Zounds, a blasphemous oath.

If Hampton Court these eyes had never seen! 150
Yet am not I the first mistaken maid,
By love of courts to numerous ills betrayed.
Oh had I rather un-admired remained
In some lone isle, or distant Northern land;
Where the gilt chariot never marks the way,
Where none learn ombre, none e'er taste bohea!
There kept my charms concealed from mortal eye,
Like roses, that in deserts bloom and die.
What moved my mind with youthful lords to roam?
Oh had I stayed, and said my prayers at home! 160
'Twas this, the morning omens seemed to tell,
Thrice from my trembling hand the patch-box fell;
The tott'ring china shook without a wind,
Nay, Poll sat mute, and Shock was most unkind!
A sylph too warned me of the threats of fate,
In mystic visions, now believed too late!
See the poor remnants of these slighted hairs!
My hands shall rend what even thy rapine spares:
These in two sable ringlets taught to break,
Once gave new beauties to the snowy neck; 170
The sister-lock now sits uncouth, alone,
And in its fellow's fate foresees its own;
Uncurled it hangs, the fatal shears demands,
And tempts once more, thy sacrilegious hands.
Oh hadst thou, cruel! been content to seize
Hairs less in sight, or any hairs but these!"

CANTO V

She said: the pitying audience melt in tears.
But Fate and Jove had stopped the Baron's ears.
In vain Thalestris with reproach assails,
For who can move when fair Belinda fails?
Not half so fixed the Trojan could remain,
While Anna begged and Dido raged in vain.
Then grave Clarissa graceful waved her fan;
Silence ensued, and thus the nymph began.
    "Say why are beauties praised and honored most,
The wise man's passion, and the vain man's toast? 10
Why decked with all that land and sea afford,
Why angels called, and angel-like adored?
Why round our coaches crowd the white-gloved beaux,

---

156. **bohea:** a kind of tea.
164. **Poll:** Belinda's parrot.

5. **Trojan:** Aeneas, who disregarded his sister Anna and abandoned Dido.

Why bows the side-box from its inmost rows;
How vain are all these glories, all our pains,
Unless good sense preserve what beauty gains:
That men may say, when we the front-box grace:
'Behold the first in virtue as in face!'
Oh! if to dance all night, and dress all day,   20
Charmed the small-pox, or chased old-age away;
Who would not scorn what housewife's cares produce,
Or who would learn one earthly thing of use?
To patch, nay ogle, might become a saint,
Nor could it sure be such a sin to paint.
But since, alas! frail beauty must decay,
Curled or uncurled, since locks will turn to grey;
Since painted, or not painted, all shall fade,
And she who scorns a man, must die a maid;
What then remains but well our power to use,
And keep good-humor still whate'er we lose?   30
And trust me, dear! good-humor can prevail,
When airs, and flights, and screams, and scolding fail.
Beauties in vain their pretty eyes may roll;
Charms strike the sight, but merit wins the soul."
     So spoke the Dame, but no applause ensued;
Belinda frowned, Thalestris called her prude.
"To arms, to arms!" the fierce virago cries,
And swift as lightning to the combat flies.
All side in parties, and begin th' attack;
Fans clap, silks rustle, and tough whalebones crack;   40
Heroes' and heroines' shouts confus'dly rise,
And bass and treble voices strike the skies.
No common weapons in their hands are found,
Like gods they fight, nor dread a mortal wound.
     So when bold Homer makes the gods engage,
And heavenly breasts with human passions rage;
'Gainst Pallas, Mars; Latona, Hermes arms;
And all Olympus rings with loud alarms:
Jove's thunder roars, heaven trembles all around,
Blue Neptune storms, the bellowing deeps resound: 50
Earth shakes her nodding towers, the ground gives way,
And the pale ghosts start at the flash of day!
     Triumphant Umbriel on a sconce's height
Clapped his glad wings, and sat to view the fight:
Propped on their bodkin spears, the sprites survey
The growing combat, or assist the fray,
     While through the press enraged Thalestris flies,

37. **virago:** quarrelsome woman.
53. **sconce:** candle-holder.

And scatters death around from both her eyes.
A beau and witling perished in the throng,
One died in metaphor, and one in song.   60
"O cruel nymph! a living death I bear,"
Cried Dapperwit, and sunk beside his chair.
A mournful glance Sir Fopling upwards cast,
"Those eyes are made so killing"—was his last.
Thus on Mæander's flowery margin lies
Th' expiring swan, and as he sings he dies.
    When bold Sir Plume had drawn Clarissa down,
Chloe stepped in, and killed him with a frown;
She smiled to see the doughty hero slain,
But, at her smile, the beau revived again.   70
    Now Jove suspends his golden scales in air,
Weighs the men's wits against the lady's hair;
The doubtful beam long nods from side to side;
At length the wits mount up, the hairs subside.
    See, fierce Belinda on the Baron flies,
With more than usual lightning in her eyes:
Nor feared the chief th' unequal fight to try,
Who sought no more than on his foe to die.
    But this bold lord with manly strength endued,
She with one finger and a thumb subdued: 80
Just where the breath of life his nostrils drew,
A charge of snuff the wily virgin threw;
The gnomes direct, to every atom just,
The pungent grains of titillating dust.
Sudden, with starting tears each eye o'erflows,
And the high dome re-echoes to his nose.
    "Now meet thy fate," incensed Belinda cried,
And drew a deadly bodkin from her side.
(The same, his ancient personage to deck,
Her great great grandsire wore about his neck,   90
In three seal-rings; which after, melted down,
Formed a vast buckle for his widow's gown:
Her infant grandame's whistle next it grew,
The bells she jingled, and the whistle blew;
Then in a bodkin graced her mother's hairs,
Which long she wore, and now Belinda wears.)
    "Boast not my fall" (he cried) "insulting foe!
Thou by some other shalt be laid as low,
Nor think, to die dejects my lofty mind:

---

74. **wits mount up:** in a beam balance, the lighter side rises.
88. **deadly bodkin:** an ornamental stiletto. Note the exact parallel here—as elsewhere
in the poem—with elements of *The Iliad* (in this instance, the genealogy of Agamem-
non's scepter).

All that I dread is leaving you behind!   100
Rather than so, ah let me still survive,
And burn in Cupid's flames—but burn alive."
    "Restore the lock!" she cries; and all around,
"Restore the lock!" the vaulted roofs rebound.
Not fierce Othello in so loud a strain
Roared for the handkerchief that caused his pain.
But see how oft ambitious aims are crossed,
And chiefs contend till all the prize is lost!
The lock, obtained with guilt, and kept with pain,
In every place is sought, but sought in vain: 110
With such a prize no mortal must be blest,
So heaven decrees! with heaven who can contest?
    Some thought it mounted to the lunar sphere,
Since all things lost on earth are treasured there.
There heroes' wits are kept in pond'rous vases,
And beaux in snuff-boxes and tweezer-cases.
There broken vows and death-bed alms are found,
And lovers' hearts with ends of riband bound,
The courtier's promises, and sick man's prayers,
The smiles of harlots, and the tears of heirs,   120
Cages for gnats, and chains to yoke a flea,
Dried butterfles, and tomes of casuistry.
    But trust the Muse—she saw it upward rise,
Though marked by none but quick, poetic eyes:
(So Rome's great founder to the heavens withdrew,
To Proculus alone confessed in view)
A sudden star, it shot through liquid air,
And drew behind a radiant trail of hair.
Not Berenice's locks first rose so bright,
The heavens bespangling with disheveled light.   130
The sylphs behold it kindling as it flies,
And pleased pursue its progress through the skies.
    This the beau monde shall from the Mall survey,
And hail with music its propitious ray.
This the blest lover shall for Venus take,
And send up vows from Rosamonda's lake.
This Partridge soon shall view in cloudless skies,

113. **lunar sphere:** that sphere on which the moon, symbol of chastity, is fixed.
125. **Rome's . . . founder:** Romulus, translated directly to heaven, later appeared to Proculus, a Roman senator.
129. **Berenice's:** the wife of Ptolemy III pledged a lock of her hair in return for her husband's safety. The lock became a constellation.
133. **beau monde:** the fashionable world.
133–136. **Mall . . . Rosamonda's lake:** both are in St. James's Park.
137. **Partridge:** an astrologer ridiculed by the Pope-Swift group.

When next he looks through Galileo's eyes;
And hence th' egregious wizard shall foredoom
The fate of Louis, and the fall of Rome.   140
    Then cease, bright nymph! to mourn thy ravished hair,
Which adds new glory to the shining sphere!
Not all the tresses that fair head can boast,
Shall draw such envy as the lock you lost.
For, after all the murders of your eye,
When, after millions slain, yourself shall die:
When those fair suns shall set, as set they must,
And all those tresses shall be laid in dust,
This lock, the Muse shall consecrate to fame,
And 'midst the stars inscribe Belinda's name.   150

THOMAS GRAY

❧ *Elegy Written in a Country Churchyard*

THE Curfew tolls the knell of parting day,
The lowing herd wind slowly o'er the lea,
The plowman homeward plods his weary way,
And leaves the world to darkness and to me.

Now fades the glimmering landscape on the sight,
And all the air a solemn stillness holds,
Save where the beetle wheels his droning flight,
And drowsy tinklings lull the distant folds;

Save that from yonder ivy-mantled tower
The moping owl does to the moon complain   10
Of such, as wandering near her secret bower,
Molest her ancient solitary reign.

Beneath those rugged elms, that yew-tree's shade,
Where heaves the turf in many a mouldering heap,
Each in his narrow cell for ever laid,
The rude forefathers of the hamlet sleep.

The breezy call of incense-breathing morn,
The swallow twittering from the straw-built shed,

16. **hamlet:** small village.

The cock's shrill clarion, or the echoing horn,
No more shall rouse them from their lowly bed.   20

For them no more the blazing hearth shall burn,
Or busy housewife ply her evening care;
No children run to lisp their sire's return,
Or climb his knees the envied kiss to share.

Oft did the harvest to their sickle yield,
Their furrow oft the stubborn glebe has broke;
How jocund did they drive their team afield!
How bowed the woods beneath their sturdy stroke!

Let not Ambition mock their useful toil,
Their homely joys, and destiny obscure;
Nor Grandeur hear with a disdainful smile   30
The short and simple annals of the poor.

The boast of heraldry, the pomp of power,
And all that beauty, all that wealth e'er gave,
Awaits alike the inevitable hour.
The paths of glory lead but to the grave.

Nor you, ye proud, impute to these the fault,
If Memory o'er their tomb no trophies raise,
Where through the long-drawn aisle and fretted vault
The pealing anthem swells the note of praise.   40

Can storied urn or animated bust
Back to its mansion call the fleeting breath?
Can Honor's voice provoke the silent dust,
Or Flattery soothe the dull cold ear of Death?

Perhaps in this neglected spot is laid
Some heart once pregnant with celestial fire;
Hands, that the rod of empire might have swayed,
Or waked to ecstasy the living lyre.

But Knowledge to their eyes her ample page
Rich with the spoils of time did ne'er unroll;   50
Chill Penury repressed their noble rage,
And froze the genial current of the soul.

41. **storied:** inscribed.
41. **animated:** lifelike.
43. **provoke:** inspire to action.
51. **Penury:** poverty.

Full many a gem of purest ray serene,
The dark unfathomed caves of ocean bear;
Full many a flower is born to blush unseen,
And waste its sweetness on the desert air.

Some village-Hampden, that with dauntless breast
The little tyrant of his fields withstood;
Some mute inglorious Milton here may rest,
Some Cromwell guiltless of his country's blood.   60

The applause of listening senates to command,
The threats of pain and ruin to despise,
To scatter plenty o'er a smiling land,
And read their history in a nation's eyes,

Their lot forbade: nor circumscribed alone
Their growing virtues, but their crimes confined;
Forbade to wade through slaughter to a throne,
And shut the gates of mercy on mankind,

The struggling pangs of conscious truth to hide,
To quench the blushes of ingenuous shame,   70
Or heap the shrine of Luxury and Pride
With incense kindled at the Muse's flame.

Far from the madding crowd's ignoble strife,
Their sober wishes never learned to stray;
Along the cool sequestered vale of life
They kept the noiseless tenor of their way.

Yet even these bones from insult to protect,
Some frail memorial still erected nigh,
With uncouth rhymes and shapeless sculpture decked,
Implores the passing tribute of a sigh.   80

Their name, their years, spelt by th' unlettered muse,
The place of fame and elegy supply:
And many a holy text around she strews,
That teach the rustic moralist to die.

57. **Hampden:** John Hampden (1595–1643) withstood the power of Charles I, refusing to pay taxes he thought unjust.
60. **Cromwell:** Oliver Cromwell (1599–1658), Lord Protector of England (1653–1658) following the execution of Charles I.
76. **tenor:** course.

For who to dumb Forgetfulness a prey,
This pleasing anxious being e'er resigned,
Left the warm precincts of the cheerful day,
Nor cast one longing lingering look behind?

On some fond breast the parting soul relies,
Some pious drops the closing eye requires;   90
Ev'n from the tomb the voice of Nature cries,
Ev'n in our ashes live their wonted fires.

For thee, who mindful of the unhonoured dead
Dost in these lines their artless tale relate,
If chance, by lonely contemplation led,
Some kindred spirit shall inquire thy fate,

Haply some hoary-headed swain may say,
"Oft have we seen him at the peep of dawn
Brushing with hasty steps the dews away
To meet the sun upon the upland lawn.   100

"There at the foot of yonder nodding beech
That wreathes its old fantastic roots so high,
His listless length at noontide would he stretch,
And pore upon the brook that babbles by.

"Hard by yon wood, now smiling as in scorn,
Muttering his wayward fancies he would rove,
Now drooping, woeful wan, like one forlorn,
Or crazed with care, or crossed in hopeless love.

"One morn I missed him on the customed hill,
Along the heath and near his favorite tree;   110
Another came; nor yet beside the rill,
Nor up the lawn, nor at the wood was he;

"The next with dirges due in sad array
Slow through the church-way path we saw him borne.
Approach and read (for thou can'st read) the lay,
Graved on the stone beneath yon agèd thorn."

THE EPITAPH

Here rests his head upon the lap of earth
A youth to fortune and to fame unknown.
Fair Science frowned not on his humble birth,
And Melancholy marked him for her own.   120

Large was his bounty, and his soul sincere,
Heaven did a recompense as largely send:
He gave to Misery all he had, a tear,
He gained from Heaven ('twas all he wished) a friend.

No farther seek his merits to disclose,
Or draw his frailties from their dread abode
(There they alike in trembling hope repose),
The bosom of his Father and his God.

WILLIAM BLAKE

❧ *A Divine Image*

CRUELTY has a human heart,
And Jealousy a human face;
Terror the human form divine,
And Secrecy the human dress.

The human dress is forgèd iron,
The human form a fiery forge,
The human face a furnace sealed,
The human heart its hungry gorge.

❧ *The Lamb*

LITTLE lamb, who made thee?
Dost thou know who made thee?
Gave thee life, and bid thee feed
By the stream and o'er the mead;
Gave thee clothing of delight,
Softest clothing, wooly, bright;
Gave thee such a tender voice,
Making all the vales rejoice?
Little lamb, who made thee?
Dost thou know who made thee?

8. **gorge:** throat, possibly stomach.

Little lamb, I'll tell thee.
Little lamb, I'll tell thee:
He is callèd by thy name,
For he calls himself a lamb.
He is meek, and he is mild;
He became a little child.
I a child, and thou a lamb,
We are callèd by his name.
Little lamb, God bless thee!
Little lamb, God bless thee!

❧ The Tyger

Tyger! Tyger! burning bright
In the forests of the night,
What immortal hand or eye
Could frame thy fearful symmetry?

In what distant deeps or skies
Burnt the fire of thine eyes?
On what wings dare he aspire?
What the hand dare seize the fire?

And what shoulder, and what art,
Could twist the sinews of thy heart?
And when thy heart began to beat,
What dread hand? and what dread feet?

What the hammer? what the chain?
In what furnace was thy brain?
What the anvil? what dread grasp
Dare its deadly terrors clasp?

When the stars threw down their spears,
And watered heaven with their tears,
Did he smile his work to see?
Did he who made the Lamb make thee?

Tyger! Tyger! burning bright
In the forests of the night,
What immortal hand or eye,
Dare frame thy fearful symmetry?

🌿 *The Chimney Sweeper*

[*Songs of Innocence*]

WHEN my mother died I was very young,
And my father sold me while yet my tongue
Could scarcely cry "weep! weep! weep! weep!"
So your chimneys I sweep, and in soot I sleep.

There's little Tom Dacre, who cried when his head,
That curled like a lamb's back, was shaved: so I said
"Hush, Tom! never mind it, for when your head's bare
You know that the soot cannot spoil your white hair."

And so he was quiet, and that very night,
As Tom was a-sleeping, he had such a sight!
That thousands of sweepers, Dick, Joe, Ned, and Jack,
Were all of them locked up in coffins of black.

And by came an Angel who had a bright key,
And he opened the coffins and set them all free;
Then down a green plain leaping, laughing, they run,
And wash in a river, and shine in the sun.

Then naked and white, all their bags left behind,
They rise upon clouds and sport in the wind;
And the Angel told Tom, if he'd be a good boy,
He'd have God for his father, and never want joy.

And so Tom awoke; and we rose in the dark,
And got with our bags and our brushes to work.
Tho' the morning was cold, Tom was happy and warm;
So if all do their duty they need not fear harm,

🌿 *The Chimney Sweeper*

[*Songs of Experience*]

A LITTLE black thing among the snow,
Crying "weep! weep!" in notes of woe!
"Where are thy father and mother, say?"—
"They are both gone up to the church to pray.

"Because I was happy upon the hearth,
And smiled among the winter's snow,
They clothed me in the clothes of death,
And taught me to sing the notes of woe.

"And because I am happy and dance and sing,
They think they have done me no injury,
And are gone to praise God and his priest and king,
Who make up a heaven of our misery."

❧ Infant Joy

"I HAVE no name:
I am but two days old."
What shall I call thee?
"I happy am,
Joy is my name."
Sweet joy befall thee!

Pretty joy!
Sweet joy but two days old,
Sweet joy I call thee:
Thou dost smile,
I sing the while,
Sweet joy befall thee!

❧ Infant Sorrow

MY mother groaned! my father wept.
Into the dangerous world I leapt:
Helpless, naked, piping loud:
Like a fiend hid in a cloud.

Struggling in my father's hands,
Striving against my swaddling-bands,
Bound and weary I thought best
To sulk upon my mother's breast.

6. **swaddling bands:** long narrow bands of cloth formerly used to prevent an infant's
movement.

❧ *Ah, Sun-Flower!*

Ah, Sun-flower! weary of time,
Who countest the steps of the sun;
Seeking after that sweet golden clime
Where the traveller's journey is done;

Where the youth pined away with desire,
And the pale virgin shrouded in snow,
Arise from their graves, and aspire
Where my Sun-flower wishes to go.

❧ *London*

I wander thro' each chartered street,
Near where the chartered Thames does flow,
And mark in every face I meet
Marks of weakness, marks of woe.

In every cry of every man,
In every infant's cry of fear,
In every voice, in every ban,
The mind-forged manacles I hear.

How the chimney-sweeper's cry
Every blackening church appalls;
And the hapless soldier's sigh
Runs in blood down palace walls.

But most thro' midnight streets I hear
How the youthful harlot's curse
Blasts the new born infant's tear,
And blights with plagues the marriage hearse.

❧ *A Poison Tree*

I was angry with my friend:
I told my wrath, my wrath did end.
I was angry with my foe:
I told it not, my wrath did grow.

And I watered it in fears,
Night and morning with my tears:
And I sunnèd it with smiles,
And with soft deceitful wiles.

And it grew both day and night,
Till it bore an apple bright;
And my foe beheld it shine,
And he knew that it was mine,

And into my garden stole
When the night had veiled the pole:
In the morning glad I see
My foe outstretched beneath the tree.

ROBERT BURNS

❦ *Holy Willie's Prayer*

"And send the godly in a pet to pray."—Pope

O THOU wha in the heavens does dwell,
Wha, as it pleases best thysel',
Sends ane to heaven an' ten to hell
A' for thy glory,
And no for onie guid or ill
They've done before thee!

I bless and praise thy matchless might
When thousands thou hast left in night,
That I am here before thy sight,
For gifts an' grace   10
A burning and a shining light
To a' this place.

What was I, or my generation,
What I should get sic exaltation?
I, wha deserv'd most just damnation
For broken laws
Sax thousand years ere my creation,
Through Adam's cause!

When from my mither's womb I fell,
Thou might hae plung'd me deep in hell,   20
To gnash my gooms, and weep, and wail
In burning lakes,
Where damned devils roar and yell,
Chained to their stakes.

Yet I am here, a chosen sample,
To show thy grace is great and ample;
I'm here a pillar in thy temple,
Strong as a rock,
A guide, a buckler, and example
To a' thy flock.   30

O Lord, thou kens what zeal I bear,
When drinkers drink, and swearers swear,
And singin' there and dancin' here,
Wi' great an' sma':
For I am keepit by thy fear,
Free frae them a'.

But yet, O Lord! confess I must:
At times I'm fash'd wi' fleshly lust;
An' sometimes, too, wi' warldly trust,
Vile self gets in;   40
But thou remembers we are dust,
Defil'd in sin.

O Lord! yestreen, thou kens, wi' Meg—
Thy pardon I sincerely beg,
O! may it ne'er be a livin' plague
To my dishonor!
An' I'll ne'er lift a lawless leg
Again upon her.

Besides, I farther maun allow,
Wi' Lizzie's lass, three times, I trow;   50
But, Lord, that Friday I was fou,
When I came near her,

31. **kens:** knows.
36. **frae:** from.
38. **fash'd:** troubled.
43. **yestreen:** yesterday evening.
49. **maun allow:** must admit.
51. **fou:** drunk.

Or else, thou kens thy servant true
Wad ne'er hae steered her.

May be thou lets this fleshly thorn
Beset thy servant e'en and morn,
Lest he owre high and proud should turn,
'Cause he's sae gifted;
If sae, thy hand maun e'en be borne,
Until thou lift it.   60

Lord, bless thy chosen in this place,
For here thou hast a chosen race;
But God confound their stubborn face,
And blast their name,
Wha bring thy elders to disgrace
An' public shame!

Lord, mind Gau'n Hamilton's deserts:
He drinks, an' swears, an' plays at cartes,
Yet has sae monie takin' arts
Wi grit and sma',   70
Frae God's ain priest the people's hearts
He steals awa'.

An' whan we chasten'd him therefore,
Thou kens how he bred sic a splore,
As set the warld in a roar
O' laughin' at us;
Curse thou his basket and his store,
Kail and potatoes!

Lord, hear my earnest cry an' pray'r
Against that Presbyt'ry o' Ayr!   80
Thy strong right hand, Lord, make it bare
Upo' their heads;
Lord, weigh it down, an' dinna spare,
For their misdeeds!

O Lord my God! that glib-tongu'd Aiken,
My very heart and flesh are quakin',
To think how we stood sweatin', shakin',
An' piss'd wi' dread,

54. **steered:** stirred.
65. **elders:** elders of the church.
74. **splore:** riot.
78. **Kail:** cabbage or greens.

While he, wi' hingin' lip an' snakin',
Held up his head.   90

Lord, in the day of vengeance try him;
Lord, visit them wha did empty him,
And pass not in thy mercy by 'em,
Nor hear their pray'r:
But, for thy people's sake, destry 'em,
An' dinna spare.

But Lord, remember me and mine
Wi' mercies temp'ral and divine,
That I for gear and grace may shine,
Excelled by nane;   100
And a' the glory shall be thine,
Amen, Amen.

❧ *John Anderson My Jo*

JOHN ANDERSON my jo, John,
When we were first acquent,
Your locks were like the raven,
Your bonnie brow was brent;
But now your brow is beld, John,
Your locks are like the snow;
But blessings on your frosty pow,
John Anderson, my jo.

John Anderson my jo, John,
We clamb the hill thegither;   10
And mony a canty day, John,
We've had wi' ane anither:
Now we maun totter down, John,
And hand in hand we'll go,
And sleep thegither at the foot,
John Anderson, my jo.

89. **snakin':** sneering.
99. **gear:** wealth, goods.

 4. **brent:** bright.
 5. **beld:** bald.
 7. **pow:** head, "noggin."
11. **canty:** cheerful.

❧ *Edward, Edward*

"Why does your brand sae drop wi' blude,
Edward, Edward?
Why does your brand sae drop wi' blude,
And why sae sad gang ye, O?"—
"O I hae kill'd my hawk sae gude,
Mither, mither;
O I hae kill'd my hawk sae gude,
And I had nae mair but he, O."

"Your hawk's blude was never sae red,
Edward, Edward;   10
Your hawk's blude was never sae red,
My dear son, I tell thee, O."—
"O I hae kill'd my red-roan steed,
Mither, mither;
O I hae kill'd my red-roan steed,
That erst was sae fair and free, O."

"Your steed was auld, and ye hae got mair,
Edward, Edward;
Your steed was auld, and ye hae got mair;
Some other dule ye dree, O."   20
"O I hae kill'd my father dear,
Mither, mither;
O I hae kill'd my father dear,
Alas, and wae is me, O!"

"And whatten penance will ye dree for that,
Edward, Edward?
Whatten penance will ye dree for that?
My dear son, now tell me, O."—
"I'll set my feet in yonder boat,
Mither, mither;   30
I'll set my feet in yonder boat,
And I'll fare over the sea, O."

1. **brand:** sword.
20. **dule ye dree:** sorrow you suffer.

"And what will ye do wi' your tow'rs and your ha',
Edward, Edward?
And what will ye do wi' your tow'rs and your ha',
That were sae fair to see, O?"—
"I'll let them stand till they doun fa',
Mither, mither;
I'll let them stand till they doun fa',
For here never mair maun I be, O." 40

"And what will ye leave to your bairns and your wife,
Edward, Edward?
And what will ye leave to your bairns and your wife,
When ye gang owre the sea, O?"—
"The warld's room, let them beg through life,
Mither, mither;
The warld's room, let them beg through life;
For them never mair will I see, O."

"And what will ye leave to your ain mither dear,
Edward, Edward? 50
And what will ye leave to your ain mither dear,
My dear son, now tell me, O?"—
"The curse of hell frae me sall ye bear,
Mither, mither;
The curse of hell frae me sall ye bear:
Sic counsels ye gave to me, O!"

❧ Sir Patrick Spens

THE king sits in Dumferling toune,
Drinking the blude-reid wine:
"O quhar will I get guid sailor,
To sail this schip of mine?"

Up and spak an eldern knicht,
Sat at the king's richt knee:
"Sir Patrick Spens is the best sailor
That sails upon the sea."

The king has written a braid letter,
And signed it wi' his hand; 10

3. **quhar:** where.
9. **braid:** broad.

And sent it to Sir Patrick Spens,
Was walking on the sand.

The first line that Sir Patrick red,
A loud lauch lauchèd he:
The next line that Sir Patrick red,
The teir blinded his ee.

"O quha is this has don this deid,
This ill deid don to me;
To send me out this time o' the yeir,
To sail upon the sea?   20

"Mak haste, mak haste, my mirry men all,
Our good schip sails the morn."
"O say na sae, my master deir,
For I feir a deadlie storme.

"Late late yestreen I saw the new moone
Wi' the auld moone in his arme;
And I feir, I feir, my deir master,
That we will come to harme."

O our Scots nobles wer richt laith
To weet their cork-heild schoone;   30
But lang owre a' the play were played,
Their hats they swam aboone.

O lang, lang may the ladies stand
Wi' their fans in their hand,
Or e'er they see Patrick Spens
Come sailing to the land.

O lang, lang may the ladies stand
Wi' their gold kems in their hair,
Waiting for their ain deir lords,
For they'll see them na mair.   40

Have owre, have owre to Aberdour,
It's fifty fadom deip:
And thair lies guid Sir Patrick Spens,
Wi' the Scots lords at his feit.

14. **lauch:** laugh.
17. **quha:** who.
29. **laith:** loath, unwilling.
30. **schoone:** shoes.
32. **aboone:** above.
38. **kems:** combs.
41. **owre:** over.

❧ *The Wife of Usher's Well*

THERE lived a wife at Usher's Well,
And a wealthy wife was she;
She had three stout and stalwart sons,
And sent them oer the sea.

They hadna been a week from her,
A week but barely ane,
Whan word came to the carlin wife
That her three sons were gane.

They hadna been a week from her,
A week but barely three,   10
Whan word came to the carlin wife
That her sons she'd never see.

"I wish the wind may never cease,
Nor fashes in the flood,
Till my three sons come hame to me,
In earthly flesh and blood."

It fell about the Martinmass,
When nights are lang and mirk,
The carlin wife's three sons came hame,
And their hats were o' the birk.   20

It neither grew in syke nor ditch,
Nor yet in ony sheugh;
But at the gates o' Paradise,
That birk grew fair eneugh.

"Blow up the fire, my maidens,
Bring water from the well;
For a' my house shall feast this night,
Since my three sons are well."

 7. **carlin:** stout and old.
14. **fashes:** troubles.
17. **Martinmass:** November 11.
20. **birk:** birch.
21. **syke:** trench.
22. **sheugh:** furrow.

And she has made to them a bed,
She's made it large and wide,   30
And she's taen her mantle her about,
Sat down at the bed-side.

Up then crew the red, red cock,
And up and crew the gray;
The eldest to the youngest said,
"Tis time we were away."

The cock he hadna crawd but once,
And clapped his wings at a',
When the youngest to the eldest said,
"Brother, we must awa.   40

"The cock doth craw, the day doth daw,
The channerin' worm doth chide;
Gin we be mist out o' our place,
A sair pain we maun bide.

"Faer ye weel, my mother dear!
Fareweel to barn and byre!
And fare ye weel, the bonny lass
That kindles my mother's fire!"

❧ *Bonnie George Campbell*

HIE upon Hielands
And low upon Tay,
Bonnie George Campbell
Rode out on a day.
And low upon Tay,
And gallant rade he;
Hame cam his gude horse,
But never cam he!

Out cam his auld mither
Greeting fu' sair,   10
And out cam his bonnie bride

41. **daw:** dawn.
42. **channerin':** fretting.
43. **Gin:** if.

10. **Greeting:** weeping.

Rivin' her hair.
Saddled and bridled
And booted rade he;
Toom hame cam the saddle,
But never cam he!

"My meadow lies green,
And my corn is unshorn;
My barn is too big,
And my baby's unborn."   20
Saddled and bridled
And booted rade he;
Toom hame cam the saddle,
But never cam he!

WILLIAM WORDSWORTH

❧ Lines: Composed a Few Miles Above Tintern Abbey

FIVE years have past; five summers, with the length
Of five long winters; and again I hear
These waters, rolling from their mountain-springs
With a soft inland murmur.—Once again
Do I behold these steep and lofty cliffs,
That on a wild secluded scene impress
Thoughts of more deep seclusion, and connect
The landscape with the quiet of the sky.
The day is come when I again repose
Here, under this dark sycamore, and view   10
These plots of cottage-ground, these orchard-tufts,
Which at this season, with their unripe fruits,
Are clad in one green hue, and lose themselves
'Mid groves and copses. Once again I see
These hedge-rows, hardly hedge-rows, little lines
Of sportive wood run wild: these pastoral farms,
Green to the very door; and wreaths of smoke
Sent up, in silence, from among the trees!
With some uncertain notice, as might seem

12. **Rivin':** tearing.
19. **too big:** still to be built.

Of vagrant dwellers in the houseless woods,   20
Or of some Hermit's cave, where by his fire
The Hermit sits alone.
                                    These beauteous forms,
Through a long absence, have not been to me
As is a landscape to a blind man's eye:
But oft, in lonely rooms, and 'mid the din
Of towns and cities, I have owed to them
In hours of weariness, sensations sweet,
Felt in the blood, and felt along the heart;
And passing even into my purer mind,
With tranquil restoration—feelings too   30
Of unremembered pleasure: such, perhaps,
As have no slight or trivial influence
On that best portion of a good man's life,
His little, nameless, unremembered acts
Of kindness and of love. Nor less, I trust,
To them I may have owed another gift,
Of aspect more sublime; that blessed mood,
In which the burden of the mystery,
In which the heavy and the weary weight
Of all this unintelligible world,   40
Is lightened—that serene and blessed mood,
In which the affections gently lead us on—
Until, the breath of this corporeal frame
And even the motion of our human blood
Almost suspended, we are laid asleep
In body, and become a living soul:
While with an eye made quiet by the power
Of harmony, and the deep power of joy,
We see into the life of things.
                                                    If this
Be but a vain belief, yet, oh!—how oft—   50
In darkness and amid the many shapes
Of joyless daylight; when the fretful stir
Unprofitable, and the fever of the world,
Have hung upon the beatings of my heart—
How oft, in spirit, have I turned to thee,
O sylvan Wye! thou wanderer thro' the woods,
How often has my spirit turned to thee!
And now, with gleams of half extinguished thought,
With many recognitions dim and faint,
And somewhat of a sad perplexity,   60
The picture of the mind revives again:
While here I stand, not only with the sense
Of present pleasure, but with pleasing thoughts
That in this moment there is life and food

For future years. And so I dare to hope,
Though changed, no doubt, from what I was when first
I came among these hills; when like a roe
I bounded o'er the mountains, by the sides
Of the deep rivers, and the lonely streams,
Wherever nature led: more like a man   70
Flying from something that he dreads, than one
Who sought the thing he loved. For nature then
(The coarser pleasures of my boyish days,
And their glad animal movements all gone by)
To me was all in all.—I cannot paint
What then I was. The sounding cataract
Haunted me like a passion: the tall rock,
The mountain, and the deep and gloomy wood,
Their colours and their forms, were then to me
An appetite; a feeling and a love,   80
That had no need of a remoter charm,
By thought supplied, nor any interest
Unborrowed from the eye.—That time is past,
And all its aching joys are now no more,
And all its dizzy raptures. Not for this
Faint I, nor mourn nor murmur; other gifts
Have followed; for such loss, I would believe,
Abundant recompense. For I have learned
To look on nature, not as in the hour
Of thoughtless youth; but hearing oftentimes   90
The still, sad music of humanity,
Nor harsh nor grating, though of ample power
To chasten and subdue. And I have felt
A presence that disturbs me with the joy
Of elevated thoughts; a sense sublime
Of something far more deeply interfused,
Whose dwelling is the light of setting suns,
And the round ocean, and the living air,
And the blue sky, and in the mind of man;
A motion and a spirit, that impels   100
All thinking things, all objects of all thought,
And rolls through all things. Therefore am I still
A lover of the meadows and the woods,
And mountains; and of all that we behold
From this green earth; of all the mighty world
Of eye, and ear—both what they half create,
And what perceive; well pleased to recognize
In nature and the language of the sense,
The anchor of my purest thoughts, the nurse,
The guide, the guardian of my heart, and soul   110
Of all my moral being.

                              Nor perchance,
If I were not thus taught, should I the more
Suffer my genial spirits to decay:
For thou art with me here upon the banks
Of this fair river; thou my dearest friend,
My dear, dear friend; and in thy voice I catch
The language of my former heart, and read
My former pleasures in the shooting lights
Of thy wild eyes. Oh! yet a little while
May I behold in thee what I was once,   120
My dear, dear sister! and this prayer I make,
Knowing that Nature never did betray
The heart that loved her; 'tis her privilege,
Through all the years of this our life, to lead
From joy to joy: for she can so inform
The mind that is within us, so impress
With quietness and beauty, and so feed
With lofty thoughts, that neither evil tongues,
Rash judgments, nor the sneers of selfish men,
Nor greetings where no kindness is, nor all   130
The dreary intercourse of daily life,
Shall e'er prevail against us, or disturb
Our cheerful faith that all which we behold
Is full of blessings. Therefore let the moon
Shine on thee in thy solitary walk;
And let the misty mountain-winds be free
To blow against thee: and, in after years,
When these wild ecstasies shall be matured
Into a sober pleasure; when thy mind
Shall be a mansion for all lovely forms,   140
Thy memory be as a dwelling-place
For all sweet sounds and harmonies; oh! then,
If solitude, or fear, or pain, or grief,
Should be thy portion, with what healing thoughts
Of tender joy wilt thou remember me,
And these my exhortations! Nor, perchance—
If I should be where I no more can hear
Thy voice, nor catch from thy wild eyes these gleams
Of past existence—wilt thou then forget
That on the banks of this delightful stream   150
We stood together; and that I, so long
A worshipper of Nature, hither came
Unwearied in that service: rather say
With warmer love—oh! with far deeper zeal
Of holier love. Nor wilt thou then forget,

116. **friend:** Dorothy, the poet's sister.

That after many wanderings, many years
Of absence, these steep woods and lofty cliffs,
And this green pastoral landscape, were to me
More dear, both for themselves and for thy sake!

❧ She Dwelt Among the Untrodden Ways

SHE dwelt among the untrodden ways
Beside the springs of Dove,
A maid whom there were none to praise
And very few to love:

A violet by a mossy stone
Half hidden from the eye!
Fair as a star, when only one
Is shining in the sky.

She lived unknown, and few could know
When Lucy ceased to be;   10
But she is in her grave, and, oh,
The difference to me!

❧ Three Years She Grew

THREE years she grew in sun and shower,
Then Nature said, "A lovelier flower
On earth was never sown;
This child I to myself will take;
She shall be mine, and I will make
A lady of my own.

"Myself will to my darling be
Both law and impulse: and with me
The girl, in rock and plain,
In earth and heaven, in glade and bower,
Shall feel an overseeing power
To kindle or restrain.

"She shall be sportive as the fawn
That wild with glee across the lawn

2. **Dove:** no exact identification of this stream is possible—Wordsworth knew at least three.

Or up the mountain springs;
And hers shall be the breathing balm,
And hers the silence and the calm
Of mute insensate things.

"The floating clouds their state shall lend
To her; for her the willow bend;
Nor shall she fail to see
Even in the motions of the storm
Grace that shall mold the maiden's form
By silent sympathy.

"The stars of midnight shall be dear
To her; and she shall lean her ear
In many a secret place
Where rivulets dance their wayward round,
And beauty born of murmuring sound
Shall pass into her face.

"And vital feelings of delight
Shall rear her form to stately height,
Her virgin bosom swell;
Such thoughts to Lucy I will give
While she and I together live
Here in this happy dell."

Thus Nature spake. The work was done.
How soon my Lucy's race was run!
She died, and left to me
This heath, this calm and quiet scene;
The memory of what has been,
And never more will be.

❧ *A Slumber Did My Spirit Seal*

A SLUMBER did my spirit seal;
I had no human fears:
She seemed a thing that could not feel
The touch of earthly years.

No motion has she now, no force;
She neither hears nor sees;
Rolled round in earth's diurnal course,
With rocks, and stones, and trees.

7. **diurnal:** daily.

❧ Composed upon Westminster Bridge

EARTH has not anything to show more fair:
Dull would he be of soul who could pass by
A sight so touching in its majesty:
This city now doth, like a garment, wear
The beauty of the morning; silent, bare,
Ships, towers, domes, theatres, and temples lie
Open unto the fields, and to the sky,
All bright and glittering in the smokeless air.
Never did sun more beautifully steep
In his first splendour, valley, rock, or hill;
Ne'er saw I, never felt, a calm so deep!
The river glideth at his own sweet will:
Dear God! the very houses seem asleep;
And all that mighty heart is lying still!

❧ It Is a Beauteous Evening, Calm and Free

IT IS a beauteous evening, calm and free;
The holy time is quiet as a nun
Breathless with adoration; the broad sun
Is sinking down in its tranquillity;
The gentleness of heaven broods o'er the sea:
Listen! the mighty Being is awake,
And doth with his eternal motion make
A sound like thunder—everlastingly.
Dear child! dear girl! that walkest with me here,
If thou appear untouched by solemn thought,   10
Thy nature is not therefore less divine:
Thou liest in Abraham's bosom all the year,
And worship'st at the temple's inner shrine,
God being with thee when we know it not.

9. **child, girl:** Wordsworth's natural daughter, Caroline, and her mother, Annette Vallon.
12. **Abraham's bosom:** Abraham was the father of the Hebrew people; to be in his bosom was to be both secure and close to God.

❧ *London, 1802*

MILTON! thou shouldst be living at this hour;
England hath need of thee; she is a fen
Of stagnant waters: altar, sword, and pen,
Fireside, the heroic wealth of hall and bower,
Have forfeited their ancient English dower
Of inward happiness. We are selfish men;
Oh! raise us up, return to us again;
And give us manners, virtue, freedom, power.
Thy soul was like a star, and dwelt apart:
Thou hadst a voice whose sound was like the sea: 10
Pure as the naked heavens, majestic, free,
So didst thou travel on life's common way,
In cheerful godliness; and yet thy heart
The lowliest duties on herself did lay.

❧ *Stepping Westward*

While my fellow-traveller and I were walking by the side of Loch Ketterine, one
fine evening after sunset, in our road to a hut where, in the course of our tour, we
had been hospitably entertained some weeks before, we met in one of the loneliest
parts of that solitary region, two well-dressed women, one of whom said to us, by
way of greeting, "What, you are stepping westward?"—Wordsworth

"What, you are stepping westward?"—"Yea."
—'T would be a *wildish* destiny,
If we, who thus together roam
In a strange land, and far from home,
Were in this place the guests of Chance:
Yet who would stop, or fear to advance,
Though home or shelter he had none,
With such a sky to lead him on?

The dewy ground was dark and cold;
Behind, all gloomy to behold;

4. **bower:** cottage.

And stepping westward seemed to be
A kind of *heavenly* destiny:
I liked the greeting; 'twas a sound
Of something without place or bound;
And seemed to give me spiritual right
To travel through that region bright.

The voice was soft, and she who spake
Was walking by her native lake:
The salutation had to me
The very sound of courtesy:
Its power was felt; and while my eye
Was fixed upon the glowing sky,
The echo of the voice enwrought
A human sweetness with the thought
Of travelling through the world that lay
Before me in my endless way.

❧ *Ode: Intimations of Immortality from Recollections of Early Childhood*

I

THERE was a time when meadow, grove, and stream,
The earth, and every common sight,
To me did seem
Apparelled in celestial light,
The glory and the freshness of a dream.
It is not now as it hath been of yore—
Turn wheresoe'er I may,
By night or day,
The things which I have seen I now can see no more.

II

The rainbow comes and goes,   10
And lovely is the rose;
The moon doth with delight
Look round her when the heavens are bare;
Waters on a starry night
Are beautiful and fair;
The sunshine is a glorious birth;
But yet I know, where'er I go,
That there hath past away a glory from the earth.

III

Now, while the birds thus sing a joyous song,
And while the young lambs bound   20
As to the tabor's sound,
To me alone there came a thought of grief:
A timely utterance gave that thought relief,
And I again am strong:
The cataracts blow their trumpets from the steep;
No more shall grief of mine the season wrong;
I hear the echoes through the mountains throng,
The winds come to me from the fields of sleep,
And all the earth is gay;
Land and sea   30
Give themselves up to jollity,
And with the heart of May
Doth every beast keep holiday—
Thou child of joy,
Shout round me, let me hear thy shouts, thou
          happy shepherd-boy!

IV

Ye blessed creatures, I have heard the call
Ye to each other make; I see
The heavens laugh with you in your jubilee;
My heart is at your festival,
My head hath its coronal,   40
The fulness of your bliss, I feel—I feel it all.
Oh evil day! if I were sullen
While Earth herself is adorning,
This sweet May-morning,
And the children are culling
On every side,
In a thousand valleys far and wide,
Fresh flowers; while the sun shines warm,
And the babe leaps up on his mother's arm—
I hear, I hear, with joy I hear!   50
—But there's a tree, of many, one,
A single field which I have looked upon,
Both of them speak of something that is gone;
The pansy at my feet
Doth the same tale repeat:
Whither is fled the visionary gleam?
Where is it now, the glory and the dream?

21. **tabor:** a small drum.
40. **coronal:** garland or crown.

V

Our birth is but a sleep and a forgetting:
The soul that rises with us, our life's star,
Hath had elsewhere its setting,   60
And cometh from afar:
Not in entire forgetfulness,
And not in utter nakedness,
But trailing clouds of glory do we come
From God, who is our home:
Heaven lies about us in our infancy!
Shades of the prison-house begin to close
Upon the growing boy,
But he beholds the light, and whence it flows,
He sees it in his joy;   70
The youth, who daily farther from the east
Must travel, still is nature's priest,
And by the vision splendid
Is on his way attended;
At length the man perceives it die away,
And fade into the light of common day.

VI

Earth fills her lap with pleasures of her own;
Yearnings she hath in her own natural kind,
And, even with something of a mother's mind,
And no unworthy aim,   80
The homely Nurse doth all she can
To make her foster-child, her inmate man,
Forget the glories he hath known,
And that imperial palace whence he came.

VII

Behold the child among his new-born blisses,
A six years' darling of a pigmy size!
See, where 'mid work of his own hand he lies,
Fretted by sallies of his mother's kisses,
With light upon him from his father's eyes!
See, at his feet, some little plan or chart,   90
Some fragment from his dream of human life,
Shaped by himself with newly-learnèd art;
A wedding or a festival,
A mourning or a funeral;
And this hath now his heart,
And unto this he frames his song:
Then will he fit his tongue
To dialogues of business, love, or strife;

But it will not be long
Ere this be thrown aside,   100
And with new joy and pride
The little actor cons another part;
Filling from time to time his "humorous stage"
With all the persons, down to palsied Age,
That Life brings with her in her equipage;
As if his whole vocation
Were endless imitation.

VIII

Thou, whose exterior semblance doth belie
Thy soul's immensity;
Thou best philosopher, who yet dost keep   110
Thy heritage, thou eye among the blind,
That, deaf and silent, read'st the eternal deep,
Haunted for ever by the eternal mind—
Mighty prophet! Seer blest!
On whom those truths do rest,
Which we are toiling all our lives to find,
In darkness lost, the darkness of the grave;
Thou, over whom thy immortality
Broods like the day, a master o'er a slave,
A presence which is not to be put by;   120
Thou little child, yet glorious in the might
Of heaven-born freedom on thy being's height,
Why with such earnest pains dost thou provoke
The years to bring the inevitable yoke,
Thus blindly with thy blessedness at strife?
Full soon thy soul shall have her earthly freight,
And custom lie upon thee with a weight,
Heavy as frost, and deep almost as life!

IX

O joy! that in our embers
Is something that doth live,   130
That nature yet remembers
What was so fugitive!
The thought of our past years in me doth breed
Perpetual benediction: not indeed
For that which is most worthy to be blest—
Delight and liberty, the simple creed
Of childhood, whether busy or at rest,
With new-fledged hope still fluttering in his breast—

103. **humorous**: suggests both a bitter irony and the concept of single governing traits, or *humours*, in dramatic writing.

                    Not for these I raise
                    The song of thanks and praise;   140
                    But for those obstinate questionings
                    Of sense and outward things,
                    Fallings from us, vanishings;
                    Blank misgivings of a creature
                    Moving about in worlds not realised,
                    High instincts before which our mortal nature
                    Did tremble like a guilty thing surprised:
                    But for those first affections,
                    Those shadowy recollections,
                    Which, be they what they may,   150
                    Are yet the fountain-light of all our day,
                    Are yet a master-light of all our seeing;
                    Uphold us, cherish, and have power to make
                    Our noisy years seem moments in the being
                    Of the eternal Silence: truths that wake,
                    To perish never:
                    Which neither listlessness, nor mad endeavour,
                    Nor man nor boy,
                    Nor all that is at enmity with joy,
                    Can utterly abolish or destroy!   160
                    Hence in a season of calm weather
                    Though inland far we be,
                    Our souls have sight of that immortal sea
                    Which brought us hither,
                    Can in a moment travel thither,
                    And see the children sport upon the shore,
                    And hear the mighty waters rolling evermore.

          X

                    Then sing, ye birds, sing, sing a joyous song!
                    And let the young lambs bound
                    As to the tabor's sound!   170
                    We in thought will join your throng,
                    Ye that pipe and ye that play,
                    Ye that through your hearts to-day
                    Feel the gladness of the May!
                    What though the radiance which was once so bright
                    Be now for ever taken from my sight,
                    Though nothing can bring back the hour
                    Of splendour in the grass, of glory in the flower;
                    We will grieve not, rather find
                    Strength in what remains behind;   180

148. **affections:** in the psychological system of David Hartley, to whom Wordsworth
was much indebted, the affections, derived from the understanding, are impulses exciting
us to pursue pleasure and avoid pain.

In the primal sympathy
Which having been must ever be;
In the soothing thoughts that spring
Out of human suffering;
In the faith that looks through death,
In years that bring the philosophic mind.

XI

And O, ye fountains, meadows, hills, and groves,
Forebode not any severing of our loves!
Yet in my heart of hearts I feel your might;
I only have relinquished one delight   190
To live beneath your more habitual sway.
I love the brooks which down their channels fret,
Even more than when I tripped lightly as they;
The innocent brightness of a new-born day
Is lovely yet;
The clouds that gather round the setting sun
Do take a sober colouring from an eye
That hath kept watch o'er man's mortality;
Another race hath been, and other palms are won.
Thanks to the human heart by which we live,   200
Thanks to its tenderness, its joys, and fears,
To me the meanest flower that blows can give
Thoughts that do often lie too deep for tears.

SAMUEL TAYLOR COLERIDGE

❧ Kubla Khan: Or, A Vision in a Dream

In Xanadu did Kubla Khan
A stately pleasure-dome decree:
Where Alph, the sacred river, ran
Through caverns measureless to man
Down to a sunless sea.
So twice five miles of fertile ground
With walls and towers were girdled round:
And here were gardens bright with sinuous rills
Where blossomed many an incense-bearing tree;
And here were forests ancient as the hills,   10
Enfolding sunny spots of greenery.
But oh! that deep romantic chasm which slanted
Down the green hill athwart a cedarn cover!

A savage place! as holy and enchanted
As e'er beneath a waning moon was haunted
By woman wailing for her demon-lover!
And from this chasm, with ceaseless turmoil seething,
As if this earth in fast thick pants were breathing,
A mighty fountain momently was forced;
Amid whose swift half-intermitted burst   20
Huge fragments vaulted like rebounding hail,
Or chaffy grain beneath the thresher's flail:
And 'mid these dancing rocks at once and ever
It flung up momently the sacred river.
Five miles meandering with a mazy motion
Through wood and dale the sacred river ran,
Then reached the caverns measureless to man,
And sank in tumult to a lifeless ocean:
And 'mid this tumult Kubla heard from far
Ancestral voices prophesying war!   30

The shadow of the dome of pleasure
Floated midway on the waves;
Where was heard the mingled measure
From the fountain and the caves.
It was a miracle of rare device,
A sunny pleasure-dome with caves of ice!

A damsel with a dulcimer
In a vision once I saw:
It was an Abyssinian maid,
And on her dulcimer she played,   40
Singing of Mount Abora.
Could I revive within me
Her symphony and song,
To such a deep delight 'twould win me,
That with music loud and long,
I would build that dome in air,
That sunny dome! those caves of ice!
And all who heard should see them there,
And all should cry, Beware! Beware!
His flashing eyes, his floating hair!   50
Weave a circle round him thrice,
And close your eyes with holy dread,
For he on honey-dew hath fed,
And drunk the milk of Paradise.

41. **Mt. Abora:** probably the idyllic mountain in Abyssinia where kings sent their sons for safety.

❦ *This Lime-Tree Bower My Prison*

In the June of 1797 some long-expected friends paid a visit to the author's cottage; and on the morning of their arrival, he met with an accident, which disabled him from walking during the whole time of their stay. One evening, when they had left him for a few hours, he composed the following lines in the garden-bower.— Coleridge.

WELL, they are gone, and here must I remain,
This lime-tree bower my prison! I have lost
Beauties and feelings, such as would have been
Most sweet to my remembrance even when age
Had dimmed mine eyes to blindness! They meanwhile,
Friends, whom I never more may meet again,
On springy heath, along the hill-top edge,
Wander in gladness, and wind down, perchance,
To that still roaring dell, of which I told;
The roaring dell, o'erwooded, narrow, deep,   10
And only speckled by the mid-day sun;
Where its slim trunk the ash from rock to rock
Flings arching like a bridge—that branchless ash,
Unsunned and damp, whose few poor yellow leaves
Ne'er tremble in the gale, yet tremble still,
Fanned by the water-fall! And there my friends
Behold the dark green file of long lank weeds,
That all at once (a most fantastic sight!)
Still nod and drip beneath the dripping edge
Of the blue clay-stone.   20
                Now, my friends emerge
Beneath the wide wide Heaven—and view again
The many-steepled tract magnificent
Of hilly fields and meadows, and the sea,
With some fair bark, perhaps, whose sails light up
The slip of smooth clear blue betwixt two isles
Of purple shadow! Yes! they wander on
In gladness all; but thou, methinks, most glad,
My gentle-hearted Charles! for thou hast pined
And hungered after nature, many a year,   30
In the great city pent, winning thy way
With sad yet patient soul, through evil and pain
And strange calamity! Ah! slowly sink

6. **Friends:** Charles Lamb, Dorothy and William Wordsworth.

Behind the western ridge, thou glorious sun!
Shine in the slant beams of the sinking orb,
Ye purple heath-flowers! richlier burn, ye clouds!
Live in the yellow light, ye distant groves!
And kindle, thou blue ocean! So my friend
Struck with deep joy may stand, as I have stood,
Silent with swimming sense; yea, gazing round   40
On the wide landscape, gaze till all doth seem
Less gross than bodily; and of such hues
As veil the Almighty Spirit, when yet He makes
Spirits perceive His presence.
                   A delight
Comes sudden on my heart, and I am glad
As I myself were there! Nor in this bower,
This little lime-tree bower, have I not marked
Much that has soothed me. Pale beneath the blaze
Hung the transparent foliage; and I watched   50
Some broad and sunny leaf, and loved to see
The shadow of the leaf and stem above
Dappling its sunshine! And that walnut-tree
Was richly tinged, and a deep radiance lay
Full on the ancient ivy, which usurps
Those fronting elms, and now with blackest mass
Makes their dark branches gleam a lighter hue
Through the late twilight; and though now the bat
Wheels silent by, and not a swallow twitters,
Yet still the solitary humble-bee   60
Sings in the bean-flower! Henceforth I shall know
That Nature ne'er deserts the wise and pure;
No plot so narrow, be but Nature there,
No waste so vacant, but may well employ
Each faculty of sense, and keep the heart
Awake to love and beauty! and sometimes
'Tis well to be bereft of promised good,
That we may lift the soul, and contemplate
With lively joy the joys we cannot share.
My gentle-hearted Charles! when the last rook   70
Beat its straight path along the dusky air
Homewards, I blest it! deeming its black wing
(Now a dim speck, now vanishing in light)
Had crossed the mighty orb's dilated glory,
While thou stood'st gazing; or, when all was still,
Flew creeking o'er thy head, and had a charm
For thee, my gentle-hearted Charles, to whom
No sound is dissonant which tells of life.

42. **Less . . . bodily:** less inanimate than organic, living, and capable of containing a soul.

WALTER SAVAGE LANDOR

❧ *Mother, I Cannot Mind My Wheel*

MOTHER, I cannot mind my wheel;
My fingers ache, my lips are dry:
Oh! if you felt the pain I feel!
But oh, who ever felt as I?
No longer could I doubt him true—
All other men may use deceit;
He always said my eyes were blue,
And often swore my lips were sweet.

GEORGE GORDON, LORD BYRON

❧ *When We Two Parted*

WHEN we two parted
In silence and tears,
Half broken-hearted
To sever for years,
Pale grew thy cheek and cold,
Colder thy kiss;
Truly that hour foretold
Sorrow to this.

The dew of the morning
Sunk chill on my brow—
It felt like the warning
Of what I feel now.
Thy vows are all broken,
And light is thy fame:
I hear thy name spoken,
And share in its shame.

They name thee before me,
A knell to mine ear;
A shudder comes o'er me—
Why wert thou so dear?
They know not I knew thee,
Who knew thee too well—

Long, long shall I rue thee,
Too deeply to tell.

In secret we met—
In silence I grieve,
That thy heart could forget,
Thy spirit deceive.
If I should meet thee
After long years,
How should I greet thee?—
With silence and tears.

❧ *Written After Swimming from Sestos to Abydos*

If, in the month of dark December,
Leander, who was nightly wont
(What maid will not the tale remember?)
To cross thy stream, broad Hellespont!

If, when the wintry tempest roared,
He sped to Hero, nothing loth,
And thus of old thy current poured,
Fair Venus! how I pity both!

For *me*, degenerate modern wretch,
Though in the genial month of May,   10
My dripping limbs I faintly stretch,
And think I've done a feat to-day.

But since he crossed the rapid tide,
According to the doubtful story,
To woo—and—Lord knows what beside,
And swam for love, as I for glory;

'T were hard to say who fared the best:
Sad mortals! thus the gods still plague you!
He lost his labour, I my jest;
For he was drowned, and I've the ague.   20

2. **Leander:** a youth of Abydos who nightly swam the Hellespont to rendezvous with Hero, a priestess of Aphrodite at Sestos. He drowned; she leaped to her death in the sea.
20. **ague:** a severe chill.

❧ On This Day I Complete My Thirty-Sixth Year

'Tis time this heart should be unmoved,
Since others it hath ceased to move:
Yet, though I cannot be beloved,
Still let me love!

My days are in the yellow leaf;
The flowers and fruits of love are gone;
The worm, the canker, and the grief
Are mine alone!

The fire that on my bosom preys
Is lone as some volcanic isle;
No torch is kindled at its blaze—
A funeral pile.

The hope, the fear, the jealous care,
The exalted portion of the pain
And power of love, I cannot share,
But wear the chain.

But 'tis not *thus*—and 'tis not *here*—
Such thoughts should shake my soul, nor *now*,
Where glory decks the hero's bier,
Or binds his brow.

The sword, the banner, and the field,
Glory and Greece, around me see!
The Spartan, borne upon his shield,
Was not more free.

Awake! (not Greece—she *is* awake!)
Awake, my spirit! Think through *whom*
The life-blood tracks its parent lake,
And then strike home!

"On This Day": composed January 22, 1824, in the military camp of Mavrocordato, where Byron had gone to assist the cause of Greek independence. His health was not strong; on April 19, he died.

Tread those reviving passions down,
Unworthy manhood!—unto thee
Indifferent should the smile or frown
Of beauty be.

If thou regrett'st thy youth, *why live?*
The land of honourable death
Is here—up to the field, and give
Away thy breath!

Seek out—less often sought than found—
A soldier's grave, for thee the best;
Then look around, and choose thy ground,
And take thy rest.

❧ *Don Juan: Canto I,* CIV-CXVII

'Twas on the sixth of June, about the hour
Of half-past six—perhaps still nearer seven—
When Julia sate within as pretty a bower
As e'er held houri in that heathenish heaven
Described by Mahomet, and Anacreon Moore,
To whom the lyre and laurels have been given,
With all the trophies of triumphant song—
He won them well, and may he wear them long!

She sate, but not alone; I know not well
How this same interview had taken place,   10
And even if I knew, I should not tell—
People should hold their tongues in any case;
No matter how or why the thing befell,
But there were she and Juan, face to face—
When two such faces are so, 'twould be wise,
But very difficult, to shut their eyes.

3. **Julia:** Dona Julia is a beautiful young woman married to Don Alfonso, thirty years her senior. Through her friendship with Don Juan's mother, Dona Julia meets the innocent sixteen-year-old Don Juan, with the result that the young man is soon forced to set out on his notorious travels to avoid Don Alfonso's vengeance.
4. **houri:** a virgin provided for the Mohammedan faithful in paradise.
5. **Anacreon Moore:** Thomas Moore (1779–1852), a close friend of Byron's, published a translation of Anacreon's *Odes*.

How beautiful she looked! her conscious heart
Glowed in her cheek, and yet she felt no wrong.
Oh Love! how perfect is thy mystic art,
Strengthening the weak, and trampling on the strong!   20
How self-deceitful is the sagest part
Of mortals whom thy lure hath led along!—
The precipice she stood on was immense,
So was her creed in her own innocence.

She thought of her own strength, and Juan's youth,
And of the folly of all prudish fears,
Victorious virtue, and domestic truth,
And then of Don Alfonso's fifty years:
I wish these last had not occurred, in sooth,
Because that number rarely much endears,   30
And through all climes, the snowy and the sunny,
Sounds ill in love, whate'er it may in money.

When people say, "I've told you *fifty* times,"
They mean to scold, and very often do;
When poets say, "I've written *fifty* rhymes,"
They make you dread that they'll recite them too;
In gangs of *fifty*, thieves commit their crimes;
At *fifty* love for love is rare, 'tis true,
But then, no doubt, it equally as true is,
A good deal may be bought for *fifty* louis.   40

Julia had honour, virtue, truth, and love
For Don Alfonso; and she inly swore,
By all the vows below to powers above,
She never would disgrace the ring she wore,
Nor leave a wish which wisdom might reprove;
And while she pondered this, besides much more,
One hand on Juan's carelessly was thrown,
Quite by mistake—she thought it was her own.

Unconsciously she leaned upon the other,
Which played within the tangles of her hair;   50
And to contend with thoughts she could not smother,
She seemed, by the distraction of her air.
'Twas surely very wrong in Juan's mother
To leave together this imprudent pair,
She who for many years had watched her son so—
I'm very certain *mine* would not have done so.

24. **creed:** credence.
40. **louis:** French gold coin worth $4.50.

The hand which still held Juan's, by degrees
Gently, but palpably confirmed its grasp,
As if it said, "Detain me, if you please";
Yet there's no doubt she only meant to clasp 60
His fingers with a pure Platonic squeeze;
She would have shrunk as from a toad, or asp,
Had she imagined such a thing could rouse
A feeling dangerous to a prudent spouse.

I cannot know what Juan thought of this,
But what he did, is much what you would do;
His young lip thanked it with a grateful kiss,
And then, abashed at its own joy, withdrew
In deep despair, lest he had done amiss—
Love is so very timid when 'tis new: 70
She blushed, and frowned not, but she strove to speak,
And held her tongue, her voice was grown so weak.

The sun set, and up rose the yellow moon:
The devil's in the moon for mischief; they
Who called her *chaste*, methinks, began too soon
Their nomenclature; there is not a day,
The longest, not the twenty-first of June,
Sees half the business in a wicked way,
On which three single hours of moonshine smile—
And then she looks so modest all the while. 80

There is a dangerous silence in that hour,
A stillness, which leaves room for the full soul
To open all itself, without the power
Of calling wholly back its self-control;
The silver light which, hallowing tree and tower,
Sheds beauty and deep softness o'er the whole,
Breathes also to the heart, and o'er it throws
A loving languor, which is not repose.

And Julia sate with Juan, half embraced
And half retiring from the glowing arm, 90
Which trembled like the bosom where 'twas placed,
Yet still she must have thought there was no harm,
Or else 'twere easy to withdraw her waist;
But then the situation had its charm,
And then—God knows what next—I can't go on;
I'm almost sorry that I e'er begun.

Oh Plato! Plato! you have paved the way,
With your confounded fantasies, to more

Immoral conduct by the fancied sway
Your system feigns o'er the controlless core   100
Of human hearts, than all the long array
Of poets and romancers: You're a bore,
A charlatan, a coxcomb—and have been,
At best, no better than a go-between.

And Julia's voice was lost, except in sighs,
Until too late for useful conversation;
The tears were gushing from her gentle eyes;
I wish, indeed, they had not had occasion;
But who, alas! can love, and then be wise?
Not that remorse did not oppose temptation;   110
A little still she strove, and much repented,
And whispering "I will ne'er consent"—consented.

PERCY BYSSHE SHELLEY

❧ Ozymandias

I MET a traveller from an antique land
Who said: Two vast and trunkless legs of stone
Stand in the desert. Near them, on the sand,
Half sunk, a shattered visage lies, whose frown,
And wrinkled lip, and sneer of cold command,
Tell that its sculptor well those passions read
Which yet survive, stamped on these lifeless things,
The hand that mocked them and the heart that fed;
And on the pedestal these words appear:
"My name is Ozymandias, king of kings:
Look on my works, ye Mighty, and despair!"
Nothing beside remains. Round the decay
Of that colossal wreck, boundless and bare
The lone and level sands stretch far away.

❧ Sonnet: England in 1819

AN OLD, mad, blind, despised, and dying king,
Princes, the dregs of their dull race, who flow
Through public scorn—mud from a muddy spring—
Rulers who neither see, nor feel, nor know,

1. king: George III.

But leech-like to their fainting country cling,
Till they drop, blind in blood, without a blow;
A people starved and stabbed in the untilled field;
An army, which liberticide and prey
Makes as a two-edged sword to all who wield
Golden and sanguine laws which tempt and slay;   10
Religion Christless, Godless—a book sealed;
A Senate—time's worst statute unrepealed—
Are graves, from which a glorious phantom may
Burst, to illumine our tempestuous day.

❧ *Ode to the West Wind*

I

O WILD West Wind, thou breath of Autumn's being,
Thou, from whose unseen presence the leaves dead
Are driven, like ghosts from an enchanter fleeing,

Yellow, and black, and pale, and hectic red,
Pestilence-stricken multitudes: O thou,
Who chariotest to their dark wintry bed

The wingèd seeds, where they lie cold and low,
Each like a corpse within its grave, until
Thine azure sister of the spring shall blow

Her clarion o'er the dreaming earth, and fill   10
(Driving sweet buds like flocks to feed in air)
With living hues and odours plain and hill;

Wild Spirit, which art moving everywhere;
Destroyer and preserver; hear, Oh hear!

II

Thou on whose stream, 'mid the steep sky's commotion,
Loose clouds like earth's decaying leaves are shed,
Shook from the tangled boughs of heaven and ocean,

Angels of rain and lightning: there are spread
On the blue surface of thine airy surge,
Like the bright hair uplifted from the head   20

Of some fierce Mænad, even from the dim verge
Of the horizon to the zenith's height,
The locks of the approaching storm. Thou dirge

21. **Mænad:** one of the mad women who served Bacchus.

Of the dying year, to which this closing night
Will be the dome of a vast sepulchre,
Vaulted with all thy congregated might

Of vapours, from whose solid atmosphere
Black rain, and fire, and hail will burst: Oh hear!

III

Thou who didst waken from his summer dreams
The blue Mediterranean, where he lay,   30
Lulled by the coil of his crystalline streams,

Beside a pumice isle in Baiæ's bay,
And saw in sleep old palaces and towers
Quivering within the wave's intenser day,

All overgrown with azure moss and flowers
So sweet, the sense faints picturing them! Thou
For whose path the Atlantic's level powers

Cleave themselves into chasms, while far below
The sea-blooms and the oozy woods which wear
The sapless foliage of the ocean, know   40

Thy voice, and suddenly grow gray with fear,
And tremble and despoil themselves: Oh hear!

IV

If I were a dead leaf thou mightest bear;
If I were a swift cloud to fly with thee;
A wave to pant beneath thy power, and share

The impulse of thy strength, only less free
Than thou, O uncontrollable! If even
I were as in my boyhood, and could be

The comrade of thy wanderings over heaven,
As then, when to outstrip thy skiey speed   50
Scarce seemed a vision; I would ne'er have striven

As thus with thee in prayer in my sore need.
Oh! lift me as a wave, a leaf, a cloud!
I fall upon the thorns of life! I bleed!

32. **Baiæ:** city in southwest Italy.

A heavy weight of hours has chained and bowed
One too like thee; tameless, and swift, and proud.

V

Make me thy lyre, even as the forest is:
What if my leaves are falling like its own!
The tumult of thy mighty harmonies

Will take from both a deep, autumnal tone,   60
Sweet though in sadness. Be thou, spirit fierce,
My spirit! Be thou me, impetuous one!

Drive my dead thoughts over the universe
Like withered leaves to quicken a new birth!
And, by the incantation of this verse,

Scatter, as from an unextinguished hearth
Ashes and sparks, my words among mankind!
Be through my lips to unawakened earth

The trumpet of a prophecy! O, wind,
If Winter comes, can Spring be far behind?   70

❧ Lines: "When the Lamp Is Shattered"

When the lamp is shattered
The light in the dust lies dead—
When the cloud is scattered
The rainbow's glory is shed.
When the lute is broken,
Sweet tones are remembered not;
When the lips have spoken,
Loved accents are soon forgot.

As music and splendour
Survive not the lamp and the lute,   10
The heart's echoes render
No song when the spirit is mute—
No song but sad dirges,
Like the wind through a ruined cell,
Or the mournful surges
That ring the dead seaman's knell.

16. **knell:** the image is of a bell-buoy.

When hearts have once mingled,
Love first leaves the well-built nest;
The weak one is singled
To endure what it once possessed.   20
O Love! who bewailest
The frailty of all things here,
Why choose you the frailest
For your cradle, your home, and your bier?

Its passions will rock thee
As the storms rock the ravens on high;
Bright reason will mock thee,
Like the sun from a wintry sky.
From thy nest every rafter
Will rot, and thine eagle home   30
Leave thee naked to laughter,
When leaves fall and cold winds come.

WILLIAM CULLEN BRYANT

❧ *To a Waterfowl*

WHITHER, midst falling dew,
While glow the heavens with the last steps of day,
Far, through their rosy depths, dost thou pursue
Thy solitary way?

Vainly the fowler's eye
Might mark thy distant flight to do thee wrong,
As, darkly seen against the crimson sky,
Thy figure floats along.

Seek'st thou the plashy brink
Of weedy lake, or marge of river wide,
Or where the rocking billows rise and sink
On the chafed ocean-side?

There is a Power whose care
Teaches thy way along that pathless coast—
The desert and illimitable air—
Lone wandering, but not lost.

25. **Its passions:** the human passions of "the frailest," where Love chooses to nest.

All day thy wings have fanned,
At that far height, the cold, thin atmosphere,
Yet stoop not, weary, to the welcome land,
Though the dark night is near.

And soon that toil shall end;
Soon shalt thou find a summer home, and rest,
And scream among thy fellows; reeds shall bend,
Soon, o'er thy sheltered nest.

Thou'rt gone, the abyss of heaven
Hath swallowed up thy form; yet, on my heart
Deeply hath sunk the lesson thou hast given,
And shall not soon depart.

He who, from zone to zone,
Guides through the boundless sky thy certain flight,
In the long way that I must tread alone,
Will lead my steps aright.

JOHN KEATS

❧ *On First Looking into Chapman's Homer*

Much have I travelled in the realms of gold,
And many goodly states and kingdoms seen;
Round many western islands have I been
Which bards in fealty to Apollo hold.
Oft of one wide expanse had I been told
That deep-browed Homer ruled as his demesne;
Yet did I never breathe its pure serene
Till I heard Chapman speak out loud and bold:
Then felt I like some watcher of the skies
When a new planet swims into his ken;   10
Or like stout Cortez when with eagle eyes
He stared at the Pacific—and all his men
Looked at each other with a wild surmise—
Silent, upon a peak in Darien.

"Chapman": George Chapman (1559?–1634?) published verse translations of *The Iliad* in 1611, *The Odyssey* in 1615.

4. **fealty to Apollo:** in obedience to the god of poetry.
6. **demesne:** domain, in the feudal sense.
11. **Cortez:** in fact, it was Balboa.
14. **Darien:** the Isthmus of Panama.

❧ *On Seeing the Elgin Marbles*

My spirit is too weak—mortality
Weighs heavily on me like unwilling sleep,
And each imagined pinnacle and steep
Of godlike hardship, tells me I must die
Like a sick eagle looking at the sky.
Yet 'tis a gentle luxury to weep
That I have not the cloudy winds to keep,
Fresh for the opening of the morning's eye.
Such dim-conceivèd glories of the brain
Bring round the heart an undescribable feud;
So do these wonders a most dizzy pain,
That mingles Grecian grandeur with the rude
Wasting of old Time—with a billowy main—
A sun—a shadow of a magnitude.

❧ *On the Sea*

It keeps eternal whisperings around
Desolate shores, and with its mighty swell
Gluts twice ten thousand caverns, till the spell
Of Hecate leaves them their old shadowy sound.
Often 'tis in such gentle temper found,
That scarcely will the very smallest shell
Be moved for days from where it sometime fell,
When last the winds of heaven were unbound.
Oh ye! who have your eye-balls vexed and tired,
Feast them upon the wideness of the sea;   10
Oh ye! whose ears are dinned with uproar rude,
Or fed too much with cloying melody—
Sit ye near some old cavern's mouth, and brood
Until ye start, as if the sea-nymphs quired!

"Elgin": The Earl of Elgin (1766–1841) brought to England parts of the Parthenon frieze and pediment, which were placed in the British Museum in 1816.

4. **Hecate:** a witchlike goddess of the moon.
14. **quired:** choired, sang together in harmony.

❧ *Ode to a Nightingale*

My heart aches, and a drowsy numbness pains
My sense, as though of hemlock I had drunk,
Or emptied some dull opiate to the drains
One minute past, and Lethe-wards had sunk:
'Tis not through envy of thy happy lot,
But being too happy in thine happiness—
That thou, light wingèd Dryad of the trees,
In some melodious plot
Of beechen green, and shadows numberless,
Singest of summer in full-throated ease.   10

O, for a draught of vintage! that hath been
Cool'd a long age in the deep-delvèd earth,
Tasting of Flora and the country green,
Dance, and Provençal song, and sunburnt mirth!
O for a beaker full of the warm South,
Full of the true, the blushful Hippocrene,
With beaded bubbles winking at the brim,
And purple-stainèd mouth;
That I might drink, and leave the world unseen,
And with thee fade away into the forest dim: 20

Fade far away, dissolve, and quite forget
What thou among the leaves hast never known,
The weariness, the fever, and the fret
Here, where men sit and hear each other groan;
Where palsy shakes a few, sad, last gray hairs,
Where youth grows pale, and spectre-thin, and dies;
Where but to think is to be full of sorrow
And leaden-eyed despairs,
Where Beauty cannot keep her lustrous eyes,
Or new Love pine at them beyond to-morrow.   30

Away! away! for I will fly to thee,
Not charioted by Bacchus and his pards,

---

2. **hemlock:** a kind of poison.
4. **Lethe-wards:** toward the river of forgetfulness in Hades.
7. **Dryad:** a nymph or goddess inhabiting trees.
16. **Hippocrene:** spring on Mt. Helicon, which gave poetic inspiration.
32. **Bacchus:** God of Wine.

But on the viewless wings of poesy,
Though the dull brain perplexes and retards:
Already with thee! tender is the night,
And haply the Queen-Moon is on her throne,
Clustered around by all her starry fays;
But here there is no light,
Save what from heaven is with the breezes blown
Through verdurous glooms and winding mossy ways.   40

I cannot see what flowers are at my feet,
Nor what soft incense hangs upon the boughs,
But, in embalmèd darkness, guess each sweet
Wherewith the seasonable month endows
The grass, the thicket, and the fruit-tree wild:
White hawthorn, and the pastoral eglantine;
Fast fading violets covered up in leaves;
And mid-May's eldest child,
The coming musk-rose, full of dewy wine,
The murmurous haunt of flies on summer eves.   50

Darkling I listen; and, for many a time
I have been half in love with easeful Death,
Called him soft names in many a musèd rhyme,
To take into the air my quiet breath;
Now more than ever seems it rich to die,
To cease upon the midnight with no pain,
While thou art pouring forth thy soul abroad
In such an ecstasy!
Still wouldst thou sing, and I have ears in vain—
To thy high requiem become a sod.   60

Thou wast not born for death, immortal bird!
No hungry generations tread thee down;
The voice I hear this passing night was heard
In ancient days by emperor and clown:
Perhaps the self-same song that found a path
Through the sad heart of Ruth, when, sick for home,
She stood in tears amid the alien corn;
The same that oft-times hath
Charmed magic casements, opening on the foam
Of perilous seas, in faery lands forlorn.   70

37. **fays:** fairies.
51. **Darkling:** in the dark.
60. **sod:** in the negative sense of *clod*(?) If so, the poem turns sharply here.
64. **clown:** peasant.
66. **Ruth:** the widowed daughter of Naomi, exiled in the kingdom of Boaz.

Forlorn! the very word is like a bell
To toll me back from thee to my sole self!
Adieu! the fancy cannot cheat so well
As she is famed to do, deceiving elf.
Adieu! adieu! thy plaintive anthem fades
Past the near meadows, over the still stream,
Up the hill-side; and now 'tis buried deep
In the next valley-glades:
Was it a vision, or a waking dream?
Fled is that music:—Do I wake or sleep?   80

❧ *Ode on a Grecian Urn*

THOU still unravished bride of quietness,
Thou foster-child of silence and slow time,
Sylvan historian, who canst thus express
A flowery tale more sweetly than our rhyme:
What leaf-fringed legend haunts about thy shape
Of deities or mortals, or of both,
In Tempe or the dales of Arcady?
What men or gods are these? What maidens loth?
What mad pursuit? What struggle to escape?
What pipes and timbrels? What wild ecstasy?   10

Heard melodies are sweet, but those unheard
Are sweeter; therefore, ye soft pipes, play on;
Not to the sensual ear, but, more endeared,
Pipe to the spirit ditties of no tone:
Fair youth, beneath the trees, thou canst not leave
Thy song, nor ever can those trees be bare;
Bold lover, never, never canst thou kiss
Though winning near the goal—yet, do not grieve;
She cannot fade, though thou hast not thy bliss;
Forever wilt thou love, and she be fair!   20

Ah, happy, happy boughs! that cannot shed
Your leaves, nor ever bid the Spring adieu;
And, happy melodist, unwearied,
Forever piping songs forever new;
More happy love! more happy, happy love!

79. **vision . . . dream:** i.e., was it a revelation of truth or a momentary illusion?
7. **Tempe:** beautiful valley in Thessaly, near Mt. Olympus.
7. **Arcady:** district in the Peloponnesus.
10. **timbrels:** tambourines.

Forever warm and still to be enjoyed,
Forever panting, and forever young;
All breathing human passion far above,
That leaves a heart high-sorrowful and cloyed,
A burning forehead, and a parching tongue.   30

Who are these coming to the sacrifice?
To what green altar, O mysterious priest,
Lead'st thou that heifer lowing at the skies,
And all her silken flanks with garlands dressed?
What little town by river or sea shore,
Or mountain-built with peaceful citadel,
Is emptied of this folk, this pious morn?
And, little town, thy streets for evermore
Will silent be; and not a soul to tell
Why thou art desolate, can e'er return.   40

O Attic shape! Fair attitude! with brede
Of marble men and maidens overwrought
With forest branches and the trodden weed;
Thou, silent form, dost tease us out of thought
As doth eternity: cold pastoral!
When old age shall this generation waste,
Thou shalt remain, in midst of other woe
Than ours, a friend to man, to whom thou say'st,
"Beauty is truth, truth beauty"—that is all
Ye know on earth, and all ye need to know.   50

❧ *To Autumn*

SEASON of mists and mellow fruitfulness,
Close bosom-friend of the maturing sun;
Conspiring with him how to load and bless
With fruit the vines that round the thatch-eaves run;
To bend with apples the mossed cottage-trees,
And fill all fruit with ripeness to the core;
To swell the gourd, and plump the hazel shells
With a sweet kernel; to set budding more,
And still more, later flowers for the bees,
Until they think warm days will never cease,   10
For Summer has o'er-brimmed their clammy cells.

41. **Attic:** Greek.
41. **brede:** braid, embroidery; but a pun on *breed* as well(?).

Who hath not seen thee oft amid thy store?
Sometimes whoever seeks abroad may find
Thee sitting careless on a granary floor,
Thy hair soft-lifted by the winnowing wind;
Or on a half-reaped furrow sound asleep,
Drowsed with the fume of poppies, while thy hook
Spares the next swath and all its twined flowers:
And sometimes like a gleaner thou dost keep
Steady thy laden head across a brook;   20
Or by a cider-press, with patient look,
Thou watchest the last oozings hours by hours.

Where are the songs of Spring? Ay, where are they?
Think not of them, thou hast thy music too—
While barred clouds bloom the soft-dying day,
And touch the stubble-plains with rosy hue;
Then in a wailful choir the small gnats mourn
Among the river sallows, borne aloft
Or sinking as the light wind lives or dies;
And full-grown lambs loud bleat from hilly bourn;   30
Hedge-crickets sing; and now with treble soft
The red-breast whistles from a garden-croft;
And gathering swallows twitter in the skies.

ALFRED, LORD TENNYSON

❧ *Break, Break, Break*

BREAK, break, break,
On thy cold gray stones, O Sea!
And I would that my tongue could utter
The thoughts that arise in me.

O well for the fisherman's boy,
That he shouts with his sister at play!
O well for the sailor lad,
That he sings in his boat on the bay!

And the stately ships go on
To their haven under the hill;
But O for the touch of a vanished hand,
And the sound of a voice that is still!

32. **garden-croft:** small piece of fenced ground.

Break, break, break,
At the foot of thy crags, O Sea!
But the tender grace of a day that is dead
Will never come back to me.

❧ *Tears, Idle Tears*

TEARS, idle tears, I know not what they mean,
Tears from the depth of some divine despair
Rise in the heart, and gather to the eyes,
In looking on the happy Autumn-fields,
And thinking of the days that are no more.

Fresh as the first beam glittering on a sail
That brings our friends up from the underworld,
Sad as the last which reddens over one
That sinks with all we love below the verge;
So sad, so fresh, the days that are no more.   10

Ah, sad and strange as in dark summer dawns
The earliest pipe of half-awakened birds
To dying ears, when unto dying eyes
The casement slowly grows a glimmering square;
So sad, so strange, the days that are no more.

Dear as remembered kisses after death,
And sweet as those by hopeless fancy feigned
On lips that are for others; deep as love,
Deep as first love, and wild with all regret;
O Death in Life, the days that are no more!   20

❧ *Ulysses*

IT little profits that an idle king,
By this still hearth, among these barren crags,
Matched with an aged wife, I mete and dole
Unequal laws unto a savage race,
That hoard, and sleep, and feed, and know not me.

---

7. **underworld:** in two senses, as the world below the horizon and as Hades, the world
of the dead to which Ulysses was able to sail.

I cannot rest from travel: I will drink
Life to the lees; all times I have enjoyed
Greatly, have suffered greatly, both with those
That loved me, and alone; on shore, and when
Through scudding drifts the rainy Hyades   10
Vext the dim sea. I am become a name;
For always roaming with a hungry heart
Much have I seen and known; cities of men,
And manners, climates, councils, governments,
Myself not least, but honoured of them all;
And drunk delight of battle with my peers,
Far on the ringing plains of windy Troy.
I am a part of all that I have met;
Yet all experience is an arch wherethrough
Gleams that untravelled world, whose margin fades   20
For ever and for ever when I move.
How dull it is to pause, to make an end,
To rust unburnished, not to shine in use!
As though to breathe were life. Life piled on life
Were all too little, and of one to me
Little remains; but every hour is saved
From that eternal silence, something more,
A bringer of new things; and vile it were
For some three suns to store and hoard myself,
And this grey spirit yearning in desire   30
To follow knowledge like a sinking star,
Beyond the utmost bound of human thought.
This is my son, mine own Telemachus,
To whom I leave the sceptre and the isle—
Well-loved of me, discerning to fulfil
This labour, by slow prudence to make mild
A rugged people, and through soft degrees
Subdue them to the useful and the good.
Most blameless is he, centered in the sphere
Of common duties, decent not to fail   40
In offices of tenderness, and pay
Meet adoration to my household gods,
When I am gone. He works his work, I mine.
There lies the port; the vessel puffs her sail;
There gloom the dark broad seas. My mariners,
Souls that have toiled, and wrought, and thought with me—
That ever with a frolic welcome took
The thunder and the sunshine, and opposed
Free hearts, free foreheads—you and I are old;
Old age hath yet his honour and his toil;   50
Death closes all; but something ere the end,

10. **Hyades:** a moving cluster of stars supposed to indicate rain.

Some work of noble note, may yet be done,
Not unbecoming men that strove with Gods.
The lights begin to twinkle from the rocks;
The long day wanes; the slow moon climbs; the deep
Moans round with many voices. Come, my friends,
'Tis not too late to seek a newer world.
Push off, and sitting well in order smite
The sounding furrows; for my purpose holds
To sail beyond the sunset, and the baths   60
Of all the western stars, until I die.
It may be that the gulfs will wash us down;
It may be we shall touch the Happy Isles,
And see the great Achilles, whom we knew.
Though much is taken, much abides; and though
We are not now that strength which in old days
Moved earth and heaven; that which we are, we are;
One equal temper of heroic hearts,
Made weak by time and fate, but strong in will
To strive, to seek, to find, and not to yield.   70

❧ I Held It Truth, With Him Who Sings

[IN MEMORIAM: 1]

I HELD it truth, with him who sings
To one clear harp in divers tones,
That men may rise on stepping-stones
Of their dead selves to higher things.

But who shall so forecast the years
And find in loss a gain to match?
Or reach a hand thro' time to catch
The far-off interest of tears?

Let Love clasp Grief lest both be drowned,
Let darkness keep her raven gloss: 10

63. **Happy Isles:** a paradise for heroes, supposed to be in the Atlantic beyond Gibraltar.

"I Held It Truth": This is the first in a sequence of 131 poems concerned with the poet's grief at the death of his friend A. H. Hallam. The sequence illustrates the gradual resolution of grief and comments widely on the intellectual currents of the Victorian period.
1. **him who sings:** Goethe.
8. **interest:** in the monetary sense.

Ah, sweeter to be drunk with loss,
To dance with death, to beat the ground,

Than that the victor Hours should scorn
The long result of love, and boast,
"Behold the man that loved and lost,
But all he was is overworn."

❧ *By Night We Lingered on the Lawn*

[IN MEMORIAM: XCV]

By night we lingered on the lawn,
For underfoot the herb was dry;
And genial warmth; and o'er the sky
The silvery haze of summer drawn;

And calm that let the tapers burn
Unwavering: not a cricket chirred:
The brook alone far-off was heard,
And on the board the fluttering urn:

And bats went round in fragrant skies,
And wheeled or lit the filmy shapes   10
That haunt the dusk, with ermine capes
And woolly breasts and beaded eyes;

While now we sang old songs that pealed
From knoll to knoll, where, couched at ease,
The white kine glimmered, and the trees
Laid their dark arms about the field.

But when those others, one by one,
Withdrew themselves from me and night,
And in the house light after light
Went out, and I was all alone,   20

A hunger seized my heart; I read
Of that glad year which once had been,
In those fall'n leaves which kept their green,
The noble letters of the dead:

15. **kine:** cattle.

And strangely on the silence broke
The silent-speaking words, and strange
Was love's dumb cry defying change
To test his worth; and strangely spoke

The faith, the vigour, bold to dwell
On doubts that drive the coward back,   30
And keen thro' wordy snares to track
Suggestion to her inmost cell.

So word by word, and line by line,
The dead man touched me from the past,
And all at once it seemed at last
The living soul was flashed on mine.

And mine in this was wound, and whirled
About empyreal heights of thought,
And came on that which is, and caught
The deep pulsations of the world.   40

Aeonian music measuring out
The steps of Time—the shocks of Chance—
The blows of Death. At length my trance
Was cancelled, stricken thro' with doubt.

Vague words! but ah, how hard to frame
In matter-moulded forms of speech,
Or even for intellect to reach
Thro' memory that which I became:

Till now the doubtful dusk revealed
The knolls once more where, couched at ease,   50
The white kine glimmered, and the trees
Laid their dark arms about the field:

And sucked from out the distant gloom
A breeze began to tremble o'er
The large leaves of the sycamore,
And fluctuate all the still perfume,

And gathering freshlier overhead,
Rocked the full foliaged elms, and swung
The heavy-folded rose, and flung
The lilies to and fro, and said   60

38. **empyreal:** the highest celestial level.
41. **Aeonian:** eternal.

"The dawn, the dawn," and died away;
And East and West, without a breath,
Mixt their dim lights, like life and death,
To broaden into boundless day.

❧ *The Oak*

Live thy life,
Young and old,
Like yon oak,
Bright in spring,
Living gold;

Summer-rich
Then; and then
Autumn-changed,
Soberer-hued
Gold again.

All his leaves
Fallen at length,
Look, he stands,
Trunk and bough,
Naked strength.

ROBERT BROWNING

❧ *My Last Duchess*

FERRARA

That's my last Duchess painted on the wall,
Looking as if she were alive. I call
That piece a wonder, now: Frà Pandolf's hands
Worked busily a day, and there she stands.
Will't please you sit and look at her? I said
"Frà Pandolf" by design, for never read
Strangers like you that pictured countenance,
The depth and passion of its earnest glance,
But to myself they turned (since none puts by

The curtain I have drawn for you, but I)
And seemed as they would ask me, if they durst,
How such a glance came there; so, not the first
Are you to turn and ask thus. Sir, 'twas not
Her husband's presence only, called that spot
Of joy into the Duchess' cheek; perhaps
Frà Pandolf chanced to say, "Her mantle laps
Over my lady's wrist too much," or "Paint
Must never hope to reproduce the faint
Half-flush that dies along her throat": such stuff
Was courtesy, she thought, and cause enough
For calling up that spot of joy. She had
A heart—how shall I say?—too soon made glad,
Too easily impressed: she liked whate'er
She looked on, and her looks went everywhere.
Sir, 'twas all one! My favour at her breast,
The dropping of the daylight in the West,
The bough of cherries some officious fool
Broke in the orchard for her, the white mule
She rode with round the terrace—all and each
Would draw from her alike the approving speech,
Or blush, at least. She thanked men—good! but thanked
Somehow—I know not how—as if she ranked
My gift of a nine-hundred-years-old name
With anybody's gift. Who'd stoop to blame
This sort of trifling? Even had you skill
In speech—which I have not—to make your will
Quite clear to such an one, and say, "Just this
Or that in you disgusts me; here you miss,
Or there exceed the mark"—and if she let
Herself be lessoned so, nor plainly set
Her wits to yours, forsooth, and made excuse,
—E'en then would be some stooping; and I choose
Never to stoop. Oh sir, she smiled, no doubt,
Whene'er I passed her; but who passed without
Much the same smile? This grew; I gave commands;
Then all smiles stopped together. There she stands
As if alive. Will't please you rise? We'll meet
The company below, then. I repeat,
The Count your master's known munificence
Is ample warrant that no just pretence
Of mine for dowry will be disallowed;
Though his fair daughter's self, as I avowed
At starting, is my object. Nay, we'll go
Together down, sir. Notice Neptune, though,
Taming a sea-horse, thought a rarity,
Which Claus of Innsbruck cast in bronze for me!

❧ The Bishop Orders His Tomb at Saint Praxed's Church

ROME, 15—

VANITY, saith the preacher, vanity!
Draw round my bed: is Anselm keeping back?
Nephews—sons mine . . . ah God, I know not! Well—
She, men would have to be your mother once,
Old Gandolf envied me, so fair she was!
What's done is done, and she is dead beside,
Dead long ago, and I am Bishop since,
And as she died so must we die ourselves,
And thence ye may perceive the world's a dream.
Life, how and what is it? As here I lie   10
In this state-chamber, dying by degrees,
Hours and long hours in the dead night, I ask,
"Do I live, am I dead?" Peace, peace seems all.
Saint Praxed's ever was the church for peace;
And so, about this tomb of mine. I fought
With tooth and nail to save my niche, ye know:
—Old Gandolf cozened me, despite my care;
Shrewd was that snatch from out the corner South
He graced his carrion with, God curse the same!
Yet still my niche is not so cramped but thence   20
One sees the pulpit o' the epistle-side,
And somewhat of the choir, those silent seats,
And up into the aery dome where live
The angels, and a sunbeam's sure to lurk;
And I shall fill my slab of basalt there,
And 'neath my tabernacle take my rest,
With those nine columns round me, two and two,
The odd one at my feet where Anselm stands:
Peach-blossom marble all, the rare, the ripe
As fresh-poured red wine of a mighty pulse.   30

5. **Gandolf:** a rival churchman, the bishop's predecessor.
17. **cozened:** outwitted.
21. **epistle-side:** the right, facing the altar.
25. **basalt:** a dark-colored stone.
26. **tabernacle:** canopy.
30. **pulse:** mashed grapes from which wine is made.

—Old Gandolf with his paltry onion-stone,
Put me where I may look at him! True peach,
Rosy and flawless: how I earned the prize!
Draw close: that conflagration of my church
—What then? So much was saved if aught were missed!
My sons, ye would not be my death? Go dig
The white-grape vineyard where the oil-press stood,
Drop water gently till the surface sink,
And if ye find . . . Ah God, I know not, I! . . .
Bedded in store of rotten fig-leaves soft,   40
And corded up in a tight olive-frail,
Some lump, ah God, of *lapis lazuli*,
Big as a Jew's head cut off at the nape,
Blue as a vein o'er the Madonna's breast . . .
Sons, all have I bequeathed you, villas, all,
That brave Frascati villa with its bath,
So, let the blue lump poise between my knees,
Like God the Father's globe on both his hands
Ye worship in the Jesu Church so gay,
For Gandolf shall not choose but see and burst!   50
Swift as a weaver's shuttle fleet our years:

Man goeth to the grave, and where is he?
Did I say basalt for my slab, sons? Black—
'Twas ever antique-black I meant! How else
Shall ye contrast my frieze to come beneath?
The bas-relief in bronze ye promised me,
Those Pans and Nymphs ye wot of, and perchance
Some tripod, thyrsus, with a vase or so,
The Savior at his sermon on the mount,
Saint Praxed in a glory, and one Pan   60
Ready to twitch the Nymph's last garment off,
And Moses with the tables . . . but I know
Ye mark me not! What do they whisper thee,
Child of my bowels, Anselm? Ah, ye hope
To revel down my villas while I gasp
Bricked o'er with beggar's moldy travertine

31. **onion-stone:** inferior green marble.
41. **olive-frail:** a basket.
42. **lapis lazuli:** a precious blue stone.
46. **Frascati:** resort near Rome.
49. **Jesu Church:** a Jesuit church in Rome, with an image of God holding a globe of lapis lazuli.
51. **weaver's shuttle:** see Job 7:6.
54. **antique-black:** a black marble, more expensive than the others mentioned.
58. **tripod:** a stool used in pre-Christian times.
58. **thyrsus:** the staff carried as Bacchus' symbol.
66. **travertine:** limestone.

Which Gandolf from his tomb-top chuckles at!
Nay, boys, ye love me—all of jasper, then!
'Tis jasper ye stand pledged to, lest I grieve
My bath must needs be left behind, alas!   70
One block, pure green as a pistachio-nut—
There's plenty jasper somewhere in the world—
And have I not Saint Praxed's ear to pray
Horses for ye, and brown Greek manuscripts,
And mistresses with great smooth marbly limbs?
—That's if ye carve my epitaph aright,
Choice Latin, picked phrase, Tully's every word,
No gaudy ware like Gandolf's second line—
Tully, my masters? Ulpian serves his need!
And then how I shall lie through centuries,   80
And hear the blessed mutter of the mass,
And see God made and eaten all day long,
And feel the steady candle-flame, and taste
Good, strong, thick, stupefying incense-smoke!
For as I lie here, hours of the dead night,
Dying in state and by such slow degrees,
I fold my arms as if they clasped a crook,
And stretch my feet forth straight as stone can point,
And let the bedclothes, for a mortcloth, drop
Into great laps and folds of sculptor's-work: 90
And as yon tapers dwindle, and strange thoughts
Grow, with a certain humming in my ears,
About the life before I lived this life,
And this life too, popes, cardinals and priests,
Saint Praxed at his sermon on the mount,
Your tall pale mother with her talking eyes,
And new-found agate urns as fresh as day,
And marble's language, Latin pure, discreet,
—Aha, ELUCESCEBAT quoth our friend?
No Tully, said I, Ulpian at the best!   100
Evil and brief hath been my pilgrimage.
All *lapis*, all, sons! Else I give the Pope
My villas! Will ye ever eat my heart?
Ever your eyes were as a lizard's quick,
They glitter like your mother's for my soul,
Or ye would heighten my impoverished frieze,

68. **jasper:** a dark-green stone, more expensive than antique-black.
77. **Tully's:** Cicero's, i.e., classic Latin.
79. **Ulpian:** Domitius Ulpianus, whose language was less elegant than Cicero's.
87. **crook:** the shepherd's crook, symbol of a bishop.
89. **mortcloth:** a pall for a corpse.
99. **ELUCESCEBAT:** the better form for "he was famous" is *elucebat*.

Piece out its starved design, and fill my vase
With grapes, and add a visor and a term,
And to the tripod ye would tie a lynx
That in his struggle throws the thyrsus down,   110
To comfort me on my entablature
Whereon I am to lie till I must ask,
"Do I live, am I dead?" There, leave me, there!
For ye have stabbed me with ingratitude
To death—ye wish it—God, ye wish it! Stone—
Gritstone, a-crumble! Clammy squares which sweat
As if the corpse they keep were oozing through—
And no more *lapis* to delight the world!
Well, go! I bless ye. Fewer tapers there,
But in a row: and, going, turn your backs   120
—Aye, like departing altar-ministrants,
And leave me in my church, the church for peace,
That I may watch at lesiure if he leers—
Old Gandolf—at me, from his onion-stone,
As still he envied me, so fair she was!

❧ *"Childe Roland to the Dark Tower Came"*

My first thought was, he lied in every word,
That hoary cripple, with malicious eye
Askance to watch the working of his lie
On mine, and mouth scarce able to afford
Suppression of the glee that pursed and scored
Its edge at one more victim gained thereby.

What else should he be set for, with his staff?
What, save to waylay with his lies, ensnare
All travellers that might find him posted there,
And ask the road? I guessed what skull-like laugh   10
Would break, what crutch 'gin write my epitaph
For pastime in the dusty thoroughfare,

If at his counsel I should turn aside
Into that ominous tract which, all agree,

108. **visor:** mask.
108. **term:** bust and pedestal.
111. **entablature:** the platform on which the reclining statue of the bishop will rest.
The body itself will be beneath.
116. **gritstone:** sandstone.

Hides the Dark Tower. Yet acquiescingly
I did turn as he pointed; neither pride
Nor hope rekindling at the end descried,
So much as gladness that some end might be.

For, what with my whole world-wide wandering,
What with my search drawn out thro' years, my hope   20
Dwindled into a ghost not fit to cope
With that obstreperous joy success would bring—
I hardly tried now to rebuke the spring
My heart made, finding failure in its scope.

As when a sick man very near to death
Seems dead indeed, and feels begin and end
The tears, and takes the farewell of each friend,
And hears one bid the other go, draw breath
Freelier outside ("since all is o'er," he saith,
"And the blow fallen no grieving can amend");   30

While some discuss if near the other graves
Be room enough for this, and when a day
Suits best for carrying the corpse away,
With care about the banners, scarves and staves—
And still the man hears all, and only craves
He may not shame such tender love and stay.

Thus, I had so long suffered in this quest,
Heard failure prophesied so oft, been writ
So many times among "The Band!"—to wit,
The knights who to the Dark Tower's search addressed   40
Their steps—that just to fail as they, seemed best.
And all the doubt was now—should I be fit.

So, quiet as despair, I turned from him,
That hateful cripple, out of his highway
Into the path he pointed. All the day
Had been a dreary one at best, and dim
Was settling to its close, yet shot one grim
Red leer to see the plain catch its estray.

For mark! no sooner was I fairly found
Pledged to the plain, after a pace or two,   50
Than, pausing to throw backward a last view
To the safe road, 'twas gone; grey plain all round:

48. **estray:** stray—with sense of a strayed animal.

Nothing but plain to the horizon's bound.
I might go on; nought else remained to do.

So, on I went. I think I never saw
Such starved ignoble nature; nothing throve:
For flowers—as well expect a cedar grove!
But cockle, spurge, according to their law
Might propagate their kind, with none to awe,
You'd think; a burr had been a treasure-trove.   60

No! penury, inertness and grimace,
In some strange sort, were the land's portion. "See
Or shut your eyes," said Nature peevishly,
"It nothing skills: I cannot help my case:
'Tis the Last Judgment's fire must cure this place,
Calcine its clods and set my prisoners free."

If there pushed any ragged thistle-stalk
Above its mates, the head was chopped—the bents
Were jealous else. What made those holes and rents
In the dock's harsh swarth leaves—bruised as to baulk   70
All hope of greenness? 'tis a brute must walk
Pashing their life out, with a brute's intents.

As for the grass, it grew as scant as hair
In leprosy; thin dry blades pricked the mud
Which underneath looked kneaded up with blood.
One stiff blind horse, his every bone a-stare,
Stood stupefied, however he came there:
Thrust out past service from the devil's stud!

Alive? he might be dead for aught I know,
With that red, gaunt and colloped neck a-strain,   80
And shut eyes underneath the rusty mane;
Seldom went such grotesqueness with such woe;
I never saw a brute I hated so;
He must be wicked to deserve such pain.

I shut my eyes and turned them on my heart.
As a man calls for wine before he fights,

58. **cockle, spurge:** common weeds.
64. **skills:** matters.
66. **calcine:** burn up.
68. **bents:** grasses.
70. **dock:** a coarse weed.
80. **colloped:** loose-skinned.

I asked one draught of earlier, happier sights,
Ere fitly I could hope to play my part.
Think first, fight afterwards—the soldier's art:
One taste of the old time sets all to rights!   90

Not it! I fancied Cuthbert's reddening face
Beneath its garniture of curly gold,
Dear fellow, till I almost felt him fold
An arm in mine to fix me to the place,
That way he used. Alas! one night's disgrace!
Out went my heart's new fire and left it cold.

Giles, then, the soul of honour—there he stands
Frank as ten years ago when knighted first.
What honest men should dare (he said) he durst.
Good—but the scene shifts—faugh! what hangman's hands   100
Pin to his breast a parchment? his own bands
Read it. Poor traitor, spit upon and curst!

Better this present than a past like that;
Back therefore to my darkening path again.
No sound, no sight as far as eye could strain.
Will the night send a howlet or a bat?
I asked: when something on the dismal flat
Came to arrest my thoughts and change their train.

A sudden little river crossed my path
As unexpected as a serpent comes.   110
No sluggish tide congenial to the glooms—
This, as it frothed by, might have been a bath
For the fiend's glowing hoof—to see the wrath
Of its black eddy bespate with flakes and spumes.

So petty yet so spiteful! all along,
Low scrubby alders kneeled down over it;
Drenched willows flung them headlong in a fit
Of mute despair, a suicidal throng:
The river which had done them all the wrong,
Whate'er that was, rolled by, deterred no whit.   120

Which, while I forded—good saints, how I feared
To set my foot upon a dead man's cheek,
Each step, or feel the spear I thrust to seek
For hollows, tangled in his hair or beard!
—It may have been a water-rat I speared,
But, ugh! it sounded like a baby's shriek.

Glad was I when I reached the other bank.
Now for a better country. Vain presage!
Who were the strugglers, what war did they wage,
Whose savage trample thus could pad the dank   130
Soil to a plash? toads in a poisoned tank,
Or wild cats in a red-hot iron cage—

The fight must so have seemed in that fell cirque.
What penned them there, with all the plain to choose?
No footprint leading to that horrid mews,
None out of it. Mad brewage set to work
Their brains, no doubt, like galley-slaves the Turk
Pits for his pastime, Christians against Jews.

And more than that—a furlong on—why, there!
What bad use was that engine for, that wheel,   140
Or brake, not wheel—that harrow fit to reel
Men's bodies out like silk? with all the air
Of Tophet's tool, on earth left unaware,
Or brought to sharpen its rusty teeth of steel.

Then came a bit of stubbed ground, once a wood,
Next a marsh, it would seem, and now mere earth
Desperate and done with—so a fool finds mirth,
Makes a thing and then mars it, till his mood
Changes and off he goes!—within a rood—
Bog, clay and rubble, sand and stark black dearth.   150

Now blotches rankling, coloured gay and grim,
Now patches where some leanness of the soil's
Broke into moss or substances like boils;
Then came some palsied oak, a cleft in him
Like a distorted mouth that splits its rim
Gaping at death, and dies while it recoils.

And just as far as ever from the end!
Nought in the distance but the evening, nought
To point my footsteps further! At the thought,
A great black bird, Apollyon's bosom-friend,   160
Sailed past, nor beat his wide wing dragon-penned
That brushed my cap—perchance the guide I sought.

133. **cirque:** natural amphitheater.
135. **mews:** stables.
141. **brake:** torture instrument.
160. **Apollyon:** the devil.

For, looking up, aware I somehow grew,
'Spite of the dusk, the plain had given place
All round to mountains—with such name to grace
Mere ugly heights and heaps now stolen in view.
How thus they had surprised me—solve it, you!
How to get from them was no clearer case.

Yet half I seemed to recognize some trick
Of mischief happened to me, God knows when—   170
In a bad dream perhaps. Here ended, then,
Progress this way. When, in the very nick
Of giving up, one time more, came a click
As when a trap shuts—you're inside the den!

Burningly it came on me all at once,
This was the place! those two hills on the right,
Crouched like two bulls locked horn in horn in fight;
While to the left, a tall scalped mountain . . . Dunce,
Fool, to be dozing at the very nonce,
After a life spent training for the sight!   180

What in the midst lay but the Tower itself?
The round squat turret, blind as the fool's heart,
Built of brown stone, without a counterpart
In the whole world. The tempest's mocking elf
Points to the shipman thus the unseen shelf
He strikes on, only when the timbers start.

Not see? because of night perhaps?—Why, day
Came back again for that! before it left,
The dying sunset kindled through a cleft:
The hills, like giants at a hunting, lay,   190
Chin upon hand, to see the game at bay—
"Now stab and end the creature—to the heft!"

Not hear? when noise was everywhere! it tolled
Increasing like a bell. Names in my ears
Of all the lost adventurers my peers—
How such a one was strong, and such was bold,
And such was fortunate, yet each of old
Lost, lost! one moment knelled the woe of years.

There they stood, ranged along the hillsides, met
To view the last of me, a living frame   200

179. **nonce:** moment.

For one more picture! in a sheet of flame
I saw them and I knew them all. And yet
Dauntless the slug-horn to my lips I set,
And blew. *"Childe Roland to the Dark Tower came."*

❧ *Fra Lippo Lippi*

I AM poor brother Lippo, by your leave!
You need not clap your torches to my face.
Zooks, what's to blame? you think you see a monk!
What, 'tis past midnight, and you go the rounds,
And here you catch me at an alley's end
Where sportive ladies leave their doors ajar?
The Carmine's my cloister: hunt it up,
Do—harry out, if you must show your zeal,
Whatever rat, there, haps on his wrong hole,
And nip each softling of a wee white mouse,   10
Weke, weke, that's crept to keep him company!
Aha, you know your betters! Then, you'll take
Your hand away that's fiddling on my throat,
And please to know me likewise. Who am I?
Why, one, sir, who is lodging with a friend
Three streets off—he's a certain . . . how d'ye call?
Master—a . . . Cosimo of the Medici,
I' the house that caps the corner. Boh! you were best!
Remember and tell me, the day you're hanged,
How you affected such a gullet's-gripe!   20
But you, sir, it concerns you that your knaves
Pick up a manner nor discredit you:
Zooks, are we pilchards, that they sweep the streets
And count fair prize what comes into their net?
He's Judas to a tittle, that man is!
Just such a face! Why, sir, you make amends.
Lord, I'm not angry! Bid your hangdogs go
Drink out this quarter-florin to the health
Of the munificent House that harbors me
(And many more beside, lads! more beside!)   30
And all's come square again. I'd like his face—

203. **slug-horn:** trumpet.

   1. **Lippo:** Fra Lippo Lippi (1406–1469), a famous painter of Florence.
   7. **Carmine:** a Carmelite monastery in Florence.
  17. **Cosimo:** Cosimo de' Medici (1389–1464) was one of the most famous members
of the family that ruled Florence.
  23. **pilchards:** cheap fish, sardines.

His, elbowing on his comrade in the door
With the pike and lantern—for the slave that holds
John Baptist's head a-dangle by the hair
With one hand ("Look you, now," as who should say)
And his weapon in the other, yet unwiped!
It's not your chance to have a bit of chalk,
A wood-coal or the like? or you should see!
Yes, I'm the painter, since you style me so.
What, brother Lippo's doings, up and down,   40
You know them and they take you? like enough!
I saw the proper twinkle in your eye—
Tell you, I liked your looks at very first.
Let's sit and set things straight now, hip to haunch.
Here's spring come, and the nights one makes up bands
To roam the town and sing out carnival,
And I've been three weeks shut within my mew,
A-painting for the great man, saints and saints
And saints again. I could not paint all night—
Ouf! I leaned out of window for fresh air.   50
There came a hurry of feet and little feet,
A sweep of lute-strings, laughs, and whifts of song—
Flower o' the broom,
Take away love, and our earth is a tomb!
Flower o' the quince,
I let Lisa go, and what good in life since?
Flower o' the thyme—and so on. Round they went.
Scarce had they turned the corner when a titter
Like the skipping of rabbits by moonlight—three slim shapes,
And a face that looked up . . . Zooks, sir, flesh and blood,   60
That's all I'm made of! Into shreds it went,
Curtain and counterpane and coverlet,
All the bed-furniture—a dozen knots,
There was a ladder! Down I let myself,
Hands and feet, scrambling somehow, and so dropped,
And after them. I came up with the fun
Hard by Saint Laurence, hail fellow, well met—
Flower o' the rose,
If I've been merry, what matter who knows?
And so as I was stealing back again   70
To get to bed and have a bit of sleep
Ere I rise up to-morrow and go work
On Jerome knocking at his poor old breast

---

46. **carnival:** celebration preceding Lent.
47. **mew:** stable or pen.
67. **Saint Laurence:** Church of San Lorenzo.
73. **Jerome:** Saint Jerome (340?–420), an ascetic Father of the Church who lived in
the desert as penance for his sins.

With his great round stone to subdue the flesh,
You snap me of the sudden. Ah, I see!
Though your eye twinkles still, you shake your head—
Mine's shaved—a monk, you say—the sting's in that!
If Master Cosimo announced himself,
Mum's the word naturally; but a monk!
Come, what am I a beast for? tell us, now!   80
I was a baby when my mother died
And father died and left me in the street.
I starved there, God knows how, a year or two
On fig-skins, melon-parings, rinds and shucks,
Refuse and rubbish. One fine frosty day,
My stomach being empty as your hat,
The wind doubled me up and down I went.
Old Aunt Lapaccia trussed me with one hand,
(Its fellow was a stinger as I knew)
And so along the wall, over the bridge,   90
By the straight cut to the convent. Six words there,
While I stood munching my first bread that month:
"So boy, you're minded," quoth the good fat father,
Wiping his own mouth, 'twas refection-time—
"To quit this very miserable world?
Will you renounce" . . . "the mouthful of bread?" thought I;
By no means! Brief, they made a monk of me;
I did renounce the world, its pride and greed,
Palace, farm, villa, shop, and banking-house,
Trash, such as these poor devils of Medici   100
Have given their hearts to—all at eight years old.
Well, sir, I found in time, you may be sure,
'Twas not for nothing—the good bellyful,
The warm serge and the rope that goes all 'round,
And day-long blessed idleness beside!
"Let's see what the urchin's fit for"—that came next.
Not overmuch their way, I must confess.
Such a to-do! They tried me with their books;
Lord, they'd have taught me Latin in pure waste!
Flower o' the clove,   110
All the Latin I construe is "amo," I love!
But, mind you, when a boy starves in the streets
Eight years together, as my fortune was,
Watching folk's faces to know who will fling
The bit of half-stripped grape-bunch he desires,
And who will curse or kick him for his pains—
Which gentleman processional and fine,
Holding a candle to the Sacrament,

117. **processional:** in a religious procession through the streets.

Will wink and let him lift a plate and catch
The droppings of the wax to sell again,   120
Or holla for the Eight and have him whipped—
How say I?—nay, which dog bites, which lets drop
His bone from the heap of offal in the street—
Why, soul and sense of him grow sharp alike,
He learns the look of things, and none the less
For admonition from the hunger-pinch.
I had a store of such remarks, be sure,
Which, after I found leisure, turned to use.
I drew men's faces on my copy-books,
Scrawled them within the antiphonary's marge,   130
Joined legs and arms to the long music-notes,
Found eyes and nose and chin for A's and B's,
And made a string of pictures of the world
Betwixt the ins and outs of verb and noun,
On the wall, the bench, the door. The monks looked black.
"Nay," quoth the Prior, "turn him out, d'ye say?
In no wise. Lose a crow and catch a lark.
What if at last we get our man of parts,
We Carmelites, like those Camaldolese
And Preaching Friars, to do our church up fine   140
And put the front on it that ought to be!"
And hereupon he bade me daub away.
Thank you! my head being crammed, the walls a blank,
Never was such prompt disemburdening.
First, every sort of monk, the black and white,
I drew them, fat and lean: then, folk at church,
From good old gossips waiting to confess
Their cribs of barrel-droppings, candle-ends—
To the breathless fellow at the altar-foot,
Fresh from his murder, safe and sitting there   150
With the little children round him in a row
Of admiration, half for his beard and half
For that white anger of his victim's son
Shaking a fist at him with one fierce arm,
Signing himself with the other because of Christ
(Whose sad face on the cross sees only this
After the passion of a thousand years)
Till some poor girl, her apron o'er her head,
(Which the intense eyes looked through) came at eve

---

121. **Eight:** the governing magistrates.
122. **How say I?:** Here, Lippo fears he has given the captain an idea of doing the same.
130. **antiphonary:** hymn book.
139. **Camaldolese:** from the convent of Camaldoli, outside Florence.
140. **Preaching Friars:** Dominicans.

On tiptoe, said a word, dropped in a loaf,   160
Her pair of earrings and a bunch of flowers
(The brute took growling), prayed, and so was gone.
I painted all, then cried " 'Tis ask and have;
Choose, for more's ready!"—laid the ladder flat,
And showed my covered bit of cloister-wall.
The monks closed in a circle and praised loud
Till checked, taught what to see and not to see,
Being simple bodies—"That's the very man!
Look at the boy who stoops to pat the dog!
That woman's like the Prior's niece who comes   170
To care about his asthma: it's the life!"
But there my triumph's straw-fire flared and funked;
Their betters took their turn to see and say:
The Prior and the learned pulled a face
And stopped all that in no time. "How? what's here?
Quite from the mark of painting, bless us all!
Faces, arms, legs, and bodies like the true
As much as pea and pea! it's devil's game!
Your business is not to catch men with show,
With homage to the perishable clay,   180
But lift them over it, ignore it all,
Make them forget there's such a thing as flesh.
Your business is to paint the souls of men—
Man's soul, and it's a fire, smoke . . . no, it's not . . .
It's vapor done up like a new-born babe—
(In that shape when you die it leaves your mouth)
It's . . . well, what matters talking, it's the soul!
Give us no more of body than shows soul!
Here's Giotto, with his Saint a-praising God,
That sets us praising—why not stop with him?   190
Why put all thoughts of praise out of our head
With wonder at lines, colors, and what not?
Paint the soul, never mind the legs and arms!
Rub all out, try at it a second time.
Oh, that white smallish female with the breasts,
She's just my niece . . . Herodias, I would say—
Who went and danced and got men's heads cut off!
Have it all out!" Now, is this sense, I ask?
A fine way to paint soul, by painting body
So ill, the eye can't stop there, must go further   200
And can't fare worst! Thus, yellow does for white
When what you put for yellow's simply black,

189. **Giotto:** Giotto di Bondone (1276–1337), who preceded Lippo, was anything but
a realistic painter.
201. **yellow does for white:** color tones are relative—yellow will look white if contrasted
with black.

And any sort of meaning looks intense
When all beside itself means and looks naught.
Why can't a painter lift each foot in turn,
Left foot and right foot, go a double step,
Make his flesh liker and his soul more like,
Both in their order? Take the prettiest face,
The Prior's niece . . . patron-saint—is it so pretty
You can't discover if it means hope, fear,   210
Sorrow or joy? won't beauty go with these?
Suppose I've made her eyes all right and blue,
Can't I take breath and try to add life's flash,
And then add soul and heighten them three-fold?
Or say there's beauty with no soul at all—
(I never saw it—put the case the same—)
If you get simple beauty and naught else,
You get about the best thing God invents:
That's somewhat: and you'll find the soul you have missed,
Within yourself, when you return him thanks.   220
"Rub all out!" Well, well, there's my life, in short,
And so the thing has gone on ever since.
I'm grown a man no doubt, I've broken bounds:
You should not take a fellow eight years old
And make him swear to never kiss the girls.
I'm my own master, paint now as I please—
Having a friend, you see, in the Corner-house!
Lord, it's fast holding by the rings in front—
Those great rings serve more purposes than just
To plant a flag in, or tie up a horse!   230
And yet the old schooling sticks, the old grave eyes
Are peeping o'er my shoulder as I work,
The heads shake still—"It's art's decline, my son!
You're not of the true painters, great and old;
Brother Angelico's the man, you'll find;
Brother Lorenzo stands his single peer:
Fag on at flesh, you'll never make the third!"
Flower o' the pine,
You keep your mistr . . . manners, and I'll stick to mine!
I'm not the third, then: bless us, they must know!   240
Don't you think they're the likeliest to know,
They with their Latin? So, I swallow my rage,
Clench my teeth, suck my lips in tight, and paint
To please them—sometimes do and sometimes don't;
For, doing most, there's pretty sure to come
A turn, some warm eve finds me at my saints—

235. **Angelico:** Fra Angelico (1387–1455), a great medieval religious painter.
236. **Lorenzo:** Fra Lorenzo Monaco (1380?–1425?), like Lippo a Camaldolese monk.

A laugh, a cry, the business of the world—
(*Flower o' the peach,*
Death for us all, and his own life for each!)
And my whole soul revolves, the cup runs over,   250
The world and life's too big to pass for a dream,
And I do these wild things in sheer despite,
And play the fooleries you catch me at,
In pure rage! The old mill-horse, out at grass
After hard years, throws up his stiff heels so,
Although the miller does not preach to him
The only good of grass is to make chaff.
What would men have? Do they like grass or no—
May they or mayn't they? all I want's the thing
Settled for ever one way. As it is,   260
You tell too many lies and hurt yourself:
You don't like what you only like too much,
You do like what, if given you at your word,
You find abundantly detestable.
For me, I think I speak as I was taught;
I always see the garden and God there
A-making man's wife; and, my lesson learned,
The value and significance of flesh,
I can't unlearn ten minutes afterwards.

You understand me: I'm a beast, I know.   270
But see, now—why, I see as certainly
As that the morning-star's about to shine,
What will hap some day. We've a youngster here
Comes to our convent, studies what I do,
Slouches and stares and lets no atom drop:
His name is Guidi—he'll not mind the monks—
They call him Hulking Tom, he lets them talk—
He picks my practice up—he'll paint apace,
I hope so—though I never live so long,
I know what's sure to follow. You be judge!   280
You speak no Latin more than I, belike;
However, you're my man, you've seen the world
—The beauty and the wonder and the power,
The shapes of things, their colors, lights and shades,
Changes, surprises—and God made it all!
—For what? Do you feel thankful, ay or no,
For this fair town's face, yonder river's line,

262. **You don't like:** you pretend to renounce what you really desire; you pursue things you really would not want.
276. **Guidi:** Tommaso Guidi, known as Masaccio (1401–1428) was in fact Lippo's master, not his apprentice.

The mountain round it and the sky above,
Much more the figures of man, woman, child,
These are the frame to? What's it all about?   290
To be passed over, despised? or dwelt upon,
Wondered at? oh, this last of course!—you say.
But why not do as well as say—paint these
Just as they are, careless what comes of it?
God's works—paint any one, and count it crime
To let a truth slip. Don't object, "His works

Are here already; nature is complete:
Suppose you reproduce her—(which you can't)
There's no advantage! you must beat her, then."
For, don't you mark? we're made so that we love   300
First when we see them painted, things we have passed
Perhaps a hundred times nor cared to see;
And so they are better, painted—better to us,
Which is the same thing. Art was given for that;
God uses us to help each other so,
Lending our minds out. Have you noticed, now,
Your cullion's hanging face? A bit of chalk,
And trust me but you should, though! How much more,
If I drew higher things with the same truth!
That were to take the Prior's pulpit-place,   310
Interpret God to all of you! Oh, oh,
It makes me mad to see what men shall do
And we in our graves! This world's no blot for us,
Nor blank; it means intensely, and means good:
To find its meaning is my meat and drink.
"Ay, but you don't so instigate to prayer!"
Strikes in the Prior: "when your meaning's plain
It does not say to folk—remember matins,
Or, mind you fast next Friday!" Why, for this
What need of art at all? A skull and bones,   320
Two bits of stick nailed crosswise, or, what's best,
A bell to chime the hour with, does as well.
I painted a Saint Laurence six months since
At Prato, splashed the fresco in fine style:
"How looks my painting, now the scaffold's down?"
I ask a brother: "Hugely," he returns—
"Already not one phiz of your three slaves
Who turn the Deacon off his toasted side,
But's scratched and prodded to our heart's content,

307. **cullion:** any low person.
307. **hanging face:** a face suggesting that its owner will someday be hanged for something.
323. **Saint Laurence:** St. Laurence was burned to death on a gridiron.
324. **Prato:** Cathedral of Prato, near Florence.

The pious people have so eased their own   330
With coming to say prayers there in a rage:
We get on fast to see the bricks beneath.
Expect another job this time next year,
For pity and religion grow i' the crowd—
Your painting serves its purpose!" Hang the fools!

—That is—you'll not mistake an idle word
Spoke in a huff by a poor monk, God wot,
Tasting the air this spicy night which turns
The unaccustomed head like Chianti wine!
Oh, the church knows! don't misreport me, now!   340
It's natural a poor monk out of bounds
Should have his apt word to excuse himself:
And hearken how I plot to make amends.
I have bethought me: I shall paint a piece
. . . There's for you! Give me six months, then go, see
Something in Sant' Ambrogio's! Bless the nuns!
They want a cast o' my office. I shall paint
God in the midst, Madonna and her babe,
Ringed by a bowery, flowery angel-brood,
Lilies and vestments and white faces, sweet   350
As puff on puff of grated orris-root
When ladies crowd to Church at midsummer.
And then i' the front, of course a saint or two—
Saint John, because he saves the Florentines,
Saint Ambrose, who puts down in black and white
The convent's friends and gives them a long day,
And Job, I must have him there past mistake,
The man of Uz (and Us without the z,
Painters who need his patience). Well, all these
Secured at their devotion, up shall come   360
Out of a corner when you least expect,
As one by a dark stair into a great light,
Music and talking, who but Lippo! I!—
Mazed, motionless, and moonstruck—I'm the man!
Back I shrink—what is this I see and hear?
I, caught up with my monk's-things by mistake,
My old serge gown and rope that goes all round,
I, in this presence, this pure company!
Where's a hole, where's a corner for escape?

335. **Hang the fools!:** Lippo immediately realizes that he has gone too far and perhaps offended the captain.
346. **Sant' Ambrogio's:** a church in Florence.
347. **I shall paint:** Lippo describes his *Coronation of the Virgin*, which exists as
described here.
351. **orris-root:** a fragrant species of iris, grated and used as face powder.

Then steps a sweet angelic slip of a thing   370
Forward, puts out a soft palm—"Not so fast!"
—Addresses the celestial presence, "nay—
He made you and devised you, after all,
Though he's none of you! Could Saint John there draw—
His camel-hair make up a painting-brush?
We come to brother Lippo for all that,
Iste perfecit opus!" So, all smile—
I shuffle sideways with my blushing face
Under the cover of a hundred wings
Thrown like a spread of kirtles when you're gay   380
And play hot cockles, all the doors being shut,
Till, wholly unexpected, in there pops
The hothead husband! Thus I scuttle off
To some safe bench behind, not letting go
The palm of her, the little lily thing
That spoke the good word for me in the nick,
Like the Prior's niece . . . Saint Lucy, I would say.
And so all's saved for me, and for the church
A pretty picture gained. Go, six months hence!
Your hand, sir, and good-by: no lights, no lights!   390
The street's hushed, and I know my own way back,
Don't fear me! There's the gray beginning. Zooks!

WALT WHITMAN

❧ *Out of the Cradle Endlessly Rocking*

OUT of the cradle endlessly rocking,
Out of the mocking-bird's throat, the musical shuttle,
Out of the Ninth-month midnight,
Over the sterile sands, and the fields beyond, where the child, leaving his
    bed, wandered alone, bareheaded, barefoot,
Down from the showered halo,
Up from the mystic play of shadows, twining and twisting as if they were
    alive,
Out from the patches of briers and blackberries,
From the memories of the bird that chanted to me,
From your memories, sad brother—from the fitful risings and fallings I heard,

375. **camel-hair:** St. John wore a hair shirt.
377. **Iste perfecit opus:** The inscription, "This one did the work," appears in the
painting.
380. **kirtles:** skirts.
381. **hot cockles:** a not so innocent variant of blind man's buff.

From under that yellow half-moon, late-risen, and swollen as if with tears, 10
From those beginning notes of sickness and love, there in the transparent mist,
From the thousand responses of my heart, never to cease,
From the myriad thence-aroused words,
From the word stronger and more delicious than any,
From such, as now they start, the scene revisiting,
As a flock, twittering, rising, or overhead passing,
Borne hither—ere all eludes me, hurriedly,
A man—yet by these tears a little boy again,
Throwing myself on the sand, confronting the waves,
I, chanter of pains and joys, uniter of here and hereafter,   20
Taking all hints to use them—but swiftly leaping beyond them,
A reminiscence sing.

Once, Paumanok,
When the snows had melted—when the lilac-scent was in the air, and the
        Fifth-month grass was growing,
Up this sea-shore, in some briers,
Two guests from Alabama—two together,
And their nest, and four light-green eggs, spotted with brown,
And every day the he-bird, to and fro, near at hand,
And every day the she-bird, crouched on her nest, silent, with bright eyes,
And every day I, a curious boy, never too close, never disturbing them, 30
Cautiously peering, absorbing, translating.

Shine! shine! shine!
Pour down your warmth, great Sun!
While we bask—we two together.

Two together!
Winds blow South, or winds blow North,
Day come white, or night come black,
Home, or rivers and mountains from home,
Singing all time, minding no time,
While we two keep together.   40

Till of a sudden,
May-be killed, unknown to her mate,
One forenoon the she-bird crouched not on the nest,
Nor returned that afternoon, nor the next,
Nor ever appeared again.
And thenceforward, all summer, in the sound of the sea,
And at night, under the full of the moon, in calmer weather,

23. **Paumanok:** Long Island.

Over the hoarse surging of the sea,
Or flitting from brier to brier by day,
I saw, I heard at intervals, the remaining one, the he-bird,   50
The solitary guest from Alabama.

Blow! blow! blow!
Blow up, sea-winds, along Paumanok's shore!
I wait and I wait, till you blow my mate to me.

Yes, when the stars glistened,
All night long, on the prong of a moss-scalloped stake,
Down, almost amid the slapping waves,
Sat the lone singer, wonderful, causing tears.

He called on his mate;
He poured forth the meanings which I, of all men, know.   60

Yes, my brother, I know;
The rest might not—but I have treasured every note;
For once, and more than once, dimly, down to the beach gliding,
Silent, avoiding the moonbeams, blending myself with the shadows,
Recalling now the obscure shapes, the echoes, the sounds and sights after
      their sorts,
The white arms out in the breakers tirelessly tossing,
I, with bare feet, a child, the wind wafting my hair,
Listened long and long.

Listened, to keep, to sing—now translating the notes,
Following you, my brother.   70

Soothe! soothe! soothe!
Close on its wave soothes the wave behind,
And again another behind, embracing and lapping, every one close,
But my love soothes not me, not me.

Low hangs the moon—it rose late;
O it is lagging—O I think it is heavy with love, with love.

O madly the sea pushes, pushes upon the land,
With love—with love.

O night! do I not see my love fluttering out there among the breakers?

What is that little black thing I see there in the white?   80
Loud! loud! loud!
Loud I call to you, my love!

High and clear I shoot my voice over the waves;
Surely you must know who is here, is here;
You must know who I am, my love.

Low-hanging moon!
What is that dusky spot in your brown yellow?
O it is the shape, the shape of my mate!
O moon, do not keep her from me any longer.

Land! land! O land!   90
Whichever way I turn, O I think you could give me my mate back again,
    if you only would;
For I am almost sure I see her dimly whichever way I look.

O rising stars!
Perhaps the one I want so much will rise, will rise with some of you.

O throat! O trembling throat!
Sound clearer through the atmosphere!
Pierce the woods, the earth;
Somewhere listening to catch you, must be the one I want.

Shake out, carols!
Solitary here—the night's carols!   100
Carols of lonesome love! Death's carols!
Carols under that lagging, yellow, waning moon!
O, under that moon, where she droops almost down into the sea!
O reckless, despairing carols.

But soft! sink low;
Soft! let me just murmur;
And do you wait a moment, you husky-noised sea;
For somewhere I believe I heard my mate responding to me,
So faint—I must be still, be still to listen;
But not altogether still, for then she might not come immediately to me.   110

Hither, my love!
Here I am! Here!
With this just-sustained note I announce myself to you;
This gentle call is for you, my love, for you.

Do not be decoyed elsewhere!
That is the whistle of the wind—it is not my voice;
That is the fluttering, the fluttering of the spray;
Those are the shadows of leaves.

O darkness! O in vain!
O I am very sick and sorrowful.   120

O brown halo in the sky, near the moon, drooping upon the sea!
O troubled reflection in the sea!
O throat! O throbbing heart!
O all—and I singing uselessly, uselessly all the night.

Yet I murmur, murmur on!
O murmurs—you yourselves make me continue to sing, I know not why.
O past! O life! O songs of joy!
In the air—in the woods—over fields;
Loved! loved! loved! loved! loved!
But my love no more, no more with me!   130
We two together no more.

The aria sinking;
All else continuing—the stars shining,
The winds blowing—the notes of the bird continuous echoing,
With angry moans the fierce old mother incessantly moaning,
On the sands of Paumanok's shore, grey and rustling;
The yellow half-moon enlarged, sagging down, drooping, the face of the sea
    almost touching;
The boy ecstatic—with his bare feet the waves, with his hair the atmosphere
    dallying,
The love in the heart long pent, now loose, now at last tumultuously bursting,
The aria's meaning, the ears, the Soul, swiftly depositing,   140
The strange tears down the cheeks coursing,
The colloquy there—the trio—each uttering,
The undertone—the savage old mother, incessantly crying,
To the boy's Soul's questions sullenly timing—some drowned secret hissing,
To the outsetting bard of love.

Demon or bird! (said the boy's soul,)
Is it indeed toward your mate you sing? or is it mostly to me?
For I, that was a child, my tongue's use sleeping,
Now I have heard you,
Now in a moment I know what I am for—I awake,   150
And already a thousand singers—a thousand songs, clearer, louder and
    more sorrowful than yours,
A thousand warbling echoes have started to life within me,
Never to die.

O you singer, solitary, singing by yourself—projecting me;
O solitary me, listening—never more shall I cease perpetuating you;
Never more shall I escape, never more the reverberations,
Never more the cries of unsatisfied love be absent from me,
Never again leave me to be the peaceful child I was before what there, in
    the night,
By the sea, under the yellow and sagging moon,
The messenger there aroused—the fire, the sweet hell within,   160

The unknown want, the destiny of me.
O give me the clue! (it lurks in the night here somewhere;)
O if I am to have so much, let me have more!
O a word! O what is my destination? (I fear it is henceforth chaos;)
O how joys, dreads, convolutions, human shapes, and all shapes, spring as
    from graves around me!
O phantoms! you cover all the land and all the sea!
O I cannot see in the dimness whether you smile or frown upon me;
O vapour, a look, a word! O well-beloved!
O you dear women's and men's phantoms!
A word then, (for I will conquer it),   170
The word final, superior to all,
Subtle, sent up—what is it?—I listen;
Are you whispering it, and have been all the time, you sea-waves?
Is that it from your liquid rims and wet sands?

Whereto answering, the sea,
Delaying not, hurrying not,
Whispered me through the night, and very plainly before daybreak,
Lisped to me the low and delicious word Death;
And again Death—ever Death, Death, Death,
Hissing melodious, neither like the bird, nor like my aroused child's heart, 180
But edging near, as privately for me, rustling at my feet,
Creeping thence steadily up to my ears, and laving me softly all over,
Death, Death, Death, Death, Death.

Which I do not forget,
But fuse the song of my dusky demon and brother,
That he sang to me in the moonlight on Paumanok's grey beach,
With the thousand responsive songs, at random,
My own songs, awaked from that hour;
And with them the key, the word up from the waves,
The word of the sweetest song, and all songs,   190
That strong and delicious word which, creeping to my feet,
The sea whispered me.

❧ As Toilsome I Wandered Virginia's Woods

As toilsome I wandered Virginia's woods,
To the music of rustling leaves kicked by my feet (for 'twas autumn),
I marked at the foot of a tree the grave of a soldier;
Mortally wounded he and buried on the retreat (easily all could I understand),
The halt of a mid-day hour, when up! no time to lose—yet this sign left,
On a tablet scrawled and nailed on the tree by the grave,
Bold, cautious, true, and my loving comrade.

Long, long I muse, then on my way go wandering,
Many a changeful season to follow, and many a scene of life,
Yet at times through changeful season and scene, abrupt, alone, or in the
  crowded street,
Comes before me the unknown soldier's grave, comes the inscription rude in
  Virginia's woods,
Bold, cautious, true, and my loving comrade.

ARTHUR HUGH CLOUGH

❧ *The Latest Decalogue*

THOU shalt have one God only; who
Would be at the expense of two?
No graven images may be
Worshipped, except the currency;
Swear not at all; for, for thy curse
Thine enemy is none the worse;
At church on Sunday to attend
Will serve to keep the world thy friend;
Honour thy parents; that is, all
From whom advancement may befall;
Thou shalt not kill; but need'st not strive
Officiously to keep alive;
Do not adultery commit;
Advantage rarely comes of it;
Thou shalt not steal; an empty feat,
When it's so lucrative to cheat;
Bear not false witness; let the lie
Have time on its own wings to fly;
Thou shalt not covet, but tradition
Approves all forms of competition.

MATTHEW ARNOLD

❧ *Isolation: To Marguerite*

WE were apart; yet, day by day,
I bade my heart more constant be.
I bade it keep the world away,
And grow a home for only thee;
Nor feared but thy love likewise grew,
Like mine, each day, more tried, more true.

The fault was grave! I might have known,
What far too soon, alas! I learned—
The heart can bind itself alone,
And faith may oft be unreturned.   10
Self-swayed our feelings ebb and swell—
Thou lov'st no more—Farewell! Farewell!

Farewell!—and thou, thou lonely heart,
Which never yet without remorse
Even for a moment didst depart
From thy remote and spherèd course
To haunt the place where passions reign—
Back to thy solitude again!

Back! with the conscious thrill of shame
Which Luna felt, that summer-night,   20
Flash through her pure immortal frame,
When she forsook the starry height
To hang over Endymion's sleep
Upon the pine-grown Latmian steep.

Yet she, chaste queen, had never proved
How vain a thing is mortal love,
Wandering in Heaven, far removed.
But thou hast long had place to prove
This truth—to prove, and make thine own:
"Thou hast been, shalt be, art, alone."   30

Or, if not quite alone, yet they
Which touch thee are unmating things—
Ocean and clouds and night and day;
Lorn autumns and triumphant springs;
And life, and others' joy and pain,
And love, if love, of happier men.

Of happier men—for they, at least,
Have *dreamed* two human hearts might blend
In one, and were through faith released
From isolation without end   40
Prolonged; nor knew, although not less
Alone than thou, their loneliness.

13. **thou lonely heart:** he is addressing his own heart.
20. **Luna:** Diana, Goddess of the moon and hunting, who fell in love with the mortal Endymion, who lived on Mt. Latmos.

❧ To Marguerite—Continued

YES! in the sea of life enisled,
With echoing straits between us thrown,
Dotting the shoreless watery wild,
We mortal millions live *alone*.
The islands feel the enclasping flow,
And then their endless bounds they know.

But when the moon their hollows lights,
And they are swept by balms of spring,
And in their glens, on starry nights,
The nightingales divinely sing;
And lovely notes, from shore to shore,
Across the sounds and channels pour—

Oh! then a longing like despair
Is to their farthest caverns sent;
For surely once, they feel, we were
Parts of a single continent!
Now round us spreads the watery plain—
Oh might our marges meet again!

Who ordered, that their longing's fire
Should be, as soon as kindled, cooled?
Who renders vain their deep desire?—
A God, a God their severance ruled!
And bade betwixt their shores to be
The unplumbed, salt, estranging sea.

❧ Thyrsis

A Monody, to Commemorate the Author's Friend,
Arthur Hugh Clough, Who Died at Florence, 1861.

How changed is here each spot man makes or fills!
In the two Hinkseys nothing keeps the same;
The village street its haunted mansion lacks,
And from the sign is gone Sibylla's name,
And from the roofs the twisted chimney-stacks—

"**A Monody**": this poem is in the form of a pastoral elegy (see Glossary) with some surprising modifications in treatment. Compare "Lycidas."
4. **Sibylla's**: Sibylla was a tavern keeper.

Are ye too changed, ye hills?
See, 'tis no foot of unfamiliar men
Tonight from Oxford up your pathway strays!
Here came I often, often, in old days—
Thyrsis and I; we still had Thyrsis then.   10

Runs it not here, the track by Childsworth Farm,
Past the high wood, to where the elmtree crowns
The hill behind whose ridge the sunset flames?
The signal-elm, that looks on Ilsley Downs,
The Vale, the three lone weirs, the youthful Thames?—
This winter-eve is warm,
Humid the air! leafless, yet soft as spring,
The tender purple spray on copse and briers!
And that sweet city with her dreaming spires,
She needs not June for beauty's heightening.   20

Lovely all times she lies, lovely tonight!—
Only, methinks, some loss of habit's power
Befalls me wandering through this upland dim.
Once passed I blindfold here, at any hour;
Now seldom come I, since I came with him.
That single elmtree bright
Against the west—I miss it! is it gone?
We prized it dearly; while it stood, we said,
Our friend, the Gipsy-Scholar, was not dead;
While the tree lived, he in these fields lived on.   30

Too rare, too rare, grow now my visits here,
But once I knew each field, each flower, each stick;
And with the country-folk acquaintance made
By barn in threshing-time, by new-built rick.
Here, too, our shepherd-pipes we first assayed.
Ah me! this many a year
My pipe is lost, my shepherd's holiday!
Needs must I lose them, needs with heavy heart
Into the world and wave of men depart;
But Thyrsis of his own will went away.   40

10. **Thyrsis:** a pastoral name for Clough.
19. **sweet city:** Oxford.
29. **Gipsy-Scholar:** Arnold had earlier written a poem on the myth of an Oxford
scholar turned gipsy.
35. **assayed:** tried to play.
40. **his own will:** Clough had resigned his fellowship in a dispute over the Thirty-Nine
Articles of the church.

It irked him to be here, he could not rest.
He loved each simple joy the country yields,
He loved his mates; but yet he could not keep,
For that a shadow loured on the fields,
Here with the shepherds and the silly sheep.
Some life of men unblessed
He knew, which made him droop, and filled his head.
He went; his piping took a troubled sound
Of storms that rage outside our happy ground;
He could not wait their passing, he is dead.   50

So, some tempestuous morn in early June,
When the year's primal burst of bloom is o'er,
Before the roses and the longest day—
When garden-walks and all the grassy floor
With blossoms red and white of fallen May
And chestnut-flowers are strewn—
So have I heard the cuckoo's parting cry,
From the wet field, through the vext garden-trees,
Come with the volleying rain and tossing breeze:
The bloom is gone, and with the bloom go I!   60

Too quick despairer, wherefore wilt thou go?
Soon will the high Midsummer pomps come on,
Soon will the musk carnations break and swell,
Soon shall we have gold-dusted snapdragon,
Sweet-William with his homely cottage-smell,
And stocks in fragrant blow;
Roses that down the alleys shine afar,
And open, jasmine-muffled lattices,
And groups under the dreaming garden trees,
And the full moon, and the white evening-star.   70

He harkens not! light comer, he is flown!
What matters it? next year he will return,
And we shall have him in the sweet spring-days,
With whitening hedges, and uncrumpling fern,
And blue-bells trembling by the forest-ways,
And scent of hay new-mown.
But Thyrsis never more we swains shall see;
See him come back, and cut a smoother reed,
And blow a strain the world at last shall heed—
For Time, not Corydon, hath conquered thee!   80

45. **silly:** innocent.
80. **Corydon:** a pastoral name for Arnold.

Alack, for Corydon no rival now!—
But when Sicilian shepherds lost a mate,
Some good survivor with his flute would go,
Piping a ditty sad for Bion's fate;
And cross the unpermitted ferry's flow,
And relax Pluto's brow,
And make leap up with joy the beauteous head
Of Proserpine, among whose crownèd hair
Are flowers, first opened on Sicilian air,
And flute his friend, like Orpheus, from the dead.   90

O easy access to the hearer's grace
When Dorian shepherds sang to Proserpine!
For she herself had trod Sicilian fields,
She knew the Dorian water's gush divine,
She knew each lily white which Enna yields,
Each rose with blushing face;
She loved the Dorian pipe, the Dorian strain.
But ah, of our poor Thames she never heard!
Her foot the Cumner cowslips never stirred;
And we should tease her with our plaint in vain!   100

Well! wind-dispersed and vain the words will be,
Yet, Thyrsis, let me give my grief its hour
In the old haunt, and find our tree-topped hill!
Who, if not I, for questing here hath power?
I know the wood which hides the daffodil,
I know the Fyfield tree,
I know what white, what purple fritillaries
The grassy harvest of the river-fields,
Above by Ensham, down by Sandford, yields,
And what sedged brooks are Thames's tributaries;   110

I know these slopes; who knows them if not I?—
But many a dingle on the loved hill-side,
With thorns once studded, old, white-blossomed trees,

84. **Bion:** refers to the poet Moschus' "Lament for Bion" (150 B.C.).
85. **unpermitted ferry:** the crossing of the River Styx, barred to the living.
86–88. **Pluto, Proserpine:** the God of the Underworld and his mortal bride.
90. **Orpheus:** with his music, Orpheus charmed Pluto into releasing his wife Eurydice from Hades.
95. **Enna:** Proserpine lived in Enna, Sicily, before Pluto carried her away.
99. **Cumner:** an area near Oxford.
106. **Fyfield:** an elm in the village of Fyfield.
107. **fritillaries:** flowers of the lily family.
109. **Ensham, Sandford:** villages near Oxford.
112. **dingle:** a narrow wooded valley.

Where thick the cowslips grew, and far descried
High towered the spikes of purple orchises,
Hath since our day put by
The coronals of that forgotten time;
Down each green bank hath gone the ploughboy's team,
And only in the hidden brookside gleam
Primroses, orphans of the flowery prime. 120

Where is the girl, who by the boatman's door,
Above the locks, above the boating throng,
Unmoored our skiff when through the Wytham flats,
Red loosestrife and blond meadow-sweet among,
And darting swallows and light water-gnats,
We tracked the shy Thames shore?
Where are the mowers, who, as the tiny swell
Of our boat passing heaved the river-grass,
Stood with suspended scythe to see us pass?—
They all are gone, and thou art gone as well! 130

Yes, thou art gone! and round me too the night
In ever-nearing circle weaves her shade.
I see her veil draw soft across the day,
I feel her slowly chilling breath invade
The cheek grown thin, the brown hair sprent with grey;
I feel her finger light
Laid pausefully upon life's headlong train—
The foot less prompt to meet the morning dew,
The heart less bounding at emotion new,
And hope, once crushed, less quick to spring again. 140

And long the way appears, which seemed so short
To the less practised eye of sanguine youth;
And high the mountain-tops, in cloudy air,
The mountain-tops where is the throne of Truth,
Tops in life's morning-sun so bright and bare!
Unbreachable the fort
Of the long-battered world uplifts its wall;
And strange and vain the earthly turmoil grows,
And near and real the charm of thy repose,
And night as welcome as a friend would fall. 150

But hush! the upland hath a sudden loss
Of quiet!—Look, adown the dusk hill-side,

115. **orchises:** a variety of orchid.
117. **coronals:** garlands.
123. **Wytham flats:** marshes on the Thames.
124. **loosestrife, meadow-sweet:** primrose and spirea.

A troop of Oxford hunters going home,
As in old days, jovial and talking, ride!
From hunting with the Berkshire hounds they come.
Quick! let me fly, and cross
Into yon further field!—'Tis done, and see,
Backed by the sunset, which doth glorify
The orange and pale violet evening-sky,
Bare on its lonely ridge, the Tree! the Tree!   160

I take the omen! Eve lets down her veil,
The white fog creeps from bush to bush about,
The west unflushes, the high stars grow bright,
And in the scattered farms the lights come out.
I cannot reach the signal-tree tonight,
Yet, happy omen, hail!
Hear it from thy broad lucent Arno vale
(For there thine earth-forgetting eyelids keep
The morningless and unawakening sleep
Under the flowery oleanders pale),   170

Hear it, O Thyrsis, still our tree is there!—
Ah, vain! These English fields, this upland dim,
These brambles pale with mist engarlanded,
That lone, sky-pointing tree, are not for him;
To a boon southern country he is fled,
And now in happier air,
Wandering with the great Mother's train divine
(And purer or more subtle soul than thee,
I trow, the mighty Mother doth not see)
Within a folding of the Apennine,   180

Thou hearest the immortal chants of old!—
Putting his sickle to the perilous grain
In the hot cornfield of the Phrygian king,
For thee the Lityerses-song again
Young Daphnis with his silver voice doth sing;
Sings his Sicilian fold,
His sheep, his hapless love, his blinded eyes—

167. **Arno:** a river near Clough's burial place, Florence.
175. **boon:** bounteous.
177. **Mother's train:** the band following Cybele, Goddess of Nature and mother of the Gods.
184. **Lityerses-song:** a harvest song commemorating the reaping contest (with life as the stake) between the Sicilian boy, Daphnis, and the Phrygian king, Lityerses.
187. **blinded eyes:** Daphnis, in another story, was struck blind for infidelity to a nymph of his acquaintance. When he was translated to heaven by his father, Hermes, a fountain sprang from the spot where he had been standing.

And how a call celestial round him rang,
And heavenward from the fountain-brink he sprang,
And all the marvel of the golden skies. 190

There thou art gone, and me thou leavest here
Sole in these fields! yet will I not despair.
Despair I will not, while I yet descry
'Neath the mild canopy of English air
That lonely tree against the western sky.
Still, still these slopes, 'tis clear,
Our Gipsy-Scholar haunts, outliving thee!
Fields where soft sheep from cages pull the hay,
Woods with anemones in flower till May,
Know him a wanderer still; then why not me? 200

A fugitive and gracious light he seeks,
Shy to illumine; and I seek it too.
This does not come with houses or with gold,
With place, with honor, and a flattering crew;
'Tis not in the world's market bought and sold—
But the smooth-slipping weeks
Drop by, and leave its seeker still untired;
Out of the heed of mortals he is gone,
He wends unfollowed, he must house alone;
Yet on he fares, by his own heart inspired. 210

Thou too, O Thyrsis, on like quest wast bound;
Thou wanderedst with me for a little hour!
Men gave thee nothing; but this happy quest,
If men esteemed thee feeble, gave thee power,
If men procured thee trouble, gave thee rest.
And this rude Cumner ground,
Its fir-topped Hurst, its farms, its quiet fields,
Here cam'st thou in thy jocund youthful time,
Here was thine height of strength, thy golden prime!
And still the haunt beloved a virtue yields. 220

What though the music of thy rustic flute
Kept not for long its happy, country tone;
Lost it too soon, and learnt a stormy note
Of men contention-tossed, of men who groan,
Which tasked thy pipe too sore, and tired thy throat—
It failed, and thou wast mute!
Yet hadst thou always visions of our light,
And long with men of care thou couldst not stay,

217. **Hurst:** a hill in Cumner.

And soon thy foot resumed its wandering way,
Left human haunt, and on alone till night.   230

Too rare, too rare, grow now my visits here!
'Mid city-noise, not, as with thee of yore,
Thyrsis! in reach of sheep-bells is my home.
—Then through the great town's harsh, heart-wearying roar,
Let in thy voice a whisper often come,
To chase fatigue and fear:
Why faintest thou? I wandered till I died.
Roam on! The light we sought is shining still.
Dost thou ask proof? Our tree yet crowns the hill,
Our Scholar travels yet the loved hill-side.   240

❧ Dover Beach

THE sea is calm to-night.
The tide is full, the moon lies fair
Upon the straits; on the French coast the light
Gleams and is gone; the cliffs of England stand,
Glimmering and vast, out in the tranquil bay.
Come to the window, sweet is the night air!
Only, from the long line of spray
Where the sea meets the moon-blanched land,
Listen! you hear the grating roar
Of pebbles which the waves draw back, and fling,   10
At their return, up the high strand,
Begin, and cease, and then again begin,
With tremulous cadence slow, and bring
The eternal note of sadness in.

Sophocles long ago
Heard it on the Ægean, and it brought
Into his mind the turbid ebb and flow
Of human misery; we
Find also in the sound a thought,
Hearing it by this distant northern sea.   20
The Sea of Faith
Was once, too, at the full, and round earth's shore
Lay like the folds of a bright girdle furled.
But now I only hear
Its melancholy, long, withdrawing roar,
Retreating, to the breath
Of the night wind, down the vast edges drear
And naked shingles of the world.

Ah, love, let us be true
To one another! for the world, which seems 30
To lie before us like a land of dreams,
So various, so beautiful, so new,
Hath really neither joy, nor love, nor light,
Nor certitude, nor peace, nor help for pain;
And we are here as on a darkling plain
Swept with confused alarms of struggle and flight,
Where ignorant armies clash by night.

❧ *Growing Old*

WHAT is it to grow old?
Is it to lose the glory of the form,
The luster of the eye?
Is it for beauty to forego her wreath?
—Yes, but not this alone.

Is it to feel our strength—
Not our bloom only, but our strength—decay?
Is it to feel each limb
Grow stiffer, every function less exact,
Each nerve more loosely strung?

Yes, this, and more; but not,
Ah, 'tis not what in youth we dreamed 'twould be!
'Tis not to have our life
Mellowed and softened as with sunset-glow,
A golden day's decline.

'Tis not to see the world
As from a height, with rapt prophetic eyes,
And heart profoundly stirred;
And weep, and feel the fullness of the past,
The years that are no more.

It is to spend long days
And not once feel that we were ever young;
It is to add, immured
In the hot prison of the present, month
To month with weary pain.

It is to suffer this,
And feel but half, and feebly, what we feel.

Deep in our hidden heart
Festers the dull remembrance of a change,
But no emotion—none.

It is—last stage of all—
When we are frozen up within, and quite
The phantom of ourselves,
To hear the world applaud the hollow ghost
Which blamed the living man.

GEORGE MEREDITH

❧ Lucifer in Starlight

On a starred night Prince Lucifer uprose.
Tired of his dark dominion swung the fiend
Above the rolling ball in cloud part screened,
Where sinners hugged their spectre of repose.
Poor prey to his hot fit of pride were those.
And now upon his western wing he leaned,
Now his huge bulk o'er Afric's sands careened,
Now the black planet shadowed Arctic snows.
Soaring through wider zones that pricked his scars
With memory of the old revolt from Awe,
He reached a middle height, and at the stars,
Which are the brain of heaven, he looked, and sank.
Around the ancient track marched rank on rank,
The army of unalterable law.

EMILY DICKINSON

❧ Because I Could Not Stop for Death

Because I could not stop for Death,
He kindly stopped for me;
The carriage held but just ourselves
And Immortality.

We slowly drove, he knew no haste,
And I had put away
My labor, and my leisure too,
For his civility.

We passed the school where children played
At wrestling in a ring;
We passed the fields of gazing grain,
We passed the setting sun.

We paused before a house that seemed
A swelling of the ground;
The roof was scarcely visible,
The cornice but a mound.

Since then 'tis centuries; but each
Feels shorter than the day
I first surmised the horses' heads
Were toward eternity.

❧ *After Great Pain a Formal Feeling Comes*

AFTER great pain a formal feeling comes—
The nerves sit ceremonious like tombs;
The stiff heart questions—was it he that bore?
And yesterday—or centuries before?

The feet mechanical
Go round a wooden way,
Of ground or air or Ought, regardless grown,
A quartz contentment like a stone.

This is the hour of lead,
Remembered if outlived,
As freezing persons recollect the snow—
First chill, then stupor, then the letting go.

❧ *The Thought Beneath So Slight a Film*

THE thought beneath so slight a film
Is more distinctly seen—
As laces just reveal the surge,
Or mists the Appenine.

3. **surge:** of a woman's breast.

❧ *There's a Certain Slant of Light*

THERE'S a certain slant of light,
On winter afternoons,
That oppresses, like the weight
Of cathedral tunes.

Heavenly hurts it gives us;
We can find no scar,
But internal difference
Where the meanings are.

None may teach it anything;
'Tis the seal, despair—
An imperial affliction
Sent us of the air.

When it comes, the landscape listens,
Shadows hold their breath;
When it goes, 'tis like the distance
On the look of death.

❧ *A Narrow Fellow in the Grass*

A NARROW fellow in the grass
Occasionally rides;
You may have met him—did you not?
His notice sudden is.

The grass divides as with a comb,
A spotted shaft is seen;
And then it closes at your feet
And opens further on.

He likes a boggy acre,
A floor too cool for corn.
Yet when a child, and barefoot,
I more than once, at morn,

Have passed, I thought, a whip-lash
Unbraiding in the sun—

When, stooping to secure it,
It wrinkled, and was gone.

Several of nature's people
I know, and they know me;
I feel for them a transport
Of cordiality;

But never met this fellow,
Attended or alone,
Without a tighter breathing,
And zero at the bone.

❧ *I Know That He Exists*

I KNOW that He exists
Somewhere, in silence.
He has hid His rare life
From our gross eyes.

'Tis an instant's play,
'Tis a fond ambush,
Just to make bliss
Earn her own surprise!

But should the play
Prove piercing earnest,
Should the glee glaze
In death's stiff stare,

Would not the fun
Look too expensive?
Would not the jest
Have crawled too far?

❧ *It Dropped So Low in My Regard*

IT dropped so low in my regard
I heard it hit the ground,
And go to pieces on the stones
At bottom of my mind;

Yet blamed the fate that fractured, less
Than I reviled myself
For entertaining plated wares
Upon my silver shelf.

❧ *Much Madness Is Divinest Sense*

Much madness is divinest sense
To a discerning eye;
Much sense the starkest madness.
'Tis the majority
In this, as all, prevails.
Assent, and you are sane;
Demur—you're straightway dangerous,
And handled with a chain.

LEWIS CARROLL
[CHARLES LUTWIDGE DODGSON]

❧ *Jabberwocky*

'Twas brillig, and the slithy toves
Did gyre and gimble in the wabe;
All mimsy were the borogoves,
And the mome raths outgrabe.

"Beware the Jabberwock, my son!
The jaws that bite, the claws that catch!
Beware the jubjub bird, and shun
The frumious Bandersnatch!"

He took his vorpal sword in hand:
Long time the manxome foe he sought—
So rested he by the Tumtum tree,
And stood awhile in thought.

And as in uffish thought he stood,
The Jabberwock, with eyes of flame,
Came whiffling through the tulgey wood,
And burbled as it came!

One, two! One, two! And through and through
The vorpal blade went snicker-snack!
He left it dead, and with its head
He went galumphing back.

"And hast thou slain the Jabberwock?
Come to my arms, my beamish boy!
O frabjous day! Callooh! Callay!"
He chortled in his joy.

'Twas brillig, and the slithy toves
Did gyre and gimble in the wabe;
All mimsy were the borogoves,
And the mome raths outgrabe.

WILLIAM MORRIS

❦ *The Haystack in the Floods*

HAD she come all the way for this,
To part at last without a kiss?
Yea, had she borne the dirt and rain
That her own eyes might see him slain
Beside the haystack in the floods?
Along the dripping leafless woods,
The stirrup touching either shoe,
She rode astride as troopers do;
With kirtle kilted to her knee,
To which the mud splashed wretchedly;   10
And the wet dripped from every tree
Upon her head and heavy hair,
And on her eyelids broad and fair;
The tears and rain ran down her face.

By fits and starts they rode apace,
And very often was his place
Far off from her; he had to ride
Ahead, to see what might betide
When the roads crossed; and sometimes, when
There rose a murmuring from his men,   20
Had to turn back with promises;
Ah me! she had but little ease;
And often for pure doubt and dread
She sobbed, made giddy in the head
By the swift riding; while, for cold,

Her slender fingers scarce could hold
The wet reins; yea, and scarcely, too,
She felt the foot within her shoe
Against the stirrup: all for this,
To part at last without a kiss   30
Beside the haystack in the floods.

For when they neared that rain-soaked hay,
They saw across the only way
That Judas, Godmar; and the three
Red running lions dismally
Grinned from his pennon, under which
In one straight line along the ditch,
They counted thirty heads.

So then,
While Robert turned round to his men,   40
She saw at once the wretched end,
And, stooping down, tried hard to rend
Her coif the wrong way from her head,
And hid her eyes; while Robert said:
"Nay, love, 'tis scarcely two to one,
At Poictiers where we made them run
So fast—why, sweet my love, good cheer,
The Gascon frontier is so near,
Nought after this."
But, "O," she said,   50
"My God! my God! I have to tread
The long way back without you; then
The court at Paris; those six men;
The gratings of the Chatelet;
The swift Seine on some rainy day
Like this, and people standing by,
And laughing, while my weak hands try
To recollect how strong men swim.
All this, or else a life with him,
For which I should be damned at last.   60
Would God that this next hour were past!"

He answered not, but cried his cry,
"St. George for Marny!" cheerily;

43. **coif:** headdress.
46. **Poictiers:** at Poitiers, in 1356, the English, though vastly outnumbered, defeated the French.
53. **six men:** judges in a witchcraft trial at the Grand Chatelet prison. The test would be in the Seine: if Jehane is able to swim, she will be judged guilty since the devil will have helped her; if she drowns, she will be innocent.
63. **Marny:** Robert's last name.

And laid his hand upon her rein.
Alas! no man of all his train
Gave back that cheery cry again;
And, while for rage his thumb beat fast
Upon his sword-hilt, some one cast
About his neck a kerchief long,
And bound him.   70
Then they went along
To Godmar; who said: "Now, Jehane,
Your lover's life is on the wane
So fast, that, if this very hour
You yield not as my paramour,
He will not see the rain leave off—
Nay, keep your tongue from gibe and scoff,
Sir Robert, or I slay you now."

She laid her hand upon her brow,
Then gazed upon the palm, as though   80
She thought her forehead bled, and—"No,"
She said, and turned her head away,
As there were nothing else to say,
And everything were settled; red
Grew Godmar's face from chin to head:
"Jehane, on yonder hill there stands
My castle, guarding well my lands;
What hinders me from taking you,
And doing that I list to do
To your fair wilful body, while   90
Your knight lies dead?"

A wicked smile
Wrinkled her face, her lips grew thin,
A long way out she thrust her chin:
"You know that I should strangle you
While you were sleeping; or bite through
Your throat, by God's help: ah!" she said,
"Lord Jesus, pity your poor maid!
For in such wise they hem me in,
I cannot choose but sin and sin,   100
Whatever happens: yet I think
They could not make me eat or drink,
And so should I just reach my rest."

"Nay, if you do not my behest,
O Jehane! though I love you well,"
Said Godmar, "would I fail to tell
All that I know?" "Foul lies," she said.

"Eh? lies, my Jehane? by God's head,
At Paris folks would deem them true!
Do you know, Jehane, they cry for you,   110
'Jehane the brown! Jehane the brown!
Give us Jehane to burn or drown!'
Eh—gag me Robert!—sweet my friend,
This were indeed a piteous end
For those long fingers, and long feet,
And long neck, and smooth shoulders sweet;
An end that few men would forget
That saw it. So, an hour yet:
Consider, Jehane, which to take,
Or life or death!"   120

So, scarce awake,
Dismounting, did she leave that place,
And totter some yards: with her face
Turned upward to the sky she lay,
Her head on a wet heap of hay,
And fell asleep: and while she slept,
And did not dream, the minutes crept
Round to the twelve again; but she,
Being waked at last, sighed quietly,
And strangely childlike came, and said: 130
"I will not." Straightway Godmar's head,
As though it hung on strong wires, turned
Most sharply round, and his face burned.

For Robert—both his eyes were dry,
He could not weep, but gloomily
He seemed to watch the rain; yea, too,
His lips were firm; he tried once more
To touch her lips; she reached out, sore
And vain desire so tortured them,
The poor grey lips, and now the hem   140
Of his sleeve brushed them.

With a start
Up Godmar rose, thrust them apart;
From Robert's throat he loosed the bands
Of silk and mail; with empty hands
Held out, she stood and gazed, and saw,
The long bright blade without a flaw
Glide out from Godmar's sheath, his hand
In Robert's hair; she saw him bend
Back Robert's head; she saw him send   150

The thin steel down; the blow told well,
Right backward the knight Robert fell,

And moaned as dogs do, being half dead,
Unwitting, as I deem: so then
Godmar turned grinning to his men,
Who ran, some five or six, and beat
His head to pieces at their feet.

Then Godmar turned again and said:
"So, Jehane, the first fitte is read!
Take note, my lady, that your way   160
Lies backward to the Chatelet!"
She shook her head and gazed awhile
At her cold hands with a rueful smile,
As though this thing had made her mad.

This was the parting that they had
Beside the haystack in the floods.

❧ In Prison

WEARILY, drearily,
Half the day long,
Flap the great banners
High over the stone;
Strangely and eerily
Sounds the wind's song,
Bending the banner-poles.

While, all alone,
Watching the loophole's spark,
Lie I, with life all dark,
Feet tethered, hands fettered
Fast to the stone,
The grim wall, square lettered
With prisoned men's groan.

Still strain the banner-poles
Through the wind's song;
Westward the banner rolls
Over my wrong.

HENRY AUSTIN DOBSON

❧ *"You Bid Me Try"*

You bid me try, BLUE-EYES, to write
A Rondeau. What!—forthwith?—tonight?
Reflect. Some skill I have, 'tis true;
But thirteen lines!—and rimed on two!
"Refrain," as well. Ah, hapless plight!

Still, there are five lines—ranged aright.
These Gallic bonds, I feared, would fright
My easy Muse. They did, till you—
You bid me try!

That makes them eight. The port's in sight—   10
'Tis all because your eyes are bright!
Now just a pair to end in "oo"—
When maids command, what can't we do?
Behold—the RONDEAU, tasteful, light,
You bid me try!

JOHN ADDINGTON SYMONDS

❧ *An Episode*

VASARI tells that Luca Signorelli,
The morning star of Michael Angelo,
Had but one son, a youth of seventeen summers,
Who died. That day the master at his easel
Wielded the liberal brush wherewith he painted
At Orvieto, on the Duomo's walls,

2. **Rondeau:** see Glossary.
4. **thirteen lines:** the refrain is not counted here.
7. **Gallic:** French.
8. **easy:** easygoing.

1. **Vasari:** Giorgio Vasari (1511–1574) wrote *Lives of the Most Excellent Architects, Painters, and Sculptors*, a source book used also by Browning.
1. **Luca Signorelli:** Italian painter who preceded **Michael Angelo** Buonarroti (1475–1564) in powerfully detailed treatment of nude figures. The model for Luca's figure of the dead Christ at Cortona is said to have been the body of his own son.
6. **At . . . walls:** refers to Luca's *The Last Judgment* in the cathedral (duomo) at the town of Orvieto.

Stern forms of Death and Heaven and Hell and Judgment.
Then came they to him, and cried: "Thy son is dead,
Slain in a duel; but the bloom of life
Yet lingers round red lips and downy cheek." 10
Luca spoke not, but listened. Next they bore
His dead son to the silent painting-room,
And left on tiptoe son and sire alone.
Still Luca spoke and groaned not; but he raised
The wonderful dead youth, and smoothed his hair,
Washed his red wounds, and laid him on a bed,
Naked and beautiful, where rosy curtains
Shed a soft glimmer of uncertain splendor
Life-like upon the marble limbs below.
Then Luca seized his palette. Hour by hour 20
Silence was in the room; none durst approach.
Morn wore to noon, and noon to eve, when shyly
A little maid peeped in, and saw the painter
Painting his dead son with unerring handstroke,
Firm and dry-eyed before the lordly canvas.

THOMAS HARDY

❧ *An Ancient to Ancients*

WHERE once we danced, where once we sang,
Gentleman,
The floors are sunken, cobwebs hang,
And cracks creep; worms have fed upon
The doors. Yea, sprightlier times were then
Than now, with harps and tabrets gone,
Gentlemen!

Where once we rowed, where once we sailed,
Gentlemen,
And damsels took the tiller, veiled 10
Against too strong a stare (God wot
Their fancy, then or anywhen!)
Upon that shore we are clean forgot,
Gentlemen!

We have lost somewhat, afar and near,
Gentlemen,

6. **tabrets:** taborets, very small drums.
11. **God wot:** God knows.

The thinning of our ranks each year
Affords a hint we are nigh undone,
That we shall not be ever again
The marked of many, loved of one,   20
Gentlemen.

In dance the polka hit our wish,
Gentlemen,
The paced quadrille, the spry schottische,
"Sir Roger."—And in opera spheres
The "Girl" (the famed "Bohemian"),
And "Trovatore," held the ears,
Gentlemen.

This season's paintings do not please,
Gentlemen,   30
Like Etty, Mulready, Maclise;
Throbbing romance has waned and wanned;
No wizard yields the witching pen
Of Bulwer, Scott, Dumas, and Sand,
Gentlemen.

The bower we shrined to Tennyson,
Gentlemen,
Is roof-wrecked; damps there drip upon
Sagged seats, the creeper-nails are rust,
The spider is sole denizen;   40
Even she who voiced those rhymes is dust,
Gentlemen!

We who met sunrise sanguine-souled,
Gentlemen,
Are wearing weary. We are old;
These younger press; we feel our rout
Is imminent to Aïdes' den—
That evening shades are stretching out,
Gentlemen!

And yet, though ours be failing frames,   50
Gentlemen,

24. **quadrille . . . schottische:** dances, the first a kind of square dance, the second a
polka.
26. **The Girl . . . Bohemian: The Bohemian Girl** (1843), an opera.
27. **Trovatore:** *Il Trovatore* (1853), an opera by Verdi.
31. **Etty, etc.:** early nineteenth-century painters.
34. **Bulwer, etc.:** early nineteenth-century novelists.
36. **Tennyson:** became English poet laureate in 1850.
43. **sanguine-souled:** cheerful, hopeful.
47. **Aïdes:** Hades, God of the Underworld.

So were some others history names,
Who trode their track light-limbed and fast
As these youth, and not alien
From enterprise, to their long last,
Gentlemen.

Sophocles, Plato, Socrates,
Gentlemen,
Pythagoras, Thucydides,
Herodotus, and Homer—yea,   60
Clement, Augustin, Origen,
Burnt brightlier toward their setting-day,
Gentlemen.

And ye, red-lipped and smooth-browed; list,
Gentlemen;
Much is there waits you we have missed;
Much lore we leave you worth the knowing,
Much, much has lain outside our ken:
Nay, rush not: time serves: we are going,
Gentlemen.   70

❧ In Tenebris

"Percussus sum sicut foenum, et aruit cor meum."

WINTERTIME nighs;
But my bereavement-pain
It cannot bring again:
Twice no one dies.

Flower-petals flee;
But, since it once hath been,

52. **others:** others *whom.*
53. **trode:** archaic past of *tread.*
57–60. **Sophocles . . . Homer:** Greek playwrights, philosophers, historians, and poets who lived between the fifth and tenth centuries, B.C.
64. **And ye:** the young men who are being addressed for the first time in the poem.

"In Tenebris": in darkness.
"Percussus . . .": this is the beginning of Psalm 101 of the Latin Vulgate Bible, translated as Psalms 102:4 (King James version), "My heart is smitten, and withered like grass."
2. **bereavement-pain:** probably refers to the loss of belief in a benevolently ordered universe rather than to loss of a friend.

No more that severing scene
Can harrow me.

Birds faint in dread;
I shall not lose old strength   10
In the lone frost's black length:
Strength long since fled!

Leaves freeze to dun;
But friends can not turn cold
This season as of old
For him with none.

Tempests may scath;
But love can not make smart
Again this year his heart
Who no heart hath.   20

Black is night's cope;
But death will not appal
One who, past doubtings all,
Waits in unhope.

GERARD MANLEY HOPKINS

❧ *God's Grandeur*

The world is charged with the grandeur of God.
It will flame out, like shining from shook foil;
It gathers to a greatness, like the ooze of oil
Crushed. Why do men then now not reck his rod?
Generations have trod, have trod, have trod;
And all is seared with trade; bleared, smeared with toil;
And wears man's smudge and shares man's smell: the soil
Is bare now, nor can foot feel, being shod.
And for all this, nature is never spent;
There lives the dearest freshness deep down things;   10
And though the last lights off the black West went

17. **scath[e]:** injure.
21. **cope:** a covering like a cloak or canopy.
22. **appal:** horrify, but originally, "to make pale."

4. **reck his rod:** an archaic phrase suggesting "pay attention to his *rod* (a cane used for punishment), his *rōd* (Old English for 'cross'), and perhaps, his *ræd* (Old English for 'counsel' or 'advice')."

Oh, morning, at the brown brink eastward, springs—
Because the Holy Ghost over the bent
World broods with warm breast and with ah! bright wings.

❧ *The Windhover*

To Christ Our Lord

I CAUGHT this morning morning's minion, king-
        dom of daylight's dauphin, dapple-dawn-drawn Falcon, in his riding
Of the rolling level underneath him steady air, and striding
High there, how he rung upon the rein of a wimpling wing
In his ecstasy! then off, off forth on swing,
As a skate's heel sweeps smooth on a bow-bend: the hurl and gliding
Rebuffed the big wind. My heart in hiding
Stirred for a bird—the achieve of, the mastery of the thing!

Brute beauty and valor and act, oh, air, pride, plume, here
Buckle! AND the fire that breaks from thee then, a billion   10
Times told lovelier, more dangerous, O my chevalier!

No wonder of it: shéer plód makes plow down sillion
Shine, and blue-bleak embers, ah my dear,
Fall, gall themselves, and gash gold-vermilion.

❧ *Felix Randal*

FELIX RANDAL the farrier, O he is dead then? my duty all ended,
Who have watched his mould of man, big-boned and hardy-handsome
Pining, pining, till time when reason rambled in it and some
Fatal four disorders, fleshed there, all contended?

1. **caught:** saw.
1. **minion:** a favorite.
2. **dauphin:** eldest son of the King of France.
4. **rung:** spiraled upward.
4. **wimpling:** rippling.
6. **skate:** an ice skate.
6. **bow-bend:** a "figure eight."
10. **Buckle!:** come together, or possibly "set to work together," as in "buckle down."
12. **sillion:** a furrow.

1. **farrier:** blacksmith.
1. **my duty:** as a Jesuit priest.

Sickness broke him. Impatient he cursed at first, but mended
Being anointed and all; though a heavenlier heart began some
Months earlier, since I had our sweet reprieve and ransom
Tendered to him. Ah well, God rest him all road ever he offended!
This seeing the sick endears them to us, us too it endears.
My tongue had taught thee comfort, touch had quenched thy tears,   10
Thy tears that touched my heart, child, Felix, poor Felix Randal;
How far from then forethought of, all thy more boisterous years,
When thou at the random grim forge, powerful amidst peers,
Didst fettle for the great grey drayhorse his bright and battering sandal!

❧ *Spring and Fall: To a Young Child*

MÁRGARÉT, are you gríeving
Over Goldengrove unleaving?
Leáves, líke the things of man, you
With your fresh thoughts care for, can you?
Ah! ás the heart grows older
It will come to such sights colder
By and by, nor spare a sigh
Though worlds of wanwood leafmeal lie;
And yet you wíll weep and know why.
Now no matter, child, the name: 10
Sórrow's spríngs áre the same.
Nor mouth had, no nor mind, expressed
What heart heard of, ghost guessed:
It ís the blight man was born for,
It is Margaret you mourn for.

❧ *Carrion Comfort*

NOT, I'll not, carrion comfort, Despair, not feast on thee;
Not untwist—slack they may be—these last strands of man
In me ór, most weary, cry *I can no more*. I can;
Can something, hope, wish day come, not choose not to be.

6. **anointed:** as part of the sacrament of extreme unction given the dying.
14. **fettle:** dialect, to put in order; also, to beat, as on an anvil.

2. **unleaving:** losing its leaves.
8. **wanwood:** coined word—*wan* is "pallid, sickly."
8. **leafmeal:** suggests finely ground dead leaves.
13. **ghost:** spirit.

1. **carrion:** dead flesh; note the ambiguity of its use here.

But ah, but O thou terrible, why wouldst thou rude on me
Thy wring-world right foot rock? lay a lion limb against me? scan
With darksome devouring eyes my bruisèd bones? and fan,
O in turns of tempest, me heaped there; me frantic to avoid thee and flee?
Why? That my chaff might fly; my grain lie, sheer and clear.
Nay in all that toil, that coil, since (seems) I kissed the rod,   10
Hand rather, my heart lo! lapped strength, stole joy, would laugh, chéer.
Cheer whom though? the hero whose heaven-handling flung me, fóot tród
Me? or me that fought him? O which one? is it each one? That night, that year
Of now done darkness I wretch lay wrestling with (my God!) my God.

ROBERT BRIDGES

❧ *When First We Met*

WHEN first we met we did not guess
That Love would prove so hard a master;
Of more than common friendliness
When first we met we did not guess.
Who could foretell this sore distress,
This irretrievable disaster,
When first we met?—We did not guess
That Love would prove so hard a master.

❧ *London Snow*

WHEN men were all asleep the snow came flying,
In large white flakes falling on the city brown,
Stealthily and perpetually settling and loosely lying,
Hushing the latest traffic of the drowsy town;
Deadening, muffling, stifling its murmurs failing;
Lazily and incessantly floating down and down:
Silently sifting and veiling road, roof and railing;
Hiding difference, making unevenness even,
Into angles and crevices softly drifting and sailing.
All night it fell, and when full inches seven   10

10. **coil:** tumult, confused argument. Hopkins became a Roman Catholic in 1866, entered the Jesuit order two years later, and was ordained a priest in 1877.

"**When . . . Met**": This poem is a triolet. See Glossary.

It lay in the depth of its uncompacted lightness,
The clouds blew off from a high and frosty heaven;
And all woke earlier for the unaccustomed brightness
Of the winter dawning, the strange unheavenly glare:
The eye marvelled—marvelled at the dazzling whiteness;
The ear hearkened to the stillness of the solemn air;
No sound of wheel rumbling nor of foot falling,
And the busy morning cries came thin and spare.
Then boys I heard, as they went to school, calling,
They gathered up the crystal manna to freeze   20
Their tongues with tasting, their hands with snowballing;
Or rioted in a drift, plunging up to the knees;
Or peering up from under the white-mossed wonder,
"O look at the trees!" they cried, "O look at the trees!"
With lessened load a few carts creak and blunder,
Following along the white deserted way,
A country company long dispersed asunder:
When now already the sun, in pale display
Standing by Paul's high dome, spread forth below
His sparkling beams, and awoke the stir of the day.   30
For now doors open, and war is waged with the snow;
And trains of somber men, past tale of number,
Tread long brown paths, as toward their toil they go:
But even for them awhile no cares encumber
Their minds diverted; the daily word is unspoken,
The daily thoughts of labour and sorrow slumber
At the sight of the beauty that greets them, for the charm
    they have broken.

❧ Low Barometer

THE south-wind strengthens to a gale,
Across the moon the clouds fly fast,
The house is smitten as with a flail,
The chimney shudders to the blast.

On such a night, when Air has loosed
Its guardian grasp on blood and brain,
Old terrors then of god or ghost
Creep from their caves to life again;

18. **spare:** meager.
20. **manna:** the food miraculously supplied in Exodus 16:14–36.
29. **Paul's:** St. Paul's Cathedral.
32. **tale:** enumeration.

And Reasons kens he herits in
A haunted house. Tenants unknown 10
Assert their squalid lease of sin
With earlier title than his own.

Unbodied presences, the packed
Pollution and remorse of Time,
Slipped from oblivion reënact
The horrors of unhouseled crime.

Some men would quell the thing with prayer
Whose sightless footsteps pad the floor,
Whose fearful trespass mounts the stair
Or bursts the locked forbidden door. 20

Some have seen corpses long interred
Escape from hallowing control,
Pale charnel forms—nay even have heard
The shrilling of a troubled soul,

That wanders till the dawn hath crossed
The dolorous dark, or Earth hath wound
Closer her storm-spredd cloke, and thrust
The baleful phantoms underground.

WILLIAM ERNEST HENLEY

❧ *Ballade of Dead Actors*

WHERE are the passions they essayed,
And where are the tears they made to flow?
Where the wild humors they portrayed
For laughing worlds to see and know?
Othello's wrath and Juliet's woe?

9. **kens:** perceives.
9. **herits in:** lives in his inheritance.
16. **unhouseled:** beyond redemption by the church sacraments.
22. **hallowing:** blessing, consecrating.
23. **charnel:** from the tomb.
28. **baleful:** menacing.

"**Ballade**": see Glossary.
1. **essayed:** attempted to perform.
3. **humors:** refers to the comedy of humors, in which each character represents a single pronounced trait.
5–7. **Othello's . . . Romeo:** characters in *Othello, Romeo and Juliet*, Sheridan's *School for Scandal*, Shakespeare's *Timon of Athens*, Congreve's *The Way of the World*.

Sir Peter's whims and Timon's gall?
And Millamant and Romeo?
Into the night go one and all.

Where are the braveries, fresh or frayed?
The plumes, the armors—friend and foe?   10
The cloth of gold, the rare brocade,
The mantles glittering to and fro?
The pomp, the pride, the royal show?
The cries of war and festival?
The youth, the grace, the charm, the glow?
Into the night go one and all.

The curtain falls, the play is played:
The Beggar packs beside the Beau;
The Monarch troops, and troops the Maid;
The Thunder huddles with the Snow.   20
Where are the revelers high and low?
The clashing swords? The lover's call?
The dancers gleaming row on row?
Into the night go one and all.

ENVOY

Prince, in one common overthrow
The Hero tumbles with the Thrall;
As dust that drives, as straws that blow,
Into the night go one and all.

ROBERT LOUIS STEVENSON

❧ Bright Is the Ring of Words

BRIGHT is the ring of words
When the right man rings them,
Fair the fall of songs
When the singer sings them.
Still they are caroled and said—
On wings they are carried—
After the singer is dead
And the maker buried.

9. **braveries:** showy splendors.
18. **packs:** crowds up closely.
19. **troops:** walks by in review, as at a curtain call.

8. **maker:** note that Stevenson distinguishes two kinds of poetry, *singing* and *making.*
Poet comes from a Greek word meaning *to make.*

Low as the singer lies
In the field of heather,   10
Songs of his fashion bring
The swains together.
And when the west is red
With the sunset embers,
The lover lingers and sings,
And the maid remembers.

A. E. HOUSMAN

❧ *Terence, This Is Stupid Stuff*

"TERENCE, this is stupid stuff;
You eat your victuals fast enough;
There can't be much amiss, 'tis clear,
To see the rate you drink your beer.
But oh, good Lord, the verse you make,
It gives a chap the belly-ache.
The cow, the old cow, she is dead;
It sleeps well, the horned head:
We poor lads, 'tis our turn now
To hear such tunes as killed the cow.   10
Pretty friendship 'tis to rhyme
Your friends to death before their time
Moping melancholy mad:
Come, pipe a tune to dance to, lad."
Why, if 'tis dancing you would be,
There's brisker pipes than poetry.
Say, for what were hop-yards meant,
Or why was Burton built on Trent?
Oh, many a peer of England brews
Livelier liquor than the Muse,   20
And malt does more than Milton can
To justify God's ways to man.
Ale, man, ale's the stuff to drink
For fellows whom it hurts to think:
Look into the pewter pot
To see the world as the world's not.
And faith, 'tis pleasant till 'tis past:
The mischief is that 'twill not last.
Oh, I have been to Ludlow fair

11. **Songs . . . fashion:** of his fashioning or making.
18. **Burton . . . Trent:** Burton on Trent is a great brewing center.

And left my necktie God knows where,   30
And carried half way home, or near,
Pints and quarts of Ludlow beer:
Then the world seemed none so bad,
And I myself a sterling lad;
And down in lovely muck I've lain,

Happy till I woke again.
Then I saw the morning sky:
Heigho, the tale was all a lie;
The world, it was the old world yet,
I was I, my things were wet,   40
And nothing now remained to do
But begin the game anew.

Therefore, since the world has still
Much good, but much less good than ill,
And while the sun and moon endure,
Luck's a chance, but trouble's sure,
I'd face it as a wise man would,
And train for ill and not for good.
'Tis true, the stuff I bring for sale
Is not so brisk a brew as ale: 50
Out of a stem that scored the hand
I wrung it in a weary land.
But take it: if the smack is sour,
The better for the embittered hour;
It should do good to heart and head
When your soul is in my soul's stead;
And I will friend you, if I may,
In the dark and cloudy day.

There was a king reigned in the East:
There, when kings will sit to feast,   60
They get their fill before they think
With poisoned meat and poisoned drink.
He gathered all that springs to birth
From the many-venomed earth;
First a little, thence to more,
He sampled all her killing store;
And easy, smiling, seasoned sound,
Sate the king when healths went round.
They put arsenic in his meat
And stared aghast to watch him eat;   70

51. **a stem:** metaphorically, the poet's brew is wrung from painful experience.
59. **a king:** to foil his enemies, Mithridates VI (120–63 B.C.) carefully built up a
tolerance for poison.

They poured strychnine in his cup
And shook to see him drink it up:
They shook, they stared as white's their shirt:
Them it was their poison hurt.
—I tell the tale that I heard told.
Mithridates, he died old.

❧ *With Rue My Heart Is Laden*

WITH rue my heart is laden
For golden friends I had,
For many a rose-lipped maiden
And many a lightfoot lad.

By brooks too broad for leaping
The lightfoot boys are laid;
The rose-lipped girls are sleeping
In fields where roses fade.

❧ *On Moonlit Heath and Lonesome Bank*

ON moonlit heath and lonesome bank
The sheep beside me graze;
And yon the gallows used to clank
Fast by the four cross ways.

A careless shepherd once would keep
The flocks by moonlight there,
And high amongst the glimmering sheep
The dead man stood on air.

They hang us now in Shrewsbury jail:
The whistles blow forlorn,   10
And trains all night groan on the rail
To men that die at morn.

There sleeps in Shrewsbury jail to-night,
Or wakes, as may betide,

5. **a careless shepherd:** "Hanging in chains was called 'keeping sheep by moonlight.' "
[Housman's note].

A better lad, if things went right,
Than most that sleep outside.

And naked to the hangman's noose
The morning clocks will ring
A neck God made for other use
Than strangling in a string.   20

And sharp the link of life will snap,
And dead on air will stand
Heels that held up as straight a chap
As treads upon the land.

So here I'll watch the night and wait
To see the morning shine,
When he will hear the stroke of eight
And not the stroke of nine;

And wish my friend as sound a sleep
As lads' I did not know,   30
That shepherded the moonlit sheep
A hundred years ago.

RUDYARD KIPLING

❧ *Sestina of the Tramp-Royal*

SPEAKIN' in general, I 'ave tried 'em all—
The 'appy roads that take you o'er the world.
Speakin' in general, I 'ave found them good
For such as cannot use one bed too long,
But must get 'ence, the same as I 'ave done,
An' go observin' matters till they die.

What do it matter where or 'ow we die,
So long as we've our 'ealth to watch it all—
The different ways that different things are done,
An' men an' women lovin' in this world;
Takin' our chances as they come along,
An' when they ain't, pretendin' they are good?

"Sestina": see Glossary.

In cash or credit—no, it aren't no good;
You 'ave to 'ave the 'abit or you'd die,
Unless you lived your life but one day long,
Nor didn't prophesy nor fret at all,
But drew your tucker some'ow from the world,
An' never bothered what you might ha' done.

But, Gawd, what things are they I 'aven't done!
I've turned my 'and to most, an' turned it good,
In various situations round the world—
For 'im that doth not work must surely die;
But that's no reason man should labour all
'Is life on one same shift—life's none so long.

Therefore, from job to job I've moved along.
Pay couldn't 'old me when my time was done,
For something in my 'ead upset it all,
Till I 'ad dropped whatever 't was for good,
An', out at sea, be'eld the dock-lights die,
An' met my mate—the wind that tramps the world!

It's like a book, I think, this bloomin' world,
Which you can read and care for just so long,
But presently you feel that you will die
Unless you get the page you're readin' done,
An' turn another—likely not so good;
But what you're after is to turn 'em all.

Gawd bless this world! Whatever she 'ath done—
Excep' when awful long—I've found it good.
So write, before I die, " 'E liked it all!"

WILLIAM BUTLER YEATS

❧ The Second Coming

TURNING and turning in the widening gyre
The falcon cannot hear the falconer;
Things fall apart; the center cannot hold;
Mere anarchy is loosed upon the world,
The blood-dimmed tide is loosed, and everywhere
The ceremony of innocence is drowned;

1. **gyre:** spiral. The image also alludes to Yeats' theory of history, in which ages of spirituality alternate with ages of materialism and brutality.

The best lack all conviction, while the worst
Are full of passionate intensity.

Surely some revelation is at hand;
Surely the Second Coming is at hand.   10
The Second Coming! Hardly are those words out
When a vast image out of *Spiritus Mundi*
Troubles my sight: somewhere in sands of the desert
A shape with lion body and the head of a man,
A gaze blank and pitiless as the sun,
Is moving its slow thighs, while all about it
Reel shadows of the indignant desert birds.
The darkness drops again; but now I know
That twenty centuries of stony sleep
Were vexed to nightmare by a rocking cradle,   20
And what rough beast, its hour come round at last,
Slouches towards Bethlehem to be born?

❧ *Sailing to Byzantium*

THAT is no country for old men. The young
In one another's arms, birds in the trees
—Those dying generations—at their song,
The salmon-falls, the mackerel-crowded seas,
Fish, flesh, or fowl, commend all summer long
Whatever is begotten, born, and dies.
Caught in that sensual music all neglect
Monuments of unaging intellect.

An aged man is but a paltry thing,
A tattered coat upon a stick, unless   10
Soul clap its hands and sing, and louder sing
For every tatter in its mortal dress,
Nor is there singing school but studying
Monuments of its own magnificence;
And therefore I have sailed the seas and come
To the holy city of Byzantium.

12. **Spiritus Mundi:** the single great soul of the world, repository of man's collective memory.
14. **A shape:** the sphinx, symbol of the era preceding the Christian.

"Byzantium": an ancient city (became Constantinople in A.D. 330), capital of the Eastern Roman Empire and symbol for Yeats of the world of art and intellect.

O sages standing in God's holy fire
As in the gold mosaic of a wall,
Come from the holy fire, perne in a gyre,
And be the singing-masters of my soul.   20
Consume my heart away, sick with desire
And fastened to a dying animal
It knows not what it is; and gather me
Into the artifice of eternity.

Once out of nature I shall never take
My bodily form from any natural thing,
But such a form as Grecian goldsmiths make
Of hammered gold and gold enamelling
To keep a drowsy Emperor awake;
Or set upon a golden bough to sing   30
To lords and ladies of Byzantium
Of what is past, or passing, or to come.

❧ *Lapis Lazuli*

I HAVE heard that hysterical women say
They are sick of the palette and fiddlebow,
Of poets that are always gay,
For everybody knows or else should know
That if nothing drastic is done
Aeroplane and Zeppelin will come and
Pitch like King Billy bomb-balls in
Until the town lie beaten flat.

All perform their tragic play,
There struts Hamlet, there is Lear,   10
That's Ophelia, that Cordelia;
Yet they, should the last scene be there,
The great stage curtain about to drop,
If worthy their prominent part in the play,
Do not break up their lines to weep.
They know that Hamlet and Lear are gay;

17. **God's holy fire:** the golden halos against which these figures are set in the mosaic suggests that they are close to God.
19. **perne:** spool; hence, "wind downward in a spiral [to me]."

7. **King Billy:** William III bombarded towns in Ireland in 1690.

Gaiety transfiguring all that dread.
All men have aimed at found and lost;
Black out; Heaven blazing into the head:
Tragedy wrought to its uttermost.   20
Though Hamlet rambles and Lear rages,
And all the drop-scenes drop at once
Upon a hundred thousand stages,
It cannot grow by an inch or an ounce.

On their own feet they came, or on shipboard,
Camel-back, horse-back, ass-back, mule-back,
Old civilisations put to the sword.
Then they and their wisdom went to rack:
No handiwork of Callimachus,
Who handled marble as if it were bronze,   30
Made draperies that seemed to rise
When sea-wind swept the corner, stands;
His long lamp-chimney shaped like the stem
Of a slender palm, stood but a day;
All things fall and are built again,
And those that build them again are gay.

Two Chinamen, behind them a third,
Are carved in lapis lazuli,
Over them flies a long-legged bird,
A symbol of longevity;   40
The third, doubtless a serving-man,
Carries a musical instrument.

Every discoloration of the stone,
Every accidental crack or dent,
Seems a water-course or an avalanche,
Or lofty slope where it still snows
Though doubtless plum or cherry-branch
Sweetens the little half-way house
Those Chinamen climb towards, and I
Delight to imagine them seated there;   50
There, on the mountain and the sky,
On all the tragic scene they stare.
One asks for mournful melodies;
Accomplished fingers begin to play.
Their eyes mid many wrinkles, their eyes,
Their ancient, glittering eyes, are gay.

29. **Callimachus**: Greek sculptor (450? B.C.).
37. **Two Chinamen**: carved in a piece of lapis lazuli the poet has before him.

❦ *Crazy Jane Talks with the Bishop*

I MET the Bishop on the road
And much said he and I.
"Those breasts are flat and fallen now,
Those veins must soon be dry;
Live in a heavenly mansion,
Not in some foul sty."

"Fair and foul are near of kin,
And fair needs foul," I cried.
"My friends are gone, but that's a truth
Nor grave nor bed denied,
Learned in bodily lowliness
And in the heart's pride.

"A woman can be proud and stiff
When on love intent;
But Love has pitched his mansion in
The place of excrement;
For nothing can be sole or whole
That has not been rent."

❦ *Among School Children*

I WALK through the long schoolroom questioning,
A kind old nun in a white hood replies;
The children learn to cipher and to sing,
To study reading-books and history,
To cut and sew, be neat in everything
In the best modern way—the children's eyes
In momentary wonder stare upon
A sixty year old smiling public man.

I dream of a Ledæan body, bent
Above a sinking fire, a tale that she   10

8. **public man:** In 1922, Yeats was made a senator in the Irish Free State.
9. **Ledaean:** *of Leda,* whose union with Zeus (in the form of a swan) produced the beautiful Helen of Troy. Yeats is probably thinking here of Maud Gonne, a fiery revolutionist whom he loved deeply.

Told of a harsh reproof, or trivial event
That changed some childish day to tragedy—
Told, and it seemed that our two natures blent
Into a sphere from youthful sympathy,
Or else, to alter Plato's parable,
Into the yolk and white of the one shell.

And thinking of that fit of grief or rage
I look upon one child or t'other there
And wonder if she stood so at that age—
For even daughters of the swan can share   20
Something of every paddler's heritage—
And had that color upon cheek or hair;
And thereupon my heart is driven wild:
She stands before me as a living child.

Her present image floats into the mind—
Did quattrocento finger fashion it
Hollow of cheek as though it drank the wind
And took a mess of shadows for its meat?
And I though never of Ledæan kind
Had pretty plumage once—enough of that,   30
Better to smile on all that smile, and show
There is a comfortable kind of old scarecrow.

What youthful mother, a shape upon her lap
Honey of generation had betrayed,
And that must sleep, shriek, struggle to escape
As recollection or the drug decide,
Would think her son, did she but see that shape
With sixty or more winters on its head,
A compensation for the pang of his birth,
Or the uncertainty of his setting forth?   40

Plato thought nature but a spume that plays
Upon a ghostly paradigm of things;

15. **Plato's parable:** in the *Symposium,* it is suggested that male and female are each halves of a single sphere.
21. **paddler:** ducklings as distinct from the swanlike woman he is thinking of.
26. **quattrocento:** the fifteenth century in Italy was a high point in art.
34. **Honey of generation:** the delight of being born, which betrays the child into moving from its ideal pre-existent state into this life; also a drug which blots out memory of that pre-existence in the baby; and finally, of course, sexual desire which leads to the birth of a child.
42. **paradigm:** the essential scheme or outline of reality. Plato, Aristotle, and Pythagoras each suggested a different view of reality.

Solider Aristotle played the taws
Upon the bottom of a king of kings;
World-famous golden-thighed Pythagoras
Fingered upon a fiddle stick or strings
What a star sang and careless Muses heard:
Old clothes upon old sticks to scare a bird.

Both nuns and mothers worship images,
But those the candles light are not as those   50
That animate a mother's reveries,
But keep a marble or a bronze repose.
And yet they too break hearts—O Presences
That passion, piety or affection knows,
And that all heavenly glory symbolize—
O self-born mockers of man's enterprise;

Labor is blossoming or dancing where
The body is not bruised to pleasure soul,
Nor beauty born out of its own despair,
Nor blear-eyed wisdom out of midnight oil.   60
O chestnut tree, great rooted blossomer,
Are you the leaf, the blossom or the bole?
O body swayed to music, O brightening glance,
How can we know the dancer from the dance?

ERNEST DOWSON

❧ *Villanelle of the Poet's Road*

WINE and woman and song,
Three things garnish our way;
Yet is day over long.

Lest we do our youth wrong,
Gather them while we may:
Wine and woman and song.

43. **played the taws:** as tutor to the young Alexander the Great, Aristotle used a leather strap (taws) on his pupil's bottom—a startling thought in view of the fact that Alexander later conquered the world.
45. **Pythagoras:** thought by his followers to have a golden thigh as a mark of his divinity, Pythagoras was concerned with mathematics and the harmony of the spheres.
48. **Old clothes:** all three philosophies are dismissed as no more than scarecrows.
54. **passion, piety, or affection:** that lovers, nuns, or mothers know.
56. **self-born mockers:** man-created, these ideal "presences" mock man's efforts to discover and present the truth.

"Villanelle": see Glossary.

Three things render us strong,
Vine leaves, kisses, and bay;
Yet is day over long.

Unto us they belong,
Us the bitter and gay,
Wine and woman and song.

We, as we pass along,
Are sad that they will not stay;
Yet is day over long.

Fruits and flowers among,
What is better than they:
Wine and woman and song?
Yet is day over long.

EDWIN ARLINGTON ROBINSON

❦ *Mr. Flood's Party*

OLD Eben Flood, climbing alone one night
Over the hill between the town below
And the forsaken upland hermitage
That held as much as he should ever know
On earth again of home, paused warily.
The road was his with not a native near;
And Eben, having leisure, said aloud,
For no man else in Tilbury Town to hear:

"Well, Mr. Flood, we have the harvest moon
Again, and we may not have many more;   10
The bird is on the wing, the poet says,
And you and I have said it here before.
Drink to the bird." He raised up to the light
The jug that he had gone so far to fill,
And answered huskily: "Well, Mr. Flood,
Since you propose it, I believe I will."

Alone, as if enduring to the end
A valiant armor of scarred hopes outworn,
He stood there in the middle of the road

Like Roland's ghost winding a silent horn.   20
Below him, in the town among the trees,
Where friends of other days had honored him,
A phantom salutation of the dead
Rang thinly till old Eben's eyes were dim.

Then, as a mother lays her sleeping child
Down tenderly, fearing it may awake,
He set the jug down slowly at his feet
With trembling care, knowing that most things break;
And only when assured that on firm earth
It stood, as the uncertain lives of men   30
Assuredly did not, he paced away,
And with his hand extended paused again:

"Well, Mr. Flood, we have not met like this
In a long time; and many a change has come
To both of us, I fear, since last it was
We had a drop together. Welcome home!"
Convivially returning with himself,
Again he raised the jug up to the light
And with an acquiescent quaver said:
"Well, Mr. Flood, if you insist, I might.   40

"Only a very little, Mr. Flood—
For auld lang syne. No more, sir; that will do."
So, for the time, apparently it did,
And Eben evidently thought so too;
For soon amid the silver loneliness
Of night he lifted up his voice and sang,
Secure, with only two moons listening,
Until the whole harmonious landscape rang—

"For auld lang syne." The weary throat gave out,
The last word wavered; and the song being done,   50
He raised again the jug regretfully
And shook his head, and was again alone.
There was not much that was ahead of him,
And there was nothing in the town below—
Where strangers would have shut the many doors
That many friends had opened long ago.

---

20. **Roland's ghost:** Roland was commander of Charlemagne's rear guard in the pass
of Ronceveaux in 778. Set upon by a pagan army, he sounded his trumpet for help, but
too late.

❧ *Eros Turannos*

SHE fears him, and will always ask
What fated her to choose him;
She meets in his engaging mask
All reasons to refuse him;
But what she meets and what she fears
Are less than are the downward years,
Drawn slowly to the foamless weirs
Of age, were she to lose him.

Between a blurred sagacity
That once had power to sound him,   10
And Love, that will not let him be
The Judas that she found him,
Her pride assuages her almost,
As if it were alone the cost.
He sees that he will not be lost,
And waits and looks around him.

A sense of ocean and old trees
Envelops and allures him;
Tradition, touching all he sees,
Beguiles and reassures him;   20
And all her doubts of what he says
Are dimmed with what she knows of days—
Till even prejudice delays
And fades, and she secures him.

The falling leaf inaugurates
The reign of her confusion;
The pounding wave reverberates
The dirge of her illusion;
And home, where passion lived and died,
Becomes a place where she can hide,   30
While all the town and harbor side
Vibrate with her seclusion.

"Eros Turannos": "Love, the Tyrant"—here used as a title, like *Oedipus Rex*.
7. **weirs:** fish traps set in a stream.

We tell you, tapping on our brows,
The story as it should be—
As if the story of a house
Were told, or ever could be;
We'll have no kindly veil between
Her visions and those we have seen—
As if we guessed what hers have been,
Or what they are or would be.   40

Meanwhile we do no harm; for they
That with a god have striven,
Not hearing much of what we say,
Take what the god has given;
Though like waves breaking it may be,
Or like a changed familiar tree,
Or like a stairway to the sea
Where down the blind are driven.

WALTER DE LA MARE

❧ *The Listeners*

"Is there anybody there?" said the Traveller,
Knocking on the moonlit door;
And his horse in the silence champed the grasses
Of the forest's ferny floor:
And a bird flew up out of the turret,
Above the Traveller's head:
And he smote upon the door again a second time;
"Is there anybody there?" he said.
But no one descended to the Traveller;
No head from the leaf-fringed sill
Leaned over and looked into his grey eyes,
Where he stood perplexed and still.
But only a host of phantom listeners
That dwelt in the lone house then
Stood listening in the quiet of the moonlight
To that voice from the world of men:
Stood thronging the faint moonbeams on the dark stair,

---

33. **We tell you:** here, "we" seems to mean the town gossips, the public in general.
Note the many shifts in point of view throughout this poem.

That goes down to the empty hall,
Hearkening in an air stirred and shaken
By the lonely Traveller's call.
And he felt in his heart their strangeness,
Their stillness answering his cry,
While his horse moved, cropping the dark turf,
'Neath the starred and leafy sky;
For he suddenly smote on the door, even
Louder, and lifted his head:
"Tell them I came, and no one answered,
That I kept my word!" he said.
Never the least stir made the listeners,
Though every word he spake
Fell echoing through the shadowiness of the still house
From the one man left awake;
Ay, they heard his foot upon the stirrup,
And the sound of iron on stone,
And how the silence surged softly backward,
When the plunging hoofs were gone.

ROBERT FROST

❧ *Stopping by Woods on a Snowy Evening*

Whose woods these are I think I know.
His house is in the village though;
He will not see me stopping here
To watch his woods fill up with snow.

My little horse must think it queer
To stop without a farmhouse near
Between the woods and frozen lake
The darkest evening of the year.

He gives his harness bells a shake
To ask if there is some mistake.
The only other sound's the sweep
Of easy wind and downy flake.

The woods are lovely, dark and deep.
But I have promises to keep,
And miles to go before I sleep,
And miles to go before I sleep.

❧ Desert Places

Snow falling and night falling fast, oh, fast
In a field I looked into going past,
And the ground almost covered smooth in snow,
But a few weeds and stubble showing last.

The woods around it have it—it is theirs.
All animals are smothered in their lairs.
I am too absent-spirited to count;
The loneliness includes me unawares.

And lonely as it is that loneliness
Will be more lonely ere it will be less—
A blanker whiteness of benighted snow
With no expression, nothing to express.

They cannot scare me with their empty spaces
Between stars—on stars where no human race is.
I have it in me so much nearer home
To scare myself with my own desert places.

❧ Design

I found a dimpled spider, fat and white,
On a white heal-all, holding up a moth
Like a white piece of rigid satin cloth—
Assorted characters of death and blight
Mixed ready to begin the morning right,
Like the ingredients of a witch's broth—
A snow-drop spider, a flower like froth,
And dead wings carried like a paper kite.

What had that flower to do with being white,
The wayside blue and innocent heal-all?
What brought the kindred spider to that height,
Then steered the white moth thither in the night?
What but design of darkness to appall?
If design govern in a thing so small.

❧ *The Tuft of Flowers*

I WENT to turn the grass once after one
Who mowed it in the dew before the sun.

The dew was gone that made his blade so keen
Before I came to view the leveled scene.

I looked for him behind an isle of trees;
I listened for his whetstone on the breeze.

But he had gone his way, the grass all mown,
And I must be, as he had been—alone,

"As all must be," I said within my heart,
"Whether they work together or apart."

But as I said it, swift there passed me by
On noiseless wing a bewildered butterfly,

Seeking with memories grown dim o'er night
Some resting flower of yesterday's delight.

And once I marked his flight go round and round,
As where some flower lay withering on the ground.

And then he flew as far as eye could see,
And then on tremulous wing came back to me.

I thought of questions that have no reply,
And would have turned to toss the grass to dry;

But he turned first, and led my eye to look
At a tall tuft of flowers beside a brook,

A leaping tongue of bloom the scythe had spared
Beside a reedy brook the scythe had bared.

I left my place to know them by their name,
Finding them butterfly-weed when I came.

The mower in the dew had loved them thus,
By leaving them to flourish, not for us,

Nor yet to draw one thought of ours to him,
But from sheer morning gladness at the brim.

The butterfly and I had lit upon,
Nevertheless, a message from the dawn,

That made me hear the wakening birds around,
And hear his long scythe whispering to the ground,

And feel a spirit kindred to my own;
So that henceforth I worked no more alone;

But glad with him, I worked as with his aid,
And weary, sought at noon with him the shade;

And dreaming, as it were, held brotherly speech
With one whose thought I had not hoped to reach.

"Men work together," I told him from the heart,
"Whether they work together or apart."

❧ *The Road Not Taken*

Two roads diverged in a yellow wood,
And sorry I could not travel both
And be one traveler, long I stood
And looked down one as far as I could
To where it bent in the undergrowth;

Then took the other, as just as fair,
And having perhaps the better claim,
Because it was grassy and wanted wear;
Though as for that the passing there
Had worn them really about the same,

And both that morning equally lay
In leaves no step had trodden black.
Oh, I kept the first for another day!
Yet knowing how way leads on to way,
I doubted if I should ever come back.

I shall be telling this with a sigh
Somewhere ages and ages hence:

Two roads diverged in a wood, and I—
I took the one less traveled by,
And that has made all the difference.

WALLACE STEVENS

❧ Peter Quince at the Clavier

I

JUST as my fingers on these keys
Make music, so the self-same sounds
On my spirit make a music, too.

Music is feeling, then, not sound;
And thus it is that what I feel,
Here in this room, desiring you,

Thinking of your blue-shadowed silk,
Is music. It is like the strain
Waked in the elders by Susanna;

Of a green evening, clear and warm,   10
She bathed in her still garden, while
The red-eyed elders, watching, felt
The basses of their being throb
In witching chords, and their thin blood
Pulse pizzicati of Hosanna.

II

In the green water, clear and warm,
Susanna lay.
She searched
The touch of springs,
And found   20
Concealed imaginings.

"Peter Quince at the Clavier": Quince was the director of the artisan's play in A
Midsummer Night's Dream. A clavier is a keyboard.
  9. Susanna: in the Apocrypha, Susanna innocently arouses the lust of two elders, or
judges, who have been peeping at her. When she refuses their attentions, they accuse
her of adultery—which carries a death sentence. Daniel discovers the truth, saves her,
and executes her accusers.
15. pizzicati: notes played by plucking the strings of a violin.
15. Hosanna: a shout of praise.

She sighed
For so much melody.

Upon the bank she stood
In the cool
Of spent emotions.
She felt, among the leaves,
The dew
Of old devotions.

She walked upon the grass,   30
Still quavering.
The winds were like her maids,
On timid feet,
Fetching her woven scarves,
Yet wavering.

A breath upon her hand
Muted the night.
She turned—
A cymbal crashed,
And roaring horns.   40

III

Soon, with a noise like tambourines,
Came her attendant Byzantines.

They wondered why Susanna cried
Against the elders by her side:

And as they whispered, the refrain
Was like a willow swept by rain.

Anon their lamps' uplifted flame
Revealed Susanna and her shame.

And then the simpering Byzantines,
Fled, with a noise like tambourines.   50

IV

Beauty is momentary in the mind—
The fitful tracing of a portal;
But in the flesh it is immortal.
The body dies; the body's beauty lives.

So evenings die, in their green going,
A wave, interminably flowing.

So gardens die, their meek breath scenting
The cowl of winter, done repenting.
So maidens die, to the auroral
Celebration of a maiden's choral.   60

Susanna's music touch the bawdy strings
Of those white elders; but, escaping,
Left only Death's ironic scraping.
Now, in its immortality, it plays
On the clear viol of her memory,
And makes a constant sacrament of praise.

WILLIAM CARLOS WILLIAMS

❧ *Tragic Detail*

THE day before I died
I noticed the maple tree
how its bark curled
against the November blaze

There was some work
to do and three birds
stopped awkwardly abreast
upon the bare lawn

Only the country-woman's
lip woft with down
black as her hair was black
against the white skin

comforted me but the twins
and their sister
excluded me dragging
insistent upon the loose gown.

59. **auroral**: dawn-like.

D. H. LAWRENCE

❧ *Piano*

SOFTLY, in the dusk, a woman is singing to me;
Taking me back down the vista of years, till I see
A child sitting under the piano, in the boom of the tingling strings
And pressing the small, poised feet of a mother who smiles as she sings.
In spite of myself, the insidious mastery of song
Betrays me back, till the heart of me weeps to belong
To the old Sunday evenings at home, with winter outside
And hymns in the cosy parlour, the tinkling piano our guide.
So now it is vain for the singer to burst into clamour
With the great black piano appassionato.
The glamour
Of childish days is upon me, my manhood is cast
Down in the flood of remembrance, I weep like a child for the past.

❧ *Snake*

A SNAKE came to my water-trough
On a hot, hot day, and I in pyjamas for the heat,
To drink there.

In the deep, strange-scented shade of the great dark carob-tree
I came down the steps with my pitcher
And must wait, must stand and wait, for there he was at the trough
   before me.

He reached down from a fissure in the earth-wall in the gloom
And trailed his yellow-brown slackness soft-bellied down, over the edge
   of the stone trough
And rested his throat upon the stone bottom,
And where the water had dripped from the tap, in a small clearness,   10
He sipped with his straight mouth,
Softly drank through his straight gums, into his slack long body,
Silently.

Someone was before me at my water-trough,
And I, like a second comer, waiting.

He lifted his head from his drinking, as cattle do,
And looked at me vaguely, as drinking cattle do,
And flickered his two-forked tongue from his lips, and mused a moment,
And stooped and drank a little more,
Being earth-brown, earth-golden from the burning burning bowels of
    the earth   20
On the day of Sicilian July, with Etna smoking.

The voice of my education said to me
He must be killed,
For in Sicily the black, black snakes are innocent, the gold are venomous.

And voices in me said, If you were a man
You would take a stick and break him now, and finish him off.

But must I confess how I liked him,
How glad I was he had come like a guest in quiet, to drink at my water-trough
And depart peaceful, pacified, and thankless,
Into the burning bowels of this earth?   30

Was it cowardice, that I dared not kill him?
Was it perversity, that I longed to talk to him?
Was it humility, to feel so honoured?
I felt so honoured.

And yet those voices:
If you were not afraid, you would kill him!

And truly I was afraid, I was most afraid,
But even so, honoured still more
That he should seek my hospitality
From out the dark door of the secret earth.   40

He drank enough
And lifted his head, dreamily, as one who has drunken,
And flickered his tongue like a forked night on the air, so black,
Seeming to lick his lips,
And looked around like a god, unseeing, into the air,
And slowly turned his head,
And slowly, very slowly, as if thrice adream,
Proceeded to draw his slow length curving round
And climb again the broken bank of my wall-face.

And as he put his head into that dreadful hole,   50
And as he slowly drew up, snake-easing his shoulders, and entered farther,
A sort of horror, a sort of protest against his withdrawing into that horrid
    black hole,

Deliberately going into the blackness, and slowly drawing himself after,
Overcame me now his back was turned.
I looked round, I put down my pitcher,
I picked up a clumsy log
And threw it at the water-trough with a clatter.

I think it did not hit him,
But suddenly that part of him that was left behind convulsed in
    undignified haste,
Writhed like lightning, and was gone
Into the black hole, the earth-lipped fissure in the wallfront,   60
At which, in the intense still noon, I stared with fascination.

And immediately I regretted it.
I thought how paltry, how vulgar, what a mean act!
I despised myself and the voices of my accursed human education.

And I thought of the albatross,
And I wished he would come back, my snake.

For he seemed to me again like a king,
Like a king in exile, uncrowned in the underworld,
Now due to be crowned again.   70

And so, I missed my chance with one of the lords
Of life.
And I have something to expiate;
A pettiness.

                                      EZRA POUND

❧ *Portrait d'une Femme*

YOUR mind and you are our Sargasso Sea
London has swept about you this score years
And bright ships left you this or that in fee:
Ideas, old gossip, oddments of all things,
Strange spars of knowledge and dimmed wares of price.
Great minds have sought you—lacking someone else.
You have been second always. Tragical?
No. You preferred it to the usual thing:
One dull man, dulling and uxorious,

"d'une Femme": "of a woman," with the connotation that she is not quite respectable.
9. **uxorious**: excessively fond of one's wife.

One average mind—with one thought less, each year.   10
Oh, you are patient, I have seen you sit
Hours, where something might have floated up.
And now you pay one. Yes, you richly pay.
You are a person of some interest, one comes to you
And takes strange gain away:
Trophies fished up; some curious suggestion;
Fact that leads nowhere; and a tale or two,
Pregnant with mandrakes, or with something else
That might prove useful and yet never proves,
That never fits a corner or shows use,   20
Or finds its hour upon the loom of days:
The tarnished, gaudy, wonderful old work;
Idols and ambergris and rare inlays,
These are your riches, your great store; and yet
For all this sea-hoard of deciduous things,
Strange woods half sodden, and new brighter stuff;
In the slow float of differing light and deep,
No! there is nothing! In the whole and all
Nothing that's quite your own.
Yet this is you.   30

SIEGFRIED SASSOON

❧ *They*

The Bishop tells us: "When the boys come back
They will not be the same; for they'll have fought
In a just cause: they lead the last attack
On Anti-Christ; their comrade's blood has bought
New right to breed an honorable race.
They have challenged Death and dared him face to face."

"We're none of us the same!" the boys reply.
For George lost both his legs; and Bill's stone blind;
Poor Jim's shot through the lungs and like to die;
And Bert's gone syphilitic: you'll not find
A chap who's served that hasn't found *some* change."
And the bishop said, "The ways of God are strange!"

18. **mandrakes:** the root of the mandrake, when eaten, was supposed to aid conception.
23. **ambergris:** a secretion of the sperm whale used for perfume. Usually found floating
near the shore.

MARIANNE MOORE

❧ *Poetry*

I, TOO, dislike it: there are things that are important beyond all this fiddle.
Reading it, however, with a perfect contempt for it, one discovers in
it after all, a place for the genuine.
Hands that can grasp, eyes
that can dilate, hair that can rise
if it must, these things are important not because a

high-sounding interpretation can be put upon them but because they are
useful. When they become so derivative as to become unintelligible,
the same thing may be said for all of us, that we
do not admire what   10
we cannot understand: the bat
holding on upside down or in quest of something to

eat, elephants pushing, a wild horse taking a roll, a tireless wolf under
a tree, the immovable critic twitching his skin like a horse that feels
a flea, the base-
ball fan, the statistician—
nor is it valid
to discriminate against "business documents and

school-books"; all these phenomena are important. One must make a
distinction   20
however: when dragged into prominence by half poets, the result is
not poetry,
nor till the poets among us can be
"literalists of
the imagination"—above
insolence and triviality and can present

for inspection, "imaginary gardens with real toads in them," shall we
have
it. In the meantime, if you demand on the one hand,

18. **"business documents"**: Tolstoi excluded these from consideration as poetry in the
passage from which this quote is taken.
24–25. **"literalists . . . imagination"**: Yeats criticized Blake as a "too literal realist of
the imagination."

the raw material of poetry in   30
all its rawness and
that which is on the other hand
genuine, you are interested in poetry.

❧ *To a Snail*

If "compression is the first grace of style,"
you have it. Contractility is a virtue
as modesty is a virtue.
It is not the acquisition of any one thing
that is able to adorn,
or the incidental quality that occurs
as a concomitant of something well said,
that we value in style,
but the principle that is hid:
in the absence of feet, "a method of conclusions";   10
"a knowledge of principles,"
in the curious phenomenon of your occipital horn.

EDWIN MUIR

❧ *Troy*

He all that time among the sewers of Troy
Scouring for scraps. A man so venerable
He might have been Priam's self, but Priam was dead,
Troy taken. His arms grew meagre as a boy's,
And all that flourished in that hollow famine
Was his long, white, round beard. Oh, sturdily
He swung his staff and sent the bold rats skipping
Across the scurfy hills and worm-wet valleys,
Crying: "Achilles, Ajax, turn and fight!
Stop cowards!" Till his cries, dazed and confounded,   10

12. **occipital horn:** that part of the human brain that lies at the base of the skull.

3. **Priam:** Hector's father, ruler of Troy.
9. **Achilles, Ajax:** the strongest of the Greek fighters who had attacked Troy—and destroyed it.

Flew back at him with: "Coward, turn and fight!"
And the wild Greeks yelled round him.
Yet he withstood them, a brave, mad old man,
And fought the rats for Troy. The light was rat-grey,
The hills and dells, the common drain, his Simois,
Rat-grey. Mysterious shadows fell
Affrighting him whenever a cloud offended
The sun up in the other world. The rat-hordes,
Moving, were grey dust shifting in grey dust.
Proud history has such sackends. He was taken   20
At last by some chance robber seeking treasure
Under Troy's riven roots. Dragged to the surface.
And there he saw Troy like a burial ground
With tumbled walls for tombs, the smooth sward wrinkled
As time's last wave had long since passed that way,
The sky, the sea, Mount Ida and the islands,
No sail from edge to edge, the Greeks clean gone.
They stretched him on a rock and wrenched his limbs,
Asking: "Where is the treasure?" till he died.

❧ *The Gate*

We sat, two children, warm against the wall
Outside the towering stronghold of our fathers
That frowned its stern security down upon us.
We could not enter there. That fortress life,
Our safe protection, was too gross and strong
For our unpractised palates. Yet our guardians
Cherished our innocence with gentle hands
(They, who had long since lost their innocence),
And in grave play put on a childish mask
Over their tell-tale faces, as in shame
For the fine food that plumped their lusty bodies
And made them strange as gods. We sat that day
With that great parapet behind us, safe
As every day, yet outcast, safe and outcast
As castaways thrown upon an empty shore.
Before us lay our well-worn scene, a hillock
So small and smooth and green, it seemed intended
For us alone and childhood, a still pond
That opened upon no sight a quiet eye,
A little stream that tinkled down the slope.

But suddenly all seemed old
And dull and shrunken, shut within itself
In a sullen dream. We were outside, alone.
And then behind us the huge gate swung open.

ROBINSON JEFFERS

❧ *Hurt Hawks*

I

THE broken pillar of the wing jags from the clotted shoulder,
The wing trails like a banner in defeat,
No more to use the sky forever but live with famine
And pain a few days: cat nor coyote
Will shorten the week of waiting for death, there is game without talons.
He stands under the oak-bush and waits
The lame feet of salvation; at night he remembers freedom
And flies in a dream, the dawns ruin it.
He is strong and pain is worse to the strong, incapacity is worse.
The curs of the day come and torment him
At distance, no one but death the redeemer will humble that head,
The intrepid readiness, the terrible eyes.
The wild God of the world is sometimes merciful to those
That ask mercy, not often to the arrogant.
You do not know him, you communal people, or you have forgotten him;
Intemperate and savage, the hawk remembers him;
Beautiful and wild, the hawks, and men that are dying, remember him.

II

I'd sooner, except the penalties, kill a man than a hawk; but the great redtail
Had nothing left but unable misery
From the bone too shattered for mending, the wing that trailed under his
    talons when he moved.
We had fed him six weeks, I gave him freedom,
He wandered over the foreland hill and returned in the evening, asking for
    death,
Not like a beggar, still eyed with the old
Implacable arrogance. I gave him the lead gift in the twilight. What fell was
    relaxed,
Owl-downy, soft feminine feathers; but what
Soared: the fierce rush: the night-herons by the flooded river cried fear at its
    rising
Before it was quite unsheathed from reality.

❦ *The Love Song of J. Alfred Prufrock*

S'io credesse che mia risposta fosse
A persona che mai tornasse al mondo,
Questa fiamma staria senza piu scosse.
Ma perciocche giammai di questo fondo
Non torno vivo alcum, s'i'odo il vero,
Senza tema d'infamia ti rispondo.

LET us go then, you and I,
When the evening is spread out against the sky
Like a patient etherized upon a table;
Let us go, through certain half-deserted streets,
The muttering retreats
Of restless nights in one-night cheap hotels
And sawdust restaurants with oyster-shells:
Streets that follow like a tedious argument
Of insidious intent
To lead you to an overwhelming question. . . .   10
Oh, do not ask, "What is it?"
Let us go and make our visit.

In the room the women come and go
Talking of Michelangelo.

The yellow fog that rubs its back upon the window-panes,
The yellow smoke that rubs its muzzle on the window-panes,
Licked its tongue into the corners of the evening,
Lingered upon the pools that stand in drains,
Let fall upon its back the soot that falls from chimneys,
Slipped by the terrace, made a sudden leap,   20
And seeing that it was a soft October night,
Curled once about the house, and fell asleep.

"S'io credesse . . . rispondo": "If I thought my answer were to one who might ever
return to the world, this flame would be still, but since no one ever returns alive from
this depth, if I hear correctly, I answer without fear of infamy" Dante, *Inferno,*
27:61–66.

And indeed there will be time
For the yellow smoke that slides along the street,
Rubbing its back upon the window-panes;
There will be time, there will be time
To prepare a face to meet the faces that you meet;
There will be time to murder and create,
And time for all the works and days of hands
That lift and drop a question on your plate;   30
Time for you and time for me,
And time yet for a hundred indecisions,
And for a hundred visions and revisions,
Before the taking of a toast and tea.

In the room the women come and go
Talking of Michelangelo.

And indeed there will be time
To wonder, "Do I dare?" and, "Do I dare?"
Time to turn back and descend the stair,
With a bald spot in the middle of my hair—   40
[They will say: "How his hair is growing thin!"]
My morning coat, my collar mounting firmly to the chin,
My necktie rich and modest, but asserted by a simple pin—
[They will say: "But how his arms and legs are thin!"]
Do I dare
Disturb the universe?
In a minute there is time
For decisions and revisions which a minute will reverse.

For I have known them all already, known them all—
Have known the evenings, mornings, afternoons,   50
I have measured out my life with coffee spoons;
I know the voices dying with a dying fall
Beneath the music from a farther room.
So how should I presume?

And I have known the eyes already, known them all—
The eyes that fix you in a formulated phrase,
And when I am formulated, sprawling on a pin,
When I am pinned and wriggling on the wall,
Then how should I begin
To spit out all the butt-ends of my days and ways?   60
And how should I presume?

And I have known the arms already, known them all—
Arms that are braceleted and white and bare

[But in the lamplight, downed with light brown hair!]
Is it perfume from a dress
That makes me so digress?
Arms that lie along a table, or wrap about a shawl.
And should I then presume?
And how should I begin?

.   .   .

Shall I say, I have gone at dusk through narrow streets   70
And watched the smoke that rises from the pipes
Of lonely men in shirt-sleeves, leaning out of windows? . . .

I should have been a pair of ragged claws
Scuttling across the floors of silent seas.

.   .   .

And the afternoon, the evening, sleeps so peacefully!
Smoothed by long fingers,
Asleep . . . tired . . . or it malingers,
Stretched on the floor, here beside you and me.
Should I, after tea and cakes and ices,
Have the strength to force the moment to its crisis?   80
But though I have wept and fasted, wept and prayed,
Though I have seen my head [grown slightly bald] brought in upon a platter,
I am no prophet—and here's no great matter;
I have seen the moment of my greatness flicker,
And I have seen the eternal Footman hold my coat, and snicker,
And in short, I was afraid.

And would it have been worth it, after all,
After the cups, the marmalade, the tea,
Among the porcelain, among some talk of you and me,
Would it have been worth while,   90
To have bitten off the matter with a smile,
To have squeezed the universe into a ball
To roll it toward some overwhelming question,
To say: "I am Lazarus, come from the dead,
Come back to tell you all, I shall tell you all"—
If one, settling a pillow by her head,

73. **ragged claws:** suggests the purely physical, without thought.
77. **malingers:** feigns illness.
82. **brought in . . . platter:** John the Baptist's head was delivered to Salome on a
platter at Herodias' insistence. See Matthew 14:3–12.
92. **squeezed the universe:** see Andrew Marvell, "To His Coy Mistress."
94. **Lazarus:** Lazarus was raised from the dead by Jesus. See John 11:1–46.

Should say: "That is not what I meant at all.
That is not it, at all."

And would it have been worth it, after all,
Would it have been worth while,   100
After the sunsets and the dooryards and the sprinkled streets,
After the novels, after the teacups, after the skirts that trail along the floor—
And this, and so much more?—
It is impossible to say just what I mean!
But as if a magic lantern threw the nerves in patterns on a screen:
Would it have been worth while
If one, settling a pillow or throwing off a shawl,
And turning toward the window, should say:
"That is not it at all,
That is not what I meant, at all."   110

                    .   .   .

No! I am not Prince Hamlet, nor was meant to be;
Am an attendant lord, one that will do
To swell a progress, start a scene or two,
Advise the prince; no doubt, an easy tool,
Deferential, glad to be of use,
Politic, cautious, and meticulous;
Full of high sentence, but a bit obtuse;
At times, indeed, almost ridiculous—
Almost, at times, the Fool.

I grow old. . . . I grow old. . . .   120
I shall wear the bottoms of my trousers rolled.
Shall I part my hair behind? Do I dare to eat a peach?
I shall wear white flannel trousers, and walk upon the beach.
I have heard the mermaids singing, each to each.

I do not think that they will sing to me.

I have seen them riding seaward on the waves
Combing the white hair of the waves blown back
When the wind blows the water white and black.

We have lingered in the chambers of the sea
By sea-girls wreathed with seaweed red and brown   130
Till human voices wake us, and we drown.

113. **swell a progress:** be part of a procession in a play.

❧ *Janet Waking*

BEAUTIFULLY Janet slept
Till it was deeply morning. She woke then
And thought about her dainty-feathered hen,
To see how it had kept.

One kiss she gave her mother.
Only a small one gave she to her daddy
Who would have kissed each curl of his shining baby;
No kiss at all for her brother.

"Old Chucky, old Chucky!" she cried,
Running across the world upon the grass   10
To Chucky's house, and listening. But alas,
Her Chucky had died.

It was a transmogrifying bee
Came droning down on Chucky's old bald head
And sat and put the poison. It scarcely bled,
But how exceedingly

And purply did the knot
Swell with the venom and communicate
Its rigor! Now the poor comb stood up straight
But Chucky did not.   20

So there was Janet
Kneeling on the wet grass, crying her brown hen
(Translated far beyond the daughters of men)
To rise and walk upon it.

And weeping fast as she had breath
Janet implored us, "Wake her from her sleep!"
And would not be instructed in how deep
Was the forgetful kingdom of death.

13. **transmogrifying:** transforming.

CONRAD AIKEN

❧ *Watch Long Enough, And You Will See*

WATCH long enough, and you will see the leaf
Fall from the bough. Without a sound it falls:
And soundless meets the grass. . . . And so you have
A bare bough, and a dead leaf in dead grass.
Something has come and gone. And that is all.

But what were all the tumults in this action?
What wars of atoms in the twig, what ruins,
Fiery and disastrous, in the leaf?
Timeless the tumult was, but gave no sigh.
Only, the leaf fell, and the bough is bare.

This is the world: there is no more than this.
The unseen and disastrous prelude, shaking
The trivial act from the terrific action.
Speak: and the ghosts of change, past and to come,
Throng the brief word. The maelstrom has us all.

ARCHIBALD MACLEISH

❧ *Ars Poetica*

A POEM should be palpable and mute
As a globed fruit

Dumb
As old medallions to the thumb

Silent as the sleeve-worn stone
Of casement ledges where the moss has grown—

A poem should be wordless
As the flight of birds.

A poem should be motionless in time
As the moon climbs

Leaving, as the moon releases
Twig by twig the night-entangled trees,

Leaving, as the moon behind the winter leaves,
Memory by memory the mind—

A poem should be motionless in time
As the moon climbs

A poem should be equal to:
Not true

For all the history of grief
An empty doorway and a maple leaf

For love
The leaning grasses and two lights above the sea—

A poem should not mean
But be.

❧ *The End of the World*

QUITE unexpectedly as Vasserot
The armless ambidextrian was lighting
A match between his great and second toe
And Ralph the lion was engaged in biting
The neck of Madam Sossman while the drum
Pointed, and Teeny was about to cough
In waltz-time swinging Jocko by the thumb—
Quite unexpectedly the top blew off:

And there, there overhead, there, there, hung over
Those thousands of white faces, those dazed eyes,
There in the starless dark the poise, the hover,
There with vast wings across the canceled skies,
There in the sudden blackness the black pall
Of nothing, nothing, nothing—nothing at all.

JOHN PEALE BISHOP

❦ *Speaking of Poetry*

THE ceremony must be found
that will wed Desdemona to the huge moor.

It is not enough—
to win the approval of the Senator
or to outwit his disapproval; honest Iago
can manage that: it is not enough. For then,
though she may pant again in his black arms
(his weight resilient as a Barbary stallion's)
she will be found
when the ambassadors of the Venetian state arrive
again smothered. These things have not been changed,
not in three hundred years.

(Tupping is still tupping
though that particular word is obsolete.
Naturally, the ritual would not be in Latin.)

For though Othello had his blood from kings
his ancestry was barbarous, his ways African,
his speech uncouth. It must be remembered
that though he valued an embroidery—
three mulberries proper on a silk like silver—
it was not for the subtlety of the stitches,
but for the magic in it. Whereas, Desdemona
once contrived to imitate in needlework
her father's shield, and plucked it out
three times, to begin again, each time
with diminished colors. This is a small point
but indicative.

Desdemona was small and fair,
delicate as a grasshopper
at the tag-end of summer: a Venetian
to her noble finger tips.

O, it is not enough
that they should meet, naked, at dead of night

in a small inn on a dark canal. Procurers
less expert than Iago can arrange as much.

The ceremony must be found

Traditional, with all its symbols
ancient as the metaphors in dreams;
strange, with never before heard music; continuous
until the torches deaden at the bedroom door.

WILFRED OWEN

❧ *Dulce et Decorum Est*

BENT double, like old beggars under sacks,
Knock-kneed, coughing like hags, we cursed through sludge,
Till on the haunting flares we turned our backs,
And towards our distant rest began to trudge.
Men marched asleep. Many had lost their boots,
But limped on, blood-shod. All went lame, all blind;
Drunk with fatigue; deaf even to the hoots
Of gas-shells dropping softly behind.

Gas! Gas! Quick, boys!—An ecstasy of fumbling,
Fitting the clumsy helmets just in time,   10
But someone still was yelling out and stumbling
And floundering like a man in fire or lime.
Dim through the misty panes and thick green light,
As under a green sea, I saw him drowning.

In all my dreams before my helpless sight
He plunges at me, guttering, choking, drowning.

If in some smothering dreams, you too could pace
Behind the wagon that we flung him in,
And watch the white eyes writhing in his face,
His hanging face, like a devil's sick of sin;   20
If you could hear, at every jolt, the blood
Come gargling from the froth-corrupted lungs,
Bitter as the cud
Of vile, incurable sores on innocent tongues,
My friend, you would not tell with such high zest

To children ardent for some desperate glory,
The old Lie: *Dulce et decorum est*
Pro patria mori.

E. E. CUMMINGS

❧ *in Just-spring*

in Just-
spring   when the world is mud-
luscious the little
lame balloonman

whistles   far   and wee

and eddieandbill come
running from marbles and
piracies and it's
spring

when the world is puddle-wonderful

the queer
old balloonman whistles
far   and   wee
and bettyandisbel come dancing

from hop-scotch and jump-rope and

it's
spring
and
        the

            goat-footed

balloonMan   whistles
far
and
wee

27–28. **Dulce . . . mori:** "Sweet and fitting it is to die for one's country," Horace, *Odes*, III:2.

ROBERT GRAVES

❧ *The Cool Web*

CHILDREN are dumb to say how hot the day is,
How hot the scent is of the summer rose,
How dreadful the black wastes of evening sky,
How dreadful the tall soldiers drumming by.

But we have speech, to chill the angry day,
And speech, to dull the rose's cruel scent.
We spell away the overhanging night,
We spell away the soldiers and the fright.

There's a cool web of language winds us in,
Retreat from too much joy or too much fear: 10
We grow sea-green at last and coldly die
In brininess and volubility.

But if we let our tongues lose self-possession,
Throwing off language and its watery clasp
Before our death, instead of when death comes,
Facing the wide glare of the children's day,
Facing the rose, the dark sky and the drums,
We shall go mad no doubt and die that way.

KENNETH FEARING

❧ *No Credit*

WHETHER dinner was pleasant, with the windows lit by gunfire, and no one
    disagreed; or whether, later, we argued in the park, and there was a touch
    of vomit-gas in the evening air;
Whether we found a greater, deeper, more perfect love, by courtesy of Camels,
    over NBC; whether the comics amused us, or the newspapers carried a
    hunger death and a White House prayer for mother's day;

7. **spell away:** in one sense, exorcise with a magic spell.

Whether the bills were paid or not, whether or not we had our doubts, whether
we spoke our minds at Joe's, and the receipt said "Not Returnable," and
the cash-register rang up "No Sale,"
Whether the truth was then, or later, or whether the best had already gone—

Nevertheless, we know; as every turn is measured; as every unavoidable risk
is known;
As nevertheless, the flesh grows old, dies, dies in its only life, is gone;
The reflection goes from the mirror, as the shadow, of even a rebel, is gone
from the wall;
As nevertheless, the current is thrown and the wheels revolve; and nevertheless,
as the word is spoken and the wheat grows tall and the ships sail on—

None but the fool is paid in full; none but the broker, none but the scab is
certain of profit;
The sheriff alone may attend a third degree in formal attire; alone, the
academy artists multiply in dignity as trooper's bayonet guards the
door;   10
Only Steve, the side-show robot, knows content; only Steve, the mechanical
man in love with a photo-electric beam, remains aloof; only Steve, who
sits and smokes or stands in salute, is secure;
Steve, whose shoebutton eyes are blind to terror, whose painted ears are deaf
to appeal, whose welded breast will never be slashed by bullets, whose
armature soul can hold no fear.

C. DAY LEWIS

❧ *Let Us Now Praise Famous Men*

LET us now praise famous men,
Not your earth-shakers, not the dynamiters,
But who in the Home Counties or the Khyber,
Trimming their nails to meet an ill wind,
Facing the Adversary with a clean collar,
Justified the system.
Admire the venerable pile that bred them,
Bones are its foundations,
The pinnacles are stone abstractions,
Whose halls are whispering-galleries designed   10

9. **scab:** a non-union worker who ignores a strike.

3. **Home Counties:** the counties around London.
3. **Khyber:** a famous pass on the Afghanistan–Pakistan border.

To echo voices of the past, dead tongues.
White hopes of England here
Are taught to rule by learning to obey,
Bend over before vested interests,
Kiss the rod, salute the quarter-deck;
Here is no savage discipline
Of peregrine swooping, of fire destroying,
But a civil code; no capital offender
But the cool cad, the man who goes too far.
Ours the curriculum   20
Neither of building birds nor wasteful waters,
Bound in book not violent in vein:
Here we inoculate with dead ideas
Against blood-epidemics, against
The infection of faith and the excess of life.
Our methods are up to date; we teach
Through head and not by heart,
Language with gramophones and sex with cards,
Prophecy by deduction, prayer by numbers.
For honors see prospectus: those who leave us   30
Will get a post and pity the poor;
Their eyes glaze at strangeness;
They are never embarrassed, have a word for everything,
Living on credit, dying when the heart stops;
Will wear black armlets and stand a moment in silence
For the passing of an era, at their own funeral.

                              RICHARD EBERHART

❧ *The Groundhog*

          In June, amid the golden fields,
          I saw a groundhog lying dead.
          Dead lay he; my senses shook,
          And mind outshot our naked frailty.
          There lowly in the vigorous summer
          His form began its senseless change,
          And made my senses waver dim
          Seeing nature ferocious in him.
          Inspecting close his maggots' might
          And seething cauldron of his being,   10

17. **peregrine:** foreign; also, a kind of hawk.

Half with loathing, half with a strange love,
I poked him with an angry stick.
The fever arose, became a flame
And Vigour circumscribed the skies,
Immense energy in the sun,
And through my frame a sunless trembling.
My stick had done nor good nor harm.
Then stood I silent in the day
Watching the object, as before;
And kept my reverence for knowledge   20
Trying for control, to be still,
To quell the passion of the blood;
Until I had bent down on my knees
Praying for joy in the sight of decay.
And so I left; and I returned
In Autumn strict of eye, to see
The sap gone out of the groundhog,
But the bony sodden hulk remained.
But the year had lost its meaning,
And in intellectual chains   30
I lost both love and loathing,
Mured up in the wall of wisdom.
Another summer took the fields again
Massive and burning, full of life,
But when I chanced upon the spot
There was only a little hair left,
And bones bleaching in the sunlight
Beautiful as architecture;
I watched them like a geometer,
And cut a walking stick from a birch.   40
It has been three years, now.
There is no sign of the groundhog.
I stood there in the whirling summer,
My hand capped a withered heart,
And thought of China and of Greece,
Of Alexander in his tent;
Of Montaigne in his tower,
Of Saint Theresa in her wild lament.

46. **Alexander:** Alexander the Great (356–323 B.C.) conquered most of the known
world.
47. **Montaigne:** Michel Eyquem de Montaigne (1533–1592), the famous essayist,
was much interested in the meaning of death.
48. **Saint Theresa:** Spanish saint (1515–1582), famous for her visions, her books, and
her reform of the Carmelite Order.

LOUIS MACNEICE

❧ Nature Morte

(Even so it is not so easy to be dead)

As those who are not athletic at breakfast day by day
Employ and enjoy the sinews of others vicariously,
Shielded by the upheld journal from their dream-puncturing wives
And finding in the printed word a multiplication of their lives,
So we whose senses give us things misfelt and misheard
Turn also, for our adjustment, to the pretentious word
Which stabilizes the light on the sun-fondled trees
And, by photographing our ghosts, claims to put us at our ease;
Yet even so, no matter how solid and staid we contrive
Our reconstructions, even a still life is alive   10
And in your Chardin the appalling unrest of the soul
Exudes from the dried fish and the brown jug and the bowl.

W. H. AUDEN

❧ The Quarry

O WHAT is that sound which so thrills the ear
Down in the valley drumming, drumming?
Only the scarlet soldiers, dear,
The soldiers coming.

O what is that light I see flashing so clear
Over the distance brightly, brightly?
Only the sun on their weapons, dear,
As they step lightly.

O what are they doing with all that gear,
What are they doing this morning, this morning?

11. **Chardin:** Jean-Baptiste Simeon Chardin (1699–1779), French painter of still life, was particularly concerned with ordinary subjects done in sober colors, lighting.

Only their usual manoeuvres, dear,
Or perhaps a warning.

O why have they left the road down there,
Why are they suddenly wheeling, wheeling?
Perhaps a change in their orders, dear.
Why are you kneeling?

O haven't they stopped for the doctor's care,
Haven't they reined their horses, their horses?
Why, they are none of them wounded, dear,
None of these forces.

O is it the parson they want, with white hair,
Is it the parson, is it, is it?
No, they are passing his gateway, dear,
Without a visit.

O it must be the farmer who lives so near.
It must be the farmer so cunning, so cunning?
They have passed the farmyard already, dear,
And now they are running.

O where are you going? Stay with me here!
Were the vows you swore deceiving, deceiving?
No, I promised to love you, dear,
But I must be leaving.

O it's broken the lock and splintered the door,
O it's the gate where they're turning, turning;
Their boots are heavy on the floor
And their eyes are burning.

❧ *Musée des Beaux Arts*

About suffering they were never wrong,
The Old Masters: how well they understood
Its human position; how it takes place
While someone else is eating or opening a window or just walking dully along;
How, when the aged are reverently, passionately waiting
For the miraculous birth, there always must be
Children who did not specially want it to happen, skating
On a pond at the edge of the wood:

They never forgot
That even the dreadful martyrdom must run its course   10
Anyhow in a corner, some untidy spot
Where the dogs go on with their doggy life and the torturer's horse
Scratches its innocent behind on a tree.

In Brueghel's *Icarus*, for instance: how everything turns away
Quite leisurely from the disaster; the ploughman may
Have heard the splash, the forsaken cry,
But for him it was not an important failure; the sun shone
As it had to on the white legs disappearing into the green
Water; and the expensive delicate ship that must have seen
Something amazing, a boy falling out of the sky,   20
Had somewhere to get to and sailed calmly on.

❧ *The Shield of Achilles*

      SHE looked over his shoulder
      For vines and olive trees,
      Marble, well-governed cities
      And ships upon wine-dark seas;
      But there on the shining metal
      His hands had put instead
      An artificial wilderness
      And a sky like lead.

  A plain without a feature, bare and brown,
  No blade of grass, no sight of neighborhood,   10
  Nothing to eat and nowhere to sit down;
  Yet, congregated on that blankness, stood
  An unintelligible multitude,
  A million eyes, a million boots, in line,
  Without expression, waiting for a sign.

14. **Brueghel's *Icarus*:** a painting by Pieter Brueghel the Elder (1520?–1569) showing
the son of Daedalus falling into the sea. Icarus and his father had escaped from the
labyrinth of King Minos by constructing wings, but Icarus flew too high and the sun
melted the wax holding them together.

"The Shield . . .": in *The Iliad*, 18:478–616, the shield wrought by Hephaestos for
Achilles is described. It is intricately decorated with scenes of daily life—marriage
processions, the marketplace, farms, vineyards, etc.
13. **unintelligible multitude:** in *The Iliad*, the people in the marketplace are cheering
their favorites in a lively dispute.

Out of the air a voice without a face
Proved by statistics that some cause was just
In tones as dry and level as the place;
No one was cheered and nothing was discussed;
Column by column, in a cloud of dust,   20
They marched away, enduring a belief
Whose logic brought them, somewhere else, to grief.

    She looked over his shoulder
    For ritual pieties,
    White flower-garlanded heifers,
    Libation and sacrifice:
    But there on the shining metal
    Where the altar should have been
    She saw by his flickering forge-light
    Quite another scene.   30

Barbed wire enclosed an arbitrary spot
Where bored officials lounged (one cracked a joke)
And sentries sweated for the day was hot;
A crowd of ordinary decent folk
Watched from outside and neither moved nor spoke
As three pale figures were led forth and bound
To three posts driven upright in the ground.

The mass and majesty of this world, all
That carries weight and always weighs the same,
Lay in the hands of others; they were small   40
And could not hope for help, and no help came;
What their foes liked to do was done; their shame
Was all the worst could wish: they lost their pride
And died as men before their bodies died.

    She looked over his shoulder
    For athletes at their games,
    Men and women in a dance
    Moving their sweet limbs,
    Quick, quick, to music;
    But there on the shining shield   50
    His hands had set no dancing-floor
    But a weed-choked field.

31. **arbitrary spot:** again in *The Iliad*, an ambush is prepared and a battle fought, but
though bloody it is not a numb, hopeless, mechanical action like the present one.
36. **three pale figures:** on Achilles' shield, three sheaf-binders are happily at work in
the fields, watched by the king, as others are preparing a feast.

A ragged urchin, aimless and alone,
Loitered about that vacancy; a bird
Flew up to safety from his well-aimed stone:
That girls are raped, that two boys knife a third,
Were axioms to him, who'd never heard
Of any world where promises were kept
Or one could weep because another wept.

The thin-lipped armorer   60
Hephaestos hobbled away;
Thetis of the shining breasts
Cried out in dismay
At what the God had wrought
To please her son, the strong
Iron-hearted man-slaying Achilles
Who would not live long.

THEODORE ROETHKE

❧ *Elegy for Jane*

(My student, thrown by a horse)

I REMEMBER the neckcurls, limp and damp as tendrils;
And her quick look, a sidelong pickerel smile;
And how, once startled into talk, the light syllables leaped for her,
And she balanced in the delight of her thought,
A wren, happy, tail into the wind,
Her song trembling the twigs and small branches.
The shade sang with her;
The leaves, their whispers turned to kissing,
And the mould sang in the bleached valleys under the rose.

Oh, when she was sad, she cast herself down into such a pure depth,
Even a father could not find her:
Scraping her cheek against straw;
Stirring the clearest water.

53. **ragged urchin:** in the original, a boy is playing a lament for the departing summer on his viol. He is surrounded by children carrying the grape harvest and dancing as they walk.
62. **Thetis:** Achilles' mother, an immortal.

My sparrow, you are not here,
Waiting like a fern, making a spiney shadow.
The sides of wet stones cannot console me,
Nor the moss, wound with the last light.

If only I could nudge you from this sleep,
My maimed darling, my skittery pigeon.
Over this damp grave I speak the words of my love:
I, with no rights in this matter,
Neither father nor lover.

STEPHEN SPENDER

❧ My Parents Kept Me from Children Who Were Rough

My parents kept me from children who were rough
Who threw words like stones and who wore torn clothes.
Their thighs showed through rags. They ran in the street
And climbed cliffs and stripped by the country streams.

I feared more than tigers their muscles like iron
Their jerking hands and their knees tight on my arms.
I feared the salt coarse pointing of those boys
Who copied my lisp behind me on the road.

They were lithe, they sprang out behind hedges
Like dogs to bark at my world. They threw mud
While I looked the other way, pretending to smile.
I longed to forgive them, but they never smiled.

❧ The Express

AFTER the first powerful plain manifesto,
The black statement of pistons, without more fuss
But gliding like a queen, she leaves the station.
Without bowing and with restrained unconcern
She passes the houses which humbly crowd outside,
The gasworks and at last the heavy page
Of death, printed by gravestones in the cemetery.
Beyond the town there lies the open country

Where, gathering speed, she acquires mystery,
The luminous self-possession of ships on ocean.
It is now she begins to sing—at first quite low
Then loud, and at last with a jazzy madness—
The song of her whistle screaming at curves,
Of deafening tunnels, brakes, innumerable bolts.
And always light, aerial, underneath
Goes the elate meter of her wheels.
Steaming through metal landscape on her lines
She plunges new eras of wild happiness
Where speed throws up strange shapes, broad curves
And parallels clean like the steel of guns.
At last, further than Edinburgh or Rome,
Beyond the crest of the world, she reaches night
Where only a low streamline brightness
Of phosphorus on the tossing hills is white.
Ah, like a comet through flames she moves entranced
Wrapt in her music no song, no, nor bough
Breaking with honey buds, shall ever equal.

RANDALL JARRELL

❧ *The Death of the Ball Turret Gunner*

From my mother's sleep I fell into the State,
And I hunched in its belly till my wet fur froze.
Six miles from earth, loosed from its dream of life,
I woke to black flak and the nightmare fighters.
When I died they washed me out of the turret with a hose.

❧ *Losses*

It was not dying: everybody died.
It was not dying: we had died before
In the routine crashes—and our fields
Called up the papers, wrote home to our folks,
And the rates rose, all because of us.
We died on the wrong page of the almanac,

5. **rates rose:** insurance rates.
6. **wrong page of the almanac:** the deaths were recorded as accidents rather than casualties in war.

Scattered on mountains fifty miles away;
Diving on haystacks, fighting with a friend,
We blazed up on the lines we never saw.
We died like aunts or pets or foreigners.   10
(When we left high school nothing else had died
For us to figure we had died like.)

In our new planes, with our new crews, we bombed
The ranges by the desert or the shore,
Fired at towed targets, waited for our scores—
And turned into replacements and woke up
One morning, over England, operational.
It wasn't different: but if we died
It was not an accident but a mistake
(But an easy one for anyone to make).   20
We read our mail and counted up our missions—
In bombers named for girls, we burned
The cities we had learned about in school—
Till our lives wore out; our bodies lay among
The people we had killed and never seen.
When we lasted long enough they gave us medals;
When we died they said, "Our casualties were low."

They said, "Here are the maps"; we burned the cities.

It was not dying—no, not ever dying;
But the night I died I dreamed that I was dead,   30
And the cities said to me: "Why are you dying?
We are satisfied, if you are; but why did I die?"

DYLAN THOMAS

❧ *In My Craft or Sullen Art*

IN my craft or sullen art
Exercised in the still night
When only the moon rages
And the lovers lie abed
With all their griefs in their arms,
I labour by singing light
Not for ambition or bread
Or the strut and trade of charms
On the ivory stages
But for the common wages
Of their most secret heart.

Not for the proud man apart
From the raging moon I write
On these spindrift pages
Nor for the towering dead
With their nightingales and psalms
But for the lovers, their arms
Round the griefs of the ages,
Who pay no praise or wages
Nor heed my craft or art.

❧ Fern Hill

Now as I was young and easy under the apple boughs
About the lilting house and happy as the grass was green,
The night above the dingle starry,
Time let me hail and climb
Golden in the heydays of his eyes,
And honored among wagons I was prince of the apple towns
And once below a time I lordly had the trees and leaves
Trail with daisies and barley
Down the rivers of the windfall light.

And as I was green and carefree, famous among the barns   10
About the happy yard and singing as the farm was home,
In the sun that is young once only,
Time let me play and be
Golden in the mercy of his means,
And green and golden I was huntsman and herdsman, the calves
Sang to my horn, the foxes on the hills barked clear and cold,
And the sabbath rang slowly
In the pebbles of the holy streams.

All the sun long it was running, it was lovely, the hay
Fields high as the house, the tunes from the chimneys, it was air   20
And playing, lovely and watery
And fire green as grass.
And nightly under the simple stars
As I rode to sleep the owls were bearing the farm away,
All the moon long I heard, blessed among stables, the nightjars

3. **dingle:** a narrow wooded valley.
24. **bearing the farm away:** a common superstition that the birds carry the farm away
as one sleeps, then bring it back in the morning.
25. **nightjars:** a species of bird.

Flying with the ricks, and the horses
Flashing into the dark.

And then to awake, and the farm, like a wanderer white
With the dew, come back, the cock on his shoulder: it was all
Shining, it was Adam and maiden,   30
The sky gathered again
And the sun grew round that very day.
So it must have been after the birth of the simple light
In the first, spinning place, the spellbound horses walking warm
Out of the whinnying green stable
On to the fields of praise.

And honoured among foxes and pheasants by the gay house
Under the new made clouds and happy as the heart was long,
In the sun born over and over,
I ran my heedless ways,   40
My wishes raced through the house-high hay
And nothing I cared, at my sky blue trades, that time allows
In all his tuneful turning so few and such morning songs
Before the children green and golden
Follow him out of grace.

Nothing I cared, in the lamb white days, that time would take me
Up to the swallow thronged loft by the shadow of my hand,
In the moon that is always rising,
Nor that riding to sleep
I should hear him fly with the high fields   50
And wake to the farm forever fled from the childless land.
Oh as I was young and easy in the mercy of his means,
Time held me green and dying
Though I sang in my chains like the sea.

JOHN BETJEMAN

❧ *False Security*

I REMEMBER the dread with which I at a quarter past four
Let go with a bang behind me our house front door
And, clutching a present for my dear little hostess tight,
Sailed out for the children's party into the night

Or rather the gathering night. For still some boys
In the near municipal acres were making a noise
Shuffling in fallen leaves and shouting and whistling
And running past hedges of hawthorn, spikey and bristling.
And black in the oncoming darkness stood out the trees
And pink shone the ponds in the sunset ready to freeze
And all was still and ominous waiting for dark
And the keeper was ringing his closing bell in the park
And the arc lights started to fizzle and burst into mauve
As I climbed West Hill to the great big house in The Grove,
Where the children's party was and the dear little hostess.
But halfway up stood the empty house where the ghost is.
I crossed to the other side and under the arc
Made a rush for the next kind lamp-post out of the dark
And so to the next and the next till I reached the top
Where the Grove branched off to the left. Then ready to drop
I ran to the ironwork gateway of number seven
Secure at last on the lamplit fringe of Heaven.
Oh who can say how subtle and safe one feels
Shod in one's children's sandals from Daniel Neal's,
Clad in one's party clothes made of stuff from Heal's?
And who can still one's thrill at the candle shine
On cakes and ices and jelly and blackcurrant wine,
And the warm little feel of my hostess's hand in mine?
Can I forget my delight at the conjuring show?
And wasn't I proud that I was the last to go?
Too overexcited and pleased with myself to know
That the words I heard my hostess's mother employ
To a guest departing, would ever diminish my joy,
I WONDER WHERE JULIA FOUND THAT STRANGE, RATHER COMMON
    LITTLE BOY?

                                        ROBERT LOWELL

❧ *Children of Light*

        OUR fathers wrung their bread from stocks and stones
        And fenced their gardens with the Redman's bones;
        Embarking from the Nether Land of Holland,
        Pilgrims unhoused by Geneva's night,

1. **stocks:** stumps on land they cleared.
4. **unhoused:** set outside the sacraments of the church.
4. **Geneva's night:** a reference to the doctrines of John Calvin, whose theocratic rule
of Geneva was despotic; to the Geneva Bible (1560), with its marginal commentary;
and perhaps to the "Geneva gown" of black cloth worn by the Calvinist clergy.

They planted here the Serpent's seeds of light;
And here the pivoting searchlights probe to shock
The riotous glass houses built on rock,
And candles gutter by an empty altar,
And light is where the landless blood of Cain
Is burning, burning the unburied grain.   10

❧ *Mr. Edwards and the Spider*

I saw the spiders marching through the air,
Swimming from tree to tree that mildewed day
In latter August when the hay
Came creaking to the barn. But where
The wind is westerly,
Where gnarled November makes the spiders fly
Into the apparitions of the sky,
They purpose nothing but their ease and die
Urgently beating east to sunrise and the sea;

What are we in the hands of the great God?   10
It was in vain you set up thorn and brier
In battle array against the fire
And treason crackling in your blood;
For the wild thorns grow tame
And will do nothing to oppose the flame;
Your lacerations tell the losing game
You play against a sickness past your cure.
How will the hands be strong? How will the heart endure?

A very little thing, a little worm,
Or hourglass-blazoned spider, it is said,   20
Can kill a tiger. Will the dead
Hold up his mirror and affirm

5. **Serpent:** the devil.
9. **blood of Cain:** the descendants of Cain, who wandered in exile from Eden—land-less—after killing his brother Abel. See Genesis 4:1–15.

"**Mr. Edwards . . .**": Jonathan Edwards (1703–1758), the famous Puritan preacher, while still a child, wrote an essay on the flying spider.
10. **hands of the great God:** see Edwards' Enfield sermon, *Sinners in the Hands of an Angry God* (1741).
20. **hourglass-blazoned:** the black widow.

To the four winds the smell
And flash of his authority? It's well
If God who holds you to the pit of hell,
Much as one holds a spider, will destroy,
Baffle and dissipate your soul. As a small boy

On Windsor Marsh, I saw the spider die
When thrown into the bowels of fierce fire:
There's no long struggle, no desire 30
To get up on its feet and fly—
It stretches out its feet
And dies. This is the sinner's last retreat;
Yes, and no strength exerted on the heat
Then sinews the abolished will, when sick
And full of burning, it will whistle on a brick.

But who can plumb the sinking of that soul?
Josiah Hawley, picture yourself cast
Into a brick-kiln where the blast
Fans your quick vitals to a coal— 40
If measured by a glass,
How long would it seem burning! Let there pass
A minute, ten, ten trillion; but the blaze
Is infinite, eternal: this is death,
To die and know it. This is the Black Widow, death.

HOWARD NEMEROV

❧ Death and the Maiden

ONCE I saw a grown man fall from a tree
and die. That's years ago, I was a girl.
My father's house is sold into a home
for the feeble-minded gentlefolk who can't
any longer stand the world, but in those days
there was money to maintain the mile or so
of discipline that kept the hungry grass
parading to the lake, and once a year
bring men to prune the files of giant trees
whose order satisfied and stood for some 10

28. **Windsor Marsh:** at Windsor, Connecticut, where Edwards was born.

euclidean ancestor's dream about the truth:
elms, most of them, already dying of
their yellow blight, and blackened with witches' broom
in the highest branches—but they could die for years,
decades, so tall their silence, and tell you nothing.
Those men came in October every year,
and among the last leaves, the driven leaves,
would set their ladders for assault and swarm
like pirates into the shrouds, thrusting with hook
and long-handled bill against the withered members   20
of those great corporations, amputating
death away from the center. They were called
tree surgeons. On the ground they were surly-
polite and touched their caps, but in the air
they dared. I would watch one straddle a branch
on a day of rainy wind, his red shirt patched
on the elm's great fan of sky, his pruning-claw
breaking the finger-bones from the high hand
which held him, and I'd dream of voyages.
My father said: "It looks more dangerous   30
than really it is." But if your hand offend,
I thought, cut off the hand, and if your eye
offend, pluck out the eye. I looked at him
out of my window all one afternoon,
and I think he looked back once, a young man
proud and probably lecherous, while I—
was a maiden at a window. Only he died
that day. "Unlucky boy," my father said,
who then was dying himself without a word
to anyone, the crab's claw tightening   40
inside the bowel that year to the next
in a dead silence. I do not know if things
that happen can be said to come to pass,
or only happen, but when I remember
my father's house, I imagine sometimes
a dry, ruined spinster at my rainy window
trying to tally on dumb fingers a world's
incredible damage—nothing can stand it!—and
watching the red shirt patched against the sky,
so far and small in the webbed hand of the elm.

11. **euclidean:** geometry-minded.
13. **witches' broom:** an abnormal growth (suggesting cancer in this context) of small branches in clusters.
20. **bill:** pruning hook.
40. **crab:** in the zodiac, the Crab is Cancer.

RICHARD WILBUR

❧ *The Death of a Toad*

A TOAD the power mower caught,
Chewed and clipped of a leg, with a hobbling hop has got
To the garden verge, and sanctuaried him
Under the cineraria leaves, in the shade
Of the ashen heart-shaped leaves, in a dim,
Low, and a final glade.

The rare original heartsblood goes,
Spends on the earthen hide, in the folds and wizenings, flows
In the gutters of the banked and staring eyes. He lies
As still as if he would return to stone,   10
And soundlessly attending, dies
Toward some deep monotone,

Toward misted and ebullient seas
And cooling shores, toward lost Amphibia's emperies.
Day dwindles, drowning, and at length is gone
In the wide and antique eyes, which still appear
To watch, across the castrate lawn,
The haggard daylight steer.

❧ *Mind*

MIND in the purest play is like some bat
That beats about in caverns all alone,
Contriving by a kind of senseless wit
Not to conclude against a wall of stone.

4. **cineraria:** plants of the aster family.
10. **return to stone:** toads were believed to exist in stones.
14. **Amphibia:** actually, a class of amphibious vertebrates, but here suggesting a lost kingdom, like Atlantis.
14. **emperies:** imperial dominions, splendors.
17. **castrate:** emasculated.

It has no need to falter or explore;
Darkly it knows what obstacles are there,
And so may weave and flitter, dip and soar
In perfect courses through the blackest air.

And has this simile a like perfection?
The mind is like a bat. Precisely. Save
That in the very happiest intellection
A graceful error may correct the cave.

SHORT
STORIES

THE ART OF
Prose Fiction

STORYTELLING is as old as the recorded history of man, but the novel and the short story as we know them now are of relatively recent origin. The novel in English was born with the rise of the middle class in the first quarter of the eighteenth century. The short story did not make its appearance until a hundred years later, in the tales of two American writers, Nathaniel Hawthorne and Edgar Allan Poe.

Poe is commonly regarded as the father of the short story because, in addition to the skillfully constructed prose tales that he published in various magazines and annuals between 1830 and 1835, he was the first to set down a clear concept of what a short story should be: a brief tale with every word aimed to bring about a single effect, a "pre-established design."

Although the short story has had outstanding practitioners in many countries, it has had its greatest popularity and development in America. That development has taken numerous directions: the well-plotted story with a realistic portrayal of men and motives; the story with a surprise or trick ending; the "local color" story; the hard-boiled story with a strictly objective approach to its presentation of characters in action; the story with a strong emphasis upon character and a consequent playing down of plot; the "slice of life" with the virtual disappearance of any organized plot structure; the story with social implications. The short story today is in a state of flux, continual experimentation, but in the hands of skillful practitioners it is a powerful instrument for saying something significant about the world in which we live.

In spite of its diversity, we can describe the short story in the following terms. As Poe has indicated, because it is short enough to be read at one sitting, it is capable of a unity of effect that the novel is unable to achieve. A single line of action that develops a single idea, or theme, is its main characteristic. This, we say, is what the story is *about*. Also, where the novel is likely to have a multiplicity of characters, the short story has few, and always one who stands out as the central figure upon whom our attention is focused. This individual, called the *protagonist*, is engaged in a conflict of some sort, the outcome of which is crucial to him, and consequently to us; for if the story is successful, we identify with him in some measure as we follow his fortunes. The experience he undergoes is so significant that it usually leaves its mark upon him; normally, we see him at the end of the story a changed individual. The pattern is infinitely various, every story presenting its own problem, worked out by the author in his own way.

To read a story with full understanding makes certain demands upon the reader. A story is made up of characters in action, and so the reader must recognize the characters' moral nature that motivates their actions. These actions grow out of an initial situation, take place in a particular setting—a physical, a social, a psychological environment—and are presented from an angle of vision that both limits and illuminates the action. A dominant idea, or theme, unfolds as the action develops—a theme often underlined by certain symbols and enforced by the author's style.

What we are leading up to is that to read a short story intelligently requires a knowledge of the techniques of prose fiction. As we consider them in detail, let us focus upon a few of the stories in the anthology, and primarily upon one story, Wilbur Daniel Steele's "How Beautiful with Shoes."

Character

Let us first consider characters in a story. Our interest in people, the forces that move them and motivate their actions, is a primary reason for reading fiction. We are as likely to remember the characters in a story as what happened to them, for the skillful author brings to life unforgettable men and women, as real as the flesh-and-blood people we meet every day.

There is, however, one fundamental difference. A fictional character is never as complex as the people we see around us. Only a few significant traits appear in a character as he is re-created for us in the fictitious world of the short story. To use E. M. Forster's classification, the characters in a short story are "flat," not "round" (see pages 650–655); that is, they act consistently from a few well-defined traits. Why is this? No author can develop in a few thousand words many varying facets of an individual's personality. Nor is this necessary. A short story uses only those aspects of character required by the situation.

To illustrate from Steele's story, Mare Doggett, as Steele portrays her, is quite uncomplicated. She is a slow-minded, inarticulate farm girl with a natural skill in handling animals. She possesses a certain fortitude, a quiet courage when the occasion demands it. There is also the bare suggestion that she has inherited from her dead father the potential for an appreciation of beauty, symbolized by the name he gave her—Amarantha. This summarizes Mare, who is by far the most fully realized character in the story.

Ruby Herter, her fiancé, is little more than a healthy young male animal. Mrs. Doggett, Mare's mother, is merely a querulous, deaf woman. Humble Jewett, the "loony," is more complex. A demented, tortured soul, his love for beauty is at odds with his homicidal tendencies.

The simplification of the characters in a story makes them immediately intelligible and keeps their actions consistent. We expect—demand, really—the consistency that we seldom get from the people in the world around us. Calling a character in fiction "flat" is no term of reproach, no indication that he is unreal. Mare is certainly real to the reader; in fact, she is more real than if she had been presented with such a high degree of complexity that her actions would be bewildering.

Most of the characters in prose fiction are flat, even in the novel. This, as Forster goes on to state, is a great advantage to both writer and reader. "It is," says Forster, "a convenience for an author when he can strike with his full force at once, and flat characters are very useful to him, since they never need reintroducing, never run away, have not to be watched for development, and provide their own atmosphere. . . ." They are "easily remembered by the reader afterwards. They remain in his mind as unalterable, for the reason that they were not changed by circumstances; they move through circumstances, which gives them in retrospect a comforting quality, and preserves them when the book that produced them may decay."

RECOGNIZING AND EVALUATING CHARACTER

An author presents the reader with many clues for the recognition and evaluation of character in his story. These clues are comparable to the ways by which we evaluate people in the world around us. They are:

Action. We judge people by the way they act, particularly in a crucial situation. What a person *does* presents convincing evidence of what he *is*. Mare's action in quietly leading the homicidal "loony" away from the house to protect her mother indicates the firm control she has over herself, which manifests itself again, later, when she is abducted by him. And the passivity with which she receives Ruby's caresses, the matter-of-fact way in which she responds to his rough humor as he yanks her head back by her braids, shows a certain phlegmatic temperament. Ruby's actions are also revealing. His aggressive masculinity becomes apparent in his treatment of Mare at the outset of the story and by the way he immediately joins the pursuing posse when taunted with the possibility that he might be afraid.

Speech. A person's speech, like his actions, can be very revealing. In addition to showing such things as age, nationality, education—all of which serve as identification—speech can reveal habits of mind and the reaction to people and events—both sharply indicative of character. Most of us have had the experience of overhearing a conversation between people who are total strangers to us and gaining therefrom an immediate impression of their personalities. Ernest Hemingway, in the opening scene of "The Killers," lets us listen to a conversation between two strangers and the counterman in Henry's lunchroom. The contempt, the downright nastiness, the utter disregard for personality, the blatant egotism displayed in the speech of these two strangers marks them at once as cold-blooded and vicious.

In "How Beautiful with Shoes," Mare's woodenness and natural shyness are revealed, in part, by her inarticulateness; and her comments to Humble Jewett, as he recites to her verses from the Song of Solomon, reveal her simplicity. When Humble Jewett remarks, at hearing her name, "Amarantha! That's poetry," Steele tells us that "Mare knew then that she did not know him." Of course. For his speech marked him as coming from a world different from her own. Neither Ruby nor any of his companions would have spoken like that. Ruby calls out to Mare as he sees her coming toward him across the field, "Don't run yourself out o' breath, Mare; I got all night," and his speech is as characteristic of him as the way he sits motionless on the wagon seat after she does arrive, stirring only to cut himself a fresh wad of tobacco.

Description. Physical appearance can, of course, be a clue to character, but the writer of fiction seldom stresses it. Details of appearance, either of feature or dress, are more often a means of identification than a means of revealing personality. Nick Adams, for example, the main character in Hemingway's "The Killers," is not described at all. The killers are, but note that they are described as though they were "twins," with their white faces and tight lips, their too-tight black overcoats buttoned across the chest, their derby hats, silk mufflers, and gloves. The intent is clearly not to show their character but to identify them as belonging to a type: paid gunmen from a large city. In "How Beautiful with Shoes" Mare is described only as "broad-fleshed," with "bare, barn-soiled feet," suggestive of a certain stodginess and that she is a farm girl. Her "yellow hair" is mentioned because, along with her name, it suggests to Humble Jewett the lines by Lovelace.

> Amarantha sweet and fair
> Braid no more that shining hair,

the name and the hair transforming flat-faced Mare Doggett into a romantic vision to the deranged former schoolteacher. Steele pictures Ruby Herter as a "big-barrelled, heavy-limbed fellow," wearing a jumper and chewing tobacco. These details, of course, do suggest character. They depict someone quite the reverse of Paul in Willa Cather's story "Paul's Case," with his thin, cramped shoulders, narrow chest, eyes marked by a hysterical brilliancy, wearing an opal tie pin and a red carnation in his buttonhole, as he stands at bay before his teachers.

Environment. The presentation of a person's surroundings, particularly those he deliberately chooses, including the recreations he prefers and the company he keeps, contributes to an understanding of his character. Willa Cather's description of Paul, as we have seen, gives us a clue to what he is like. But a more significant clue to his character is his reaction to his environment— his overwhelming distaste for the commonplace quality of his home, his contempt for his teachers in the high school, his reveling in the artificial glitter of the theatrical. Mare, in "How Beautiful with Shoes," is also characterized by her environment. It is what she has always known, this life on the farm, close to the soil and to elemental things. But she does not, like Paul, rebel against it. Her being a farm girl is significant in the story. It accounts for the fact that "in an animal way she knew animals," sick animals; she knew "how to move so as not to fret them." As a result, she handles Jewett, the mentally sick man, as she would handle a sick animal.

Thoughts. To reveal a person's thoughts is an act of omniscience. Mental states, such as nervousness, anger, horror, can be indicated by physical re- actions, such as sweating palms, flushed face, rigid muscles. But thought itself cannot be so clinically observed, no matter how well we know an individual.

An author, however, can play God. This is one of the conventions of prose fiction. And presenting a person's thoughts is a very important means of characterizing him. Looking into the mind of a character, an author can reveal the secrets of his character's heart, the motivating force that drives him. We say that imputing motives to people is unfair, for how can one be sure? The writer of fiction can be sure and can open the mind of his characters to the reader at will.

In Steele's story, Mare is the only person whose thoughts are constantly revealed to us. We see everyone else almost entirely from the outside. This admission into Mare's mind plays a large part in making her, for us, a fully realized individual. When she leads the "loony" away from the house and her mother and we are allowed to learn that she is saying to herself, "He won't hurt her; it's me, not her," we become aware of the conspicuous bravery of her action. And because we can enter her mind through all the mad experience of that night with Humble Jewett and the aftermath, we can understand why she pushes Ruby out the door at the end of the story—an act that, to Ruby, is completely bewildering.

Explanation. Explanation is an outright statement by the author *about* his characters. It has been called "direct" characterization, in contrast to the "indirect" characterization of showing an individual in action, listening to him talk, following his thoughts, with the reader making his own inferences. Direct characterization was a common technique of the writer of prose fiction until comparatively recent times. Thackeray, for example, remarks in *Vanity Fair*: "And as we bring our characters forward, I will ask leave as a man and a brother, not only to introduce them but occasionally to step down from the platform and talk about them. . . ." Today this method of presenting char- acter is much less common, and, in the short story, is all but outmoded. The modern short-story writer tends to screen himself out of the story by identifying himself with one of the characters. We shall discuss this method of storytelling more in detail when we consider point of view.

Willa Cather, D. H. Lawrence, Katherine Mansfield, and Wilbur Daniel Steele, among others, do talk about their characters, as well as present them dramatically. Steele, for example, tells us outright that Mare is "slow-minded" and speaks of her "native timidity." Miss Cather says that Paul "was quite accustomed to lying; found it, indeed, indispensable for overcoming friction." Actually, this direct characterization is nothing more than explanation, the author telling us directly what his characters are like.

Any or all of these methods of characterization may be used by the writer of short stories to make his people—those people who inhabit the world that he has created—live for the reader. As we read, we try to discover an individual's outstanding traits, his moral disposition, the forces that motivate him. A short story cannot show the growth and development of character. The people who appear in a short story must have their character already formed, and act in a fashion consistent with what they are. Their actions are not only consistent but inevitable. Character, we say, is fate.

Point of View

Point of view is the angle from which a story is told, the intelligence through whose authority we view the characters and the action. Point of view is extremely important, for it accounts for the selection of a multitude of details: where we, as readers, go; what we see; whose consciousness we share. The author chooses what seems to him the most effective intelligence through which to relate the story, the one most likely to draw the reader in the most telling fashion into the emotional pull of the fictitious world that the author is creating. In doing so, he has a variety of choices.

OMNISCIENT POINT OF VIEW

Sanctioned by long custom is the omniscient point of view. The author, as creator, tells the story from his own vantage point. He can be anywhere at any time, enter the mind of any of his characters at will, reveal their thoughts, relate the action from their physical and mental points of view, make whatever comments about them he chooses.

This omniscient point of view, although an accepted convention, runs contrary to experience, for in life everyone is limited to the testimony of his own senses and the working of his own mind. For this reason, modern writers tend to avoid the omniscient point of view in favor of a more dramatic method, one in which they do not stand between the characters and the reader. D. H. Lawrence, however, uses the omniscient point of view with complete effectiveness in "The Rocking-Horse Winner." Although Paul is the central figure, we see not only into Paul's mind but into the mind of his mother and his uncle. At the end of the story, we find ourselves not with Paul at all, but with the mother, as she opens the door of Paul's room and sees Paul rocking back and forth madly on his rocking horse and, later still, as she sits by his bedside watching him waste away, "feeling her heart had gone, turned actually into a stone."

DRAMATIC POINT OF VIEW

At the opposite extreme from omniscience is the dramatic point of view. The writer presents the action in a purely objective fashion, as if he were at the theater watching a play. This is the point of view of the observer who relates only those details that come to him through his senses, without comment, and without entering the mind of any of his characters. Stories told from this point of view make a great demand on the reader, for he has nothing to guide his interpretation of the action. Motivation of the characters must be judged entirely by externals.

For certain types of stories and certain purposes, however, the dramatic point of view is very effective. Hemingway used the dramatic point of view in many of his early stories. Governed by a desire to avoid any explicit expression of values, Hemingway relied entirely upon the implication of the details themselves, and since dialogue is the most objective method of telling a story, leaned heavily upon dialogue. "The Killers" is a good example of the dramatic point of view. The implications of the story are not difficult to see, and yet Hemingway's objectivity is such that some readers may miss the fact that the story is Nick Adams' story.

PERSONAL POINT OF VIEW

Between these extremes is the personal point of view. The author does not pretend to see all, know all, tell all (omniscient), nor is he an outside observer, watching the action like a member of a theater audience (dramatic); rather, he identifies himself with one actor in the drama and tells the story as it appears to him. He may tell it in the first person or the third person.

Since the personal point of view limits the writer to the actions witnessed by one individual and to this individual's thoughts and emotions, it serves as a unifying factor, a principle of selection. And because it identifies the reader with one person in the story, it helps maintain the illusion of reality that the writer is trying to create.

FIRST PERSON

The first-person point of view is the most natural, because it is the point of view of someone recounting his own experiences. It carries an air of immediacy and authority; the reader gets the impression that he is in the center of the action, seeing things through the eyes and consciousness of the one most concerned. It reads like autobiography, not fiction. In fact, the reader must be careful not to confuse the two, not to identify the author with the character that he has created.

The account that filters through to the reader is, of course, biased. An individual telling a story in which he plays the major role cannot be objective. The nineteen-year-old hero of "I'm a Fool," for instance, tries to throw a certain amount of blame for his actions on the "dude" in the bar, whose cane and Windsor tie so irritated him that he pushed the dude around and then drank more whiskey than he had intended, just to put up a "good front." What he calls putting up a "good front," someone else might call by a quite different name. The first-person narrator, then, might be giving himself away without realizing it; he might also overrate himself or be overmodest. The reader, in other words, is expected to read between the lines, not to take the words of the protagonist at face value.

One variation of first-person point of view is the story told through the consciousness of a minor character. In a story of this kind, the narrator is merely an outsider to the main action who happens to be present at crucial times and through whose eyes and consciousness we see the action unfolding. This point of view enables an author to tell the story through someone who may not realize its significance, but who still furnishes the authenticity of an eye witness. The reader is expected to understand what is happening even though the narrator may not.

THIRD PERSON

The most common point of view is the third-person point of view, in which we follow the action through the eye and mind of one of the characters, usually the protagonist, who is always referred to as "he" or "she." It has been called "stream of experience" (not to be confused with stream of consciousness), for the narrator *experiences* the story as it is taking place. For example, in Truman Capote's "A Tree of Night," the story is told through the consciousness of a college sophomore named Kay, who is riding the night coach of a train on her way home from her uncle's funeral. When Kay climbs aboard the train, we climb with her; as she walks through the coach looking for a seat, we walk with her; when she gets up and goes out on the observation platform, we get up and go out with her—we see everything through her consciousness. For example:

> Kay resisted a temptation to hold her nose and threaded her way carefully down the aisle, tripping once, without disaster, over a dozing fat man's protruding leg. . . .
> Embarrassed, Kay nervously opened a pack of cigarettes and lighted one. She wondered if there might not be a seat in a car up ahead. She could not bear the woman, or, for that matter, the man, another minute. But she had never before been in a remotely comparable situation.

This third-person point of view gives the illusion of reality almost as completely as does the first-person point of view, but it allows more freedom and flexibility in the telling; for the author can be outside, as well as inside, the character and can thus describe his appearance and actions as well as his thoughts and emotions. For the most part, however, it serves as an effective way for the author to screen himself out of the story by identifying with this narrator. It is also an effective way of leading the reader into the emotional center of the story, for the protagonist in a story told from this point of view is a sympathetic character, and the reader tends to identify with him—not merely to look on, but to live the experience as he lives it, to share his doubts and fears, his joys and transports. This identification is what is meant by a vicarious experience, one of the lasting pleasures of reading prose fiction.

In "How Beautiful with Shoes" Steele uses the omniscient point of view at the beginning as he introduces the reader to the characters and the situation. In the opening paragraphs of the story we watch the action through the consciousness of various people. At the outset the point of view is Mare's: "Then in the quiet she heard a sound of hoofs on the bridge, where the road crossed the creek a hundred yards below the house, and she set the pail down on the ground beside her bare, barn-soiled feet." A little later, Mare leaves the scene and we are, for a brief moment, in the consciousness of the author: "For moments after the girl had disappeared beyond the willows the widow continued to call, unaware through long habit of how absurd it sounded, the name which that strange man her husband had put upon their daughter in one of his moods." Still later, we watch the action, briefly, through Ruby's eyes: "When he saw the girl getting over the fence under the willows he tongued the wad of tobacco out of his mouth into his palm, threw it away beyond the road, and drew a sleeve of his jumper across his lips." Once the conflict has started, however, Steele adheres strictly to the third-person point of view, letting the reader share Mare's experience by presenting all the action through Mare's consciousness: her two meetings with Jewett, the weird flight through the night, the final rescue at the hands of old man Wyker, the aftermath at her home. Steele shifts briefly to the omniscient point of view after the rescue as the neighbors gather at the Doggett home, but then once more returns to Mare's point of view and maintains it consistently until the end of the story.

Plot

The basis of every story is a conflict between the central character and some opposing force, which lies either inside or outside him, or perhaps both. The conflict may be with another person or persons, or with his environment, or with some aspect of his own personality. Conflict arises from circumstances that cause an unstable situation (the origin of suspense) and is resolved when the character either overcomes this opposing force or succumbs to it, and the situation becomes stable again. What happens beyond that point is "another story."

Thus the plot of a story is, generally, a conflict and its resolution. Plot is intimately related to character and story idea, or theme; plot is, in fact, the inexorable working-out of the story in terms of the revealed traits of the characters. The emphasis is on causality; a story is a sequence of events in time. But events do not merely happen; they happen *because*—because a certain character with a specific moral nature and disposition, placed in a specific situation, is motivated to act in a certain way.

The elements of plot may be listed as exposition; point of attack; rising action, or complication; climax, or turning point; falling action; and dénouement. *Exposition* is the antecedent information necessary to understand the forward progress of the action; it includes a knowledge of the characters and their relation to each other, the time, the place, the situation out of which the conflict develops. In some stories very little exposition is necessary. Steele, for example, devotes little space to exposition in "How Beautiful with Shoes." Once the story is located for us in the New England countryside, the characters of Mare and Ruby clarified for us, and their engagement indicated, along with a quick picture of their casual love making, we are ready to move ahead with the action. In contrast to this, Sherwood Anderson devotes a good third of "I'm a Fool" to exposition, going into considerable detail about the character of his protagonist, the nineteen-year-old lad who is telling the story, and to earlier events in his life that bear on the present action. Much of this exposition is given in a *flashback*, the insertion of antecedent details after the action of the story has started, either by description or in a scene.

The *point of attack* is the place at which the conflict begins, where the *status quo* is disturbed. In Steele's story the point of attack comes with the escape of the homicidal "loony"; this is the event that disturbs the lives of Mare and Ruby, alters the even tenor of their way. The *rising action* consists of the incident or series of incidents by which the conflict is developed; and the *climax*, or turning point, is that point where we can see how the story must inevitably end (at least we can see this in retrospect). In Steele's story the rising action consists of Mare's two encounters with Humble Jewett, the abduction, the mad experience of that night, with the climax coming at the point where Jewett is shot and killed. The *falling action* is the movement from the climax to the *dénouement*, which is the solution, or "unknotting," of the conflict. Like most short stories, "How Beautiful with Shoes" has no falling action; we move directly from climax to dénouement. The dénouement, the aftermath, comes in the wake of the adventure as Mare sits in her room reliving the experience of the night before.

Few short stories, particularly contemporary ones, have such a fully developed plot pattern. Indeed, most of the time it is unrealistic to discuss the modern story in these terms. This is not to imply that the modern story has no plot. Wherever there is conflict and resolution, if only stalemate, there is plot. The best way to analyze the structure of a story is to note what the conflict is, what causes it, how it is resolved, and how it is worked out in terms of action.

Action

Action is the physical movement of the characters in time, as well as what they think and what they say. Through action the plot is developed.

Action is presented in one of two ways: (1) by means of a *summary* or (2) by means of a *scene*. A summary, or *panorama* (as Percy Lubbock called it in *The Craft of Fiction*), is a narrative of events related in general terms, in which the reader is *told* what happened. A summary is capable of covering a good deal of ground and time in a few words and is often used as a link between scenes. For instance, in "How Beautiful with Shoes," Steele writes, at one point in the narrative: "Ruby went home, but Older Haskins stayed to supper with them, and helped Mare do the dishes afterward; it was nearly nine when he left." This is summary: we don't *see* what *takes* place; we are *told* what *took* place. Hours of time are covered in one sentence. Note, also, that we are kept at a distance from the characters; we are not close-up.

A *scene*, on the contrary, is an episode limited in time and place, with the action slowed down so that the reader can watch it take place in front of him. For instance, in the sentences that directly follow the summary sentence just quoted, Steele writes:

> The mother was already in bed, and Mare was about to sit down to get those shoes off her wretched feet at last, when she heard the cow carrying on up at the barn, lowing and kicking, and the next minute the sow was in it with a horning note. It might be a fox passing by to get at the henhouse or a weasel. Mare forgot her feet, took a broom-handle they used in boiling clothes, opened the back door, and stepped out. Blinking the lamplight from her eyes, she peered up toward the outbuildings, and saw the gable end of the barn standing like a red arrow in the dark, and the top of a butternut tree beyond it drawn in skeleton traceries, and just then a cock crowed.

This is the beginning of a scene that goes on for a number of pages. We watch Mare start to sit down, listen to the farm animals, conclude that they are perhaps being molested, pick up a broomhandle, go to the door, step outside, look toward the barn. All this action takes place in front of our eyes. Whereas the summary sentence covered several hours in twenty-five words, this portion of a scene covers several minutes in about one hundred and thirty-five words. Note, also, that we are close-up, watching the action as it happens.

Setting

Stories do not take place in a void, but in a specific place at a specific time. This time and place constitute the setting, the background for the action. In "The Boarding House," by Joyce, the action takes place in Dublin shortly after the turn of the century. In "How Beautiful with Shoes" the action takes place in rural New England in the twenties. Polly's home in Dublin and Mare's in rural New England are worlds far-removed from each other. Physical surroundings, living conditions, customs, social milieu—all contribute to make the atmosphere of the two locales as different as night from day.

Setting, then, is the environment that surrounds the characters and influences them and their actions. It is the *total* environment, even including the physical objects associated with the characters. In Steele's story it includes the cows and the pigs in the barnyard of the Doggett farm, the clods of earth that Mare feels breaking between her bare toes, her bedroom off the kitchen in the farmhouse, the woods and the undergrowth on the hillside through which she struggles with Humble Jewett, the two-dollar shoes with cloth tops that hurt her feet. More than this, it is the atmosphere of the rural countryside that makes Mare's putting on her shoes an event in itself and that leads directly into the theme of the story.

Sometimes, the setting of a story is not important. There are stories in which the action is independent of any environment. But usually, it plays a distinct role in the action and contributes markedly to the total meaning. The heath in Thomas Hardy's novel *The Return of the Native* is as important as Eustacia Vye, who hates it, and Clym Yeobright, who loves it. It is a dominant factor in shaping the pattern of their lives, and Hardy makes this clear by devoting the initial chapter of the novel to the heath and its moods. Untamable, unchangeable, it remains as always, Hardy says, appealing to "a subtler and scarcer instinct, to a more recently learnt emotion, than that which responds to the sort of beauty called charming and fair." In the stories in this anthology, note the importance of setting in Conrad's story "The Lagoon," suggested by the fact that the setting gives the story its name.

Story Idea (Theme)

A short story does more than merely present clearly defined characters acting in a particular environment, however interesting those characters may be, however absorbing their actions. Underlying the action, and controlling it, is always one idea, or theme, the unifying element that gives the story meaning. It is the author's commentary on life, his insight into the principles that govern human behavior. This is another way of saying that a short story is always *about* something, comes to some conclusion about life. And this is the governing factor in the author's selection of characters, the situation in which he places them, the actions he gives to them, and the very words in which he presents them.

This idea, or theme, is not necessarily a moral, such as "crime does not pay," or a message, "fortune favors the brave," although it may be; the story idea is an observation. If it poses a problem, that problem need not be solved, only observed. The theme may be specifically stated by the author, as in Katherine Anne Porter's "The Circus," or left to be inferred by the reader.

But the theme is there all the time, illuminating and giving significance to all the details. If the story is well-written, the reader will find himself absorbed by the action, engrossed by the characters; but by the time he lays the story down, he should be aware of the author's vision of the world.

The grandmother in Miss Porter's story had qualms about allowing the children to attend the circus. When her son remarks that the children do not seem to be "much damaged" by the experience, she answers: "The fruits of their present are in a future so far off, neither of us may live to know whether harm has been done or not." In that remark lies the theme of the story, which governs every detail of character, plot, action, setting: Miranda's reactions to the crowd under the big tent, the noise, the flaring lights, the clowns, her leaving the circus in hysterics, her bursting into tears at the supper table, her waking up in the dark with nightmares, screaming in her sleep.

"How Beautiful with Shoes" is not merely the story of a farm girl, abducted by a dangerous lunatic, rescued and returned after a night of terror. The significance of the story resides in the theme that underlies the experience. Mare is betrothed to Ruby Herter, whose love-making, as we are shown at the outset, is casual and awkward and matter-of-fact. Steele makes a point of this, suggesting an almost animal relationship: "They were used to handling animals, both of them." Mare responds to Ruby with a passive mouth and a slow warmth, "formless, nameless, almost impersonal." Ruby's technique of showing Mare that she is his true love consists of yanking her head back by her braided hair, sticking his chin out pugnaciously, and blurting, "Listen, Mare, you wouldn't leave nobody else hug and kiss you, dang you!"

Humble Jewett, who abducts her, is bizarre and demented, but he races with her through a moonlit night in a world filled with loveliness that he makes her see. He holds her tenderly in his arms, breathes poetry into her ears: "Amarantha sweet and fair—Ah, braid no more that shining hair. . . . How beautiful are thy feet with shoes, O prince's daughter!" After she is restored to her home, all this comes back to Mare. Only then, Steele tells us, did the "conscious part of her brain begin to make words of the whispering," only then did she "smell the groundpine." And Mare begins to wonder, "Is it only crazy folks ever run like that and talk that way? . . . Is it only crazy folks ever say such things? . . . Or call you that?" With this experience, then, she awakens to the wonder and the beauty of love.

The immediate results of Mare's discovery are dramatic as she pushes Ruby out the door when he comes once more, wiping his mouth on his jumper sleeve and saying, "Come on, give us a kiss, babe!"

We can see in retrospect how everything in the story is aimed at bringing out Mare's awakened sensibilities; how theme is the governing factor for all the details. When the details click into place like this, then we can be sure that we have grasped the theme, know what the story is about.

Intimately related to the theme, and at times important in underlining it, are the symbols that an author uses.

Symbolism

A symbol is something that stands for something else, over and above what it is in itself. For instance, a lily is a white flower, but it is also symbolic of purity; and since it blooms normally in the spring, it is associated with Easter and has acquired a religious connotation. The cross is a common religious symbol; the flag is a symbol of nationalism, love of country. Other symbols are less conventional but still easily understood, such as twilight, the approach of night, as a symbol of the end of life; the ocean as the restless ebb and flow of life itself. Still other symbols, such as those used by William Blake and William Butler Yeats and T. S. Eliot in their poetry, may be called "private" symbols, for they carry no such commonly accepted significance; and the reader must be initiated into their meaning, perhaps by the poet's expressed statement, in order to understand them.

Prose fiction, as well as poetry, makes use of symbols. In "Paul's Case" Willa Cather uses symbols to enforce her theme. Cordelia Street, where Paul lives, becomes the symbol of all that is ugly and commonplace. Note how often Cordelia Street is mentioned, how Paul "felt the waters close above his head" when he turned into Cordelia Street as he returned from the dream world of the concert hall. In New York, immersed in his dream world, he doubts the existence of Cordelia Street. Later, when reality closes in, "all the world had become Cordelia Street." Paul's red carnation is also symbolic; he wears it flauntingly in his buttonhole as he faces his teachers in his ordeal at school. The flower symbolizes all that Cordelia Street is not. And at the end of the story, he carefully buries the red carnations he is then wearing in the snow before he jumps in front of the train.

"The Rocking-Horse Winner" is symbolic throughout in its suggestion that society in its feverish search for money as a substitute for love is driving itself to destruction; for the story is surely more than a mere fantasy, a tale of supernatural powers in a young boy. The rocking horse itself is a symbol, in its furious mad rush, getting nowhere. Paul says that he does get where he wants to go, but it is all an illusion. Where he gets is the yawning gates of death, oblivion.

The selection and juxtaposition of concrete details in the mere description of a place can also have symbolic suggestion. Note the following passage:

> The funeral procession had departed. We were alone. Before us lay a yellow mound of soggy clay, partly covered with huge wreaths of flowers and ferns. In front of the mound was the grave, cut clean and sheer to that wooden box five feet below. A fine, pattering rain splashed dirty yellow specks on the white blossoms of the lilies and the green of the ferns. It trickled along in the footprints on the edge of the grave, and finally fell, a yellow, sluggish stream, down into the grave itself.

Here the details of the soiling of the flowers (dirty specks on the white blossoms), the water trickling along in the footprints (someone was here, is now gone), and its final sluggish fall over the edge suggest the decay of the powers of the human body and its eventual descent into the grave.

But symbol hunting can be a dangerous habit, since there is no sure equation of object and symbolic significance. On the other hand, missing the symbols that the author used to enforce his theme could well mean missing half of what the author set out to convey. Reading "Bartleby the Scrivener" as nothing but the story of a curious clerk in a law office who was, perhaps, a psychopathic case is surely missing what Melville was saying. To read intelligently is to recognize everything that an author put into a story. It is also the refusal to read *into* a story something that the author did *not* put there.

Style

With a discussion of style we come to the last of the techniques of prose fiction that contribute to the total meaning of a story. Style is the author's characteristic way of using language or the way he uses language in a particular story for a particular effect. A writer's style is the words he chooses, the images he selects, both literal and figurative, the sound of the word in the phrase, the rhythm and structure of his sentences. Style, in other words, is *how* a writer expresses himself over and above *what* he says.

"Style is the man himself," according to Count Georges Buffon (1707–1788). Certainly, the individuality of expression that marks one author from another is one of the things we mean by style. All mature writers of fiction have style in this sense, a characteristic mode of expression distinctively their own. Faulkner does not write like Hemingway, and Katherine Anne Porter does not write like Katherine Mansfield. Yet each is a craftsman in his own right, using language in his own way to gain certain effects.

Miss Mansfield was an immensely conscious craftsman, choosing sentence rhythm as carefully and deliberately as she chose words to portray her characters. About one of her stories, "Miss Brill," she said:

> I chose not only the length of every sentence, but even the sound of every sentence. I chose the rise and fall of every paragraph to fit her, and to fit her on that day at that moment. After I'd written it I read it aloud—numbers of times—just as one would *play over* a musical composition, trying to get it nearer and nearer to the expression of Miss Brill, until it fitted her.

In "The Doll's House" note how she expresses Aunt Beryl's opinion of the smell of paint clinging to the doll's house in comparison with the children's:

> [Aunt Beryl:] For, really, the smell of paint coming from that doll's house . . . was quite enough to make any one seriously ill, in Aunt Beryl's opinion. Even before the sacking was taken off. And when it was. . . .

[Children:] But perfect, perfect little house! Who could possibly mind the smell? It was part of the joy, part of the newness.

And when she speaks of the mother's permission to allow the girls at school to come, two at a time, to look at the doll's house, the prose sounds like a direct quotation: "Not to stay to tea, of course, or to come traipsing through the house. But just to stand quietly in the courtyard. . . ."

Hemingway, like Miss Mansfield, was painfully conscious of his style. He said that when he was young he wrote like Kipling, whom he admired, but that later on he knew he "had to break the language down and start new." In doing so, he developed a very distinct style, marked by the following: a simple sentence structure with a striking lack of subordinate elements; the piling-up of statement after statement, joined, if at all, with the conjunction "and"; the free use of concrete details, a vivid re-creation of the sense world; but few comparisons, few figures of speech, and those usually of the simplest sort; a heavy dependence upon dialogue, an excellent transcript of colloquial rhythms. Hemingway's style, widely imitated by writers of the hard-boiled school of fiction, effectively reflected the attitude toward life that one associates with him, the attitude of a spectator who looks and depicts, but refuses to comment. "The Killers" is typical Hemingway of the early period, its style devoid of ornament—simple, spare, elemental. In the opening the sentence structure is so primitive that it sounds almost like a first-grade reader:

> The door of Henry's lunchroom opened and two men came in. They sat down at the counter.
> "What's yours?" George asked them.
> "I don't know," one of the men said. "What do you want to eat, Al?"
> "I don't know," said Al. "I don't know what I want to eat."
> Outside it was getting dark The street-light came on outside the window. The two men at the counter read the menu.

This is about as direct and elemental as expression can be. It is as though Hemingway were saying, "I'm giving it to you as straight and direct as I can. This is it."

Steele too is a superb craftsman whose sentences reflect any mood, intensify any emotion. Note the matter-of-fact quality of the following:

> Then in the quiet she heard a sound of hoofs on the bridge, where the road crossed the creek a hundred yards below the house, and she set the pail down on the ground beside her bare, barn-soiled feet. She picked it up again. She set it down. It was as if she calculated its weight.

Late in the story, when Mare is recalling what seems to her, in retrospect, the loveliness of the experience of the night before, Steele uses rhythms in his prose so close to poetry that it can almost be scanned:

Mare ran. She ran through a wind white with moonlight and wet with "the small rain." And the wind she ran through, it ran through her, and made her shiver as she ran. And the man beside her leaped high over the waves of the dead grasses and gathered the wind in his arms, and her hair was heavy and his was tossing, and a little fox ran before them across the top of the world. And the world spread down around in waves of black and silver, more immense than she had ever known the world could be, and more beautiful.

Style, then, is an aid to the meaning. It should, however, be unobtrusive. The most effective style is one that so fits the subject that the reader is unaware of it until he looks closely to see where the impact of the passage lies. It is like the background music to a first-rate motion picture, so much a part of the mood that it loses its own identity.

Let us look again at Steele's story, "How Beautiful with Shoes," to summarize what our examination of the various techniques of the short story has brought to light. Steele, we see, has written a story about a farm girl named Amarantha by her father, now dead, but who is called Mare by everyone except her deaf mother. The name Mare is symbolic; certainly, it fits her better than Amarantha. For she is large, slow-minded, inarticulate, close to the soil, skilled in handling animals, passive in her acceptance of things, rather phlegmatic in temperament. Her surname, Doggett, is also symbolic, suggesting the word "dogged."

The story is about her awakening to the wonder and beauty of love by way of a frightening, yet revealing, experience with an escaped homicidal lunatic, who developed a sudden attraction to her. This is the controlling idea, we see in retrospect. The lunatic's tender and poetic love-making turns him into a curious rival of her fiancé, Ruby Herter. He becomes a kind of foil for Ruby, whose own love-making displays itself in manifestations of aggressive masculinity.

Steele sets the story in New England, and opens it with a scene on the Doggett farm, which lies next door to that of Mare's fiancé. In this scene he characterizes both Mare and Ruby, and brings out the situation: they are betrothed; their love-making is casual and clumsy.

A complication enters their lives with the news that a homicidal lunatic, Humble Jewett, has escaped from a nearby asylum. This news leads at once to a physical separation between Mare and Ruby—Ruby immediately joins a posse engaged in hunting the lunatic down—a separation that will be more profound and significant before the story is over.

Action now begins with the appearance of the lunatic, who has eluded the pursuing posse and shows up at the Doggett farm. He is attracted to Mare by her name (he hears her deaf mother call her "Amarantha") and her yellow hair, both of which remind him of Lovelace's lines: "Amarantha, sweet and fair,/Ah, braid no more that shining hair." Mare is not the beauty that the lunatic, hypnotized by her name, declares her to be. But she shows her courage in leading him away from her mother into an open field, where he is captured by the returning posse.

This is the first stage of the action, and it accomplishes a number of things essential to the story: (1) Mare, temporizing with the lunatic, agrees that she loves him and will go away with him. This leads to his later return to the farm and to the abduction. (2) The aftermath of the capture, which brings a number of people to the farmhouse, brings about a natural revelation of information about the lunatic: he is college bred and taught in an academy before his mind gave way; thus his sensitivity to beauty and his love of poetry become clearly understandable. (3) The presence of Judge North and the later lingering of Older Haskins result in Mare's putting on her new shoes and leaving them on.

The second phase of the action is the abduction. Escaping from the jail after setting it on fire and killing the jailer, Jewett returns to the Doggett farm and makes off with Mare. The abduction is adequately motivated by the lunatic's attraction to Mare and her earlier forced declaration that she loves him and will go away with him. Ruby had joked about this: "Know the only thing they can get him to say, Mare? Only God thing he'll say is, 'Amarantha, she's goin' with me.'" Mare's presence on top of the rock pile, away from the house, is also logically accounted for in her natural desire to see more of the fire that drew her out of doors. So, also, is the lunatic's gentleness with her, in spite of the ever-present threat to her safety.

The action continues in a succession of scenes—the hiding from their pursuers; the mad dash through the countryside; the breaking into Wyker's cabin—scenes that hold us constantly in suspense, fraught as they are with the imminent possibility at all times that Mare will be raped or killed. Upon several occasions, with the lunatic's changing moods, one or the other seems near at hand. Ever present, also, is the strange love-making—the hand on the throat while the lips recite the poetry of Lovelace or the Song of Solomon; the strange tenderness and the beauty that she has never known; the gentle fingers caressing her hair; the hands softly exploring her body.

The climax comes with Mare's rescue by Wyker. A blast of a shotgun and Mare is returned to her home and her fiancé. The threat to the romance between her and Ruby is over. The *status quo* is restored. The lives of Mare and Ruby are back once more into their even groove.

But are they? Mare is physically unharmed. But she is not unchanged. In the aftermath of that frightful experience, she sits alone in her room recalling all that had happened. In retrospect, the terror drops away, and she remembers only the strange and wonderful love-making of her captor, which, in turn, makes her conscious of the shortcomings of Ruby, her fiancé, as a lover. This is brought home to us when Ruby, who is exactly the same as he was at the beginning of the story, wipes his mouth on his jumper sleeve as he had done only a few hours earlier and says, "Come on, give us a kiss, babe!" Before, she had yielded to him passively, "a slow warmth" pervading her. Her response now is to push him out the door crying, "Go 'way! Lea' me be!"

The story, of course, is Mare's story. She is the protagonist with whom we sympathize. And since the story deals with a discovery by Mare that changes her, Steele presents the story largely from her point of view. It is Mare's mind that we enter, Mare's feelings that we explore, Mare's reactions that we share. The conflict has been a significant one for the girl. She acts always within the bounds of her revealed character (as, indeed, do Ruby and Humble Jewett). And at the end of the story, the experience has left its mark on her. She will never be quite the same again, although she may get over her first revulsion for her fiancé.

Steele's style enhances the mounting tensions and suspense as vivid scenes depict the physical and emotional worlds through which Mare moves. Because both Mare and Humble Jewett's motivations are clear, there is a logical chain of cause and effect in the action. It is a bizarre story in some ways—a curious kind of love-making between an uneducated, phlegmatic, inarticulate girl and a demented, beauty-mad, former schoolteacher. But the characters are not mere freaks; they are made eminently understandable to us, and their story has universal significance that gives its theme validity.

NATHANIEL HAWTHORNE

❧ *Young Goodman Brown*

YOUNG GOODMAN BROWN came forth at sunset into the street of Salem village, but put his head back, after crossing the threshold, to exchange a parting kiss with his young wife. And Faith, as the wife was aptly named, thrust her own pretty head into the street, letting the wind play with the pink ribbons of her cap, while she called to Goodman Brown.

"Dearest heart," whispered she, softly and rather sadly, when her lips were close to his ear, "prithee, put off your journey until sunrise and sleep in your own bed to-night. A lone woman is troubled with such dreams and such thoughts that she's afeard of herself sometimes. Pray tarry with me this night, dear husband, of all nights in the year."

"My love and my Faith," replied young Goodman Brown, "of all nights in the year, this one must I tarry away from thee. My journey, as thou callest it, forth and back again, must needs be done 'twixt now and sunrise. What, my sweet, pretty wife, doest thou doubt me already, and we but three months married?"

"Then God bless you!" said Faith, with the pink ribbons; "and may you find all well when you come back."

"Amen!" cried Goodman Brown. "Say thy prayers, dear Faith, and go to bed at dusk, and no harm will come to thee."

So they parted; and the young man pursued his way until, being about to turn the corner by the meeting-house, he looked back and saw the head of Faith still peeping after him with a melancholy air, in spite of her pink ribbons.

"Poor little Faith!" thought he, for his heart smote him. "What a wretch am I, to leave her on such an errand! She talks of dreams, too. Methought as she spoke there was trouble in her face, as if a dream had warned her what work is to be done to-night. But no, no; t'would kill her to think it. Well, she's a blessed angel on earth; and after this one night I'll cling to her skirts and follow her to heaven."

With this excellent resolve for the future, Goodman Brown felt himself justified in making more haste on his present evil purpose. He had taken a dreary road, darkened by all the gloomiest trees of the forest, which barely stood aside to let the narrow path creep through, and closed immediately behind. It was all as lonely as could be; and there is this peculiarity in such a solitude, that the traveler knows not who may be concealed by the innumerable trunks and the thick boughs overhead; so that with lonely footsteps he may yet be passing through an unseen multitude.

"There may be a devilish Indian behind every tree," said Goodman Brown to himself; and he glanced fearfully behind him as he added, "What if the devil himself should be at my very elbow!"

His head being turned back, he passed a crook of the road, and, looking forward again, beheld the figure of a man, in grave and decent attire, seated at the foot of an old tree. He arose at Goodman's approach and walked onward side by side with him.

"You are late, Goodman Brown," said he. "The clock of the Old South was striking as I came through Boston, and that is full fifteen minutes agone."

"Faith kept me back awhile," replied the young man, with a tremor in his voice caused by the sudden appearance of his companion, though not wholly unexpected.

It was now deep dusk in the forest, and deepest in that part of it where these two were journeying. As nearly as could be discerned, the second traveler was about fifty years old, apparently in the same rank of life as Goodman Brown, and bearing a considerable resemblance to him, though perhaps more in expression than features. Still they might have been taken for father and son. And yet, though the elder person was as simply clad as the younger, and as simple in manner too, he had an indescribable air of one who knew the world, and who would not have felt abashed at the governor's dinner table or in King William's court, were it possible that his affairs should call him thither. But the only thing about him that could be fixed upon as remarkable was his staff, which bore the likeness of a great black snake, so curiously wrought that it might almost be seen to twist and wriggle itself like a living serpent. This, of course, must have been an ocular deception, assisted by the uncertain light.

"Come, Goodman Brown!" cried his fellow-traveler, "this is a dull pace for the beginning of a journey. Take my staff, if you are so soon weary."

"Friend," said the other, exchanging his slow pace for a full stop, "having kept covenant by meeting thee here, it is my purpose now to return from whence I came. I have scruples touching the matter thou wot'st of."

"Sayest thou so?" replied he of the serpent, smiling apart. "Let us walk on, nevertheless, reasoning as we go; and if I convince thee not thou shalt turn back. We are but a little way in the forest yet."

"Too far! Too far!" exclaimed the good man, unconsciously resuming his walk. "My father never went into the woods on such an errand, nor his father before him. We have been a race of honest men and good Christians since the days of the martyrs; and shall I be the first of the name of Brown that ever took this path and kept—"

"Such company, thou wouldst say," observed the elder person, interrupting his pause. "Well said, Goodman Brown! I have been as well acquainted with your family as with ever a one among the Puritans; and that's no trifle to say. I helped your grandfather, the constable, when he lashed the Quaker woman so smartly through the streets of Salem; and it was I who brought your father a pitch-pine knot, kindled at my own hearth, to set fire to an Indian village, in

King Philip's war. They were my good friends, both; and many a pleasant walk have we had along this path, and returned merrily after midnight. I would fain be friends with you for their sake."

"If it be as thou sayest," replied Goodman Brown, "I marvel they never spoke of these matters; or, verily, I marvel not, seeing that the least rumor of the sort would have driven them from New England. We are a people of prayer, and good works to boot, and abide no such wickedness."

"Wickedness or not," said the traveler with the twisted staff, "I have a very general acquaintance here in New England. The deacons of many a church have drunk the communion wine with me; the selectmen of divers towns make me their chairman; and a majority of the Great and General Court are firm supporters of my interest. The governor and I, too—But these are state secrets."

"Can this be so?" cried Goodman Brown, with a stare of amazement at his undisturbed companion. "Howbeit, I have nothing to do with the governor and council; they have their own ways, and are no rule for a simple husbandman like me. But, were I to go on with thee, how should I meet the eye of that good old man, our minister, at Salem village? Oh, his voice would make me tremble both Sabbath day and lecture day."

Thus far the elder traveler had listened with due gravity; but now burst into a fit of irrepressible mirth, shaking himself so violently that his snake-like staff actually seemed to wriggle in sympathy.

"Ha! ha! ha!" shouted he again and again; then, composing himself, "Well, go on, Goodman Brown, go on; but prithee don't kill me with laughing!"

"Well, then, to end the matter at once," said Goodman Brown, considerably nettled, "there is my wife, Faith. It would break her dear little heart, and I'd rather break my own."

"Nay, if that be the case," answered the other, "e'en go thy ways, Goodman Brown. I would not for twenty old women like the one hobbling before us that Faith should come to any harm."

As he spoke he pointed his staff at a female figure on the path, in whom Goodman Brown recognized a very pious and exemplary dame, who had taught him his catechism in youth, and was still his moral and spiritual adviser, jointly with the minister and Deacon Gookin.

"A marvel, truly, that Goody Cloyse should be so far in the wilderness at nightfall," said he. "But with your leave, friend, I shall take a cut through the woods until we have left this Christian woman behind. Being a stranger to you, she might ask whom I was consorting with and whither I was going."

"Be it so," said his fellow-traveler. "Betake you to the woods and let me keep the path."

Accordingly the young man turned aside, but took care to watch his companion, who advanced softly along the road until he had come within a staff's length of the old dame. She, meanwhile, was making the best of her way with singular speed for so aged a woman and mumbling some indistinct words—a prayer, doubtless—as she went. The traveler put forth his staff and touched her withered neck with what seemed the serpent's tail.

"The devil!" screamed the pious old lady.

"Then Goody Cloyse knows her old friend?" observed the traveler, confronting her and leaning on his writhing stick.

"Ah, forsooth, and is it your worship, indeed?" cried the good dame. "Yea, truly is it, and in the very image of my old gossip, Goodman Brown, the grandfather of the silly fellow that now is. But—would your worship believe it?—my broomstick hath strangely disappeared, stolen, as I suspect, by that unhanged witch, Goody Cory, and that, too, when I was all anointed with the juice of smallage, and cinquefoil, and wolf's bane—"

"Mingled with fine wheat and the fat of a new-born babe," said the shape of old Goodman Brown.

"Ah, your worship knows the recipe," cried the old lady, cackling aloud. "So, as I was saying, being all ready for the meeting, and no horse to ride on, I made up my mind to foot it; for they tell me there is a nice young man to be taken into communion to-night. But now your good worship will lend me your arm, and we shall be there in a twinkling."

"That can hardly be," answered her friend. "I may not spare you my arm, Goody Cloyse; but here is my staff, if you will."

So saying, he threw it down at her feet, where, perhaps, it assumed life, being one of the rods which its owner had formerly lent to the Egyptian magi. Of this fact, however, Goodman Brown could not take cognizance. He had cast up his eyes in astonishment, and, looking down again, beheld neither Goody Cloyse nor the serpentine staff, but his fellow-traveler alone, who waited for him as calmly as if nothing had happened.

"That old woman taught me my catechism," said the young man; and there was a world of meaning in this simple comment.

They continued to walk onward, while the elder traveler exhorted his companion to make good speed and persevere in the path, discoursing so aptly that his arguments seemed rather to spring up in the bosom of his auditor than to be suggested by himself. As they went, he plucked a branch of maple to serve for a walking stick, and began to strip it of the twigs and little boughs, which were wet with evening dew. The moment his fingers touched them they became strangely withered and dried up, as with a week's sunshine. Thus the pair proceeded, at a good free pace, until suddenly, in a gloomy hollow of the road, Goodman Brown sat himself down on the stump of a tree and refused to go any farther.

"Friend," said he, stubbornly, "my mind is made up. Not another step will I budge on this errand. What if a wretched old woman do choose to go to the devil when I thought she was going to heaven? Is that any reason why I should quit my dear Faith and go after her?"

"You will think better of this by and by," said his acquaintance, composedly. "Sit here and rest yourself awhile; and when you feel like moving again, there is my staff to help you along." Without more words, he threw his companion the maple stick, and was as speedily out of sight as if he had vanished into the deepening gloom.

The young man sat a few moments by the roadside, applauding himself greatly, and thinking with how clear a conscience he should meet the minister in his morning walk, nor shrink from the eye of good old Deacon Gookin. And what calm sleep would be his that very night, which was to have been spent so wickedly, but so purely and sweetly now, in the arms of Faith! Amidst these pleasant and praiseworthy meditations, Goodman Brown heard the tramp of horses along the road, and deemed it advisable to conceal himself within the verge of the forest, conscious of the guilty purpose that had brought him thither, though now so happily turned from it.

On came the hoof tramps and the voices of the riders, two grave old voices conversing soberly as they drew near. These mingled sounds appeared to pass along the road, within a few yards of the young man's hiding-place; but, owing doubtless to the depth of the gloom at that particular spot, neither the travelers nor their steeds were visible. Though their figures brushed the small boughs by the wayside, it could not be seen that they intercepted, even for a moment, the faint gleam from the strip of bright sky athwart which they must have passed. Goodman Brown alternately crouched and stood on tiptoe, pulling aside the branches and thrusting forth his head as far as he durst, without discerning so much as a shadow. It vexed him the more, because he could have sworn, were such a thing possible, that he recognized the voices of the minister and Deacon Gookin, jogging along quietly, as they were wont to do when bound to some ordination or ecclesiastical council. While yet within hearing, one of the riders stopped to pluck a switch.

"Of the two, reverend sir," said the voice like the deacon's, "I had rather miss an ordination dinner than to-night's meeting. They tell me that some of our community are to be here from Falmouth and beyond, and others from Connecticut and Rhode Island, besides several of the Indian powwows, who, after their fashion, know almost as much deviltry as the best of us. Moreover, there is a goodly young woman to be taken into communion."

"Mighty well, Deacon Gookin!" replied the solemn old tones of the minister. "Spur up, or we shall be late. Nothing can be done, you know, until I get on the ground."

The hoofs clattered again; and the voices, talking so strangely in the empty air, passed on through the forest, where no church had ever been gathered or solitary Christian prayed. Whither, then, could these holy men be journeying so deep into the heathen wilderness? Young Goodman Brown caught hold of a tree for support, being ready to sink down on the ground, faint and over-burdened with the heavy sickness of his heart. He looked up to the sky, doubting whether there really was a heaven above him. Yet there was the blue arch, and the stars brightening in it.

"With heaven above and Faith below, I will yet stand firm against the devil!" cried Goodman Brown.

While he still gazed upward into the deep arch of the firmament and had lifted his hands to pray, a cloud, though no wind was stirring, hurried across the zenith and hid the brightening stars. The blue sky was still visible, except directly overhead, where this black mass of cloud was sweeping swiftly north-ward. Aloft in the air, as if from the depths of the cloud, came a confused and doubtful sound of voices. Once the listener fancied that he could distinguish the accents of towns-people of his own, men and women, both pious and ungodly, many of whom he had met at the communion table, and had seen others rioting at the tavern. The next moment, so indistinct were the sounds, he doubted whether he had heard aught but the murmur of the old forest, whispering without a wind. Then came a stronger swell of those familiar tones, heard daily in the sunshine at Salem village, but never until now from a cloud of night. There was one voice, of a young woman, uttering lamentations, yet with an uncertain sorrow, and entreating for some favor, which, perhaps, it would grieve her to obtain; and all the unseen multitude, both saints and sinners, seemed to encourage her onward.

"Faith!" shouted Goodman Brown, in a voice of agony and desperation; the echoes of the forest mocked him, crying, "Faith! Faith!" as if bewildered wretches were seeking her all through the wilderness.

The cry of grief, rage, and terror was yet piercing the night, when the unhappy husband held his breath for a response. There was a scream, drowned immediately in a louder murmur of voices, fading into far-off laughter, as the dark cloud swept away, leaving the clear and silent sky above Goodman Brown. But something fluttered lightly down through the air and caught on the branch of a tree. The young man seized it, and beheld a pink ribbon.

"My Faith is gone!" cried he, after one stupefied moment. "There is no good on earth; and sin is but a name! Come, devil; for to thee is this world given."

And, maddened with despair, so that he laughed loud and long, did Goodman Brown grasp his staff and set forth again, at such a rate that he seemed to fly along the forest path rather than to walk or run. The road grew wilder and drearier and more faintly traced, and vanished at length, leaving him in the heart of the dark wilderness, still rushing onward with the instinct that guides mortal man to evil. The whole forest was peopled with frightful sounds—the creaking of the trees, the howling of wild beasts, and the yell of Indians; while sometimes the wind tolled like a distant church bell, and sometimes gave a broad roar around the traveler, as if all Nature were laughing him to scorn. But he was himself the chief horror of the scene, and shrank not from its other horrors.

"Ha! ha! ha!" roared Goodman Brown when the wind laughed at him. "Let us hear which will laugh loudest. Think not to frighten me with your deviltry. Come witch, come wizard, come Indian powwow, come devil himself, and here comes Goodman Brown. You may as well fear him as he fear you."

In truth, all through the haunted forest there could be nothing more frightful than the figure of Goodman Brown. On he flew among the black pines, brandishing his staff with frenzied gestures, now giving vent to an inspiration of horrid blasphemy, and now shouting forth such laughter as set all the echoes of the forest laughing like demons around him. The fiend in his own shape is less hideous than when he rages in the breast of man. Thus sped the demoniac on his course, until, quivering among the trees, he saw a red light before him, as when the felled trunks and branches of a clearing have been set on fire, and throw up their lurid blaze against the sky at the hour of midnight. He paused, in a lull of the tempest that had driven him onward, and heard the swell of what seemed a hymn, rolling solemnly from a distance with the weight of many voices. He knew the tune; it was a familiar one in the choir of the village meeting-house. The verse died heavily away, and was lengthened by a chorus, not of human voices, but of all the sounds of the benighted wilderness pealing in awful harmony together. Goodman Brown cried out, and his cry was lost to his own ear by its unison with the cry of the desert.

In the interval of silence he stole forward until the light glared full upon his eyes. At one extremity of an open space, hemmed in by the dark wall of the forest, arose a rock, bearing some rude natural resemblance either to an altar or a pulpit, and surrounded by four blazing pines, their tops aflame, their stems untouched, like candles at an evening meeting. The mass of foliage that had overgrown the summit of the rock was all on fire, blazing high into the night and fitfully illuminating the whole field. Each pendant twig and leafy festoon was in a blaze. As the red light arose and fell, a numerous congregation alternately shone forth, then disappeared in shadow, and again grew, as it were, out of the darkness, peopling the heart of the solitary woods at once.

"A grave and dark-clad company," quoth Goodman Brown.

In truth they were such. Among them, quivering to and fro between gloom and splendor, appeared faces that would be seen next day at the council board of the province, and others which, Sabbath after Sabbath, looked devoutly heavenward, and benignantly over the crowded pews, from the holiest pulpits in the land. Some affirm that the lady of the governor was there. At least there were high dames well known to her, and wives of honored husbands, and widows, a great multitude, and ancient maidens, all of excellent repute, and fair young girls, who trembled lest their mothers should espy them. Either the sudden gleams of light flashing over the obscure field bedazzled Goodman Brown, or he recognized a score of the church members of Salem village famous for their especial sancity. Good old Deacon Gookin had arrived, and waited at the skirts of that venerable saint, his reverend pastor. But irreverently consorting with these grave, reputable, and pious people, these elders of the church, these chaste dames and dewy virgins, there were men of dissolute lives and women of spotted fame, wretches given over to all mean and filthy vice, and suspected even of horrid crimes. It was strange to see that the good shrank not from the wicked, nor were the sinners abashed by the saints. Scattered also among their pale-faced enemies were the Indian priests, or powwows, who had often scared their native forest with more hideous incantations than any known to English witchcraft.

"But where is Faith?" thought Goodman Brown; and, as hope came into his heart, he trembled.

Another verse of the hymn arose, a slow and mournful strain, such as the pious love, but joined to words which expressed all that our nature can conceive of sin, and darkly hinted at far more. Unfathomable to mere mortals is the lore of fiends. Verse after verse was sung; and still the chorus of the desert swelled between like the deepest tone of a mighty organ; and with the final peal of that dreadful anthem there came a sound, as if the roaring wind, the rushing streams, the howling beasts, and every other voice of the unconcerted wilderness were mingling and according with the voice of guilty man in homage to the prince of all. The four blazing pines threw up a loftier flame, and obscurely discovered shapes and visages of horror on the smoke wreaths above the impious assembly. At the same moment the fire on the rock shot redly forth and formed a glowing arch above its base, where now appeared a figure. With reverence be it spoken, the figure bore no slight similitude, both in garb and manner, to some grave divine of the New England churches.

"Bring forth the converts!" cried a voice that echoed through the field and rolled into the forest.

At the word, Goodman Brown stepped forth from the shadow of the trees and approached the congregation, with whom he felt a loathful brotherhood by the sympathy of all that was wicked in his heart. He could have well-nigh sworn that the shape of his own dead father beckoned him to advance, looking downward from a smoke wreath, while a woman, with dim features of despair, threw out her hand to warn him back. Was it his mother? But he had no power to retreat one step, nor to resist, even in thought, when the minister and good old Deacon Gookin seized his arms and led him to the blazing rock. Thither came, also, the slender form of a veiled female, led between Goody Cloyse, that pious teacher of the catechism, and Martha Carrier, who had received the devil's promise to be queen of hell. A rampant hag was she! And there stood the proselytes beneath the canopy of fire.

"Welcome, my children," said the dark figure, "to the communion of your race. Ye have found thus young your nature and your destiny. My children, look behind you!"

They turned; and, flashing forth, as it were, in a sheet of flame, the fiend worshipers were seen; the smile of welcome gleamed darkly on every visage.

"There," resumed the sable form, "are all whom ye have reverenced from youth. Ye deemed them holier than yourselves and shrank from your own sin, contrasting it with their lives of righteousness and prayerful aspirations heavenward. Yet here are they all in my worshiping assembly! This night it shall be granted you to know their secret deeds: how hoary-bearded elders of the church have whispered wanton words to the young maids of their households; how many a woman, eager for widows' weeds, has given her husband a drink at bedtime and let him sleep his last sleep in her bosom; how beardless youths have made haste to inherit their fathers' wealth; and how fair damsels—blush not, sweet ones—have dug little graves in the garden, and bidden me, the sole guest, to an infant's funeral. By the sympathy of your human hearts for sin ye shall scent out all the places—whether in church, bed-chamber, street, field, or forest—where crime has been committed, and shall exult to behold the whole earth one stain of guilt, one mighty blood spot. Far more than this. It shall be yours to penetrate, in every bosom, the deep mystery of sin, the fountain of all wicked arts, and which inexhaustibly supplies more evil impulses than human power—than my power at its utmost—can make manifest in deeds. And now, my children, look upon each other."

They did so; and, by the blaze of the hell-kindled torches, the wretched man beheld his Faith, and the wife her husband, trembling before that unhallowed altar.

"Lo, there ye stand, my children," said the figure, in a deep and solemn tone, almost sad with its despairing awfulness, as if his once angelic nature could yet mourn for our miserable race. "Depending upon one another's hearts, ye had still hoped that virtue were not all a dream. Now are ye undeceived. Evil is the nature of mankind. Evil must be your only happiness. Welcome again, my children, to the communion of your race!"

"Welcome," repeated the fiend worshipers, in one cry of despair and triumph.

And there they stood, the only pair, as it seemed, who were yet hesitating on the verge of wickedness in this dark world. A basin was hollowed, naturally, in the rock. Did it contain water, reddened by the lurid light? or was it blood? or, perchance, a liquid flame? Herein did the shape of evil dip his hand and prepare to lay the mark of baptism upon their foreheads, that they might be partakers of the mystery of sin, more conscious of the secret guilt of others, both in deed and thought, then they could now be of their own. The husband cast one look at his pale wife, and Faith at him. What polluted wretches would the next glance show them to each other, shuddering alike at what they disclosed and what they saw!

"Faith! Faith!" cried the husband, "Look up to heaven, and resist the wicked one."

Whether Faith obeyed he knew not. Hardly had he spoken when he found himself amid calm night and solitude, listening to a roar of the wind which died heavily away through the forest. He staggered against the rock, and felt it chill and damp; while a hanging twig, that had been all on fire, besprinkled his cheek with the coldest dew.

The next morning young Goodman Brown came slowly into the street of Salem village, staring around him like a bewildered man. The good old minister was taking a walk along the graveyard to get an appetite for breakfast and meditate his sermon, and bestowed a blessing, as he passed, on Goodman

Brown. He shrank from the venerable saint as if to avoid an anathema. Old Deacon Gookin was at domestic worship, and the holy words of his prayer were heard through the open window. "What God doth the wizard pray to?" quoth Goodman Brown. Goody Cloyse, that excellent old Christian, stood in the early sunshine at her own lattice, catechising a little girl who had brought her a pint of morning's milk. Goodman Brown snatched away the child as from the grasp of the fiend himself. Turning the corner by the meeting-house, he spied the head of Faith, with the pink ribbons, gazing anxiously forth, and bursting into such joy at sight of him that she skipped along the street and almost kissed her husband before the whole village. But Goodman Brown looked sternly and sadly into her face, and passed on without a greeting.

Had Goodman Brown fallen asleep in the forest and only dreamed a wild dream of a witch-meeting? Be it so if you will; but, alas! it was a dream of evil omen for young Goodman Brown. A stern, a sad, a darkly meditative, a distrustful, if not a desperate man did he become from the night of that fearful dream. On the Sabbath day, when the congregation were singing a holy psalm, he could not listen because an anthem of sin rushed loudly upon his ear and drowned all the blessed strain. When the minister spoke from the pulpit with power and fervid eloquence, and, with his hand on the open Bible, of the sacred truths of our religion, and of saint-like lives and triumphant deaths, and of future bliss or misery unutterable, then did Goodman Brown turn pale, dreading lest the roof should thunder down upon the gray blasphemer and his hearers. Often, awaking suddenly at midnight, he shrank from the bosom of Faith; and at morning or eventide, when the family knelt down at prayer, he scowled and muttered to himself, and gazed sternly at his wife, and turned away. And when he had lived long, and was borne to his grave a hoary corpse, followed by Faith, an aged woman, and children and grandchildren, a goodly procession, besides neighbors not a few, they carved no hopeful verse upon his tombstone, for his dying hour was gloom.

EDGAR ALLAN POE

❧ *The Black Cat*

FOR THE most wild, yet most homely narrative which I am about to pen, I neither expect nor solicit belief. Mad indeed would I be to expect it, in a case where my very senses reject their own evidence. Yet, mad am I not—and very surely do I not dream. But tomorrow I die, and today I would unburden my soul. My immediate purpose is to place before the world, plainly, succinctly,

and without comment, a series of mere household events. In their consequences, these events have terrified—have tortured—have destroyed me. Yet I
will not attempt to expound them. To me, they have presented little but
Horror; to many they will seem less terrible than *baroques* [strange]. Hereafter,
perhaps, some intellect may be found which will reduce my phantasm to the
commonplace: some intellect more calm, more logical, and far less excitable
than my own, which will perceive, in the circumstances I detail with awe,
nothing more than an ordinary succession of very natural causes and effects.

From my infancy I was noted for the docility and humanity of my disposition. My tenderness of heart was even so conspicuous as to make me the jest of
my companions. I was especially fond of animals, and was indulged by my
parents with a great variety of pets. With these I spent most of my time, and
never was so happy as when feeding and caressing them. This peculiarity of
character grew with my growth, and in my manhood I derived from it one of
my principal sources of pleasure. To those who have cherished an affection for a
faithful and sagacious dog, I need hardly be at the trouble of explaining the
nature or the intensity of the gratification thus derivable. There is something in
the unselfish and self-sacrificing love of a brute which goes directly to the heart
of him who has had frequent occasion to test the paltry friendship and
gossamer fidelity of mere *Man*.

I married early, and was happy to find in my wife a disposition not
uncongenial with my own. Observing my partiality for domestic pets, she lost
no opportunity of procuring those of the most agreeable kind. We had birds,
goldfish, a fine dog, rabbits, a small monkey, and *a cat*.

This latter was a remarkably large and beautiful animal, entirely black, and
sagacious to an astonishing degree. In speaking of his intelligence, my wife, who
at heart was not a little tinctured with superstition, made frequent allusion to
the ancient popular notion which regarded all black cats as witches in disguise.
Not that she was ever *serious* upon this point—and I mention the matter at all
for no better reason than that it happens, just now, to be remembered.

Pluto—this was the cat's name—was my favorite pet and playmate. I alone
fed him, and he attended me wherever I went about the house. It was even
with difficulty that I could prevent him from following me through the streets.

Our friendship lasted, in this manner, for several years, during which my
general temperament and character, through the instrumentality of the Fiend
Intemperance, had (I blush to confess it) experienced a radical alteration for
the worse. I grew, day by day, more moody, more irritable, more regardless of
the feelings of others. I suffered myself to use intemperate language to my wife.
At length, I even offered her personal violence. My pets, of course, were made
to feel the change in my disposition. I not only neglected, but ill-used them.
For Pluto, however, I still retained sufficient regard to restrain me from
maltreating him, as I made no scruple of maltreating the rabbits, the monkey,
or even the dog, when by accident or through affection, they came in my way.
But my disease grew upon me—for what disease is like Alcohol!—and at length

even Pluto, who was now becoming old, and consequently somewhat peevish—
even Pluto began to experience the effects of my ill-temper.

One night, returning home, much intoxicated, from one of my haunts
about town I fancied that the cat avoided my presence. I seized him; when, in
his fright at my violence, he inflicted a slight wound upon my hand with his
teeth. The fury of a demon instantly possessed me. I knew myself no longer.
My original soul seemed, at once, to take its flight from my body; and a more
than fiendish malevolence, gin-nurtured, thrilled every fibre of my frame. I took
from my waistcoat-pocket a pen-knife, opened it, grasped the poor beast by the
throat, and deliberately cut one of its eyes from the socket! I blush, I burn, I
shudder, while I pen the damnable atrocity.

When reason returned with the morning—when I had slept off the fumes
of the night's debauch—I experienced a sentiment half of horror, half of
remorse, for the crime of which I had been guilty; but it was, at best, a feeble
and equivocal feeling, and the soul remained untouched. I again plunged into
excess, and soon drowned in wine all memory of the deed.

In the meantime the cat slowly recovered. The socket of the lost eye
presented, it is true, a frightful appearance, but he no longer appeared to suffer
any pain. He went about the house as usual, but, as might be expected, fled in
extreme terror at my approach. I had so much of my old heart left, as to be at
first grieved by this evident dislike on the part of a creature which had once so
loved me. But this feeling soon gave place to irritation. And then came, as if to
my final and irrevocable overthrow, the spirit of PERVERSENESS. Of this
spirit philosophy takes no account. Yet I am not more sure that my soul lives
than I am that perverseness is one of the primitive impulses of the human heart:
one of the indivisible primary faculties, or sentiments, which give direction to
the character of Man. Who has not, a hundred times, found himself committing
a vile or a silly action, for no other reason that because he knows he should *not?*
Have we not a perpetual inclination, in the teeth of our best judgment, to
violate that which is *Law,* merely because we understand it to be such? This
spirit of perverseness, I say, came to my final overthrow. It was this unfathomable longing of the soul *to vex itself*—to offer violence to its own nature—to do
wrong for the wrong's sake only—that urged me to continue and finally to
consummate the injury I had inflicted upon the unoffending brute. One
morning, in cool blood, I slipped a noose about its neck and hung it to the limb
of a tree; hung it with the tears streaming from my eyes, and with the bitterest
remorse at my heart; hung it *because* I knew that it had loved me, and *because*
I felt it had given me no reason of offence; hung it *because* I knew that in so
doing I was committing a sin—a deadly sin that would so jeopardize my
immortal soul as to place it, if such a thing were possible, even beyond the
reach of the infinite mercy of the Most Merciful and Most Terrible God.

On the night of the day on which this cruel deed was done, I was aroused
from sleep by the cry of fire. The curtains of my bed were in flames. The whole
house was blazing. It was with great difficulty that my wife, a servant, and
myself, made our escape from the conflagration. The destruction was complete.

My entire worldly wealth was swallowed up, and I resigned myself thenceforward to despair.

I am above the weakness of seeking to establish a sequence of cause and effect, between the disaster and the atrocity. But I am detailing a chain of facts, and wish not to leave even a possible link imperfect. On the day succeeding the fire, I visited the ruins. The walls, with one exception, had fallen in. This exception was found in a compartment wall, not very thick, which stood about the middle of the house and against which had rested the head of my bed. The plastering had here, in great measure, resisted the action of fire—a fact which I attributed to its having been recently spread. About this wall a dense crowd were collected, and many persons seemed to be examining a particular portion of it with very minute and eager attention. The words "strange!" "singular!" and other similar expressions, excited my curiosity. I approached and saw, as if graven in *bas relief* upon the white surface, the figure of a gigantic *cat*. The impression was given with an accuracy truly marvellous. There was a rope about the animal's neck.

When I first beheld this apparition—for I could scarcely regard it as less—my wonder and terror were extreme. But at length reflection came to my aid. The cat, I remembered, had been hung in a garden adjacent to the house. Upon the alarm of fire, this garden had been immediately filled by the crowd—by some one of whom the animal must have been cut from the tree and thrown, through an open window, into my chamber. This had probably been done with the view of arousing me from sleep. The falling of other walls had compressed the victim of my cruelty into the substance of the freshly-spread plaster; the lime of which, with the flames, and the ammonia from the carcass, had then accomplished the portraiture as I saw it.

Although I thus readily accounted to my reason, if not altogether to my conscience, for the startling fact just detailed, it did not the less fail to make a deep impression upon my fancy. For months I could not rid myself of the phantasm of the cat; and during this period there came back into my spirit a half-sentiment that seemed, but was not, remorse. I went so far as to regret the loss of the animal, and to look about me, among the vile haunts which I now habitually frequented, for another pet of the same species, and of somewhat similar appearance, with which to supply its place.

One night as I sat, half stupefied, in a den of more than infamy, my attention was suddenly drawn to some black object, reposing upon the head of one of the immense hogsheads of Gin, or of Rum, which constituted the chief furniture of the apartment. I had been looking steadily at the top of this hogshead for some minutes, and what now caused me surprise was the fact that I had not sooner perceived the object thereupon. I approached it and touched it with my hand. It was a black cat—a very large one—fully as large as Pluto, and closely resembling him in every respect but one. Pluto had not a white hair upon any portion of his body; but this cat had a large, although indefinite splotch of white, covering nearly the whole region of the breast.

Upon my touching him, he immediately arose, purred loudly, rubbed against my hand, and appeared delighted with my notice. This, then, was the very creature of which I was in search. I at once offered to purchase it of the landlord; but this person made no claim to it—knew nothing of it—had never seen it before.

I continued my caresses, and, when I prepared to go home, the animal evinced a disposition to accompany me. I permitted it to do so; occasionally stooping and patting it as I proceeded. When it reached the house, it domesticated itself at once, and became immediately a great favorite with my wife.

For my own part, I soon found a dislike to it arising within me. This was just the reverse of what I had anticipated; but—I know not how or why it was—its evident fondness for myself rather disgusted and annoyed. By slow degrees, these feelings of disgust and annoyance rose into the bitterness of hatred; I avoided the creature, a certain sense of shame, and the remembrance of my former deed of cruelty, preventing me from physically abusing it. I did not, for some weeks, strike, or otherwise violently ill use it; but gradually—very gradually—I came to look upon it with unutterable loathing, and to flee silently from its odious presence, as from the breath of a pestilence.

What added, no doubt, to my hatred of the beast, was the discovery, on the morning after I brought it home, that, like Pluto, it also had been deprived of one of its eyes. This circumstance, however, only endeared it to my wife, who, as I have already said, possessed, in a high degree, that humanity of feeling which had once been my distinguishing trait, and the source of many of my simplest and purest pleasures.

With my aversion to this cat, however, its partiality for myself seemed to increase. It followed my footsteps with a pertinacity which it would be difficult to make the reader comprehend. Whenever I sat, it would crouch beneath my chair, or spring upon my knees, covering me with its loathsome caresses. If I arose to walk, it would get between my feet and thus nearly throw me down, or, fastening its long and sharp claws in my dress, clamber in this manner, to my breast. At such times, although I longed to destroy it with a blow, I was yet withheld from so doing, partly by a memory of my former crime, but chiefly— let me confess it at once—by absolute *dread* of the beast.

This dread was not exactly a dread of physical evil—and yet I should be at a loss how otherwise to define it. I am almost ashamed to own—yes, even in this felon's cell, I am almost ashamed to own—that the terror and horror with which the animal inspired me, had been heightened by one of the merest chimeras it would be possible to conceive. My wife had called my attention, more than once, to the character of the mark of white hair, of which I have spoken, and which constituted the sole visible difference between the strange beast and the one I had destroyed. The reader will remember that this mark, although large, had been originally very indefinite; but, by slow degrees—degrees nearly imperceptible, and which for a long time my Reason struggled to reject as fanciful—it had, at length, assumed a rigorous distinctness of outline. It was now the representation of an object that I shudder to name; and for this, above all, I loathed, and dreaded, and would have rid myself of the monster *had I dared*; it was now, I say, the image of a hideous—of a ghastly thing—of the GALLOWS!—oh, mournful and terrible engine of Horror and of Crime, of Agony and of Death!

And now was I indeed wretched beyond the wretchedness of mere Humanity. And a brute beast—whose fellow I had contemptuously destroyed—*a brute beast* to work out for *me*—for me a man, fashioned in the image of the High God—so much of insufferable woe! Alas! neither by day nor by night knew I the blessing of Rest any more! During the former the creature left me no moment alone; and, in the latter, I started, hourly, from dreams of unutterable fear, to find the hot breath of *the thing* upon my face, and its vast weight—an incarnate Nightmare that I had no power to shake off—incumbent eternally upon my *heart!*

Beneath the pressure of torments such as these, the feeble remnant of the good within me succumbed. Evil thoughts became my sole intimates—the darkest and most evil of thoughts. The moodiness of my usual temper increased to hatred of all things and of all mankind; while, from the sudden, frequent, and ungovernable outbursts of a fury to which I now blindly abandoned myself, my uncomplaining wife, alas! was the most usual and the most patient of sufferers.

One day she accompanied me, upon some household errand, into the cellar of the old building which our poverty compelled us to inhabit. The cat followed me down the steep stairs, and, nearly throwing me headlong, exasperated me to madness. Uplifting an axe, and forgetting, in my wrath, the childish dread which had hitherto stayed my hand, I aimed a blow at the animal which, of course, would have proved instantly fatal had it descended as I wished. But this blow was arrested by the hand of my wife. Goaded, by the interference, into a rage more than demoniacal, I withdrew my arm from her grasp and buried the axe in her brain. She fell dead upon the spot, without a groan.

This hideous murder accomplished, I set myself forthwith, and with entire deliberation, to the task of concealing the body. I knew that I could not remove it from the house, either by day or by night, without the risk of being observed by the neighbors. Many projects entered my mind. At one period I thought of cutting the corpse into minute fragments, and destroying them by fire. At another, I resolved to dig a grave for it in the floor of the cellar. Again, I deliberated about casting it in the well in the yard—about packing it in a box, as if merchandise, with the usual arrangements, and so getting a porter to take it from the house. Finally I hit upon what I considered a far better expedient than either of these. I determined to wall it up in the cellar—as the monks of the Middle Ages are recorded to have walled up their victims.

For a purpose such as this the cellar was well adapted. Its walls were loosely constructed, and had lately been plastered throughout with a rough plaster, which the dampness of the atmosphere had prevented from hardening. Moreover, in one of the walls was a projection, caused by a false chimney, or fireplace, that had been filled up, and made to resemble the rest of the cellar. I made no doubt that I could readily displace the bricks at this point, insert the corpse, and wall the whole up as before, so that no eye could detect anything suspicious.

And in this calculation I was not deceived. By means of a crow-bar I easily dislodged the bricks, and, having carefully deposited the body against the inner wall, I propped it in that position, while, with little trouble, I re-laid the whole structure as it originally stood. Having procured mortar, sand, and hair, with every possible precaution, I prepared a plaster which could not be distinguished from the old, and with this I very carefully went over the new brickwork. When I had finished, I felt satisfied that all was right. The wall did not present the slightest appearance of having been disturbed. The rubbish on the floor was picked up with the minutest care. I looked around triumphantly, and said to myself—"Here at least, then, my labor has not been in vain."

My next step was to look for the beast which had been the cause of so much wretchedness; for I had, at length, firmly resolved to put it to death. Had I been able to meet with it, at the moment, there could have been no doubt of its fate; but it appeared that the crafty animal had been alarmed at the violence of my previous anger, and forbore to present itself in my present mood. It is impossible to describe, or to imagine, the deep, the blissful sense of relief which the absence of the detested creature occasioned in my bosom. It did not make its appearance during the night—and thus for one night at least, since its introduction into the house, I soundly and tranquilly slept; ay, *slept* even with the burden of murder upon my soul!

The second and the third day passed, and still my tormentor came not. Once again I breathed as a free man. The monster, in terror, had fled the premises forever! I should behold it no more! My happiness was supreme! The guilt of my dark deed disturbed me but little. Some few inquiries had been made, but these had been readily answered. Even a search had been instituted —but of course nothing was to be discovered. I looked upon my future felicity as secured.

Upon the fourth day of the assassination, a party of the police came, very unexpectedly, into the house, and proceeded again to make rigorous investigation of the premises. Secure, however, in the inscrutability of my place of concealment, I felt no embarrassment whatever. The officers bade me accompany them in their search. They left no nook or corner unexplored. At length, for the third or fourth time, they descended into the cellar. I quivered not in a muscle. My heart beat calmly as that of one who slumbers in innocence. I walked the cellar from end to end. I folded my arms upon my bosom, and roamed easily to and fro. The police were thoroughly satisfied and prepared to depart. The glee at my heart was too strong to be restrained. I burned to say if but one word, by way of triumph, and to render doubly sure their assurance of my guiltlessness.

"Gentlemen," I said at last, as the party ascended the steps. "I delight to have allayed your suspicions. I wish you all health, and a little more courtesy. By the bye, gentlemen, this—this is a very well constructed house." (In the rabid desire to say something easily, I scarcely knew what I uttered at all) "I may say an *excellently* well constructed house. These walls—are you going, gentlemen?—these walls are solidly put together"; and here, through the mere frenzy of bravado, I rapped heavily, with a cane which I held in my hand, upon that very portion of the brick-work behind which stood the corpse of the wife of my bosom.

But may God shield and deliver me from the fangs of the Arch-Fiend! No sooner had the reverberation of my blows sunk into silence, than I was answered by a voice from within the tomb!—by a cry, at first muffled and broken, like the sobbing of a child, and then quickly swelling into one long, loud, and continuous scream, utterly anomalous and inhuman—a howl—a wailing shriek, half of horror and half of triumph, such as might have arisen only out of hell, conjointly from the throats of the damned in their agony and of the demons that exult in the damnation.

Of my own thoughts it is folly to speak. Swooning, I staggered to the opposite wall. For one instant the party upon the stairs remained motionless, through extremity of terror and of awe. In the next, a dozen stout arms were toiling at the wall. It fell bodily. The corpse, already greatly decayed and clotted with gore, stood erect before the eyes of the spectators. Upon its head, with red extended mouth and solitary eye of fire, sat the hideous beast whose craft had seduced me into murder, and whose informing voice had consigned me to the hangman. I had walled the monster up within the tomb!

HERMAN MELVILLE

❧ *Bartleby the Scrivener*

I AM a rather elderly man. The nature of my avocations, for the last thirty years, has brought me into more than ordinary contact with what would seem an interesting and somewhat singular set of men, of whom, as yet, nothing, that I know of, has ever been written—I mean, the law-copyists, or scriveners. I have known very many of them, professionally and privately, and, if I pleased, could relate divers histories, at which good-natured gentlemen might smile, and sentimental souls might weep. But I waive the biographies of all other scriveners, for a few passages in the life of Bartleby, who was a scrivener, the strangest I ever saw, or heard of. While, of other law-copyists, I might write the complete life, of Bartleby nothing of that sort can be done. I believe that no materials exist for a full and satisfactory biography of this man. It is an irreparable loss to literature. Bartleby was one of those beings of whom nothing is ascertainable, except from the original sources, and, in his case, those are very small. What my own astonished eyes saw of Bartleby, *that* is all I know of him, except, indeed, one vague report, which will appear in the sequel.

Ere introducing the scrivener, as he first appeared to me, it is fit I make some mention of myself, my *employés*, my business, my chambers, and general surroundings; because some such description is indispensable to an adequate understanding of the chief character about to be presented. Imprimis: I am a man who, from his youth upwards, has been filled with a profound conviction that the easiest way of life is the best. Hence, though I belong to a profession proverbially energetic and nervous, even to turbulence, at times, yet nothing of that sort have I ever suffered to invade my peace. I am one of those unambitious lawyers who never address a jury, or in any way draw down public applause; but, in the cool tranquillity of a snug retreat, do a snug business among rich men's bonds, and mortgages, and title-deeds. All who know me, consider me an eminently *safe* man. The late John Jacob Astor, a personage little given to poetic enthusiasm, had no hesitation in pronouncing my first grand point to be prudence; my next, method. I do not speak it in vanity, but simply record the fact, that I was not unemployed in my profession by the late John Jacob Astor; a name which, I admit, I love to repeat; for it hath a rounded and orbicular sound to it, and rings like unto bullion. I will freely add, that I was not insensible to the late John Jacob Astor's good opinion.

Some time prior to the period at which this little history begins, my avocations had been largely increased. The good old office, now extinct in the State of New York, of a Master in Chancery, had been conferred upon me. It was not a very arduous office, but very pleasantly remunerative. I seldom lose my temper; much more seldom indulge in dangerous indignation at wrongs and outrages; but I must be permitted to be rash here and declare that I consider the sudden and violent abrogation of the office of Master in Chancery, by the new Constitution, as a —— premature act; inasmuch as I had counted upon a life-lease of the profits, whereas I only received those of a few short years. But this is by the way.

My chambers were up stairs, at No. – Wall Street. At one end, they looked upon the white wall of the interior of a spacious sky-light shaft, penetrating the building from top to bottom.

This view might have been considered rather tame than otherwise, deficient in what landscape painters call "life." But, if so, the view from the other end of my chambers offered, at least, a contrast, if nothing more. In that direction, my windows commanded an unobstructed view of a lofty brick wall, black by age and everlasting shade; which wall required no spy-glass to bring out its lurking beauties, but, for the benefit of all near-sighted spectators, was pushed up to within ten feet of my window-panes. Owing to the great height of the surrounding buildings, and my chambers being on the second floor, the interval between this wall and mine not a little resembled a huge square cistern.

At the period just preceding the advent of Bartleby, I had two persons as copyists in my employment, and a promising lad as an office-boy. First, Turkey; second, Nippers; third, Ginger Nut. These may seem names, the like of which are not usually found in the Directory. In truth, they were nicknames, mutually conferred upon each other by my three clerks, and were deemed expressive of their respective persons or characters. Turkey was a short, pursy Englishman, of about my own age—that is, somewhere not far from sixty. In the morning, one might say, his face was of a fine florid hue, but after twelve o'clock, meridian— his dinner hour—it blazed like a grate full of Christmas coals; and continued blazing—but, as it were, with a gradual wane—till six o'clock, P.M., or thereabouts; after which, I saw no more of the proprietor of the face, which, gaining its meridian with the sun, seemed to set with it, to rise, culminate, and decline the following day, with the like regularity and undiminished glory. There are many singular coincidences I have known in the course of my life, not the least among which was the fact, that, exactly when Turkey displayed his fullest beams from his red and radiant countenance, just then, too, at that critical moment, began the daily period when I considered his business capacities as seriously disturbed for the remainder of the twenty-four hours. Not that he was absolutely idle, or averse to business then; far from it. The difficulty was, he was apt to be altogether too energetic. There was a strange, inflamed, flurried, flighty recklessness of activity about him. He would be incautious in dipping his pen into his inkstand. All his blots upon my documents were dropped there after twelve o'clock, meridian. Indeed, not only would he be reckless, and sadly given to making blots in the afternoon, but, some days, he went further, and was rather noisy. At such times, too, his face flamed with augmented blazonry, as if cannel coal had been heaped on anthracite. He made an unpleasant racket with his chair; spilled his sand-box; in mending his pens, impatiently split them all to pieces, and threw them on the floor in a sudden passion; stood up and leaned over his table, boxing his papers about in a most indecorous manner, very sad to behold in an elderly man like him. Nevertheless, as he was in many ways a most valuable person to me, and all the time before twelve o'clock, meridian, was the quickest, steadiest creature, too, accomplishing a great deal of work in a style not easily to be matched—for these reasons, I was willing to overlook his eccentricities, though, indeed, occasionally, I remonstrated with him. I did this very gently, however, because, though the civilest, nay, the blandest and most reverential of men in the morning, yet, in the afternoon, he was disposed, upon provocation, to be slightly rash with his tongue—in fact, insolent. Now, valuing his morning services as I did, and resolved not to lose them—yet, at the same time, made uncomfortable by his inflamed ways after twelve o'clock—and being a man of peace, unwilling by my admonitions to call forth unseemly retorts from him, I took upon me, one Saturday noon (he was always worse on Saturdays) to hint to him, very kindly, that, perhaps, now that he was growing old, it might be well to abridge his labours; in short, he need not come to my chambers after twelve o'clock, but, dinner over, had best go home to his lodgings, and rest himself till tea-time. But no; he insisted upon his afternoon devotions. His countenance became intolerably fervid, as he oratorically assured me—gesticulating with a long ruler at the other end of the room—that if his services in the morning were useful, how indispensable, then, in the afternoon?

"With submission, sir," said Turkey, on this occasion, "I consider myself your right-hand man. In the morning I but marshal and deploy my columns; but in the afternoon I put myself at their head, and gallantly charge the foe, thus"—and he made a violent thrust with the ruler.

"But the blots, Turkey," intimated I.

"True; but, with submission, sir, behold these hairs! I am getting old. Surely, sir, a blot or two of a warm afternoon is not to be severely urged against grey hairs. Old age—even if it blot the page—is honourable. With submission, sir, we *both* are getting old."

This appeal to my fellow-feeling was hardly to be resisted. At all events, I saw that go he would not. So, I made up my mind to let him stay, resolving, nevertheless, to see to it that, during the afternoon, he had to do with my less important papers.

Nippers, the second on my list, was a whiskered, sallow, and, upon the whole, rather piratical-looking young man, of about five-and-twenty. I always deemed him the victim of two evil powers—ambition and indigestion. The ambition was evinced by a certain impatience of the duties of a mere copyist, an unwarrantable usurpation of strictly professional affairs, such as the original drawing up of legal documents. The indigestion seemed betokened in an occasional nervous testiness and grinning irritability, causing the teeth to audibly grind together over mistakes committed in copying; unnecessary maledictions, hissed, rather than spoken, in the heat of business; and especially by a continual discontent with the height of the table where he worked. Though of a very ingenious mechanical turn, Nippers could never get this table to suit him. He put chips under it, blocks of various sorts, bits of pasteboard, and at last went so far as to attempt an exquisite adjustment, by final pieces of folded blotting-paper. But no invention would answer. If, for the sake of easing his back, he brought the table-lid at a sharp angle well up towards his chin, and wrote there like a man using the steep roof of a Dutch house for his desk, then he declared that it stopped the circulation in his arms. If now he lowered the table to his waistbands, and stooped over it in writing, then there was a sore aching in his back. In short, the truth of the matter was, Nippers knew not what he wanted. Or, if he wanted anything, it was to be rid of a scrivener's table altogether. Among the manifestations of his diseased ambition was a fondness he had for receiving visits from certain ambiguous-looking fellows in seedy coats, whom he called his clients. Indeed, I was aware that not only was he, at times, considerable of a ward-politician, but he occasionally did a little business at the Justices' courts, and was not unknown on the steps of the Tombs. I have good reason to believe, however, that one individual who called upon him at my chambers, and who, with a grand air, he insisted was his client, was no other than a dun, and the alleged title-deed, a bill. But with all his failings, and the annoyances he caused me, Nippers, like his compatriot Turkey, was a very useful man to me; wrote a neat, swift hand; and, when he chose, was not deficient in a gentlemanly sort of deportment. Added to this, he always dressed in a gentlemanly sort of way; and so, incidentally, reflected credit upon my chambers. Whereas, with respect to Turkey, I had much ado to keep him from being a reproach to me. His clothes were apt to look oily, and smell of eating-houses. He wore his pantaloons very loose and baggy in summer. His coats were execrable; his hat not to be handled. But while the hat was a thing of indifference to me, inasmuch as his natural civility and deference, as a dependent Englishman, always led him to doff it the moment he entered the room, yet his coat was another matter. Concerning his coats, I reasoned with him; but with no effect. The truth was, I suppose, that a man with so small an income could not afford to sport such a lustrous face and a lustrous coat at one and the same time. As Nippers once observed, Turkey's money went chiefly for red ink. One winter day, I presented Turkey with a highly respectable-looking coat of my own—a padded grey coat, of a most comfortable warmth, and which buttoned straight up from the knee to the neck. I thought Turkey would appreciate the favour, and abate his rashness and obstreperousness of afternoons. But no; I verily believe that buttoning himself up in so downy and blanket-like a coat had a pernicious effect upon him—upon the same principle that too much oats are bad for horses. In fact, precisely as a rash, restive horse is said to feel his oats, so Turkey felt his coat. It made him insolent. He was a man whom prosperity harmed.

Though, concerning the self-indulgent habits of Turkey, I had my own private surmises, yet, touching Nippers, I was well persuaded that, whatever might be his faults in other respects, he was, at least, a temperate young man. But, indeed, nature herself seemed to have been his vintner, and, at his birth, charged him so thoroughly with an irritable, brandy-like disposition, that all subsequent potations were needless. When I consider how, amid the stillness of my chambers, Nippers would sometimes impatiently rise from his seat, and stooping over his table, spread his arms wide apart, seize the whole desk, and move it, and jerk it, with a grim, grinding motion on the floor, as if the table were a perverse voluntary agent, intent on thwarting and vexing him, I plainly perceive that, for Nippers, brandy-and-water were altogether superfluous.

It was fortunate for me that, owing to its peculiar cause—indigestion—the irritability and consequent nervousness of Nippers were mainly observable in the morning, while in the afternoon he was comparatively mild. So that, Turkey's paroxysms only coming on about twelve o'clock, I never had to do with their eccentricities at one time. Their fits relieved each other, like guards.

When Nippers's was on, Turkey's was off and *vice versa*. This was a good natural arrangement, under the circumstances.

Ginger Nut, the third on my list, was a lad, some twelve years old. His father was a car-man, ambitious of seeing his son on the bench instead of a cart, before he died. So he sent him to my office, as student at law, errand-boy, cleaner and sweeper, at the rate of one dollar a week. He had a little desk to himself, but he did not use it much. Upon inspection, the drawer exhibited a great array of the shells of various sorts of nuts. Indeed, to this quick-witted youth, the whole noble science of the law was contained in a nutshell. Not the least among the employments of Ginger Nut, as well as one which he discharged with the most alacrity, was his duty as cake and apple purveyor for Turkey and Nippers. Copying law-papers being proverbially a dry, husky sort of business, my two scriveners were fain to moisten their mouths very often with Spitzenbergs, to be had at the numerous stalls nigh the Custom House and Post Office. Also, they sent Ginger Nut very frequently for that peculiar cake— small, flat, round, and very spicy—after which he had been named by them. Of a cold morning, when business was but dull, Turkey would gobble up scores of these cakes, as if they were mere wafers—indeed, they sell them at the rate of six or eight for a penny—the scrape of his pen blending with the crunching of the crisp particles in his mouth. Of all the fiery afternoon blunders and flurried rashnesses of Turkey, was his once moistening a ginger-cake between his lips, and clapping it on to a mortgage, for a seal. I came within an ace of dismissing him then. But he mollified me by making an oriental bow, and saying—

"With submission, sir, it was generous of me to find you in stationery on my own account."

Now my original business—that of a conveyancer and title hunter, and drawer-up of recondite documents of all sorts—was considerably increased by receiving the Master's office. There was now great work for scriveners. Not only must I push the clerks already with me, but I must have additional help.

In answer to my advertisement, a motionless young man one morning stood upon my office threshold, the door being open, for it was summer. I can see that figure now—pallidly neat, pitiably respectable, incurably forlorn! It was Bartleby.

After a few words touching his qualifications, I engaged him, glad to have among my corps of copyists a man of so singularly sedate an aspect, which I thought might operate beneficially upon the flighty temper of Turkey, and the fiery one of Nippers.

I should have stated before that ground-glass folding-doors divided my premises into two parts, one of which was occupied by my scriveners, the other by myself. According to my humour, I threw open these doors, or closed them. I resolved to assign Bartleby a corner by the folding-doors, but on my side of them, so as to have this quiet man within easy call, in case any trifling thing was to be done. I placed his desk close up to a small side-window in that part of the room, a window which originally had afforded a lateral view of certain grimy backyards and bricks, but which, owing to subsequent erections, commanded at present no view at all, though it gave some light. Within three feet of the panes was a wall, and the light came down from far above, between two lofty buildings, as from a very small opening in a dome. Still further to a satisfactory arrangement, I procured a high green folding screen, which might entirely isolate Bartleby from my sight, though not remove him from my voice. And thus, in a manner, privacy and society were conjoined.

At first, Bartleby did an extraordinary quantity of writing. As if long famishing for something to copy, he seemed to gorge himself on my documents. There was no pause for digestion. He ran a day and night line, copying by sunlight and by candle-light. I should have been quite delighted with his application, had he been cheerfully industrious. But he wrote on silently, palely, mechanically.

It is, of course, an indispensable part of a scrivener's business to verify the accuracy of his copy, word by word. Where there are two or more scriveners in an office, they assist each other in this examination, one reading from the copy, the other holding the original. It is a very dull, wearisome, and lethargic affair. I can readily imagine that, to some sanguine temperaments, it would be altogether intolerable. For example, I cannot credit that the mettlesome poet, Byron, would have contentedly sat down with Bartleby to examine a law document of, say five hundred pages, closely written in a crimpy hand.

Now and then, in the haste of business, it had been my habit to assist in comparing some brief document myself, calling Turkey or Nippers for this purpose. One object I had, in placing Bartleby so handy to me behind the screen, was to avail myself of his services on such trivial occasions. It was on the third day, I think, of his being with me, and before any necessity had arisen for having his own writing examined, that, being much hurried to complete a small affair I had in hand, I abruptly called to Bartleby. In my haste and natural expectancy of instant compliance, I sat with my head bent over the original on my desk, and my right hand sideways, and somewhat nervously extended with the copy, so that, immediately upon emerging from his retreat, Bartleby might snatch it and proceed to business without the least delay.

In this very attitude did I sit when I called to him, rapidly stating what it was I wanted him to do—namely, to examine a small paper with me. Imagine my surprise, nay, my consternation, when, without moving from his privacy, Bartleby, in a singularly mild, firm voice, replied, "I would prefer not to."

I sat awhile in perfect silence, rallying my stunned faculties. Immediately it occurred to me that my ears had deceived me, or Bartleby had entirely misunderstood my meaning. I repeated my request in the clearest tone I could assume; but in quite as clear a one came the previous reply, "I would prefer not to."

"Prefer not to," echoed I, rising in high excitement, and crossing the room with a stride. "What do you mean? Are you moon-struck? I want you to help me compare this sheet here—take it," and I thrust it towards him.

"I would prefer not to," he said.

I looked at him steadfastly. His face was leanly composed; his grey eye dimly calm. Not a wrinkle of agitation rippled him. Had there been the least uneasiness, anger, impatience or impertinence in his manner; in other words, had there been anything ordinarily human about him, doubtless I should have violently dismissed him from the premises. But as it was, I should have as soon thought of turning my pale plaster-of-paris bust of Cicero out of doors. I stood gazing at him awhile, as he went on with his own writing, and then reseated myself at my desk. This is very strange, thought I. What had one best do? But my business hurried me. I concluded to forget the matter for the present, reserving it for my future leisure. So, calling Nippers from the other room, the paper was speedily examined.

A few days after this, Bartleby concluded four lengthy documents, being quadruplicates of a week's testimony taken before me in my High Court of Chancery. It became necessary to examine them. It was an important suit, and great accuracy was imperative. Having all things arranged, I called Turkey, Nippers, and Ginger Nut from the next room, meaning to place the four copies in the hands of my four clerks, while I should read from the original. Accordingly, Turkey, Nippers, and Ginger Nut had taken their seats in a row, each with his document in his hand, when I called to Bartleby to join this interesting group.

"Bartleby! quick, I am waiting."

I heard a slow scrape of his chair legs on the uncarpeted floor, and soon he appeared standing at the entrance of his hermitage.

"What is wanted?" said he, mildly.

"The copies, the copies," said I, hurriedly. "We are going to examine them. There"—and I held towards him the fourth quadruplicate.

"I would prefer not to," he said, and gently disappeared behind the screen.

For a few moments I was turned into a pillar of salt, standing at the head of my seated column of clerks. Recovering myself, I advanced towards the screen, and demanded the reason for such extraordinary conduct.

"*Why* do you refuse?"

"I would prefer not to."

With any other man I should have flown outright into a dreadful passion, scorned all further words, and thrust him ignominiously from my presence. But there was something about Bartleby that not only strangely disarmed me, but, in a wonderful manner, touched and disconcerted me. I began to reason with him.

"These are your own copies we are about to examine. It is labour saving to you, because one examination will answer for your four papers. It is common usage. Every copyist is bound to help examine his copy. Is it not so? Will you not speak? Answer!"

"I prefer not to," he replied in a flute-like tone. It seemed to me that, while I had been addressing him, he carefully revolved every statement that I made; fully comprehended the meaning; could not gainsay the irresistible conclusion;

but, at the same time, some paramount consideration prevailed with him to reply as he did.

"You are decided, then, not to comply with my request—a request made according to common usage and common sense?"

He briefly gave me to understand, that on that point my judgment was sound. Yes: his decision was irreversible.

It is not seldom the case that, when a man is brow-beaten in some unprecedented and violently unreasonable way, he begins to stagger in his own plainest faith. He begins, as it were, vaguely to surmise that, wonderful as it may be, all the justice and all the reason is on the other side. Accordingly, if any disinterested persons are present, he turns to them for some reinforcement for his own faltering mind.

"Turkey," said I, "what do you think of this? Am I not right?"

"With submission, sir," said Turkey, in his blandest tone, "I think that you are."

"Nippers," said I, "what do *you* think of it?"

"I think I should kick him out of the office."

(The reader of nice perceptions will here perceive that, it being morning, Turkey's answer is couched in polite and tranquil terms, but Nippers replies in ill-tempered ones. Or, to repeat a previous sentence, Nippers's ugly mood was on duty, and Turkey's off.)

"Ginger Nut," said I, willing to enlist the smallest suffrage in behalf, "what do *you* think of it?"

"I think, sir, he's a little *luny*," replied Ginger Nut, with a grin.

"You hear what they say," said I, turning towards the screen, "come forth and do your duty."

But he vouchsafed no reply. I pondered a moment in sore perplexity. But once more business hurried me. I determined again to postpone the consideration of this dilemma to my future leisure. With a little trouble we made out to examine the papers without Bartleby, though at every page or two Turkey deferentially dropped his opinion, that this proceeding was quite out of the common; while Nippers, twitching in his chair with a dyspeptic nervousness, ground out, between his set teeth, occasional hissing maledictions against the stubborn oaf behind the screen. And for his (Nippers's) part, this was the first and the last time he would do another man's business without pay.

Meanwhile Bartleby sat in his hermitage, oblivious to everything but his own peculiar business there.

Some days passed, the scrivener being employed upon another lengthy work. His late remarkable conduct led me to regard his ways narrowly. I observed that he never went to dinner; indeed, that he never went anywhere. As yet I had never, of my personal knowledge, known him to be outside of my office. He was a perpetual sentry in the corner. At about eleven o'clock though, in the morning, I noticed that Ginger Nut would advance toward the opening in Bartleby's screen, as if silently beckoned thither by a gesture invisible to me where I sat. The boy would then leave the office, jingling a few pence, and reappear with a handful of ginger-nuts, which he delivered in the hermitage, receiving two of the cakes for his trouble.

He lives, then, on ginger-nuts, thought I; never eats a dinner, properly speaking; he must be a vegetarian, then; but no; he never eats even vegetables, he eats nothing but ginger-nuts. My mind then ran on in reveries concerning the probable effects upon the human constitution of living entirely on ginger-nuts. Ginger-nuts are so called, because they contain ginger as one of their peculiar constituents, and the final flavouring one. Now, what was ginger? A hot, spicy thing. Was Bartleby hot and spicy? Not at all. Ginger, then, had no effect upon Bartleby. Probably he preferred it should have none.

Nothing so aggravates an earnest person as a passive resistance. If the individual so resisted be of a not inhumane temper, and the resisting one perfectly harmless in his passivity, then, in the better moods of the former, he will endeavour charitably to construe to his imagination what proves impossible to be solved by his judgment. Even so, for the most part, I regarded Bartleby and his ways. Poor fellow! thought I, he means no mischief; it is plain he intends no insolence; his aspect sufficiently evinces that his eccentricities are involuntary. He is useful to me. I can get along with him. If I turn him away, the chances are he will fall in with some less indulgent employer, and then he will be rudely treated, and perhaps driven forth miserably to starve. Yes. Here I can cheaply purchase a delicious self-approval. To befriend Bartleby; to humour him in his strange wilfulness, will cost me little or nothing, while I lay up in my soul what will eventually prove a sweet morsel for my conscience. But this mood was not invariable with me. The passiveness of Bartleby sometimes irritated me. I felt strangely goaded on to encounter him in new opposition—to elicit some angry spark from him answerable to my own. But, indeed, I might as well have essayed to strike fire with my knuckles against a bit of Windsor soap. But one afternoon the evil impulse in me mastered me, and the following little scene ensued:

"Bartleby," said I, "when those papers are all copied, I will compare them with you."

"I would prefer not to."

"How? Surely you do not mean to persist in that mulish vagary?"

No answer.

I threw open the folding-doors near by, and turning upon Turkey and Nippers, exclaimed:

"Bartleby a second time says, he won't examine his papers. What do you think of it, Turkey?"

It was afternoon, be it remembered. Turkey sat glowing like a brass boiler; his bald head steaming; his hands reeling among his blotted papers.

"Think of it?" roared Turkey. "I'll just step behind his screen, and black his eyes for him!"

So saying, Turkey rose to his feet and threw his arms into a pugilistic position. He was hurrying away to make good his promise, when I detained him, alarmed at the effect of incautiously rousing Turkey's combativeness after dinner.

"Sit down, Turkey," said I, "and hear what Nippers has to say. What do you think of it, Nippers? Would I not be justified in immediately dismissing Bartleby?"

"Excuse me, that is for you to decide, sir. I think his conduct quite unusual, and, indeed, unjust, as regards Turkey and myself. But it may only be a passing whim."

"Ah," exclaimed I, "you have strangely changed your mind, then—you speak very gently of him now."

"All beer," cried Turkey; "gentleness is effects of beer—Nippers and I dined together to-day. You see how gentle I am, sir. Shall I go and black his eyes?"

"You refer to Bartleby, I suppose. No, not to-day, Turkey," I replied, "pray, put up your fists."

I closed the doors, and again advanced towards Bartleby. I felt additional incentives tempting me to my fate. I burned to be rebelled against again. I remembered that Bartleby never left the office.

"Bartleby," said I, "Ginger Nut is away; just step around to the Post Office, won't you?" (it was but a three minutes' walk) "and see if there is anything for me."

"I would prefer not to."

"You *will* not?"

"I *prefer* not."

I staggered to my desk, and sat there in a deep study. My blind inveteracy returned. Was there any other thing in which I could procure myself to be ignominiously repulsed by this lean, penniless wight?—my hired clerk? What added thing is there, perfectly reasonable, that he will be sure to refuse to do?

"Bartleby!"

No answer.

"Bartleby," in a louder tone.

No answer.

"Bartleby," I roared.

Like a very ghost, agreeably to the laws of magical invocation at the third summons, he appeared at the entrance of his hermitage.

"Go to the next room, and tell Nippers to come to me."

"I prefer not to," he respectfully and slowly said, and mildly disappeared.

"Very good, Bartleby," said I, in a quiet sort of serenely-severe, self-possessed tone, intimating the unalterable purpose of some terrible retribution very close at hand. At the moment I half intended something of the kind. But upon the whole, as it was drawing towards my dinner-hour, I thought it best to put on my hat and walk home for the day, suffering much from perplexity and distress of mind.

Shall I acknowledge it? The conclusion of this whole business was, that it soon became a fixed fact of my chambers, that a pale young scrivener, by the name of Bartleby, had a desk there; that he copied for me at the usual rate of four cents a folio (one hundred words); but he was permanently exempt from examining the work done by him, that duty being transferred to Turkey and Nippers, out of compliment, doubtless, to their superior acuteness; moreover, said Bartleby was never, on any account, to be dispatched on the most trivial errand of any sort; and that even if entreated to take upon him such a matter, it was generally understood that he would "prefer not to"—in other words, that he would refuse point-blank.

As days passed on, I became considerably reconciled to Bartleby. His steadiness, his freedom from all dissipation, his incessant industry (except when he chose to throw himself into a standing reverie behind his screen), his great stillness, his unalterableness of demeanour under all circumstances, made him a valuable acquisition. One prime thing was this—*he was always there*—first in the morning, continually through the day, and the last at night. I had a singular confidence in his honesty. I felt my most precious papers perfectly safe in his hands. Sometimes, to be sure, I could not, for the very soul of me, avoid falling into sudden spasmodic passions with him. For it was exceeding difficult to bear in mind all the time those strange peculiarities, privileges, and unheard-of exemptions, forming the tacit stipulations on Bartleby's part under which he remained in my office. Now and then, in the eagerness of dispatching pressing business, I would inadvertently summon Bartleby, in a short, rapid tone, to put his finger, say, on the incipient tie of a bit of red tape with which I was about compressing some papers. Of course, from behind the screen the usual answer, "I prefer not to," was sure to come, and then, how could a human creature, with the common infirmities of our nature, refrain from bitterly exclaiming upon such perverseness—such unreasonableness? However, every added repulse of this sort which I received only tended to lessen the probability of my repeating the inadvertence.

Here it must be said, that, according to the custom of most legal gentlemen occupying chambers in densely-populated law buildings, there were several keys to my door. One was kept by a woman residing in the attic, which person weekly scrubbed and daily swept and dusted my apartments. Another was kept by Turkey for convenience' sake. The third I sometimes carried in my own pocket. The fourth I knew not who had.

Now, one Sunday morning I happened to go to Trinity Church, to hear a celebrated preacher, and finding myself rather early on the ground I thought I would walk around to my chambers for a while. Luckily I had my key with me; but upon applying it to the lock, I found it resisted by something inserted from the inside. Quite surprised, I called out; when to my consternation a key was turned from within; and thrusting his lean visage at me, and holding the door ajar, the apparition of Bartleby appeared, in his shirt-sleeves, and otherwise in a strangely tattered deshabille, saying quietly that he was sorry, but he was deeply engaged just then, and—preferred not admitting me at present. In a brief word or two, he moreover added, that perhaps I had better walk round the block two or three times, and by that time he would probably have concluded his affairs.

Now, the utterly unsurmised appearance of Bartleby, tenanting my law-chambers of a Sunday morning, with his cadaverously gentlemanly *noncha-lance*, yet withal firm and self-possessed, had such a strange effect upon me, that incontinently I slunk away from my own door, and did as desired. But not without sundry twinges of impotent rebellion against the mild effrontery of this unaccountable scrivener. Indeed, it was his wonderful mildness chiefly, which not only disarmed me, but unmanned me, as it were. For I consider that one, for the time, is somehow unmanned when he tranquilly permits his hired clerk to dictate to him, and order him away from his own premises. Furthermore, I was full of uneasiness as to what Bartleby could possibly be doing in my office in his shirt-sleeves, and in an otherwise dismantled condition of a Sunday morning. Was anything amiss going on? Nay, that was out of the question. It was not to be thought of for a moment that Bartleby was an immoral person. But what could he be doing there?—copying? Nay again, whatever might be his eccentricities, Bartleby was an eminently decorous person. He would be the last man to sit down to his desk in any state approaching to nudity. Besides, it was Sunday; and there was something about Bartleby that forbade the supposition that he would by any secular occupation violate the proprieties of the day.

Nevertheless, my mind was not pacified; and full of a restless curiosity, at last I returned to the door. Without hindrance I inserted my key, opened it, and entered. Bartleby was not to be seen. I looked round anxiously, peeped behind his screen; but it was very plain that he was gone. Upon more closely examining the place, I surmised that for an indefinite period Bartleby must have ate, dressed, and slept in my office, and that too without plate, mirror, or bed. The cushioned seat of a rickety old sofa in one corner bore the faint impress of a lean, reclining form. Rolled away under his desk, I found a blanket; under the empty grate, a blacking box and brush; on a chair, a tin basin, with soap and a ragged towel; in a newspaper a few crumbs of ginger-nuts and a morsel of cheese. Yes, thought I, it is evident enough that Bartleby has been making his home here, keeping bachelor's hall all by himself. Immediately then the thought came sweeping across me, what miserable friendlessness and loneliness are here revealed! His poverty is great; but his solitude, how horrible! Think of it. Of a Sunday, Wall Street is deserted as Petra; and every night of every day it is an emptiness. This building, too, which of week-days hums with industry and life, at nightfall echoes with sheer vacancy, and all through Sunday is forlorn. And here Bartleby makes his home; sole spectator of a solitude which he has seen all populous—a sort of innocent and transformed Marius brooding among the ruins of Carthage! [Gaius Marius Victorinus; Latin philosopher and writer of the fourth century A.D.]

For the first time in my life a feeling of overpowering stinging melancholy seized me. Before, I had never experienced aught but a not unpleasing sadness. The bond of a common humanity now drew me irresistibly to gloom. A fraternal melancholy! For both I and Bartleby were sons of Adam. I remembered the bright silks and sparkling faces I had seen that day, in gala trim, swan-like sailing down the Mississippi of Broadway; and I contrasted them with the pallid copyist, and thought to myself, Ah, happiness courts the light, so we deem the world is gay; but misery hides aloof, so we deem that misery there is none. These sad fancyings—chimeras, doubtless, of a sick and silly brain—led on to other and more special thoughts, concerning the eccentricities of Bartleby. Presentiments of strange discoveries hovered round me. The scrivener's pale form appeared to me laid out, among uncaring strangers, in its shivering winding-sheet.

Suddenly I was attracted by Bartleby's closed desk, the key in open sight left in the lock.

I mean no mischief, seek the gratification of no heartless curiosity, thought I; besides, the desk is mine, and its contents, too, so I will make bold to look within. Everything was methodically arranged, the papers smoothly placed. The pigeon-holes were deep, and removing the files of documents, I groped into their recesses. Presently I felt something there, and dragged it out. It was an old bandanna handkerchief, heavy and knotted. I opened it, and saw it was a savings bank.

I now recalled all the quiet mysteries which I had noted in the man. I remembered that he never spoke but to answer; that, though at intervals he had considerable time to himself, yet I had never seen him reading—no, not even a newspaper, that for long periods he would stand looking out, at his pale window behind the screen, upon the dead brick wall; I was quite sure he never visited any refectory or eating-house; while his pale face clearly indicated that he never drank beer like Turkey, or tea and coffee even, like other men; that he never went anywhere in particular that I could learn; never went out for a walk, unless, indeed, that was the case at present; that he had declined telling who he was, or whence he came, or whether he had any relatives in the world; that though so thin and pale, he never complained of ill-health. And more than all, I remembered a certain unconscious air of pallid—how shall I call it?—of pallid haughtiness, say, or rather an austere reserve about him, which had positively awed me into my tame compliance with his eccentricites, when I had feared to ask him to do the slightest incidental thing for me, even though I might know, from his long-continued motionlessness, that behind his screen he must be standing in one of those dead-wall reveries of his.

Revolving all these things, and coupling them with the recently discovered fact, that he made my office his constant abiding place and home, and not forgetful of his morbid moodiness; revolving all these things, a prudential feeling began to steal over me. My first emotions had been those of pure melancholy and sincerest pity; but just in proportion as the forlornness of Bartleby grew and grew to my imagination, did that same melancholy merge into fear, that pity into repulsion. So true it is, and so terrible, too, that up to a certain point the thought or sight of misery enlists our best affections; but, in certain special cases, beyond that point it does not. They err who would assert that invariably this is owing to the inherent selfishness of the human heart. It rather proceeds from a certain hopelessness of remedying excessive and organic ill. To a sensitive being, pity is not seldom pain. And when at last it is perceived that such pity cannot lead to effectual succour, common sense bids the soul be rid of it. What I saw that morning persuaded me that the scrivener was the victim of innate and incurable disorder. I might give alms to his body; but his body did not pain him; it was his soul that suffered, and his soul I could not reach.

I did not accomplish the purpose of going to Trinity Church that morning. Somehow, the things I had seen disqualified me for the time from church-going. I walked homeward, thinking what I would do with Bartleby. Finally, I resolved upon this—I would put certain calm questions to him the next morning, touching his history, etc., and if he declined to answer them openly and unreservedly (and I supposed he would prefer not), then to give him a twenty dollar bill over and above whatever I might owe him, and tell him his services were no longer required; but that if in any other way I could assist him, I would be happy to do so, especially if he desired to return to his native place, wherever that might be, I would willingly help to defray the expenses. More-over, if, after reaching home, he found himself at any time in want of aid, a letter from him would be sure of a reply.

The next morning came.

"Bartleby," said I, gently calling to him behind his screen.

No reply.

"Bartleby," said I, in a still gentler tone, "come here; I am not going to ask you to do anything you would prefer not to do—I simply wish to speak to you."

Upon this he noiselessly slid into view.

"Will you tell me, Bartleby, where you were born?"

"I would prefer not to."

"Will you tell me *anything* about yourself?"

"I would prefer not to."

"But what reasonable objection can you have to speak to me? I feel friendly towards you."

He did not look at me while I spoke, but kept his glance fixed upon my bust of Cicero, which, as I then sat, was directly behind me, some six inches above my head.

"What is your answer, Bartleby?" said I, after waiting a considerable time for a reply, during which his countenance remained immovable, only there was the faintest conceivable tremor of the white attenuated mouth.

"At present I prefer to give no answer," he said, and retired into his hermitage.

It was rather weak in me I confess, but his manner, on this occasion, nettled me. Not only did there seem to lurk in it a certain calm disdain, but his perverseness seemed ungrateful, considering the undeniable good usage and indulgence he had received from me.

Again I sat ruminating what I should do. Mortified as I was at his behaviour, and resolved as I had been to dismiss him when I entered my office, nevertheless I strangely felt something superstitious knocking at my heart, and forbidding me to carry out my purpose, and denouncing me for a villain if I dared to breathe one bitter word against this forlornest of mankind. At last, familiarly drawing my chair behind his screen, I sat down and said: "Bartleby, never mind, then, about revealing your history; but let me entreat you, as a friend, to comply as far as may be with the usages of this office. Say now, you will help to examine papers to-morrow or next day; in short, say now, that in a day or two you will begin to be a little reasonable—say so, Bartleby."

"At present I would prefer not to be a little reasonable," was his mildly cadaverous reply.

Just then the folding-doors opened, and Nippers approached. He seemed suffering from an unusually bad night's rest, induced by severer indigestion than common. He overheard those final words of Bartleby.

"*Prefer not,* eh?" gritted Nippers—"I'd *prefer* him, if I were you, sir," addressing me—"I'd *prefer* him; I'd give him preferences, the stubborn mule! What is it, sir, pray, that he *prefers* not to do now?"

Bartleby moved not a limb.

"Mr. Nippers," said I, "I'd prefer that you would withdraw for the present."

Somehow, of late, I had got into the way of involuntarily using this word "prefer" upon all sorts of not exactly suitable occasions. And I trembled to think that my contact with the scrivener had already and seriously affected me in a mental way. And what further and deeper aberration might it not yet produce? This apprehension had not been without efficacy in determining me to summary measures.

As Nippers, looking very sour and sulky, was departing, Turkey blandly and deferentially approached.

"With submission, sir," said he, "yesterday I was thinking about Bartleby here, and I think that if he would but prefer to take a quart of good ale every day, it would do much towards mending him, and enabling him to assist in examining his papers."

"So you have got the word, too," said I slightly excited.

"With submission, what word, sir?" asked Turkey, respectfully crowding himself into the contracted space behind the screen, and by so doing, making me jostle the scrivener. "What word, sir?"

"I would prefer to be left alone here," said Bartleby, as if offended at being mobbed in his privacy.

"*That's* the word, Turkey," said I—"*that's* it."

"Oh, *prefer?* oh yes—queer word. I never use it myself. But, sir, as I was saying, if he would but prefer——"

"Turkey," interrupted I, "you will please withdraw."

"Oh certainly, sir, if you prefer that I should."

As he opened the folding-door to retire, Nippers at his desk caught a glimpse of me, and asked whether I would prefer to have a certain paper copied on blue paper or white. He did not in the least roguishly accent the word "prefer." It was plain that it involuntarily rolled from his tongue. I thought to myself, surely I must get rid of a demented man, who already has in some degree turned the tongues, if not the heads of myself and clerks. But I thought it prudent not to break the dismission at once.

The next day I noticed that Bartleby did nothing but stand at his window in his dead-wall reverie. Upon asking him why he did not write, he said that he had decided upon doing no more writing.

"Why, how now? what next?" exclaimed I, "do no more writing?"

"No more."

"And what is the reason?"

"Do you not see the reason for yourself?" he indifferently replied.

I looked steadfastly at him, and perceived that his eyes looked dull and glazed. Instantly it occurred to me, that his unexampled diligence in copying by his dim window for the first few weeks of his stay with me might have temporarily impaired his vision.

I was touched. I said something in condolence with him. I hinted that of course he did wisely in abstaining from writing for a while; and urged him to embrace that opportunity of taking wholesome exercise in the open air. This, however, he did not do. A few days after this, my other clerks being absent, and being in a great hurry to dispatch certain letters by the mail, I thought that, having nothing else earthly to do, Bartleby would surely be less inflexible than usual, and carry these letters to the post-office. But he blankly declined. So, much to my inconvenience, I went myself.

Still added days went by. Whether Bartleby's eyes improved or not, I could not say. To all appearance, I thought they did. But when I asked him if they did, he vouchsafed no answer. At all events, he would do no copying. At last, in reply to my urgings, he informed me that he had permanently given up copying.

"What!" exclaimed I; "suppose your eyes should get entirely well—better than ever before—would you not copy then?"

"I have given up copying," he answered, and slid aside.

He remained as ever, a fixture in my chamber. Nay—if that were possible—he became still more of a fixture than before. What was to be done? He would do nothing in the office; why should he stay there? In plain fact, he had now become a millstone to me, not only useless as a necklace, but afflictive to bear. Yet I was sorry for him. I speak less than truth when I say that, on his own account, he occasioned me uneasiness. If he would but have named a single relative or friend, I would instantly have written, and urged their taking the poor fellow away to some convenient retreat. But he seemed alone, absolutely alone in the universe. A bit of wreck in the mid-Atlantic. At length, necessities connected with my business tyrannized over all other considerations. Decently as I could, I told Bartleby that in six days' time he must unconditionally leave the office. I warned him to take measures, in the interval, for procuring some other abode. I offered to assist him in this endeavour, if he himself would but take the first step towards a removal. "And when you finally quit me, Bartleby," added I, "I shall see that you go not away entirely unprovided. Six days from this hour, remember."

At the expiration of that period, I peeped behind the screen, and lo! Bartleby was there.

I buttoned up my coat, balanced myself; advanced slowly towards him, touched his shoulder, and said, "The time has come; you must quit this place; I am sorry for you; here is money; but you must go."

"I would prefer not," he replied, with his back still towards me.

"You *must*."

He remained silent.

Now I had an unbounded confidence in this man's common honesty. He had frequently restored to me sixpences and shillings carelessly dropped upon the floor, for I am apt to be very reckless in such shirt-button affairs. The proceeding, then, which followed will not be deemed extraordinary.

"Bartleby," said I, "I owe you twelve dollars on account; here are thirty-two; the odd twenty are yours—Will you take it?" and I handed the bills towards him.

But he made no motion.

"I will leave them here, then," putting them under a weight on the table. Then taking my hat and cane and going to the door, I tranquilly turned and added—"After you have removed your things from these offices, Bartleby, you will of course lock the door—since every one is now gone for the day but you—and if you please, slip your key underneath the mat, so that I may have it in the morning. I shall not see you again; so good-bye to you. If, hereafter, in your new place of abode, I can be of any service to you, do not fail to advise me by letter. Good-bye, Bartleby, and fare you well."

But he answered not a word; like the last column of some ruined temple, he remained standing mute and solitary in the middle of the otherwise deserted room.

As I walked home in a pensive mood, my vanity got the better of my pity. I could not but highly plume myself on my masterly management in getting rid of Bartleby. Masterly I call it, and such it must appear to any dispassionate thinker. The beauty of my procedure seemed to consist in its perfect quietness. There was no vulgar bullying, no bravado of any sort, no choleric hectoring, and striding to and fro across the apartment, jerking out vehement commands for Bartleby to bundle himself off with his beggarly traps. Nothing of the kind. Without loudly bidding Bartleby depart—as an inferior genius might have done—I *assumed* the ground that depart he must; and upon that assumption built all I had to say. The more I thought over my procedure, the more I was charmed with it. Nevertheless, next morning, upon awakening, I had my doubts—I had somehow slept off the fumes of vanity. One of the coolest and wisest hours a man has, is just after he awakes in the morning. My procedure seemed as sagacious as ever—but only in theory. How it would prove in practice—there was the rub. It was truly a beautiful thought to have assumed Bartleby's departure; but, after all, that assumption was simply my own, and none of Bartleby's. The great point was, not whether I had assumed that he would quit me, but whether he would prefer so to do. He was more a man of preferences than assumptions.

After breakfast, I walked down town, arguing the probabilities *pro* and *con*. One moment I thought it would prove a miserable failure, and Bartleby would be found all alive at my office as usual; the next moment it seemed certain that I should find his chair empty. And so I kept veering about. At the corner of Broadway and Canal Street, I saw quite an excited group of people standing in earnest conversation.

"I'll take odds he doesn't," said a voice I passed.

"Doesn't go?—done!" said I, "put up your money."

I was instinctively putting my hand in my pocket to produce my own, when I remembered that this was an election day. The words I had overheard bore no reference to Bartleby, but to the success or non-success of some candidate for the mayoralty. In my intent frame of mind, I had, as it were, imagined that all Broadway shared in my excitement, and were debating the same question with me. I passed on, very thankful that the uproar of the street screened my momentary absent-mindedness.

As I had intended, I was earlier than usual at my office door. I stood listening for a moment. All was still. He must be gone. I tried the knob. The door was locked. Yes, my procedure had worked to a charm; he indeed must be vanished. Yet a certain melancholy mixed with this: I was almost sorry for my brilliant success. I was fumbling under the door mat for the key, which Bartleby was to have left there for me, when accidentally my knee knocked against a panel, producing a summoning sound, and in response a voice came to me from within—"Not yet; I am occupied."

It was Bartleby.

I was thunderstruck. For an instant I stood like the man who, pipe in mouth, was killed one cloudless afternoon long ago in Virginia, by summer lightning; at his own warm open window he was killed, and remained leaning out there upon the dreamy afternoon, till some one touched him, when he fell.

"Not gone!" I murmured at last. But again obeying that wondrous ascendancy which the inscrutable scrivener had over me, and from which ascendancy, for all my chafing, I could not completely escape, I slowly went downstairs and out into the street, and while walking round the block, considered what I should next do in this unheard-of perplexity. Turn the man out by an actual thrusting I could not; to drive him away by calling him hard names would not do; calling in the police was an unpleasant idea; and yet, permit him to enjoy his cadaverous triumph over me—this, too, I could not think of. What was to be done? or, if nothing could be done, was there anything further that I could *assume* in the matter? Yes, as before I had prospectively assumed that Bartleby would depart, so now I might retrospectively assume that departed he was. In the legitimate carrying out of this assumption, I might enter my office in a great hurry, and pretending not to see Bartleby at all, walk straight against him as if he were air. Such a proceeding would in a singular degree have the appearance of a home-thrust. It was hardly possible that Bartleby could withstand such an application of the doctrine of assumptions. But upon second thoughts the success of the plan seemed rather dubious. I resolved to argue the matter over with him again.

"Bartleby," said I, entering the office, with a quietly severe expression, "I am seriously displeased. I am pained, Bartleby. I thought better of you. I had imagined you of such a gentlemanly organization, that in any delicate dilemma a slight hint would suffice—in short, an assumption. But it appears I am deceived. Why," I added, unaffectedly starting, "you have not even touched that money yet," pointing to it, just where I had left it the evening previous.

He answered nothing.

"Will you, or will you not, quit me?" I now demanded in a sudden passion, advancing close to him.

"I would prefer *not* to quit you," he replied, gently emphasizing the *not*.

"What earthly right have you to stay here? Do you pay any rent? Do you pay my taxes? Or is this property yours?"

He answered nothing.

"Are you ready to go on and write now? Are your eyes recovered? Could you copy a small paper for me this morning? or help examine a few lines? or step round to the post-office? In a word, will you do anything at all, to give a colouring to your refusal to depart the premises?"

He silently retired into his hermitage.

I was now in such a state of nervous resentment that I thought it but prudent to check myself at present from further demonstrations. Bartleby and I were alone. I remembered the tragedy of the unfortunate Adams and the still more unfortunate Colt in the solitary office of the latter; and how poor Colt, being dreadfully incensed by Adams, and imprudently permitting himself to get wildly excited, was at unawares hurried into his fatal act—an act which certainly no man could possibly deplore more than the actor himself. Often it had occurred to me in my ponderings upon the subject that had that altercation taken place in the public street, or at a private residence, it would not have terminated as it did. It was the circumstance of being alone in a solitary office, up stairs, of a building entirely unhallowed by humanizing domestic associations—an uncarpeted office, doubtless, of a dusty, haggard sort of appearance—

this it must have been, which greatly helped to enhance the irritable desperation of the hapless Colt.

But when this old Adam of resentment rose in me and tempted me concerning Bartleby, I grappled him and threw him. How? Why, simply by recalling the divine injunction: "A new commandment give I unto you, that ye love one another." Yes, this it was that saved me. Aside from higher considerations, charity often operates as a vastly wise and prudent principle—a great safeguard to its possessor. Men have committed murder for jealousy's sake, and anger's sake, and hatred's sake, and selfishness' sake, and spiritual pride's sake; but no man, that ever I heard of, ever committed a diabolical murder for sweet charity's sake. Mere self-interest, then, if no better motive can be enlisted, should, especially with high-tempered men, prompt all beings to charity and philanthropy. At any rate, upon the occasion in question, I strove to drown my exasperated feelings towards the scrivener by benevolently construing his conduct. Poor fellow, poor fellow! thought I, he don't mean anything; and besides, he has seen hard times, and ought to be indulged.

I endeavoured, also, immediately to occupy myself, and at the same time to comfort my despondency. I tried to fancy, that in the course of the morning, at such time as might prove agreeable to him, Bartleby, of his own free accord, would emerge from his hermitage and take up some decided line of march in the direction of the door. But no. Half-past twelve o'clock came; Turkey began to glow in the face, overturn his inkstand, and become generally obstreperous; Nippers abated down into quietude and courtesy; Ginger Nut munched his noon apple; and Bartleby remained standing at his window in one of his profoundest dead-wall reveries. Will it be credited? Ought I to acknowledge it? That afternoon I left the office without saying one further word to him.

Some days now passed, during which, at leisure intervals I looked a little into "Edwards on the Will," and "Priestly on Necessity." Under the circumstances, those books induced a salutary feeling. Gradually I slid into the persuasion that these troubles of mine, touching the scrivener, had been all predestinated from eternity, and Bartleby was billeted upon me for some mysterious purpose of an all-wise Providence, which it was not for a mere mortal like me to fathom. Yes, Bartleby, stay there behind your screen, thought I; I shall persecute you no more; you are harmless and noiseless as any of these old chairs; in short, I never feel so private as when I know you are here. At last I see it, I feel it; I penetrate to the predestinated purpose of my life. I am content. Others may have loftier parts to enact; but my mission in this world, Bartleby, is to furnish you with office-room for such period as you may see fit to remain.

I believe that this wise and blessed frame of mind would have continued with me, had it not been for the unsolicited and uncharitable remarks obtruded upon me by my professional friends who visited the rooms. But thus it often is, that the constant friction of illiberal minds wears out at last the best resolves of the more generous. Though to be sure, when I reflected upon it, it was not strange that people entering my office should be struck by the peculiar aspect of the unaccountable Bartleby, and so be tempted to throw out some sinister observations concerning him. Sometimes an attorney, having business with me, and calling at my office, and finding no one but the scrivener there, would undertake to obtain some sort of precise information from him touching my whereabouts; but without heeding his idle talk, Bartleby would remain standing immovable in the middle of the room. So after contemplating him in that position for a time, the attorney would depart, no wiser than he came.

Also, when a reference was going on, and the room full of lawyers and witnesses, and business driving fast, some deeply-occupied legal gentleman present, seeing Bartleby wholly unemployed, would request him to run round to his (the legal gentleman's) office and fetch some papers for him. Thereupon, Bartleby would tranquilly decline, and yet remain idle as before. Then the lawyer would give a great stare, and turn to me. And what could I say? At last I was made aware that all through the circle of my professional acquaintance, a whisper of wonder was running round, having reference to the strange creature I kept at my office. This worried me very much. And as the idea came upon me of his possibly turning out a long-lived man, and keep occupying my chambers, and denying my authority; and perplexing my visitors; and scandalizing my professional reputation; and casting a general gloom over the premises; keeping soul and body together to the last upon his savings (for doubtless he spent but half a dime a day), and in the end perhaps outlive me, and claim possession of my office by right of his perpetual occupancy: as all these dark anticipations crowded upon me more and more, and my friends continually intruded their relentless remarks upon the apparition in my room; a great change was wrought in me. I resolved to gather all my faculties together, and forever rid me of this intolerable incubus.

Ere resolving any complicated project, however, adapted to this end, I first simply suggested to Bartleby the propriety of his permanent departure. In a calm and serious tone, I commended the idea to his careful and mature consideration. But, having taken three days to meditate upon it, he apprised me, that his original determination remained the same; in short, that he still preferred to abide with me.

What shall I do? I now said to myself, buttoning up my coat to the last button. What shall I do? what ought I to do? what does conscience say I *should* do with this man, or, rather, ghost? Rid myself of him, I must; go, he shall. But how? You will not thrust him, the poor, pale, passive mortal—you will not thrust such a helpless creature out of your door? you will not dishonour yourself by such cruelty? No, I will not, I cannot do that. Rather would I let him live and die here, and then mason up his remains in the wall. What, then, will you do? For all your coaxing, he will not budge. Bribes he leaves under your own paper-weight on your table; in short, it is quite plain that he prefers to cling to you.

Then something severe, something unusual must be done. What! surely you

will not have him collared by a constable, and commit his innocent pallor to
the common jail? And upon what ground could you procure such a thing to be
done?—a vagrant, is he? What! he a vagrant, a wanderer, who refuses to
budge? It is because he will *not* be a vagrant, then, that you seek to count him
as a vagrant. That is too absurd. No visible means of support: there I have him.
Wrong again: for indubitably he *does* support himself, and that is the only
unanswerable proof that any man can show of his possessing the means so to
do. No more, then. Since he will not quit me, I must quit him. I will change
my offices; I will move elsewhere, and give him fair notice, that if I find him on
my new premises I will then proceed against him as a common trespasser.

Acting accordingly, next day I thus addressed him: "I find these chambers
too far from the City Hall; the air is unwholesome. In a word, I propose to
remove my offices next week, and shall no longer require your services. I tell you
this now, in order that you may seek another place."

He made no reply, and nothing more was said.

On the appointed day I engaged carts and men, proceeded to my chambers,
and, having but little furniture, everything was removed in a few hours.
Throughout, the scrivener remained standing behind the screen, which I
directed to be removed the last thing. It was withdrawn; and, being folded up
like a huge folio, left him the motionless occupant of a naked room. I stood in
the entry watching him a moment, while something from within me upbraided
me.

I re-entered, with my hand in my pocket—and—and my heart in my
mouth.

"Good-bye, Bartleby; I am going—good-bye, and God some way bless you;
and take that," slipping something in his hand. But it dropped upon the floor,
and then—strange to say—I tore myself from him whom I had so longed to be
rid of.

Established in my new quarters, for a day or two I kept the door locked,
and started at every footfall in the passages. When I returned to my rooms,
after any little absence, I would pause at the threshold for an instant, and
attentively listen, ere applying my key. But these fears were needless. Bartleby
never came nigh me.

I thought all was going well, when a perturbed-looking stranger visited me,
inquiring whether I was the person who had recently occupied rooms at
No. — Wall Street.

Full of forebodings, I replied that I was.

"Then, sir," said the stranger, who proved a lawyer, "you are responsible for
the man you left there. He refuses to do any copying; he refuses to do anything;
he says he prefers not to; and he refuses to quit the premises."

"I am very sorry, sir," said I, with assumed tranquillity, but an inward
tremor, "but, really, the man you allude to is nothing to me—he is no relation
or apprentice of mine, that you should hold me responsible for him."

"In mercy's name, who is he?"

"I certainly cannot inform you. I know nothing about him. Formerly I employed him as a copyist; but he has done nothing for me now for some time past."

"I shall settle him, then—good morning, sir."

Several days passed, and I heard nothing more; and, though I often felt charitable promptings to call at the place and see poor Bartleby, yet a certain squeamishness, of I know not what, withheld me.

All is over with him, by this time, thought I, at last, when, through another week, no further intelligence reached me. But, coming to my room the day after, I found several persons waiting at my door in a high state of nervous excitement.

"That's the man—here he comes," cried the foremost one, whom I recognized as the lawyer who had previously called upon me alone.

"You must take him away, sir, at once," cried a portly person among them, advancing upon me, and whom I knew to be the landlord of No. — Wall Street. "These gentlemen, my tenants, cannot stand it any longer; Mr. B——," pointing to the lawyer, "has turned him out of his room, and he now persists in haunting the building generally, sitting upon the banisters of the stairs by day, and sleeping in the entry by night. Everybody is concerned; clients are leaving the offices; some fears are entertained of a mob; something you must do, and that without delay."

Aghast at this torrent, I fell back before it, and would fain have locked myself in my new quarters. In vain I persisted that Bartleby was nothing to me—no more than to any one else. In vain—I was the last person known to have anything to do with him, and they held me to the terrible account. Fearful, then, of being exposed in the papers (as one person present obscurely threatened), I considered the matter, and, at length, said, that if the lawyer would give me a confidential interview with the scrivener, in his (the lawyer's) own room, I would, that afternoon, strive my best to rid them of the nuisance they complained of.

Going up stairs to my old haunt, there was Bartleby silently sitting upon the banister at the landing.

"What are you doing here, Bartleby?" said I.

"Sitting upon the banister," he mildly replied.

I motioned him into the lawyer's room, who then left us.

"Bartleby," said I, "are you aware that you are the cause of great tribulation to me, by persisting in occupying the entry after being dismissed from the office?"

No answer.

"Now one of two things must take place. Either you must do something, or something must be done to you. Now what sort of business would you like to engage in? Would you like to re-engage in copying for some one?"

"No; I would prefer not to make any change."

"Would you like a clerkship in a dry-goods store?"

"There is too much confinement about that. No, I would not like a clerk-ship; but I am not particular."

"Too much confinement," I cried, "why, you keep yourself confined all the time!"

"I would prefer not to take a clerkship," he rejoined, as if to settle that little item at once.

"How would a bar-tender's business suit you? There is no trying of the eye-sight in that."

"I would not like it at all; though, as I said before, I am not particular."

His unwonted wordiness inspirited me. I returned to the charge.

"Well, then, would you like to travel through the country collecting bills for the merchants? That would improve your health."

"No, I would prefer to be doing something else."

"How, then, would going as a companion to Europe, to entertain some young gentleman with your conversation—how would that suit you?"

"Not at all. It does not strike me that there is anything definite about that. I like to be stationary. But I am not particular."

"Stationary you shall be, then," I cried, now losing all patience, and, for the first time in all my exasperating connection with him, fairly flying into a passion. "If you do not go away from these premises before night, I shall feel bound—indeed, I *am* bound—to—to—to quit the premises myself!" I rather absurdly concluded, knowing not with what possible threat to try to frighten his immobility into compliance. Despairing of all further efforts, I was precipitately leaving him, when a final thought occurred to me—one which had not been wholly unindulged before.

"Bartleby," said I, in the kindest tone I could assume under such exciting circumstances, "will you go home with me now—not to my office, but my dwelling—and remain there till we can conclude upon some convenient arrangement for you at our leisure? Come, let us start now, right away."

"No: at present I would prefer not to make any change at all."

I answered nothing; but, effectually dodging every one by the suddenness and rapidity of my flight, rushed from the building, ran up Wall Street towards Broadway, and, jumping into the first omnibus, was soon removed from pursuit. As soon as tranquillity returned, I distinctly perceived that I had now done all that I possibly could, both in respect to the demands of the landlord and his tenants, and with regard to my own desire and sense of duty, to benefit Bartleby, and shield him from rude persecution. I now strove to be entirely care-free and quiescent; and my conscience justified me in the attempt; though, indeed, it was not so successful as I could have wished. So fearful was I of being again hunted out by the incensed landlord and his exasperated tenants, that, surrendering my business to Nippers, for a few days, I drove about the upper part of the town and through the suburbs, in my rockaway; crossed over to Jersey City and Hoboken, and paid fugitive visits to Manhattanville and Astoria. In fact, I almost lived in my rockaway for the time.

When again I entered my office, lo, a note from the landlord lay upon the desk. I opened it with trembling hands. It informed me that the writer had sent to the police, and had Bartleby removed to the Tombs as a vagrant. Moreover, since I knew more about him than any one else, he wished me to appear at that place, and make a suitable statement of the facts. These tidings had a conflicting effect upon me. At first I was indignant; but, at last, almost approved. The landlord's energetic, summary disposition, had led him to adopt a procedure which I do not think I would have decided upon myself; and yet, as a last resort, under such peculiar circumstances, it seemed the only plan.

As I afterwards learned, the poor scrivener, when told that he must be conducted to the Tombs, offered not the slightest obstacle, but, in his pale, unmoving way, silently acquiesced.

Some of the compassionate and curious by-standers joined the party; and headed by one of the constables arm-in-arm with Bartleby, the silent procession filed its way through all the noise, and heat, and joy of the roaring thorough-fares at noon.

The same day I received the note, I went to the Tombs, or, to speak more properly, the Halls of Justice. Seeking the right officer, I stated the purpose of my call, and was informed that the individual I described was, indeed, within. I then assured the functionary that Bartleby was a perfectly honest man, and greatly to be compassioned, however unaccountably eccentric. I narrated all I knew, and closed by suggesting the idea of letting him remain in as indulgent confinement as possible, till something less harsh might be done—though, indeed, I hardly knew what. At all events, if nothing else could be decided upon, the almshouse must receive him. I then begged to have an interview.

Being under no disgraceful charge, and quite serene and harmless in all his ways, they had permitted him freely to wander about the prison, and, especially, in the inclosed grass-platted yards thereof. And so I found him there, standing all alone in the quietest of the yards, his face towards a high wall, while all around, from the narrow slits of the jail windows, I thought I saw peering out upon him the eyes of murderers and thieves.

"Bartleby!"

"I know you," he said, without looking round—"and I want nothing to say to you."

"It was not I that brought you here, Bartleby," said I, keenly pained at his implied suspicion. "And to you, this should not be so vile a place. Nothing reproachful attaches to you by being here. And see, it is not so sad a place as one might think. Look, there is the sky, and here is the grass."

"I know where I am," he replied, but would say nothing more, and so I left him.

As I entered the corridor again, a broad meat-like man, in an apron, accosted me, and, jerking his thumb over his shoulder, said—"Is that your friend?"

"Yes."

"Does he want to starve? If he does, let him live on the prison fare, that's all."

"Who are you?" asked I, not knowing what to make of such an unofficially speaking person in such a place.

"I am the grub-man. Such gentlemen as have friends here, hire me to provide them with something good to eat."

"Is this so?" said I, turning to the turnkey.

He said it was.

"Well, then," said I, slipping some silver into the grub-man's hands (for so they called him), "I want you to give particular attention to my friend there; let him have the best dinner you can get. And you must be as polite to him as possible."

"Introduce me, will you?" said the grub-man, looking at me with an expression which seemed to say he was all impatience for an opportunity to give a specimen of his breeding.

Thinking it would prove of benefit to the scrivener, I acquiesced; and, asking the grub-man his name went up with him to Bartleby.

"Bartleby, this is a friend; you will find him very useful to you."

"Your sarvant, sir, your sarvant," said the grub-man, making a low salutation behind his apron. "Hope you find it pleasant here, sir; nice grounds—cool apartments—hope you'll stay with us some time—try to make it agreeable. What will you have for dinner to-day?"

"I prefer not to dine to-day," said Bartleby, turning away. "It would disagree with me; I am unused to dinners." So saying, he slowly moved to the other side of the inclosure, and took up a position fronting the dead-wall.

"How's this?" said the grub-man, addressing me with a stare of astonishment. "He's odd, ain't he?"

"I think he is a little deranged," said I, sadly.

"Deranged? deranged is it? Well, now, upon my word, I thought that friend of yourn was a gentleman forger; they are always pale and genteel-like, them forgers. I can't help pity 'em—can't help it, sir. Did you know Monroe Edwards?" he added, touchingly, and paused. Then, laying his hand piteously on my shoulder, sighed, "He died of consumption at Sing-Sing. So you weren't acquainted with Monroe?"

"No, I was never socially acquainted with any forgers. But I cannot stop longer. Look to my friend yonder. You will not lose by it. I will see you again."

Some few days after this, I again obtained admission to the Tombs, and went through the corridors in quest of Bartleby; but without finding him.

"I saw him coming from his cell not long ago," said a turnkey, "may be he's gone to loiter in the yards."

So I went in that direction.

"Are you looking for the silent man?" said another turnkey, passing me. "Yonder he lies—sleeping in the yard there. 'Tis not twenty minutes since I saw him lie down."

The yard was entirely quiet. It was not accessible to the common prisoners. The surrounding walls, of amazing thickness, kept off all sounds behind them. The Egyptian character of the masonry weighed upon me with its gloom. But a soft imprisoned turf grew under foot. The heart of the eternal pyramids, it seemed, wherein, by some strange magic, through the clefts, grass-seed, dropped by birds, had sprung.

Strangely huddled at the base of the wall, his knees drawn up, and lying on his side, his head touching the cold stones, I saw the wasted Bartleby. But nothing stirred. I paused; then went close up to him; stooped over, and saw that his dim eyes were open; otherwise he seemed profoundly sleeping. Something prompted me to touch him. I felt his hand, when a tingling shiver ran up my arm and down my spine to my feet.

The round face of the grub-man peered upon me now. "His dinner is ready. Won't he dine to-day, either? Or does he live without dining?"

"Lives without dining," said I, and closed the eyes.

"Eh!—He's asleep, ain't he?"

"With kings and counsellors," murmured I.

There would seem little need for proceeding further in this history. Imagination will readily supply the meagre recital of poor Bartleby's interment. But, ere parting with the reader, let me say, that if this little narrative has sufficiently interested him, to awaken curiosity as to who Bartleby was, and what manner of life he led prior to the present narrator's making his acquaintance, I can only reply, that in such curiosity I fully share, but am wholly unable to gratify it. Yet here I hardly know whether I should divulge one little item of rumour, which came to my ear a few months after the scrivener's decease. Upon what basis it rested, I could never ascertain; and hence, how true it is I cannot now tell. But, inasmuch as this vague report has not been without a certain suggestive interest to me, however sad, it may prove the same with some others; and so I will briefly mention it. The report was this: that Bartleby had been a subordinate clerk in the Dead Letter Office at Washington, from which he had been suddenly removed by a change in the administration. When I think over this rumour, hardly can I express the emotions which seize me. Dead letters! does it not sound like dead men? Conceive a man by nature and misfortune prone to a pallid hopelessness, can any business seem more fitted to heighten it than that of continually handling these dead letters, and assorting them for the flames? For by the cart-load they are annually burned. Sometimes from out the folded paper the pale clerk takes a ring—the finger it was meant for, perhaps, moulders in the grave; a bank-note sent in swiftest charity—he whom it would relieve, nor eats nor hungers any more; pardon for those who died despairing; hope for those who died unhoping; good tidings for those who died stifled by unrelieved calamities. On errands of life, these letters speed to death.

Ah, Bartleby! Ah, humanity!

GUY DE MAUPASSANT

❧ *La Mère Sauvage*

I HAD not been at Virelogne for fifteen years. I went back there in the autumn, to shoot with my friend Serval, who had at last rebuilt his château, which had been destroyed by the Prussians.

I loved that district very much. It is one of those corners of the world which have a sensuous charm for the eyes. You love it with a bodily love. We, whom the country seduces, we keep tender memories for certain springs, for certain woods, for certain pools, for certain hills, seen very often, and which have stirred us like joyful events. Sometimes our thoughts turn back towards a corner in a forest, or the end of a bank, or an orchard powdered with flowers, seen but a single time, on some gay day; yet remaining in our hearts like the images of certain women met in the street on a spring morning, with bright transparent dresses; and leaving in soul and body an unappeased desire which is not to be forgotten, a feeling that you have just rubbed elbows with happiness.

At Virelogne I loved the whole countryside, dotted with little woods, and crossed by brooks which flashed in the sun and looked like veins, carrying blood to the earth. You fished in them for crawfish, trout, and eels! Divine happiness! You could bathe in places, and you often found snipe among the high grass which grew along the borders of these slender watercourses.

I was walking, lightly as a goat, watching my two dogs ranging before me. Serval, a hundred metres to my right, was beating a field of lucern. I turned the thicket which forms the boundary of the wood of Sandres, and I saw a cottage in ruins.

All of a sudden, I remembered it as I had seen it the last time, in 1869, neat, covered with vines, with chickens before the door. What is sadder than a dead house, with its skeleton standing upright, bare and sinister?

I also remembered that in it, one very tiring day, the good woman had given me a glass of wine to drink, and that Serval had then told me the history of its inhabitants. The father, an old poacher, had been killed by the gendarmes. The son, whom I had once seen, was a tall, dry fellow who also passed for a ferocious destroyer of game. People called them *"les Sauvages."*

Was that a name or a nickname?

I hailed Serval. He came up with his long strides like a crane.

I asked him:

Translated by Jonathan Sturges.

"What's become of those people?"

And he told me this story:

When war was declared, the son Sauvage, who was then thirty-three years old, enlisted, leaving his mother alone in the house. People did not pity the old woman very much because she had money; they knew it.

But she remained quite alone in that isolated dwelling so far from the village, on the edge of the wood. She was not afraid, however, being of the same strain as her menfolk; a hardy old woman, tall and thin, who laughed seldom, and with whom one never jested. The women of the fields laugh but little in any case; that is men's business, that! But they themselves have sad and narrowed hearts, leading a melancholy, gloomy life. The peasants learn a little boisterous merriment at the tavern, but their helpmates remain grave, with countenances which are always severe. The muscles of their faces have never learned the movements of the laugh.

La Mère Sauvage continued her ordinary existence in her cottage, which was soon covered by the snows. She came to the village once a week, to get bread and a little meat; then she returned into her house. As there was talk of wolves, she went out with a gun upon her back—her son's gun, rusty, and with the butt worn by the rubbing of the hand; and she was strange to see, the tall "*Sauvage*," a little bent, going with slow strides over the snow, the muzzle of the piece extending beyond the black head-dress, which pressed close to her head and imprisoned her white hair, which no one had ever seen.

One day a Prussian force arrived. It was billeted upon the inhabitants, according to the property and resources of each. Four were allotted to the old woman, who was known to be rich.

They were four great boys with blond skin, with blond beards, with blue eyes, who had remained stout notwithstanding the fatigues which they had endured already, and who also, though in a conquered country, had remained kind and gentle. Alone with this aged woman, they showed themselves full of consideration, sparing her, as much as they could, all expenses and fatigue. They would be seen, all four of them, making their toilet round the well, of a morning, in their shirt-sleeves, splashing with great swishes of water, under the crude daylight of the snowy weather, their pink-white Northman's flesh, while *La Mère Sauvage* went and came, making ready the soup. Then they would be seen cleaning the kitchen, rubbing the tiles, splitting wood, peeling potatoes, doing up all the housework, like four good sons about their mother.

But the old woman thought always of her own, so tall and thin, with his hooked nose and his brown eyes and his heavy mustache which made a roll of black hairs upon his lip. She asked each day of each of the soldiers who were installed beside her hearth:

"Do you know where the French Marching Regiment No. 23 was sent? My boy is in it."

They answered, "No, not know, not know at all." And, understanding her pain and her uneasiness (they, who had mothers too, there at home), they rendered her a thousand little services. She loved them well, moreover, her four enemies, since the peasantry feels no patriotic hatred; that belongs to the upper class alone. The humble, those who pay the most, because they are poor, and because every new burden crushes them down; those who are killed in masses, who make the true cannon's-meat, because they are so many; those, in fine, who suffer most cruelly the atrocious miseries of war, because they are the feeblest, and offer least resistance—they hardly understand at all those bellicose ardors, that excitable sense of honor, or those pretended political combinations which in six months exhaust two nations, the conqueror with the conquered.

They said on the country-side, in speaking of the Germans of *La Mère Sauvage*:

"There are four who have found a soft place."

Now, one morning, when the old woman was alone in the house, she perceived far off on the plain a man coming towards her dwelling. Soon she recognized him; it was the postman charged to distribute the letters. He gave her a folded paper, and she drew out of her case the spectacles which she used for sewing; then she read:

"MADAME SAUVAGE,—The present letter is to tell you sad news. Your boy Victor was killed yesterday by a shell which near cut him in two. I was just by, seeing that we stood next each other in the company, and he would talk to me about you to let you know on the same day if anything happened to him.

"I took his watch, which was in his pocket, to bring it back to you when the war is done.

"I salute you very friendly.
"Césaire Rivot,
"Soldier of the 2d class, March. Reg. No. 23."

The letter was dated three weeks back.

She did not cry at all. She remained motionless, so seized and stupefied that she did not even suffer as yet. She thought: "V'la [*voilà*] Victor who is killed now." Then little by little the tears mounted to her eyes, and the sorrow caught her heart. The ideas came to her, one by one, dreadful, torturing. She would never kiss him again, her child, her big boy, never again! The gendarmes had killed the father, the Prussians had killed the son. He had been cut in two by a cannon-ball. She seemed to see the thing, the horrible thing: the head falling, the eyes open, while he chewed the corner of his big mustache as he always did in moments of anger.

What had they done with his body afterwards? If they had only let her have her boy back as they had given her back her husband—with the bullet in the middle of his forehead!

But she heard a noise of voices. It was the Prussians returning from the village. She hid her letter very quickly in her pocket, and she received them quietly, with her ordinary face, having had time to wipe her eyes.

They were laughing, all four, delighted, since they brought with them a fine rabbit—stolen, doubtless—and they made signs to the old woman that there was to be something good to eat.

She set herself to work at once to prepare breakfast; but when it came to killing the rabbit, her heart failed her. And yet it was not the first. One of the soldiers struck it down with a blow of his fist behind the ears.

The beast once dead, she separated the red body from the skin; but the sight of the blood which she was touching, and which covered her hands, of the warm blood which she felt cooling and coagulating, made her tremble from head to foot; and she kept seeing her big boy cut in two, and quite red also, like this still palpitating animal.

She set herself at table with the Prussians, but she could not eat, not even a mouthful. They devoured the rabbit without troubling themselves about her. She looked at them askance, without speaking, ripening a thought, and with a face so impassible that they perceived nothing.

All of a sudden, she said: "I don't even know your names, and here's a whole month that we've been together." They understood, not without difficulty, what she wanted, and told their names. That was not sufficient; she had them written for her on a paper, with the addresses of their families, and, resting her spectacles on her great nose, she considered that strange handwriting, then folded the sheet and put it in her pocket, on top of the letter which told her of the death of her son.

When the meal was ended, she said to the men:

"I am going to work for you."

And she began to carry up hay into the loft where they slept.

They were astonished at her taking all this trouble; she explained to them that thus they would not be so cold; and they helped her. They heaped the trusses of hay as high as the straw roof; and in that manner they made a sort of great chamber with four walls of fodder, warm and perfumed, where they should sleep splendidly.

At dinner, one of them was worried to see that *La Mère Sauvage* still ate nothing. She told him that she had the cramps. Then she kindled a good fire to warm herself up, and the four Germans mounted to their lodging-place by the ladder which served them every night for this purpose.

As soon as they closed the trap, the old woman removed the ladder, then opened the outside door noiselessly, and went back to look for more bundles of straw, with which she filled her kitchen. She went barefoot in the snow, so softly that no sound was heard. From time to time she listened to the sonorous and unequal snorings of the four soldiers who were fast asleep.

When she judged her preparations to be sufficient, she threw one of the bundles into the fireplace, and when it was alight she scattered it over all the others. Then she went outside again and looked.

In a few seconds the whole interior of the cottage was illumined with a violent brightness and became a dreadful brasier, a gigantic fiery furnace, whose brilliance spouted out of the narrow window and threw a glittering beam upon the snow.

Then a great cry issued from the summit of the house; it was a clamor of human shriekings, heart-rending calls of anguish and of fear. At last, the trap having fallen in, a whirlwind of fire shot up into the loft, pierced the straw roof, rose to the sky like the immense flame of a torch; and all the cottage flared.

Nothing more was heard therein but the crackling of the fire, the crackling sound of the walls, the falling of the rafters. All of a sudden the roof fell in, and the burning carcass of the dwelling hurled a great plume of sparks into the air, amid a cloud of smoke.

The country, all white, lit up by the fire, shone like a cloth of silver tinted with red.

A bell, far off, began to toll.

The old *"Sauvage"* remained standing before her ruined dwelling, armed with her gun, her son's gun, for fear lest one of those men might escape.

When she saw that it was ended, she threw her weapon into the brasier. A loud report rang back.

People were coming, the peasants, the Prussians.

They found the woman seated on the trunk of a tree, calm and satisfied.

A German officer, who spoke French like a son of France, demanded of her:

"Where are your soldiers?"

She extended her thin arm towards the red heap of fire which was gradually going out, and she answered with a strong voice:

"There!"

They crowded around her. The Prussian asked:

"How did it take fire?"

She said:

"It was I who set it on fire."

They did not believe her, they thought that the sudden disaster had made her crazy. So, while all pressed round and listened, she told the thing from one end to the other, from the arrival of the letter to the last cry of the men who were burned with her house. She did not forget a detail of all which she had felt, nor of all which she had done.

When she had finished, she drew two pieces of paper from her pocket, and, to distinguish them by the last glimmers of the fire, she again adjusted her spectacles; then she said, showing one: "That, that is the death of Victor." Showing the other, she added, indicating the red ruins with a bend of the head: "That, that is their names, so that you can write home." She calmly held the white sheet out to the officer, who held her by the shoulders, and she continued:

"You must write how it happened, and you must say to their mothers that it was I who did that, Victoire Simon, *la Sauvage*! Do not forget."

The officer shouted some orders in German. They seized her, they threw her against the walls of her house, still hot. Then twelve men drew quickly up before her, at twenty paces. She did not move. She had understood; she waited.

An order rang out, followed instantly by a long report. A belated shot went off by itself, after the others.

The old woman did not fall. She sank as though they had mowed off her legs.

The Prussian officer approached. She was almost cut in two, and in her withered hand she held her letter bathed with blood.

My friend Serval added:

"It was by way of reprisal that the Germans destroyed the château of the district, which belonged to me."

As for me, I thought of the mothers of those four gentle fellows burned in that house; and of the atrocious heroism of that other mother shot against the wall.

And I picked up a little stone, still blackened by the flames.

JOSEPH CONRAD

❧ *The Lagoon*

THE white man, leaning with both arms over the roof of the little house in the stern of the boat, said to the steersman—

"We will pass the night in Arsat's clearing. It is late."

The Malay only grunted, and went on looking fixedly at the river. The white man rested his chin on his crossed arms and gazed at the wake of the boat. At the end of the straight avenue of forests cut by the intense glitter of the river, the sun appeared unclouded and dazzling, poised low over the water that shone smoothly like a band of metal. The forests, sombre and dull, stood motionless and silent on each side of the broad stream. At the foot of big, towering trees, trunkless nipa palms rose from the mud of the bank, in bunches of leaves enormous and heavy, that hung unstirring over the brown swirl of eddies. In the stillness of the air every tree, every leaf, every bough, every tendril of creeper and every petal of minute blossoms seemed to have been bewitched into an immobility perfect and final. Nothing moved on the river but the eight paddles that rose flashing regularly, dipped together with a single splash; while the steersman swept right and left with a periodic and sudden flourish of his blade describing a glinting semicircle above his head. The churned-up water frothed alongside with a confused murmur. And the white man's canoe, advancing upstream in the short-lived disturbance of its own making, seemed to enter the portals of a land from which the very memory of motion had forever departed.

The white man, turning his back upon the setting sun, looked along the empty and broad expanse of the sea-reach. For the last three miles of its course the wandering, hesitating river, as if enticed irresistibly by the freedom of an open horizon, flows straight into the sea, flows straight to the east—to the east that harbours both light and darkness. Astern of the boat the repeated call of some bird, a cry discordant and feeble, skipped along over the smooth water and lost itself, before it could reach the other shore, in the breathless silence of the world.

The steersman dug his paddle into the stream, and held hard with stiffened arms, his body thrown forward. The water gurgled aloud; and suddenly the long straight reach seemed to pivot on its centre, the forests swung in a semicircle, and the slanting beams of sunset touched the broadside of the canoe with a fiery glow, throwing the slender and distorted shadows of its crew upon the streaked glitter of the river. The white man turned to look ahead. The course of the boat had been altered at right-angles to the stream, and the carved dragon-head of its prow was pointing now at a gap in the fringing bushes of the bank. It glided through, brushing the overhanging twigs, and disappeared from the river like some slim and amphibious creature leaving the water for its lair in the forests.

The narrow creek was like a ditch: tortuous, fabulously deep; filled with gloom under the thin strip of pure and shining blue of the heaven. Immense trees soared up, invisible behind the festooned draperies of creepers. Here and there, near the glistening blackness of the water, a twisted root of some tall tree showed amongst the tracery of small ferns, black and dull, writhing and motionless, like an arrested snake. The short words of the paddlers reverberated loudly between the thick and sombre walls of vegetation. Darkness oozed out from between the trees, through the tangled maze of the creepers, from behind the great fantastic and unstirring leaves; the darkness, mysterious and invincible; the darkness scented and poisonous of impenetrable forests.

The men poled in the shoaling water. The creek broadened, opening out into a wide sweep of a stagnant lagoon. The forests receded from the marshy bank, leaving a level strip of bright green, reedy grass to frame the reflected blueness of the sky. A fleecy pink cloud drifted high above, trailing the delicate colouring of its image under the floating leaves and the silvery blossoms of the lotus. A little house, perched on high piles, appeared black in the distance. Near it, two tall nibong palms, that seemed to have come out of the forests in the background, leaned slightly over the ragged roof, with a suggestion of sad tenderness and care in the droop of their leafy and soaring heads.

The steersman, pointing with his paddle, said, "Arsat is there. I see his canoe fast between the piles."

The polers ran along the sides of the boat glancing over their shoulders at the end of the day's journey. They would have preferred to spend the night somewhere else than on this lagoon of weird aspect and ghostly reputation. Moreover, they disliked Arsat, first as a stranger, and also because he who repairs a ruined house, and dwells in it, proclaims that he is not afraid to live amongst the spirits that haunt the places abandoned by mankind. Such a man can disturb the course of fate by glances or words; while his familiar ghosts are not easy to propitiate by casual wayfarers upon whom they long to wreak the malice of their human master. White men care not for such things, being unbelievers and in league with the Father of Evil, who leads them unharmed through the invisible dangers of this world. To the warnings of the righteous they oppose an offensive pretence of disbelief. What is there to be done?

So they thought, throwing their weight on the end of their long poles. The big canoe glided on swiftly, noiselessly, and smoothly, towards Arsat's clearing, till, in a great rattling of poles thrown down and the loud murmurs of "Allah be praised!" it came with a gentle knock against the crooked piles below the house.

The boatmen with uplifted faces shouted discordantly, "Arsat! O Arsat!" Nobody came. The white man began to climb the rude ladder giving access to the bamboo platform before the house. The juragan [steersman] of the boat said sulkily, "We will cook in the sampan, and sleep on the water."

"Pass my blankets and the basket," said the white man, curtly.

He knelt on the edge of the platform to receive the bundle. Then the boat shoved off, and the white man, standing up, confronted Arsat, who had come out through the low door of his hut. He was a man young, powerful, with broad chest and muscular arms. He had nothing on but his sarong. His head was bare. His big, soft eyes stared eagerly at the white man, but his voice and demeanour were composed as he asked, without any words of greeting—

"Have you medicine, Tuan [Sir]?"

"No," said the visitor in a startled tone. "No. Why? Is there sickness in the house?"

"Enter and see," replied Arsat, in the same calm manner, and turning short round, passed again through the small doorway. The white man, dropping his bundles, followed.

In the dim light of the dwelling he made out on a couch of bamboos a woman stretched on her back under a broad sheet of red cotton cloth. She lay still, as if dead; but her big eyes, wide open, glittered in the gloom, staring upwards at the slender rafters, motionless and unseeing. She was in a high fever, and evidently unconscious. Her cheeks were sunk slightly, her lips were partly open, and on the young face there was the ominous and fixed expression—the absorbed, contemplating expression of the unconscious who are going to die. The two men stood looking down at her in silence.

"Has she been long ill?" asked the traveller.

"I have not slept for five nights," answered the Malay, in a deliberate tone. "At first she heard voices calling her from the water and struggled against me who held her. But since the sun of to-day rose she hears nothing—she hears not me. She sees nothing. She sees not me—me!"

He remained silent for a minute, then asked softly—

"Tuan, will she die?"

"I fear so," said the white man, sorrowfully. He had known Arsat years ago, in a far country in times of trouble and danger, when no friendship is to be despised. And since his Malay friend had come unexpectedly to dwell in the hut on the lagoon with a strange woman, he had slept many times there, in his journeys up and down the river. He liked the man who knew how to keep faith in council and how to fight without fear by the side of his white friend. He liked him—not so much perhaps as a man likes his favourite dog—but still he liked him well enough to help and ask no questions, to think sometimes vaguely and hazily in the midst of his own pursuits, about the lonely man and the long-haired woman with audacious face and triumphant eyes, who lived together hidden by the forests—alone and feared.

The white man came out of a hut in time to see the enormous conflagration of sunset put out by the swift and stealthy shadows that, rising like a black and impalpable vapour above the tree-tops, spread over the heaven, extinguishing the crimson glow of floating clouds and the red brilliance of departing daylight. In a few moments all the stars came out above the intense blackness of the earth and the great lagoon gleaming suddenly with reflected lights resembled an oval patch of night sky flung down into the hopeless and abysmal night of the wilderness. The white man had some supper out of the basket, then collecting a few sticks that lay about the platform, made up a small fire, not for warmth, but for the sake of the smoke, which would keep off the mosquitos. He wrapped himself in the blankets and sat with his back against the reed wall of the house, smoking thoughtfully.

Arsat came through the doorway with noiseless steps and squatted down by the fire. The white man moved his outstretched legs a little.

"She breathes," said Arsat in a low voice, anticipating the expected question. "She breathes and burns as if with a great fire. She speaks not; she hears not—and burns!"

He paused for a moment, then asked in a quiet, incurious tone—

"Tuan . . . will she die?"

The white man moved his shoulders uneasily and muttered in a hesitating manner—

"If such is her fate."

"No, Tuan," said Arsat, calmly. "If such is my fate. I hear, I see, I wait. I remember . . . Tuan, do you remember the old days? Do you remember my brother?"

"Yes," said the white man. The Malay rose suddenly and went in. The other, sitting still outside, could hear the voice in the hut. Arsat said: "Hear me! Speak!" His words were succeeded by a complete silence. "O Diamelen!" he cried, suddenly. After that cry there was a deep sigh. Arsat came out and sank down again in his old place.

They sat in silence before the fire. There was no sound within the house, there was no sound near them; but far away on the lagoon they could hear the voices of the boatmen ringing fitful and distinct on the calm water. The fire in the bows of the sampan shone faintly in the distance with a hazy red glow. Then it died out. The voices ceased. The land and the water slept invisible, unstirring and mute. It was as though there had been nothing left in the world but the glitter of stars streaming, ceaseless and vain, through the black stillness of the night.

The white man gazed straight before him into the darkness with wide-open eyes. The fear and fascination, the inspiration and the wonder of death—of death near, unavoidable, and unseen, soothed the unrest of his race and stirred the most indistinct, the most intimate of his thoughts. The ever-ready suspicion of evil, the gnawing suspicion that lurks in our hearts, flowed out into the stillness around him—into the stillness profound and dumb, and made it appear untrustworthy and infamous, like the placid and impenetrable mask of an unjustifiable violence. In that fleeting and powerful disturbance of his being the earth enfolded, in the starlight peace became a shadowy country of inhuman strife, a battlefield of phantoms terrible and charming, august or ignoble, struggling ardently for the possession of our helpless hearts. An unquiet and mysterious country of inextinguishable desires and fears.

A plaintive murmur rose in the night; a murmur saddening and startling, as if the great solitudes of surrounding woods had tried to whisper into his ear the wisdom of their immense and lofty indifference. Sounds hesitating and vague floated in the air round him, shaped themselves slowly into words; and at last flowed on gently in a murmuring stream of soft and monotonous sentences. He stirred like a man waking up and changed his position slightly. Arsat, motionless and shadowy, sitting with bowed head under the stars, was speaking in a low and dreamy tone—

". . . for where can we lay down the heaviness of our trouble but in a friend's heart? A man must speak of war and of love. You, Tuan, know what war is, and you have seen me in time of danger seek death as other men seek life! A writing may be lost; a lie may be written; but what the eye has seen is truth and remains in the mind!"

"I remember," said the white man, quietly. Arsat went on with mournful composure—

"Therefore I shall speak to you of love. Speak in the night. Speak before both night and love are gone—and the eye of day looks upon my sorrow and my shame; upon my blackened face; upon my burnt-up heart."

A sigh, short and faint, marked an almost imperceptible pause, and then his words flowed on, without a stir, without a gesture.

"After the time of trouble and war was over and you went away from my country in the pursuit of your desires, which we, men of the islands, cannot understand, I and my brother became again, as we had been before, the sword-bearers of the Ruler. You know we were men of family, belonging to a ruling race, and more fit than any to carry on our right shoulder the emblem of power. And in the time of prosperity Si Dendring showed us favour, as we, in time of sorrow, had showed to him the faithfulness of our courage. It was a time of peace. A time of deer-hunts and cock-fights; of idle talks and foolish squabbles between men whose bellies are full and weapons are rusty. But the sower watched the young rice-shoots grow up without fear, and the traders came and went, departed lean and returned fat into the river of peace. They brought news, too. Brought lies and truth mixed together, so that no man knew when to rejoice and when to be sorry. We heard from them about you also. They had seen you here and had seen you there. And I was glad to hear, for I remembered the stirring times, and I always remembered you, Tuan, till the time came when my eyes could see nothing in the past, because they had looked upon the one who is dying there—in the house."

He stopped to exclaim in an intense whisper, "O Mara bahia! O Calamity!" then went on speaking a little louder:

"There's no worse enemy and no better friend than a brother, Tuan, for one brother knows another, and in perfect knowledge is strength for good or evil. I loved my brother. I went to him and told him that I could see nothing but one face, near nothing but one voice. He told me: 'Open your heart so that she can see what is in it—and wait. Patience is wisdom. Inchi Midah may die or our Ruler may throw off his fear of a woman!' . . . I waited! . . . You remember the lady with the veiled face, Tuan, and the fear of our Ruler before her cunning and temper. And if she wanted her servant, what could I do? But I fed the hunger of my heart on short glances and stealthy words. I loitered on the path to the bath-houses in the daytime, and when the sun had fallen behind the forest I crept along the jasmine hedges of the women's courtyard. Unseeing, we spoke to one another through the scent of flowers, through the veil of leaves, through the blades of long grass that stood still before our lips; so great was our prudence, so faint was the murmur of our great longing. The time passed swiftly . . . and there were whispers amongst women—and our enemies watched—my brother was gloomy, and I began to think of killing and of a fierce death. . . . We are of a people who take what they want—like you whites. There is a time when a man should forget loyalty and respect. Might and authority are given to rulers, but to all men is given love and strength and courage. My brother said, 'You shall take her from their midst. We are two who are like one.' And I answered, 'Let it be soon, for I find no warmth in sunlight that does not shine upon her.' Our time came when the Ruler and all the great people went to the mouth of the river to fish by torchlight. There were hundreds of boats, and on the white sand, between the water and the forests, dwellings of leaves were built for the households of the Rajahs. The smoke of cooking-fires was like a blue mist of the evening, and many voices rang in it joyfully. While they were making the boats ready to beat up the fish, my brother came to me and said, 'To-night!' I looked to my weapons, and when the time came our canoe took its place in the circle of boats carrying the torches. The lights blazed on the water, but behind the boats there was darkness. When the shouting began and the excitement made them like mad we dropped out. The water swallowed our fire, and we floated back to the shore that was dark with only here and there the glimmer of embers. We could hear the talk of slave-girls amongst the sheds. Then we found a place deserted and silent. We waited there. She came. She came running along the shore, rapid and leaving no trace, like a leaf driven by the wind into the sea. My brother said gloomily, 'Go and take her; carry her into our boat.' I lifted her in my arms. She panted. Her heart was beating against my breast. I said, 'I take you from those people. You came to the cry of my heart, but my arms take you into my boat against the will of the great!' 'It is right,' said my brother. 'We are men who take what we want and can hold it against many. We should have taken her in daylight.' I said, 'Let us be off'; for since she was in my boat I began to think of our Ruler's many men. 'Yes. Let us be off,' said my brother. 'We are cast out and this boat is our country now—and the sea is our refuge.' He lingered with his foot on the shore, and I entreated him to hasten, for I remembered the strokes of her heart against my breast and thought that two men cannot withstand a hundred. We left, paddling downstream close to the bank; and as we passed by the creek where they were fishing, the great shouting had ceased, but the murmur of voices was loud like the humming of insects flying at noonday. The boats floated, clustered together, in the red light of torches, under a black roof of smoke; and men talked of their sport. Men that boasted, and praised, and jeered—men that would have been our friends in the morning, but on that night were already our enemies. We paddled swiftly past. We had no more friends in the country of our birth. She sat in the middle of the canoe with covered face; silent as she is now; unseeing as she is now—and I had no regret at what I was leaving because I could hear her breathing close to me—as I can hear her now."

He paused, listened with his ear turned to the doorway, then shook his head and went on:

"My brother wanted to shout the cry of challenge—one cry only—to let the people know we were freeborn robbers who trusted our arms and the great sea. And again I begged him in the name of our love to be silent. Could I not hear her breathing close to me? I knew the pursuit would come quick enough. My brother loved me. He dipped his paddle without a splash. He only said, 'There is half a man in you now—the other half is in that woman. I can wait. When you are a whole man again, you will come back with me here to shout defiance. We are sons of the same mother.' I made no answer. All my strength and all my spirit were in my hands that held the paddle—for I longed to be with her in a safe place beyond the reach of men's anger and of women's spite. My love was so great, that I thought it could guide me to a country where death was unknown, if I could only escape from Inchi Midah's fury and from our Ruler's sword. We paddled with haste, breathing through our teeth. The blades bit deep into the smooth water. We passed out of the river; we flew in clear channels amongst the shallows. We skirted the black coast; we skirted the sand beaches where the sea speaks in whispers to the land; and the gleam of white sand flashed back past our boat, so swiftly she ran upon the water. We spoke not. Only once I said, 'Sleep, Diamelen, for soon you may want all your strength.' I heard the sweetness of her voice, but I never turned my head. The sun rose and still we went on. Water fell from my face like rain from a cloud. We flew in the light and heat. I never looked back, but I knew that my brother's eyes, behind me, were looking steadily ahead, for the boat went as straight as a bushman's dart, when it leaves the end of the sumpitan [blow-gun]. There was no better paddler, no better steersman than my brother. Many times, together, we had won races in that canoe. But we never had put out our strength as we did then—then, when for the last time we paddled together! There was no braver or stronger man in our country than my brother. I could not spare the strength to turn my head and look at him, but every minute I heard the hiss of his breath getting louder behind me. Still he did not speak. The sun was high. The heat clung to my back like a flame of fire. My ribs were ready to burst, but I could no longer get enough air into my chest. And then I felt I must cry out with my last breath, 'Let us rest!' . . . 'Good!' he answered; and his voice was firm. He was strong. He was brave. He knew not fear and no fatigue . . . My brother!"

A murmur powerful and gentle, a murmur vast and faint; the murmur of trembling leaves, of stirring boughs, ran through the tangled depths of the forests, ran over the starry smoothness of the lagoon, and the water between the piles lapped the slimy timber once with a sudden splash. A breath of warm air touched the two men's faces and passed on with a mournful sound—a breath loud and short like an uneasy sigh of the dreaming earth.

Arsat went on in an even, low voice.

"We ran our canoe on the white beach of a little bay close to a long tongue of land that seemed to bar our road; a long wooded cape going far into the sea. My brother knew that place. Beyond the cape a river has its entrance, and through the jungle of that land there is a narrow path. We made a fire and cooked rice. Then we lay down to sleep on the soft sand in the shade of our canoe, while she watched. No sooner had I closed my eyes than I heard her cry of alarm. We leaped up. The sun was halfway down the sky already, and coming in sight in the opening of the bay we saw a prau[1] manned by many paddlers. We knew it at once; it was one of our Rajah's praus. They were watching the shore, and saw us. They beat the gong, and turned the head of the prau into the bay. I felt my heart become weak within my breast. Diamelen

---

[1] A swift Malayan canoe, with sail and outrigger. [Eds.]

sat on the sand and covered her face. There was no escape by sea. My brother laughed. He had the gun you had given him, Tuan, before you went away, but there was only a handful of powder. He spoke to me quickly: 'Run with her along the path. I shall keep them back, for they have no firearms, and landing in the face of a man with a gun is certain death for some. Run with her. On the other side of that wood there is a fisherman's house—and a canoe. When I have fired all the shots I will follow. I am a great runner, and before they can come up we shall be gone. I will hold out as long as I can, for she is but a woman—that can neither run nor fight, but she has your heart in her weak hands.' He dropped behind the canoe. The prau was coming. She and I ran, and as we rushed along the path I heard shots. My brother fired—once—twice—and the booming of the gong ceased. There was silence behind us. That neck of land is narrow. Before I heard my brother fire the third shot I saw the shelving shore, and I saw the water again; the mouth of a broad river. We crossed a grassy glade. We ran down to the water. I saw a low hut above the black mud, and a small canoe hauled up. I heard another shot behind me. I thought, 'That is his last charge.' We rushed down to the canoe; a man came running from the hut, but I leaped on him, and we rolled together in the mud. Then I got up, and he lay still at my feet. I don't know whether I had killed him or not. I and Diamelen pushed the canoe afloat. I heard yells behind me, and I saw my brother run across the glade. Many men were bounding after him, I took her in my arms and threw her into the boat, then leaped in myself. When I looked back I saw that my brother had fallen. He fell and was up again, but the men were closing round him. He shouted, 'I am coming!' The men were close to him. I looked. Many men. Then I looked at her. Tuan, I pushed the canoe! I pushed it into deep water. She was kneeling forward looking at me, and I said, 'Take your paddle,' while I struck the water with mine. Tuan, I heard him cry. I heard him cry my name twice; and I heard voices shouting, 'Kill! Strike!' I never turned back. I heard him calling my name again with a great shriek, as when life is going out together with the voice—and I never turned my head. My own name! . . . My brother! Three times he called—but I was not afraid of life. Was she not there in that canoe? And could I not with her find a country where death is forgotten—where death is unknown!"

The white man sat up. Arsat rose and stood, an indistinct and silent figure above the dying embers of the fire. Over the lagoon a mist drifting and low had crept, erasing slowly the glittering images of the stars. And now a great expanse of white vapour covered the land: it flowed cold and gray in the darkness, eddied in noiseless whirls round the tree-trunks and about the platform of the house, which seemed to float upon a restless and impalpable illusion of a sea. Only far away the tops of the trees stood outlined on the twinkle of heaven, like a sombre and forbidding shore—a coast deceptive, pitiless and black.

Arsat's voice vibrated loudly in the profound peace.

"I had her there! I had her! To get her I would have faced all mankind. But I had her—and—"

His words went out ringing into the empty distances. He paused, and seemed to listen to them dying away very far—beyond help and beyond recall. Then he said quietly—

"Tuan, I loved my brother."

A breath of wind made him shiver. High above his head, high above the silent sea of mist the drooping leaves of the palms rattled together with a mournful and expiring sound. The white man stretched his legs. His chin rested on his chest, and he murmured sadly without lifting his head—

"We all love our brothers."

Arsat burst out with an intense whispering violence—

"What did I care who died? I wanted peace in my own heart."

He seemed to hear a stir in the house—listened—then stepped in noise-lessly. The white man stood up. A breeze was coming in fitful puffs. The stars shone paler as if they had retreated into the frozen depths of immense space. After a chill gust of wind there were a few seconds of perfect calm and absolute silence. Then from behind the black and wavy line of the forests a column of golden light shot up into the heavens and spread over the semicircle of the eastern horizon. The sun had risen. The mist lifted, broke into drifting patches, vanished into thin flying wreaths; and the unveiled lagoon lay, polished and black, in the heavy shadows at the foot of the wall of trees. A white eagle rose over it with a slanting and ponderous flight, reached the clear sunshine and appeared dazzlingly brilliant for a moment, then soaring higher, became a dark and motionless speck before it vanished into the blue as if it had left the earth forever. The white man, standing gazing upwards before the doorway, heard in the hut a confused and broken murmur of distracted words ending with a loud groan. Suddenly Arsat stumbled out with outstretched hands, shivered, and stood still for some time with fixed eyes. Then he said—

"She burns no more."

Before his face the sun showed its edge above the tree-tops rising steadily. The breeze freshened; a great brilliance burst upon the lagoon, sparkled on the rippling water. The forests came out of the clear shadows of the morning, became distinct, as if they had rushed nearer—to stop short in a great stir of leaves, of nodding boughs, of swaying branches. In the merciless sunshine the whisper of unconscious life grew louder, speaking in an incomprehensible voice round the dumb darkness of that human sorrow. Arsat's eyes wandered slowly, then stared at the rising sun.

"I can see nothing," he said half aloud to himself.

"There is nothing," said the white man, moving to the edge of the platform and waving his hand to his boat. A shout came faintly over the lagoon and the sampan began to glide towards the abode of the friend of ghosts.

"If you want to come with me, I will wait all the morning," said the white man, looking away upon the water.

"No, Tuan," said Arsat, softly. "I shall not eat or sleep in this house, but I must first see my road. Now I can see nothing—see nothing! There is no light and no peace in the world; but there is death—death for many. We are sons of the same mother—and I left him in the midst of enemies; but I am going back now."

He drew a long breath and went on in a dreamy tone:

"In a little while I shall see clear enough to strike—to strike. But she has died, and . . . now . . . darkness."

He flung his arms wide open, let them fall along his body, then stood still with unmoved face and stony eyes, staring at the sun. The white man got down into his canoe. The polers ran smartly along the sides of the boat, looking over their shoulders at the beginning of a weary journey. High in the stern, his head muffled up in white rags, the juragan sat moody, letting his paddle trail in the water. The white man, leaning with both arms over the grass roof of the little cabin, looked back at the shining ripple of the boat's wake. Before the sampan passed out of the lagoon into the creek he lifted his eyes. Arsat had not moved. He stood lonely in the searching sunshine; and he looked beyond the great light of a cloudless day into the darkness of a world of illusions.

ANTON CHEKHOV

❧ The Lady with the Dog

It was said that a new person had appeared on the sea-front: a lady with a little dog. Dmitri Dmitritch Gurov, who had by then been a fortnight at Yalta, and so was fairly at home there, had begun to take an interest in new arrivals. Sitting in Verney's pavilion, he saw, walking on the sea-front, a fair-haired young lady of medium height, wearing a *béret*; a white Pomeranian dog was running behind her.

And afterwards he met her in the public gardens and in the square several times a day. She was walking alone, always wearing the same *béret*, and always with the same white dog; no one knew who she was, and every one called her simply "the lady with the dog."

"If she is here alone without a husband or friends, it wouldn't be amiss to make her acquaintance," Gurov reflected.

He was under forty, but he had a daughter already twelve years old, and two sons at school. He had been married young, when he was a student in his

Translated by Constance Garnett.

second year, and by now his wife seemed half as old again as he. She was a tall, erect woman with dark eyebrows, staid and dignified, and, as she said of herself, intellectual. She read a great deal, used phonetic spelling, called her husband, not Dmitri, but Dimitri, and he secretly considered her unintelligent, narrow, inelegant, was afraid of her, and did not like to be at home. He had begun being unfaithful to her long ago—had been unfaithful to her often, and, probably on that account, almost always spoke ill of women, and when they were talked about in his presence, used to call them "the lower race."

It seemed to him that he had been so schooled by bitter experience that he might call them what he liked, and yet he could not get on for two days together without "the lower race." In the society of men he was bored and not himself, with them he was cold and uncommunicative; but when he was in the company of women he felt free, and knew what to say to them and how to behave; and he was at ease with them even when he was silent. In his appearance, in his character, in his whole nature, there was something attractive and elusive which allured women and disposed them in his favour; he knew that, and some force seemed to draw him, too, to them.

Experience often repeated, truly bitter experience, had taught him long ago that with decent people, especially Moscow people—always slow to move and irresolute—every intimacy, which at first so agreeably diversifies life and appears a light and charming adventure, inevitably grows into a regular problem of extreme intricacy, and in the long run the situation becomes unbearable. But at every fresh meeting with an interesting woman this experience seemed to slip out of his memory, and he was eager for life, and everything seemed simple and amusing.

One evening he was dining in the gardens, and the lady in the *béret* came up slowly to take the next table. Her expression, her gait, her dress, and the way she did her hair told him that she was a lady, that she was married, that she was in Yalta for the first time and alone, and that she was dull there. . . . The stories told of the immorality in such places as Yalta are to a great extent untrue; he despised them, and knew that such stories were for the most part made up by persons who would themselves have been glad to sin if they had been able; but when the lady sat down at the next table three paces from him, he remembered these tales of easy conquests, of trips to the mountains, and the tempting thought of a swift, fleeting love affair, a romance with an unknown woman, whose name he did not know, suddenly took possession of him.

He beckoned coaxingly to the Pomeranian, and when the dog came up to him he shook his finger at it. The Pomeranian growled: Gurov shook his finger at it again.

The lady looked at him and at once dropped her eyes.

"He doesn't bite," she said, and blushed.

"May I give him a bone?" he asked; and when she nodded he asked courteously, "Have you been long in Yalta?"

"Five days."

"And I have already dragged out a fortnight here."

There was a brief silence.

"Time goes fast, and yet it is so dull here!" she said, not looking at him.

"That's only the fashion to say it is dull here. A provincial will live in Belyov or Zhidra and not be dull, and when he comes here it's 'Oh, the dullness! Oh, the dust!' One would think he came from Grenada."

She laughed. Then both continued eating in silence, like strangers, but after dinner they walked side by side; and there sprang up between them the light jesting conversation of people who are free and satisfied, to whom it does not matter where they go or what they talk about. They walked and talked of the strange light on the sea: the water was of a soft warm lilac hue, and there was a golden streak from the moon upon it. They talked of how sultry it was after a hot day. Gurov told her that he came from Moscow, that he had taken his degree in Arts, but had a post in a bank; that he had trained as an opera-singer, but had given it up, that he owned two houses in Moscow. . . And from her he learnt that she had grown up in Petersburg, but had lived in S—— since her marriage two years before, that she was staying another month in Yalta, and that her husband, who needed a holiday too, might perhaps come and fetch her. She was not sure whether her husband had a post in a Crown Department or under the Provincial Council—and was amused by her own ignorance. And Gurov learnt, too, that she was called Anna Sergeyevna.

Afterwards he thought about her in his room at the hotel—thought she would certainly meet him next day; it would be sure to happen. As he got into bed he thought how lately she had been a girl at school, doing lessons like his own daughter; he recalled the diffidence, the angularity, that was still manifest in her laugh and her manner of talking with a stranger. This must have been the first time in her life she had been alone in surroundings in which she was followed, looked at, and spoken to merely from a secret motive which she could hardly fail to guess. He recalled her slender, delicate neck, her lovely grey eyes.

"There's something pathetic about her, anyway," he thought, and fell asleep.

II

A week had passed since they had made acquaintance. It was a holiday. It was sultry indoors, while in the street the wind whirled the dust round and round, and blew people's hats off. It was a thirsty day, and Gurov often went into the pavilion, and pressed Anna Sergeyevna to have syrup and water or an ice. One did not know what to do with oneself.

In the evening when the wind had dropped a little, they went out on the groyne [wooden breakwater] to see the steamer come in. There were a great many people walking about the harbour; they had gathered to welcome someone, bringing bouquets. And two peculiarities of a well-dressed Yalta crowd were very conspicuous: the elderly ladies were dressed like young ones, and there were great numbers of generals.

Owing to the roughness of the sea, the steamer arrived late, after the sun had set, and it was a long time turning about before it reached the groyne. Anna Sergeyevna looked through her lorgnette at the steamer and the passengers as though looking for acquaintances, and when she turned to Gurov her eyes were shining. She talked a great deal and asked disconnected questions, forgetting next moment what she had asked; then she dropped her lorgnette in the crush.

The festive crowd began to disperse; it was too dark to see people's faces. The wind had completely dropped, but Gurov and Anna Sergeyevna still stood as though waiting to see someone else come from the steamer. Anna Sergeyevna was silent now, and sniffed the flowers without looking at Gurov.

"The weather is better this evening," he said. "Where shall we go now? Shall we drive somewhere?"

She made no answer.

Then he looked at her intently, and all at once put his arm round her and kissed her on the lips, and breathed in the moisture and the fragrance of the flowers; and he immediately looked round him, anxiously wondering whether any one had seen them.

"Let us go to your hotel," he said softly. And both walked quickly.

The room was close and smelt of the scent she had bought at the Japanese shop. Gurov looked at her and thought: "What different people one meets in the world!" From the past he preserved memories of careless, good-natured women, who loved cheerfully and were grateful to him for the happiness he gave them, however brief it might be; and of women like his wife who loved without any genuine feeling, with superfluous phrases, affectedly, hysterically, with an expression that suggested that it was not love nor passion, but something more significant; and of two or three others, very beautiful, cold women, on whose faces he had caught a glimpse of a rapacious expression—an obstinate desire to snatch from life more than it could give, and these were capricious, unreflecting, domineering, unintelligent women not in their first youth, and when Gurov grew cold to them their beauty excited his hatred, and the lace on their linen seemed to him like scales.

But in this case there was still the diffidence, the angularity of inexperienced youth, an awkward feeling; and there was a sense of consternation as though someone had suddenly knocked at the door. The attitude of Anna Sergeyevna —"the lady with the dog"—to what had happened was somehow peculiar, very grave, as though it were her fall—so it seemed, and it was strange and inappropriate. Her face dropped and faded, and on both sides of it her long hair hung down mournfully; she mused in a dejected attitude like "the woman who was a sinner" in an old-fashioned picture.

"It's wrong," she said. "You will be the first to despise me now."

There was a watermelon on the table. Gurov cut himself a slice and began eating it without haste. There followed at least half an hour of silence.

Anna Sergeyevna was touching; there was about her the purity of a good, simple woman who had seen little of life. The solitary candle burning on the table threw a faint light on her face, yet it was clear that she was very unhappy.

"How could I despise you?" asked Gurov. "You don't know what you are saying."

"God forgive me," she said, and her eyes filled with tears. "It's awful."

"You seem to feel you need to be forgiven."

"Forgiven? No. I am a bad, low woman; I despise myself and don't attempt to justify myself. It's not my husband but myself I have deceived. And not only just now; I have been deceiving myself for a long time. My husband may be a good honest man, but he is a flunkey! I don't know what he does there, what his work is, but I know he is a flunkey! I was twenty when I was married to him. I have been tormented by curiosity; I wanted something better. 'There must be a different sort of life,' I said to myself. I wanted to live! To live, to live! . . . I was fired by curiosity . . . you don't understand it, but, I swear to God, I could not control myself; something happened to me: I could not be restrained. I told my husband I was ill, and came here. . . . And here I have been walking about as though I were dazed, like a mad creature; . . . and now I have become a vulgar, contemptible woman whom any one may despise."

Gurov felt bored already, listening to her. He was irritated by the naïve tone, by this remorse, so unexpected and inopportune; but for the tears in her eyes, he might have thought she was jesting or playing a part.

"I don't understand," he said softly. "What is it you want?"

She hid her face on his breast and pressed close to him.

"Believe me, believe me, I beseech you . . ." she said. "I love a pure, honest life, and sin is loathsome to me. I don't know what I am doing. Simple people say: 'The Evil One has beguiled me.' And I may say of myself now that the Evil One has beguiled me."

"Hush, hush! . . ." he muttered.

He looked at her fixed, scared eyes, kissed her, talked softly and affectionately, and by degrees she was comforted, and her gaiety returned; they both began laughing.

Afterwards when they went out there was not a soul on the sea-front. The town with its cypresses had quite a deathlike air, but the sea still broke noisily on the shore; a single barge was rocking on the waves, and a lantern was blinking sleepily on it.

They found a cab and drove to Oreanda.

"I found out your surname in the hall just now: it was written on the board—Von Diderits," said Gurov. "Is your husband a German?"

"No; I believe his grandfather was a German, but he is an Orthodox Russian himself."

At Oreanda they sat on a seat not far from the church, looked down at the sea, and were silent. Yalta was hardly visible through the morning mist; white clouds stood motionless on the mountain-tops. The leaves did not stir on the trees, grasshoppers chirruped, and the monotonous hollow sound of the sea rising up from below, spoke of the peace, of the eternal sleep awaiting us. So it must have sounded when there was no Yalta, no Oreanda here; so it sounds now, and it will sound as indifferently and monotonously when we are all no more. And in this constancy, in this complete indifference to the life and death of each of us, there lies hid, perhaps, a pledge of our eternal salvation, of the unceasing movement of life upon earth, of unceasing progress towards perfection. Sitting beside a young woman who in the dawn seemed so lovely, soothed and spellbound in these magical surroundings—the sea, mountains, clouds, the open sky—Gurov thought how in reality everything is beautiful in this world when one reflects: everything except what we think or do ourselves when we forget our human dignity and the higher aims of our existence.

A man walked up to them—probably a keeper—looked at them and walked away. And this detail seemed mysterious and beautiful, too. They saw a steamer come from Theodosia [seaport, southeast Crimea], with its lights out in the glow of dawn.

"There is dew on the grass," said Anna Sergeyevna, after a silence.

"Yes. It's time to go home."

They went back to the town.

Then they met every day at twelve o'clock on the sea-front, lunched and dined together, went for walks, admired the sea. She complained that she slept badly, that her heart throbbed violently; asked the same questions, troubled now by jealousy and now by the fear that he did not respect her sufficiently. And often in the square or gardens, when there was no one near them, he suddenly drew her to him and kissed her passionately. Complete idleness, these kisses in broad daylight while he looked round in dread of someone's seeing them, the heat, the smell of the sea, and the continual passing to and fro before him of idle, well-dressed, well-fed people, made a new man of him; he told Anna Sergeyevna how beautiful she was, how fascinating. He was impatiently passionate, he would not move a step away from her, while she was often pensive and continually urged him to confess that he did not respect her, did not love her in the least, and thought of her as nothing but a common woman. Rather late almost every evening they drove somewhere out of town, to Oreanda or to the waterfall; and the expedition was always a success, the scenery invariably impressed them as grand and beautiful.

They were expecting her husband to come, but a letter came from him, saying that there was something wrong with his eyes, and he entreated his wife to come home as quickly as possible. Anna Sergeyevna made haste to go.

"It's a good thing I am going away," she said to Gurov. "It's the finger of destiny!"

She went by coach and he went with her. They driving the whole day. When she had got into a compartment of the express, and when the second bell had rung, she said:

"Let me look at you once more . . . look at you once again. That's right."

She did not shed tears, but was so sad that she seemed ill, and her face was quivering.

"I shall remember you . . . think of you," she said. "God be with you; be happy. Don't remember evil against me. We are parting forever—it must be so, for we ought never to have met. Well, God be with you."

The train moved off rapidly, its lights soon vanished from sight, and a minute later there was no sound of it, as though everything had conspired together to end as quickly as possible that sweet delirium, that madness. Left alone on the platform, and gazing into the dark distance, Gurov listened to the chirrup of the grasshoppers and the hum of the telegraph wires, feeling as though he had only just waked up. And he thought, musing, that there had been another episode or adventure in his life, and it, too, was at an end, and nothing was left of it but a memory. . . . He was moved, sad, and conscious of a slight remorse. This young woman whom he would never meet again had not been happy with him; he was genuinely warm and affectionate with her, but yet in his manner, his tone, and his caresses there had been a shade of light irony, the coarse condescension of a happy man who was, besides, almost twice her age. All the time she had called him kind, exceptional, lofty; obviously he had seemed to her different from what he really was, so he had unintentionally deceived her. . . .

Here at the station was already a scent of autumn; it was a cold evening.

"It's time for me to go north," thought Gurov as he left the platform. "High time!"

III

At home in Moscow everything was in its winter routine; the stoves were heated, and in the morning it was still dark when the children were having breakfast and getting ready for school, and the nurse would light the lamp for a short time. The frosts had begun already. When the first snow has fallen, on the first day of sledge-driving it is pleasant to see the white earth, the white roofs, to draw soft, delicious breath, and the season brings back the days of one's youth. The old limes and birches, white with hoar-frost, have a good-natured expression; they are nearer to one's heart than cypresses and palms, and near them one doesn't want to be thinking of the sea and the mountains.

Gurov was Moscow born; he arrived in Moscow on a fine frosty day, and when he put on his fur coat and warm gloves, and walked along Petrovka, and when on Saturday evening he heard the ringing of the bells, his recent trip and the places he had seen lost all charm for him. Little by little he became absorbed in Moscow life, greedily read three newspapers a day, and declared he did not read the Moscow papers on principle! He already felt a longing to go to restaurants, clubs, dinner-parties, anniversary celebrations, and he felt flattered at entertaining distinguished lawyers and artists, and at playing cards with a professor at the doctors' club. He could already eat a whole plateful of salt fish and cabbage. . . .

In another month, he fancied, the image of Anna Sergeyevna would be shrouded in a mist in his memory, and only from time to time would visit him in his dreams with a touching smile as others did. But more than a month passed, real winter had come, and everything was still clear in his memory as though he had parted with Anna Sergeyevna only the day before. And his memories glowed more and more vividly. When in the evening stillness he heard from his study the voices of his children, preparing their lessons, or when he listened to a song or the organ at the restaurant, or the storm howled in the chimney, suddenly everything would rise up in his memory: what had happened on the groyne, and the early morning with the mist on the mountains, and the steamer coming from Theodosia, and the kisses. He would pace a long time about his room, remembering it all and smiling; then his memories passed into dreams, and in his fancy the past was mingled with what was to come. Anna Sergeyevna did not visit him in dreams, but followed him about everywhere like a shadow and haunted him. When he shut his eyes he saw her as though she were living before him, and she seemed to him lovelier, younger, tenderer than she was; and he imagined himself finer than he had been in Yalta. In the evening she peeped out at him from the bookcase, from the fireplace, from the corner—he heard her breathing, the caressing rustle of her dress. In the street he watched the women, looking for some one like her.

He was tormented by an intense desire to confide his memories to someone. But in his home it was impossible to talk of his love, and he had no one outside; he could not talk to his tenants nor to any one at the bank. And what had he to talk of? Had he been in love, then? Had there been anything beautiful, poetical, or edifying or simply interesting in his relations with Anna Serge-yevna? And there was nothing for him but to talk vaguely of love, of women, and no one guessed what it meant; only his wife twitched her black eyebrows, and said: "The part of a lady-killer does not suit you at all, Dimitri."

One evening, coming out of the doctors' club with an official with whom he had been playing cards, he could not resist saying:

"If only you knew what a fascinating woman I made the acquaintance of in Yalta!"

The official got into his sledge and was driving away, but turned suddenly and shouted:

"Dmitri Dmitritch!"

"What?"

"You were right this evening: the sturgeon was a bit too strong!"

These words, so ordinary, for some reason moved Gurov to indignation, and struck him as degrading and unclean. What savage manners, what people! What senseless nights, what uninteresting, uneventful days! The rage for card-playing, the gluttony, the drunkenness, the continual talk always about the same thing. Useless pursuits and conversations always about the same things absorb the better part of one's time, the better part of one's strength, and in the end there is left a life grovelling and curtailed, worthless and trivial, and there is no escaping or getting away from it—just as though one were in a madhouse or a prison.

Gurov did not sleep all night, and was filled with indignation. And he had a headache all next day. And the next night he slept badly; he sat up in bed, thinking, or paced up and down his room. He was sick of his children, sick of the bank; he had no desire to go anywhere or to talk of anything.

In the holidays in December he prepared for a journey, and told his wife he was going to Petersburg to do something in the interests of a young friend— and he set off for S——. What for? He did not very well know himself. He wanted to see Anna Sergeyevna and to talk with her—to arrange a meeting, if possible.

He reached S—— in the morning, and took the best room at the hotel, in which the floor was covered with grey army cloth, and on the table was an inkstand, grey with dust and adorned with a figure on horseback, with its hat in its hand and its head broken off. The hotel porter gave him the necessary information; Von Diderits lived in a house of his own in Old Gontcharny Street—it was not far from the hotel: he was rich and lived in good style, and had his own horses; every one in the town knew him. The porter pronounced the name "Dridirits."

Gurov went without haste to Old Gontcharny Street and found the house. Just opposite the house stretched a long grey fence adorned with nails.

"One would run away from a fence like that," thought Gurov, looking from the fence to the windows of the house and back again.

He considered: today was a holiday, and the husband would probably be at home. And in any case it would be tactless to go into the house and upset her. If he were to send her a note it might fall into her husband's hands, and then it might ruin everything. The best thing was to trust to chance. And he kept walking up and down the street by the fence, waiting for the chance. He saw a beggar go in at the gate and dogs fly at him; then an hour later he heard a piano, and the sounds were faint and indistinct. Probably it was Anna Serge-yevna playing. The front door suddenly opened, and an old woman came out, followed by the familiar white Pomeranian. Gurov was on the point of calling to the dog, but his heart began beating violently, and in his excitement he could not remember the dog's name.

He walked up and down, and loathed the grey fence more and more, and by now he thought irritably that Anna Sergeyevna had forgotten him, and was perhaps already amusing herself with someone else, and that that was very natural in a young woman who had nothing to look at from morning till night but that confounded fence. He went back to his hotel room and sat for a long while on the sofa, not knowing what to do, then he had dinner and a long nap.

"How stupid and worrying it is!" he thought when he woke and looked at the dark windows: it was already evening. "Here I've had a good sleep for some reason. What shall I do in the night?"

He sat on the bed, which was covered by a cheap grey blanket, such as one sees in hospitals, and he taunted himself in his vexation:

"So much for the lady with the dog . . . so much for the adventure. . . . You're in a nice fix. . . ."

That morning at the station a poster in large letters had caught his eye. "The Geisha" was to be performed for the first time. He thought of this and went to the theatre.

"It's quite possible she may go to the first performance," he thought.

The theatre was full. As in all provincial theatres, there was a fog above the chandelier, the gallery was noisy and restless; in the front row the local dandies were standing up before the beginning of the performance, with their hands behind them; in the Governor's box the Governor's daughter, wearing a boa, was sitting in the front seat, while the Governor himself lurked modestly behind the curtain with only his hands visible; the orchestra was a long time tuning up; the stage curtain swayed. All the time the audience were coming in and taking their seats Gurov looked at them eagerly.

Anna Sergeyevna, too, came in. She sat down in the third row, and when Gurov looked at her his heart contracted, and he understood clearly that for him there was in the whole world no creature so near, so precious, and so important to him; she, this little woman, in no way remarkable, lost in a provincial crowd, with a vulgar lorgnette in her hand, filled his whole life now, was his sorrow and his joy, the one happiness that he now desired for himself, and to the sounds of the inferior orchestra, of the wretched provincial violins, he thought how lovely she was. He thought and dreamed.

A young man with small side-whiskers, tall and stooping, came in with Anna Sergeyevna and sat down beside her; he bent his head at every step and seemed to be continually bowing. Most likely this was the husband whom at Yalta, in a rush of bitter feeling, she had called a flunkey. And there really was in his long figure, his side-whiskers, and the small bald patch on his head, something of the flunkey's obsequiousness; his smile was sugary, and in his buttonhole there was some badge of distinction like the number of a waiter.

During the first interval the husband went away to smoke; she remained alone in her stall. Gurov, who was sitting in the stalls, too, went up to her and said in a trembling voice, with a forced smile:

"Good-evening."

She glanced at him and turned pale, then glanced again with horror, unable to believe her eyes, and tightly gripped the fan and the lorgnette in her hands, evidently struggling with herself not to faint. Both were silent. She was sitting, he was standing, frightened by her confusion and not venturing to sit down beside her. The violins and the flute began tuning up. He felt suddenly frightened; it seemed as though all the people in the boxes were looking at them. She got up and went quickly to the door; he followed her, and both walked senselessly along passages, and up and down stairs, and figures in legal, scholastic, and civil service uniforms, all wearing badges, flitted before their eyes. They caught glimpses of ladies, of fur coats hanging on pegs; the draughts blew on them, bringing a smell of stale tobacco. And Gurov, whose heart was beating violently, thought:

"Oh, heavens! Why are these people here and this orchestra! . . ."

And at that instant he recalled how when he had seen Anna Sergeyevna off at the station he had thought that everything was over and they would never meet again. But how far they were still from the end!

On the narrow, gloomy staircase over which was written "To the Amphitheatre," she stopped.

"How you have frightened me!" she said, breathing hard, still pale and overwhelmed. "Oh, how you have frightened me! I am half dead. Why have you come? Why?"

"But do understand, Anna, do understand . . ." he said hastily in a low voice. "I entreat you to understand. . . ."

She looked at him with dread, with entreaty, with love; she looked at him intently, to keep his features more distinctly in her memory.

"I am so unhappy," she went on, not heeding him. "I have thought of nothing but you all the time; I live only in the thought of you. And I wanted to forget you; but why, or, why, have you come?"

On the landing above them two schoolboys were smoking and looking down, but that was nothing to Gurov; he drew Anna Sergeyevna to him, and began kissing her face, her cheeks, and her hands.

"What are you doing, what are you doing!" she cried in horror, pushing him away. "We are mad. Go away to-day; go away at once. . . . I beseech you by all that is sacred, I implore you. . . . There are people coming this way!"

Someone was coming up the stairs.

"You must go away," Anna Sergeyevna went on in a whisper. "Do you hear, Dmitri Dmitritch? I will come and see you in Moscow. I have never been happy; I am miserable now, and I never, never shall be happy, never! Don't make me suffer still more! I swear I'll come to Moscow. But now let us part. My precious, good, dear one, we must part!"

She pressed his hand and began rapidly going downstairs, looking round at him, and from her eyes he could see that she really was unhappy. Gurov stood for a little while, listened, then, when all sound had died away, he found his coat and left the theatre.

IV

And Anna Sergeyevna began coming to see him in Moscow. Once in two or three months she left S——, telling her husband that she was going to consult a doctor about an internal complaint—and her husband believed her, and did not believe her. In Moscow she stayed at the Slaviansky Bazaar hotel, and at once sent a man in a red cap to Gurov. Gurov went to see her, and no one in Moscow knew of it.

Once he was going to see her in this way on a winter morning (the messenger had come the evening before when he was out). With him walked his daughter, whom he wanted to take to school: it was on the way. Snow was falling in big wet flakes.

"It's three degrees above freezing-point, and yet it is snowing," said Gurov to his daughter. "The thaw is only on the surface of the earth; there is quite a different temperature at a greater height in the atmosphere."

"And why are there no thunderstorms in the winter, father?"

He explained that, too. He talked, thinking all the while that he was going to see *her,* and no living soul knew of it, and probably never would know. He had two lives: one, open, seen, and known by all who cared to know, full of relative truth and of relative falsehood, exactly like the lives of his friends and acquaintances; and another life running its course in secret. And through some strange, perhaps accidental, conjunction of circumstances, everything that was essential, of interest and of value to him, everything in which he was sincere and did not deceive himself, everything that made the kernel of his life, was hidden from other people; and all that was false in him, the sheath in which he hid himself to conceal the truth—such, for instance, as his work in the bank, his discussions at the club, his "lower race," his presence with his wife at anniversary festivities—all that was open. And he judged of others by himself, not believing in what he saw, and always believing that every man had his real, most interesting life under the cover of secrecy and under the cover of night. All personal life rested on secrecy, and possibly it was partly on that account that civilised man was so nervously anxious that personal privacy should be respected.

After leaving his daughter at school, Gurov went on to the Slaviansky Bazaar. He took off his fur coat below, went upstairs, and softly knocked at the door. Anna Sergeyevna, wearing his favourite grey dress, exhausted by the journey and the suspense, had been expecting him since the evening before. She was pale; she looked at him, and did not smile, and he had hardly come in when she fell on his breast. Their kiss was slow and prolonged, as though they had not met for two years.

"Well, how are you getting on there?" he asked. "What news?"

"Wait; I'll tell you directly. . . . I can't talk."

She could not speak; she was crying. She turned away from him, and pressed her handkerchief to her eyes.

"Let her have her cry out. I'll sit down and wait," he thought, and he sat down in an arm-chair.

Then he rang and asked for tea to be brought him, and while he drank his tea she remained standing at the window with her back to him. She was crying from emotion, from the miserable consciousness that their life was so hard for them; they could only meet in secret, hiding themselves from people, like thieves! Was not their life shattered?

"Come, do stop!" he said.

It was evident to him that this love of theirs would not soon be over, that he could not see the end of it. Anna Sergeyevna grew more and more attached to him. She adored him, and it was unthinkable to say to her that it was bound to have an end some day; besides, she would not have believed it!

He went up to her and took her by the shoulders to say something affectionate and cheering, and that moment he saw himself in the looking-glass.

His hair was already beginning to turn grey. And it seemed strange to him that he had grown so much older, so much plainer during the last few years. The shoulders on which his hands rested were warm and quivering. He felt compassion for this life, still so warm and lovely, but probably already not far from beginning to fade and wither like his own. Why did she love him so much? He always seemed to women different from what he was, and they loved in him not himself, but the man created by their imagination, whom they had been eagerly seeking all their lives; and afterwards, when they noticed their mistake; they loved him all the same. And not one of them had been happy with him. Time passed, he had made their acquaintance, got on with them, parted, but he had never once loved; it was anything you like, but not love.

And only now when his head was grey he had fallen properly, really in love—for the first time in his life.

Anna Sergeyevna and he loved each other like people very close and akin, like husband and wife, like tender friends; it seemed to them that fate itself had meant them for one another, and they could not understand why he had a wife and she a husband; and it was as though they were a pair of birds of passage, caught and forced to live in different cages. They forgave each other for what they were ashamed of in their past, they forgave everything in the present, and felt that this love of theirs had changed them both.

In moments of depression in the past he had comforted himself with any arguments that came into his mind, but now he no longer cared for arguments; he felt profound compassion, he wanted to be sincere and tender. . . .

"Don't cry, my darling," he said. "You've had your cry; that's enough. . . . Let us talk now, let us think of some plan."

Then they spent a long while taking counsel together, talked of how to avoid the necessity for secrecy, for deception, for living in different towns and not seeing each other for long at a time. How could they be free from this intolerable bondage?

"How? How?" he asked, clutching his head. "How?"

And it seemed as though in a little while the solution would be found, and then a new and splendid life would begin; and it was clear to both of them that they had still a long, long road before them, and that the most complicated and difficult part of it was only just beginning.

SHERWOOD ANDERSON

❧ *I'm a Fool*

It was a hard jolt for me, one of the most bitterest I ever had to face. And it all came about through my own foolishness too. Even yet, sometimes, when I think of it, I want to cry or swear or kick myself. Perhaps, even now, after all this time, there will be a kind of satisfaction in making myself look cheap by telling of it.

It began at three o'clock one October afternoon as I sat in the grandstand at the fall trotting and pacing meet at Sandusky, Ohio.

To tell the truth, I felt a little foolish that I should be sitting in the grandstand at all. During the summer before I had left my home town with Harry Whitehead and, with a nigger named Burt, had taken a job as swipe with one of the two horses Harry was campaigning through the fall race meets that year. Mother cried and my sister Mildred, who wanted to get a job as school teacher in our town that fall, stormed and scolded about the house all during the week before I left. They both thought it something disgraceful that one of our family should take a place as a swipe with race horses. I've an idea Mildred thought my taking the place would stand in the way of her getting the job she'd been working so long for.

But after all I had to work and there was no other work to be got. A big lumbering fellow of nineteen couldn't just hang around the house and I had got too big to mow people's lawns and sell newspapers. Little chaps who could get next to people's sympathies by their sizes were always getting jobs away from me. There was one fellow who kept saying to everyone who wanted a lawn mowed or a cistern cleaned that he was saving money to work his way through college, and I used to lay awake nights thinking up ways to injure him without being found out. I kept thinking of wagons running over him and bricks falling on his head as he walked along the street. But never mind him.

I got the place with Harry and I liked Burt fine. We got along splendid together. He was a big nigger with a lazy sprawling body and soft kind eyes, and when it came to a fight he could hit like Jack Johnson. He had Bucephalus, a big black pacing stallion that could do 2.09 or 2.10 if he had to, and I had a little gelding named Doctor Fritz that never lost a race all fall when Harry wanted him to win.

We set out from home late in July in a box car with the two horses, and after that, until late November, we kept moving along to the race meets and the fairs. It was a peachy time for me, I'll say that. Sometimes, now, I think that boys who are raised regular in houses, and never have a fine nigger like Burt for best friend, and go to high schools and college, and never steal anything or get drunk a little, or learn to swear from fellows who know how, or come walking up in front of a grandstand in their shirt sleeves and with dirty horsey pants on when the races are going on and the grandstand is full of people all dressed up—What's the use talking about it? Such fellows don't know nothing at all. They've never had no opportunity.

But I did. Burt taught me how to rub down a horse and put the bandages on after a race and steam a horse out and a lot of valuable things for any man to know. He could wrap a bandage on a horse's leg so smooth that if it had been the same color you would think it was his skin, and I guess he'd have been a big driver, too, and got to the top like Murphy and Walter Cox and the others if he hadn't been black.

Gee whizz, it was fun. You got to a county seat town maybe, say, on a Saturday or Sunday, and the fair began the next Tuesday and lasted until Friday afternoon. Doctor Fritz would be, say, in the 2.25 trot on Tuesday afternoon and on Thursday afternoon Bucephalus would knock 'em cold in the "free-for-all" pace. It left you a lot of time to hang around and listen to horse talk, and see Burt knock some yap cold that got too gay, and you'd find out about horses and men and pick up a lot of stuff you could use all the rest of your life if you had some sense and salted down what you heard and felt and saw.

And then at the end of the week when the race meet was over, and Harry had run home to tend up to his livery stable business, you and Burt hitched the two horses to carts and drove slow and steady across country to the place for the next meeting so as not to overheat the horses, etc., etc., you know.

Gee whizz, gosh amighty, the nice hickorynut and beechnut and oaks and other kinds of trees along the roads, all brown and red, and the good smells, and Burt singing a song that was called Deep River, and the country girls at the windows of houses and everything. You can stick your colleges up your nose for all me. I guess I know where I got my education.

Why, one of those little burgs of towns you come to on the way, say now, on a Saturday afternoon, and Burt says, "let's lay up here." And you did.

And you took the horses to a livery stable and fed them and you got your good clothes out of a box and put them on.

And the town was full of farmers gaping, because they could see you were race horse people, and the kids maybe never see a nigger before and was afraid and run away when the two of us walked down their main street.

And that was before prohibition and all that foolishness, and so you went into a saloon, the two of you, and all the yaps come and stood around, and there was always someone pretended he was horsey and knew things and spoke up and began asking questions, and all you did was to lie and lie all you could about what horses you had, and I said I owned them, and then some fellow said, "Will you have a drink of whisky?" and Burt knocked his eye out the way he could say, offhand like, "Oh, well, all right, I'm agreeable to a little nip. I'll split a quart with you." Gee whizz.

But that isn't what I want to tell my story about. We got home late in November and I promised mother I'd quit the race horses for good. There's a lot of things you've got to promise a mother because she don't know any better.

And so, there not being any work in our town any more than when I left there to go to the races, I went off to Sandusky and got a pretty good place taking care of the horses for a man who owned a teaming and delivery and storage business there. It was a pretty good place with good eats and a day off each week and sleeping on a cot in the big barn, and mostly just shoveling in hay and oats to a lot of big good-enough skates of horses that couldn't have trotted a race with a toad. I wasn't dissatisfied and I could send money home.

And then, as I started to tell you, the fall races come to Sandusky and I got the day off and I went. I left the job at noon and had on my good clothes and my new brown derby hat I'd just bought the Saturday before, and a stand-up collar.

First of all I went downtown and walked about with the dudes. I've always thought to myself, "put up a good front," and so I did it. I had forty dollars in my pocket and so I went into the West House, a big hotel, and walked up to the cigar stand. "Give me three twenty-five cent cigars," I said. There was a lot of horse men and strangers and dressed-up people from other towns standing around in the lobby and in the bar, and I mingled amongst them. In the bar there was a fellow with a cane and a Windsor tie on, that it made me sick to look at him. I like a man to be a man and dress up, but not to go put on that kind of airs. So I pushed him aside, kind of rough, and had me a drink of whisky. And then he looked at me as though he thought he'd get gay, but he changed his mind and didn't say anything. And then I had another drink of whisky, just to show him something, and went out and had a hack out to the races all to myself, and when I got there I bought myself the best seat I could get up in the grandstand, but didn't go in for any of these boxes. That's putting on too many airs.

And so there I was, sitting up in the grandstand as gay as you please and looking down on the swipes coming out with their horses and with their dirty horsey pants on and the horse blankets swung over their shoulders same as I had been doing all the year before. I liked one thing about the same as the other, sitting up there and feeling grand and being down there and looking up at the yaps and feeling grander and more important too. One thing's about as good as another if you take it just right. I've often said that.

Well, right in front of me, in the grandstand that day, there was a fellow with a couple of girls and they was about my age. The young fellow was a nice guy all right. He was the kind maybe that goes to college and then comes to be a lawyer or maybe a newspaper editor or something like that, but he wasn't stuck on himself. There are some of that kind are all right and he was one of the ones.

He had his sister with him and another girl and the sister looked around over his shoulder, accidental at first, not intending to start anything—she wasn't that kind—and her eyes and mine happened to meet.

You know how it is. Gee, she was a peach. She had on a soft dress, kind of a blue stuff, and it looked carelessly made, but was well sewed and made and everything. I knew that much. I blushed when she looked right at me and so did she. She was the nicest girl I've ever seen in my life. She wasn't stuck on herself and she could talk proper grammar without being like a school teacher or something like that. What I mean is, she was O.K. I think maybe her father was well-to-do, but not rich to make her chesty because she was his daughter, as some are. Maybe he owned a drug store or a dry goods store in their home town, or something like that. She never told me and I never asked.

My own people are all O.K. too, when you come to that. My grandfather was Welsh and over in the old country, in Wales, he was—but never mind that.

The first heat of the first race come off and the young fellow setting there with the two girls left them and went down to make a bet. I knew what he was up to, but he didn't talk big and noisy and let everyone around know he was a sport, as some do. He wasn't that kind. Well, he come back and I heard him tell the two girls what horse he'd bet on, and when the heat was trotted they all half got to their feet and acted in the excited, sweaty way people do when they've got money down on a race, and the horse they bet on is up there pretty close at the end, and they think maybe he'll come on with a rush, but he never does because he hasn't got the old juice in him, come right down to it.

And, then, pretty soon, the horses came out for the 2.18 pace and there was a horse in it I knew. He was a horse Bob French had in his string, but Bob didn't own him. He was a horse owned by a Mr. Mathers down at Marietta, Ohio.

This Mr. Mathers had a lot of money and owned a coal mine or something, and he had a swell place out in the country, and he was stuck on race horses, but was a Presbyterian or something, and I think more than likely his wife was one, too, maybe a stiffer one than himself. So he never raced his horses hisself, and the story round the Ohio race tracks was that when one of his horses got ready to go to the races he turned him over to Bob French and pretended to his wife he was sold.

So Bob had the horses and he did pretty much as he pleased and you can't blame Bob; at least, I never did. Sometimes he was out to win and sometimes he wasn't. I never cared much about that when I was swiping a horse. What I did want to know was that my horse had the speed and could go out in front if you wanted him to.

And, as I'm telling you, there was Bob in this race with one of Mr. Mathers' horses, was named "About Ben Ahem" or something like that, and was fast as a streak. He was a gelding and had a mark of 2.21, but could step in .08 or .09.

Because when Burt and I were out, as I've told you, the year before, there was a nigger Burt knew, worked for Mr. Mathers, and we went out there one day when we didn't have no race on at the Marietta Fair and our boss Harry had gone home.

And so everyone was gone to the fair but just this one nigger, and he took us all through Mr. Mathers' swell house and he and Burt tapped a bottle of wine Mr. Mathews had hid in his bedroom, back in a closet, without his wife knowing, and he showed us this Ahem horse. Burt was always stuck on being a driver, but didn't have much chance to get to the top, being a nigger, and he and the other nigger gulped that whole bottle of wine and Burt got a little lit up.

So the nigger let Burt take this About Ben Ahem and step him a mile in a track Mr. Mathers had all to himself, right there on the farm. And Mr. Mathers had one child, a daughter, kinda sick and not very good-looking, and she came home and we had to hustle and get About Ben Ahem stuck back in the barn.

I'm only telling you to get everything straight. At Sandusky, that afternoon I was at the fair, this young fellow with the two girls was fussed, being with the girls and losing his bet. You know how a fellow is that way. One of them was his girl and the other his sister. I had figured that out.

"Gee whizz" I says to myself, "I'm going to give him the dope."

He was mighty nice when I touched him on the shoulder. He and the girls were nice to me right from the start and clear to the end. I'm not blaming them.

And so he leaned back and I gave him the dope on About Ben Ahem. "Don't bet a cent on this first heat because he'll go like an oxen hitched to a plough, but when the first heat is over go right down and lay on your pile." That's what I told him.

Well, I never saw a fellow treat any one sweller. There was a fat man sitting beside the little girl that had looked at me twice by this time, and I at her, and both blushing, and what did he do but have the nerve to turn and ask the fat man to get up and change places with me so I could set with his crowd.

Gee whizz, amighty. There I was. What a chump I was to go and get gay up there in the West House bar, and just because that dude was standing there with a cane and that kind of a necktie on, to go and get all balled up and drink that whisky, just to show off.

Of course, she would know, me setting right beside her and letting her smell of my breath. I could have kicked myself right down out of that grandstand and all around that race track and made a faster record than most of the skates of horses they had there that year.

Because that girl wasn't any mutt of a girl. What wouldn't I have given right then for a stick of chewing gum to chew, or a lozenger, or some licorice, or most anything. I was glad I had those twenty-five cent cigars in my pocket, and right away I give that fellow one and lit one myself. Then that fat man got up and we changed places and there I was plunked down beside her.

They introduced themselves, and the fellow's best girl he had with him, was named Miss Elinor Woodbury, and her father was a manufacturer of barrels from a place called Tiffin, Ohio. And the fellow himself was named Wilbur Wessen and his sister was Miss Lucy Wessen.

I suppose it was their having such swell names got me off my trolley. A fellow, just because he has been a swipe with a race horse, and works taking care of horses for a man in the teaming, delivery and storage business, isn't any better or worse than anyone else. I've often thought that, and said it, too.

But you know how a fellow is. There's something in that kind of nice clothes, and the kind of nice eyes she had, and the way she looked at me, awhile before, over her brother's shoulder, and me looking back at her, and both of us blushing.

I couldn't show her up for a boob, could I?

I made a fool of myself, that's what I did. I said my name was Walter Mathers from Marietta, Ohio, and then I told all three of them the smashingest lie you ever heard. What I said was that my father owned the horse About Ben Ahem, and that he had let him out to this Bob French for racing purposes, because our family was proud and had never gone into racing that way, in our own name, I mean. Then I had got started, and they were all leaning over and listening, and Miss Lucy Wessen's eyes were shining, and I went the whole hog.

I told about our place down at Marietta, and about the big stables and the grand brick house we had on a hill, up above the Ohio River, but I knew enough not to do it in no bragging way. What I did was to start things and then let them drag the rest out of me. I acted just as reluctant to tell as I could. Our family hasn't got any barrel factory, and, since I've known us, we've always been pretty poor, but not asking anything of anyone at that, and my grandfather, over in Wales—but never mind that.

We set there talking like we had known each other for years and years, and I went and told them that my father had been expecting maybe this Bob French wasn't on the square, and had sent me up to Sandusky on the sly to find out what I could.

And I bluffed it through I had found out all about the 2.18 pace in which About Ben Ahem was to start.

I said he would lose the first heat by pacing like a lame cow and then he would come back and skin 'em alive after that. And to back up what I said I took thirty dollars out of my pocket and handed it to Mr. Wilbur Wessen and asked him would he mind, after the first heat, to go down and place it on About Ben Ahem for whatever odds he could get. What I said was that I didn't want Bob French to see me and none of the swipes.

Sure enough the first heat come off and About Ben Ahem went off his stride, up the back stretch, and looked like a wooden horse or a sick one, and come in to be last. Then this Wilbur Wessen went down to the betting place under the grandstand and there I was with the two girls, and when that Miss Woodbury was looking the other way once, Lucy Wessen kinda, with her shoulder you know, kinda touched me. Not just tucking down, I don't mean. You know how a woman can do. They get close, but not getting gay either. You know what they do. Gee whizz.

And then they give me a jolt. What they had done when I didn't know, was to get together, and they had decided Wilbur Wessen would bet fifty dollars, and the two girls had gone and put in ten dollars each of their own money, too. I was sick then, but I was sicker later.

About the gelding, About Ben Ahem, and their winning their money I wasn't worried a lot about that. It come out O.K. Ahem stepped the next three heats like a bushel of spoiled eggs going to market before they could be found out, and Wilbur Wessen had got nine to two for the money. There was something else eating at me.

Because Wilbur come back after he had bet the money, and after that he spent most of his time talking to that Miss Woodbury, and Lucy Wessen and I was left alone together like on a desert island. Gee, if I'd only been on the square or if there had been any way of getting myself on the square. There ain't any Walter Mathers, like I said to her and them, and there hasn't ever been one, but if there was, I bet I'd go to Marietta, Ohio, and shoot him tomorrow.

There I was, big boob that I am. Pretty soon the race was over, and Wilbur had gone down and collected our money, and we had a hack down town, and he stood us a swell dinner at the West House, and a bottle of champagne beside.

And I was with that girl and she wasn't saying much, and I wasn't saying much either. One thing I know. She wasn't stuck on me because of the lie about my father being rich and all that. There's a way you know. . . . Craps amighty. There's a kind of girl you see just once in your life, and if you don't get busy and make hay then you're gone for good and all and might as well go jump off a bridge. They give you a look from inside of them somewhere, and it ain't no vamping, and what it means is—you want that girl to be your wife, and you want nice things around her like flowers and swell clothes, and you want her to have the kids you're going to have, and you want good music played and no ragtime. Gee whizz.

There's a place over near Sandusky, across a kind of bay, and it's called Cedar Point. And when we had had that dinner we went over to it in a launch, all by ourselves. Wilbur and Miss Lucy and that Miss Woodbury had to catch a ten o'clock train back to Tiffin, Ohio, because when you're out with girls like that you can't get careless and miss any trains and stay out all night like you can with some kinds of Janes.

And Wilbur blowed himself to the launch and it cost him fifteen cold plunks, but I wouldn't ever have knew it if I hadn't listened. He wasn't no tin horn kind of a sport.

Over at the Cedar Point place we didn't stay around where there was a gang of common kind of cattle at all.

There was big dance halls and dining places for yaps, and there was a beach you could walk along and get where it was dark, and we went there.

She didn't talk hardly at all and neither did I, and I was thinking how glad I was my mother was all right, and always made us kids learn to eat with a fork at table and not swill soup and not be noisy and rough like a gang you see around a race track that way.

Then Wilbur and his girl went away up the beach and Lucy and I set down in a dark place where there was some roots of old trees the water had washed up, and after that, the time, till we had to go back in the launch and they had to catch their trains, wasn't nothing at all. It went like winking your eye.

Here's how it was. The place we were setting in was dark, like I said, and there was the roots from that old stump sticking up like arms, and there was a watery smell, and the night was like—as if you could put your hand out and feel it—so warm and soft and dark and sweet like an orange.

I most cried and I most swore and I most jumped up and danced, I was so mad and happy and sad.

When Wilbur come back from being alone with his girl, and she saw him coming, Lucy she says, "We got to go to the train now," and she was most crying, too, but she never knew nothing I knew, and she couldn't be so all busted up. And then, before Wilbur and Miss Woodbury got up to where we was, she put her face up and kissed me quick and put her head up against me and she was all quivering and—Gee whizz.

Sometimes I hope I have cancer and die. I guess you know what I mean. We went in the launch across the bay to the train like that, and it was dark too. She whispered and said it was like she and I could get out of the boat and walk on the water, and it sounded foolish, but I knew what she meant.

And then quick, we were right at the depot, and there was a big gang of yaps, the kind that goes to the fairs, and crowded and milling around like cattle, and how could I tell her? "It won't be long because you'll write and I'll write to you." That's all she said.

I got a chance like a hay barn afire. A swell chance I got.

And maybe she would write me, down at Marietta that way, and the letter would come back, and stamped on the front of it by the U.S.A. "there ain't any such guy," or something like that, whatever they stamp on a letter that way.

And me trying to pass myself off for a bigbug and a swell—to her, as decent a little body as God ever made. Craps amighty. A swell chance I got.

And then the train come and she got on, and Wilbur Wessen come and shook hands with me, and that Miss Woodbury was nice too, and bowed to me and I at her and the train went and I busted out and cried like a kid.

Gee, I could have run after that train and made Dan Patch look like a freight train after a wreck, but socks amighty, what was the use? Did you ever see such a fool?

I'll bet you what—if I had an arm broke right now or a train had run over my foot—I wouldn't go to no doctor at all. I'd go set down and let her hurt and hurt—that's what I 'd do.

I'll bet you what—if I hadn't a drunk that booze I'd a never been such a boob as to go tell such a lie—that couldn't never be made straight to a lady like her.

I wish I had that fellow right here that had on a Windsor tie and carried a cane. I'd smash him for fair. Gosh darn his eyes. He's a big fool—that's what he is.

And if I'm not another you just go find me one and I'll quit working and be a bum and give him my job. I don't care nothing for working and earning money and saving it for no such boob as myself.

WILLA CATHER

❧ *Paul's Case*

IT WAS Paul's afternoon to appear before the faculty of the Pittsburgh High School to account for his various misdemeanors. He had been suspended a week ago, and his father had called at the Principal's office and confessed his perplexity about his son. Paul entered the faculty room suave and smiling. His clothes were a trifle outgrown, and the tan velvet on the collar of his open overcoat was frayed and worn; but for all that there was something of the dandy about him, and he wore an opal pin in his neatly knotted black four-in-hand, and a red carnation in his buttonhole. This latter adornment the faculty somehow felt was not properly significant of the contrite spirit befitting a boy under the ban of suspension.

Paul was tall for his age and very thin, with high, cramped shoulders and a narrow chest. His eyes were remarkable for a certain hysterical brilliancy, and he continually used them in a conscious, theatrical sort of way, peculiarly offensive in a boy. The pupils were abnormally large, as though he were addicted to belladonna, but there was a glassy glitter about them which that drug does not produce.

When questioned by the Principal as to why he was there, Paul stated, politely enough, that he wanted to come back to school. This was a lie, but Paul was quite accustomed to lying; found it, indeed, indispensable for overcoming friction. His teachers were asked to state their respective charges against him, which they did with such a rancor and aggrievedness as evinced that this was not a usual case. Disorder and impertinence were among the offenses named, yet each of his instructors felt that it was scarcely possible to put into words the real cause of the trouble, which lay in a sort of hysterically defiant manner of the boy's; in the contempt which they all knew he felt for them, and which he seemingly made not the least effort to conceal. Once, when he had been making a synopsis of a paragraph at the blackboard, his English teacher had stepped to his side and attempted to guide his hand. Paul had started back with a shudder and thrust his hands violently behind him. The astonished woman could scarcely have been more hurt and embarrassed had he struck at her. The insult was so involuntary and definitely personal as to be unforgettable. In one way and another, he had made all his teachers, men and women alike, conscious of the same feeling of physical aversion. In one class he habitually sat with his hand shading his eyes; in another he always looked out of the window during the recitation; in another he made a running commentary on the lecture, with humorous intent.

His teachers felt this afternoon that his whole attitude was symbolized by his shrug and his flippantly red carnation flower, and they fell upon him without mercy, his English teacher leading the pack. He stood through it smiling, his pale lips parted over his white teeth. (His lips were continually twitching, and he had a habit of raising his eyebrows that was contemptuous and irritating to the last degree.) Older boys than Paul had broken down and shed tears under that ordeal, but his set smile did not once desert him, and his only sign of discomfort was the nervous trembling of the fingers that toyed with the buttons of his overcoat, and an occasional jerking of the other hand which held his hat. Paul was always smiling, always glancing about him, seeming to feel that people might be watching him and trying to detect something. This conscious expression, since it was as far as possible from boyish mirthfulness, was usually attributed to insolence or "smartness."

As the inquisition proceeded, one of his instructors repeated an impertinent remark of the boy's, and the Principal asked him whether he thought that a courteous speech to make to a woman. Paul shrugged his shoulders slightly and his eyebrows twitched.

"I don't know," he replied. "I didn't mean to be polite or impolite, either. I guess it's a sort of way I have, of saying things regardless."

The Principal asked him whether he didn't think that a way it would be well to get rid of. Paul grinned and said he guessed so. When he was told that he could go, he bowed gracefully and went out. His bow was like a repetition of the scandalous red carnation.

His teachers were in despair, and his drawing master voiced the feeling of them all when he declared there was something about the boy which none of them understood. He added: "I don't really believe that smile of his comes altogether from insolence; there's something sort of haunted about it. The boy is not strong, for one thing. There is something wrong about the fellow."

The drawing master had come to realize that, in looking at Paul, one saw only his white teeth and the forced animation of his eyes. One warm afternoon the boy had gone to sleep at his drawing board, and his master had noted with amazement what a white, blue-veined face it was; drawn and wrinkled like an old man's about the eyes, the lips twitching even in his sleep.

His teachers left the building dissatisfied and unhappy; humiliated to have felt so vindictive toward a mere boy, to have uttered this feeling in cutting terms, and to have set each other on, as it were, in the gruesome game of intemperate reproach. One of them remembered having seen a miserable street cat set at bay by a ring of tormentors.

As for Paul, he ran down the hill whistling the Soldiers' Chorus from *Faust*, looking wildly behind him now and then to see whether some of his teachers were not there to witness his light-heartedness. As it was now late in the afternoon and Paul was on duty that evening as usher at Carnegie Hall, he decided that he would not go home to supper.

When he reached the concert hall the doors were not yet open. It was chilly outside, and he decided to go up into the picture gallery—always deserted at this hour—where there were some of Raffaelli's [1850–1924; French impressionist painter] gay studies of Paris streets and an airy blue Venetian scene or two that always exhilarated him. He was delighted to find no one in the gallery but the old guard, who sat in the corner, a newspaper on his knee, a black patch over one eye and the other closed. Paul possessed himself of the place and walked confidently up and down, whistling under his breath. After a while he sat down before a blue Rico [1833–1908; Spanish landscape artist] and lost himself. When he bethought him to look at his watch, it was after seven o'clock, and he rose with a start and ran downstairs, making a face at Augustus Caesar, peering out from the cast-room, and an evil gesture at the Venus of Milo as he passed her on the stairway.

When Paul reached the ushers' dressing-room half a dozen boys were there already, and he began excitedly to tumble into his uniform. It was one of the few that at all approached fitting, and Paul thought it very becoming—though he knew the tight, straight coat accentuated his narrow chest, about which he was exceedingly sensitive. He was always excited while he dressed, twanging all over to the tuning of the strings and the preliminary flourishes of the horns in the music-room; but tonight he seemed quite beside himself, and he teased and plagued the boys until, telling him that he was crazy, they put him down on the floor and sat on him.

Somewhat calmed by his suppression, Paul dashed out to the front of the house to seat the early comers. He was a model usher. Gracious and smiling he ran up and down the aisles. Nothing was too much trouble for him; he carried messages and brought programs as though it were his greatest pleasure in life, and all the people in his section thought him a charming boy, feeling that he remembered and admired them. As the house filled, he grew more and more vivacious and animated, and the color came to his cheeks and lips. It was very much as though this were a great reception and Paul were the host. Just as the musicians came out to take their places, his English teacher arrived with checks for the seats which a prominent manufacturer had taken for the season. She betrayed some embarrassment when she handed Paul the tickets, and a *hauteur* which subsequently made her feel very foolish. Paul was startled for a moment, and had the feeling of wanting to put her out; what business had she here among all these fine people and gay colors? He looked her over and decided that she was not appropriately dressed and must be a fool to sit downstairs in such togs. The tickets had probably been sent her out of kindness, he reflected, as he put down a seat for her, and she had about as much right to sit there as he had.

When the symphony began Paul sank into one of the rear seats with a long sigh of relief, and lost himself as he had done before the Rico. It was not that symphonies, as such, meant anything in particular to Paul, but the first sigh of the instruments seemed to free some hilarious spirit within him; something that struggled there like the Genius in the bottle found by the Arab fisherman. He felt a sudden zest of life; the lights danced before his eyes and the concert hall blazed into unimaginable splendor. When the soprano soloist came on, Paul forgot even the nastiness of his teacher's being there, and gave himself up to the peculiar intoxication such personages always had for him. The soloist chanced to be a German woman, by no means in her first youth, and the mother of many children; but she wore a satin gown and a tiara, and she had that indefinable air of achievement, that world-shine upon her, which always blinded Paul to any possible defects.

After a concert was over, Paul was often irritable and wretched until he got to sleep,—and tonight he was even more than usually restless. He had the feeling of not being able to let down; of its being impossible to give up this delicious excitement which was the only thing that could be called living at all. During the last number he withdrew and, after hastily changing his clothes in the dressing-room, slipped out to the side door where the singer's carriage stood. Here he began pacing rapidly up and down the walk, waiting to see her come out.

Over yonder the Schenley, in its vacant stretch, loomed big and square through the fine rain, the windows of its twelve stories glowing like those of a lighted cardboard house under a Christmas tree. All the actors and singers of any importance stayed there when they were in the city, and a number of the big manufacturers of the place lived there in the winter. Paul had often hung about the hotel, watching the people go in and out, longing to enter and leave schoolmasters and dull care behind him forever.

At last the singer came out, accompanied by the conductor, who helped her into her carriage and closed the door with a cordial *auf wiedersehen,*—which set Paul to wondering whether she were not an old sweetheart of his. Paul followed the carriage over to the hotel, walking so rapidly as not to be far from the entrance when the singer alighted and disappeared behind the swinging glass doors which were opened by a Negro in a tall hat and a long coat. In the moment that the door was ajar, it seemed to Paul that he, too, entered. He seemed to feel himself go after her up the steps, into the warm, lighted building, into an exotic, a tropical world of shiny, glistening surfaces and basking ease. He reflected upon the mysterious dishes that were brought into the dining-room, the green bottles in buckets of ice, as he had seen them in the supper party pictures of the Sunday supplement. A quick gust of wind brought the rain down with sudden vehemence, and Paul was startled to find that he was still outside in the slush of the gravel driveway; that his boots were letting in the water and his scanty overcoat was clinging wet about him; that the lights in front of the concert hall were out, and that the rain was driving in sheets between him and the orange glow of the windows above him. There it was, what he wanted—tangibly before him, like the fairy world of a Christmas pantomime; as the rain beat in his face, Paul wondered whether he were destined always to shiver in the black night outside, looking up at it.

He turned and walked reluctantly toward the car tracks. The end had to come some time; his father in his night-clothes at the top of the stairs, explanations that did not explain, hastily improvised fictions that were forever tripping him up, his upstairs room and its horrible yellow wall paper, the creaking bureau with the greasy plush collar-box, and over his painted wooden bed the pictures of George Washington and John Calvin, and the framed motto, "Feed my Lambs," which had been worked in red worsted by his mother, whom Paul could not remember.

Half an hour later, Paul alighted from the Negley Avenue car and went slowly down one of the side streets off the main thoroughfare. It was a highly respectable street, where all the houses were exactly alike, and where business men of moderate means begot and reared large families of children, all of whom went to Sabbath-school and learned the shorter catechism, and were interested in arithmetic; all of whom were as exactly alike as their homes, and of a piece with the monotony in which they lived. Paul never went up Cordelia Street without a shudder of loathing. His home was next the house of the Cumberland minister. He approached it tonight with the nerveless sense of defeat, the hopeless feeling of sinking back forever into ugliness and commonness that he had always had when he came home. The moment he turned into Cordelia Street he felt the waters close above his head. After each of these orgies of living, he experienced all the physical depression which follows a debauch; the loathing of respectable beds, of common food, of a house permeated by kitchen odors; a shuddering repulsion for the flavorless, colorless mass of everyday existence; a morbid desire for cool things and soft lights and fresh flowers.

The nearer he approached the house, the more absolutely unequal Paul felt to the sight of it all; his ugly sleeping chamber; the cold bathroom with the grimy zinc tub, the cracked mirror, the dripping spiggots; his father, at the top of the stairs, his hairy legs sticking out from his nightshirt, his feet thrust into carpet slippers. He was so much later than usual that there would certainly be inquiries and reproaches. Paul stopped short before the door. He felt that he could not be accosted by his father tonight; that he could not toss again on that miserable bed. He would not go in. He would tell his father that he had no car fare, and it was raining so hard he had gone home with one of the boys and stayed all night.

Meanwhile, he was wet and cold. He went around to the back of the house and tried one of the basement windows, found it open, raised it cautiously, and scrambled down the cellar wall to the floor. There he stood, holding his breath, terrified by the noise he had made; but the floor above him was silent, and there was no creak on the stairs. He found a soap-box, and carried it over to the soft ring of light that streamed from the furnace door, and sat down. He was horribly afraid of rats, so he did not try to sleep, but sat looking distrustfully at the dark, still terrified lest he might have awakened his father. In such reactions, after one of the experiences which made days and nights out of the dreary blanks of the calendar, when his senses were deadened, Paul's head was always singularly clear. Suppose his father had heard him getting in at the window and had come down and shot him for a burglar? Then, again, suppose his father had come down, pistol in hand, and he had cried out in time to save himself, and his father had been horrified to think how nearly he had killed him? Then, again, suppose a day should come when his father would remember that night, and wish there had been no warning cry to stay his hand? With this last supposition Paul entertained himself until daybreak.

The following Sunday was fine; the sodden November chill was broken by the last flash of autumnal summer. In the morning Paul had to go to church and Sabbath-school, as always. On seasonable Sunday afternoons the burghers of Cordelia Street usually sat out on their front "stoops," and talked to their neighbors on the next stoop, or called to those across the street in neighborly fashion. The men sat placidly on gay cushions placed upon the steps that led down to the sidewalk, while the women, in their Sunday "waists," sat in rockers on the cramped porches, pretending to be greatly at their ease. The children played in the streets; there were so many of them that the place resembled the recreation grounds of a kindergarten. The men on the steps—all in their shirt sleeves, their vests unbuttoned—sat with their legs well apart, their stomachs comfortably protruding, and talked of the prices of things, or told anecdotes of the sagacity of their various chiefs and overlords. They occasionally looked over the multitude of squabbling children, listened affectionately to their high-pitched, nasal voices, smiling to see their own proclivities reproduced in their offspring, and interspersed their legends of the iron kings with remarks about their sons' progress at school, their grades in arithmetic, and the amounts they had saved in their toy banks. On this last Sunday of November, Paul sat all the afternoon on the lowest step of his stoop, staring into the street, while his sisters, in their rockers, were talking to the minister's daughters next door about how many shirtwaists they had made in the last week, and how many waffles someone had eaten at the last church supper. When the weather was warm, and his father was in a particularly jovial frame of mind, the girls made lemonade, which was always brought out in a red-glass pitcher, ornamented with forget-me-nots in blue enamel. This the girls thought very fine, and the neighbors joked about the suspicious color of the pitcher.

Today Paul's father, on the top step, was talking to a young man who shifted a restless baby from knee to knee. He happened to be the young man who was daily held up to Paul as a model, and after whom it was his father's dearest hope that he would pattern. This young man was of a ruddy complexion, with a compressed, red mouth, and faded, nearsighted eyes, over which he wore thick spectacles, with gold bows that curved about his ears. He was clerk to one of the magnates of a great steel corporation, and was looked upon in Cordelia Street as a young man with a future. There was a story that, some five years ago—he was now barely twenty-six—he had been a trifle "dissipated," but in order to curb his appetites and save the loss of time and strength that a sowing of wild oats might have entailed, he had taken his chief's advice, oft reiterated to his employees, and at twenty-one had married the first woman whom he could persuade to share his fortunes. She happened to be an angular school mistress, much older than he, who also wore thick glasses, and who had now borne him four children, all near-sighted, like herself.

The young man was relating how his chief, now cruising in the Mediterranean, kept in touch with all the details of the business, arranging his office hours on his yacht just as though he were at home, and "knocking off work enough to keep two stenographers busy." His father told, in turn, the plan his corporation was considering, of putting in an electric railway plant at Cairo. Paul snapped his teeth; he had an awful apprehension that they might spoil it all before he got there. Yet he rather liked to hear these legends of the iron kings, that were told and retold on Sundays and holidays; these stories of palaces in Venice, yachts on the Mediterranean, and high play at Monte Carlo appealed to his fancy, and he was interested in the triumphs of cash boys[2] who had become famous, though he had no mind for the cash-boy stage.

After supper was over, and he had helped to dry the dishes, Paul nervously asked his father whether he could go to George's to get some help in his geometry, and still more nervously asked for car fare. This latter request he had to repeat, as his father, on principle, did not like to hear requests for money, whether much or little. He asked Paul whether he could not go to some boy who lived nearer, and told him that he ought not to leave his school work until Sunday; but he gave him the dime. He was not a poor man, but he had a worthy ambition to come up in the world. His only reason for allowing Paul to usher was that he thought a boy ought to be earning a little.

Paul bounded upstairs, scrubbed the greasy odor of the dishwater from his hands with the ill-smelling soap he hated, and then shook over his fingers a few

---

[2] Messengers who carry money or chips from the gambling table to the cashier and back. [Eds.]

drops of violet water from the bottle he kept hidden in his drawer. He left the house with his geometry conspicuously under his arm, and the moment he got out of Cordelia Street and boarded a downtown car, he shook off the lethargy of two deadening days, and began to live again.

The leading juvenile of the permanent stock company which played at one of the downtown theaters was an acquaintance of Paul's, and the boy had been invited to drop in at the Sunday night rehearsals whenever he could. For more than a year Paul had spent every available moment loitering about Charley Edwards's dressing-room. He had won a place among Edwards's following not only because the young actor, who could not afford to employ a dresser, often found him useful, but because he recognized in Paul something akin to what churchmen term "vocation."

It was at the theater and at Carnegie Hall that Paul really lived; the rest was but a sleep and a forgetting. This was Paul's fairy tale, and it had for him all the allurement of a secret love. The moment he inhaled the gassy, painty, dusty odor behind the scenes, he breathed like a prisoner set free, and felt within him the possibility of doing or saying splendid, brilliant things. The moment the cracked orchestra beat out the overture from *Martha*, or jerked at the serenade from *Rigoletto*, all stupid and ugly things slid from him, and his senses were deliciously, yet delicately fired.

Perhaps it was because, in Paul's world, the natural nearly always wore the guise of ugliness, that a certain element of artificiality seemed to him necessary in beauty. Perhaps it was because his experience of life elsewhere was so full of Sabbath-school picnics, petty economies, wholesome advice as to how to succeed in life, and the unescapable odors of cooking that he found this existence so alluring, these smartly-clad men and women so attractive, that he was so moved by these starry apple orchards that bloomed perennially under the limelight.

It would be difficult to put it strongly enough how convincingly the stage entrance of that theater was for Paul the actual portal of Romance. Certainly none of the company ever suspected it, least of all Charley Edwards. It was very like the old stories that used to float about London of fabulously rich Jews, who had subterranean halls, with palms, and fountains, and soft lamps and richly apparelled women who never saw the disenchanting light of London day. So, in the midst of that smoke-palled city, enamored of figures and grimy toil, Paul had his secret temple, his wishing-carpet, his bit of blue-and-white Mediterranean shore bathed in perpetual sunshine.

Several of Paul's teachers had a theory that his imagination had been perverted by garish fiction; but the truth was, he scarcely ever read at all. The books at home were not such as would either tempt or corrupt a youthful mind, and as for reading the novels that some of his friends urged upon him—well, he got what he wanted much more quickly from music; any sort of music, from an orchestra to a barrel organ. He needed only the spark, the indescribable thrill that made his imagination master of his senses, and he could make plots and pictures enough of his own. It was equally true that he was not stage-struck—not, at any rate, in the usual acceptation of that expression. He had no desire to become an actor, any more than he had to become a musician. He felt no necessity to do any of these things; what he wanted was to see, to be in the atmosphere, float on the wave of it, to be carried out, blue league after blue league, away from everything.

After a night behind the scenes, Paul found the schoolroom more than ever repulsive; the bare floors and naked walls; the prosy men who never wore frock coats, or violets in their buttonholes; the women with their dull gowns, shrill voices, and pitiful seriousness about prepositions that govern the dative. He could not bear to have the other pupils think, for a moment, that he took these people seriously; he must convey to them that he considered it all trivial, and was there only by way of a joke, anyway. He had autograph pictures of all the members of the stock company which he showed his classmates, telling them the most incredible stories of his familiarity with these people, of his acquaintance with the soloists who came to Carnegie Hall, his suppers with them and the flowers he sent them. When these stories lost their effect, and his audience grew listless, he would bid all the boys good-by, announcing that he was going to travel for a while; going to Naples, to California, to Egypt. Then, next Monday, he would slip back, conscious and nervously smiling; his sister was ill, and he would have to defer his voyage until spring.

Matters went steadily worse with Paul at school. In the itch to let his instructors know how heartily he despised them, and how thoroughly he was appreciated elsewhere, he mentioned once or twice that he had no time to fool with theorems; adding—with a twitch of the eyebrows and a touch of that nervous bravado which so perplexed them—that he was helping the people down at the stock company; they were old friends of his.

The upshot of the matter was, that the Principal went to Paul's father, and Paul was taken out of school and put to work. The manager at Carnegie Hall was told to get another usher in his stead; the doorkeeper at the theater was warned not to admit him to the house; and Charley Edwards remorsefully promised the boy's father not to see him again.

The members of the stock company were vastly amused when some of Paul's stories reached them—especially the women. They were hard-working women, most of them supporting indolent husbands or brothers, and they laughed rather bitterly at having stirred the boy to such fervid and florid inventions. They agreed with the faculty and with his father, that Paul's was a bad case.

The east-bound train was plowing through a January snowstorm; the dull dawn was beginning to show gray when the engine whistled a mile out of Newark. Paul started up from the seat where he had lain curled in uneasy slumber, rubbed the breath-misted window glass with his hand, and peered out. The snow was whirling in curling eddies above the white bottom lands, and the drifts lay already deep in the fields and along the fences, while here and there the long dead grass and dried weed stalks protruded black above it. Lights shone from the scattered houses, and a gang of laborers who stood beside the track waved their lanterns.

Paul had slept very little, and he felt grimy and uncomfortable. He had made the all-night journey in a day coach because he was afraid if he took a Pullman he might be seen by some Pittsburgh business man who had noticed him in Denny & Carson's office. When the whistle woke him, he clutched quickly at his breast pocket, glancing about him with an uncertain smile. But the little, clay-bespattered Italians were still sleeping, the slatternly women across the aisle were in open-mouthed oblivion, and even the crumby, crying babies were for the nonce stilled. Paul settled back to struggle with his impatience as best he could.

When he arrived at the Jersey City station, he hurried through his breakfast, manifestly ill at ease and keeping a sharp eye about him. After he reached the Twenty-third Street station, he consulted a cabman, and had himself driven to a men's furnishing establishment which was just opening for the day. He spent upward to two hours there, buying with endless reconsidering and great care. His new street suit he put on in the fitting-room; the frock coat and dress clothes he had bundled into the cab with his new shirts. Then he drove to a hatter's and a shoe house. His next errand was at Tiffany's, where he selected silver-mounted brushes and a scarf-pin. He would not wait to have his silver marked, he said. Lastly, he stopped at a trunk shop on Broadway, and had his purchases packed into various traveling bags.

It was a little after one o'clock when he drove up to the Waldorf, and, after settling with the cabman, went into the office. He registered from Washington; said his mother and father had been abroad, and that he had come down to await the arrival of their steamer. He told his story plausibly and had no trouble, since he offered to pay for them in advance, in engaging his rooms; a sleeping-room, sitting room and bath.

Not once, but a hundred times Paul had planned this entry into New York. He had gone over every detail of it with Charley Edwards, and in his scrap book at home there were pages of description about New York hotels, cut from the Sunday papers.

When he was shown to his sitting room on the eighth floor, he saw at a glance that everything was as it should be; there was but one detail in his mental picture that the place did not realize, so he rang for the bell boy and sent him down for flowers. He moved about nervously until the boy returned, putting away his new linen and fingering it delightedly as he did so. When the flowers came, he put them hastily into water, and then tumbled into a hot bath. Presently he came out of his white bathroom, resplendent in his new silk underwear, and playing with the tassels of his red robe. The snow was whirling so fiercely outside his windows that he could scarcely see across the street; but within, the air was deliciously soft and fragrant. He put the violets and jonquils on the tabouret beside the couch, and threw himself down with a long sigh, covering himself with a Roman blanket. He was thoroughly tired; he had been in such haste, he had stood up to such a strain, covered so much ground in the last twenty-four hours, that he wanted to think how it had all come about. Lulled by the sound of the wind, the warm air, and the cool fragrance of the flowers, he sank into deep, drowsy retrospection.

It had been wonderfully simple; when they had shut him out of the theater and concert hall, when they had taken away his bone, the whole thing was virtually determined. The rest was a mere matter of opportunity. The only thing that at all surprised him was his own courage—for he realized well enough that he had always been tormented by fear, a sort of apprehensive dread that, of late years, as the meshes of the lies he had told closed about him, had been pulling the muscles of his body tighter and tighter. Until now, he could not remember a time when he had not been dreading something. Even when he was a little boy, it was always there—behind him, or before, or on either side. There had always been the shadowed corner, the dark place into which he dared not look but from which something seemed always to be watching him—and Paul had done things that were not pretty to watch, he knew.

But now he had a curious sense of relief, as though he had at last thrown down the gauntlet to the thing in the corner.

Yet it was but a day since he had been sulking in the traces; but yesterday afternoon that he had been sent to the bank with Denny & Carson's deposit, as usual—but this time he was instructed to leave the book to be balanced. There was above two thousand dollars in checks, and nearly a thousand in the bank notes which he had taken from the book and quietly transferred to his pocket. At the bank he had made out a new deposit slip. His nerves had been steady enough to permit of his returning to the office, where he had finished his work and asked for a full day's holiday tomorrow, Saturday, giving a perfectly reasonable pretext. The bank book, he knew, would not be returned before Monday or Tuesday, and his father would be out of town for the next week. From the time he slipped the bank notes into his pocket until he boarded the night train for New York, he had not known a moment's hesitation.

How astonishingly easy it had all been; here he was, the thing done; and this time there would be no awakening, no figure at the top of the stairs. He watched the snowflakes whirling by his window until he fell asleep.

When he awoke, it was four o'clock in the afternoon. He bounded up with a start; one of his precious days gone already! He spent nearly an hour in dressing, watching every stage of his toilet carefully in the mirror. Everything was quite perfect; he was exactly the kind of boy he had always wanted to be.

When he went downstairs, Paul took a carriage and drove up Fifth Avenue toward the Park. The snow had somewhat abated; carriages and tradesmen's wagons were hurrying soundlessly to and fro in the winter twilight; boys in woolen mufflers were shoveling off the doorsteps; the avenue stages made fine spots of color against the white street. Here and there on the corners whole flower gardens blooming behind glass windows, against which the snowflakes stuck and melted; violets, roses, carnations, lilies of the valley—somehow vastly more lovely and alluring that they blossomed thus unnaturally in the snow. The Park itself was a wonderful stage winter-piece.

When he returned, the pause of the twilight had ceased, and the tune of the streets had changed. The snow was falling faster, lights streamed from the hotels that reared their many stories fearlessly up into the storm, defying the raging Atlantic winds. A long, black stream of carriages poured down the avenue, intersected here and there by other streams, tending horizontally. There were a score of cabs about the entrance of his hotel, and his driver had to wait. Boys in livery were running in and out of the awning stretched across the sidewalk, up and down the red velvet carpet laid from the door to the street. Above, about, within it all, was the rumble and roar, the hurry and toss of thousands of human beings as hot for pleasure as himself, and on every side of him towered the glaring affirmation of the omnipotence of wealth.

The boy set his teeth and drew his shoulders together in a spasm of realization; the plot of all dramas, the text of all romances, the nerve-stuff of all sensations was whirling about him like the snowflakes. He burnt like a faggot in a tempest.

When Paul came down to dinner, the music of the orchestra floated up the elevator shaft to greet him. As he stepped into the thronged corridor, he sank back into one of the chairs against the wall to get his breath. The lights, the chatter, the perfumes, the bewildering medley of color—he had, for a moment, the feeling of not being able to stand it. But only for a moment; these were his own people, he told himself. He went slowly about the corridors, through the writing-rooms, smoking-rooms, reception-rooms, as though he were exploring the chambers of an enchanted palace, built and peopled for him alone.

When he reached the dining room he sat down at a table near a window. The flowers, the white linen, the many-colored wine glasses, the gay toilettes of the women, the low popping of corks, the undulating repetitions of the *Blue Danube* from the orchestra, all flooded Paul's dream with bewildering radiance. When the roseate tinge of his champagne was added—that cold, precious, bubbling stuff that creamed and foamed in his glass—Paul wondered that there were honest men in the world at all. This was what all the world was fighting for, he reflected; this was what all the struggle was about. He doubted the reality of his past. Had he ever known a place called Cordelia Street, a place where fagged-looking business men boarded the early car? Mere rivets in a machine they seemed to Paul,—sickening men, with combings of children's hair always hanging to their coats, and the smell of cooking in their clothes. Cordelia Street—Ah, that belonged to another time and country! Had he not always been thus, had he not sat here night after night, from as far back as he could remember, looking pensively over just such shimmering textures, and slowly twirling the stem of a glass like this one between his thumb and middle finger? He rather thought he had.

He was not in the least abashed or lonely. He had no especial desire to meet or to know any of these people; all he demanded was the right to look on and conjecture, to watch the pageant. The mere stage properties were all he contended for. Nor was he lonely later in the evening, in his loge at the Opera. He was entirely rid of his nervous misgivings, of his forced aggressiveness, of the imperative desire to show himself different from his surroundings. He felt now that his surroundings explained him. Nobody questioned the purple; he had only to wear it passively. He had only to glance down at his dress coat to reassure himself that here it would be impossible for anyone to humiliate him.

He found it hard to leave his beautiful sitting room to go to bed that night, and sat long watching the raging storm from his turret window. When he went to sleep, it was with the lights turned on in his bedroom; partly because of his old timidity, and partly so that, if he should wake in the night, there would be no wretched moment of doubt, no horrible suspicion of yellow wall paper, or of Washington and Calvin above his bed.

On Sunday morning the city was practically snow-bound. Paul breakfasted late, and in the afternoon he fell in with a wild San Francisco boy, a freshman at Yale, who said he had run down for a "little flyer" [reckless adventure] over Sunday. The young man offered to show Paul the night side of the town, and the two boys went off together after dinner, not returning to the hotel until seven o'clock the next morning. They had started out in the confiding warmth of a champagne friendship, but their parting in the elevator was singularly cool. The freshman pulled himself together to make his train, and Paul went to bed. He awoke at two o'clock in the afternoon, very thirsty and dizzy, and rang for ice water, coffee, and the Pittsburgh papers.

On the part of the hotel management, Paul excited no suspicion. There was this to be said for him, that he wore his spoils with dignity and in no way made himself conspicuous. His chief greediness lay in his ears and eyes, and his excesses were not offensive ones. His dearest pleasures were the gray winter twilights in his sitting room; his quiet enjoyment of his flowers, his clothes, his wide divan, his cigarette and his sense of power. He could not remember a time when he had felt so at peace with himself. The mere release from the necessity of petty lying, lying every day and every day, restored his self-respect. He had never lied for pleasure, even at school; but to make himself noticed and admired, to assert his difference from other Cordelia Street boys; and he felt a good deal more manly, more honest, even, now that he had no need for boastful pretensions, now that he could, as his actor friends used to say, "dress the part." It was characteristic that remorse did not occur to him. His golden days went by without a shadow, and he made each as perfect as he could.

On the eighth day after his arrival in New York, he found the whole affair exploited in the Pittsburgh papers, exploited with a wealth of detail which indicated that local news of a sensational nature was at a low ebb. The firm of Denny & Carson announced that the boy's father had refunded the full amount of his theft, and that they had no intention of prosecuting. The Cumberland minister had been interviewed, and expressed his hope of yet reclaiming the motherless lad, and Paul's Sabbath-school teacher declared that she would spare no effort to that end. The rumor had reached Pittsburgh that the boy had been seen in a New York hotel, and his father had gone East to find him and bring him home.

Paul had just come in to dress for dinner; he sank into a chair, weak in the knees, and clasped his head in his hands. It was to be worse than jail, even; the tepid waters of Cordelia Street were to close over him finally and forever. The gray monotony stretched before him in hopeless, unrelieved years; Sabbath-school, Young People's Meeting, the yellow-papered room, the damp dish-towels; it all rushed back upon him with sickening vividness. He had the old feeling that the orchestra had suddenly stopped, the sinking sensation that the play was over. The sweat broke out on his face, and he sprang to his feet, looked about him with his white, conscious smile, and winked at himself in the mirror. With something of the childish belief in miracles with which he had so often gone to class, all his lessons unlearned, Paul dressed and dashed whistling down the corridor to the elevator.

He had no sooner entered the dining room and caught the measure of the music, than his remembrance was lightened by his old elastic power of claiming the moment, mounting with it, and finding it all sufficient. The glare and glitter about him, the mere scenic accessories had again, and for the last time, their old potency. He would show himself that he was game, he would finish the thing splendidly. He doubted, more than ever, the existence of Cordelia Street, and for the first time he drank his wine recklessly. Was he not, after all, one of these fortunate beings? Was he not still himself, and in his own place? He drummed a nervous accompaniment to the music and looked about him, telling himself over and over that it had paid.

He reflected drowsily, to the swell of the violin and the chill sweetness of his wine, that he might have done it more wisely. He might have caught an outbound steamer and been well out of their clutches before now. But the other side of the world had seemed too far away and too uncertain then; he could not have waited for it; his need had been too sharp. If he had to choose over again, he would do the same thing tomorrow. He looked affectionately about the dining room, now gilded with a soft mist. Ah, it had paid indeed!

Paul was awakened next morning by a painful throbbing in his head and feet. He had thrown himself across the bed without undressing, and had slept with his shoes on. His limbs and hands were lead heavy, and his tongue and throat were parched. There came upon him one of those fateful attacks of clear-headedness that never occurred except when he was physically exhausted and his nerves hung loose. He lay still and closed his eyes and let the tide of realities wash over him.

His father was in New York; "stopping at some joint or other," he told himself. The memory of successive summers on the front stoop fell upon him like a weight of black water. He had not a hundred dollars left; and he knew now, more than ever, that money was everything, the wall that stood between all he loathed and all he wanted. The thing was winding itself up; he had thought of that on his first glorious day in New York, and had even provided a way to snap the thread. It lay on his dressing-table now; he had got it out last night when he came blindly up from dinner,—but the shiny metal hurt his eyes, and he disliked the look of it, anyway.

He rose and moved about with a painful effort, succumbing now and again to attacks of nausea. It was the old depression exaggerated; all the world had become Cordelia Street. Yet somehow he was not afraid of anything, was absolutely calm; perhaps because he had looked into the dark corner at last, and knew. It was bad enough, what he saw there; but somehow not so bad as his long fear of it had been. He saw everything clearly now. He had a feeling that he had made the best of it, that he had lived the sort of life he was meant to live, and for half an hour he sat staring at the revolver. But he told himself that was not the way, so he went downstairs and took a cab to the ferry.

When Paul arrived at Newark, he got off the train and took another cab, directing the driver to follow the Pennsylvania tracks out of the town. The snow lay heavy on the roadways and had drifted deep in the open fields. Only here and there the dead grass or dried weed stalks projected, singularly black, above it. Once well into the country, Paul dismissed the carriage and walked, floundering along the tracks, his mind a medley of irrelevant things. He seemed to hold in his brain an actual picture of everything he had seen that morning. He remembered every feature of both his drivers, the toothless old woman from whom he had bought the red flowers in his coat, the agent from whom he had got his ticket, and all of his fellow-passengers on the ferry. His mind, unable to cope with vital matters near at hand, worked feverishly and deftly at sorting and grouping these images. They made for him a part of the ugliness of the world, of the ache in his head, and the bitter burning on his tongue. He stooped and put a handful of snow into his mouth as he walked, but that, too, seemed hot. When he reached a little hillside, where the tracks ran through a cut some twenty feet below him, he stopped and sat down.

The carnations in his coat were drooping with the cold, he noticed; all their red glory over. It occurred to him that all the flowers he had seen in the show windows that first night must have gone the same way, long before this. It was only one splendid breath they had, in spite of their brave mockery at the winter outside the glass. It was a losing game in the end, it seemed, this revolt against the homilies by which the world is run. Paul took one of the blossoms carefully from his coat and scooped a little hole in the snow, where he covered it up. Then he dozed a while, from his weak condition, seeming insensible to the cold.

The sound of an approaching train woke him, and he started to his feet, remembering only his resolution, and afraid lest he should be too late. He stood watching the approaching locomotive, his teeth chattering, his lips drawn away from them in a frightened smile; once or twice he glanced nervously sidewise, as though he were being watched. When the right moment came, he jumped. As he fell, the folly of his haste occurred to him with merciless clearness, the vastness of what he had left undone. There flashed through his brain, clearer than ever before, the blue of Adriatic water, the yellow of Algerian sands.

He felt something strike his chest,—his body was being thrown swiftly through the air, on and on, immeasurably far and fast, while his limbs gently relaxed. Then, because the picture-making mechanism was crushed, the disturbing visions flashed into black, and Paul dropped back into the immense design of things.

JAMES JOYCE

❧ The Boarding House

MRS. MOONEY was a butcher's daughter. She was a woman who was quite able to keep things to herself: a determined woman. She had married her father's foreman and opened a butcher's shop near Spring Gardens. But as soon as his father-in-law was dead Mr. Mooney began to go to the devil. He drank, plundered the till, ran headlong into debt. It was no use making him take the pledge: he was sure to break out again a few days after. By fighting his wife in the presence of customers and by buying bad meat he ruined his business. One night he went for his wife with the cleaver and she had to sleep in a neighbour's house.

After that they lived apart. She went to the priest and got a separation from him with care of the children. She would give him neither money nor food nor house-room; and so he was obliged to enlist himself as a sheriff's man. He was a shabby stooped little drunkard with a white face and a white moustache and white eyebrows, pencilled above his little eyes, which were pink-veined and raw; and all day long he sat in the bailiff's room, waiting to be put on a job. Mrs. Mooney, who had taken what remained of her money out of the butcher business and set up a boarding house in Hardwicke Street, was a big imposing woman. Her house had a floating population made up of tourists from Liverpool and the Isle of Man and, occasionally, *artistes* from the music halls. Its resident population was made up of clerks from the city. She governed the house cunningly and firmly, knew when to give credit, when to be stern and when to let things pass. All the resident young men spoke of her as *The Madam*.

Mrs. Mooney's young men paid fifteen shillings a week for board and lodgings (beer or stout at dinner excluded). They shared in common tastes and occupations and for this reason they were very chummy with one another. They discussed with one another the chances of favourites and outsiders. Jack Mooney, the Madam's son, who was clerk to a commission agent in Fleet Street, had the reputation of being a hard case. He was fond of using soldiers' obscenities: usually he came home in the small hours. When he met his friends he had always a good one to tell them and he was always sure to be on to a good thing—that is to say, a likely horse or a likely *artiste*. He was also handy with the mitts and sang comic songs. On Sunday nights there would often be a reunion in Mrs. Mooney's front drawing-room. The music-hall *artistes* would oblige; and Sheridan played waltzes and polkas and vamped accompaniments. Polly Mooney, the Madam's daughter, would also sing. She sang:

> "I'm a . . . naughty girl,
> You needn't sham:
> You know I am."

Polly was a slim girl of nineteen; she had light soft hair and a small full mouth. Her eyes, which were grey with a shade of green through them, had a habit of glancing upwards when she spoke with anyone, which made her look like a little perverse madonna. Mrs. Mooney had first sent her daughter to be a typist in a corn-factor's office but, as a disreputable sheriff's man used to come every other day to the office, asking to be allowed to say a word to his daughter, she had taken her daughter home again and set her to do housework. As Polly was very lively the intention was to give her the run of the young men. Besides, young men like to feel that there is a young woman not very far away. Polly, of course, flirted with the young men but Mrs. Mooney, who was a shrewd judge, knew that the young men were only passing the time away: none of them meant business. Things went on so for a long time and Mrs. Mooney began to think of sending Polly back to typewriting when she noticed that something was going on between Polly and one of the young men. She watched the pair and kept her own counsel.

Polly knew that she was being watched, but still her mother's persistent silence could not be misunderstood. There had been no open complicity between mother and daughter, no open understanding but, though people in the house began to talk of the affair, still Mrs. Mooney did not intervene. Polly began to grow a little strange in her manner and the young man was evidently perturbed. At last, when she judged it to be the right moment, Mrs. Mooney intervened. She dealt with moral problems as a cleaver deals with meat: and in this case she had made up her mind.

It was a bright Sunday morning of early summer, promising heat, but with a fresh breeze blowing. All the windows of the boarding house were open and the lace curtains ballooned gently towards the street beneath the raised sashes. The belfry of George's Church sent out constant peals and worshippers, singly or in groups, traversed the little circus before the church, revealing their purpose by their self-contained demeanour no less than by the little volumes in their gloved hands. Breakfast was over in the boarding house and the table of the breakfast-room was covered with plates on which lay yellow streaks of eggs with morsels of bacon-fat and bacon-rind. Mrs. Mooney sat in the straw arm-chair and watched the servant Mary remove the breakfast things. She made Mary collect the crusts and pieces of broken bread to help to make Tuesday's bread-pudding. When the table was cleared, the broken bread collected, the sugar and butter safe under lock and key, she began to reconstruct the interview which she had had the night before with Polly. Things were as she had suspected: she had been frank in her questions and Polly had been frank in her answers. Both had been somewhat awkward, of course. She had been made awkward by her not wishing to receive the news in too cavalier a fashion or to seem to have connived and Polly had been made awkward not merely because allusions of that kind always made her awkward but also because she did not wish it to be thought that in her wise innocence she had divined the intention behind her mother's tolerance.

Mrs. Mooney glanced instinctively at the little gilt clock on the mantelpiece as soon as she had become aware through her revery that the bells of George's Church had stopped ringing. It was seventeen minutes past eleven: she would have lots of time to have the matter out with Mr. Doran and then catch short twelve at Marlborough Street. She was sure she would win. To begin with she had all the weight of social opinion on her side: she was an outraged mother. She had allowed him to live beneath her roof, assuming that he was a man of honour, and he had simply abused her hospitality. He was thirty-four or thirty-five years of age, so that youth could not be pleaded as his excuse; nor could ignorance be his excuse since he was a man who had seen something of the world. He had simply taken advantage of Polly's youth and inexperience: that was evident. The question was: What reparation would he make?

There must be reparation made in such case. It is all very well for the man: he can go his ways as if nothing had happened, having had his moment of pleasure, but the girl has to bear the brunt. Some mothers would be content to patch up such an affair for a sum of money; she had known cases of it. But she would not do so. For her only one reparation could make up for the loss of her daughter's honour: marriage.

She counted all her cards again before sending Mary up to Mr. Doran's room to say that she wished to speak with him. She felt sure she would win. He was a serious young man, not rakish or loud-voiced like the others. If it had been Mr. Sheridan or Mr. Meade or Bantam Lyons her task would have been much harder. She did not think he would face publicity. All the lodgers in the house knew something of the affair; details had been invented by some. Besides, he had been employed for thirteen years in a great Catholic wine-merchant's office and publicity would mean for him, perhaps, the loss of his job. Whereas if he agreed all might be well. She knew he had a good screw for one thing and she suspected he had a bit of stuff put by.

Nearly the half-hour! She stood up and surveyed herself in the pier-glass. The decisive expression of her great florid face satisfied her and she thought of some mothers she knew who could not get their daughters off their hands.

Mr. Doran was very anxious indeed this Sunday morning. He had made two attempts to shave but his hand had been so unsteady that he had been obliged to desist. Three days' reddish beard fringed his jaws and every two or three minutes a mist gathered on his glasses so that he had to take them off and polish them with his pocket-handkerchief. The recollection of his confession of the night before was a cause of acute pain to him; the priest had drawn out every ridiculous detail of the affair and in the end had so magnified his sin that he was almost thankful at being afforded a loophole of reparation. The harm was done. What could he do now but marry her or run away? He could not brazen it out. The affair would be sure to be talked of and his employer would be certain to hear of it. Dublin is such a small city: everyone knows everyone else's business. He felt his heart leap warmly in his throat as he heard in his excited imagination old Mr. Leonard calling out in his rasping voice: "Send Mr. Doran here, please."

All his long years of service gone for nothing! All his industry and diligence thrown away! As a young man he had sown his wild oats, of course; he had boasted of his free-thinking and denied the existence of God to his companions in public-houses. But that was all passed and done with . . . nearly. He still bought a copy of *Reynold's Newspaper* every week but he attended to his religious duties and for nine-tenths of the year lived a regular life. He had money enough to settle down on; it was not that. But the family would look down on her. First of all there was her disreputable father and then her mother's boarding house was beginning to get a certain fame. He had a notion that he was being had. He could imagine his friends talking of the affair and laughing. She *was* a little vulgar; some times she said "I seen" and "If I had've known." But what would grammar matter if he really loved her? He could not make up his mind whether to like her or despise her for what she had done. Of course he had done it too. His instinct urged him to remain free, not to marry. Once you are married you are done for, it said.

While he was sitting helplessly on the side of the bed in shirt and trousers she tapped lightly at his door and entered. She told him all, that she had made a clean breast of it to her mother and that her mother would speak with him that morning. She cried and threw her arms round his neck, saying:

"O Bob! Bob! What am I to do? What am I to do at all?"

She would put an end to herself, she said.

He comforted her feebly, telling her not to cry, that it would be all right, never fear. He felt against his shirt the agitation of her bosom.

It was not altogether his fault that it had happened. He remembered well, with the curious patient memory of the celibate, the first casual caresses her dress, her breath, her fingers had given him. Then late one night as he was undressing for bed she had tapped at his door, timidly. She wanted to relight her candle at his for hers had been blown out by a gust. It was her bath night. She wore a loose open combing jacket of printed flannel. Her white instep shone in the opening of her furry slippers and the blood glowed warmly behind her perfumed skin. From her hands and wrists too as she lit and steadied her candle a faint perfume arose.

On nights when he came in very late it was she who warmed up his dinner. He scarcely knew what he was eating feeling her beside him alone, at night, in the sleeping house. And her thoughtfulness! If the night was any way cold or wet or windy there was sure to be a little tumbler of punch ready for him. Perhaps they could be happy together. . . .

They used to go upstairs together on tiptoe, each with a candle, and on the third landing exchange reluctant good-nights. They used to kiss. He remembered well her eyes, the touch of her hand and his delirium. . . .

But delirium passes. He echoed her phrase, applying it to himself: "*What am I to do?*" The instinct of the celibate warned him to hold back. But the sin was there; even his sense of honour told him that reparation must be made for such a sin.

While he was sitting with her on the side of the bed Mary came to the door and said that the missus wanted to see him in the parlour. He stood up to put on his coat and waistcoat, more helpless than ever. When he was dressed he went over to her to comfort her. It would be all right, never fear. He left her crying on the bed and moaning softly: "*O my God!*"

Going down the stairs his glasses became so dimmed with moisture that he had to take them off and polish them. He longed to ascend through the roof and fly away to another country where he would never hear again of his trouble, and yet a force pushed him downstairs step by step. The implacable faces of his employer and of the Madam stared upon his discomfiture. On the last flight of stairs he passed Jack Mooney who was coming up from the pantry nursing two bottles of *Bass*. They saluted coldly; and the lover's eyes rested for a second or two on a thick bulldog face and a pair of thick short arms. When he reached the foot of the staircase he glanced up and saw Jack regarding him from the door of the return-room.

Suddenly he remembered the night when one of the music-hall *artistes*, a little blond Londoner, had made a rather free allusion to Polly. The reunion had been almost broken up on account of Jack's violence. Everyone tried to quiet him. The music-hall *artiste*, a little paler than usual, kept smiling and saying that there was no harm meant: but Jack kept shouting at him that if any fellow tried that sort of a game on with his sister he'd bloody well put his teeth down his throat, so he would.

Polly sat for a little time on the side of the bed, crying. Then she dried her eyes and went over to the looking-glass. She dipped the end of the towel in the water-jug and refreshed her eyes with the cool water. She looked at herself in profile and readjusted a hairpin above her ear. Then she went back to the bed again and sat at the foot. She regarded the pillows for a long time and the sight of them awakened in her mind secret, amiable memories. She rested the nape of her neck against the cool iron bed-rail and fell into a revery. There was no longer any perturbation visible on her face.

She waited on patiently, almost cheerfully, without alarm, her memories gradually giving place to hopes and visions of the future. Her hopes and visions were so intricate that she no longer saw the white pillows on which her gaze was fixed or remembered that she was waiting for anything.

At last she heard her mother calling. She started to her feet and ran to the banisters.

"Polly! Polly!"

"Yes, mama?"

"Come down, dear. Mr. Doran wants to speak to you."

Then she remembered what she had been waiting for.

D. H. LAWRENCE

❦ *The Rocking-Horse Winner*

THERE WAS a woman who was beautiful, who started with all the advantages, yet she had no luck. She married for love, and the love turned to dust. She had bonny children, yet she felt they had been thrust upon her, and she could not love them. They looked at her coldly, as if they were finding fault with her. And hurriedly she felt she must cover up some fault in herself. Yet what it was that she must cover up she never knew. Nevertheless, when her children were present, she always felt the center of her heart go hard. This troubled her, and in her manner she was all the more gentle and anxious for her children, as if she loved them very much. Only she herself knew that at the center of her heart was a hard little place that could not feel love, no, not for anybody. Everybody else said of her: "She is such a good mother. She adores her children." Only she herself, and her children themselves, knew it was not so. They read it in each other's eyes.

There were a boy and two little girls. They lived in a pleasant house, with a garden, and they had discreet servants, and felt themselves superior to anyone in the neighborhood.

Although they lived in style, they felt always an anxiety in the house. There was never enough money. The mother had a small income, and the father had a small income, but not nearly enough for the social position which they had to keep up. The father went into town to some office. But though he had good prospects, these prospects never materialized. There was always the grinding sense of the shortage of money, though the style was always kept up.

At last the mother said: "I will see if *I* can't make something." But she did not know where to begin. She racked her brains, and tried this thing and the other, but could not find anything successful. The failure made deep lines come into her face. Her children were growing up, they would have to go to school. There must be more money, there must be more money. The father, who was always very handsome and expensive in his tastes, seemed as if he never *would* be able to do anything worth doing. And the mother, who had a great belief in herself, did not succeed any better, and her tastes were just as expensive.

And so the house came to be haunted by the unspoken phrase: *There must be more money! There must be more money!* The children could hear it all the time, though nobody said it aloud. They heard it at Christmas, when the expensive and splendid toys filled the nursery. Behind the shining modern rocking-horse, behind the smart doll's house, a voice would start whispering: "There *must* be more money! There *must* be more money!" And the children would stop playing, to listen for a moment. They would look into each other's eyes, to see if they had all heard. And each one saw in the eyes of the other two that they too had heard. "There *must* be more money! There *must* be more money!"

It came whispering from the springs of the still-swaying rocking-horse, and even the horse, bending his wooden, champing head, heard it. The big doll, sitting so pink and smirking in her new pram, could hear it quite plainly, and seemed to be smirking all the more self-consciously because of it. The foolish puppy, too, that took the place of the teddy-bear, he was looking so extraordinarily foolish for no other reason but that he heard the secret whisper all over the house: "There *must* be more money!"

Yet nobody ever said it aloud. The whisper was everywhere, and therefore no one spoke it. Just as no one ever says: "We are breathing!" in spite of the fact that breath is coming and going all the time.

"Mother," said the boy Paul one day, "why don't we keep a car of our own? Why do we always use uncle's, or else a taxi?"

"Because we're the poor members of the family," said the mother.

"But why *are* we, mother?"

"Well—I suppose," she said slowly and bitterly, "it's because your father has no luck."

The boy was silent for some time.

"Is luck money, mother?" he asked, rather timidly.

"No, Paul. Not quite. It's what causes you to have money."

"Oh!" said Paul vaguely. "I thought when Uncle Oscar said *filthy lucker*, it meant money."

"*Filthy lucre* does mean money," said the mother. "But it's lucre, not luck."

"Oh!" said the boy. "Then what *is* luck, mother?"

"It's what causes you to have money. If you're lucky you have money. That's why it's better to be born lucky than rich. If you're rich, you may lose your money. But if you're lucky, you will always get more money."

"Oh! Will you? And is father not lucky?"

"Very unlucky, I should say," she said bitterly.

The boy watched her with unsure eyes.

"Why?" he asked.

"I don't know. Nobody ever knows why one person is lucky and another unlucky."

"Don't they? Nobody at all? Does *nobody* know?"

"Perhaps God. But He never tells."

"He ought to, then. And aren't you lucky either, mother?"

"I can't be, if I married an unlucky husband."

"But by yourself, aren't you?"

"I used to think I was, before I married. Now I think I am very unlucky indeed."

"Why?"

"Well—never mind! Perhaps I'm not really," she said.

The child looked at her to see if she meant it. But he saw, by the lines of her mouth, that she was only trying to hide something from him.

"Well, anyhow," he said stoutly, "I'm a lucky person."

"Why?" said his mother, with a sudden laugh.

He stared at her. He didn't even know why he had said it.

"God told me," he asserted, brazening it out.

"I hope He did, dear!" she said, again with a laugh, but rather bitter.

"He did, mother!"

"Excellent!" said the mother, using one of her husband's exclamations.

The boy saw she did not believe him; or rather, that she paid no attention to his assertion. This angered him somewhat, and made him want to compel her attention.

He went off by himself, vaguely, in a childish way, seeking for the clue to "luck." Absorbed, taking no heed of other people, he went about with a sort of stealth, seeking inwardly for luck. He wanted luck, he wanted it, he wanted it. When the two girls were playing dolls in the nursery, he would sit on his big rocking-horse, charging madly into space, with a frenzy that made the little girls peer at him uneasily. Wildly the horse careered, the waving dark hair of the boy tossed, his eyes had a strange glare in them. The little girls dared not speak to him.

When he had ridden to the end of his mad little journey, he climbed down and stood in front of his rocking-horse, staring fixedly into its lowered face. Its red mouth was slightly open, its big eye was wide and glassy-bright.

"Now!" he would silently command the snorting steed. "Now, take me to where there is luck! Now take me!"

And he would slash the horse on the neck with the little whip he had asked

Uncle Oscar for. He *knew* the horse could take him to where there was luck, if only he forced it. So he would mount again and start on his furious ride, hoping at last to get there. He knew he could get there.

"You'll break your horse, Paul!" said the nurse.

"He's always riding like that! I wish he'd leave off!" said his elder sister Joan.

But he only glared down on them in silence. Nurse gave him up. She could make nothing of him. Anyhow, he was growing beyond her.

One day his mother and his Uncle Oscar came in when he was on one of his furious rides. He did not speak to them.

"Hallo, you young jockey! Riding a winner?" said his uncle.

"Aren't you growing too big for a rocking-horse? You're not a very little boy any longer, you know," said his mother.

But Paul only gave a blue glare from his big, rather close-set eyes. He would speak to nobody when he was in full tilt. His mother watched him with an anxious expression on her face.

At last he suddenly stopped forcing his horse into the mechanical gallop and slid down.

"Well, I got there!" he announced fiercely, his blue eyes still flaring, and his sturdy long legs straddling apart.

"Where did you get to?" asked his mother.

"Where I wanted to go," he flared back at her.

"That's right, son!" said Uncle Oscar. "Don't you stop till you get there. What's the horse's name?"

"He doesn't have a name," said the boy.

"Gets on without all right?" asked the uncle.

"Well, he has different names. He was called Sansovino last week."

"Sansovino, eh? Won the Ascot. How did you know his name?"

"He always talks about horse-races with Bassett," said Joan.

The uncle was delighted to find that his small nephew was posted with all the racing news. Bassett, the young gardener, who had been wounded in the left foot in the war and had got his present job through Oscar Cresswell, whose batman he had been, was a perfect blade of the "turf." He lived in the racing events, and the small boy lived with him.

Oscar Cresswell got it all from Bassett.

"Master Paul comes and asks me, so I can't do more than tell him, sir," said Bassett, his face terribly serious, as if he were speaking of religious matters.

"And does he ever put anything on a horse he fancies?"

"Well—I don't want to give him away—he's a young sport, a fine sport, sir. Would you mind asking him himself? He sort of takes a pleasure in it, and perhaps he'd feel I was giving him away, sir, if you don't mind."

Bassett was serious as a church.

The uncle went back to his nephew and took him off for a ride in the car.

"Say, Paul, old man, do you ever put anything on a horse?" the uncle asked.

The boy watched the handsome man closely.

"Why, do you think I oughtn't to?" he parried.

"Not a bit of it! I thought perhaps you might give me a tip for the Lincoln."

The car sped on into the country, going down to Uncle Oscar's place in Hampshire.

"Honor bright?" said the nephew.

"Honor bright, son!" said the uncle.

"Well, then, Daffodil."

"Daffodil! I doubt it, sonny. What about Mirza?"

"I only know the winner," said the boy. "That's Daffodil."

"Daffodil, eh?"

There was a pause. Daffodil was an obscure horse comparatively.

"Uncle!"

"Yes, son?"

"You won't let it go any further, will you? I promised Bassett."

"Bassett be damned, old man! What's he got to do with it?"

"We're partners. We've been partners from the first. Uncle, he lent me my first five shillings, which I lost. I promised him, honor bright, it was only between me and him; only you gave me that ten-shilling note I started winning with, so I thought you were lucky. You won't let it go any further, will you?"

The boy gazed at his uncle from those big, hot, blue eyes, set rather close together. The uncle stirred and laughed uneasily.

"Right you are, son! I'll keep your tip private. Daffodil, eh? How much are you putting on him?"

"All except twenty pounds," said the boy. "I keep that in reserve."

The uncle thought it a good joke.

"You keep twenty pounds in reserve, do you, you young romancer? What are you betting, then?"

"I'm betting three hundred," said the boy gravely. "But it's between you and me, Uncle Oscar! Honor bright?"

The uncle burst into a roar of laughter.

"It's between you and me all right, you young Nat Gould [a novelist who wrote 130 books about horse racing]," he said, laughing. "But where's your three hundred?"

"Bassett keeps it for me. We're partners."

"You are, are you! And what is Bassett putting on Daffodil?"

"He won't go quite as high as I do, I expect. Perhaps he'll go a hundred and fifty."

"What, pennies?" laughed the uncle.

"Pounds," said the child, with a surprised look at his uncle. "Bassett keeps a bigger reserve than I do."

Between wonder and amusement Uncle Oscar was silent. He pursued the matter no further, but he determined to take his nephew with him to the Lincoln races.

"Now, son," he said, "I'm putting twenty on Mirza, and I'll put five on for you on any horse you fancy. What's your pick?"

"Daffodil, uncle."

"No, not the fiver on Daffodil!"

"I should if it was my own fiver," said the child.

"Good! Good! Right you are! A fiver for me and a fiver for you on Daffodil."

The child had never been to a race-meeting before, and his eyes were blue fire. He pursed his mouth tight and watched. A Frenchman just in front had put his money on Lancelot. Wild with excitement, he flayed his arms up and down, yelling *"Lancelot! Lancelot!"* in his French accent.

Daffodil came in first, Lancelot second, Mirza third. The child, flushed and with eyes blazing, was curiously serene. His uncle brought him four five-pound notes, four to one.

"What am I to do with these?" he cried, waving them before the boy's eyes.

"I suppose we'll talk to Bassett," said the boy. "I expect I have fifteen hundred now; and twenty in reserve; and this twenty."

His uncle studied him for some moments.

"Look here, son!" he said. "You're not serious about Bassett and that fifteen hundred, are you?"

"Yes, I am. But it's between you and me, uncle. Honor bright?"

"Honor bright all right, son! But I must talk to Bassett."

"If you'd like to be a partner, uncle, with Bassett and me, we could all be partners. Only, you'd have to promise, honor bright, uncle, not to let it go beyond us three. Bassett and I are lucky, and you must be lucky, because it was your ten shillings I started winning with. . . ."

Uncle Oscar took both Bassett and Paul into Richmond Park for an afternoon, and there they talked.

"It's like this, you see, sir," Bassett said. "Master Paul would get me talking about racing events, spinning yarns, you know, sir. And he was always keen on knowing if I'd made or if I'd lost. It's about a year since, now, that I put five shillings on Blush of Dawn for him: and we lost. Then the luck turned, with that ten shillings he had from you: that we put on Singhalese. And since that time, it's been pretty steady, all things considering. What do you say, Master Paul?"

"We're all right when we're sure," said Paul. "It's when we're not quite sure that we go down."

"Oh, but we're careful then," said Bassett.

"But when are you *sure?*" smiled Uncle Oscar.

"It's Master Paul, sir," said Bassett in a secret, religious voice. "It's as if he had it from heaven. Like Daffodil, now, for the Lincoln. That was as sure as eggs."

"Did you put anything on Daffodil?" asked Oscar Cresswell.

"Yes, sir. I made my bit."

"And my nephew?"

Bassett was obstinately silent, looking at Paul.

"I made twelve hundred, didn't I, Bassett? I told uncle I was putting three hundred on Daffodil."

"That's right," said Bassett, nodding.

"But where's the money?" asked the uncle.

"I keep it safe locked up, sir. Master Paul he can have it any minute he likes to ask for it."

"What, fifteen hundred pounds?"

"And twenty! And *forty*, that is, with the twenty he made on the course."

"It's amazing!" said the uncle.

"If Master Paul offers you to be partners, sir, I would, if I were you: if you'll excuse me," said Bassett.

Oscar Cresswell thought about it.

"I'll see the money," he said.

They drove home again, and, sure enough, Bassett came round to the garden-house with fifteen hundred pounds in notes. The twenty pounds reserve was left with Joe Glee, in the Turf Commission deposit.

"You see, it's all right, uncle, when I'm *sure!* Then we go strong, for all we're worth. Don't we, Bassett?"

"We do that, Master Paul."

"And when are you sure?" said the uncle, laughing.

"Oh, well, sometimes I'm *absolutely* sure, like about Daffodil," said the boy; "and sometimes I have an idea; and sometimes I haven't even an idea, have I, Bassett? Then we're careful, because we mostly go down."

"You do, do you! And when you're sure, like about Daffodil, what makes you sure, sonny?"

"Oh, well, I don't know," said the boy uneasily. "I'm sure, you know, uncle; that's all."

"It's as if he had it from heaven, sir," Bassett reiterated.

"I should say so!" said the uncle.

But he became a partner. And when the Leger was coming on Paul was "sure" about Lively Spark, which was a quite inconsiderable horse. The boy insisted on putting a thousand on the horse, Bassett went for five hundred, and Oscar Cresswell two hundred. Lively Spark came in first, and the betting had been ten to one against him. Paul had made ten thousand.

"You see," he said, "I was absolutely sure of him."

Even Oscar Cresswell had cleared two thousand.

"Look here, son," he said, "this sort of thing makes me nervous."

"It needn't, uncle! Perhaps I shan't be sure again for a long time."

"But what are you going to do with your money?" asked the uncle.

"Of course," said the boy, "I started it for mother. She said she had no luck, because father is unlucky, so I thought if I was lucky, it might stop whispering."

"What might stop whispering?"

"Our house. I *hate* our house for whispering."

"What does it whisper?"

"Why—why"—the boy fidgeted—"why, I don't know. But it's always short of money, you know, uncle."

"I know it, son, I know it."

"You know people send mother writs, don't you, uncle?"

"I'm afraid I do," said the uncle.

"And then the house whispers, like people laughing at you behind your back. It's awful, that is! I thought if I was lucky—"

"You might stop it," added the uncle.

The boy watched him with big blue eyes, that had an uncanny cold fire in them, and he said never a word.

"Well, then!" said the uncle. "What are we doing?"

"I shouldn't like mother to know I was lucky," said the boy.

"Why not, son?"

"She'd stop me."

"I don't think she would."

"Oh!"—and the boy writhed in an odd way—"I *don't* want her to know, uncle."

"All right, son! We'll manage it without her knowing."

They managed it very easily. Paul, at the other's suggestion, handed over five thousand pounds to his uncle, who deposited it with the family lawyer, who was then to inform Paul's mother that a relative had put five thousand pounds into his hands, which sum was to be paid out a thousand pounds at a time, on the mother's birthday, for the next five years.

"So she'll have a birthday present of a thousand pounds for five successive years," said Uncle Oscar. "I hope it won't make it all the harder for her later."

Paul's mother had her birthday in November. The house had been "whispering" worse than ever lately, and, even in spite of his luck, Paul could not bear up against it. He was very anxious to see the effect of the birthday letter, telling his mother about the thousand pounds.

When there were no visitors, Paul now took his meals with his parents, as he was beyond the nursery control. His mother went into town nearly every day. She had discovered that she had an odd knack of sketching furs and dress materials, so she worked secretly in the studio of a friend who was the chief "artist" for the leading drapers. She drew the figures of ladies in furs and ladies in silk and sequins for the newspaper advertisements. This young woman artist earned several thousand pounds a year, but Paul's mother only made several hundreds, and she was again dissatisfied. She so wanted to be first in something, and she did not succeed, even in making sketches for drapery advertisements.

She was down to breakfast on the morning of her birthday. Paul watched her face as she read her letters. He knew the lawyer's letter. As his mother read it, her face hardened and became more expressionless. Then a cold, determined look came on her mouth. She hid the letter under the pile of others, and said not a word about it.

"Didn't you have anything nice in the post for your birthday, mother?" said Paul.

"Quite moderately nice," she said, her voice cold and absent.

She went away to town without saying more.

But in the afternoon Uncle Oscar appeared. He said Paul's mother had had a long interview with the lawyer, asking if the whole five thousand could not be advanced at once, as she was in debt.

"What do you think, uncle?" said the boy.

"I leave it to you, son."

"Oh, let her have it, then! We can get some more with the other," said the boy.

"A bird in the hand is worth two in the bush, laddie!" said Uncle Oscar.

"But I'm sure to *know* for the Grand National; or the Lincolnshire; or else the Derby. I'm sure to know for *one* of them," said Paul.

So Uncle Oscar signed the agreement, and Paul's mother touched the whole five thousand. Then something very curious happened. The voices in the house suddenly went mad, like a chorus of frogs on a spring evening. There were certain new furnishings, and Paul had a tutor. He was *really* going to Eton, his father's school, in the following autumn. There were flowers in the winter, and a blossoming of the luxury Paul's mother had been used to. And yet the voices in the house, behind the sprays of mimosa and almond-blossom, and from under the piles of iridescent cushions, simply trilled and screamed in a sort of ecstasy: "There *must* be more money! Oh-h-h; there *must* be more money. Oh, now, now-w! Now-w-w—there *must* be more money!—more than ever! More than ever!"

It frightened Paul terribly. He studied away at his Latin and Greek with his tutor. But his intense hours were spent with Bassett. The Grand National had gone by: he had not "known," and had lost a hundred pounds. Summer was at hand. He was in agony for the Lincoln. But even for the Lincoln he didn't "know," and he lost fifty pounds. He became wild-eyed and strange, as if something were going to explode in him.

"Let it alone, son! Don't you bother about it!" urged Uncle Oscar. But it was as if the boy couldn't really hear what his uncle was saying.

"I've got to know for the Derby! I've got to know for the Derby!" the child reiterated, his big blue eyes blazing with a sort of madness.

His mother noticed how overwrought he was.

"You'd better go to the seaside. Wouldn't you like to go now to the seaside, instead of waiting? I think you'd better," she said, looking down at him anxiously, her heart curiously heavy because of him.

But the child lifted his uncanny blue eyes.

"I couldn't possibly go before the Derby, mother!" he said. "I couldn't possibly!"

"Why not?" she said, her voice becoming heavy when she was opposed. "Why not? You can still go from the seaside to see the Derby with your Uncle Oscar, if that's what you wish. No need for you to wait here. Besides, I think you care too much about these races. It's a bad sign. My family has been a gambling family, and you won't know till you grow up how much damage it has done. But it has done damage. I shall have to send Bassett away, and ask Uncle Oscar not to talk racing to you, unless you promise to be reasonable about it: go away to the seaside and forget it. You're all nerves!"

"I'll do what you like, mother, so long as you don't send me away till after the Derby," the boy said.

"Send you away from where? Just from this house?"

"Yes," he said, gazing at her.

"Why, you curious child, what makes you care about this house so much, suddenly? I never knew you loved it."

He gazed at her without speaking. He had a secret within a secret, something he had not divulged, even to Bassett or to his Uncle Oscar.

But his mother, after standing undecided and a little bit sullen for some moments, said:

"Very well, then! Don't go to the seaside till after the Derby, if you don't wish it. But promise me you won't let your nerves go to pieces. Promise you won't think so much about horse-racing and *events*, as you call them!"

"Oh no," said the boy casually. "I won't think much about them, mother. You needn't worry. I wouldn't worry, mother, if I were you."

"If you were me and I were you," said his mother, "I wonder what we *should* do!"

"But you know you needn't worry, mother, don't you?" the boy repeated.

"I should be awfully glad to know it," she said wearily.

"Oh, well, you *can*, you know. I mean, you *ought* to know you needn't worry," he insisted.

"Ought I? Then I'll see about it," she said.

Paul's secret of secrets was his wooden horse, that which had no name. Since he was emancipated from a nurse and a nursery-governess, he had had his rocking-horse removed to his own bedroom at the top of the house.

"Surely you're too big for a rocking-horse!" his mother had remonstrated.

"Well, you see, mother, till I can have a *real* horse, I like to have *some* sort of animal about," had been his quaint answer.

"Do you feel he keeps you company?" she laughed.

"Oh yes! He's very good, he always keeps me company, when I'm there," said Paul.

So the horse, rather shabby, stood in an arrested prance in the boy's bedroom.

The Derby was drawing near, and the boy grew more and more tense. He hardly heard what was spoken to him, he was very frail, and his eyes were really uncanny. His mother had sudden strange seizures of uneasiness about him. Sometimes, for half an hour, she would feel a sudden anxiety about him that was almost anguish. She wanted to rush to him at once, and know he was safe.

Two nights before the Derby, she was at a big party in town, when one of her rushes of anxiety about her boy, her first-born, gripped her heart till she could hardly speak. She fought with the feeling, might and main, for she believed in common sense. But it was too strong. She had to leave the dance and go downstairs to telephone to the country. The children's nursery-governess was terribly surprised and startled at being rung up in the night.

"Are the children all right, Miss Wilmot?"

"Oh yes, they are quite all right."

"Master Paul? Is he all right?"

"He went to bed as right as a trivet. Shall I run up and look at him?"

"No," said Paul's mother reluctantly. "No! Don't trouble. It's all right. Don't sit up. We shall be home fairly soon." She did not want her son's privacy intruded upon.

"Very good," said the governess.

It was about one o'clock when Paul's mother and father drove up to their house. All was still. Paul's mother went to her room and slipped off her white fur cloak. She had told her maid not to wait up for her. She heard her husband downstairs, mixing a whisky and soda.

And then, because of the strange anxiety at her heart, she stole upstairs to her son's room. Noiselessly she went along the upper corridor. Was there a faint noise? What was it?

She stood, with arrested muscles, outside his door, listening. There was a strange, heavy, and yet not loud noise. Her heart stood still. It was a soundless noise, yet rushing and powerful. Something huge, in violent, hushed motion. What was it? What in God's name was it? She ought to know. She felt that she knew the noise. She knew what it was.

Yet she could not place it. She couldn't say what it was. And on and on it went, like a madness.

Softly, frozen with anxiety and fear, she turned the doorhandle.

The room was dark. Yet in the space near the window, she heard and saw something plunging to and fro. She gazed in fear and amazement.

Then suddenly she switched on the light, and saw her son, in his green pyjamas, madly surging on the rocking-horse. The blaze of light suddenly lit him up, as he urged the wooden horse, and lit her up, as she stood, blonde, in her dress of pale green and crystal, in the doorway.

"Paul!" she cried. "Whatever are you doing?"

"It's Malabar!" he screamed in a powerful, strange voice. "It's Malabar!"

His eyes blazed at her for one strange and senseless second, as he ceased urging his wooden horse. Then he fell with a crash to the ground, and she, all her tormented motherhood flooding upon her, rushed to gather him up.

But he was unconscious, and unconscious he remained, with some brain-fever. He talked and tossed, and his mother sat stonily by his side.

"Malabar! It's Malabar! Bassett, Bassett, I *know*! It's Malabar!"

So the child cried, trying to get up and urge the rocking-horse that gave him his inspiration.

"What does he mean by Malabar?" asked the heart-frozen mother.

"I don't know," said the father stonily.

"What does he mean by Malabar?" she asked her brother Oscar.

"It's one of the horses running for the Derby," was the answer.

And, in spite of himself, Oscar Cresswell spoke to Bassett, and himself put a thousand on Malabar: at fourteen to one.

The third day of the illness was critical: they were waiting for a change. The boy, with his rather long, curly hair, was tossing ceaselessly on the pillow. He neither slept nor regained consciousness, and his eyes were like blue stones. His mother sat, feeling her heart had gone, turned actually into a stone.

In the evening, Oscar Cresswell did not come, but Bassett sent a message, saying could he come up for one moment, just one moment? Paul's mother was very angry at the intrusion, but on second thought she agreed. The boy was the same. Perhaps Bassett might bring him to consciousness.

The gardener, a shortish fellow with a little brown moustache and sharp little brown eyes, tiptoed into the room, touched his imaginary cap to Paul's mother, and stole to the bedside, staring with glittering, smallish eyes at the tossing, dying child.

"Master Paul!" he whispered. "Master Paul! Malabar came in first all right, a clean win. I did as you told me. You've made over seventy thousand pounds, you have; you've got over eighty thousand. Malabar came in all right, Master Paul."

"Malabar! Malabar! Did I say Malabar, mother? Did I say Malabar? Do you think I'm lucky, mother? I knew Malabar, didn't I? Over eighty thousand pounds! I call that lucky, don't you, mother? Over eighty thousand pounds! I knew, didn't I know I knew? Malabar came in all right. If I ride my horse till I'm sure, then I tell you, Bassett, you can go as high as you like. Did you go for all you were worth, Bassett?"

"I went a thousand on it, Master Paul."

"I never told you, mother, that if I can ride my horse, and *get there*, then I'm absolutely sure—oh, absolutely! Mother, did I ever tell you? I *am* lucky!"

"No, you never did," said his mother.

But the boy died in the night.

And even as he lay dead, his mother heard her brother's voice saying to her: "My God, Hester, you're eighty-odd thousand to the good, and a poor devil of a son to the bad. But, poor devil, poor devil, he's best gone out of a life where he rides his rocking-horse to find a winner."

WILBUR DANIEL STEELE

❧ *How Beautiful with Shoes*

By the time the milking was finished, the sow, which had farrowed the past week, was making such a row that the girl spilled a pint of the warm milk down the trough-lead to quiet the animal before taking the pail to the well-house. Then in the quiet she heard a sound of hoofs on the bridge, where the road crossed the creek a hundred yards below the house, and she set the pail down on the ground beside her bare, barn-soiled feet. She picked it up again. She set it down. It was as if she calculated its weight.

That was what she was doing, as a matter of fact, setting off against its pull toward the well-house the pull of that wagon team in the road, with little more of personal will or wish in the matter than has a wooden weather-vane between two currents in the wind. And as with the vane, so with the wooden girl—the added behest of a whip-lash cracking in the distance was enough; leaving the pail at the barn door, she set off in a deliberate, docile beeline through the cow-yard, over the fence, and down in a diagonal across the farm's one tilled field toward the willow brake that walled the road at the dip. And once under way, though her mother came to the kitchen door and called in her high, flat voice, "Amarantha, where you goin', Amarantha?" the girl went on apparently unmoved, as though she had been as deaf as the woman in the doorway; indeed, if there was emotion in her it was the purely sensuous one of feeling the clods of the furrows breaking softly between her toes. It was springtime in the mountains.

"Amarantha, why don't you answer me, Amarantha?"

For moments after the girl had disappeared beyond the willows the widow continued to call, unaware through long habit of how absurd it sounded, the name which that strange man her husband had put upon their daughter in one of his moods. Mrs. Doggett had been deaf so long she did not realize that nobody else ever thought of it for the broad-fleshed, slow-minded girl, but called her Mary or, even more simply, Mare.

Ruby Herter had stopped his team this side of the bridge, the mules' heads turned into the lane to his father's farm beyond the road. A big-barreled, heavy-limbed fellow with a square, sallow, not unhandsome face, he took out youth in ponderous gestures of masterfulness; it was like him to have cracked his whip above his animals' ears the moment before he pulled them to a halt. When he saw the girl getting over the fence under the willows he tongued the wad of tobacco out of his mouth into his palm, threw it away beyond the road, and drew a sleeve of his jumper across his lips.

"Don't run yourself out o' breath, Mare; I got all night."

"I was comin'." It sounded sullen only because it was matter of fact.

"Well, keep a-comin' and give us a smack." Hunched on the wagon seat, he remained motionless for some time after she had arrived at the hub, and when he stirred it was but to cut a fresh bit of tobacco, as if already he had forgotten why he threw the old one away. Having satisfied his humor, he unbent, climbed down, kissed her passive mouth, and hugged her up to him, roughly and loosely, his hands careless of contours. It was not out of the way; they were used to handling animals, both of them; and it was spring. A slow warmth pervaded the girl, formless, nameless, almost impersonal.

Her betrothed pulled her head back by the braid of her yellow hair. He studied her face, his brows gathered and his chin out.

"Listen, Mare, you wouldn't leave nobody else hug and kiss you, dang you!"

She shook her head, without vehemence or anxiety.

"Who's that?" She hearkened up the road. "Pull your team out," she added, as a Ford came in sight around the bend above the house, driven at speed. "Geddap!" she said to the mules herself.

But the car came to a halt near them, and one of the five men crowded in it called, "Come on, Ruby, climb in. They's a loony loose out o' Dayville Asylum, and they got him trailed over somewheres on Split Ridge and Judge North phoned up to Slosson's store for ever'body come help circle him—come on, hop the runnin'-board!"

Ruby hesitated, an eye on his team.

"Scared, Ruby?" The driver raced his engine. "They say this boy's a killer."

"Mare, take the team in and tell pa." The car was already moving when Ruby jumped in. A moment after it had sounded on the bridge it was out of sight.

"Amarantha, Amarantha, why don't you come, Amarantha?"

Returning from her errand, fifteen minutes later, Mare heard the plaint lifted in the twilight. The sun had dipped behind the back ridge, and though the sky was still bright with day, the dusk began to smoke up out of the plowed field like a ground-fog. The girl had returned through it, got the milk, and started toward the well-house before the widow saw her.

"Daughter, seems to me you might!" she expostulated without change of key. "Here's some young man friend o' yourn stopped to say howdy, and I been rackin' my lungs out after you. . . . Put that milk in the cool and come!"

Some young man friend? But there was no good to be got from puzzling. Mare poured the milk in the pan in the dark of the low house over the well, and as she came out, stooping, she saw a figure waiting for her, black in silhouette against the yellowing sky.

"Who are you?" she asked, a native timidity making her sound sulky.

"Amarantha!" the fellow mused. "That's poetry." And she knew then that she did not know him.

She walked past, her arms straight down and her eyes front. Strangers always affected her with a kind of muscular terror simply by being strangers. So she gained the kitchen steps, aware by his tread that he followed. There, taking courage at sight of her mother in the doorway, she turned on him, her eyes at the level of his knees.

"Who are you and what d' y' want?"

He still mused. "Amarantha! Amarantha in Carolina! That makes me happy!"

Mare hazarded one upward look. She saw that he had red hair, brown eyes, and hollows under his cheekbones, and though the green sweater he wore on top of a gray overall was plainly not meant for him, sizes too large as far as girth went, yet he was built so long of limb that his wrists came inches out of the sleeves and made his big hands look even bigger.

Mrs. Doggett complained. "Why don't you introduce us, daughter?"

The girl opened her mouth and closed it again. Her mother, unaware that no sound had come out of it, smiled and nodded, evidently taking to the tall, homely fellow and tickled by the way he could not seem to get his eyes off her daughter. But the daughter saw none of it, all her attention centered upon the stranger's hands.

Restless, hard-fleshed, and chap-bitten, they were like a countryman's hands; but the fingers were longer than the ordinary, and slightly spatulate at their ends, and these ends were slowly and continuously at play among themselves.

The girl could not have explained how it came to her to be frightened and at the same time to be calm, for she was inept with words. It was simply that in an animal way she knew animals, knew them in health and ailing, and when they were ailing she knew by instinct, as her father had known, how to move so as not to fret them.

Her mother had gone in to light up; from beside the lampshelf she called back, "If he's aimin' to stay to supper you should've told me, Amarantha, though I guess there's plenty of the side-meat to go 'round, if you'll bring me in a few more turnips and potatoes, though it is late."

At the words the man's cheeks moved in and out. "I'm very hungry," he said.

Mare nodded deliberately. Deliberately, as if her mother could hear her, she said over her shoulder, "I'll go get the potatoes and turnips, ma." While she spoke she was moving, slowly, softly, at first, toward the right of the yard, where the fence gave over into the field. Unluckily her mother spied her through the window.

"Amarantha, where *are* you goin'?"

"I'm goin' to get the potatoes and turnips." She neither raised her voice nor glanced back, but lengthened her stride. "He won't hurt her," she said to herself. "He won't hurt her; it's me, not her," she kept repeating, while she got over the fence and down into the shadow that lay more than ever like a fog on the field.

The desire to believe that it actually did hide her, the temptation to break from her rapid but orderly walk grew till she could no longer fight it. She saw the road willows only a dash ahead of her. She ran, her feet floundering among the furrows.

She neither heard nor saw him, but when she realized he was with her she knew he had been with her all the while. She stopped, and he stopped, and so they stood, with the dark open of the field all around. Glancing sidewise presently, she saw he was no longer looking at her with those strangely importunate brown eyes of his, but had raised them to the crest of the wooded ridge behind her.

By and by, "What does it make you think of?" he asked. And when she made no move to see, "Turn around and look!" he said, and though it was low and almost tender in its tone, she knew enough to turn.

A ray of the sunset hidden in the west struck through the tops of the topmost trees, far and small up there, a thin, bright hem.

"What does it make you think of, Amarantha? . . . Answer!"

"Fire," she made herself say.

"Or blood."

"Or blood, yeh. That's right, or blood." She had heard a Ford going up the road beyond the willows, and her attention was not on what she said.

The man soliloquized. "Fire and blood, both; spare one or the other, and where is beauty, the way the world is? It's an awful thing to have to carry, but Christ had it. Christ came with a sword. I love beauty, Amarantha. . . . I say, I love beauty!"

"Yeh, that's right, I hear." What she heard was the car stopping at the house.

"Not prettiness. Prettiness'll have to go with ugliness, because it's only ugliness trigged up. But beauty!" Now again he was looking at her. "Do you know how beautiful you are, Amarantha, 'Amarantha sweet and fair'?" Of a sudden, reaching behind her, he began to unravel the meshes of her hair-braid, the long, flat-tipped fingers at once impatient and infinitely gentle. " 'Braid no more that shining hair!' "

Flat-faced Mare Doggett tried to see around those glowing eyes so near to hers, but wise in her instinct, did not try too hard. "Yeh," she temporized. "I mean, no, I mean."

"Amarantha, I've come a long, long way for you. Will you come away with me now?"

"Yeh—that is—in a minute I will, mister—yeh . . ."

"Because you want to, Amarantha? Because you love me as I love you? Answer!"

"Yeh—sure—uh . . . *Ruby!*"

The man tried to run, but there were six against him, coming up out of the dark that lay in the plowed ground. Mare stood where she was while they knocked him down and got a rope around him; after that she walked back toward the house with Ruby and Older Haskins, her father's cousin.

Ruby wiped his brow and felt of his muscles. "Gees, you're lucky we come, Mare. We're no more'n past the town, when they come hollerin' he'd broke over this way."

When they came to the fence the girl sat on the rail for a moment and rebraided her hair before she went into the house, where they were making her mother smell ammonia.

Lots of cars were coming. Judge North was coming, somebody said. When Mare heard this she went into her bedroom off the kitchen and got her shoes and put them on. They were brand new two-dollar shoes with cloth tops, and she had only begun to break them in last Sunday; she wished afterwards she had put her stockings on too, for they would have eased the seams. Or else that she had put on the old button pair, even though the soles were worn through.

Judge North arrived. He thought first of taking the loony straight through to Dayville that night, but then decided to keep him in the lock-up at the courthouse till morning and make the drive by day. Older Haskins stayed in, gentling Mrs. Doggett, while Ruby went out to help get the man into the Judge's sedan. Now that she had them on, Mare didn't like to take the shoes off till Older went; it might make him feel small, she thought.

Older Haskins had a lot of facts about the loony.

"His name's Humble Jewett," he told them. "They belong back in Breed County, all them Jewetts, and I don't reckon there's none of 'em that's not a mite unbalanced. He went to college though, worked his way, and he taught somethin' 'rother in some academy-school a spell, till he went off his head all of a sudden and took after folks with an axe. I remember it in the paper at the time. They give out one while how the Principal wasn't goin' to live, and there was others—there was a girl he tried to strangle. That was four—five year back."

Ruby came in guffawing. "Know the only thing they can get 'im to say, Mare? Only God thing he'll say is, 'Amarantha, she's goin' with me.' . . . Mare!"

"Yeh, I know."

The cover of the kettle the girl was handling slid off the stove with a clatter. A sudden sick wave passed over her. She went out to the back, out into the air. It was not till now she knew how frightened she had been.

Ruby went home, but Older Haskins stayed to supper with them, and helped Mare do the dishes afterward; it was nearly nine when he left. The mother was already in bed, and Mare was about to sit down to get those shoes off her wretched feet at last, when she heard the cow carrying on up at the barn, lowing and kicking, and next minute the sow was in it with a horning note. It might be a fox passing by to get at the hen-house, or a weasel. Mare forgot her feet, took a broom-handle they used in boiling clothes, opened the back door, and stepped out. Blinking the lamplight from her eyes, she peered up toward the outbuildings, and saw the gable end of the barn standing like a red arrow in the dark, and the top of a butternut tree beyond it drawn in skeleton traceries, and just then a cock crowed.

She went to the right corner of the house and saw where the light came from, ruddy above the woods down the valley. Returning into the house, she bent close to her mother's ear and shouted, "Somethin's a-fire down to the town, looks like," then went out again and up to the barn. "Soh! Soh!" she called to the animals. She climbed up and stood on the top rail of the cow-pen fence, only to find she could not locate the flame even there.

Ten rods behind the buildings a mass of rock mounted higher than their ridgepoles, a chopped-off buttress of the back ridge, covered with oak scrub and wild grapes and blackberries, whose thorny ropes the girl beat away from her skirt with the broom-handle as she scrambled up in the wine-colored dark. Once at the top, and the brush held aside, she could see the tongue-tip of the conflagration half a mile away at the town. And she knew by the bearing of the two church steeples that it was the building where the lock-up was that was burning.

There is a horror in knowing animals trapped in a fire, no matter what the animals.

"Oh, my God!" Mare said.

A car went down the road. Then there was a horse galloping. That would be Older Haskins probably. People were out at Ruby's father's farm; she could hear their voices raised. There must have been another car up from the other way, for lights wheeled and shouts were exchanged in the neighborhood of the bridge. Next thing she knew, Ruby was at the house below, looking for her probably.

He was telling her mother. Mrs. Doggett was not used to him, so he had to shout even louder than Mare had to.

"What y' reckon he done, the hellion! he broke the door and killed Lew Fyke and set the courthouse afire! . . . Where's Mare?"

Her mother would not know. Mare called. "Here, up the rock here."

She had better go down. Ruby would likely break his bones if he tried to climb the rock in the dark, not knowing the way. But the sight of the fire fascinated her simple spirit, the fearful element, more fearful than ever now, with the news. "Yes, I'm comin'," she called sulkily, hearing feet in the brush. "You wait; I'm comin'."

When she turned and saw it was Humble Jewett, right behind her among the branches, she opened her mouth to screech. She was not quick enough. Before a sound came out he got one hand over her face and the other arm around her body.

Mare had always thought she was strong, and the loony looked gangling, yet she was so easy for him that he need not hurt her. He made no haste and little noise as he carried her deeper into the undergrowth. Where the hill began to mount it was harder though. Presently he set her on her feet. He let the hand that had been over her mouth slip down to her throat, where the broad-tipped fingers wound, tender as yearning, weightless as caress.

"I was afraid you'd scream before you knew who 'twas, Amarantha. But I didn't want to hurt your lips, dear heart, your lovely, quiet lips."

It was so dark under the trees she could hardly see him, but she felt his breath on her mouth, near to. But then, instead of kissing her, he said, "No! No!" took from her throat for an instant the hand that had held her mouth, kissed its palm, and put it back softly against her skin.

"Now, my love, let's go before they come."

She stood stock still. Her mother's voice was to be heard in the distance, strident and meaningless. More cars were on the road. Nearer, around the rock, there were sounds of tramping and thrashing. Ruby fussed and cursed. He shouted, "Mare, dang you, where are you, Mare?" his voice harsh with uneasy anger. Now, if she aimed to do anything, was the time to do it. But there was neither breath nor power in her windpipe. It was as if those yearning fingers had paralyzed the muscles.

"Come!" The arm he put around her shivered against her shoulder blades. It was anger. "I hate killing. It's a dirty, ugly thing. It makes me sick." He gagged, judging by the sound. But then he ground his teeth. "Come away, my love!"

She found herself moving. Once when she broke a branch underfoot with an instinctive awkwardness he chided her. "Quiet, my heart, else they'll hear!" She made herself heavy. He thought she grew tired and bore more of her weight till he was breathing hard.

Men came up the hill. There must have been a dozen spread out, by the angle of their voices as they kept touch. Always Humble Jewett kept caressing Mare's throat with one hand; all she could do was hang back.

"You're tired and you're frightened," he said at last. "Get down here."

There were twigs in the dark, the overhang of a thicket of some sort. He thrust her in under this, and lay beside her on the bed of groundpine. The hand that was not in love with her throat reached across her; she felt the weight of its forearm on her shoulder and its fingers among the strands of her hair, eagerly, but tenderly, busy. Not once did he stop speaking, no louder than breathing, his lips to her ear.

" 'Amarantha sweet and fair—Ah, braid no more that shining hair . . .' "

Mare had never heard of Lovelace, the poet; she thought the loony was just going on, hardly listened, got little sense. But the cadence of it added to the lethargy of all her flesh.

" 'Like a clew of golden thread—Most excellently ravelléd . . .' "

Voices loudened; feet came tramping; a pair went past not two rods away.

" '. . . Do not then wind up the light—In ribbands, and o'ercloud in night . . .' "

The search went on up the woods, men shouting to one another and beating the brush.

" '. . . *But shake your head and scatter day!' I've* never loved, Amarantha. They've tried me with prettiness, but prettiness is too cheap, yes, it's too cheap."

Mare was cold, and the coldness made her lazy. All she knew was that he talked on.

"But dogwood blowing in the spring isn't cheap. The earth of a field isn't cheap. Lots of time I've laid down and kissed the earth of a field, Amarantha. That's beauty, and a kiss for beauty." His breath moved up her cheek. He trembled violently. "No, no, not yet!" He got to his knees and pulled her by an arm. "We can go now."

They went back down the slope, but at an angle, so that when they came to the level they passed two hundred yards to the north of the house, and crossed the road there. More and more, her walking was like sleepwalking, the feet numb in their shoes. Even where he had to let go of her, crossing the creek on stones, she stepped where he stepped with an obtuse docility. The voices of the searchers on the back ridge were small in distance when they began to climb the face of Coward Hill, on the opposite side of the valley.

There is an old farm on top of Coward Hill, big hayfields as flat as tables. It had been half-past nine when Mare stood on the rock above the barn; it was toward midnight when Humble Jewett put aside the last branches of the woods and let her out on the height, and half a moon had risen. And a wind blew there, tossing the withered tops of last year's grasses, and mists ran with the wind, and ragged shadows with the mists, and mares'-tails of clear moonlight among the shadows, so that now the boles of birches on the forest's edge beyond the fences were but opal blurs and now cut alabaster. It struck so cold against the girl's cold flesh, this wind, that another wind of shivers blew through her, and she put her hands over her face and eyes. But the madman stood with his eyes wide open and his mouth open, drinking the moonlight and the wet wind.

His voice, when he spoke at last, was thick in his throat.

"Get down on your knees." He got down on his and pulled her after. "And pray!"

Once in England a poet sang four lines. Four hundred years have forgotten his name, but they have remembered his lines. The daft man knelt upright, his face raised to the wild scud, his long wrists hanging to the dead grass. He began simply:

" 'O western wind, when wilt thou blow
That the small rain down can rain?' "

The Adam's-apple was big in his bent throat. As simply he finished.

" 'Christ, that my love were in my arms
And I in my bed again!' "

Mare got up and ran. She ran without aim or feeling in the power of the wind. She told herself again that the mists would hide her from him, as she had done at dusk. And again, seeing that he ran at her shoulder, she knew he had been there all the while, making a race of it, flailing the air with his long arms for joy of play in the cloud of spring, throwing his knees high, leaping the moon-blue waves of the brown grass, shaking his bright hair; and her own hair was a weight behind her, lying level on the wind. Once a shape went bounding ahead of them for instants; she did not realize it was a fox till it was gone.

She never thought of stopping; she never thought anything, except once, "Oh, my God, I wish I had my shoes off!" And what would have been the good in stopping or in turning another way, when it was only play? The man's ecstasy magnified his strength. When a snake-fence came at them he took the top rail in flight, like a college hurdler, and, seeing the girl hesitate and half turn as if to flee, he would have releaped it without touching a hand. But then she got a loom of buildings, climbed over quickly, before he should jump, and ran along the lane that ran with the fence.

Mare had never been up there, but she knew that the farm and the house belonged to a man named Wyker, a kind of cousin of Ruby Herter's, a violent, bearded old fellow who lived by himself. She could not believe her luck. When she had run half the distance and Jewett had not grabbed her, doubt grabbed her instead. "Oh, my God, go careful!" she told herself. "Go slow!" she implored herself, and stopped running, to walk.

Here was a misgiving the deeper in that it touched her special knowledge. She had never known an animal so far gone that its instincts failed it; a starving rat will scent the trap sooner than a fed one. Yet, after one glance at the house they approached, Jewett paid it no further attention, but walked with his eyes to the right, where the cloud had blown away, and wooded ridges, like black waves rimmed with silver, ran down away toward the Valley of Virginia.

"I've never lived!" In his single cry there were two things, beatitude and pain.

Between the bigness of the falling world and his eyes the flag of her hair blew. He reached out and let it whip between his fingers. Mare was afraid it would break the spell then, and he would stop looking away and look at the house again. So she did something almost incredible; she spoke.

"It's a pretty—I mean—a beautiful view down that-away."

"God Almighty beautiful, to take your breath away. I knew I'd never loved, Beloved—" He caught a foot under the long end of one of the boards that covered the well and went down heavily on his hands and knees. It seemed to make no difference. "But I never knew I'd never lived," he finished in the same tone of strong rapture, quadruped in the grass, while Mare ran for the door and grabbed the latch.

When the latch would not give, she lost what little sense she had. She pounded with her fists. She cried with all her might: "Oh—hey—in there—hey—in there!" Then Jewett came and took her gently between his hands and drew her away, and then, though she was free, she stood in something like an awful embarrassment while he tried shouting.

"Hey! Friend! whoever you are, wake up and let my love and me come in!"

"No!" wailed the girl.

He grew peremptory. "Hey, wake up!" He tried the latch. He passed to full fury in a wink's time; he cursed, he kicked, he beat the door till Mare thought he would break his hands. Withdrawing, he ran at it with his shoulder; it burst at the latch, went slamming in, and left a black emptiness. His anger dissolved in a big laugh. Turning in time to catch her by a wrist, he cried joyously, "Come, my Sweet One!"

"No! No! Please—aw—listen. There ain't nobody there. He ain't to home. It wouldn't be right to go in anybody's house if they wasn't to home, you know that."

His laugh was blither than ever. He caught her high in his arms.

"I'd do the same by his love and him if 'twas my house, I would." At the threshold he paused and thought, "That is, if she was the true love of his heart forever."

The room was the parlor. Moonlight slanted in at the door, and another shaft came through a window and fell across a sofa, its covering dilapidated, showing its wadding in places. The air was sour, but both of them were farm-bred.

"Don't, Amarantha!" His words were pleading in her ear. "Don't be so frightened."

He set her down on the sofa. As his hands let go of her they were shaking.

"But look, I'm frightened too." He knelt on the floor before her, reached out his hands, withdrew them. "See, I'm afraid to touch you." He mused, his eyes rounded. "Of all the ugly things there are, fear is the ugliest. And yet, see, it can be the very beautifulest. That's a strange queer thing."

The wind blew in and out of the room, bringing the thin, little bitter sweetness of new April at night. The moonlight that came across Mare's shoulders fell full upon his face, but hers it left dark, ringed by the aureole of her disordered hair.

"Why do you wear a halo, Love?" He thought about it. "Because you're an angel, is that why?" The swift, untempered logic of the mad led him to dismay. His hands came flying to hers, to make sure they were of earth; and he touched her breast, her shoulders, and her hair. Peace returned to his eyes as his fingers twined among the strands.

" 'Thy hair is as a flock of goats that appear from Gilead . . .' " He spoke like a man dreaming. " 'Thy temples are like a piece of pomegranate within thy locks.' "

Mare never knew that he could not see her for the moonlight.

"Do you remember, Love?"

She dared not shake her head under his hand. "Yeh, I reckon," she temporized.

"You remember how I sat at your feet, long ago, like this, and made up a song? And all the poets in all the world have never made one to touch it, have they, Love?"

"Ugh-ugh—never."

" 'How beautiful are thy feet with shoes . . .' Remember?"

"Oh, my God, what's he sayin' now?" she wailed to herself.

> " 'How beautiful are thy feet with shoes, O prince's daughter! the joints of thy thighs are like jewels, the work of the hands of a cunning workman.
>
> Thy navel is like a round goblet, which wanteth not liquor; thy belly is like an heap of wheat set about with lilies.
> Thy two breasts are like two young roes that are twins.' "

Mare had not been to church since she was a little girl, when her mother's black dress wore out. "No, no!" she wailed under her breath. "You're awful to say such awful things." She might have shouted it; nothing could have shaken the man now, rapt in the immortal, passionate periods of Solomon's song.

> " '. . . now also thy breasts shall be as clusters of the vine, and the smell of thy nose like apples.' "

Hotness touched Mare's face for the first time. "Aw, no, don't talk so!"

> " 'And the roof of thy mouth like the best wine for my belovéd . . . causing the lips of them that are asleep to speak.' "

He had ended. His expression changed. Ecstasy gave place to anger, love to hate. And Mare felt the change in the weight of the fingers in her hair.

"What do you mean, I mustn't say it like that?" But it was not to her his fury spoke, for he answered himself straightway. "Like poetry, Mr. Jewett; I won't have blasphemy around my school."

"Poetry! My God! if that isn't poetry—if that isn't music—" . . . "It's Bible, Jewett. What you're paid to teach here is *literature*."

"Doctor Ryeworth, you're the blasphemer and you're an ignorant man." . . . "And your Principal. And I won't have you going around reading sacred allegory like earthly love."

"Ryeworth, you're an old man, a dull man, a dirty man, and you'd be better dead."

Jewett's hand had slid down from Mare's head. "Then I went to put my fingers around his throat, so. But my stomach turned, and I didn't do it. I went to my room. I laughed all the way to my room. I sat in my room at my table and I laughed. I laughed all afternoon and long after dark came. And then, about ten, somebody came and stood beside me in my room."

" 'Wherefore dost thou laugh, son?'

"Then I knew who He was, He was Christ.

" 'I was laughing about that dirty, ignorant, crazy old fool, Lord.'

" 'Wherefore dost thou laugh?'

"I didn't laugh any more. He didn't say any more. I kneeled down, bowed my head.

" 'Thy will be done! Where is he, Lord?'

" 'Over at the girls' dormitory, waiting for Blossom Sinckley.'

"Brassy Blossom, dirty Blossom . . ."

It had come so suddenly it was nearly too late. Mare tore at his hands with hers, tried with all her strength to pull her neck away.

"Filthy Blossom! and him an old filthy man, Blossom! and you'll find him in Hell when you reach there, Blossom . . ."

It was more the nearness of his face than the hurt of his hands that gave her power of fright to choke out three words.

"I—ain't—Blossom!"

Light ran in crooked veins. Through the veins she saw his face bewildered. His hands loosened. One fell down and hung; the other he lifted and put over his eyes, took away again and looked at her.

"Amarantha!" His remorse was fearful to see. "What have I done!" His hands returned to hover over the hurts, ravening with pity, grief and tenderness. Tears fell down his cheeks. And with that, dammed desire broke its dam.

"Amarantha, my love, my dove, my beautiful love—"

"And I ain't Amarantha neither, I'm Mary! Mary, that's my name!"

She had no notion what she had done. He was like a crystal crucible that a chemist watches, changing hue in a wink with one adeptly added drop; but hers was not the chemist's eye. All she knew was that she felt light and free of him; all she could see of his face as he stood away above the moonlight were the whites of his eyes.

"Mary!" he muttered. A slight paroxysm shook his frame. So in the transparent crucible desire changed its hue. He retreated farther, stood in the dark by some tall piece of furniture. And still she could see the whites of his eyes.

"Mary! Mary Adorable!" A wonder was in him. "Mother of God!"

Mare held her breath. She eyed the door, but it was too far. And already he came back to go on his knees before her, his shoulders so bowed and his face so lifted that it must have cracked his neck, she thought; all she could see on the face was pain.

"Mary Mother, I'm sick to my death. I'm so tired."

She had seen a dog like that, one she had loosed from a trap after it had been there three days, its caught leg half gnawed free. Something about the eyes.

"Mary Mother, take me in your arms . . ."

Once again her muscles tightened. But he made no move.

". . . and give me sleep."

No, they were worse than the dog's eyes.

"Sleep, sleep! why won't they let me sleep? Haven't I done it all yet,

Mother? Haven't I washed them yet of all their sins? I've drunk the cup that was given me; is there another? They've mocked me and reviled me, broken my brow with thorns and my hands with nails, and I've forgiven them, for they knew not what they did. Can't I go to sleep now, Mother?"

Mare could not have said why, but now she was more frightened than she had ever been. Her hands lay heavy on her knees, side by side, and she could not take them away when he bowed his head and rested his face upon them.

After a moment he said one thing more. "Take me down gently when you take me from the Tree."

Gradually the weight of his body came against her shins, and he slept.

The moon streak that entered by the eastern window crept north across the floor, thinner and thinner; the one that fell through the southern doorway traveled east and grew fat. For a while Mare's feet pained her terribly and her legs too. She dared not move them, though, and by and by they did not hurt so much.

A dozen times, moving her head slowly on her neck, she canvassed the shadows of the room for a weapon. Each time her eyes came back to a heavy earthenware pitcher on a stand some feet to the left of the sofa. It would have had flowers in it when Wyker's wife was alive; probably it had not been moved from its dust-ring since she died. It would be a long grab, perhaps too long; still, it might be done if she had her hands.

To get her hands from under the sleeper's head was the task she set herself. She pulled first one, then the other, infinitesimally. She waited. Again she tugged a very, very little. The order of his breathing was not disturbed. But at the third trial he stirred.

"Gently! gently!" His own muttering waked him more. With some drowsy instinct of possession he threw one hand across her wrists, pinning them together between thumb and fingers. She kept dead quiet, shut her eyes, lengthened her breathing, as if she too slept.

There came a time when what was pretense grew to be a peril; strange as it was, she had to fight to keep her eyes open. She never knew whether or not she really napped. But something changed in the air, and she was wide awake again. The moonlight was fading on the doorsill, and the light that runs before dawn waxed in the window behind her head.

And then she heard a voice in the distance, lifted in maundering song. It was old man Wyker coming home after a night, and it was plain he had had some whisky.

Now a new terror laid hold of Mare.

"Shut up, you fool you!" she wanted to shout. "Come quiet, quiet!" She might have chanced it now to throw the sleeper away from her and scramble and run, had his powers of strength and quickness not taken her simple imagination utterly in thrall.

Happily the singing stopped. What had occurred was that the farmer had espied the open door and, even befuddled as he was, wanted to know more about it quietly. He was so quiet that Mare began to fear he had gone away. He had the squirrel-hunter's foot, and the first she knew of him was when she looked and saw his head in the doorway, his hard, soiled, whiskery face half-up-side-down with craning.

He had been to the town. Between drinks he had wandered in and out of the night's excitement; had even gone a short distance with one search party himself. Now he took in the situation in the room. He used his forefinger. First he held it to his lips. Next he pointed it with a jabbing motion at the sleeper. Then he tapped his own forehead and described wheels. Lastly, with his whole hand, he made pushing gestures, for Mare to wait. Then he vanished as silently as he had appeared.

The minutes dragged. The light in the east strengthened and turned rosy. Once she thought she heard a board creaking in another part of the house, and looked down sharply to see if the loony stirred. All she could see of his face was a temple with freckles on it and the sharp ridge of a cheekbone, but even from so little she knew how deeply and peacefully he slept. The door darkened. Wyker was there again. In one hand he carried something heavy; with the other he beckoned.

"Come jumpin'!" he said out loud.

Mare went jumping, but her cramped legs threw her down half way to the sill; the rest of the distance she rolled and crawled. Just as she tumbled through the door it seemed as if the world had come to an end above her; two barrels of a shotgun discharged into a room make a noise. Afterwards all she could hear in there was something twisting and bumping on the floor-boards. She got up and ran.

Mare's mother had gone to pieces; neighbor women put her to bed when Mare came home. They wanted to put Mare to bed, but she would not let them. She sat on the edge of her bed in her lean-to bedroom off the kitchen, just as she was, her hair down all over her shoulders and her shoes on, and stared away from them, at a place in the wallpaper.

"Yeh, I'll go myself. Lea' me be!"

The women exchanged quick glances, thinned their lips, and left her be. "God knows," was all they would answer to the questionings of those that had not gone in, "but she's gettin' herself to bed."

When the doctor came through he found her sitting just as she had been, still dressed, her hair down on her shoulders and her shoes on.

"What d' y' want?" she muttered and stared at the place in the wallpaper.

How could Doc Paradise say, when he did not know himself?

"I didn't know if you might be—might be feeling very smart, Mary."

"I'm all right. Lea' me be."

It was a heavy responsibility. Doc shouldered it. "No, it's all right," he said to the men in the road. Ruby Herter stood a little apart, chewing sullenly and looking another way. Doc raised his voice to make certain it carried. "Nope, nothing."

Ruby's ears got red, and he clamped his jaws. He knew he ought to go in and see Mare, but he was not going to do it while everybody hung around waiting to see if he would. A mule tied near him reached out and mouthed his sleeve in idle innocence; he wheeled and banged a fist against the side of the animal's head.

"Well, what d' y' aim to do 'bout it?" he challenged its owner.

He looked at the sun then. It was ten in the morning. "Hell, I got work!" he flared, and set off down the road for home. Doc looked at Judge North, and the Judge started after Ruby. But Ruby shook his head angrily. "Lea' me be!" He went on, and the Judge came back.

It got to be eleven and then noon. People began to say, "Like enough she'd be as thankful if the whole neighborhood wasn't camped here." But none went away.

As a matter of fact they were no bother to the girl. She never saw them. The only move she made was to bend her ankles over and rest her feet on edge; her shoes hurt terribly and her feet knew it, though she did not. She sat all the while staring at that one figure in the wallpaper, and she never saw the figure.

Strange as the night had been, this day was stranger. Fright and physical pain are perishable things once they are gone. But while pain merely dulls and telescopes in memory and remains diluted pain, terror looked back upon has nothing of terror left. A gambling chance taken, at no matter what odds, and won was a sure thing since the world's beginning; perils come through safely were never perilous. But what fright does do in retrospect is this—it heightens each sensuous recollection, like a hard, clear lacquer laid on wood, bringing out the color and grain of it vividly.

Last night Mare had lain stupid with fear on groundpine beneath a bush, loud foot-falls and light whispers confused in her ear. Only now, in her room, did she smell the groundpine.

Only now did the conscious part of her brain begin to make words of the whispering.

"Amarantha," she remembered, "*Amarantha sweet and fair*." That was as far as she could go for the moment, except that the rhyme with "fair" was "hair." But then a puzzle, held in abeyance, brought other words. She wondered what "ravel Ed" could mean. "*Most excellently ravelléd*." It was left to her mother to bring the end.

They gave up trying to keep her mother out at last. The poor woman's prostration took the form of fussiness.

"Good gracious, daughter, you look a sight. Them new shoes, half ruined; ain't your feet *dead*? And look at your hair, all tangled like a wild one!"

She got a comb.

"Be quiet, daughter; what's ailin' you. Don't shake your head!"

" '*But shake your head and scatter day.*' "

"What you say, Amarantha?" Mrs. Doggett held an ear down.

"Go 'way! Lea' me be!"

Her mother was hurt and left. And Mare ran, as she stared at the wallpaper. *"Christ, that my love were in my arms . . ."*

Mare ran. She ran through a wind white with moonlight and wet with "the small rain." And the wind she ran through, it ran through her, and made her shiver as she ran. And the man beside her leaped high over the waves of the dead grasses and gathered the wind in his arms, and her hair was heavy and his was tossing, and a little fox ran before them across the top of the world. And the world spread down around in waves of black and silver, more immense than she had ever known the world could be, and more beautiful.

"God Almighty beautiful, to take your breath away!"

Mare wondered, and she was not used to wondering. "Is it only crazy folks ever run like that and talk that way?"

She no longer ran; she walked; for her breath was gone. And there was some other reason, some other reason. Oh, yes, it was because her feet were hurting her. So, at last, and roundabout, her shoes had made contact with her brain.

Bending over the side of the bed, she loosened one of them mechanically. She pulled it half off. But then she looked down at it sharply, and she pulled it on again.

"How beautiful . . ."

Color overspread her face in a slow wave.

"How beautiful are thy feet with shoes . . ."

"Is it only crazy folks ever say such things?"

"O prince's daughter!"

"Or call you that?"

By and by there was a knock at the door. It opened, and Ruby Herter came in.

"Hello, Mare old girl!" His face was red. He scowled and kicked at the floor. "I'd 'a' been over sooner, except we got a mule down sick." He looked at his dumb betrothed. "Come on, cheer up, forget it! He won't scare you no more, not that boy, not what's left o' him. What you lookin' at, sourface? Ain't you glad to see me?"

Mare quit looking at the wallpaper and looked at the floor.

"Yeh," she said.

"That's more like it, babe." He came and sat beside her; reached down behind her and gave her a spank. "Come on, give us a kiss, babe!" He wiped his mouth on his jumper sleeve, a good farmer's sleeve, spotted with milking. He put his hands on her; he was used to handling animals. "Hey, you, warm up a little, reckon I'm goin' to do all the lovin'?"

"Ruby, lea' me be!"

"What!"

She was up, twisting. He was up, purple.

"What's ailin' you, Mare? What you bawlin' about?"

"Nothin'—only go 'way!"

She pushed him to the door and through it with all her strength, and closed it in his face, and stood with her weight against it, crying, "Go 'way! Go 'way! Lea' me be!"

KATHERINE MANSFIELD

❧ *The Doll's House*

WHEN dear old Mrs. Hay went back to town after staying with the Burnells she sent the children a doll's house. It was so big that the carter and Pat carried it into the courtyard, and there it stayed, propped up on two wooden boxes beside the feed-room door. No harm could come of it; it was summer. And perhaps the smell of paint would have gone off by the time it had to be taken in. For, really, the smell of paint coming from that doll's house ("Sweet of old Mrs. Hay, of course; most sweet and generous!")—but the smell of paint was quite enough to make any one seriously ill, in Aunt Beryl's opinion. Even before the sacking was taken off. And when it was. . . .

There stood the doll's house, a dark, oily, spinach green, picked out with bright yellow. Its two solid little chimneys, glued on to the roof, were painted red and white, and the door, gleaming with yellow varnish, was like a little slab of toffee. Four windows, real windows, were divided into panes by a broad streak of green. There was actually a tiny porch, too, painted yellow, with big lumps of congealed paint hanging along the edge.

But perfect, perfect little house! Who could possibly mind the smell? It was part of the joy, part of the newness.

"Open it quickly, some one!"

The hook at the side was stuck fast. Pat pried it open with his penknife, and the whole house-front swung back, and—there you were, gazing at one and the same moment into the drawing-room and dining-room, the kitchen and two bed-rooms. That is the way for a house to open! Why don't all houses open like that? How much more exciting than peering through the slit of a door into a mean little hall with a hatstand and two umbrellas! That is—isn't it?—what you long to know about a house when you put your hand on the knocker. Perhaps it is the way God opens houses at dead of night when He is taking a quiet turn with an angel. . . .

"O-oh!" The Burnell children sounded as though they were in despair. It was too marvellous; it was too much for them. They had never seen anything like it in their lives. All the rooms were papered. There were pictures on the walls, painted on the paper, with gold frames complete. Red carpet covered all the floors except the kitchen; red plush chairs in the drawing-room, green in the dining-room; tables, beds with real bedclothes, a cradle, a stove, a dresser with tiny plates and one big jug. But what Kezia liked more than anything, what she liked frightfully, was the lamp. It stood in the middle of the dining-room table, an exquisite little amber lamp with a white globe. It was even filled all ready for lighting, though, of course, you couldn't light it. But there was something inside that looked like oil, and that moved when you shook it.

The father and mother dolls, who sprawled very stiff as though they had fainted in the drawing-room, and their two little children asleep upstairs, were really too big for the doll's house. They didn't look as though they belonged. But the lamp was perfect. It seemed to smile at Kezia, to say, "I live here." The lamp was real.

The Burnell children could hardly walk to school fast enough the next morning. They burned to tell everybody, to describe, to—well—to boast about their doll's house before the school-bell rang.

"I'm to tell," said Isabel, "because I'm the eldest. And you two can join in after. But I'm to tell first."

There was nothing to answer. Isabel was bossy, but she was always right, and Lottie and Kezia knew too well the powers that went with being eldest. They brushed through the thick buttercups at the road edge and said nothing.

"And I'm to choose who's to come and see it first. Mother said I might."

For it had been arranged that while the doll's house stood in the courtyard they might ask the girls at school, two at a time, to come and look. Not to stay to tea, of course, or to come traipsing through the house. But just to stand quietly in the courtyard while Isabel pointed out the beauties, and Lottie and Kezia looked pleased. . . .

But hurry as they might, by the time they had reached the tarred palings of the boys' playground the bell had begun to jangle. They only just had time to whip off their hats and fall into line before the roll was called. Never mind. Isabel tried to make up for it by looking very important and mysterious and by whispering behind her hand to the girls near her, "Got something to tell you at playtime."

Playtime came and Isabel was surrounded. The girls of her class nearly fought to put their arms round her, to walk away with her, to beam flatteringly, to be her special friend. She held quite a court under the huge pine trees at the side of the playground. Nudging, giggling together, the little girls pressed up close. And the only two who stayed outside the ring were the two who were always outside, the little Kelveys. They knew better than to come anywhere near the Burnells.

For the fact was, the school the Burnell children went to was not at all the kind of place their parents would have chosen if there had been any choice. But there was none. It was the only school for miles. And the consequence was all the children in the neighborhood, the Judge's little girls, the doctor's daughters, the storekeeper's children, the milkman's, were forced to mix together. Not to speak of there being an equal number of rude, rough little boys as well. But the line had to be drawn somewhere. It was drawn at the Kelveys. Many of the children, including the Burnells, were not allowed even to speak to them. They walked past the Kelveys with their heads in the air, and as they set the fashion in all matters of behaviour, the Kelveys were shunned by everybody. Even the teacher had a special voice for them, and a special smile for the other children when Lil Kelvey came up to her desk with a bunch of dreadfully common-looking flowers.

They were the daughters of a spry, hardworking little washerwoman, who went about from house to house by the day. This was awful enough. But where was Mr. Kelvey? Nobody knew for certain. But everybody said he was in prison. So they were the daughters of a washerwoman and a gaolbird. Very nice company for other people's children! And they looked it. Why Mrs. Kelvey made them so conspicuous was hard to understand. The truth was they were dressed in "bits" given to her by the people for whom she worked. Lil, for instance, who was a stout, plain child, with big freckles, came to school in a dress made from a green art-serge tablecloth of the Burnells', with red plush sleeves from the Logans' curtains. Her hat, perched on top of her high forehead, was a grown-up woman's hat, once the property of Miss Lecky, the post-mistress. It was turned up at the back and trimmed with a large scarlet quill. What a little guy she looked! It was impossible not to laugh. And her little sister, our Else, wore a long white dress, rather like a nightgown, and a pair of little boy's boots. But whatever our Else wore she would have looked strange. She was a tiny wishbone of a child, with cropped hair and enormous solemn eyes—a little white owl. Nobody had ever seen her smile; she scarcely ever spoke. She went through life holding on to Lil, with a piece of Lil's skirt screwed up in her hand. Where Lil went our Else followed. In the playground, on the road going to and from the school, there was Lil marching in front and our Else holding on behind. Only when she wanted anything, or when she was out of breath, our Else gave Lil a tug, a twitch, and Lil stopped and turned round. The Kelveys never failed to understand each other.

Now they hovered at the edge; you couldn't stop them listening. When the little girls turned round and sneered, Lil, as usual, gave her silly, shamefaced smile, but our Else only looked.

And Isabel's voice, so very proud, went on telling. The carpet made a great sensation, but so did the beds with real bedclothes, and the stove with an oven door.

When she finished Kezia broke in. "You've forgotten the lamp, Isabel."

"Oh, yes," said Isabel, "and there's a teeny little lamp, all made of yellow glass, with a white globe that stands on the dining-room table. You couldn't tell it from a real one."

"The lamp's best of all," cried Kezia. She thought Isabel wasn't making half enough of the little lamp. But nobody paid any attention. Isabel was choosing the two who were to come back with them that afternoon and see it. She chose Emmie Cole and Lena Logan. But when the others knew they were all to have a chance, they couldn't be nice enough to Isabel. One by one they put their arms round Isabel's waist and walked her off. They had something to whisper to her, a secret. "Isabel's *my* friend."

Only the little Kelveys moved away forgotten; there was nothing more for them to hear.

Days passed, and as more children saw the doll's house, the fame of it spread. It became the one subject, the rage. The one question was, "Have you seen Burnells' doll's house? Oh, ain't it lovely!" "Haven't you seen it? Oh, I say!"

Even the dinner hour was given up to talking about it. The little girls sat under the pines eating their thick mutton sandwiches and big slabs of johnny cake spread with butter. While always, as near as they could get, sat the Kelveys, our Else holding on to Lil, listening too, while they chewed their jam sandwiches out of a newspaper soaked with large red blobs. . . .

"Mother," said Kezia, "can't I ask the Kelveys just once?"

"Certainly not, Kezia."

"But why not?"

"Run away, Kezia; you know quite well why not."

At last everybody had seen it except them. On that day the subject rather flagged. It was the dinner hour. The children stood together under the pine trees, and suddenly, as they looked at the Kelveys eating out of their paper, always by themselves, always listening, they wanted to be horrid to them. Emmie Cole started the whisper.

"Lil Kelvey's going to be a servant when she grows up."

"O-oh, how awful!" said Isabel Burnell, and she made eyes at Emmie.

Emmie swallowed in a very meaning way and nodded to Isabel as she'd seen her mother do on those occasions.

"It's true—it's true—it's true," she said.

Then Lena Logan's little eyes snapped. "Shall I ask her?" she whispered.

"Bet you don't," said Jessie May.

"Pooh, I'm not frightened," said Lena. Suddenly she gave a little squeal and danced in front of the other girls. "Watch! Watch me! Watch me now!" said Lena. And sliding, gliding, dragging one foot, giggling behind her hand, Lena went over to the Kelveys.

Lil looked up from her dinner. She wrapped the rest quickly away. Our Else stopped chewing. What was coming now?

"Is it true you're going to be a servant when you grow up, Lil Kelvey?" shrilled Lena.

Dead silence. But instead of answering, Lil only gave her silly, shamefaced smile. She didn't seem to mind the question at all. What a sell for Lena! The girls began to titter.

Lena couldn't stand that. She put her hands on her hips; she shot forward. "Yah, yer father's in prison!" she hissed, spitefully.

This was such a marvellous thing to have said that the little girls rushed away in a body, deeply, deeply excited, wild with joy. Some one found a long rope, and they began skipping. And never did they skip so high, run in and out so fast or do such daring things as on that morning.

In the afternoon Pat called for the Burnell children with the buggy and they drove home. There were visitors. Isabel and Lottie, who liked visitors, went upstairs to change their pinafores. But Kezia thieved out at the back. Nobody was about; she began to swing on the big white gates of the courtyard. Presently, looking along the road, she saw two little dots. They grew bigger, they were coming towards her. Now she could see that one was in front and one close behind. Now she could see that they were the Kelveys. Kezia stopped swinging. She slipped off the gate as if she was going to run away. Then she hesitated. The Kelveys came nearer, and beside them walked their shadows, very long, stretching right across the road with their heads in the buttercups. Kezia clambered back on the gate; she had made up her mind; she swung out.

"Hullo," she said to the passing Kelveys.

They were so astounded that they stopped. Lil gave her silly smile. Our Else stared.

"You can come and see our doll's house if you want to," said Kezia, and she dragged one toe on the ground. But at that Lil turned red and shook her head quickly.

"Why not?" asked Kezia.

Lil gasped, then she said, "Your ma told our ma you wasn't to speak to us."

"Oh, well," said Kezia. She didn't know what to reply. "It doesn't matter. You can come and see our doll's house all the same. Come on. Nobody's looking."

But Lil shook her head still harder.

"Don't you want to?" asked Kezia.

Suddenly there was a twitch, a tug at Lil's skirt. She turned round. Our Else was looking at her with big, imploring eyes; she was frowning; she wanted to go. For a moment Lil looked at our Else very doubtfully. But then our Else twitched her skirt again. She started forward. Kezia led the way. Like two little stray cats they followed across the courtyard to where the doll's house stood.

"There it is," said Kezia.

There was a pause. Lil breathed loudly, almost snorted; our Else was still as a stone.

"I'll open it for you," said Kezia kindly. She undid the hook and they looked inside.

"There's the drawing-room and the dining-room, and that's the—"

"Kezia!"

Oh, what a start they gave!

"Kezia!"

It was Aunt Beryl's voice. They turned round. At the back door stood Aunt Beryl, staring as if she couldn't believe what she saw.

"How dare you ask the little Kelveys into the courtyard?" said her cold, furious voice. "You know as well as I do, you're not allowed to talk to them. Run away, children, run away at once. And don't come back again," said Aunt Beryl. And she stepped into the yard and shooed them out as if they were chickens.

"Off you go immediately!" she called, cold and proud.

They did not need telling twice. Burning with shame, shrinking together, Lil huddling along like her mother, our Else dazed, somehow they crossed the big courtyard and squeezed through the white gate.

"Wicked, disobedient little girl!" said Aunt Beryl bitterly to Kezia, and she slammed the doll's house to.

The afternoon had been awful. A letter had come from Willie Brent, a terrifying, threatening letter, saying if she did not meet him that evening in Pulman's Bush, he'd come to the front door and ask the reason why! But now that she had frightened those little rats of Kelveys and given Kezia a good scolding, her heart felt lighter. That ghastly pressure was gone. She went back to the house humming.

When the Kelveys were well out of sight of Burnells', they sat down to rest on a big red drain-pipe by the side of the road. Lil's cheeks were still burning; she took off the hat with the quill and held it on her knee. Dreamily they looked over the hay paddocks, past the creek, to the group of wattles where Logan's cows stood waiting to be milked. What were their thoughts?

Presently our Else nudged up close to her sister. But now she had forgotten the cross lady. She put out a finger and stroked her sister's quill; she smiled her rare smile.

"I seen the little lamp," she said, softly.

Then both were silent once more.

KATHERINE ANNE PORTER

❧ The Circus

THE long planks set on trestles rose one above the other to a monstrous height and stretched dizzyingly in a wide oval ring. They were packed with people—"lak fleas on a dog's ear," said Dicey, holding Miranda's hand firmly

and looking about her with disapproval. The white billows of enormous canvas
sagged overhead, held up by three poles set evenly apart down the center. The
family, when seated, occupied almost a whole section on one level.

On one side of them in a long row sat Father, sister Maria, brother Paul,
Grandmother; great-aunt Keziah, cousin Keziah, and second-cousin Keziah,
who had just come down from Kentucky on a visit; uncle Charles Breaux,
cousin Charles Breaux, and aunt Marie-Anne Breaux. On the other side sat
small cousin Lucie Breaux, big cousin Paul Gay, great-aunt Sally Gay (who
took snuff and was therefore a disgrace to the family); two strange, extremely
handsome young men who might be cousins but who were certainly in love with
cousin Miranda Gay; and cousin Miranda Gay herself, a most dashing young
lady with crisp silk skirts, a half dozen of them at once, a lovely perfume and
wonderful black curly hair above enormous wild gray eyes, "like a colt's," Father
said. Miranda hoped to be exactly like her when she grew up. Hanging to
Dicey's arm she leaned out and waved to cousin Miranda, who waved back
smiling, and the strange young men waved to her also. Miranda was most
fearfully excited. It was her first circus; it might also be her last because the
whole family had combined to persuade Grandmother to allow her to come
with them. "Very well, this once," Grandmother said, "since it's a family
reunion."

This once! This once! She could not look hard enough at everything. She
even peeped down between the wide crevices of the piled-up plank seats, where
she was astonished to see odd-looking, roughly dressed little boys peeping up
from the dust below. They were squatted in little heaps, staring up quietly. She
looked squarely into the eyes of one, who returned her a look so peculiar she
gazed and gazed, trying to understand it. It was a bold grinning stare without
any kind of friendliness in it. He was a thin, dirty little boy with a floppy old
checkerboard cap pulled over crumpled red ears and dust-colored hair. As she
gazed he nudged the little boy next to him, whispered, and the second little boy
caught her eye. This was too much. Miranda pulled Dicey's sleeve. "Dicey,
what are those little boys doing down there?" "Down where?" asked Dicey, but
she seemed to know already, for she bent over and looked through the crevice,
drew her knees together and her skirts around her, and said severely: "You jus
mind yo' own business and stop throwin' yo' legs around that way. Don't you
pay any mind. Plenty o' monkeys right here in the show widout you studyin' dat
kind."

An enormous brass band seemed to explode right at Miranda's ear. She
jumped, quivered, thrilled blindly and almost forgot to breathe as sound and
color and smell rushed together and poured through her skin and hair and beat
in her head and hands and feet and pit of her stomach. "Oh," she called out in
her panic, closing her eyes and seizing Dicey's hand hard. The flaring lights
burned through her lids, a roar of laughter like rage drowned out the steady
raging of the drums and horns. She opened her eyes . . . A creature in a
blousy white overall with ruffles at the neck and ankles, with bone-white skull

and chalk-white face, with tufted eyebrows far apart in the middle of his forehead, the lids in a black sharp angle, a long scarlet mouth stretching back into sunken cheeks, turned up at the corners in a perpetual bitter grimace of pain, astonishment, not smiling, pranced along a wire stretched down the center of the ring, balancing a long thin pole with little wheels at either end. Miranda thought at first he was walking on air, or flying, and this did not surprise her; but when she saw the wire, she was terrified. High above their heads the inhuman figure pranced, spinning the little wheels. He paused, slipped, the flapping white leg waved in space; he staggered, wobbled, slipped sidewise, plunged, and caught the wire with frantic knee, hanging there upside down, the other leg waving like a feeler above his head; slipped once more, caught by one frenzied heel, and swung back and forth like a scarf. . . . The crowd roared with savage delight, shrieks of dreadful laughter like devils in delicious torment. . . . Miranda shrieked too, with real pain, clutching at her stomach with her knees drawn up. . . . The man on the wire, hanging by his foot, turned his head like a seal from side to side and blew sneering kisses from his cruel mouth. Then Miranda covered her eyes and screamed, the tears pouring over her cheeks and chin.

"Take her home," said her father, "get her out of here at once," but the laughter was not wiped from his face. He merely glanced at her and back to the ring. "Take her away, Dicey," called the Grandmother, from under her half-raised crepe veil. Dicey, rebelliously, very slowly, without taking her gaze from the white figure swaying on the wire, rose, seized the limp, suffering bundle, prodded and lumped her way over knees and feet, through the crowd, down the levels of the scaffolding, across a space of sandy tanbark, out through a flap in the tent. Miranda was crying steadily with an occasional hiccough. A dwarf was standing in the entrance, wearing a little woolly beard, a pointed cap, tight red breeches, long shoes with turned-up toes. He carried a thin white wand. Miranda almost touched him before she saw him, her distorted face with its open mouth and glistening tears almost level with his. He leaned forward and peered at her with kind, not-human golden eyes, like a near-sighted dog: then made a horrid grimace at her, imitating her own face. Miranda struck at him in sheer ill temper, screaming. Dicey drew her away quickly, but not before Miranda had seen in his face, suddenly, a look of haughty, remote displeasure, a true grown-up look. She knew it well. It chilled her with a new kind of fear: she had not believed he was really human.

"Raincheck, get your raincheck!" said a very disagreeable-looking fellow as they passed. Dicey turned toward him almost in tears herself. "Mister, caint you see I won't be able to git back? I got this young un to see to. . . . What good dat lil piece of paper goin to do *me?*" All the way home she was cross, and grumbled under her breath: little ole meany . . . little ole scare-cat . . . gret big baby . . . never go nowhere . . . never see nothin . . . come on here now, hurry up—always ruinin everything for othah folks . . . won't let anybody rest a minute, won't let anybody have any good times . . . come on here now, you wanted to go home and you're going there . . . snatching Miranda along, vicious but cautious, careful not to cross the line where Miranda could say outright: "Dicey did this or said this to me . . ." Dicey was allowed a certain freedom up to a point.

The family trooped into the house just before dark and scattered out all over it. From every room came the sound of chatter and laughter. The other children told Miranda what she had missed: wonderful little ponies with plumes and bells on their bridles, ridden by darling little monkeys in velvet jackets and peaked hats . . . trained white goats that danced . . . a baby elephant that crossed his front feet and leaned against his cage and opened his mouth to be fed, *such* a baby! . . . more clowns, funnier than the first one even . . . beautiful ladies with bright yellow hair, wearing white silk tights with red satin sashes, had performed on white trapezes; they also had hung by their toes, but how gracefully, like flying birds! Huge white horses had lolloped around and round the ring with men and women dancing on their backs! One man had swung by his teeth from the top of the tent and another had put his head in a lion's mouth. Ah, what she had not missed! Everybody had been enjoying themselves while she was missing her first big circus and spoiling the day for Dicey. Poor Dicey. Poor dear Dicey. The other children who hadn't thought of Dicey until that moment, mourned over her with sad mouths, their malicious eyes watching Miranda squirm. Dicey had been looking forward for weeks to this day! And then Miranda must get scared—"Can you *imagine* being afraid of that funny old clown?" each one asked the other, and then they smiled pityingly on Miranda. . . .

Then too, it had been a very important occasion in another way: it was the first time Grandmother had ever allowed herself to be persuaded to go to the circus. One could not gather, from her rather generalized opinions, whether there had been no circuses when she was young, or there had been and it was not proper to see them. At any rate for her usual sound reasons, Grandmother had never approved of circuses, and though she would not deny she had been amused somewhat, still there had been sights and sounds in this one which she maintained were, to say the least, not particularly edifying to the young. Her son Harry, who came in while the children made an early supper, looked at their illuminated faces, all the brothers and sisters and visiting cousins, and said, "This basket of young doesn't seem too much damaged." His mother said, "The fruits of their present are in a future so far off, neither of us may live to know whether harm has been done or not. That is the trouble," and she went on ladling out hot milk to pour over their buttered toast. Miranda was sitting silent, her underlip drooping. Her father smiled at her. "You missed it, Baby," he said softly, "and what good did that do you?"

Miranda burst again into tears: had to be taken away at last, and her supper was brought up to her. Dicey was exasperated and silent. Miranda could not eat. She tried, as if she were really remembering them, to think of the beautiful wild beings in white satin and spangles and red sashes who danced and frolicked on the trapezes; of the sweet little furry ponies and the lovely pet monkeys in their comical clothes. She fell asleep, and her invented memories gave way before her real ones, the bitter terrified face of the man in blowsy white falling to his death—ah, the cruel joke!—and the terrible grimace of the unsmiling dwarf. She screamed in her sleep and sat up crying for deliverance from her torments.

Dicey came, her cross, sleepy eyes half-closed, her big dark mouth pouted, thumping the floor with her thick bare feet. "I *swear*," she said, in a violent hoarse whisper. "What the matter with you? You need a good spankin, I *swear!* Wakin everybody up like this . . ."

Miranda was completely subjugated by her fears. She had a way of answering Dicey back. She would say, "Oh, hush up, Dicey." Or she would say, "I don't have to mind *you*. I don't have to mind anybody but my grand-mother," which was provokingly true. And she would say, "You don't know what you're talking about." The day just past had changed that. Miranda sincerely did not want anybody, not even Dicey, to be cross with her. Ordinarily she did not care how cross she made the harassed adults around her. Now if Dicey must be cross, she still did not really care, if only Dicey might not turn out the lights and leave her to the fathomless terrors of the darkness where sleep could overtake her once more. She hugged Dicey with both arms, crying, "Don't, don't leave me. *Don't* be so angry! I c-c-can't b-bear it!"

Dicey lay down beside her with a long moaning sigh, which meant that she was collecting her patience and making up her mind to remember that she was a Christian and must bear her cross. "Now you go to sleep," she said, in her usual warm being-good voice. "Now you jes shut yo eyes and go to sleep. I ain't going to leave you. Dicey ain't mad at nobody . . . *nobody* in the whole worl'. . . ."

F. SCOTT FITZGERALD

❧ *The Ice Palace*

I

THE sunlight dripped over the house like golden paint over an art jar, and the freckling shadows here and there only intensified the rigor of the bath of light. The Butterworth and Larkin houses flanking were intrenched behind great stodgy trees; only the Happer house took the full sun, and all day long faced the dusty road-street with a tolerant kindly patience. This was the city of Tarleton in southernmost Georgia, September afternoon.

Up in her bedroom window Sally Carrol Happer rested her nineteen-year-old chin on a fifty-two–year–old sill and watched Clark Darrow's ancient Ford turn the corner. The car was hot—being partly metallic it retained all the heat it absorbed or evolved—and Clark Darrow sitting bolt upright at the wheel wore a pained, strained expression as though he considered himself a spare part, and rather likely to break. He laboriously crossed two dust ruts, the wheels squeaking indignantly at the encounter, and then with a terrifying expression he gave the steering-gear a final wrench and deposited self and car approximately in front of the Happer steps. There was a plaintive heaving sound, a death-rattle, followed by a short silence; and then the air was rent by a startling whistle.

Sally Carrol gazed down sleepily. She started to yawn, but finding this quite impossible unless she raised her chin from the window-sill, changed her mind and continued silently to regard the car, whose owner sat brilliantly if perfunctorily at attention as he waited for an answer to his signal. After a moment the whistle once more split the dusty air.

"Good mawnin'."

With difficulty Clark twisted his tall body round and bent a distorted glance on the window.

" 'Tain't mawnin', Sally Carrol."

"Isn't it, sure enough?"

"What you doin'?"

"Eatin' 'n apple."

"Come on go swimmin'—want to?"

"Reckon so."

"How 'bout hurryin' up?"

"Sure enough."

Sally Carrol sighed voluminously and raised herself with profound inertia from the floor, where she had been occupied in alternately destroying parts of a green apple and painting paper dolls for her younger sister. She approached a mirror, regarded her expression with a pleased and pleasant languor, dabbed two spots of rouge on her lips and a grain of powder on her nose, and covered her bobbed corn-colored hair with a rose-littered sunbonnet. Then she kicked over the painting water, said, "Oh, damn!"—but let it lay—and left the room.

"How you, Clark?" she inquired a minute later as she slipped nimbly over the side of the car.

"Mighty fine, Sally Carrol."

"Where we go swimmin'?"

"Out to Walley's Pool. Told Marylyn we'd call by an' get her an' Joe Ewing."

Clark was dark and lean, and when on foot was rather inclined to stoop. His eyes were ominous and his expression somewhat petulant except when startlingly illuminated by one of his frequent smiles. Clark had "a income"—just enough to keep himself in ease and his car in gasoline—and he had spent the two years since he graduated from Georgia Tech in dozing round the lazy streets of his home town, discussing how he could best invest his capital for an immediate fortune.

Hanging round he found not at all difficult; a crowd of little girls had grown up beautifully, the amazing Sally Carroll foremost among them; and they enjoyed being swum with and danced with and made love to in the flower-filled summery evenings—and they all liked Clark immensely. When feminine company palled there were half a dozen other youths who were always just about to do something, and meanwhile were quite willing to join him in a few holes of golf, or a game of billiards, or the consumption of a quart of "hard yella licker." Every once in a while one of these contemporaries made a farewell round of calls before going up to New York or Philadelphia or Pittsburgh to go into business, but mostly they just stayed round in this languid paradise of dreamy skies and firefly evenings and noisy niggery street fairs—and especially of gracious, soft-voiced girls, who were brought up on memories instead of money.

The Ford having been excited into a sort of restless resentful life, Clark and Sally Carrol rolled and rattled down Valley Avenue into Jefferson Street, where the dust road became a pavement; along opiate Millicent Place, where there were half a dozen prosperous, substantial mansions; and on into the down-town section. Driving was perilous here, for it was shopping time; the population idled casually across the streets and a drove of low-moaning oxen were being urged along in front of a placid street-car; even the shops seemed only yawning their doors and blinking their windows in the sunshine before retiring into a state of utter and finite coma.

"Sally Carrol," said Clark suddenly, "it a fact that you're engaged?"

She looked at him quickly.

"Where'd you hear that?"

"Sure enough, you engaged?"

" 'At's a nice question!"

"Girl told me you were engaged to a Yankee you met up in Asheville last summer."

Sally Carrol sighed.

"Never saw such an old town for rumors."

"Don't marry a Yankee, Sally Carrol. We need you round here." Sally Carrol was silent a moment.

"Clark," she demanded suddenly, "who on earth shall I marry?"

"I offer my services."

"Honey, you couldn't support a wife," she answered cheerfully. "Anyway, I know you too well to fall in love with you."

" 'At doesn't mean you ought to marry a Yankee," he persisted.

"S'pose I love him?"

He shook his head.

"You couldn't. He'd be a lot different from us, every way."

He broke off as he halted the car in front of a rambling, dilapidated house. Marylyn Wade and Joe Ewing appeared in the doorway.

" 'Lo, Sally Carrol."

"Hi!"

"How you-all?"

"Sally Carrol," demanded Marylyn as they started off again, "you engaged?"

"Lawdy, where'd all this start? Can't I look at a man 'thout everybody in town engagin' me to him?"

Clark stared straight in front of him at a bolt on the clattering windshield.

"Sally Carrol," he said with a curious intensity, "don't you like us?"

"What?"

"Us down here?"

"Why, Clark, you know I do. I adore all you boys."

"Then why you gettin' engaged to a Yankee?"

"Clark, I don't know. I'm not sure what I'll do, but—well, I want to go places and see people. I want my mind to grow. I want to live where things happen on a big scale."

"What you mean?"

"Oh, Clark, I love you, and I love Joe here, and Ben Arrot, and you-all, but you'll—you'll—"

"We'll all be failures?"

"Yes. I don't mean only money failures, but just sort of—of ineffectual and sad, and—oh, how can I tell you?"

"You mean because we stay here in Tarleton?"

"Yes, Clark; and because you like it and never want to change things or think or go ahead."

He nodded and she reached over and pressed his hand.

"Clark," she said softly, "I wouldn't change you for the world. You're sweet the way you are. The things that'll make you fail I'll love always—the living in the past, the lazy days and nights you have, and all your carelessness and generosity."

"But you're goin' away?"

"Yes—because I couldn't ever marry you. You've a place in my heart no one else ever could have, but tied down here I'd get restless. I'd feel I was— wastin' myself. There's two sides to me, you see. There's the sleepy old side you love; an' there's a sort of energy—the feelin' that makes me do wild things. That's the part of me that may be useful somewhere, that'll last when I'm not beautiful any more."

She broke off with characteristic suddenness and sighed, "Oh, sweet cooky!" as her mood changed.

Half closing her eyes and tipping back her head till it rested on the seat-back she let the savory breeze fan her eyes and ripple the fluffy curls of her bobbed hair. They were in the country now, hurrying between tangled growths of bright-green coppice and grass and tall trees that sent sprays of foliage to hang a cool welcome over the road. Here and there they passed a battered Negro cabin, its oldest white-haired inhabitant smoking a corncob pipe beside the door, and half a dozen scantily clothed pickaninnies parading tattered dolls on the wild-grown grass in front. Farther out were lazy cotton-fields, where even the workers seemed intangible shadows lent by the sun to the earth, not for toil, but to while away some age-old tradition in the golden September fields. And round the drowsy picturesqueness, over the trees and shacks and muddy rivers, flowed the heat, never hostile, only comforting, like a great warm nourishing bosom for the infant earth.

"Sally Carrol, we're here!"

"Poor chile's soun' asleep."

"Honey, you dead at last outa sheer laziness?"

"Water, Sally Carrol! Cool water waitin' for you!"

Her eyes opened sleepily.

"Hi!" she murmured, smiling.

II

In November Harry Bellamy, tall, broad, and brisk, came down from his Northern city to spend four days. His intention was to settle a matter that had been hanging fire since he and Sally Carrol had met in Asheville, North Carolina, in midsummer. The settlement took only a quiet afternoon and an evening in front of a glowing open fire, for Harry Bellamy had everything she wanted; and, besides, she loved him—loved him with that side of her she kept especially for loving. Sally Carrol had several rather clearly defined sides.

On his last afternoon they walked, and she found their steps tending half-unconsciously toward one of her favorite haunts, the cemetery. When it came in sight, gray-white and golden-green under the cheerful late sun, she paused, irresolute, by the iron gate.

"Are you mournful by nature, Harry?" she asked with a faint smile.

"Mournful? Not I."

"Then let's go in here. It depresses some folks, but I like it."

They passed through the gateway and followed a path that led through a wavy valley of graves—dusty-gray and mouldy for the fifties; quaintly carved with flowers and jars for the seventies; ornate and hideous for the nineties, with fat marble cherubs lying in sodden sleep on stone pillows, and great impossible growths of nameless granite flowers. Occasionally they saw a kneeling figure with tributary flowers, but over most of the graves lay silence and withered leaves with only the fragrance that their own shadowy memories could waken in living minds.

They reached the top of a hill where they were fronted by a tall, round headstone, freckled with dark spots of damp and half grown over with vines.

"Margery Lee," she read, "1844–1873. Wasn't she nice? She died when she was twenty-nine. Dear Margery Lee," she added softly. "Can't you see her, Harry?"

"Yes, Sally Carrol."

He felt a little hand insert itself into his.

"She was dark, I think; and she always wore her hair with a ribbon in it, and gorgeous hoop-skirts of alice blue and old rose."

"Yes."

"Oh, she was sweet, Harry! And she was the sort of girl born to stand on a wide, pillared porch and welcome folks in. I think perhaps a lot of men went away to war meanin' to come back to her; but maybe none of 'em ever did."

He stooped down close to the stone, hunting for any record of marriage.

"There's nothing here to show."

"Of course not. How could there be anything there better than just 'Margery Lee,' and that eloquent date?"

She drew close to him and an unexpected lump came into his throat as her yellow hair brushed his cheek.

"You see how she was, don't you, Harry?"

"I see," he agreed gently. "I see through your precious eyes. You're beautiful now, so I know she must have been."

Silent and close they stood, and he could feel her shoulders trembling a little. An ambling breeze swept up the hill and stirred the brim of her floppidy hat.

"Let's go down there!"

She was pointing to a flat stretch on the other side of the hill where along the green turf were a thousand grayish-white crosses stretching in endless, ordered rows like the stacked arms of a battalion.

"Those are the Confederate dead," said Sally Carrol simply.

They walked along and read the inscriptions, always only a name and a date, sometimes quite indecipherable.

"The last row is the saddest—see, 'way over there. Every cross has just a date on it, and the word 'Unknown.' "

She looked at him and her eyes brimmed with tears.

"I can't tell you how real it is to me, darling—if you don't know."

"How you feel about it is beautiful to me."

"No, no, it's not me, it's them—that old time that I've tried to have live in me. These were just men, unimportant evidently or they wouldn't have been 'unknown'; but they died for the most beautiful thing in the world—the dead South. You see," she continued, her voice still husky, her eyes glistening with tears, "people have these dreams they fasten onto things, and I've always grown up with that dream. It was so easy because it was all dead and there weren't any disillusions comin' to me. I've tried in a way to live up to those past standards of noblesse oblige—there's just the last remnants of it, you know, like the roses of an old garden dying all round us—streaks of strange courtliness and chivalry in some of these boys an' stories I used to hear from a Confederate soldier who lived next door, and a few old darkies. Oh, Harry, there was something, there was something! I couldn't ever make you understand, but it was there."

"I understand," he assured her again quietly.

Sally Carrol smiled and dried her eyes on the tip of a handkerchief protruding from his breast pocket.

"You don't feel depressed, do you, lover? Even when I cry I'm happy here, and I get a sort of strength from it."

Hand in hand they turned and walked slowly away. Finding soft grass she drew him down to a seat beside her with their backs against the remnants of a low broken wall.

"Wish those three old women would clear out," he complained. "I want to kiss you, Sally Carrol."

"Me, too."

They waited impatiently for the three bent figures to move off, and then she kissed him until the sky seemed to fade out and all her smiles and tears to vanish in an ecstasy of eternal seconds.

Afterward they walked slowly back together, while on the corners twilight played at somnolent black-and-white checkers with the end of day.

"You'll be up about mid-January," he said, "and you've got to stay a month at least. It'll be slick. There's a winter carnival on, and if you've never really seen snow it'll be like fairy-land to you. There'll be skating and skiing and tobogganing and sleigh-riding, and all sorts of torchlight parades on snowshoes. They haven't had one for years, so they're going to make it a knock-out."

"Will I be cold, Harry?" she asked suddenly.

"You certainly won't. You may freeze your nose, but you won't be shivery cold. It's hard and dry, you know."

"I guess I'm a summer child. I don't like any cold I've ever seen."

She broke off and they were silent for a minute.

"Sally Carrol," he said very slowly, "what do you say to—March?"

"I say I love you."

"March?"

"March, Harry."

III

All night in the Pullman it was very cold. She rang for the porter to ask for another blanket, and when he couldn't give her one she tried vainly, by squeezing down into the bottom of her berth and doubling back the bedclothes, to snatch a few hours' sleep. She wanted to look her best in the morning.

She rose at six and sliding uncomfortably into her clothes stumbled up to the diner for a cup of coffee. The snow had filtered into the vestibules and covered the floor with a slippery coating. It was intriguing, this cold, it crept in everywhere. Her breath was quite visible and she blew into the air with a naïve enjoyment. Seated in the diner she stared out the window at white hills and valleys and scattered pines whose every branch was a green platter for a cold feast of snow. Sometimes a solitary farmhouse would fly by, ugly and bleak and lone on the white waste; and with each one she had an instant of chill compassion for the souls shut in there waiting for spring.

As she left the diner and swayed back into the Pullman she experienced a surging rush of energy and wondered if she was feeling the bracing air of which Harry had spoken. This was the North, the North—her land now!

> "Then blow, ye winds, heigh-ho!
> A-roving I will go,"

she chanted exultantly to herself.

"What's 'at?" inquired the porter politely.

"I said: 'Brush me off.' "

The long wires of the telegraph-poles doubled; two tracks ran up beside the train—three—four; came a succession of white-roofed houses, a glimpse of a trolly car with frosted windows, streets—more streets—the city.

She stood for a dazed moment in the frosty station before she saw three fur-bundled figures descending upon her.

"There she is!"

"Oh, Sally Carrol!"

Sally Carrol dropped her bag.

"Hi!"

A faintly familiar icy-cold face kissed her, and then she was in a group of faces all apparently emitting great clouds of heavy smoke; she was shaking hands. There were Gordon, a short, eager man of thirty who looked like an amateur knocked-about model for Harry, and his wife, Myra, a listless lady with flaxen hair under a fur automobile cap. Almost immediately Sally Carrol thought of her as vaguely Scandinavian. A cheerful chauffeur adopted her bag, and amid ricochets of half-phrases, exclamations, and perfunctory listless "my dears" from Myra, they swept each other from the station.

Then they were in a sedan bound through a crooked succession of snowy streets where dozens of little boys were hitching sleds behind grocery wagons and automobiles.

"Oh," cried Sally Carrol, "I want to do that! Can we, Harry?"

"That's for kids. But we might—"

"It looks like such a circus!" she said regretfully.

Home was a rambling frame house set on a white lap of snow, and there she met a big, gray-haired man of whom she approved, and a lady who was like an egg, and who kissed her—these were Harry's parents. There was a breathless indescribable hour crammed full of half-sentences, hot water, bacon and eggs and confusion; and after that she was alone with Harry in the library, asking him if she dared smoke.

It was a large room with a Madonna over the fireplace and rows upon rows of books in covers of light gold and dark gold and shiny red. All the chairs had little lace squares where one's head should rest, the couch was just comfortable, the books looked as if they had been read—some—and Sally Carrol had an instantaneous vision of the battered old library at home, with her father's huge medical books, and the oil-paintings of her three great-uncles, and the old couch that had been mended up for forty-five years and was still luxurious to dream in. This room struck her as being neither attractive nor particularly otherwise. It was simply a room with a lot of fairly expensive things in it that all looked about fifteen years old.

"What do you think of it up here?" demanded Harry eagerly. "Does it surprise you? Is it what you expected, I mean?"

"You are, Harry," she said quietly, and reached out her arms to him.

But after a brief kiss he seemed anxious to extort enthusiasm from her.

"The town, I mean. Do you like it? Can you feel the pep in the air?"

"Oh, Harry," she laughed, "you'll have to give me time. You can't just fling questions at me."

She puffed at her cigarette with a sigh of contentment.

"One thing I want to ask you," he began rather apologetically; "you Southerners put quite an emphasis on family, and all that—not that it isn't quite all right, but you'll find it a little different here. I mean—you'll notice a lot of things that'll seem to you sort of vulgar display at first, Sally Carrol; but just remember that this is a three-generation town. Everybody has a father, and about half of us have grandfathers. Back of that we don't go."

"Of course," she murmured.

"Our grandfathers, you see, founded the place, and a lot of them had to take some pretty queer jobs while they were doing the founding. For instance, there's one woman who at present is about the social model for the town; well, her father was the first public ash man—things like that."

"Why," said Sally Carrol, puzzled, "did you s'pose I was goin' to make remarks about people?"

"Not at all," interrupted Harry; "and I'm not apologizing for any one either. "It's just that—well, a Southern girl came up here last summer and said some unfortunate things, and—oh, I just thought I'd tell you."

Sally Carrol felt suddenly indignant—as though she had been unjustly spanked—but Harry evidently considered the subject closed, for he went on with a great surge of enthusiasm.

"It's carnival time, you know. First in ten years. And there's an ice palace they're building now that's the first they've had since eighty-five. Built out of blocks of the clearest ice they could find—on a tremendous scale."

She rose and walking to the window pushed aside the heavy Turkish portières and looked out.

"Oh!" she cried suddenly. "There's two little boys makin' a snow man! Harry, do you reckon I can go out an' help 'em?"

"You dream! Come here and kiss me."

She left the window rather reluctantly.

"I don't guess this is a very kissable climate, is it? I mean, it makes you so you don't want to sit round, doesn't it?"

"We're not going to. I've got a vacation for the first week you're here, and there's a dinner-dance to-night."

"Oh, Harry," she confessed, subsiding in a heap, half in his lap, half in the pillows, "I sure do feel confused. I haven't got an idea whether I'll like it or not, an' I don't know what people expect, or anythin'. You'll have to tell me, honey."

"I'll tell you," he said softly, "if you'll just tell me you're glad to be here."

"Glad—just awful glad!" she whispered, insinuating herself into his arms in her own peculiar way. "Where you are is home for me, Harry."

And as she said this she had the feeling for almost the first time in her life that she was acting a part.

That night, amid the gleaming candles of a dinner-party, where the men seemed to do most of the talking while the girls sat in a haughty and expensive aloofness, even Harry's presence on her left failed to make her feel at home.

"They're a good-looking crowd, don't you think?" he demanded. "Just look round. There's Spud Hubbard, tackle at Princeton last year, and Junie Morton—he and the red-haired fellow next to him were both Yale hockey captains; Junie was in my class. Why, the best athletes in the world come from these States round here. This is a man's country, I tell you. Look at John J. Fishburn!"

"Who's he?" asked Sally Carrol innocently.

"Don't you know?"

"I've heard the name."

"Greatest wheat man in the Northwest, and one of the greatest financiers in the country."

She turned suddenly to a voice on her right.

"I guess they forgot to introduce us. My name's Roger Patton."

"My name is Sally Carrol Happer," she said graciously.

"Yes, I know. Harry told me you were coming."

"You a relative?"

"No, I'm a professor."

"Oh," she laughed.

"At the university. You're from the South, aren't you?"

"Yes; Tarleton, Georgia."

She liked him immediately—a reddish-brown mustache under watery blue eyes that had something in them that these other eyes lacked, some quality of appreciation. They exchanged stray sentences through dinner, and she made up her mind to see him again.

After coffee she was introduced to numerous good-looking young men who danced with conscious precision and seemed to take it for granted that she wanted to talk about nothing except Harry.

"Heavens," she thought, "they talk as if my being engaged made me older than they are—as if I'd tell their mothers on them!"

In the South an engaged girl, even a young married woman, expected the same amount of half-affectionate badinage and flattery that would be accorded a débutante, but here all that seemed banned. One young man, after getting well started on the subject of Sally Carrol's eyes, and how they had allured him ever since she entered the room, went into a violent confusion when he found she was visiting the Bellamys—was Harry's fiancée. He seemed to feel as though he had made some risqué and inexcusable blunder, became immediately formal, and left her at the first opportunity.

She was rather glad when Roger Patton cut in on her and suggested that they sit out a while.

"Well," he inquired, blinking cheerily, "how's Carmen from the South?"

"Mighty fine. How's—how's Dangerous Dan McGrew? Sorry, but he's the only Northerner I know much about."

He seemed to enjoy that.

"Of course," he confessed, "as a professor of literature I'm not supposed to have read Dangerous Dan McGrew."

"Are you a native?"

"No, I'm a Philadelphian. Imported from Harvard to teach French. But I've been here ten years."

"Nine years, three hundred an' sixty-four days longer than me."

"Like it here?"

"Uh-huh. Sure do!"

"Really?"

"Well, why not? Don't I look as if I were havin' a good time?"

"I saw you look out the window a minute ago—and shiver."

"Just my imagination," laughed Sally Carrol. "I'm used to havin' everythin' quiet outside, an' sometimes I look out an' see a flurry of snow, an' it's just as if somethin' dead was movin'."

He nodded appreciatively.

"Ever been North before?"

"Spent two Julys in Asheville, North Carolina."

"Nice-looking crowd, aren't they?" suggested Patton, indicating the swirling floor.

Sally Carrol started. This had been Harry's remark.

"Sure are! They're canine."

"What?"

She flushed.

"I'm sorry; that sounded worse than I meant it. You see I always think of people as feline or canine, irrespective of sex."

"Which are you?"

"I'm feline. So are you. So are most Southern men an' most of these girls here."

"What's Harry?"

"Harry's canine distinctly. All the men I've met to-night seem to be canine."

"What does 'canine' imply? A certain conscious masculinity as opposed to subtlety?"

"Reckon so. I never analyzed it—only I just look at people an' say 'canine' or 'feline' right off. It's right absurd, I guess."

"Not at all. I'm interested. I used to have a theory about these people. I think they're freezing up."

"What?"

"I think they're growing like Swedes—Ibsenesque, you know. Very gradually getting gloomy and melancholy. It's these long winters. Ever read any Ibsen?"

She shook her head.

"Well, you find in his characters a certain brooding rigidity. They're righteous, narrow, and cheerless, without infinite possibilities for great sorrow or joy."

"Without smiles or tears?"

"Exactly. That's my theory. You see there are thousands of Swedes up here. They come, I imagine, because the climate is very much like their own, and there's been a gradual mingling. There're probably not half a dozen here tonight, but—we've had four Swedish governors. Am I boring you?"

"I'm mighty interested."

"Your future sister-in-law is half Swedish. Personally I like her, but my theory is that Swedes react rather badly on us as a whole. Scandinavians, you know, have the largest suicide rate in the world."

"Why do you live here if it's so depressing?"

"Oh, it doesn't get me. I'm pretty well cloistered, and I suppose books mean more than people to me anyway."

"But writers all speak about the South being tragic. You know—Spanish señoritas, black hair and daggers an' haunting music."

He shook his head.

"No, the Northern races are the tragic races—they don't indulge in the cheering luxury of tears."

Sally Carrol thought of her graveyard. She supposed that that was vaguely what she had meant when she said it didn't depress her.

"The Italians are about the gayest people in the world—but it's a dull subject," he broke off. "Anyway, I want to tell you you're marrying a pretty fine man."

Sally Carrol was moved by an impulse of confidence.

"I know. I'm the sort of person who wants to be taken care of after a certain point, and I feel sure I will be."

"Shall we dance? You know," he continued as they rose, "it's encouraging to find a girl who knows what she's marrying for. Nine-tenths of them think of it as a sort of walking into a moving-picture sunset."

She laughed, and liked him immensely.

Two hours later on the way home she nestled near Harry in the back seat.

"Oh, Harry," she whispered, "it's so co-old!"

"But it's warm in here, darling girl."

"But outside it's cold; and oh, that howling wind!"

She buried her face deep in his fur coat and trembled involuntarily as his cold lips kissed the tip of her ear.

IV

The first week of her visit passed in a whirl. She had her promised toboggan-ride at the back of an automobile through a chill January twilight. Swathed in furs she put in a morning tobogganing on the country-club hill; even tried skiing, to sail through the air for a glorious moment and then land in a tangled laughing bundle on a soft snowdrift. She liked all the winter sports, except an afternoon spent snow-shoeing over a glaring plain under pale yellow sunshine, but she soon realized that these things were for children—that she was being humored and that the enjoyment round her was only a reflection of her own.

At first the Bellamy family puzzled her. The men were reliable and she liked them; to Mr. Bellamy especially, with his iron-gray hair and energetic dignity, she took an immediate fancy, once she found that he was born in Kentucky; this made of him a link between the old life and the new. But toward the women she felt a definite hostility. Myra, her future sister-in-law, seemed the essence of spiritless conventionality. Her conversation was so utterly devoid of personality that Sally Carrol, who came from a country where a certain amount of charm and assurance could be taken for granted in the women, was inclined to despise her.

"If those women aren't beautiful," she thought, "they're nothing. They just fade out when you look at them. They're glorified domestics. Men are the centre of every mixed group."

Lastly there was Mrs. Bellamy, whom Sally Carrol detested. The first day's impression of an egg had been confirmed—an egg with a cracked, veiny voice and such an ungracious dumpiness of carriage that Sally Carrol felt that if she once fell she would surely scramble. In addition, Mrs. Bellamy seemed to typify the town in being innately hostile to strangers. She called Sally Carrol "Sally," and could not be persuaded that the double name was anything more than a tedious ridiculous nickname. To Sally Carrol this shortening of her name was like presenting her to the public half clothed. She loved "Sally Carroll"; she loathed "Sally." She knew also that Harry's mother disapproved of her bobbed hair; and she had never dared smoke down-stairs after that first day when Mrs. Bellamy had come into the library sniffing violently.

Of all the men she met she preferred Roger Patton, who was a frequent visitor at the house. He never again alluded to the Ibsenesque tendency of the populace, but when he came in one day and found her curled upon the sofa bent over "Peer Gynt" he laughed and told her to forget what he'd said—that it was all rot.

And then one afternoon in her second week she and Harry hovered on the edge of a dangerously steep quarrel. She considered that he precipitated it entirely, though the Serbian in the case was an unknown man who had not had his trousers pressed.

They had been walking homeward between mounts of high-piled snow and under a sun which Sally Carrol scarcely recognized. They passed a little girl done up in gray wool until she resembled a small Teddy bear, and Sally Carrol could not resist a gasp of maternal appreciation.

"Look! Harry!"

"What?"

"That little girl—did you see her face?"

"Yes, why?"

"It was red as a little strawberry. Oh, she was cute!"

"Why, your own face is almost as red as that already! Everybody's healthy here. We're out in the cold as soon as we're old enough to walk. Wonderful climate!"

She looked at him and had to agree. He was mighty healthy-looking; so was his brother. And she had noticed the new red in her own cheeks that very morning.

Suddenly their glances were caught and held, and they stared for a moment at the street-corner ahead of them. A man was standing there, his knees bent, his eyes gazing upward with a tense expression as though he were about to make a leap toward the chilly sky. And then they both exploded into a shout of laughter, for coming closer they discovered it had been a ludicrous momentary illusion produced by the extreme bagginess of the man's trousers.

"Reckon that's one on us," she laughed.

"He must be a Southerner, judging by those trousers," suggested Harry mischievously.

"Why, Harry!"

Her surprised look must have irritated him.

"Those damn Southerners!"

Sally Carrol's eyes flashed.

"Don't call 'em that!"

"I'm sorry, dear," said Harry, malignantly apologetic, "but you know what I think of them. They're sort of—sort of degenerates—not at all like the old Southerners. They've lived so long down there with all the colored people that they've gotten lazy and shiftless."

"Hush your mouth, Harry!" she cried angrily. "They're not! They may be lazy—anybody would be in that climate—but they're my best friends, an' I don't want to hear 'em criticised in any such sweepin' way. Some of 'em are the finest men in the world."

"Oh, I know. They're all right when they come North to college, but of all the hangdog, ill-dressed, slovenly lot I ever saw, a bunch of small-town Southerners are the worst!"

Sally Carrol was clinching her gloved hands and biting her lip furiously.

"Why," continued Harry, "there was one in my class at New Haven, and we all thought that at last we'd found the true type of Southern aristocrat, but it turned out that he wasn't an aristocrat at all—just the son of a Northern carpetbagger, who owned about all the cotton round Mobile."

"A Southerner wouldn't talk the way you're talking now," she said evenly.

"They haven't the energy!"

"Or the somethin' else."

"I'm sorry, Sally Carrol, but I've heard you say yourself that you'd never marry—"

"That's quite different. I told you I wouldn't want to tie my life to any of the boys that are round Tarleton now, but I never made any sweepin' generalities."

They walked along in silence.

"I probably spread it on a bit thick, Sally Carrol. I'm sorry."

She nodded but made no answer. Five minutes later as they stood in the hallway she suddenly threw her arms round him.

"Oh, Harry," she cried, her eyes brimming with tears, "let's get married next week. I'm afraid of having fusses like that. I'm afraid, Harry. It wouldn't be that way if we were married."

But Harry, being in the wrong, was still irritated.

"That'd be idiotic. We decided on March."

The tears in Sally Carrol's eyes faded; her expression hardened slightly.

"Very well—I suppose I shouldn't have said that."

Harry melted.

"Dear little nut!" he cried. "Come and kiss me and let's forget."

That very night at the end of a vaudeville performance the orchestra played "Dixie" and Sally Carrol felt something stronger and more enduring than her tears and smiles of the day brim up inside her. She leaned forward gripping the arms of her chair until her face grew crimson.

"Sort of get you, dear?" whispered Harry.

But she did not hear him. To the spirited throb of the violins and the inspiring beat of the kettledrums her own old ghosts were marching by and on into the darkness, and as fifes whistled and sighed in the low encore they seemed so nearly out of sight that she could have waved good-by.

> "Away, away,
>   Away down South in Dixie!
> Away, away,
>   Away down South in Dixie!"

V

It was a particularly cold night. A sudden thaw had nearly cleared the streets the day before, but now they were traversed again with a powdery wraith of loose snow that travelled in wavy lines before the feet of the wind, and filled the lower air with a fine-particled mist. There was no sky—only a dark, ominous tent that draped in the tops of the streets and was in reality a vast approaching army of snowflakes—while over it all, chilling away the comfort from the brown-and-green glow of lighted windows and muffling the steady trot of the horse pulling their sleigh, interminably washed the north wind. It was a dismal town after all, she thought—dismal.

Sometimes at night it had seemed to her as though no one lived here—they had all gone long ago—leaving lighted houses to be covered in time by tombing heaps of sleet. Oh, if there should be snow on her grave! To be beneath great piles of it all winter long, where even her headstone would be a light shadow against light shadows. Her grave—a grave that should be flower-strewn and washed with sun and rain.

She thought again of those isolated country houses that her train had passed, and of the life there the long winter through—the ceaseless glare through the windows, the crust forming on the soft drifts of snow, finally the slow, cheerless melting, and the harsh spring of which Roger Patton had told her. Her spring—to lose it forever—with its lilacs and the lazy sweetness it stirred in her heart. She was laying away that spring—afterward she would lay away that sweetness.

With a gradual insistence the storm broke. Sally Carrol felt a film of flakes melt quickly on her eyelashes, and Harry reached over a furry arm and drew down her complicated flannel cap. Then the small flakes came in skirmish-line, and the horse bent his neck patiently as a transparency of white appeared momentarily on his coat.

"Oh, he's cold, Harry," she said quickly.

"Who? The horse? Oh, no, he isn't. He likes it!"

After another ten minutes they turned a corner and came in sight of their destination. On a tall hill outlined in vivid glaring green against the wintery sky stood the ice palace. It was three stories in the air, with battlements and embrasures and narrow icicled windows, and the innumerable electric lights inside made a gorgeous transparency of the great central hall. Sally Carrol clutched Harry's hand under the fur robe.

"It's beautiful!" he cried excitedly. "My golly, it's beautiful, isn't it! They haven't had one here since eighty-five!"

Somehow the notion of there not having been one since eighty-five oppressed her. Ice was a ghost, and this mansion of it was surely peopled by those shades of the eighties, with pale faces and blurred snow-filled hair.

"Come on, dear," said Harry.

She followed him out of the sleigh and waited while he hitched the horse. A party of four—Gordon, Myra, Roger Patton, and another girl—drew up beside them with a mighty jingle of bells. There were quite a crowd already, bundled in fur or sheepskin, shouting and calling to each other as they moved through the snow, which was now so thick that people could scarcely be distinguished a few yards away.

"It's a hundred and seventy feet tall," Harry was saying to a muffled figure beside him as they trudged toward the entrance; "covers six thousand square yards."

She caught snatches of conversation: "One main hall"—"walls twenty to forty inches thick"—"and the ice cave has almost a mile of—"—"this Canuck who built it—"

They found their way inside, and dazed by the magic of the great crystal walls Sally Carrol found herself repeating over and over two lines from "Kubla Khan":

> "It was a miracle of rare device,
> A sunny pleasure-dome with caves of ice!"

In the great glittering cavern with the dark shut out she took a seat on a wooden bench, and the evening's oppression lifted. Harry was right—it was beautiful; and her gaze travelled the smooth surface of the walls, the blocks for which had been selected for their purity and clearness to obtain this opalescent, translucent effect.

"Look! Here we go—oh, boy!" cried Harry.

A band in a far corner struck up "Hail, Hail, the Gang's All Here!" which echoed over to them in wild muddled acoustics, and then the lights suddenly went out; silence seemed to flow down the icy sides and sweep over them. Sally Carrol could still see her white breath in the darkness, and a dim row of pale faces over on the other side.

The music eased to a sighing complaint, and from outside drifted in the full-throated resonant chant of the marching clubs. It grew louder like some pæan a viking tribe traversing an ancient wild; it swelled—they were coming nearer; then a row of torches appeared, and another and another, and keeping time with their moccasined feet a long column of gray-mackinawed figures swept in, snowshoes slung at their shoulders, torches soaring and flickering as their voices rose along the great walls.

The gray column ended and another followed, the light streaming luridly this time over red toboggan caps and flaming crimson mackinaws, and as they entered they took up the refrain; then came a long platoon of blue and white, of green, of white, of brown and yellow.

"Those white ones are the Wacouta Club," whispered Harry eagerly. "Those are the men you've met round at dances."

The volume of the voices grew; the great cavern was a phantasmagoria of torches waving in great banks of fire, of colors and the rhythm of soft-leather steps. The leading column turned and halted, platoon deployed in front of platoon until the whole procession made a solid flag of flame, and then from thousands of voices burst a mighty shout that filled the air like a crash of thunder, and sent the torches wavering. It was magnificent, it was tremendous! To Sally Carrol it was the North offering sacrifice on some mighty altar to the gray pagan God of Snow. As the shout died the band struck up again and there came more singing, and then long reverberating cheers by each club. She sat very quiet listening while the staccato cries rent the stillness; and then she started, for there was a volley of explosion, and great clouds of smoke went up here and there through the cavern—the flash-light photographers at work—and the council was over. With the band at their head the clubs formed in column once more, took up their chant, and began to march out.

"Come on!" shouted Harry. "We want to see the labyrinths downstairs before they turn the lights off!"

They all rose and started toward the chute—Harry and Sally Carrol in the lead, her little mitten buried in his big fur gauntlet. At the bottom of the chute was a long empty room of ice, with the ceiling so low that they had to stoop—and their hands were parted. Before she realized what he intended Harry had darted down one of the half-dozen glittering passages that opened into the room and was only a vague receding blot against the green shimmer.

"Harry!" she called.

"Come on!" he cried back.

She looked round the empty chamber; the rest of the party had evidently decided to go home, were already outside somewhere in the blundering snow. She hesitated and then darted in after Harry.

"Harry!" she shouted.

She had reached a turning-point thirty feet down; she heard a faint muffled answer far to the left, and with a touch of panic fled toward it. She passed another turning, two more yawning alleys.

"Harry!"

No answer. She started to run straight forward, and then turned like lightening and sped back the way she had come, enveloped in a sudden icy terror.

She reached a turn—was it here?—took the left and came to what should have been the outlet into the long, low room, but it was only another glittering passage with darkness at the end. She called again but the walls gave back a flat, lifeless echo with no reverberations. Retracing her steps she turned another corner, this time following a wide passage. It was like the green lane between the parted waters of the Red Sea, like a damp vault connecting empty tombs.

She slipped a little now as she walked, for ice had formed on the bottom of her overshoes; she had to run her gloves along the half-slippery, half-sticky walls to keep her balance.

"Harry!"

Still no answer. The sound she made bounced mockingly down to the end of the passage.

Then on an instant the lights went out, and she was in complete darkness. She gave a small, frightened cry, and sank down into a cold little heap on the ice. She felt her left knee do something as she fell, but she scarcely noticed it as some deep terror far greater than any fear of being lost settled upon her. She was alone with this presence that came out of the North, the dreary loneliness that rose from ice-bound whalers in the Arctic seas, from smokeless, trackless wastes where were strewn the whitened bones of adventure. It was an icy breath of death; it was rolling down low across the land to clutch at her.

With a furious, despairing energy she rose again and started blindly down the darkness. She must get out. She might be lost in here for days, freeze to death and lie embedded in the ice like corpses she had read of, kept perfectly preserved until the melting of a glacier. Harry probably thought she had left with the others—he had gone by now; no one would know until late next day. She reached pitifully for the wall. Forty inches thick, they had said—forty inches thick!

"Oh!"

On both sides of her along the walls she felt things creeping, damp souls that haunted this palace, this town, this North.

"Oh, send somebody—send somebody!" she cried aloud.

Clark Darrow—he would understand; or Joe Ewing; she couldn't be left here to wander forever—to be frozen, heart, body, and soul. This her—this Sally Carrol! Why, she was a happy thing. She was a happy little girl. She liked warmth and summer and Dixie. These things were foreign—foreign.

"You're not crying," something said aloud. "You'll never cry any more. Your tears would just freeze; all tears freeze up here!"

She sprawled full length on the ice.

"Oh, God!" she faltered.

A long single file of minutes went by, and with a great weariness she felt her eyes closing. Then some one seemed to sit down near her and take her face in warm, soft hands. She looked up gratefully.

"Why, it's Margery Lee," she crooned softly to herself. "I knew you'd come." It really was Margery Lee, and she was just as Sally Carrol had known she would be, with a young, white brow, and wide, welcoming eyes, and a hoop-skirt of some soft material that was quite comforting to rest on.

"Margery Lee."

It was getting darker now and darker—all those tombstones ought to be repainted, sure enough, only that would spoil 'em, of course. Still, you ought to be able to see 'em.

Then after a succession of moments that went fast and then slow, but seemed to be ultimately resolving themselves into a multitude of blurred rays converging toward a pale-yellow sun, she heard a great cracking noise break her new-found stillness.

It was the sun, it was a light; a torch, and a torch beyond that, and another one, and voices; a face took flesh below the torch, heavy arms raised her, and she felt something on her cheek—it felt wet. Someone had seized her and was rubbing her face with snow. How ridiculous—with snow!

"Sally Carrol! Sally Carrol!"

It was Dangerous Dan McGrew; and two other faces she didn't know.

"Child, child! We've been looking for you two hours! Harry's half-crazy!"

Things came rushing back into place—the singing, the torches, the great shout of the marching clubs. She squirmed in Patton's arms and gave a long low cry.

"Oh, I want to get out of here! I'm going back home. Take me home"— her voice rose to a scream that sent a chill to Harry's heart as he came racing down the next passage—"to-morrow!" she cried with delirious, unrestrained passion—"To-morrow! To-morrow! To-morrow!"

VI

The wealth of golden sunlight poured a quite enervating yet oddly comforting heat over the house where day long it faced the dusty stretch of road. Two birds were making a great to-do in a cool spot found among the branches of a tree next door, and down the street a colored woman was announcing herself melodiously as a purveyor of strawberries. It was April afternoon.

Sally Carrol Happer, resting her chin on her arm, and her arm on an old window-seat gazed sleepily down over the spangled dust whence the heat waves were rising for the first time this spring. She was watching a very ancient Ford turn a perilous corner and rattle and groan to a jolting stop at the end of the walk. She made no sound, and in a minute a strident familiar whistle rent the air. Sally Carrol smiled and blinked.

"Good mawnin'."

A head appeared tortuously from under the car-top below.

" 'Tain't mawnin', Sally Carrol."

"Sure enough!" she said in affected surprise. "I guess maybe not."

"What you doin'?"

"Eatin' green peach. 'Spect to die any minute."

Clark twisted himself a last impossible notch to get a view of her face.

"Water's warm as a kettla steam, Sally Carrol. Wanta go swimmin'?"

"Hate to move," sighed Sally Carrol lazily, "but I reckon so."

WILLIAM FAULKNER

❧ *A Rose for Emily*

I

WHEN Miss Emily Grierson died, our whole town went to her funeral: the men through a sort of respectful affection for a fallen monument, the women mostly out of curiosity to see the inside of her house, which no one save an old manservant—a combined gardener and cook—had seen in at least ten years.

It was a big, squarish frame house that had once been white, decorated with cupolas and spires and scrolled balconies in the heavily lightsome style of the seventies, set on what had once been our most select street. But garages and cotton gins had encroached and obliterated even the august names of that neighborhood; only Miss Emily's house was left, lifting its stubborn and coquettish decay above the cotton wagons and the gasoline pumps—an eyesore among eyesores. And now Miss Emily had gone to join the representatives of those august names where they lay in the cedar-bemused cemetery among the ranked and anonymous graves of Union and Confederate soldiers who fell at the battle of Jefferson.

Alive, Miss Emily had been a tradition, a duty, and a care; a sort of hereditary obligation upon the town, dating from that day in 1894 when Colonel Sartoris, the mayor—he who fathered the edict that no Negro woman should appear on the streets without an apron—remitted her taxes, the dispensation dating from the death of her father on into perpetuity. Not that Miss Emily would have accepted charity. Colonel Sartoris invented an involved tale to the effect that Miss Emily's father had loaned money to the town, which the town, as a matter of business, preferred this way of repaying. Only a man of Colonel Sartoris' generation and thought could have invented it, and only a woman could have believed it.

When the next generation, with its more modern ideas, became mayors and aldermen, this arrangement created some little dissatisfaction. On the first of the year they mailed her a tax notice. February came, and there was no reply. They wrote her a formal letter, asking her to call at the sheriff's office at her convenience. A week later the mayor wrote her himself, offering to call or to send his car for her, and received in reply a note on paper of an archaic shape, in a thin, flowing calligraphy in faded ink, to the effect that she no longer went out at all. The tax notice was also enclosed, without comment.

They called a special meeting of the Board of Aldermen. A deputation waited upon her, knocked at the door through which no visitor had passed since she ceased giving china-painting lessons eight or ten years earlier. They were admitted by the old Negro into a dim hall from which a stairway mounted into still more shadow. It smelled of dust and disuse—a close, dank smell. The Negro led them into the parlor. It was furnished in heavy, leather-covered furniture. When the Negro opened the blinds of one window, they could see that the leather was cracked; and when they sat down, a faint dust rose sluggishly about their thighs, spinning with slow motes in the single sun-ray. On a tarnished gilt easel before the fireplace stood a crayon portrait of Miss Emily's father.

They rose when she entered—a small, fat woman in black, with a thin gold chain descending to her waist and vanishing into her belt, leaning on an ebony cane with a tarnished gold head. Her skeleton was small and spare; perhaps that was why what would have been merely plumpness in another was obesity in her. She looked bloated, like a body long submerged in motionless water, and of that pallid hue. Her eyes, lost in the fatty ridges of her face, looked like two small pieces of coal pressed into a lump of dough as they moved from one face to another while the visitors stated their errand.

She did not ask them to sit. She just stood in the door and listened quietly until the spokesman came to a stumbling halt. Then they could hear the invisible watch ticking at the end of the gold chain.

Her voice was dry and cold. "I have no taxes in Jefferson. Colonel Sartoris explained it to me. Perhaps one of you can gain access to the city records and satisfy yourselves."

"But we have. We are the city authorities, Miss Emily. Didn't you get a notice from the sheriff, signed by him?"

"I received a paper, yes," Miss Emily said. "Perhaps he considers himself the sheriff . . . I have no taxes in Jefferson."

"But there is nothing on the books to show that, you see. We must go by the—"

"See Colonel Sartoris. I have no taxes in Jefferson."

"But, Miss Emily—"

"See Colonel Sartoris." (Colonel Sartoris had been dead almost ten years.) "I have no taxes in Jefferson. Tobe!" The Negro appeared. "Show these gentlemen out."

II

So she vanquished them, horse and foot, just as she had vanquished their fathers thirty years before about the smell. That was two years after her father's death and a short time after her sweetheart—the one we believed would marry her—had deserted her. After her father's death she went out very little; after her sweetheart went away, people hardly saw her at all. A few of the ladies had the temerity to call, but were not received, and the only sign of life about the place was the Negro man—a young man then—going in and out with a market basket.

"Just as if a man—any man—could keep a kitchen properly," the ladies said; so they were not surprised when the smell developed. It was another link between the gross, teeming world and the high and mighty Griersons.

A neighbor, a woman, complained to the mayor, Judge Stevens, eighty years old.

"But what will you have me do about it, madam?" he said.

"Why, send her word to stop it," the woman said. "Isn't there a law?"

"I'm sure that won't be necessary," Judge Stevens said. "It's probably just a snake or a rat that nigger of hers killed in the yard. I'll speak to him about it."

The next day he received two more complaints, one from a man who came in diffident deprecation. "We really must do something about it, Judge. I'd be the last one in the world to bother Miss Emily, but we've got to do something." That night the Board of Aldermen met—three graybeards and one younger man, a member of the rising generation.

"It's simple enough," he said. "Send her word to have her place cleaned up. Give her a certain time to do it in, and if she don't . . ."

"Dammit, sir," Judge Stevens said, "will you accuse a lady to her face of smelling bad?"

So the next night, after midnight, four men crossed Miss Emily's lawn and slunk about the house like burglars, sniffing along the base of the brickwork and at the cellar openings while one of them performed a regular sowing motion with his hand out of a sack slung from his shoulder. They broke open the cellar door and sprinkled lime there, and in all the outbuildings. As they re-crossed the lawn, a window that had been dark was lighted and Miss Emily sat in it, the light behind her, and her upright torso motionless as that of an idol. They crept quietly across the lawn and into the shadow of the locusts that lined the street. After a week or two the smell went away.

That was when people had begun to feel really sorry for her. People in our town, remembering how old lady Wyatt, her great-aunt, had gone completely crazy at last, believed that the Griersons held themselves a little too high for what they really were. None of the young men were quite good enough for Miss Emily and such. We had long thought of them as a tableau: Miss Emily a slender figure in white in the background, her father a spraddled silhouette in the foreground, his back to her and clutching a horsewhip, the two of them framed by the back-flung front door. So when she got to be thirty and was still single, we were not pleased exactly, but vindicated; even with insanity in the family she wouldn't have turned down all of her chances if they had really materialized.

When her father died, it got about that the house was all that was left to her; and in a way, people were glad. At last they could pity Miss Emily. Being left alone, and a pauper, she had become humanized. Now she too would know the old thrill and the old despair of a penny more or less.

The day after his death all the ladies prepared to call at the house and offer condolence and aid, as is our custom. Miss Emily met them at the door, dressed as usual and with no trace of grief on her face. She told them that her father was not dead. She did that for three days, with the ministers calling on her, and the doctors, trying to persuade her to let them dispose of the body. Just as they were about to resort to law and force, she broke down, and they buried her father quickly.

We did not say she was crazy then. We believed she had to do that. We remembered all the young men her father had driven away, and we knew that with nothing left, she would have to cling to that which had robbed her, as people will.

III

She was sick for a long time. When we saw her again, her hair was cut short, making her look like a girl, with a vague resemblance to those angels in colored church windows—sort of tragic and serene.

The town had just let the contracts for paving the sidewalks, and in the summer after her father's death they began the work. The construction company came with niggers and mules and machinery, and a foreman named Homer Barron, a Yankee—a big, dark, ready man, with a big voice and eyes lighter than his face. The little boys would follow in groups to hear him cuss the niggers, and the niggers singing in time to the rise and fall of picks. Pretty soon he knew everybody in town. Whenever you heard a lot of laughing anywhere about the square, Homer Barron would be in the center of the group. Presently we began to see him and Miss Emily on Sunday afternoons driving in the yellow-wheeled buggy and the matched team of bays from the livery stable.

At first we were glad that Miss Emily would have an interest, because the ladies all said, "Of course a Grierson would not think seriously of a Northerner, a day laborer." But there were still others, older people, who said that even grief could not cause a real lady to forget *noblesse oblige*—without calling it *noblesse oblige*. They just said, "Poor Emily. Her kinsfolk should come to her." She had some kin in Alabama; but years ago her father had fallen out with them over the estate of old lady Wyatt, the crazy woman, and there was no communication between the two families. They had not even been represented at the funeral.

And as soon as the old people said, "Poor Emily," the whispering began. "Do you suppose it's really so?" they said to one another. "Of course it is. What else could . . ." This behind their hands; rustling of craned silk and satin behind jalousies closed upon the sun of Sunday afternoon as the thin, swift clop-clop-clop of the matched team passed: "Poor Emily."

She carried her head high enough—even when we believed that she was fallen. It was as if she demanded more than ever the recognition of her dignity as the last Grierson; as if it had wanted that touch of earthiness to reaffirm her imperviousness. Like when she bought the rat poison, the arsenic. That was over a year after they had begun to say "Poor Emily," and while the two female cousins were visiting her.

"I want some poison," she said to the druggist. She was over thirty then, still a slight woman, though thinner than usual, with cold, haughty black eyes in a face the flesh of which was strained across the temples and about the eyesockets as you imagine a lighthouse-keeper's face ought to look. "I want some poison," she said.

"Yes, Miss Emily. What kind? For rats and such? I'd recom—"

"I want the best you have. I don't care what kind."

The druggist named several. "They'll kill anything up to an elephant. But what you want is—"

"Arsenic," Miss Emily said. "Is that a good one?"

"Is . . . arsenic? Yes, ma'am. But what you want—"

"I want arsenic."

The druggist looked down at her. She looked back at him, erect, her face like a strained flag. "Why, of course," the druggist said. "If that's what you want. But the law requires you to tell what you are going to use it for."

Miss Emily just stared at him, her head tilted back in order to look him eye for eye, until he looked away and went and got the arsenic and wrapped it up. The Negro delivery boy brought her the package; the druggist didn't come back. When she opened the package at home there was written on the box, under the skull and bones: "For rats."

IV

So the next day we all said, "She will kill herself"; and we said it would be the best thing. When she had first begun to be seen with Homer Barron, we had said, "She will marry him." Then we said, "She will persuade him yet," because Homer himself had remarked—he liked men, and it was known that he drank with the younger men in the Elks' Club—that he was not a marrying man. Later we said, "Poor Emily," behind the jalousies as they passed on Sunday afternoon in the glittering buggy, Miss Emily with her head high and Homer Barron with his hat cocked and a cigar in his teeth, reins and whip in a yellow glove.

Then some of the ladies began to say that it was a disgrace to the town and a bad example to the young people. The men did not want to interfere, but at last the ladies forced the Baptist minister—Miss Emily's people were Episcopal —to call upon her. He would never divulge what happened during that inter-view, but he refused to go back again. The next Sunday they again drove about the streets, and the following day the minister's wife wrote to Miss Emily's relations in Alabama.

So she had blood-kin under her roof again and we sat back to watch developments. At first nothing happened. Then we were sure that they were to be married. We learned that Miss Emily had been to the jeweler's and ordered a man's toilet set in silver, with the letters H.B. on each piece. Two days later we learned that she had bought a complete outfit of men's clothing, including a nightshirt, and we said, "They are married." We were really glad. We were glad because the two female cousins were even more Grierson than Miss Emily had ever been.

So we were not surprised when Homer Barron—the streets had been finished some time since—was gone. We were a little disappointed that there was not a public blowing-off, but we believed that he had gone on to prepare for Miss Emily's coming, or to give her a chance to get rid of the cousins. (By that time it was a cabal, and we were all Miss Emily's allies to help circumvent the cousins.) Sure enough, after another week they departed. And, as we had expected all along, within three days Homer Barron was back in town. A neighbor saw the Negro man admit him at the kitchen door at dusk one evening.

And that was the last we saw of Homer Barron. And of Miss Emily for some time. The Negro man went in and out with the market basket, but the front door remained closed. Now and then we would see her at a window for a moment, as the men did that night when they sprinkled the lime, but for almost six months she did not appear on the streets. Then we knew that this was to be expected too; as if that quality of her father which had thwarted her woman's life so many times had been too virulent and too furious to die.

When we next saw Miss Emily, she had grown fat and her hair was turning gray. During the next few years it grew grayer and grayer until it attained an even pepper-and-salt iron-gray, when it ceased turning. Up to the day of her death at seventy-four it was still that vigorous iron-gray, like the hair of an active man.

From that time on her front door remained closed, save for a period of six or seven years, when she was about forty, during which she gave lessons in china-painting. She fitted up a studio in one of the downstairs rooms, where the daughters and granddaughters of Colonel Sartoris' contemporaries were sent to her with the same regularity and in the same spirit that they were sent on Sundays with a twenty-five cent piece for the collection plate. Meanwhile her taxes had been remitted.

Then the newer generation became the backbone and the spirit of the town, and the painting pupils grew up and fell away and did not send their children to her with boxes of color and tedious brushes and pictures cut from the ladies' magazines. The front door closed upon the last one and remained closed for good. When the town got free postal delivery Miss Emily alone refused to let them fasten the metal numbers above her door and attach a mailbox to it. She would not listen to them.

Daily, monthly, yearly we watched the Negro grow grayer and more stooped, going in and out with the market basket. Each December we sent her a tax notice, which would be returned by the post office a week later, unclaimed. Now and then we would see her in one of the downstairs windows—she had evidently shut up the top floor of the house—like the carven torso of an idol in a niche, looking or not looking at us, we could never tell which. Thus she passed from generation to generation—dear, inescapable, impervious, tranquil, and perverse.

And so she died. Fell ill in the house filled with dust and shadows, with only a doddering Negro man to wait on her. We did not even know she was sick; we had long since given up trying to get any information from the Negro. He talked to no one, probably not even to her, for his voice had grown harsh and rusty, as if from disuse.

She died in one of the downstairs rooms, in a heavy walnut bed with a curtain, her gray head propped on a pillow yellow and moldy with age and lack of sunlight.

V

The Negro met the first of the ladies at the front door and let them in, with their hushed, sibilant voices and their quick, curious glances, and then he disappeared. He walked right through the house and out the back and was not seen again.

The two female cousins came at once. They held the funeral on the second day, with the town coming to look at Miss Emily beneath a mass of bought flowers, with the crayon face of her father musing profoundly above the bier and the ladies sibilant and macabre; and the very old men—some in their brushed Confederate uniforms—on the porch and the lawn, talking of Miss Emily as if she had been a contemporary of theirs, believing that they had danced with her and courted her perhaps, confusing time with its mathematical progression, as the old do, to whom all the past is not a diminishing road, but, instead, a huge meadow which no winter ever quite touches, divided from them now by the narrow bottle-neck of the most recent decade of years.

Already we knew that there was one room in that region above stairs which no one had seen in forty years, and which would have to be forced. They waited until Miss Emily was decently in the ground before they opened it.

The violence of breaking down the door seemed to fill this room with pervading dust. A thin, acrid pall as of the tomb seemed to lie everywhere upon this room decked and furnished as for a bridal: upon the valance curtains of faded rose color, upon the rose-shaded lights, upon the dressing table, upon the delicate array of crystal and the man's toilet things backed with tarnished silver, silver so tarnished that the monogram was obscured. Among them lay a collar and tie, as if they had just been removed, which, lifted, left upon the surface a pale crescent in the dust. Upon a chair hung the suit, carefully folded; beneath it the two mute shoes and the discarded socks.

The man himself lay in the bed.

For a long while we just stood there, looking down at the profound and fleshless grin. The body had apparently once lain in the attitude of an embrace, but now the long sleep that outlasts love, that conquers even the grimace of love, had cuckolded him. What was left of him, rotted beneath what was left of the nightshirt, had become inextricable from the bed in which he lay; and upon him and upon the pillow beside him lay that even coating of the patient and biding dust.

Then we noticed that in the second pillow was the indentation of a head. One of us lifted something from it, and leaning forward, that faint and invisible dust dry and acrid in the nostrils, we saw a long strand of iron-gray hair.

ERNEST HEMINGWAY

❧ *The Killers*

THE DOOR of Henry's lunchroom opened and two men came in. They sat down at the counter.

"What's yours?" George asked them.

"I don't know," one of the men said. "What do you want to eat, Al?"

"I don't know," said Al. "I don't know what I want to eat."

Outside it was getting dark. The street-light came on outside the window. The two men at the counter read the menu. From the other end of the counter Nick Adams watched them. He had been talking to George when they came in.

"I'll have a roast pork tenderloin with apple sauce and mashed potatoes," the first man said.

"It isn't ready yet."

"What the hell do you put it on the card for?"

"That's the dinner," George explained. "You can get that at six o'clock."

George looked at the clock on the wall behind the counter.

"It's five o'clock."

"The clock says twenty minutes past five," the second man said.

"It's twenty minutes fast."

"Oh, to hell with the clock," the first man said. "What have you got to eat?"

"I can give you any kind of sandwiches," George said. "You can have ham and eggs, bacon and eggs, liver and bacon, or a steak."

"Give me chicken croquettes with green peas and cream sauce and mashed potatoes."

"That's the dinner."

"Everything we want's the dinner, eh? That's the way you work it."

"I can give you ham and eggs, bacon and eggs, liver—"

"I'll take ham and eggs," the man called Al said. He wore a derby hat and a black overcoat buttoned across the chest. His face was small and white and he had tight lips. He wore a silk muffler and gloves.

"Give me bacon and eggs," said the other man. He was about the same size as Al. Their faces were different, but they were dressed like twins. Both wore overcoats too tight for them. They sat leaning forward, their elbows on the counter.

"Got anything to drink?" Al asked.

"Silver beer, bevo, ginger-ale," George said.

"I mean you got anything to *drink?*"

"Just those I said."

"This is a hot town," said the other. "What do they call it?"

"Summit."

"Ever hear of it?" Al asked his friend.

"No," said the friend.

"What do you do here nights?" Al asked.

"They eat the dinner," his friend said. "They all come here and eat the big dinner."

"That's right," George said.

"So you think that's right?" Al asked George.

"Sure."

"You're a pretty bright boy, aren't you?"

"Sure," said George.

"Well, you're not," said the other little man. "Is he, Al?"

"He's dumb," said Al. He turned to Nick. "What's your name?"

"Adams."

"Another bright boy," Al said. "Ain't he a bright boy, Max?"

"The town's full of bright boys," Max said.

George put the two platters, one of ham and eggs, the other of bacon and eggs, on the counter. He set down two side-dishes of fried potatoes and closed the wicket into the kitchen.

"Which is yours?" he asked Al.

"Don't you remember?"

"Ham and eggs."

"Just a bright boy," Max said. He leaned forward and took the ham and eggs. Both men ate with their gloves on. George watched them eat.

"What are *you* looking at?" Max looked at George.

"Nothing."

"The hell you were. You were looking at me."

"Maybe the boy meant it for a joke, Max," Al said.

George laughed.

"*You* don't have to laugh," Max said to him. "*You* don't have to laugh at all, see?"

"All right," said George.

"So he thinks it's all right." Max turned to Al. "He thinks it's all right. That's a good one."

"Oh, he's a thinker," Al said. They went on eating.

"What's the bright boy's name down the counter?" Al asked Max.

"Hey, bright boy," Max said to Nick. "You go around on the other side of the counter with your boy friend."

"What's the idea?" Nick asked.

"There isn't any idea."

"You better go around, bright boy," Al said. Nick went around behind the counter.

"What's the idea?" George asked.

"None of your damn business," Al said. "Who's out in the kitchen?"

"The nigger."

"What do you mean the nigger?"

"The nigger that cooks."

"Tell him to come in."

"What's the idea?"

"Tell him to come in."

"Where do you think you are?"

"We know damn well where we are," the man called Max said. "Do we look silly?"

"You talk silly," Al said to him. "What the hell do you argue with this kid for? Listen," he said to George, "tell the nigger to come out here."

"What are you going to do to him?"

"Nothing. Use your head, bright boy. What would we do to a nigger?"

George opened the slit that opened back into the kitchen. "Sam," he called. "Come in here a minute."

The door to the kitchen opened and the nigger came in. "What was it?" he asked. The two men at the counter took a look at him.

"All right, nigger. You stand right there," Al said.

Sam, the nigger, standing in his apron, looked at the two men sitting at the counter. "Yes, sir," he said. Al got down from his stool.

"I'm going back to the kitchen with the nigger and bright boy," he said. "Go on back to the kitchen, nigger. You go with him, bright boy." The little man walked after Nick and Sam, the cook, back into the kitchen. The door shut after them. The man called Max sat at the counter opposite George. He didn't look at George but looked in the mirror that ran along back of the counter. Henry's had been made over from a saloon into a lunch counter.

"Well, bright boy," Max said, looking into the mirror, "why don't you say something?"

"What's it all about?"

"Hey, Al," Max called, "bright boy wants to know what it's all about."

"Why don't you tell him?" Al's voice came from the kitchen.

"What do you think it's all about?"

"I don't know."

"What do you think?"

Max looked into the mirror all the time he was talking.

"I wouldn't say."

"Hey, Al, bright boy says he wouldn't say what he thinks it's all about."

"I can hear you, all right," Al said from the kitchen. He had propped open the slit that dishes passed through into the kitchen with a catsup bottle. "Listen, bright boy," he said from the kitchen to George. "Stand a little further along the bar. You move a little to the left, Max." He was like a photographer arranging for a group picture.

"Talk to me, bright boy," Max said. "What do you think's going to happen?"

George did not say anything.

"I'll tell you," Max said. "We're going to kill a Swede. Do you know a big Swede named Ole Andreson?"

"Yes."

"He comes here to eat every night, don't he?"

"Sometimes he comes here."

"He comes here at six o'clock, don't he?"

"If he comes."

"We know all that, bright boy," Max said. "Talk about something else. Ever go to the movies?"

"Once in a while."

"You ought to go to the movies more. The movies are fine for a bright boy like you."

"What are you going to kill Ole Andreson for? What did he ever do to you?"

"He never had a chance to do anything to us. He never even seen us."

"And he's only going to see us once," Al said from the kitchen.

"What are you going to kill him for, then?" George asked.

"We're killing him for a friend. Just to oblige a friend, bright boy."

"Shut up," said Al from the kitchen. "You talk too goddam much."

"Well, I got to keep bright boy amused. Don't I, bright boy?"

"You talk too damn much," Al said. "The nigger and my bright boy are amused by themselves. I got them tied up like a couple of girl friends in the convent."

"I suppose you were in a convent."

"You never know."

"You were in a kosher convent. That's where you were."

George looked up at the clock.

"If anybody comes in you tell them the cook is off, and if they keep after it, you tell them you'll go back and cook yourself. Do you get that, bright boy?"

"All right," George said. "What you going to do with us afterward?"

"That'll depend," Max said. "That's one of those things you never know at the time."

George looked up at the clock. It was a quarter past six. The door from the street opened. A street-car motorman came in.

"Hello, George," he said. "Can I get supper?"

"Sam's gone out," George said. "He'll be back in about half an hour."

"I'd better go up the street," the motorman said. George looked at the clock. It was twenty minutes past six.

"That was nice, bright boy," Max said. "You're a regular little gentleman."

"He knew I'd blow his head off," Al said from the kitchen.

"No," said Max. "It ain't that. Bright boy is nice. He's a nice boy. I like him."

At six-fifty-five George said: "He's not coming."

Two other people had been in the lunch-room. Once George had gone out to the kitchen and made a ham-and-egg sandwich "to go" that a man wanted to take with him. Inside the kitchen he saw Al, his derby hat tipped back, sitting on a stool beside the wicket with the muzzle of a sawed-off shotgun resting on the ledge. Nick and the cook were back to back in the corner, a towel tied in each of their mouths. George had cooked the sandwich, wrapped it up in oiled paper, put it in a bag, brought it in, and the man had paid for it and gone out.

"Bright boy can do everything." Max said. "He can cook and everything. You'd make some girl a nice wife, bright boy."

"Yes?" George said. "Your friend, Ole Andreson, isn't going to come."

"We'll give him ten minutes," Max said.

Max watched the mirror and the clock. The hands of the clock marked seven o'clock, and then five minutes past seven.

"Come on, Al," said Max. "We better go. He's not coming."

"Better give him five minutes," Al said from the kitchen.

In the five minutes a man came in, and George explained that the cook was sick.

"Why the hell don't you get another cook?" the man asked. "Aren't you running a lunch-counter?" He went out.

"Come on, Al," Max said.

"What about the two bright boys and the nigger?"

"They're all right."

"You think so?"

"Sure. We're through with it."

"I don't like it," said Al. "It's sloppy. You talk too much."

"Oh, what the hell," said Max. "We got to keep amused, haven't we?"

"You talk too much, all the same," Al said. He came out from the kitchen. The cut-off barrels of the shotgun made a slight bulge under the waist of his too tight-fitting overcoat. He straightened his coat with his gloved hands.

"So long, bright boy," he said to George. "You got a lot of luck."

"That's the truth," Max said. "You ought to play the races, bright boy."

The two of them went out the door. George watched them, through the window, pass under the arc-light and across the street. In their tight overcoats and derby hats they looked like a vaudeville team. George went back through the swinging door into the kitchen and untied Nick and the cook.

"I don't want any more of that," said Sam, the cook, "I don't want any more of that."

Nick stood up. He had never had a towel in his mouth before. "Say," he said. "What the hell?" He was trying to swagger it off.

"They were going to kill Ole Andreson," George said. "They were going to shoot him when he came in to eat."

"Ole Andreson?"

"Sure."

The cook felt the corners of his mouth with his thumbs.

"They all gone?" he asked.

"Yeah," said George. "They're gone now."

"I don't like it," said the cook. "I don't like any of it at all."

"Listen," George said to Nick. "You better go see Ole Andreson."

"All right."

"You better not have anything to do with it at all," Sam, the cook, said. "You better stay way out of it."

"Don't go if you don't want to," George said.

"Mixing up in this ain't going to get you anywhere," the cook said. "You stay out of it."

"I'll go see him," Nick said to George. "Where does he live?" The cook turned away.

"Little boys always know what they want to do," he said.

"He lives up at Hirsch's rooming-house," George said to Nick.

"I'll go up there."

Outside the arc-light shone through the bare branches of a tree. Nick walked up the street beside the car-tracks and turned at the next arc-light down a side-street. Three houses up the street was Hirsch's rooming-house. Nick walked up the two steps and pushed the bell. A woman came to the door.

"Is Ole Andreson here?"

"Do you want to see him?"

"Yes, if he's in."

Nick followed the woman up a flight of stairs and back to the end of a corridor. She knocked on the door.

"Who is it?"

"It's somebody to see you, Mr. Andreson," the woman said.

"It's Nick Adams."

"Come in."

Nick opened the door and went into the room. Ole Andreson was lying on the bed with all his clothes on. He had been a heavyweight prizefighter and he was too long for the bed. He lay with his head on two pillows. He did not look at Nick.

"What was it?" he asked.

"I was up at Henry's," Nick said, "and two fellows came in and tied up me and the cook, and they said they were going to kill you."

It sounded silly when he said it. Ole Andreson said nothing.

"They put us out in the kitchen," Nick went on. "They were going to shoot you when you came in to supper."

Ole Andreson looked at the wall and did not say anything.

"George thought I better come and tell you about it."

"There isn't anything I can do about it," Ole Andreson said.

"I'll tell you what they were like,"

"I don't want to know what they were like," Ole Andreson said. He looked at the wall. "Thanks for coming to tell me about it."

"That's all right."

Nick looked at the big man lying on the bed.

"Don't you want me to go and see the police?"

"No," Ole Andreson said. "That wouldn't do any good."

"Isn't there something I could do?"

"No. There ain't anything to do."

"Maybe it was just a bluff."

"No. It ain't just a bluff."

Ole Andreson rolled over toward the wall.

"The only thing is," he said, talking toward the wall, "I just can't make up my mind to go out. I been in here all day."

"Couldn't you get out of town?"

"No," Ole Andreson said. "I'm through with all that running around."

He looked at the wall.

"There ain't anything to do now."

"Couldn't you fix it up some way?"

"No, I got in wrong." He talked in the same flat voice. "There ain't anything to do. After a while I'll make up my mind to go out."

"I better go back and see George," Nick said.

"So long," said Ole Andreson. He did not look toward Nick. "Thanks for coming around."

Nick went out. As he shut the door he saw Ole Andreson with all his clothes on, lying on the bed looking at the wall.

"He's been in his room all day," the landlady said downstairs. "I guess he don't feel well. I said to him: 'Mr. Andreson, you ought to go out and take a walk on a nice fall day like this,' but he didn't feel like it."

"He doesn't want to go out."

"I'm sorry he don't feel well," the woman said. "He's an awfully nice man. He was in the ring, you know."

"I know it."

"You'd never know it except from the way his face is," the woman said. They stood talking just inside the street door. "He's just as gentle."

"Well, good night, Mrs. Hirsch," Nick said.

"I'm not Mrs. Hirsch," the woman said. "She owns the place. I just look after it for her. I'm Mrs. Bell."

"Well, good night, Mrs. Bell," Nick said.

"Good night," the woman said.

Nick walked up the dark street to the corner under the arc-light, and then along the car-tracks to Henry's eating-house. George was inside, back of the counter. "Did you see Ole?"

"Yes," said Nick. "He's in his room and he won't go out."

The cook opened the door from the kitchen when he heard Nick's voice.

"I don't even listen to it," he said and shut the door.

"Did you tell him about it?" George asked.

"Sure. I told him but he knows what it's all about."

"What's he going to do?"

"Nothing."

"They'll kill him."

"I guess they will."

"He must have got mixed up in something in Chicago."

"I guess so," said Nick.

"It's a hell of a thing."

"It's an awful thing," Nick said.

They did not say anything. George reached down for a towel and wiped the counter.

"I wonder what he did?" Nick said.

"Double-crossed somebody. That's what they kill them for."

"I'm going to get out of this town," Nick said.

"Yes," said George. "That's a good thing to do."

"I can't stand to think about him waiting in the room and knowing he's going to get it. It's too damned awful."

"Well," said George, "you better not think about it."

JOHN STEINBECK

❧ *The Great Mountains*

IN THE humming heat of a midsummer afternoon the little boy Jody listlessly looked about the ranch for something to do. He had been to the barn, had thrown rocks at the swallows' nests under the eaves until every one of the little mud houses broke open and dropped its lining of straw and dirty feathers. Then at the ranch house he baited a rat trap with stale cheese and set it where Doubletree Mutt, that good big dog, would get his nose snapped. Jody was not moved by an impulse of cruelty; he was bored with the long hot afternoon. Doubletree Mutt put his stupid nose in the trap and got it smacked, and shrieked with agony and limped away with blood on his nostrils. No matter where he was hurt, Mutt limped. It was just a way he had. Once when he was young, Mutt got caught in a coyote trap, and always after that he limped, even when he was scolded.

When Mutt yelped, Jody's mother called from inside the house, "Jody! Stop torturing that dog and find something to do."

Jody felt mean then, so he threw a rock at Mutt. Then he took his slingshot from the porch and walked up toward the brush line to try to kill a bird. It was a good slingshot, with store-bought rubbers, but while Jody had often shot at birds, he had never hit one. He walked up through the vegetable patch, kicking his bare toes into the dust. And on the way he found the perfect slingshot stone, round and slightly flattened and heavy enough to carry through the air. He fitted it into the leather pouch of his weapon and proceeded to the brush line. His eyes narrowed, his mouth worked strenuously; for the first time that afternoon he was intent. In the shade of the sagebrush the little birds were working, scratching in the leaves, flying restlessly a few feet and scratching again. Jody pulled back the rubbers of the sling and advanced cautiously. One little thrush paused and looked at him and crouched, ready to fly. Jody sidled nearer, moving one foot slowly after the other. When he was twenty feet away, he carefully raised the sling and aimed. The stone whizzed; the thrush started up and flew right into it. And down the little bird went with a broken head. Jody ran to it and picked it up.

"Well, I got you," he said.

The bird looked much smaller dead than it had alive. Jody felt a little mean pain in his stomach, so he took out his pocket-knife and cut off the bird's head. Then he disemboweled it, and took off its wings; and finally he threw all the pieces into the brush. He didn't care about the bird, or its life, but he knew what older people would say if they had seen him kill it; he was ashamed because of their potential opinion. He decided to forget the whole thing as quickly as he could, and never to mention it.

The hills were dry at this season, and the wild grass was golden, but where the spring-pipe filled the round tub and the tub spilled over, there lay a stretch of fine green grass, deep and sweet and moist. Jody drank from the mossy tub and washed the bird's blood from his hands in cold water. Then he lay on his back in the grass and looked up at the dumpling summer clouds. By closing one eye and destroying perspective he brought them down within reach so that he could put up his fingers and stroke them. He helped the gentle wind push them down the sky; it seemed to him that they went faster for his help. One fat white cloud he helped clear to the mountain rims and pressed it firmly over, out of sight. Jody wondered what it was seeing, then. He sat up the better to look at the great mountains where they went piling back, growing darker and more savage until they finished with one jagged ridge, high up against the west. Curious secret mountains; he thought of the little he knew about them.

"What's on the other side?" he asked his father once.

"More mountains, I guess. Why?"

"And on the other side of them?"

"More mountains. Why?"

"More mountains on and on?"

"Well, no. At last you come to the ocean."

"But what's in the mountains?"

"Just cliffs and brush and rocks and dryness."

"Were you ever there?"

"No."

"Has anybody ever been there?"

"A few people, I guess. It's dangerous, with cliffs and things. Why, I've read there's more unexplored country in the mountains of Monterey County [California] than any place in the United States." His father seemed proud that this should be so.

"And at last the ocean?"

"At last the ocean."

"But," the boy insisted, "but in between? No one knows?"

"Oh, a few people do, I guess. But there's nothing there to get. And not much water. Just rocks and cliffs and greasewood. Why?"

"It would be good to go."

"What for? There's nothing there."

Jody knew something was there, something very wonderful because it wasn't known, something secret and mysterious. He could feel within himself that this was so. He said to his mother, "Do you know what's in the big mountains?"

She looked at him and then back at the ferocious range, and she said, "Only the bear, I guess."

"What bear?"

"Why the one that went over the mountain to see what he could see."

Jody questioned Billy Buck, the ranch hand, about the possibility of ancient cities lost in the mountains, but Billy agreed with Jody's father.

"It ain't likely," Billy said. "There'd be nothing to eat unless a kind of people that can eat rocks live there."

That was all the information Jody ever got, and it made the mountains dear to him, and terrible. He thought often of the miles of ridge after ridge until at last there was the sea. When the peaks were pink in the morning they invited him among them: and when the sun had gone over the edge in the evening and the mountains were a purple-like despair, then Jody was afraid of them; then they were so impersonal and aloof that their very imperturbality was a threat.

Now he turned his head toward the mountains of the east, the Gabilans, and they were jolly mountains, with hill ranches in their creases, and with pine trees growing on the crests. People lived there, and battles had been fought against the Mexicans on the slopes. He looked back for an instant at the Great Ones and shivered a little at the contrast. The foothill cup of the home ranch below him was sunny and safe. The house gleamed with white light and the barn was brown and warm. The red cows on the farther hill ate their way slowly toward the north. Even the dark cypress tree by the bunkhouse was usual and safe. The chickens scratched about in the dust of the farmyard with quick waltzing steps.

Then a moving figure caught Jody's eye. A man walked slowly over the brow of the hill, on the road from Salinas [capital of Monterey County], and he was headed toward the house. Jody stood up and moved down toward the house too, for if someone was coming, he wanted to be there to see. By the time the boy had got to the house the walking man was only halfway down the road, a lean man, very straight in the shoulders. Jody could tell he was old only because his heels struck the ground with hard jerks. As he approached nearer, Jody saw that he was dressed in blue jeans and in a coat of the same material. He wore clodhopper shoes and an old flat-brimmed Stetson hat. Over his shoulder he carried a gunny sack, lumpy and full. In a few moments he had trudged close enough so that his face could be seen. And his face was as dark as dried beef. A mustache, blue-white against the dark skin, hovered over his mouth, and his hair was white, too, where it showed at his neck. The skin of his face had shrunk back against the skull until it defined bone, not flesh, and made the nose and chin seem sharp and fragile. The eyes were large and deep and dark, with eyelids stretched tightly over them. Irises and pupils were one, and very black, but the eyeballs were brown. There were no wrinkles in the face at all. This old man wore a blue denim coat buttoned to the throat with brass buttons, as all men do who wear no shirts. Out of the sleeves came strong bony wrists and hands gnarled and knotted and hard as peach branches. The nails were flat and blunt and shiny.

The old man drew close to the gate and swung down his sack when he confronted Jody. His lips fluttered a little and a soft impersonal voice came from between them.

"Do you live here?"

Jody was embarrassed. He turned and looked at the house, and he turned back and looked toward the barn where his father and Billy Buck were. "Yes," he said, when no help came from either direction.

"I have come back," the old man said. "I am Gitano, and I have come back."

Jody could not take all this responsibility. He turned abruptly, and ran into the house for help, and the screen door banged after him. His mother was in the kitchen poking out the clogged holes of a colander with a hairpin, and biting her lower lip with concentration.

"It's an old man," Jody cried excitedly. "It's an old *paisano* man, and he says he's come back."

His mother put down the colander and stuck the hairpin behind the sink board. "What's the matter now?" she asked patiently.

"It's an old man outside. Come on out."

"Well, what does he want?" She untied the strings of her apron and smoothed her hair with her fingers.

"I don't know. He came walking."

His mother smoothed down her dress and went out, and Jody followed her. Gitano had not moved.

"Yes?" Mrs. Tiflin asked.

Gitano took off his old black hat and held it with both hands in front of him. He repeated, "I am Gitano, and I have come back."

"Come back? Back where?"

Gitano's whole straight body leaned forward a little. His right hand described the circle of the hills, the sloping fields and the mountains, and ended at his hat again. "Back to the rancho. I was born here, and my father, too."

"Here?" she demanded. "This isn't an old place."

"No, there," he said, pointing to the western ridge. "On the other side there, in a house that is gone."

At last she understood. "The old 'dobe that's washed almost away, you mean?"

"Yes, señora. When the rancho broke up they put no more lime on the 'dobe, and the rains washed it down."

Jody's mother was silent for a little, and curious homesick thoughts ran through her mind, but quickly she cleared them out. "And what do you want here now, Gitano?"

"I will stay here," he said quietly, "until I die."

"But we don't need an extra man here."

"I can not work hard any more, señora. I can milk a cow, feed chickens, cut a little wood; no more. I will stay here." He indicated the sack on the ground beside him. "Here are my things."

She turned to Jody. "Run down to the barn and call your father."

Jody dashed away, and he returned with Carl Tiflin and Billy Buck behind him. The old man was standing as he had been, but he was resting now. His whole body had sagged into a timeless repose.

"What is it?" Carl Tiflin asked. "What's Jody so excited about?"

Mrs. Tiflin motioned to the old man. "He wants to stay here. He wants to do a little work and stay here."

"Well, we can't have him. We don't need any more men. He's too old. Billy does everything we need."

They had been talking over him as though he did not exist, and now, suddenly, they both hesitated and looked at Gitano and were embarrassed.

He cleared his throat. "I am too old to work. I come back where I was born."

"You weren't born here," Carl said sharply.

"No. In the 'dobe house over the hill. It was all one rancho before you came."

"In the mud house that's all melted down?"

"Yes, I and my father. I will stay here now on the rancho."

"I tell you you won't stay," Carl said angrily. "I don't need an old man. This isn't a big ranch. I can't afford food and doctor bills for an old man. You must have relatives and friends. Go to them. It is like begging to come to strangers."

"I was born here," Gitano said patiently and inflexibly.

Carl Tiflin didn't like to be cruel, but he felt he must. "You can eat here tonight," he said. "You can sleep in the little room of the old bunkhouse. We'll give you your breakfast in the morning, and then you'll have to go along. Go to your friends. Don't come to die with strangers."

Gitano put on his black hat and stooped for the sack. "Here are my things," he said.

Carl turned away. "Come on, Billy, we'll finish down at the barn. Jody, show him the little room in the bunkhouse."

He and Billy turned back toward the barn. Mrs. Tiflin went into the house, saying over her shoulder, "I'll send some blankets down."

Gitano looked questioningly at Jody. "I'll show you where it is," Jody said.

There was a cot with a shuck mattress, an apple box holding a tin lantern, and a backless rocking-chair in the little room of the bunkhouse. Gitano laid his sack carefully on the floor and sat down on the bed. Jody stood shyly in the room, hesitating to go. At last he said,

"Did you come out of the big mountains?"

Gitano shook his head slowly. "No, I worked down the Salinas Valley."

The afternoon thought would not let Jody go. "Did you ever go into the big mountains back there?"

The old dark eyes grew fixed, and their light turned inward on the years that were living in Gitano's head. "Once—when I was a little boy. I went with my father."

"Way back, clear into the mountains?"

"Yes."

"What was there?" Jody cried. "Did you see any people or any houses?"

"No."

"Well, what was there?"

Gitano's eyes remained inward. A little wrinkled strain came between his brows.

"What did you see in there?" Jody repeated.

"I don't know," Gitano said. "I don't remember."

"Was it terrible and dry?"

"I don't remember."

In his excitement, Jody had lost his shyness. "Don't you remember anything about it?"

Gitano's mouth opened for a word, and remained open while his brain sought the word. "I think it was quiet—I think it was nice."

Gitano's eyes seemed to have found something back in the years, for they grew soft and a little smile seemed to come and go in them.

"Didn't you ever go back in the mountains again?" Jody insisted.

"No."

"Didn't you ever want to?"

But now Gitano's face became impatient. "No," he said in a tone that told Jody he didn't want to talk about it any more. The boy was held by a curious fascination. He didn't want to go away from Gitano. His shyness returned.

"Would you like to come down to the barn and see the stock?" he asked.

Gitano stood up and put on his hat and prepared to follow.

It was almost evening now. They stood near the watering trough while the horses sauntered in from the hillsides for an evening drink. Gitano rested his big twisted hands on the top rail of the fence. Five horses came down and drank, and then stood about, nibbling at the dirt or rubbing their sides against the polished wood of the fence. Long after they had finished drinking an old horse appeared over the brow of the hill and came painfully down. It had long yellow teeth; its hoofs were flat and sharp as spades, and its ribs and hip-bones jutted out under its skin. It hobbled up to the trough and drank water with a loud sucking noise.

"That's old Easter," Jody explained. "That's the first horse my father ever had. He's thirty years old." He looked up into Gitano's old eyes for some response.

"No good any more," Gitano said.

Jody's father and Billy Buck came out of the barn and walked over.

"Too old to work," Gitano repeated. "Just eats and pretty soon dies."

Carl Tiflin caught the last words. He hated his brutality toward old Gitano, and so he became brutal again.

"It's a shame not to shoot Easter," he said. "It'd save him a lot of pains and rheumatism." He looked secretly at Gitano, to see whether he noticed the parallel, but the big bony hands did not move, nor did the dark eyes turn from the horse. "Old things ought to be put out of their misery," Jody's father went on. "One shot, a big noise, one big pain in the head maybe, and that's all. That's better than stiffness and sore teeth."

Billy Buck broke in. "They got a right to rest after they worked all their life. Maybe they like to just walk around."

Carl had been looking steadily at the skinny horse. "You can't imagine now what Easter used to look like," he said softly. "High neck, deep chest, fine barrel. He could jump a five-bar gate in stride. I won a flat race on him when I was fifteen years old. I could of got two hundred dollars for him any time. You wouldn't think how pretty he was." He checked himself, for he hated softness. "But he ought to be shot now," he said.

"He's got a right to rest," Billy Buck insisted.

Jody's father had a humorous thought. He turned to Gitano. "If ham and eggs grew on a side-hill I'd turn you out to pasture too," he said. "But I can't afford to pasture you in my kitchen."

He laughed to Billy Buck about it as they went on toward the house. "Be a good thing for all of us if ham and eggs grew on the side-hills."

Jody knew how his father was probing for a place to hurt Gitano. He had been probed often. His father knew every place in the boy where a word would fester.

"He's only talking," Jody said. "He didn't mean it about shooting Easter. He likes Easter. That was the first horse he ever owned."

The sun sank behind the high mountains as they stood there, and the ranch was hushed. Gitano seemed to be more at home in the evening. He made a curious sharp sound with his lips and stretched one of his hands over the fence. Old Easter moved stiffly to him, and Gitano rubbed the lean neck under the mane.

"You like him?" Jody asked softly.

"Yes—but he's no damn good."

The triangle sounded at the ranch house. "That's supper," Jody cried. "Come on up to supper."

As they walked up toward the house Jody noticed again that Gitano's body was as straight as that of a young man. Only by a jerkiness in his movements and by the scuffling of his heels could it be seen that he was old.

The turkeys were flying heavily into the lower branches of the cypress tree by the bunkhouse. A fat sleek ranch cat walked across the road carrying a rat so large that its tail dragged on the ground. The quail on the side-hills were still sounding the clear water call.

Jody and Gitano came to the back steps and Mrs. Tiflin looked out through the screen door at them.

"Come running, Jody. Come in to supper, Gitano."

Carl and Billy Buck had started to eat at the long oilcloth-covered table. Jody slipped into his chair without moving it, but Gitano stood holding his hat until Carl looked up and said, "Sit down, sit down. You might as well get your belly full before you go on." Carl was afraid he might relent and let the old man stay, and so he continued to remind himself that this couldn't be.

Gitano laid his hat on the floor and diffidently sat down. He wouldn't reach for food. Carl had to pass it to him. "Here, fill yourself up." Gitano ate very slowly, cutting tiny pieces of meat and arranging little pats of mashed potato on his plate.

The situation would not stop worrying Carl Tiflin. "Haven't you got any relatives in this part of the country?" he asked.

Gitano answered with some pride, "My brother-in-law is in Monterey. I have cousins there, too."

"Well, you can go and live there, then."

"I was born here," Gitano said in gentle rebuke.

Jody's mother came in from the kitchen, carrying a large bowl of tapioca pudding.

Carl chuckled to her, "Did I tell you what I said to him? I said if ham and eggs grew on the side-hills I'd put him out to pasture, like old Easter."

Gitano stared unmoved at his plate.

"It's too bad he can't stay," said Mrs. Tiflin.

"Now don't you start anything," Carl said crossly.

When they had finished eating, Carl and Billy Buck and Jody went into the living-room to sit for a while, but Gitano, without a word of farewell or thanks, walked through the kitchen and out the back door. Jody sat and secretly watched his father. He knew how mean his father felt.

"This country's full of these old *paisanos*," Carl said to Billy Buck.

"They're damn good men," Billy defended them. "They can work older than white men. I saw one of them a hundred and five years old, and he could still ride a horse. You don't see any white men as old as Gitano walking twenty or thirty miles."

"Oh, they're tough all right," Carl agreed. "Say, are you standing up for him too? Listen, Billy," he explained, "I'm having a hard enough time keeping this ranch out of the Bank of Italy without taking on anybody else to feed. You know that, Billy."

"Sure, I know," said Billy. "If you was rich, it'd be different."

"That's right, and it isn't like he didn't have relatives to go to. A brother-in-law and cousins right in Monterey. Why should I worry about him?"

Jody sat quietly listening, and he seemed to hear Gitano's gentle voice and its unanswerable, "But I was born here." Gitano was mysterious like the mountains. There were ranges back as far as you could see, but behind the last range piled up against the sky there was a great unknown country. And Gitano was an old man, until you got to the dull dark eyes. And in behind them was some unknown thing. He didn't ever say enough to let you guess what was inside, under the eyes. Jody felt himself irresistibly drawn toward the bunkhouse. He slipped from his chair while his father was talking and he went out the door without making a sound.

The night was very dark and far-off noises carried in clearly. The hamebells of a wood team sounded from way over the hill on the country road. Jody picked his way across the dark yard. He could see a light through the window of the little room of the bunkhouse. Because the night was secret he walked quietly up to the window and peered in. Gitano sat in the rocking-chair and his back was toward the window. His right arm moved slowly back and forth in front of him. Jody pushed the door open and walked in. Gitano jerked upright and, seizing a piece of deerskin, he tried to throw it over the thing in his lap, but the skin slipped away. Jody stood overwhelmed by the thing in Gitano's hand, a lean and lovely rapier with a golden basket hilt. The blade was like a thin ray of dark light. The hilt was pierced and intricately carved.

"What is it?" Jody demanded.

Gitano only looked at him with resentful eyes, and he picked up the fallen deerskin and firmly wrapped the beautiful blade in it.

Jody put out his hand. "Can't I see it?"

Gitano's eyes smoldered angrily and he shook his head.

"Where'd you get it? Where'd it come from?"

Now Gitano regarded him profoundly, as though he pondered. "I got it from my father."

"Well, where'd he get it?"

Gitano looked down at the long deerskin parcel in his hand. "I don' know?"

"Didn't he ever tell you?"

"No."

"What do you do with it?"

Gitano looked slightly surprised. "Nothing. I just keep it."

"Can't I see it again?"

The old man slowly unwrapped the shining blade and let the lamplight slip along it for a moment. Then he wrapped it up again. "You go now. I want to go to bed." He blew out the lamp almost before Jody had closed the door.

As he went back toward the house, Jody knew one thing more sharply than he had ever known anything. He must never tell anyone about the rapier. It would be a dreadful thing to tell anyone about it, for it would destroy some fragile structure of truth. It was a truth that might be shattered by division.

On the way across the dark yard Jody passed Billy Buck. "They're wondering where you are," Billy said.

Jody slipped into the living-room, and his father turned to him. "Where have you been?"

"I just went out to see if I caught any rats in my new trap."

"It's time you went to bed," his father said.

Jody was first at the breakfast table in the morning. Then his father came in, and last, Billy Buck. Mrs. Tiflin looked in from the kitchen.

"Where's the old man, Billy?" she asked.

"I guess he's out walking," Billy said. "I looked in his room and he wasn't there."

"Maybe he started early to Monterey," said Carl. "It's a long walk."

"No," Billy explained. "His sack is in the little room."

After breakfast Jody walked down to the bunkhouse. Flies were flashing about in the sunshine. The ranch seemed especially quiet this morning. When he was sure no one was watching him, Jody went into the little room, and looked into Gitano's sack. An extra pair of long cotton underwear was there, an extra pair of jeans and three pairs of worn socks. Nothing else was in the sack. A sharp loneliness fell on Jody. He walked slowly back toward the house. His father stood on the porch talking to Mrs. Tiflin.

"I guess old Easter's dead at last," he said. "I didn't see him come down to water with the other horses."

In the middle of the morning Jess Taylor from the ridge ranch rode down.

"You didn't sell that old gray crowbait of yours, did you, Carl?"

"No, of course not. Why?"

"Well," Jess said. "I was out this morning early, and I saw a funny thing. I saw an old man on an old horse, no saddle, only a piece of rope for a bridle. He wasn't on the road at all. He was cutting right up straight through the brush. I think he had a gun. At least I saw something shine in his hand."

"That's old Gitano," Carl Tiflin said. "I'll see if any of my guns are missing." He stepped into the house for a second. "Nope, all here. Which way was he heading, Jess?"

"Well, that's the funny thing. He was heading straight back into the mountains."

Carl laughed. "They never get too old to steal," he said. "I guess he stole old Easter."

"Want to go after him, Carl?"

"Hell no, just save me burying that horse. I wonder where he got the gun. I wonder what he wants back there."

Jody walked up through the vegetable patch, toward the brush line. He looked searchingly at the towering mountains—ridge after ridge after ridge until at last there was the ocean. For a moment he thought he could see a black speck crawling up the farthest ridge. Jody thought of the rapier and of Gitano. And he thought of the great mountains. A longing caressed him, and it was so sharp that he wanted to cry to get it out of his breast. He lay down in the green grass near the round tub at the brush line. He covered his eyes with his crossed arms and lay there a long time, and he was full of a nameless sorrow.

ALBERT CAMUS

❧ *The Guest*

THE schoolmaster was watching the two men climb toward him. One was on horseback, the other on foot. They had not yet tackled the abrupt rise leading to the schoolhouse built on the hillside. They were toiling onward, making slow progress in the snow, among the stones, on the vast expanse of the high, deserted plateau. From time to time the horse stumbled. Without hearing anything yet, he could see the breath issuing from the horse's nostrils. One of the men, at least, knew the region. They were following the trail although it

Translated by Justin O'Brien.

had disappeared days ago under a layer of dirty white snow. The schoolmaster calculated that it would take them half an hour to get onto the hill. It was cold; he went back into the school to get a sweater.

He crossed the empty, frigid classroom. On the blackboard the four rivers of France, drawn with four different colored chalks, had been flowing toward their estuaries for the past three days. Snow had suddenly fallen in mid-October after eight months of drought without the transition of rain, and the twenty pupils, more or less, who lived in the villages scattered over the plateau had stopped coming. With fair weather they would return. Daru now heated only the single room that was his lodging, adjoining the classroom and giving also onto the plateau to the east. Like the class windows, his window looked to the south too. On that side the school was a few kilometers from the point where the plateau began to slope toward the south. In clear weather could be seen the purple mass of the mountain range where the gap opened onto the desert.

Somewhat warmed, Daru returned to the window from which he had first seen the two men. They were no longer visible. Hence they must have tackled the rise. The sky was not so dark, for the snow had stopped falling during the night. The morning had opened with a dirty light which had scarcely become brighter as the ceiling of clouds lifted. At two in the afternoon it seemed as if the day were merely beginning. But still this was better than those three days when the thick snow was falling amidst unbroken darkness with little gusts of wind that rattled the double door of the classroom. Then Daru had spent long hours in his room, leaving it only to go to the shed and feed the chickens or get some coal. Fortunately the delivery truck from Tadjid, the nearest village to the north, had brought his supplies two days before the blizzard. It would return in forty-eight hours.

Besides, he had enough to resist a siege, for the little room was cluttered with bags of wheat that the administration left as a stock to distribute to those of his pupils whose families had suffered from the drought. Actually they had all been victims because they were all poor. Every day Daru would distribute a ration to the children. They had missed it, he knew, during these bad days. Possibly one of the fathers or big brothers would come this afternoon and he could supply them with grain. It was just a matter of carrying them over to the next harvest. Now shiploads of wheat were arriving from France and the worst was over. But it would be hard to forget that poverty, that army of ragged ghosts wandering in the sunlight, the plateaus burned to a cinder month after month, the earth shriveled up little by little, literally scorched, every stone bursting into dust under one's foot. The sheep had died then by thousands and even a few men, here and there, sometimes without anyone's knowing.

In contrast with such poverty, he who lived almost like a monk in his remote schoolhouse, nonetheless satisfied with the little he had and with the rough life, had felt like a lord with his white-washed walls, his narrow couch, his unpainted shelves, his well, and his weekly provision of water and food. And suddenly this snow, without warning, without the foretaste of rain. This is the way the region was, cruel to live in, even without men—who didn't help matters either. But Daru had been born here. Everywhere else, he felt exiled.

He stepped out onto the terrace in front of the schoolhouse. The two men were now halfway up the slope. He recognized the horseman as Balducci, the old gendarme he had known for a long time. Balducci was holding on the end of a rope an Arab who was walking behind him with hands bound and head lowered. The gendarme waved a greeting to which Daru did not reply, lost as he was in contemplation of the Arab dressed in a faded blue jellaba,[3] his feet in sandals but covered with socks of heavy raw wool, his head surmounted by a narrow, short chèche.[4] They were approaching. Balducci was holding back his horse in order not to hurt the Arab, and the group was advancing slowly.

Within earshot, Balducci shouted: "One hour to do the three kilometers from El Ameur!" Daru did not answer. Short and square in his thick sweater, he watched them climb. Not once had the Arab raised his head. "Hello," said Daru when they got up onto the terrace. "Come in and warm up." Balducci painfully got down from his horse without letting go the rope. From under his bristling mustache he smiled at the schoolmaster. His little dark eyes, deep-set under a tanned forehead, and his mouth surrounded with wrinkles made him look attentive and studious. Daru took the bridle, led the horse to the shed, and came back to the two men, who were now waiting for him in the school. He led them into his room. "I am going to heat up the classroom," he said. "We'll be more comfortable there." When he entered the room again, Balducci was on the couch. He had undone the rope tying him to the Arab, who had squatted near the stove. His hands still bound, the chèche pushed back on his head, he was looking toward the window. At first Daru noticed only his huge lips, fat, smooth, almost Negroid; yet his nose was straight, his eyes were dark and full of fever. The chèche revealed an obstinate forehead and, under the weathered skin now rather discolored by the cold, the whole face had a restless and rebellious look that struck Daru when the Arab, turning his face toward him, looked him straight in the eyes. "Go into the other room," said the schoolmaster, "and I'll make you some mint tea." "Thanks," Balducci said. "What a chore! How I long for retirement." And addressing his prisoner in Arabic: "Come on, you." The Arab got up and, slowly, holding his bound wrists in front of him, went into the classroom.

With the tea, Daru brought a chair. But Balducci was already enthroned on the nearest pupil's desk and the Arab had squatted against the teacher's platform facing the stove, which stood between the desk and the window. When he held out the glass of tea to the prisoner, Daru hesitated at the sight of his bound hands. "He might perhaps be untied." "Sure," said Balducci. "That was for the trip." He started to get to his feet. But Daru, setting the glass on the floor, had knelt beside the Arab. Without saying anything, the

---

[3] A wide short-sleeved cloak with a hood, worn by natives of North Africa. [Eds.]
[4] A cylindrical, tufted skull-cap, worn by Arabs. [Eds.]

Arab watched him with his feverish eyes. Once his hands were free, he rubbed his swollen wrists against each other, took the glass of tea, and sucked up the burning liquid in swift little sips.

"Good," said Daru. "And where are you headed?"

Balducci withdrew his mustache from the tea. "Here, son."

"Odd pupils! And you're spending the night?"

"No. I'm going back to El Ameur. And you will deliver this fellow to Tinguit. He is expected at police headquarters."

Balducci was looking at Daru with a friendly little smile.

"What's this story?" asked the schoolmaster. "Are you pulling my leg?"

"No, son. Those are the orders."

"The orders? I'm not . . ." Daru hesitated, not wanting to hurt the old Corsican. "I mean, that's not my job."

"What! What's the meaning of that? In wartime people do all kinds of jobs."

"Then I'll wait for the declaration of war!"

Balducci nodded.

"O.K. But the orders exist and they concern you too. Things are brewing, it appears. There is talk of a forthcoming revolt. We are mobilized, in a way."

Daru still had his obstinate look.

"Listen, son," Balducci said. "I like you and you must understand. There's only a dozen of us at El Ameur to patrol throughout the whole territory of a small department and I must get back in a hurry. I was told to hand this guy over to you and return without delay. He couldn't be kept there. His village was beginning to stir; they wanted to take him back. You must take him to Tinguit tomorrow before the day is over. Twenty kilometers shouldn't faze a husky fellow like you. After that, all will be over. You'll come back to your pupils and your comfortable life."

Behind the wall the horse could be heard snorting and pawing the earth. Daru was looking out the window. Decidedly, the weather was clearing and the light was increasing over the snowy plateau. When all the snow was melted, the sun would take over again and once more would burn the fields of stone. For days, still, the unchanging sky would shed its dry light on the solitary expanse where nothing had any connection with man.

"After all," he said, turning around toward Balducci, "what did he do?" And, before the gendarme had opened his mouth, he asked: "Does he speak French?"

"No, not a word. We had been looking for him for a month, but they were hiding him. He killed his cousin."

"Is he against us?"

"I don't think so. But you can never be sure."

"Why did he kill?"

"A family squabble, I think. One owed the other grain, it seems. It's not at all clear. In short, he killed his cousin with a billhook. You know, like a sheep, *kreezk!*"

Balducci made the gesture of drawing a blade across his throat and the Arab, his attention attracted, watched him with a sort of anxiety. Daru felt a sudden wrath against the man, against all men with their rotten spite, their tireless hates, their blood lust.

But the kettle was singing on the stove. He served Balducci more tea, hesitated, then served the Arab again, who, a second time, drank avidly. His raised arms made the jellaba fall open and the schoolmaster saw his thin, muscular chest.

"Thanks, kid," Balducci said. "And now, I'm off."

He got up and went toward the Arab, taking a small rope from his pocket.

"What are you doing?" Daru asked dryly.

Balducci, disconcerted, showed him the rope.

"Don't bother."

The old gendarme hesitated. "It's up to you. Of course, you are armed?"

"I have my shotgun."

"Where?"

"In the trunk."

"You ought to have it near your bed."

"Why? I have nothing to fear."

"You're crazy, son. If there's an uprising, no one is safe, we're all in the same boat."

"I'll defend myself. I'll have time to see them coming."

Balducci began to laugh, then suddenly the mustache covered the white teeth.

"You'll have time? O.K. That's just what I was saying. You have always been a little cracked. That's why I like you, my son was like that."

At the same time he took out his revolver and put it on the desk.

"Keep it; I don't need two weapons from here to El Ameur."

The revolver shone against the black paint of the table. When the gendarme turned toward him, the schoolmaster caught the smell of leather and horseflesh.

"Listen, Balducci," Daru said suddenly, "every bit of this disgusts me, and first of all your fellow here. But I won't hand him over. Fight, yes, if I have to. But not that."

The old gendarme stood in front of him and looked at him severely.

"You're being a fool," he said slowly. "I don't like it either. You don't get used to putting a rope on a man even after years of it, and you're even ashamed—yes, ashamed. But you can't let them have their way."

"I won't hand him over," Daru said again.

"It's an order, son, and I repeat it."

"That's right. Repeat to them what I've said to you: I won't hand him over."

Balducci made a visible effort to reflect. He looked at the Arab and at Daru. At last he decided.

"No, I won't tell them anything. If you want to drop us, go ahead; I'll not denounce you. I have an order to deliver the prisoner and I'm doing so. And now you'll just sign this paper for me."

"There's no need. I'll not deny that you left him with me."

"Don't be mean with me. I know you'll tell the truth. You're from hereabouts and you are a man. But you must sign, that's the rule."

Daru opened his drawer, took out a little square bottle of purple ink, the red wooden penholder with the "sergeant-major" pen he used for making models of penmanship, and signed. The gendarme carefully folded the paper and put it into his wallet. Then he moved toward the door.

"I'll see you off," Daru said.

"No," said Balducci. "There's no use being polite. You insulted me."

He looked at the Arab, motionless in the same spot, sniffed peevishly, and turned away toward the door. "Good-by, son," he said. The door shut behind him. Balducci appeared suddenly outside the window and then disappeared. His footsteps were muffled by the snow. The horse stirred on the other side of the wall and several chickens fluttered in fright. A moment later Balducci reappeared outside the window leading the horse by the bridle. He walked toward the little rise without turning around and disappeared from sight with the horse following him. A big stone could be heard bouncing down. Daru walked back toward the prisoner, who, without stirring, never took his eyes off him. "Wait," the schoolmaster said in Arabic and went toward the bedroom. As he was going through the door, he had a second thought, went to the desk, took the revolver, and stuck it in his pocket. Then, without looking back, he went into his room.

For some time he lay on his couch watching the sky gradually close over, listening to the silence. It was this silence that had seemed painful to him during the first days here, after the war. He had requested a post in the little town at the base of the foothills separating the upper plateaus from the desert. There, rocky walls, green and black to the north, pink and lavender to the south, marked the frontier of eternal summer. He had been named to a post farther north, on the plateau itself. In the beginning, the solitude and the silence had been hard for him on these wastelands peopled only by stones. Occasionally, furrows suggested cultivation, but they had been dug to uncover a certain kind of stone good for building. The only plowing here was to harvest rocks. Elsewhere a thin layer of soil accumulated in the hollows would be scraped out to enrich paltry village gardens. This is the way it was: bare rock covered three quarters of the region. Towns sprang up, flourished, then disappeared; men came by, loved one another or fought bitterly, then died. No one in this desert, neither he nor his guest, mattered. And yet, outside this desert neither of them, Daru knew, could have really lived.

When he got up, no noise came from the classroom. He was amazed at the unmixed joy he derived from the mere thought that the Arab might have fled and that he would be alone with no decision to make. But the prisoner was there. He had merely stretched out between the stove and the desk. With eyes open, he was staring at the ceiling. In that position, his thick lips were particularly noticeable, giving him a pouting look. "Come," said Daru. The Arab got up and followed him. In the bedroom, the schoolmaster pointed to a chair near the table under the window. The Arab sat down without taking his eyes off Daru.

"Are you hungry?"

"Yes," the prisoner said.

Daru set the table for two. He took flour and oil, shaped a cake in a frying-pan, and lighted the little stove that functioned on bottled gas. While the cake was cooking, he went out to the shed to get cheese, eggs, dates, and condensed milk. When the cake was done he set it on the window sill to cool, heated some condensed milk diluted with water, and beat up the eggs into an omelette. In one of his motions he knocked against the revolver stuck in his right pocket. He set the bowl down, went into the classroom, and put the revolver in his desk drawer. When he came back to the room, night was falling. He put on the light and served the Arab. "Eat," he said. The Arab took a piece of the cake, lifted it eagerly to his mouth, and stopped short.

"And you?" he asked.

"After you. I'll eat too."

The thick lips opened slightly. The Arab hesitated, then bit into the cake determinedly.

The meal over, the Arab looked at the schoolmaster. "Are you the judge?"

"No, I'm simply keeping you until tomorrow."

"Why do you eat with me?"

"I'm hungry."

The Arab fell silent. Daru got up and went out. He brought back a folding bed from the shed, set it up between the table and the stove, perpendicular to his own bed. From a large suitcase which, upright in a corner, served as a shelf for papers, he took two blankets and arranged them on the camp bed. Then he stopped, felt useless, and sat down on his bed. There was nothing more to do or to get ready. He had to look at this man. He looked at him, therefore, trying to imagine his face bursting with rage. He couldn't do so. He could see nothing but the dark yet shining eyes and the animal mouth.

"Why did you kill him?" he asked in a voice whose hostile tone surprised him.

The Arab looked away.

"He ran away. I ran after him."

He raised his eyes to Daru again and they were full of a sort of woeful interrogation. "Now what will they do to me?"

"Are you afraid?"

He stiffened, turning his eyes away.

"Are you sorry?"

The Arab stared at him openmouthed. Obviously he did not understand. Daru's annoyance was growing. At the same time he felt awkward and self-conscious with his big body wedged between the two beds.

"Lie down there," he said impatiently. "That's your bed."

The Arab didn't move. He called to Daru:

"Tell me!"

The schoolmaster looked at him.

"Is the gendarme coming back tomorrow?"

"I don't know."

"Are you coming with us?"

"I don't know. Why?"

The prisoner got up and stretched out on top of the blankets, his feet toward the window. The light from the electric bulb shone straight into his eyes and he closed them at once.

"Why?" Daru repeated, standing beside the bed.

The Arab opened his eyes under the blinding light and looked at him, trying not to blink.

"Come with us," he said.

In the middle of the night, Daru was still not asleep. He had gone to bed after undressing completely; he generally slept naked. But when he suddenly realized that he had nothing on, he hesitated. He felt vulnerable and the temptation came to him to put his clothes back on. Then he shrugged his shoulders; after all, he wasn't a child and, if need be, he could break his adversary in two. From his bed he could observe him, lying on his back, still motionless with his eyes closed under the harsh light. When Daru turned out the light, the darkness seemed to coagulate all of a sudden. Little by little, the night came back to life in the window where the starless sky was stirring gently. The schoolmaster soon made out the body lying at his feet. The Arab still did not move, but his eyes seemed open. A faint wind was prowling around the schoolhouse. Perhaps it would drive away the clouds and the sun would reappear.

During the night the wind increased. The hens fluttered a little and then were silent. The Arab turned over on his side with his back to Daru, who thought he heard him moan. Then he listened for his guest's breathing, which had become heavier and more regular. He listened to that breath so close to him and mused without being able to go to sleep. In this room where he had been sleeping alone for a year, this presence bothered him. But it bothered him also by imposing on him a sort of brotherhood he knew well but refused to accept in the present circumstances. Men who share the same rooms, soldiers or prisoners, develop a strange alliance as if, having cast off their armor with their clothing, they fraternized every evening, over and above their differences, in the ancient community of dream and fatigue. But Daru shook himself; he didn't like such musings, and it was essential to sleep.

A little later, however, when the Arab stirred slightly, the schoolmaster was still not asleep. When the prisoner made a second move, he stiffened, on the alert. The Arab was lifting himself slowly on his arms with almost the motion of a sleepwalker. Seated upright in bed, he waited motionless without turning his head toward Daru, as if he were listening attentively. Daru did not stir; it had just occurred to him that the revolver was still in the drawer of his desk. It was better to act at once. Yet he continued to observe the prisoner, who, with the same slithery motion, put his feet on the ground, waited again, then began to stand up slowly. Daru was about to call out to him when the Arab began to walk, in a quite natural but extraordinarily silent way. He was heading toward the door at the end of the room that opened into the shed. He lifted the latch with precaution and went out, pushing the door behind him but without shutting it. Daru had not stirred. "He is running away," he merely thought. "Good riddance!" Yet he listened attentively. The hens were not fluttering; the guest must be on the plateau. A faint sound of water reached him, and he didn't know what it was until the Arab again stood framed in the doorway, closed the door carefully, and came back to bed without a sound. Then Daru turned his back on him and fell asleep. Still later, he seemed, from the depths of his sleep, to hear furtive steps around the schoolhouse. "I'm dreaming! I'm dreaming!" he repeated to himself. And he went on sleeping.

When he awoke, the sky was clear; the loose window let in a cold, pure air. The Arab was asleep, hunched up under the blankets now, his mouth open, utterly relaxed. But when Daru shook him, he started dreadfully, staring at Daru with wild eyes as if he had never seen him and such a frightened expression that the schoolmaster stepped back. "Don't be afraid. It's me. You must eat." The Arab nodded his head and said yes. Calm had returned to his face, but his expression was vacant and listless.

The coffee was ready. They drank it seated together on the folding bed as they munched their pieces of the cake. Then Daru led the Arab under the shed and showed him the faucet where he washed. He went back into the room, folded the blankets and the bed, made his own bed and put the room in order. Then he went through the classroom and out onto the terrace. The sun was already rising in the blue sky; a soft, bright light was bathing the deserted plateau. On the ridge the snow was melting in spots. The stones were about to reappear. Crouched on the edge of the plateau, the schoolmaster looked at the deserted expanse. He thought of Balducci. He had hurt him, for he had sent him off in a way as if he didn't want to be associated with him. He could still hear the gendarme's farewell and, without knowing why, he felt strangely empty and vulnerable. At that moment, from the other side of the schoolhouse, the prisoner coughed. Daru listened to him almost despite himself and then, furious, threw a pebble that whistled through the air before sinking into the snow. That man's stupid crime revolted him, but to hand him over was contrary to honor. Merely thinking of it made him smart with humiliation. And he cursed at one and the same time his own people who had sent him this Arab and the Arab too who had dared to kill and not managed to get away. Daru got up, walked in a circle on the terrace, waited motionless, and then went back into the schoolhouse.

The Arab, leaning over the cement floor of the shed, was washing his teeth with two fingers. Daru looked at him and said: "Come." He went back into the room ahead of the prisoner. He slipped a hunting-jacket on over his sweater and put on walking-shoes. Standing, he waited until the Arab had put on his *chèche* and sandals. They went into the classroom and the schoolmaster pointed to the exit, saying: "Go ahead." The fellow didn't budge. "I'm coming," said Daru. The Arab went out. Daru went back into the room and made a package of pieces of rusk, dates, and sugar. In the classroom, before going out, he hesitated a second in front of his desk, then crossed the threshold and locked the door. "That's the way," he said. He started toward the east, followed by the prisoner. But, a short distance from the schoolhouse, he thought he heard a slight sound behind them. He retraced his steps and examined the surroundings of the house; there was no one there. The Arab watched him without seeming to understand. "Come on," said Daru.

They walked for an hour and rested beside a sharp peak of limestone. The snow was melting faster and faster and the sun was drinking up the puddles at once, rapidly cleaning the plateau, which gradually dried and vibrated like the air itself. When they resumed walking, the ground rang under their feet. From time to time a bird rent the space in front of them with a joyful cry. Daru breathed in deeply the fresh morning light. He felt a sort of rapture before the vast familiar expanse, now almost entirely yellow under its dome of blue sky. They walked an hour more, descending toward the south. They reached a level height made up of crumbly rocks. From there on, the plateau sloped down, eastward, toward a low plain where there were a few spindly trees and, to the south, toward outcroppings of rock that gave the landscape a chaotic look.

Daru surveyed the two directions. There was nothing but the sky on the horizon. Not a man could be seen. He turned toward the Arab, who was looking at him blankly. Daru held out the package to him. "Take it," he said. "There are dates, bread, and sugar. You can hold out for two days. Here are a thousand francs too." The Arab took the package and the money but kept his full hands at chest level as if he didn't know what to do with what was being given him. "Now look," the schoolmaster said as he pointed in the direction of the east, "there's the way to Tinguit. You have a two-hour walk. At Tinguit you'll find the administration and the police. They are expecting you." The Arab looked toward the east, still holding the package and the money against his chest. Daru took his elbow and turned him rather roughly toward the south. At the foot of the height on which they stood could be seen a faint path. "That's the trail across the plateau. In a day's walk from here you'll find pasturelands and the first nomads. They'll take you in and shelter you according to their law." The Arab had now turned toward Daru and a sort of panic was visible in his expression. "Listen," he said. Daru shook his head: "No, be quiet.

Now I'm leaving you." He turned his back on him, took two long steps in the direction of the school, looked hesitantly at the motionless Arab, and started off again. For a few minutes he heard nothing but his own step resounding on the cold ground and did not turn his head. A moment later, however, he turned around. The Arab was still there on the edge of the hill, his arms hanging now, and he was looking at the schoolmaster. Daru felt something rise in his throat. But he swore with impatience, waved vaguely, and started off again. He had already gone some distance when he again stopped and looked. There was no longer anyone on the hill.

Daru hesitated. The sun was now rather high in the sky and was beginning to beat down on his head. The schoolmaster retraced his steps, at first somewhat uncertainly, then with decision. When he reached the little hill, he was bathed in sweat. He climbed it as fast as he could and stopped, out of breath, at the top. The rock-fields to the south stood out sharply against the blue sky, but on the plain to the east a steamy heat was already rising. And in that slight haze, Daru, with heavy heart, made out the Arab walking slowly on the road to prison.

A little later, standing before the window of the classroom, the schoolmaster was watching the clear light bathing the whole surface of the plateau, but he hardly saw it. Behind him on the blackboard, among the winding French rivers, sprawled the clumsily chalked-up words he had just read: "You handed over our brother. You will pay for this." Daru looked at the sky, the plateau, and, beyond, the invisible lands stretching all the way to the sea. In this vast landscape he had loved so much, he was alone.

J. F. POWERS

❧ *Zeal*

SOUTH of St. Paul the conductor appeared at the head of the coach, held up his ticket punch, and clicked it.

The Bishop felt for his ticket. It was there.

"I know it's not a pass," said Father Early. He had been talking across the aisle to one of the pilgrims he was leading to Rome, but now he was back on the subject of the so-called clergy pass. "But it is a privilege."

The Bishop said nothing. He'd meant to imply by his silence before, when Father Early brought up the matter, that there was nothing wrong with an arrangement which permitted the clergy to travel in parlor cars at coach rates.

The Bishop wished the arrangement were in effect in all parts of the country, and on all trains.

"But on a run like this, Bishop, with these fine coaches, I daresay there aren't many snobs who'll go to the trouble of filling out the form."

The Bishop looked away. Father Early had a nose like a parrot's and something on it like psoriasis that held the Bishop's attention—unfortunately, for Father Early seemed to think it was his talk. The Bishop had a priest or two in his diocese like Father Early.

"Oh, the railroads, I daresay, mean well."

"Yes," said the Bishop distantly. The voice at his right ear went on without him. He gazed out the window, up at the limestone scarred by its primeval intercourse with the Mississippi, now shrunk down into itself, and there he saw a cave, another cave, and another. Criminals had been discovered in them, he understood, and ammunition from the Civil War, and farther down the river, in the high bluffs, rattlesnakes were said to be numerous still.

"Bishop, I don't think I'm one to strain at a gnat." (The Bishop glanced at Father Early's nose with interest.) "But I must say I fear privilege more than persecution. Of course the one follows the other, as the night the day."

"Is it true, Father, that there are rattlesnakes along here?"

"Very likely," said Father Early, hardly bothering to look out the window. "Bishop, I was dining in New York, in a crowded place, observed by all and sundry, when the management tried to present me with a bottle of wine. Well!"

The Bishop, spying a whole row of caves, thought of the ancient Nile. Here, though, the country was too fresh and frigid. Here the desert fathers would've married early and gone fishing. The aborigines, by their fruits, pretty much proved that. He tried again to interrupt Father Early. "There must be a cave for you up there, somewhere, Father."

Father Early responded with a laugh that sounded exactly like ha-ha, no more or less. "I'll tell you a secret, Bishop. When I was in seminary, they called me Crazy Early. I understand they still do. Perhaps you knew."

"No," said the Bishop. Father Early flattered himself. The Bishop had never heard of him until that day.

"I thought perhaps Monsignor Reed had told you."

"I seldom see him." He saw Reed only by accident, at somebody's funeral or jubilee celebration or, it seemed, in railroad stations, which had happened again in Minneapolis that morning. It was Reed who had introduced Father Early to him then. Had Reed known what he was doing? It was six hours to Chicago, hours of this. . . .

"I suppose you know Macaulay's [*History of*] *England*, Bishop."

"No." There was something to be gained by a frank admission of ignorance when it was assumed anyway.

"Read the section dealing with the status of the common clergy in the eighteenth century. I'm talking about the Anglican clergy. Hardly the equal of servants, knaves, figures of fun! The fault of the Reformation, you say? Yes, of course"—the Bishop had in no way signified assent—"but I say it could happen anywhere, everywhere, any time! Take what's going on in parts of Europe today. When you consider the status of the Church there in the past, and the overwhelmingly Catholic population even now. I wonder, though, if it doesn't take something to bring us to our senses from time to time—*now* what do you say, Bishop?"

If the conductor hadn't been upon them, the Bishop would've said there was probably less danger of the clergy getting above themselves than there was of their being accepted for less than they were; or at least for less than they were supposed to be; or was that what Father Early was saying?

The conductor took up their tickets, placed two receipts overhead, one white and one blue. Before he moved on, he advised the Bishop to bring his receipt with him, the blue one, when he moved into the parlor car.

The Bishop nodded serenely.

Beside him, Father Early was full of silence, and opening his breviary.

The Bishop, who had expected to be told apologetically that it was a matter of no importance if he'd used his clergy pass, had an uncomfortable feeling that Father Early was praying for him.

At Winona, the train stopped for a minute. The Bishop from his window saw Father Early on the platform below talking to an elderly woman. In parting, they pecked at each other, and she handed him a box. Returning to his seat, he said he'd had a nice visit with his sister. He went to the head of the coach with the box, and came slowly back down the aisle, offering the contents to the pilgrims. "Divinity? Divinity?" The Bishop, when his turn came, took a piece, and consumed it. Then he felt committed to stay with Father Early until Chicago.

It was some time before Father Early returned to his seat—from making the acquaintance of Monsignor Reed's parishioners. "What we did was split the responsibility. Miss Culhane's in charge of Monsignor's people. Of course, the ultimate responsibility is mine." Peering up the aisle at two middle-aged women drawing water from the cooler, Father Early said, "The one coming this way now," and gazed out the window.

Miss Culhane, a paper cup in each hand, smiled at the Bishop. He smiled back.

When Miss Culhane had passed, Father Early said, "She's been abroad once, and that's more than most of 'em can say. She's a secretary in private life, and it's hard to find a man with much sense of detail. But I don't know . . . From what I've heard already I'd say the good people don't like the idea. I'm afraid they think she stands between them and me."

The other woman, also carrying paper cups, came down the aisle, and again Father Early gazed out the window. So did the Bishop. When the woman had gone by, Father Early commented dryly, "Her friend, whose name escapes me.

Between the two of 'em, Bishop . . . Oh, it'll be better for all concerned when Monsignor joins us."

The Bishop knew nothing about this. Reed had told him nothing. "*Monsignor?*"

"Claims he's allergic to trains."

"*Reed?*"

Again Father Early treated the question as rhetorical. "His plane doesn't arrive until noon tomorrow. We sail at four. That doesn't give us much time in New York."

The Bishop was putting it all together. Evidently Reed was planning to have as much privacy as he could on the trip. Seeing his little flock running around loose in the station, though, he must have felt guilty—and then the Bishop had happened along. Would Reed do this to him? Reed had done this to him. Reed had once called the Bishop's diocese the next thing to a titular see.

"I'm sorry he isn't sailing with us," said Father Early.

"Isn't he?"

"He's got business of some kind—stained glass, I believe—that'll keep him in New York for a few days. He may have to go to Boston. So he's flying over. I wonder, Bishop, if he isn't allergic to boats too." Father Early smiled at the Bishop as one good sailor to another.

The Bishop wasn't able to smile back. He was thinking how much he preferred to travel alone. When he was being hustled into the coach by Reed and Father Early, he hadn't considered the embarrassment there might be in the end; together on the train to Chicago and again on the one to New York and then crossing on the same liner, apart, getting an occasional glimpse of each other across the barriers. The perfidious Reed had united them, knowing full well that the Bishop was traveling first class and that Father Early and the group were going tourist. The Bishop hoped there would be time for him to see Reed in New York. According to Father Early, though, Reed didn't want them to look for him until they saw him. The Bishop wouldn't.

Miss Culhane, in the aisle again, returned with more water. When she passed, the Bishop and Father Early were both looking out the window. "You can't blame 'em," Father Early said. "I wish he'd picked a man for the job. No, they want more than a man, Bishop. They want a priest."

"They've got you," said the Bishop. "And Monsignor will soon be with you."

"Not until we reach Rome."

"No?" The Bishop was rocked by this new evidence of Reed's ruthlessness. Father Early and the group were going to Ireland and England first, as the Bishop was, but they'd be spending more time in those countries, about two weeks.

"No," said Father Early. "He won't."

The Bishop got out his breviary. He feared that Father Early would not be easily discouraged. The Bishop, if he could be persuaded to join the group, would more than make up for the loss of Reed. To share the command with such a man as Father Early, however, would be impossible. It would be to serve under him—as Reed may have realized. The Bishop would have to watch out. It would be dangerous for him to offer Father Early plausible excuses, to point out, for instance, that they'd be isolated from each other once they sailed from New York. Such an excuse, regretfully tendered now, could easily commit him to service on this train, and on the next one, and in New York—and the Bishop wasn't at all sure that Father Early wouldn't find a way for him to be with the group aboard ship. The Bishop turned a page.

When Father Early rose and led the pilgrims in the recitation of the rosary, the Bishop put aside his breviary, took out his beads and prayed along with them. After that, Father Early directed the pilgrims in the singing of "Onward, Christian Soldiers"—which was *not* a Protestant hymn, not originally, he said. Monsignor Reed's parishioners didn't know the words, but Father Early got around that difficulty by having everyone sing the notes of the scale, the ladies *la*, the men *do*. The Bishop cursed his luck and wouldn't even pretend to sing. Father Early was in the aisle, beating time with his fist, exhorting some by name to contribute more to the din, clutching others (males) by the shoulders until they did. The Bishop grew afraid that even he might not be exempt, and again sought the protection of his breviary.

He had an early lunch. When he returned to his seat, it was just past noon, and Father Early was waiting in the aisle for him.

"How about a bite to eat, Bishop?"

"I've eaten, Father."

"You eat early, Bishop."

"I couldn't wait."

Father Early did his little ha-ha laugh. "By the way, Bishop, are you planning anything for the time we'll have in Chicago between trains?" Before the Bishop, who was weighing the significance of the question, could reply, Father Early told him that the group was planning a visit to the Art Institute. "The Art Treasures of Vienna are there now."

"I believe I've seen them, Father."

"In Vienna, Bishop?"

"Yes."

"Well, they should be well worth seeing again."

"Yes. But I don't think I'll be seeing them." Not expecting the perfect silence that followed—this from Father Early was more punishing than his talk—the Bishop added, "Not today." Then, after more of that silence, "I've nothing planned, Father." Quickly, not liking the sound of that, "I do have a few things I might do."

Father Early nodded curtly and went away.

The Bishop heard him inviting some of the group to have lunch with him.

During the rest of the afternoon, the indefatigable voice of Father Early came to the Bishop from all over the coach, but the man himself didn't return to his seat. And when the train pulled into the station, Father Early wasn't in the coach. The Bishop guessed he was with the conductor, to whom he had a lot to say, or with the other employees of the railroad, who never seem to be around at the end of a journey. Stepping out of the coach, the Bishop felt like a free man.

Miss Culhane, however, was waiting for him. She introduced him to an elderly couple, the Doyles, who were the only ones in the group not planning to visit the Art Institute. Father Early, she said, understood that the Bishop wasn't planning to do anything in Chicago and would be grateful if the Bishop would keep an eye on the Doyles there. They hadn't been there before.

The Bishop showed them Grant Park from a taxicab, and pointed out the Planetarium, the Aquarium, the Field Museum. "Thought it was the stock-yards," Mr. Doyle commented on Soldier Field, giving Mrs. Doyle a laugh. "I'm afraid there isn't time to go there," the Bishop said. He was puzzled by the Doyles. They didn't seem to realize the sight-seeing was for them. He tried them on foot in department stores until he discovered from something Mrs. Doyle said that they were bearing with him. Soon after that they were standing across the street from the Art Institute, with the Bishop asking if they didn't want to cross over and join the group inside. Mr. Doyle said he didn't think they could make it over there alive—a reference to the heavy traffic, serious or not, the Bishop couldn't tell, but offered to take them across. The Doyles could not be tempted. So the three of them wandered around some more, the Doyles usually a step or two behind the Bishop. At last, in the lobby of the Congress Hotel, Mrs. Doyle expressed a desire to sit down. And there they sat, three in a row, in silence, until it was time to take a cab to the station. On the way over, Mr. Doyle, watching the meter, said, "These things could sure cost you."

In the station the Bishop gave the Doyles a gentle shove in the direction of the gate through which some members of the group were passing. A few minutes later, after a visit to the newsstand, he went through the gate unaccompanied. As soon as he entered his Pullman his ears informed him that he'd reckoned without Mr. Hope, the travel agent in Minneapolis. Old pastors wise in the ways of the world and to the escapist urge to which so many of the men, sooner or later, succumbed, thinking it only a love of travel, approved of Mr. Hope's system. If Mr. Hope had a priest going somewhere, he tried to make it a pair; dealt two, he worked for three of a kind; and so on—and nuns, of course, were wild, their presence eminently sobering. All day the Bishop had thought the odds safely against their having accommodations in the same Pullman car, but he found himself next door to Father Early.

They had dinner together. In the Bishop's view, it was fortunate that the young couple seated across the table was resilient from drink. Father Early opened up on the subject of tipping.

"These men," he said, his glance taking in several waiters, and his mouth almost in the ear of the one who was serving them, a cross-looking colored man, "are in a wonderful position to assert their dignity as human beings—which dignity, being from God, may not be sold with impunity. And for a mere pittance at that! Or, what's worse, bought!"

The Bishop, laying down his soup spoon, sat gazing out the window, for which he was again grateful. It was getting dark. The world seen from a train always looked sadder then. Indiana. Ohio next, but he wouldn't see it. Pennsylvania, perhaps, in the early morning, if he didn't sleep well.

"I see what you mean," he heard the young woman saying, "but I just charge it up to expenses."

"Ah, ha," said Father Early. "Then you don't see what I mean."

"Oh, don't I? Well, it's not important. And *please*—don't explain."

The Bishop, coloring, heard nothing from Father Early and thanked God for that. They had been coming to this, or something like it, inevitably they had. And again the Bishop suffered the thought that the couple was associating him with Father Early.

When he had served dessert across the table, the waiter addressed himself to Father Early. "As far as I'm concerned, sir, you're right," he said, and moved off.

The young woman, watching the waiter go, said, "He can't do that to me."

Airily, Father Early was saying, "And this time tomorrow we'll be on our way to Europe."

The Bishop was afraid the conversation would lapse entirely—which might have been the best thing for it in the long run—but the young man was nodding.

"Will this be your first trip?" asked the young woman. She sounded as though she thought it would be.

"My fifth, God willing," Father Early said. "I don't mean that as a commentary on the boat we're taking. Only as a little reminder to myself that we're all of us hanging by a thread here, only a heart's beat from eternity. Which doesn't mean we shouldn't do our best while here. On the contrary. Some people think Catholics oppose progress here below. Look on your garbage can and what do you see? Galvanized. Galvan was a Catholic. Look on your light bulb. Watts. Watt was a Catholic. The Church never harmed Galileo."

Father Early, as if to see how he was doing, turned to the Bishop. The Bishop, however, was dining with his reflection in the window. He had displayed a spark of interest when Father Early began to talk of the trip, believing there was to be a change of subject matter, but Father Early had tricked him.

"And how long in Rome?" asked the young woman.

"Only two days. Some members of the group intend to stay longer, but they won't return with me. Two days doesn't seem long enough, does it? Well, I can't say that I care for Rome. I didn't feel at home there, or anywhere on the Continent. We'll have two good weeks in the British Isles."

"Some people don't travel to feel at home," said the young woman.

To this Father Early replied, "Ireland first and then England. It may interest you to know that about half of the people in the group are carrying the complete works of Shakespeare. I'm hoping the rest of the group will manage to secure copies of the plays and read them before we visit Stratford."

"It sounds like a large order," said the young woman.

"Paperback editions are to be had everywhere," Father Early said with enthusiasm. "By the way, what book would you want if you were shipwrecked on a desert island?"

Apparently the question had novelty for the young man. "That's a hard one," he said.

"Indeed it is. Chesterton, one of the great Catholic writers, said he'd like a manual of shipbuilding, but I don't consider that a serious answer to the question. I'll make it two books because, of course, you'd want the Bible. Some people think Catholics don't read the Bible. But who preserved Scripture in the Dark Ages? Holy monks. Now what do you say? No. Ladies first."

"I think I'd like that book on shipbuilding," said the young woman.

Father Early smiled. "And you, sir?"

"Shakespeare, I guess."

"I was hoping you'd say that."

Then the Bishop heard the young woman inquiring:

"Shakespeare wasn't a Catholic, was he?"

The Bishop reached for his glass of water, and saw Father Early observing a moment of down-staring silence. When he spoke his voice was deficient. "As a matter of fact, we don't know. Arguments both ways. But we just don't know. Perhaps it's better that way," he said, and that was all he said. At last he was eating his dinner.

When the young couple rose to leave, the Bishop, who had been waiting for this moment, turned in time to see the young man almost carry out Father Early's strict counsel against tipping. With one look, however, the young woman prevailed over him. The waiter came at once and removed the tip. With difficulty, the Bishop put down the urge to comment. He wanted to say that he believed people should do what they could do, little though it might be, and shouldn't be asked to attempt what was obviously beyond them. The young woman, who probably thought Father Early was just tight, was better off than the young man.

After the waiter came and went again, Father Early sat back and said, "I'm always being surprised by the capacity ordinary people have for sacrifice."

The Bishop swallowed what—again—would have been his comment. Evidently Father Early was forgetting about the young man.

"Thanks for looking after the Doyles. I would've asked you myself but I was in the baggage car. Someone wanted me to say hello to a dog that's going to South Bend. No trouble, were they? What'd you see?"

The Bishop couldn't bring himself to answer either question. "It's hard to know what other people want to do," he said. "They might've had a better guide."

"I can tell you they enjoyed your company, Bishop."

"Oh?" The Bishop, though touched, had a terrible vision of himself doing the capitals of the world with the Doyles.

Father Early handed the Bishop a cigar. "Joe Quirke keeps me well supplied with these," he said, nodding to a beefy middle-aged man two tables away who looked pleased at having caught Father Early's eye. "I believe you know him."

"I met him," the Bishop said, making a distinction. Mr. Quirke had sat down next to him in the club car before dinner, taken up a magazine, put it down after a minute, and offered to buy the Bishop a drink. When the Bishop (who'd been about to order one) refused, Mr. Quirke had apparently taken him for a teetotaler with a past. He said he'd had a little problem until Father Early got hold of him.

Father Early was discussing the youth eating with Mr. Quirke. "Glenn's been in a little trouble at home—and at school. Three schools, I believe. Good family. I have his father's permission to leave him with the Christian Brothers in Ireland, if they'll have him."

When Glenn got up from the table, the Bishop decided he didn't like the look of him. Glenn was short-haired, long-legged, a Doberman pinscher of a boy. He loped out of the diner, followed by Mr. Quirke.

Two problems, thought the Bishop, getting ready to happen—and doubtless there were more of them in the group. Miss Culhane, in her fashion, could make trouble.

"There's something I'd like to discuss with you, Bishop."

The Bishop stiffened. Now it was coming, he feared, the all-out attempt to recruit him.

Father Early was looking across the table, at the empty places there. "You realize they'd been drinking?"

The Bishop refused to comment. *Now what?*

"It wouldn't surprise me if they met on this train."

"Yes, well . . ."

"Bishop, in my opinion, the boy is or has been a practicing Catholic."

In the Bishop's opinion, it was none of Father Early's business. He knew what Father Early was getting at, and he didn't like it. Father Early was thinking of taking on more trouble.

"I believe the boy's in danger," Father Early said. "Real danger."

The Bishop opened his mouth to tell Father Early off, but not much came out. "I wouldn't call him a boy." The Bishop felt that Father Early had expected something of the sort from him, nothing, and no support. Father Early had definitely gone into one of his silences. The Bishop, fussing with his cuffs, suddenly reached, but Father Early beat him to the checks.

Father Early complimented the waiter on the service and food, rewarding him with golden words.

The Bishop was going to leave a tip, to be on the safe side, but apparently the waiter was as good as his word. They left the diner in the blaze of his hospitality.

The Bishop had expected to be asked where in New York he'd be saying Mass in the morning, but when they arrived at their doors, Father Early smiled and put out his hand. It certainly looked like good-by.

They shook hands

And then, suddenly, Father Early was on his knees, his head bowed and waiting for the Bishop's blessing.

His mind was full of the day and he was afraid he was in for one of those nights he'd had on trains before. He kept looking at his watch in the dark, listening for sounds of activity next door, and finally admitted to himself that he was waiting for Father Early to come in. So he gave Father Early until midnight—and then he got dressed and went out to look for him.

Up ahead he saw Glenn step into the corridor from an end room and go around the corner. The Bishop prepared to say hello. But when he was about to pass, the atmosphere filled up with cigarette smoke. The Bishop hurried through it, unrecognized, he hoped, considering the lateness of the hour and the significance of another visit to the club car, as it might appear to Glenn, who could have observed him there earlier in the evening.

The club car was empty except for a man with a magazine in the middle of the car, the waiter serving him a drink, and the young man and Father Early at the tail end of the train, seated on a sofa facing upon the tracks. The Bishop advanced with difficulty to the rear. The train was traveling too fast.

Father Early glanced around. He moved over on the sofa to make room for the Bishop, and had the young man move. The Bishop sat down beside the young man, who was now in the middle.

One I went to—we're talking about fairs, Bishop—had an educated donkey, as the fellow called it. This donkey could tell one color from another—knew them all by name. The fellow had these paddles, you've seen them, painted different colors. Red, green, blue, brown, black, orange, yellow, white—oh, all colors . . ."

The Bishop, from the tone of this, sensed that nothing had been resolved and that Father Early's objective was to keep the young man up all night with him. It was a siege.

"The fellow would say, 'Now, Trixie'—I remember the little donkey's name. You might've seen her at some time."

The young man shook his head.

" 'Now, Trixie,' the fellow would say, 'bring me the yellow paddle,' and that's what she'd do. She'd go to the rack, where all the paddles were hanging, pick out the yellow one, and carry it to the fellow. Did it with her teeth, of course. Then the fellow would say, 'Trixie, bring me the green paddle.' "

"And she brought the green one," said the young man patiently.

"That's right. The fellow would say, 'Now, Trixie, bring me the paddles that are the colors of the flag.' " Father Early addressed the Bishop: "Red, white, and blue."

"Yes," said the Bishop. What an intricate instrument for good a simple man could be! Perhaps Father Early was only a fool, a ward of heaven, not subject to the usual penalties for meddling. No, it was zeal, and people, however far gone, still expected it from a man of God. But, even so, Father Early ought to be more careful, humbler before the mystery of iniquity. And still . . .

"My, that was a nice little animal, that Trixie." Father Early paused, giving his attention to the signal lights blinking down the tracks, and continued. "Red, green, all colors. Most fairs have little to recommend them. Some fairs, however, are worth while." Father Early stood up. "I'll be right back," he said, and went to the lavatory.

The Bishop was about to say something—to keep the ball rolling—when the young man got up and left, without a word.

The Bishop sat where he was until he heard the lavatory door open and shut. Then he got up to meet Father Early. Father Early looked beyond the Bishop, toward the place where the young man had been, and then at the Bishop. He didn't appear to blame the Bishop at all. Nothing was said.

They walked in the direction from which Father Early had just come. The Bishop thought they were calling it a day, but Father Early was onto something else, trying the waiter on baseball.

"Good night, Father."

"Oh?" said Father Early, as if he'd expected the Bishop to stick around for it.

"Good night, Father." The Bishop had a feeling that baseball wouldn't last, that the sermon on tipping was due again.

"Good night, Bishop."

The Bishop moved off comically, as the train made up for lost time. Entering his Pullman car, he saw the young man, who must have been kept waiting, disappear into the room Glenn had come out of earlier.

The Bishop slept well that night, after all, but not before he thought of Father Early still out there, on his feet and trying, which was what counted in the sight of God, not success. *Thinkest thou that I cannot ask my Father, and he will give me presently more than twelve legions of angels?*

"Would you like me to run through these names with you, Bishop, or do you want to familiarize yourself with the people as we go along?"

"I'd prefer that, I think. And I wish you'd keep the list, Miss Culhane."

"I don't think Father Early would want you to be without it, Bishop."

"No? Very well, I'll keep it then."

TRUMAN CAPOTE

❧ *A Tree of Night*

IT WAS winter. A string of naked light bulbs, from which it seemed all warmth had been drained, illuminated the little depot's cold, windy platform. Earlier in the evening it had rained, and now icicles hung along the stationhouse eaves like some crystal monster's vicious teeth. Except for a girl, young and rather tall, the platform was deserted. The girl wore a gray flannel suit, a raincoat, and a plaid scarf. Her hair, parted in the middle and rolled up neatly on the sides, was rich blondish-brown; and, while her face tended to be too thin and narrow, she was, though not extraordinarily so, attractive. In addition to an assortment of magazines and a gray suede purse on which elaborate brass letters spelled Kay, she carried conspicuously a green Western guitar.

When the train, spouting steam and glaring with light, came out of the darkness and rumbled to a halt, Kay assembled her paraphernalia and climbed up into the last coach.

The coach was a relic with a decaying interior of ancient red-plush seats, bald in spots, and peeling iodine-colored woodwork. An old-time copper lamp, attached to the ceiling, looked romantic and out of place. Gloomy dead smoke sailed the air; and the car's heated closeness accentuated the stale odor of discarded sandwiches, apple cores, and orange hulls: this garbage, including Lily cups, soda-pop bottles, and mangled newspapers, littered the long aisle. From a water cooler, embedded in the wall, a steady stream trickled to the floor. The passengers, who glanced up wearily when Kay entered, were not, it seemed, at all conscious of any discomfort.

Kay resisted a temptation to hold her nose and threaded her way carefully down the aisle, tripping once, without disaster, over a dozing fat man's protruding leg. Two nondescript men turned an interested eye as she passed; and a kid stood up in his seat squalling, "Hey, Mama, look at de banjo! Hey, lady, lemme play ya banjo!" till a slap from Mama quelled him.

There was only one empty place. She found it at the end of the car in an isolated alcove occupied already by a man and woman who were sitting with their feet settled lazily on the vacant seat opposite. Kay hesitated a second then said, "Would you mind if I sat here?"

The woman's head snapped up as if she had not been asked a simple question, but stabbed with a needle, too. Nevertheless, she managed a smile. "Can't say as I see what's to stop you, honey," she said, taking here feet down and also, with a curious impersonality, removing the feet of the man who was staring out the window, paying no attention whatsoever.

Thanking the woman, Kay took off her coat, sat down, and arranged herself with purse and guitar at her side, magazines in her lap: comfortable enough, though she wished she had a pillow for her back.

The train lurched; a ghost of steam hissed against the window; slowly the dingy lights of the lonesome depot faded past.

"Boy, what a jerkwater dump," said the woman. "No town, no nothin'."

Kay said, "The town's a few miles away."

"That so? Live there?"

No. Kay explained she had been at the funeral of an uncle. An uncle who, though she did not of course mention it, had left her nothing in his will but the green guitar. Where was she going? Oh, back to college.

After mulling this over, the woman concluded, "What'll you ever learn in a place like that? Let me tell you, honey, I'm plenty educated and I never saw the inside of no college."

"You didn't?" murmured Kay politely and dismissed the matter by opening one of her magazines. The light was dim for reading and none of the stories looked in the least compelling. However, not wanting to become involved in a conversational marathon, she continued gazing at it stupidly till she felt a furtive tap on her knee.

"Don't read," said the woman. "I need somebody to talk to. Naturally, it's no fun talking to *him*." She jerked a thumb toward the silent man. "He's afflicted: deaf and dumb, know what I mean?"

Kay closed the magazine and looked at her more or less for the first time. She was short; her feet barely scraped the floor. And like many undersized people she had a freak of structure, in her case an enormous, really huge head. Rouge so brightened her sagging, flesh-featured face it was difficult even to guess at her age: perhaps fifty, fifty-five. Her big sheep eyes squinted, as if distrustful of what they saw. Her hair was an obviously dyed red, and twisted into parched, fat corkscrew curls. A once-elegant lavender hat of impressive size flopped crazily on the side of her head, and she was kept busy brushing back a drooping cluster of celluloid cherries sewed to the brim. She wore a plain, somewhat shabby blue dress. Her breath had a vividly sweetish gin smell.

"You do wanna talk to me, don't you honey?"

"Sure," said Kay, moderately amused.

"Course you do. You bet you do. That's what I like about a train. Bus people are a close-mouthed buncha dopes. But a train's the place for putting your cards on the table, that's what I always say." Her voice was cheerful and booming, husky as a man's. "But on accounta *him,* I always try to get us this here seat; it's more private, like a swell compartment, see?"

"It's very pleasant," Kay agreed. "Thanks for letting me join you."

"Only too glad to. We don't have much company; it makes some folks nervous to be around him."

As if to deny it, the man made a queer, furry sound deep in his throat and plucked the woman's sleeve. "Leave me alone, dear-heart," she said, as if she were talking to an inattentive child. "I'm O.K. We're just having us a nice little ol' talk. Now behave yourself or this pretty girl will go away. She's very rich; she goes to college." And winking, she added, "He thinks I'm drunk."

The man slumped in the seat, swung his head sideways, and studied Kay intently from the corners of his eyes. These eyes, like a pair of clouded milky-blue marbles, were thickly lashed and oddly beautiful. Now, except for a certain remoteness, his wide, hairless face had no real expression. It was as if he were incapable of experiencing or reflecting the slightest emotion. His gray hair was clipped close and combed forward into uneven bangs. He looked like a child aged abruptly by some uncanny method. He wore a frayed blue serge suit, and he had anointed himself with a cheap, vile perfume. Around his wrist was strapped a Mickey Mouse watch.

"He thinks I'm drunk," the woman repeated. "And the real funny part is, I am. Oh, shoot—you gotta do something, ain't that right?" She bent closer. "Say, ain't it?"

Kay was still gawking at the man; the way he was looking at her made her squeamish, but she could not take her eyes off him. "I guess so," she said.

"Then let's us have us a drink," suggested the woman. She plunged her hand into an oilcloth satchel and pulled out a partially filled gin bottle. She began to unscrew the cap, but, seeming to think better of this, handed the bottle to Kay. "Gee, I forgot about you being company," she said. "I'll go get us some nice paper cups."

So, before Kay could protest that she did not want a drink, the woman had risen and started none too steadily down the aisle toward the water cooler.

Kay yawned and rested her forehead against the windowpane, her fingers idly strumming the guitar: the strings sang a hollow, lulling tune, as monotonously soothing as the Southern landscape, smudged in darkness, flowing past the window. An icy winter moon rolled above the train across the night sky like a thin white wheel.

And then, without warning, a strange thing happened: the man reached out and gently stroked Kay's cheek. Despite the breathtaking delicacy of this movement, it was such a bold gesture Kay was at first too startled to know what to make of it: her thoughts shot in three or four fantastic directions. He leaned forward till his queer eyes were very near her own; the reek of his perfume was sickening. The guitar was silent while they exchanged a searching gaze. Suddenly, from some spring of compassion, she felt for him a keen sense of pity; but also, and this she could not suppress, an overpowering disgust, an absolute loathing: something about him, an elusive quality she could not quite put a finger on, reminded her of—of what?

After a little, he lowered his hand solemnly and sank back in the seat, an asinine grin transfiguring his face, as if he had performed a clever stunt for which he wished applause.

"Giddyup! Giddyup! my little bucker-ROOS . . ." shouted the woman. And she sat down, loudly proclaiming to be, "Dizzy as a witch! Dog tired! Whew!" From a handful of Lily cups she separated two and casually thrust the rest down her blouse. "Keep 'em safe and dry, ha ha ha. . . ." A coughing spasm seized her, but when it was over she appeared calmer. "Has my boy friend been entertaining?" she asked, patting her bosom reverently. "Ah, he's so sweet." She looked as if she might pass out. Kay rather wished she would.

"I don't want a drink," Kay said, returning the bottle. "I never drink: I hate the taste."

"Mustn't be a kill-joy," said the woman firmly. "Here now, hold your cup like a good girl."

"No please . . ."

"Formercysake, hold it still. Imagine, nerves at your age! Me, I can shake like a leaf, I've got reasons. Oh, Lordy, have I got 'em."

"But . . ."

A dangerous smile tipped the woman's face hideously awry. "What's the matter? Don't you think I'm good enough to drink with?"

"Please, don't misunderstand," said Kay, a tremor in her voice. "It's just that I don't like being forced to do something I don't want to. So look, couldn't I give this to the gentleman?"

"Him? No sirree: he needs what little sense he's got. Come on, honey, down the hatch."

Kay, seeing it was useless, decided to succumb and avoid a possible scene. She sipped and shuddered. It was terrible gin. It burned her throat till her eyes watered. Quickly, when the woman was not watching, she emptied the cup out into the sound hole of the guitar. It happened, however, that the man saw; and Kay, realizing it, recklessly signaled to him with her eyes a plea not to give her away. But she could not tell from his clear-blank expression how much he understood.

"Where you from, kid?" resumed the woman presently.

For a bewildered moment, Kay was unable to provide an answer. The names of several cities came to her all at once. Finally, from this confusion, she extracted: "New Orleans. My home is in New Orleans."

The woman beamed. "N.O.'s where I wanna go when I kick off. One time, oh, say 1923, I ran me a sweet little fortune-teller parlor there. Let's see, that was on St. Peter Street." Pausing, she stooped and set the empty gin bottle on the floor. It rolled into the aisle and rocked back and forth with a drowsy sound. "I was raised in Texas—on a big ranch—my papa was rich. Us kids always had the best; even Paris, France, clothes. I'll bet you've got a big swell house, too. Do you have a garden? Do you grow flowers?"

"Just lilacs."

A conductor entered the coach, preceded by a cold gust of wind that rattled the trash in the aisle and briefly livened the dull air. He lumbered along, stopping now and then to punch a ticket or talk with a passenger. It was after midnight. Someone was expertly playing a harmonica. Someone else was arguing the merits of a certain politician. A child cried out in his sleep.

"Maybe you wouldn't be so snotty if you knew who we was," said the woman, bobbing her tremendous head. "We ain't nobodies, not by a long shot."

Embarrassed, Kay nervously opened a pack of cigarettes and lighted one. She wondered if there might not be a seat in a car up ahead. She could not bear the woman, or, for that matter, the man, another minute. But she had never before been in a remotely comparable situation. "If you'll excuse me now," she said, "I have to be leaving. It's been very pleasant, but I promised to meet a friend on the train. . . ."

With almost invisible swiftness the woman grasped the girl's wrist. "Didn't your mama ever tell you it was sinful to lie?" she stage-whispered. The lavender hat tumbled off her head but she made no effort to retrieve it. Her tongue flicked out and wetted her lips. And, as Kay stood up, she increased the pressure of her grip. "Sit down, dear . . . there ain't any friend . . . Why, we're your only friends and we wouldn't have you leave us for the world."

"Honestly, I wouldn't lie."

"Sit down, dear."

Kay dropped her cigarette and the man picked it up. He slouched in the corner and became absorbed in blowing a chain of lush smoke rings that mounted upward like hollow eyes and expanded into nothing.

"Why, you wouldn't want to hurt his feelings by leaving us, now, would you, dear?" crooned the woman softly. "Sit down—down—now, that's a good girl. My, what a pretty guitar. What a pretty, pretty guitar . . ." Her voice faded before the sudden whooshing, static noise of a second train. And for an instant the lights in the coach went off; in the darkness the passing train's golden windows winked black-yellow-black-yellow-black-yellow. The man's cigarette pulsed like the glow of a firefly, and his smoke rings continued rising tranquilly. Outside, a bell pealed wildly.

When the lights came on again, Kay was massaging her wrist where the woman's strong fingers had left a painful bracelet mark. She was more puzzled than angry. She determined to ask the conductor if he would find her a different seat. But when he arrived to take her ticket, the request stuttered on her lips incoherently.

"Yes, miss?"

"Nothing," she said.

And he was gone.

The trio in the alcove regarded one another in mysterious silence till the woman said, "I've got something here I wanna show you, honey." She rummaged once more in the oilcloth satchel. "You won't be so snotty after you get a gander at this."

What she passed to Kay was a handbill, published on such yellowed, antique paper it looked as if it must be centuries old. In fragile, overly fancy lettering, it read:

LAZARUS
The Man Who Is Buried Alive
A MIRACLE
SEE FOR YOURSELF
Adults, 25¢—Children, 10¢

"I always sing a hymn and read a sermon," said the woman. "It's awful sad: some folks cry, especially the old ones. And I've got me a perfectly elegant costume: a black veil and a black dress, oh, very becoming. *He* wears a gorgeous made-to-order bridegroom suit and a turban and lotsa talcum on his face. See, we try to make it as much like a bonafide funeral as we can. But shoot, nowadays you're likely to get just a buncha smart alecks come for laughs—so sometimes I'm real glad he's afflicted like he is on accounta otherwise his feelings would be hurt, maybe."

Kay said, "You mean you're with a circus or a side-show or something like that?"

"Nope, us alone," said the woman as she reclaimed the fallen hat. "We've been doing it for years and years—played every tank town in the South: Singasong, Mississippi—Spunky, Louisiana—Eureka, Alabama . . ." these and other names rolled off her tongue musically, running together like rain. "After the hymn, after the sermon, we bury him."

"In a coffin?"

"Sort of. Its gorgeous, it's got silver stars painted all over the lid."

"I should think he would suffocate," said Kay, amazed. "How long does he stay buried?"

"All told it takes maybe an hour—course that's not counting the lure."

"The lure?"

"Uh huh. It's what we do the night before the show. See, we hunt up a store, any ol' store with a big glass window'll do, and get the owner to let *him* sit inside this window, and, well, hypnotize himself. Stays there all night stiff as a poker and people come and look: scares the livin' hell out of 'em. . . ." While she talked she jiggled a finger in her ear, withdrawing it occasionally to examine her find. "And one time this ol' bindlestiff Mississippi sheriff tried to . . ."

The tale that followed was baffling and pointless: Kay did not bother to listen. Nevertheless, what she had heard already inspired a reverie, a vague recapitulation of her uncle's funeral; an event which, to tell the truth, had not much affected her since she had scarcely known him. And so, while gazing abstractedly at the man, an image of her uncle's face, white next the pale silk casket pillow, appeared in her mind's eye. Observing their faces simultaneously, both the man's and uncle's, as it were, she thought she recognized an odd parallel: there was about the man's face the same kind of shocking, embalmed, secret stillness, as though, in a sense, he were truly an exhibit in a glass cage, complacent to be seen, uninterested in seeing.

"I'm sorry, what did you say?"

"I said: I sure wish they'd lend us the use of a regular cemetery. Like it is now we have to put on the show wherever we can . . . mostly in empty lots that are nine times outa ten smack up against some smelly fillin' station which ain't exactly a big help. But like I say, we got us a swell act, the best. You oughta come see it if you get a chance."

"Oh, I should love to," Kay said, absently.

"Oh, I should love to," mimicked the woman. "Well, who asked you? Anybody ask you?" She hoisted up her skirt and enthusiastically blew her nose on the ragged hem of a petticoat. "Bu-leeve me, it's a hard way to turn a dollar. Know what our take was last month? Fifty-three bucks! Honey, you try living on that sometime." She sniffed and rearranged her skirt with considerable primness. "Well, one of these days my sweet boy's sure enough going to die down there; and even then somebody'll say it was a gyp."

At this point the man took from his pocket what seemed to be a finely shellacked peach seed and balanced it on the palm of his hand. He looked across at Kay and, certain of her attention, opened his eyelids wide and began to squeeze and caress the seed in an undefinably obscene manner.

Kay frowned. "What does he want?"

"He wants you to buy it."

"But what is it?"

"A charm," said the woman. "A love charm."

Whoever was playing the harmonica stopped. Other sounds, less unique, became at once prominent: someone snoring, the gin bottle seesaw rolling, voices in sleepy argument, the train wheels' distant hum.

"Where could you get love cheaper, honey?"

"It's nice. I mean it's cute. . . ." Kay said, stalling for time. The man rubbed and polished the seed on his trouser leg. His head was lowered at a supplicating, mournful angle, and presently he stuck the seed between his teeth and bit it, as if it were a suspicious piece of silver. "Charms always bring me bad luck. And besides . . . please, can't you make him stop acting that way?"

"Don't look so scared," said the woman, more flat-voiced than ever. "He ain't gonna hurt you."

"Make him stop, damn it!"

"What can I do?" asked the woman, shrugging her shoulders. "You're the one that's got money. You're rich. All he wants is a dollar, one dollar."

Kay tucked her purse under her arm. "I have just enough to get back to school," she lied, quickly rising and stepping out into the aisle. She stood there a moment, expecting trouble. But nothing happened.

The woman, with rather deliberate indifference, heaved a sigh and closed her eyes; gradually the man subsided and stuck the charm back in his pocket. Then his hand crawled across the seat to join the woman's in a lax embrace.

Kay shut the door and moved to the front of the observation platform. It was bitterly cold in the open air, and she had left her raincoat in the alcove. She loosened her scarf and draped it over her head.

Although she had never made this trip before, the train was traveling through an area strangely familiar: tall trees, misty, painted pale by malicious moonshine, towered steep on either side without a break or clearing. Above, the sky was a stark, unexplorable blue thronged with stars that faded here and there. She could see streamers of smoke trailing from the train's engine like long clouds of ectoplasm. In one corner of the platform a red kerosene lantern cast a colorful shadow.

She found a cigarette and tried to light it: the wind snuffed match after match till only one was left. She walked to the corner where the lantern burned and cupped her hands to protect the last match: the flame caught, sputtered, died. Angrily she tossed away the cigarette and empty folder; all the tension in her tightened to an exasperating pitch and she slammed the wall with her fist and began to whimper softly, like an irritable child.

The intense cold made her head ache, and she longed to go back inside the warm coach and fall asleep. But she couldn't, at least not yet; and there was no sense in wondering why, for she knew the answer very well. Aloud, partly to keep her teeth from chattering and partly because she needed the reassurance of her own voice, she said: "We're in Alabama now, I think, and tomorrow we'll be in Atlanta and I'm nineteen and I'll be twenty in August and I'm a sophomore. . . ." She glanced around at the darkness, hoping to see a sign of dawn, and finding the same endless wall of trees, the same frosty moon. "I hate him, he's horrible and I hate him. . . ." She stopped, ashamed of her foolishness and too tired to evade the truth: she was afraid.

Suddenly she felt an eerie compulsion to kneel down and touch the lantern. Its graceful glass funnel was warm, and the red glow seeped through her hands, making them luminous. The heat thawed her fingers and tingled along her arms.

She was so preoccupied she did not hear the door open. The train wheels roaring clickety-clack-clackety-click hushed the sound of the man's footsteps.

It was a subtle zero sensation that warned her finally; but some seconds passed before she dared look behind.

He was standing there with mute detachment, his head tilted, his arms dangling at his sides. Staring up into his harmless, vapid face, flushed brilliant by the lantern light, Kay knew of what she was afraid: it was a memory, a childish memory of terrors that once, long ago, had hovered above her like haunted limbs on a tree of night. Aunts, cooks, strangers—each eager to spin a tale or teach a rhyme of spooks and death, omens, spirits, demons. And always there had been the unfailing threat of the wizard man: stay close to the house, child, else a wizard man'll snatch you and eat you alive! He lived everywhere, the wizard man, and everywhere was danger. At night, in bed, hear him tapping at the window? Listen!

Holding onto the railing, she inched upward till she was standing erect. The man nodded and waved his hand toward the door. Kay took a deep breath and stepped forward. Together they went inside.

The air in the coach was numb with sleep: a solitary light now illuminated the car, creating a kind of artificial dusk. There was no motion but the train's sluggish sway, and the stealthy rattle of discarded newspapers.

The woman alone was wide awake. You could see she was greatly excited: she fidgeted with her curls and celluloid cherries, and her plump little legs, crossed at the ankles, swung agitatedly back and forth. She paid no attention when Kay sat down. The man settled in the seat with one leg tucked beneath him and his arms folded across his chest.

In an effort to be casual, Kay picked up a magazine. She realized the man was watching her, not removing his gaze an instant; she knew this though she was afraid to confirm it, and she wanted to cry out and waken everyone in the coach. But suppose they did not hear? What if they were not really *asleep?* Tears started in her eyes, magnifying and distorting the print on a page till it became a hazy blur. She shut the magazine with fierce abruptness and looked at the woman.

"I'll buy it," she said. "The charm, I mean. I'll buy it, if that's all—just all you want."

The woman made no response. She smiled apathetically as she turned toward the man.

As Kay watched, the man's face seemed to change form and recede before her like a moon-shaped rock sliding downward under a surface of water. A warm laziness relaxed her. She was dimly conscious of it when the woman took away her purse, and when she gently pulled the raincoat like a shroud above her head.

FLANNERY O'CONNOR

❧ A Late Encounter with the Enemy

GENERAL SASH was a hundred and four years old. He lived with his granddaughter, Sally Poker Sash, who was sixty-two years old and who prayed every night on her knees that he would live until her graduation from college. The General didn't give two slaps for her graduation but he never doubted he would live for it. Living had got to be such a habit with him that he couldn't conceive of any other condition. A graduation exercise was not exactly his idea of a good time, even if, as she said, he would be expected to sit on the stage in his uniform. She said there would be a long procession of teachers and students in their robes but that there wouldn't be anything to equal *him* in his uniform. He knew this well enough without her telling him, and as for the damn procession, it could march to hell and back and not cause him a quiver. He liked parades with floats full of Miss Americas and Miss Daytona Beaches and Miss Queen Cotton Products. He didn't have any use for processions, and a procession full of schoolteachers was about as deadly as the River Styx to his way of thinking. However, he was willing to sit on the stage in his uniform so that they could see him.

Sally Poker was not as sure as he was that he would live until her graduation. There had not been any perceptible change in him for the last five years, but she had the sense that she might be cheated out of her triumph because she so often was. She had been going to summer school every year for the past twenty because when she started teaching, there were no such things as degrees. In those times, she said, everything was normal but nothing had been normal since she was sixteen, and for the past twenty summers, when she should have been resting, she had had to take a trunk in the burning heat to the state teacher's college; and though when she returned in the fall, she always taught in the exact way she had been taught not to teach, this was a mild revenge that didn't satisfy her sense of justice. She wanted the General at her graduation because she wanted to show what she stood for, or, as she said, "what all was behind her," and was not behind them. This *them* was not anybody in particular. It was just all the upstarts who had turned the world on its head and unsettled the ways of decent living.

She meant to stand on that platform in August with the General sitting in his wheel chair on the stage behind her and she meant to hold her head very high as if she were saying, "See him! See him! My kin, all you upstarts! Glorious upright old man standing for the old traditions! Dignity! Honor!

Courage! See him!" One night in her sleep she screamed, "See him! See him!" and turned her head and found him sitting in his wheel chair behind her with a terrible expression on his face and with all his clothes off except the general's hat and she had waked up and had not dared to go back to sleep again that night.

For his part, the General would not have consented even to attend her graduation if she had not promised to see to it that he sit on the stage. He liked to sit on any stage. He considered that he was still a very handsome man. When he had been able to stand up, he had measured five feet four inches of pure gamecock. He had white hair that reached to his shoulders behind and he would not wear teeth because he thought his profile was more striking without them. When he put on his full-dress general's uniform, he knew well enough that there was nothing to match him anywhere.

This was not the same uniform he had worn in the War Between the States. He had not actually been a general in that war. He had probably been a foot soldier; he didn't remember what he had been; in fact, he didn't remember that war at all. It was like his feet, which hung down now shriveled at the very end of him, without feeling, covered with a blue-gray afghan that Sally Poker had crocheted when she was a little girl. He didn't remember the Spanish-American War in which he had lost a son; he didn't even remember the son. He didn't have any use for history because he never expected to meet it again. To his mind, history was connected with processions and life with parades and he liked parades. People were always asking him if he remembered this or that—a dreary black procession of questions about the past. There was only one event in the past that had any significance for him and that he cared to talk about: that was twelve years ago when he had received the general's uniform and had been in the premiere.

"I was in that preemy they had in Atlanta," he would tell visitors sitting on his front porch. "Surrounded by beautiful guls. It wasn't a thing local about it. Listen here. It was a nashnul event and they had me in it—up onto the stage. There was no bob-tails at it. Every person at it had paid ten dollars to get in and had to wear his tuxseeder. I was in this uniform. A beautiful gul presented me with it that afternoon in a hotel room."

"It was in a suite in the hotel and I was in it too, Papa," Sally Poker would say, winking at the visitors. "You weren't alone with any young lady in a hotel room."

"Was, I'd a known what to do," the old General would say with a sharp look and the visitors would scream with laughter. "This was a Hollywood, California, gul," he'd continue. "She was from Hollywood, California, and didn't have any part in the pitcher. Out there they have so many beautiful guls that they don't need that they call them a extra and they don't use them for nothing but presenting people with things and having their pitchers taken. They took my pitcher with her. No, it was two of them. One on either side and me in the middle with my arms around each of them's waist and their waist ain't any bigger than a half a dollar."

Sally Poker would interrupt again. "It was Mr. Govisky that gave you the uniform, Papa, and he gave me the most exquisite corsage. Really, I wish you could have seen it. It was made with gladiola petals taken off and painted gold and put back together to look like a rose. It was exquisite. I wish you could have seen it, it was . . ."

"It was as big as her head," the General would snarl. "I was tellin it. They gimme this uniform and they gimme this soward and they say, 'Now General, we don't want you to start a war on us. All we want you to do is march right up on that stage when you're innerduced tonight and answer a few questions. Think you can do that?' 'Think I can do it!' I say. 'Listen here. I was doing things before you were born,' and they hollered."

"He was the hit of the show," Sally Poker would say, but she didn't much like to remember the premiere on account of what had happened to her feet at it. She had bought a new dress for the occasion—a long black crepe dinner dress with a rhinestone buckle and a bolero—and a pair of silver slippers to wear with it, because she was supposed to go up on the stage with him to keep him from falling. Everything was arranged for them. A real limousine came at ten minutes to eight and took them to the theater. It drew up under the marquee at exactly the right time, after the big stars and the director and the author and the governor and the mayor and some less important stars. The police kept traffic from jamming and there were ropes to keep the people off who couldn't go. All the people who couldn't go watched them step out of the limousine into the lights. Then they walked down the red and gold foyer and an usherette in a Confederate cap and little short skirt conducted them to their special seats. The audience was already there and a group of UDC [United Daughters of the Confederacy] members began to clap when they saw the General in his uniform and that started everybody to clap. A few more celebrities came after them and then the doors closed and the lights went down.

A young man with blond wavy hair who said he represented the motion-picture industry came out and began to introduce everybody and each one who was introduced walked up on the stage and said how really happy he was to be here for this great event. The General and his granddaughter were introduced sixteenth on the program. He was introduced as General Tennessee Flintrock Sash of the Confederacy, though Sally Poker had told Mr. Govisky that his name was George Poker Sash and that he had only been a major. She helped him up from his seat but her heart was beating so fast she didn't know whether she'd make it herself.

The old man walked up the aisle slowly with his fierce white head high and his hat held over his heart. The orchestra began to play the Confederate Battle Hymn very softly and the UDC members rose as a group and did not sit down again until the General was on the stage. When he reached the center of the stage with Sally Poker just behind him guiding his elbow, the orchestra burst out in a loud rendition of the Battle Hymn and the old man, with real stage presence, gave a vigorous trembling salute and stood at attention until the last blast had died away. Two of the usherettes in Confederate caps and short skirts held a Confederate and a Union flag crossed behind them.

The General stood in the exact center of the spotlight and it caught a weird moon-shaped slice of Sally Poker—the corsage, the rhinestone buckle and one hand clenched around a white glove and handkerchief. The young man with the blond wavy hair inserted himself into the circle of light and said he was *really* happy to have here tonight for this great event, one, he said, who had fought and bled in the battles they would soon see daringly re-acted on the screen, and "Tell me, General," he asked, "how old are you?"

"Niiiiiinntety-two!" the General screamed.

The young man looked as if this were just about the most impressive thing that had been said all evening. "Ladies and gentlemen," he said, "let's give the General the biggest hand we've got!" and there was applause immediately and the young man indicated to Sally Poker with a motion of his thumb that she could take the old man back to his seat now so that the next person could be introduced; but the General had not finished. He stood immovable in the exact center of the spotlight, his neck thrust forward, his mouth slightly open, and his voracious gray eyes drinking in the glare and the applause. He elbowed his granddaughter roughly away. "How I keep so young," he screeched, "I kiss all the pretty guls!"

This was met with a great din of spontaneous applause and it was at just that instant that Sally Poker looked down at her feet and discovered that in the excitement of getting ready she had forgotten to change her shoes: two brown Girl Scout oxfords protruded from the bottom of her dress. She gave the General a yank and almost ran with him off the stage. He was very angry that he had not got to say how glad he was to be here for this event and on the way back to his seat, he kept saying as loud as he could, "I'm glad to be here at this preemy with all these beautiful guls!" but there was another celebrity going up the other aisle and nobody paid any attention to him. He slept through the picture, muttering fiercely every now and then in his sleep.

Since then, his life had not been very interesting. His feet were completely dead now, his knees worked like old hinges, his kidneys functioned when they would, but his heart persisted doggedly to beat. The past and the future were the same thing to him, one forgotten and the other not remembered; he had no more notion of dying than a cat. Every year on Confederate Memorial Day, he was bundled up and lent to the Capitol City Museum where he was displayed from one to four in a musty room full of old photographs, old uniforms, old artillery, and historic documents. All these were carefully preserved in glass cases so that children would not put their hands on them. He wore his general's uniform from the premiere and sat, with a fixed scowl, inside a small roped area. There was nothing about him to indicate that he was alive except an occasional movement in his milky gray eyes, but once when a bold child touched his sword, his arm shot forward and slapped the hand off in an instant. In the spring when the old homes were opened for pilgrimages, he was invited to wear his uniform and sit in some conspicuous spot and lend atmosphere to the scene. Some of these times he only snarled at the visitors but sometimes he told about the premiere and the beautiful girls.

If he had died before Sally Poker's graduation, she thought she would have died herself. At the beginning of the summer term, even before she knew if she would pass, she told the Dean that her grandfather, General Tennessee Flintrock Sash of the Confederacy, would attend her graduation and that he was a hundred and four years old and that his mind was still clear as a bell. Distinguished visitors were always welcome and could sit on the stage and be introduced. She made arrangements with her nephew, John Wesley Poker Sash, a Boy Scout, to come wheel the General's chair. She thought how sweet it would be to see the old man in his courageous gray and the young boy in his clean khaki—the old and the new, she thought appropriately—they would be behind her on the stage when she received her degree.

Everything went almost exactly as she had planned. In the summer while she was away at school, the General stayed with other relatives and they brought him and John Wesley, the Boy Scout, down to the graduation. A reporter came to the hotel where they stayed and took the General's picture with Sally Poker on one side of him and John Wesley on the other. The General, who had had his picture taken with beautiful girls, didn't think much of this. He had forgotten precisely what kind of event this was he was going to attend but he remembered that he was to wear his uniform and carry the sword.

On the morning of the graduation, Sally Poker had to line up in the academic procession with the B.S.'s in Elementary Education and she couldn't see to getting him on the stage herself—but John Wesley, a fat blond boy of ten with an executive expression, guaranteed to take care of everything. She came in her academic gown to the hotel and dressed the old man in his uniform. He was as frail as a dried spider. "Aren't you just thrilled, Papa?" she asked. "I'm just thrilled to death!"

"Put the soward acrost my lap, damm you," the old man said, "where it'll shine."

She put it there and then stood back looking at him. "You look just grand," she said.

"God damm it," the old man said in a slow monotonous certain tone as if he were saying it to the beating of his heart. "God damm every goddam thing to hell."

"Now, now," she said and left happily to join the procession.

The graduates were lined up behind the Science building and she found her place just as the line started to move. She had not slept much the night before and when she had, she had dreamed of the exercises, murmuring, "See him, see him?" in her sleep but waking up every time before she turned her head to look at him behind her. The graduates had to walk three blocks in the hot sun in their black wool robes and as she plodded stolidly along she thought that if anyone considered this academic procession something impressive to behold, they need only wait until they saw that old General in his courageous gray and that clean young Boy Scout stoutly wheeling his chair across the stage with the sunlight catching the sword. She imagined that John Wesley had the old man ready now behind the stage.

The black procession wound its way up the two blocks and started on the main walk leading to the auditorium. The visitors stood on the grass, picking out their graduates. Men were pushing back their hats and wiping their foreheads and women were lifting their dresses slightly from the shoulders to keep them from sticking to their backs. The graduates in their heavy robes looked as if the last beads of ignorance were being sweated out of them. The sun blazed off the fenders of automobiles and beat from the columns of the buildings and pulled the eye from one spot of glare to another. It pulled Sally Poker's toward the big red Coca-Cola machine that had been set up by the side of the auditorium. Here she saw the General parked, scowling and hatless in his chair in the blazing sun while John Wesley, his blouse loose behind, his hip and cheek pressed to the red machine, was drinking a Coca-Cola. She broke from the line and galloped to them and snatched the bottle away. She shook the boy and thrust in his blouse and put the hat on the old man's head. "Now get him in there!" she said, pointing one rigid finger to the side door of the building.

For his part the General felt as if there were a little hole beginning to widen in the top of his head. The boy wheeled him rapidly down a walk and up a ramp and into a building and bumped him over the stage entrance and into position where he had been told and the General glared in front of him at heads that all seemed to flow together and eyes that moved from one face to another. Several figures in black robes came and picked up his hand and shook it. A black procession was flowing up each aisle and forming to stately music in a pool in front of him. The music seemed to be entering his head through the little hole and he thought for a second that the procession would try to enter it too.

He didn't know what procession this was but there was something familiar about it. It must be familiar to him since it had come to meet him, but he didn't like a black procession. Any procession that came to meet him, he thought irritably, ought to have floats with beautiful guls on them like the floats before the preemy. It must be something connected with history like they were always having. He had no use for any of it. What happened then wasn't anything to a man living now and he was living now.

When all the procession had flowed into the black pool, a black figure began orating in front of it. The figure was telling something about history and the General made up his mind he wouldn't listen, but the words kept seeping in through the little hole in his head. He heard his own name mentioned and his chair was shuttled forward roughly and the Boy Scout took a big bow. They called his name and the fat brat bowed. Goddam you, the old man tried to say, get out of my way, I can stand up!—but he was jerked back again before he could get up and take the bow. He supposed the noise they made was for him. If he was over, he didn't intend to listen to any more of it. If it hadn't been for the little hole in the top of his head, none of the words would have got to him. He thought of putting his finger up there into the hole to block them but the hole was a little wider than his finger and it felt as if it were getting deeper.

Another black robe had taken the place of the first one and was talking now and he heard his name mentioned again but they were not talking about him, they were still talking about history. "If we forget our past," the speaker was saying, "we won't remember our future and it will be as well for we won't have one." The General heard some of these words gradually. He had forgotten history and he didn't intend to remember it again. He had forgotten the name and face of his wife and the names and faces of his children or even if he had a wife and children, and he had forgotten the names of places and the places themselves and what had happened at them.

He was considerably irked by the hole in his head. He had not expected to have a hole in his head at this event. It was the slow black music that had put it there and though most of the music had stopped outside, there was still a little of it in the hole, going deeper and moving around in his thoughts, letting the words he heard into the dark places of his brain. He heard the words, Chicka-mauga, Shiloh, Johnston, Lee, and he knew he was inspiring all these words that meant nothing to him. He wondered if he had been a general at Chicka-mauga or at Lee. Then he tried to see himself and the horse mounted in the middle of a float full of beautiful girls, being driven slowly through downtown Atlanta. Instead, the old words began to stir in his head as if they were trying to wrench themselves out of place and come to life.

The speaker was through with that war and had gone on to the next one and now he was approaching another and all his words, like the black procession, were vaguely familiar and irritating. There was a long finger of music in the General's head, probing various spots that were words, letting in a little light on the words and helping them to live. The words began to come toward him and he said, Dammit! I ain't going to have it! and started edging backwards to get out of the way. Then he saw the figure in the black robe sit down and there was a noise and the black pool in front of him began to rumble and to flow toward him from either side to the black slow music, and he said, Stop dammit! I can't do but one thing at a time! He couldn't protect himself from the words and attend to the procession too and the words were coming at him fast. He felt that he was running backwards and the words were coming at him like musket fire, just escaping him but getting nearer and nearer. He turned around and began to run as fast as he could but he found himself running toward the words. He was running into a regular volley of them and meeting them with quick curses. As the music swelled toward him, the entire past opened up on him out of nowhere and he felt his body riddled in a hundred places with sharp stabs of pain and he fell down, returning a curse for every hit. He saw his wife's narrow face looking at him critically through her round gold-rimmed glasses; he saw one of his squinting bald-headed sons; and his mother ran toward him with an anxious look; then a succession of places—Chickamauga, Shiloh, Marthasville—rushed at him as if the past were the only future now and he had to endure it. Then suddenly he saw that the black procession was almost on him. He recognized it, for it had been dogging all his days. He made such a desperate effort to see over it and find out what comes after the past that his hand clenched the sword until the blade touched bone.

The graduates were crossing the stage in a long file to receive their scrolls and shake the president's hand. As Sally Poker, who was near the end, crossed, she glanced at the General and saw him sitting fixed and fierce, his eyes wide open, and she turned her head forward again and held it a perceptible degree higher and received her scroll. Once it was all over and she was out of the auditorium in the sun again, she located her kin and they waited together on a bench in the shade for John Wesley to wheel the old man out. That crafty scout had bumped him out the back way and rolled him at high speed down a flagstone path and was waiting now, with the corpse, in the long line at the Coca-Cola machine.

JOHN UPDIKE

❧ *Pigeon Feathers*

WHEN they moved to Firetown, things were upset, displaced, rearranged. A red cane-back sofa that had been the chief piece in the living room at Olinger was here banished, too big for the narrow country parlor, to the barn, and shrouded under a tarpaulin. Never again would David lie on its length all afternoon eating raisins and reading mystery novels and science fiction and P. G. Wodehouse. The blue wing chair that had stood for years in the ghostly, immaculate guest bedroom in town, gazing through windows curtained with dotted swiss at the telephone wires and horse-chestnut trees and opposite houses, was here established importantly in front of the smutty little fireplace that supplied, in those first cold April days, their only heat. As a child, David had always been afraid of the guest bedroom—it was there that he, lying sick with the measles, had seen a black rod the size of a yardstick jog along at a slight slant beside the edge of the bed, and vanish when he screamed—and it was disquieting to have one of the elements of its haunted atmosphere basking by the fire, in the center of the family, growing sooty with use. The books that at home had gathered dust in the case beside the piano were here hastily stacked, all out of order, in the shelves that the carpenters had built low along one wall. David, at fourteen, had been more moved than a mover; like the furniture, he had to find a new place, and on the Saturday of the second week tried to work off some of his disorientation by arranging the books.

It was a collection obscurely depressing to him, mostly books his mother had acquired when she was young: college anthologies of Greek plays and Romantic poetry; Will Durant's *Story of Philosophy*; a soft-leather set of Shakespeare with string bookmarks sewed to the bindings; *Green Mansions* [by W. H. Hudson], boxed and illustrated with woodcuts; *I, the Tiger*, by Manuel Komroff; novels by names like Galsworthy and Ellen Glasgow [1874–1945; American novelist] and Irvin S. Cobb [1876–1944; American journalist] and Sinclair Lewis and "Elizabeth." The odor of faded taste made him feel the ominous gap between himself and his parents, the insulting gulf of time that existed before he was born. Suddenly he was tempted to dip into this time. From the heaps of books around him on the broad old floorboards, he picked up Volume II of a four-volume set of *An Outline of History*, by H. G. Wells. The book's red binding had faded to orange-pink on the spine. When he lifted the cover, there was a sweetish, atticlike smell, and his mother's maiden name written in unfamiliar handwriting on the flyleaf—an upright, bold, yet careful signature, bearing a faint relation to the quick scrunched backslant that flowed with marvelous consistency across her shopping lists and budget accounts and notes on Christmas cards to college friends from this same, vaguely menacing long ago.

He leafed through, pausing at drawings, done in an old-fashioned stippled style, of bas-reliefs, masks, Romans without pupils in their eyes, articles of ancient costume, fragments of pottery found in unearthed homes. The print was determinedly legible, and smug, like a lesson book. As he bent over the pages, yellow at the edges, they were like rectangles of dusty glass through which he looked down into unreal and irrelevant worlds. He could see things sluggishly move, and an unpleasant fullness came into his throat. His mother and grandmother fussed in the kitchen; the puppy, which they had just acquired, "for protection in the country," was cowering, with a sporadic panicked scrabble of claws, under the dining table that in their old home had been reserved for special days but that here was used for every meal.

Then, before he could halt his eyes, David slipped into Wells's account of Jesus. He had been an obscure political agitator, a kind of hobo, in a minor colony of the Roman Empire. By an accident impossible to reconstruct, he (the small *h* horrified David) survived his own crucifixion and presumably died a few weeks later. A religion was founded on the freakish incident. The credulous imagination of the times retrospectively assigned miracles and supernatural pretensions to Jesus; a myth grew, and then a church, whose theology at most points was in direct contradiction of the simple, rather communistic teachings of the Galilean.

It was as if a stone that for weeks and even years had been gathering weight in the web of David's nerves snapped them, plunged through the page, and a hundred layers of paper underneath. These fantastic falsehoods (plainly untrue; churches stood everywhere, the entire nation was founded "under God") did not at first frighten him; it was the fact that they had been permitted to exist in an actual human brain. This was the initial impact—that at a definite spot in time and space a brain black with the denial of Christ's divinity had been suffered to exist; that the universe had not spit out this ball of tar but allowed it to continue in its blasphemy, to grow old, win honors, wear a hat, write books that, if true, collapsed everything into a jumble of horror. The world outside the deep-silled windows—a rutted lawn, a whitewashed barn, a walnut tree frothy with fresh green—seemed a haven from which he was forever sealed off. Hot washrags seemed pressed against his cheeks.

He read the account again. He tried to supply out of his ignorance objections that would defeat the complacent march of these black words, and found none. Survivals and misunderstandings more farfetched were reported daily in the papers. But none of them caused churches to be built in every town. He tried to work backwards through the churches, from their brave high fronts through their shabby, ill-attended interiors back into the events at Jerusalem, and felt himself surrounded by shifting gray shadows, centuries of history, where he knew nothing. The thread dissolved in his hands. Had Christ ever come to him, David Kern, and said, "Here. Feel the wound in My side"? No; but prayers had been answered. What prayers? He had prayed that Rudy Mohn, whom he had purposely tripped so he cracked his head on their radiator, not die, and he had not died. But for all the blood, it was just a cut; Rudy came back the same day, wearing a bandage and repeating the same teasing words. He could never have died. Again, David had prayed for two separate photographs of movie stars he had sent away for to arrive tomorrow, and though they did not, they did arrive, some days later, together, popping through the clacking letter slot like a rebuke from God's mouth: *I answer your prayers in My way, in My time.* After that, he had made his prayers less definite, less susceptible of being twisted into a scolding. But what a tiny, ridiculous coincidence this was, after all, to throw into battle against H. G. Wells's engines of knowledge! Indeed, it proved the enemy's point: Hope bases vast premises on foolish accidents, and reads a word where in fact only a scribble exists.

His father came home. They had supper. It got dark. He had to go to the bathroom, and took a flashlight down through the wet grass to the outhouse. For once, his fear of spiders there felt trivial. He set the flashlight, burning, beside him, and an insect alighted on its lens, a tiny insect, a mosquito or flea, so fragile and fine that the weak light projected its X-ray onto the wall boards; the faint rim of its wings, the blurred strokes, magnified, of its long hinged legs, the dark cone at the heart of its anatomy. The tremor must be its heart beating.

Without warning, David was visited by an exact vision of death: a long hole in the ground, no wider than your body, down which you are drawn while the white faces above recede. You try to reach them but your arms are pinned. Shovels pour dirt into your face. There you will be forever, in an upright position, blind and silent, and in time no one will remember you, and you will never be called. As strata of rock shift, your fingers elongate, and your teeth are distended sidewise in a great underground grimace indistinguishable from a strip of chalk. And the earth tumbles on, and the sun expires, and unaltering darkness reigns where once there were stars.

Sweat broke out on his back. His mind seemed to rebound off of a solidness. Such extinction was not another threat, a graver sort of danger, a kind of pain; it was qualitatively different. It was not even a conception that could be voluntarily pictured; it entered you from outside. His protesting nerves swarmed on its surface like lichen on a meteor. The skin of his chest was soaked with the effort of rejection. At the same time that the fear was dense and internal, it was dense and all around him; a tide of clay had swept up to the stars; space was crushed into a mass. When he stood up, automatically hunching his shoulders to keep his head away from the spider webs, it was with a numb sense of being cramped between two huge volumes of rigidity. That he had even this small freedom to move surprised him. In the narrow shelter of that rank shack, adjusting his pants, he felt—his first spark of comfort—too small to be crushed.

But in the open, as the beam of the flashlight skidded with frightened quickness across the remote surfaces of the barn wall and the grape arbor and the giant pine that stood by the path to the woods, the terror descended. He raced up through the clinging grass pursued not by one of the wild animals the woods might hold, or one of the goblins his superstitious grandmother had communicated to his childhood, but by specters out of science fiction, where gigantic cinder moons fill half the turquoise sky. As David ran, a gray planet rolled inches behind his neck. If he looked back, he would be buried. And in the momentum of his terror, hideous possibilities—the dilation of the sun, the triumph of the insects—wheeled out of the vacuum of make-believe and added their weight to his impending oblivion.

He wrenched the door open; the lamps within the house flared. The wicks burning here and there seemed to mirror one another. His mother was washing the dishes in a little pan of heated pump water; Granmom fluttered near her elbow apprehensively. In the living room—the downstairs of the little square house was two long rooms—his father sat in front of the black fireplace restlessly folding and unfolding a newspaper.

David took from the shelf, where he had placed it this afternoon, the great unabridged Webster's Dictionary that his grandfather had owned. He turned the big thin pages, floppy as cloth, to the entry he wanted, and read:

soul . . . 1. An entity conceived as the essence, substance, animating principle, or actuating cause of life, or of the individual life, esp. of life manifested in physical activities; the vehicle of individual existence, separate in nature from the body and usually held to be separable in existence.

The definition went on, into Greek and Egyptian conceptions, but David stopped short on the treacherous edge of antiquity. He needed to read no farther. The careful overlapping words shingled a temporary shelter for him. "Usually held to be separable in existence"—what could be fairer, more judicious, surer?

Upstairs, he seemed to be lifted above his fears. The sheets on his bed were clean. Granmom had ironed them with a pair of flatirons saved from the Olinger attic; she plucked them hot off the stove alternately, with a wooden handle called a goose. It was a wonder, to see how she managed. In the next room, his parents made comforting scratching noises as they carried a little lamp back and forth. Their door was open a crack, so he saw the light shift and swing. Surely there would be, in the last five minutes, in the last second, a crack of light, showing the door from the dark room to another, full of light. Thinking of it this vividly frightened him. His own dying, in a specific bed in a specific room, specific walls mottled with wallpaper, the dry whistle of his breathing, the murmuring doctors, the nervous relatives going in and out, but for him no way out but down into the funnel. Never touch a doorknob again. A whisper, and his parents' light was blown out. David prayed to be reassured. Though the experiment frightened him, he lifted his hands high into the darkness above his face and begged Christ to touch them. Not hard or long; the faintest, quickest grip would be final for a lifetime. His hands waited in the air, itself a substance, which seemed to move through his fingers; or was it the pressure of his pulse? He returned his hands to beneath the covers uncertain if they had been touched or not. For would not Christ's touch *be* infinitely gentle?

Through all the eddies of its aftermath, David clung to this thought about his revelation of extinction: that there, in the outhouse, he had struck a solidness *qualitatively different*, a rock of horror firm enough to support any height of construction. All he needed was a little help; a word, a gesture, a nod of certainty and he would be sealed in, safe. The assurance from the dictionary had melted in the night. Today was Sunday, a hot fair day. Across a mile of clear air the church bells called, *Celebrate, celebrate*. Only Daddy went. He put on a coat over his rolled-up shirtsleeves and got into the little old black Plymouth parked by the barn and went off, with the same pained, hurried grimness of all his actions. His churning wheels, as he shifted too hastily into second, raised plumes of red dust on the dirt road. Mother walked to the far field, to see what bushes needed cutting. David, though he usually preferred to stay in the house, went with her. The puppy followed at a distance, whining as it picked its way through the stubble but floundering off timidly if one of them went back to pick it up and carry it. When they reached the crest of the far field, his mother asked, "David, what's troubling you?"

"Nothing. Why?"

She looked at him sharply. The greening woods crosshatched the space beyond her half-gray hair. Then she turned her profile and gestured toward the house, which they had left a half mile behind them. "See how it sits in the land? They don't know how to build with the land any more. Pop always said the foundations were set with the compass. We must try to get a compass and see. It's supposed to face due south; but south feels a little more *that* way to me." From the side, as she said these things, she seemed handsome and young. The smooth sweep of her hair over her ear seemed white with a purity and calm that made her feel foreign to him. He had never regarded his parents as consolers of his troubles; from the beginning they had seemed to have more troubles than he. Their confusion had flattered him into an illusion of strength; so now on this high clear ridge he jealously guarded the menace all around them, blowing like a breeze on his fingertips, the possibility of all this wide scenery sinking into darkness. The strange fact that though she came to look at the brush she carried no clippers, for she had a fixed prejudice against working on Sundays, was the only consolation he allowed her to offer.

As they walked back, the puppy whimpering after them, the rising dust behind a distant line of trees announced that Daddy was speeding home from church. When they reached the house he was there. He had brought back the Sunday paper and the vehement remark "Dobson's too intelligent for these farmers. They just sit there with their mouths open and don't hear a thing he's saying."

David hid in the funny papers and sports section until one-thirty. At two the catechetical class met at the Firetown church. He had transferred from the catechetical class of the Lutheran church in Olinger, a humiliating comedown. In Olinger they met on Wednesday nights, spiffy and spruce, in the atmosphere of a dance. Afterward, blessed by the brick-faced minister from whose lips the word "Christ" fell like a burning stone, the more daring of them went with their Bibles to a luncheonette and smoked. Here in Firetown, the girls were dull white cows and the boys narrow-faced brown goats in old men's suits, herded on Sunday afternoons into a threadbare church basement that smelled of stale hay. Because his father had taken the car on one of his countless errands to Olinger, David walked, grateful for the open air and the silence. The catechetical class embarrassed him, but today he placed hope in it, as the source of the nod, the gesture, that was all he needed.

Reverend Dobson was a delicate young man with great dark eyes and small white shapely hands that flickered like protesting doves when he preached; he seemed a bit misplaced in the Lutheran ministry. This was his first call. It was a split parish; he served another rural church twelve miles away. His iridescent green Ford, new six months ago, was spattered to the windows with red mud and rattled from bouncing on the rude back roads, where he frequently got lost, to the malicious satisfaction of many. But David's mother liked him, and, more pertinent to his success, the Haiers, the sleek family of feed merchants and innkeepers and tractor salesmen who dominated the Firetown church, liked him. David liked him, and felt liked in turn; sometimes in class, after some special stupidity, Dobson directed toward him out of those wide black eyes a mild look of disbelief, a look that, though flattering, was also delicately disquieting.

Catechetical instruction consisted of reading aloud from a work booklet answers to problems prepared during the week, problems like "I am the ———, the ———, and the ———, saith the Lord." Then there was a question period in which no one ever asked any questions. Today's theme was the last third of the Apostles' Creed. When the time came for questions, David blushed and asked, "About the Resurrection of the Body—are we conscious between the time when we die and the Day of Judgment?"

Dobson blinked, and his fine little mouth pursed, suggesting that David was making difficult things more difficult. The faces of the other students went blank, as if an indiscretion had been committed.

"No, I suppose not," Reverend Dobson said.

"Well, where is our soul, then, in this gap?"

The sense grew, in the class, of a naughtiness occurring. Dobson's shy eyes watered, as if he were straining to keep up the formality of attention, and one of the girls, the fattest, simpered toward her twin, who was a little less fat. Their chairs were arranged in a rough circle. The current running around the circle panicked David. Did everybody know something he didn't know?

"I suppose you could say our souls are asleep," Dobson said.

"And then they wake up, and there is the earth like it always is, and all the people who have ever lived? Where will Heaven be?"

Anita Haier giggled. Dobson gazed at David intently, but with an awkward, puzzled flicker of forgiveness, as if there existed a secret between them that David was violating. But David knew of no secret. All he wanted was to hear Dobson repeat the words he said every Sunday morning. This he would not do. As if these words were unworthy of the conversational voice.

"David, you might think of Heaven this way: as the way the goodness Abraham Lincoln did lives after him."

"But is Lincoln conscious of it living on?" He blushed no longer with embarrassment but in anger; he had walked here in good faith and was being made a fool.

"Is he conscious now? I would have to say no; but I don't think it matters." Dobson's voice had a coward's firmness; he was hostile now.

"You don't?"

"Not in the eyes of God, no." The unction, the stunning impudence, of this reply sprang tears of outrage in David's eyes. He bowed them to his book, where short words like Duty, Love, Obey, Honor were stacked in the form of a cross.

"Were there any other questions, David?" Dobson asked with renewed gentleness. The others were rustling, collecting their books.

"No." He made his voice firm, though he could not bring up his eyes.

"Did I answer your question fully enough?"

"Yes."

In the minister's silence the shame that should have been his crept over David: the burden and fever of being a fraud were placed upon *him*, who was innocent, and it seemed, he knew, a confession of this guilt that on the way out he was unable to face Dobson's stirred gaze, though he felt it probing the side of his head.

Anita Haier's father gave him a ride down the highway as far as the dirt road. David said he wanted to walk the rest, and figured that his offer was accepted because Mr. Haier did not want to dirty his bright blue Buick with dust. This was all right; everything was all right, as long as it was clear. His indignation at being betrayed, at seeing Christianity betrayed, had hardened him. The straight dirt road reflected his hardness. Pink stones thrust up through its packed surface. The April sun beat down from the center of the afternoon half of the sky; already it had some of summer's heat. Already the fringes of weeds at the edges of the road were bedraggled with dust. From the reviving grass and scruff of the fields he walked between, insects were sending up a monotonous, automatic chant. In the distance a tiny figure in his father's coat was walking along the edge of the woods. His mother. He wondered what joy she found in such walks; to him the brown stretches of slowly rising and falling land expressed only a huge exhaustion.

Flushed with fresh air and happiness, she returned from her walk earlier than he had expected, and surprised him at his grandfather's Bible. It was a stumpy black book, the boards worn thin where the old man's fingers had held them; the spine hung by one weak hinge of fabric. David had been looking for the passage where Jesus says to the one thief on the cross "Today shalt thou be with me in paradise." He had never tried reading the Bible for himself before. What was so embarrassing about being caught at it was that he detested the apparatus of piety. Fusty churches, creaking hymns, ugly Sunday-school teachers and their stupid leaflets—he hated everything about them but the promise they held out, a promise that in the most perverse way, as if the homeliest crone in the kingdom were given the prince's hand, made every good and real thing, ball games and jokes and big-breasted girls, possible. He couldn't explain this to his mother. Her solicitude was upon him.

"David, what are you doing at Granpop's Bible?"

"Trying to read it. This is supposed to be a Christian country, isn't it?"

She sat down on the green sofa that used to be in the sun parlor at Olinger, under the fancy mirror. A little smile still lingered on her face from the walk. "David, I wish you'd talk to me."

"What about?"

"About whatever it is that's troubling you. Your father and I have both noticed it."

"I asked Reverend Dobson about Heaven and he said it was like Abraham Lincoln's goodness living after him."

He waited for the shock to strike her. "Yes?" she said, expecting more.

"That's all."

"And why didn't you like it?"

"Well; don't you see? It amounts to saying there isn't any Heaven at all."

"I don't see that it amounts to that. What do you want Heaven to be?"

"Well, I don't know. I want it to be *something*. I thought *he'd* tell me what it was. I thought that was his job." He was becoming angry, sensing her surprise at him. She had assumed that Heaven had faded from his head years ago. She had imagined that he had already entered, in the secrecy of silence, the conspiracy that he now knew to be all around him.

"David," she asked gently, "don't you ever want to rest?"

"No. Not forever."

"David, you're so young. When you get older, you'll feel differently."

"Grandpa didn't. Look how tattered this book is."

"I never understood your grandfather."

"Well, I don't understand ministers who say it's like Lincoln's memory going on and on. Suppose you're not Lincoln?"

"I think Reverend Dobson made a mistake. You must try to forgive him."

"It's not a *question* of his making a mistake! It's a question of dying and never moving or seeing or hearing anything ever again."

"But"—in exasperation—"darling, it's so *greedy* of you to want more. When God has given us this wonderful April day, and given us this farm, and you have your whole life ahead of you—"

"You think, then, that there is God?"

"Of course I do"—with deep relief that smoothed her features into a reposeful oval. He was standing, and above her, too near for his comfort. He was afraid she would reach out and touch him.

"He made everything? You feel that?"

"Yes."

"Then who made Him?"

"Why, Man. Man." The happiness of this answer lit up her face radiantly, until she saw his gesture of disgust.

"Well that amounts to saying there is none."

Her hand reached for his wrist but he backed away. "David, it's a mystery. A miracle. It's a miracle more beautiful than any Reverend Dobson could have told you about. You don't say houses don't exist because Man made them."

"No. God has to be different."

"But, David, you have the *evidence*. Look out the window at the sun; at the fields."

"Mother, good grief. Don't you see"—he gasped away the roughness in his throat—"if when we die there's nothing, all your sun and fields and what not are all, ah, *horror?* It's just an ocean of horror."

"But, David, it's not. It's so clearly not that." And she made an urgent opening gesture with her hands that expressed, with its suggestion of a willingness to receive his helplessness, all her grace, her gentleness, her love of beauty gathered into a passive intensity that made him intensely hate her. He would not be wooed away from the truth. *I am the Way, the Truth—*

"No," he told her. "Just let me alone."

He found his tennis ball behind the piano and went outside to throw it against the side of the house. There was a patch high up where the brown stucco that had been laid over the sandstone masonry was crumbling away; he kept trying with the tennis ball to chip more pieces off. Superimposed upon his deep ache was a smaller but more immediate worry that he had hurt his mother. He heard his father's car rattling on the straightaway, and went into the house, to make peace before he arrived. To his relief she was not giving off the stifling damp heat of her anger but instead was cool, decisive, maternal. She handed him an old green book, her college text of Plato.

"I want you to read the Parable of the Cave," she said.

"All right," he said, though he knew it would do no good. Some story by a dead Greek just vague enough to please her. "Don't worry about it, Mother."

"I *am* worried. Honestly, David, I'm sure there will be something for us. As you get older, these things seem to matter a great deal less."

"That may be. It's a dismal thought, though."

His father bumped at the door. The locks and jambs stuck here. But before Granmom could totter to the catch and let him in, he had knocked it open. Although Mother usually kept her talks with David a confidence, a treasure between them, she called instantly, "George, David is worried about death!"

He came to the doorway of the living room, his shirt pocket bristling with pencils, holding in one hand a pint box of melting ice cream and in the other the knife with which he was about to divide it into four sections, their Sunday treat. "Is the kid worried about death? Don't give it a thought, David. I'll be lucky if I live till tomorrow, and I'm not worried. If they'd taken a buckshot gun and shot me in the cradle I'd be better off. The *world'*d be better off. Hell, I think death is a wonderful thing. I look forward to it. Get the garbage out of the way. If I had the man here who invented death, I'd pin a medal on him."

"Hush, George. You'll frighten the child worse than he is."

This was not true; he never frightened David. There was no harm in his father, no harm at all. Indeed, in the man's steep self-disgust the boy felt a kind of ally. A distant ally. He saw his position with a certain strategic coldness. Nowhere in the world of other people would he find the hint, the nod, he needed to begin to build his fortress against death. They none of them believed. He was alone. In a deep hole.

In the months that followed, his position changed little. School was some comfort. All those sexy, perfumed people, wisecracking, chewing gum, all of them doomed to die, and none of them noticing. In their company David felt that they would carry him along into the bright, cheap paradise reserved for them. In any crowd, the fear ebbed a little; he had reasoned that somewhere in the world there must exist a few people who believed what was necessary, and the larger the crowd, the greater the chance that he was near such a soul, within calling distance, if only he was not too ignorant, too ill-equipped, to spot him. The sight of clergymen cheered him; whatever they themselves thought, their collars were still a sign that somewhere, at some time, someone had recognized that we cannot, *cannot*, submit to death. The sermon topics posted outside churches, the flip hurried pieties of disc jockeys, the cartoons in magazines showing angels or devils—on such scraps he kept alive the possibility of hope.

For the rest, he tried to drown his hopelessness in clatter and jostle. The pinball machine at the luncheonette was a merciful distraction; as he bent over its buzzing, flashing board of flippers and cushions, the weight and constriction in his chest lightened and loosened. He was grateful for all the time his father wasted in Olinger. Every delay postponed the moment when they must ride together down the dirt road into the heart of the dark farmland, where the only light was the kerosene lamp waiting on the dining-room table, a light that made their food shadowy, scrabbled, sinister.

He lost his appetite for reading. He was afraid of being ambushed again. In mystery novels people died like dolls being discarded; in science fiction enormities of space and time conspired to crush the humans; and even in P. G. Wodehouse he felt a hollowness, a turning away from reality that was implicitly bitter and became explicit in the comic figures of futile clergymen. All gaiety seemed minced out on the skin of a void. All quiet hours seemed invitations to dread.

School stopped. His father took the car in the opposite direction, to a construction job where he had been hired for the summer as a timekeeper, and David was stranded in the middle of acres of heat and greenery and blowing pollen and the strange, mechanical humming that lay invisibly in the weeds and alfalfa and dry orchard grass.

For his fifteenth birthday his parents gave him, with jokes about his being a hillbilly now, a Remington .22. It was somewhat like a pinball machine to take it out to the old kiln in the woods, where they dumped their trash, and set up tin cans on the kiln's sandstone shoulder and shoot them off one by one. He'd take the puppy, who had grown long legs and a rich coat of reddish fur—he was part chow. Copper hated the gun but loved David enough to accompany him. When the flat acrid crack rang out, he would race in terrified circles that would tighten and tighten until they brought him, shivering, against David's legs. Depending upon his mood, David would shoot again or drop to his knees and comfort the dog. Giving this comfort to a degree returned comfort to him. The dog's ears, laid flat against his skull in fear, were folded so intricately, so—he groped for the concept—*surely*. Where the dull-studded collar made his fur stand up, each hair showed a root of soft white under the length, black-tipped, of the metal color that had given the dog its name. In his agitation Copper panted through nostrils that were elegant slits, like two healed cuts, or like the keyholes of a dainty lock of black, grained wood. His whole whorling, knotted, jointed body was a wealth of such embellishments. And in the smell of the dog's hair David seemed to descend through many finely differentiated layers of earth: mulch, soil, sand, clay, and the glittering mineral base.

But when he returned to the house, and saw the books arranged on the low shelves, fear returned. The four adamant volumes of Wells like four thin bricks, the green Plato that had puzzled him with its queer softness and tangled purity, the dead Galsworthy and "Elizabeth," Grandpa's mammoth dictionary, Grandpa's Bible, the Bible that he himself had received on becoming a member of the Firetown Lutheran Church—at the sight of these, the memory of his fear reawakened and came around him. He had grown stiff and stupid in its embrace. His parents tried to think of ways to entertain him.

"David, I have a job for you to do," his mother said one evening at the table.

"What?"

"If you're going to take that tone perhaps we'd better not talk."

"What tone? I didn't take any tone."

"Your grandmother thinks there are too many pigeons in the barn."

"Why?" David turned to look at his grandmother, but she sat there staring at the orange flame of the burning lamp with her usual expression of bewilderment.

Mother shouted, "Mom, he wants to know why?"

Granmom made a jerky, irritable motion with her bad hand, as if generating the force for utterance, and said. "They foul the furniture."

"That's right," Mother said. "She's afraid for that old Olinger furniture that we'll never use. David, she's been after me for a month about those poor pigeons. She wants you to shoot them."

"I don't want to kill anything especially," David said.

Daddy said, "The kid's like you are, Elsie. He's too good for this world. Kill or be killed, that's my motto."

His mother said loudly, "Mother, he doesn't want to do it."

"Not?" The old lady's eyes distended as if in horror, and her claw descended slowly to her lap.

"Oh, I'll do it, I'll do it tomorrow," David snapped, and a pleasant crisp taste entered his mouth with the decision.

"And I had thought, when Boyer's men made the hay, it would be better if the barn doesn't look like a rookery," his mother added needlessly.

A barn, in day, is a small night. The splinters of light between the dry shingles pierce the high roof like stars, and the rafters and crossbeams and built-in ladders seem, until your eyes adjust, as mysterious as the branches of a haunted forest. David entered silently, the gun in one hand. Copper whined desperately at the door, too frightened to come in with the gun yet unwilling to leave the boy. David stealthily turned, said, "Go away," shut the door on the dog, and slipped the bolt across. It was a door within a door; the double door for wagons and tractors was as high and wide as the face of a house.

The smell of old straw scratched his sinuses. The red sofa, half hidden under its white-splotched tarpaulin, seemed assimilated into this smell, sunk in it, buried. The mouths of empty bins gaped like caves. Rusty oddments of farming—coils of baling wire, some spare tines for a harrow, a handleless shovel—hung on nails driven here and there in the thick wood. He stood stock-still a minute; it took a while to separate the cooing of the pigeons from the rustling in his ears. When he had focused on the cooing, it flooded the vast interior with its throaty, bubbling outpour: there seemed no other sound. They were up behind the beams. What light there was leaked through the shingles and the dirty glass windows at the far end and the small round holes, about as big as basketballs, high on the opposite stone side walls, under the ridge of the roof.

A pigeon appeared in one of these holes, on the side toward the house. It flew in, with a battering of wings, from the outside, and waited there, silhouetted against its pinched bit of sky, preening and cooing in a throbbing, thrilled, tentative way. David tiptoed four steps to the side, rested his gun against the lowest rung of a ladder pegged between two upright beams, and lowered the gunsight into the bird's tiny, jauntily cocked head. The slap of the report seemed to come off the stone wall behind him, and the pigeon did not fall. Neither did it fly. Instead it stuck in the round hole, pirouetting rapidly and nodding its head as if in frantic agreement. David shot the bolt back and forth and had aimed again before the spent cartridge stopped jingling on the boards by his feet. He eased the tip of the sight a little lower, into the bird's breast, and took care to squeeze the trigger with perfect evenness. The slow contraction of his hand abruptly sprang the bullet; for a half second there was doubt, and then the pigeon fell like a handful of rags, skimming down the barn wall into the layer of straw that coated the floor of the mow on this side.

Now others shook loose from the rafters, and whirled in the dim air with a great blurred hurtle of feathers and noise. They would go for the hole; he fixed his sights on the little moon of blue, and when a pigeon came to it, shot him as he was walking the ten inches or so of stone that would carry him into the open air. This pigeon lay down in that tunnel of stone, unable to fall either one way or the other, although he was alive enough to lift one wing and cloud the light. It would sink back, and he would suddenly lift it again, the feathers flaring. His body blocked that exit. David raced to the other side of the barn's main aisle, where a similar ladder was symmetrically placed, and rested his gun on the same rung. Three birds came together to this hole; he got one, and two got through. The rest resettled in the rafters.

There was a shallow triangular space behind the crossbeams supporting the roof. It was here they roosted and hid. But either the space was too small, or they were curious, for now that his eyes were at home in the dusty gloom David could see little dabs of gray popping in and out. The cooing was shriller now; its apprehensive tremolo made the whole volume of air seem liquid. He noticed one little smudge of a head that was especially persistent in peeking out; he marked the place, and fixed his gun on it, and when the head appeared again, had his finger tightened in advance on the trigger. A parcel of fluff slipped off the beam and fell the barn's height onto a canvas covering some Olinger furniture, and where its head had peeked out there was a fresh prick of light in the shingles.

Standing in the center of the floor, fully master now, disdaining to steady the barrel with anything but his arm, he killed two more that way. He felt like a beautiful avenger. Out of the shadowy ragged infinity of the vast barn roof these impudent things dared to thrust their heads, presumed to dirty its starred silence with their filthy timorous life, and he cut them off, tucked them back neatly into the silence. He had the sensations of a creator; these little smudges and flickers that he was clever to see and even cleverer to hit in the dim recesses of the rafters—out of each of them he was making a full bird. A tiny peek, probe, dab of life, when he hit it, blossomed into a dead enemy, falling with good, final weight.

The imperfection of the second pigeon he had shot, who was still lifting his wing now and then up in the round hole, nagged him. He put a new clip into the stock. Hugging the gun against his body, he climbed the ladder. The barrel sight scratched his ear; he had a sharp, bright vision, like a color slide, of shooting himself and being found tumbled on the barn floor among his prey. He locked his arm around the top rung—a fragile, gnawed rod braced between uprights—and shot into the bird's body from a flat angle. The wing folded, but the impact did not, as he had hoped, push the bird out of the hole. He fired again, and again, and still the little body, lighter than air when alive, was too heavy to budge from its high grave. From up here he could see green trees and a brown corner of the house through the hole. Clammy with the cobwebs that gathered between the rungs, he pumped a full clip of eight bullets into the stubborn shadow, with no success. He climbed down, and was struck by the silence in the barn. The remaining pigeons must have escaped out the other hole. That was all right; he was tired of it.

He stepped with his rifle into the light. His mother was coming to meet him, and it amused him to see her shy away from the carelessly held gun. "You took a chip out of the house," she said. "What were those last shots about?"

"One of them died up in that little round window and I was trying to shoot it down."

"Copper's hiding behind the piano and won't come out. I had to leave him."

"Well, don't blame me. *I* didn't want to shoot the poor devils."

"Don't smirk. You look like your father. How many did you get?"

"Six."

She went into the barn, and he followed. She listened to the silence. Her hair was scraggly, perhaps from tussling with the dog. "I don't suppose the others will be back," she said wearily. "Indeed, I don't know why I let Mother talk me into it. Their cooing was such a comforting noise." She began to gather up the dead birds. Though he didn't want to touch them, David went into the mow and picked up by its tepid, horny, coral-colored feet the first bird he had killed. Its wings unfolded disconcertingly, as if the creature had been held together by threads that now were slit. It did not weigh much. He retrieved the one on the other side of the barn; his mother got the three in the middle, and led the way across the road to the little southern slope of land that went down toward the foundations of the vanished tobacco shed. The ground was too steep to plant or mow; wild strawberries grew in the tangled grass. She put her burden down and said, "We'll have to bury them. The dog will go wild."

He put his two down on her three; the slick feathers let the bodies slide liquidly on one another. He asked, "Shall I get you the shovel?"

"Get it for yourself; *you* bury them. They're your kill," she said. "And be sure to make the hole deep enough so he won't dig them up."

While he went to the tool shed for the shovel, she went into the house. Unlike her, she did not look up, either at the orchard to the right of her or at the meadow on her left, but instead held her head rigidly, tilted a little, as if listening to the ground.

He dug the hole, in a spot where there were no strawberry plants, before he studied the pigeons. He had never seen a bird this close before. The feathers were more wonderful than dog's hair; for each filament was shaped within the shape of the feather, and the feathers in turn were trimmed to fit a pattern that flowed without error across the bird's body. He lost himself in the geometrical tides as the feathers now broadened and stiffened to make an edge for flight, now softened and constricted to cup warmth around the mute flesh. And across the surface of the infinitely adjusted yet somehow effortless mechanics of the feathers played idle designs of color, no two alike, designs executed, it seemed, in a controlled rapture, with a joy that hung level in the air above and behind him. Yet these birds bred in the millions and were exterminated as pests. Into the fragrant, open earth he dropped one broadly banded in shades of slate blue, and on top of it another, mottled all over with rhythmic patches of lilac and gray. The next was almost wholly white, yet with a salmon glaze at the throat. As he fitted the last two, still pliant, on the top, and stood up, crusty coverings were lifted from him, and with a feminine, slipping sensation along his nerves that seemed to give the air hands, he was robed in this certainty: that the God who had lavished such craft upon these worthless birds would not destroy His whole Creation by refusing to let David live forever.

CRITICAL ESSAYS

INTRODUCTION TO THE
Essay

THE ESSAY as a literary form received its name from Michel de Montaigne, who called the personal, rambling discourses that he published in 1580 *Essais*, or "attempts," to distinguish them from the formal treatises of his contemporaries. Francis Bacon was the first to use the name in English when, in 1597, he called his brief epigrammatic compositions *Essays*.

From the time of Bacon to the present, the essay has been a recognized literary genre: a short composition of expository prose dealing with a limited subject. Essays have commonly been divided into two categories: formal and informal. The informal essay, highly personal and confidential, is a sort of intimate conversation between equals, marked by a relaxed and easy approach to its subject, a graceful style, and often a rambling and unconventional form. The formal essay aims to teach as much as to entertain, and it argues a thesis soberly and, at times, with passion.

One type of formal essay is the "literary," or "critical," essay, which aims, as Cleanth Brooks has said, "to put the reader in possession of a work of art." Criticism is almost as old as the poetry that first called it forth. Aristotle's analysis of epic and dramatic poetry in *The Poetics* dates back to the fourth century B.C. Since Aristotle, men of letters have written searching and brilliant analyses of literature, which have shed light on their own or their fellow artists' productions. These critical essays have assisted countless readers to understand and evaluate works of literature. And when the critical essay has distinction of form and style, it becomes literature in its own right.

The essays in this anthology are all critical essays. The rationale behind their inclusion in an introduction to literature is twofold: (1) they are representative examples of a well-established literary genre—they cover a period of four centuries—and (2) they furnish useful commentaries upon the poetry, drama, and prose fiction that make up the rest of this anthology. Aristotle's commentaries on tragedy, for example, are a valuable aid to understanding tragic drama; and the essays by Addison, Edith Hamilton, Bradley, and Bernard Knox offer illuminating commentaries on tragedy and on specific dramatists, Sophocles and Shakespeare, whose plays appear in the anthology. The essays by Coleridge, Wordsworth, Ruskin, Eliot, and Frost serve, in the same way, to illuminate the study of poetry; and those by Fielding, Johnson, Conrad, Henry James, Forster, and Northrop Frye, the study of prose fiction.

A critic is not absolutely indispensable to the reading of literature. Anyone is privileged to read a short story or a poem or a play and make of it what he will. The critic, however, skilled in literary appreciation, remarks, in effect: Have you noticed this? Sometimes the reader has; often he has not. Thus the critic can open the door to new and fascinating vistas.

Over and above their aid to an increased understanding and appreciation of literature, the twenty-three essays in this anthology serve as examples of literary prose distinguished in substance and style. As such, they offer excellent models for analysis and discussion, and for a student's own attempts at writing expository prose.

To Read an Essay

Reading an essay with full understanding, like reading any literary genre, is an acquired experience. An essay is expository prose, requiring certain techniques from the reader, as do prose fiction or drama or poetry. How does one go about it? Let us analyze an essay by Samuel Johnson published in *The Rambler*, No. 4, March 31, in 1750 (see pages 563–566).

BACKGROUND INFORMATION

The first things to consider are the author, title, and date the piece was written. Samuel Johnson, one learns from a reference book like *The Oxford Companion to English Literature* or *The Cambridge History of English Literature,* was a moralizing "literary dictator" of the mid-eighteenth century, who founded *The Rambler* to instruct his contemporaries "in wisdom and piety." He was a contemporary of Fielding and Richardson, who were among the earliest English novelists. Johnson was a great admirer of Richardson, whose novel *Pamela, or Virtue Rewarded,* published in 1740, had been widely popular, but he disapproved of Fielding, calling *Tom Jones,* published in 1749, a "vicious book," adding that "he scarcely knew a more corrupt work." Johnson's essay, "The Novel and Morality," was published the year after *Tom Jones.*

The more information we have about the author, the times, the circumstances of publication, the more intelligently we will read the essay. Everyone brings to what he reads a background of experience, sometimes broad, sometimes narrow. Obviously, the broader the better. This is one reason why a well-informed critic has an advantage over a poorly informed reader. The more one reads, the broader his background for understanding and critical appreciation. An editor often supplies biographical notes expressly to aid the reader.

SPOTTING THE GENERALIZATIONS

The author, title, and date having given some insight into the occasion and the subject of the essay, we turn to the text, reading carefully to discover the thesis the author is developing. The central problem in understanding any expository prose is to locate the main and subordinate generalizations that carry the argument, distinguishing them from the supporting particulars. Locating the generalizations is not always easy.

The quotation from Horace that precedes Johnson's essay suggests its tenor: literature should yield profit along with delight. In reading the essay we notice that Johnson is talking about a new type of fiction popular in his day ("fiction with which the present generation seems more particularly delighted"). He sets out to define it, and he calls it "the comedy of romance." Notice that he never uses the word "*novel*," nor does Fielding, whose preface to *Joseph Andrews* (see pages 558–562), with its reference to a "comic epic poem in prose," reminds us of Johnson's remark that this new type of fiction is "conducted nearly by the rules of comic poetry." Johnson helps to clarify what this new fiction, with its accurate exhibition of the living world, is like by contrasting it with heroic romance, made up of incredible actions and fantastic personages.

As we follow the argument we recognize the generalizations as *inclusive* statements. That is, they include the particulars and details by which they are developed and clarified. Thus the generalization stated in Paragraph One of Johnson's essay covers the particulars that make up the next four paragraphs. These paragraphs do not *advance* the idea; they merely clarify it by contrasting the new fiction with heroic romance and then by elaborating the idea (in Paragraph Five) that the authors of this new fiction must draw upon "observations of the living world."

The final sentence of Paragraph Five, however, brings in a new note: the danger inherent in this new type of fiction is a failure to copy nature accurately. And the opening sentence of Paragraph Six indicates that Johnson is now moving ahead to a new generalization: "But the danger of not being approved as just copiers of human manners is not the most important concern that an author of this sort ought to have before him." The conjunction "but" at the beginning of the sentence calls the reader's attention to a change in the direction of the thought. The next two sentences state this new generalization, which might be summarized as follows: Since these books copy nature, they "serve as lectures of conduct and introductions into life." Knowing what a moral individual Johnson was, we are not surprised at this statement and stand ready to believe that it may be of considerable importance in the essay, may possibly be the thesis, the main generalization he intends to develop. As we read on, we are led to believe that this *is* his main generalization, his thesis.

Our reasoning follows somewhat along these lines: Paragraph Seven does not advance the argument; it merely brings in "authority," in terms of an "ancient writer," to support it. The next three paragraphs, Eight, Nine, and Ten, develop a subgeneralization—*why* "familiar histories" serve as models for the young, whereas historical romances do not. Phrases like "for this reason," the opening phrase in paragraph ten, aid the reader to follow the argument; this phrase is retrospective reference, a looking-back to the material already discussed before moving ahead.

The argument does move ahead in the next paragraph, Eleven, beginning: "The chief advantages which these fictions have over real life." But this argument is clearly another subgeneralization. It discusses *how* the author of these familiar histories can protect the young from indecencies, while at the same time presenting an "accurate observation of the living world." Although an author may not *invent*, he may *select* the objects and the individuals about whom he is to write. The key word in this generalization is clearly "*select*."

The two following paragraphs, Twelve and Thirteen, develop this idea by indicating what is to be selected. Writers should avoid particularly what is discolored by passion and deformed by wickedness.

Paragraph Fourteen, beginning "Many writers for the sake of following nature," brings in another subgeneralization. No longer is Johnson developing the idea of what is to be selected. He is now concerned with showing how writers of these familiar histories have erred: by mingling good and bad qualities in their heroes, making both equally conspicuous.

There is no further progress, no further generalization, in the argument for five paragraphs, Fourteen through Eighteen. The concluding sentence of paragraph Eighteen, the next to last paragraph in the essay, is still referring to the "fatal error" of those who confound right and wrong and "mix them with so much art that no common mind is able to disunite them." These five paragraphs, therefore, are made up of particulars developing this subgeneralization.

The final paragraph, Nineteen, ends the essay by stating unequivocally a positive concept: realistic fiction, which is not concerned with historical truth, should always exhibit "the most perfect idea of virtue"; and where vice is shown, it "should always disgust." Fiction must teach virtue.

If we have spotted the generalizations—the main generalization, or thesis, and the subgeneralizations—we can put them together and get the heart of the essay, a kind of précis: The works of fiction with which the present generation seems more particularly delighted are such as exhibit life in its true state, diversified only by accidents that daily happen in the world and influenced by passions and qualities that are really found in conversing with mankind. Since these books copy nature, they serve as lectures of conduct and introductions into life for the young and ignorant and idle who read them. These fictions have an advantage over life in that their authors may select the objects and individuals presented as models. In mingling good and bad qualities in the characters they imitate, they make a fatal error: they confound the two so that the common mind cannot disunite them and is consequently corrupted. Realistic fiction should teach virtue by always exhibiting the most perfect idea of virtue and by presenting vice in such a way that it always disgusts.

UNDERSTANDING WORDS IN CONTEXT

To follow the argument of an essay, to make sure of its thesis and distinguish the subgeneralizations from the supporting particulars, to understand the meaning of all words and phrases in context, the reader must recognize figurative language, including irony, be familiar with the persons and places referred to, and be aware of all literary allusions. In these matters, reading an essay intelligently is no different from reading a lyrical poem or a classical tragedy. We are reading words, and we must know their denotative and connotative meanings, their emotional overtones, and their symbolic significance.

Take, for example, Johnson's reference to "machines and expedients of the heroic romance" in the second paragraph of his essay. Machines in this context are supernatural agents and have nothing to do with complicated mechanisms. If we fail to recognize this meaning, we would not understand what Johnson is saying. Understanding a familiar word used in an unfamiliar way, like "machines," is always a problem, particularly when one is reading an essay written in another century, for words shift their meaning with the years. Thus, when a seventeenth-century writer speaks of a *coy* maiden, he does not mean "bashful," but "disdainful." Consulting a good dictionary is the only recourse when faced with unfamiliar words or words that look out of place in a particular context. A dictionary that lists definitions in an historical order often helps, for the earliest meanings listed will most likely be the meanings in use during the sixteenth or seventeenth century. But there is really no substitute for the *Oxford English Dictionary*, which defines words in their historical context, with specific dates given for the quotations in which the word appears.

FIGURATIVE LANGUAGE

Figurative language, irony in particular, sometimes offers difficulties to the reader. For a full consideration of metaphor, simile, and other common figures of speech see The Study of Poetry (pages 3–34). A figure of speech is, by definition, an expression that says one thing and means another. When we say, "He flies through the air with the greatest of ease—the daring young man on the flying trapeze," which is a metaphor, we do not mean that he literally flew, but that he moved through the air quickly, like a bird. Or when we say that the furnace is out, which is metonymy, we do not mean that the furnace is no longer in the basement, but that the fire inside the furnace has ceased burning. These examples offer no difficulty, but some figures of speech do, and to misunderstand their meaning is to miss what the author is saying.

Irony presents a special problem. There is no sure way of recognizing irony, of realizing that the author means the opposite of what he is saying. We depend upon the context and the writer's attitude to know when he is being ironic. Take an instance from Matthew Arnold's essay "Sweetness and Light." Arnold borrows the terms "sweetness" and "light" from Swift, who uses them in *The Battle of the Books* as synonyms for beauty and intelligence, two attributes of a finely tempered nature. At one point in his essay, Arnold refers to the *Nonconformist*, the organ of a religious organization called the Independents, and its motto: "The Dissidence of Dissent and the Protestantism of the Protestant Religion." "There is sweetness and light," Arnold comments, "and an ideal of complete harmonious human perfection." Certainly, the context makes it apparent that Arnold is being ironic; what he really means is that this motto represents anything but sweetness and light.

CRITICAL TERMS, PEOPLE

Johnson's reference to "heroic romance" and to "the rules of comic poetry" also requires elucidation. Terms of this sort appear constantly in critical essays, and the best place to find an explanation is in a glossary of literary terms. Certain terms, like "poetic justice," might also be found in the dictionary. Every subject has its own terminology, and literature is no exception. The student of literature would do well to familiarize himself with literary terms that are used frequently.

In his third paragraph Johnson refers to a "remark made by Scaliger upon Pontanus" to the effect that "all his writings are filled with the same images." From the context it seems clear that Scaliger is a critic and Pontanus a poet. In this particular instance, knowing what Pontanus wrote or that Scaliger was a famous Renaissance scholar of the sixteenth century who was called the "founder of historical criticism" is not necessary to understand Johnson's meaning. For it does not affect the force of the illustration. Normally, however, biographical information of this sort is highly desirable, if not essential. We can find minimal information about prominent people in a dictionary. Reference books, biographical dictionaries, and encyclopedias contain more information. For the student of literature *The Oxford Companion to English Literature*, *The Oxford Companion to Classical Literature*, and *The Oxford Companion to American Literature* are all valuable.

CLEAR THINKING: LOGIC

There remains the question of logic, which is more a matter of judgment than of understanding. The two are not to be confused, although the author of the critical essay is constantly making judgments that the reader accepts or rejects on the basis of his past experience and the evidence brought forward.

We should always be asking ourselves: How pertinent are the arguments advanced? How valid are the conclusions reached? How relevant and how adequate are the illustrations and examples, the particulars and details, by which the author supports his generalizations? If he brings in the statements of others to support him, are these people authorities whose words carry weight?

What are the assumptions underlying his argument? Are they valid or controversial? Is the author guilty of faulty reasoning, building his argument upon a false syllogism, begging the question, arguing from false analogy, etc.?

In Johnson's essay the reader is asked to accept certain assumptions: that youth should be carefully protected; that the artist's aim is to inculcate virtue; and that art should imitate nature. The bulk of his argument, therefore, is concerned with showing why these familiar histories are likely to be an influence for good or bad upon the young, and how they have become corrupters of youth in the writers who fail to select only virtuous examples for representation and who insist that men's vices should be displayed along with their virtues.

Inevitably, the reader accepts or rejects Johnson's dictum on the basis not only of his arguments but of the reader's own experience with prose fiction. If he is familiar with *Tom Jones*, he will realize that Johnson had Fielding's novel in mind, and the reader's opinion of the novel, coupled with all he has read about it, will color his opinion of Johnson's argument. If he is familiar with Stevenson's and Carlyle's attack on *Tom Jones* and Coleridge's and Bulwer-Lytton's defense of it, he may call them to mind. He may remember the famous tribute to Fielding by Thackeray in his preface to *Pendennis*. And playing an important part in his judgment will be his attitude toward the contemporary novel, with its free and open handling of sexual relations.

MENTAL BLOCKS

In the way of a reader's understanding are two common mental blocks. The first is prejudice. Everyone has his own pet prejudices, certain opinions and beliefs grounded not on reason but on feeling. These prejudices can rise up and shut out comprehension, so that extra care must be taken in reading to keep the mind open, to listen to what the author is saying. Politics and religion, for example, are notorious for closing a mind completely to the words of a writer or distorting them beyond recognition. And the agitation over racial or minority issues presents another instance of prejudice resulting in completely different interpretations of the written word.

The second mental block is the habit of reading one's own ideas *into* what an author is saying, rather than reading the author's ideas *from* what he has said. Literary critics themselves are liable to this error. This reading into, not from, manifests itself in many ways and for many reasons. One *expects* a writer to say certain things because of what one knows of him, or thinks he knows of him; and behold! the reader finds it, whether it is there or not. This danger attaches itself to what is usually a virtue: knowing about the author, his background, the circumstances of the essay, as we discussed earlier, particularly if the information is sketchy and possibly inaccurate. Again, the reader may know something of the subject under discussion and thus read what he knows into what the author is saying, consequently missing the author's statement. When he agrees with the author up to a point, he may nod his head in accord and lose the fact that the author has gone on to develop a quite different thesis.

IN SUMMARY

These are aspects of the problem of reading expository prose intelligently. To read an essay intelligently, one must bring to what he reads some background information about the author, the occasion, the subject under discussion. The reader must be able to identify the main thesis of the essay and the subordinate generalizations that help to develop it, distinguishing them from the details that do not move the thought forward. He must be able to understand words and phrases in context, their connotative as well as their denotative meanings, figurative language as well as literal language; he must also recognize the people and places referred to. He must be prepared to criticize the logic of the arguments advanced, recognizing the author's assumptions and implications and whether his reasoning is sound or faulty. And finally, the reader must allow no mental block, such as prejudice or reading into, instead of from, an author's statements, to stand in the way of his full comprehension.

❦ On Tragedy

. . . A TRAGEDY . . . is the imitation of an action that is serious and also, as having magnitude, complete in itself; in language with pleasurable accessories, each kind brought in separately in the parts of the work; in a dramatic, not in a narrative form; with incidents arousing pity and fear, wherewith to accomplish its catharsis of such emotions. Here by "language with pleasurable accessories" I mean that with rhythm and harmony or song superadded; and by "the kinds separately" I mean that some portions are worked out with verse only, and others in turn with song.

As they act the stories, it follows that in the first place the Spectacle (or stage-appearance of the actors) must be some part of the whole; and in the second Melody and Diction, these two being the means of their imitation. Here by "Diction" I mean merely this, the composition of the verses; and by "Melody," what is too completely understood to require explanation. But further: the subject represented also is an action; and the action involves agents, who must necessarily have their distinctive qualities both of character and thought, since it is from these that we ascribe certain qualities to their actions. There are in the natural order of things, therefore, two causes, Thought and Character, of their actions, and consequently of their success or failure in their lives. Now the action (that which was done) is represented in the play by the Fable or Plot. The Fable, in our present sense of the term, is simply this, the combination of the incidents, or things done in the story; whereas Character is what makes us ascribe certain moral qualities to the agents; and Thought is shown in all they say when proving a particular point or, it may be, enunciating a general truth. There are six parts consequently of every tragedy, as a whole (that is) of such or such quality, viz., a Fable or Plot, Characters, Diction, Thought, Spectacle, and Melody; two of them arising from the means, one from the manner, and three from the objects of the dramatic imitation; and there is nothing else besides these six. Of these, its formative elements, then, not a few of the dramatists have made due use, as every play, one may say, admits of Spectacle, Character, Fable, Diction, Melody, and Thought.

The most important of the six is the combination of the incidents of the story. Tragedy is essentially an imitation not of persons but of action and life, or happiness and misery. All human happiness or misery takes the form of action; the end for which we live is a certain kind of activity, not a quality.

Translated by Ingram Bywater.

Character gives us qualities, but it is in our actions—what we do—that we are happy or the reverse. In a play accordingly they do not act in order to portray the Characters; they include the Characters for the sake of the action. So that it is the action in it, i.e., its Fable or Plot, that is the end and purpose of the tragedy; and the end is everywhere the chief thing. Besides this, a tragedy is impossible without action, but there may be one without Character. The tragedies of most of the moderns are characterless—a defect common among poets of all kinds, and with its counterpart in painting in Zeuxis as compared with Polygnotus; for whereas the latter is strong in character, the work of Zeuxis is devoid of it. And again: one may string together a series of character-istic speeches of the utmost finish as regards Diction and Thought, and yet fail to produce the true tragic effect; but one will have much better success with a tragedy which, however inferior in these respects, has a Plot, a combination of incidents, in it. And again: the most powerful elements of attraction in Tragedy, the Peripeties and Discoveries, are parts of the Plot. A further proof is in the fact that beginners succeed earlier with the Diction and Characters than with the construction of a story; and the same may be said of nearly all the early dramatists. We maintain, therefore, that the first essential, the life and soul, so to speak, of Tragedy is the Plot; and that the Characters come second—compare the parallel in painting, where the most beautiful colours laid on without order will not give one the same pleasure as a simple black-and-white sketch of a portrait. We maintain that Tragedy is primarily an imitation of action, and that it is mainly for the sake of the action that it imitates the personal agents. Third comes the element of Thought, i.e., the power of saying whatever can be said, or what is appropriate to the occasion. This is what, in the speeches in Tragedy, falls under the arts of Politics and Rhetoric; for the older poets make their personages discourse like statesmen, and the modern like rhetoricians. One must not confuse it with Character. Character in a play is that which reveals the moral purpose of the agents, i.e., the sort of thing they seek or avoid, where that is not obvious—hence there is no room for Character in a speech on a purely indifferent subject. Thought, on the other hand, is shown in all they say when proving or disproving some particular point, or enunciating some universal proposition. Fourth among the literary elements is the Diction of the personages, i.e., as before explained, the expression of their thoughts in words, which is practically the same thing with verse as with prose. As for the two remaining parts, the Melody is the greatest of the pleasurable accessories of Tragedy. The Spectacle, though an attraction, is the least artistic of all the parts, and has least to do with the art of poetry. The tragic effect is quite possible without a public performance and actors; and besides, the getting-up of the Spectacle is more a matter for the costumier than the poet.

. . . Having thus distinguished the parts, let us now consider the proper construction of the Fable or Plot, as that is at once the first and the most important thing in Tragedy. We have laid it down that a tragedy is an imitation of an action that is complete in itself, as a whole of some magnitude; for a whole may be of no magnitude to speak of. Now a whole is that which has beginning, middle, and end. A beginning is that which is not itself necessarily after anything else, and which has naturally something else after it; an end is that which is naturally after something itself, either as its necessary or usual consequent, and with nothing else after it; and a middle, that which is by nature after one thing and has also another after it. A well-constructed Plot, therefore, cannot either begin or end at any point one likes; beginning and end in it must be of the forms just described. Again: to be beautiful, a living creature, and every whole made up of parts, must not only present a certain order in its arrangement of parts, but also be of a certain definite magnitude. Beauty is a matter of size and order, and therefore impossible either (1) in a very minute creature, since our perception becomes distinct as it approaches instantaneity; or (2) in a creature of vast size—one, say, 1,000 miles long—as in that case, instead of the object being seen all at once, the unity and wholeness of it is lost to the beholder. Just in the same way, then, as a beautiful whole made up of parts, or a beautiful living creature, must be of some size, but a size to be taken in by the eye, so a story or Plot must be of some length, but of a length to be taken in by the memory. As for the limit of its length, so far as that is relative to public performances and spectators, it does not fall within the theory of poetry. If they had to perform a hundred tragedies, they would be timed by water-clocks, as they are said to have been at one period. The limit, however, set by the actual nature of the thing is this: the longer the story, consistently with its being comprehensible as a whole, the finer it is by reason of its magnitude. As a rough general formula, "a length which allows of the hero passing by a series of probable or necessary stages from misfortune to happiness, or from happiness to misfortune," may suffice as a limit for the magnitude of the story.

. . . The Unity of a Plot does not consist, as some suppose, in its having one man as its subject. An infinity of things befall that one man, some of which it is impossible to reduce to unity; and in like manner there are many actions of one man which cannot be made to form one action. One sees, therefore, the mistake of all the poets who have written a *Heracleid*, a *Theseid*, or similar poems; they suppose that, because Heracles was one man, the story also of Heracles must be one story. Homer, however, evidently understood this point quite well, whether by art or instinct, just in the same way as he excels the rest in every other respect. In writing an *Odyssey*, he did not make the poem cover all that ever befell his hero—it befell him, for instance, to get wounded on Parnassus and also to feign madness at the time of the call to arms, but the two incidents had no necessary or probable connexion with one another—instead of doing that, he took as the subject of the *Odyssey*, as also of the *Iliad*, an action with a Unity of the kind we are describing. The truth is that, just as in the other imitative arts one imitation is always of one thing, so in poetry the story, as an imitation of action, must represent one action, a complete whole, with its several incidents so closely connected that the transposal or withdrawal of any one of them will disjoin and dislocate the whole. For that which makes no perceptible difference by its presence or absence is no real part of the whole.

. . . From what we have said it will be seen that the poet's function is to describe, not the thing that has happened, but a kind of thing that might happen, i.e., what is possible as being probable or necessary. The distinction between historian and poet is not in the one writing prose and the other verse—you might put the work of Herodotus into verse, and it would still be a species of history; it consists really in this, that the one describes the thing that has been, and the other a kind of thing that might be. Hence poetry is something more philosophic and of graver import than history, since its statements are of the nature rather of universals, whereas those of history are singulars. By a universal statement I mean one as to what such or such a kind of man will probably or necessarily say or do—which is the aim of poetry, though it affixes proper names to the characters; by a singular statement, one as to what, say Alcibiades did or had done to him. In Comedy this has become clear by this time; it is only when their plot is already made up of probable incidents that they give it a basis of proper names, choosing for the purpose any names that may occur to them, instead of writing like the old iambic poets about particular persons. In Tragedy, however, they still adhere to the historic names; and for this reason: what convinces is the possible; now whereas we are not yet sure as to the possibility of that which has not happened, that which has happened is manifestly possible, else it would not have come to pass. Nevertheless even in Tragedy, there are some plays with but one or two known names in them, the rest being inventions; and there are some without a single known name, e.g., Agathon's [Athenian tragic poet of late fifth century B.C.] *Antheus*, in which both incidents and names are of the poet's invention; and it is no less delightful on that account. So that one must not aim at a rigid adherence to the traditional stories on which tragedies are based. It would be absurd, in fact, to do so, as even the known stories are only known to a few, though they are a delight none the less to all.

It is evident from the above that the poet must be more the poet of his stories or Plots than of his verses, inasmuch as he is a poet by virtue of the imitative element in his work, and it is actions that he imitates. And if he should come to take a subject from actual history, he is none the less a poet for that; since some historic occurrences may very well be in the probable and possible order of things; and it is in that aspect of them that he is their poet.

Of simple Plots and actions the episodic are the worst. I call a Plot episodic when there is neither probability nor necessity in the sequence of its episodes. Actions of this sort bad poets construct through their own fault, and good ones on account of the players. His work being for public performance, a good poet often stretches out a Plot beyond its capabilities, and is thus obliged to twist the sequence of incident.

Tragedy, however, is an imitation not only of a complete action, but also of incidents arousing pity and fear. Such incidents have the very greatest effect on the mind when they occur unexpectedly and at the same time in consequence of one another; there is more of the marvellous in them then than if they happened of themselves or by mere chance. Even matters of chance seem most marvellous if there is an appearance of design as it were in them; as for instance the statue of Mitys at Argos killed the author of Mitys' death by falling down on him when a looker-on at a public spectacle; for incidents like that we think to be not without a meaning. A Plot, therefore, of this sort is necessarily finer than others.

. . . Plots are either simple or complex, since the actions they represent are naturally of this twofold description. The action, proceeding in the way defined, as one continuous whole, I call simple, when the change in the hero's fortunes takes place without Peripety or Discovery; and complex, when it involves one or the other, or both. These should each of them arise out of the structure of the Plot itself, so as to be the consequence, necessary or probable, of the antecedents. There is a great difference between a thing happening *propter hoc* [because of this] and *post hoc* [after this].

. . . A Peripety is the change of the kind described from one state of things within the play to its opposite, and that too in the way we are saying, in the probable or necessary sequence of events; as it is for instance in *Oedipus*: here the opposite state of things is produced by the Messenger, who, coming to gladden Oedipus and to remove his fears as to his mother, reveals the secret of his birth. And in *Lynceus*: just as he is being led off for execution, with Danaus at his side to put him to death, the incidents preceding this bring it about that he is saved and Danaus put to death. A Discovery is, as the very word implies, a change from ignorance to knowledge, and thus to either love or hate, in the personages marked for good or evil fortune. The finest form of Discovery is one attended by Peripeties, like that which goes with the Discovery in *Oedipus*. There are no doubt other forms of it; what we have said may happen in a way in reference to inanimate things, even things of a very casual kind; and it is also possible to discover whether some one has done or not done something. But the form most directly connected with the Plot and the action of the piece is the first-mentioned. This, with a Peripety, will arouse either pity or fear—actions of that nature being what Tragedy is assumed to represent; and it will also serve to bring about the happy or unhappy ending. The Discovery, then, being of persons, it may be that of one party only to the other, the latter being already known; or both the parties may have to discover themselves. Iphigenia, for instance, was discovered to Orestes by sending the letter; and another Discovery was required to reveal him to Iphigenia.

Two parts of the Plot, then, Peripety and Discovery, are on matters of this sort. A third part is Suffering; which we may define as an action of a destructive or painful nature, such as murders on the stage, tortures, woundings, and the like. The other two have been already explained.

. . . The parts of Tragedy to be treated as formative elements in the whole were mentioned in a previous Chapter. From the point of view, however, of its quantity, i.e., the separate sections into which it is divided, a tragedy has the following parts: Prologue, Episode, Exode, and a choral portion, distinguished into Parode and Stasimon; these two are common to all tragedies, whereas songs from the stage and *Commoe* are only found in some. The Prologue is all that precedes the Parode of the chorus; an Episode all that comes in between two whole choral songs; the Exode all that follows after the last choral song. In the choral portion the Parode is the whole first statement of the chorus; a Stasimon, a song of the chorus without anapaests or trochees; a *Commos*, a lamentation sung by chorus and actor in concert. The parts of Tragedy to be used as formative elements in the whole we have already mentioned; the above are its parts from the point of view of its quantity, or the separate sections into which it is divided.

. . . The next points after what we have said above will be these: (1) What is the poet to aim at, and what is he to avoid, in constructing his Plots? and (2) What are the conditions on which the tragic effect depends?

We assume that, for the finest form of Tragedy, the Plot must be not simple but complex; and further, that it must imitate actions arousing fear and pity, since that is the distinctive function of this kind of imitation. It follows, therefore, that there are three forms of Plot to be avoided. (1) A good man must not be seen passing from happiness to misery, or (2) a bad man from misery to happiness. The first situation is not fear-inspiring or piteous, but simply odious to us. The second is the most untragic that can be; it has no one of the requisites of Tragedy; it does not appeal either to the human feeling in us, or to our pity, or to our fears. Nor, on the other hand, should (3) an extremely bad man be seen falling from happiness into misery. Such a story may arouse the human feeling in us, but it will not move us to either pity or fear; pity is occasioned by undeserved misfortune, and fear by that of one like ourselves; so that there will be nothing either piteous or fear-inspiring in the situation. There remains, then, the intermediate kind of personage, a man not pre-eminently virtuous and just, whose misfortune, however, is brought upon him not by vice and depravity but by some error of judgment, of the number of those in the enjoyment of great reputation and prosperity; e.g., Oedipus, Thyestes, and the men of note of similar families. The perfect Plot, accordingly, must have a single, and not (as some tell us) a double issue; the change in the hero's fortunes must be not from misery to happiness, but on the contrary from happiness to misery; and the cause of it must lie not in any depravity, but in some great error on his part; the man himself being either such as we have described, or better, not worse, than that.

❧ *Of Studies*

STUDIES serve for delight, for ornament, and for ability. Their chief use for delight is in privateness and retiring; for ornament, is in discourse; and for ability, is in the judgment and disposition of business; for expert men can execute, and perhaps judge of particulars, one by one; but the general counsels, and the plots and marshaling of affairs come best from those that are learned. To spend too much time in studies is sloth; to use them too much for ornament is affectation; to make judgment wholly by their rules is the humor of a scholar. They perfect nature, and are perfected by experience; for natural abilities are like natural plants, that need pruning by study; and studies themselves do give forth directions too much at large, except they be bounded in by experience. Crafty men contemn studies, simple men admire them, and wise men use them; for they teach not their own use; but that is a wisdom without them and above them, won by observation. Read not to contradict and confute, nor to believe and take for granted, nor to find talk and discourse, but to weigh and consider. Some books are to be tasted, others to be swallowed, and some few to be chewed and digested; that is, some books are to be read only in parts; others to be read but not curiously, and some few to be read wholly, and with diligence and attention. Some books also may be read by deputy, and extracts made of them by others; but that would be only in the less important arguments and the meaner sort of books; else distilled books are, like common distilled waters, flashy things. Reading maketh a full man; conference a ready man; and writing an exact man. And, therefore, if a man write little, he had need have a great memory; if he confer little, he had need have a present wit; and if he read little, he had need have much cunning, to seem to know that he doth not. Histories make men wise; poets, witty; the mathematics, subtle; natural philosophy, deep; moral, grave; logic and rhetoric, able to contend; *Abeunt studia in mores* [studies form manners]. Nay, there is no stand or impediment in the wit but may be wrought out by fit studies, like as diseases of the body may have appropriate exercises: bowling is good for the stone and reins, shooting for the lungs and breast, gentle walking for the stomach, riding for the head and the like. So if a man's wit be wandering, let him study the mathematics, for in demonstrations, if his wit be called away never so little, he must begin again. If his wit be not apt to distinguish or find differences, let him study the school-men, for they are *cymini sectores* [hairsplitters]. If he be not apt to beat over matters, and to call up one thing to prove and illustrate another, let him study the lawyers' cases: so every defect of the mind may have a special receipt.

JOSEPH ADDISON

❧ Poetic Justice

Ac ne forte putes me, quae facere ipse recusem,
cum recte tractent alii, laudare maligne;
ille per extentum funem mihi posse videtur
ire poeta, meum qui pectus inaniter angit,
irritat, mulcet, falsis terroribus implet,
ut magus, et modo me Thebis, modo ponit Athenis.[1]

HORACE

THE English writers of tragedy are possessed with a notion that when they represent a virtuous or innocent person in distress, they ought not to leave him till they have delivered him out of his troubles or made him triumph over his enemies. This error they have been led into by a ridiculous doctrine in modern criticism that they are obliged to an equal distribution of rewards and punishments, and an impartial execution of poetical justice. Who were the first that established this rule I know not, but I am sure it has no foundation in nature, in reason, or in the practice of the ancients. We find that good and evil happen alike to all men on this side the grave, and as the principal design of tragedy is to raise commiseration and terror in the minds of the audience, we shall defeat this great end if we always make virtue and innocence happy and successful. Whatever crosses and disappointments a good man suffers in the body of the tragedy, they will make but small impression on our minds when we know that in the last act he is to arrive at the end of his wishes and desires. When we see him engaged in the depth of his afflictions, we are apt to comfort ourselves because we are sure he will find his way out of them, and that his grief, how great soever it may be at present, will soon terminate in gladness. For this reason the ancient writers of tragedy treated men in their plays as they are dealt with in the world, by making virtue sometimes happy and sometimes miserable, as they found it in the fable which they made choice of, or as it might affect their audience in the most agreeable manner. Aristotle considers the tragedies that were written in either of these kinds, and observes that those

[1] And lest, perchance, you may think that I withhold praise
When others are handling well what I decline to try myself,
I think that poet is able to walk a tightrope
Who with airy nothings wrings my heart, inflames, soothes,
Fills it with vain alarms like a magician,
And sets me down now at Thebes, now at Athens.
EPISTLES II, 1:208–213. [Eds.]

which ended unhappily had always pleased the people and carried away the prize, in the public disputes of the stage, from those that ended happily. Terror and commiseration leave a pleasing anguish in the mind and fix the audience in such a serious composure of thought as is much more lasting and delightful than any little transient starts of joy and satisfaction. Accordingly we find that more of our English tragedies have succeeded in which the favorites of the audience sink under their calamities than those in which they recover themselves out of them. The best plays of this kind are *The Orphan* [by Thomas Otway], *Venice Preserved* [by Thomas Otway], *Alexander the Great, Theodosius, All for Love* [by John Dryden and Nathaniel Lee], *Oedipus* [by Dryden], *Oroonoko* [by Thomas Southerne], *Othello* [by William Shakespeare], etc. *King Lear* is an admirable tragedy of the same kind, as Shakespeare wrote it, but as it is reformed according to the chimerical notion of poetical justice, in my humble opinion it has lost half its beauty. At the same time I must allow that there are very noble tragedies which have been framed upon the other plan, and have ended happily, as indeed most of the good tragedies which have been written since the starting of the above-mentioned criticism have taken this turn, as *The Mourning Bride* [by William Congreve], *Tamerlane* [by Nicholas Rowe], *Ulysses, Phaedra and Hippolitus,* with most of Mr. Dryden's. I must also allow that many of Shakespeare's and several of the celebrated tragedies of antiquity are cast in the same form. I do not therefore dispute against this way of writing tragedies, but against the criticism that would establish this as the only method and by that means would very much cramp the English tragedy and perhaps give a wrong bent to the genius of our writers.

The tragicomedy, which is the product of the English theater, is one of the most monstrous inventions that ever entered into a poet's thoughts. An author might as well think of weaving the adventures of Aeneas and Hudibras into one poem as of writing such a motley piece of mirth and sorrow. But the absurdity of these performances is so very visible that I shall not insist upon it.

The same objections which are made to tragicomedy may in some measure be applied to all tragedies that have a double plot in them, which are likewise more frequent upon the English stage than upon any other. For though the grief of the audience in such performances be not changed into another passion, as in tragicomedies, it is diverted upon another object, which weakens their concern for the principal action and breaks the tide of sorrow by throwing it into different channels. This inconvenience, however, may in a great measure be cured, if not wholly removed, by the skillful choice of an underplot which may bear such a near relation to the principal design as to contribute towards the completion of it and be concluded by the same catastrophe.

There is also another particular which may be reckoned among the blemishes, or rather the false beauties, of our English tragedy: I mean those particular speeches which are commonly known by the name of *rants*. The warm and passionate parts of a tragedy are always the most taking with the audience, for which reason we often see the players pronouncing in all the violence of action several parts of the tragedy which the author writ with great temper and designed that they should have been so acted. I have seen Powell very often raise himself a loud clap by this artifice. The poets that were acquainted with this secret have given frequent occasion for such emotions in the actor by adding vehemence to words where there was no passion, or inflaming a real passion into fustian. This hath filled the mouths of our heroes with bombast and given them such sentiments as proceed rather from a swelling than a greatness of mind. Unnatural exclamations, curses, vows, blasphemies, a defiance of mankind, and an outraging of the gods frequently pass upon the audience for towering thoughts, and have accordingly met with infinite applause.

I shall here add a remark which I am afraid our tragic writers may make an ill use of. As our heroes are generally lovers, their swelling and blustering upon the stage very much recommends them to the fair part of their audience. The ladies are wonderfully pleased to see a man insulting kings or affronting the gods in one scene, and throwing himself at the feet of his mistress in another. Let him behave himself insolently towards the men and abjectly towards the fair one, and it is ten to one but he proves a favorite of the boxes. Dryden and Lee [1653?–1692; English actor and playwright], in several of their tragedies, have practiced this secret with good success.

But to show how a rant pleases beyond the most just and natural thought that is not pronounced with vehemence, I would desire the reader, when he sees the tragedy of *Oedipus,* to observe how quietly the hero is dismissed at the end of the third act, after having pronounced the following lines, in which the thought is very natural, and apt to move compassion:

> To you, good Gods, I make my last appeal;
> Or clear my Virtues, or my Crime reveal:
> If wandering in the maze of Fate I run,
> And backward trod the paths I sought to shun,
> Impute my Errors to your own Decree;
> My hands are guilty, but my heart is free.

Let us then observe with what thunderclaps of applause he leaves the stage after the impieties and execrations at the end of the fourth act, and you will wonder to see an audience so cursed and so pleased at the same time.

> O that, as oft I have at *Athens* seen
>   (Where, by the way, there was no stage till many years after Oedipus.)
> The Stage arise, and the big Clouds descend;
> So now in very deed I might behold
> The pond'rous Earth, and all yon marble Roof,
> Meet, like the hands of *Jove,* and crush Mankind:
>   For all the Elements, etc. . . .

RICHARD STEELE

❧ *On Story Telling*

Tom Lizard told us a story the other day, of some persons which our family know very well, with so much humour and life, that it caused a great deal of mirth at the tea-table. His brother Will, the Templar, was highly delighted with it, and the next day being with some of his inns-of-court acquaintances, resolved (whether out of the benevolence, or the pride of his heart, I will not determine) to entertain them with what he called "a pleasant humour enough." I was in great pain for him when I heard him begin, and was not at all surprised to find the company very little moved by it. Will blushed, looked round the room, and with a forced laugh, "Faith, gentlemen," said he, "I do not know what makes you look so grave, it was an admirable story when I heard it."

When I came home I fell into a profound contemplation upon story-telling, and as I have nothing so much at heart as the good of my country, I resolved to lay down some precautions upon this subject.

I have often thought that a story-teller is born, as well as a poet. It is, I think, certain, that some men have such a peculiar cast of mind, that they see things in another light, than men of grave dispositions. Men of a lively imagination, and a mirthful temper, will represent things to their hearers in the same manner as they themselves were affected with them; and whereas serious spirits might perhaps have been disgusted at the sight of some odd occurrences in life; yet the very same occurrences shall please them in a well-told story, where the disagreeable parts of the images are concealed, and those only which are pleasing exhibited to the fancy. Story-telling is therefore not an art, but what we call a "knack"; it doth not so much subsist upon wit as upon humour; and I will add, that it is not perfect without proper gesticulations of the body, which naturally attend such merry emotions of the mind. I know very well, that a certain gravity of countenance sets some stories off to advantage, where the hearer is to be surprised in the end; but this is by no means a general rule; for it is frequently convenient to aid and assist by cheerful looks, and whimsical agitations. I will go yet further, and affirm that the success of a story very often depends upon the make of the body, and formation of the features, of him who relates it. I have been of this opinion ever since I criticised upon the chin of Dick Dewlap. I very often had the weakness to repine at the prosperity of his conceits, which made him pass for a wit with the widow at the coffee-house, and the ordinary mechanics that frequent it; nor could I myself forbear laughing at them most heartily, though upon examination I thought most of them very flat and insipid. I found after some time, that the merit of his wit was founded upon the shaking of a fat paunch, and the tossing up of a pair of rosy jowls. Poor Dick had a fit of sickness, which robbed him of his fat and his fame at once; and it was full three months before he regained his reputation, which rose in proportion to his floridity. He is now very jolly and ingenious, and hath a good constitution for wit.

Those, who are thus adorned with the gifts of nature, are apt to shew their parts with too much ostentation: I would therefore advise all the professors of this art never to tell stories but as they seem to grow out of the subject-matter of the conversation, or as they serve to illustrate, or enliven it. Stories, that are very common, are generally irksome; but may be aptly introduced, provided they be only hinted at, and mentioned by way of allusion. Those, that are altogether new, should never be ushered in, without a short and pertinent character of the chief persons concerned; because, by that means, you make the company acquainted with them; and it is a certain rule, that slight and trivial accounts of those who are familiar to us administer more mirth, than the brightest points of wit in unknown characters. A little circumstance, in the complexion or dress of the man you are talking of, sets his image before the hearer, if it be chosen aptly for the story. Thus, I remember Tom Lizard, after having made his sisters merry with an account of a formal old man's way of complimenting, owned very frankly, that his story would not have been worth one farthing, if he had made the hat of him whom he represented one inch narrower. Besides the marking distinct characters, and selecting pertinent circumstances, it is likewise necessary to leave off in time, and end smartly. So that there is a kind of drama in the forming of a story, and the manner of conducting and pointing it, is the same as in an epigram. It is a miserable thing, after one hath raised the expectation of the company by humourous characters, and a pretty conceit, to pursue the matter too far. There is no retreating, and how poor it is for a story-teller to end his relation by saying, "that's all!"

As the choosing of pertinent circumstances is the life of a story, and that wherein humour principally consists; so the collectors of impertinent particulars are the very bane and opiates of conversation. Old men are great transgressors this way. Poor Ned Poppy,—he's gone—was a very honest man, but was so excessively tedious over his pipe, that he was not to be endured. He knew so exactly what they had for dinner, when such a thing happened; in what ditch his bay stone-horse [a horse not castrated, a stallion] had his sprain at that time, and how his man John,—no! it was William, started a hare in the common-field; that he never got to the end of his tale. Then he was extremely particular in marriages and inter-marriages, and cousins twice or thrice removed; and whether such a thing happened at the latter end of July, or the beginning of August. He had a marvellous tendency likewise to digressions; insomuch that if a considerable person was mentioned in his story, he would straightway launch out into an episode on him; and again, if in that person's story he had occasion to remember a third man, he broke off, and gave us his history, and so on. He always put me in mind of what Sir William Temple informs us of the tale-tellers in the north of Ireland, who are hired to tell stories of giants and enchanters to lull people asleep. These historians are obliged, by their bargain, to go on without stopping; so that after the patient hath by this benefit enjoyed a long nap, he is sure to find the operator proceeding in his work. Ned procured the like effect in me the last time I was with him. As he was in the third hour of his story, and very thankful that his memory did not fail him, I fairly nodded in the elbow chair. He was much affronted at this, till I told him, "Old friend, you have your infirmity, and I have mine."

But of all evils in story-telling, the humour of telling tales one after another, in great numbers, is the least supportable. Sir Harry Pandolf and his son gave my lady Lizard great offence in this particular. Sir Harry hath what they call a string of stories, which he tells over every Christmas. When our family visits there, we are constantly, after supper, entertained with the Glastonbury Thorn.[2] When we have wondered at that a little, "Ay, but, father," saith the son, "let us have the spirit in the wood." After that hath been laughed at, "Ay, but, father," cries the booby again, "tell us how you served the robber." "Alack-a-day," said Sir Harry, with a smile, and rubbing his forehead, "I have almost forgot that: but it is a pleasant conceit, to be sure." Accordingly he tells that and twenty more in the same independent order; and without the least varia-tion, at this day, as he hath done, to my knowledge, ever since the [Crom-wellian] revolution. I must not forget a very odd compliment that Sir Harry always makes my lady when he dines here. After dinner he strokes his belly, and says with a feigned concern in his countenance, "Madam, I have lost by you to-day." "How so, Sir Harry," replies my lady. "Madam," says he, "I have lost an excellent stomach." At this, his son and heir laughs immoderately, and winks upon Mrs. Annabella. This is the thirty-third time that Sir Harry hath been thus arch, and I can bear it no longer.

As the telling of stories is a great help and life to conversation, I always encourage them, if they are pertinent and innocent; in opposition to those gloomy mortals, who disdain everything but matter of fact. Those grave fellows are my aversion, who sift every thing with the utmost nicety, and find the malignity of a lie in a piece of humour, pushed a little beyond exact truth. I likewise have a poor opinion of those, who have got a trick of keeping a steady countenance, that cock their hats, and look glum when a pleasant thing is said, and ask, "Well! and what then?" Men of wit and parts should treat one another with benevolence: and I will lay it down as a maxim, that if you seem to have a good opinion of another man's wit, he will allow you to have judgment.

2 Glastonbury is a town and borough of Somersetshire, England. Legend holds that Joseph of Arimathea planted at Glastonbury a thorn of a distinct variety, flowering twice a year. Specimens of this variety do exist in various parts of England. [Eds.]

HENRY FIELDING

❧ *Preface to* Joseph Andrews

As IT IS possible the mere English reader may have a different idea of romance from the author of these little[3] volumes, and may consequently expect a kind of entertainment not to be found, nor which was even intended, in the following pages, it may not be improper to premise a few words concerning this kind of writing, which I do not remember to have seen hitherto attempted in our language.

The EPIC, as well as the DRAMA, is divided into tragedy and comedy. HOMER, who was the father of this species of poetry, gave us a pattern of both these, though that of the latter kind is entirely lost; which Aristotle tells us, bore the same relation to comedy which his *Iliad* bears to tragedy. And perhaps, that we have no more instances of it among the writers of antiquity, is owing to the loss of this great pattern, which, had it survived, would have found its imitators equally with the other poems of this great original.

And farther, as this poetry may be tragic or comic, I will not scruple to say it may be likewise either in verse or prose: for though it wants one particular, which the critic enumerates in the constituent parts of an epic poem, namely metre; yet, when any kind of writing contains all its other parts, such as fable, action, characters, sentiments, and diction, and is deficient in metre only, it seems, I think, reasonable to refer it to the epic; at least, as no critic hath thought proper to range it under any other head, or to assign it a particular name to itself.

Thus the Telemachus of the archbishop of Cambray[4] appears to me of the epic kind, as well as the Odyssey of Homer; indeed, it is much fairer and more reasonable to give it a name common with that species from which it differs only in a single instance, than to confound it with those which it resembles in no other. Such are those voluminous works, commonly called romances, namely, *Cledia, Cleopatra* [by La Calprenède], *Astraea, Cassandra* [by La Calprenède], the *Grand Cyrus*,[5] and innumerable others, which contain, as I apprehend, very little instruction or entertainment.

Now, a comic romance is a comic epic poem in prose; differing from comedy, as the serious epic from tragedy: its action being more extended and

---

[3] Originally, *Joseph Andrews* was published in two volumes. [Eds.]
[4] François Fénelon (1651–1715): *Télémaque.* [Eds.]
[5] *Artamène ou le Grand Cyrus,* by Mlle. Madeleine de Scudéry (1607–1701), was the most popular of the French romances. [Eds.]

comprehensive; containing a much larger circle of incidents, and introducing a greater variety of characters. It differs from the serious romance in its fable and action, in this; that as in the one these are grave and solemn, so in the other they are light and ridiculous: it differs in its characters by introducing persons of inferior rank, and consequently, of inferior manners, whereas the grave romance sets the highest before us: lastly, in its sentiments and diction; by preserving the ludicrous instead of the sublime. In the diction, I think burlesque itself may be sometimes admitted; of which many instances will occur in this work, as in the description of the battles, and some other places, not necessary to be pointed out to the classical reader, for whose entertainment those parodies or burlesque imitations are chiefly calculated.

But though we have sometimes admitted this in our diction, we have carefully excluded it from our sentiments and characters; for there it is never properly introduced, unless in writings of the burlesque kind, which this is not intended to be. Indeed, no two species of writing can differ more widely than the comic and the burlesque; for as the latter is ever the exhibition of what is monstrous and unnatural, and where our delight, if we examine it, arises from the surprising absurdity, as in appropriating the manners of the highest to the lowest, or *è converso* [in reverse]; so in the former we should ever confine ourselves strictly to nature, from the just imitation of which will flow all the pleasure we can this way convey to a sensible reader. And perhaps there is one reason why a comic writer should of all others be the least excused for deviating from nature, since it may not be always so easy for a serious poet to meet with the great and the admirable; but life everywhere furnishes an accurate observer with the ridiculous.

I have hinted this little concerning burlesque, because I have often heard that name given to performances which have been truly of the comic kind, from the author's having sometimes admitted it in his diction only; which, as it is the dress of poetry, doth, like the dress of men, establish characters (the one of the whole poem, and the other of the whole man), in vulgar opinion, beyond any of their greater excellences: but surely, a certain drollery in style, where characters and sentiments are perfectly natural, no more constitutes the burlesque, than an empty pomp and dignity of words, where everything else is mean and low, can entitle any performance to the appellation of the true sublime.

And I apprehend my Lord Shaftesbury's opinion of mere burlesque agrees with mine, when he asserts, There is no such thing to be found in the writings of the ancients. But perhaps I have less abhorrence than he professes for it; and that, not because I have had some little success on the stage this way, but rather as it contributes more to exquisite mirth and laughter than any other; and these are probably more wholesome physic for the mind, and conduce better to purge away spleen, melancholy, and ill affections, than is generally imagined. Nay, I will appeal to common observation, whether the same companies are not found more full of good-humour and benevolence, after they have been sweetened for two or three hours with entertainments of this kind, than when soured by a tragedy or a grave lecture.

But to illustrate all this by another science, in which, perhaps, we shall see the distinction more clearly and plainly, let us examine the works of a comic history painter, with those performances which the Italians call *Caricatura*, where we shall find the true excellence of the former to consist in the exactest copying of nature; insomuch that a judicious eye instantly rejects anything *outré*, any liberty which the painter hath taken with the features of that *alma mater*; whereas in the *Caricatura* we allow all license—its aim is to exhibit monsters, not men; and all distortions and exaggerations whatever are within its proper province.

Now, what *Caricatura* is in painting, Burlesque is in writing; and in the same manner the comic writer and painter correlate to each other. And here I shall observe, that, as in the former the painter seems to have the advantage; so it is in the latter infinitely on the side of the writer; for the *Monstrous* is much easier to paint than describe, and the *Ridiculous* to describe than paint.

And though perhaps this latter species doth not in either science so strongly affect and agitate the muscles as the other; yet it will be owned, I believe, that a more rational and useful pleasure arises to us from it. He who should call the ingenious Hogarth a burlesque painter, would, in my opinion, do him very little honour; for sure it is much easier, much less the subject of admiration, to paint a man with a nose, or any other feature, of a preposterous size, or to expose him in some absurd or monstrous attitude, than to express the affections of men on canvas. It hath been thought a vast commendation of a painter to say his figures *seem to breathe*; but surely it is a much greater and nobler applause, *that they appear to think*.

But to return. The ridiculous only, as I have before said, falls within my province in the present work. Nor will some explanation of this word be thought impertinent by the reader, if he considers how wonderfully it hath been mistaken, even by writers who have professed it: for to what but such a mistake can we attribute the many attempts to ridicule the blackest villainies, and, what is yet worse, the most dreadful calamities? What could exceed the absurdity of an author, who should write *the Comedy of Nero, with the merry Incident of ripping up his Mother's Belly?* or what would give a greater shock to humanity than an attempt to expose the miseries of poverty and distress to ridicule? And yet the reader will not want much learning to suggest such instances to himself.

Besides, it may seem remarkable, that Aristotle, who is so fond and free of definitions, hath not thought proper to define the Ridiculous. Indeed, where he tells us it is proper to comedy, he hath remarked that villainy is not its object: but he hath not, as I remember, positively asserted what is. Nor doth the Abbé Bellegarde, who hath written a treatise on this subject, though he shows us many species of it, once trace it to its fountain.

The only source of the true Ridiculous (as it appears to me) is affectation.

But though it arises from one spring only, when we consider the infinite streams into which this one branches, we shall presently cease to admire at the copious field it affords to an observer. Now, affectation proceeds from one of these two causes, vanity or hypocrisy: for as vanity puts us on affecting false characters, in order to purchase applause; so hypocrisy sets us on an endeavour to avoid censure, by concealing our vices under an appearance of their opposite virtues. And though these two causes are often confounded (for there is some difficulty in distinguishing them), yet, as they proceed from very different motives, so they are as clearly distinct in their operations: for indeed, the affectation which arises from vanity is nearer to truth than the other, as it hath not that violent repugnancy of nature to struggle with, which that of the hypocrite hath. It may be likewise noted, that affectation doth not imply an absolute negation of those qualities which are affected; and, therefore, though, when it proceeds from hypocrisy, it be nearly allied to deceit; yet when it comes from vanity only, it partakes of the nature of ostentation: for instance, the affectation of liberality in a vain man differs visibly from the same affectation in the avaricious; for though the vain man is not what he would appear, or hath not the virtue he affects, to the degree he would be thought to have it; yet it sits less awkwardly on him than on the avaricious man, who is the very reverse of what he would *seem* to be.

From the discovery of this affectation arises the Ridiculous, which always strikes the reader with surprise and pleasure; and that in a higher and stronger degree when the affectation arises from hypocrisy, than when from vanity; for to discover any one to be the exact reverse of what he affects, is more surprising, and consequently more ridiculous, than to find him a little deficient in the quality he desires the reputation of. I might observe that our Ben Jonson, who of all men understood the Ridiculous the best, hath chiefly used the hypocritical affectation.

Now, from affectation only, the misfortunes and calamities of life, or the imperfection of nature, may become the objects of ridicule. Surely he hath a very ill-framed mind who can look on ugliness, infirmity, or poverty, as ridiculous in themselves: nor do I believe any man living, who meets a dirty fellow riding through the streets in a cart, is struck with an idea of the Ridiculous from it; but if he should see the same figure descend from his coach and six, or bolt from his chair with his hat under his arm, he would then begin to laugh, and with justice. In the same manner, were we to enter a poor house and behold a wretched family shivering with cold and languishing with hunger, it would not incline us to laughter (at least we must have very diabolical natures if it would); but should we discover there a grate, instead of coals, adorned with flowers, empty plate or china dishes on the sideboard, or any other affectation of riches and finery, either on their persons or in their furniture, we might then indeed be excused for ridiculing so fantastical an appearance. Much less are natural imperfections the object of derision; but when ugliness aims at the applause of beauty, or lameness endeavours to display agility, it is then that these unfortunate circumstances, which at first moved our compassion, tend only to raise our mirth.

The poet carries this very far:

> None are for being what they are in fault,
> But for not being what they would be thought.[6]

Where if the metre would suffer the word ridiculous to close the first line, the thought would be rather more proper. Great vices are the proper objects of our destestation, smaller faults, of our pity; but affectation appears to me the only true source of the ridiculous.

But perhaps it may be objected to me, that I have against my own rules introduced vices, and of a very black kind, into this work. To which I shall answer: first, that it is very difficult to pursue a series of human actions, and keep clear from them. Secondly, that the vices to be found here are rather the accidental consequences of some human frailty or foible, than causes habitually existing in the mind. Thirdly, that they are never set forth as the objects of ridicule, but detestation. Fourthly, that they are never the principal figure at that time on the scene: and, lastly, they never produce the intended evil.

Having thus distinguished *Joseph Andrews* from the productions of romance writers on the one hand and burlesque writers on the other, and given some few very short hints (for I intended no more) of this species of writing, which I have affirmed to be hitherto unattempted in our language; I shall leave to my good-natured reader to apply my piece to my observations, and will detain him no longer than with a word concerning the characters in this work.

And here I solemnly protest I have no intention to vilify or asperse any one; for though everything is copied from the book of nature, and scarce a character or action produced which I have not taken from my own observations and experience; yet I have used the utmost care to obscure the persons by such different circumstances, degrees, and colours, that it will be impossible to guess at them with any degree of certainty; and if it ever happens otherwise, it is only where the failure characterised is so minute, that it is a foible only which the party himself may laugh at as well as any other.

As to the character of Adams, as it is the most glaring in the whole, so I conceive it is not to be found in any book now extant. It is designed a character of perfect simplicity; and as the goodness of his heart will recommend him to the good-natured, so I hope it will excuse me to the gentlemen of his cloth; for whom, while they are worthy of their sacred order, no man can possibly have a greater respect. They will therefore excuse me, notwithstanding the low adventures in which he is engaged, that I have made him a clergyman; since no other office could have given him so many opportunities of displaying his worthy inclinations.

[6] William Congreve: "Of Pleasing." [Eds.]

SAMUEL JOHNSON

❧ *The Novel and Morality**

Simul et jucunda et idonea dicere vitae.[7]

HORACE [*Ars Poetica*]

And join both profit and delight in one.

CREECH

1 THE WORKS of fiction with which the present generation seems more particularly delighted are such as exhibit life in its true state, diversified only by accidents that daily happen in the world, and influenced by passions and qualities which are really to be found in conversing with mankind.

2 This kind of writing may be termed not improperly the comedy of romance, and is to be conducted nearly by the rules of comic poetry. Its province is to bring about natural events by easy means and keep up curiosity without the help of wonder; it is therefore precluded from the machines and expedients of the heroic romance, and can neither employ giants to snatch away a lady from the nuptial rites nor knights to bring her back from captivity; it can neither bewilder its personages in deserts nor lodge them in imaginary castles.

3 I remember a remark made by Scaliger upon Pontanus, that all his writings are filled with the same images and that if you take from him his lilies and his roses, his satyrs and his dryads, he will have nothing left that can be called poetry. In like manner almost all the fictions of the last age will vanish if you deprive them of a hermit and a wood, a battle and a shipwreck.

4 Why this wild strain of imagination found reception so long in polite and learned ages it is not easy to conceive, but we cannot wonder that, while readers could be procured, the authors were willing to continue it, for when a man had by practice gained some fluency of language, he had no further care than to retire to his closet, let loose his invention, and heat his mind with incredibilities; a book was thus produced without fear of criticism, without the toil of study, without knowledge of nature or acquaintance with life.

5 The task of our present writers is very different; it requires, together with that learning which is to be gained from books, that experience which can never be attained by solitary diligence but must arise from general converse and accurate observation of the living world. Their performances have, as Horace

* Editor's title.
7 To speak of life is at once both pleasant and fit. [Eds.]

expresses it, *plus oneris quanto veniae minus,* little indulgence, and therefore more difficulty. They are engaged in portraits of which everyone knows the original and can detect any deviation from exactness of resemblance. Other writings are safe, except from the malice of learning, but these are in danger from every common reader, as the slipper ill executed was censured by a shoemaker who happened to stop in his way at the Venus of Apelles.

⁶ But the danger of not being approved as just copiers of human manners is not the most important concern that an author of this sort ought to have before him. These books are written chiefly to the young, the ignorant, and the idle, to whom they serve as lectures of conduct and introductions into life. They are the entertainment of minds unfurnished with ideas and therefore easily susceptible of impressions, not fixed by principles and therefore easily following the current of fancy, not informed by experience and consequently open to every false suggestion and partial account.

⁷ That the highest degree of reverence should be paid to youth and that nothing indecent should be suffered to approach their eyes or ears are precepts extorted by sense and virtue from an ancient writer by no means eminent for chastity of thought. The same kind, though not the same degree of caution, is required in everything which is laid before them, to secure them from unjust prejudices, perverse opinions, and incongruous combinations of images.

⁸ In the romances formerly written, every transaction and sentiment was so remote from all that passes among men that the reader was in very little danger of making any applications to himself. The virtues and crimes were equally beyond his sphere of activity, and he amused himself with heroes and with traitors, deliverers and persecutors, as with beings of another species, whose actions were regulated upon motives of their own and who had neither faults nor excellencies in common with himself.

⁹ But when an adventurer is leveled with the rest of the world and acts in such scenes of the universal drama as may be the lot of any other man, young spectators fix their eyes upon him with closer attention and hope by observing his behavior and success to regulate their own practices when they shall be engaged in the like part.

¹⁰ For this reason these familiar histories may perhaps be made of greater use than the solemnities of professed morality, and convey the knowledge of vice and virtue with more efficacy than axioms and definitions. But if the power of example is so great as to take possession of the memory by a kind of violence, and produce effects almost without the intervention of the will, care ought to be taken that, when the choice is unrestrained, the best examples only should be exhibited, and that which is likely to operate so strongly should not be mischievous, or uncertain in its effects.

¹¹ The chief advantage which these fictions have over real life is that their authors are at liberty, though not to invent, yet to select objects and to cull from the mass of mankind those individuals upon which the attention ought most to be employed, as a diamond, though it cannot be made, may be polished

by art and placed in such a situation as to display that luster which before was buried among common stones.

12 It is justly considered as the greatest excellency of art to imitate nature, but it is necessary to distinguish those parts of nature which are most proper for imitation. Greater care is still required in representing life, which is so often discolored by passion or deformed by wickedness. If the world be promiscuously described, I cannot see of what use it can be to read the account or why it may not be as safe to turn the eye immediately upon mankind, as upon a mirror which shows all that presents itself without discrimination.

13 It is therefore not a sufficient vindication of a character that it is drawn as it appears, for many characters ought never to be drawn; nor of a narrative, that the train of events is agreeable to observation and experience, for that observation which is called knowledge of the world will be found much more frequently to make men cunning than good. The purpose of these writings is surely not only to show mankind, but to provide that they may be seen hereafter with less hazard; to teach the means of avoiding the snares which are laid by Treachery for Innocence, without infusing any wish for that superiority with which the betrayer flatters his vanity; to give the power of counteracting fraud, without the temptation to practice it; to initiate youth by mock encounters in the art of necessary defense; and to increase prudence without impairing virtue.

14 Many writers for the sake of following nature so mingle good and bad qualities in their principal personages that they are both equally conspicuous, and as we accompany them through their adventures with delight, and are led by degrees to interest ourselves in their favor, we lose the abhorrence of their faults because they do not hinder our pleasure, or, perhaps, regard them with some kindness for being united with so much merit.

15 There have been men indeed splendidly wicked whose endowments threw a brightness on their crimes and whom scarce any villainy made perfectly detestable, because they never could be wholly divested of their excellencies; but such have been in all ages the great corrupters of the world, and their resemblance ought no more to be preserved than the art of murdering without pain.

16 Some have advanced, without due attention to the consequences of this notion, that certain virtues have their correspondent faults and therefore that to exhibit either apart is to deviate from probability. Thus men are observed by Swift to be "grateful in the same degree as they are resentful." This principle, with others of the same kind, supposes man to act from a brute impulse and pursue a certain degree of inclination without any choice of the object, for otherwise, though it should be allowed that gratitude and resentment arise from the same constitution of the passions, it follows not that they will be equally indulged when reason is consulted; yet unless that consequence be admitted, this sagacious maxim becomes an empty sound, without any relation to practice or to life.

17 Nor is it evident that even the first motions to these effects are always in the same proportion. For pride, which produces quickness of resentment, will

frequently obstruct gratitude by unwillingness to admit that inferiority which obligation implies; and it is very unlikely that he who cannot think he receives a favor will ever acknowledge or repay it.

¹⁸ It is of the utmost importance to mankind that positions of this tendency should be laid open and confuted, for while men consider good and evil as springing from the same root, they will spare the one for the sake of the other, and in judging, if not of others at least of themselves, will be apt to estimate their virtues by their vices. To this fatal error all those will contribute who confound the colors of right and wrong, and instead of helping to settle their boundaries, mix them with so much art that no common mind is able to disunite them.

¹⁹ In narratives where historical veracity has no place I cannot discover why there should not be exhibited the most perfect idea of virtue, of virtue not angelical, nor above probability, for what we cannot credit we shall never imitate, but the highest and purest that humanity can reach, which, exercised in such trials as the various revolutions of things shall bring upon it, may, by conquering some calamities and enduring others, teach us what we may hope and what we can perform. Vice (for vice is necessary to be shown) should always disgust, nor should the graces of gaiety or the dignity of courage be so united with it as to reconcile it to the mind. Wherever it appears, it should raise hatred by the malignity of its practices, and contempt by the meanness of its stratagems, for while it is supported by either parts or spirit, it will be seldom heartily abhorred. The Roman tyrant was content to be hated if he was but feared, and there are thousands of the readers of romances willing to be thought wicked if they may be allowed to be wits. It is therefore to be steadily inculcated that virtue is the highest proof of understanding and the only solid basis of greatness, and that vice is the natural consequence of narrow thoughts, that it begins in mistake and ends in ignominy.

WILLIAM WORDSWORTH

❧ The Language of Poetry

THE principal object . . . proposed in these Poems was to choose incidents and situations from common life, and to relate or describe them, throughout, as far as was possible, in a selection of language really used by men, and, at the same time, to throw over them a certain colouring of imagination, whereby ordinary things should be presented to the mind in an unusual aspect; and further, and above all, to make these incidents and situations interesting by tracing in them, truly though not ostentatiously, the primary laws of our nature: chiefly, as far as regards the manner in which we associate ideas in a state of excitement. Humble and rustic life was generally chosen, because, in that condition, the essential passions of the heart find a better soil in which they can attain their maturity, are less under restraint, and speak a plainer and more emphatic language; because in that condition of life our elementary feelings co-exist in a state of great simplicity, and, consequently, may be more accurately contemplated, and more forcibly communicated; because the manners of rural life germinate from those elementary feelings, and, from the necessary character of rural occupations, are more easily comprehended, and are more durable; and, lastly, because in that condition the passions of men are incorporated with the beautiful and permanent forms of nature. The language, too, of these men has been adopted (purified indeed from what appear to be its real defects, from all lasting and rational causes of dislike or disgust) because such men hourly communicate with the best objects from which the best part of language is originally derived; and because, from their rank in society and the sameness and narrow circle of their intercourse, being less under the influence of social vanity, they convey their feelings and notions in simple and unelaborated expressions. Accordingly, such a language, arising out of repeated experience and regular feelings, is a more permanent, and a far more philosophical language than that which is frequently substituted for it by poets, who think that they are conferring honor upon themselves and their art, in proportion as they separate themselves from the sympathies of men, and indulge in arbitrary and capricious habits of expression, in order to furnish food for fickle tastes, and fickle appetites, of their own creation.

I cannot, however, be insensible to the present outcry against the triviality and meanness, both of thought and language, which some of my contemporaries have occasionally introduced into their metrical compositions; and I acknowledge that this defect, where it exists, is more dishonorable to the writer's own character than false refinement or arbitrary innovation, though I should contend at the same time it is far less pernicious in the sum of its consequences. From such verses the poems in these volumes will be found distinguished at least by one mark of difference, that each of them has a worthy *purpose*. Not that I always began to write with a distinct purpose formally conceived; but habits of meditation have, I trust, so prompted and regulated my feelings, that my descriptions of such objects as strongly excite those feelings will be found to carry along with them a *purpose*. If this opinion be erroneous, I can have little right to the name of a poet. For all good poetry is the spontaneous overflow of powerful feelings: and though this be true, poems to which any value can be attached were never produced on any variety of subjects but by a man who, being possessed of more than usual organic sensibility, had also thought long and deeply. For our continued influxes of feeling are modified and directed by our thoughts, which are indeed the representatives of all our past feelings; and, as by contemplating the relation of these general representatives to each other, we discover what is really important to men, so, by the repetition and continuance of this act, our feelings will be connected with important subjects, till at length, if we be originally possessed of much sensibility, such habits of mind will be produced that, by obeying blindly and mechanically the impulses of those habits, we shall describe objects, and utter sentiments, of such a nature, and in such connection with each other, that the understanding of the reader must necessarily be in some degree enlightened, and his affections strengthened and purified.

It has been said that each of these poems has a purpose. Another circumstance must be mentioned which distinguishes these poems from the popular poetry of the day; it is this, that the feeling therein developed gives importance to the action and situation, and not the action and situation to the feeling.

SAMUEL TAYLOR COLERIDGE

❦ Occasion of the Lyrical Ballads

DURING the first year that Mr. Wordsworth and I were neighbours, our conversations turned frequently on the two cardinal points of poetry, the power of exciting the sympathy of the reader by a faithful adherence to the truth of nature, and the power of giving the interest of novelty by the modifying colors of imagination. The sudden charm, which accidents of light and shade, which moon-light or sun-set diffused over a known and familiar landscape, appeared to represent the practicability of combining both. These are the poetry of nature. The thought suggested itself (to which of us I do not recollect) that a series of poems might be composed of two sorts. In the one, the incidents and agents were to be, in part at least, supernatural; and the excellence aimed at was to consist in the interesting of the affections by the dramatic truth of such emotions, as would naturally accompany such situations, supposing them real. And real in *this* sense they have been to every human being who, from whatever source of delusion, has at any time believed himself under supernatural agency. For the second class, subjects were to be chosen from ordinary life; the characters and incidents were to be such, as will be found in every village and its vicinity, where there is a meditative and feeling mind to seek after them, or to notice them, when they present themselves.

In this idea originated the plan of the "Lyrical Ballads"; in which it was agreed, that my endeavours should be directed to persons and characters supernatural, or at least romantic; yet so as to transfer from our inward nature a human interest and a semblance of truth sufficient to procure for these shadows of imagination that willing suspension of disbelief for the moment, which constitutes poetic faith. Mr. Wordsworth, on the other hand, was to propose to himself as his object, to give the charm of novelty to things of every day, and to excite a feeling analogous to the supernatural, by awakening the mind's attention from the lethargy of custom, and directing it to the loveliness and the wonders of the world before us; an inexhaustible treasure, but for which, in consequence of the film of familiarity and selfish solicitude, we have eyes, yet see not, ears that hear not, and hearts that neither feel nor understand.

With this view I wrote "The Ancient Mariner," and was preparing among other poems, "The Dark Ladie," and the "Christabel," in which I should have more nearly realized my ideal, than I had done in my first attempt. But Mr. Wordsworth's industry had proved so much more successful, and the number of his poems so much greater, that my compositions, instead of forming a balance, appeared rather an interpolation of heterogeneous matter. Mr. Wordsworth added two or three poems written in his own character, in the impassioned, lofty, and sustained diction, which is characteristic of his genius. In this form the "Lyrical Ballads" were published; and were presented by him, as an *experiment*, whether subjects, which from their nature rejected the usual ornaments and extra-colloquial style of poems in general, might not be so managed in the language of ordinary life as to produce the pleasureable interest, which it is the peculiar business of poetry to impart. To the second edition he added a preface of considerable length; in which, notwithstanding some passages of apparently a contrary import, he was understood to contend for the extension of this style to poetry of all kinds, and to reject as vicious and indefensible all phrases and forms of style that were not included in what he (unfortunately, I think, adopting an equivocal expression) called the language of *real* life. From this preface, prefixed to poems in which it was impossible to deny the presence of original genius, however mistaken its direction might be deemed, arose the whole long-continued controversy. For from the conjunction of perceived power with supposed heresy I explain the inveteracy and in some instances, I grieve to say, the acrimonious passions, with which the controversy has been conducted by the assailants.

Had Mr. Wordsworth's poems been the silly, the childish things, which they were for a long time described as being; had they been really distinguished from the compositions of other poets merely by meanness of language and inanity of thought; had they indeed contained nothing more than what is found in the parodies and pretended imitations of them; they must have sunk at once, a dead weight, into the slough of oblivion, and have dragged the preface along with them. But year after year increased the number of Mr. Wordsworth's admirers. They were found too not in the lower classes of the reading public, but chiefly among young men of strong sensibility and meditative minds; and their admiration (inflamed perhaps in some degree by opposition) was distinguished by its intensity, I might almost say, by its *religious* fervor. These facts, and the intellectual energy of the author, which was more or less consciously felt, where it was outwardly and even boisterously denied, meeting with sentiments of aversion to his opinions, and of alarm at their consequences, produced an eddy of criticism, which would of itself have borne up the poems by the violence, with which it whirled them round and round. With many parts of this preface, in the sense attributed to them, and which the words undoubtedly seem to authorize, I never concurred; but on the contrary objected to them as erroneous in principle, and as contradictory (in appearance at least) both to other parts of the same preface, and to the author's own practice in the greater number of the poems themselves. Mr. Wordsworth in his recent collection has, I find, degraded this prefatory disquisition to the end of his second volume, to be read or not at the reader's choice. But he has not, as far as I can discover, announced any change in his poetic creed. At all events, considering it as the source of a controversy, in which I have been honored more than I deserve by the frequent conjunction of my name with his, I think it expedient to declare once for all, in what points I coincide with his opinions, and in what points I altogether differ. But in order to render myself intelligible I must previously, in as few words as possible, explain my ideas, first, of a poem; and secondly, of poetry itself, in *kind*, and in *essence*.

The office of philosophical *disquisition* consists in just *distinction*; while it is the privilege of the philosopher to preserve himself constantly aware, that distinction is not division. In order to obtain adequate notions of any truth, we must intellectually separate its distinguishable parts; and this is the technical *process* of philosophy. But having so done, we must then restore them in our conceptions to the unity, in which they actually co-exist; and this is the *result* of philosophy. A poem contains the same elements as a prose composition; the difference therefore must consist in a different combination of them, in consequence of a different object being proposed. According to the difference of the object will be the difference of the combination. It is possible, that the object may be merely to facilitate the recollection of any given facts or observations by artificial arrangement; and the composition will be a poem, merely because it is distinguished from prose by metre, or by rhyme, or by both conjointly. In this, the lowest sense, a man might attribute the name of a poem to the well-known enumeration of the days in the several months;

> "Thirty days hath September,
> April, June, and November," &c.

and others of the same class and purpose. And as a particular pleasure is found in anticipating the recurrence of sounds and quantities, all compositions that have this charm super-added, whatever be their contents, *may* be entitled poems.

So much for the superficial *form*. A difference of object and contents supplies an additional ground of distinction. The immediate purpose may be the communication of truths; either of truth absolute and demonstrable, as in works of science; or of facts experienced and recorded, as in history. Pleasure, and that of the highest and most permanent kind, may *result* from the *attainment* of the end; but it is not itself the immediate end. In other works the communication of pleasure may be the immediate purpose; and though truth, either moral or intellectual, ought to be the *ultimate* end, yet this will distinguish the character of the author, not the class to which the work belongs. Blest indeed is that state of society, in which the immediate purpose would be baffled by the perversion of the proper ultimate end; in which no charm of diction or imagery could exempt the Bathyllus [beautiful youth of Samos] even of an Anacreon, or the Alexis of Virgil, from disgust and aversion!

But the communication of pleasure may be the immediate object of a work not metrically composed; and that object may have been in a high degree attained, as in novels and romances. Would then the mere superaddition of metre, with or without rhyme, entitle *these* to the name of poems? The answer is, that nothing can permanently please, which does not contain in itself the reason why it is so, and not otherwise. If metre be superadded, all other parts must be made consonant with it. They must be such, as to justify the perpetual and distinct attention to each part, which an exact correspondent recurrence of accent and sound are calculated to excite. The final definition then, so deduced, may be thus worded. A poem is that species of composition, which is opposed to works of science, by proposing for its *immediate* object pleasure, not truth; and from all other species (having *this* object in common with it) it is discriminated by proposing to itself such delight from the *whole*, as is compatible with a distinct gratification from each component *part*.

Controversy is not seldom excited in consequence of the disputants attaching each a different meaning to the same word; and in few instances has this been more striking, than in disputes concerning the present subject. If a man chooses to call every composition a poem, which is rhyme, or measure, or both, I must leave his opinion uncontroverted. The distinction is at least competent to characterize the writer's intention. If it were subjoined, that the whole is likewise entertaining or affecting, as a tale, or as a series of interesting reflections, I of course admit this as another fit ingredient of a poem, and an additional merit. But if the definition sought for be that of a *legitimate* poem, I answer, it must be one, the parts of which mutually support and explain each other; all in their proportion harmonizing with, and supporting the purpose and known influences of metrical arrangement. The philosophic critics of all ages coincide with the ultimate judgement of all countries, in equally denying the praises of a just poem, on the one hand, to a series of striking lines or distichs, each of which, absorbing the whole attention of the reader to itself, disjoins it from its context, and makes it a separate whole, instead of an harmonizing part; and on the other hand, to an unsustained composition, from which the reader collects rapidly the general result, unattracted by the component parts. The reader should be carried forward, not merely or chiefly by the mechanical impulse of curiosity, or by a restless desire to arrive at the final solution; but by the pleasurable activity of mind excited by the attractions of the journey itself. Like the motion of a serpent, which the Egyptians made the emblem of intellectual power; or like the path of sound through the air; at every step he pauses and half recedes, and from the retrogressive movement collects the force which again carries him onward. "Praecipitandus *est liber* spiritus [a free mind is a hastening one]," says Petronius Arbiter [Roman exquisite of first century A.D.] most happily. The epithet, *liber*, here balances the preceding verb; and it is not easy to conceive more meaning condensed in fewer words.

But if this should be admitted as a satisfactory character of a poem, we have still to seek for a definition of poetry. The writings of Plato, and Bishop Taylor, and the "Theoria Sacra" [*The Sacred Theory of the Earth*] of Burnet [1635?–1715; English divine and author], furnish undeniable proofs that poetry of the highest kind may exist without metre, and even without the contra-distinguishing objects of a poem. The first chapter of Isaiah (indeed a very large portion of the whole book) is poetry in the most emphatic sense; yet it would be not less irrational than strange to assert, that pleasure, and not truth, was the immediate object of the prophet. In short, whatever *specific* import we attach to the word, poetry, there will be found involved in it, as a necessary consequence, that a poem of any length neither can be, or ought to be, all poetry. Yet if an harmonious whole is to be produced, the remaining parts must be preserved *in keeping* with the poetry; and this can be no otherwise effected than by such a studied selection and artificial arrangement, as will partake of *one*, though not a *peculiar* property of poetry. And this again can be no other than the property of exciting a more continuous and equal attention than the language of prose aims at, whether colloquial or written.

My own conclusions on the nature of poetry, in the strictest use of the word, have been in part anticipated in the preceding disquisition on the fancy and imagination. What is poetry? is so nearly the same question with, what is a poet? that the answer to the one is involved in the solution of the other. For it is a distinction resulting from the poetic genius itself, which sustains and modifies the images, thoughts, and emotions of the poet's own mind.

The poet, described in *ideal* perfection, brings the whole soul of man into activity, with the subordination of its faculties to each other, according to their relative worth and dignity. He diffuses a tone and spirit of unity, that blends, and (as it were) *fuses*, each into each, by that synthetic and magical power, to which we have exclusively appropriated the name of imagination. This power, first put in action by the will and understanding, and retained under their irremissive, though gentle and unnoticed, control (*laxis effertur habenis* [brought about by loose reins]) reveals itself in the balance or reconciliation of opposite or discordant qualities: of sameness, with difference; of the general, with the concrete; the idea, with the image; the individual, with the representative; the sense of novelty and freshness, with old and familiar objects; a more than usual state of emotion, with more than usual order; judgement ever awake and steady self-possession, with enthusiasm and feeling profound or vehement; and while it blends and harmonizes the natural and the artificial, still subordinates art to nature; the manner to the matter; and our admiration of the poet to our sympathy with the poetry. "Doubtless," as Sir John Davies [1569–1626; English jurist and poet] observes of the soul (and his words may with slight alteration be applied, and even more appropriately, to the poetic imagination)

"Doubtless this could not be, but that she turns
    Bodies to spirit by sublimation strange,
As fire converts to fire the things it burns,
    As we our food into our nature change.

From their gross matter she abstracts their forms,
    And draws a kind of quintessence from things;
Which to her proper nature she transforms,
    To bear them light on her celestial wings.

Thus does she, when from individual states
    She doth abstract the universal kinds;
Which then re-clothed in divers names and fates
    Steal access through our senses to our minds."

Finally, good sense is the body of poetic genius, fancy its drapery, motion its life, and imagination the soul that is everywhere, and in each; and forms all into one graceful and intelligent whole.

JOHN HENRY NEWMAN

❧ *The Definition of "Literature"*

. . . By Letters or Literature is meant the expression of thought in language, where by "thought" I mean the ideas, feelings, views, reasonings, and other operations of the human mind. And the Art of Letters is the method by which a speaker or writer brings out in words, worthy of his subject, and sufficient for his audience or readers, the thoughts which impress him. Literature, then, is of a personal character; it consists in the enunciations and teachings of those who have a right to speak as representatives of their kind, and in whose words their brethren find an interpretation of their own sentiments, a record of their own experience, and a suggestion for their own judgments. A great author, Gentlemen, is not one who merely has a *copia verborum* [abundance of words], whether in prose or verse, and can, as it were, turn on at his will any number of splendid phrases and swelling sentences; but he is one who has something to say and knows how to say it. I do not claim for him, as such, any great depth of thought, or breadth of view, or philosophy, or sagacity, or knowledge of human nature, or experience of human life, though these additional gifts he may have, and the more he has of them the greater he is; but I ascribe to him, as his characteristic gift, in a large sense, the faculty of Expression. He is master of the twofold Logos, the thought and the word, distinct, but inseparable from each other. He may, if so be, elaborate his compositions, or he may pour out his improvisations, but in either case he has but one aim, which he keeps steadily before him, and is conscientious and single-minded in fulfilling. That aim is to give forth what he has within him; and from his very earnestness it comes to pass that, whatever be the splendour of his diction or the harmony of his periods, he has with him the charm of an incommunicable simplicity. Whatever be his subject, high or low, he treats it suitably and for its own sake. If he is a poet, "nil molitur *ineptè* [nothing is undertaken unsuitably]." If he is an orator, then too he speaks, not only "distinctè [distinctly]" and "splendidé [nobly]," but also "*aptè* [suitably]." His page is the lucid mirror of his mind and life—

> Quo fit, ut omnis
> Votivâ pateat veluti descripta tabellâ
> Vita senis.[8]

He writes passionately, because he feels keenly; forcibly, because he conceives vividly; he sees too clearly to be vague; he is too serious to be otiose; he can analyze his subject, and therefore he is rich; he embraces it as a whole and in its parts, and therefore he is consistent; he has a firm hold of it, and therefore he is luminous. When his imagination wells up, it overflows in ornament; when his heart is touched, it thrills along his verse. He always has the right word for the right idea, and never a word too much. If he is brief, it is because few words suffice; when he is lavish of them, still each word has its mark, and aids, not embarrasses, the vigorous march of his elocution. He expresses what all feel, but all cannot say; and his sayings pass into proverbs among his people, and his phrases become household words and idioms of their daily speech, which is tesselated with the rich fragments of his language, as we see in foreign lands the marbles of Roman grandeur worked into the walls and pavements of modern palaces.

Such pre-eminently is Shakespeare among ourselves; such pre-eminently Virgil among the Latins; such in their degree are all those writers who in every nation go by the name of Classics. To particular nations they are necessarily attached from the circumstance of the variety of tongues, and the peculiarities of each; but so far they have a catholic and ecumenical character, that what they express is common to the whole race of man, and they alone are able to express it.

If then the power of speech is a gift as great as any that can be named,—if the origin of language is by many philosophers even considered to be nothing short of divine,—if by means of words the secrets of the heart are brought to light, pain of soul is relieved, hidden grief is carried off, sympathy conveyed, counsel imparted, experience recorded, and wisdom perpetuated,—if by great authors the many are drawn up into unity, national character is fixed, a people speaks, the past and the future, the East and the West are brought into communication with each other,—if such men are, in a word, the spokesmen

---

[8] He so acts that in his old age his entire life appears as if engraved upon votive tablets. [Eds.]

and prophets of the human family,—it will not answer to make light of Literature or to neglect its study; rather we may be sure that, in proportion as we master it in whatever language, and imbibe its spirit, we shall ourselves become in our own measure the ministers of like benefits to others, be they many or few, be they in the obscurer or the more distinguished walks of life,—who are united to us by social ties, and are within the sphere of our personal influence.

JOHN RUSKIN

❧ *Of the Pathetic Fallacy*

1. German dulness, and English affectation, have of late much multiplied among us the use of two of the most objectionable words that were ever coined by the troublesomeness of metaphysicians—namely, "objective," and "subjective."

No words can be more exquisitely, and in all points, useless; and I merely speak of them that I may, at once and for ever, get them out of my way, and out of my reader's. But to get that done, they must be explained.

The word "blue," say certain philosophers, means the sensation of colour which the human eye receives in looking at the open sky, or at a bell gentian.

Now, say they farther, as this sensation can only be felt when the eye is turned to the object, and as, therefore, no such sensation is produced by the object when nobody looks at it, therefore the thing, when it is not looked at, is not blue; and thus (say they) there are many qualities of things which depend as much on something else as on themselves. To be sweet, a thing must have a taster; it is only sweet while it is being tasted, and if the tongue had not the capacity of taste, then the sugar would not have the quality of sweetness.

And then they agree that the qualities of things which thus depend upon our perception of them, and upon our human nature as affected by them, shall be called subjective; and the qualities of things which they always have, irrespective of any other nature, as roundness or squareness, shall be called objective.

From these ingenious views the step is very easy to a farther opinion, that it does not much matter what things are in themselves, but only what they are to us; and that the only real truth of them is their appearance to, or effect upon, us. From which position, with a hearty desire for mystification, and much egotism, selfishness, shallowness, and impertinence, a philosopher may easily go so far as to believe, and say, that everything in the world depends upon his seeing or thinking of it, and that nothing, therefore, exists, but what he sees or thinks of.

2. Now, to get rid of all these ambiguities and troublesome words at once, be it observed that the word "blue" does *not* mean the *sensation* caused by a gentian on the human eye; but it means the *power* of producing that sensation: and this power is always there, in the thing, whether we are there to experience it or not, and would remain there though there were not left a man on the face of the earth. Precisely in the same way gunpowder has a power of exploding. It will not explode if you put no match to it. But it has always the power of so exploding, and is therefore called an explosive compound, which it very positively and assuredly is, whatever philosophy may say to the contrary.

In like manner, a gentian does not produce the sensation of blueness if you don't look at it. But it has always the power of doing so; its particles being everlastingly so arranged by its Maker. And, therefore, the gentian and the sky are always verily blue, whatever philosophy may say to the contrary; and if you do not see them blue when you look at them, it is not their fault, but yours.[9]

3. Hence I would say to these philosophers: If, instead of using the sonorous phrase, "It is objectively so," you will use the plain old phrase, "It *is* so," and if instead of the sonorous phrase, "It is subjectively so," you will say, in plain old English, "It does so," or "It seems so to me," you will, on the whole, be more intelligible to your fellow-creatures; and besides, if you find that a thing which generally "does so" to other people (as a gentian looks blue to most men), does *not* so to you, on any particular occasion, you will not fall into the impertinence of saying, that the thing is not so, or did not so, but you will say simply (what you will be all the better for speedily finding out), that something is the matter with you. If you find that you cannot explode the gunpowder, you will not declare that all gunpowder is subjective, and all explosion imaginary, but you will simply suspect and declare yourself to be an ill-made match. Which, on the whole, though there may be a distant chance of a mistake about it, is, nevertheless, the wisest conclusion you can come to until further experiment.[10]

---

[9] It is quite true, that in all qualities involving sensation, there may be a doubt whether different people receive the same sensation from the same thing . . . ; but, though this makes such facts not distinctly explicable, it does not alter the facts themselves. I derive a certain sensation, which I call sweetness, from sugar. That is a fact. Another person feels a sensation, which *he* also calls sweetness, from sugar. That is also a fact. The sugar's power to produce these two sensations, which we suppose to be, and which are, in all probability, very nearly the same in both of us, and, on the whole, in the human race, is its sweetness.

[10] In fact (for I may as well, for once, meet our German friends in their own style), all that has been subjected to us on the subject seems object to this great objection; that the subjection of all things (subject to no exceptions) to senses which are, in us, both subject and object, and objects of perpetual contempt, cannot but make it our ultimate object to subject ourselves to the senses, and to remove whatever objections existed to such subjection. So that, finally, that which is the subject of examination or object of attention, uniting thus in itself the characters of subness and obness (so that, that which has no obness in it should be called sub-subjective, or a sub-subject, and that which has no subness in it should be called upper or ober-objective, or an ob-object); and we also, who suppose ourselves the objects of every arrangement, and are certainly the subjects of every sensual impression, thus uniting in ourselves, in an obverse or adverse manner, the characters of obness and subness, must both become

4. Now, therefore, putting these tiresome and absurd words quite out of our way, we may go on at our ease to examine the point in question—namely, the difference between the ordinary, proper, and true appearances of things to us; and the extraordinary, or false appearances, when we are under the influence of emotion, or contemplative fancy;[11] false appearances, I say, as being entirely unconnected with any real power or character in the object, and only imputed to it by us.

For instance—

> The spendthrift crocus, bursting through the mould
> Naked and shivering, with his cup of gold.[12]

This is very beautiful, and yet very untrue. The crocus is not a spendthrift, but a hardy plant; its yellow is not gold, but saffron. How is it that we enjoy so much the having it put into our heads that it is anything else than a plain crocus?

It is an important question. For, throughout our past reasonings about art, we have always found that nothing could be good or useful, or ultimately pleasurable, which was untrue. But here is something pleasurable in written poetry, which is nevertheless *un*true. And what is more, if we think over our favourite poetry, we shall find it full of this kind of fallacy, and that we like it all the more for being so.

5. It will appear also, on consideration of the matter, that this fallacy is of two principal kinds. Either, as in this case of the crocus, it is the fallacy of wilful fancy, which involves no real expectation that it will be believed; or else it is a fallacy caused by an excited state of the feelings, making us, for the time, more or less irrational. Of the cheating of the fancy we shall have to speak presently; but in this chapter, I want to examine the nature of the other error, that which the mind admits when affected strongly by emotion. Thus, for instance, in *Alton Locke*—

> They rowed her in across the rolling foam—
> The cruel, crawling foam.

The foam is not cruel, neither does it crawl. The state of mind which attributes to it these characters of a living creature is one in which the reason is unhinged by grief. All violent feelings have the same effect. They produce in us a falseness in all our impressions of external things, which I would generally characterize as the "pathetic fallacy."

6. Now we are in the habit of considering this fallacy as eminently a

---

metaphysically dejected or rejected, nothing remaining in *us* objective, but subjectivity, and the very objectivity of the object being lost in the abyss of this subjectivity of the Human.

There is, however, some meaning in the above sentence, if the reader cares to make it out; but in a pure German sentence of the highest style there is often none whatever.

[11] Contemplative, in the sense explained in Part III. sec. ii. chap. iv. (of *Modern Painters*).

[12] Holmes (Oliver Wendell), quoted by Miss Mitford in her *Recollections of a Literary Life*.

character of poetical description, and the temper of mind in which we allow it, as one eminently poetical, because passionate. But I believe, if we look well into the matter, that we shall find the greatest poets do not often admit this kind of falseness—that it is only the second order of poets who much delight in it.[13]

Thus, when Dante describes the spirits falling from the bank of Acheron "as dead leaves flutter from a bough," he gives the most perfect image possible of their utter lightness, feebleness, passiveness, and scattering agony of despair, without, however, for an instant losing his own clear perception that *these* are souls, and *those* are leaves; he makes no confusion of one with the other. But when Coleridge speaks of

> The one red leaf, the last of its clan,
> That dances as often as dance it can,

he has a morbid, that is to say, a so far false, idea about the leaf; he fancies a life in it, and will, which there are not; confuses its powerlessness with choice, its fading death with merriment, and the wind that shakes it with music. Here, however, there is some beauty, even in the morbid passage; but take an instance in Homer and Pope. Without the knowledge of Ulysses, Elpenor, his youngest follower, has fallen from an upper chamber in the Circean palace, and has been left dead, unmissed by his leader or companions, in the haste of their departure. They cross the sea to the Cimmerian land; and Ulysses summons the shades from Tartarus. The first which appears is that of the lost Elpenor. Ulysses, amazed, and in exactly the spirit of bitter and terrified lightness which is seen in Hamlet,[14] addresses the spirit with the simple, startled words—

> "Elpenor! How camest thou under the shadowy darkness? Hast thou come faster on foot than I in my black ship?"

[13] I admit two orders of poets, but no third; and by these two orders I mean the creative (Shakespeare, Homer, Dante), and reflective or perceptive (Wordsworth, Keats, Tennyson). But both of these must be *first*-rate in their range, though their range is different; and with poetry second-rate in *quality* no one ought to be allowed to trouble mankind. There is quite enough of the best,—much more than we can ever read or enjoy in the length of a life; and it is a literal wrong or sin in any person to encumber us with inferior work. I have no patience with apologies made by young pseudo-poets, "that they believe there is *some* good in what they have written: that they hope to do better in time," etc. *Some* good! If there is not *all* good, there is no good. If they ever hope to do better, why do they trouble us now? Let them rather courageously burn all they have done, and wait for the better days. There are few men, ordinarily educated, who in moments of strong feeling could not strike out a poetical thought, and afterwards polish it so as to be presentable. But men of sense know better than so to waste their time; and those who sincerely love poetry, know the touch of the master's hand on the chords too well to fumble among them after him. Nay, more than this, all inferior poetry is an injury to the good, inasmuch as it takes away the freshness of rhymes, blunders upon and gives a wretched commonalty to good thoughts; and, in general, adds to the weight of human weariness in a most woeful and culpable manner. There are few thoughts likely to come across ordinary men, which have not already been expressed by greater men in the best possible way; and it is a wiser, more generous, more noble thing to remember and point out the perfect words, than to invent poorer ones, wherewith to encumber temporarily the world.

[14] "Well said, old mole! canst work i' the ground so fast?"

Which Pope renders thus—

> O, say, what angry power Elpenor led
> To glide in shades, and wander with the dead?
> How could thy soul, by realms and seas disjoined,
> Outfly the nimble sail, and leave the lagging wind?

I sincerely hope the reader finds no pleasure here, either in the nimbleness of the sail, or the laziness of the wind! And yet how is it that these conceits are so painful now, when they have been pleasant to us in the other instances?

7. For a very simple reason. They are not a *pathetic* fallacy at all, for they are put into the mouth of the wrong passion—a passion which never could possibly have spoken them—agonized curiosity. Ulysses wants to know the facts of the matter; and the very last thing his mind could do at the moment would be to pause, or suggest in any wise what was *not* a fact. The delay in the first three lines, and conceit in the last, jar upon us instantly like the most frightful discord in music. No poet of true imaginative power could possibly have written the passage. It is worth while comparing the way a similar question is put by the exquisite sincerity of Keats—

> He wept, and his bright tears
> Went trickling down the golden bow he held.
> Thus, with half-shut, suffused eyes, he stood;
> While from beneath some cumbrous boughs hard by
> With solemn step an awful goddess came,
> And there was purport in her looks for him,
> Which he with eager guess began to read
> Perplex'd, the while melodiously he said,
> *"How camest thou over the unfooted sea?"*
> (*Hyperion*, Book III)

Therefore we see that the spirit of truth must guide us in some sort, even in our enjoyment of fallacy. Coleridge's fallacy has no discord in it, but Pope's has set our teeth on edge. Without farther questioning, I will endeavour to state the main bearings of this matter.

8. The temperament which admits the pathetic fallacy, is, as I said above, that of a mind and body in some sort too weak to deal fully with what is before them or upon them; borne away, or over-clouded, or over-dazzled by emotion, and it is a more or less noble state, according to the force of the emotion which has induced it. For it is no credit to a man that he is not morbid or inaccurate in his perceptions, when he has no strength of feeling to warp them; and it is in general a sign of higher capacity and stand in the ranks of being, that the emotions should be strong enough to vanquish, partly, the intellect, and make it believe what they choose. But it is still a grander condition when the intellect also rises, till it is strong enough to assert its rule against, or together with, the utmost efforts of the passions; and the whole man stands in an iron glow, white hot, perhaps, but still strong, and in no wise evaporating; even if he melts, losing none of his weight.

So, then, we have the three ranks: the man who perceives rightly, because he does not feel, and to whom the primrose is very accurately the primrose, because he does not love it. Then, secondly, the man who perceives wrongly, because he feels, and to whom the primrose is anything else than a primrose: a star, or a sun, or a fairy's shield, or a forsaken maiden. And then, lastly, there is the man who perceives rightly in spite of his feelings, and to whom the primrose is for ever nothing else than itself—a little flower apprehended in the very plain and leafy fact of it, whatever and how many soever the associations and passions may be that crowd around it. And, in general, these three classes may be rated in comparative order, as the men who are not poets at all, and the poets of the second order, and the poets of the first; only however great a man may be, there are always some subjects which *ought* to throw him off his balance; some, by which his poor human capacity of thought should be conquered, and brought into the inaccurate and vague state of perception, so that the language of the highest inspiration becomes broken, obscure, and wild in metaphor, resembling that of the weaker man, overborne by weaker things.

9. And thus, in full, there are four classes: the men who feel nothing, and therefore see truly; the men who feel strongly, think weakly, and see untruly (second order of poets); the men who feel strongly, think strongly, and see truly (the first order of poets); and the men who, strong as human creatures can be, are yet submitted to influences stronger than they, and see in a sort untruly, because what they see is inconceivably above them. This last is the usual condition of prophetic inspiration.

10. I separate these classes, in order that their character may be clearly understood; but of course they are united each to the other by imperceptible transitions, and the same mind, according to the influences to which it is subjected, passes at different times into the various states. Still, the difference between the great and less man is, on the whole, chiefly in this point of *alterability*. That is to say, the one knows too much, and perceives and feels too much of the past and future, and of all things beside and around that which immediately affects him, to be in any wise shaken by it. His mind is made up; his thoughts have an accustomed current; his ways are steadfast; it is not this or that new sight which will at once unbalance him. He is tender to impression at the surface, like a rock with deep moss upon it; but there is too much mass of him to be moved. The smaller man, with the same degree of sensibility, is at once carried off his feet; he wants to do something he did not want to do before; he views all the universe in a new light through his tears; he is gay or enthusiastic, melancholy or passionate, as things come and go to him. Therefore the high creative poet might even be thought, to a great extent, impassive (as shallow people think Dante stern), receiving indeed all feelings to the full, but having a great centre of reflection and knowledge in which he stands serene, and watches the feeling, as it were, from afar off.

Dante, in his most intense moods, has entire command of himself, and can look around calmly, at all moments, for the image or the word that will best tell what he sees to the upper or lower world. But Keats and Tennyson, and the poets of the second order, are generally themselves subdued by the feelings under which they write, or, at least, write as choosing to be so, and therefore admit certain expressions and modes of thought which are in some sort diseased or false.

11. Now so long as we see that the *feeling* is true, we pardon, or are even pleased by, the confessed fallacy of sight which it induces: we are pleased, for instance, with those lines of Kingsley's above quoted, not because they fallaciously describe foam, but because they faithfully describe sorrow. But the moment the mind of the speaker becomes cold, that moment every such expression becomes untrue, as being for ever untrue in the external facts. And there is no greater baseness in literature than the habit of using these metaphorical expressions in cool blood. An inspired writer, in full impetuosity of passion, may speak wisely and truly of "raging waves of the sea foaming out their own shame"; but it is only the basest writer who cannot speak of the sea without talking of "raging waves," "remorseless floods," "ravenous billows," etc.; and it is one of the signs of the highest power in a writer to check all such habits of thought, and to keep his eyes fixed firmly on the *pure fact*, out of which if any feeling comes to him or his reader, he knows it must be a true one.

To keep to the waves, I forget who it is who represents a man in despair desiring that his body may be cast into the sea,

> *Whose changing mound, and foam that passed away,*
> Might mock the eyes that questioned where I lay.

Observe, there is not here a single false, or even overcharged, expression. "Mound" of the sea wave is perfectly simple and true; "Changing" is as familiar as may be; "foam that passed away," strictly literal; and the whole line descriptive of the reality with a degree of accuracy which I know not any other verse, in the range of poetry, that altogether equals. For most people have not a distinct idea of the clumsiness and massiveness of a large wave. The word "wave" is used too generally of ripples and breakers, and bendings in light drapery or grass: it does not by itself convey a perfect image. But the word "mound" is heavy, large, dark, definite; there is no mistaking the kind of wave meant, nor missing the sight of it. Then the term "changing" has a peculiar force also. Most people think of waves as rising and falling. But if they look at the sea carefully, they will perceive that the waves do not rise and fall. They change. Change both place and form, but they do not fall; one wave goes on, and on, and still on; now lower, now higher, now tossing its mane like a horse, now building itself together like a wall, now shaking, now steady, but still the same wave, till at last it seems struck by something, and changes, one knows not how—becomes another wave.

The close of the line insists on this image, and paints it still more perfectly—"foam that passed away." Not merely melting, disappearing, but passing on, out of sight, on the career of the wave. Then, having put the absolute ocean fact as far as he may before our eyes, the poet leaves us to feel about it as we may, and to trace for ourselves the opposite fact—the image of the green mounds that do not change, and the white and written stones that do not pass away; and thence to follow out also the associated images of the calm life with the quiet grave, and the despairing life with the fading foam—

> Let no man move his bones.
> As for Samaria, her king is cut off like the foam upon the water.

But nothing of this is actually told or pointed out, and the expressions, as they stand, are perfectly severe and accurate, utterly uninfluenced by the firmly governed emotion of the writer. Even the word "mock" is hardly an exception, as it may stand merely for "deceive" or "defeat," without implying any impersonation of the waves.

12. It may be well, perhaps, to give one or two more instances to show the peculiar dignity possessed by all passages, which thus limit their expression to the pure fact, and leave the hearer to gather what he can from it. Here is a notable one from the *Iliad*. Helen, looking from the Scæan gate of Troy over the Grecian host, and telling Priam the names of its captains, says at last—

> "I see all the other dark-eyed Greeks; but two I cannot see—Castor and Pollux,—whom one mother bore with me. Have they not followed from fair Lacedæmon, or have they indeed come in their sea-wandering ships, but now will not enter into the battle of men, fearing the shame and the scorn that is in me?"

Then Homer—

> "So she spoke. But them, already, the life-giving earth possessed, there in Lacedæmon, in the dear fatherland."

Note, here, the high poetical truth carried to the extreme. The poet has to speak of the earth in sadness, but he will not let that sadness affect or change his thoughts of it. No; though Castor and Pollux be dead, yet the earth is our mother still, fruitful, life-giving. These are the facts of the thing. I see nothing else than these. Make what you will of them.

13. Take another very notable instance from Casimir de la Vigne's terrible ballad, "La Toilette de Constance." I must quote a few lines out of it here and there, to enable the reader who has not the book by him, to understand its close.

> *Vite, Anna, vite; au miroir,*
>   *Plus vite, Anna. L'heure s'avance,*
> *Et je vais au bal ce soir*
>   *Chez l'ambassadeur de France.*
>
> *Y pensez-vous? ils sont fanés, ces nœuds;*
>   *Ils sont d'hier; mon Dieu, comme tout passe!*

Que du réseau qui retient mes cheveux
  Les glands d'azur retombent avec grâce.
Plus haut! Plus bas! Vous ne comprenez rien!
  Que sur mon front ce saphir étincelle:
Vous me piquez, maladroite. Ah, c'est bien,
  Bien—chère Anna! Je t'aime, je suis belle.

Celui qu'en vain je voudrais oublier . . .
  (Anna, ma robe) il y sera, j'espère.
(Ah, fi! profane, est-ce là mon collier?
  Quoi! ces grains d'or bénits par le Saint-Père!)
Il y sera; Dieu; s'il pressait ma main,
  En y pensant à peine je respire:
Frère Anselmo doit m'entendre demain,
  Comment ferai-je, Anna, pour tout lui dire? . . .

    Vite! un coup d'œil au miroir,
      Le dernier.—J'ai l'assurance
    Qu'on va m'adorer ce soir
      Chez l'ambassadeur de France.

Près du foyer, Constance s'admirait.
  Dieu! sur sa robe il vole une étincelle!
Au feu! Courez! Quand l'espoir l'enivrait
  Tout perdre ainsi! Quoi! Mourir—et si belle!
L'horrible feu ronge avec volupté
  Ses bras, son sein, et l'entoure, et s'élève,
Et sans pitié dévore sa beauté,
  Ses dix-huit ans, hélas, et son doux rêve!

    Adieu, bal, plaisir, amour!
      On disait, Pauvre Constance!
    Et on dansait, jusqu'au jour,
      Chez l'ambassadeur de France.[15]

[15] Quick, Anna, quick; the mirror,
Faster, Anna. It's getting late,
And this evening I am going to the ball
At the French ambassador's.

What are you thinking of? these ribbons are faded;
  They are yesterday's; my God, nearly everything goes wrong!
Let the blue tassels of my hair net
  Hang gracefully.
Higher! Lower! You don't understand anything!
  Let this sapphire sparkle on my forehead:
You're sticking me, clumsy. Ah, it's all right,
  All right—dear Anna! I love you, I am beautiful.

The one whom I am vainly trying to forget . . .
  (Anna, my dress) he will be there, I hope.
(Ah, damn! sacrilegious creature, is this my necklace?
  What! these gold beads blessed by the Pope!)

Yes, that is the fact of it. Right or wrong, the poet does not say. What you may think about it, he does not know. He has nothing to do with that. There lie the ashes of the dead girl in her chamber. There they danced, till the morning, at the Ambassador's of France. Make what you will of it.

If the reader will look through the ballad, of which I have quoted only about the third part, he will find that there is not, from beginning to end of it, a single poetical (so called) expression, except in one stanza. The girl speaks as simple prose as may be; there is not a word she would not have actually used as she was dressing. The poet stands by, impassive as a statue, recording her words just as they come. At last the doom seizes her, and in the very presence of death, for an instant, his own emotions conquer him. He records no longer the facts only, but the facts as they seem to him. The fire gnaws with *voluptuousness—without pity*. It is soon past. The fate is fixed for ever; and he retires into his pale and crystalline atmosphere of truth. He closes all with the calm veracity,

"They said, 'Poor Constance!' "

14. Now in this there is the exact type of the consummate poetical temperament. For, be it clearly and constantly remembered, that the greatness of a poet depends upon the two facilities, acuteness of feeling, and command of it. A poet is great, first in proportion to the strength of his passion, and then, that strength being granted, in proportion to his government of it; there being, however, always a point beyond which it would be inhuman and monstrous if he pushed this government, and, therefore, a point at which all feverish and wild fancy becomes just and true. Thus the destruction of the kingdom of Assyria cannot be contemplated firmly by a prophet of Israel. The fact is too

---

He will be there; God, if he should squeeze my hand,
  Thinking about it, I can scarcely breathe:
Brother Anselmo must hear my confession tomorrow,
  Anna, how will I tell him everything? . . .

    Quick, a glance in the mirror,
      The last.—I'm sure
    They'll adore me this evening
      At the French ambassador's.

Next to the fireplace, Constance is admiring herself.
  God! a spark flies onto her dress!
Fire! Run! Just when hope was intoxicating her,
  To lose everything this way! What! To die—so beautiful, too!
The horrible fire gnaws with voluptuousness
  At her arms, her breasts, it surrounds her and grows higher,
And pitilessly devours her beauty,
  Her eighteen years, alas, and her tender dream!

    Goodbye ball, pleasure, love!
      They said, "Poor Constance!"
    And they danced till dawn,
      At the French ambassador's.
  [Eds.]

great, too wonderful. It overthrows him, dashes him into a confused element of dreams. All the world is, to his stunned thought, full of strange voices. "Yea, the fir-trees rejoice at thee, and the cedars of Lebanon, saying, 'Since thou art gone down to the grave, no feller is come up against us.' " So, still more, the thought of the presence of Deity cannot be borne without this great astonishment. "The mountains and the hills shall break forth before you into singing, and all the trees of the field shall clap their hands."

15. But by how much this feeling is noble when it is justified by the strength of its cause, by so much it is ignoble when there is not cause enough for it; and beyond all other ignobleness is the mere affectation of it, in hardness of heart. Simply bad writing may almost always, as above noticed, be known by its adoption of these fanciful metaphorical expressions as a sort of current coin; yet there is even a worse, at least a more harmful condition of writing than this, in which such expressions are not ignorantly and feelinglessly caught up, but, by some master, skilful in handling, yet insincere, deliberately wrought out with chill and studied fancy; as if we should try to make an old lava-stream look red hot again, by covering it with dead leaves, or white-hot, with hoar-frost.

When Young is lost in veneration, as he dwells on the character of truly good and holy man, he permits himself for a moment to be overborne by the feeling so far as to exclaim—

> Where shall I find him? angels, tell me where
> You know him; he is near you; point him out.
> Shall I see glories beaming from his brow,
> Or trace his footsteps by the rising flowers?

This emotion has a worthy cause, and is thus true and right. But now hear the cold-hearted Pope say to a shepherd girl—

> Where'er you walk, cool gales shall fan the glade;
> Trees, where you sit, shall crowd into a shade;
> Your praise the birds shall chant in every grove,
> And winds shall waft it to the powers above.
> But would you sing, and rival Orpheus' strain,
> The wondering forests soon should dance again;
> The moving mountains hear the powerful call,
> And headlong streams hang, listening, in their fall.

This is not, nor could it for a moment be mistaken for, the language of passion. It is simple falsehood, uttered by hypocrisy; definite absurdity, rooted in affectation, and coldly asserted in the teeth of nature and fact. Passion will indeed go far in deceiving itself; but it must be a strong passion, not the simple wish of a lover to tempt his mistress to sing. Compare a very closely parallel passage in Wordsworth, in which the lover has lost his mistress:

Three years had Barbara in her grave been laid,
When thus his moan he made—

"Oh, move, thou cottage, from behind yon oak,
   Or let the ancient tree uprooted lie,
That in some other way yon smoke
   May mount into the sky.

If still behind yon pine-tree's ragged bough,
   Headlong, the waterfall must come,
   Oh, let it, then, be dumb—
Be anything, sweet stream, but that which thou art now."

Here is a cottage to be moved, if not a mountain, and a waterfall to be silent, if it is not to hang listening: but with what different relation to the mind that contemplates them! Here, in the extremity of its agony, the soul cries out wildly for relief, which at the same moment it partly knows to be impossible, but partly believes possible, in a vague impression that a miracle *might* be wrought to give relief even to a less sore distress—that nature is kind, and God is kind, and that grief is strong: it knows not well what *is* possible to such grief. To silence a stream, to move a cottage wall—one might think it could do as much as that!

16. I believe these instances are enough to illustrate the main point I insist upon respecting the pathetic fallacy—that so far as it *is* a fallacy, it is always the sign of a morbid state of mind, and comparatively of a weak one. Even in the most inspired prophet it is a sign of the incapacity of his human sight or thought to bear what has been revealed to it. In ordinary poetry, if it is found in the thoughts of the poet himself, it is at once a sign of his belonging to the inferior school; if in the thoughts of the characters imagined by him, it is right or wrong according to the genuineness of the emotion from which it springs; always, however, implying necessarily *some* degree of weakness in the character.

Take two most exquisite instances from master hands. The Jessy of Shenstone, and the Ellen of Wordsworth, have both been betrayed and deserted. Jessy, in the course of her most touching complaint, says:

If through the garden's flowery tribes I stray,
   Where bloom the jasmines that could once allure,
"Hope not to find delight in us," they say,
   "For we are spotless, Jessy, we are pure."

Compare this with some of the words of Ellen:

"Ah, why," said Ellen, sighing to herself,
"Why do not words, and kiss, and solemn pledge,
And nature, that is kind in woman's breast,
And reason, that in man is wise and good,
And fear of Him Who is a righteous Judge—

Why do not these prevail for human life,
To keep two hearts together, that began
Their springtime with one love, and that have need
Of mutual pity and forgiveness sweet
To grant, or be received; while that poor bird—
O, come and hear him! Thou who hast to me
Been faithless, hear him—though a lowly creature,
One of God's simple children that yet know not
The Universal Parent, *how* he sings!
As if he wished the firmament of heaven
Should listen, and give back to him the voice
Of his triumphant constancy and love;
The proclamation that he makes, how far
His darkness doth transcend our fickle light."

The perfection of both these passages, as far as regards truth and tenderness of imagination in the two poets, is quite insuperable. But of the two characters imagined, Jessy is weaker than Ellen, exactly in so far as something appears to her to be in nature which is not. The flowers do not really reproach her. God meant them to comfort her, not to taunt her; they would do so if she saw them rightly.

Ellen, on the other hand, is quite above the slightest erring emotion. There is not the barest film of fallacy in all her thoughts. She reasons as calmly as if she did not feel. And, although the singing of the bird suggests to her the idea of its desiring to be heard in heaven, she does not for an instant admit any veracity in the thought. "As if," she says—"I know he means nothing of the kind; but it does verily seem as if." The reader will find, by examining the rest of the poem, that Ellen's character is throughout consistent in this clear though passionate strength.

It then being, I hope, now made clear to the reader in all respects that the pathetic fallacy is powerful only so far as it is pathetic, feeble so far as it is fallacious, and, therefore, that the dominion of Truth is entire, over this, as over every other natural and just state of the human mind, we may go on to the subject for the dealing with which this prefatory inquiry became necessary; and why necessary, we shall see forthwith.[16]

[16] I cannot quit this subject without giving two more instances, both exquisite, of the pathetic fallacy, which I have just come upon, in *Maud* [by Alfred Tennyson]:

For a great speculation had fail'd;
And ever he mutter'd and madden'd, and ever wann'd with despair;
And out he walk'd, when the wind like a broken worldling wail'd,
And the *flying gold of the ruin'd woodlands drove thro' the air.*

There has fallen a splendid tear
From the passion-flower at the gate.
The red rose cries, "She is near, she is near!"
And the white rose weeps, "She is late."
The larkspur listens, "I hear, I hear!"
And the lily whispers, "I wait."

MATTHEW ARNOLD

❧ *Literature and Science*

PRACTICAL people talk with a smile of Plato and of his absolute ideas; and it is impossible to deny that Plato's ideas do often seem unpractical and impracticable, and especially when one views them in connection with the life of a great work-a-day world like the United States. The necessary staple of the life of such a world Plato regards with disdain; handicraft and trade and the working professions he regards with disdain; but what becomes of the life of an industrial modern community if you take handicraft and trade and the working professions out of it? The base mechanic arts and handicrafts, says Plato, bring about a natural weakness in the principle of excellence in a man, so that he cannot govern the ignoble growths in him, but nurses them, and cannot understand fostering any other. Those who exercise such arts and trades, as they have their bodies, he says, marred by their vulgar businesses, so they have their souls, too, bowed and broken by them. And if one of these uncomely people has a mind to seek self-culture and philosophy, Plato compares him to a bald little tinker, who has scraped together money, and has got his release from service, and has had a bath, and bought a new coat, and is rigged out like a bridegroom about to marry the daughter of his master who has fallen into poor and helpless estate.

Nor do the working professions fare any better than trade at the hands of Plato. He draws for us an inimitable picture of the working lawyer, and of his life of bondage; he shows how this bondage from his youth up has stunted and warped him, and made him small and crooked of soul, encompassing him with difficulties which he is not man enough to rely on justice and truth as means to encounter, but has recourse, for help out of them, to falsehood and wrong. And so, says Plato, this poor creature is bent and broken, and grows up from boy to man without a particle of soundness in him, although exceedingly smart and clever in his own esteem.

One cannot refuse to admire the artist who draws these pictures. But we say to ourselves that his ideas show the influence of a primitive and obsolete order of things, when the warrior caste and the priestly caste were alone in honour and the humble work of the world was done by slaves. We have now changed all that; the modern majority consists in work, as Emerson declares; and in work, we may add, principally of such plain and dusty kind as the work of cultivators of the ground, handicraftsmen, men of trade and business, men of the working professions. Above all is this true in a great industrious community such as that of the United States.

Now education, many people go on to say, is still mainly governed by the ideas of men like Plato, who lived when the warrior caste and the priestly or philosophical class were alone in honour, and the really useful part of the community were slaves. It is an education fitted for persons of leisure in such a community. This education passed from Greece and Rome to the feudal communities of Europe, where also the warrior caste and the priestly caste were alone held in honour and where the really useful and working part of the community, though not nominally slaves as in the pagan world, were practically not much better off than slaves, and not more seriously regarded. And how absurd it is, people end by saying, to inflict this education upon an industrious modern community, where very few indeed are persons of leisure, and the mass to be considered has not leisure, but is bound, for its own great good, and for the great good of the world at large, to plain labour and to industrial pursuits, and the education in question tends necessarily to make men dissatisfied with these pursuits and unfitted for them!

That is what is said. So far I must defend Plato, as to plead that his view of education and studies is in the general, as it seems to me, sound enough, and fitted for all sorts and conditions of men, whatever their pursuits may be. "An intelligent man," says Plato, "will prize those studies which result in his soul getting soberness, righteousness, and wisdom, and will less value the others." I cannot consider *that* a bad description of the aim of education, and of the motives which should govern us in the choice of studies, whether we are preparing ourselves for an hereditary seat in the English House of Lords or for the pork trade in Chicago.

Still I admit that Plato's world was not ours, that his scorn of trade and handicraft is fantastic, that he had no conception of a great industrial community such as that of the United States, and that such a community must and will shape its education to suit its own needs. If the usual education handed down to it from the past does not suit it, it will certainly before long drop this and try another. The usual education in the past has been mainly literary. The question is whether the studies which were long supposed to be the best for all of us are practically the best now; whether others are not better. The tyranny of the past, many think, weighs on us injuriously in the predominance given to letters in education. The question is raised whether, to meet the needs of our modern life, the predominance ought not now to pass from letters to science; and naturally the question is nowhere raised with more energy than here in the United States. The design of abasing what is called "mere literary instruction and education," and of exalting what is called "sound, extensive, and practical scientific knowledge," is, in this intensely modern world of the United States, even more perhaps than in Europe, a very popular design, and makes great and rapid progress.

I am going to ask whether the present movement for ousting letters from their old predominance in education, and for transferring the predominance in education to the natural sciences, whether this brisk and flourishing movement ought to prevail, and whether it is likely that in the end it really will prevail. An objection may be raised which I will anticipate. My own studies have been almost wholly in letters, and my visits to the field of the natural sciences have been very slight and inadequate, although those sciences have always strongly moved my curiosity. A man of letters, it will perhaps be said, is not competent to discuss the comparative merits of letters and natural science as means of education. To this objection I reply, first of all, that his incompetence, if he attempts the discussion but is really incompetent for it, will be abundantly visible; nobody will be taken in; he will have plenty of sharp observers and critics to save mankind from that danger. But the line I am going to follow is, as you will soon discover, so extremely simple, that perhaps it may be followed without failure even by one who for a more ambitious line of discussion would be quite incompetent.

Some of you may possibly remember a phrase of mine which has been the object of a good deal of comment; an observation to the effect that in our culture, the aim being *to know ourselves and the world*, we have, as the means to this end, *to know the best which has been thought and said in the world*. A man of science, who is also an excellent writer and the very prince of debaters, Professor [Thomas Henry] Huxley, in a discourse at the opening of Sir Josiah Mason's college at Birmingham, laying hold of this phrase, expanded it by quoting some more words of mine, which are these: "The civilized world is to be regarded as now being, for intellectual and spiritual purposes, one great confederation, bound to a joint action and working to a common result; and whose members have for their proper outfit a knowledge of Greek, Roman, and Eastern antiquity, and of one another. Special local and temporary advantages being put out of account, that modern nation will in the intellectual and spiritual sphere make most progress, which most thoroughly carries out this programme."

Now on my phrase, thus enlarged, Professor Huxley remarks that when I speak of the above-mentioned knowledge as enabling us to know ourselves and the world, I assert *literature* to contain the materials which suffice for thus making us know ourselves and the world. But it is not by any means clear, says he, that after having learnt all which ancient and modern literatures have to tell us, we have laid a sufficiently broad and deep foundation for that criticism of life, that knowledge of ourselves and the world, which constitutes culture. On the contrary, Professor Huxley declares that he finds himself "wholly unable to admit that either nations or individuals will really advance, if their outfit draws nothing from the stores of physical science. An army without weapons of precision, and with no particular base of operations, might more hopefully enter upon a campaign on the Rhine, than a man, devoid of a knowledge of what physical science has done in the last century, upon a criticism of life."

This shows how needful it is for those who are to discuss any matter together, to have a common understanding as to the sense of the terms they employ—how needful, and how difficult. What Professor Huxley says, implies just the reproach which is so often brought against the study of *belles lettres*, as they are called: that the study is an elegant one, but slight and ineffectual; a smattering of Greek and Latin and other ornamental things, of little use for any one whose object is to get at truth, and to be a practical man. So, too, M. Renan talks of the "superficial humanism" of a school-course which treats us as if we were all going to be poets, writers, preachers, orators, and he opposes this humanism to positive science, or the critical search after truth. And there is always a tendency in those who are remonstrating against the predominance of letters in education, to understand by letters *belles lettres*, and by *belles lettres* a superficial humanism the opposite of science or true knowledge.

But when we talk of knowing Greek and Roman antiquity, for instance, which is the knowledge people have called the humanities, I for my part mean a knowledge which is something more than a superficial humanism, mainly decorative. "I call all teaching *scientific*," says Wolf [1759–1824; German philologist], the critic of Homer, "which is systematically laid out and followed up to its original sources. For example: a knowledge of classical antiquity is scientific when the remains of classical antiquity are correctly studied in the original languages." There can be no doubt that Wolf is perfectly right; that all learning is scientific which is systematically laid out and followed up to its original sources, and that a genuine humanism is scientific.

When I speak of knowing Greek and Roman antiquity, therefore, as a help to knowing ourselves and the world, I mean more than a knowledge of so much vocabulary, so much grammar, so many portions of authors in the Greek and Latin languages, I mean knowing the Greeks and Romans, and their life and genius, and what they were and did in the world; what we get from them, and what is its value. That, at least, is the ideal; and when we talk of endeavouring to know Greek and Roman antiquity, as a help to knowing ourselves and the world, we mean endeavouring so to know them as to satisfy this ideal, however much we may still fall short of it.

The same also as to knowing our own and other modern nations, with the like aim of getting to understand ourselves and the world. To know the best that has been thought and said by the modern nations, is to know, says Professor Huxley, "only what modern *literatures* have to tell us; it is the criticism of life contained in modern literature." And yet "the distinctive character of our times," he urges, "lies in the vast and constantly increasing part which is played by natural knowledge." And how, therefore, can a man, devoid of knowledge of what physical science has done in the last century, enter hopefully upon a criticism of modern life?

Let us, I say, be agreed about the meaning of the terms we are using. I talk of knowing the best which has been thought and uttered in the world; Professor Huxley says this means knowing *literature*. Literature is a large word; it may mean everything written with letters or printed in a book. Euclid's *Elements* and Newton's *Principia* are thus literature. All knowledge that reaches us through books is literature. But by literature Professor Huxley means *belles lettres*. He means to make me say, that knowing the best which has been thought and said by the modern nations is knowing their *belles lettres* and no more. And this is no sufficient equipment, he argues, for a criticism of modern life. But as I do not mean, by knowing ancient Rome, knowing merely more or less of Latin *belles lettres*, and taking no account of Rome's military, and political, and legal, and administrative work in the world; and as, by knowing ancient Greece, I understand knowing her as the giver of Greek art, and the guide to a free and right use of reason and to scientific method, and the founder of our mathematics and physics and astronomy and biology—I understand knowing her as all this, and not merely knowing certain Greek poems, and histories, and treatises, and speeches—so as to the knowledge of modern nations also. By knowing modern nations, I mean not merely knowing their *belles lettres*, but knowing also what has been done by such men as Copernicus, Galileo, Newton, Darwin. "Our ancestors learned," says Professor Huxley, "that the earth is the centre of the visible universe, and that man is the cynosure of things terrestrial; and more especially was it inculcated that the course of nature had no fixed order, but that it could be, and constantly was, altered." But for us now, continues Professor Huxley, "the notions of the beginning and the end of the world entertained by our forefathers are no longer credible. It is very certain that the earth is not the chief body in the material universe, and that the world is not subordinated to man's use. It is even more certain that nature is the expression of a definite order, with which nothing interferes." "And yet," he cries, "the purely classical education advocated by the representatives of the humanists in our day gives no inkling of all this!"

In due place and time I will just touch upon that vexed question of classical education; but at present the question is as to what is meant by knowing the best which modern nations have thought and said. It is not knowing their *belles lettres* merely which is meant. To know Italian *belles lettres*, is not to know Italy, and to know English *belles lettres* is not to know England. In knowing Italy and England there comes a great deal more, Galileo and Newton amongst it. The reproach of being a superficial humanism, a tincture of *belles lettres*, may attach rightly enough to some other disciplines; but to the particular discipline recommended when I proposed knowing the best that has been thought and said in the world, it does not apply. In that best I certainly include what in modern times has been thought and said by the great observers and knowers of nature.

There is, therefore, really no question between Professor Huxley and me as to whether knowing the great results of the modern scientific study of nature is not required as a part of our culture, as well as knowing the products of literature and art. But to follow the processes by which those results are reached, ought, say the friends of physical science, to be made the staple of education for the bulk of mankind. And here there does arise a question between those whom Professor Huxley calls with playful sarcasm "the Levites of culture," and those whom the poor humanist is sometimes apt to regard as its Nebuchadnezzars.

The great results of the scientific investigation of nature we are agreed upon knowing, but how much of our study are we bound to give to the processes by which those results are reached? The results have their visible bearing on human life. But all the processes, too, all the items of fact, by which those results are reached and established, are interesting. All knowledge is interesting to a wise man, and the knowledge of nature is interesting to all men. It is very interesting to know, that, from the albuminous white of the egg, the chick in the egg gets the materials for its flesh, bones, blood, and feathers; while from the fatty yolk of the egg, it gets the heat and energy which enable it at length to break its shell and begin the world. It is less interesting, perhaps, but still it is interesting, to know that when a taper burns, the wax is converted into carbonic acid and water. Moreover, it is quite true that the habit of dealing with facts, which is given by the study of nature, is, as the friends of physical science praise it for being, an excellent discipline. The appeal, in the study of nature, is constantly to observation and experiment; not only is it said that the thing is so, but we can be made to see that it is so. Not only does a man tell us that when a taper burns the wax is converted into carbonic acid and water, as a man may tell us, if he likes, that Charon is punting his ferry-boat on the river Styx, or that Victor Hugo is a sublime poet, or Mr. Gladstone the most admirable of statesmen; but we are made to see that the conversion into carbonic acid and water does actually happen. This reality of natural knowledge it is, which makes the friends of physical science contrast it, as a knowledge of things, with the humanist's knowledge, which is, say they, a knowledge of words. And hence Professor Huxley is moved to lay it down that, "for the purpose of attaining real culture, an exclusively scientific education is at least as effectual as an exclusively literary education." And a certain President of the Section for Mechanical Science in the British Association is, in Scripture phrase, "very bold," and declares that if a man, in his mental training, "has substituted literature and history for natural science, he has chosen the less useful alternative." But whether we go these lengths or not, we must all admit that in natural science the habit gained of dealing with facts is a most valuable discipline, and that every one should have some experience of it.

More than this, however, is demanded by the reformers. It is proposed to make the training in natural science the main part of education, for the great majority of mankind at any rate. And here, I confess, I part company with the friends of physical science, with whom up to this point I have been agreeing. In differing from them, however, I wish to proceed with the utmost caution and diffidence. The smallness of my own acquaintance with the disciplines of natural science is ever before my mind, and I am fearful of doing these diciplines an injustice. The ability and pugnacity of the partisans of natural science make them formidable persons to contradict. The tone of tentative inquiry, which befits a being of dim faculties and bounded knowledge, is the tone I would wish to take and not to depart from. At present it seems to me, that those who are for giving to natural knowledge, as they call it, the chief place in the education of the majority of mankind, leave one important thing out of their account: the constitution of human nature. But I put this forward on the strength of some facts not at all recondite, very far from it; facts capable of being stated in the simplest possible fashion, and to which, if I so state them, the man of science will, I am sure, be willing to allow their due weight.

Deny the facts altogether, I think, he hardly can. He can hardly deny, that when we set ourselves to enumerate the powers which go to the building up of human life, and say that they are the power of conduct, the power of intellect and knowledge, the power of beauty, and the power of social life and manners—he can hardly deny that this scheme, though drawn in rough and plain lines enough, and not pretending to scientific exactness, does yet give a fairly true representation of the matter. Human nature is built up by these powers; we have the need for them all. When we have rightly met and adjusted the claims of them all, we shall then be in a fair way for getting soberness and righteousness, with wisdom. This is evident enough, and the friends of physical science would admit it.

But perhaps they may not have sufficiently observed another thing: namely, that the several powers just mentioned are not isolated, but there is, in the generality of mankind, a perpetual tendency to relate them one to another in divers ways. With one such way of relating them I am particularly concerned now. Following our instinct for intellect and knowledge, we acquire pieces of knowledge; and presently, in the generality of men, there arises the desire to relate these pieces of knowledge to our sense for conduct, to our sense for beauty—and there is weariness and dissatisfaction if the desire is baulked. Now in this desire lies, I think, the strength of that hold which letters have upon us.

All knowledge is, as I said just now, interesting; and even items of knowledge which from the nature of the case cannot well be related, but must stand isolated in our thoughts, have their interest. Even lists of exceptions have their interest. If we are studying Greek accents it is interesting to know that *pais* and *pas*, and some other monosyllables of the same form of declension, do not take the circumflex upon the last syllable of the genitive plural, but vary, in this respect, from the common rule. If we are studying physiology, it is interesting to know that the pulmonary artery carries dark blood and the pulmonary vein carries bright blood, departing in this respect from the common rule for the division of labour between the veins and the arteries. But every one knows how we seek naturally to combine the pieces of our knowledge together, to bring them under general rules, to relate them to principles; and how unsatisfactory and tiresome it would be to go on forever learning lists of exceptions, or accumulating items of fact which must stand isolated.

Well, that same need of relating our knowledge, which operates here within the sphere of our knowledge itself, we shall find operating, also, outside that sphere. We experience, as we go on learning and knowing—the vast majority of us experience—the need of relating what we have learnt and known to the sense which we have in us for conduct, to the sense which we have in us for beauty.

A certain Greek prophetess of Mantineia in Arcadia, Diotima by name, once explained to the philosopher Socrates that love, and impulse, and bent of all kinds, is, in fact, nothing else but the desire in men that good should forever be present to them. This desire for good, Diotima assured Socrates, is our fundamental desire, of which fundamental desire every impulse in us is only some one particular form. And therefore this fundamental desire it is, I suppose—this desire in men that good should be forever present to them—which acts in us when we feel the impulse for relating our knowledge to our sense for conduct and to our sense for beauty. At any rate, with men in general the instinct exists. Such is human nature. And the instinct, it will be admitted, is innocent, and human nature is preserved by our following the lead of its innocent instincts. Therefore, in seeking to gratify this instinct in question, we are following the instinct of self-preservation in humanity.

But, no doubt, some kinds of knowledge cannot be made to directly serve the instinct in question, cannot be directly related to the sense for beauty, to the sense for conduct. These are instrument-knowledges; they lead on to other knowledges, which can. A man who passes his life in instrument-knowledges is a specialist. They may be invaluable as instruments to something beyond, for those who have the gift thus to employ them; and they may be disciplines in themselves wherein it is useful for every one to have some schooling. But it is inconceivable that the generality of men should pass all their mental life with Greek accents or with formal logic. My friend Professor Sylvester, who is one of the first mathematicians in the world, holds transcendental doctrines as to the virtue of mathematics, but those doctrines are not for common men. In the very Senate House and heart of our English Cambridge I once ventured, though not without an apology for my profaneness, to hazard the opinion that for the majority of mankind a little of mathematics, even, goes a long way. Of course this is quite consistent with their being of immense importance as an instrument to something else; but it is the few who have the aptitude for thus using them, not the bulk of mankind.

The natural sciences do not, however, stand on the same footing with these instrument-knowledges. Experience shows us that the generality of men will find more interest in learning that, when a taper burns, the wax is converted into carbonic acid and water, or in learning the explanation of the phenomenon of dew, or in learning how the circulation of the blood is carried on, than they find in learning that the genitive plural of *pais* and *pas* does not take the circumflex on the termination. And one piece of natural knowledge is added to another, and others are added to that, and at last we come to propositions so interesting as Mr. Darwin's famous proposition that "our ancestor was a hairy quadruped furnished with a tail and pointed ears, probably arboreal in his habits." Or we come to propositions of such reach and magnitude as those which Professor Huxley delivers, when he says that the notions of our fore-fathers about the beginning and the end of the world were all wrong, and that nature is the expression of a definite order with which nothing interferes.

Interesting, indeed, these results of science are, important they are, and we should all of us be acquainted with them. But what I now wish you to mark is, that we are still, when they are propounded to us and we receive them, we are still in the sphere of intellect and knowledge. And for the generality of men there will be found, I say, to arise, when they have duly taken in the proposition that their ancestor was "a hairy quadruped furnished with a tail and pointed ears, probably arboreal in his habits," there will be found to arise an invincible desire to relate this proposition to the sense in us for conduct, and to the sense in us for beauty. But this the men of science will not do for us, and will hardly even profess to do. They will give us other pieces of knowledge, other facts, about other animals and their ancestors, or about plants, or about stones, or about stars; and they may finally bring us to those great "general conceptions of the universe, which are forced upon us all," says Professor Huxley, "by the progress of physical science." But still it will be *knowledge* only which they give us; knowledge not put for us into relation with our sense for conduct, our sense for beauty, and touched with emotion by being so put; not thus put for us, and therefore, to the majority of mankind, after a certain while, unsatisfying, wearying.

Not to the born naturalist, I admit. But what do we mean by a born naturalist? We mean a man in whom the zeal for observing nature is so uncommonly strong and eminent, that it marks him off from the bulk of mankind. Such a man will pass his life happily in collecting natural knowledge and reasoning upon it, and will ask for nothing, or hardly anything, more. I have heard it said that the sagacious and admirable naturalist whom we lost not very long ago, Mr. Darwin, once owned to a friend that for his part he did not experience the necessity for two things which most men find so necessary to them—religion and poetry; science and the domestic affections, he thought, were enough. To a born naturalist, I can well understand that this should seem so. So absorbing is his occupation with nature, so strong his love for his occupation, that he goes on acquiring natural knowledge and reasoning upon it, and has little time or inclination for thinking about getting it related to the desire in man for conduct, the desire in man for beauty. He relates it to them for himself as he goes along, so far as he feels the need; and he draws from the domestic affections all the additional solace necessary. But then Darwins are extremely rare. Another great and admirable master of natural knowledge, Faraday, was a Sandemanian. That is to say, he related his knowledge to his instinct for conduct and to his instinct for beauty, by the aid of that respectable Scottish sectary, Robert Sandeman. And so strong, in general, is the demand of religion and poetry to have their share in a man, to associate themselves with his knowing, and to relieve and rejoice it, that, probably, for one man amongst us with the disposition to do as Darwin did in this respect, there are at least fifty with the disposition to do as Faraday.

Education lays hold upon us, in fact, by satisfying this demand. Professor Huxley holds up to scorn medieval education, with its neglect of the knowledge of nature, its poverty even of literary studies, its formal logic devoted to "showing how and why that which the Church said was true must be true." But the great medieval Universities were not brought into being, we may be sure, by the zeal for giving a jejune and contemptible education. Kings have been their nursing fathers, and queens have been their nursing mothers, but not for this. The medieval Universities came into being, because the supposed knowledge, delivered by Scripture and the Church, so deeply engaged men's hearts, by so simply, easily, and powerfully relating itself to their desire for conduct, their desire for beauty. All other knowledge was dominated by this supposed knowledge and was subordinated to it, because of the surpassing strength of the hold which it gained upon the affections of men, by allying itself profoundly with their sense for conduct, their sense for beauty.

But now, says Professor Huxley, conceptions of the universe fatal to the notions held by our forefathers have been forced upon us by physical science. Grant to him that they are thus fatal, that the new conceptions must and will soon become current everywhere, and that every one will finally perceive them to be fatal to the beliefs of our forefathers. The need of humane letters, as they are truly called, because they serve the paramount desire in men that good should be forever present to them—the need of humane letters, to establish a relation between the new conceptions, and our instinct for beauty, our instinct for conduct, is only the more visible. The Middle Age could do without humane letters, as it could do without the study of nature, because its supposed knowledge was made to engage its emotions so powerfully. Grant that the supposed knowledge disappears, its power of being made to engage the emotions will of course disappear along with it—but the emotions themselves, and their claim to be engaged and satisfied, will remain. Now if we find by experience that humane letters have an undeniable power of engaging the emotions, the importance of humane letters in a man's training becomes not less, but greater, in proportion to the success of modern science in extirpating what it calls "medieval thinking."

Have humane letters, then, have poetry and eloquence, the power here attributed to them of engaging the emotions, and do they exercise it? And if they have it and exercise it, *how* do they exercise it, so as to exert an influence upon man's sense for conduct, his sense for beauty? Finally, even if they both can and do exert an influence upon the senses in question, how are they to relate to them the results—the modern results—of natural science? All these questions may be asked. First, have poetry and eloquence the power of calling out the emotions? The appeal is to experience. Experience shows that for the vast majority of men, for mankind in general, they have the power. Next, do they exercise it? They do. But then, *how* do they exercise it so as to affect man's sense for conduct, his sense for beauty? And this is perhaps a case for applying the Preacher's words: "Though a man labour to seek it out, yet he shall not find it; yea, farther, though a wise man think to know it, yet shall he not be able to find it." [Eccles. 8:17] Why should it be one thing, in its effect upon the emotions, to say, "Patience is a virtue," and quite another thing, in its effect upon the emotions, to say with Homer,

τλητὸν γὰρ Μοῖραι θυμὸν θέσαν ἀνθρώποισιν—[Iliad, 24:49]

"for an enduring heart have the destinies appointed to the children of men"? Why should it be one thing, in its effect upon the emotions, to say with the philosopher Spinoza, Felicitas in ea consistit quod homo suum esse conservare potest—"Man's happiness consists in his being able to preserve his own essence," and quite another thing, in its effect upon the emotions, to say with the Gospel, "What is a man advantaged, if he gain the whole world, and lose himself, forfeit himself?" How does this difference of effect arise? I cannot tell, and I am not much concerned to know; the important thing is that it does arise, and that we can profit by it. But how, finally, are poetry and eloquence to exercise the power of relating the modern results of natural science to man's instinct for conduct, his instinct for beauty? And here again I answer that I do not know how they will exercise it, but that they can and will exercise it I am sure. I do not mean that modern philosophical poets and modern philosophical moralists are to come and relate for us, in express terms, the results of modern scientific research to our instinct for conduct, our instinct for beauty. But I mean that we shall find, as a matter of experience, if we know the best that has been thought and uttered in the world, we shall find that the art and poetry and eloquence of men who lived, perhaps, long ago, who had the most limited natural knowledge, who had the most erroneous conceptions about many important matters, we shall find that this art, and poetry, and eloquence, have in fact not only the power of refreshing and delighting us, they have also the power—such is the strength and worth, in essentials, of their authors' criticism of life—they have a fortifying, and elevating, and quickening, and suggestive power, capable of wonderfully helping us to relate the results of modern science to our need for conduct, our need for beauty. Homer's conceptions of the physical universe were, I imagine, grotesque; but really, under the shock of hearing from modern science that "the world is not subordinated to man's use, and that man is not the cynosure of things terrestrial," I could, for my own part, desire no better comfort than Homer's line which I quoted just now,

τλητὸν γὰρ Μοῖραι θυμὸν θέσαν ἀνθρώποισιν—

"for an enduring heart have the destinies appointed to the children of men"!

And the more that men's minds are cleared, the more that the results of science are frankly accepted, the more that poetry and eloquence come to be received and studied as what in truth they really are—the criticism of life by gifted men, alive and active with extraordinary power at an unusual number of points—so much the more will the value of humane letters, and of art also, which is an utterance having a like kind of power with theirs, be felt and acknowledged, and their place in education be secured.

Let us therefore, all of us, avoid indeed as much as possible any invidious comparison between the merits of humane letters, as means of education, and the merits of the natural sciences. But when some President of a Section for Mechanical Science insists on making the comparison, and tells us that "he who in his training has substituted literature and history for natural science has chosen the less useful alternative," let us make answer to him that the student of humane letters only, will, at least, know also the great general conceptions brought in by modern physical science; for science, as Professor Huxley says, forces them upon us all. But the student of the natural sciences only, will, by our very hypothesis, know nothing of humane letters; not to mention that in setting himself to be perpetually accumulating natural knowledge, he sets himself to do what only specialists have in general the gift for doing genially. And so he will probably be unsatisfied, or at any rate incomplete, and even more incomplete than the student of humane letters only.

I once mentioned in a school-report, how a young man in one of our English training colleges having to paraphrase the passage in *Macbeth* beginning,

Can'st thou not minister to a mind diseased?

turned this line into, "Can you not wait upon the lunatic?" And I remarked what a curious state of things it would be, if every pupil of our national schools knew, let us say, that the moon is two thousand one hundred and sixty miles in diameter, and thought at the same time that a good paraphrase for

Can'st thou not minister to a mind diseased?

was, "Can you not wait upon the lunatic?" If one is driven to choose, I think I would rather have a young person ignorant about the moon's diameter, but aware that "Can you not wait upon the lunatic?" is bad, than a young person whose education had been such as to manage things the other way.

Or to go higher than the pupils of our national schools. I have in my mind's eye a member of our British Parliament who comes to travel here in America, who afterwards relates his travels, and who shows a really masterly knowledge of the geology of this great country and of its mining capabilities, but who ends by gravely suggesting that the United States should borrow a prince from our Royal Family, and should make him their king, and should create a House of Lords of great landed proprietors after the pattern of ours; and then America, he thinks, would have her future happily and perfectly secured. Surely, in this case, the President of the Section for Mechanical Science would himself hardly say that our member of Parliament, by concentrating himself upon geology and mineralogy, and so on, and not attending to literature and history, had "chosen the more useful alternative."

If then there is to be separation and option between humane letters on the one hand, and the natural sciences on the other, the great majority of mankind, all who have not exceptional and overpowering aptitudes for the study of nature, would do well, I cannot but think, to choose to be educated in humane letters rather than in the natural sciences. Letters will call out their being at more points, will make them live more.

I said that before I ended I would just touch on the question of classical education, and I will keep my word. Even if literature is to retain a large place in our education, yet Latin and Greek, say the friends of progress, will certainly have to go. Greek is the grand offender in the eyes of these gentlemen. The attackers of the established course of study think that against Greek, at any rate, they have irresistible arguments. Literature may perhaps be needed in education, they say; but why on earth should it be Greek literature? Why not French or German? Nay, "has not an Englishman models in his own literature of every kind of excellence?" As before, it is not on any weak pleadings of my own that I rely for convincing the gainsayers; it is on the constitution of human nature itself, and on the instinct of self-preservation in humanity. The instinct for beauty is set in human nature, as surely as the instinct for knowledge is set there, or the instinct for conduct. If the instinct for beauty is served by Greek literature and art as it is served by no other literature and art, we may trust to the instinct of self-preservation in humanity for keeping Greek as part of our culture. We may trust to it for even making the study of Greek more prevalent than it is now. Greek will come, I hope, some day to be studied more rationally than at present; but it will be increasingly studied as men increasingly feel the need in them for beauty, and how powerfully Greek art and Greek literature can serve this need. Women will again study Greek, as Lady Jane Grey did; I believe that in that chain of forts, with which the fair host of the Amazons are now engirdling our English universities, I find that here in America, in colleges like Smith College in Massachusetts, and Vassar College in the State of New York, and in the happy families of the mixed universities out West, they are studying it already.

Defuit una mihi symmetria prisca—"The antique symmetry was the one thing wanting to me," said Leonardo da Vinci; and he was an Italian. I will not presume to speak for the Americans, but I am sure that, in the Englishman, the want of this admirable symmetry of the Greeks is a thousand times more great and crying than in any Italian. The results of the want show themselves most glaringly, perhaps, in our architecture, but they show themselves, also, in all our art. *Fit details strictly combined, in view of a large general result nobly conceived:* that is just the beautiful *symmetria prisca* ["antique symmetry"] of the Greeks, and it is just where we English fail, where all our art fails. Striking ideas we have, and well executed details we have; but that high symmetry which, with satisfying and delightful effect, combines them, we seldom or never have. The glorious beauty of the Acropolis at Athens did not come from single fine things stuck about on that hill, a statue here, a gateway there—no, it arose from all things being perfectly combined for a supreme total effect. What must not an Englishman feel about our deficiencies in this respect, as the sense for beauty, whereof this symmetry is an essential element, awakens and strengthens within him! what will not one day be his respect and desire for Greece and its *symmetria prisca*, when the scales drop from his eyes as he walks the London streets, and he sees such a lesson in meanness, as the Strand, for instance, in its true deformity! But here we are coming to our friend Mr. Ruskin's province, and I will not intrude upon it, for he is its very sufficient guardian.

And so we at last find, it seems, we find flowing in favour of the humanities the natural and necessary stream of things, which seemed against them when we started. The "hairy quadruped furnished with a tail and pointed ears, probably arboreal in his habits," this good fellow carried hidden in his nature, apparently, something destined to develop into a necessity for humane letters. Nay, more; we seem finally to be even led to the further conclusion that our hairy ancestor carried in his nature, also, a necessity for Greek.

And, therefore, to say the truth, I cannot really think that humane letters are in much actual danger of being thrust out from their leading place in education, in spite of the array of authorities against them at this moment. So long as human nature is what it is, their attractions will remain irresistible. As with Greek, so with letters generally: they will some day come, we may hope, to be studied more rationally, but they will not lose their place. What will happen will rather be that there will be crowded into education other matters besides, far too many; there will be, perhaps, a period of unsettlement and confusion and false tendency; but letters will not in the end lose their leading place. If they lose it for a time, they will get it back again. We shall be brought back to them by our wants and aspirations. And a poor humanist may possess his soul in patience, neither strive nor cry, admit the energy and brilliancy of the partisans of physical science, and their present favour with the public, to be far greater than his own, and still have a happy faith that the nature of things works silently on behalf of the studies which he loves, and that, while we shall all have to acquaint ourselves with the great results reached by modern science, and to give ourselves as much training in its disciplines as we can conveniently carry, yet the majority of men will always require humane letters; and so much the more, as they have the more and the greater results of science to relate to the need in man for conduct, and to the need in him for beauty.

THOMAS H. HUXLEY

❧ *Science and Culture*

SIX YEARS ago, as some of my present hearers may remember, I had the privilege of addressing a large assemblage of the inhabitants of this city [Birmingham], who had gathered together to do honour to the memory of their famous townsman, Joseph Priestley; and, if any satisfaction attaches to posthumous glory, we may hope that the names of the burnt-out philosopher were then finally appeased.

No man, however, who is endowed with a fair share of common sense, and not more than a fair share of vanity, will identify either contemporary or posthumous fame with the highest good; and Priestley's life leaves no doubt that he, at any rate, set a much higher value upon the advancement of knowledge, and the promotion of that freedom of thought which is at once the cause and the consequence of intellectual progress.

Hence I am disposed to think that, if Priestley could be amongst us to-day, the occasion of our meeting would afford him even greater pleasure than the proceedings which celebrated the centenary of his chief discovery. The kindly heart would be moved, the high sense of social duty would be satisfied, by the spectacle of well-earned wealth neither squandered in tawdry luxury and vainglorious show, nor scattered with the careless charity which blesses neither him that gives nor him that takes, but expended in the execution of a well-considered plan for the aid of present and future generations of those who are willing to help themselves.

We shall all be of one mind thus far. But it is needful to share Priestley's keen interest in physical science; and to have learned, as he had learned, the value of scientific training in fields of inquiry apparently far remote from physical science; in order to appreciate, as he would have appreciated, the value of the noble gift which Sir Josiah Mason has bestowed upon the inhabitants of the Midland district.

For us children of the nineteenth century, however, the establishment of a college under the conditions of Sir Josiah Mason's Trust, has a significance apart from any which it could have possessed a hundred years ago. It appears to be an indication that we are reaching the crisis of the battle, or rather of the long series of battles, which have been fought over education in a campaign which began long before Priestley's time, and will probably not be finished just yet.

In the last century, the combatants were the champions of ancient literature on the one side, and those of modern literature on the other; but, some thirty years ago, the contest became complicated by the appearance of a third army, ranged round the banner of Physical Science.

I am not aware that any one has authority to speak in the name of this new host. For it must be admitted to be somewhat of a guerilla force, composed largely of irregulars, each of whom fights pretty much for his own hand. But the impressions of a full private, who has seen a good deal of service in the ranks, respecting the present position of affairs and the conditions of a permanent peace, may not be devoid of interest; and I do not know that I could make a better use of the present opportunity than by laying them before you.

From the time that the first suggestion to introduce physical science into ordinary education was timidly whispered, until now, the advocates of scientific education have met with opposition of two kinds. On the one hand, they have been pooh-poohed by the men of business who pride themselves on being the representatives of practicality; while, on the other hand, they have been excommunicated by the classical scholars, in their capacity of Levites in charge of the ark of culture and monopolists of liberal education.

The practical men believed that the idol whom they worship—rule of thumb—has been the source of the past prosperity, and will suffice for the future welfare of the arts and manufactures. They were of opinion that science is speculative rubbish; that theory and practice have nothing to do with one another; and that the scientific habit of mind is an impediment, rather than an aid, in the conduct of ordinary affairs.

I have used the past tense in speaking of the practical men—for although they were very formidable thirty years ago, I am not sure that the pure species has not been extirpated. In fact, so far as mere argument goes, they have been subjected to such a *feu d'enfer* [hell-fire] that it is a miracle if any have escaped. But I have remarked that your typical practical man has an unexpected resemblance to one of Milton's angels. His spiritual wounds, such as are inflicted by logical weapons, may be as deep as a well and as wide as a church door, but beyond shedding a few drops of ichor, celestial or otherwise, he is no whit the worse. So, if any of these opponents be left, I will not waste time in vain repetition of the demonstrative evidence of the practical value of science; but knowing that a parable will sometimes penetrate where syllogisms fail to effect an entrance, I will offer a story for their consideration.

Once upon a time, a boy, with nothing to depend upon but his own vigorous nature, was thrown into the thick of the struggle for existence in the midst of a great manufacturing population. He seems to have had a hard fight, inasmuch as, by the time he was thirty years of age, his total disposable funds amounted to twenty pounds. Nevertheless, middle life found him giving proof of his comprehension of the practical problems he had been roughly called upon to solve, by a career of remarkable prosperity.

Finally, having reached old age with its well-earned surroundings of "honour, troops of friends," the hero of my story bethought himself of those who were making a like start in life, and how he could stretch out a helping hand to them.

After long and anxious reflection this successful practical man of business could devise nothing better than to provide them with the means of obtaining "sound, extensive, and practical scientific knowledge." And he devoted a large part of his wealth and five years of incessant work to this end.

I need not point the moral of a tale which, as the solid and spacious fabric of the Scientific College assures us, is no fable, nor can anything which I could say intensify the force of this practical answer to practical objections.

We may take it for granted then, that, in the opinion of those best qualified to judge, the diffusion of thorough scientific education is an absolutely essential condition of industrial progress; and that the College which has been opened to-day will confer an inestimable boon upon those whose livelihood is to be gained by the practise of the arts and manufactures of the district.

The only question worth discussion is, whether the conditions, under which the work of the College is to be carried out, are such as to give it the best possible chance of achieving permanent success.

Sir Josiah Mason, without doubt most wisely, has left large freedom of action to the trustees, to whom he proposes ultimately to commit the administration of the College, so that they may be able to adjust its arrangements in accordance with the changing conditions of the future. But, with respect to three points, he has laid most explicit injunctions upon both administrators and teachers.

Party politics are forbidden to enter into the minds of either, so far as the work of the College is concerned; theology is as sternly banished from its precincts; and finally, it is especially declared that the College shall make no provision for "mere literary instruction and education."

It does not concern me at present to dwell upon the first two injunctions any longer than may be needful to express my full conviction of their wisdom. But the third prohibition brings us face to face with those other opponents of scientific education, who are by no means in the moribund condition of the practical man, but alive, alert, and formidable.

It is not impossible that we shall hear this express exclusion of "literary instruction and education" from a College which, nevertheless, professes to give a high and efficient education, sharply criticised. Certainly the time was that the Levites of culture would have sounded their trumpets against its walls as against an educational Jericho.

How often have we not been told that the study of physical science is incompetent to confer culture; that it touches none of the higher problems of life; and, what is worse, that the continual devotion to scientific studies tends to generate a narrow and bigoted belief in the applicability of scientific methods to the search after truth of all kinds? How frequently one has reason to observe that no reply to a troublesome argument tells so well as calling its author a "mere scientific specialist." And, as I am afraid it is not permissible to speak of this form of opposition to scientific education in the past tense; may we not expect to be told that this, not only omission, but prohibition, of "mere literary instruction and education" is a patent example of scientific narrow-mindedness? I am not acquainted with Sir Josiah Mason's reasons for the action which he has taken; but if, as I apprehend is the case, he refers to the ordinary classical course of our schools and universities by the name of "mere literary instruction and education," I venture to offer sundry reasons of my own in support of that action.

For I hold very strongly by two convictions—The first is, that neither the discipline nor the subject-matter of classical education is of such direct value to the student of physical science as to justify the expenditure of valuable time upon either; and the second is, that for the purpose of attaining real culture, an exclusively scientific education is at least as effectual as an exclusively literary education.

I need hardly point out to you that these opinions, especially the latter, are diametrically opposed to those of the great majority of educated Englishmen, influenced as they are by school and university traditions. In their belief, culture is obtainable only by a liberal education; and a liberal education is synonymous, not merely with education and instruction in literature, but in one particular form of literature, namely, that of Greek and Roman antiquity. They hold that the man who has learned Latin and Greek, however little, is educated; while he who is versed in other branches of knowledge, however deeply, is a more or less respectable specialist, not admissible into the cultured caste. The stamp of the educated man, the University degree, is not for him.

I am too well acquainted with the generous catholicity of spirit, the true sympathy with scientific thought, which pervades the writings of our chief apostle of culture to identify him with these opinions; and yet one may cull from one and another of those epistles to the Philistines, which so much delight all who do not answer to that name, sentences which lend them some support.

Mr. Arnold tells us that the meaning of culture is "to know the best that has been thought and said in the world." It is the criticism of life contained in literature. That criticism regards "Europe as being, for intellectual and spiritual purposes, one great confederation, bound to a joint action and working to a common result; and whose members have, for their common outfit, a knowledge of Greek, Roman, and Eastern antiquity, and of one another. Special, local, and temporary advantages being put out of account, that modern nation will in the intellectual and spiritual sphere make most progress, which most thoroughly carries out this programme. And what is that but saying that we too, all of us, as individuals, the more thoroughly we carry it out, shall make the more progress?"

We have here to deal with two distinct propositions. The first, that a criticism of life is the essence of culture; the second, that literature contains the materials which suffice for the construction of such criticism.

I think that we must all assent to the first proposition. For culture certainly means something quite different from learning or technical skill. It implies the possession of an ideal, and the habit of critically estimating the value of things by comparison with a theoretic standard. Perfect culture should supply a complete theory of life, based upon a clear knowledge alike of its possibilities and of its limitations.

But we may agree to all this, and yet strongly dissent from the assumption that literature alone is competent to supply this knowledge. After having learnt all that Greek, Roman, and Eastern antiquity have thought and said, and all that modern literature have to tell us, it is not self-evident that we have laid a sufficiently broad and deep foundation for the criticism of life, which constitutes culture.

Indeed, to any one acquainted with the scope of physical science, it is not at all evident. Considering progress only in the "intellectual and spiritual sphere," I find myself wholly unable to admit that either nations or individuals will really advance, if their common outfit draws nothing from the stores of physical science. I should say that an army, without weapons of precision and with no particular base of operations, might more hopefully enter upon a campaign on the Rhine, than a man, devoid of a knowledge of what physical science has done in the last century, upon a criticism of life.

When a biologist meets with an anomaly, he instinctively turns to the study of development to clear it up. The rationale of contradictory opinions may with equal confidence be sought in history.

It is, happily, no new thing that Englishmen should employ their wealth in building and endowing institutions for educational purposes. But, five or six hundred years ago, deeds of foundation expressed or implied conditions as nearly as possible contrary to those which have been thought expedient by Sir Josiah Mason. That is to say, physical science was practically ignored, while a certain literary training was enjoined as a means to the acquirement of knowledge which was essentially theological.

The reason of this singular contradiction between the actions of men alike animated by a strong and disinterested desire to promote the welfare of their fellows, is easily discovered.

At that time, in fact, if any one desired knowledge beyond such as could be obtained by his own observation, or by common conversation, his first necessity was to learn the Latin language, inasmuch as all the higher knowledge of the western world was contained in works written in that language. Hence, Latin grammar, with logic and rhetoric, studied through Latin, were the fundamentals of education. With respect to the substance of the knowledge imparted through this channel, the Jewish and Christian Scriptures, as interpreted and supplemented by the Romish Church, were held to contain a complete and infallibly true body of information.

Theological dicta were, to the thinkers of those days, that which the axioms and definitions of Euclid are to the geometers of these. The business of the philosophers of the middle ages was to deduce from the data furnished by the theologians, conclusions in accordance with ecclesiastical decrees. They were allowed the high privilege of showing, by logical process, how and why that which the Church said was true, must be true. And if their demonstrations fell short of or exceeded this limit, the Church was maternally ready to check their aberrations; if need were by the help of the secular arm.

Between the two, our ancestors were furnished with a compact and complete criticism of life. They were told how the world began and how it would end; they learned that all material existence was but a base and insignificant blot upon the fair face of the spiritual world, and that nature was, to all intents and purposes, the playground of the devil; they learned that the earth is the centre of the visible universe, and that man is the cynosure of things terrestrial, and more especially was it inculcated that the course of nature had no fixed order, but that it could be, and constantly was, altered by the agency of innumerable spiritual beings, good and bad, according as they were moved by the deeds and prayers of men. The sum and substance of the whole doctrine was to produce the conviction that the only thing really worth knowing in this world was how to secure that place in a better which, under certain conditions, the Church promised.

Our ancestors had a living belief in this theory of life, and acted upon it in their dealings with education, as in all other matters. Culture meant saintliness—after the fashion of the saints of those days; the education that led to it was, of necessity, theological; and the way to theology lay through Latin.

That the study of nature—further than was requisite for the satisfaction of everyday wants—should have any bearing on human life was far from the thoughts of men thus trained. Indeed, as nature had been cursed for man's sake, it was an obvious conclusion that those who meddled with nature were likely to come into pretty close contact with Satan. And, if any born scientific investigator followed his instincts, he might safely reckon upon earning the reputation, and probably upon suffering the fate, of a sorcerer.

Had the western world been left to itself in Chinese isolation, there is no saying how long this state of things might have endured. But, happily, it was not left to itself. Even earlier than the thirteenth century, the development of Moorish civilisation in Spain and the great movement of the Crusades had introduced the leaven which, from that day to this, has never ceased to work. At first, through the intermediation of Arabic translations, afterwards by the study of the originals, the western nations of Europe became acquainted with the writings of the ancient philosophers and poets, and, in time, with the whole of the vast literature of antiquity.

Whatever there was of high intellectual aspiration or dominant capacity in

Italy, France, Germany, and England, spent itself for centuries in taking possession of the rich inheritance left by the dead civilisations of Greece and Rome. Marvellously aided by the invention of printing, classical learning spread and flourished. Those who possessed it prided themselves on having attained the highest culture then within the reach of mankind.

And justly. For, saving Dante on his solitary pinnacle, there was no figure in modern literature at the time of the Renascence to compare with the men of antiquity; there was no art to compete with their sculpture; there was no physical science but that which Greece had created. Above all, there was no other example of perfect intellectual freedom—of the unhesitating acceptance of reason as the sole guide to truth and the supreme arbiter of conduct.

The new learning necessarily soon exerted a profound influence upon education. The language of the monks and schoolmen seemed little better than gibberish to scholars fresh from Virgil and Cicero, and the study of Latin was placed upon a new foundation. Moreover, Latin itself ceased to afford the sole key to knowledge. The student who sought the highest thought of antiquity, found only a second-hand reflection of it in Roman literature, and turned his face to the full light of the Greeks. And after a battle, not altogether dissimilar to that which is at present being fought over the teaching of physical science, the study of Greek was recognised as an essential element of all higher education.

Then the Humanists, as they were called, won the day; and the great reform which they effected was of incalculable service to mankind. But the Nemesis of all reformers is finality; and the reformers of education, like those of religion, fell into the profound, however common, error of mistaking the beginning for the end of the work of reformation.

The representatives of the Humanists, in the nineteenth century, take their stand upon classical education as the sole avenue to culture, as firmly as if we were still in the age of Renascence. Yet, surely, the present intellectual relations of the modern and the ancient worlds are profoundly different from those which obtained three centuries ago. Leaving aside the existence of a great and characteristically modern literature, of modern painting, and, especially, of modern music, there is one feature of the present state of the civilised world which separates it more widely from the Renascence, than the Renascence was separated from the middle ages.

This distinctive character of our own times lies in the vast and constantly increasing part which is played by natural knowledge. Not only is our daily life shaped by it, not only does the prosperity of millions of men depend upon it, but our whole theory of life has long been influenced, consciously or unconsciously, by the general conceptions of the universe, which have been forced upon us by physical science.

In fact, the most elementary acquaintance with the results of scientific investigation shows us that they offer a broad and striking contradiction to the opinion so implicitly credited and taught in the middle ages.

The notions of the beginning and the end of the world entertained by our forefathers are no longer credible. It is very certain that the earth is not the chief body in the material universe, and that the world is not subordinated to man's use. It is even more certain that nature is the expression of a definite order with which nothing interferes, and that the chief business of mankind is to learn that order and govern themselves accordingly. Moreover this scientific "criticism of life" presents itself to us with different credentials from any other. It appeals not to authority, nor to what anybody may have thought or said, but to nature. It admits that all our interpretations of natural fact are more or less imperfect and symbolic, and bids the learner seek for truth not among words but among things. It warns us that the assertion which outstrips evidence is not only a blunder but a crime.

The purely classical education advocated by the representatives of the Humanists in our day, gives no inkling of all this. A man may be a better scholar than Erasmus, and know no more of the chief causes of the present intellectual fermentation than Erasmus did. Scholarly and pious persons, worthy of all respect, favour us with allocutions upon the sadness of the antagonism of science to their mediaeval way of thinking, which betray an ignorance of the first principles of scientific investigation, an incapacity for understanding what a man of science means by veracity, and an unconsciousness of the weight of established scientific truths, which is almost comical.

There is no great force in the *tu quoque* argument, or else the advocates of scientific education might fairly enough retort upon the modern Humanists that they may be learned specialists, but that they possess no such sound foundation for a criticism of life as deserves the name of culture. And, indeed, if we were disposed to be cruel, we might urge that the Humanists have brought this reproach upon themselves, not because they are too full of the spirit of the ancient Greek, but because they lack it.

The period of the Renascence is commonly called that of the "Revival of Letters," as if the influences then brought to bear upon the mind of Western Europe had been wholly exhausted in the field of literature. I think it is very commonly forgotten that the revival of science, effected by the same agency, although less conspicuous, was not less momentous.

In fact, the few and scattered students of nature of that day picked up the clue to her secrets exactly as it fell from the hands of the Greeks a thousand years before. The foundations of mathematics were so well laid by them, that our children learn their geometry from a book written for the school of Alexandria two thousand years ago. Modern astronomy is the natural continuation and development of the work of Hipparchus and of Ptolemy; modern physics of that of Democritus and of Archimedes; it was long before modern biological science outgrew the knowledge bequeathed to us by Aristotle, by Theophrastus, and by Galen.

We cannot know all the best thoughts and sayings of the Greeks unless we know what they thought about natural phenomena. We cannot fully apprehend their criticism of life unless we understand the extent to which that criticism was affected by scientific conceptions. We falsely pretend to be the inheritors of their culture, unless we are penetrated, as the best minds among them were, with an unhesitating faith that the free employment of reason, in accordance with scientific method, is the sole method of reaching truth.

Thus I venture to think that the pretensions of our modern Humanists to the possession of the monopoly of culture and to the exclusive inheritance of the spirit of antiquity must be abated, if not abandoned. But I should be very sorry that anything I have said should be taken to imply a desire on my part to depreciate the value of classical education, as it might be and as it sometimes is. The native capacities of mankind vary no less than their opportunities; and while culture is one, the road by which one man may best reach it is widely different from that which is most advantageous to another. Again, while scientific education is yet inchoate and tentative, classical education is thoroughly well organised upon the practical experience of generations of teachers. So that, given ample time for learning and estimation for ordinary life, or for a literary career, I do not think that a young Englishman in search of culture can do better than follow the course usually marked out for him, supplementing its deficiencies by his own efforts.

But for those who mean to make science their serious occupation; or who intend to follow the profession of medicine; or who have to enter early upon the business of life; for all these, in my opinion, classical education is a mistake; and it is for this reason that I am glad to see "mere literary education and instruction" shut out from the curriculum of Sir Josiah Mason's College, seeing that its inclusion would probably lead to the introduction of the ordinary smattering of Latin and Greek.

Nevertheless, I am the last person to question the importance of genuine literary education, or to suppose that intellectual culture can be complete without it. An exclusively scientific training will bring about a mental twist as surely as an exclusively literary training. The value of the cargo does not compensate for a ship's being out of trim; and I should be very sorry to think that the Scientific College would turn out none but lopsided men.

There is no need, however, that such a catastrophe should happen. Instruction in English, French, and German is provided, and thus the three greatest literatures of the modern world are made accessible to the student.

French and German, and especially the latter language, are absolutely indispensable to those who desire full knowledge in any department of science. But even supposing that the knowledge of these languages acquired is not more than sufficient for purely scientific purposes, every Englishman has, in his native tongue, an almost perfect instrument of literary expression; and, in his own literature, models of every kind of literary excellence. If an Englishman cannot get literary culture out of his Bible, his Shakespeare, his Milton, neither, in my belief, will the profoundest study of Homer and Sophocles, Virgil and Horace, give it to him.

Thus, since the constitution of the College makes sufficient provision for literary as well as for scientific education, and since artistic instruction is also contemplated, it seems to me that a fairly complete culture is offered to all who are willing to take advantage of it.

But I am not sure that at this point the "practical" man, scotched but not slain, may ask what all this talk about culture has to do with an Institution, the object of which is defined to be "to promote the prosperity of the manufactures and the industry of the country." He may suggest that what is wanted for this end is not culture, nor even a purely scientific discipline, but simply a knowledge of applied science.

I often wish that this phrase, "applied science," had never been invented. For it suggests that there is a sort of scientific knowledge of direct practical use, which can be studied apart from another sort of scientific knowledge, which is of no practical utility, and which is termed "pure science." But there is no more complete fallacy than this. What people call applied science is nothing but the application of pure science to particular classes of problems. It consists of deductions from those general principles, established by reasoning and observation, which constitute pure science. No one can safely make these deductions until he has a firm grasp of the principles; and he can obtain that grasp only by personal experience of the operations of observation and of reasoning on which they are founded.

Almost all the processes employed in the arts and manufactures fall within the range either of physics or of chemistry. In order to improve them, one must thoroughly understand them; and no one has a chance of really understanding them, unless he has obtained that mastery of principles and that habit of dealing with facts, which is given by long-continued and well-directed purely scientific training in the physical and the chemical laboratory. So that there really is no question as to the necessity of purely scientific discipline, even if the work of the College were limited by the narrowest interpretation of its stated aims.

And, as to the desirableness of a wider culture than that yielded by science alone, it is to be recollected that the improvement of manufacturing processes is only one of the conditions which contribute to the prosperity of industry. Industry is a means and not an end; and mankind work only to get something which they want. What that something is depends partly on their innate, and partly on their acquired, desires.

If the wealth resulting from prosperous industry is to be spent upon the gratification of unworthy desires, if the increasing perfection of manufacturing processes is to be accompanied by an increasing debasement of those who carry them on, I do not see the good of industry and prosperity.

Now it is perfectly true that men's views of what is desirable depend upon their characters; and that the innate proclivities to which we give that name are not touched by any amount of instruction. But it does not follow that even mere intellectual education may not, to an indefinite extent, modify the practical manifestation of the characters of men in their actions, by supplying them with motives unknown to the ignorant. A pleasure-loving character will have pleasure of some sort; but, if you give him the choice, he may prefer pleasures which do not degrade him to those which do. And this choice is offered to every man, who possesses in literary or artistic culture a never-failing source of pleasures, which are neither withered by age, nor staled by custom, nor embittered in the recollection by the pangs of self-reproach.

If the Institution opened to-day fulfils the intention of its founder, the picked intelligences among all classes of the population of this district will pass through it. No child born in Birmingham, henceforward, if he have the capacity to profit by the opportunities offered to him, first in the primary and other schools, and afterwards in the Scientific College, need fail to obtain, not merely the instruction, but the culture most appropriate to the conditions of his life.

Within these walls, the future employer and the future artisan may sojourn together for a while, and carry, through all their lives, the stamp of the influences then brought to bear upon them. Hence, it is not beside the mark to remind you, that the prosperity of industry depends not merely upon the improvement of manufacturing processes, not merely upon the ennobling of the individual character, but upon a third condition, namely, a clear understanding of the conditions of social life, on the part of both the capitalist and the operative, and their agreement upon common principles of social action. They must learn that social phenomena are as much the expression of natural laws as any others; that no social arrangements can be permanent unless they harmonise with the requirements of social statics and dynamics; and that, in the nature of things, there is an arbiter whose decisions execute themselves.

But this knowledge is only to be obtained by the application of the methods of investigation adopted in physical researches to the investigation of the phenomena of society. Hence, I confess, I should like to see one addition made to the excellent scheme of education propounded for the College, in the shape of provision for the teaching of Sociology. For though we are all agreed that party politics are to have no place in the instruction of the College; yet in this country, practically governed as it is now by universal suffrage, every man who does his duty must exercise political functions. And, if the evils which are inseparable from the good of political liberty are to be checked, if the perpetual oscillation of nations between anarchy and despotism is to be replaced by the steady march of self-restraining freedom; it will be because men will gradually bring themselves to deal with political, as they now deal with scientific, questions; to be as ashamed of undue haste and partisan prejudice in the one case as in the other; and to believe that the machinery of society is at least as delicate as that of a spinning-jenny, and as little likely to be improved by the meddling of those who have not taken the trouble to master the principles of its action.

In conclusion, I am sure that I make myself the mouthpiece of all present in offering to the venerable founder of the Institution, which now commences its beneficent career, our congratulations on the completion of his work; and in expressing the conviction, that the remotest posterity will point to it as a crucial instance of the wisdom which natural piety leads all men to ascribe to their ancestors.

WALTER PATER

❧ *Conclusion to* The Renaissance

To REGARD all things and principles of things as inconstant modes or fashions has more and more become the tendency of modern thought. Let us begin with that which is without—our physical life. Fix upon it in one of its more exquisite intervals, the moment, for instance, of delicious recoil from the flood of water in summer heat. What is the whole physical life in that moment but a combination of natural elements to which science gives their names? But those elements, phosphorus and lime and delicate fibres, are present not in the human body alone: we detect them in places most remote from it. Our physical life is a perpetual motion of them—the passage of the blood, the wasting and repairing of the lenses of the eye, the modification of the tissues of the brain under every ray of light and sound—processes which science reduces to simpler and more elementary forces. Like the elements of which we are composed, the action of these forces extends beyond us: it rusts iron and ripens corn. Far out on every side of us those elements are broadcast, driven in many currents; and birth and gesture and death and the springing of violets from the grave are but a few out of ten thousand resultant combinations. That clear, perpetual outline of face and limb is but an image of ours, under which we group them—a design in a web, the actual threads of which pass out beyond it. This at least of flamelike our life has, that it is but the concurrence, renewed from moment to moment, of forces parting sooner or later on their ways.

Or if we begin with the inward world of thought and feeling, the whirlpool is still more rapid, the flame more eager and devouring. There it is no longer the gradual darkening of the eye, the gradual fading of colour from the wall— movements of the shore-side, where the water flows down indeed, though in apparent rest—but the race of the midstream, a drift of momentary acts of sight and passion and thought. At first sight experience seems to bury us under a flood of external objects, pressing upon us with a sharp and importunate reality, calling us out of ourselves in a thousand forms of action. But when reflection begins to play upon those objects they are dissipated under its influence; the cohesive force seems suspended like some trick of magic; each object is loosed into a group of impressions—colour, odour, texture—in the mind of the observer. And if we continue to dwell in thought on this world, not of objects in the solidity with which language invests them, but of impressions, unstable, flickering, inconsistent, which burn and are extinguished with our consciousness of them, it contracts still further: the whole scope of observation is dwarfed into the narrow chamber of the individual mind. Experience, already reduced to a group of impressions, is ringed round for each one of us by that thick wall of personality through which no real voice has ever pierced on its way to us, or from us to that which we can only conjecture to be without. Every one of those impressions is the impression of the individual in his isolation, each mind keeping as a solitary prisoner its own dream of a world. Analysis goes a step farther still, and assures us that those impressions of the individual mind to which, for each one of us, experience dwindles down, are in perpetual flight; that each of them is limited by time, and that as time is infinitely divisible, each of them is infinitely divisible also; all that is actual in it being a single moment, gone while we try to apprehend it, of which it may ever be more truly said that it has ceased to be than that it is. To such a tremulous wisp constantly reforming itself on the stream, to a single sharp impression, with a sense in it, a relic more or less fleeting, of such moments gone by, what is real in our life fines itself down. It is with this movement, with the passage and dissolution of impressions, images, sensations, that analysis leaves off—that continual vanishing away, that strange, perpetual weaving and unweaving of ourselves.

Philosophiren, says Novalis, *ist dephlegmatisiren vivificiren.* The service of philosophy, of speculative culture, towards the human spirit, is to rouse, to startle it to a life of constant and eager observation. Every moment some form grows perfect in hand or face; some tone on the hills or the sea is choicer than the rest; some mood of passion or insight or intellectual excitement is irresistibly real and attractive to us—for that moment only. Not the fruit of experience, but experience itself, is the end. A counted number of pulses only is given to us of a variegated, dramatic life. How may we see in them all that is to be seen in them by the finest senses? How shall we pass most swiftly from point to point, and be present always at the focus where the greatest number of vital forces unite in their purest energy?

To burn always with this hard, gemlike flame, to maintain this ecstasy, is success in life. In a sense it might even be said that our failure is to form habits: for, after all, habit is relative to a stereotyped world, and meantime it is only the roughness of the eye that makes any two persons, things, situations, seem alike. While all melts under our feet, we may well grasp at any exquisite passion, or any contribution to knowledge that seems by a lifted horizon to set the spirit free for a moment, or any stirring of the senses, strange dyes, strange colours, and curious odours, or work of the artist's hands, or the face of one's friend. Not to discriminate every moment some passionate attitude in those about us, and in the very brilliancy of their gifts some tragic dividing of forces on their ways, is, on this short day of frost and sun, to sleep before evening. With this sense of the splendour of our experience and of its awful brevity, gathering all we are into one desperate effort to see and touch, we shall hardly have time to make theories about the things we see and touch. What we have to do is to be for ever curiously testing new opinions and courting new impressions, never acquiescing in a facile orthodoxy of Comte, or of Hegel, or of our own. Philosophical theories or ideas, as points of view, instruments of criticism, may help us to gather up what might otherwise pass unregarded by us. "Philosophy is the microscope of thought." The theory or idea or system which requires of us the sacrifice of any part of this experience, in consideration of some interest into which we cannot enter, or some abstract theory we have not identified with ourselves, or of what is only conventional, has no real claim upon us.

One of the most beautiful passages of Rousseau is that in the sixth book of the *Confessions,* where he describes the awakening in him of the literary sense. An undefinable taint of death had always clung about him, and now in early manhood he believed himself smitten by mortal disease. He asked himself how he might make as much as possible of the interval that remained; and he was not biased by anything in his previous life when he decided that it must be by intellectual excitement, which he found just then in the clear, fresh writings of Voltaire. Well! we are all *condamnés,* as Victor Hugo says: we are all under sentence of death but with a sort of indefinite reprieve—*les hommes sont tous condamnés à mort avec des sursis indéfinis:* we have an interval, and then our place knows us no more. Some spend this interval in listlessness, some in high passions, the wisest, at least among "the children of this world," in art and song. For our one chance lies in expanding that interval, in getting as many pulsations as possible into the given time. Great passions may give us this quickened sense of life, ecstasy and sorrow of love, the various forms of enthusiastic activity, disinterested or otherwise, which come naturally to many of us. Only be sure it is passion—that it does yield you this fruit of a quickened, multiplied consciousness. Of such wisdom, the poetic passion, the desire of beauty, the love of art for its own sake, has most. For art comes to you proposing frankly to give nothing but the highest quality to your moments as they pass, and simply for those moments' sake.

HENRY JAMES

❧ *The Art of Fiction*

I SHOULD not have affixed so comprehensive a title to these few remarks, necessarily wanting in any completeness upon a subject the full consideration of which would carry us far, did I not seem to discover a pretext for my temerity in the interesting pamphlet lately published under this name by Mr. Walter Besant. Mr. Besant's lecture at the Royal Institution—the original form of his pamphlet—appears to indicate that many persons are interested in the art of fiction, and are not indifferent to such remarks, as those who practice it may attempt to make about it. I am therefore anxious not to lose the benefit of this favorable association, and to edge in a few words under cover of the attention which Mr. Besant is sure to have excited. There is something very encouraging in his having put into form certain of his ideas on the mystery of story-telling.

It is a proof of life and curiosity—curiosity on the part of the brotherhood of novelists as well as on the part of their readers. Only a short time ago it might have been supposed that the English novel was not what the French call *discutable* [debatable]. It had no air of having a theory, a conviction, a consciousness of itself behind it—of being the expression of an artistic faith, the result of choice and comparison. I do not say it was necessarily the worse for that: it would take much more courage than I possess to intimate that the form of the novel as Dickens and Thackeray (for instance) saw it had any taint of incompleteness. It was, however, *naïf* (if I may help myself out with another French word); and evidently if it be destined to suffer in any way for having lost its *naïveté* it has now an idea of making sure of the corresponding advantages. During the period I have alluded to there was a comfortable, good-humored feeling abroad that a novel is a novel, as a pudding is a pudding, and that our only business with it could be to swallow it. But within a year or two, for some reason or other, there have been signs of returning animation—the era of discussion would appear to have been to a certain extent opened. Art lives upon discussion, upon experiment, upon curiosity, upon variety of attempt, upon the exchange of views and the comparison of standpoints; and there is a presumption that those times when no one has anything particular to say about it, and has no reason to give for practice or preference, though they may be times of honor, are not times of development—are times, possibly even, a little of dullness. The successful application of any art is a delightful spectacle, but the theory too is interesting; and though there is a great deal of the latter without the former I suspect there has never been a genuine success that has not had a latent core of conviction. Discussion, suggestion, formulation, these things are fertilizing when they are frank and sincere. Mr. Besant has set an excellent example in saying what he thinks, for his part, about the way in which fiction should be written, as well as about the way in which it should be published; for his view of the "art," carried on into an appendix, covers that too. Other laborers in the same field will doubtless take up the argument, they will give it the light of their experience, and the effect will surely be to make our interest in the novel a little more what it had for some time threatened to fail to be—a serious, active, inquiring interest, under protection of which this delightful study may, in moments of confidence, venture to say a little more what it thinks of itself.

It must take itself seriously for the public to take it so. The old superstition about fiction being "wicked" has doubtless died out in England; but the spirit of it lingers in a certain oblique regard directed toward any story which does not more or less admit that it is only a joke. Even the most jocular novel feels in some degree the weight of the proscription that was formerly directed against literary levity: the jocularity does not always succeed in passing for orthodoxy. It is still expected, though perhaps people are ashamed to say it, that a production which is after all only a "make-believe" (for what else is a "story"?) shall be in some degree apologetic—shall renounce the pretension of attempting really to represent life. This, of course, any sensible, wide-awake story declines to do, for it quickly perceives that the tolerance granted to it on such a condition is only an attempt to stifle it disguised in the form of generosity. The old evangelical hostility to the novel, which was as explicit as it was narrow, and which regarded it as little less favorable to our immortal part than a stage play, was in reality far less insulting. The only reason for the existence of a novel is that it does attempt to represent life. When it relinquishes this attempt, the same attempt that we see on the canvas of the painter, it will have arrived at a very strange pass. It is not expected of the picture that it will make itself humble in order to be forgiven; and the analogy between the art of the painter and the art of the novelist is, so far as I am able to see, complete. Their inspiration is the same, their process (allowing for the different quality of the vehicle) is the same, their success is the same. They may learn from each other, they may explain and sustain each other. Their cause is the same, and the honor of one is the honor of another. The Mahometans think a picture an unholy thing, but it is a long time since any Christian did, and it is therefore the more odd that in the Christian mind the traces (dissimulated though they may be) of a suspicion of the sister art should linger to this day. The only effectual way to lay it to rest is to emphasize the analogy to which I just alluded—to insist on the fact that as the picture is reality, so the novel is history. That is the only general description (which does it justice) that we may give of the novel. But history also is allowed to represent life; it is not, any more than painting, expected to apologize. The subject-matter of fiction is stored up likewise in documents and records, and if it will not give itself away, as they say in California, it must speak with assurance, with the tone of the historian. Certain accomplished novelists have a habit of giving themselves away which must often bring tears to the eyes of people who take their fiction seriously. I was lately struck, in reading over many pages of Anthony Trollope, with his want of discretion in this particular. In a digression, a parenthesis or an aside, he concedes to the reader that he and this trusting friend are only "making believe." He admits that the events he narrates have not really happened, and that he can give his narrative any turn the reader may like best. Such a betrayal of a sacred office seems to me, I confess, a terrible crime; it is what I mean by the attitude of apology, and it shocks me every whit as much in Trollope as it would have shocked me in Gibbon or Macaulay. It implies that the novelist is less occupied in looking for the truth (the truth, of course I mean, that he assumed, the premises that we grant him, whatever they may be) than the historian, and in doing so it deprives him at a stroke of all his standing room. To represent and illustrate the past, the actions of men, is the task of either writer, and the only difference that I can see is, in proportion as he succeeds, to the honor of the novelist, consisting as it does in his having more difficulty in collecting his evidence, which is so far from being purely literary. It seems to me to give him a great character, the fact that he has at once so much in common with the philosopher and the painter; this double analogy is a magnificent heritage.

It is of all this evidently that Mr. Besant is full when he insists upon the fact that fiction is one of the *fine* arts, deserving in its turn of all the honors and emoluments that have hitherto been reserved for the successful profession of music, poetry, painting, architecture. It is impossible to insist too much on so important a truth, and the place that Mr. Besant demands for the work of the novelist may be represented, a trifle less abstractly, by saying that he demands not only that it shall be reputed artistic, but that it shall be reputed very artistic indeed. It is excellent that he should have struck this note, for his doing so indicates that there was need of it, that his proposition may be to many people a novelty. One rubs one's eyes at the thought; but the rest of Mr. Besant's essay confirms the revelation. I suspect in truth that it would be possible to confirm it still further, and that one would not be far wrong in saying that in addition to the people to whom it has never occurred that a novel ought to be artistic, there are a great many others who, if this principle were urged upon them, would be filled with an indefinable mistrust. They would find it difficult to explain their repugnance, but it would operate strongly to put them on their guard. "Art," in our Protestant communities, where so many things have got so strangely twisted about, is supposed in certain circles to have some vaguely injurious effect upon those who make it an important consideration, who let it weigh in the balance. It is assumed to be opposed in some mysterious manner to morality, to amusement, to instruction. When it is embodied in the work of the painter (the sculptor is another affair!) you know what it is: it stands there before you, in the honesty of pink and green and a gilt frame; you can see the worst of it at a glance, and you can be on your guard. But when it is introduced into literature it becomes more insidious—there is danger of its hurting you before you know it. Literature should be either instructive or amusing, and there is in many minds an impression that these artistic preoccupations, the search for form, contribute to neither end, interfere indeed with both. They are too frivolous to be edifying, and too serious to be diverting; and they are moreover priggish and paradoxical and superfluous. That, I think, represents the manner in which the latent thought of many people who read novels as an exercise in skipping would explain itself if it were to become articulate. They would argue, of course, that a novel ought to be "good," but they would interpret this term in a fashion of their own, which indeed would vary considerably from one critic to another. One would say that being good means representing virtuous and aspiring characters, placed in prominent positions; another would say that it depends on a "happy ending," on a distribution at the last of prizes, pensions, husbands, wives, babies, millions, appended paragraphs, and cheerful remarks. Another still would say that it means being full of incident and movement, so that we shall wish to jump ahead, to see who was the mysterious stranger, and if the stolen will was ever found, and shall not be distracted from this pleasure by any tiresome analysis or "description." But they would all agree that the "artistic" idea would spoil some of their fun. One would hold it accountable for all the description, another would see it revealed in the absence of sympathy. Its hostility to a happy ending would be evident, and it might even in some cases render any ending at all impossible. The "ending" of a novel is, for many persons, like that of a good dinner, a course of dessert and ices, and the artist in fiction is regarded as a sort of meddlesome doctor who forbids agreeable after-tastes. It is therefore true that this conception of Mr. Besant's of the novel as a superior form encounters not only a negative but a positive indifference. It matters little that as a work of art it should really be as little or as much of its essence to supply happy endings, sympathetic characters, and an objective tone, as if it were a work of mechanics: the association of ideas, however incongruous, might easily be too much for it if an eloquent voice were not sometimes raised to call attention to the fact that it is at once as free and as serious a branch of literature as any other.

Certainly this might sometimes be doubted in presence of the enormous number of works of fiction that appeal to the credulity of our generation, for it might easily seem that there could be no great character in a commodity so quickly and easily produced. It must be admitted that good novels are much compromised by bad ones, and that the field at large suffers discredit from overcrowding. I think, however, that this injury is only superficial, and that the superabundance of written fiction proves nothing against the principle itself. It has been vulgarized, like all other kinds of literature, like everything else today, and it has proved more than some kinds accessible to vulgarization. But there is as much difference as there ever was between a good novel and a bad one: the bad is swept with all the daubed canvases and spoiled marble into some unvisited limbo, or infinite rubbish-yard beneath the back-windows of the world, and the good subsists and emits its light and stimulates our desire for perfection. As I shall take the liberty of making but a single criticism of Mr. Besant, whose tone is so full of the love of his art, I may as well have done with it at once. He seems to me to mistake in attempting to say so definitely beforehand what sort of an affair the good novel will be. To indicate the danger of such an error as that has been the purpose of these few pages; to suggest that certain traditions on the subject, applied *a priori*, have already had much to answer for, and that the good health of an art which undertakes so immediately to reproduce life must demand that it be perfectly free. It lives upon exercise, and the very meaning of exercise is freedom. The only obligation to which in advance we may hold a novel, without incurring the accusation of being arbitrary, is that it be interesting. That general responsibility rests upon it, but it is the only one I can think of. The ways in which it is at liberty to accomplish this result (of interesting us) strike me as innumerable, and such as can only suffer from being marked out or fenced in by prescription. They are as various as the temperament of man, and they are successful in proportion as they reveal a particular mind, different from others. A novel is in its broadest definition a personal, a direct impression of life: that, to begin with, constitutes its value, which is greater or less according to the intensity of the impression. But there will be no intensity at all, and therefore no value, unless there is freedom to feel and say. The tracing of a line to be followed, of a tone to be taken, of a form to be filled out, is a limitation of that freedom and a suppression of the very thing that we are most curious about. The form, it seems to me, is to be appreciated after the fact: then the author's choice has been made, his standard has been indicated; then we can follow lines and directions and compare tones and resemblances. Then in a word we can enjoy one of the most charming of pleasures, we can estimate quality, we can apply the test of execution. The execution belongs to the author alone; it is what is most personal to him, and we measure him by that. The advantage, the luxury, as well as the torment and responsibility of the novelist, is that there is no limit to what he may attempt as an executant—no limit to his possible experiments, efforts, discoveries, successes. Here it is especially that he works, step by step, like his brother of the brush, of whom we may always say that he has painted his picture in a manner best known to himself. His manner is his secret, not necessarily a jealous one. He cannot disclose it as a general thing if he would; he would be at a loss to teach it to others. I say this with a due recollection of having insisted on the community of method of the artist who paints a picture and the artist who writes a novel. The painter *is* able to teach the rudiments of his practice, and it is possible, from the study of good work (granted the aptitude), both to learn how to paint and to learn how to write. Yet it remains true, without injury to the *rapprochement*, that the literary artist would be obliged to say to his pupil much more than the other, "Ah, well, you must do it as you can!" It is a question of degree, a matter of delicacy. If there are exact sciences, there are also exact arts, and the grammar of painting is so much more definite that it makes the difference.

I ought to add, however, that if Mr. Besant says at the beginning of his essay that the "laws of fiction may be laid down and taught with as much precision and exactness as the laws of harmony, perspective, and proportion," he mitigates what might appear to be an extravagance by applying his remark to "general" laws, and by expressing most of these rules in a manner with which it would certainly be unaccommodating to disagree. That the novelist must write from his experience, that his "characters must be real and such as might be met with in actual life"; that "a young lady brought up in a quiet country village should avoid descriptions of garrison life," and "a writer whose friends and personal experiences belong to the lower middle-class should carefully avoid introducing his characters into society"; that one should enter one's notes in a common-place book; that one's figures should be clear in outline; that making them clear by some trick of speech or of carriage is a bad method, and "describing them at length" is a worse one; that English Fiction should have a "conscious moral purpose"; that "it is almost impossible to estimate too highly the value of careful workmanship—that is, of style"; that "the most important point of all is the story," that "the story is everything": these are principles with most of which it is surely impossible not to sympathize. That remark about the lower middle-class writer and his knowing his place is perhaps rather chilling; but for the rest I should find it difficult to dissent from any one of these recommendations. At the same time, I should find it difficult positively to assent to them, with the exception, perhaps, of the injunction as to entering one's notes in a common-place book. They scarcely seem to me to have the quality that Mr. Besant attributes to the rules of the novelist—the "precision and exactness" of "the laws of harmony, perspective, and proportion." They are suggestive, they are even inspiring, but they are not exact, though they are doubtless as much so as the case admits of: which is a proof of that liberty of interpretation for which I just contended. For the value of these different injunctions—so beautiful and so vague—is wholly in the meaning one attaches to them. The characters, the situation, which strike one as real will be those that touch and interest one most, but the measure of reality is very difficult to fix. The reality of Don Quixote or of Mr. Micawber is a very delicate shade; it is a reality so colored by the author's vision that, vivid as it may be, one would hesitate to propose it as a model: one would expose one's self to some very embarrassing questions on the part of a pupil. It goes without saying that you will not write a good novel unless you possess the sense of reality; but it will be difficult to give you a recipe for calling that sense into being. Humanity is immense, and reality has a myriad forms; the most one can affirm is that some of the flowers of fiction have the odor of it, and others have not; as for telling you in advance how your nosegay should be composed, that is another affair. It is equally excellent and inconclusive to say that one must write from experience;

to our suppositious aspirant such a declaration might savor of mockery. What kind of experience is intended, and where does it begin and end? Experience is never limited, and it is never complete; it is an immense sensibility, a kind of huge spider-web of the finest silken threads suspended in the chamber of consciousness, and catching every air-borne particle in its tissue. It is the very atmosphere of the mind; and when the mind is imaginative—much more when it happens to be that of a man of genius—it takes to itself the faintest hints of life, it converts the very pulses of the air into revelations. The young lady living in a village has only to be a damsel upon whom nothing is lost to make it quite unfair (as it seems to me) to declare to her that she shall have nothing to say about the military. Greater miracles have been seen than that, imagination assisting, she should speak the truth about some of these gentlemen. I remember an English novelist, a woman of genius, telling me that she was much commended for the impression she had managed to give in one of her tales of the nature and way of life of the French Protestant youth. She had been asked where she learned so much about this recondite being, she had been congratulated on her peculiar opportunities. These opportunities consisted in her having once, in Paris, as she ascended a staircase, passed an open door where, in the household of a *pasteur* [pastor], some of the young Protestants were seated at table round a finished meal. The glimpse made a picture; it lasted only a moment, but that moment was experience. She had got her direct personal impression, and she turned out her type. She knew what youth was, and what Protestantism; she also had the advantage of having seen what it was to be French, so that she converted these ideas into a concrete image and produced a reality. Above all, however, she was blessed with the faculty which when you give it an inch takes an ell, and which for the artist is a much greater source of strength than any accident of residence or of place in the social scale. The power to guess the unseen from the seen, to trace the implication of things, to judge the whole piece by the pattern, the condition of feeling life in general so completely that you are well on your way to knowing any particular corner of it—this cluster of gifts may almost be said to constitute experience, and they occur in country and in town, and in the most differing stages of education. If experience consists of impressions, it may be said that impressions *are* experience, just as (have we not seen it?) they are the very air we breathe. Therefore, if I should certainly say to a novice, "Write from experience and experience only," I should feel that this was rather a tantalizing monition if I were not careful immediately to add, "Try to be one of the people on whom nothing is lost!"

I am far from intending by this to minimize the importance of exactness— of truth of detail. One can speak best from one's own taste, and I may therefore venture to say that the air of reality (solidity of specification) seems to me to be the supreme virtue of a novel—the merit on which all its other merits (including that conscious moral purpose of which Mr. Besant speaks) helplessly and submissively depend. If it be not there, they are all as nothing, and if these be there, they owe their effect to the success with which the author has produced the illusion of life. The cultivation of this success, the study of this exquisite process, form, to my taste, the beginning and the end of the art of the novelist. They are his inspiration, his despair, his reward, his torment, his delight. It is here in very truth that he competes with life; it is here that he competes with his brother the painter in *his* attempt to render the look of things, the look that conveys their meaning, to catch the color, the relief, the expression, the surface, the substance of the human spectacle. It is in regard to this that Mr. Besant is well inspired when he bids him take notes. He cannot possibly take too many, he cannot possibly take enough. All life solicits him, and to "render" the simplest surface, to produce the most momentary illusion, is a very complicated business. His case would be easier, and the rule would be more exact, if Mr. Besant had been able to tell him what notes to take. But this, I fear, he can never learn in any manual; it is the business of his life. He has to take a great many in order to select a few, he has to work them up as he can, and even the guides and philosophers who might have most to say to him must leave him alone when it comes to the application of precepts, as we leave the painter in communion with his palette. That his characters "must be clear in outline," as Mr. Besant says—he feels that down to his boots; but how he shall make them so is a secret between his good angel and himself. It would be absurdly simple if he could be taught that a great deal of "description" would make them so, or that on the contrary the absence of description and the cultivation of dialogue, or the absence of dialogue and the multiplication of "incident," would rescue him from his difficulties. Nothing, for instance, is more possible than that he be of a turn of mind for which this odd, literal opposition of description and dialogue, incident and description, has little meaning and light. People often talk of these things as if they had a kind of internecine distinctness, instead of melting into each other at every breath, and being intimately associated parts of one general effort of expression. I cannot imagine composition existing in a series of blocks, nor conceive, in any novel worth discussing at all, of a passage of description that is not in its intention narrative, a passage of dialogue that is not in its intention descriptive, a touch of truth of any sort that does not partake of the nature of incident, or an incident that derives its interest from any other source than the general and only source of the success of a work of art—that of being illustrative. A novel is a living thing, all one and continuous, like any other organism, and in proportion as it lives will it be found, I think, that in each of the parts there is something of each of the other parts. The critic who over the close texture of a finished work shall pretend to trace a geography of items will mark some frontiers as artificial, I fear, as any that have been known to history. There is an old-fashioned distinction between the novel of character and the novel of incident which must have cost many a smile to the intending fabulist who was keen about his work. It appears to me as little to the point as the equally celebrated distinction between the novel and the romance—to answer as little to any reality. There are bad novels and good

novels, as there are bad pictures and good pictures; but that is the only distinction in which I see any meaning, and I can as little imagine speaking of a novel
of character as I can imagine speaking of a picture of character. When one says
picture one says of character, when one says novel one says of incident, and the
terms may be transposed at will. What is character but the determination of
incident? What is incident but the illustration of character? What is either a
picture or a novel that is *not* of character? What else do we seek in it and find
in it? It is an incident for a woman to stand up with her hand resting on a table
and look out at you in a certain way; or if it be not an incident I think it will be
hard to say what it is. At the same time it is an expression of character. If you
say you don't see it (character in *that—allons donc* [nonsense]!), this is
exactly what the artist who has reasons of his own for thinking he *does* see it
undertakes to show you. When a young man makes up his mind that he has
not faith enough after all to enter the church as he intended, that is an
incident, though you may not hurry to the end of the chapter to see whether
perhaps he doesn't change once more. I do not say that these are extraordinary
or startling incidents. I do not pretend to estimate the degree of interest
proceeding from them, for this will depend upon the skill of the painter. It
sounds almost puerile to say that some incidents are intrinsically much more
important than others, and I need not take this precaution after having professed my sympathy for the major ones in remarking that the only classification
of the novel that I can understand is into that which has life and that which
has it not.

The novel and the romance, the novel of incident and that of character—
these clumsy separations appear to me to have been made by critics and readers
for their own convenience, and to help them out of some of their occasional
queer predicaments, but to have little reality or interest for the producer, from
whose point of view it is of course that we are attempting to consider the art of
fiction. The case is the same with another shadowy category which Mr. Besant
apparently is disposed to set up—that of "modern English novel"; unless
indeed it be that in this matter he has fallen into an accidental confusion of
standpoints. It is not quite clear whether he intends the remarks in which he
alludes to it to be didactic or historical. It is as difficult to suppose a person
intending to write a modern English as to suppose him writing an ancient
English novel: that is a label which begs the question. One writes the novel,
one paints the picture, of one's language and of one's time, and calling it
modern English will not, alas! make the difficult task any easier. No more,
unfortunately, will calling this or that work of one's fellow-artist a romance—
unless it be, of course, simply for the pleasantness of the thing, as for instance
when Hawthorne gave this heading to his story of *Blithedale*. The French, who
have brought the theory of fiction to remarkable completeness, have but one
name for the novel, and have not attempted smaller things in it, that I can see,
for that. I can think of no obligation to which the "romancer" would not be
held equally with the novelist; the standard of execution is equally high for

each. Of course it is of execution that we are talking—that being the only point of a novel that is open to contention. This is perhaps too often lost sight of, only to produce interminable confusions and cross-purposes. We must grant the artist his subject, his idea, his *donnée* [premises]: our criticism is applied only to what he makes of it. Naturally I do not mean that we are bound to like it or find it interesting: in case we do not our course is perfectly simple—to let it alone. We may believe that of a certain idea even the most sincere novelist can make nothing at all, and the event may perfectly justify our belief; but the failure will have been a failure to execute, and it is in the execution that the fatal weakness is recorded. If we pretend to respect the artist at all, we must allow him his freedom of choice, in the face, in particular cases, of innumerable presumptions that the choice will not fructify. Art derives a considerable part of its beneficial exercise from flying in the face of presumptions, and some of the most interesting experiments of which it is capable are hidden in the bosom of common things. Gustave Flaubert has written a story about the devotion of a servant-girl to a parrot, and the production, highly finished as it is, cannot on the whole be called a success. We are perfectly free to find it flat, but I think it might have been interesting; and I, for my part, am extremely glad he should have written it; it is a contribution to our knowledge of what can be done—or what cannot. Ivan Turgenev has written a tale about a deaf and dumb serf and a lap-dog, and the thing is touching, loving, a little masterpiece. He struck the note of life where Gustave Flaubert missed it—he flew in the face of a presumption and achieved a victory.

Nothing, of course, will ever take the place of the good old fashion of "liking" a work of art or not liking it: the most improved criticism will not abolish that primitive, that ultimate test. I mention this to guard myself from the accusation of intimating that the idea, the subject, of a novel or a picture, does not matter. It matters, to my sense, in the highest degree, and if I might put up a prayer it would be that artists should select none but the richest. Some, as I have already hastened to admit, are much more remunerative than others, and it would be a world happily arranged in which persons intending to treat them should be exempt from confusions and mistakes. This fortunate condition will arrive only, I fear, on the same day that critics become purged from error. Meanwhile, I repeat, we do not judge the artist with fairness unless we say to him,

"Oh, I grant you your starting-point, because if I did not I should seem to prescribe to you, and heaven forbid I should take that responsibility. If I pretend to tell you what you must not take, you will call upon me to tell you then what you must take; in which case I shall be prettily caught. Moreover, it isn't till I have accepted your data that I can begin to measure you. I have the standard, the pitch; I have no right to tamper with your flute and then criticize your music. Of course I may not care for your idea at all; I may think it silly, or stale, or unclean; in which case I wash my hands of you altogether. I may content myself with believing that you will not have succeeded in being interesting, but I shall, of course, not attempt to demonstrate it, and you will be as indifferent to me as I am to you. I needn't remind you that there are all sorts of tastes: who can know it better? Some people, for excellent reasons, don't like to read about carpenters; others, for reasons even better, don't like to read about courtesans. Many object to Americans. Others (I believe they are mainly editors and publishers) won't look at Italians. Some readers don't like quiet subjects; others don't like bustling ones. Some enjoy a complete illusion, others the consciousness of large concessions. They choose their novels accordingly, and if they don't care about your idea they won't, *a fortiori*, care about your treatment."

So that it comes back very quickly, as I have said, to the liking: in spite of M. Zola, who reasons less powerfully than he represents, and who will not reconcile himself to this absoluteness of taste, thinking that there are certain things that people ought to like, and that they can be made to like. I am quite at a loss to imagine anything (at any rate in this matter of fiction) that people *ought* to like or to dislike. Selection will be sure to take care of itself, for it has a constant motive behind it. That motive is simply experience. As people feel life, so they will feel the art that is most closely related to it. This closeness of relation is what we should never forget in talking of the effort of the novel. Many people speak of it as a factitious, artificial form, a product of ingenuity, the business of which is to alter and arrange the things that surround us, to translate them into conventional, traditional moulds. This, however, is a view of the matter which carries us but a very short way, condemns the art to an eternal repetition of a few familiar *clichés*, cuts short its development, and leads us straight up to a dead wall. Catching the very note and trick, the strange irregular rhythm of life, that is the attempt whose strenuous force keeps Fiction upon her feet. In proportion as in what she offers us we see life *without* rearrangement do we feel that we are touching the truth; in proportion as we see it *with* rearrangement do we feel that we are being put off with a substitute, a compromise and convention. It is not uncommon to hear an extraordinary assurance of remark in regard to this matter of rearranging, which is often spoken of as if it were the last word of art. Mr. Besant seems to me in danger of falling into the great error with his rather unguarded talk about "selection." Art is essentially selection, but it is a selection whose main care is to be typical, to be inclusive. For many people art means rose-colored window-panes, and selection means picking a bouquet for Mrs. Grundy. They will tell you glibly that artistic considerations have nothing to do with the disagreeable, with the ugly; they will rattle off shallow commonplaces about the province of art and the limits of art till you are moved to some wonder in return as to the province and the limits of ignorance. It appears to me that no one can ever have made a seriously artistic attempt without becoming conscious of an immense increase—a kind of revelation—of freedom. One perceives in that case—by the light of a heavenly ray—that the province of art is all life, all feeling, all observation, all vision. As Mr. Besant so justly intimates, it is all experience. That is a sufficient answer to those who maintain that it must not touch the sad things of life, who stick into its divine unconscious bosom little prohibitory inscriptions on the end of sticks, such as we see in public gardens—"It is forbidden to walk on the grass; it is forbidden to touch the flowers; it is not allowed to introduce dogs or to remain after dark; it is requested to keep to the right." The young aspirant in the line of fiction whom we continue to imagine will do nothing without taste, for in that case his freedom would be of little use to him; but the first advantage of his taste will be to reveal to him the absurdity of the little sticks and tickets. If he have taste, I must add, of course he will have ingenuity, and my disrespectful reference to that quality just now was not meant to imply that it is useless in fiction. But it is only a secondary aid; the first is a capacity for receiving straight impressions.

Mr. Besant has some remarks on the question of "the story" which I shall not attempt to criticize, though they seem to me to contain a singular ambiguity, because I do not think I understand them. I cannot see what is meant by talking as if there were a part of a novel which is the story and part of it which for mystical reasons is not—unless indeed the distinction be made in a sense in which it is difficult to suppose that any one should attempt to convey anything. "The story," if it represents anything, represents the subject, the idea, the *donnée* of the novel; and there is surely no "school"—Mr. Besant speaks of a school—which urges that a novel should be all treatment and no subject. There must assuredly be something to treat; every school is intimately conscious of that. This sense of the story being the idea, the starting-point, of the novel, is the only one that I see in which it can be spoken of as something different from its organic whole; and since in proportion as the work is successful the idea permeates and penetrates it, informs and animates it, so that every word and every punctuation-point contribute directly to the expression, in that proportion do we lose our sense of the story being a blade which may be drawn more or less out of its sheath. The story and the novel, the idea and the form, are the needle and thread, and I never heard of a guild of tailors who recommended the use of the thread without the needle, or the needle without the thread. Mr. Besant is not the only critic who may be observed to have spoken as if there were certain things in life which constitute stories, and certain others which do not. I find the same odd implication in an entertaining article in the *Pall Mall Gazette*, devoted, as it happens, to Mr. Besant's lecture. "The story is the thing!" says this graceful writer, as if with a tone of opposition to some other idea. I should think it was, as every painter who, as the time for "sending in" his picture looms in the distance, finds himself still in quest of a subject—as every belated artist not fixed about his theme will heartily agree. There are some subjects which speak to us and others which do not, but he would be a clever man who should undertake to give a rule—an *index expurgatorius*—by which the story and the no-story should be known apart. It is impossible (to me at least) to imagine any such rule which shall not be altogether arbitrary. The writer in the *Pall Mall* opposes the delightful (as I suppose) novel of *Margot la Balafrée* to certain tales in which "Bostonian nymphs" appear to have "rejected English dukes for psychological reasons." I am not acquainted with the romance just designated, and can scarcely forgive the *Pall Mall* critic for not mentioning the name of the author, but the title appears to refer to a lady who may have received a scar in some heroic adventure. I am inconsolable at not being acquainted with this episode, but am utterly at a loss to see why it is a story when the rejection (or acceptance) of a duke is not, and why a reason, psychological or other, is not a subject when a cicatrix is. They are all particles of the multitudinous life with which the novel deals, and surely no dogma which pretends to make it lawful to touch the one and unlawful to touch the other will stand for a moment on its feet. It is the special picture that must stand or fall, according as it seems to possess truth or to lack it. Mr. Besant does not, to my sense, light up the subject by intimating that a story must, under penalty of not being a story, consist of "adventures." Why of adventures more than of green spectacles? He mentions a category of impossible things, and among them he places "fiction without adventure." Why without adventure, more than without matrimony, or celibacy, or parturition, or cholera, or hydropathy, or Jansenism? This seems to me to bring the novel back to the hapless little *rôle* of being an artificial, ingenious thing—bring it down from its large, free character of an immense and exquisite correspondence with life. And what *is* adventure, when it comes to that, and by what sign is the listening pupil to recognize it? It is an adventure—an immense one—for me to write this little article; and for a Bostonian nymph to reject an English duke is an adventure only less stirring, I should say, than for an English duke to be rejected by a Bostonian nymph. I see dramas within dramas in that, and innumerable points of view. A psychological reason is, to my imagination, an object adorably pictorial; to catch the tint of its complexion—I feel as if that idea inspires one to Titianesque efforts. There are few things more exciting to me, in short, than a psychological reason, and yet, I protest, the novel seems to me the most magnificent form of art. I have just been reading, at the same time, the delightful story of *Treasure Island*, by Mr. Robert Louis Stevenson and, in a manner less consecutive, the last tale from M. Edmond de Goncourt, which is entitled *Chérie*. One of these works treats of murders, mysteries, islands of dreadful renown, hairbreadth escapes, miraculous coincidences and buried doubloons. The other treats of a little French girl who lived in a fine house in Paris, and died of wounded sensibility because no one would marry her. I call *Treasure Island* delightful, because it appears to me to have succeeded wonderfully in what it attempts; and I venture to bestow no epithet upon *Chérie*, which strikes me as having failed deplorably in what it attempts—that is in tracing the development of the moral consciousness of a child. But one of these productions strikes me as exactly as much of a novel as the other, and as having a "story" quite as much. The moral consciousness of a child is as much a part of life as the islands of the Spanish Main, and the one sort of geography seems to me to have those "surprises" of which Mr. Besant speaks quite as much as the other. For myself (since it comes back in the last resort, as I say, to the preference of the individual), the picture of the child's experience has the advantage that I can at successive steps (an immense luxury, near to the "sensual pleasure" of which Mr. Besant's critic in the *Pall Mall* speaks) say Yes or No, as it may be, to what the artist puts before me. I have been a child in fact, but I have been on a quest for a buried treasure only in supposition, and it is a simple accident that with M. de Goncourt I should have for the most part to say No. With George Eliot, when she painted that country with a far other intelligence, I always said Yes.

The most interesting part of Mr. Besant's lecture is unfortunately the briefest passage—his very cursory allusion to the "conscious moral purpose" of the novel. Here again it is not very clear whether he can be recording a fact or laying down a principle; it is a great pity that in the latter case he should not have developed his idea. This branch of the subject is of immense importance, and Mr. Besant's few words point to considerations of the widest reach, not to be lightly disposed of. He will have treated the art of fiction but superficially who is not prepared to go every inch of the way that these considerations will carry him. It is for this reason that at the beginning of these remarks I was careful to notify the reader that my reflections on so large a theme have no pretension to be exhaustive. Like Mr. Besant, I have left the question of the morality of the novel till the last, and at the last I find I have used up my space. It is a question surrounded with difficulties, as witness the very first that meets us, in the form of a definite question, on the threshold. Vagueness, in such a discussion, is fatal, and what is the meaning of your morality and your conscious moral purpose? Will you not define your terms and explain how (a novel being a picture) a picture can be either moral or immoral? You wish to paint a moral picture or carve a moral statue: will you not tell us how you would set about it? We are discussing the Art of Fiction; questions of art are questions (in the widest sense) of execution; questions of morality are quite another affair, and will you not let us see how it is that you find it so easy to mix them up? These things are so clear to Mr. Besant that he has deduced from them a law which he sees embodied in English Fiction, and which is "a truly admirable thing and a great cause for congratulation." It is a great cause for congratulation indeed when such thorny problems become as smooth as silk. I may add that in so far as Mr. Besant perceives that in point of fact English Fiction has addressed itself preponderantly to these delicate questions he will appear to many people to have made a vain discovery. They will have been positively struck, on the contrary, with the moral timidity of the usual English novelist; with his (or with her) aversion to face the difficulties with which on every side the treatment of reality bristles. He is apt to be extremely shy (whereas the picture that Mr. Besant draws is a picture of boldness), and the sign of his work, for the most part, is a cautious silence on certain subjects. In the English novel (by which of course I mean the American as well), more than in any other, there is a traditional difference between that which people know and that which they agree to admit that they know, that which they see, that which they speak of, that which they feel to be a part of life and that which they allow to enter into literature. There is the great difference, in short, between what they talk of in conversation and what they talk of in print. The essence of moral energy is to survey the whole field, and I should directly reverse Mr. Besant's remark and say not that the English novel has a purpose, but that it has a diffidence. To what degree a purpose in a work of art is a source of corruption I shall not attempt to inquire; the one that seems to me least dangerous is the purpose of making a perfect work. As for our novel, I may say lastly on this score that as we find it in England today it strikes me as addressed in a large degree to "young people," and that this in itself constitutes a presumption that it will be rather shy. There are certain things which it is generally agreed not to discuss, not even to mention, before young people. That is very well, but the absence of discussion is not a symptom of the moral passion. The purpose of the English novel—"a truly admirable thing, and a great cause for congratulation"—strikes me therefore as rather negative.

There is one point at which the moral sense and the artistic sense lie very near together; that is in the light of the very obvious truth that the deepest quality of a work of art will always be the quality of the mind of the producer. In proportion as that intelligence is fine will the novel, the picture, the statue partake of the substance of beauty and truth. To be constituted of such elements is, to my vision, to have purpose enough. No good novel will ever proceed from a superficial mind; that seems to me an axiom which, for the artist in fiction, will cover all needful moral ground: If the youthful aspirant take it to heart it will illuminate for him any of the mysteries of "purpose." There are many other useful things that might be said to him, but I have come to the end of my article, and can only touch them as I pass. The critic in the *Pall Mall Gazette*, whom I have already quoted, draws attention to the danger, in speaking of the art of fiction, of generalizing. The danger that he has in mind is rather, I imagine, that of particularizing, for there are some comprehensive remarks which, in addition to those embodied in Mr. Besant's suggestive lecture, might without fear of misleading him be addressed to the ingenuous student. I should remind him first of the magnificence of the form that is open to him, which offers to sight so few restrictions and such innumerable opportunities. The other arts, in comparison, appear confined and hampered; the various conditions under which they are exercised are so rigid and definite. But the only condition that I can think of attaching to the composition of the novel is, as I have already said, that it be sincere. This freedom is a splendid privilege, and the first lesson of the young novelist is to learn to be worthy of it.

"Enjoy it as it deserves (I should say to him); take possession of it, explore it to its utmost extent, publish it, rejoice in it. All life belongs to you, and do not listen either to those who would shut you up into corners of it and tell you that it is only here and there that art inhabits, or to those who would persuade you that this heavenly messenger wings her way outside of life altogether, breathing a superfine air, and turning away her head from the truth of things. There is no impression of life, no manner of seeing it and feeling it, to which the plan of the novelist may not offer a place; you have only to remember that talents so dissimilar as those of Alexandre Dumas and Jane Austen, Charles Dickens and Gustave Flaubert have worked in this field with equal glory. Do not think too much about optimism and pessimism; try and catch the color of life itself. In France today we see a prodigious effort (that of Emile Zola, to whose solid and serious work no explorer of the capacity of the novel can allude without respect), we see an extraordinary effort vitiated by a spirit of pessimism on a narrow basis. M. Zola is magnificent, but he strikes an English reader as ignorant; he has an air of working in the dark; if he had as much light as energy, his results would be of the highest value. As for the aberrations of a shallow optimism, the ground (of English fiction especially) is strewn with their brittle particles as with broken glass. If you must indulge in conclusions, let them have the taste of a wide knowledge. Remember that your first duty is to be as complete as possible—to make as perfect a work. Be generous and delicate and pursue the prize."

A. C. BRADLEY

❧ The Ultimate Power in
Shakespeare's Tragic World

In [Shakespeare's] tragic world, . . . where individuals, however great they may be and however decisive their actions may appear, are so evidently not the ultimate power, what is this power? What account can we give of it which will correspond with the imaginative impressions we receive? . . .

The variety of the answers given to this question shows how difficult it is. And the difficulty has many sources. Most people, even among those who know Shakespeare well and come into real contact with his mind, are inclined to isolate and exaggerate some one aspect of the tragic fact. Some are so much influenced by their own habitual beliefs that they import them more or less into their interpretation of every author who is 'sympathetic' to them. And even where neither of these causes of error appears to operate, another is present from which it is probably impossible wholly to escape. What I mean is this.

Any answer we give to the question proposed ought to correspond with, or to represent in terms of the understanding, our imaginative and emotional experience in reading the tragedies. We have, of course, to do our best by study and effort to make this experience true to Shakespeare; but, that done to the best of our ability, the experience is the matter to be interpreted, and the test by which the interpretation must be tried. But it is extremely hard to make out exactly what this experience is, because, in the very effort to make it out, our reflecting mind, full of everyday ideas, is always tending to transform it by the application of these ideas, and so to elicit a result which, instead of representing the fact, conventionalises it. And the consequence is not only mistaken theories; it is that many a man will declare that he feels in reading a tragedy what he never really felt, while he fails to recognise what he actually did feel. It is not likely that we shall escape all these dangers in our effort to find an answer to the question regarding the tragic world and the ultimate power in it.

It will be agreed, however, first, that this question must not be answered in 'religious' language. For although this or that *dramatis persona* may speak of gods or of God, of evil spirits or of Satan, of heaven and of hell, and although the poet may show us ghosts from another world, these ideas do not materially influence his representation of life, nor are they used to throw light on the mystery of its tragedy. The Elizabethan drama was almost wholly secular; and while Shakespeare was writing he practically confined his view to the world of non-theological observation and thought, so that he represents it substantially in one and the same way whether the period of the story is pre-Christian or Christian. He looked at this 'secular' world most intently and seriously; and he painted it, we cannot but conclude, with entire fidelity, without the wish to enforce an opinion of his own, and, in essentials, without regard to anyone's hopes, fears, or beliefs. His greatness is largely due to this fidelity in a mind of extraordinary power; and if, as a private person, he had a religious faith, his tragic view can hardly have been in contradiction with this faith, but must have been included in it, and supplemented, not abolished, by additional ideas.

Two statements, next, may at once be made regarding the tragic fact as he represents it: one, that it is and remains to us something piteous, fearful and mysterious; the other, that the representation of it does not leave us crushed, rebellious or desperate. These statements will be accepted, I believe, by any reader who is in touch with Shakespeare's mind and can observe his own. Indeed such a reader is rather likely to complain that they are painfully obvious. But if they are true as well as obvious, something follows from them in regard to our present question.

From the first it follows that the ultimate power in the tragic world is not adequately described as a law or order which we can see to be just and benevolent,—as, in that sense, a 'moral order': for in that case the spectacle of suffering and waste could not seem to us so fearful and mysterious as it does. And from the second it follows that this ultimate power is not adequately described as a fate, whether malicious and cruel, or blind and indifferent to human happiness and goodness: for in that case the spectacle would leave us desperate or rebellious. Yet one or other of these two ideas will be found to govern most accounts of Shakespeare's tragic view or world. These accounts isolate and exaggerate single aspects, either the aspect of action or that of suffering; either the close and unbroken connection of character, will, deed and catastrophe, which, taken alone, shows the individual simply as sinning against, or failing to conform to, the moral order and drawing his just doom on his own head; or else that pressure of outward forces, that sway of accident, and those blind and agonised struggles, which, taken alone, show him as the mere victim of some power which cares neither for his sins nor for his pain. Such views contradict one another, and no third view can unite them; but the several aspects from whose isolation and exaggeration they spring are both present in the fact, and a view which would be true to the fact and to the whole of our imaginative experience must in some way combine these aspects.

Let us begin, then, with the idea of fatality and glance at some of the impressions which give rise to it, without asking at present whether this idea is their natural or fitting expression. There can be no doubt that they do arise and that they ought to arise. If we do not feel at times that the hero is, in some sense, a doomed man; that he and others drift struggling to destruction like helpless creatures borne on an irresistible flood towards a cataract; that, faulty as they may be, their fault is far from being the sole or sufficient cause of all they suffer; and that the power from which they cannot escape is relentless and immovable, we have failed to receive an essential part of the full tragic effect.

The sources of these impressions are various, and I will refer only to a few. One of them is put into words by Shakespeare himself when he makes the player-king in *Hamlet* say:

> Our thoughts are ours, their ends none of our own;

'their ends' are the issues or outcomes of our thoughts, and these, says the speaker, are not our own. The tragic world is a world of action, and action is the translation of thought into reality. We see men and women confidently attempting it. They strike into the existing order of things in pursuance of their ideas. But what they achieve is not what they intended; it is terribly unlike it. They understand nothing, we say to ourselves, of the world on which they operate. They fight blindly in the dark, and the power that works through them makes them the instrument of a design which is not theirs. They act freely, and yet their action binds them hand and foot. And it makes no difference whether they meant well or ill. No one could mean better than Brutus, but he contrives misery for his country and death for himself. No one could mean worse than Iago, and he too is caught in the web he spins for others. Hamlet, recoiling from the rough duty of revenge, is pushed into blood-guiltiness he never dreamed of, and forced at last the revenge he could not will. His adversary's murders, and no less his adversary's remorse, bring about the opposite of what they sought. Lear follows an old man's whim, half generous, half selfish; and in a moment it looses all the powers of darkness upon him. Othello agonises over an empty fiction, and, meaning to execute solemn justice, butchers innocence and strangles love. They understand themselves no better than the world about them. Coriolanus thinks that his heart is iron, and it melts like snow before a fire. Lady Macbeth, who thought she could dash out her own child's brains, finds herself hounded to death by the smell of a stranger's blood. Her husband thinks that to gain a crown he would jump the life to come, and finds that the crown has brought him all the horrors of that life. Everywhere, in this tragic world, man's thought, translated into act, is transformed into the opposite of itself. His act, the movement of a few ounces of matter in a moment of time, becomes a monstrous flood which spreads over a kingdom. And whatsoever he dreams of doing, he achieves that which he least dreamed of, his own destruction.

All this makes us feel the blindness and helplessness of man. Yet by itself it would hardly suggest the idea of fate, because it shows man as in some degree, however slight, the cause of his own undoing. But other impressions come to aid it. It is aided by everything which makes us feel that a man is, as we say, terribly unlucky; and of this there is, even in Shakespeare, not a little. Here come in some of the accidents already considered, Juliet's waking from her trance a minute too late, Desdemona's loss of her handkerchief at the only moment when the loss would have mattered, that insignificant delay which cost Cordelia's life. Again, men act, no doubt, in accordance with their characters; but what is it that brings them just the one problem which is fatal to them and would be easy to another, and sometimes brings it to them just when they are least fitted to face it? How is it that Othello comes to be the companion of the one man in the world who is at once able enough, brave enough, and vile enough to ensnare him? By what strange fatality does it happen that Lear has such daughters and Cordelia such sisters? Even character itself contributes to these feelings of fatality. How could men escape, we cry, such vehement propensities as drive Romeo, Antony, Coriolanus, to their doom? And why is it that a man's virtues help to destroy him, and that his weakness or defect is so intertwined with everything that is admirable in him that we can hardly separate them even in imagination?

If we find in Shakespeare's tragedies the source of impressions like these, it is important, on the other hand, to notice what we do *not* find there. We find practically no trace of fatalism in its more primitive, crude and obvious forms. Nothing, again, makes us think of the actions and sufferings of the persons as somehow arbitrarily fixed beforehand without regard to their feelings, thoughts and resolutions. Nor, I believe, are the facts ever so presented that it seems to us as if the supreme power, whatever it may be, had a special spite against a family or an individual. Neither, lastly, do we receive the impression (which, it must be observed, is not purely fatalistic) that a family, owing to some hideous crime or impiety in early days, is doomed in later days to continue a career of portentous calamities and sins. Shakespeare, indeed, does not appear to have taken much interest in heredity, or to have attached much importance to it.

What, then, is this 'fate' which the impressions already considered lead us to describe as the ultimate power in the tragic world? It appears to be a mythological expression for the whole system or order, of which the individual characters form an inconsiderable and feeble part; which seems to determine, far more than they, their native dispositions and their circumstances, and, through these, their action; which is so vast and complex that they can scarcely at all understand it or control its workings; and which has a nature so definite and fixed that whatever changes take place in it produce other changes inevitably and without regard to men's desires and regrets. And whether this system or order is best called by the name of fate or no,[17] it can hardly be denied that it does appear as the ultimate power in the tragic world, and that it has such characteristics as these. But the name 'fate' may be intended to imply something more—to imply that this order is a blank necessity, totally regardless alike of human weal and of the difference between good and evil or right and wrong. And such an implication many readers would at once reject. They would maintain, on the contrary, that this order shows characteristics of quite another kind from those which made us give it the name of fate, characteristics which certainly should not induce us to forget those others, but which would lead us to describe it as a moral order and its necessity as a moral necessity.

Let us turn, then, to this idea. It brings into the light those aspects of the tragic fact which the idea of fate throws into the shade. And the argument which leads to it in its simplest form may be stated briefly thus: 'Whatever may be said of accidents, circumstances and the like, human action is, after all, presented to us as the central fact in tragedy, and also as the main cause of the catastrophe. That necessity which so much impresses us is, after all, chiefly the necessary connection of actions and consequences. For these actions we, without even raising a question on the subject, hold the agents responsible; and the tragedy would disappear for us if we did not. The critical action is, in greater or less degree, wrong or bad. The catastrophe is, in the main, the return of this action on the head of the agent. It is an example of justice; and that order which, present alike within the agents and outside them, infallibly brings it about, is therefore just. The rigour of its justice is terrible, no doubt, for a

---

[17] I have raised no objection to the use of the idea of fate, because it occurs so often both in conversation and in books about Shakespeare's tragedies that I must suppose it to be natural to many readers. Yet I doubt whether it would be so if Greek tragedy had never been written; and I must in candour confess that to me it does not often occur while I am reading, or when I have just read, a tragedy of Shakespeare. Wordsworth's lines, for example, about

> poor humanity's afflicted will
> Struggling in vain with ruthless destiny

do not represent the impression I receive; much less to images which compare man to a puny creature helpless in the claws of a bird of prey. The reader should examine himself closely on this matter.

tragedy is a terrible story; but, in spite of fear and pity, we acquiesce, because our sense of justice is satisfied.'

Now, if this view is to hold good, the 'justice' of which it speaks must be at once distinguished from what is called 'poetic justice.' 'Poetic justice' means that prosperity and adversity are distributed in proportion to the merits of the agents. Such 'poetic justice' is in flagrant contradiction with the facts of life, and it is absent from Shakespeare's tragic picture of life; indeed, this very absence is a ground of constant complaint on the part of Dr. Johnson. Δράσαντι παθεῖν, 'the doer must suffer'—this we find in Shakespeare. We also find that villainy never remains victorious and prosperous at the last. But an assignment of amounts of happiness and misery, an assignment even of life and death, in proportion to merit, we do not find. No one who thinks of Desdemona and Cordelia; or who remembers that one end awaits Richard III and Brutus, Macbeth and Hamlet; or who asks himself which suffered most, Othello or Iago; will ever accuse Shakespeare of representing the ultimate power as 'poetically' just.

And we must go further. I venture to say that it is a mistake to use at all these terms of justice and merit or desert. And this for two reasons. In the first place, essential as it is to recognize the connection between act and consequence, and natural as it may seem in some cases (e.g. Macbeth's) to say that the doer only gets what he deserves, yet in very many cases to say this would be quite unnatural. We might not object to the statement that Lear deserved to suffer for his folly, selfishness and tyranny; but to assert that he deserved to suffer what he did suffer is to do violence not merely to language but to any healthy moral sense. It is, moreover, to obscure the tragic fact that the consequences of action cannot be limited to that which would appear to us to follow 'justly' from them. And, this being so, when we call the order of the tragic world just, we are either using the word in some vague and unexplained sense, or we are going beyond what is shown us of this order, and are appealing to faith.

But, in the second place, the ideas of justice and desert are, it seems to me, in *all* cases—even those of Richard III and of Macbeth and Lady Macbeth— untrue to our imaginative experience. When we are immersed in a tragedy, we feel towards dispositions, actions, and persons such emotions as attraction and repulsion, pity, wonder, fear, horror, perhaps hatred; but we do not *judge*. This is a point of view which emerges only when, in reading a play, we slip, by our own fault or the dramatist's, from the tragic position, or when, in thinking about the play afterwards, we fall back on our everyday legal and moral notions. But tragedy does not belong, any more than religion belongs, to the sphere of these notions; neither does the imaginative attitude in the presence of it. While we are in its world we watch what is, seeing that so it happened and must have happened, feeling that it is piteous, dreadful, awful, mysterious, but neither passing sentence on the agents, nor asking whether the behaviour of the ultimate power towards them is just. And, therefore, the use of such language in attempts to render our imaginative experience in terms of the understanding is, to say the least, full of danger.[18]

Let us attempt then to re-state the idea that the ultimate power in the tragic world is a moral order. Let us put aside the ideas of justice and merit, and speak simply of good and evil. Let us understand by these words, primarily, moral good and evil, but also everything else in human beings which we take to be excellent or the reverse. Let us understand the statement that the ultimate power or order is 'moral' to mean that it does not show itself indifferent to good and evil, or equally favourable or unfavourable to both, but shows itself akin to good and alien from evil. And, understanding the statement thus, let us ask what grounds it has in the tragic fact as presented by Shakespeare.

Here, as in dealing with the grounds on which the idea of fate rests, I choose only two or three out of many. And the most important is this. In Shakespearean tragedy the main source of the convulsion which produces suffering and death is never good: good contributes to this convulsion only from its tragic implication with its opposite in one and the same character. The main source, on the contrary, is in every case evil; and, what is more (though this seems to have been little noticed), it is in almost every case evil in the fullest sense, not mere imperfection but plain moral evil. The love of Romeo and Juliet conducts them to death only because of the senseless hatred of their houses. Guilty ambition, seconded by diabolic malice and issuing in murder, opens the action in *Macbeth*. Iago is the main source of the convulsion in *Othello*; Goneril, Regan and Edmund in *King Lear*. Even when this plain moral evil is not the obviously prime source within the play, it lies behind it: the situation with which Hamlet has to deal has been formed by adultery and murder. *Julius Caesar* is the only tragedy in which one is even tempted to find an exception to this rule. And the inference is obvious. If it is chiefly evil that violently disturbs the order of the world, this order cannot be friendly to evil or indifferent between evil and good, any more than a body which is convulsed by poison is friendly to it or indifferent to the distinction between poison and food.

Again, if we confine our attention to the hero, and to those cases where the gross and palpable evil is not in him but elsewhere, we find that the comparatively innocent hero still shows some marked imperfection or defect,—irresolution, precipitancy, pride, credulousness, excessive simplicity, excessive susceptibility to sexual emotions, and the like. These defects or imperfections are

---

[18] It is dangerous, I think, in reference to all really good tragedies, but I am dealing here only with Shakespeare's. In not a few Greek tragedies it is almost inevitable that we should think of justice and retribution, not only because the *dramatis personae* often speak of them, but also because there is something casuistical about the tragic problem itself. The poet treats the story in such a way that the question, Is the hero doing right or wrong? is almost forced upon us. But this is not so with Shakespeare. *Julius Caesar* is probably the only one of his tragedies in which the question suggests itself to us, and this is one of the reasons why that play has something of a classic air. Even here, if we ask the question, we have no doubt at all about the answer.

certainly, in the wide sense of the word, evil, and they contribute decisively to the conflict and catastrophe. And the inference is again obvious. The ultimate power which shows itself disturbed by this evil and reacts against it, must have a nature alien to it. Indeed its reaction is so vehement and 'relentless' that it would seem to be bent on nothing short of good in perfection, and to be ruthless in its demand for it.

To this must be added another fact, or another aspect of the same fact. Evil exhibits itself everywhere as something negative, barren, weakening, destructive, a principle of death. It isolates, disunites, and tends to annihilate not only its opposite but itself. That which keeps the evil man[19] prosperous, makes him succeed, even permits him to exist, is the good in him (I do not mean only the obviously 'moral' good). When the evil in him masters the good and has its way, it destroys other people through him, but it also destroys *him*. At the close of the struggle he has vanished, and has left behind him nothing that can stand. What remains is a family, a city, a country, exhausted, pale and feeble, but alive through the principle of good which animates it; and, within it, individuals who, if they have not the brilliance or greatness of the tragic character, still have won our respect and confidence. And the inference would seem clear. If existence in an order depends on good, and if the presence of evil is hostile to such existence, the inner being or soul of this order must be akin to good.

These are aspects of the tragic world at least as clearly marked as those which, taken alone, suggest the idea of fate. And the idea which they in their turn, when taken alone, may suggest, is that of an order which does not indeed award 'poetic justice,' but which reacts through the necessity of its own 'moral' nature both against attacks made upon it and against failure to conform to it. Tragedy, on this view, is the exhibition of that convulsive reaction; and the fact that the spectacle does not leave us rebellious or desperate is due to a more or less distinct perception that the tragic suffering and death arise from collision, not with a fate or blank power, but with a moral power, a power akin to all that we admire and revere in the characters themselves. This perception produces something like a feeling of acquiescence in the catastrophe, though it neither leads us to pass judgment on the characters nor diminishes the pity, the fear, and the sense of waste, which their struggle, suffering and fall evoke. And, finally, this view seems quite able to do justice to those aspects of the tragic fact which give rise to the idea of fate. They would appear as various expressions of the fact that the moral order acts not capriciously or like a human being, but from the necessity of its nature, or, if we prefer the phrase, by general laws,—a necessity or law which of course knows no exception and is as 'ruthless' as fate.

---

[19] It is most essential to remember that an evil man is much more than the evil in him. I may add that in this paragraph I have, for the sake of clearness, considered evil in its most pronounced form; but what is said would apply, *mutatis mutandis*, to evil as imperfection, etc.

It is impossible to deny to this view a large measure of truth. And yet without some amendment it can hardly satisfy. For it does not include the whole of the facts, and therefore does not wholly correspond with the impressions they produce. Let it be granted that the system or order which shows itself omnipotent against individuals is, in the sense explained, moral. Still—at any rate for the eye of sight—the evil against which it asserts itself, and the persons whom this evil inhabits, are not really something outside the order, so that they can attack it or fail to conform to it; they are within it and a part of it. It itself produces them,—produces Iago as well as Desdemona, Iago's cruelty as well as Iago's courage. It is not poisoned, it poisons itself. Doubtless it shows by its violent reaction that the poison *is* poison, and that its health lies in good. But one significant fact cannot remove another, and the spectacle we witness scarcely warrants the assertion that the order is responsible for the good in Desdemona, but Iago for the evil in Iago. If we make this assertion, we make it on grounds other than the facts as presented in Shakespeare's tragedies.

Nor does the idea of a moral order asserting itself against attack or want of conformity answer in full to our feelings regarding the tragic character. We do not think of Hamlet merely as failing to meet its demand, of Antony as merely sinning against it, or even of Macbeth as simply attacking it. What we feel corresponds quite as much to the idea that they are *its* parts, expressions, products; that in their defect or evil *it* is untrue to its soul of goodness, and falls into conflict and collision with itself; that, in making them suffer and waste themselves, *it* suffers and wastes itself; and that when, to save its life and regain peace from this intestinal struggle, it casts them out, it has lost a part of its own substance,—a part more dangerous and unquiet, but far more valuable and nearer to its heart, than that which remains,—a Fortinbras, a Malcolm, an Octavius. There is no tragedy in its expulsion of evil: the tragedy is that this involves the waste of good.

Thus we are left at last with an idea showing two sides or aspects which we can neither separate nor reconcile. The whole or order against which the individual part shows itself powerless seems to be animated by a passion for perfection: we cannot otherwise explain its behaviour towards evil. Yet it appears to engender this evil within itself, and in its effort to overcome and expel it it is agonised with pain, and driven to mutilate its own substance and to lose not only evil but priceless good. That this idea, though very different from the idea of a blank fate, is no solution of the riddle of life is obvious; but why should we expect it to be such a solution? Shakespeare was not attempting to justify the ways of God to men, or to show the universe as a Divine Comedy. He was writing tragedy, and tragedy would not be tragedy if it were not a painful mystery. Nor can he be said even to point distinctly, like some writers of tragedy, in any direction where a solution might lie. We find a few references to gods or God, to the influence of the stars, to another life: some of them certainly, all of them perhaps, merely dramatic—appropriate to the person from whose lips they fall. A ghost comes from Purgatory to impart a secret out of the reach of its hearer—who presently meditates on the question whether the sleep of death is dreamless. Accidents once or twice remind us strangely of the words, 'There's a divinity that shapes our ends.' More important are other impressions. Sometimes from the very furnace of affliction a conviction seems borne to us that somehow, if we could see it, this agony counts as nothing against the heroism and love which appear in it and thrill our hearts. Sometimes we are driven to cry out that these mighty or heavenly spirits who perish are too great for the little space in which they move, and that they vanish not into nothingness but into freedom. Sometimes from these sources and from others comes a presentiment, formless but haunting and even profound, that all the fury of conflict, with its waste and woe, is less than half the truth, even an illusion, 'such stuff as dreams are made on.' But these faint and scattered intimations that the tragic world, being but a fragment of a whole beyond our vision, must needs be a contradiction and no ultimate truth, avail nothing to interpret the mystery. We remain confronted with the inexplicable fact, or the no less inexplicable appearance, of a world travailing for perfection, but bringing to birth, together with glorious good, an evil which it is able to overcome only by self-torture and self-waste. And this fact or appearance is tragedy.

JOSEPH CONRAD

❧ *Preface to*
The Nigger of the Narcissus

A WORK that aspires, however humbly, to the condition of art should carry its justification in every line. And art itself may be defined as a single-minded attempt to render the highest kind of justice to the visible universe, by bringing to light the truth, manifold and one, underlying its every aspect. It is an attempt to find in its forms, in its colours, in its light, in its shadows, in the aspects of matter and in the facts of life what of each is fundamental, what is enduring and essential—their one illuminating and convincing quality—the very truth of their existence. The artist, then, like the thinker or the scientist, seeks the truth and makes his appeal. Impressed by the aspect of the world the thinker plunges into ideas, the scientist into facts—whence, presently, emerging they make their appeal to those qualities of our being that fit us best for the hazardous enterprise of living. They speak authoritatively to our common-sense, to our intelligence, to our desire of peace or to our desire of unrest; not seldom to our prejudices, sometimes to our fears, often to our egoism—but always to our credulity. And their words are heard with reverence, for their concern is with weighty matters: with the cultivation of our minds and the proper care of our bodies, with the attainment of our ambitions, with the perfection of the means and the glorification of our precious aims.

It is otherwise with the artist.

Confronted by the same enigmatical spectacle the artist descends within himself, and in that lonely region of stress and strife, if he be deserving and fortunate, he finds the terms of his appeal. His appeal is made to our less obvious capacities: to that part of our nature which, because of the warlike conditions of existence, is necessarily kept out of sight within the more resisting and hard qualities—like the vulnerable body within a steel armour. His appeal is less loud, more profound, less distinct, more stirring—and sooner forgotten. Yet its effect endures forever. The changing wisdom of successive generations discards ideas, questions facts, demolishes theories. But the artist appeals to that part of our being which is not dependent on wisdom; to that in us which is a gift and not an acquisition—and, therefore, more permanently enduring. He speaks to our capacity for delight and wonder, to the sense of mystery surrounding our lives; to our sense of pity, and beauty, and pain; to the latent feeling of fellowship with all creation—and to the subtle but invincible conviction of solidarity that knits together the loneliness of innumerable hearts, to the solidarity in dreams, in joy, in sorrow, in aspirations, in illusions, in hope, in fear, which binds men to each other, which binds together all humanity—the dead to the living and the living to the unborn.

It is only some such train of thought, or rather of feeling, that can in a measure explain the aim of the attempt, made in the tale which follows, to present an unrestful episode in the obscure lives of a few individuals out of all the disregarded multitude of the bewildered, the simple and the voiceless. For, if any part of truth dwells in the belief confessed above, it becomes evident that there is not a place of splendour or a dark corner of the earth that does not deserve, if only a passing glance of wonder and pity. The motive then, may be held to justify the matter of the work; but this preface, which is simply an avowal of endeavour, cannot end here—for the avowal is not yet complete.

Fiction—if it at all aspires to be art—appeals to temperament. And in truth it must be, like painting, like music, like all art, the appeal of one temperament to all the other innumerable temperaments whose subtle and resistless power endows passing events with their true meaning, and creates the moral, the emotional atmosphere of the place and time. Such an appeal to be effective must be an impression conveyed through the senses; and, in fact, it cannot be made in any other way, because temperament, whether individual or collective, is not amenable to persuasion. All art, therefore, appeals primarily to the senses, and the artistic aim when expressing itself in written words must also make its appeal through the senses, if its high desire is to reach the secret spring of responsive emotions. It must strenuously aspire to the plasticity of sculpture, to the colour of painting, and to the magic suggestiveness of music—which is the art of arts. And it is only through complete, unswerving devotion to the perfect blending of form and substance; it is only through an unremitting never-discouraged care for the shape and ring of sentences that an approach can be made to plasticity, to colour, and that the light of magic suggestiveness may be brought to play for an evanescent instant over the commonplace surface of words: of the old, old words, worn thin, defaced by ages of careless usage.

The sincere endeavour to accomplish that creative task, to go as far on that road as his strength will carry him, to go undeterred by faltering, weariness or reproach, is the only valid justification for the worker in prose. And if his conscience is clear, his answer to those who in the fulness of a wisdom which looks for immediate profit, demand specifically to be edified, consoled, amused; who demand to be promptly improved, or encouraged, or frightened, or shocked, or charmed, must run thus:—My task which I am trying to achieve is, by the power of the written word to make you hear, to make you feel—it is, before all, to make you *see*. That—and no more, and it is everything. If I succeed, you shall find there according to your deserts: encouragement, con-solation, fear, charm—all you demand—and, perhaps, also that glimpse of truth for which you have forgotten to ask.

To snatch in a moment of courage, from the remorseless rush of time, a passing phase of life, is only the beginning of the task. The task approached in tenderness and faith is to hold up unquestioningly, without choice and without fear, the rescued fragment before all eyes in the light of a sincere mood. It is to show its vibration, its colour, its form; and through its movement, its form, and its colour, reveal the substance of its truth—disclose its inspiring secret: the stress and passion within the core of each convincing moment. In a single-minded attempt of that kind, if one be deserving and fortunate, one may perchance attain to such clearness of sincerity that at last the presented vision of regret or pity, of terror or mirth, shall awaken in the hearts of the beholders that feeling of unavoidable solidarity; of the solidarity in mysterious origin, in toil, in joy, in hope, in uncertain fate, which binds men to each other and all mankind to the visible world.

It is evident that he who, rightly or wrongly, holds by the convictions expressed above cannot be faithful to any one of the temporary formulas of his craft. The enduring part of them—the truth which each only imperfectly veils—should abide with him as the most precious of his possessions, but they all: Realism, Romanticism, Naturalism, even the unofficial sentimentalism (which like the poor, is exceedingly difficult to get rid of), all these gods must, after a short period of fellowship, abandon him—even on the very threshold of the temple—to the stammerings of his conscience and to the outspoken consciousness of the difficulties of his work. In that uneasy solitude the supreme cry of Art for Art itself, loses the exciting ring of its apparent immorality. It sounds far off. It has ceased to be a cry, and is heard only as a whisper, often incomprehensible, but at times and faintly encouraging.

Sometimes, stretched at ease in the shade of a roadside tree, we watch the motions of a labourer in a distant field, and after a time, begin to wonder languidly as to what the fellow may be at. We watch the movements of his body, the waving of his arms, we see him bend down, stand up, hesitate, begin again. It may add to the charm of an idle hour to be told the purpose of his exertions. If we know he is trying to lift a stone, to dig a ditch, to uproot a stump, we look with a more real interest at his efforts; we are disposed to condone the jar of his agitation upon the restfulness of the landscape; and even, if in a brotherly frame of mind, we may bring ourselves to forgive his failure. We understood his object, and, after all, the fellow has tried, and perhaps he had not the strength—and perhaps he had not the knowledge. We forgive, go on our way—and forget.

And so it is with the workman of art. Art is long and life is short, and success is very far off. And thus, doubtful of strength to travel so far, we talk a little about the aim—the aim of art, which, like life itself, is inspiring, difficult—obscured by mists. It is not in the clear logic of a triumphant conclusion; it is not in the unveiling of one of those heartless secrets which are called the Laws of Nature. It is not less great, but only more difficult.

To arrest, for the space of a breath, the hands busy about the work of the earth, and compel men entranced by the sight of distant goals to glance for a moment at the surrounding vision of form and colour, of sunshine and shadows; to make them pause for a look, for a sigh, for a smile—such is the aim, difficult and evanescent, and reserved only for a very few to achieve. But sometimes, by the deserving and the fortunate, even that task is accomplished. And when it is accomplished—behold!—all the truth of life is there: a moment of vision, a sigh, a smile—and the return to an eternal rest.

EDITH HAMILTON

❧ *The Idea of Tragedy*

THE great tragic artists of the world are four, and three of them are Greek. It is in tragedy that the pre-eminence of the Greeks can be seen most clearly. Except for Shakespeare, the great three, Aeschylus, Sophocles, Euripides, stand alone. Tragedy is an achievement peculiarly Greek. They were the first to perceive it and they lifted it to its supreme height. Nor is it a matter that directly touches only the great artists who wrote tragedies; it concerns the entire people as well, who felt the appeal of the tragic to such a degree that they would gather thirty thousand strong to see a performance. In tragedy the

Greek genius penetrated farthest and it is the revelation of what was most profound in them.

The special characteristic of the Greeks was their power to see the world clearly and at the same time as beautiful. Because they were able to do this, they produced art distinguished from all other art by an absence of struggle, marked by a calm and serenity which is theirs alone. There is, it seems to assure us, a region where beauty is truth, truth beauty. To it their artists would lead us, illumining life's dark confusions by gleams fitful indeed and wavering compared with the fixed light of religious faith, but by some magic of their own, satisfying, affording a vision of something inconclusive and yet of incalculable significance. Of all the great poets this is true, but truest of the tragic poets, for the reason that in them the power of poetry confronts the inexplicable.

Tragedy was a Greek creation because in Greece thought was free. Men were thinking more and more deeply about human life, and beginning to perceive more and more clearly that it was bound up with evil and that injustice was of the nature of things. And then, one day, this knowledge of something irremediably wrong in the world came to a poet with his poet's power to see beauty in the truth of human life, and the first tragedy was written. As the author of a most distinguished book on the subject says: "The spirit of inquiry meets the spirit of poetry and tragedy is born." Make it concrete: early Greece with her god-like heroes and hero gods fighting far on the ringing plains of windy Troy; with her lyric world, where every common thing is touched with beauty—her twofold world of poetic creation. Then a new age dawns, not satisfied with beauty of song and story, an age that must try to know and to explain. And for the first time tragedy appears. A poet of surpassing magnitude, not content with the old sacred conventions, and of a soul great enough to bear new and intolerable truth—that is Aeschylus, the first writer of tragedy.

Tragedy belongs to the poets. Only they have "trod the sunlit heights and from life's dissonance struck one clear chord." None but a poet can write a tragedy. For tragedy is nothing less than pain transmuted into exaltation by the alchemy of poetry, and if poetry is true knowledge and the great poets guides safe to follow, this transmutation has arresting implications.

Pain changed into, or, let us say, charged with, exaltation. It would seem that tragedy is a strange matter. There is indeed none stranger. A tragedy shows us pain and gives us pleasure thereby. The greater the suffering depicted, the more terrible the events, the more intense our pleasure. The most monstrous and appalling deeds life can show are those the tragedian chooses, and by the spectacle he thus offers us, we are moved to a very passion of enjoyment. There is food for wonder here, not to be passed over, as the superficial have done, by pointing out that the Romans made a holiday of a gladiator's slaughter, and that even to-day fierce instincts, savage survivals, stir in the most civilized. Grant all that, and we are not a step advanced on the way to explaining the mystery of tragic pleasure. It has no kinship with cruelty or the lust for blood.

On this point it is illuminating to consider our every-day use of the words tragedy and tragic. Pain, sorrow, disaster, are always spoken of as depressing, as dragging down—the dark abyss of pain, a crushing sorrow, an overwhelming disaster. But speak of tragedy and extraordinarily the metaphor changes. Lift us to tragic heights, we say, and never anything else. The depths of pathos but never of tragedy. Always the height of tragedy. A word is no light matter. Words have with truth been called fossil poetry, each, that is, a symbol of a creative thought. The whole philosophy of human nature is implicit in human speech. It is a matter to pause over, that the instinct of mankind has perceived a difference, not of degree but of kind, between tragic pain and all other pain. There is something in tragedy which marks it off from other disaster so sharply that in our common speech we bear witness to the difference.

All those whose attention has been caught by the strange contradiction of pleasure through pain agree with this instinctive witness, and some of the most brilliant minds the world has known have concerned themselves with it. Tragic pleasure, they tell us, is in a class by itself. "Pity and awe," Aristotle called it, "and a sense of emotion purged and purified thereby." "Reconciliation," said Hegel, which we may understand in the sense of life's temporary dissonance resolved into eternal harmony. "Acceptance," said Schopenhauer, the temper of mind that says, "Thy will be done." "The reaffirmation of the will to live in the face of death," said Nietzsche, "and the joy of its inexhaustibility when so reaffirmed."

Pity, awe, reconciliation, exaltation—these are the elements that make up tragic pleasure. No play is a tragedy that does not call them forth. So the philosophers say, all in agreement with the common judgment of mankind, that tragedy is something above and beyond the dissonance of pain. But what it is that causes a play to call forth these feelings, what is the essential element in a tragedy, Hegel alone seeks to define. In a notable passage he says that the only tragic subject is a spiritual struggle in which each side has a claim upon our sympathy. But, as his critics have pointed out, he would thus exclude the tragedy of the suffering of the innocent, and a definition which does not include the death of Cordelia or of Deianira cannot be taken as final.

The suffering of the innocent, indeed, can itself be so differently treated as to necessitate completely different categories. In one of the greatest tragedies, the *Prometheus* of Aeschylus, the main actor is an innocent sufferer, but, beyond this purely formal connection, that passionate rebel, defying God and all the powers of the universe, has no relationship whatever to the lovely, loving Cordelia. An inclusive definition of tragedy must cover cases as diverse in circumstance and in the character of the protagonist as the whole range of life and letters can afford it. It must include such opposites as Antigone, the high-souled maiden who goes with open eyes to her death rather than leave her brother's body unburied, and Macbeth, the ambition-mad, the murderer of his king and guest. These two plays, seemingly so totally unlike, call forth the same response. Tragic pleasure of the greatest intensity is caused by them both. They have something in common, but the philosophers do not tell us what it is. Their concern is with what a tragedy makes us feel, not with what makes a tragedy.

Only twice in literary history has there been a great period of tragedy, in the Athens of Pericles and in Elizabethan England. What these two periods had in common, two thousand years and more apart in time, that they expressed themselves in the same fashion, may give us some hint of the nature of tragedy, for far from being periods of darkness and defeat, each was a time when life was seen exalted, a time of thrilling and unfathomable possibilities. They held their heads high, those men who conquered at Marathon and Salamis, and those who fought Spain and saw the Great Armada sink. The world was a place of wonder; mankind was beauteous; life was lived on the crest of the wave. More than all, the poignant joy of heroism had stirred men's hearts. Not stuff for tragedy, would you say? But on the crest of the wave one must feel either tragically or joyously; one cannot feel tamely. The temper of mind that sees tragedy in life has not for its opposite the temper that sees joy. The opposite pole to the tragic view of life is the sordid view. When humanity is seen as devoid of dignity and significance, trivial, mean, and sunk in dreary hopelessness, then the spirit of tragedy departs. "Sometime let gorgeous tragedy in sceptred pall come sweeping by." At the opposite pole stands Gorki with *The Lower Depths.*

Other poets may, the tragedian must, seek for the significance of life. An error strangely common is that this significance for tragic purposes depends, in some sort, upon outward circumstance, on

> pomp and feast and revelry,
> With mask, and antique pageantry—

Nothing of all that touches tragedy. The surface of life is comedy's concern; tragedy is indifferent to it. We do not, to be sure, go to Main Street or to Zenith for tragedy, but the reason has nothing to do with their dull familiarity. There is no reason inherent in the house itself why Babbitt's home in Zenith [scene of Sinclair Lewis' *Babbitt*] should not be the scene of a tragedy quite as well as the Castle of Elsinore [scene of Shakespeares' *Hamlet*]. The only reason it is not is Babbitt himself. "That singular swing toward elevation" which Schopenhauer discerned in tragedy, does not take any of its impetus from outside things.

The dignity and the significance of human life—of these, and of these alone, tragedy will never let go. Without them there is no tragedy. To answer the question, what makes a tragedy, is to answer the question wherein lies the essential significance of life, what the dignity of humanity depends upon in the last analysis. Here the tragedians speak to us with no uncertain voice. The great tragedies themselves offer the solution to the problem they propound. It is by our power to suffer, above all, that we are of more value than the sparrows. Endow them with a greater or as great a potentiality of pain and our foremost place in the world would no longer be undisputed. Deep down, when we search out the reason for our conviction of the transcendent worth of each human being, we know that it is because of the possibility that each can suffer so terribly. What do outside trappings matter, Zenith or Elsinore? Tragedy's preoccupation is with suffering.

But, it is to be well noted, not with all suffering. There are degrees in our high estate of pain. It is not given to all to suffer alike. We differ in nothing more than in our power to feel. There are souls of little and of great degree, and upon that degree the dignity and significance of each life depend. There is no dignity like the dignity of a soul in agony.

> Here I and sorrows sit;
> Here is my throne, bid kings come bow to it.

Tragedy is enthroned, and to her realm those alone are admitted who belong to the only true aristocracy, that of all passionate souls. Tragedy's one essential is a soul that can feel greatly. Given such a one and any catastrophe may be tragic. But the earth may be removed and the mountains be carried into the midst of the sea, and if only the small and shallow are confounded, tragedy is absent.

One dark page of Roman history tells of a little seven-year-old girl, daughter of a man judged guilty of death and so herself condemned to die, and how she passed through the staring crowds sobbing and asking, "What had she done wrong? If they would tell her, she would never do it again"—and so on to the black prison and the executioner. That breaks the heart, but is not tragedy, it is pathos. No heights are there for the soul to mount to, but only the dark depths where there are tears for things. Undeserved suffering is not in itself tragic. Death is not tragic in itself, not the death of the beautiful and the young, the lovely and beloved. Death felt and suffered as Macbeth feels and suffers is tragic. Death felt as Lear feels Cordelia's death is tragic. Ophelia's death is not a tragedy. She being what she is, it could be so only if Hamlet's and Laertes' grief were tragic grief. The conflicting claims of the law of God and the law of man are not what make the tragedy of the *Antigone* [by Sophocles]. It is Antigone herself, so great, so tortured. Hamlet's hesitation to kill his uncle is not tragic. The tragedy is his power to feel. Change all the circumstances of the drama and Hamlet in the grip of any calamity would be tragic, just as Polonius would never be, however awful the catastrophe. The suffering of a soul that can suffer greatly—that and only that, is tragedy.

It follows, then, that tragedy has nothing to do with the distinction between Realism and Romanticism. The contrary has always been maintained. The Greeks went to the myths for their subjects, we are told, to insure remoteness from real life which does not admit of high tragedy. "Realism is the ruin of tragedy," says the latest writer on the subject. It is not true. If indeed Realism were conceived of as dealing only with the usual, tragedy would be ruled out, for the soul capable of a great passion is not usual. But if nothing human is alien to Realism, then tragedy is of her domain, for the unusual is as real as the usual. When the Moscow Art Players presented the *Brothers Karamazoff* [by Feodor Dostoevsky] there was seen on the stage an absurd little man in dirty clothes who waved his arms about and shuffled and sobbed, the farthest possible remove from the traditional figures of tragedy, and yet tragedy was there in his person, stripped of her gorgeous pall, but sceptred truly, speaking the authentic voice of human agony in a struggle past the power of the human heart to bear. A drearier setting, a more typically realistic setting, it would be hard to find, but to see the play was to feel pity and awe before a man dignified by one thing only, made great by what he could suffer. Ibsen's plays are not tragedies. Whether Ibsen is a realist or not—the Realism of one generation is apt to be the Romanticism of the next—small souls are his dramatis personae and his plays are dramas with an unhappy ending. The end of *Ghosts* leaves us with a sense of shuddering horror and cold anger against a society where such things can be, and these are not tragic feelings.

The greatest realistic works of fiction have been written by the French and the Russians. To read one of the great Frenchmen's books is to feel mingled despair and loathing for mankind, so base, so trivial and so wretched. But to read a great Russian novel is to have an altogether different experience. The baseness, the beast in us, the misery of life, are there as plain to see as in the French book, but what we are left with is not despair and not loathing, but a sense of pity and wonder before mankind that can so suffer. The Russian sees life in that way because the Russian genius is primarily poetical; the French genius is not. *Anna Karénina* [by Leo Tolstoy] is a tragedy; *Madame Bovary* [by Gustave Flaubert] is not. Realism and Romanticism, or comparative degrees of Realism, have nothing to do with the matter. It is a case of the small soul against the great soul and the power of a writer whose special endowment is *"voir clair dans ce qui est"* [to see clearly into what is] against the intuition of a poet.

If the Greeks had left no tragedies behind for us, the highest reach of their power would be unknown. The three poets who were able to sound the depths of human agony were able also to recognize and reveal it as tragedy. The mystery of evil, they said, curtains that of which "every man whose soul is not a clod hath visions." Pain could exalt and in tragedy for a moment men could have sight of a meaning beyond their grasp. "Yet had God not turned us in his hand and cast to earth our greatness," Euripides makes the old Trojan queen say in her extremity, "we would have passed away giving nothing to men. They would have found no theme for song in us nor made great poems from our sorrows."

Why is the death of the ordinary man a wretched, chilling thing which we turn from, while the death of the hero, always tragic, warms us with a sense of quickened life? Answer this question and the enigma of tragic pleasure is solved. "Never let me hear that brave blood has been shed in vain," said Sir Walter Scott; "it sends an imperious challenge down through all the generations." So the end of a tragedy challenges us. The great soul in pain and in death transforms pain and death. Through it we catch a glimpse of the Stoic Emperor's [Marcus Aurelius Antoninus] Dear City of God, of a deeper and more ultimate reality than that in which our lives are lived.

ROBERT FROST

❧ *The Poetry of Amy Lowell*

IT IS absurd to think that the only way to tell if a poem is lasting is to wait and see if it lasts. The right reader of a good poem can tell the moment it strikes him that he has taken an immortal wound—that he will never get over it. That is to say, permanence in poetry as in love is perceived instantly. It hasn't to await the test of time. The proof of a poem is not that we have never forgotten it, but that we knew at sight that we never could forget it. There was a barb to it and a toxin that we owned to at once. How often I have heard it in the voice and seen it in the eyes of this generation that Amy Lowell had lodged poetry with them to stay.

The most exciting movement in nature is not progress, advance, but expansion and contraction, the opening and shutting of the eye, the hand, the heart, the mind. We throw our arms wide with a gesture of religion to the universe; we close them around a person. We explore and adventure for a while and then we draw in to consolidate our gains. The breathless swing is between subject matter and form. Amy Lowell was distinguished in a period of dilation when poetry, in the effort to include a larger material, stretched itself almost to the breaking of the verse. Little ones with no more apparatus than a teacup looked on with alarm. She helped make it stirring times for a decade to those immediately concerned with art and to many not so immediately.

The water in our eyes from her poetry is not warm with any suspicion of tears; it is water flung cold, bright and many-colored from flowers gathered in her formal garden in the morning. Her Imagism lay chiefly in images to the eye. She flung flowers and everything else. Her poetry was forever a clear resonant calling off of things seen.

E. M. FORSTER

❧ *Flat and Round Characters*

WE MAY divide characters into flat and round.

Flat characters were called "humours" in the seventeenth century, and are sometimes called types, and sometimes caricatures. In their purest form, they are constructed round a single idea or quality: when there is more than one factor in them, we get the beginning of the curve towards the round. The really flat character can be expressed in one sentence such as "I never will desert Mr. Micawber." There is Mrs. Micawber—she says she won't desert Mr. Micawber, she doesn't, and there she is. Or: "I must conceal, even by subterfuges, the poverty of my master's house." There is Caleb Balderstone in *The Bride of Lammermoor* [by Sir Walter Scott]. He does not use the actual phrase, but it completely describes him; he has no existence outside it, no pleasures, none of the private lusts and aches that must complicate the most consistent of servitors. Whatever he does, wherever he goes, whatever lies he tells or plates he breaks, it is to conceal the poverty of his master's house. It is not his *idée fixe*, because there is nothing in him into which the idea can be fixed. He is the idea, and such life as he possesses radiates from its edges and from the scintillations it strikes when other elements in the novel impinge. Or take Proust. There are numerous flat characters in Proust, such as the Princess of Parma, or Legrandin.[20] Each can be expressed in a single sentence, the Princess's sentence being, "I must be particularly careful to be kind." She does nothing except to be particularly careful, and those of the other characters who are more complex than herself easily see through the kindness, since it is only a by-product of the carefulness.

One great advantage of flat characters is that they are easily recognized whenever they come in—recognized by the reader's emotional eye, not by the visual eye, which merely notes the recurrence of a proper name. In Russian novels, where they so seldom occur, they would be a decided help. It is a convenience for an author when he can strike with his full force at once, and flat characters are very useful to him, since they never need reintroducing, never run away, have not to be watched for development, and provide their own atmosphere—little luminous disks of a pre-arranged size, pushed hither and thither like counters across the void or between the stars; most satisfactory.

A second advantage is that they are easily remembered by the reader

---

[20] Proust wrote a series of volumes grouped under the title À *la Recherche du Temps Perdu* (*Remembrance of Things Past*). [Eds.]

afterwards. They remain in his mind as unalterable for the reason that they were not changed by circumstances; they moved through circumstances, which gives them in retrospect a comforting quality, and preserves them when the book that produced them may decay. The Countess in *Evan Harrington* [by George Meredith] furnishes a good little example here. Let us compare our memories of her with our memories of Becky Sharp [in William Thackeray's *Vanity Fair*]. We do not remember what the Countess did or what she passed through. What is clear is her figure and the formula that surrounds it, namely, "Proud as we are of dear papa, we must conceal his memory." All her rich humour proceeds from this. She is a flat character. Becky is round. She, too, is on the make, but she cannot be summed up in a single phrase, and we remember her in connection with the great scenes through which she passed and as modified by those scenes—that is to say, we do not remember her so easily because she waxes and wanes and has facets like a human being. All of us, even the sophisticated, yearn for permanence, and to the unsophisticated permanence is the chief excuse for a work of art. We all want books to endure, to be refuges, and their inhabitants to be always the same, and flat characters tend to justify themselves on this account.

All the same, critics who have their eyes fixed severely upon daily life—as were our eyes last week—have very little patience with such renderings of human nature. Queen Victoria, they argue, cannot be summed up in a single sentence, so what excuse remains for Mrs. Micawber? One of our foremost writers, Mr. Norman Douglas, is a critic of this type, and the passage from him which I will quote puts the case against flat characters in a forcible fashion. The passage occurs in an open letter to D. H. Lawrence, with whom he is quarrelling: a doughty pair of combatants, the hardness of whose hitting makes the rest of us feel like a lot of ladies up in a pavilion. He complains that Lawrence, in a biography, has falsified the picture by employing "the novelist's touch," and he goes on to define what this is:

It consists, I should say, in a failure to realize the complexities of the ordinary human mind; it selects for literary purposes two or three facets of a man or woman, generally the most spectacular, and therefore useful ingredients of their character and disregards all the others. Whatever fails to fit in with these specially chosen traits is eliminated—must be eliminated, for otherwise the description would not hold water. Such and such are the data: everything incompatible with those data has to go by the board. It follows that the novelist's touch argues, often logically, from a wrong premise: it takes what it likes and leaves the rest. The facts may be correct as far as they go but there are too few of them: what the author says may be true and yet by no means the truth. That is the novelist's touch. It falsifies life.

Well, the novelist's touch as thus defined is, of course, bad in biography, for no human being is simple. But in a novel it has its place: a novel that is at all complex often requires flat people as well as round, and the outcome of their collisions parallels life more accurately than Mr. Douglas implies. The case of Dickens is significant. Dickens' people are nearly all flat (Pip [Philip Pirrip in *Great Expectations*] and David Copperfield attempt roundness, but so diffidently that they seem more like bubbles than solids). Nearly every one can be summed up in a sentence, and yet there is this wonderful feeling of human depth. Probably the immense vitality of Dickens causes his characters to vibrate a little, so that they borrow his life and appear to lead one of their own. It is a conjuring trick; at any moment we may look at Mr. Pickwick edgeways and find him no thicker than a gramophone record. But we never get the sideway view. Mr. Pickwick is far too adroit and well trained. He always has the air of weighing something, and when he is put into the cupboard of the young ladies' school he seems as heavy as Falstaff in the buck-basket [wash bucket] at Windsor. Part of the genius of Dickens is that he does use types and caricatures, people whom we recognize the instant they re-enter, and yet achieves effects that are not mechanical and a vision of humanity that is not shallow. Those who dislike Dickens have an excellent case. He ought to be bad. He is actually one of our big writers, and his immense success with types suggests that there may be more in flatness than the severer critics admit.

Or take H. G. Wells. With the possible exception of Kipps and the aunt in *Tono Bungay*, all Wells' characters are as flat as a photograph. But the photographs are agitated with such vigour that we forget their complexities lie on the surface and would disappear if it was scratched or curled up. A Wells character cannot indeed be summed up in a single phrase; he is tethered much more to observation, he does not create types. Nevertheless his people seldom pulsate by their own strength. It is the deft and powerful hands of their maker that shake them and trick the reader into a sense of depth. Good but imperfect novelists, like Wells and Dickens, are very clever at transmitting force. The part of their novel that is alive galvanizes the part that is not, and causes the characters to jump about and speak in a convincing way. They are quite different from the perfect novelist who touches all his material directly, who seems to pass the creative finger down every sentence and into every word. Richardson, Defoe, Jane Austen, are perfect in this particular way; their work may not be great but their hands are always upon it; there is not the tiny interval between the touching of the button and the sound of the bell which occurs in novels where the characters are not under direct control.

For we must admit that flat people are not in themselves as big achievements as round ones, and also that they are best when they are comic. A serious or tragic flat character is apt to be a bore. Each time he enters crying "Revenge!" or "My heart bleeds for humanity!" or whatever his formula is, our hearts sink. One of the romances of a popular contemporary writer is constructed round a Sussex farmer who says, "I'll plough up that bit of gorse." There is the farmer, there is the gorse; he says he'll plough it up, he does plough it up, but it is not like saying "I'll never desert Mr. Micawber," because we are so bored by his consistency that we do not care whether he succeeds with the gorse or fails. If his formula was analysed and connected up with the rest of the human outfit, we should not be bored any longer, the formula would cease to be the man and become an obsession in the man; that is to say he would have turned from a flat farmer into a round one. It is only round people who are fit to perform tragically for any length of time and can move us to any feelings except humour and appropriateness.

So now let us desert these two-dimensional people, and by way of transition to the round, let us go to *Mansfield Park* [by Jane Austen], and look at Lady Bertram, sitting on her sofa with pug. Pug is flat, like most animals in fiction. He is once represented as straying into a rose-bed in a cardboard kind of way, but that is all, and during most of the book his mistress seems to be cut out of the same simple material as her dog. Lady Bertram's formula is, "I am kindly, but must not be fatigued," and she functions out of it. But at the end there is a catastrophe. Her two daughters come to grief—to the worst grief known to Miss Austen's universe, far worse than the Napoleonic wars. Julia elopes; Maria, who is unhappily married, runs off with a lover. What is Lady Bertram's reaction? The sentence describing it is significant: "Lady Bertram did not think deeply, but, guided by Sir Thomas, she thought justly on all important points, and she saw therefore in all its enormity, what had happened, and neither endeavoured herself, nor required Fanny to advise her, to think little of guilt and infamy." These are strong words and they used to worry me because I thought Jane Austen's moral sense was getting out of hand. She may, and of course does, deprecate guilt and infamy herself, and she duly causes all possible distress in the minds of Edmund and Fanny, but has she any right to agitate calm, consistent Lady Bertram? Is it not like giving pug three faces and setting him to guard the gates of Hell? Ought not her ladyship to remain on the sofa saying, "This is a dreadful and sadly exhausting business about Julia and Maria, but where is Fanny gone? I have dropped another stitch"?

I used to think this, through misunderstanding Jane Austen's method— exactly as Scott misunderstood it when he congratulated her for painting on a square of ivory. She is a miniaturist, but never two-dimensional. All her characters are round, or capable of rotundity. Even Miss Bates has a mind, even Elizabeth Eliot a heart, and Lady Bertram's moral fervour ceases to vex us when we realize this: The disk has suddenly extended and become a little globe. When the novel is closed, Lady Bertram goes back to the flat, it is true; the dominant impression she leaves can be summed up in a formula. But that is not how Jane Austen conceived her, and the freshness of her reappearances are due to this. Why do the characters in Jane Austen give us a slightly new pleasure each time they come in, as opposed to the merely repetitive pleasure that is caused by a character in Dickens? Why do they combine so well in a conversation, and draw one another out without seeming to do so, and never perform?

The answer to this question can be put in several ways: that, unlike Dickens, she was a real artist, that she never stooped to caricature, etc. But the best reply is that her characters though smaller than his are more highly organized. They function all round, and even if her plot made greater demands on them than it does, they would still be adequate. Suppose that Louisa Musgrove had broken her neck on the Cobb. The description of her death would have been feeble and ladylike—physical violence is quite beyond Miss Austen's powers—but the survivors would have reacted properly as soon as the corpse was carried away, they would have brought into view new sides of their character, and though *Persuasion* would have been spoiled as a book, we should know more than we do about Captain Wentworth and Anne. All the Jane Austen characters are ready for an extended life, for a life which the scheme of her books seldom requires them to lead, and that is why they lead their actual lives so satisfactorily. Let us return to Lady Bertram and the crucial sentence. See how subtly it modulates from her formula into an area where the formula does not work. "Lady Bertram did not think deeply." Exactly: as per formula. "But guided by Sir Thomas she thought justly on all important points." Sir Thomas' guidance, which is part of the formula, remains, but it pushes her ladyship towards an independent and undesired morality. "She saw therefore in all its enormity what had happened." This is the moral fortissimo—very strong but carefully introduced. And then follows a most artful decrescendo, by means of negatives. "She neither endeavoured herself, nor required Fanny to advise her, to think little of guilt or infamy." The formula is reappearing, because as a rule she does try to minimize trouble, and does require Fanny to advise her how to do this; indeed Fanny has done nothing else for the last ten years. The words, though they are negatived, remind us of this, her normal state is again in view, and she has in a single sentence been inflated into a round character and collapsed back into a flat one. How Jane Austen can write! In a few words she has extended Lady Bertram, and by so doing she has increased the probability of the elopements of Maria and Julia. I say probability because the elopements belong to the domain of violent physical action, and here, as already indicated, Jane Austen is feeble and ladylike. Except in her school-girl novels, she cannot stage a crash. Everything violent has to take place "off"—Louisa's accident and Marianne Dashwood's putrid throat are the nearest exceptions—and consequently all the comments on the elopement must be sincere and convincing, otherwise we should doubt whether it occurred. Lady Bertram helps us to believe that her daughters have run away, and they have to run away, or there would be no apotheosis for Fanny. It is a little point, and a little sentence, yet it shows us how delicately a great novelist can modulate into the round.

All through her works we find these characters, apparently so simple and flat, never needing reintroduction and yet never out of their depth—Henry Tilney [in *Northanger Abbey*], Mr. Woodhouse [in *Emma*], Charlotte Lucas [in *Pride and Prejudice*]. She may label her characters "Sense," "Pride," "Sensibility," "Prejudice," but they are not tethered to those qualities.

As for the round characters proper, they have already been defined by implication and no more need be said. All I need do is to give some examples of people in books who seem to me round so that the definition can be tested afterwards:

All the principal characters in *War and Peace* [by Leo Tolstoy], all the Dostoevsky characters, and some of the Proust—for example, the old family servant, the Duchess of Guermantes, M. de Charlus, and Saint Loup; Madame Bovary—who, like Moll Flanders, has her book to herself [by Gustave Flaubert and Daniel Defoe, respectively], and can expand and secrete unchecked; some people in Thackeray—for instance, Becky and Beatrix [in *Henry Esmond*]; some in Fielding—Parson Adams [in *Joseph Andrews*], Tom Jones; and some in Charlotte Brontë, most particularly Lucy Snowe [in *Villette*]. (And many more —this is not a catalogue.) The test of a round character is whether it is capable of surprising in a convincing way. If it never surprises, it is flat. If it does not convince, it is a flat pretending to be round. It has the incalculability of life about it—life within the pages of a book. And by using it sometimes alone, more often in combination with the other kind, the novelist achieves his task of acclimatization and harmonizes the human race with the other aspects of his work.

T. S. ELIOT

❧ *The Metaphysical Poets*

BY COLLECTING these poems from the work of a generation more often named than read, and more often read than profitably studied, Professor Grierson [1866–1960; English scholar] has rendered a service of some importance. Certainly the reader will meet with many poems already preserved in other anthologies, at the same time that he discovers poems such as those of Aurelian Townshend or Lord Herbert of Cherbury [1583–1648; English philosopher, poet, historian, and diplomat] here included. But the function of such an anthology as this is neither that of Professor Saintsbury's [1845–1933; English critic and historian] admirable edition of Caroline poets nor that of the *Oxford Book of English Verse*. Mr. Grierson's book is in itself a piece of criticism and a provocation of criticism; and we think that he was right in including so many poems of Donne, elsewhere (though not in many editions) accessible, as documents in the case of "metaphysical poetry." The phrase has long done duty as a term of abuse or as the label of a quaint and pleasant taste. The question is to what extent the so-called metaphysicals formed a school (in our own time we should say a "movement"), and how far this so-called school or movement is a digression from the main current.

Not only is it extremely difficult to define metaphysical poetry, but difficult to decide what poets practise it and in which of their verses. The poetry of Donne (to whom Marvell and Bishop King [1592–1669; English prelate and man of letters] are sometimes nearer than any of the other authors) is late Elizabethan, its feeling often very close to that of Chapman. The "courtly" poetry is derivative from Jonson, who borrowed liberally from the Latin; it expires in the next century with the sentiment and witticism of Prior. There is finally the devotional verse of Herbert, Vaughan, and Crashaw (echoed long after by Christina Rossetti and Francis Thompson); Crashaw, sometimes more profound and less sectarian than the others, has a quality which returns through the Elizabethan period to the early Italians. It is difficult to find any precise use of metaphor, simile, or other conceit, which is common to all the poets and at the same time important enough as an element of style to isolate these poets as a group. Donne, and often Cowley, employ a device which is sometimes considered characteristically "metaphysical"; the elaboration (contrasted with the condensation) of a figure of speech to the farthest stage to which ingenuity can carry it. Thus Cowley develops the commonplace comparison of the world to a chess-board through long stanzas (*To Destiny*), and Donne, with more grace, in A V*alediction*, the comparison of two lovers to a pair of compasses. But elsewhere we find, instead of the mere explication of the content of a comparison, a development by rapid association of thought which requires considerable agility on the part of the reader.

> On a round ball
> A workman that hath copies by, can lay
> An Europe, Afrique, and an Asia,
> And quickly make that, which was nothing, All,
> So doth each teare,
> Which thee doth weare,
> A globe, yea, world by that impression grow,
> Till thy tears mixt with mine doe overflow
> This world, by waters sent from thee, my heaven dissolved so.

Here we find at least two connexions which are not implicit in the first figure, but are forced upon it by the poet: from the geographer's globe to the tear, and the tear to the deluge. On the other hand, some of Donne's most successful and characteristic effects are secured by brief words and sudden contrasts:

> A bracelet of bright hair about the bone,

where the most powerful effect is produced by the sudden contrast of associations of "bright hair" and of "bone." This telescoping of images and multiplied associations is characteristic of the phrase of some of the dramatists of the period which Donne knew: not to mention Shakespeare, it is frequent in

Middleton, Webster, and Tourneur, and is one of the sources of the vitality of their language.

Johnson, who employed the term "metaphysical poets," apparently having Donne, Cleveland [1613–1658; English poet and satirist], and Cowley chiefly in mind, remarks of them that "the most heterogeneous ideas are yoked by violence together." The force of this impeachment lies in the failure of the conjunction, the fact that often the ideas are yoked but not united; and if we are to judge of styles of poetry by their abuse, enough examples may be found in Cleveland to justify Johnson's condemnation. But a degree of heterogeneit of material compelled into unity by the operation of the poet's mind is omnipresent in poetry. We need not select for illustration such a line as:

Notre âme est un trois-mâts cherchant son Icarie;[21]

we may find it in some of the best lines of Johnson himself (*The Vanity of Human Wishes*):

> His fate was destined to a barren strand,
> A petty fortress, and a dubious hand;
> He left a name at which the world grew pale,
> To point a moral, or adorn a tale.

where the effect is due to a contrast of ideas, different in degree but the same in principle, as that which Johnson mildly reprehended. And in one of the finest poems of the age (a poem which could not have been written in any other age), the *Exequy* of Bishop King, the extended comparison is used with perfect success: the idea and the simile become one, in the passage in which the Bishop illustrates his impatience to see his dead wife, under the figure of a journey:

> Stay for me there; I will not faile
> To meet thee in that hollow Vale.
> And think not much of my delay;
> I am already on the way,
> And follow thee with all the speed
> Desire can make, or sorrows breed.
> Each minute is a short degree,
> And ev'ry houre a step towards thee.
> At night when I betake to rest,
> Next morn I rise nearer my West
> Of life, almost by eight houres sail,
> Than when sleep breath'd his drowsy gale. . . .
> But heark! My Pulse, like a soft Drum
> Beats my approach, tells *Thee* I come;
> And slow howere my marches be,
> I shall at last sit down by *Thee.*

[21] Our soul is a three-masted ship looking for its Icarus. [Eds.]

(In the last few lines there is that effect of terror which is several times attained by one of Bishop King's admirers, Edgar Poe.) Again, we may justly take these quatrains from Lord Herbert's *Ode*, stanzas which would, we think, be immediately pronounced to be of the metaphysical school:

> So when from hence we shall be gone,
>> And be no more, nor you, nor I,
>> As one another's mystery,
> Each shall be both, yet both but one.

> This said, in her up-lifted face,
>> Her eyes, which did that beauty crown,
>> Were like two starrs, that having fal'n down,
> Look up again to find their place:

> While such a moveless silent peace
>> Did seize on their becalmed sense,
>> One would have thought some influence
> Their ravished spirits did possess.

There is nothing in these lines (with the possible exception of the stars, a simile not at once grasped, but lovely and justified) which fits Johnson's general observations on the metaphysical poets in his essay on Cowley. A good deal resides in the richness of association which is at the same time borrowed from and given to the word "becalmed"; but the meaning is clear, the language simple and elegant. It is to be observed that the language of these poets is as a rule simple and pure; in the verse of George Herbert this simplicity is carried as far as it can go—a simplicity emulated without success by numerous modern poets. The *structure* of the sentences, on the other hand, is sometimes far from simple, but this is not a vice; it is a fidelity to thought and feeling. The effect, at its best, is far less artificial than that of an ode by Gray. And as this fidelity induces variety of thought and feeling, so it induces variety of music. We doubt whether, in the eighteenth century, could be found two poems in nominally the same metre, so dissimilar as Marvell's *Coy Mistress* and Crashaw's *Saint Teresa*; the one producing an effect of great speed by the use of short syllables, and the other an ecclesiastical solemnity by the use of long ones:

> Love, thou art absolute sole lord
> Of life and death.

If so shrewd and sensitive (though so limited) a critic as Johnson failed to define metaphysical poetry by its faults, it is worth while to inquire whether we may not have more success by adopting the opposite method: by assuming that the poets of the seventeenth century (up to the Revolution) were the direct and normal development of the precedent age; and, without prejudicing their case by the adjective "metaphysical," consider whether their virtue was not something permanently valuable, which subsequently disappeared, but ought not to have disappeared. Johnson has hit, perhaps by accident, on one of their peculiarities, when he observes that "their attempts were always analytic"; he would not agree that, after the dissociation, they put the material together again in a new unity.

It is certain that the dramatic verse of the later Elizabethan and early Jacobean poets expresses a degree of development of sensibility which is not found in any of the prose, good as it often is. If we except Marlowe, a man of prodigious intelligence, these dramatists were directly or indirectly (it is at least a tenable theory) affected by Montaigne. Even if we except also Jonson and Chapman, these two were notably erudite, and were notably men who incorporated their erudition into their sensibility: their mode of feeling was directly and freshly altered by their reading and thought. In Chapman especially there is a direct sensuous apprehension of thought, or a recreation of thought into feeling, which is exactly what we find in Donne:

> in this one thing, all the discipline
> Of manners and of manhood is contained;
> A man to join himself with th' Universe
> In his main sway, and make in all things fit
> One with that All, and go on, round as it;
> Not plucking from the whole his wretched part,
> And into straits, or into nought revert,
> Wishing the complete Universe might be
> Subject to such a rag of it as he;
> But to consider great Necessity.

We compare this with some modern passage:

> No, when the fight begins within himself,
> A man's worth something. God stoops o'er his head,
> Satan looks up between his feet—both tug—
> He left, himself, i' the middle; the soul wakes
> And grows. Prolong that battle through his life!

It is perhaps somewhat less fair, though very tempting (as both poets are concerned with the perpetuation of love by offspring), to compare with the stanzas already quoted from Lord Herbert's *Ode* the following from Tennyson:

> One walked between his wife and child,
> With measured footfall firm and mild,
> And now and then he gravely smiled.
> > The prudent partner of his blood
> > Leaned on him, faithful, gentle, good,
> > Wearing the rose of womanhood.
> And in their double love secure,
> The little maiden walked demure,
> Pacing with downward eyelids pure.
> > These three made unity so sweet,
> > My frozen heart began to beat,
> > Remembering its ancient heat.

The difference is not a simple difference of degree between poets. It is something which had happened to the mind of England between the time of Donne or Lord Herbert of Cherbury and the time of Tennyson and Browning; it is the difference between the intellectual poet and the reflective poet. Tennyson and Browning are poets, and they think; but they do not feel their thought as immediately as the odour of a rose. A thought to Donne was an experience; it modified his sensibility. When a poet's mind is perfectly equipped for its work, it is constantly amalgamating disparate experience; the ordinary man's experience is chaotic, irregular, fragmentary. The latter falls in love, or reads Spinoza, and these two experiences have nothing to do with each other, or with the noise of the typewriter or the smell of cooking; in the mind of the poet these experiences are always forming new wholes.

We may express the difference by the following theory: The poets of the seventeenth century, the successors of the dramatists of the sixteenth, possessed a mechanism of sensibility which could devour any kind of experience. They are simple, artificial, difficult, or fantastic, as their predecessors were; no less nor more than Dante, Guido Cavalcanti [1250–1300; Italian poet and philosopher], Guinizelli [1240?–1274; Italian poet], or Cino [1270–1336; Italian poet and jurist]. In the seventeenth century a dissociation of sensibility set in, from which we have never recovered; and this dissociation, as is natural, was aggravated by the influence of the two most powerful poets of the century, Milton and Dryden. Each of these men performed certain poetic functions so magnificently well that the magnitude of the effect concealed the absence of others. The language went on and in some respects improved; the best verse of Collins, Gray, Johnson and even Goldsmith satisfies some of our fastidious demands better than that of Donne or Marvell or King. But while the language became more refined, the feeling became more crude. The feeling, the sensibility, expressed in the *Country Churchyard* [Gray] (to say nothing of Tennyson and Browning) is cruder than that in the *Coy Mistress* [Marvell].

The second effect of the influence of Milton and Dryden followed from the first, and was therefore slow in manifestation. The sentimental age began early in the eighteenth century, and continued. The poets revolted against the ratiocinative, the descriptive; they thought and felt by fits, unbalanced; they reflected. In one or two passages of Shelley's *Triumph of Life*, in the second *Hyperion*, there are traces of a struggle toward unification of sensibility. But Keats and Shelley died, and Tennyson and Browning ruminated.

After this brief exposition of a theory—too brief, perhaps, to carry conviction—we may ask, what would have been the fate of the "metaphysical" had the current of poetry descended in a direct line from them, as it descended in a direct line to them? They would not, certainly, be classified as metaphysical. The possible interests of a poet are unlimited; the more intelligent he is the better; the more intelligent he is the more likely that he will have interests: our only condition is that he turn them into poetry, and not merely meditate on them poetically. A philosophical theory which has entered into poetry is established, for its truth or falsity in one sense ceases to matter, and its truth in another sense is proved. The poets in question have, like other poets, various faults. But they were, at best, engaged in the task of trying to find the verbal equivalent for states of mind and feeling. And this means both that they are more mature, and that they wear better, than later poets of certainly not less literary ability.

It is not a permanent necessity that poets should be interested in philosphy, or in any other subject. We can only say that it appears likely that poets in our civilization, as it exists at present, must be *difficult*. Our civilization comprehends great variety and complexity, and this variety and complexity, playing upon a refined sensibility, must produce various and complex results. The poet must become more and more comprehensive, more allusive, more direct, in order to force, to dislocate if necessary, language into his meaning. (A brilliant and extreme statement of this view, with which it is not requisite to associate oneself, is that of M. Jean Epstein, *La Poésie d'aujourd'hui* [*The Poetry of Today*].) Hence we get something which looks very much like the conceit—we get, in fact, a method curiously similar to that of the "metaphysical poets," similar also in its use of obscure words and of simple phrasing.

> *O géraniums diaphanes, guerroyeurs sortilèges,*
> *Sacrilèges monomanes!*
> *Emballages, dévergondages, douches! O pressoirs*
> *Des vendanges des grands soirs!*
> *Layettes aux abois,*
> *Thyrses au fond des bois!*
> *Transfusions, représailles,*
> *Relevailles, compresses et l'éternel potion,*
> *Angélus! n'en pouvoir plus*
> *De débâcles nuptiales! de débâcles nuptiales!*[22]

The same poet could write also simply:

> *Elle est bien loin, elle pleure,*
> *Le grand vent se lamente aussi.*[23]

Jules Laforgue [1860–1887; French symbolist poet], and Tristan Corbière [1845–1875; French symbolist poet] in many of his poems, are nearer to the

---

[22] O diaphanous geraniums, bewitched warriors,
   Sacrilegious monomaniacs!
   Wrappings, indecencies, douches! O wine presses
   Of the vintages of the long evenings!
   Desperate baby-clothes,
   Thyrsi in the far reaches of the forest!
   Transfusions, retaliations,
   Prayers, compresses and the everlasting drink,
   Angelus! to be overwhelmed
   With nuptial disasters! with nuptial disasters!
     [23] She is very far away, she is crying,
     The far-reaching wind mourns too.

"school of Donne" than any modern English poet. But poets more classical than they have the same essential quality of transmuting ideas into sensations, of transforming an observation into a state of mind.

> Pour l'enfant, amoureux de cartes et d'estampes,
> L'univers est égal à son vaste appétit.
> Ah, que le monde est grand à la clarté des lampes!
> Aux yeux du souvenir que le monde est petit![24]

In French literature the great master of the seventeenth century—Racine—and the great master of the nineteenth—Baudelaire—are in some ways more like each other than they are like any one else. The greatest two masters of diction are also the greatest two psychologists, the most curious explorers of the soul. It is interesting to speculate whether it is not a misfortune that two of the greatest masters of diction in our language, Milton and Dryden, triumph with a dazzling disregard of the soul. If we continued to produce Miltons and Drydens it might not so much matter, but as things are it is a pity that English poetry has remained so incomplete. Those who object to the "artificiality" of Milton or Dryden sometimes tell us to "look into our hearts and write." But that is not looking deep enough; Racine or Donne looked into a good deal more than the heart. One must look into the cerebral cortex, the nervous system, and the digestive tracts.

May we not conclude, then, that Donne, Crashaw, Vaughan, Herbert and Lord Herbert, Marvell, King, Cowley at his best, are in the direct current of English poetry, and that their faults should be reprimanded by this standard rather than coddled by antiquarian affection? They have been enough praised in terms which are implicit limitations because they are "metaphysical" or "witty," "quaint" or "obscure," though at their best they have not these attributes more than other serious poets. On the other hand, we must not reject the criticism of Johnson (a dangerous person to disagree with) without having mastered it, without having assimilated the Johnsonian canons of taste. In reading the celebrated passage in his essay on Cowley we must remember that by wit he clearly means something more serious than we usually mean today; in his criticism of their versification we must remember in what a narrow discipline he was trained, but also how well trained; we must remember that Johnson tortures chiefly the chief offenders, Cowley and Cleveland. It would be a fruitful work, and one requiring a substantial book, to break up the classification of Johnson (for there has been none since) and exhibit these poets in all their difference of kind and of degree, from the massive music of Donne to the faint, pleasing tinkle of Aurelian Townshend whose *Dialogue Between a Pilgrim and Time* is one of the few regrettable omissions from the excellent anthology of Professor Grierson.

[24] For the child, lovers of cards and stamps,
The universe is indifferent in its vast hunger.
Ah, how large is the world in the light of lamps!
How small is the world in the eyes of memory!

JAMES THURBER

❧ *The Case for Comedy*

THE ROBIN in my apple tree sings as cheerily now as if he were living in the Gay Nineties, when there never was a cakewalk or a band concert in the park that ended in a knife fight, the throwing of beer cans and bottles, the calling out of the National Guard, and the turning of fire hoses on youthful rioters. Through it all the robin sings, "Summertime, and the living is easy," and I wish I could sit down and have a heart-to-heart talk with the merry moron. I would tell him that it is easy enough to be lighthearted if you have not got yourself involved in the Broadway theater. And if that cued him into "Give my regards to Broadway," I should probably make a pass at him with a fly swatter and order him out of the house, or the tree.

Editors, and other busy minds, keep asking me what I think about the future of the American theater. If they telephone me in the country to ask this question, I always say, with a sigh of relief, "Then you mean it's still alive!" Naturally, I worry about the fabulous invalid, which has got into a far worse state since the 1920s than I have. In 1928, Philip Barry's *Holiday* opened on Broadway on a Monday night in November, and there were four other openings that night, and twelve in all during the week.

Later the legitimate theater acquired a slow wasting ailment. It began to develop the nightmares and matineemares that now afflict the drama. Once, last summer, when the robin woke me with his Gershwin tune, I lay there retitling certain plays to fit the temper and trend of the present day, and came up with these: *Abie's Irish Neurosis, The Bitter and Ache Man, Ned Macabre's Daughter, I Dismember Mama, They Slew What They Wanted, Toys in the Psychosomatic, The Glands Menagerie, Destroy Writes Again, The Maniac Who Came to Dinner*, and, a title calculated to pop you out of bed and into a cold tub, *Oklahomosexual*.

It seems to me that this year's extensive arguments and debates about the morbid and decadent state of so-called serious modern drama skim the surface like skipping stones because they fail to take into consideration the dying out of humor and comedy, and the consequent process of dehumanization, both on stage and off. There were literally dozens of comedies to lighten the heart and quicken the step between, say, *The First Year* and *Life With Father*. These were comedies of American life, familial and familiar, but they seem like ancient history now, something to be discussed solemnly by a present-day

Aristotle. They could be more cogently and amusingly discussed by a new Robert Benchley, but, alas, there isn't any.

The decline of humor and comedy in our time has had a multiplicity of causes, a principal one being the ideological beating they have taken from both the intellectual left and the political right. The latter came about through the intimidation of writers and playwrights under McCarthyism. The former is more complex. Humor has long been a target of leftist intellectuals, and the reason is simple enough in itself. Humor, as Lord Boothby has said, is the only solvent of terror and tension, and terror and tension are among the chief ideological weapons of Communism. The leftists have made a concerted attack on humor as an antisocial, antiracial, antilabor, antiproletarian stereotype, and they have left no stereotype unused in their attack, from "no time for comedy" to the grim warnings that humor is a sickness, a sign of inferiority complex, a shield and not a weapon.

The modern morbid playwrights seem to have fallen for the false argument that only tragedy is serious and has importance, whereas the truth is that comedy is just as important, and often more serious in its approach to truth, and, what few writers seem to realize or to admit, usually more difficult to write.

It is not a curious but a natural thing that arrogant intellectual critics condemn humor and comedy, for while they can write about Greek Old Comedy, Middle Comedy, and New Comedy with all the flourishes of pretension, they avoid a simple truth, succinctly expressed by the *Oxford Classical Dictionary* in its discussion of Middle Comedy. "Before long the realistic depiction of daily life became the chief aim in Comedy. Ordinary, commonplace life is no easy subject to treat interestingly on the stage; and Antiphanes contrasts the comic poet's more difficult lot with the tragedian's, whose plot is already familiar, and the *deus ex machina* at hand—the comic writer has no such resources."

The history of stage comedy, in both Greece and Rome, begins with cheap and ludicrous effects. In Greek Old Comedy there were the padded costumes of the grotesque comedian, the paunch and the leather phallus. The Roman Plautus, in freely translating Greek New Comedy, stuck in gags to make his rough and restless audiences guffaw, so that in the beginning comedy was, to use a medical term, exogenous—that is, not arising from within the human being, but dragged in from the outside. The true balance of life and art, the saving of the human mind as well as of the theater, lies in what has long been known as tragicomedy, for humor and pathos, tears and laughter are, in the highest expression of human character and achievement, inseparable. Many dictionaries, including the *OED*, wrongly hyphenate tragicomedy, as if the two integral parts were warring elements that must be separated.

I think the first play that ever sent me out of the American theater in a mood of elation and of high hope for our stage was *What Price Glory?* [by Maxwell Anderson and Laurence Stallings]. Amidst all the blood and slaughter there ran the recurring sound of congruous laughter. I still vividly remember the scene in which the outraged French father of an outraged daughter babbles his grievance for a full minute to the bewildered Captain Flagg, who then asks a French-speaking American lieutenant, "What did he say?"

"Rape," says the lieutenant.

That scene fairly shines with humanity when compared to an episode in the recent *There Was a Little Girl* in which the raped little girl solemnly asks her seducer if he had enjoyed the experience. And I can still recall the gleams of humor in R. C. Sherriff's *Journey's End*, as bitter a war play as any.

"What kind of soup *is* this, Sergeant?" asks Captain Stanhope.

"Yellow soup, sir," says the mess sergeant, apologetically.

Screen writers, as well as playwrights, seem reluctant, or unable, to use the devices of comedy out of fear of diluting suspense. A few years ago, in a movie about a bank clerk who stole a million dollars, crammed it into a suitcase, got into a taxi with his unaware and bewildered wife, and headed for an airport to flee the country, there came a scene in which he handed the driver a fifty-dollar bill and told him to "Step on it." Now I submit that the wife of an American male of modest income would have gone into a comedy scene at this point, but the writer or writers of the script must have been afraid that such an interlude would ruin the terror and tension, and terror and tension must be preserved nowadays, even at the expense of truth.

Katherine Hepburn recently said that our playwrights should "rise above their time," but, if they tried that, they would simply sink below themselves, or sit there staring at the blank paper in their typewriters. Separate molds turn out unvarying shapes. You can't make a Tennessee Ernie out of a Tennessee Williams, any more than you can turn a callin' back into a trough cleanin'. A callin' back, if you don't know, is a gatherin' of folks at the bedside of a dyin' man, to call him back. I hope this doesn't inspire one of the morbid playmakers to make a play in which the dyin' man drags all the other folks down with him.

It will be said, I suppose, that I couldn't write such a tragedy because of the limitation of my tools and the nature of my outlook. (Writers of comedy have outlook, whereas writers of tragedy have, according to them, insight.) It is true, I confess, that if a male character of my invention started across the stage to disrobe a virgin criminally (ah, euphemism to end euphemisms!), he would probably catch his foot in the piano stool and end up playing *Button up Your Overcoat* on the black keys. There are more ways than one, including, if you will, a Freudian stumble, to get from tragedy into tragicomedy. Several years ago a book reviewer in the New York Sunday *Times* wrote: "The tragedy of age is not that a man grows old, but that he stays young," and, indeed, there is the basis of a good tragedy in that half-truth. The other half might be stated, in a reverse Shavian paraphrase, "The trouble with youth is that it is wasted on the old." There is where the comedy would come in to form a genuine tragicomedy. At sixty-five, going on sixty-six, I think I can speak with a touch of authority.

Miss Hepburn (to get back to her) is devoted to the great plays of Shakespeare, who didn't rise above his time, but merely above the ability of his contemporaries. He often wrote about a time worse than his own, such as the period of Macbeth. In that drama he could proclaim that life is a tale told by an idiot, full of sound and fury, signifying nothing, but say it in a play told by a genius, full of soundness and fury, signifying many things. The distinguished Mr. Williams and his contemporaries are not so much expressers of their time as expressions of it, and, for that matter, aren't we all? The playwright of today likes to believe that he is throwing light upon his time, or upon some part of it, when his time is actually throwing light upon him. This, it seems to me, has always been the case, but it happens more intensely now, perhaps, than ever before. Moreover, there are two kinds of light, the glow that illumines and the glare that obscures, and the former seems to be dimming.

The American family, in spite of all its jitters and its loss of cohesion, still remains in most of its manifestations as familiar as ever, and it is our jumpy fancy to believe that all fathers are drunkards, all mothers kookies, and all children knife wielders planning to knock off their parents. Our loss of form in literature is, in large part, the result of an Oral Culture into which we began descending quite a while back. This is the age of the dragged-out interview, the endless discussion panels on television; an age in which photographers, calling on writers in their homes, stay around the house as long as the paper hanger or the roofer. Everything is tending to get longer and longer, and more and more shapeless. Telephone calls last as long as half an hour, or even forty minutes by my own count; women, saying goodby at front doors, linger longer than ever, saying, "Now I *must* go," and, eventually, "Now, I *really* must go." But nothing is accomplished simply any more. Writers of letters finish what they have to say on page two and then keep on going. Khrushchev talks for five hours at press conferences and may even have got it up to ten by the time this survey appears. (Moral: Great oafs from little icons grow.)

As brevity is the soul of wit, form, it seems to me, is the heart of humor and the salvation of comedy. "You are a putter in, and I am a taker out," Scott Fitzgerald once wrote to Thomas Wolfe. Fitzgerald was not a master of comedy, but in his dedication to taking out, he stated the case for form as against flow. It is up to our writers, in this era of Oral Culture, to bring back respect for form and for the innate stature and dignity of comedy. We cannot, to be sure, evoke humorists, or writers of comedy, by prayer or pleading or argument, but we can, and must, hope for a renascence of recognizable American comedy. The trend of the modern temper is toward gloom, resignation, and even surrender, and there is a great wailing of the word "Decadence!" on all sides. But for twenty-five hundred years decadence has come and decadence has gone. Reading Webster on the subject might make a newly arrived visitor from Mars believe that everything in art and literature came to a morose end as the nineteenth century closed out. It was a period of Decadence and of the

Decadents, led by Baudelaire, Verlaine, and Mallarmé in France. Writes old Noah [Webster]: "They cultivated the abnormal, artificial, and neurotic in subject and treatment, tending to the morbid or eccentric, and to the mystically sensuous and symbolic."

Well, we are still going on, and we have four decades left in this battered and bloody century. Walter Lippmann said last summer, in his first television appearance, that he did not believe the world is coming apart. It is heartening to know that he selected as the foremost leader of our time Sir Winston Churchill, a man also respected for his wit and humor, but one who, like Lincoln, had to survive suspicion and attack for his gift of comedy. I think it was Booth Tarkington who once said, "Sobersides looks at humor the way a duchess looks at bugs." It is high time that Sobersides came of age and realized that, like Emily Dickinson's hope, humor is a feathered thing that perches in the soul.

THEODORE SPENCER

❧ *How to Criticize a Poem*

(IN THE MANNER OF CERTAIN
CONTEMPORARY CRITICS)

1

I PROPOSE to examine the following poem:

> Thirty days hath September,
> April, June and November:
> All the rest have thirty-one,
> Excepting February alone,
> Which has only eight and a score
> Till leap-year gives it one day more.

2

The previous critics who have studied this poem, Coleridge among them, have failed to explain what we may describe as its fundamental *dynamic*. This I now propose to do. The first thing to observe is the order in which the names (or verbal constructs) of the months are presented. According to the prose meaning—what I shall henceforth call the *prose-demand*—"September" should not precede, it should follow "April," as a glance at the calendar will show. Indeed "September" should follow not only "April," it should also follow

"June" if the prose-demand is to be properly satisfied. The prose order of the first two lines should therefore read: "Thirty days hath April, June, September and November." That is the only sequence consonant with prose logic.

3

Why, then, we ask ourselves, did the poet violate what educated readers know to be the facts? Was he ignorant of the calendar, believing that September preceded April in the progress of the seasons? It is difficult to imagine that such was the case. We must find another explanation. It is here that the principle of dynamic analysis comes to our aid.

4

Dynamic analysis proves that the most successful poetry achieves its effect by producing an *expectation* in the reader's mind before his sensibility is fully prepared to receive the full impact of the poem. The reader makes a *proto-response* which preconditions him to the total response toward which his fully equilibrized organs of apperception subconsciously tend. It is this proto-response which the poet has here so sensitively manipulated. The ordinary reader, trained only to prose-demands, expects the usual order of the months. But the poet's sensibility knows that poetic truth is more immediately effective than the truth of literal chronology. He does not *state* the inevitable sequence; he *prepares* us for it. In his profound analysis of the two varieties of mensual time, he puts the *gentlest* month first. (Notice how the harsh sound of "pt" in "September" is softened by the "e" sound on either side of it.) It is the month in which vegetation first begins to fade, but which does not as yet give us a sense of tragic fatality.

5

Hence the poet prepares us, dynamically, for what is to follow. By beginning his list of the months *in medias res*, he is enabled to return later to the beginning of the series of contrasts which is the subject of his poem. The analogy to the "Oedipus Rex" of Euripides and the "Iliad" of Dante at once becomes clear. Recent criticism has only too often failed to observe that these works also illustrate the dynamic method by beginning in the middle of things. It is a striking fact, hitherto (I believe) unnoticed, that a Latin poem called the "Aeneid" does much the same thing. We expect the author of that poem to begin with the departure of his hero from Troy, just as we expect the author of our poem to begin with "April." But in neither case is our expectation fulfilled. Cato, the author of the "Aeneid," creates dynamic suspense by beginning with Aeneas in Carthage; our anonymous poet treats his readers' sensibilities in a similar fashion by beginning with "September," and then *going back* to "April" and "June."

6

But the sensibility of the poet does not stop at this point. Having described what is true of *four* months, he disposes of *seven* more with masterly
economy. In a series of pungent constructs his sensibility sums up their inexorable limitations: they *All* (the capitalization should be noted) "have
thirty-one." The poet's sensibility communicates a feeling to the sensibility of
the reader so that the sensibility of both, with reference to their previous but
independent sensibilities, is fused into that momentary communion of sensibility which is the final sensibility that poetry can give both to the sensibility
of the poet and the sensibility of the reader. The texture and structure of the
poem have erupted into a major reaction. The ambiguity of equilibrium is
achieved.

7

Against these two groups of spatial, temporal and numerical measure-
ments—one consisting of four months, the other of seven—the tragic individual,
the sole exception, "February," is dramatically placed. February is "alone," is
cut off from communion with his fellows. The tragic note is struck the moment
"February" is mentioned. For the initial sound of the word "excepting" is "X,"
and as that sound strikes the sensibility of the reader's ear a number of associations subconsciously accumulate. We think of the spot, the murderous and
lonely spot, which "X" has so frequently marked; we remember the examina-
tions of our childhood where the wrong answers were implacably signaled with
"X"; we think of ex-kings and exile, of lonely crossroads and executions, of the
inexorable anonymity of those who cannot sign their names. . . .

8

And yet the poet gives us one ray of hope, though it eventually proves to
be illusory. The lonely "February" (notice how the "alone" in line four is
echoed by the "only" in line five), the solitary and maladjusted individual who
is obviously the hero and crucial figure of the poem, is not condemned to the
routine which his fellows, in their different ways, must forever obey. Like
Hamlet, he has a capacity for change. He is a symbol of individualism, and the
rhythm of the lines which are devoted to him signalize a gayety, however
desperate, which immediately wins our sympathy and reverberates profoundly
in our sensibility.

9

But (and this is the illusion to which I have previously referred) in spite
of all his variety, his capacity for change, "February" cannot quite accomplish
(and in this his tragedy consists) the *quantitative* value of the society in which
circumstances have put him. No matter how often he may alternate from

twenty-eight to twenty-nine (the poet, with his exquisite sensibility, does not actually *mention* those humiliating numbers), he can never achieve the bourgeois, if anonymous, security of "thirty-one," nor equal the more modest and aristocratic assurance of "thirty." Decade after decade, century after century, millennium after millennium, he is eternally frustrated. The only symbol of change in a changeless society, he is continually beaten down. Once every four years he tries to rise, to achieve the high, if delusive, level of his dreams. But he fails. He is always one day short, and the three years before the recurrence of his next effort are a sad interval in which the remembrance of previous disappointment melts into the futility of hope, only to sink back once more into the frustration of despair. Like Tantalus he is forever stretched upon a wheel.

10

So far I have been concerned chiefly with the dynamic *analysis* of the poem. Further study should reveal the *synthesis* which can be made on the basis of the analysis which my thesis has tentatively attempted to bring to an emphasis. This, perhaps, the reader with a proper sensibility can achieve for himself.

NORTHROP FRYE

❧ *The Four Forms of Fiction*

In ASSIGNING the term fiction to the genre of the written word in which prose tends to become the predominating rhythm, we collide with the view that the real meaning of fiction is falsehood or unreality. Thus an autobiography coming into a library would be classified as non-fiction if the librarian believed the author, and as fiction if she thought he was lying. It is difficult to see what use such a distinction can be to a literary critic. Surely the word fiction, which, like poetry, means etymologically something made for its own sake, could be applied in criticism to any work of literary art in a radically continuous form, which almost always means a work of art in prose. Or, if that is too much to ask, at least some protest can be entered against the sloppy habit of identifying fiction with the one genuine form of fiction which we know as the novel.

Let us look at a few of the unclassified books lying on the boundary of "non-fiction" and "literature." Is *Tristram Shandy* [by Laurence Sterne] a novel? Nearly everyone would say yes, in spite of its easygoing disregard of "story values." Is *Gulliver's Travels* [by Jonathan Swift] a novel? Here most would demur, including the Dewey decimal system, which puts it under "Satire and

Humor." But surely everyone would call it fiction, and if it is fiction, a distinction appears between fiction as a genus and the novel as a species of that genus. Shifting the ground to fiction, then, is *Sartor Resartus* [by Thomas Carlyle] fiction? If not, why not? If it is, is *The Anatomy of Melancholy* [by Robert Burton] fiction? Is it a literary form or only a work of "non-fiction" written with "style"? Is Borrow's *Lavengro* fiction? Everyman's Library says yes; the World's Classics puts it under "Travel and Topography."

The literary historian who identifies fiction with the novel is greatly embarrassed by the length of time that the world managed to get along without the novel, and until he reaches his great deliverance in Defoe, his perspective is intolerably cramped. He is compelled to reduce Tudor fiction to a series of tentative essays in the novel form, which works well enough for Deloney but makes nonsense of Sidney. He postulates a great fictional gap in the seventeenth century which exactly covers the golden age of rhetorical prose. He finally discovers that the word novel, which up to about 1900 was still the name of a more or less recognizable form, has since expanded into a catchall term which can be applied to practically any prose book that is not "on" something. Clearly, this novel-centered view of prose fiction is a Ptolemaic perspective which is now too complicated to be any longer workable, and some more relative and Copernican view must take its place.

When we start to think seriously about the novel, not as fiction, but as a form of fiction, we feel that its characteristics, whatever they are, are such as make, say, Defoe, Fielding, Austen, and James central in its tradition, and Borrow, Peacock, Melville, and Emily Brontë somehow peripheral. This is not an estimate of merit: we may think *Moby Dick* "greater" than *The Egoist* and yet feel that Meredith's book is closer to being a typical novel. Fielding's conception of the novel as a comic epic in prose seems fundamental to the tradition he did so much to establish. In novels that we think of as typical, like those of Jane Austen, plot and dialogue are closely linked to the conventions of the comedy of manners. The conventions of *Wuthering Heights* are linked rather with the tale and the ballad. They seem to have more affinity with tragedy, and the tragic emotions of passion and fury, which would shatter the balance of tone in Jane Austen, can be safely accommodated here. So can the supernatural, or the suggestion of it, which is difficult to get into a novel. The shape of the plot is different: instead of manoeuvring around a central situation, as Jane Austen does, Emily Brontë tells her story with linear accents, and she seems to need the help of a narrator, who would be absurdly out of place in Jane Austen. Conventions so different justify us in regarding *Wuthering Heights* as a different form of prose fiction from the novel, a form which we shall here call the romance. Here again we have to use the same word in several different contexts, but romance seems on the whole better than tale, which appears to fit a somewhat shorter form.

The essential difference between novel and romance lies in the conception of characterization. The romancer does not attempt to create "real people" so much as stylized figures which expand into psychological archetypes. It is in the romance that we find Jung's libido, anima, and shadow reflected in the hero, heroine, and villain respectively. That is why the romance so often radiates a glow of subjective intensity that the novel lacks, and why a suggestion of allegory is constantly creeping in around its fringes. Certain elements of character are released in the romance which make it naturally a more revolutionary form than the novel. The novelist deals with personality, with characters wearing their *personae* or social masks. He needs the framework of a stable society, and many of our best novelists have been conventional to the verge of fussiness. The romancer deals with individuality, with characters *in vacuo* idealized by revery, and, however conservative he may be, something nihilistic and untamable is likely to keep breaking out of his pages.

The prose romance, then, is an independent form of fiction to be distinguished from the novel and extracted from the miscellaneous heap of prose works now covered by that term. Even in the other heap known as short stories one can isolate the tale form used by Poe, which bears the same relation to the full romance that the stories of Chekhov or Katherine Mansfield do to the novel. "Pure" examples of either form are never found; there is hardly any modern romance that could not be made out to be a novel, and vice versa. The forms of prose fiction are mixed, like racial strains in human beings, not separable like the sexes. In fact the popular demand in fiction is always for a mixed form, a romantic novel just romantic enough for the reader to project his libido on the hero and his anima on the heroine, and just novel enough to keep these projections in a familiar world. It may be asked, therefore, what is the use of making the above distinction, especially when, though undeveloped in criticism, it is by no means unrealized. It is no surprise to hear that Trollope wrote novels and William Morris romances.

The reason is that a great romancer should be examined in terms of the conventions he chose. William Morris should not be left on the side lines of prose fiction merely because the critic has not learned to take the romance form seriously. Nor, in view of what has been said about the revolutionary nature of the romance, should his choice of that form be regarded as an "escape" from his social attitude. If Scott has any claims to be a romancer, it is not good criticism to deal only with his defects as a novelist. The romantic qualities of *The Pilgrim's Progress* [by John Bunyan], too, its archetypal characterization and its revolutionary approach to religious experience, make it a well-rounded example of a literary form: it is not merely a book swallowed by English literature to get some religious bulk in its diet. Finally, when Hawthorne, in the preface to *The House of the Seven Gables*, insists that his story should be read as romance and not as novel, it is possible that he meant what he said, even though he indicates that the prestige of the rival form has induced the romancer to apologize for not using it.

Romance is older than the novel, a fact which has developed the historical illusion that it is something to be outgrown, a juvenile and undeveloped form. The social affinities of the romance, with its grave idealizing of heroism and purity, are with the aristocracy. . . . It revived in the period we call Romantic as part of the Romantic tendency to archaic feudalism and a cult of the hero, or idealized libido. In England the romances of Scott and, in less degree, the Brontës, are part of a mysterious Northumbrian renaissance, a Romantic reaction against the new industrialism in the Midlands, which also produced the poetry of Wordsworth and Burns and the philosophy of Carlyle. It is not surprising, therefore, that an important theme in the more bourgeois novel should be the parody of the romance and its ideals. The tradition established by *Don Quixote* continues in a type of novel which looks at a romantic situation from its own point of view, so that the conventions of the two forms make up an ironic compound instead of a sentimental mixture. Examples range from *Northanger Abbey* to *Madame Bovary* and *Lord Jim* [by Joseph Conrad].

The tendency to allegory in the romance may be conscious, as in *The Pilgrim's Progress*, or unconscious, as in the very obvious sexual mythopoeia in William Morris. The romance, which deals with heroes, is intermediate between the novel, which deals with men, and the myth, which deals with gods. Prose romance first appears as a late development of Classical mythology, and the prose Sagas of Iceland follow close on the mythical Eddas. The novel tends rather to expand into a fictional approach to history. The soundness of Fielding's instinct in calling *Tom Jones* a history is confirmed by the general rule that the larger the scheme of a novel becomes, the more obviously its historical nature appears. As it is creative history, however, the novelist usually prefers his material in a plastic, or roughly contemporary state, and feels cramped by a fixed historical pattern. *Waverley* [by Sir Walter Scott] is dated about sixty years back from the time of writing and *Little Dorrit* [by Charles Dickens] about forty years, but the historical pattern is fixed in the romance and plastic in the novel, suggesting the general principle that most "historical novels" are romances. Similarly a novel becomes more romantic in its appeal when the life it reflects has passed away: thus the novels of Trollope were read primarily as romances during the Second World War. It is perhaps the link with history and a sense of temporal context that has confined the novel, in striking contrast to the worldwide romance, to the alliance of time and Western man.

Autobiography is another form which merges with the novel by a series of insensible gradations. Most autobiographies are inspired by a creative, and therefore fictional, impulse to select only those events and experiences in the writer's life that go to build up an integrated pattern. This pattern may be something larger than himself with which he has come to identify himself, or simply the coherence of his character and attitudes. We may call this very important form of prose fiction the confession form, following St. Augustine, who appears to have invented it, and Rousseau, who established a modern type of it. The earlier tradition gave *Religio Medici* [by Sir Thomas Browne], *Grace Abounding* [by John Bunyan], and Newman's *Apologia* to English literature, besides the related but subtly different type of confession favored by the mystics.

Here again, as with the romance, there is some value in recognizing a distinct prose form in the confession. It gives several of our best prose works a definable place in fiction instead of keeping them in a vague limbo of books which are not quite literature because they are "thought," and not quite religion or philosophy because they are Examples of Prose Style. The confession, too, like the novel and the romance, has its own short form, the familiar essay, and Montaigne's *livre de bonne foy* [book of good faith] is a confession made up of essays in which only the continuous narrative of the longer form is missing. Montaigne's scheme is to the confession what a work of fiction made up of short stories, such as Joyce's *Dubliners* or Boccaccio's *Decameron*, is to the novel or romance.

After Rousseau—in fact in Rousseau—the confession flows into the novel, and the mixture produces the fictional autobiography, the *Künstler-roman* [artist-novel], and kindred types. There is no literary reason why the subject of a confession should always be the author himself, and dramatic confessions have been used in the novel at least since *Moll Flanders*. The "stream of consciousness" technique permits of a much more concentrated fusion of the two forms, but even here the characteristics peculiar to the confession form show up clearly. Nearly always some theoretical and intellectual interest in religion, politics, or art plays a leading role in the confession. It is his success in integrating his mind on such subjects that makes the author of a confession feel that his life is worth writing about. But this interest in ideas and theoretical statements is alien to the genius of the novel proper, where the technical problem is to dissolve all theory into personal relationships. In Jane Austen, to take a familiar instance, church, state, and culture are never examined except as social data, and Henry James has been described as having a mind so fine that no idea could violate it. The novelist who cannot get along without ideas, or has not the patience to digest them in the way that James did, instinctively resorts to what Mill calls a "mental history" of a single character. And when we find that a technical discussion of a theory of aesthetics forms the climax of Joyce's *Portrait*, we realize that what makes this possible is the presence in that novel of another tradition of prose fiction.

The novel tends to be extroverted and personal; its chief interest is in human character as it manifests itself in society. The romance tends to be introverted and personal: it also deals with characters, but in a more subjective way. (Subjective here refers to treatment, not subject-matter. The characters of romance are heroic and therefore inscrutable; the novelist is freer to enter his characters' minds because he is more objective.) The confession is also introverted, but intellectualized in content. Our next step is evidently to discover a fourth form of fiction which is extroverted and intellectual.

We remarked earlier that most people would call *Gulliver's Travels* fiction but not a novel. It must then be another form of fiction, as it certainly has a form, and we feel that we are turning from the novel to this form, whatever it is, when we turn from Rousseau's *Emile* to Voltaire's *Candide*, or from Butler's *The Way of All Flesh* to the Erewhon books, or from Huxley's *Point Counter Point* to *Brave New World*. The form thus has its own traditions, and, as the examples of Butler and Huxley show, has preserved some integrity even under the ascendancy of the novel. Its existence is easy enough to demonstrate, and no one will challenge the statement that the literary ancestry of *Gulliver's Travels* and *Candide* runs through Rabelais and Erasmus to Lucian. But while much has been said about the style and thought of Rabelais, Swift, and Voltaire, very little has been made of them as craftsmen working in a specific medium, a point no one dealing with a novelist would ignore. Another great writer in this tradition, Huxley's master Peacock, has fared even worse, for, his form not being understood, a general impression has grown up that his status in the development of prose fiction is that of a slapdash eccentric. Actually, he is as exquisite and precise an artist in his medium as Jane Austen is in hers.

The form used by these authors is the Menippean satire, also more rarely called the Varronian satire, allegedly invented by a Greek cynic named Menippus. His works are lost, but he had two great disciples, the Greek Lucian and the Roman Varro, and the tradition of Varro, who has not survived either except in fragments, was carried on by Petronius and Apuleius. The Menippean satire appears to have developed out of verse satire through the practice of adding prose interludes, but we know it only as a prose form, though one of its recurrent features (seen in Peacock) is the use of incidental verse.

The Menippean satire deals less with people as such than with mental attitudes. Pedants, bigots, cranks, parvenus, virtuosi, enthusiasts, rapacious and incompetent professional men of all kinds, are handled in terms of their occupational approach to life as distinct from their social behavior. The Menippean satire thus resembles the confession in its ability to handle abstract ideas and theories, and differs from the novel in its characterization, which is stylized rather than naturalistic, and presents people as mouthpieces of the ideas they represent. Here again no sharp boundary lines can or should be drawn, but if we compare a character in Jane Austen with a similar character in Peacock we can immediately feel the difference between the two forms. Squire Western belongs to the novel, but Thwackum and Square [characters in *Tom Jones*] have Menippean blood in them. A constant theme in the tradition is the ridicule of the *philosophus gloriosus* [glorious philosopher]. The novelist sees evil and folly as social diseases, but the Menippean satirist sees them as diseases of the intellect, as a kind of maddened pedantry which the *philosophus gloriosus* at once symbolizes and defines.

Petronius, Apuleius, Rabelais, Swift, and Voltaire all use a loose-jointed narrative form often confused with the romance. It differs from the romance, however (though there is a strong admixture of romance in Rabelais), as it is not primarily concerned with the exploits of heroes, but relies on the free play of intellectual fancy and the kind of humorous observation that produces caricature. It differs also from the picaresque form, which has the novel's interest in the actual structure of society. At its most concentrated the Menippean satire presents us with a vision of the world in terms of a single intellectual pattern. The intellectual structure built up from the story makes for violent dislocations in the customary logic of narrative, though the appearance of carelessness that results reflects only the carelessness of the reader or his tendency to judge by a novel-centered conception of fiction.

The word "satire," in Roman and Renaissance times, meant either of two specific literary forms of that name, one (this one) prose and the other verse. Now it means a structural principle or attitude, . . . a *mythos*. In the Menippean satires we have been discussing, the name of the form also applies to the attitude. As the name of an attitude, satire is, we have seen, a combination of fantasy and morality. But as the name of a form, the term satire, though confined to literature (for as a *mythos* it may appear in any art, a cartoon, for example), is more flexible, and can be either entirely fantastic or entirely moral. The Menippean adventure story may thus be pure fantasy, as it is in the literary fairy tale. The Alice books are perfect Menippean satires, and so is *The Water-Babies* [by Charles Kingsley], which has been influenced by Rabelais. The purely moral type is a serious vision of society as a single intellectual pattern, in other words a Utopia.

The short form of the Menippean satire is usually a dialogue or colloquy, in which the dramatic interest is in a conflict of ideas rather than of character. This is the favorite form of Erasmus, and is common in Voltaire. Here again the form is not invariably satiric in attitude, but shades off into more purely fanciful or moral discussions, like the *Imaginary Conversations* of Landor or the "dialogue of the dead." Sometimes this form expands to full length, and more than two speakers are used: the setting then is usually a *cena* [dinner] or symposium, like the one that looms so large in Petronius. Plato, though much earlier in the field than Menippus, is a strong influence on this type, which stretches in an unbroken tradition down through those urbane and leisurely conversations which define the ideal courtier in Castiglione or the doctrine and discipline of angling in Walton. A modern development produces the country-house weekends in Peacock, Huxley, and their imitators in which the opinions and ideas and cultural interests expressed are as important as the lovemaking.

The novelist shows his exuberance either by an exhaustive analysis of human relationships, as in Henry James, or of social phenomena, as in Tolstoy. The Menippean satirist, dealing with intellectual themes and attitudes, shows his exuberance in intellectual ways, by piling up an enormous mass of erudition about his theme or in overwhelming his pedantic targets with an avalanche of their own jargon. A species, or rather sub-species, of the form is the kind of encyclopaedic farrago represented by Althenaeus' *Deipnosophists* and Macrobius' [Latin grammarian of late fourth and early fifth century] *Saturnalia*, where people sit at a banquet and pour out a vast mass of erudition on every subject that might conceivably come up in a conversation. The display of erudition had probably been associated with the Menippean tradition by Varro, who was enough of a polymath [a person having a wide range of knowledge] to make Quintilian, if not stare and gasp, at any rate call him *vir Romanorum eruditissimus* [the most learned of the Romans]. The tendency to expand into an encyclopaedic farrago is clearly marked in Rabelais, notably in the great catalogues of torcheculs [medieval equivalent of toilet paper] and epithets of codpieces and methods of divination. The encyclopaedic compilations produced in the line of duty by Erasmus and Voltaire suggest that a magpie instinct to collect facts is not unrelated to the type of ability that has made them famous as artists. Flaubert's encyclopaedic approach to the construction of *Bouvard et Pecuchet* is quite comprehensible if we explain it as marking an affinity with the Menippean tradition.

This creative treatment of exhaustive erudition is the organizing principle of the greatest Menippean satire in English before Swift, Burton's *Anatomy of Melancholy*. Here human society is studied in terms of the intellectual pattern provided by the conception of melancholy, a symposium of books replaces dialogue, and the result is the most comprehensive survey of human life in one book that English literature had seen since Chaucer, one of Burton's favorite authors. We may note in passing, the Utopia in his introduction and his "digressions," which when examined turn out to be scholarly distillations of Menippean forms: the digression of air, of the marvellous journey; the digression of spirits, of the ironic use of erudition; the digression of the miseries of scholars, of the satire on the *philosophus gloriosus*. The word "anatomy" in Burton's title means a dissection or analysis, and expresses very accurately the intellectualized approach of his form. We may as well adopt it as a convenient name to replace the cumbersome and in modern times rather misleading "Menippean satire."

The anatomy, of course, eventually begins to merge with the novel, producing various hybrids including the *roman à thèse* [a novel that advances, illustrates, or defends a thesis] and novels in which the characters are symbols of social or other ideas, like the proletarian novels of the thirties in this century. It was Sterne, however, the disciple of Burton and Rabelais, who combined them with greatest success. *Tristram Shandy* may be, as was said at the beginning, a novel, but the digressing narrative, the catalogues, the stylizing of character along "humor" lines, the marvellous journey of the great nose, the symposium discussions, and the constant ridicule of philosophers and pedantic critics are all features that belong to the anatomy.

A clearer understanding of the form and traditions of the anatomy would make a good many elements in the history of literature come into focus. Boethius' *Consolation of Philosophy*, with its dialogue form, its verse interludes and its pervading tone of contemplative irony, is a pure anatomy, a fact of considerable importance for the understanding of its vast influence. *The Compleat Angler* is an anatomy because of its mixture of prose and verse, its rural *cena* setting, its dialogue form, its deipnosophistical [of one who discourses learnedly at meals] interest in food, and its gentle Menippean raillery of a society which considers everything more important than fishing and yet has discovered very few better things to do. In nearly every period of literature there are many romances, confessions, and anatomies that are neglected only because the categories to which they belong are unrecognized. In the period between Sterne and Peacock, for example, we have, among romances, *Melmoth the Wanderer* [by Charles Maturin]; among confessions, Hogg's *Confessions of a Justified Sinner;* among anatomies, Southey's *Doctor,* Amory's [1691?–1788; English writer] *John Buncle,* and the *Noctes Ambrosianae* [a series of papers appearing in *Blackwood's Magazine,* 1822–1835].

To sum up then: when we examine fiction from the point of view of form, we can see four chief strands binding it together, novel, confession, anatomy, and romance. The six possible combinations of these forms all exist, and we have shown how the novel has combined with each of the other three. Exclusive concentration on one form is rare: the early novels of George Eliot, for instance, are influenced by the romance, and the later ones by the anatomy. The romance-confession hybrid is found, naturally, in the autobiography of a romantic temperament, and is represented in English by the extroverted George Borrow and the introverted De Quincey. The romance-anatomy one we have noticed in Rabelais; a later example is *Moby Dick,* where the romantic theme of the wild hunt expands into an encyclopaedic anatomy of the whale. Confession and anatomy are united in *Sartor Resartus* and in some of Kierkegaard's strikingly original experiments in prose fiction form, including *Either/Or.* More comprehensive fictional schemes usually employ at least three forms: we can see strains of novel, romance, and confession in *Pamela,* of novel, romance, and anatomy in *Don Quixote,* of novel, confession, and anatomy in Proust, and of romance, confession, and anatomy in Apuleius.

I deliberately make this sound schematic in order to suggest the advantage of having a simple and logical explanation for the form of, say, *Moby Dick* or *Tristram Shandy.* The usual critical approach to the form of such works resembles that of the doctors in Brobdingnag, who after great wrangling finally pronounced Gulliver a *lusus naturae* [freak of nature]. It is the anatomy in particular that has baffled critics, and there is hardly any fiction writer deeply influenced by it who has not been accused of disorderly conduct. The reader may be reminded here of Joyce, for describing Joyce's books as monstrous has become a nervous tic. I find "demogorgon," "behemoth," and "white elephant" in good critics; the bad ones could probably do much better. The care that Joyce took to organize *Ulysses* and *Finnegans Wake* amounted to nearly obsession, but as they are not organized on familiar principles of prose fiction, the impression of shapelessness remains. Let us try our formulas on him.

If a reader were asked to set down a list of the things that had most impressed him about *Ulysses,* it might reasonably be somewhat as follows. First, the clarity with which the sights and sounds and smells of Dublin come to life, the rotundity of the character-drawing, and the naturalness of the dialogue. Second, the elaborate way that the story and characters are parodied by being set against archetypal heroic patterns, notably the one provided by the *Odyssey*. Third, the revelation of character and incident through the searching use of the stream-of-consciousness technique. Fourth, the constant tendency to be encyclopaedic and exhaustive both in technique and in subject matter, and to see both in highly intellectualized terms. It should not be too hard for us by now to see that these four points describe elements in the book which relate to the novel, romance, confession, and anatomy respectively. *Ulysses*, then, is a complete prose epic with all four forms employed in it, all of practically equal importance, and all essential to one another, so that the book is a unity and not an aggregate.

This unity is built up from an intricate scheme of parallel contrasts. The romantic archetypes of Hamlet and Ulysses are like remote stars in a literary heaven looking down quizzically on the shabby creatures of Dublin obediently intertwining themselves in the patterns set by their influences. In the "Cyclops" and "Circe" episodes particularly there is a continuous parody of realistic patterns by romantic ones which reminds us, though the irony leans in the opposite direction, of *Madame Bovary*. The relation of novel and confession techniques is similar; the author jumps into his characters' minds to follow their stream of consciousness, and out again to describe them externally. In the novel-anatomy combination, too, found in the "Ithaca" chapter, the sense of lurking antagonism between the personal and intellectual aspects of the scene accounts for much of its pathos. The same principle of parallel contrast holds good for the other three combinations: of romance and confession in "Nausicaa" and "Penelope," of confession and anatomy in "Proteus" and "The Lotos-Eaters," of romance and anatomy (a rare and fitful combination) in "Sirens" and parts of "Circe."

In *Finnegans Wake* the unity of design goes far beyond this. The dingy story of the sodden HCE and his pinched wife is not contrasted with the archetypes of Tristram and the divine king; HCE is himself Tristram and the divine king. As the setting is a dream, no contrast is possible between confession and novel, between a stream of consciousness inside the mind and the appearances of other people outside it. Nor is the experiential world of the novel to be separated from the intelligible world of the anatomy. The forms we have been isolating in fiction, and which depend for their existence on the commonsense dichotomies of the daylight consciousness, vanish in *Finnegans Wake* into a fifth and quintessential form. This form is the one traditionally associated with scriptures and sacred books, and treats life in terms of the fall and awakening of the human soul and the creation and apocalypse of nature. The Bible is the definitive example of it; the Egyptian Book of the Dead and the Icelandic Prose Edda, both of which have left deep imprints on *Finnegans Wake*, also belong to it.

BERNARD KNOX

❧ *Sophocles'* Oedipus

SOPHOCLES' *Oedipus* is not only the greatest creation of a major poet and the classic representative figure of his age: he is also one of the long series of tragic protagonists who stand as symbols of human aspiration and despair before the characteristic dilemma of Western civilization—the problem of man's true nature, his proper place in the universe.

In the earlier of the two Sophoclean plays which deal with the figure of Oedipus, this fundamental problem is raised at the very beginning of the prologue by the careful distinctions which the priest makes in defining his attitude toward Oedipus, the former savior of Thebes, its absolute ruler, and its last hope of rescue from the plague. "We beg your help," he says, "regarding you not as one equated to the gods, θεοῖσι . . . οὐκ ἰσούμενον, but as first of men."

"Not equated to the gods, but first of men." The positive part of the statement at any rate is undeniably true. Oedipus is *tyrannos* of Thebes, its despotic ruler. The Greek word corresponds neither to Shelley's "Tyrant" nor to Yeats' "King": tyrannos is an absolute ruler, who may be a bad ruler, or a good one (as Oedipus clearly is), but in either case he is a ruler who has seized power, not inherited it. He is not a king, for a king succeeds only by birth; the tyrannos succeeds by brains, force, influence. "This absolute power, τυραννίς," says Oedipus in the play "is a prize won with masses and money." This title of Oedipus, tyrannos, is one of the most powerful ironies of the play, for, although Oedipus does not know it, he is not only tyrannos, the outsider who came to power in Thebes, he is also the legitimate king by birth, for he was born the son of Laius. Only when his identity is revealed can he properly be called king: and the chorus refers to him by this title for the first time in the great ode which it sings after Oedipus knows the truth.

But the word tyrannos has a larger significance. Oedipus, to quote that same choral ode, is a παράδειγμα, a paradigm, an example to all men; and the fact that he is tyrannos, self-made ruler, the proverbial Greek example of worldly success won by individual intelligence and exertion, makes him an appropriate symbol of civilized man, who was beginning to believe, in the 5th century B.C., that he could seize control of his environment and make his own destiny, become, in fact, equated to the gods. "Oedipus shot his arrow far beyond the range of others"—the choral ode again—"and accomplished the conquest of complete prosperity and happiness."

Oedipus became tyrannos by answering the riddle of the Sphinx. It was no easy riddle, and he answered it, as he proudly asserts, without help from prophets, from bird-signs, from gods; he answered it alone, with his intelligence. The answer won him a city and the hand of a queen. And the answer to the Sphinx's riddle was—Man. In Sophocles' own century the same answer had been proposed to a greater riddle. "Man," said Protagoras the sophist, "is the measure of all things."

Protagoras' famous statement is the epitome of the critical and optimistic spirit of the middle years of the 5th century; its implications are clear—man is the center of the universe, his intelligence can overcome all obstacles, he is master of his own destiny, tyrannos, self-made ruler who has the capacity to attain complete prosperity and happiness.

In an earlier Sophoclean play, *Antigone*, the chorus sings a hymn to this man the conqueror. "Many are the wonders and terrors, and nothing more wonderful and terrible than man." He has conquered the sea, "this creature goes beyond the white sea pressing forward as the swell crashes about him"; and he has conquered the land, "earth, highest of the gods . . . he wears away with the turning plough." He has mastered not only the elements, sea and land, but the birds, beasts, and fishes; "through knowledge and technique," sings the chorus, he is yoker of the horse, tamer of the bull. "And he has taught himself speech and thought swift as the wind and attitudes which enable him to live in communities and means to shelter himself from the frost and rain. Full of resources he faces the future, nothing will find him at a loss. Death, it is true, he will not avoid, yet he has thought out ways of escape from desperate diseases. His knowledge, ingenuity and technique are beyond anything that could have been foreseen." These lyrics describe the rise to power of *anthropos tyrannos*; self-taught he seizes control of his environment, he is master of the elements, the animals, the arts and sciences of civilization. "Full of resources he faces the future"—an apt description of Oedipus at the beginning of our play.

And it is not the only phrase of this ode which is relevant; for Oedipus is connected by the terms he uses, and which are used to and about him, with the whole range of human achievement which has raised man to his present level. All the items of this triumphant catalogue recur in the *Oedipus Tyrannos*; the images of the play define him as helmsman, conqueror of the sea, and ploughman, conqueror of the land, as hunter, master of speech and thought, inventor, legislator, physician. Oedipus is faced in the play with an intellectual problem, and as he marshals his intellectual resources to solve it, the language of the play suggests a comparison between Oedipus' methods in the play and the whole range of sciences and techniques which have brought man to mastery, made him tyrannos of the world.

Oedipus' problem is apparently simple: "Who is the murderer of Laius?" but as he pursues the answer the question changes shape. It becomes a different problem: "Who am I?" And the answer to this problem involves the gods as well as man. The answer to the question is not what he expected, it is in fact a reversal, that *peripeteia* which Aristotle speaks of in connection with this play. The state of Oedipus is reversed from "first of men" to "most accursed of men"; his attitude from the proud ἀρκτέον "I must rule" to the humble πειστέον, "I must obey." "Reversal" says Aristotle, "is a change of the action into the opposite," and one meaning of this much disputed phrase is that the action produces the opposite of the actor's intentions. So Oedipus curses the murderer of Laius and it turns out that he has cursed himself. But this reversal is not confined to the action; it is also the process of all the great images of the play which identify Oedipus as the inventive, critical spirit of his century. As the images unfold, the enquirer turns into the object of enquiry, the hunter into the prey, the doctor into the patient, the investigator into the criminal, the revealer into the thing revealed, the finder into the thing found, the savior into the thing saved ("I was saved, for some dreadful destiny"), the liberator into the thing released ("I released your feet from the bonds which pierced your ankles" says the Corinthian messenger), the accuser becomes the defendant, the ruler the subject, the teacher not only the pupil but also the object lesson, the example. A change of the action into its opposite, from active to passive.

And the two opening images of the Antigone ode recur with hideous effect. Oedipus the helmsman, who steers the ship of state, is seen, in Tiresias' words, as one who "steers his ship into a nameless anchorage," "who" in the chorus' words "shared the same great harbour with his father." And Oedipus the ploughman—"How," asks the chorus, "how could the furrows which your father ploughed bear you in silence for so long?"

This reversal is the movement of the play, parallel in the imagery and the action: it is the overthrow of the tyrannos, of man who seized power and thought himself "equated to the gods." The bold metaphor of the priest introduces another of the images which parallel in their development the reversal of the hero, and which suggest that Oedipus is a figure symbolic of human intelligence and achievement in general. He is not only helmsman, ploughman, inventor, legislator, liberator, revealer, doctor—he is also equator, mathematician, calculator; "equated" is a mathematical term, and it is only one of a whole complex of such terms which present Oedipus in yet a fresh aspect of man tyrannos. One of Oedipus' favorite words is "measure" and this is of course a significant metaphor: measure, mensuration, number, calculation—these are among the most important inventions which have brought man to power. Aeschylus' Prometheus, the mythical civilizer of human life, counts number among the foremost of his gifts to man. "And number, too, I invented, outstanding among clever devices." In the river valleys of the East generations of mensuration and calculation had brought man to an understanding of the movements of the stars and of time: in the histories of his friend Herodotus, Sophocles had read of the calculation and mensuration which had gone into the building of the pyramids. "Measure"—it is Protagoras' word: "Man is the measure of all things." In this play man's measure is taken, his true equation found. The play is full of equations, some of them incomplete, some false; the final equation shows man equated not to the gods but to himself, as Oedipus is finally equated to himself. For there are in the play not one Oedipus but two.

One is the magnificent figure set before us in the opening scenes, tyrannos, the man of wealth and power, first of men, the intellect and energy which drives on the search. The other is the object of the search, a shadowy figure who has violated the most fundamental human taboos, an incestuous parricide, "most accursed of men." And even before the one Oedipus finds the other, they are connected and equated in the name which they both bear, Oedipus. Oedipus—Swollen-foot; it emphasizes the physical blemish which scars the body of the splendid tyrannos, a defect which he tries to forget but which reminds us of the outcast child this tyrannos once was and the outcast man he is soon to be. The second half of the name πούς, "foot," recurs throughout the play, as a mocking phrase which recalls this other Oedipus. "The Sphinx forced us to look at what was at our feet," says Creon. Tiresias invokes "the dread-footed curse of your father and mother." And the choral odes echo and re-echo with this word. "Let the murderer of Laius set his foot in motion in flight." "The murderer is a man alone with forlorn foot." "The laws of Zeus are high-footed." "The man of pride plunges down into doom where he cannot use his foot."

These mocking repetitions of one-half the name invoke the unknown Oedipus who will be revealed: the equally emphatic repetition of the first half emphasizes the dominant attitude of the man before us. *Oidi*—"swell," but it is also *Oida*, "I know," and this word is often, too often, in Oedipus' mouth. His knowledge is what makes him tyrannos, confident and decisive; knowledge has made man what he is, master of the world. Οἶδα, "I know"—it runs through the play with the same mocking persistence as πούς, "foot," and sometimes reaches an extreme of macabre punning emphasis.

When the messenger, to take one example of many, comes to tell Oedipus that his father, Polybus, is dead, he enquires for Oedipus, who is in the palace, in the following words:

> "Strangers, from you might I learn where
> is the palace of the tyrannos Oedipus,
> best of all, where he is himself if you know where."

Here it is in the Greek:

> ἆρ' ἄν παρ' ὑμῶν ὦρξένοι μάθοιμ' ὅπου (oimopou)
> τὰ τοῦ τυράννου δώματ' ἐστὶν Οἰδίπου (oidipou)
> μάλιστα δ' αὐτὸν εἴπατ' εἰ κάτισθ' ὅπου (isthopou)

Those punning rhyming line-endings, μάθοιμ' ὅπου, Οἰδίπου, κάτισθ' ὅπου, "learn where," "Oedipus," "know where," unparalleled elsewhere in Greek tragedy, are a striking example of the boldness with which Sophocles uses language: from the "sweet singer of Colonus" they are somewhat unexpected, they might almost have been written by the not-so-sweet singer of Trieste-Zürich-Paris.

Οἶδα, the knowledge of the tyrannos, πούς, the swollen foot of Laius' son—in the hero's name the basic equation is already symbolically present, the equation which Oedipus will finally solve. But the priest in the prologue is speaking of a different equation, ἰσούμενον, "We beg your help, not as one equated to the gods. . . ." It is a warning, and the warning is needed. For although Oedipus in the opening scenes is a model of formal and verbal piety, the piety is skin-deep. And even before he declares his true religion, he can address the chorus, which has been praying to the gods, with godlike words. "What you pray for you will receive, if you will listen to and accept what I am about to say."

The priest goes on to suggest a better equation: he asks Oedipus to equate himself to the man he was when he saved Thebes from the Sphinx. "You saved us then, be now the equal of the man you were." This is the first statement of the theme, the double Oedipus; here there is a contrast implied between the present Oedipus who is failing to save his city from the plague and the successful Oedipus of the past who answered the riddle of the Sphinx. He must answer a riddle again, be his old self, but the answer to this riddle will not be as simple as the answer to the first. When it is found, he will be equated, not to the foreigner who saved the city and became tyrannos, but to the native-born king, the son of Laius and Jocasta.

Oedipus repeats the significant word, "equal," ὅστις ἐξ ἴσου νοσεῖ. "Sick as you are, not one of you has sickness equal to mine," and he adds a word of his own, his characteristic metaphor. He is impatient at Creon's absence. "Measuring the day against the time (ξυμμετρούμενον χρόνῳ), I am worried. . . ." And then as Creon approaches, "He is now commensurate with the range of our voices"—ξύμμετρος γὰρ ὡς κλύειν.

Here is Oedipus the equator and measurer, this is the method by which he will reach the truth: calculation of time and place, measurement and comparison of age and number and description—these are the techniques which will solve the equation, establish the identity of the murderer of Laius. The tightly organized and relentless process by which Oedipus finds his way to the truth is the operation of the human intellect in many aspects; it is the investigation of the officer of the law who identifies the criminal, the series of diagnoses of the physician who identifies the disease—it has even been compared by Freud to the process of psychoanalysis—and it is also the working out of a mathematical problem which will end with the establishment of a true equation.

The numerical nature of the problem is emphasized at once with Creon's entry. "One man of Laius' party escaped," says Creon, "he had only one thing to say." "What is it?" asks Oedipus. "One thing might find a way to learn many." The one thing is that Laius was killed not by one man but by many. This sounds like a problem in arithmetic, and Oedipus undertakes to solve it. But the chorus which now comes on stage has no such confidence: it sings of the plague with despair, but it makes this statement in terms of the same metaphor; it has its characteristic word which, like the priest and like Oedipus, it pronounces twice. The chorus' word is ἀνάριθμος, "numberless," "uncountable." "My sorrows are beyond the count of number," and later, "uncountable the deaths of which the city is dying." The plague is something beyond the power of "number . . . outstanding among clever devices."

The prologue and the first stasimon, besides presenting the customary exposition of the plot, present also the exposition of the metaphor. And with the entry of Tiresias, the development of the metaphor begins, its terrible potentialities are revealed. "Even though you are tyrannos," says the prophet at the height of his anger, "you and I must be made equal in one thing, at least, the chance for an equal reply," ἐξισωστέον τὸ γοῦν ἴσ' ἀντιλέξαι. Tiresias is blind, and Oedipus will be made equal to him in this before the play is over. But there is more still. "There is a mass of evil of which you are unconscious which shall equate you to yourself and your children."

ἅ σ' ἐξισώσει σοί τε καὶ τοῖς σοῖς τέκνοις.

This is not the equation the priest desired to see, Oedipus present equated with Oedipus past, the deliverer from the Sphinx, but a more terrible equation reaching farther back into the past, Oedipus son of Polybus and Merope equated to Oedipus son of Laius and Jocasta; "equate you with your own children," for Oedipus is the brother of his own sons and daughters. In his closing words Tiresias explains this mysterious line, and connects it with the unknown murderer of Laius. "He will be revealed, a native Theban, one who in his relationship with his own children is both brother and father, with his mother both son and husband, with his father, both marriage-partner and murderer. Go inside and reckon this up, λογίζου, and if you find me mistaken in my reckoning, ἐψευσμένον, then say I have no head for prophecy."

Tiresias adopts the terms of Oedipus' own science and throws them in his face. But these new equations are beyond Oedipus' understanding, he dismisses them as the ravings of an unsuccessful conspirator with his back to the wall. Even the chorus, though disturbed, rejects the prophet's words and resolves to stand by Oedipus.

After Tiresias, Creon: after the prophet, the politician. In Tiresias, Oedipus faced a blind man who saw with unearthly sight; but Creon's vision, like that of Oedipus, is of this world. They are two of a kind, and Creon talks Oedipus' language. It is a quarrel between two calculators. "Hear an equal reply," says Creon, and "Long time might be measured since Laius' murder." "You and Jocasta rule in equality of power." And finally "Am I not a third party equated, ἰσοῦμαι, to you two?" Creon and Oedipus are not equal now, for Creon is at the mercy of Oedipus, begging for a hearing; but before the play is over Oedipus will be at the mercy of Creon, begging kindness for his daughters, and he then uses the same word. "Do not equate them with my misfortunes."

μηδ' ἐξισώσῃς τάσδε τοῖς ἐμοῖς κακοῖς

With Jocasta's intervention the enquiry changes direction. In her attempt to comfort Oedipus, whose only accuser is a prophet, she indicts prophecy in general, using as an example the unfulfilled prophecy about her own child, who was supposed to kill Laius. The child was abandoned on the mountainside and Laius was killed by robbers where three wagon roads meet. "Such were the definitions, διώρισαν, made by prophetic voices," and they were incorrect. But Oedipus is not, for the moment, interested in prophetic voices. "Where three wagon roads meet." He once killed a man at such a place and now in a series of swift questions he determines the relation of these two events. The place, the time, the description of the victim, the number in his party, five, all correspond exactly. His account of the circumstances includes Apollo's prophecy that he would kill his father and be his mother's mate. But this does not disturb him now. That prophecy has not been fulfilled, for his father and mother are in Corinth, where he will never go again. "I measure the distance to Corinth by the stars," ἄστροις . . . ἐκμετρούμενος. What does disturb him is that he may be the murderer of Laius, the cause of the plague, the object of his own solemn excommunication. But he has some slight ground for hope. There is a discrepancy in the two events. It is the same numerical distinction which was discussed before, whether Laius was killed by one man or many. Jocasta said robbers and Oedipus was alone. This distinction is now all-important, the key to the solution of the equation. Oedipus sends for the survivor who can confirm or deny the saving detail. "If he says the same number as you then I am not the murderer. For one cannot equal many."

οὐ γὰρ γένοιτ' ἂν εἷς γε τοῖς πολλοῖς ἴσος

which may fairly be rendered, "In no circumstances can one be equal to more than one." Oedipus' guilt or innocence rests now on a mathematical axiom.

But a more fundamental equation has been brought into question, the relation of the oracles to reality. Here are two oracles, both the same, both unfulfilled; the same terrible destiny was predicted for Jocasta's son, who is dead, and for Oedipus, who has avoided it. One thing is clear to Jocasta. Whoever turns out to be Laius' murderer, the oracles are wrong. "From this day forward I would not, for all prophecy can say, turn my head this way or that." If the equation of the oracles with reality is a false equation, then religion is meaningless. Neither Jocasta nor Oedipus can allow the possibility that the oracles are right, and they accept the consequences, as they proceed to make clear. But the chorus cannot, and it now abandons Oedipus the calculator and turns instead to those "high-footed laws, which are the children of Olympus and not a creation of mortal man." It calls on Zeus to fulfill the oracles. "If these things do not coincide," ἁρμόσει, if the oracles do not equal reality, then "the divine order is overthrown," ἔρρει τὰ θεῖα. The situation and future of two individuals has become a test of divine power: if they are right, sings the chorus, "why reverence Apollo's Delphi, the center of the world? Why join the choral dance?" τί δεῖ με χορεύειν; and with this phrase the issue is brought out of the past into the present moment in the theater of Dionysus. For this song itself is also a dance, the choral stasimon which is the nucleus of tragedy and which reminds us that tragedy itself is an act of religious worship. If the oracles and the truth are not equated the performance of the play has no meaning, for tragedy is a religious ritual. This phrase is a tour de force which makes the validity of the performance itself depend on the dénouement of the play.

The oracles are now the central issue; the murder of Laius fades into the background. A messenger from Corinth brings news, news which will be greeted, he announces, "with an equal amount of sorrow and joy." "What is it," asks Jocasta, "which has such double power?" Polybus is dead. The sorrow equal to the joy will come later; for the moment there is only joy. The oracles are proved wrong again: Oedipus' father is dead. Oedipus can no more kill his father than the son of Laius killed his. "Oracles of the gods, where are you now?" Oedipus is caught up in Jocasta's exaltation, but it does not last. Only half his burden has been lifted from him. His mother still lives. He must still measure the distance to Corinth by the stars, still fear the future.

Both Jocasta and the messenger now try to relieve him of this last remaining fear. Jocasta makes her famous declaration in which she rejects fear, providence, divine and human alike, and indeed any idea of order or plan. Her declaration amounts almost to a rejection of the law of cause and effect: and it certainly attacks the basis of human calculation. For her, the calculation has gone far enough: it has produced an acceptable result; let it stop here. "Why should man fear?" she asks. "His life is governed by the operation of chance. Nothing can be accurately foreseen. The best rule is to live blindly, at random, εἰκῆ, as best one can." It is a statement which recognizes and accepts a meaningless universe. And Oedipus would agree, but for one thing. His mother lives. He must still fear.

Where Jocasta failed the messenger succeeds. He does it by destroying the equation on which Oedipus' life is based. And he uses familiar terms. "Polybus is no more your father than I, but equally so." Oedipus' question is indignant: "How can my father be equal to a nobody, to zero? τῷ μηδενί" The answer—"Polybus is not your father, neither am I." But that is as far as the Corinthian's knowledge goes; he was given the child Oedipus by another, a shepherd, one of Laius' men. And now the two separate equations begin to merge. "I think," says the chorus, "that that shepherd was the same man that you already sent for." The eyewitness to the death of Laius. He was sent for to say whether Laius was killed by one or many, but he will bring more important news. He will finally lift from Oedipus' shoulders the burden of fear he has carried since he left Delphi. Chance governs all. Oedipus' life history is the operation of chance; found by one shepherd, passed on to another, given to Polybus who was childless, brought up as heir to a kingdom, self-exiled from Corinth he came to Thebes a homeless wanderer, answered the riddle of the Sphinx, and won a city and the hand of a queen. And that same guiding chance will now reveal to him his real identity. Jocasta was right. Why should he fear?

But Jocasta has already seen the truth. Not chance, but the fulfillment of the oracle; the prophecy and the facts coincide (ἁρμόσει), as the chorus prayed they would. Jocasta is lost, but she tries to save Oedipus, to stop the enquiry. But nothing can stop him now. Her farewell to him expresses her agony and knowledge by its omissions: she recognizes but cannot formulate the dreadful equation which Tiresias stated. "ἰοὺ, ἰού, δύστηνε, Unfortunate. This is the only name I can call you." She cannot call him husband. The three-day-old child she sent out to die on the mountain-side has been restored to her, and she cannot call him son.

Oedipus hardly listens. He in his turn has scaled the same heights of confidence from which she has toppled, and he goes higher still. "I will know my origin, burst forth what will." He knows that it will be good. Chance governs the universe and Oedipus is her son. Not the son of Polybus, nor of any mortal man but the son of fortunate chance. In his exaltation he rises in imagination above human stature. "The months, my brothers, have defined, διώρισαν, my greatness and smallness"; he has waned and waxed like the moon, he is one of the forces of the universe, his family is time and space. It is a religious, a mystical conception; here is Oedipus' real religion, he is equal to the gods, the son of chance, the only real goddess. Why should he not establish his identity?

The solution is only a few steps ahead. The shepherd is brought on. "If I, who never met the man, may make an estimate (σταθμᾶσθαι), I think this is the shepherd who has been the object of our investigation (ζητοῦμεν). In age he is commensurate σύμμετρος with the Corinthian here." With this significant prologue he plunges into the final calculation.

The movement of the next sixty lines is the swift ease of the last stages of the mathematical proof: the end is half foreseen, the process an automatic sequence from one step to the next until Oedipus tyrannos and Oedipus the accursed, the knowledge and the swollen foot, are equated. "It all comes out clear," he cries. τὰ πάντ' ἂν ἐξήκοι σαφῆς. The prophecy has been fulfilled. Oedipus knows himself for what he is. He is not the measurer but the thing measured, not the equator but the thing equated. He is the answer to the problem he tried to solve. The chorus sees in Oedipus a παράδειγμα, an example to mankind. In this self-recognition of Oedipus, man recognizes himself. Man measures himself and the result is not that man is the measure of all things. The chorus, which rejected number and all that it stood for, has learned to count; and states the result of the great calculation. "Generations of man that must die, I add up the total of your life and find it equal to zero" ἴσα καὶ τὸ μηδὲν ζώσας ἐναριθμῶ.

The overthrow of the tyrannos is complete. When Oedipus returns from the palace he is blind, and, by the terms of his own proclamation, an outcast. It is a terrible reversal, and it raises the question, "Is it deserved? How far is he responsible for what he has done? Were the actions for which he is now paying not predestined?" No. They were committed in ignorance, but they were not predestined, merely predicted. An essential distinction, as essential for Milton's Adam [in *Paradise Lost*] as for Sophocles' Oedipus. His will was free, his actions his own, but the pattern of his action is the same as that of the Delphic prophecy. The relation between the prophecy and Oedipus' actions is not that of cause and effect. It is the relation suggested by the metaphor, the relation of two independent entities which are equated.

Yet no man can look on Oedipus without sympathy. In his moment of exaltation—"I am the son of fortune"—he is man at his blindest, but he is also man at his most courageous and heroic: "Burst forth what will, I will know." And he has served, as the chorus says, to point a moral. He is a paradigm, a demonstration. True, Oedipus, the independent being, was a perfectly appropriate subject for the demonstration. But we cannot help feeling that the gods owe Oedipus a debt. Sophocles felt it too, and in his last years wrote the play which shows us the nature of the payment, *Oedipus at Colonus*.

This play deals with Oedipus' reward, and the reward is a strange one. How strange can be seen clearly if we compare Oedipus with another great figure who also served as the subject of a divine demonstration, Job. After his torment Job had it all made up to him. "The Lord gave Job twice as much as he had before. For he had 14,000 sheep, and 6,000 camels and 1,000 yoke of oxen and 1,000 she-asses. He had also 7 sons and 3 daughters. And after this lived Job an hundred and forty years, and saw his sons and his sons' sons, even four generations." This is the kind of reward we can understand—14,000 sheep, 6,000 camels—Job, to use an irreverent comparison, hit the patriarchal jackpot. Oedipus' reward includes no camels or she-asses, no long life, in fact no life at all, his reward is death. But a death which Job could never imagine. For in death Oedipus becomes equated to the gods. The ironic phrase with which the first play began has here a literal fulfillment. Oedipus becomes something superhuman, a spirit which lives on in power in the affairs of men after the death of the body. His tomb is to be a holy place, for the city in whose territory his body lies will win a great victory on the field where Oedipus lies buried. By his choice of a burial place he thus influences history, becomes a presence to be feared by some and thanked by others. But it is not only in his grave that he will be powerful. In the last hours of his life he begins to assume the attributes of the divinity he is to become; the second play, *Oedipus at Colonus*, puts on stage the process of Oedipus' transition from human to divine.

"Equated to the gods." We have not seen the gods, but we know from the first play what they are. That play demonstrated that the gods have knowledge, full complete knowledge, the knowledge which Oedipus thought he had. He was proved ignorant; real knowledge is what distinguishes god from man. Since the gods have knowledge their action is confident and sure. They act with the swift decision which was characteristic of Oedipus but which was in him misplaced. Only a god can be sure, not a man. And their action is just. It is a justice based on perfect knowledge, is exact and appropriate, and therefore allows no room for forgiveness—but it can be angry. The gods can even mock the wrongdoer as Athene does Ajax, as the echoes of his name mocked Oedipus. This sure, full, angry justice is what Oedipus tried to administer to Tiresias, to Creon, but his justice was based on ignorance and was injustice. These attributes of divinity—knowledge, certainty, justice—are the qualities Oedipus thought he possessed—and that is why he was the perfect example of the inadequacy of human knowledge, certainty, and justice. But in the second play Oedipus is made equal to the gods, he assumes the attributes of divinity, the attributes he once thought his, he becomes what he once thought he was. This old Oedipus seems to be equal to the young, confident in his knowledge, fiercely angry in his administration of justice, utterly sure of himself—but this time he is justified. These are not the proper attitudes for a man, but Oedipus is turning into something more than man; now he knows surely, sees clearly, the gods give Oedipus back his eyes, but they are eyes of superhuman vision. Now in his transformation, as then, in his reversal, he serves still as an example. The rebirth of the young, confident Oedipus in the tired old man emphasizes the same lesson; it defines once more the limits of man and the power of gods, states again that the possession of knowledge, certainty, and justice is what distinguishes god from man.

The opening statement of Oedipus shows that as a man he has learned the lesson well. "I have learned acquiescence, taught by suffering and long time." As a man Oedipus has nothing more to learn. With this statement he comes to the end of a long road. The nearby city whose walls he cannot see is Athens, and here is the place of his reward, his grave, his home. The welcome he receives is to be ordered off by the first arrival; he has trespassed on holy ground, the grove of the Eumenides. He knows what this means, this is the resting place he was promised by Apollo, and he refuses to move. His statement recalls the tyrannos, a characteristic phrase: "In no circumstances will I leave this place." The terms of his prayer to the goddesses of the grave foreshadow his transition from body to spirit. "Pity this wretched ghost of Oedipus the man, this body that is not what it once was long ago."

As a body, as a man, he is a thing to be pitied; he is blind, feeble, ragged, dirty. But the transformation has already begun. The first comer spoke to him with pity, even condescension, but the chorus of citizens which now enters feels fear. "Dreadful to see, dreadful to hear." When they know his identity their fear changes to anger, but Oedipus defends his past. He sees himself as one who was ignorant, who suffered rather than acted. But now he is actor, not sufferer.

He comes with knowledge, and power. "I come bringing advantage to this city."

He does not yet know what advantage. His daughter Ismene comes to tell him what it is, that his grave will be the site of a victory for the city that shelters him. And to tell him that his sons and Creon, all of whom despised and rejected him, now need him, and will come to beg his help. Oedipus has power over the future and can now reward his friends and punish his enemies. He chooses to reward Athens, to punish Creon and his own sons. He expresses his choice in terms which show a recognition of human limitations; Athens' reward, something which lies within his will, as an intention; his sons' punishment, something over which he has no sure control, as a wish. "May the issue of the battle between them lie in my hands. If that were to be, the one would not remain king, nor the other win the throne."

Theseus, the king of Athens, welcomes him generously, but when he learns that Thebes wants Oedipus back and that he refuses to go, Theseus reproaches the old man. "Anger is not what your misfortune calls for." And the answer is a fiery rebuke from a superior. "Wait till you hear what I say, before you reproach me." Oedipus tells Theseus that he brings victory over Thebes at some future time, and Theseus, the statesman, is confident that Athens will never be at war with Thebes. Oedipus reproaches him in his turn. Such confidence is misplaced. No man should be so sure of the future: "Only to the gods comes no old age or death. Everything else is dissolved by all-powerful time. The earth's strength decays, the body decays, faith dies, mistrust flowers and the wind of friendship changes between man and man, city and city." No man can be confident of the future. Man's knowledge is ignorance. It is the lesson Oedipus learned in his own person and he reads it to Theseus now with all the authority of his blind eyes and dreadful name—but he does not apply it to himself. For he goes on to predict the future. He hands down the law of human behavior to Theseus speaking already as a *daemon*, not one subject to the law but one who administers it. And with his confident prediction, his assumption of sure knowledge, goes anger, but not the old human anger of Oedipus *tyrannos*. As he speaks of Thebes' future defeat on the soil where he will be buried, the words take on an unearthly quality, a daemonic wrath.

> ἵν' οὑμὸς εὕδων καὶ κεκρυμμένος νεκύς
> ψυχρὸς ποτ' αὐτῶν θερμὸν αἷμα πίεται
> εἰ Ζεὺς ἔτι Ζεὺς χὡ Διὸς Φοῖβος σαφής.

"There my sleeping and hidden corpse, cold though it be, will drink their warm blood, if Zeus is still Zeus and Apollo a true prophet." What before was wish and prayer is now prediction. But the prediction is qualified: "if Apollo be a true prophet." He does not yet speak in the authority of his own name. That will be the final stage.

And when it comes, he speaks face to face with the objects of his anger. Creon's condescending and hypocritical speech is met with a blast of fury that surpasses the anger he had to face long ago in Thebes. The final interview is a repetition of the first. In both Creon is condemned, in both with the same swift vindictive wrath, but this time the condemnation is just. Oedipus sees through to the heart of Creon, he knows what he is: and Creon proceeds to show the justice of Oedipus' rejection by revealing that he has already kidnapped Ismene, by kidnapping Antigone, and laying hands on Oedipus himself. Oedipus is helpless, and only the arrival of Theseus saves him. This is the man who is being equated to the gods, not the splendid tyrannos, the man of power, vigor, strength, but a blind old man, the extreme of physical weakness, who cannot even see, much less prevent, the violence that is done him.

Physical weakness, but a new height of spiritual strength. This Oedipus judges justly and exactly, knows fully, sees clearly—his power is power over the future, the defeat of Thebes, the death of his sons, the terrible reversal of Creon. One thing Creon says to Oedipus clarifies the nature of the process we are witnessing. "Has not time taught you wisdom?" Creon expected to find the Oedipus of the opening scene of the play, whom time had taught acquiescence, but he finds what seems to be the tyrannos he knew and feared. "You harm yourself now as you did then," he says, "giving way to that anger which has always been your defeat." He sees the old Oedipus as equal to the young. In one sense they are, but in a greater sense they are no more equal than man is equal to the gods.

With the next scene the whole story comes full circle. A suppliant begs Oedipus for help. Our last sight of Oedipus is like our first. This suppliant is Polynices, his son, and the comparison with the opening scene of the first play is emphasized by the repetitions of the priest's speech—words, phrases, even whole lines—which appear in Polynices' appeal to his father. It is a hypocritical speech which needs no refutation. It is met with a terrible indictment which sweeps from accusation through prophecy to a climax which, with its tightly packed explosive consonants resembles not so much human speech as a burst of daemonic anger:

θανεῖν κτανεῖν θ'ὑφ' οὗπερ ἐξελήλασαι
τοιαῦτ' ἀρῶμαι καὶ καλῶ τὸ Ταρτάρου
στυγνὸν πατρῷον ἔρεβος ὥς σ' ἀποικίαη

"Kill and be killed by the brother who drove you out. This is my curse, I call on the hideous darkness of Tartarus where your fathers lie, to prepare a place for you. . . ." This is a superhuman anger welling from the outraged sense of justice not of a man but of the forces of the universe themselves.

Creon could still argue and resist, but to this speech no reply is possible. There can be no doubt of its authority. When Polynices discusses the speech with his sisters, the right word for it is found. Oedipus speaks with the voice of an oracle. "Will you go to Thebes and fulfill his prophecies? (μαντεύματα)" says Antigone. Oedipus who fought to disprove an oracle has become one himself. And his son now starts on the same road his father trod. "Let him prophesy. I do not have to fulfill it." Polynices leaves with a phrase that repeats his mother's denunciation of prophets. "All this is in the power of the divinity, ἐν τω δαίμονι, it may turn out this way or that." In the power of a god—in the power of chance—whatever he means, he does not realize the sense in which the words are true. The daemon, the divinity, in whose power it lies is Oedipus himself.

Oedipus has stayed too long. Power such as this should not walk the earth in the shape of a man. The thunder and lightning summon him, and the gods reproach him for his delay. "You Oedipus, you, why do we hesitate to go? You have delayed too long."

> ὦ οὗτος οὗτος Οἰδίπους τί μέλλομεν
> χωρεῖν; πάλαι δὴ τἀπὸ σοῦ βραδύνεται.

These strange words are the only thing the gods say in either play. And as was to be expected of so long delayed and awful a statement, it is complete and final. The hesitation for which they reproach Oedipus is the last shred of his humanity, which he must now cast off. Where he is going vision is clear, knowledge certain, action instantaneous and effective; between the intention and the act there falls no shadow of hesitation or delay. The divine "we"— "Why do *we* hesitate to go"—completes and transcends the equation of Oedipus with the gods; his identity is merged with theirs. And in this last moment of his bodily life they call him by his name, *Oidipous*, the name which contains in itself the lesson of which not only his action and suffering but also his apotheosis serve as the great example—*oida*—that man's knowledge, which makes him master of the world, should never allow him to think that he is equated to the gods, should never allow him to forget the foot, *pous*, the reminder of his true measurement, his real identity.

STANTON MILLET

ꙮ *The Structure of* Measure for Measure

ALTHOUGH there is much critical disagreement about such problems as the Duke's ethics and function, Angelo's character, the quality of Isabella's virtue, and the relevance and taste of the low scenes in *Measure for Measure*, a surprisingly large number of critics agree that the play is seriously defective in structure. The last two acts, they insist, not only fail to satisfy the audience's outraged moral sense, but simply do not fit with the rest of the plot. The reason for this failure, V. K. Whitaker suggests, is that Shakespeare attempted to make a philosophical play "by loading philosophical analysis upon a simple source plot which he patched up in the easy-going fashion of the romantic comedies."[25] L. C. Knights recognizes the same fault and dismisses the last two acts as little more than a hasty drawing out and resolution of the plot.[26] And finally, Murray Kreiger condemns the entire play, saying that "its unified significance as drama must elude us as, indeed, it may have eluded even Shakespeare."[27]

If one attempts to explain the action in terms of a central character (Isabella, Claudio, the Duke, and Angelo have all been suggested), these criticisms are fully justified, but if one searches instead for a central theme, the unity of the play emerges rather clearly. One main theme, certainly, is that of government, involving such problems as the purpose of the laws, the balance between liberty and restraint, the relationship of the judge to the laws he enforces, and the effect of power on the individual magistrate. In the play, this theme is carefully and fully developed by a contrast between (1) the false conception of justice and imperfect administration of the law represented variously by Angelo, Isabella, and Claudio and (2) the true conception of justice, involving a qualification of the law by the judge, which is represented by the Duke. Further, there is a contrast between two sorts of mercy, the one corrupt because it arises from partiality in the judge, either to the vice or to himself, and the other true mercy because it springs from holiness, used not only in the sense of piety, but also in its original meaning of "whole" or "sound." A reading of *Measure for Measure* as an exposition of this theme not only justifies the last two acts and the low scenes, but explains many of the apparent inconsistencies in character, as well.

I

Angelo relies on strict adherence to the letter of the law to make moral choices simple, if not to eliminate them completely. This is made clear early in the play when, in answer to Escalus' suggestion that he qualify the law by reference to his own experience, he insists that law and judge are separate and distinct. It makes no difference that the jury contains thieves; justice will still be done. Of course the error of this belief is immediately, and hilariously, pointed out by the entrance of Elbow, who cries, "If it please your honor, I am the poor Duke's constable, and my name is Elbow, I do lean upon justice, sir, and do bring in here before your good honor two notorious benefactors" (II.i.45–47). The entire episode is devoted to reducing Angelo's position to the

---

[25] "Philosophy and Romance in Shakespeare's 'Problem' Comedies," *The Seventeenth Century*, ed. R. F. Jones (Stanford University Press, 1951), p. 354.

[26] "The Ambiguity of 'Measure for Measure'," *The Importance of Scrutiny*, ed. Eric Bentley (New York: George Stewart, 1948), p. 149.

[27] " 'Measure for Measure' and Elizabethan Comedy," *PMLA*, LXVI (1951), 784.

absurd. Like Elbow, Angelo "leans upon justice," but how ridiculous his beliefs seem when we are shown an official who is *really* separate from the law he administers! If Angelo were right, if law were entirely independent of the official, it would make no difference that Elbow were incompetent. But the lesson is lost on Angelo, who goes on putting all his trust in the unqualified, unquestioning acceptance of the letter of the law, regardless of circumstances. Consider, for example, the following dialogue, when Isabella is pleading for Claudio's life:

> ISABELLA: Yes; I do think that you might pardon him,
>   And neither heaven nor man grieve at the mercy.
> ANGELO: I will not do't.
> ISABELLA: But can you, if you would?
> ANGELO: Look, what I will not, that I cannot do.
>   (ii.ii.50–53)

The inversion in the last line is important. What Angelo means, of course, is that he decrees what he is bound by law to decree. But the inverted order in the sentence points up the inverted order in Angelo's mind. Others might wish to do a thing, find it against the law, and decide, as a result, not to follow their inclinations; but Angelo has submerged his own will in the law, and he identifies adherence to regulations with inclination itself.

Actually, this is not in accord with the Duke's commands. The Duke had told him:

> Your scope is as mine own,
> So to enforce or qualify the laws
> As to your soul seems good.   (i.i.64–66)

But the point is that Angelo cannot qualify the laws, for he is without soul, or at least without any idea of a greater good than strict adherence to the regulations. It becomes abundantly clear in the course of the play that Angelo is just such a hollow man as Lucio had described earlier, one who is "so sound as things that are hollow. Thy bones are hollow; impiety has made a feast of thee" (i.ii.45–47). His virtue is based only on external characteristics, on appearances. In at least one place he admits, for example, that virtue is a matter of chance, not choice:

>   'Tis very pregnant,
>   The jewel that we find, we stoop and take 't
>   Because we see it; but what we do not see
>   We tread upon, and never think of it.
>   You may not so extenuate his offense
>   For I have had such faults; but rather tell me,
>   When I that censure him do so offend,

> Let mine own judgment pattern out my death,
> And nothing come in partial. Sir, he must die.
>   (II.i.23–31)

This is, as Angelo says, "pregnant"—with an irony that he does not suspect. This is not a true law, but a warning not to lose opportunities, and Angelo's proposal that his present judgment pattern out his own death is anything but adequate, since true judgment must be made in the light of the full situation. Then, too, Angelo's use of the word "extenuate" shows his lack of understanding of government. "Extenuate" implies a weakening of the law, but "qualify" (the Duke's term) implies a strengthening, or at least an adjustment to the situation.

Angelo's hollowness becomes apparent after he is tempted by Isabella. When opportunity presents itself, his shell of virtue crumbles and he attempts to disregard the law:

> O, let her brother live:
> Thieves for their robbery have authority
> When judges steal themselves.   (II.ii.176–178)

He has become the "sanctimonious pirate" of Lucio's description, who "went to sea with the Ten Commandments, but scraped one out of the table" (I.ii.7–8).

Isabella, too, shows the same sort of hollowness. Her first words in the play (I.iv.3–5) are a demand for stricter laws; and when she goes to Angelo to plead for her brother's life, she begins by affirming her own uncritical belief in the law:

> There is a vice that most I do abhor,
> And most desire should meet the blow of justice,
> For which I would not plead, but that I must,
> For which I must not plead, but that I am
> At war 'twixt will and will not.   (II.ii.29–33)

Her dilemma is resolved with remarkable ease. At Angelo's first objection, she readily gives up the cause, and it is only with constant urging from Lucio that she warms up in her arguments. She manages to pierce to the heart of Angelo's beliefs, hitting hard at his reliance on ceremony and stressing mercy. She even affirms that the judge and laws are not separate, but bound up together:

> If he had been as you, and you as he,
> You would have slipped like him, but he, like you,
> Would not have been so stern.   (II.ii.65–67)

But, perhaps because she is urging an extenuation of the law rather than a just qualification, she never fully convinces herself, much less Angelo, that she is right. When she returns again, she has no Lucio to urge her on and abandons her pleading almost immediately. When Angelo, giving his "sensual race the rein" (ii.iv.160), offers her the choice between chastity and her brother's life, she scarcely considers the alternatives. Instead, she condemns Claudio and admits that when she was asking for mercy she was trying to weaken the law out of partiality to her brother:

> O pardon me, my lord; It oft falls out
> To have what we would have, we speak not what we mean.
> I something do excuse the thing I hate
> For his advantage that I dearly love.   (ii.iv.117–120)

Like Angelo's, her attitude seems to be "what I will not, that I cannot do." All she knows is that religious law demands that she remain chaste, and she is unable even to *wish* that she could save her brother if it involves breaking the law.

It is this attitude which accounts, perhaps, for her fierce denunciation of Claudio which has caused so much critical difficulty. The scene in which this occurs is oddly parallel to the scene in which Isabella begs Angelo to extenuate the laws, but here Isabella has become the judge and Claudio the pleader. In one of the most beautiful poetic passages that Shakespeare ever wrote, Claudio begs his sister to let him live, and Isabella, outraged that anyone should question the law on which she relies—and perhaps panic-stricken at the thought of choosing—denies him in a fiery speech. She shows no more mercy than Angelo, and for the same reason. At this point, at least, she is no better able to qualify the laws by reference to her own soul than was Angelo.

Not so obvious as this parallel, but perhaps of greater significance to the play, is the similarity between Angelo's fall and the very crime he condemned in Claudio and Juliet. Not only does he attempt to duplicate Claudio's offense, but, figuratively speaking, he duplicates Juliet's, as well. He is seduced by Isabella, with Lucio as the bawd: "She speaks, and 'tis / Such sense that my sense breeds with it" (ii.ii.142–143). And, like Juliet with an illegitimate child, he is pregnant with an illegitimate thought: "And in my heart the strong and swelling evil / Of my conception" (ii.iv.6–7). There is also a dissimilarity, however. While Juliet's repentance is sincere, coming from a love of God, not from fear of His laws, Angelo's attempt to arraign his conscience is a failure:

> When I would pray and think, I think and pray
> To several subjects: Heaven hath my empty words,
> Whilst my invention, hearing not my tongue,
> Anchors on Isabel.   (ii.iv.1–4)

By comparison with the Duke's examination of Juliet's conscience (which immediately precedes these lines) we see that Angelo's penitence is "hollowly put on." Without a sincere love of some higher good, he has nothing to inspire remorse or to govern his actions once he has thrown over the laws.

This is also, of course, the trouble with Claudio, whose view of the law is the same as Angelo's and Isabella's. In the second scene of the play, when Lucio asks him why he has been arrested, he replies:

> From too much liberty, my Lucio, liberty.
> As surfeit is the father of much fast,
> So every scope by the immoderate use
> Turns to restraint. Our natures do pursue,
> Like rats that ravin down their proper bane,
> A thirsty evil, and when we drink we die.
>   (i.ii.107–112)

L. C. Knights (p. 144) finds this speech somehow "odd and inappropriate" because of the rat and poison image, maintaining that there is nothing shameful enough in Claudio's relationship with Juliet to warrant such strong words. But the point is that Claudio's view of law is just as limited as Angelo's and Isabella's. Like them, he assumes that mankind habitually pursues evil instead of good, and he forgets the corrective, or teaching, function of the laws in favor of the restraining function. Given this limited view, the rat image follows naturally. Indeed, it seems an appropriate image for any one of the three to use in explaining their ideas of law.

II

Angelo, Isabella, and Claudio are surprisingly alike; but although the first part of the play, through Act II, is almost entirely devoted to them, we are not really aware of the hollowness of their virtue or the errors in their conception of the law until Act III, which reveals, in striking contrast, the Duke's sound virtue and true justice. We already know, from his remarks to Friar Thomas in the first act, that the Duke thinks of laws as "The needful bits and curbs to headstrong wills" (i.iii.20) or as "the threatening twigs of birch" (i.iii.24) that a parent uses to discipline his child. We also know, from the prison scene with Juliet in Act II (iii.10–42), that he believes one's motive for penitence—and, by implication, obedience to law—should be love of good rather than fear of retribution. In Act III, however, a number of elements combine to give us a much deeper insight into his character and his theories.

At the very beginning of this section of the play, when he eloquently prepares Claudio for death by pointing out that all we hold dear in life—nobility, courage, individuality, happiness, certainty, riches, friendship, and youth—are vain, he also reveals his own humility and distrust of mere appearances (iii.i.5–41). The speech is admirably suited to appeal to Claudio's naturalistic view of life, and it also forms an effective contrast with the speech in the preceding scene in which Angelo reveals (ii.iv.9–12) that he could exchange his gravity (to him, only an appearance, but one that he is proud of) for an "idle plume" (a still more frivolous appearance).

A more fundamental contrast emerges when we find the Duke willing to circumvent the strict enforcement of the law, even to the extent of becoming a seeming bawd, in order to bring about greater good than strict adherence to law could produce. By bringing Mariana and Angelo together, Claudio will be saved, Mariana "advantaged" and "the corrupt deputy scaled" (iii.i.236–237). Yet it is immediately made clear, when the Duke berates Pompey (iii.ii.16–24), that he despises a bawd. This double view is not hypocrisy, however. The remainder of the act, in which the Duke's character is put on trial by Lucio and Escalus, proves that his motives are sound. Lucio is a devil's advocate, admitting that the Duke was merciful, but attributing his mercy to a full and personal knowledge of the vices. He accuses the Duke of fornication: "He had some feeling of the sport; he knew the service, and that instructed him to mercy" (iii.ii.100–101); drunkenness; shallow thinking, "A very superficial, ignorant, unweighing fellow" (iii.ii.117); and impiety, "The Duke, I say to thee again, would eat mutton on Fridays" (iii.ii.149–150). But what we know of Lucio's character, together with our knowledge of the Duke's, is enough to make the testimony ridiculous, as it is intended to be. It only remains for Escalus to describe him as "One that, above all other strifes, contended especially to know himself" (iii.ii.194–195), "a gentleman of all temperance" (iii.ii.198) and thus completely to discredit Lucio's imputation.

Lucio assumes that the Duke's mercy is grounded on knowledge of sin in himself—the same grounds for mercy that Isabella urged, less blatantly, in her arguments with Angelo. This is the common, but inadequate, view that the judge extenuates the law because of personal weakness. But the Duke, in an important soliloquy at the end of the act, maintains just the opposite:

> He who the sword of heaven will bear
> Should be as holy as severe;
> Pattern in himself to know,
> Grace to stand, and virtue go;
> More nor less to others paying
> Than by self-offenses weighing.
> Shame to him whose cruel striking
> Kills for faults of his own liking.
> (iii.ii.217–224)

The phrase "sword of *heaven*" indicates that the Duke thinks of the laws not as secular regulations complete in themselves, but as a means to guide (or even drive) men to a truer and more embracing goodness than simple adherence to the law could produce. The implication is reinforced by the requirement that the judge be "as *holy* as severe," that he be a deputy not only of the state but of heaven, and also, in another sense of the word, that he be of sound or whole character. Thus, when the Duke speaks of "More nor less to others paying /

Than by self-offenses weighing," he means that Angelo is disqualified as a competent judge because he is not above the vice he condemns. He certainly does not mean that mercy should be shown only if the judge is himself vicious.

It is evident in the play that there are two sorts of mercy: an extenuation of the laws because of the judge's weakness, and a qualification of the laws based on the judge's soundness or holiness. The Duke comments on the first kind when, expecting Claudio's pardon from Angelo, he says:

> This is his pardon, purchased by such sin
> For which the pardoner himself is in:
> Hence hath offense his quick celerity,
> When it is borne in high authority.
> When vice makes mercy, mercy's so extended
> That for the fault's love is th' offender friended.
> (iv.ii.95–100)

And he demonstrates the true mercy himself. It has already been established that he is holy in both senses of the word: he is serving as a friar, ministering to men's souls, and he is of good character. Thus, the mercy that he shows in the last act is a true qualification of the laws made by a sound judge.

III

The last six lines of the Duke's soliloquy at the end of Act iii foreshadow the action of the remainder of the play, and, I believe, explain the title:

> Craft against vice I must apply;
> With Angelo to-night shall lie
> His old betrothed, but despised:
> So disguise, shall, by th' disguised
> Pay with falsehood, false exacting,
> And perform an old contracting.
> (iii.ii.233–238)

It will become clear that the "measure for measure" of the play is not so much the penalty that should be imposed on Angelo as it is the opposition of the Duke's craft to Angelo's vice, of the Duke's and Mariana's disguises to Angelo's disguised vice, and of the Duke's pious falsehood to Angelo's false piety in arguing his demands on Isabella. The false idea of government represented by Angelo, Isabella, and Claudio, and the Duke's true conception have so far been developed separately; but in the last two acts they are brought in direct opposition, with the true judge pronouncing sentence on the false judges and demonstrating a kind of mercy of which they had been unaware.

The actual business of arranging the trap for Angelo is accomplished, of course, in the series of short, swiftly-moving scenes which comprise Act iv; and we need not discuss them here. Much more important to this discussion is the great judgment scene of Act v.

The problem confronting us is the Duke's mercy. Numerous critics have professed dissatisfaction at his seemingly excessive pardons, and they have been particularly disturbed at Angelo's escape from punishment. In examining this problem, there are a number of points to keep in mind. In the first place, Angelo had been commanded by the Duke to enforce the laws; and if, as was actually the case, his justice was too severe, it was technically legal. His neglect to qualify the laws according to his own soul was a serious fault, but it was remedied by the Duke's craftiness: Claudio was not actually put to death and Isabella's chastity was not actually violated. Angelo does not know it, but the Duke has already saved him from some of his crimes. These are only technicalities, however. The most serious crime, as we might expect from an understanding of the Duke's philosophy, is that Angelo, who was *himself guilty* of "violation / Of sacred chastity, and of promise-breach" (v.i.395–396), which disqualified him as an adequate judge, nevertheless condemned Claudio. For this crime, he is not pardoned on the basis of technicalities, but because he is truly repentant, sorry not for his own shame, but for the sorrow he has caused others (v.i.465–468). This, of course, agrees with the Duke's definition of true repentance stated earlier in the scene with Juliet (ii.iii.30–34). Then, too, as we know from his speech in Act iv, Angelo has lost his evil desire (been made "unpregnant"), and has realized that grace, the divine influence in man acting to make him pure and strong, is the most important characteristic of a good judge: "Alack, when once our grace we have forgot, / Nothing goes right; we would, and we would not" (iv.iv.31–32). As Mariana points out, he has come to know himself, and his crime may be the means of future improvement. The Duke, more interested in correction and instruction than in enforcing a death penalty, pardons him for this reason, which in the light of his philosophy is adequate.

Isabella, too, has learned from her experience. The Duke in a sense puts her on trial with the others by letting her think her brother dead and watching her narrowly to see whether her view of the laws has changed. He even goads her a bit by telling Mariana, who has just asked for her help, that if Isabella should plead for mercy for Angelo, "Her brother's ghost his paved bed would break, / And take her hence in horror" (v.i.426–427). When, even in the face of this, Isabella does ask mercy for Angelo, her speech shows an important change in her attitude. To be sure, she is still willing to accept the law without much question, admitting that Claudio "had but justice" (v.i.439), and using legal technicalities such as the fact that Angelo's "act did not o'ertake his bad intent" (v.i.442). At the same time, she shows a great deal more true mercy than she demonstrated earlier when, for example, she condemned her brother violently for a "bad intent" to live at the expense of her chastity.

As for Barnardine and Lucio, the Duke handles them much as he handled Angelo, circumventing the punishment that severe law enforcement would impose, because that punishment would be inadequate under the circumstances. Barnardine was well described by the Provost:

A man that apprehends death no more dreadfully but as a drunken sleep; careless, reckless, and fearless of what's past, present, or to come; insensible of mortality, and desperately mortal.   (iv.ii.126–128)

He is the Renaissance idea of a beast, "unfit to live or die . . . [,a] gravel heart" (iv.iii.53); and executing him in his present state would be inadequate punishment. The Duke realizes that Barnardine is condemned in a religious sense, unless he change his outlook; so he quits him of his earthly faults that he may have time to atone for his spiritual faults, and assigns a friar to instruct him (v.i.470–477). Finally, Lucio is punished for his loose conduct by being forced to marry the woman he had wronged, as Claudio and Angelo were similarly directed. It is clear that Lucio considers this the harshest punishment that could be meted out to him.

In each of these cases, the strict application of the law—an eye for an eye, a measure for a measure—would be unjust. Instead, the Duke has qualified the laws according to the circumstances and according to his own sound conception of justice. More important, each punishment carries with it an opportunity for the culprit to improve: instead of merely restraining, the Duke's law guides and instructs.

Looking at *Measure for Measure* in simplest outline form makes the real unity of structure apparent. Act I presents all of the problems involved in the theme of government; Act II is devoted to Angelo's and Isabella's false ideas of law and judgment; Act III, by way of contrast, presents the Duke's true understanding of government; and Acts IV and V bring together the two opposing theories which have so far been developed separately. This extended contrast and comparison develops and explains all of the questions posed in Act I. The contrast between the Duke's and Angelo's laws shows us that they should indeed be "the needful bits and curbs to headstrong steeds" rather than "bane" for "rats." The problem of the relationship between the judge and the laws is resolved by the same contrast: Angelo and the laws are separate, and tyrannous; the Duke and the laws are one, and just. The judge must be "as holy as severe"; he must "enforce or qualify the laws as to his soul seems good." And this in turn answers another question: how power affects the magistrate. If the judge is a complete man, one who knows himself and others, who has enough power of mind and soul to decide wisely, then power will not harm him; if, on the other hand, he is a hollow man, like Angelo, power will destroy him. It is simply a matter of the workman being big enough to handle his tools.

Basically, the theme of *Measure for Measure* as treated in this study is the same as the theme of Sonnet xciv, "They that have power to hurt and will do none." There may be other levels of meaning in the play, as Wilson Knight and R. W. Battenhouse (the latter of whom offered several valuable suggestions for the present essay) have shown; but on this level, read as the development of a theme by contrast and comparison, *Measure for Measure* emerges as a unified work of art.

DRAMA

THE ART OF
Reading Drama

WHILE it may seem curious to begin discussion of drama by examining a scene drawn from a novel, such a beginning will be useful in defining several of the basic problems that are presented to us by a play we read rather than see on the stage. Let us consider, then, a dialogue from Chapter III of *Great Expectations*, the chapter in which young Pip brings food to an escaped convict who has been hiding in the marshes waiting for the frightened boy's arrival. In order to enlist Pip's aid, the convict had threatened him the day before with a visit from a wholly imaginary, vicious young man who would, if Pip failed to follow instructions, tear out Pip's heart and liver, roast them, and eat them.

This is how the scene might appear in a dramatic script:

ACT ONE

The place, England, flat marsh country intersected with dikes, mounds, and gates. It is morning. A heavy mist obscures all but the outlines of a few large objects. Back and forth in the center of an open area of rank grass limps a tattered man dressed in gray, with a chain fastened to his leg. Philip Pirrip, a boy perhaps six or eight years old, enters from the right, hands the man a heavy file such as blacksmiths use, opens a bundle of food, and empties his pockets of still more food.

CONVICT: What's in the bottle, boy?

PIP: Brandy.

[*The convict shakily sets the bottle to his lips.*]

PIP: I think you have got the ague.

CONVICT: I'm much of your opinion, boy.

PIP: It's bad about here. You've been lying out on the meshes, and they're dreadful aguish. Rheumatic, too.

CONVICT: I'll eat my breakfast afore they're the death of me. I'd do that if I was going to be strung up to that there gallows as there is over there, directly afterwards. I'll beat the shivers so far, I'll bet you. [*He starts suddenly.*] You're not a deceiving imp? You brought no one with you?

PIP: No, sir! No!

CONVICT: Nor give no one the office to follow you?

PIP: No!

CONVICT: Well, I believe you. You'd be but a fierce young hound indeed, if at your time of life you could help to hunt a wretched varmint, hunted as near death and dunghill as this poor wretched varmint is!

PIP: [*Watching intently as the convict eats.*] I am glad you enjoy it.

CONVICT: Did you speak?

PIP: I said, I was glad you enjoyed it.

CONVICT: Thankee, my boy. I do.

PIP: I am afraid you won't leave any of it for him. There's no more to be got where that came from.

CONVICT: Leave any for him? Who's him?

PIP: The young man. That you spoke of. That was hid with you.

CONVICT: Oh, ah! [*He laughs.*] Him? Yes, yes! *He* don't want no vittles.

PIP: I thought he looked as if he did.

CONVICT: Looked? When?

PIP: Just now.

CONVICT: Where?

PIP: Yonder, over there, where I found him nodding asleep, and thought it was you. Dressed like you, you know, only with a hat, and—and—and with—the same reason for wanting to borrow a file. Didn't you hear the cannon last night?

CONVICT: Then, there *was* firing!

PIP: He had a badly bruised face.

CONVICT: [*Striking his left cheek*]   Not here?

PIP: Yes, there!

CONVICT: Where is he? Show me the way he went. I'll pull him down, like a bloodhound. Curse this iron on my sore leg! Give us hold of the file, boy. [*Muttering, he sits and begins filing at the chain.*]

PIP: [*Hesitantly*]   I must go.

[*The convict does not answer. Pip slips away a few paces, pauses momentarily, then disappears into the mist.*]

What is to be derived from a reasonably careful reading of this scene? First, we discover that certain elements may be categorized as *exposition*. Information is conveyed to us about the past and the future as well as the present. We learn of an earlier encounter between the convict and Pip ("The young man. That you spoke of. That was hid with you.") We know, too, that there was an escape the night before, that there is another convict in the marshes, and that Pip's convict, after the conclusion of the present scene, will pursue the other man and "pull him down, like a bloodhound." Certain details of setting and general atmosphere, beyond those established in the brief stage directions, are also presented. We find that the convict has been "lying out on the meshes," that "they're dreadful aguish," that there is a gallows nearby, and a prison (actually a floating hulk in the river) from which a cannon has been fired to warn of the escape.

The speeches of the two provide *characterization*, as well. Pip appears to be an intelligent, conventionally polite little boy whose diction suggests a lower class English background. He is, of course, frightened of the convict. This is made clear by the emphasis of his response to the convict's suspicious, "You brought no one with you?" and by his apprehensive reminder that the convict's companion must also be fed. Pip is clearly afraid that he will have to find food for still another terrifying outlaw. But though frightened, and perhaps naturally timid and rather apologetic, Pip is also deeply compassionate. His pity for the convict wars with his fear throughout the scene. It is implicit in his comment, "I think you have got the ague," and it is also suggested by his remark, "I am glad you enjoy it," although some part of his motive here may be relief in seeing that the convict will not threaten him further. It is established, above all, by his pausing to look back for a moment after he has been forgotten by the convict and has slipped away. Notice how different his attitude would seem if he moved carefully away and then, when he was beyond the convict's reach, ran frantically for home.

The convict similarly emerges as a human being rather than a mere figure on stage. We see him in a way that might have made him appear dehumanized, flat, merely representative of "the poor" or "the social outcast." While he does, in fact, suggest some of this—he *is* an outcast symbolically hiding in an uninhabitable marsh beyond the limits of Pip's village, beyond the law, beyond even the reach of ordinary human pity—he is nevertheless presented as a unique person with his own manner of speech, his own particular attitudes and qualities. He sees himself as a pathetic "varmint," "hunted as near death and dunghill" as it is possible to be. He sees life as little more than basic self-preservation, and he expects nothing better than fierce hunting followed by death on the gallows. Yet despite this grim and hopeless view, he apparently recognizes in children a natural compassion that will later be destroyed by a fierceness society will teach: "Well, I believe you. You'd be but a fierce young hound indeed, if at your time of life you could help to hunt a wretched varmint." And rounding out his character are both a sense of humor and a rage for vengeance, the first suggested by the laugh he utters when Pip mentions the imaginary young man with whom he had been threatened, the second by the frenzy of his speech and action when Pip tells him of the other convict's presence on the marsh.

We note, too, that there is *dramatic conflict* in the scene. The characters are not developed, nor do they act, individually. They have a direct effect on one another. The convict's attitude toward Pip at the beginning of the scene is abrupt, threatening. Pip reacts fearfully. But then his pity (and perhaps his curiosity) begin to overcome his fear. His generous comment, "I am glad you enjoy it," is met by the convict's genuinely grateful, "Thankee, my boy. I do." By the time the scene draws to a close, the convict has forgotten Pip in his determination to find and "pull down" the other man, while Pip, absorbed by pity and curiosity, stands looking at the convict rather than fleeing for his life.

Finally, the scene possesses both *plot* and *theme* functions. In the total context of the work from which the scene is drawn, we discover that this encounter between Pip and the convict sets in train a series of events by which the convict becomes Pip's secret benefactor, providing him with the money to grow up as "a gentleman" and to move from a village blacksmith's forge, to an aimless life of leisure in London, to a useful position as clerk in the foreign office of a British company. In terms of theme, Pip moves in the novel from the simple world of childhood in which natural feeling is possible, to the unfeelingly competitive world of middle-class trade and aristocratic indifference, to an intermediate world in which there is at least the possibility of reconciling what has been called "the world of the heart" with "the world of competition." The convict, the marsh, Pip's compassion for the convict—all these elements of the scene we have just read are, we discover, directly related to the theme of *Great Expectations* as well as to its plot.

If all this is to be derived from such a brief dialogue, what can be missing? A number of things. For one, we have very little material in the lines, or even in the stage directions, that enables us to visualize *precisely* what is happening on stage. We are told, for example, that our convict is dressed in gray, that he limps and hugs himself—presumably from cold or the ague—and that he wears a heavy leg iron. We do not know how old he is, whether short or tall, of villainous or ordinary appearance. We know, too, that he eats, gestures, sits down, files at the chain on his leg. But how does he eat? Slowly, with enjoyment? Ravenously? How does he really look, and what does he do, when he gives a start and asks Pip whether he has brought anyone with him? At the beginning of the scene, how rapidly delivered are the questions and answers? Later, how long does Pip watch the convict eat before he says, "I am glad you enjoy it"? In short, we are not provided with quite enough material to determine the *tempo* of the scene, the rate at which the action moves. Nor are we easily able to visualize the action as a continuous series of physical movements—the gestures, reactions, facial expressions that are often called simply *stage business*. All of these elements have serious implications for the meaning as well as for our enjoyment of the scene. For instance, when the convict says to Pip, "Thankee, my boy. I do," *how* does he say it, what does he really mean? Is it said indifferently, while the convict's attention is directed elsewhere, toward the soldiers who may be pursuing him? Is it said with elaborate politeness and sarcastic intent? Or is it said with deep emotion? Is the convict genuinely surprised and touched by Pip's concern?

Let us take a moment to compare the scene with the actual passage from which it has been extracted. This will provide the author's own authoritative answers to these and other questions, and it will illustrate the precise nature of the task confronting us in reading drama. For the point is, the additional material and the interpretive comments (here italicized) that Dickens provides his reader in the novel are the same sort of imaginary context and interpretive comment we must provide *for ourselves* when we have only the text of a play before us.

> *I was soon at the Battery, after that, and there was the right man—hugging himself and limping to and fro, as if he had never all night left off hugging and limping—waiting for me. He was awfully cold, to be sure. I half expected to see him drop down before my face and die of deadly cold. His eyes looked so awfully hungry, too, that when I handed him the file and he laid it down on the grass, it occurred to me he would have tried to eat it, if he had not seen my bundle. He did not turn me upside down this time, to get at what I had, but left me right side upwards while I opened the bundle and emptied my pockets.*
> "What's in the bottle, boy?" said he.
> "Brandy," said I.
> *He was already handing mincemeat down his throat in the most curious manner—more like a man who was putting it away somewhere in a violent hurry, than a man who was eating it—but he left off to take some of the liquor. He shivered all the while so violently, that it was quite as much as*

*he could do to keep the neck of the bottle between his teeth, without bit-
ing it off.*

"I think you have got the ague," said I.

"I'm much of your opinion, boy," said he.

"It's bad about here," I told him. "You've been lying out on the
meshes, and they're dreadful aguish. Rheumatic, too."

"I'll eat my breakfast afore they're the death of me," said he. "I'd do
that if I was going to be strung up to that there gallows as there is over
there, directly afterwards. I'll beat the shivers so far, I'll bet you."

*He was gobbling mincemeat, meat bone, bread, cheese, and pork pie,
all at once: staring distrustfully while he did so at the mist all round us,
and often stopping—even stopping his jaws—to listen. Some real or fancied
sound, some clink upon the river or breathing of beast upon the marsh,
now gave him a start, and he said, suddenly—*

"You're not a deceiving imp? You brought no one with you?"

"No, sir! No!"

"Nor give no one the office to follow you?"

"No!"

"Well," said he, "I believe you. You'd be but a fierce young hound indeed, if at your time of life you could help to hunt a wretched varmint,
hunted as near death and dunghill as this poor wretched varmint is!"

*Something clicked in his throat as if he had works in him like a clock,
and was going to strike. And he smeared his ragged rough sleeve over his
eyes.*

*Pitying his desolation, and watching him as he gradually settled down
upon the pie, I made bold to say,* "I am glad you enjoy it."

"Did you speak?"

"I said, I was glad you enjoyed it."

"Thankee, my boy. I do."

*I had often watched a large dog of ours eating his food; and I now
noticed a decided similarity between the dog's way of eating and the man's.
The man took strong sharp sudden bites, just like the dog. He swallowed,
or rather snapped up, every mouthful, too soon and too fast, and he looked
sideways here and there while he ate, as if he thought there was danger in
every direction of somebody's coming to take the pie away. He was altogether too unsettled in his mind over it, to appreciate it comfortably, I
thought, or to have anybody to dine with him, without making a chop with
his jaws at the visitor. In all of which particulars he was very like the dog.*

"I am afraid you won't leave any of it for him," *said I, timidly; after a
silence during which I had hesitated as to the politeness of making the remark.* "There's no more to be got where that came from." *It was the certainty of this fact that impelled me to offer the hint.*

"Leave any for him? Who's him?" *said my friend, stopping in his
crunching of pie-crust.*

"The young man. That you spoke of. That was hid with you."

"Oh, ah!" *he returned, with something like a gruff laugh.* "Him? Yes,
yes! He don't want no vittles."

"I thought he looked as if he did," said I.

The man stopped eating, and regarded me with the keenest scrutiny and the greatest surprise.

"Looked? When?"

"Just now."

"Where?"

"Yonder," *said I, pointing;* "over there, where I found him nodding asleep, and thought it was you."

He held me by the collar, and stared at me so, that I began to think his first idea about cutting my throat had revived.

"Dressed like you, you know, only with a hat," *I explained, trembling;* "and—and"—*I was very anxious to put this delicately—*" and with—the same reason for wanting to borrow a file. Didn't you hear the cannon last night?"

"Then, there *was* firing!" *he said to himself.* . . .

"He had a badly bruised face," *said I, recalling what I hardly knew I knew.*

"Not here?" *exclaimed the man, striking his left cheek mercilessly with the flat of his hand.*

"Yes, there!"

"Where is he?" *He crammed what little food was left, into the breast of his grey jacket.* "Show me the way he went. I'll pull him down, like a bloodhound. Curse this iron on my sore leg! Give us hold of the file, boy."

I indicated in what direction the mist had shrouded the other man, and he looked up at it for an instant. But he was down on the rank wet grass, filing at his iron like a madman, and not minding me or minding his own leg, which had an old chafe upon it and was bloody, but which he handled as roughly as if it had no more feeling in it than the file. I was very much afraid of him again, now that he had worked himself into this fierce hurry, and I was likewise very much afraid of keeping away from home any longer. I told him I must go, but he took no notice, so I thought the best thing I could do was to slip off. The last I saw of him, his head was bent over his knee and he was working hard at his fetter, muttering impatient imprecations at it and his leg. The last I heard of him, I stopped in the mist to listen, and the file was still going.

As this comparison makes clear, the elements of drama—character, setting, plot, tempo, tone, theme—are not really different from the elements of another literary form. But it should also be apparent that the dramatic script is not as self-sufficient, as complete, as a passage of prose fiction. The example from *Great Expectations* consists of dialogue and alternating passages of commentary and description that specify the precise reactions of each character, continually remind us of the particular action taking place, and give us a clear conception of tempo. A few lines from the end of the scene, for instance, when Pip reveals that he has actually met another man on the marsh, a single line of description accomplishes all three of these objectives: "*He held me by the collar, and stared at me so, that I began to think his first idea about cutting my throat had revived.*" (To understand what is meant by control of tempo, notice that the line requires about the same time for us to read as it would take an actor, on stage, to register surprise and to grab Pip's collar. When we read the passage, it is not possible for us to hurry the dialogue along faster than Dickens intended.)

Now, the play, if it is to convey all that the scene from the novel presents to us, requires a stage, scenery, actors, costumes and lighting, and above all, a skillful director. To be sure, the dramatist creates and controls the inner qualities of his characters, the verbal conflicts in which they engage, and the thematic meaning that is to emerge from these conflicts, but the director does the rest. He first interprets, then produces the play. He gives concrete form to the innumerable details and nuances of meaning that are only implicit in the script. Everything that Dickens has "added" to the basic scene between Pip and the convict that we took as our first example would have to be provided in some other way in a stage production. For instance, at the point where Dickens interpolates his long passage describing how the convict eats, the director would invent stage business that would show, directly to the audience, what Dickens describes for us. He would insist that the actor taking the part of the convict eat "like a dog," snapping at his food, glaring suspiciously, gulping down his meal like a hungry animal. He would suggest, too, that the actor taking Pip's part react to this with a subtle mixture of curiosity and repulsion, pity and fear. If properly done, the bit of action on stage would control the tempo of the scene just as the descriptive paragraph in the novel does; and it would suggest to us, at least as powerfully as in the novel, the same elements of meaning and characterization. In fact, if the play is properly produced, it may appear before us with a vitality and an illusion of reality greater even than that of the novel. As part of a theater audience, we suspend our disbelief and accept the characters and the action with neither hesitation nor conscious thought. When Othello is palpably standing over Desdemona's bed less than fifty feet from us, we do not require comments from the author to make the scene believable or to make Othello seem a "round" rather than a "flat" character. We are eyewitnesses. We do not question the testimony of our own senses.

On the other hand, if the play is not produced, but presented as dialogue and stage directions to be read, we may feel that it falls short of the novel in both clarity and power. Gone are the living actors, the fully developed setting, and the stage business that helps us to interpret or even to establish the meaning of particular lines and scenes. As members of the theater audience, we were able to load the burden of interpretation on the shoulders of professionals; as readers, we cannot do so. In the sections that follow, then, as we discuss a number of general problems and characteristics of drama, let us keep this primary requirement in mind. Critical discussions furnish useful approaches, but when we sit down to read any of the plays in this anthology, each of us will be faced with the necessity of actually producing the play for himself, in the theater of his own mind. The quality of his production, and therefore the excitement it holds for him, will be directly proportional to the amount of imagination, critical insight, and attention to detail that are brought to bear on the reading.

Dramatic Speech

Drama, as we have suggested, is a kind of imaginative communication. Like other types of literature, its core is a theme that may be anything from a broad vision of man and society to a few penetrating questions about a particular problem. This abstract idea is presented in specific, concrete terms. The playwright creates a group of individual men and women—his characters. He builds for them a particular setting in time and place. He involves them in a plot, a carefully selected series of incidents building toward a climax of conflict and a resolution of it. Like the novelist, who may use a convict to represent an entire social class and way of life, or like the poet, who may represent the abstract idea of "choosing a course" by showing us two tangible roads diverging in a forest, the playwright may use a character, an incident, or a part of the setting as a symbol to convey part of his meaning. Like other writers, too, he works with contrast, comparison, and various kinds of irony, arranging insights and revelations for us by setting characters and scenes side by side so that we may judge one against another and by allowing us to see chasms separating what a character says from what he means, or what he thinks he is accomplishing from what he is really doing to himself and others. Because of these general similarities, it is possible to transfer to the analysis of a play many of the critical techniques we apply to other genres. But if we wish to accomplish more than a crude analysis, we must pay particular attention to the nature of dramatic speech, the one crucial element that modifies and controls every other technique in drama.

Three qualities differentiate dramatic speech from ordinary talk, whether monologue or conversation. The first of these is *conflict*, the opposition of one force to another. In the play, this conflict may take several forms: the protagonist may be opposed by such vast forces as nature, fate, or "the gods"; by human society or some part of it; by another individual with a different set of goals and values; or even by a part of the protagonist's own mind and personality. These kinds of conflict are not really different from those that motivate plot, characterization, and thematic structure in other types of literature, but the techniques of presentation are clearly more limited in the drama than in other forms. Since everything in the play must be presented externally, in observable speech and action, the conflict cannot be *discussed* by the author, nor can it be revealed in the *unspoken* thoughts and reactions of a character. Thus, each force in the dramatic conflict is likely to be represented by a human spokesman—a Teiresias speaking for the gods Oedipus offends, a George Tesman representing the dull conventionality that destroys Hedda Gabler—or by some particular event that symbolizes the opposing force. Even when the character is in conflict with himself, the soliloquy that reveals his struggle is likely to suggest two characters rather than one. Consider the two contradictory attitudes in Othello's words as he prepares to murder Desdemona:

> *It is the cause, it is the cause, my soul.*
> Let me not name it to you, you chaste stars!
> It is the cause. *Yet I'll not shed her blood,*
> Nor scar that whiter skin of hers than snow,
> And smooth as monumental alabaster.
> *Yet she must die, else she'll betray more men.*
> Put out the light, and then put out the light.

Here, Othello is torn between killing Desdemona, an act motivated by his ideal of chastity, and letting her live because she is so beautiful and because, after all, he loves her. Earlier, he had suggested the same conflict when he had cried out:

> O thou black weed, why art so lovely fair?
> Thou smell'st so sweet that the sense aches at thee.
> Would thou hadst ne'er been born!

Conflict in dramatic speech may vary in intensity as well as kind, ranging from the overwhelming opposition of Oedipus and his fate to the trivial introductory arguments of Roderigo and Iago. Nor does the conflict have to be complete and explicit in a single dramatic scene. The primary opposition of forces in a play may be broken up and presented in a series of minor conflicts that almost escape our notice, at least on a first reading. The simplest passage of exposition, seemingly concerned only with factual values, may turn out to have been subtly controlled by a conflict that only becomes explicit in a later scene. The full force of the struggle between Oedipus and fate, for example, is not revealed until the end of the play, yet when we look back to the beginning, we discover that the major conflict has modified and controlled even the first, really minor, encounter between Oedipus and Creon, when Oedipus interrogates Creon a little too arrogantly and suspiciously, with too little regard for the possibility that he might be opposing the will of the gods:

OEDIPUS: And was there no one,
       No witness, no companion, to tell what happened?

CREON: They were all killed but one, and he got away
       So frightened that he could remember one thing only.

OEDIPUS: What was that one thing? One may be the key
       To everything, if we resolve to use it.

CREON: He said that a band of highwaymen attacked them,
Outnumbered them, and overwhelmed the King.

OEDIPUS: Strange, that a highwayman should be so daring—
Unless some faction here bribed him to do it.

CREON: We thought of that. But after Laïos' death
New troubles arose and we had no avenger.

OEDIPUS: What troubles could prevent you hunting down the killers?

CREON: The riddling Sphinx's song
Made us deaf to all mysteries but her own.

Here, we could scarcely hold that Oedipus and Creon are in conscious *argument* with one another. Nevertheless, there is an implicit opposition of attitudes—the one cautious, patient, and judicious; the other proudly self-confident, impatient of any resistance or delay, and rapidly decisive. Generally speaking, it is this kind of implicit opposition, rather than open controversy, that we are referring to when we speak of conflict in dramatic speech.

The second distinguishing characteristic of dramatic speech is a much greater degree of rhetorical complexity and significance than ordinary talk exhibits. This complexity and significance springs directly from the conflict, for a dramatic character, in the presence of another person, speaks "strategically" rather than directly and openly. He may have a conscious, though hidden, purpose that he hopes to achieve through disguise and indirection. If so, he will choose his words carefully to achieve this purpose, and our attention must focus not only on what he says, but on his purposes for saying it and on the effect his words have on other characters in the play. In Act II, Scene iii of *Othello*, for instance, Iago attempts to bolster Cassio's spirits after Othello has dismissed him for being drunk. If Iago is to set a trap that will destroy Othello, he must encourage Cassio to make a strong effort to regain his position rather than simply accepting the dismissal as just, and he must encourage him to do so by winning favor with Othello's wife. With these objectives in mind, he lectures Cassio, in a hearty, man-of-the-world tone, on the meaning of reputation:

CASSIO: Reputation, reputation, reputation! O! I have lost my reputation. I have lost the immortal part of myself, and what remains is bestial. My reputation, Iago, my reputation!

IAGO: As I am an honest man, I thought you had received some bodily wound. There is more sense in that than in reputation. Reputation is an idle and most false imposition, oft got without merit, and lost without deserving. You have lost no reputation at all, unless you repute yourself such a loser. What, man! there are ways to recover the general again.

You are but now cast in his mood (a punishment more in policy than in malice), even so as one would beat his offenceless dog to affright an imperious lion. Sue to him again, and he is yours.

Soon after this, in Act III, Scene iii, Iago sets about planting seeds of suspicion in Othello's mind, suggesting by apparently innocent questions that Desdemona and Cassio are carrying on an affair. His manner now is serious, cautious, suggesting that he is deeply troubled by something he has seen, but that he is unwilling to alarm Othello. Othello, worked up to an agony of apprehension, begs Iago to reveal his suspicions, whatever they may be, and Iago again speaks of reputation, eloquently stating just the opposite of what he had told Cassio:

IAGO: I do beseech you,
    Though I perchance am vicious in my guess
    (As, I confess, it is my nature's plague
    To spy into abuses, and oft my jealousy
    Shapes faults that are not)—I entreat you then,
    From one that so imperfectly conjects,
    You'd take no notice nor build yourself a trouble
    Out of my scattering and unsure observance.
    It were not for your quiet nor your good,
    Nor for my manhood, honesty, or wisdom,
    To let you know my thoughts.

OTHELLO: What dost thou mean?

IAGO: Good name in man, and woman, my dear lord,
    Is the immediate jewel of our souls.
    Who steals my purse steals trash. 'Tis something, nothing;
    'Twas mine, 'tis his, and has been slave to thousands;
    But he that filches from me my good name
    Robs me of that which not enriches him,
    And makes me poor indeed.

OTHELLO: By heaven, I'll know your thought.

IAGO: You cannot, if my heart were in your hand;
    Nor shall not, whilst 'tis in my custody.

In this speech, Iago accomplishes precisely what he had hoped. He convinces Othello that he is a man of deep principle, that he is devoted to Othello, that his suspicions are grave, and that his only reason for not accusing Cassio and Desdemona is that it would ruin their good names and make Othello's life miserable. He accuses most effectively by conscientiously refusing to accuse and at the same time makes himself appear a devoted, honorable friend. His utterance is thus the shrewd maneuvering of a man in conflict with another force. His talk is intensely meaningful because it is consciously strategic.

The greater than ordinary significance of dramatic speech is not limited to the consciously strategic passages, however. It is present even in scenes in which the conflict is so slight as to be scarcely noticed, and in which there is no devious purpose at all. In the brief exchange between Oedipus and Creon that was quoted earlier, Oedipus is not consciously maneuvering in the manner of Iago, yet he is unquestionably reacting to Creon's presence and adjusting his words to the particular situation in which he finds himself. If Creon were less cautious and reticent, Oedipus might be less suspicious and aggressive than he appears to be when he says, "What was that one thing? One may be the key/ To everything, *if we resolve to use it* [my italics]." Furthermore, if Creon were a servant rather than a brother of the queen, Oedipus would probably not think it necessary to explain *why* he wants to know "that one thing"—explanation is reserved for equals whom one does not wish to offend. And if Creon were a seer, with a presumed knowledge of divine plans, Oedipus would probably treat him with the elaborate courtesy he at first tenders Teiresias. What is true of this brief example is true of countless other scenes in all plays. Almost without exception, the conflict that is an essential quality of dramatic discourse generates rhetorical strategy, and this strategy, in turn, imparts greater than ordinary significance. As we read, we are forced to pause, to ponder, to estimate motives, effects, and deeper implications.

The third general characteristic of dramatic speech is its thematic significance. In all the examples to which we have referred, the speech of the characters contributes to the development of a meaning that goes far beyond the specific conflict. On the level of character and event, the exchange between Oedipus and Creon furnishes information necessary to our comprehension of the plot, and it suggests both the strengths and the weaknesses of Oedipus' character. On the level of theme, the encounter is one of several capsule presentations of the abstract problem with which Sophocles is concerned throughout the play—that is, man's proper relationship to the divine forces governing his world. Much the same may be said of the scenes from *Othello*, and in fact, of every dramatic speech. All the dialogue in a good play contributes in some way to the development of the theme. But to understand how this is so, we must turn to the larger question of dramatic structure, and particularly, the problem of the relationship between a concrete event or bit of dialogue and the abstract idea that is essential to dramatic structure.

Structure and Theme

Elsewhere in this volume, in the essay on poetry, we have discussed the relationship between the specific image or figure of speech and the idea that it defines and epitomizes. The simile, metaphor, and symbol, we pointed out, involve three degrees of comparison between an abstraction like "love" or "pleasure" or "the soul" and a concrete object, something as real, as perceptible to our senses as, let us say, a flower. The author may tell us that A is *like* B, "My love is like a red, red rose"; that A *is* B, "Gather ye rosebuds while ye may"; or, if he chooses to express his idea in symbolic terms, he may omit all reference to the first elements of the comparison, speak only of term B, and leave it to us to recognize an implicit comparison with term A, which is really what he is talking about. In "Songs of Experience," for example, William Blake describes the condition of the soul by speaking of a pest-ridden rose:

> O rose, thou art sick!
> The invisible worm
> That flies in the night,
> In the howling storm,
>
> Has found out thy bed
> Of crimson joy;
> And his dark secret love
> Does thy life destroy.

In this poem, our attention is focused on the literal rose and the real worm that destroys it, yet we also sense an implicit meaning far more serious and important than the complaint of a horticulturalist.

In a play, the relationship between the dramatic action and the theme it represents is analogous to this symbolic relationship between the particular rose and the abstraction it represents. In *Oedipus*, Sophocles does not tell us that hubris, or sacrilegious disregard of the divine will, is *similar to* the attitude of Oedipus, or even that hubris *is* the attitude he exhibits when, for instance, he leaps to a conclusion that Creon might have been negligent and plunges ahead in a blind search for the murderer. Instead, we are allowed to observe the particulars of term B of the comparison. We are presented with symbolic action. We watch a specific individual involved in a series of conflicts that motivate a series of specific reactions, physical as well as rhetorical. Our first concern is with the protagonist and the action in which he is involved, yet when we have finished the play, we realize that we have also been concerned with an idea, an abstract, general meaning that lies within and beyond the concrete, specific action in Thebes.

Notice we say "within" as well as "beyond." The relationship between the general theme and the specific form is not allegorical. Individual characters and conflicts do not each "stand for" some part of the theme, and critical reading is emphatically not a process of translating a series of events into a series of abstractions. The critic who tries to go beyond literary message-hunting remains as deeply concerned with the level of concrete events as he is with the level of abstract meaning. This double interest seems to be rooted in the relationship between event and meaning, observable in real life, that accounts for the very existence of plot in literature. According to one common misconception, only the extraordinary incident can be interesting. "Dogs bite men every day," runs the journalistic adage, "but when a man bites a dog, that's news." It is also true, however, that an event is interesting if it possesses a measure of general significance, if it suggests some meaning beyond itself. While this essay was being written, a woman was stabbed to death on a city street, in full view of thirty-eight people, not one of whom made a move to assist her, even to the extent of shouting for the police. The event has been deeply disturbing to many people, not because of any extraordinary quality in the crime itself, but because of the meaning it seems to convey, an intolerable element of cowardice and indifference in our society. Notice, however, that the murder and the meaning, which is to say, the levels of plot and theme in the incident, are inseparable from one another. Without the "thematic" revelation of our cowardice and indifference, the murder would be no more significant than thousands of similar crimes; and without the particulars of this actual murder, the meaning it reveals would have no more precision, and no more power over our minds, than thousands of general criticisms of our society.

Although the basic connection between an event and its meaning seems to be natural rather than artificial (no author or critic can simply command that an incident shall have a particular meaning), the meaning suggested by an incident is unquestionably conditioned by the values of the particular society in which it takes place and by the individual values of the author who relates it. Times change, and Oedipus' disregard of Teiresias' advice, or Hedda Gabler's revolt against the conventional view of woman's place in society were inevitably more meaningful to the original audiences than they can be for us. Furthermore, Sophocles and Ibsen have selected particular incidents and have presented them in the light of their own unique perceptions, emphasizing and subordinating various elements in order to present the meaning *as they saw it*. Because of these conditioning influences, the reader's task is difficult but rewarding. If the author has presented an action adequate to represent his meaning, the reader ought to be able to enjoy the action itself, to perceive the theme within the action, and to appreciate the techniques used by the author to make the action adequately represent the theme. In the process, one often gains comprehension of some of the values of the age for which the play was originally written. *Antigone, Measure for Measure, Hedda Gabler,* and *Pygmalion* reveal many details and demonstrate many specific values of the society for which each was written.

In order to develop a complex theme, a series of incidents, which is to say, individual conflicts, must be presented and unified in a plot. In a well-known definition, E. M. Forster suggests that the difference between a story and a plot depends on the way events are linked with one another. The story, he says, is a sequence of events simply following one another in time, whereas the plot is a series of events related to one another by cause and effect: X *causes* Y, which then *causes* Z. This definition does not go quite far enough, however. If what we have said about the relationship of meaning and event is true, we must suppose that it would be possible to have as a plot a series of quite dull, relatively meaningless events related to each other by cause and effect but almost useless for the purposes of serious literature. The truth seems to be that events of a plot, at least in the literature that endures, are really held together by a common thread of *meaning* more basic than the cause and effect relationship. Indeed, when we investigate the causal relationship of one incident to another, we are really searching for the meaning behind the relationship. We want to know how X caused Y, but we also want to know the meaning suggested by that fact and how the knowledge affects us. It is this coherence of meaning or thematic development—rather than any clear cause and effect linking of events in the plot—that enables us to see unity in certain *avant-garde* modern plays. The plot may be an illogical collection of fantastic events, or there may be no plot at all in the usual sense; yet we recognize that the play is a serious, unified work of art because we recognize that what is taking place on stage dramatizes a serious, unified idea or theme.

The relationship between the events of a plot, on the one hand, and the meaning that both controls and reveals itself through plot, on the other, represents the spinal column of dramatic structure. Every element of a great play, including even details that appear to be trivial ornaments, is finally dependent upon the central theme. Whether the dramatist is attempting a panoramic account of a character's life and times, as in a history play, or a sharply focused presentation of a single crisis and the incidents immediately pertaining to it, as in a play like *Oedipus*, he selects each conflict, shapes it, and relates it to other conflicts according to the pattern suggested by the central line of meaning.

Plot, Character, Setting

At this point, however, we had better leave the rarified atmosphere of theory and descend to a more practical level, for when we read a particular play, our immediate concern must be with the characters, the setting in which they move, and the plot in which they are caught up.

Generally speaking, when we survey the events of any play in an attempt to comprehend and summarize the plot, we discover that it may be divided into certain major parts. Since the characters themselves must provide all the information necessary to our understanding and must provide, too, a total context for the action, including such intangibles as "atmosphere," several of the first speeches and scenes are primarily *exposition*. The first few dramatic encounters in *Oedipus*, for example, establish a mood of fearful confusion, reveal to us that the plague in Thebes has been brought about by the city's failure to cleanse itself of a defilement (the presence of the former king's unknown murderer), and let us know both who the characters are and what they have been doing in the immediate past. We learn that Oedipus became king of Thebes shortly after the murder of Laïos, having won the gratitude of the city by freeing it from the ravages of the Sphinx. We find, too, that he is now married to Jocasta, sister of Creon and widow of the murdered king. In *Othello* and *Hedda Gabler*, necessary information is presented with equal rapidity. Brief conversations in *Othello* establish the relationships of Iago, Roderigo, Desdemona, Othello, and Cassio; in *Hedda Gabler*, we learn in similar fashion about the less complicated relationships of George Tesman, his aunt, and Hedda. In the one play, the plot is set moving by Othello's choice of Cassio as his lieutenant and by his elopement with Desdemona; in the other, by Hedda's surprising marriage to George Tesman, an unexciting scholar.

The brief scenes in which this information is conveyed also contribute, however, to the unified sequence of conflicts known as the *rising action*. These conflicts, linked by cause and effect and by their contribution to a single developing meaning, broaden our understanding of individual characters and of the forces to which the protagonist, or main character, is exposed. The ultimate confrontation of these forces, the single struggle for which the rising action carefully prepares, is the *climax*. It is usually at this point that the full meaning of the struggle between the protagonist and the forces of opposition becomes clear. The sequence of scenes immediately following this climax, the *falling action*, is a dramatic presentation of the results attendant on the climax, and thus, a further development of the thematic implications. There may also be a brief *dénouement* in which all the loose ends of plot, characterization, and theme are neatly and quickly tied. In the last hundred and fifty lines of *Othello*, for instance, Iago's treachery is exposed, and he is taken prisoner to be tortured and executed; Cassio explains how he came to have the fatal hand-kerchief; Emilia is killed, and Othello commits suicide; Cassio is placed in charge at Cyprus; and the Venetian party leaves for home.

Within this general pattern of rising and falling action, other principles of structure may operate. The play may consist of from one to five acts, and these may be divided into any number of scenes, each marking a chronological division of the action or a new conflict created by a new grouping of characters (in classical French drama, a new scene may be announced with every entrance and exit of a character). Since the dramatist may never intrude with direct commentary in the manner of the omniscient novelist and since the degree of control he may exercise through the quality of his narration and description is also markedly limited, the arrangement of these scenes becomes extremely important. Contrasts and comparisons of one scene with another furnish an effective technique for controlling the meaning and for implicitly commenting on it. In *Othello*, when we see Iago plotting with Roderigo and rousing Desdemona's father to vengeance, then telling Othello of Roderigo's villainy, then accepting the responsibility for escorting Desdemona to Cyprus, and finally plotting once more with Roderigo, we scarcely need Iago's asides and soliloquies to comprehend his villainy or to sense the atmosphere of passion and deceit in which Othello will play out his tragedy. In *Measure for Measure*, the central principle of structure is a contrast between two attitudes toward law and morality—the one epitomized by Angelo, the other, by the Duke.

Then too, individual acts may have a structure of their own, each building to a minor climax and ending with an emphatic "curtain line" that clearly marks a complete stage in the action. In *Hedda Gabler*, Act I ends with Hedda taking up General Gabler's pistols: they will, she says, furnish a means of "killing time" that will compensate for her failure to secure what she had hoped to find in her marriage. Act II ends as she awaits the results of a more dangerous pastime, her meddling in the destiny of Eilert Loveborg. At the end of Act III, when Loveborg has failed her, she gives him the pistol with which he kills himself, and symbolically destroys him by destroying the manuscript that is his life's work. At the end of Act IV, she destroys herself. Each of these acts, then, is both a part of the larger rising or falling action and a structured unit more or less complete in itself.

As we have implied throughout preceding sections of this essay, the drama is a highly compressed form demanding of the author great economy of means and demanding of the reader a vigorous imaginative contribution so that what is only suggested in a script may become vitally real in our minds. Nowhere are these demands more obvious than in the area of dramatic characterization. Let us recall for a moment the passage from *Great Expectations* with which we began this discussion. Characterization of the convict was accomplished with the aid of all the major techniques of prose fiction. We heard the convict talk; we saw him act; he was described; his thoughts were revealed in a variety of ways, though not directly; he was placed in a particular environment that helped us understand his desolation; Pip's comments were, at certain points, nearly explicit explanations of his character. In fact, Dickens had at his disposal every technique of characterization available to the writer of prose fiction, nor was he limited in using them, except by his own artistic judgment of the best ways to produce particular effects. He could—and often did—set the plot completely aside in order to develop at great length a character that caught his fancy. The playwright, on the other hand, is absolutely tied to the demands of a tightly unified, rapidly moving plot. Since no audience can be expected to sit for more than about three hours, he is limited by time. Finally, he is limited by the fact that drama is not description or explanation or comment or the unusual use of language, but direct representation of action—the script will be converted into real people on stage, "acting out" the plot as they would do in real life. These requirements sharply restrict the dramatist. Essentially, he must accomplish characterization through speech and action alone. Description and explanation, if used at all, must be presented by another character rather than by the author, who obviously has no place on stage. The passages of description or explanation must be as brief as they would be in normal conversation, and perhaps most important, they must not interfere with the steady progress of the action that is taking place. It is worth remembering that as long as the description or explanation continues, dramatic action is nearly suspended. We have exposition rather than conflict, conversation rather than dramatic speech. Then too, the comments on environment that can assist in the characterization of a person in prose fiction must be handled with great brevity in the play. In real life we do not, after all, go about giving extensive descriptions to another person of a scene that both of us are looking at. Similarly, there is something hopelessly artificial about a character's speaking aloud his inmost thoughts —as he must do if they are to be represented on stage. For this reason, soliloquies and asides must be reserved for those moments when there is no other way for the thoughts to be shown.

Despite these restrictions, a playwright's characters do come alive for us if we learn to pick up and develop even the smallest suggestions contained in their speech and action, paying particular attention to the "strategy" of their talk and to various contrasts in which they are involved. These contrasts are of two kinds, those involving parallel and diverging actions or attitudes by the same character in different scenes, and those involving another person, or "foil," whose attitudes may partly parallel, partly diverge from, the attitudes of the character under study. But to see what all this means in specific terms, let us examine the manner in which Isabella is presented in *Measure for Measure*. She is a key figure, representing one of several attitudes toward law, morality, the proper use of power, the relationship of the judge to the laws he applies. To understand the play, we must understand her. Yet the fact is, only about one-half of the four hundred lines she speaks in the play can be said to contribute directly to her characterization. She is introduced in Act I, Scene iv, after Angelo, intent on stamping out vice in the city, has applied the law in its very strictest interpretation and has condemned her brother Claudio to death for having slept with Juliet, to whom he is not yet formally betrothed, and having gotten her with child. Lucio, who seems to have no morals whatever, and who acts as a foil to Isabella, goes to the convent to inform her. Isabella enters, and her first words, significantly, are a demand for greater legal restraints:

ISABELLA: And have you nuns no farther privileges?

NUN: Are not these large enough?

ISABELLA: Yes, truly. I speak not as desiring more,
But rather wishing a more strict restraint
Upon the sisterhood, the votarists of Saint Clare.

Urged by Lucio, she appears before Angelo to plead for her brother's life but begins her discourse with another affirmation of her uncritical acceptance of the law:

ISABELLA: There is a vice that most I do abhor,
             And most desire should meet the blow of justice,
             For which I would not plead, but that I must,
             For which I must not plead, but that I am
             At war 'twixt will and will not.

At Angelo's first objection, she gives up the fight: "O just, but severe law!" she
says, "I had a brother then; heaven keep your honor." At Lucio's constant urging, she pleads at greater length and with far greater force, insisting on the
value of mercy above all else and striking hard at Angelo's reliance on the mere
outward forms of law, on the letter rather than the spirit. But despite her zeal,
it becomes clear to us that she is not, herself, convinced that she is right. She
is a woman in conflict, "At war 'twixt will and will not." Whatever she says
about the value of mercy is largely negated by her earlier insistence on stricter
laws. In two brief scenes, she emerges as a woman who is no more capable than
Angelo of modifying the law according to the demands of mercy and justice.
When Angelo offers her the choice between her own chastity and her brother's
life, she does not even consider the alternatives, but admits that she had been
trying to weaken the law out of partiality to her brother:

ISABELLA: O pardon me, my lord! It oft falls out
             To have what we would have, we speak not what we mean.
             I something do excuse the thing I hate
             For his advantage that I dearly love.

    It is not surprising, then, that in the next major scene in which she ap-
pears, when Claudio pathetically pleads for his life and suggests that the law
might be modified in the light of these special circumstances, she denounces
him outrageously:

CLAUDIO: Sweet sister, let me live.
             What sin you do to save a brother's life,
             Nature dispenses with the deed so far
             That it becomes a virtue.

ISABELLA: O you beast,
             O faithless coward, O dishonest wretch!
             Wilt thou be made a man out of my vice?
             Is't not a kind of incest, to take life
             From thine own sister's shame? What should I think?
             . . . Take my defiance,
             Die, perish. Might but my bending down
             Reprieve thee from thy fate, it should proceed.
             I'll pray a thousand prayers for thy death,
             No word to save thee.

This brief survey of Isabella's first three appearances in the play enables us to summarize, in specific terms, three major points about dramatic characterization. First, it should be noted that Isabella is presented solely through her speech and action in several contrasting scenes. In her first encounter with Angelo, she pleads eloquently for a kind of justice and mercy in which she does not really believe. We judge her attitude by her admission of the conflict between "will and will not," by comparison with her earlier demand for more severe restrictions in the convent, and by comparison with both the rigidity of Angelo and the cynical immorality of Lucio. In the scene with Claudio, we notice a clear reversal of earlier roles. In this scene, Isabella has become the judge, Claudio the pleader. Though his words to her are different from hers to Angelo, the request is the same: show mercy, modify or extenuate the strictest application of the law, judge by the spirit and the ends to be achieved rather than by the letter of the regulations. And Isabella reacts precisely as Angelo had earlier reacted to her plea for mercy, though with more heat since she is more deeply shaken than Angelo had been. Almost all of our judgments about her, we realize, are based on these comparisons and contrasts, and on the implications of her brief words to others. Second, we should note that Isabella exists primarily for her contribution to the theme of *Measure for Measure* and to its plot, rather than because of any intrinsic interest in her as a person. She is characterized, and she acts and speaks, only to the extent that she adds to the action of the play and the theme behind that action. Nothing about her is extraneous to that purpose. And the third point, linked with this, is that the characterization is really quite limited, surprisingly so. In fact, we know nothing about her apart from the one major characteristic of her attitude toward law. Everything else that makes her appear to be a real person in the play is something that we have inferred from the existence of this major trait or that we have invented in order to visualize her. We read her words, but we imagine her appearance, age, gestures, her thoughts, and the inflections of her voice—all the traits that the writer of prose fiction provides in so much greater detail than the dramatist. The characterization of other persons in the plays of this volume, it will be found, is handled in ways not very different from the manner in which Shakespeare presents Isabella.

Attention to the setting of the play is far less important than creative interpretation of character, conflict, and theme. Until comparatively recent times, few dramatists attempted to do much more than suggest, in a few words, the physical environment in which the action takes place. This is largely due to the characteristics of the theater available to each dramatist. Sophocles, writing for an audience seated in a huge amphitheater with no scenery whatever and no props but an altar and a building behind the actors, does no more than locate the action in "Thebes" or on "steps in front of the palace." Shakespeare, working in the Globe playhouse with its all-purpose inner and platform stages, its balcony, turret, and doors leading anywhere one wished, could shift the action from street to street in Venice and from wharf to street to citadel in

Cyprus. More important, he suggests physical characteristics of the scene in the speech of his characters and makes elements such as midnight darkness or a hurricane sea contribute to his theme of deceit and passionate action. Ibsen and Shaw, working in small theaters with a proscenium stage suggesting a room with only three sides, with artificial lighting and all the resources of the modern set designer at their command, were able to make their settings infinitely more detailed, though less flexible, than earlier dramatists had done.

It has been suggested that as we move from classical, to Shakespearean, to modern tragedy, the playwright's emphasis correspondingly shifts from man's struggle with fate, to his struggle with himself, to his struggle and defeat by forces in his immediate environment. Whatever the validity of this generalization, it is certainly true that the role of setting has shifted and been enlarged in ways that are consistent with such a theory. Oedipus' tragedy could be played anywhere, and the revelation of Othello's disastrous jealousy could be adequately reinforced by a rather general atmosphere of darkness and storm. But Hedda Gabler's tragedy depends on her struggle with a specific environment, the late nineteenth-century middle-class milieu, with unique costumes, attitudes, and furnishings. Because the costumes and furniture are directly relevant to the attitudes, props like a bonnet, pistols, or a painting of General Gabler become for Ibsen symbolic objects capable of carrying a great deal more meaning than one might expect. And a stage set that has both a glass door from which the protagonist may look out at the world and a small inner room into which she can retreat from it, is not a casual coincidence. The modern play, at least, demands that the reader make some attempt to reconstruct the stage set in detail while visualizing the characters who move in it.

Those who wish to go beyond a rudimentary consideration of the physical stage and its settings will find that the study is both fascinating and rewarding. One criterion of excellence in a dramatist is his ability to make the most effective use of the stage available to him, and our appreciation of the plays in this volume would probably be intensified if we were able to develop enough historical perspective to visualize each play as it was presented to the original audience. But this question is beyond the province of an introductory essay. Our immediate concern is with drama as a literary form, not as an example of stagecraft. To comprehend and enjoy a play by Shakespeare or Sophocles, it is not really imperative that we know all the details of their stages.

Tragedy and Comedy

The theme of a play, the general pattern of rising and falling action, the characterization, even the handling of individual scenes are all controlled by the larger patterns of the tragic and comic views of the human condition. Since these imply psychological as well as technical questions, their nature has been endlessly debated. Technically, in such matters as the nature and handling of the action, characterization of the protagonist, tone, and, of course, the ultimate resolution of the plot, the one seems to be distinguishable from the other; but philosophically, considered as two attitudes toward man and his problems, they begin to drift toward a middle ground, as in such "dark comedies" as *Measure for Measure.* Sharp technical distinctions tend to blur when we recognize that not all comedy is light and funny and not all tragedy ends with the hero's death. The differences become questions of degree rather than kind. Both comedy and tragedy spring from a conflict between the protagonist and another force. Both are concerned with the protagonist's reaction to this conflict, and in both, the conflict is finally resolved in a satisfying way: the audience is made to feel that it has experienced a carefully structured, completed action that has far more meaning than the ordinary experiences of real life. Furthermore, while the protagonist in comedy is never "defeated" in quite the manner of the tragic hero, he (and the audience with him) may experience something of the tragic hero's recognition of the forces opposing him; and there may be, at the end of the comedy, an aesthetic pleasure akin to the *catharsis* of tragedy, the purging of emotions that have been awakened by the action or the understanding that comes with our perception of the total meaning.

The important distinctions between the two forms develop from subtle distinctions in the quality of the force opposing the protagonist, the quality of his struggle with it, and the tone of its presentation. In tragedy, the force opposing the protagonist is not only overwhelming, but it is inscrutable, awesome, universal. The dramatic exploration of this force reveals problems that are both fundamental to man and finally beyond his control. In comedy, the force may be extremely powerful, and it may be of great significance, but it is not *crucially* significant, as the tragic force always seems to be. Nor is it inscrutable and awesome: the problems it presents are not insoluble. If the comic protagonist can be brought to comprehend the forces opposing him, he can, and usually does, resolve the conflict in a "happy" way. While Oedipus is destroyed by the strange fate divinely ordained for him; Othello, by the evil in mankind, as well as by the passions within himself; and Hedda Gabler, by the entire force of conventional middle-class views of woman's place; Eliza Doolittle finds herself in conflict with a social standard that depends on pronunciation—she learns to speak properly and triumphs over the forces that had opposed her.

As a result of these differences in the quality of the conflict, tragedy forces us to recognize the hopelessly uncorrectable flaws in ourselves and the immense, darkly frightening problems we all must face. The tragic hero becomes a representative of all mankind, bearing the defeat that all men suffer in a manner both courageous and dignified. The comic protagonist, on the other hand, is neither particularly dignified nor wisely courageous. His flaw is likely to be a correctable foible, a relatively minor weakness or failure to comprehend, and the force with which he must contend is more often than not a social rather than a metaphysical force, a generally acceptable standard of behavior or a "common sense" way of doing things that everyone except the protagonist can readily understand. Angelo, in *Measure for Measure*, furnishes an excellent illustration.

In the plays of this volume, we will encounter three significantly different views of tragedy. The first, of course, is illustrated by the two plays of Sophocles we have included. Aristotle's commentary in the *Poetics* is pertinent to them—indeed, it is largely based on the example of *Oedipus Rex*. For Aristotle, the essential quality of tragedy was action. Because his emphasis was almost entirely on the inscrutable forces *outside* man, with which we all must contend, character was for him of little importance except as a vehicle for the action and a means of exciting pity and fear in the audience. In order to excite our fear, the tragic protagonist was to be a man like ourselves (modern psychologists would say a man with whom we could identify); and in order to excite our pity, he was to be an unusually good and just man who brought unmerited misfortune on himself through a particular weakness—not a vice. The remaining characteristics of Aristotle's definition—including such parts of the plot as reversal of the situation, recognition, and the scene of suffering, as well as diction, thought, spectacle, and song—all have to do with reinforcement of the action, for the essence of tragedy was to be found there. For Shakespeare, in *Othello* and even in *Measure for Measure*, the forces with which man has to contend are not external but internal, not powers of fate or divinity but human weakness and passion. Tragedy for Shakespeare, therefore, seems to be less a matter of plot than of character. His greatest tragedies are dedicated not to showing what may *happen to* man, but what man *is*. Although the plot does not really become subservient to the characterization, the action of the play is much more closely related to character, and dependent on it, than in either of Sophocles' plays. One feels that any noble protagonist might replace Oedipus in the tragic action that destroys him, but only Othello, with his particular background and characteristics, could carry out the action of Shakespeare's play.

In our own time, there is a new emphasis. The tragic protagonist has become the absolutely ordinary, not to say mediocre, common man. Gone are the complexities of his character and his tragic flaw. He is once again the victim of forces almost totally outside himself, but these are now the pressures of his society and his general environment rather than the overwhelming powers of fate and the gods. Hedda Gabler is an excellent example, but Willie Loman, in Arthur Miller's *Death of a Salesman*, is perhaps even more definitive of the modern view. The tragic hero's character is no longer a mysterious entity, but merely the sum of his experiences, a shape formed by environmental influences and, in some instances, psychological drives that are neither conscious nor unique.

Within this general progression, numerous varieties of tragedy are distinguishable, together with nearly a dozen types of comedy. These have been relegated to the Glossary, along with such terms as "tragicomedy," "farce," "melodrama," and the "problem play," for what concerns us here is the relationship between the general patterns and the specific play, between the dramatist's overall conception of man and the specific techniques of *Antigone* or *Measure for Measure* or *Hedda Gabler*. It is not possible to lay down strict rules for the analysis of this relationship, for what may be called a metaphysical conception of man controls the other elements of the play in ways that are extremely subtle and elusive, and different in each play. Rather than generalize further, we had better study the problem in specific terms as we criticize each scene of a particular tragedy or comedy. Yet a tentative hypothesis about the principles on which the play is based will help us see how both a tragedy and a comedy may utilize the structure of exposition, rising action, climax, falling action, and catastrophe or dénouement, while differing so markedly from one another in their effects on the audience; or how the irony of *Oedipus* forces us to a terrible realization of man's helplessness in the grip of fate, while the irony of *Pygmalion* serves the purposes of light-hearted comedy and social satire.

Dramatic Criticism

In summary, a play may be regarded as an interrelated series of elements widening out from the specific and concrete to the general and abstract. A group of characters encounter one another in any number of conflicts taking place in a particular setting. These individual conflicts relate to one another in a causal sequence, the plot extending through one to five acts. More important, the events of the plot, taken together, develop and reveal a thematic statement. Beyond the theme, and controlling at least its general outlines, lies a conception of man and human action that may be characterized as tragic or comic, or more specifically as some combination or variation of the two, including revenge tragedy, comedy of manners, tragicomedy, farce, and melodrama. Involved in and partly controlling this conception are the values of the age—the Greek view of fate, for instance, or Renaissance views of human nature—and the values of the individual dramatists—Sophocles' view of the gods, Shakespeare's conception of man's capabilities, Shaw's particular views on society.

Although an adequate critical approach to drama demands some attention to each of these levels, we ordinarily find ourselves focusing on one. *Othello* may be discussed as a brilliant characterization of Iago and Othello, as an exploration of jealousy, as tragedy, as a revelation of Renaissance ideas of man, or as a revelation of Shakespeare's own interests and skills. It is best to begin at the level of conflict and character. Visualize each encounter as fully as possible, analyzing its details with an eye to fitting it into the larger patterns of plot and theme. Consider the relationship of each scene to others, paying particular attention to comparisons and contrasts within the total plot structure and, above all, searching for the common thread of meaning that lies within the sequence of conflicts. At some point in this preliminary reading, a tentative statement of theme will begin to emerge. Perhaps it will be no more than a suspicion that the play is about "the gods" or "woman's place in society"; but however vague the hypothesis, it will be possible to test individual scenes and the entire plot structure by reference to it and to bring into focus details that might otherwise have escaped our notice or our comprehension. It will also be possible, by reference to these details, to clarify our statement of theme or to substitute a better hypothesis if that seems necessary.

When this preliminary reading has produced a reasonably clear statement of theme, it is then possible to place the work in a larger frame of reference, comparing it with other plays dealing with similar themes, evaluating it as a representative of its particular comic or tragic mode, and placing it in both a biographical and historical perspective. We will find that the plays in this volume provide material for extremely interesting comparisons of structure, technique, theme, and dramatic type. *Antigone, Measure for Measure, Hedda Gabler,* and *Pygmalion,* for example, are all concerned with variations on the theme of man's proper relationship to his society, with *Antigone* and *Measure for Measure* directly comparable in their explorations into the meaning of law and justice, and in their emphasis on man's duty to a higher law than that contained in the statute books or the edicts of a temporal ruler. We will find a fascinating variety of examples of dramatic structure—in fact, structure is probably the major critical problem in *Measure for Measure*—and we will find, too, a complete range of dramatic types from classical tragedy through Shakespearean, to tragicomedy and the pure comedy of Shaw. It will be useful to explore at least a few of the possible comparisons as a final step in our reading of a particular play.

Laid out in this manner, the task of the critical reader may seem hopelessly complicated. In practice, however, we find that we are able, in most plays, to explore several levels at once and to solve a great many critical problems without even thinking about them. Great dramatists project their ideas in absorbing imitations of life in which the meaning reveals itself even to the unwary. The essence of all great literature is its ability to do just this, and critical reading of drama, like critical reading of other forms, is only an attempt to articulate what we have been made to experience in the work before us.

SOPHOCLES

❧ *Oedipus Rex*

PERSONS REPRESENTED:
Oedipus
A Priest
Creon
Teiresias
Iocastê
Messenger
Shepherd of Laïos
Second Messenger
Chorus of Theban Elders

THE SCENE *Before the palace of Oedipus, King of Thebes. A central door and two lateral doors open onto a platform which runs the length of the façade. On the platform, right and left, are altars; and three steps lead down into the "orchestra," or chorus-ground. At the beginning of the action these steps are crowded by suppliants who have brought branches and chaplets of olive leaves and who lie in various attitudes of despair.* OEDIPUS *enters.*

PROLOGUE

OEDIPUS: My children, generations of the living
In the line of Kadmos, nursed at his ancient hearth:
Why have you strewn yourselves before these altars
In supplication, with your boughs and garlands?
The breath of incense rises from the city
With a sound of prayer and lamentation.

                                    Children,
I would not have you speak through messengers,
And therefore I have come myself to hear you—
I, Oedipus, who bear the famous name.

[*To a* PRIEST]
You, there, since you are eldest in the company,
Speak for them all, tell me what preys upon you,

Translated by Dudley Fitts and Robert Fitzgerald.

Whether you come in dread, or crave some blessing:
Tell me, and never doubt that I will help you
In every way I can; I should be heartless
Were I not moved to find you suppliant here.

PRIEST: Great Oedipus, O powerful King of Thebes!
You see how all the ages of our people
Cling to your altar steps: here are boys
Who can barely stand alone, and here are priests
By weight of age, as I am a priest of God,
And young men chosen from those yet unmarried;
As for the others, all that multitude,
They wait with olive chaplets in the squares,
At the two shrines of Pallas, and where Apollo
Speaks in the glowing embers.
                                    Your own eyes
Must tell you: Thebes is tossed on a murdering sea
And can not lift her head from the surge of death.
A rust consumes the buds and fruits of the earth;
The herds are sick; children die unborn,
And labor is vain. The god of plague and pyre
Raids like detestable lightning through the city,
And all the house of Kadmos is laid waste,
All emptied, and all darkened: Death alone
Battens upon the misery of Thebes.

You are not one of the immortal gods, we know;
Yet we have come to you to make our prayer
As to the man surest in mortal ways
And wisest in the ways of God. You saved us
From the Sphinx, that flinty singer, and the tribute
We paid to her so long; yet you were never
Better informed than we, nor could we teach you:
It was some god breathed in you to set us free.

Therefore, O mighty King, we turn to you:
Find us our safety, find us a remedy,
Whether by counsel of the gods or men.
A king of wisdom tested in the past
Can act in a time of troubles, and act well.
Noblest of men, restore
Life to your city! Think how all men call you
Liberator for your triumph long ago;

Ah, when your years of kingship are remembered,
Let them not say *We rose, but later fell*—
Keep the State from going down in the storm!
Once, years ago, with happy augury,
You brought us fortune; be the same again!
No man questions your power to rule the land:
But rule over men, not over a dead city!
Ships are only hulls, citadels are nothing,
When no life moves in the empty passageways.

OEDIPUS: Poor children! You may be sure I know
All that you longed for in your coming here.
I know that you are deathly sick; and yet,
Sick as you are, not one is as sick as I.
Each of you suffers in himself alone
His anguish, not another's; but my spirit
Groans for the city, for myself, for you.

I was not sleeping, you are not waking me.
No, I have been in tears for a long while
And in my restless thought walked many ways.
In all my search, I found one helpful course,
And that I have taken: I have sent Creon,
Son of Menoikeus, brother of the Queen,
To Delphi, Apollo's place of revelation,
To learn there, if he can,
What act or pledge of mine may save the city.
I have counted the days, and now, this very day,
I am troubled, for he has overstayed his time.
What is he doing? He has been gone too long.
Yet whenever he comes back, I should do ill
To scant whatever duty God reveals.

PRIEST: It is a timely promise. At this instant
They tell me Creon is here.

OEDIPUS: O Lord Apollo!
May his news be fair as his face is radiant!

PRIEST: It could not be otherwise: he is crowned with bay,
The chaplet is thick with berries.

OEDIPUS: We shall soon know;
He is near enough to hear us now.

[*Enter* CREON]

O Prince:
Brother: son of Menoikeus:
What answer do you bring us from the god?

CREON: It is favorable. I can tell you, great afflictions
Will turn out well, if they are taken well.

OEDIPUS: What was the oracle? These vague words
Leave me still hanging between hope and fear.

CREON: Is it your pleasure to hear me with all these
Gathered around us? I am prepared to speak,
But should we not go in?

OEDIPUS: Let them all hear it.
It is for them I suffer, more than for myself.

CREON: Then I will tell you what I heard at Delphi.
In plain words
The god commands us to expel from the land of Thebes
An old defilement we are sheltering.
It is a deathly thing, beyond cure;
We must not let it feed upon us longer.

OEDIPUS: What defilement? How shall we rid ourselves of it?

CREON: By exile or death, blood for blood. It was
Murder that brought the plague-wind on the city.

OEDIPUS: Murder of whom? Surely the god has named him?

CREON: My lord: long ago Laïos was our king,
Before you came to govern us.

OEDIPUS;   I know;
I learned of him from others; I never saw him.

CREON: He was murdered; and Apollo commands us now
To take revenge upon whoever killed him.

OEDIPUS: Upon whom? Where are they? Where shall we find a clue
To solve that crime, after so many years?

CREON: Here in this land, he said. If we make enquiry,
We may touch things that otherwise escape us.

OEDIPUS: Tell me: Was Laïos murdered in his house,
Or in the fields, or in some foreign country?

CREON: He said he planned to make a pilgrimage.
He did not come home again.

OEDIPUS: And was there no one,
    No witness, no companion, to tell what happened?

CREON: They were all killed but one, and he got away
    So frightened that he could remember one thing only.

OEDIPUS: What was that one thing? One may be the key
    To everything, if we resolve to use it.

CREON: He said that a band of highwaymen attacked them,
    Outnumbered them, and overwhelmed the King.

OEDIPUS: Strange, that a highwayman should be so daring—
    Unless some faction here bribed him to do it.

CREON: We thought of that. But after Laïos' death
    New troubles arose and we had no avenger.

OEDIPUS: What troubles could prevent your hunting down the killers?

CREON: The riddling Sphinx's song
    Made us deaf to all mysteries but her own.

OEDIPUS: Then once more I must bring what is dark to light.
    It is most fitting that Apollo shows,
    As you do, this compunction for the dead.
    You shall see how I stand by you, as I should,
    To avenge the city and the city's god,
    And not as though it were for some distant friend,
    But for my own sake, to be rid of evil.
    Whoever killed King Laïos might—who knows?—
    Decide at any moment to kill me as well.
    By avenging the murdered king I protect myself.

    Come, then, my children: leave the altar steps,
    Lift up your olive boughs!
                   One of you go
    And summon the people of Kadmos to gather here.
    I will do all that I can; you may tell them that.

    [*Exit a* PAGE]

    So, with the help of God,
    We shall be saved—or else indeed we are lost.

PRIEST: Let us rise, children. It was for this we came,
    And now the King has promised it himself.
    Phoibos [Apollo] has sent us an oracle; may he descend
    Himself to save us and drive out the plague.

[*Exeunt* OEDIPUS *and* CREON *into the palace by the central door. The* PRIEST *and the* SUPPLIANTS *disperse* R *and* L. *After a short pause the* CHORUS *enters the orchestra.*]

PÁRODOS

CHORUS: What is the god singing in his profound   [STROPHE 1]
      Delphi of gold and shadow?
      What oracle for Thebes, the sunwhipped city?

Fear unjoints me, the roots of my heart tremble.

Now I remember, O Healer, your power, and wonder:
Will you send doom like a sudden cloud, or weave it
Like nightfall of the past?

Ah no: be merciful, issue of holy sound:
Dearest to our expectancy: be tender!

Let me pray to Athenê, the immortal daughter of Zeus, [ANTISTROPHE 1]
And to Artemis her sister
Who keeps her famous throne in the market ring,
And to Apollo, bowman at the far butts of heaven—

O gods, descend! Like three streams leap against
The fires of our grief, the fires of darkness;
Be swift to bring us rest!

As in the old time from the brilliant house
Of air you stepped to save us, come again!

Now our afflictions have no end,   [STROPHE 2]
Now all our stricken host lies down
And no man fights off death with his mind;

The noble plowland bears no grain,
And groaning mothers can not bear—

See, how our lives like birds take wing,
Like sparks that fly when a fire soars,
To the shore of the god of evening.

The plague burns on, it is pitiless,   [ANTISTROPHE 2]
Though pallid children laden with death
Lie unwept in the stony ways,

And old gray women by every path
Flock to the strand about the altars

There to strike their breasts and cry
Worship of Phoibos in wailing prayers:
Be kind, God's golden child!

There are no swords in this attack by fire, [STROPHE 3]
No shields, but we are ringed with cries.

Send the besieger plunging from our homes
Into the vast sea-room of the Atlantic
Or into the waves that foam eastward of Thrace—

For the day ravages what the night spares—

Destroy our enemy, lord of the thunder!
Let him be riven by lightning from heaven!

Phoibos Apollo, stretch the sun's bowstring, [ANTISTROPHE 3]
That golden cord, until it sing for us,
Flashing arrows in heaven!
                                    Artemis, Huntress,
Race with flaring lights upon our mountains!

O scarlet god, O golden-banded brow,
O Theban Bacchos in a storm of Maenads,

[*Enter* OEDIPUS, C.]

Whirl upon Death, that all the Undying hate!
Come with blinding cressets, come in joy!

SCENE I

OEDIPUS: Is this your prayer? It may be answered. Come,
            Listen to me, act as the crisis demands,
            And you shall have relief from all these evils.

            Until now I was a stranger to this tale,
            As I had been a stranger to the crime.
            Could I track down the murderer without a clue?
            But now, friends,
            As one who became a citizen after the murder,
            I make this proclamation to all Thebans:

If any man knows by whose hand Laïos, son of Labdakos,
Met his death, I direct that man to tell me everything,
No matter what he fears for having so long withheld it.
Let it stand as promised that no further trouble
Will come to him, but he may leave the land in safety.

Moreover: If anyone knows the murderer to be foreign,
Let him not keep silent: he shall have his reward from me.
However, if he does conceal it; if any man
Fearing for his friend or for himself disobeys this edict,
Hear what I propose to do:

I solemnly forbid the people of this country,
Where power and throne are mine, ever to receive that man
Or speak to him, no matter who he is, or let him
Join in sacrifice, lustration, or in prayer.
I decree that he be driven from every house,
Being, as he is, corruption itself to us: the Delphic
Voice of Zeus has pronounced this revelation.
Thus I associate myself with the oracle
And take the side of the murdered king.
As for the criminal, I pray to God—
Whether it be a lurking thief, or one of a number—
I pray that that man's life be consumed in evil and wretchedness.
And as for me, this curse applies no less
If it should turn out that the culprit is my guest here,
Sharing my hearth.
                                 You have heard the penalty.
I lay it on you now to attend to this
For my sake, for Apollo's, for the sick
Sterile city that heaven has abandoned.
Suppose the oracle had given you no command:
Should this defilement go uncleansed for ever?
You should have found the murderer: your king,
A noble king, had been destroyed!
                                               Now I,
Having the power that he held before me,
Having his bed, begetting children there
Upon his wife, as he would have, had he lived—
Their son would have been my children's brother,
If Laïos had had luck in fatherhood!
(But surely ill luck rushed upon his reign)—
I say I take the son's part, just as though
I were his son, to press the fight for him

And see it won! I'll find the hand that brought
Death to Labdakos' and Polydoros' child,
Heir of Kadmos' and Agenor's line.
And as for those who fail me,
May the gods deny them the fruit of the earth,
Fruit of the womb, and may they rot utterly!
Let them be wretched as we are wretched, and worse!

For you, for loyal Thebans, and for all
Who find my actions right, I pray the favor
Of justice, and of all the immortal gods.

CHORAGOS: Since I am under oath, my lord, I swear
I did not do the murder, I can not name
The murderer. Might not the oracle
That has ordained the search tell where to find him?

OEDIPUS: An honest question. But no man in the world
Can make the gods do more than the gods will.

CHORAGOS: There is one last expedient—

OEDIPUS: Tell me what it is.
Though it seem slight, you must not hold it back.

CHORAGOS: A lord clairvoyant to the lord Apollo,
As we all know, is the skilled Teiresias.
One might learn much about this from him, Oedipus.

OEDIPUS: I am not wasting time:
Creon spoke of this, and I have sent for him—
Twice, in fact; it is strange that he is not here.

CHORAGOS: The other matter—that old report—seems useless.

OEDIPUS: Tell me. I am interested in all reports.

CHORAGOS: The King was said to have been killed by highwaymen.

OEDIPUS: I know. But we have no witnesses to that.

CHORAGOS: If the killer can feel a particle of dread,
Your curse will bring him out of hiding!

OEDIPUS: No.
The man who dared that act will fear no curse.

[*Enter the blind seer* TEIRESIAS, *led by a* PAGE]

CHORAGOS: But there is one man who may detect the criminal.
This is Teiresias, this is the holy prophet
In whom, alone of all men, truth was born.

OEDIPUS: Teiresias: seer: student of mysteries,
              Of all that's taught and all that no man tells,
              Secrets of Heaven and secrets of the earth:
              Blind though you are, you know the city lies
              Sick with plague; and from this plague, my lord,
              We find that you alone can guard or save us.

              Possibly you did not hear the messengers?
              Apollo, when we sent to him,
              Sent us back word that this great pestilence
              Would lift, but only if we established clearly
              The identity of those who murdered Laïos.
              They must be killed or exiled.
                                          Can you use
              Birdflight or any art of divination
              To purify yourself, and Thebes, and me
              From this contagion? We are in your hands.
              There is no fairer duty
              Than that of helping others in distress.

TEIRESIAS: How dreadful knowledge of the truth can be
              When there's no help in truth! I knew this well,
              But did not act on it: else I should not have come.

OEDIPUS: What is troubling you? Why are your eyes so cold?

TEIRESIAS: Let me go home. Bear your own fate, and I'll
              Bear mine. It is better so: trust what I say.

OEDIPUS: What you say is ungracious and unhelpful
              To your native country. Do not refuse to speak.

TEIRESIAS: When it comes to speech, your own is neither temperate
              Nor opportune. I wish to be more prudent.

OEDIPUS: In God's name, we all beg you—

TEIRESIAS: You are all ignorant.
              No; I will never tell you what I know.
              Now it is my misery; then, it would be yours.

OEDIPUS: What! You do know something, and will not tell us?
              You would betray us all and wreck the State?

TEIRESIAS: I do not intend to torture myself, or you.
              Why persist in asking? You will not persuade me.

OEDIPUS: What a wicked old man you are! You'd try a stone's
              Patience! Out with it! Have you no feeling at all?

TEIRESIAS: You call me unfeeling. If you could only see
              The nature of your own feelings . . .

OEDIPUS: Why,
  Who would not feel as I do? Who could endure
  Your arrogance toward the city?

TEIRESIAS: What does it matter!
  Whether I speak or not, it is bound to come.

OEDIPUS: Then, if "it" is bound to come, you are bound to tell me.

TEIRESIAS: No, I will not go on. Rage as you please.

OEDIPUS: Rage? Why not!
                          And I'll tell you what I think:
  You planned it, you had it done, you all but
  Killed him with your own hands: if you had eyes,
  I'd say the crime was yours, and yours alone.

TEIRESIAS: So? I charge you, then,
  Abide by the proclamation you have made:
  From this day forth
  Never speak again to these men or to me;
  You yourself are the pollution of this country.

OEDIPUS: You dare say that! Can you possibly think you have
  Some way of going free, after such insolence?

TEIRESIAS: I have gone free. It is the truth sustains me.

OEDIPUS: Who taught you shamelessness? It was not your craft.

TEIRESIAS: You did. You made me speak. I did not want to.

OEDIPUS: Speak what? Let me hear it again more clearly.

TEIRESIAS: Was it not clear before? Are you tempting me?

OEDIPUS: I did not understand it. Say it again.

TEIRESIAS: I say that you are the murderer whom you seek.

OEDIPUS: Now twice you have spat out infamy. You'll pay for it!

TEIRESIAS: Would you care for more? Do you wish to be really angry?

OEDIPUS: Say what you will. Whatever you say is worthless.

TEIRESIAS: I say you live in hideous shame with those
  Most dear to you. You can not see the evil.

OEDIPUS: It seems you can go on mouthing like this for ever.

TEIRESIAS: I can, if there is power in truth.

OEDIPUS: There is:
  But not for you, not for you,
  You sightless, witless, senseless, mad old man!

TEIRESIAS: You are the madman. There is no one here
     Who will not curse you soon, as you curse me.

OEDIPUS: You child of endless night! You can not hurt me
     Or any other man who sees the sun.

TEIRESIAS: True: it is not from me your fate will come.
     That lies within Apollo's competence,
     As it is his concern.

OEDIPUS: Tell me:
     Are you speaking for Creon, or for yourself?

TEIRESIAS: Creon is no threat. You weave your own doom.

OEDIPUS: Wealth, power, craft of statesmanship!
     Kingly position, everywhere admired!
     What savage envy is stored up against these,
     If Creon, whom I trusted, Creon my friend,
     For this great office which the city once
     Put in my hands unsought—if for this power
     Creon desires in secret to destroy me!

     He has bought this decrepit fortune-teller, this
     Collector of dirty pennies, this prophet fraud—
     Why, he is no more clairvoyant than I am!
                                             Tell us:
     Has your mystic mummery ever approached the truth?
     When that hellcat the Sphinx was performing here,
     What help were you to these people?
     Her magic was not for the first man who came along:
     It demanded a real exorcist. Your birds—
     What good were they? or the gods, for the matter of that?
     But I came by,
     Oedipus, the simple man, who knows nothing—
     I thought it out for myself, no birds helped me!
     And this is the man you think you can destroy,
     That you may be close to Creon when he's king!
     Well, you and your friend Creon, it seems to me,
     Will suffer most. If you were not an old man,
     You would have paid already for your plot.

CHORAGOS: We can not see that his words or yours
     Have been spoken except in anger, Oedipus,
     And of anger we have no need. How can God's will
     Be accomplished best? That is what most concerns us.

TEIRESIAS: You are a king. But where argument's concerned
     I am your man, as much a king as you.

I am not your servant, but Apollo's.
I have no need of Creon to speak for me.

Listen to me. You mock my blindness, do you?
But I say that you, with both your eyes, are blind:
You can not see the wretchedness of your life,
Nor in whose house you live, no, nor with whom.
Who are your father and mother? Can you tell me?
You do not even know the blind wrongs
That you have done them, on earth and in the world below.
But the double lash of your parents' curse will whip you
Out of this land some day, with only night
Upon your precious eyes.
Your cries then—where will they not be heard?
What fastness of Kithairon will not echo them?
And that bridal-descant of yours—you'll know it then,
The song they sang when you came here to Thebes
And found your misguided berthing.
All this, and more, that you can not guess at now,
Will bring you to yourself among your children.

Be angry, then. Curse Creon. Curse my words.
I tell you, no man that walks upon the earth
Shall be rooted out more horribly than you.

OEDIPUS: Am I to bear this from him?—Damnation
Take you! Out of this place! Out of my sight!

TEIRESIAS: I would not have come at all if you had not asked me.

OEDIPUS: Could I have told that you'd talk nonsense, that
You'd come here to make a fool of yourself, and of me?

TEIRESIAS: A fool? Your parents thought me sane enough.

OEDIPUS: My parents again!—Wait: who were my parents?

TEIRESIAS: This day will give you a father, and break your heart.

OEDIPUS: Your infantile riddles! Your damned abracadabra!

TEIRESIAS: You were a great man once at solving riddles.

OEDIPUS: Mock me with that if you like; you will find it true.

TEIRESIAS: It was true enough. It brought about your ruin.

OEDIPUS: But if it saved this town?

TEIRESIAS: [*To the* PAGE]   Boy, give me your hand.

OEDIPUS: Yes, boy; lead him away.

                                        —While you are here
        We can do nothing. Go; leave us in peace.

TEIRESIAS: I will go when I have said what I have to say.
        How can you hurt me? And I tell you again:
        The man you have been looking for all this time,
        The damned man, the murderer of Laïos,
        That man is in Thebes. To your mind he is foreign-born,
        But it will soon be shown that he is a Theban,
        A revelation that will fail to please.

                                        A blind man,
        Who has his eyes now; a penniless man, who is rich now;
        And he will go tapping the strange earth with his staff.
        To the children with whom he lives now he will be
        Brother and father—the very same; to her
        Who bore him, son and husband—the very same
        Who came to his father's bed, wet with his father's blood.

        Enough. Go think that over.
        If later you find error in what I have said,
        You may say that I have no skill in prophecy.

        [*Exit* TEIRESIAS, *led by his* PAGE. OEDIPUS *goes into the palace.*]

ODE I

CHORUS: The Delphic stone of prophecies   [STROPHE 1]
        Remembers ancient regicide
        And a still bloody hand.
        That killer's hour of flight has come.
        He must be stronger than riderless
        Coursers of untiring wind,
        For the son of Zeus armed with his father's thunder
        Leaps in lightning after him;
        And the Furies follow him, the sad Furies.

        Holy Parnassos' peak of snow   [ANTISTROPHE 1]
        Flashes and blinds that secret man,
        That all shall hunt him down:
        Though he may roam the forest shade
        Like a bull gone wild from pasture
        To rage through glooms of stone.
        Doom comes down on him; flight will not avail him;

For the world's heart calls him desolate,
And the immortal Furies follow, for ever follow.

But now a wilder thing is heard   [STROPHE 2]
From the old man skilled at hearing Fate in the wing-beat of a bird.
Bewildered as a blown bird, my soul hovers and can not find
Foothold in this debate, or any reason or rest of mind.
But no man ever brought—none can bring
Proof of strife between Thebes' royal house,
Labdakos' line, and the son of Polybos;
And never until now has any man brought word
Of Laïos' dark death staining Oedipus the King.

Divine Zeus and Apollo hold   [ANTISTROPHE 2]
Perfect intelligence alone of all tales ever told;
And well though this diviner works, he works in his own night;
No man can judge that rough unknown or trust in second sight,
For wisdom changes hands among the wise.
Shall I believe my great lord criminal
At a raging word that a blind old man let fall?
I saw him, when the carrion woman faced him of old,
Prove his heroic mind! These evil words are lies.

SCENE II

CREON: Men of Thebes:
         I am told that heavy accusations
         Have been brought against me by King Oedipus.

         I am not the kind of man to bear this tamely.

         If in these present difficulties
         He holds me accountable for any harm to him
         Through anything I have said or done—why, then,
         I do not value life in this dishonor.
         It is not as though this rumor touched upon
         Some private indiscretion. The matter is grave.
         The fact is that I am being called disloyal
         To the State, to my fellow citizens, to my friends.

CHORAGOS: He may have spoken in anger, not from his mind.

CREON: But did you not hear him say I was the one
         Who seduced the old prophet into lying?

CHORAGOS: The thing was said; I do not know how seriously.

CREON: But you were watching him! Were his eyes steady?
     Did he look like a man in his right mind?

CHORAGOS: I do not know.
     I can not judge the behavior of great men.
     But here is the King himself.

[*Enter* OEDIPUS]

OEDIPUS: So you dared come back.
     Why? How brazen of you to come to my house,
     You murderer!
                         Do you think I do not know
     That you plotted to kill me, plotted to steal my throne?
     Tell me, in God's name: am I coward, a fool,
     That you should dream you could accomplish this?
     A fool who could not see your slippery game?
     A coward, not to fight back when I saw it?
     You are the fool, Creon, are you not? hoping
     Without support or friends to get a throne?
     Thrones may be won or bought: you could do neither.

CREON: Now listen to me. You have talked; let me talk, too.
     You can not judge unless you know the facts.

OEDIPUS: You speak well: there is one fact; but I find it hard
     To learn from the deadliest enemy I have.

CREON: That above all I must dispute with you.

OEDIPUS: That above all I will not hear you deny.

CREON: If you think there is anything good in being stubborn
     Against all reason, then I say you are wrong.

OEDIPUS: If you think a man can sin against his own kind
     And not be punished for it, I say you are mad.

CREON: I agree. But tell me: what have I done to you?

OEDIPUS: You advised me to send for that wizard, did you not?

CREON: I did. I should do it again.

OEDIPUS: Very well. Now tell me:
     How long has it been since Laïos—

CREON: What of Laïos?

OEDIPUS: Since he vanished in that onset by the road?

CREON: It was long ago, a long time.

OEDIPUS: And this prophet,
   Was he practicing here then?

CREON: He was; and with honor, as now.

OEDIPUS: Did he speak of me at that time?

CREON: He never did;
   At least, not when I was present.

OEDIPUS: But . . . the enquiry?
   I suppose you held one?

CREON: We did, but we learned nothing.

OEDIPUS: Why did the prophet not speak against me then?

CREON: I do not know; and I am the kind of man
   Who holds his tongue when he has no facts to go on.

OEDIPUS: There's one fact that you know, and you could tell it.

CREON: What fact is that? If I know it, you shall have it.

OEDIPUS: If he were not involved with you, he could not say
   That it was I who murdered Laïos.

CREON: If he says that, you are the one that knows it!—
   But now it is my turn to question you.

OEDIPUS: Put your questions. I am no murderer.

CREON: First, then: You married my sister?

OEDIPUS: I married your sister.

CREON: And you rule the kingdom equally with her?

OEDIPUS: Everything that she wants she has from me.

CREON: And I am the third, equal to both of you?

OEDIPUS: That is why I call you a bad friend.

CREON: No. Reason it out, as I have done.
   Think of this first: Would any sane man prefer
   Power, with all a king's anxieties,
   To that same power and the grace of sleep?
   Certainly not I.
   I have never longed for the king's power—only his rights.
   Would any wise man differ from me in this?
   As matters stand, I have my way in everything

With your consent, and no responsibilities.
If I were king, I should be a slave to policy.

How could I desire a scepter more
Than what is now mine—untroubled influence?
No, I have not gone mad; I need no honors,
Except those with the perquisites I have now.
I am welcome everywhere; every man salutes me,
And those who want your favor seek my ear,
Since I know how to manage what they ask.
Should I exchange this ease for that anxiety?
Besides, no sober mind is treasonable.
I hate anarchy
And never would deal with any man who likes it.

Test what I have said. Go to the priestess
At Delphi, ask if I quoted her correctly.
And as for this other thing: if I am found
Guilty of treason with Teiresias,
Then sentence me to death! You have my word
It is a sentence I should cast my vote for—
But not without evidence!
                            You do wrong
When you take good men for bad, bad men for good.
A true friend thrown aside—why, life itself
Is not more precious!
                            In time you will know this well:
For time, and time alone, will show the just man,
Though scoundrels are discovered in a day.

CHORAGOS: This is well said, and a prudent man would ponder it.
        Judgments too quickly formed are dangerous.

OEDIPUS: But is he not quick in his duplicity?
        And shall I not be quick to parry him?
        Would you have me stand still, hold my peace, and let
        This man win everything, through my inaction?

CREON: And you want—what is it, then? To banish me?

OEDIPUS: No, not exile. It is your death I want,
        So that all the world may see what treason means.

CREON: You will persist, then? You will not believe me?

OEDIPUS: How can I believe you?

CREON: Then you are a fool.

OEDIPUS: To save myself?

CREON: In justice, think of me.

OEDIPUS: You are evil incarnate.

CREON: But suppose that you are wrong?

OEDIPUS: Still I must rule.

CREON: But not if you rule badly.

OEDIPUS: O city, city!

CREON: It is my city, too!

CHORAGOS: Now, my lords, be still. I see the Queen,
Iocastê, coming from her palace chambers;
And it is time she came, for the sake of you both.
This dreadful quarrel can be resolved through her.

[*Enter* IOCASTE]

IOCASTE: Poor foolish men, what wicked din is this?
With Thebes sick to death, is it not shameful
That you should rake some private quarrel up?
[*To* OEDIPUS] Come into the house.
—And you, Creon, go now:
Let us have no more of this tumult over nothing.

CREON: Nothing? No, sister: what your husband plans for me
Is one of two great evils: exile or death.

OEDIPUS: He is right.
Why, woman I have caught him squarely
Plotting against my life.

CREON: No! Let me die
Accurst if ever I have wished you harm!

IOCASTE: Ah, believe it, Oedipus!
In the name of the gods, respect this oath of his
For my sake, for the sake of these people here!

[STROPHE 1]

CHORAGOS: Open your mind to her, my lord. Be ruled by her, I beg you!

OEDIPUS: What would you have me do?

CHORAGOS: Respect Creon's word. He has never spoken like a fool,
And now he has sworn an oath.

OEDIPUS: You know what you ask?

CHORAGOS: I do.

OEDIPUS: Speak on, then.

CHORAGOS: A friend so sworn should not be baited so,
In blind malice, and without final proof.

OEDIPUS: You are aware, I hope, that what you say
Means death for me, or exile at the least.

CHORAGOS: No, I swear by Helios, first in Heaven!   [STROPHE 2]
May I die friendless and accurst,
The worst of deaths, if ever I meant that!
      It is the withering fields
         That hurt my sick heart:
      Must we bear all these ills,
         And now your bad blood as well?

OEDIPUS: Then let him go. And let me die, if I must,
Or be driven by him in shame from the land of Thebes.
It is your unhappiness, and not his talk,
That touches me.
         As for him—
Wherever he is, I will hate him as long as I live.

CREON: Ugly in yielding, as you were ugly in rage!
Natures like yours chiefly torment themselves.

OEDIPUS: Can you not go? Can you not leave me?

CREON: I can.
You do not know me; but the city knows me,
And in its eyes I am just, if not in yours.

      [*Exit* CREON]

                                          [ANTISTROPHE 1]
CHORAGOS: Lady Iocastê, did you not ask the King to go to his chambers?

IOCASTE: First tell me what has happened.

CHORAGOS: There was suspicion without evidence; yet it rankled
As even false charges will.

IOCASTE: On both sides?

CHORAGOS: On both.

IOCASTE: But what was said?

CHORAGOS: Oh let it rest, let it be done with!
    Have we not suffered enough?

OEDIPUS: You see to what your decency has brought you:
    You have made difficulties where my heart saw none.

CHORAGOS: Oedipus, it is not once only I have told you—   [ANTISTROPHE 2]
    You must know I should count myself unwise
    To the point of madness, should I now forsake you—
        You, under whose hand,
          In the storm of another time,
          Our dear land sailed out free.
            But now stand fast at the helm!

IOCASTE: In God's name, Oedipus, inform your wife as well:
    Why are you so set in this hard anger?

OEDIPUS: I will tell you, for none of these men deserves
    My confidence as you do. It is Creon's work,
    His treachery, his plotting against me.

IOCASTE: Go on, if you can make this clear to me.

OEDIPUS: He charges me with the murder of Laïos.

IOCASTE: Has he some knowledge? Or does he speak from hearsay?

OEDIPUS: He would not commit himself to such a charge,
    But he has brought in that damnable soothsayer
    To tell his story.

IOCASTE: Set your mind at rest.
    If it is a question of soothsayers, I tell you
    That you will find no man whose craft gives knowledge
    Of the unknowable.

              Here is my proof:

An oracle was reported to Laïos once
(I will not say from Phoibos himself, but from
His appointed ministers, at any rate)
That his doom would be death at the hands of his own son—
His son, born of his flesh and of mine!

Now, you remember the story: Laïos was killed
By marauding strangers where three highways meet;
But his child had not been three days in this world

Before the King had pierced the baby's ankles
And had him left to die on a lonely mountain.

Thus, Apollo never caused that child
To kill his father, and it was not Laïos' fate
To die at the hands of his son, as he had feared.
This is what prophets and prophecies are worth!
Have no dread of them.
                              It is God himself
Who can show us what he wills, in his own way.

OEDIPUS: How strange a shadowy memory crossed my mind,
           Just now while you were speaking; it chilled my heart.

IOCASTE: What do you mean? What memory do you speak of?

OEDIPUS: If I understand you, Laïos was killed
           At a place where three roads meet.

IOCASTE: So it was said;
           We have no later story.

OEDIPUS: Where did it happen?

IOCASTE: Phokis, it is called: at a place where the Theban Way
           Divides into the roads toward Delphi and Daulia [Daulis].

OEDIPUS: When?

IOCASTE: We had the news not long before you came
           And proved the right to your succession here.

OEDIPUS: Ah, what net has God been weaving for me?

IOCASTE: Oedipus! Why does this trouble you?

OEDIPUS: Do not ask me yet.
           First, tell me how Laïos looked, and tell me
           How old he was.

IOCASTE: He was tall, his hair just touched
           With white; his form was not unlike your own.

OEDIPUS: I think that I myself may be accurst
           By my own ignorant edict.

IOCASTE: You speak strangely.
           It makes me tremble to look at you, my King.

OEDIPUS: I am not sure that the blind man can not see.
           But I should know better if you were to tell me—

IOCASTE: Anything—though I dread to hear you ask it.

OEDIPUS: Was the King lightly escorted, or did he ride
With a large company, as a ruler should?

IOCASTE: There were five men with him in all: one was a herald;
And a single chariot, which he was driving.

OEDIPUS: Alas, that makes it plain enough!
                                        But who—
Who told you how it happened?

IOCASTE: A household servant,
The only one to escape.

OEDIPUS: And is he still
A servant of ours?

IOCASTE: No; for when he came back at last
And found you enthroned in the place of the dead king,
He came to me, touched my hand with his, and begged
That I would send him away to the frontier district
Where only the shepherds go—
As far away from the city as I could send him.
I granted his prayer; for although the man was a slave,
He had earned more than this favor at my hands.

OEDIPUS: Can he be called back quickly?

IOCASTE: Easily.
But why?

OEDIPUS: I have taken too much upon myself
Without enquiry; therefore I wish to consult him.

IOCASTE: Then he shall come.
                              But am I not one also
To whom you might confide these fears of yours?

OEDIPUS: That is your right; it will not be denied you,
Now least of all; for I have reached a pitch
Of wild foreboding. Is there anyone
To whom I should sooner speak?

Polybos of Corinth is my father.
My mother is a Dorian: Meropê.
I grew up chief among the men of Corinth
Until a strange thing happened—
Not worth my passion, it may be, but strange.

At a feast, a drunken man maundering in his cups
Cries out that I am not my father's son!

I contained myself that night, though I felt anger
And a sinking heart. The next day I visited
My father and mother, and questioned them. They stormed,
Calling it all the slanderous rant of a fool;
And this relieved me. Yet the suspicion
Remained always aching in my mind;
I knew there was talk; I could not rest;
And finally, saying nothing to my parents,
I went to the shrine at Delphi.
The god dismissed my question without reply;
He spoke of other things.
                      Some were clear,
Full of wretchedness, dreadful, unbearable:
As, that I should lie with my own mother, breed
Children from whom all men would turn their eyes;
And that I should be my father's murderer.

I heard all this, and fled. And from that day
Corinth to me was only in the stars
Descending in that quarter of the sky,
As I wandered farther and farther on my way
To a land where I should never see the evil
Sung by the oracle. And I came to this country
Where, so you say, King Laïos was killed.

I will tell you all that happened there, my lady.

There were three highways
Coming together at a place I passed;
And there a herald came towards me, and a chariot
Drawn by horses, with a man such as you describe
Seated in it. The groom leading the horses
Forced me off the road at his lord's command;
But as this charioteer lurched over towards me
I struck him in my rage. The old man saw me
And brought his double goad down upon my head
As I came abreast.
                He was paid back, and more!
Swinging my club in this right hand I knocked him
Out of his car, and he rolled on the ground.
                          I killed him.

I killed them all.
Now if that stranger and Laïos were—kin,
Where is a man more miserable than I?
More hated by the gods? Citizen and alien alike
Must never shelter me or speak to me—
I must be shunned by all.

> And I myself
Pronounced this malediction upon myself!

Think of it: I have touched you with these hands,
These hands that killed your husband. What defilement!
Am I all evil, then? It must be so,
Since I must flee from Thebes, yet never again
See my own countrymen, my own country,
For fear of joining my mother in marriage
And killing Polybos, my father.

> Ah,
If I was created so, born to this fate,
Who could deny the savagery of God?

O holy majesty of heavenly powers!
May I never see that day! Never!
Rather let me vanish from the race of men
Than know the abomination destined me!

CHORAGOS: We too, my lord, have felt dismay at this.
But there is hope: you have yet to hear the shepherd.

OEDIPUS: Indeed, I fear no other hope is left me.

IOCASTE: What do you hope from him when he comes?

OEDIPUS: This much:
If his account of the murder tallies with yours,
Then I am cleared.

IOCASTE: What was it that I said
Of such importance?

OEDIPUS: Why, "marauders," you said,
Killed the King, according to this man's story.
If he maintains that still, if there were several,
Clearly the guilt is not mine: I was alone.
But if he says one man, singlehanded, did it,
Then the evidence all points to me.

IOCASTE: You may be sure that he said there were several;
And can he call back that story now? He cán not.

The whole city heard it as plainly as I.
But suppose he alters some detail of it:
He can not ever show that Laïos' death
Fulfilled the oracle: for Apollo said
My child was doomed to kill him; and my child—
Poor baby!—it was my child that died first.

No. From now on, where oracles are concerned,
I would not waste a second thought on any.

OEDIPUS: You may be right.
                                    But come: let someone go
For the shepherd at once. This matter must be settled.

IOCASTE: I will send for him.
            I would not wish to cross you in anything,
            And surely not in this.—Let us go in.

[*Exeunt into the palace*]

ODE II

CHORUS: Let me be reverent in the ways of right,   [STROPHE 1]
            Lowly the paths I journey on;
            Let all my words and actions keep
            The laws of the pure universe
            From highest Heaven handed down.
            For Heaven is their bright nurse,
            Those generations of the realms of light;
            Ah, never of mortal kind were they begot,
            Nor are they slaves of memory, lost in sleep:
            Their Father is greater than Time, and ages not.

            The tyrant is a child of Pride   [ANTISTROPHE 1]
            Who drinks from his great sickening cup
            Recklessness and vanity,
            Until from his high crest headlong
            He plummets to the dust of hope.
            That strong man is not strong.
            But let no fair ambition be denied;
            May God protect the wrestler for the State
            In government, in comely policy,
            Who will fear God, and on His ordinance wait.

Haughtiness and the high hand of disdain [STROPHE 2]
Tempt and outrage God's holy law;
And any mortal who dares hold
No immortal Power in awe
Will be caught up in a net of pain:
The price for which his levity is sold.
Let each man take due earnings, then,
And keep his hands from holy things,
And from blasphemy stand apart—
Else the crackling blast of heaven
Blows on his head, and on his desperate heart;
Though fools will honor impious men,
In their cities no tragic poet sings.

Shall we lose faith in Delphi's obscurities, [ANTISTROPHE 2]
We who have heard the world's core
Discredited, and the sacred wood
Of Zeus at Elis praised no more?
The deeds and the strange prophecies
Must make a pattern yet to be understood.
Zeus, if indeed you are lord of all,
Throned in light over night and day,
Mirror this in your endless mind:
Our masters call the oracle
Words on the wind, and the Delphic vision blind!
Their hearts no longer know Apollo,
And reverence for the gods has died away.

SCENE III

[*Enter* IOCASTE]

IOCASTE: Princes of Thebes, it has occurred to me
        To visit the altars of the gods, bearing
        These branches as a suppliant, and this incense.
        Our King is not himself: his noble soul
        Is overwrought with fantasies of dread,
        Else he would consider
        The new prophecies in the light of the old.
        He will listen to any voice that speaks disaster,
        And my advice goes for nothing.
        [*She approaches the altar, R.*]

To you, then, Apollo,
Lycean lord, since you are nearest, I turn in prayer.
Receive these offerings, and grant us deliverance
From defilement. Our hearts are heavy with fear
When we see our leader distracted, as helpless sailors
Are terrified by the confusion of their helmsman.

[*Enter* MESSENGER]

MESSENGER: Friends, no doubt you can direct me:
Where shall I find the house of Oedipus,
Or, better still, where is the King himself?

CHORAGOS: It is this very place, stranger; he is inside.
This is his wife and mother of his children.

MESSENGER: I wish her happiness in a happy house,
Blest in all the fulfillment of her marriage.

IOCASTE: I wish as much for you: your courtesy
Deserves a like good fortune. But now, tell me:
Why have you come? What have you to say to us?

MESSENGER: Good news, my lady, for your house and your husband.

IOCASTE: What news? Who sent you here?

MESSENGER: I am from Corinth.
The news I bring ought to mean joy for you,
Though it may be you will find some grief in it.

IOCASTE: What is it? How can it touch us in both ways?

MESSENGER: The word is that the people of the Isthmus
Intend to call Oedipus to be their king.

IOCASTE: But old King Polybos—is he not reigning still?

MESSENGER: No. Death holds him in his sepulchre.

IOCASTE: What are you saying? Polybos is dead?

MESSENGER: If I am not telling the truth, may I die myself.

IOCASTE: [*To a* MAIDSERVANT]   Go in, go quickly; tell this to your master.

O riddlers of God's will, where are you now!
This was the man whom Oedipus, long ago,
Feared so, fled so, in dread of destroying him—
But it was another fate by which he died.

[*Enter* OEDIPUS, C.]

OEDIPUS: Dearest Iocastê, why have you sent for me?

IOCASTE: Listen to what this man says, and then tell me
What has become of the solemn prophecies.

OEDIPUS: Who is this man? What is his news for me?

IOCASTE: He has come from Corinth to announce your father's death!

OEDIPUS: Is it true, stranger? Tell me in your own words.

MESSENGER: I can not say it more clearly: the King is dead.

OEDIPUS: Was it by treason? Or by an attack of illness?

MESSENGER: A little thing brings old men to their rest.

OEDIPUS: It was sickness, then?

MESSENGER: Yes, and his many years.

OEDIPUS: Ah!
Why should a man respect the Pythian hearth, or
Give heed to the birds that jangle above his head?
They prophesied that I should kill Polybos,
Kill my own father; but he is dead and buried,
And I am here—I never touched him, never,
Unless he died of grief for my departure,
And thus, in a sense, through me. No. Polybos
Has packed the oracles off with him underground.
They are empty words.

IOCASTE: Had I not told you so?

OEDIPUS: You had; it was my faint heart that betrayed me.

IOCASTE: From now on never think of those things again.

OEDIPUS: And yet—must I not fear my mother's bed?

IOCASTE: Why should anyone in this world be afraid,
Since Fate rules us and nothing can be foreseen?
A man should live only for the present day.

Have no more fear of sleeping with your mother:
How many men, in dreams, have lain with their mothers!
No reasonable man is troubled by such things.

OEDIPUS: That is true; only—
If only my mother were not still alive!
But she is alive. I can not help my dread.

IOCASTE: Yet this news of your father's death is wonderful.

OEDIPUS: Wonderful. But I fear the living woman.

MESSENGER: Tell me, who is this woman that you fear?

OEDIPUS: It is Meropê, man; the wife of King Polybos.

MESSENGER: Meropê? Why should you be afraid of her?

OEDIPUS: An oracle of the gods, a dreadful saying.

MESSENGER: Can you tell me about it or are you sworn to silence?

OEDIPUS: I can tell you, and I will.
Apollo said through his prophet that I was the man
Who should marry his own mother, shed his father's blood
With his own hands. And so, for all these years
I have kept clear of Corinth, and no harm has come—
Though it would have been sweet to see my parents again.

MESSENGER: And is this the fear that drove you out of Corinth?

OEDIPUS: Would you have me kill my father?

MESSENGER: As for that
You must be reassured by the news I gave you.

OEDIPUS: If you could reassure me, I would reward you.

MESSENGER: I had that in mind, I will confess: I thought
I could count on you when you returned to Corinth.

OEDIPUS: No: I will never go near my parents again.

MESSENGER: Ah, son, you still do not know what you are doing—

OEDIPUS: What do you mean? In the name of God tell me!

MESSENGER: —If these are your reasons for not going home.

OEDIPUS: I tell you, I fear the oracle may come true.

MESSENGER: And guilt may come upon you through your parents?

OEDIPUS: That is the dread that is always in my heart.

MESSENGER: Can you not see that all your fears are groundless?

OEDIPUS: How can you say that? They are my parents, surely?

MESSENGER: Polybos was not your father.

OEDIPUS: Not my father?

MESSENGER: No more your father than the man speaking to you.

OEDIPUS: But you are nothing to me!

MESSENGER: Neither was he.

OEDIPUS: Then why did he call me son?

MESSENGER: I will tell you:
    Long ago he had you from my hands, as a gift.

OEDIPUS: Then how could he love me so, if I was not his?

MESSENGER: He had no children, and his heart turned to you.

OEDIPUS: What of you? Did you buy me? Did you find me by chance?

MESSENGER: I came upon you in the crooked pass of Kithairon.

OEDIPUS: And what were you doing there?

MESSENGER: Tending my flocks.

OEDIPUS: A wandering shepherd?

MESSENGER: But your savior, son, that day.

OEDIPUS: From what did you save me?

MESSENGER: Your ankles should tell you that.

OEDIPUS: Ah, stranger, why do you speak of that childhood pain?

MESSENGER: I cut the bonds that tied your ankles together.

OEDIPUS: I have had the mark as long as I can remember.

MESSENGER: That was why you were given the name you bear.

OEDIPUS: God! Was it my father or my mother who did it?
    Tell me!

MESSENGER: I do not know. The man who gave you to me
    Can tell you better than I.

OEDIPUS: It was not you that found me, but another?

MESSENGER: It was another shepherd gave you to me.

OEDIPUS: Who was he? Can you tell me who he was?

MESSENGER: I think he was said to be one of Laïos' people.

OEDIPUS: You mean the Laïos who was king here years ago?

MESSENGER: Yes; King Laïos; and the man was one of his herdsmen.

OEDIPUS: Is he still alive? Can I see him?

MESSENGER: These men here
    Know best about such things.

OEDIPUS: Does anyone here
Know this shepherd that he is talking about?
Have you seen him in the fields, or in the town?
If you have, tell me. It is time things were made plain.

CHORAGOS: I think the man he means is that same shepherd
You have already asked to see. Iocastê perhaps
Could tell you something.

OEDIPUS: Do you know anything
About him, Lady? Is he the man we have summoned?
Is that the man this shepherd means?

IOCASTE: Why think of him?
Forget this herdsman. Forget it all.
This talk is a waste of time.

OEDIPUS: How can you say that,
When the clues to my true birth are in my hands?

IOCASTE: For God's love, let us have no more questioning!
Is your life nothing to you?
My own is pain enough for me to bear.

OEDIPUS: You need not worry. Suppose my mother a slave,
And born of slaves: no baseness can touch you.

IOCASTE: Listen to me, I beg you: do not do this thing!

OEDIPUS: I will not listen; the truth must be made known.

IOCASTE: Everything that I say is for your own good!

OEDIPUS: My own good
Snaps my patience, then; I want none of it.

IOCASTE: You are fatally wrong! May you never learn who you are!

OEDIPUS: Go, one of you, and bring the shepherd here.
Let us leave this woman to brag of her royal name.

IOCASTE: Ah, miserable!
That is the only word I have for you now.
That is the only word I can ever have.

[*Exit into the palace*]

CHORAGOS: Why has she left us, Oedipus? Why has she gone
In such a passion of sorrow? I fear this silence:
Something dreadful may come of it.

OEDIPUS: Let it come!
    However base my birth, I must know about it.
    The Queen, like a woman, is perhaps ashamed
    To think of my low origin. But I
    Am a child of Luck; I can not be dishonored.
    Luck is my mother; the passing months, my brothers,
    Have seen me rich and poor.
                  If this is so,
    How could I wish that I were someone else?
    How could I not be glad to know my birth?

ODE III

CHORUS: If ever the coming time were known   [STROPHE]
    To my heart's pondering,
    Kithairon, now by Heaven I see the torches
    At the festival of the next full moon,
    And see the dance, and hear the choir sing
    A grace to your gentle shade:
    Mountain where Oedipus was found,
    O mountain guard of a noble race!
    May the god who heals us lend his aid,
    And let that glory come to pass
    For our king's cradling-ground.

    Of the nymphs that flower beyond the years,   [ANTISTROPHE]
    Who bore you, royal child,
    To Pan of the hills or the Timberline Apollo,
    Cold in delight where the upland clears,
    Or Hermês for whom Kyllenê's heights are piled?
    Or flushed as evening cloud,
    Great Dionysos, roamer of mountains,
    He—was it he who found you there,
    And caught you up in his own proud
    Arms from the sweet god-ravisher
    Who laughed by the Muses' fountains?

SCENE IV

OEDIPUS: Sirs: though I do not know the man,
    I think I see him coming, this shepherd we want:
    He is old, like our friend here, and the men

Bringing him seem to be servants of my house.
But you can tell, if you have ever seen him.

[*Enter* SHEPHERD *escorted by* SERVANTS]

CHORAGOS: I know him, he was Laïos' man. You can trust him.

OEDIPUS: Tell me first, you from Corinth: is this the shepherd
We were discussing?

MESSENGER: This is the very man.

OEDIPUS: [*To* SHEPHERD]   Come here. No, look at me. You must answer
Everything I ask.—You belonged to Laïos?

SHEPHERD: Yes: born his slave, brought up in his house.

OEDIPUS: Tell me: what kind of work did you do for him?

SHEPHERD: I was a shepherd of his, most of my life.

OEDIPUS: Where mainly did you go for pasturage?

SHEPHERD: Sometimes Kithairon, sometimes the hills near-by.

OEDIPUS: Do you remember ever seeing this man out there?

SHEPHERD: What would he be doing there? This man?

OEDIPUS: This man standing here. Have you ever seen him before?

SHEPHERD: No. At least, not to my recollection.

MESSENGER: And that is not strange, my lord. But I'll refresh
His memory: he must remember when we two
Spent three whole seasons together, March to September,
On Kithairon or thereabouts. He had two flocks;
I had one. Each autumn I'd drive mine home
And he would go back with his to Laïos' sheepfold.—
Is this not true, just as I have described it?

SHEPHERD: True, yes; but it was all so long ago.

MESSENGER: Well, then: do you remember, back in those days,
That you gave me a baby boy to bring up as my own?

SHEPHERD: What if I did? What are you trying to say?

MESSENGER: King Oedipus was once that little child.

SHEPHERD: Damn you, hold your tongue!

OEDIPUS: No more of that!
It is your tongue needs watching, not this man's.

SHEPHERD: My King, my Master, what is it I have done wrong?

OEDIPUS: You have not answered his question about the boy.

SHEPHERD: He does not know . . . He is only making trouble . . .

OEDIPUS: Come, speak plainly, or it will go hard with you.

SHEPHERD: In God's name, do not torture an old man!

OEDIPUS: Come here, one of you; bind his arms behind him.

SHEPHERD: Unhappy king! What more do you wish to learn?

OEDIPUS: Did you give this man the child he speaks of?

SHEPHERD: I did.
And I would to God I had died that very day.

OEDIPUS: You will die now unless you speak the truth.

SHEPHERD: Yet if I speak the truth, I am worse than dead.

OEDIPUS: Very well; since you insist upon delaying—

SHEPHERD: No! I have told you already that I gave him the boy.

OEDIPUS: Where did you get him? From your house? From somewhere else?

SHEPHERD: Not from mine, no. A man gave him to me.

OEDIPUS: Is that man here? Do you know whose slave he was?

SHEPHERD: For God's love, my King, do not ask me any more!

OEDIPUS: You are a dead man if I have to ask you again.

SHEPHERD: Then . . . Then the child was from the palace of Laïos.

OEDIPUS: A slave child? or a child of his own line?

SHEPHERD: Ah, I am on the brink of dreadful speech!

OEDIPUS: And I of dreadful hearing. Yet I must hear.

SHEPHERD: If you must be told, then . . .
                                    They said it was Laïos' child;
But it is your wife who can tell you about that.

OEDIPUS: My wife!—Did she give it to you?

SHEPHERD: My lord, she did.

OEDIPUS: Do you know why?

SHEPHERD: I was told to get rid of it.

OEDIPUS: An unspeakable mother!

SHEPHERD: There had been prophecies . . .

OEDIPUS: Tell me.

SHEPHERD: It was said that the boy would kill his own father.

OEDIPUS: Then why did you give him over to this old man?

SHEPHERD: I pitied the baby, my King,
        And I thought that this man would take him far away
        To his own country.
                              He saved him—but for what a fate!
        For if you are what this man says you are,
        No man living is more wretched than Oedipus.

OEDIPUS: Ah God!
        It was true!
                    All the prophecies!
                                        —Now,
        O Light, may I look on you for the last time!
        I, Oedipus,
        Oedipus, damned in his birth, in his marriage damned,
        Damned in the blood he shed with his own hand!

        [*He rushes into the palace*]

ODE IV

CHORUS: Alas for the seed of men.   [STROPHE 1]

        What measure shall I give these generations
        That breathe on the void and are void
        And exist and do not exist?

        Who bears more weight of joy
        Than mass of sunlight shifting in images,
        Or who shall make his thoughts stay on
        That down time drifts away?

        Your splendor is all fallen.

        O naked brow of wrath and tears,
        O change of Oedipus!
        I who saw your days call no man blest—
        Your great days like ghósts góne.

That mind was a strong bow.

Deep, how deep you drew it then, hard archer,
At a dim fearful range,
And brought dear glory down!

You overcame the stranger—
The virgin with her hooking lion claws—
And though death sang, stood like a tower
To make pale Thebes take heart.

Fortress against our sorrows!

True king, giver of laws,
Majestic Oedipus!
No prince in Thebes had ever such renown,
No prince won such grace of power.

And now of all men ever known
Most pitiful is this man's story:
His fortunes are most changed, his state
Fallen to a low slave's
Ground under bitter fate.

O Oedipus, most royal one!
The great door that expelled you to the light
Gave at night—ah, gave night to your glory:
As to the father, to the fathering son.

All understood too late.

How could that queen whom Laïos won,
The garden that he harrowed at his height,
Be silent when that act was done?

But all eyes fail before time's eye,
All actions come to justice there.
Though never willed, though far down the deep past,
Your bed, your dread sirings,
Are brought to book at last.

Child by Laïos doomed to die,
Then doomed to lose that fortunate little death,
Would God you never took breath in this air
That with my wailing lips I take to cry:

For I weep the world's outcast.

I was blind, and now I can tell why:
Asleep, for you had given ease of breath
To Thebes, while the false years went by.

ÉXODOS

[*Enter, from the palace,* SECOND MESSENGER]

SECOND MESSENGER: Elders of Thebes, most honored in this land,
What horrors are yours to see and hear, what weight
Of sorrow to be endured, if, true to your birth,
You venerate the line of Labdakos!
I think neither Istros nor Phasis, those great rivers,
Could purify this place of the corruption
It shelters now, or soon must bring to light—
Evil not done unconsciously, but willed.

The greatest griefs are those we cause ourselves.

CHORAGOS: Surely, friend, we have grief enough already;
What new sorrow do you mean?

SECOND MESSENGER: The Queen is dead.

CHORAGOS: Iocastê? Dead? But at whose hand?

SECOND MESSENGER: Her own.
The full horror of what happened you can not know,
For you did not see it; but I, who did, will tell you
As clearly as I can how she met her death.

When she had left us,
In passionate silence, passing through the court,
She ran to her apartment in the house,
Her hair clutched by the fingers of both hands.
She closed the doors behind her; then, by that bed
Where long ago the fatal son was conceived—
That son who should bring about his father's death—
We heard her call upon Laïos, dead so many years,
And heard her wail for the double fruit of her marriage,
A husband by her husband, children by her child.

Exactly how she died I do not know:
For Oedipus burst in moaning and would not let us
Keep vigil to the end: it was by him

As he stormed about the room that our eyes were caught.
From one to another of us he went, begging a sword,
Cursing the wife who was not his wife, the mother
Whose womb had carried his own children and himself.
I do not know: it was none of us aided him,
But surely one of the gods was in control!
For with a dreadful cry
He hurled his weight, as though wrenched out of himself,
At the twin doors: the bolts gave, and he rushed in.
And there we saw her hanging, her body swaying
From the cruel cord she had noosed about her neck.
A great sob broke from him, heartbreaking to hear,
As he loosed the rope and lowered her to the ground.

I would blot out from my mind what happened next!
For the King ripped from her gown the golden brooches
That were her ornament, and raised them, and plunged them down
Straight into his own eyeballs, crying, "No more,
No more shall you look on the misery about me,
The horrors of my own doing! Too long you have known
The faces of those whom I should never have seen,
Too long been blind to those for whom I was searching!
From this hour, go in darkness!" And as he spoke,
He struck at his eyes—not once, but many times;
And the blood spattered his beard,
Bursting from his ruined sockets like red hail.

So from the unhappiness of two this evil has sprung,
A curse on the man and woman alike. The old
Happiness of the house of Labdakos
Was happiness enough: where is it today?
It is all wailing and ruin, disgrace, death—all
The misery of mankind that has a name—
And it is wholly and for ever theirs.

CHORAGOS: Is he in agony still? Is there no rest for him?

SECOND MESSENGER: He is calling for someone to lead him to the gates
So that all the children of Kadmos may look upon
His father's murderer, his mother's—no,
I can not say it!
              And then he will leave Thebes,
Self-exiled, in order that the curse
Which he himself pronounced may depart from the house.
He is weak, and there is none to lead him,

So terrible is his suffering.

But you will see:
Look, the doors are opening; in a moment
You will see a thing that would crush a heart of stone.

[*The central door is opened;* OEDIPUS, *blinded, is led in*]

CHORAGOS: Dreadful indeed for men to see.
Never have my own eyes
Looked on a sight so full of fear.

Oedipus!
What madness came upon you, what daemon
Leaped on your life with heavier
Punishment than a mortal man can bear?
No: I can not even
Look at you, poor ruined one.
And I would speak, question, ponder,
If I were able. No.
You make me shudder.

OEDIPUS: God.   God.
Is there a sorrow greater?
Where shall I find harbor in this world?
My voice is hurled far on a dark wind.
What has God done to me?

CHORAGOS: Too terrible to think of, or to see.

OEDIPUS: O cloud of night,   [STROPHE 1]
Never to be turned away: night coming on,
I can not tell how: night like a shroud!

My fair winds brought me here.
O God. Again
The pain of the spikes where I had sight,
The flooding pain
Of memory, never to be gouged out.

CHORAGOS: This is not strange.
You suffer it all twice over, remorse in pain,
Pain in remorse.

OEDIPUS: Ah dear friend   [ANTISTROPHE]
Are you faithful even yet, you alone?
Are you still standing near me, will you stay here,

Patient, to care for the blind?
                              The blind man!
Yet even blind I know who it is attends me,
By the voice's tone—
Though my new darkness hide the comforter.

CHORAGOS: Oh fearful act!
  What god was it drove you to rake black
  Night across your eyes?

OEDIPUS: Apollo. Apollo. Dear   [STROPHE 2]
  Children, the god was Apollo.
  He brought my sick, sick fate upon me.
  But the blinding hand was my own!
  How could I bear to see
  When all my sight was horror everywhere?

CHORAGOS: Everywhere; that is true.

OEDIPUS: And now what is left?
  Images? Love? A greeting even,
  Sweet to the senses? Is there anything?
  Ah, no, friends: lead me away.
  Lead me away from Thebes.
                              Lead the great wreck
  And hell of Oedipus, whom the gods hate.

CHORAGOS: Your fate is clear, you are not blind to that.
  Would God you had never found it out!

OEDIPUS: Death take the man who unbound   [ANTISTROPHE 2]
  My feet on that hillside
  And delivered me from death to life! What life?
  If only I had died,
  This weight of monstrous doom
  Could not have dragged me and my darlings down.

CHORAGOS: I would have wished the same.

OEDIPUS: Oh never to have come here
  With my father's blood upon me! Never
  To have been the man they call his mother's husband!
  Oh accurst! Oh child of evil,
  To have entered that wretched bed—
                              the selfsame one!
  More primal than sin itself, this fell to me.

CHORAGOS: I do not know how I can answer you.
    You were better dead than alive and blind.

OEDIPUS: Do not counsel me any more. This punishment
    That I have laid upon myself is just.
    If I had eyes,
    I do not know how I could bear the sight
    Of my father, when I came to the house of Death,
    Or my mother: for I have sinned against them both
    So vilely that I could not make my peace
    By strangling my own life.
                    Or do you think my children,
    Born as they were born, would be sweet to my eyes?
    Ah never, never! Nor this town with its high walls,
    Nor the holy images of the gods.
                 For I,
    Thrice miserable!—Oedipus, noblest of all the line
    Of Kadmos, have condemned myself to enjoy
    These things no more, by my own malediction
    Expelling that man whom the gods declared
    To be a defilement in the house of Laïos.
    After exposing the rankness of my own guilt,
    How could I look men frankly in the eyes?
    No, I swear it,
    If I could have stifled my hearing at its source,
    I would have done it and made all this body
    A tight cell of misery, blank to light and sound:
    So I should have been safe in a dark agony
    Beyond all recollection.
                Ah Kithairon!
    Why did you shelter me? When I was cast upon you,
    Why did I not die? Then I should never
    Have shown the world my execrable birth.

    Ah Polybos! Corinth, city that I believed
    The ancient seat of my ancestors: how fair
    I seemed, your child! And all the while this evil
    Was cancerous within me!
                For I am sick
    In my daily life, sick in my origin.

    O three roads, dark ravine, woodland and way
    Where three roads met: you, drinking my father's blood,

My own blood, spilled by my own hand: can you remember
The unspeakable things I did there, and the things
I went on from there to do?

                  O marriage, marriage!
The act that engendered me, and again the act
Performed by the son in the same bed—

                       Ah, the net
Of incest, mingling fathers, brothers, sons,
With brides, wives, mothers: the last evil
That can be known by men: no tongue can say
How evil!

         No. For the love of God, conceal me
Somewhere far from Thebes; or kill me; or hurl me
Into the sea, away from men's eyes for ever.

Come, lead me. You need not fear to touch me.
Of all men, I alone can bear this guilt.

[*Enter* CREON]

CHORAGOS: We are not the ones to decide; but Creon here
          May fitly judge of what you ask. He only
          Is left to protect the city in your place.

OEDIPUS: Alas, how can I speak to him? What right have I
          To beg his courtesy whom I have deeply wronged?

CREON: I have not come to mock you, Oedipus,
          Or to reproach you, either.

     [*To* ATTENDANTS]   —You, standing there:
          If you have lost all respect for man's dignity,
          At least respect the flame of Lord Helios:
          Do not allow this pollution to show itself
          Openly here, an affront to the earth
          And Heaven's rain and the light of day. No, take him
          Into the house as quickly as you can.
          For it is proper
          That only the close kindred see his grief.

OEDIPUS: I pray you in God's name, since your courtesy
          Ignores my dark expectation, visiting
          With mercy this man of all men most execrable:
          Give me what I ask—for your good, not for mine.

CREON: And what is it that you would have me do?

OEDIPUS: Drive me out of this country as quickly as may be
　　To a place where no human voice can ever greet me.

CREON: I should have done that before now—only,
　　God's will had not been wholly revealed to me.

OEDIPUS: But his command is plain: the parricide
　　Must be destroyed. I am that evil man.

CREON: That is the sense of it, yes; but as things are,
　　We had best discover clearly what is to be done.

OEDIPUS: You would learn more about a man like me?

CREON: You are ready now to listen to the god.

OEDIPUS: I will listen. But it is to you
　　That I must turn for help. I beg you, hear me.

　　The woman in there—
　　Give her whatever funeral you think proper:
　　She is your sister.
　　　　　　　—But let me go, Creon!
　　Let me purge my father's Thebes of the pollution
　　Of my living here, and go out to the wild hills,
　　To Kithairon, that has won such fame with me,
　　The tomb my mother and father appointed for me,
　　And let me die there, as they willed I should.
　　And yet I know
　　Death will not ever come to me through sickness
　　Or in any natural way: I have been preserved
　　For some unthinkable fate. But let that be.

　　As for my sons, you need not care for them.
　　They are men, they will find some way to live.
　　But my poor daughters, who have shared my table,
　　Who never before have been parted from their father—
　　Take care of them, Creon; do this for me.

　　And will you let me touch them with my hands
　　A last time, and let us weep together?
　　Be kind, my lord,
　　Great prince, be kind!
　　　　　　　　　Could I but touch them,
　　They would be mine again, as when I had my eyes.

[*Enter* ANTIGONE *and* ISMENE, *attended*]

Ah, God!
Is it my dearest children I hear weeping?
Has Creon pitied me and sent my daughters?

CREON: Yes, Oedipus: I knew that they were dear to you
In the old days, and know you must love them still.

OEDIPUS: May God bless you for this—and be a friendlier
Guardian to you than he has been to me!

Children, where are you?
Come quickly to my hands: they are your brother's—
Hands that have brought your father's once clear eyes
To this way of seeing—
                                    Ah dearest ones,
I had neither sight nor knowledge then, your father
By the woman who was the source of his own life!
And I weep for you—having no strength to see you—
I weep for you when I think of the bitterness
That men will visit upon you all your lives.
What homes, what festivals can you attend
Without being forced to depart again in tears?
And when you come to marriageable age,
Where is the man, my daughters, who would dare
Risk the bane that lies on all my children?
Is there any evil wanting? Your father killed
His father; sowed the womb of her who bore him;
Engendered you at the fount of his own existence!
That is what they will say of you.

                                    Then, whom
Can you ever marry? There are no bridegrooms for you,
And your lives must wither away in sterile dreaming.
O Creon, son of Menoikeus!
You are the only father my daughters have,
Since we, their parents, are both of us gone for ever.
They are your own blood: you will not let them
Fall into beggary and loneliness;
You will keep them from the miseries that are mine!
Take pity on them; see, they are only children,
Friendless except for you. Promise me this,
Great Prince, and give me your hand in token of it.

[CREON *clasps his right hand*]

Children:

I could say much, if you could understand me,
But as it is, I have only this prayer for you:
Live where you can, be as happy as you can—
Happier, please God, than God has made your father!

CREON: Enough. You have wept enough. Now go within.

OEDIPUS: I must; but it is hard.

CREON: Time eases all things.

OEDIPUS: But you must promise—

CREON: Say what you desire.

OEDIPUS: Send me from Thebes!

CREON: God grant that I may!

OEDIPUS: But since God hates me . . .

CREON: No, he will grant your wish.

OEDIPUS: You promise?

CREON: I can not speak beyond my knowledge.

OEDIPUS: Then lead me in.

CREON: Come now, and leave your children.

OEDIPUS: No! Do not take them from me!

CREON: Think no longer
That you are in command here, but rather think
How, when you were, you served your own destruction.

[*Exeunt into the house all but the* CHORUS; *the* CHORAGOS *chants directly
to the audience*]

CHORAGOS: Men of Thebes: look upon Oedipus.

This is the king who solved the famous riddle
And towered up, most powerful of men.
No mortal eyes but looked on him with envy,
Yet in the end ruin swept over him.

Let every man in mankind's frailty
Consider his last day; and let none
Presume on his good fortune until he find
Life, at his death, a memory without pain.

SOPHOCLES

❧ *Antigone*

PERSONS REPRESENTED
Antigonê
Ismenê
Eurydicê
Creon
Haimon
Teiresias
A Sentry
A Messenger
Chorus

SCENE   *Before the palace of Creon, King of Thebes. A central double door,*
and two lateral doors. A platform extends the length of the façade, and from
this platform three steps lead down into the "orchestra," or chorus-ground.
TIME   *Dawn of the day after the repulse of the Argive army from the assault*
on Thebes.

PROLOGUE

[ANTIGONE *and* ISMENE *enter from the central door of the Palace*]

ANTIGONE: Ismenê, dear sister,
         You would think that we had already suffered enough
         For the curse on Oedipus:
         I cannot imagine any grief
         That you and I have not gone through. And now—
         Have they told you of the new decree of our King Creon?

ISMENE: I have heard nothing: I know
         That two sisters lost two brothers, a double death
         In a single hour; and I know that the Argive army
         Fled in the night; but beyond this, nothing.

ANTIGONE: I thought so. And that is why I wanted you
         To come out here with me. There is something we must do.

Translated by Dudley Fitts and Robert Fitzgerald.

ISMENE: Why do you speak so strangely?

ANTIGONE: Listen, Ismenê:
    Creon buried our brother Eteoclês
    With military honors, gave him a soldier's funeral,
    And it was right that he should; but Polyneicês,
    Who fought as bravely and died as miserably—
    They say that Creon has sworn
    No one shall bury him, no one mourn for him,
    But his body must lie in the fields, a sweet treasure
    For carrion birds to find as they search for food.
    That is what they say, and our good Creon is coming here
    To announce it publicly; and the penalty—
    Stoning to death in the public square!
                           There it is,
    And now you can prove what you are:
    A true sister, or a traitor to your family.

ISMENE: Antigonê, you are mad! What could I possibly do?

ANTIGONE: You must decide whether you will help me or not.

ISMENE: I do not understand you. Help you in what?

ANTIGONE: Ismenê, I am going to bury him. Will you come?

ISMENE: Bury him! You have just said the new law forbids it.

ANTIGONE: He is my brother. And he is your brother, too.

ISMENE: But think of the danger! Think what Creon will do!

ANTIGONE: Creon is not strong enough to stand in my way.

ISMENE: Ah sister!
    Oedipus died, everyone hating him
    For what his own search brought to light, his eyes
    Ripped out by his own hand; and Iocastê died,
    His mother and wife at once: she twisted the cords
    That strangled her life; and our two brothers died,
    Each killed by the other's sword. And we are left:
    But oh, Antigonê,
    Think how much more terrible than these
    Our own death would be if we should go against Creon
    And do what he has forbidden! We are only women,
    We cannot fight with men, Antigonê!
    The law is strong, we must give in to the law
    In this thing, and in worse. I beg the Dead
    To forgive me, but I am helpless: I must yield

To those in authority. And I think it is dangerous business
To be always meddling.

ANTIGONE: If that is what you think,
I should not want you, even if you asked to come.
You have made your choice, you can be what you want to be.
But I will bury him; and if I must die,
I say that this crime is holy: I shall lie down
With him in death, and I shall be as dear
To him as he to me.
                    It is the dead,
Not the living, who make the longest demands:
We die for ever . . .
                    You may do as you like,
Since apparently the laws of the gods mean nothing to you.

ISMENE: They mean a great deal to me; but I have no strength
To break laws that were made for the public good.

ANTIGONE: That must be your excuse, I suppose. But as for me,
I will bury the brother I love.

ISMENE: Antigonê,
I am so afraid for you!

ANTIGONE: You need not be:
You have yourself to consider, after all.

ISMENE: But no one must hear of this, you must tell no one!
I will keep it a secret, I promise!

ANTIGONE: Oh, tell it! Tell everyone!
Think how they'll hate you when it all comes out
If they learn that you knew about it all the time!

ISMENE: So fiery! You should be cold with fear.

ANTIGONE: Perhaps. But I am doing only what I must.

ISMENE: But can you do it? I say that you cannot.

ANTIGONE: Very well: when my strength gives out, I shall do no more.

ISMENE: Impossible things should not be tried at all.

ANTIGONE: Go away, Ismenê:
I shall be hating you soon, and the dead will too,
For your words are hateful. Leave me my foolish plan:
I am not afraid of the danger; if it means death,
It will not be the worst of deaths—death without honor.

ISMENE: Go then, if you feel that you must.
          You are unwise,
          But a loyal friend indeed to those who love you.

          [*Exit into the Palace.* ANTIGONE *goes off, L. Enter the* CHORUS]

PÁRODOS

CHORUS: Now the long blade of the sun, lying   [STROPHE 1]
          Level east to west, touches with glory
          Thebes of the Seven Gates. Open, unlidded
          Eye of golden day! O marching light
          Across the eddy and rush of Dircê's stream,
          Striking the white shields of the enemy
          Thrown headlong backward from the blaze of morning!

CHORAGOS: Polyneicês their commander
          Roused them with windy phrases,
          He the wild eagle screaming
          Insults above our land,
          His wings their shields of snow,
          His crest their marshalled helms.

CHORUS: Against our seven gates in a yawning ring   [ANTISTROPHE 1]
          The famished spears came onward in the night;
          But before his jaws were sated with our blood,
          Or pinefire took the garland of our towers,
          He was thrown back; and as he turned, great Thebes—
          No tender victim for his noisy power—
          Rose like a dragon behind him, shouting war.

CHORAGOS: For God hates utterly
          The bray of bragging tongues;
          And when he beheld their smiling,
          Their swagger of golden helms,
          The frown of his thunder blasted
          Their first man from our walls.

CHORUS: We heard his shout of triumph high in the air   [STROPHE 2]
          Turn to a scream; far out in a flaming arc
          He fell with his windy torch, and the earth struck him.,
          And others storming in fury no less than his
          Found shock of death in the dusty joy of battle.

CHORAGOS: Seven captains at seven gates
          Yielded their clanging arms to the god

That bends the battle-line and breaks it.
These two only, brothers in blood,
Face to face in matchless rage,
Mirroring each the other's death,
Clashed in long combat.

CHORUS: But now in the beautiful morning of victory   [ANTISTROPHE 2]
Let Thebes of the many chariots sing for joy!
With hearts for dancing we'll take leave of war:
Our temples shall be sweet with hymns of praise,
And the long night shall echo with our chorus.

SCENE I

CHORAGOS: But now at last our new King is coming:
Creon of Thebes, Menoikeus' son.
In this auspicious dawn of his reign
What are the new complexities
That shifting Fate has woven for him?
What is his counsel? Why has he summoned
The old men to hear him?

[*Enter* CREON *from the Palace, C. He addresses the* CHORUS *from the top step*]

CREON: Gentlemen: I have the honor to inform you that our Ship of State, which recent storms have threatened to destroy, has come safely to harbor at last, guided by the merciful wisdom of Heaven. I have summoned you here this morning because I know that I can depend upon you: your devotion to King Laïos was absolute; you never hesitated in your duty to our late ruler Oedipus; and when Oedipus died, your loyalty was transferred to his children. Unfortunately, as you know, his two sons, the princes Eteoclês and Polyneicês, have killed each other in battle; and I, as the next in blood, have succeeded to the full power of the throne.

I am aware, of course, that no Ruler can expect complete loyalty from his subjects until he has been tested in office. Nevertheless, I say to you at the very outset that I have nothing but contempt for the kind of Governor who is afraid, for whatever reason, to follow the course that he knows is best for the State; and as for the man who sets private friendship above the public welfare—I have no use for him, either. I call God to witness that if I saw my country headed for ruin, I should not be afraid to speak out plainly; and I need hardly remind you that I would never have any dealings with an enemy of the people. No one values friendship more highly than I; but we must remember that friends made at the risk of wrecking our Ship are not real friends at all.

These are my principles, at any rate, and that is why I have made the following decision concerning the sons of Oedipus: Eteoclês, who died as a man should die, fighting for his country, is to be buried with full military honors, with all the ceremony that is usual when the greatest heroes die; but his brother Polyneicês, who broke his exile to come back with fire and sword against his native city and the shrines of his fathers' gods, whose one idea was to spill the blood of his blood and sell his own people into slavery—Polyneicês, I say, is to have no burial: no man is to touch him or say the least prayer for him; he shall lie on the plain, unburied; and the birds and the scavenging dogs can do with him whatever they like.

This is my command, and you can see the wisdom behind it. As long as I am King, no traitor is going to be honored with the loyal man. But whoever shows by word and deed that he is on the side of the State—he shall have my respect while he is living, and my reverence when he is dead.

CHORAGOS: If that is your will, Creon son of Menoikeus,
You have the right to enforce it: we are yours.

CREON: That is my will. Take care that you do your part.

CHORAGOS: We are old men: let the younger ones carry it out.

CREON: I do not mean that: the sentries have been appointed.

CHORAGOS: Then what is it that you would have us do?

CREON: You will give no support to whoever breaks this law.

CHORAGOS: Only a crazy man is in love with death!

CREON: And death it is; yet money talks, and the wisest
Have sometimes been known to count a few coins too many.

[Enter SENTRY from L.]

SENTRY: I'll not say that I'm out of breath from running, King, because every time I stopped to think about what I have to tell you, I felt like going back. And all the time a voice kept saying, "You fool, don't you know you're walking straight into trouble?"; and then another voice: "Yes, but if you let somebody else get the news to Creon first, it will be even worse than that for you!" But good sense won out, at least I hope it was good sense, and here I am with a story that makes no sense at all; but I'll tell it anyhow, because, as they say, what's going to happen's going to happen, and—

CREON: Come to the point. What have you to say?

SENTRY: I did not do it. I did not see who did it. You must not punish me
for what someone else has done.

CREON: A comprehensive defense! More effective, perhaps,
If I knew its purpose. Come: what is it?

SENTRY: A dreadful thing . . . I don't know how to put it—

CREON: Out with it!

SENTRY: Well, then;
The dead man—
            Polyneicês—

[*Pause. The* SENTRY *is overcome, fumbles for words.* CREON *waits impassively*]

                                out there—
                                        someone—

New dust on the slimy flesh!

[*Pause. No sign from* CREON]

Someone has given it burial that way, and
Gone . . .

[*Long pause.* CREON *finally speaks with deadly control*]

CREON: And the man who dared do this?

SENTRY: I swear I
Do not know! You must believe me!
                                    Listen:
The ground was dry, not a sign of digging, no,
Not a wheeltrack in the dust, no trace of anyone.
It was when they relieved us this morning: and one of them,
The corporal, pointed to it.
                            There it was,
The strangest—
            Look:
The body, just mounded over with light dust: you see?
Not buried really, but as if they'd covered it
Just enough for the ghost's peace. And no sign
Of dogs or any wild animal that had been there.

And then what a scene there was! Every man of us
Accusing the other: we all proved the other man did it,

We all had proof that we could not have done it.
We were ready to take hot iron in our hands,
Walk through fire, swear by all the gods,
It was not I!
I do not know who it was, but it was not I!

[CREON's *rage has been mounting steadily, but the* SENTRY *is too intent upon his story to notice it*]

And then, when this came to nothing, someone said
A thing that silenced us and made us stare
Down at the ground: you had to be told the news,
And one of us had to do it! We threw the dice,
And the bad luck fell to me. So here I am,
No happier to be here than you are to have me:
Nobody likes the man who brings bad news.

CHORAGOS: I have been wondering, King: can it be that the gods have done this?

CREON: [*Furiously*]   Stop!
Must you doddering wrecks
Go out of your heads entirely? "The gods!"
Intolerable!
The gods favor this corpse? Why? How had he served them?
Tried to loot their temples, burn their images,
Yes, and the whole State, and its laws with it!
Is it your senile opinion that the gods love to honor bad men?
A pious thought!—
                    No, from the very beginning
There have been those who have whispered together,
Stiff-necked anarchists, putting their heads together,
Scheming against me in alleys. These are the men,
And they have bribed my own guard to do this thing.
[*Sententiously*]   Money!
There's nothing in the world so demoralizing as money.
Down go your cities,
Homes gone, men gone, honest hearts corrupted,
Crookedness of all kinds, and all for money!

[*To* SENTRY]   But you—!
I swear by God and by the throne of God,
The man who has done this thing shall pay for it!
Find that man, bring him here to me, or your death
Will be the least of your problems: I'll string you up

Alive, and there will be certain ways to make you
Discover your employer before you die;
And the process may teach you a lesson you seem to have missed:
The dearest profit is sometimes all too dear:
That depends on the source. Do you understand me?
A fortune won is often misfortune.

SENTRY: King, may I speak?

CREON: Your very voice distresses me.

SENTRY: Are you sure that it is my voice, and not your conscience?

CREON: By God, he wants to analyze me now!

SENTRY: It is not what I say, but what has been done, that hurts you.

CREON: You talk too much.

SENTRY: Maybe; but I've done nothing.

CREON: Sold your soul for some silver: that's all you've done.

SENTRY: How dreadful it is when the right judge judges wrong!

CREON: Your figures of speech
May entertain you now; but unless you bring me the man,
You will get little profit from them in the end.

[*Exit* CREON *into the Palace*]

SENTRY: "Bring me the man"—!
I'd like nothing better than bringing him the man!
But bring him or not, you have seen the last of me here.
At any rate, I am safe!

[*Exit* SENTRY]

ODE I

CHORUS: Numberless are the world's wonders, but none   [STROPHE 1]
    More wonderful than man; the stormgray sea
    Yields to his prows, the huge crests bear him high;
    Earth, holy and inexhaustible, is graven
    With shining furrows where his plows have gone
    Year after year, the timeless labor of stallions.

    The lightboned birds and beasts that cling to cover,   [ANTISTROPHE 1]
    The lithe fish lighting their reaches of dim water,

All are taken, tamed in the net of his mind;
The lion on the hill, the wild horse windy-maned,
Resign to him; and his blunt yoke has broken
The sultry shoulders of the mountain bull.

Words also, and thought as rapid as air,   [STROPHE 2]
He fashions to his good use; statecraft is his,
And his the skill that deflects the arrows of snow,
The spears of winter rain: from every wind
He has made himself secure—from all but one:
In the late wind of death he cannot stand.

O clear intelligence, force beyond all measure!   [ANTISTROPHE 2]
O fate of man, working both good and evil!
When the laws are kept, how proudly his city stands!
When the laws are broken, what of his city then?
Never may the anárchic man find rest at my hearth,
Never be it said that my thoughts are his thoughts.

SCENE II

[*Re-enter* SENTRY *leading* ANTIGONE]

CHORAGOS: What does this mean? Surely this captive woman
            Is the Princess, Antigonê. Why should she be taken?

SENTRY: Here is the one who did it! We caught her
          In the very act of burying him.—Where is Creon?

CHORAGOS: Just coming from the house.

          [*Enter* CREON, *C.*]

CREON: What has happened?
          Why have you come back so soon?

SENTRY: [*Expansively*]   O King,
          A man should never be too sure of anything:
          I would have sworn
          That you'd not see me here again: your anger
          Frightened me so, and the things you threatened me with;
          But how could I tell then
          That I'd be able to solve the case so soon?

          No dice-throwing this time: I was only too glad to come!

Here is this woman. She is the guilty one:
We found her trying to bury him.

Take her, then; question her; judge her as you will.
I am through with the whole thing now, and glad of it.

CREON: But this is Antigonê! Why have you brought her here?

SENTRY: She was burying him, I tell you!

CREON: [*Severely*]   Is this the truth?

SENTRY: I saw her with my own eyes. Can I say more?

CREON: The details: come, tell me quickly!

SENTRY: It was like this:
After those terrible threats of yours, King,
We went back and brushed the dust away from the body.
The flesh was soft by now, and stinking,
So we sat on a hill to windward and kept guard.
No napping this time! We kept each other awake.
But nothing happened until the white round sun
Whirled in the center of the round sky over us:
Then, suddenly,
A storm of dust roared up from the earth, and the sky
Went out, the plain vanished with all its trees
In the stinging dark. We closed our eyes and endured it.
The whirlwind lasted a long time, but it passed;
And then we looked, and there was Antigonê!
I have seen
A mother bird come back to a stripped nest, heard
Her crying bitterly a broken note or two
For the young ones stolen. Just so, when this girl
Found the bare corpse, and all her love's work wasted,
She wept, and cried on heaven to damn the hands
That had done this thing.
                                 And then she brought more dust
And sprinkled wine three times for her brother's ghost.

We ran and took her at once. She was not afraid,
Not even when we charged her with what she had done.
She denied nothing.
                                 And this was a comfort to me,
And some uneasiness: for it is a good thing
To escape from death, but it is no great pleasure

To bring death to a friend.
                                        Yet I always say
There is nothing so comfortable as your own safe skin!

CREON: [*Slowly, dangerously*]   And you, Antigonê,
      You with your head hanging—do you confess this thing?

ANTIGONE: I do. I deny nothing.

CREON: [*To* SENTRY]   You may go.

      [*Exit* SENTRY]

      [*To* ANTIGONE]   Tell me, tell me briefly:
      Had you heard my proclamation touching this matter?

ANTIGONE: It was public. Could I help hearing it?

CREON: And yet you dared defy the law.

ANTIGONE: I dared.
      It was not God's proclamation. That final Justice
      That rules the world below makes no such laws.

      Your edict, King, was strong,
      But all your strength is weakness itself against
      The immortal unrecorded laws of God.
      They are not merely now: they were, and shall be,
      Operative for ever, beyond man utterly.

      I knew I must die, even without your decree:
      I am only mortal. And if I must die
      Now, before it is my time to die,
      Surely this is no hardship: can anyone
      Living, as I live, with evil all about me,
      Think Death less than a friend? This death of mine
      Is of no importance; but if I had left my brother
      Lying in death unburied, I should have suffered.
      Now I do not.
                        You smile at me. Ah Creon,
      Think me a fool, if you like; but it may well be
      That a fool convicts me of folly.

CHORAGOS: Like father, like daughter: both headstrong, deaf to reason!
      She has never learned to yield.

CREON: She has much to learn.
      The inflexible heart breaks first, the toughest iron
      Cracks first, and the wildest horses bend their necks

At the pull of the smallest curb.
Pride? In a slave?

This girl is guilty of a double insolence,
Breaking the given laws and boasting of it.
Who is the man here,
She or I, if this crime goes unpunished?
Sister's child, or more than sister's child,
Or closer yet in blood—she and her sister
Win bitter death for this!

[*To* SERVANTS]   Go, some of you,
Arrest Ismenê. I accuse her equally.
Bring her: you will find her sniffling in the house there.

Her mind's a traitor: crimes kept in the dark
Cry for light, and the guardian brain shudders;
But how much worse than this
Is brazen boasting of barefaced anarchy!

ANTIGONE: Creon, what more do you want than my death?

CREON: Nothing.
That gives me everything.

ANTIGONE: Then I beg you: kill me.
This talking is a great weariness: your words
Are distasteful to me, and I am sure that mine
Seem so to you. And yet they should not seem so:
I should have praise and honor for what I have done.
All these men here would praise me
Were their lips not frozen shut with fear of you.

[*Bitterly*]   Ah the good fortune of kings,
Licensed to say and do whatever they please!

CREON: You are alone here in that opinion.

ANTIGONE: No, they are with me. But they keep their tongues in leash.

CREON: Maybe. But you are guilty, and they are not.

ANTIGONE: There is no guilt in reverence for the dead.

CREON: But Eteoclês—was he not your brother too?

ANTIGONE: My brother too.

CREON: And you insult his memory?

ANTIGONE: [*Softly*]   The dead man would not say that I insult it.

CREON: He would: for you honor a traitor as much as him.

ANTIGONE: His own brother, traitor or not, and equal in blood.

CREON: He made war on his country. Eteoclês defended it.

ANTIGONE: Nevertheless, there are honors due all the dead.

CREON: But not the same for the wicked as for the just.

ANTIGONE: Ah Creon, Creon,
    Which of us can say what the gods hold wicked?

CREON: An enemy is an enemy, even dead.

ANTIGONE: It is my nature to join in love, not hate.

CREON: [*Finally losing patience*]   Go join them, then; if you must have your
    love,
Find it in hell!

CHORAGOS: But see, Ismenê comes:

[*Enter* ISMENE, *guarded*]

    Those tears are sisterly, the cloud
    That shadows her eyes rains down gentle sorrow.

CREON: You too, Ismenê,
    Snake in my ordered house, sucking my blood
    Stealthily—and all the time I never knew
    That these two sisters were aiming at my throne!
                                    Ismenê,
    Do you confess your share in this crime, or deny it?
    Answer me.

ISMENE: Yes, if she will let me say so. I am guilty.

ANTIGONE: [*Coldly*]   No, Ismenê. You have no right to say so.
    You would not help me, and I will not have you help me.

ISMENE: But now I know what you meant; and I am here
    To join you, to take my share of punishment.

ANTIGONE: The dead man and the gods who rule the dead
    Know whose act this was. Words are not friends.

ISMENE: Do you refuse me, Antigonê? I want to die with you:
    I too have a duty that I must discharge to the dead.

ANTIGONE: You shall not lessen my death by sharing it.

ISMENE: What do I care for life when you are dead?

ANTIGONE: Ask Creon. You're always hanging on his opinions.

ISMENE: You are laughing at me. Why, Antigonê?

ANTIGONE: It's a joyless laughter, Ismenê.

ISMENE: But can I do nothing?

ANTIGONE: Yes. Save yourself. I shall not envy you.
There are those who will praise you; I shall have honor, too.

ISMENE: But we are equally guilty!

ANTIGONE: No more, Ismenê.
You are alive, but I belong to Death.

CREON: [*To the* CHORUS] Gentlemen, I beg you to observe these girls:
One has just now lost her mind; the other,
It seems, has never had a mind at all.

ISMENE: Grief teaches the steadiest minds to waver, King.

CREON: Yours certainly did, when you assumed guilt with the guilty!

ISMENE: But how could I go on living without her?

CREON: You are.
She is already dead.

ISMENE: But your own son's bride!

CREON: There are places enough for him to push his plow.
I want no wicked women for my sons!

ISMENE: O dearest Haimon, how your father wrongs you!

CREON: I've had enough of your childish talk of marriage!

CHORAGOS: Do you really intend to steal this girl from your son?

CREON: No; Death will do that for me.

CHORAGOS: Then she must die?

CREON: [*Ironically*] You dazzle me.
                     —But enough of this talk!

[*To* GUARDS] You, there, take them away and guard them well:
For they are but women, and even brave men run
When they see Death coming.

[*Exeunt* ISMENE, ANTIGONE, *and* GUARDS]

ODE II

CHORUS: Fortunate is the man who has never tasted God's   [STROPHE 1]
          vengeance!
    Where once the anger of heaven has struck, that house is shaken
    For ever: damnation rises behind each child
    Lake a wave cresting out of the black northeast,
    When the long darkness under sea roars up
    And bursts drumming death upon the windwhipped sand.

    I have seen this gathering sorrow from time long past   [ANTISTROPHE 1]
    Loom upon Oedipus' children: generation from generation
    Takes the compulsive rage of the enemy god.
    So lately this last flower of Oedipus' line
    Drank the sunlight! but now a passionate word
    And a handful of dust have closed up all its beauty.

      What mortal arrogance   [STROPHE 2]
      Transcends the wrath of Zeus?
    Sleep cannot lull him, nor the effortless long months
    Of the timeless gods: but he is young for ever,
    And his house is the shining day of high Olympos.
      All that is and shall be,
      And all the past, is his.
    No pride on earth is free of the curse of heaven.

      The straying dreams of men   [ANTISTROPHE 2]
      May bring them ghosts of joy:
    But as they drowse, the waking embers burn them;
    Or they walk with fíxed éyes, as blind men walk.
    But the ancient wisdom speaks for our own time:
      Fate works most for woe
      With Folly's fairest show.
    Man's little pleasure is the spring of sorrow.

SCENE III

CHORAGOS: But here is Haimon, King, the last of all your sons.
    Is it grief for Antigonê that brings him here,
    And bitterness at being robbed of his bride?

[*Enter* HAIMON]

CREON: We shall soon see, and no need of diviners.

> —Son,

You have heard my final judgment on that girl:
Have you come here hating me, or have you come
With deference and with love, whatever I do?

HAIMON: I am your son, father. You are my guide.
You make things clear for me, and I obey you.
No marriage means more to me than your continuing wisdom.

CREON: Good. That is the way to behave: subordinate
Everything else, my son, to your father's will.
This is what a man prays for, that he may get
Sons attentive and dutiful in his house,
Each one hating his father's enemies,
Honoring his father's friends. But if his sons
Fail him, if they turn out unprofitably,
What has he fathered but trouble for himself
And amusement for the malicious?

> So you are right

Not to lose your head over this woman.
Your pleasure with her would soon grow cold, Haimon,
And then you'd have a hellcat in bed and elsewhere.
Let her find her husband in Hell!
Of all the people in this city, only she
Has had contempt for my law and broken it.

Do you want me to show myself weak before the people?
Or to break my sworn word? No, and I will not.
The woman dies.

I suppose she'll plead "family ties." Well, let her.
If I permit my own family to rebel,
How shall I earn the world's obedience?
Show me the man who keeps his house in hand,
He's fit for public authority.

> I'll have no dealings

With law-breakers, critics of the government:
Whoever is chosen to govern should be obeyed—
Must be obeyed, in all things, great and small,
Just and unjust! O Haimon,
The man who knows how to obey, and that man only,
Knows how to give commands when the time comes.
You can depend on him, no matter how fast
The spears come: he's a good soldier, he'll stick it out.

Anarchy, anarchy! Show me a greater evil!
This is why cities tumble and the great houses rain down,
This is what scatters armies!

No, no: good lives are made so by discipline.
We keep the laws then, and the lawmakers,
And no woman shall seduce us. If we must lose,
Let's lose to a man, at least! Is a woman stronger than we?

CHORAGOS: Unless time has rusted my wits,
     What you say, King, is said with point and dignity.

HAIMON: [*Boyishly earnest*]   Father:
     Reason is God's crowning gift to man, and you are right
     To warn me against losing mine. I cannot say—
     I hope that I shall never want to say!—that you
     Have reasoned badly. Yet there are other men
     Who can reason, too; and their opinions might be helpful.
     You are not in a position to know everything
     That people say or do, or what they feel:
     Your temper terrifies them—everyone
     Will tell you only what you like to hear.
     But I, at any rate, can listen; and I have heard them
     Muttering and whispering in the dark about this girl.
     They say no woman has ever, so unreasonably,
     Died so shameful a death for a generous act:
     "She covered her brother's body. Is this indecent?
     She kept him from dogs and vultures. Is this a crime?
     Death?—She should have all the honor that we can give her!"

     This is the way they talk out there in the city.

     You must believe me:
     Nothing is closer to me than your happiness.
     What could be closer? Must not any son
     Value his father's fortune as his father does his?
     I beg you, do not be unchangeable:
     Do not believe that you alone can be right.
     The man who thinks that,
     The man who maintains that only he has the power
     To reason correctly, the gift to speak, the soul—
     A man like that, when you know him, turns out empty.

     It is not reason never to yield to reason!

In flood time you can see how some trees bend,
And because they bend, even their twigs are safe,
While stubborn trees are torn up, roots and all.
And the same thing happens in sailing:
Make your sheet fast, never slacken—and over you go,
Head over heels and under: and there's your voyage.
Forget you are angry! Let yourself be moved!
I know I am young; but please let me say this:
The ideal condition
Would be, I admit, that men should be right by instinct;
But since we are all too likely to go astray,
The reasonable thing is to learn from those who can teach.

CHORAGOS: You will do well to listen to him, King,
If what he says is sensible. And you, Haimon,
Must listen to your father.—Both speak well.

CREON: You consider it right for a man of my years and experience
To go to school to a boy?

HAIMON: It is not right
If am wrong. But if I am young, and right,
What does my age matter?

CREON: You think it right to stand up for an anarchist?

HAIMON: Not at all. I pay no respect to criminals.

CREON: Then she is not a criminal?

HAIMON: The City would deny it, to a man.

CREON: And the City proposes to teach me how to rule?

HAIMON: Ah. Who is it that's talking like a boy now?

CREON: My voice is the one voice giving orders in this City!

HAIMON: It is no City if it takes orders from one voice.

CREON: The State is the King!

HAIMON: Yes, if the State is a desert.

[*Pause*]

CREON: This boy, it seems, has sold out to a woman.

HAIMON: If you are a woman: my concern is only for you.

CREON: So? Your "concern"! In a public brawl with your father!

HAIMON: How about you, in a public brawl with justice?

CREON: With justice, when all that I do is within my rights?

HAIMON: You have no right to trample on God's right.

CREON: [*Completely out of control*] Fool, adolescent fool! Taken in by a
woman!

HAIMON: You'll never see me taken in by anything vile.

CREON: Every word you say is for her!

HAIMON: [*Quietly, darkly*] And for you.
And for me. And for the gods under the earth.

CREON: You'll never marry her while she lives.

HAIMON: Then she must die.—But her death will cause another.

CREON: Another?
Have you lost your senses? Is this an open threat?

HAIMON: There is no threat in speaking to emptiness.

CREON: I swear you'll regret this superior tone of yours!
You are the empty one!

HAIMON: If you were not my father,
I'd say you were perverse.

CREON: You girlstruck fool, don't play at words with me!

HAIMON: I am sorry. You prefer silence.

CREON: Now, by God—!
I swear, by all the gods in heaven above us,
You'll watch it, I swear you shall!

[*To the* SERVANTS]   Bring her out!
Bring the woman out! Let her die before his eyes!
Here, this instant, with her bridegroom beside her!

HAIMON: Not here, no; she will not die here, King.
And you will never see my face again.
Go on raving as long as you've a friend to endure you.

[*Exit* HAIMON]

CHORAGOS: Gone, gone.
Creon, a young man in a rage is dangerous!

CREON: Let him do, or dream to do, more than a man can.
　　　He shall not save these girls from death.

CHORAGOS: These girls?
　　　You have sentenced them both?

CREON: No, you are right.
　　　I will not kill the one whose hands are clean.

CHORAGOS: But Antigonê?

CREON: [*Somberly*]   I will carry her far away
　　　Out there in the wilderness, and lock her
　　　Living in a vault of stone. She shall have food,
　　　As the custom is, to absolve the State of her death.
　　　And there let her pray to the gods of hell:
　　　They are her only gods:
　　　Perhaps they will show her an escape from death,
　　　Or she may learn,
　　　　　　　　　though late,
　　　That piety shown the dead is pity in vain.

　　　[*Exit* CREON]

ODE III

CHORUS: Love, unconquerable   [STROPHE]
　　　Waster of rich men, keeper
　　　Of warm lights and all-night vigil
　　　In the soft face of a girl:
　　　Sea-wanderer, forest-visitor!
　　　Even the pure Immortals cannot escape you,
　　　And mortal man, in his one day's dusk,
　　　Trembles before your glory.

　　　Surely you swerve upon ruin   [ANTISTROPHE]
　　　The just man's consenting heart,
　　　As here you have made bright anger
　　　Strike between father and son—
　　　And none has conquered but Love!
　　　A girl's glánce wórking the will of heaven:
　　　Pleasure to her alone who mocks us,
　　　Merciless Aphroditê.

SCENE IV

CHORAGOS: [As ANTIGONE *enters guarded*]   But I can no longer
                stand in awe of this,
            Nor, seeing what I see, keep back my tears.
            Here is Antigonê, passing to that chamber
            Where all find sleep at last.

ANTIGONE: Look upon me, friends, and pity me   [STROPHE 1]
            Turning back at the night's edge to say
            Good-by to the sun that shines for me no longer;
            Now sleepy Death
            Summons me down to Acheron, that cold shore:
            There is no bridesong there, nor any music.

CHORUS: Yet not unpraised, not without a kind of honor,
            You walk at last into the underworld;
            Untouched by sickness, broken by no sword.
            What woman has ever found your way to death?

ANTIGONE: How often I have heard the story of Niobê,   [ANTISTROPHE 1]
            Tantalos' wretched daughter, how the stone
            Clung fast about her, ivy-close: and they say
            The rain falls endlessly
            And sifting soft snow; her tears are never done.
            I feel the loneliness of her death in mine.

CHORUS: But she was born of heaven, and you
            Are woman, woman-born. If her death is yours,
            A mortal woman's, is this not for you
            Glory in our world and in the world beyond?

ANTIGONE: You laugh at me. Ah, friends, friends,   [STROPHE 2]
            Can you not wait until I am dead? O Thebes,
            O men many-charioted, in love with Fortune,
            Dear springs of Dircê, sacred Theban grove,
            Be witnesses for me, denied all pity,
            Unjustly judged! and think a word of love
            For her whose path turns
            Under dark earth, where there are no more tears.

CHORUS: You have passed beyond human daring and come at last
            Into a place of stone where Justice sits.
            I cannot tell
            What shape of your father's guilt appears in this.

ANTIGONE: You have touched it at last: that bridal bed   [ANTISTROPHE 2]
    Unspeakable, horror of son and mother mingling:
    Their crime, infection of all our family!
    O Oedipus, father and brother!
    Your marriage strikes from the grave to murder mine.
    I have been a stranger here in my own land:
    All my life
    The blasphemy of my birth has followed me.

CHORUS: Reverence is a virtue, but strength
    Lives in established law: that must prevail.
    You have made your choice,
    Your death is the doing of your conscious hand.

ANTIGONE: Then let me go, since all your words are bitter,   [EPODE]
    And the very light of the sun is cold to me.
    Lead me to my vigil, where I must have
    Neither love nor lamentation; no song, but silence.

    [CREON *interrupts impatiently*]

CREON: If dirges and planned lamentations could put off death,
    Men would be singing for ever.

    [*To the* SERVANTS]   Take her, go!
    You know your orders: take her to the vault
    And leave her alone there. And if she lives or dies,
    That's her affair, not ours: our hands are clean.

ANTIGONE: O tomb, vaulted bride-bed in eternal rock,
    Soon I shall be with my own again
    Where Persephonê welcomes the thin ghosts underground:
    And I shall see my father again, and you, mother,
    And dearest Polyneicês—
                   dearest indeed
    To me, since it was my hand
    That washed him clean and poured the ritual wine:
    And my reward is death before my time!
    And yet, as men's hearts know, I have done no wrong,
    I have not sinned before God. Or if I have,
    I shall know the truth in death. But if the guilt
    Lies upon Creon who judged me, then, I pray,
    May his punishment equal my own.

CHORAGOS: O passionate heart,
    Unyielding, tormented still by the same winds!

CREON: Her guards shall have good cause to regret their delaying.

ANTIGONE: Ah! That voice is like the voice of death!

CREON: I can give you no reason to think you are mistaken.

ANTIGONE: Thebes, and you my fathers' gods,
         And rulers of Thebes, you see me now, the last
         Unhappy daughter of a line of kings,
         Your kings, led away to death. You will remember
         What things I suffer, and at what men's hands,
         Because I would not transgress the laws of heaven.

[*To the* GUARDS, *simply*] Come: let us wait no longer.

[*Exit* ANTIGONE, *L., guarded*]

ODE IV

CHORUS: All Danaê's beauty was locked away   [STROPHE 1]
         In a brazen cell where the sunlight could not come:
         A small room, still as any grave, enclosed her.
         Yet she was a princess too,
         And Zeus in a rain of gold poured love upon her.
         O child, child,
         No power in wealth or war
         Or tough sea-blackened ships
         Can prevail against untiring Destiny!

         And Dryas' son also, that furious king,   [ANTISTROPHE 1]
         Bore the god's prisoning anger for his pride:
         Sealed up by Dionysos in deaf stone,
         His madness died among echoes.
         So at the last he learned what dreadful power
         His tongue had mocked:
         For he had profaned the revels,
         And fired the wrath of the nine
         Implacable Sisters that love the sound of the flute.

         And old men tell a half-remembered tale   [STROPHE 2]
         Of horror done where a dark ledge splits the sea
         And a double surf beats on the gráy shóres:
         How a king's new woman, sick
         With hatred for the queen he had imprisoned,
         Ripped out his two sons' eyes with her bloody hands

While grinning Arês watched the shuttle plunge
Four times: four blind wounds crying for revenge,

Crying, tears and blood mingled.—Piteously born, [ANTISTROPHE 2]
Those sons whose mother was of heavenly birth!
Her father was the god of the North Wind
And she was cradled by gales,
She raced with young colts on the glittering hills
And walked untrammeled in the open light:
But in her marriage deathless Fate found means
To build a tomb like yours for all her joy.

SCENE V

[*Enter blind* TEIRESIAS, *led by a boy. The opening speeches of* TEIRESIAS *should be in singsong contrast to the realistic lines of* CREON]

TEIRESIAS: This is the way the blind man comes, Princes, Princes,
   Lock-step, two heads lit by the eyes of one.

CREON: What new thing have you to tell us, old Teiresias?

TEIRESIAS: I have much to tell you: listen to the prophet, Creon.

CREON: I am not aware that I have ever failed to listen.

TEIRESIAS: Then you have done wisely, King, and ruled well.

CREON: I admit my debt to you. But what have you to say?

TEIRESIAS: This, Creon: you stand once more on the edge of fate.

CREON: What do you mean? Your words are a kind of dread.

TEIRESIAS: Listen, Creon:
   I was sitting in my chair of augury, at the place
   Where the birds gather about me. They were all a-chatter,
   As is their habit, when suddenly I heard
   A strange note in their jangling, a scream, a
   Whirring fury; I knew that they were fighting,
   Tearing each other, dying
   In a whirlwind of wings clashing. And I was afraid.
   I began the rites of burnt-offering at the altar,
   But Hephaistos failed me: instead of bright flame,
   There was only the sputtering slime of the fat thigh-flesh
   Melting: the entrails dissolved in gray smoke,
   The bare bone burst from the welter. And no blaze!

This was a sign from heaven. My boy described it,
Seeing for me as I see for others.

I tell you, Creon, you yourself have brought
This new calamity upon us. Our hearths and altars
Are stained with the corruption of dogs and carrion birds
That glut themselves on the corpse of Oedipus' son.
The gods are deaf when we pray to them, their fire
Recoils from our offering, their birds of omen
Have no cry of comfort, for they are gorged
With the thick blood of the dead.

                      O my son,
These are no trifles! Think: all men make mistakes,
But a good man yields when he knows his course is wrong,
And repairs the evil. The only crime is pride.

Give in to the dead man, then: do not fight with a corpse—
What glory is it to kill a man who is dead?
Think, I beg you:
It is for your own good that I speak as I do.
You should be able to yield for your own good.

CREON: It seems that prophets have made me their especial province.
All my life long
I have been a kind of butt for the dull arrows
Of doddering fortune-tellers!

                      No, Teiresias:
If your birds—if the great eagles of God himself
Should carry him stinking bit by bit to heaven,
I would not yield. I am not afraid of pollution:
No man can defile the gods.

                  Do what you will,
Go into business, make money, speculate
In India gold or that synthetic gold from Sardis,
Get rich otherwise than by my consent to bury him.
Teiresias, it is a sorry thing when a wise man
Sells his wisdom, lets out his words for hire!

TEIRESIAS: Ah Creon! Is there no man left in the world—

CREON: To do what?—Come, let's have the aphorism!

TEIRESIAS: No man who knows that wisdom outweighs any wealth?

CREON: As surely as bribes are baser than any baseness.

TEIRESIAS: You are sick, Creon! You are deathly sick!

CREON: As you say: it is not my place to challenge a prophet.

TEIRESIAS: Yet you have said my prophecy is for sale.

CREON: The generation of prophets has always loved gold.

TEIRESIAS: The generation of kings has always loved brass.

CREON: You forget yourself! You are speaking to your King.

TEIRESIAS: I know it. You are a king because of me.

CREON: You have a certain skill; but you have sold out.

TEIRESIAS: King, you will drive me to words that—

CREON: Say them, say them!
    Only remember: I will not pay you for them.

TEIRESIAS: No, you will find them too costly.

CREON: No doubt. Speak:
    Whatever you say, you will not change my will.

TEIRESIAS: Then take this, and take it to heart!
    The time is not far off when you shall pay back
    Corpse for corpse, flesh of your own flesh.
    You have thrust the child of this world into living night,
    You have kept from the gods below the child that is theirs:
    The one in a grave before her death, the other,
    Dead, denied the grave. This is your crime:
    And the Furies and the dark gods of Hell
    Are swift with terrible punishment for you.

    Do you want to buy me now, Creon?

                           Not many days,
    And your house will be full of men and women weeping,
    And curses will be hurled at you from far
    Cities grieving for sons unburied, left to rot
    Before the walls of Thebes.

    These are my arrows, Creon: they are all for you.

    [*To* BOY] But come, child: lead me home.
    Let him waste his fine anger upon younger men.
    Maybe he will learn at last

To control a wiser tongue in a better head.

[*Exit* TEIRESIAS]

CHORAGOS: The old man has gone, King, but his words
            Remain to plague us. I am old, too,
            But I cannot remember that he was ever false.

CREON: That is true. . . . It troubles me.
         Oh it is hard to give in! but it is worse
         To risk everything for stubborn pride.

CHORAGOS: Creon: take my advice.

CREON: What shall I do?

CHORAGOS: Go quickly: free Antigonê from her vault
            And build a tomb for the body of Polyneicês.

CREON: You would have me do this?

CHORAGOS: Creon, yes!
            And it must be done at once: God moves
            Swiftly to cancel the folly of stubborn men.

CREON: It is hard to deny the heart! But I
         Will do it: I will not fight with destiny.

CHORAGOS: You must go yourself, you cannot leave it to others.

CREON: I will go.
                    —Bring axes, servants:
         Come with me to the tomb. I buried her, I
         Will set her free.
                            Oh quickly!
         My mind misgives—
         The laws of the gods are mighty, and a man must serve them
         To the last day of his life!

[*Exit* CREON]

PÆAN

CHORAGOS: God of many names   [STROPHE 1]

CHORUS: O Iacchos
                    son
         of Kadmeian Sémelê

O born of the Thunder!
Guardian of the West
Regent
of Eleusis' plain
O Prince of maenad Thebes
and the Dragon Field by rippling Ismenos:

CHORAGOS: God of many names   [ANTISTROPHE 1]

CHORUS: The flame of torches
flares on our hills
the nymphs of Iacchos
dance at the spring of Castalia:

from the vine-close mountain
come, ah come in ivy:
Evohé evohé! sings through the streets of Thebes

CHORAGOS: God of many names   [STROPHE 2]

CHORUS: Iacchos of Thebes
heavenly Child
of Sémelê bride of the Thunderer!
The shadow of plague is upon us:
come
with clement feet
oh come from Parnasos
down the long slopes
across the lamenting water

CHORAGOS: Iô Fire! Chorister of the throbbing stars!   [ANTISTROPHE 2]
O purest among the voices of the night!
Thou son of God, blaze for us!

CHORUS: Come with choric rapture of circling Maenads
Who cry *Iô Iacche!*
God of many names!

ÉXODOS

[*Enter* MESSENGER, *L.*]

MESSENGER: Men of the line of Kadmos, you who live
Near Amphion's citadel:
I cannot say
Of any condition of human life "This is fixed,

This is clearly good, or bad." Fate raises up,
And Fate casts down the happy and unhappy alike:
No man can foretell his Fate.

                            Take the case of Creon:
Creon was happy once, as I count happiness:
Victorious in battle, sole governor of the land,
Fortunate father of children nobly born.
And now it has all gone from him! Who can say
That a man is still alive when his life's joy fails?
He is a walking dead man. Grant him rich,
Let him live like a king in his great house:
If his pleasure is gone, I would not give
So much as the shadow of smoke for all he owns.

CHORAGOS: Your words hint at sorrow: what is your news for us?

MESSENGER: They are dead. The living are guilty of their death.

CHORAGOS: Who is guilty? Who is dead? Speak!

MESSENGER: Haimon.
Haimon is dead; and the hand that killed him
Is his own hand.

CHORAGOS: His father's? or his own?

MESSENGER: His own, driven mad by the murder his father had done.

CHORAGOS: Teiresias, Teiresias, how clearly you saw it all!

MESSENGER: This is my news: you must draw what conclusions
             you can from it.

CHORAGOS: But look: Eurydicê, our Queen:
    Has she overheard us?

[Enter EURYDICE from the Palace, C.]

EURYDICE: I have heard something, friends:
    As I was unlocking the gate of Pallas' shrine,
    For I needed her help today, I heard a voice
    Telling of some new sorrow. And I fainted
    There at the temple with all my maidens about me.
    But speak again: whatever it is, I can bear it:
    Grief and I are no strangers.

MESSENGER: Dearest Lady,
    I will tell you plainly all that I have seen.
    I shall not try to comfort you: what is the use,

Since comfort could lie only in what is not true?
The truth is always best.

                   I went with Creon
To the outer plain where Polyneicês was lying,
No friend to pity him, his body shredded by dogs.
We made our prayers in that place to Hecatê
And Pluto, that they would be merciful. And we bathed
The corpse with holy water, and we brought
Fresh-broken branches to burn what was left of it,
And upon the urn we heaped up a towering barrow
Of the earth of his own land.

                   When we were done, we ran
To the vault where Antigonê lay on her couch of stone.
One of the servants had gone ahead,
And while he was yet far off he heard a voice
Grieving within the chamber, and he came back
And told Creon. And as the King went closer,
The air was full of wailing, the words lost,
And he begged us to make all haste. "Am I a prophet?"
He said, weeping, "And must I walk this road,
The saddest of all that I have gone before?
My son's voice calls me on. Oh quickly, quickly!
Look through the crevice there, and tell me
If it is Haimon, or some deception of the gods!"

We obeyed; and in the cavern's farthest corner
We saw her lying:
She had made a noose of her fine linen veil
And hanged herself. Haimon lay beside her,
His arms about her waist, lamenting her,
His love lost under ground, crying out
That his father had stolen her away from him.

When Creon saw him the tears rushed to his eyes
And he called to him: "What have you done, child? Speak to me.
What are you thinking that makes your eyes so strange?
O my son, my son, I come to you on my knees!"
But Haimon spat in his face. He said not a word,
Staring—
            And suddenly drew his sword
And lunged. Creon shrank back, the blade missed; and the boy,
Desperate against himself, drove it half its length
Into his own side, and fell. And as he died

He gathered Antigonê close in his arms again,
Choking, his blood bright red on her white cheek.
And now he lies dead with the dead, and she is his
At last, his bride in the houses of the dead.

[*Exit* EURYDICE *into the Palace*]

CHORAGOS: She has left us without a word. What can this mean?

MESSENGER: It troubles me, too; yet she knows what is best,
Her grief is too great for public lamentation,
And doubtless she has gone to her chamber to weep
For her dead son, leading her maidens in his dirge.

CHORAGOS: It may be so: but I fear this deep silence.

[*Pause*]

MESSENGER: I will see what she is doing. I will go in.

[*Exit* MESSENGER *into the Palace*]

[*Enter* CREON *with* ATTENDANTS, *bearing* HAIMON'S *body*]

CHORAGOS: But here is the King himself: oh look at him,
Bearing his own damnation in his arms.

CREON: Nothing you say can touch me any more.
My own blind heart has brought me
From darkness to final darkness. Here you see
The father murdering, the murdered son—
And all my civic wisdom!

Haimon my son, so young, so young to die,
I was the fool, not you; and you died for me.

CHORAGOS: That is the truth; but you were late in learning it.

CREON: This truth is hard to bear. Surely a god
Has crushed me beneath the hugest weight of heaven.
And driven me headlong a barbaric way
To trample out the thing I held most dear.

The pains that men will take to come to pain!

[*Enter* MESSENGER *from the Palace*]

MESSENGER: The burden you carry in your hands is heavy,
But it is not all: you will find more in your house.

CREON: What burden worse than this shall I find there?

MESSENGER: The Queen is dead.

CREON: O port of death, deaf world,
Is there no pity for me? And you, Angel of evil,
I was dead, and your words are death again.
Is it true, boy? Can it be true?
Is my wife dead? Has death bred death?

MESSENGER: You can see for yourself.

[*The doors are opened, and the body of* EURYDICE *is disclosed within*]

CREON: Oh pity!
All true, all true, and more than I can bear!
O my wife, my son!

MESSENGER: She stood before the altar, and her heart
Welcomed the knife her own hand guided,
And a great cry burst from her lips for Megareus dead,
And for Haimon dead, her sons; and her last breath
Was a curse for their father, the murderer of her sons.
And she fell, and the dark flowed in through her closing eyes.

CREON: O God, I am sick with fear.
Are there no swords here? Has no one a blow for me?

MESSENGER: Her curse is upon you for the deaths of both.

CREON: It is right that it should be. I alone am guilty.
I know it, and I say it. Lead me in,
Quickly, friends.
I have neither life nor substance. Lead me in.

CHORAGOS: You are right, if there can be right in so much wrong.
The briefest way is best in a world of sorrow.

CREON: Let it come,
Let death come quickly, and be kind to me.
I would not ever see the sun again.

CHORAGOS: All that will come when it will; but we, meanwhile,
Have much to do. Leave the future to itself.

CREON: All my heart was in that prayer!

CHORAGOS: Then do not pray any more: the sky is deaf.

CREON: Lead me away. I have been rash and foolish.
I have killed my son and my wife.
I look for comfort; my comfort lies here dead.

Whatever my hands have touched has come to nothing.
Fate has brought all my pride to a thought of dust.

[As CREON *is being led into the house, the* CHORAGOS *advances and speaks
directly to the audience*]

CHORAGOS: There is no happiness where there is no wisdom;
No wisdom but in submission to the gods.
Big words are always punished,
And proud men in old age learn to be wise.

WILLIAM SHAKESPEARE

❧ *The Tragedy of Othello*
The Moor of Venice

CHARACTERS

Othello, *a noble Moor in the service of the Venetian state*
Brabantio, *a senator, father to Desdemona*
Cassio, *his lieutenant*
Iago, *his ancient*
Roderigo, *a Venetian gentleman*
Duke of Venice
Senators
Montano, *Othello's predecessor in the government of Cyprus*
Lodovico, *kinsman to Brabantio*
Gratiano, *brother to Brabantio*
Clown, *servant to Othello*
Desdemona, *daughter to Brabantio and wife to Othello*
Emilia, *wife to Iago*
Bianca, *mistress to Cassio*
Sailors, Messenger, Herald, Officers, Gentlemen, Musicians,
   and Attendants

ACT I. SCENE I

Venice. A street.

[*Enter* RODERIGO *and* IAGO]

RODERIGO: Tush never tell me! I take it much unkindly
   That thou, Iago, who hast had my purse
   As if the strings were thine, shouldst know of this.

IAGO: 'Sblood, but you will not hear me!
   If ever I did dream of such a matter,
   Abhor me.

RODERIGO: Thou told'st me thou didst hold him in thy hate.

---

3 *this* i.e. Desdemona's elopement.   4 *'Sblood* by God's blood.

IAGO: Despise me if I do not. Three great ones of the city,
        In personal suit to make me his lieutenant,
        Off-capped to him; and by the faith of man,   10
        I know my price; I am worth no worse a place.
        But he, as loving his own pride and purposes,
        Evades them with a bombast circumstance
        Horribly stuffed with epithets of war;
        And, in conclusion,
        Nonsuits my mediators; for, "Certes," says he,
        "I have already chose my officer."
        And what was he?
        Forsooth, a great arithmetician,
        One Michael Cassio, a Florentine   20
        (A fellow almost damned in a fair wife)
        That never set a squadron in the field,
        Nor the division of a battle knows
        More than a spinster; unless the bookish theoric,
        Wherein the togèd consuls can propose
        As masterly as he. Mere prattle without practice
        Is all his soldiership. But he, sir, had th' election;
        And I (of whom his eyes had seen the proof
        At Rhodes, at Cyprus, and on other grounds
        Christian and heathen) must be belee'd and calmed   30
        By debitor and creditor; this counter-caster,
        He, in good time, must his lieutenant be,
        And I—God bless the mark!—his Moorship's ancient.

RODERIGO: By heaven, I rather would have been his hangman.

IAGO: Why, there's no remedy; 'tis the curse of service.
        Preferment goes by letter and affection,
        And not by old gradation, where each second
        Stood heir to th' first. Now, sir, be judge yourself,
        Whether I in any just term am affined
        To love the Moor.

RODERIGO: I would not follow him then.   40

IAGO: O, sir, content you;
        I follow him to serve my turn upon him.
        We cannot all be masters, nor all masters

---

10 *him* i.e. Othello.   13 *a bombast circumstance* pompous circumlocutions.   16
Nonsuits rejects.   19 *arithmetician* theoretician.   21 *almost . . . wife* (an obscure
allusion; Cassio is unmarried, but see IV, i, 123).   30 *belee'd and calmed* left in the
lurch.   31 *counter-caster* bookkeeper.   33 *ancient* ensign.   36 *affection* favoritism.   39
affined obliged.

Cannot be truly followed. You shall mark
Many a duteous and knee-crooking knave
That, doting on his own obsequious bondage,
Wears out his time, much like his master's ass,
For naught but provender; and when he's old, cashiered.
Whip me such honest knaves! Others there are
Who, trimmed in forms and visages of duty,   50
Keep yet their hearts attending on themselves;
And, throwing but shows of service on their lords,
Do well thrive by them, and when they have lined their coats,
Do themselves homage. These fellows have some soul;
And such a one do I profess myself. For, sir,
It is as sure as you are Roderigo,
Were I the Moor, I would not be Iago.
In following him, I follow but myself;
Heaven is my judge, not I for love and duty,
But seeming so, for my peculiar end;   60
For when my outward action doth demonstrate
The native act and figure of my heart
In compliment extern, 'tis not long after
But I will wear my heart upon my sleeve
For daws to peck at; I am not what I am.

RODERIGO: What a full fortune does the thick-lips owe
If he can carry't thus!

IAGO: Call up her father,
Rouse him. Make after him, poison his delight,
Proclaim him in the streets. Incense her kinsmen,
And though he in a fertile climate dwell,   70
Plague him with flies; though that his joy be joy,
Yet throw such changes of vexation on't
As it may lose some color.

RODERIGO: Here is her father's house. I'll call aloud.

IAGO: Do, with like timorous accent and dire yell
As when, by night and negligence, the fire
Is spied in populous cities.

---

49 *cashiered* turned off. 50 *trimmed* dressed up. 62 *The . . . heart* what I really
believe and intend. 63 *compliment extern* outward appearance. 66 *thick-lips* (Elizabethans made no clear distinction between Moors and Negroes) *owe* own. 75
timorous terrifying.

RODERIGO: What, ho, Brabantio! Signior Brabantio, ho!

IAGO: Awake! What, ho, Brabantio! Thieves! thieves! thieves!
    Look to your house, your daughter, and your bags!   80
    Thieves! thieves!

[BRABANTIO *at a window*]

BRABANTIO: [*Above*]   What is the reason of this terrible summons?
    What is the matter there?

RODERIGO: Signior, is all your family within?

IAGO: Are your doors locked?

BRABANTIO: Why, wherefore ask you this?

IAGO: Zounds, sir, y'are robbed! For shame, put on your gown!
    Your heart is burst; you have lost half your soul.
    Even now, now, very now, an old black ram
    Is tupping your white ewe. Arise, arise!
    Awake the snorting citizens with the bell,   90
    Or else the devil will make a grandsire of you.
    Arise I say!

BRABANTIO: What, have you lost your wits?

RODERIGO: Most reverend signior, do you know my voice?

BRABANTIO: Not I. What are you?

RODERIGO: My name is Roderigo.

BRABANTIO: The worser welcome!
    I have charged thee not to haunt about my doors.
    In honest plainness thou hast heard me say
    My daughter is not for thee; and now, in madness,
    Being full of supper and distemp'ring draughts,
    Upon malicious bravery dost thou come   100
    To start my quiet.

RODERIGO: Sir, sir, sir—

BRABANTIO: But thou must needs be sure
    My spirit and my place have in them power
    To make this bitter to thee.

RODERIGO: Patience, good sir.

   90 *snorting* snoring.   100 *bravery* defiance.

BRABANTIO: What tell'st thou me of robbing? This is Venice;
My house is not a grange.

RODERIGO: Most grave Brabantio,
In simple and pure soul I come to you.

IAGO: Zounds, sir, you are one of those that will not serve God if the
devil bid you. Because we come to do you service, and you think
we are ruffians, you'll have your daughter covered with a Barbary   110
horse; you'll have your nephews neigh to you; you'll have coursers
for cousins, and gennets for germans.

BRABANTIO: What profane wretch art thou?

IAGO: I am one, sir, that comes to tell you your daughter and the Moor
are now making the beast with two backs.

BRABANTIO: Thou art a villain.

IAGO: You are—a senator.

BRABANTIO: This thou shalt answer. I know thee, Roderigo.

RODERIGO: Sir, I will answer anything. But I beseech you,
If't be your pleasure and most wise consent,
As partly I find it is, that your fair daughter,   120
At this odd-even and dull watch o' th' night,
Transported, with no worse nor better guard
But with a knave of common hire, a gondolier,
To the gross clasps of a lascivious Moor—
If this be known to you, and your allowance,
We then have done you bold and saucy wrongs;
But if you know not this, my manners tell me
We have your wrong rebuke. Do not believe
That, from the sense of all civility,
I thus would play and trifle with your reverence.   130
Your daughter, if you have not given her leave,
I say again, hath made a gross revolt,
Tying her duty, beauty, wit, and fortunes
In an extravagant and wheeling stranger
Of here and everywhere. Straight satisfy yourself.
If she be in her chamber, or your house,

106 *grange* isolated farmhouse.   111 *nephews* i.e. grandsons.   112 *gennets for germans* Spanish horses for near kinsmen.   121 *odd-even* between night and morning.   125 *allowance* approval.   129 *from the sense* in violation.   134 *extravagant and wheeling* expatriate and roving.

Let loose on me the justice of the state
For thus deluding you.

BRABANTIO: Strike on the tinder, ho!
Give me a taper! Call up all my people!
This accident is not unlike my dream.   140
Belief of it oppresses me already.
Light, I say! light!   [*Exit above*]

IAGO: Farewell, for I must leave you.
It seems not meet, nor wholesome to my place,
To be produced—as, if I stay, I shall—
Against the Moor. For I do know the state,
However this may gall him with some check,
Cannot with safety cast him; for he's embarked
With such loud reason to the Cyprus wars,
Which even now stand in act, that for their souls
Another of his fathom they have none   150
To lead their business; in which regard,
Though I do hate him as I do hell-pains,
Yet, for necessity of present life,
I must show out a flag and sign of love,
Which is indeed but sign. That you shall surely find him,
Lead to the Sagittary the raisèd search;
And there will I be with him. So farewell.   [*Exit*]

[*Enter below* BRABANTIO *in his nightgown and* SERVANTS *with torches*]

BRABANTIO: It is too true an evil. Gone she is;
And what's to come of my despisèd time
Is naught but bitterness. Now, Roderigo,   160
Where didst thou see her?—O unhappy girl!—
With the Moor, say'st thou?—Who would be a father?—
How didst thou know 'twas she?—O, she deceives me
Past thought!—What said she to you?—Get moe tapers!
Raise all my kindred!—Are they married, think you?

RODERIGO: Truly I think they are.

BRABANTIO: O heaven! How got she out? O treason of the blood!
Fathers, from hence trust not your daughters' minds
By what you see them act. Is there not charms

---

140 *accident* occurrence.   146 *check* reprimand.   147 *cast* discharge.   149 *stand
in act* are going on.   150 *fathom* capacity.   156 *Sagittary* an inn.   157 s.d. *nightgown*
dressing-gown.   164 *moe* more.

By which the property of youth and maidhood 170
May be abused? Have you not read, Roderigo,
Of some such thing?

RODERIGO: Yes, sir, I have indeed.

BRABANTIO: Call up my brother.—O, would you had had her!—
Some one way, some another.—Do you know
Where we may apprehend her and the Moor?

RODERIGO: I think I can discover him, if you please
To get good guard and go along with me.

BRABANTIO: Pray you lead on. At every house I'll call;
I may command at most.—Get weapons, ho!
And raise some special officers of night.— 180
On, good Roderigo; I'll deserve your pains.   [*Exeunt*]

SCENE II

Another street.

[*Enter* OTHELLO, IAGO, *and* ATTENDANTS *with torches*]

IAGO: Though in the trade of war I have slain men,
Yet do I hold it very stuff o' th' conscience
To do no contrived murther. I lack iniquity
Sometimes to do me service. Nine or ten times
I had thought t' have yerked him here under the ribs.

OTHELLO: 'Tis better as it is.

IAGO: Nay, but he prated,
And spoke such scurvy and provoking terms
Against your honor
That with the little godliness I have
I did full hard forbear him. But I pray you, sir, 10
Are you fast married? Be assured of this,
That the magnifico is much beloved,
And hath in his effect a voice potential
As double as the Duke's. He will divorce you,
Or put upon you what restraint and grievance
The law, with all his might to enforce it on,
Will give him cable.

---

170 *property* nature.   181 *deserve* show gratitude for.   5 *yerked* stabbed.   11 *fast* securely.   12 *magnifico* grandee (Brabantio).   13 *potential* powerful.   14 *double* doubly influential.

OTHELLO: Let him do his spite.
My services which I have done the signiory
Shall out-tongue his complaints. 'Tis yet to know—
Which, when I know that boasting is an honor,   20
I shall promulgate—I fetch my life and being
From men of royal siege; and my demerits
May speak unbonneted to as proud a fortune
As this that I have reached. For know, Iago,
But that I love the gentle Desdemona,
I would not my unhousèd free condition
Put into circumscription and confine
For the sea's worth.

[*Enter* CASSIO, *with torches,* OFFICERS]

                    But look, what lights come yond?

IAGO: Those are the raisèd father and his friends.
You were best go in.

OTHELLO: Not I; I must be found.   30
My parts, my title, and my perfect soul
Shall manifest me rightly. Is it they?

IAGO: By Janus, I think no.

OTHELLO: The servants of the Duke, and my lieutenant.
The goodness of the night upon you, friends!
What is the news?

CASSIO: The Duke does greet you, general;
And he requires your haste-post-haste appearance
Even on the instant.

OTHELLO: What's the matter, think you?

CASSIO: Something from Cyprus, as I may divine.
It is a business of some heat. The galleys   40
Have sent a dozen sequent messengers
This very night at one another's heels,
And many of the consuls, raised and met,
Are at the Duke's already. You have been hotly called for;
When, being not at your lodging to be found,

---

18 *signiory* Venetian government.   19 *yet to know* still not generally known.   22
siege rank   *demerits* deserts.   23–24 *May speak . . . reached* are equal, I modestly
assert, to those of Desdemona's family.   26 *unhousèd* unrestrained.   31 *perfect soul*
stainless conscience.   41 *sequent* consecutive.

The Senate hath sent about three several quests
To search you out.

OTHELLO: 'Tis well I am found by you.
I will but spend a word here in the house,
And go with you.   [*Exit*]

CASSIO: Ancient, what makes he here?

IAGO: Faith, he to-night hath boarded a land carack.   50
If it prove lawful prize, he's made for ever.

CASSIO: I do not understand.

IAGO: He's married.

CASSIO: To who?

[*Enter* OTHELLO]

IAGO: Marry, to—Come, captain, will you go?

OTHELLO: Have with you.

CASSIO: Here comes another troop to seek for you.

[*Enter* BRABANTIO, RODERIGO, *and others with lights and weapons*]

IAGO: It is Brabantio. General, be advised.
He comes to bad intent.

OTHELLO: Holla! stand there!

RODERIGO: Signior, it is the Moor.

BRABANTIO: Down with him, thief!

[*They draw on both sides*]

IAGO: You, Roderigo! Come, sir, I am for you.

OTHELLO: Keep up your bright swords, for the dew will rust them.
Good signior, you shall more command with years   60
Than with your weapons.

BRABANTIO: O thou foul thief, where hast thou stowed my daughter?
Damned as thou art, thou hast enchanted her!
For I'll refer me to all things of sense,
If she in chains of magic were not bound,

50 *carack* treasure ship.

Whether a maid so tender, fair, and happy,
So opposite to marriage that she shunned
The wealthy curlèd darlings of our nation,
Would ever have, 't incur a general mock,
Run from her guardage to the sooty bosom   70
Of such a thing as thou—to fear, not to delight.
Judge me the world if 'tis not gross in sense
That thou hast practiced on her with foul charms,
Abused her delicate youth with drugs or minerals
That weaken motion. I'll have't disputed on;
'Tis probable, and palpable to thinking.
I therefore apprehend and do attach thee
For an abuser of the world, a practicer
Of arts inhibited and out of warrant.
Lay hold upon him. If he do resist,   80
Subdue him at his peril.

OTHELLO: Hold your hands,
Both you of my inclining and the rest.
Were it my cue to fight, I should have known it
Without a prompter. Where will you that I go
To answer this your charge?

BRABANTIO: To prison, till fit time
Of law and course of direct session
Call thee to answer.

OTHELLO: What if I do obey?
How may the Duke be therewith satisfied,
Whose messengers are here about my side
Upon some present business of the state   90
To bring me to him?

OFFICER: 'Tis true, most worthy signior.
The Duke's in council, and your noble self
I am sure is sent for.

BRABANTIO: How? The Duke in council?
In this time of the night? Bring him away.
Mine's not an idle cause. The Duke himself,
Or any of my brothers of the state,
Cannot but feel this wrong as 'twere their own;
For if such actions may have passage free,
Bondslaves and pagans shall our statesmen be.   [*Exeunt*]

---

72 *gross in sense* obvious. 75 *motion* perception. 77 *attach* arrest. 95 *idle*
trifling.

SCENE III

A council-chamber.

[*Enter* DUKE *and* SENATORS, *set at a table, with lights and* ATTENDANTS]

DUKE: There is no composition in these news
    That gives them credit.

1. SENATOR: Indeed they are disproportioned.
    My letters say a hundred and seven galleys.

DUKE: And mine a hundred forty.

2. SENATOR: And mine two hundred.
    But though they jump not on a just account—
    As in these cases where the aim reports
    'Tis oft with difference—yet do they all confirm
    A Turkish fleet, and bearing up to Cyprus.

DUKE: Nay, it is possible enough to judgment.
    I do not so secure me in the error   10
    But the main article I do approve
    In fearful sense.

SAILOR: [*Within*]   What, ho! what, ho! what, ho!

OFFICER: A messenger from the galleys.

[*Enter* SAILOR]

DUKE: Now, what's the business?

SAILOR: The Turkish preparation makes for Rhodes.
    So was I bid report here to the state
    By Signior Angelo.

DUKE: How say you by this change?

1. SENATOR: This cannot be
    By no assay of reason. 'Tis a pageant
    To keep us in false gaze. When we consider
    Th' importancy of Cyprus to the Turk,   20
    And let ourselves again but understand
    That, as it more concerns the Turk than Rhodes,

---

1 *composition* consistency.   5 *jump* agree.   6 *aim* conjecture.   10 *so secure me* take such comfort.   11 *article* substance *approve* accept.   18 *assay* test.   19 *in false gaze* looking the wrong way.

So may he with more facile question bear it,
For that it stands not in such warlike brace,
But altogether lacks th' abilities
That Rhodes is dressed in—if we make thought of this,
We must not think the Turk is so unskillful
To leave that latest which concerns him first,
Neglecting an attempt of ease and gain
To wake and wage a danger profitless.   30

DUKE: Nay, in all confidence he's not for Rhodes.

OFFICER: Here is more news.

[*Enter a* MESSENGER]

MESSENGER: The Ottomites, reverend and gracious,
Steering with due course toward the isle of Rhodes,
Have there injointed them with an after fleet.

1. SENATOR: Ay, so I thought. How many, as you guess?

MESSENGER: Of thirty sail; and now they do restem
Their backward course, bearing with frank appearance
Their purposes toward Cyprus. Signior Montano,
Your trusty and most valiant servitor,   40
With his free duty recommends you thus,
And prays you to believe him.

DUKE: 'Tis certain then for Cyprus.
Marcus Luccicos, is not he in town?

1. SENATOR: He's now in Florence.

DUKE: Write from us to him; post, post-haste dispatch.

[*Enter* BRABANTIO, OTHELLO, CASSIO, IAGO, RODERIGO, *and* OFFICERS]

1. SENATOR: Here comes Brabantio and the valiant Moor.

DUKE: Valiant Othello, we must straight employ you
Against the general enemy Ottoman.
[*To* BRABANTIO] I did not see you. Welcome, gentle signior.   50
We lacked your counsel and your help to-night.

BRABANTIO: So did I yours. Good your grace, pardon me.
Neither my place, nor aught I heard of business,
Hath raised me from my bed; nor doth the general care

    23 *with . . . bear* more easily capture.   24 *brace* posture of defense.   30 *wake and
wage* rouse and risk.   37 *restem* steer again.

Take hold on me; for my particular grief
Is of so floodgate and o'erbearing nature
That it engluts and swallows other sorrows,
And it is still itself.

DUKE: Why, what's the matter?

BRABANTIO: My daughter! O, my daughter!

ALL: Dead?

BRABANTIO: Ay, to me.   60
She is abused, stol'n from me, and corrupted
By spells and medicines bought of mountebanks;
For nature so prepost'rously to err,
Being not deficient, blind, or lame of sense,
Sans witchcraft could not.

DUKE: Whoe'er he be that in this foul proceeding
Hath thus beguiled your daughter of herself,
And you of her, the bloody book of law
You shall yourself read in the bitter letter
After your own sense; yea, though our proper son
Stood in your action.

BRABANTIO: Humbly I thank your grace.   70
Here is the man—this Moor, whom now, it seems,
Your special mandate for the state affairs
Hath hither brought.

ALL: We are very sorry for't.

DUKE: [*To* OTHELLO]   What, in your own part, can you say to this?

BRABANTIO: Nothing, but this is so.

OTHELLO: Most potent, grave, and reverend signiors,
My very noble, and approved good masters,
That I have ta'en away this old man's daughter,
It is most true; true I have married her.
The very head and front of my offending   80
Hath this extent, no more. Rude am I in my speech,
And little blessed with the soft phrase of peace;
For since these arms of mine had seven years' pith
Till now some nine moons wasted, they have used

---

56 *floodgate* torrential.   57 *engluts* devours.   63 *deficient* feeble-minded.   69 *our proper* my own.   70 *Stood in your action* were accused by you.   77 *approved* tested by experience.   81 *Rude* unpolished.   83 *pith* strength.

Their dearest action in the tented field;
And little of this great world can I speak
More than pertains to feats of broil and battle;
And therefore little shall I grace my cause
In speaking for myself. Yet, by your gracious patience,
I will a round unvarnished tale deliver   90
Of my whole course of love—what drugs, what charms,
What conjuration, and what mighty magic
(For such proceeding am I charged withal)
I won his daughter.

BRABANTIO: A maiden never bold;
Of spirit so still and quiet that her motion
Blushed at herself; and she—in spite of nature,
Of years, of country, credit, everything—
To fall in love with what she feared to look on!
It is a judgment maimed and most imperfect
That will confess perfection so could err   100
Against all rules of nature, and must be driven
To find out practices of cunning hell
Why this should be. I therefore vouch again
That with some mixtures pow'rful o'er the blood,
Or with some dram, conjured to this effect,
He wrought upon her.

DUKE: To vouch this is no proof,
Without more certain and more overt test
Than these thin habits and poor likelihoods
Of modern seeming do prefer against him.

1. SENATOR: But, Othello, speak.   110
Did you by indirect and forcèd courses
Subdue and poison this young maid's affections?
Or came it by request, and such fair question
As soul to soul affordeth?

OTHELLO: I do beseech you,
Send for the lady to the Sagittary
And let her speak of me before her father.
If you do find me foul in her report,
The trust, the office, I do hold of you

90 *round* plain.   95–96 *her motion Blushed* her own emotions caused her to blush.
102 *practices* plots.   103 *vouch* assert.   104 *blood* passions.   108 *thin habits* slight
appearances.   109 *modern seeming* everyday supposition.   111 *forcèd* violent.   113
question conversation.

Not only take away, but let your sentence
Even fall upon my life.

DUKE: Fetch Desdemona hither.   120

OTHELLO: Ancient, conduct them; you best know the place.

[*Exit* IAGO *with two or three* ATTENDANTS]

And till she come, as truly as to heaven
I do confess the vices of my blood,
So justly to your grave ears I'll present
How I did thrive in this fair lady's love,
And she in mine.

DUKE: Say it, Othello.

OTHELLO: Her father loved me, oft invited me;
Still questioned me the story of my life
From year to year—the battles, sieges, fortunes   130
That I have passed.
I ran it through, even from my boyish days
To th' very moment that he bade me tell it.
Wherein I spake of most disastrous chances,
Of moving accidents by flood and field;
Of hairbreadth scapes i' th' imminent deadly breach;
Of being taken by the insolent foe
And sold to slavery; of my redemption thence
And portance in my travel's history;
Wherein of anters vast and deserts idle,   140
Rough quarries, rocks, and hills whose heads touch heaven,
It was my hint to speak—such was the process;
And of the Cannibals that each other eat,
The Anthropophagi, and men whose heads
Do grow beneath their shoulders. This to hear
Would Desdemona seriously incline;
But still the house affairs would draw her thence;
Which ever as she could with haste dispatch,
She'ld come again, and with a greedy ear
Devour up my discourse. Which I observing,   150
Took once a pliant hour, and found good means
To draw from her a prayer of earnest heart
That I would all my pilgrimage dilate,
Whereof by parcels she had something heard,

129 *Still* continually. 139 *portance* behavior. 140 *anters* caves. 142 *hint* occasion. 144 *Anthropophagi* man-eaters. 151 *pliant* propitious. 153 *dilate* recount in full. 154 *parcels* portions.

But not intentively. I did consent,
And often did beguile her of her tears
When I did speak of some distressful stroke
That my youth suffered. My story being done,
She gave me for my pains a world of sighs.
She swore, i' faith, 'twas strange, 'twas passing strange;   160
'Twas pitiful, 'twas wondrous pitiful.
She wished she had not heard it; yet she wished
That heaven had made her such a man. She thanked me;
And bade me, if I had a friend that loved her,
I should but teach him how to tell my story,
And that would woo her. Upon this hint I spake.
She loved me for the dangers I had passed,
And I loved her that she did pity them.
This only is the witchcraft I have used.
Here comes the lady. Let her witness it.   170

[*Enter* DESDEMONA, IAGO, ATTENDANTS]

DUKE: I think this tale would win my daughter too.
    Good Brabantio,
    Take up this mangled matter at the best.
    Men do their broken weapons rather use
    Than their bare hands.

BRABANTIO: I pray you hear her speak.
    If she confess that she was half the wooer,
    Destruction on my head if my bad blame
    Light on the man! Come hither, gentle mistress.
    Do you perceive in all this noble company
    Where most you owe obedience?

DESDEMONA: My noble father,   180
    I do perceive here a divided duty.
    To you I am bound for life and education;
    My life and education both do learn me
    How to respect you: you are the lord of duty;
    I am hitherto your daughter. But here's my husband;
    And so much duty as my mother showed
    To you, preferring you before her father,
    So much I challenge that I may profess
    Due to the Moor my lord.

    155 *intentively* with full attention. 166 *hint* opportunity. 182 *education* up-
bringing. 188 *challenge* claim the right.

BRABANTIO: God b' wi' ye! I have done.
       Please it your grace, on to the state affairs.   190
       I had rather to adopt a child than get it.
       Come hither, Moor.
       I here do give thee that with all my heart
       Which, but thou hast already, with all my heart
       I would keep from thee. For your sake, jewel,
       I am glad at soul I have no other child;
       For thy escape would teach me tyranny,
       To hang clogs on them. I have done, my lord.

DUKE: Let me speak like yourself and lay a sentence
       Which, as a grise or step, may help these lovers   200
       Into your favor.
       When remedies are past, the griefs are ended
       By seeing the worst, which late on hopes depended.
       To mourn a mischief that is past and gone
       Is the next way to draw new mischief on.
       What cannot be preserved when fortune takes,
       Patience her injury a mock'ry makes.
       The robbed that smiles steals something from the thief;
       He robs himself that spends a bootless grief.

BRABANTIO: So let the Turk of Cyprus us beguile: 210
       We lose it not so long as we can smile.
       He bears the sentence well that nothing bears
       But the free comfort which from thence he hears;
       But he bears both the sentence and the sorrow
       That to pay grief must of poor patience borrow.
       These sentences, to sugar, or to gall,
       Being strong on both sides, are equivocal.
       But words are words. I never yet did hear
       That the bruisèd heart was piecèd through the ear.
       Beseech you, now to the affairs of state.   220

DUKE: The Turk with a most mighty preparation makes for Cyprus.
Othello, the fortitude of the place is best known to you; and though
we have there a substitute of most allowed sufficiency, yet opinion,
a sovereign mistress of effects, throws a more safer voice on you.
You must therefore be content to slubber the gloss of your new
fortunes with this more stubborn and boisterous expedition.

191 *get* beget.   195 *For your sake* because of you.   197 *escape* escapade.   199 *like
yourself* as you should   *sentence* maxim.   200 *grise* step.   222 *fortitude* fortification.
223 *allowed* acknowledged   *opinion* public opinion.   225 *slubber* sully.

OTHELLO: The tyrant custom, most grave senators,
          Hath made the flinty and steel couch of war
          My thrice-driven bed of down. I do agnize
          A natural and prompt alacrity   230
          I find in hardness; and do undertake
          These present wars against the Ottomites.
          Most humbly, therefore, bending to your state,
          I crave fit disposition for my wife,
          Due reference of place, and exhibition,
          With such accommodation and besort
          As levels with her breeding.

DUKE: If you please,
          Be't at her father's.

BRABANTIO: I'll not have it so.

OTHELLO: Nor I.

DESDEMONA: Nor I. I would not there reside,
          To put my father in impatient thoughts   240
          By being in his eye. Most gracious Duke,
          To my unfolding lend your prosperous ear,
          And let me find a charter in your voice,
          To assist my simpleness.

DUKE: What would you, Desdemona?

DESDEMONA: That I did love the Moor to live with him,
          My downright violence, and storm of fortunes,
          May trumpet to the world. My heart's subdued
          Even to the very quality of my lord.
          I saw Othello's visage in his mind,   250
          And to his honors and his valiant parts
          Did I my soul and fortunes consecrate.
          So that, dear lords, if I be left behind,
          A moth of peace, and he go to the war,
          The rites for which I love him are bereft me,
          And I a heavy interim shall support
          By his dear absence. Let me go with him.

OTHELLO: Let her have your voices.
          Vouch with me, heaven, I therefore beg it not

229–31 *agnize . . . hardness* recognize in myself a natural and easy response to hardship.   235 *exhibition* allowance of money.   236 *besort* suitable company.   237 *levels* corresponds.   242 *prosperous* favorable.   244 *simpleness* lack of skill.

To please the palate of my appetite, 260
Nor to comply with heat—the young affects
In me defunct—and proper satisfaction;
But to be free and bounteous to her mind;
And heaven defend your good souls that you think
I will your serious and great business scant
For she is with me. No, when light-winged toys
Of feathered Cupid seel with wanton dullness
My speculative and officed instruments,
That my disports corrupt and taint my business,
Let housewives make a skillet of my helm, 270
And all indign and base adversities
Make head against my estimation!

DUKE: Be it as you shall privately determine,
Either for her stay or going. Th' affair cries haste,
And speed must answer it. You must hence to-night.

DESDEMONA: To-night, my lord?

DUKE: This night.

OTHELLO: With all my heart.

DUKE: At nine i' th' morning here we'll meet again.
Othello, leave some officer behind,
And he shall our commission bring to you,
With such things else of quality and respect 280
As doth import you.

OTHELLO: So please your grace, my ancient;
A man he is of honesty and trust.
To his conveyance I assign my wife,
With what else needful your good grace shall think
To be sent after me.

DUKE: Let it be so.
Good night to every one. [*To* BRABANTIO] And, noble signior,
If virtue no delighted beauty lack,
Your son-in-law is far more fair than black.

1. SENATOR: Adieu, brave Moor. Use Desdemona well.

---

261 *heat* passions   *young affects* tendencies of youth.   266 *For* because.   267 *seel* blind.   268 *My . . . instruments* my perceptive and responsible faculties.   269 *That* so that.   271 *indign* unworthy   272 *estimation* reputation.   281 *import* concern. 287 *delighted* delightful.

BRABANTIO: Look to her, Moor, if thou hast eyes to see: 290
    She has deceived her father, and may thee.

    [*Exeunt* DUKE, SENATORS, OFFICERS, &c.]

OTHELLO: My life upon her faith!—Honest Iago,
    My Desdemona must I leave to thee.
    I prithee let thy wife attend on her,
    And bring them after in the best advantage.
    Come, Desdemona. I have but an hour
    Of love, of worldly matters and direction,
    To spend with thee. We must obey the time.

    [*Exit* MOOR *and* DESDEMONA]

RODERIGO: Iago,—

IAGO: What say'st thou, noble heart?   300

RODERIGO: What will I do, think'st thou?

IAGO: Why, go to bed and sleep.

RODERIGO: I will incontinently drown myself.

IAGO: If thou dost, I shall never love thee after. Why, thou silly gen-
    tleman!

RODERIGO: It is silliness to live when to live is torment; and then have
    we a prescription to die when death is our physician.

IAGO: O villainous! I have looked upon the world for four times seven
    years; and since I could distinguish betwixt a benefit and an injury,
    I never found man that knew how to love himself. Ere I would say   310
    I would drown myself for the love of a guinea hen, I would change
    my humanity with a baboon.

RODERIGO: What should I do? I confess it is my shame to be so fond,
    but it is not in my virtue to amend it.

IAGO: Virtue? a fig! 'Tis in ourselves that we are thus or thus. Our
    bodies are our gardens, to the which our wills are gardeners; so
    that if we will plant nettles or sow lettuce, set hyssop and weed
    up thyme, supply it with one gender of herbs or distract it with
    many—either to have it sterile with idleness or manured with in-
    dustry—why, the power and corrigible authority of this lies in our   320

    295 *in the best advantage* at the best opportunity.   303 *incontinently* forthwith.
318 *gender* species.   320 *corrigible* authority corrective power.

wills. If the balance of our lives had not one scale of reason to poise another of sensuality, the blood and baseness of our natures would conduct us to most preposterous conclusions. But we have reason to cool our raging motions, our carnal stings, our unbitted lusts; whereof I take this that you call love to be a sect or scion.

RODERIGO: It cannot be.

IAGO: It is merely a lust of the blood and a permission of the will. Come, be a man! Drown thyself? Drown cats and blind puppies! I have professed me thy friend, and I confess me knit to thy deserving with cables of perdurable toughness. I could never better stead thee than now. Put money in thy purse. Follow these wars; defeat thy favor with an usurped beard. I say, put money in thy purse. It cannot be that Desdemona should long continue her love to the Moor—put money in thy purse—nor he his to her. It was a violent commencement, and thou shalt see an answerable sequestration—put but money in thy purse. These Moors are changeable in their wills—fill thy purse with money. The food that to him now is as luscious as locusts shall be to him shortly as bitter as coloquintida. She must change for youth: when she is sated with his body, she will find the error of her choice. [She must have change, she must.] Therefore put money in thy purse. If thou wilt needs damn thyself, do it a more delicate way than drowning. Make all the money thou canst. If sanctimony and a frail vow betwixt an erring barbarian and a supersubtle Venetian be not too hard for my wits and all the tribe of hell, thou shalt enjoy her. Therefore make money. A pox of drowning! 'Tis clean out of the way. Seek thou rather to be hanged in compassing thy joy than to be drowned and go without her.

RODERIGO: Wilt thou be fast to my hopes, if I depend on the issue?

IAGO: Thou art sure of me. Go, make money. I have told thee often, and I retell thee again and again, I hate the Moor. My cause is hearted; thine hath no less reason. Let us be conjunctive in our revenge against him. If thou canst cuckold him, thou dost thyself a pleasure, me a sport. There are many events in the womb of time, which will be delivered. Traverse, go, provide thy money! We will have more of this to-morrow. Adieu.

---

322 *poise* counterbalance *blood and baseness* animal instincts. 324 *motions* appetites *unbitted* uncontrolled. 325 *sect or scion* offshoot, cutting. 332 *defeat thy favor* spoil thy appearance. 335 *sequestration* estrangement. 339 *coloquintida* a medicine. 343 *Make* raise. 344 *erring* wandering. 351–52 *My cause is hearted* my heart is in it. 355 *Traverse* forward march.

RODERIGO: Where shall we meet i' th' morning?

IAGO: At my lodging.

RODERIGO: I'll be with thee betimes.

IAGO: Go to, farewell.—Do you hear me, Roderigo?   360

RODERIGO: What say you?

IAGO: No more of drowning, do you hear?

RODERIGO: I am changed.

IAGO: Go to, farewell. Put money enough in your purse.

RODERIGO: I'll sell all my land.   [*Exit*]

IAGO: Thus do I ever make my fool my purse;
   For I mine own gained knowledge should profane
   If I would time expend with such a snipe
   But for my sport and profit. I hate the Moor;
   And it is thought abroad that 'twixt my sheets   370
   H'as done my office. I know not if't be true;
   Yet I, for mere suspicion in that kind,
   Will do as if for surety. He holds me well;
   The better shall my purpose work on him.
   Cassio's a proper man. Let me see now:
   To get his place, and to plume up my will
   In double knavery—How, how?—Let's see:—
   After some time, to abuse Othello's ear
   That he is too familiar with his wife.
   He hath a person and a smooth dispose   380
   To be suspected—framed to make women false.
   The Moor is of a free and open nature
   That thinks men honest that but seem to be so;
   And will as tenderly be led by th' nose
   As asses are.
   I have't! It is engendered! Hell and night
   Must bring this monstrous birth to the world's light.   [*Exit*]

---

  368 *snipe* fool.   373 *well* in high regard.   376 *plume up* gratify.   380 *dispose*
manner.   382 *free* frank.

ACT II. SCENE I

A seaport town in Cyprus. An open place near the Quay.

[*Enter* MONTANO *and two* GENTLEMEN]

MONTANO: What from the cape can you discern at sea?

1. GENTLEMAN: Nothing at all: it is a high-wrought flood.
    I cannot 'twixt the heaven and the main
    Descry a sail.

MONTANO: Methinks the wind hath spoke aloud at land;
    A fuller blast ne'er shook our battlements.
    If it hath ruffianed so upon the sea,
    What ribs of oak, when mountains melt on them,
    Can hold the mortise? What shall we hear of this?

2. GENTLEMAN: A segregation of the Turkish fleet.   10
    For do but stand upon the foaming shore,
    The chidden billow seems to pelt the clouds;
    The wind-shaked surge, with high and monstrous mane,
    Seems to cast water on the burning Bear
    And quench the Guards of th' ever-fixèd pole.
    I never did like molestation view
    On the enchafèd flood.

MONTANO: If that the Turkish fleet
    Be not sheltered and embayed, they are drowned;
    It is impossible they bear it out.

[*Enter a third* GENTLEMAN]

3. GENTLEMAN: News, lads! Our wars are done.   20
    The desperate tempest hath so banged the Turks
    That their designment halts. A noble ship of Venice
    Hath seen a grievous wrack and sufferance
    On most part of their fleet.

MONTANO: How? Is this true?

3. GENTLEMAN: The ship is here put in,
    A Veronesa; Michael Cassio,

---

9 *hold the mortise* hold their joints together.   10 *segregation* scattering.   15 *Guards* stars near the North Star   *pole* polestar.   16 *molestation* tumult.   22 *designment halts* plan is crippled.   23 *sufferance* disaster.   26 *Veronesa* ship furnished by Verona.

Lieutenant to the warlike Moor Othello,
Is come on shore; the Moor himself at sea,
And is in full commission here for Cyprus.

MONTANO: I am glad on't. 'Tis a worthy governor.   30

3. GENTLEMAN: But this same Cassio, though he speak of comfort
Touching the Turkish loss, yet he looks sadly
And prays the Moor be safe, for they were parted
With foul and violent tempest.

MONTANO: Pray heaven he be;
For I have served him, and the man commands
Like a full soldier. Let's to the seaside, ho!
As well to see the vessel that's come in
As to throw out our eyes for brave Othello,
Even till we make the main and th' aerial blue
An indistinct regard.

3. GENTLEMAN: Come, let's do so;   40
For every minute is expectancy
Of more arrivance.

[*Enter* CASSIO]

CASSIO: Thanks, you the valiant of this warlike isle,
That so approve the Moor! O, let the heavens
Give him defense against the elements,
For I have lost him on a dangerous sea!

MONTANO: Is he well shipped?

CASSIO: His bark is stoutly timbered, and his pilot
Of very expert and approved allowance;
Therefore my hopes, not surfeited to death,   50
Stand in bold cure. [*Within*] A sail, a sail, a sail!

[*Enter a* MESSENGER]

CASSIO: What noise?

MESSENGER: The town is empty; on the brow o' th' sea
Stand ranks of people, and they cry 'A sail!'

CASSIO: My hopes do shape him for the governor. [*A shot*]

---

40 *An indistinct regard* indistinguishable.   50 *surfeited to death* overindulged.   51
in bold cure a good chance of fulfillment.

2. GENTLEMAN: They do discharge their shot of courtesy:
    Our friends at least.

CASSIO: I pray you, sir, go forth
    And give us truth who 'tis that is arrived.

2. GENTLEMAN: I shall.   [*Exit*]

MONTANO: But, good lieutenant, is your general wived?   60

CASSIO: Most fortunately. He hath achieved a maid
    That paragons description and wild fame;
    One that excels the quirks of blazoning pens,
    And in th' essential vesture of creation
    Does tire the ingener.

[*Enter* SECOND GENTLEMAN]

          How now? Who has put in?

2. GENTLEMAN: 'Tis one Iago, ancient to the general.

CASSIO: H'as had most favorable and happy speed:
    Tempests themselves, high seas, and howling winds,
    The guttered rocks and congregated sands,
    Traitors ensteeped to clog the guiltless keel,   70
    As having sense of beauty, do omit
    Their mortal natures, letting go safely by
    The divine Desdemona.

MONTANO: What is she?

CASSIO: She that I spake of, our great captain's captain,
    Left in the conduct of the bold Iago,
    Whose footing here anticipates our thoughts
    A se'nnight's speed. Great Jove, Othello guard,
    And swell his sail with thine own pow'rful breath,
    That he may bless this bay with his tall ship,
    Make love's quick pants in Desdemona's arms,   80
    Give renewed fire to our extincted spirits,
    And bring all Cyprus comfort!

[*Enter* DESDEMONA, IAGO, RODERIGO, *and* EMILIA *with* ATTENDANTS]

    62 *paragons* surpasses.   63 *quirks* ingenuities   *blazoning* describing.   64–65 And . . .
ingener merely to describe her as God made her exhausts her praiser.   69 *guttered*
jagged.   70 *ensteeped* submerged.   72 *mortal* deadly.   76 *footing* landing.   77
se'nnight's week's.

O, behold!
The riches of the ship is come on shore!
Ye men of Cyprus, let her have your knees.
Hail to thee, lady! and the grace of heaven,
Before, behind thee, and on every hand,
Enwheel thee round!

DESDEMONA: I thank you, valiant Cassio.
What tidings can you tell me of my lord?

CASSIO: He is not yet arrived; nor know I aught
But that he's well and will be shortly here.   90

DESDEMONA: O but I fear! How lost you company?

CASSIO: The great contention of the sea and skies
Parted our fellowship. [*Within*] A sail, a sail! [*A shot*]
                         But hark. A sail!

2. GENTLEMAN: They give their greeting to the citadel;
This likewise is a friend.

CASSIO: See for the news.

        [*Exit* GENTLEMAN]

Good ancient, you are welcome. [To *Emilia*] Welcome, mistress.—
Let it not gall your patience, good Iago,
That I extend my manners. 'Tis my breeding
That gives me this bold show of courtesy. [*Kisses* EMILIA]

IAGO: Sir, would she give you so much of her lips   100
As of her tongue she oft bestows on me,
You would have enough.

DESDEMONA: Alas, she has no speech!

IAGO: In faith, too much.
I find it still when I have list to sleep.
Marry, before your ladyship, I grant,
She puts her tongue a little in her heart
And chides with thinking.

EMILIA: You have little cause to say so.

IAGO: Come on, come on! You are pictures out of doors,
Bells in your parlors, wildcats in your kitchens,   110

    99 S.D. *Kisses Emilia* (kissing was a common Elizabethan form of social courtesy).

> Saints in your injuries, devils being offended,
> Players in your housewifery, and housewives in your beds.

DESDEMONA: O, fie upon thee, slanderer!

IAGO: Nay, it is true, or else I am a Turk:
> You rise to play, and go to bed to work.

EMILIA: You shall not write my praise.

IAGO: No, let me not.

DESDEMONA: What wouldst thou write of me, if thou shouldst praise
me?

IAGO: O gentle lady, do not put me to't,
> For I am nothing if not critical.

DESDEMONA: Come on, assay.—There's one gone to the harbor? 120

IAGO: Ay, madam.

DESDEMONA: I am not merry; but I do beguile
> The thing I am by seeming otherwise.—
> Come, how wouldst thou praise me?

IAGO: I am about it; but indeed my invention
> Comes from my pate as birdlime does from frieze—
> It plucks out brains and all. But my Muse labors,
> And thus she is delivered:
> If she be fair and wise, fairness and wit—
> The one's for use, the other useth it. 130

DESDEMONA: Well praised! How if she be black and witty?

IAGO: If she be black, and thereto have a wit,
> She'll find a white that shall her blackness fit.

DESDEMONA: Worse and worse!

EMILIA: How if fair and foolish?

IAGO: She never yet was foolish that was fair,
> For even her folly helped her to an heir.

DESDEMONA: These are old fond paradoxes to make fools laugh i' th'
alehouse. What miserable praise hast thou for her that's foul and
foolish? 140

---

112 *housewifery* housekeeping *housewives* hussies. 120 *assay* try. 126 *birdlime* a
sticky paste *frieze* rough cloth. 131 *black* brunette. 137 *folly* wantonness. 138
fond foolish. 139 *foul* ugly.

IAGO: There's none so foul, and foolish thereunto,
       But does foul pranks which fair and wise ones do.

DESDEMONA: O heavy ignorance! Thou praisest the worst best. But
what praise couldst thou bestow on a deserving woman indeed—
one that in the authority of her merit did justly put on the vouch
of very malice itself?

IAGO: She that was ever fair, and never proud;
       Had tongue at will, and yet was never loud;
       Never lacked gold, and yet went never gay;
       Fled from her wish, and yet said 'Now I may';   150
       She that, being angered, her revenge being nigh,
       Bade her wrong stay, and her displeasure fly;
       She that in wisdom never was so frail
       To change the cod's head for the salmon's tail;
       She that could think, and ne'er disclose her mind;
       See suitors following, and not look behind:
       She was a wight (if ever such wight were)—

DESDEMONA: To do what?

IAGO: To suckle fools and chronicle small beer.

DESDEMONA: O most lame and impotent conclusion! Do not learn of   160
him, Emilia, though he be thy husband. How say you, Cassio? Is
he not a most profane and liberal counsellor?

CASSIO: He speaks home, madam. You may relish him more in the
soldier than in the scholar.

IAGO: [Aside]   He takes her by the palm. Ay, well said, whisper! With
as little a web as this will I ensnare as great a fly as Cassio. Ay,
smile upon her, do! I will gyve thee in thine own courtship.—You
say true; 'tis so, indeed!— If such tricks as these strip you out of
your lieutenantry, it had been better you had not kissed your three
fingers so oft—which now again you are most apt to play the sir in.   170
Very good! well kissed! an excellent curtsy! 'Tis so, indeed. Yet
again your fingers to your lips? Would they were clyster pipes for
your sake! [Trumpet within] The Moor! I know his trumpet.

CASSIO: 'Tis truly so.

145 *put on the vouch* compel the approval.   154 *To . . . tail* i.e. to exchange
the good for the poor but expensive.   159 *chronicle small beer* keep petty household
accounts.   162 *profane and liberal* worldly and licentious.   163 *home* bluntly.   167
gyve . . . courtship manacle you by means of your courtly manners.   170 *sir* courtly
gentleman.   171 *curtsy* courtesy.   172 *clyster pipes* syringes.

DESDEMONA: Let's meet him and receive him.

CASSIO: Lo, where he comes.

[*Enter* OTHELLO *and* ATTENDANTS]

OTHELLO: O my fair warrior!

DESDEMONA: My dear Othello!

OTHELLO: It gives me wonder great as my content
    To see you here before me. O my soul's joy!
    If after every tempest come such calms,   180
    May the winds blow till they have wakened death!
    And let the laboring bark climb hills of seas
    Olympus-high, and duck again as low
    As hell's from heaven! If it were now to die,
    'Twere now to be most happy; for I fear
    My soul hath her content so absolute
    That not another comfort like to this
    Succeeds in unknown fate.

DESDEMONA: The heavens forbid
    But that our loves and comforts should increase
    Even as our days do grow.

OTHELLO: Amen to that, sweet powers!   190
    I cannot speak enough of this content;
    It stops me here; it is too much of joy.
    And this, and this, the greatest discords be [*They kiss*]
    That e'er our hearts shall make!

IAGO: [*Aside*]   O, you are well tuned now!
    But I'll set down the pegs that make this music,
    As honest as I am.

OTHELLO: Come, let us to the castle.
    News, friends! Our wars are done; the Turks are drowned.
    How does my old acquaintance of this isle?—
    Honey, you shall be well desired in Cyprus;   200
    I have found great love amongst them. O my sweet,
    I prattle out of fashion, and I dote
    In mine own comforts. I prithee, good Iago,
    Go to the bay and disembark my coffers.
    Bring thou the master to the citadel;

   195 *set down* loosen.   200 *well desired* warmly welcomed.   205 *master* ship captain.

He is a good one, and his worthiness
Does challenge much respect.—Come, Desdemona,
Once more well met at Cyprus.

[*Exit* OTHELLO *with all but* IAGO *and* RODERIGO]

IAGO: [*To an attendant, who goes out*] Do thou meet me presently
at the harbor. [*To* RODERIGO] Come hither. If thou be'st valiant   210
(as they say base men being in love have then a nobility in their natures more than is native to them), list me. The lieutenant to-night
watches on the court of guard. First, I must tell thee this: Desdemona is directly in love with him.

RODERIGO: With him? Why, 'tis not possible.

IAGO: Lay thy finger thus, and let thy soul be instructed. Mark me
with what violence she first loved the Moor, but for bragging and
telling her fantastical lies; and will she love him still for prating?
Let not thy discreet heart think it. Her eye must be fed; and what
delight shall she have to look on the devil? When the blood is   220
made dull with the act of sport, there should be, again to inflame
it and to give satiety a fresh appetite, loveliness in favor, sympathy
in years, manners, and beauties; all which the Moor is defective in.
Now for want of these required conveniences, her delicate tenderness will find itself abused, begin to heave the gorge, disrelish and
abhor the Moor. Very nature will instruct her in it and compel her
to some second choice. Now, sir, this granted—as it is a most pregnant and unforced position—who stands so eminent in the degree of
this fortune as Cassio does? A knave very voluble; no further conscionable than in putting on the mere form of civil and humane   230
seeming for the better compassing of his salt and most hidden loose
affection? Why, none! why, none! A slipper and subtle knave; a
finder-out of occasions; that has an eye can stamp and counterfeit
advantages, though true advantage never present itself; a devilish
knave! Besides, the knave is handsome, young, and hath all those
requisites in him that folly and green minds look after. A pestilent
complete knave! and the woman hath found him already.

RODERIGO: I cannot believe that in her; she's full of most blessed condition.

207 *challenge* deserve.   213 *court of guard* headquarters.   216 *thus* i.e. on your
lips.   224 *conveniences* compatibilities   *heave the gorge* be nauseated.   227 *pregnant*
evident.   229 *conscionable* conscientious.   230 *humane* polite.   231 *salt* lecherous.
232 *slipper* slippery.   238 *condition* character.

IAGO: Blessed fig's-end! The wine she drinks is made of grapes. If she   240
had been blessed, she would never have loved the Moor. Blessed
pudding! Didst thou not see her paddle with the palm of his hand?
Didst not mark that?

RODERIGO: Yes, that I did; but that was but courtesy.

IAGO: Lechery, by this hand! an index and obscure prologue to the
history of lust and foul thoughts. They met so near with their lips
that their breaths embraced together. Villainous thoughts, Roderigo! When these mutualities so marshal the way, hard at hand
comes the master and main exercise, th' incorporate conclusion.
Pish! But, sir, be you ruled by me: I have brought you from   250
Venice. Watch you to-night; for the command, I'll lay't upon you.
Cassio knows you not. I'll not be far from you: do you find some
occasion to anger Cassio, either by speaking too loud, or tainting
his discipline, or from what other course you please which the time
shall more favorably minister.

RODERIGO: Well.

IAGO: Sir, he is rash and very sudden in choler, and haply with his
truncheon may strike at you. Provoke him that he may; for even out
of that will I cause these of Cyprus to mutiny; whose qualification
shall come into no true taste again but by the displanting of Cassio.   260
So shall you have a shorter journey to your desires by the means I
shall then have to prefer them; and the impediment most profitably
removed without the which there were no expectation of our prosperity.

RODERIGO: I will do this if you can bring it to any opportunity.

IAGO: I warrant thee. Meet me by and by at the citadel; I must fetch
his necessaries ashore. Farewell.

RODERIGO: Adieu. [Exit]

IAGO: That Cassio loves her, I do well believe it;
That she loves him, 'tis apt and of great credit.   270
The Moor, howbeit that I endure him not,
Is of a constant, loving, noble nature,
And I dare think he'll prove to Desdemona

---

248 *mutualities* exchanges. 249 *incorporate* carnal. 253 *tainting* discrediting.
257 *sudden in choler* violent in anger. 259 *qualification* appeasement. 260 *true taste*
satisfactory state. 262 *prefer* advance. 270 *apt* probable.

A most dear husband. Now I do love her too;
Not out of absolute lust, though peradventure
I stand accountant for as great a sin,
But partly led to diet my revenge,
For that I do suspect the lusty Moor
Hath leaped into my seat; the thought whereof
Doth, like a poisonous mineral, gnaw my inwards;   280
And nothing can or shall content my soul
Till I am evened with him, wife for wife;
Or failing so, yet that I put the Moor
At least into a jealousy so strong
That judgment cannot cure. Which thing to do,
If this poor trash of Venice, whom I trash
For his quick hunting, stand the putting on,
I'll have our Michael Cassio on the hip,
Abuse him to the Moor in the rank garb
(For I fear Cassio with my nightcap too),   290
Make the Moor thank me, love me, and reward me
For making him egregiously an ass
And practicing upon his peace and quiet
Even to madness. 'Tis here, but yet confused:
Knavery's plain face is never seen till used.   [*Exit*]

SCENE II

A street.

[*Enter* OTHELLO'S HERALD, *with a proclamation*]

HERALD: It is Othello's pleasure, our noble and valiant general, that,
        upon certain tidings now arrived, importing the mere perdition of
        the Turkish fleet, every man put himself into triumph; some to
        dance, some to make bonfires, each man to what sport and revels
        his addiction leads him. For, besides these beneficial news, it is the
        celebration of his nuptial. So much was his pleasure should be
        proclaimed. All offices are open, and there is full liberty of feast-
        ing from this present hour of five till the bell have told eleven.
        Heaven bless the isle of Cyprus and our noble general Othello!

     [*Exit*]

---

   276 *accountant* accountable.   277 *diet* feed.   286 *I trash* I weight down (in order
to keep under control).   287 *For* in order to develop   *stand the putting on* responds
to my inciting.   288 *on the hip* at my mercy.   289 *rank garb* gross manner.   293
practicing upon plotting against.   2 *mere perdition* complete destruction.   7 *offices*
kitchens and storerooms.

SCENE III

A hall in the castle.

[*Enter* OTHELLO, DESDEMONA, CASSIO, *and* ATTENDANTS]

OTHELLO: Good Michael, look you to the guard to-night.
Let's teach ourselves that honorable stop,
Not to outsport discretion.

CASSIO: Iago hath direction what to do;
But not withstanding, with my personal eye
Will I look to't.

OTHELLO: Iago is most honest.
Michael, good night. To-morrow with your earliest
Let me have speech with you. [*To* DESDEMONA] Come, my dear love.
The purchase made, the fruits are to ensue;
That profit's yet to come 'tween me and you.—   10
Good night.

[*Exit* OTHELLO *with* DESDEMONA *and* ATTENDANTS]

[*Enter* IAGO]

CASSIO: Welcome, Iago. We must to the watch.

IAGO: Not this hour, lieutenant; 'tis not yet ten o' th' clock. Our general cast us thus early for the love of his Desdemona; who let us not therefore blame. He hath not yet made wanton the night with her, and she is sport for Jove.

CASSIO: She's a most exquisite lady.

IAGO: And, I'll warrant her, full of game.

CASSIO: Indeed, she's a most fresh and delicate creature.

IAGO: What an eye she has! Methinks it sounds a parley to provocation.   20

CASSIO: An inviting eye; and yet methinks right modest.

IAGO: And when she speaks, is it not an alarum to love?

CASSIO: She is indeed perfection.

IAGO: Well, happiness to their sheets! Come, lieutenant, I have a stoup of wine, and here without are a brace of Cyprus gallants that would fain have a measure to the health of black Othello.

14 *cast* dismissed.   24 *stoup* two-quart tankard.

CASSIO: Not to-night, good Iago. I have very poor and unhappy brains
for drinking; I could well wish courtesy would invent some other
custom of entertainment.

IAGO: O, they are our friends. But one cup! I'll drink for you.   30

CASSIO: I have drunk but one cup to-night, and that was craftily qualified too; and behold what innovation it makes here. I am unfortunate in the infirmity and dare not task my weakness with any more.

IAGO: What, man! 'Tis a night of revels: the gallants desire it.

CASSIO: Where are they?

IAGO: Here at the door; I pray you call them in.

CASSIO: I'll do't, but it dislikes me.   [*Exit*]

IAGO: If I can fasten but one cup upon him
With that which he hath drunk to-night already,
He'll be as full of quarrel and offense   40
As my young mistress' dog. Now my sick fool Roderigo,
Whom love hath turned almost the wrong side out,
To Desdemona hath to-night caroused
Potations pottle-deep; and he's to watch.
Three lads of Cyprus—noble swelling spirits,
That hold their honors in a wary distance,
The very elements of this warlike isle—
Have I to-night flustered with flowing cups,
And they watch too. Now, 'mongst this flock of drunkards
Am I to put our Cassio in some action   50
That may offend the isle.

[*Enter* CASSIO, MONTANO, *and* GENTLEMEN; SERVANTS *following with wine*]

But here they come.
If consequence do but approve my dream,
My boat sails freely, both with wind and stream.

CASSIO: 'Fore God, they have given me a rouse already.

MONTANO: Good faith, a little one; not past a pint, as I am a soldier.

31 *qualified* diluted *innovation* disturbance. 44 *pottle-deep* bottoms up. 46
That . . . distance very sensitive about their honor.   47 *very elements* true representatives.   54 *rouse* bumper.

IAGO: Some wine, ho!

> [*Sings*] And let me the canakin clink, clink;
> And let me the canakin clink.
>   A soldier's a man;
>   A life's but a span,
> Why then, let a soldier drink.
>   Some wine, boys!   60

CASSIO: 'Fore God, an excellent song!

IAGO: I learned it in England, where indeed they are most potent in potting. Your Dane, your German, and your swag-bellied Hollander—Drink, ho!—are nothing to your English.

CASSIO: Is your Englishman so expert in his drinking?

IAGO: Why, he drinks you with facility your Dane dead drunk; he sweats not to overthrow your Almain; he gives your Hollander a vomit ere the next pottle can be filled.   70

CASSIO: To the health of our general!

MONTANO: I am for it, lieutenant, and I'll do you justice.

IAGO: O sweet England!

> [*Sings*] King Stephen was a worthy peer;
>   His breeches cost him but a crown;
> He held 'em sixpence all too dear,
>   With that he called the tailor lown.
> He was a wight of high renown,
>   And thou art but of low degree.
> 'Tis pride that pulls the country down;   80
>   Then take thine auld cloak about thee.
>   Some wine, ho!

CASSIO: 'Fore God, this is a more exquisite song than the other.

IAGO: Will you hear't again?

CASSIO: No, for I hold him to be unworthy of his place that does those things. Well, God's above all; and there be souls must be saved, and there be souls must not be saved.

IAGO: It's true, good lieutenant.

75 *lown* rascal.

CASSIO: For mine own part—no offense to the general, nor any man of quality—I hope to be saved. 90

IAGO: And so do I too, lieutenant.

CASSIO: Ay, but, by your leave, not before me. The lieutenant is to be saved before the ancient. Let's have no more of this; let's to our affairs.—God forgive us our sins!—Gentlemen, let's look to our business. Do not think, gentlemen, I am drunk. This is my ancient; this is my right hand, and this is my left. I am not drunk now. I can stand well enough, and speak well enough.

ALL: Excellent well!

CASSIO: Why, very well then. You must not think then that I am drunk.

[Exit]

MONTANO: To th' platform, masters. Come, let's set the watch. 100

IAGO: You see this fellow that is gone before.
He is a soldier fit to stand by Caesar
And give direction; and do but see his vice.
'Tis to his virtue a just equinox,
The one as long as th' other. 'Tis pity of him.
I fear the trust Othello puts him in,
On some odd time of his infirmity,
Will shake this island.

MONTANO: But is he often thus?

IAGO: 'Tis evermore the prologue to his sleep:
He'll watch the horologe a double set 110
If drink rock not his cradle.

MONTANO: It were well
The general were put in mind of it.
Perhaps he sees it not, or his good nature
Prizes the virtue that appears in Cassio
And looks not on his evils. Is not this true?

[Enter RODERIGO]

IAGO: [Aside to him] How now, Roderigo?
I pray you after the lieutenant go! [Exit RODERIGO]

MONTANO: And 'tis great pity that the noble Moor
Should hazard such a place as his own second

---

104 *just equinox* exact equivalent. 110 *watch . . . set* stay awake twice around the clock.

With one of an ingraft infirmity.   120
It were an honest action to say
So to the Moor.

IAGO: Not I, for this fair island!
I do love Cassio well and would do much
To cure him of this evil.   [*Within*]   Help! help!
                              But hark! What noise?

[*Enter* CASSIO, *driving in* RODERIGO]

CASSIO: Zounds, you rogue! you rascal!

MONTANO: What's the matter, lieutenant?

CASSIO: A knave teach me my duty?
I'll beat the knave into a twiggen bottle.

RODERIGO: Beat me?

CASSIO: Dost thou prate, rogue?   [*Strikes him*]

MONTANO: Nay, good lieutenant!

[*Stays him*]

Pray, sir, hold your hand.

CASSIO: Let me go, sir,
Or I'll knock you o'er the mazzard.

MONTANO: Come, come, you're drunk!   130

CASSIO: Drunk?   [*They fight*]

IAGO: [*Aside to* RODERIGO]   Away, I say! Go out and cry a mutiny!

[*Exit* RODERIGO]

Nay, good lieutenant. God's will, gentlemen!
Help, ho!—lieutenant—sir—Montano—sir—
Help, masters!—Here's a goodly watch indeed!

[*A bell rung*]

Who's that which rings the bell? Diablo, ho!
The town will rise. God's will, lieutenant, hold!
You will be shamed for ever.

[*Enter* OTHELLO *and* GENTLEMEN *with weapons*]

OTHELLO: What is the matter here?

127 *twiggen* wicker-covered.   130 *mazzard* head.

MONTANO: Zounds, I bleed still. I am hurt to the death.
　　　　He dies!   140

OTHELLO: Hold for your lives!

IAGO: Hold, hold! Lieutenant—sir—Montano—gentlemen!
　　　Have you forgot all sense of place and duty?
　　　Hold! The general speaks to you. Hold, hold, for shame!

OTHELLO: Why, how now, ho? From whence ariseth this?
　　　　Are we turned Turks, and to ourselves do that
　　　　Which heaven hath forbid the Ottomites?
　　　　For Christian shame put by this barbarous brawl!
　　　　He that stirs next to carve for his own rage
　　　　Holds his soul light; he dies upon his motion.   150
　　　　Silence that dreadful bell! It frights the isle
　　　　From her propriety. What's the matter, masters?
　　　　Honest Iago, that looks dead with grieving,
　　　　Speak. Who began this? On thy love, I charge thee.

IAGO: I do not know. Friends all but now, even now,
　　　In quarter, and in terms like bride and groom
　　　Devesting them for bed; and then, but now—
　　　As if some planet had unwitted men—
　　　Swords out, and tilting one at other's breast
　　　In opposition bloody. I cannot speak   160
　　　Any beginning to this peevish odds,
　　　And would in action glorious I had lost
　　　Those legs that brought me to a part of it!

OTHELLO: How comes it, Michael, you are thus forgot?

CASSIO: I pray you pardon me; I cannot speak.

OTHELLO: Worthy Montano, you were wont be civil;
　　　　The gravity and stillness of your youth
　　　　The world hath noted, and your name is great
　　　　In mouths of wisest censure. What's the matter
　　　　That you unlace your reputation thus   170
　　　　And spend your rich opinion for the name
　　　　Of a night-brawler? Give me answer to 't.

MONTANO: Worthy Othello, I am hurt to danger.
　　　　Your officer, Iago, can inform you,

---

149 *carve for* indulge.   152 *propriety* proper self.   156 *quarter* friendliness.   161
peevish odds childish quarrel.   169 *censure* judgment.   170 *unlace* undo.   171 *rich
opinion* high reputation.

While I spare speech, which something now offends me,
Of all that I do know; nor know I aught
By me that's said or done amiss this night,
Unless self-charity be sometimes a vice,
And to defend ourselves it be a sin
When violence assails us.

OTHELLO: Now, by heaven, 180
My blood begins my safer guides to rule,
And passion, having my best judgment collied,
Assays to lead the way. If I once stir
Or do but lift this arm, the best of you
Shall sink in my rebuke. Give me to know
How this foul rout began, who set it on;
And he that is approved in this offense,
Though he had twinned with me, both at a birth,
Shall lose me. What! in a town of war,
Yet wild, the people's hearts brimful of fear, 190
To manage private and domestic quarrel?
In night, and on the court and guard of safety?
'Tis monstrous. Iago, who began't?

MONTANO: If partially affined, or leagued in office,
Thou dost deliver more or less than truth,
Thou art no soldier.

IAGO: Touch me not so near.
I had rather have this tongue cut from my mouth
Than it should do offense to Michael Cassio;
Yet I persuade myself, to speak the truth
Shall nothing wrong him. Thus it is, general. 200
Montano and myself being in speech,
There comes a fellow crying out for help,
And Cassio following him with determined sword
To execute upon him. Sir, this gentleman
Steps in to Cassio and entreats his pause.
Myself the crying fellow did pursue,
Lest by his clamor—as it so fell out—
The town might fall in fright. He, swift of foot,
Outran my purpose; and I returned the rather
For that I heard the clink and fall of swords, 210

175 *offends* pains. 181 *blood* passion. 182 *collied* darkened. 183 *Assays* tries.
187 *approved in* proved guilty of. 191 *manage* carry on. 194 *partially . . . office*
prejudiced by comradeship or official relations. 204 *execute* work his will.

And Cassio high in oath; which till to-night
I ne'er might say before. When I came back—
For this was brief—I found them close together
At blow and thrust, even as again they were
When you yourself did part them.
More of this matter cannot I report;
But men are men; the best sometimes forget.
Though Cassio did some little wrong to him,
As men in rage strike those that wish them best,
Yet surely Cassio I believe received   220
From him that fled some strange indignity,
Which patience could not pass.

OTHELLO: I know, Iago,
Thy honesty and love doth mince this matter,
Making it light to Cassio. Cassio, I love thee;
But never more be officer of mine.

[*Enter* DESDEMONA, *attended*]

Look if my gentle love be not raised up!
I'll make thee an example.

DESDEMONA: What's the matter?

OTHELLO: All's well now, sweeting; come away to bed.
[*To* MONTANO] Sir, for your hurts, myself will be your surgeon.
Lead him off. [MONTANO *is led off*]   230
Iago, look with care about the town
And silence those whom this vile brawl distracted.
Come, Desdemona: 'tis the soldiers' life
To have their balmy slumbers waked with strife.

[*Exit with all but* IAGO *and* CASSIO]

IAGO: What, are you hurt, lieutenant?

CASSIO: Ay, past all surgery.

IAGO: Marry, God forbid!

CASSIO: Reputation, reputation, reputation! O, I have lost my reputation! I have lost the immortal part of myself, and what remains is
bestial. My reputation, Iago, my reputation!   240

IAGO: As I am an honest man, I thought you had received some bodily
wound. There is more sense in that than in reputation. Reputation is
an idle and most false imposition; oft got without merit and lost

without deserving. You have lost no reputation at all unless you repute yourself such a loser. What, man! there are ways to recover the general again. You are but now cast in his mood—a punishment more in policy than in malice, even so as one would beat his offenseless dog to affright an imperious lion. Sue to him again, and he's yours.

CASSIO: I will rather sue to be despised than to deceive so good a com- 250
mander with so slight, so drunken, and so indiscreet an officer. Drunk! and speak parrot! and squabble! swagger! swear! and discourse fustian with one's own shadow! O thou invisible spirit of wine, if thou hast no name to be known by, let us call thee devil!

IAGO: What was he that you followed with your sword?
What had he done to you?

CASSIO: I know not.

IAGO: Is't possible?

CASSIO: I remember a mass of things, but nothing distinctly; a quarrel, but nothing wherefore. O God, that men should put an enemy in 260
their mouths to steal away their brains! that we should with joy, pleasance, revel, and applause transform ourselves into beasts!

IAGO: Why, but you are now well enough. How came you thus recovered?

CASSIO: It hath pleased the devil drunkenness to give place to the devil wrath. One unperfectness shows me another, to make me frankly despise myself.

IAGO: Come, you are too severe a moraler. As the time, the place, and the condition of this country stands, I could heartily wish this had not so befall'n; but since it is as it is, mend it for your own good.

CASSIO: I will ask him for my place again: he shall tell me I am a 270
drunkard! Had I as many mouths as Hydra, such an answer would stop them all. To be now a sensible man, by and by a fool, and presently a beast! O strange! Every inordinate cup is unblest, and the ingredient is a devil.

IAGO: Come, come, good wine is a good familiar creature if it be well used. Exclaim no more against it. And, good lieutenant, I think you think I love you.

245 *recover* regain favor with.   246 *cast in his mood* dismissed because of his anger.   252 *parrot* meaningless phrases.   253 *fustian* bombastic nonsense.   262 *applause* desire to please.   271 *Hydra* monster with many heads.   274 *ingredient* contents.

CASSIO: I have well approved it, sir. I drunk!

IAGO: You or any man living may be drunk at some time, man. I'll tell
you what you shall do. Our general's wife is now the general. I may   280
say so in this respect, for that he hath devoted and given up himself to the contemplation, mark, and denotement of her parts and
graces. Confess yourself freely to her; importune her help to put you
in your place again. She is of so free, so kind, so apt, so blessed a
disposition she holds it a vice in her goodness not to do more than
she is requested. This broken joint between you and her husband
entreat her to splinter; and my fortunes against any lay worth nam-
ing, this crack of your love shall grow stronger than 'twas before.

CASSIO: You advise me well.

IAGO: I protest, in the sincerity of love and honest kindness.   290

CASSIO: I think it freely; and betimes in the morning will I beseech the
virtuous Desdemona to undertake for me. I am desperate of my
fortunes if they check me here.

IAGO: You are in the right. Good night, lieutenant; I must to the watch.

CASSIO: Good night, honest Iago.   [*Exit* CASSIO]

IAGO: And what's he then that says I play the villain,
When this advice is free I give and honest,
Probal to thinking, and indeed the course
To win the Moor again? For 'tis most easy
Th' inclining Desdemona to subdue   300
In any honest suit; she's framed as fruitful
As the free elements. And then for her
To win the Moor—were't to renounce his baptism,
All seals and symbols of redeemèd sin—
His soul is so enfettered to her love
That she may make, unmake, do what she list,
Even as her appetite shall play the god
With his weak function. How am I then a villain
To counsel Cassio to this parallel course,
Directly to his good? Divinity of hell!   310
When devils will the blackest sins put on,
They do suggest at first with heavenly shows,

278 *approved* proved.   284 *free* bounteous.   287 *splinter* bind up with splints.
288 *lay* wager.   298 *Probal* probable.   300 *subdue* persuade.   309 *parallel* corresponding.   310 *Divinity* theology.   311 *put on* incite.

As I do now. For whiles this honest fool
Plies Desdemona to repair his fortunes,
And she for him pleads strongly to the Moor,
I'll pour this pestilence into his ear,
That she repeals him for her body's lust;
And by how much she strives to do him good,
She shall undo her credit with the Moor.
So will I turn her virtue into pitch,   320
And out of her own goodness make the net
That shall enmesh them all.

[*Enter* RODERIGO]

> How, now, Roderigo?

RODERIGO: I do follow here in the chase, not like a hound that hunts, but one that fills up the cry. My money is almost spent; I have been to-night exceedingly well cudgelled; and I think the issue will be—I shall have so much experience for my pains; and so, with no money at all, and a little more wit, return again to Venice.

IAGO: How poor are they that have not patience!
What wound did ever heal but by degrees?
Thou know'st we work by wit, and not by witchcraft;   330
And wit depends on dilatory time.
Does't not go well? Cassio hath beaten thee,
And thou by that small hurt hast cashiered Cassio.
Though other things grow fair against the sun,
Yet fruits that blossom first will first be ripe.
Content thyself awhile. By the mass, 'tis morning!
Pleasure and action make the hours seem short.
Retire thee; go where thou art billeted.
Away, I say! Thou shalt know more hereafter.
Nay, get thee gone!   [*Exit* RODERIGO]
                Two things are to be done: 340
My wife must move for Cassio to her mistress;
I'll set her on;
Myself the while to draw the Moor apart
And bring him jump when he may Cassio find
Soliciting his wife. Ay, that's the way!
Dull not device by coldness and delay.   [*Exit*]

---

317 *repeals him* seeks his recall.   324 *cry* pack.   333 *cashiered Cassio* maneuvered Cassio's discharge.   344 *jump* at the exact moment.

ACT III. SCENE I

Cyprus. Before the castle.

[*Enter* CASSIO, *with* MUSICIANS]

CASSIO: Masters, play here, I will content your pains:
Something that's brief; and bid 'Good morrow, general.'

[*They play*]

[*Enter the* CLOWN]

CLOWN: Why, masters, ha' your instruments been at Naples, that they
speak i' th' nose thus?

MUSICIAN: How, sir, how?

CLOWN: Are these, I pray, called wind instruments?

MUSICIAN: Ay, marry, are they, sir.

CLOWN: O, thereby hangs a tail.

MUSICIAN: Whereby hangs a tale, sir?

CLOWN: Marry, sir, by many a wind instrument that I know. But, mas-   10
ters, here's money for you; and the general so likes your music that
he desires you, for love's sake, to make no more noise with it.

MUSICIAN: Well, sir, we will not.

CLOWN: If you have any music that may not be heard, to't again: but,
as they say, to hear music the general does not greatly care.

MUSICIAN: We have none such, sir.

CLOWN: Then put up your pipes in your bag, for I'll away.
Go, vanish into air, away!   [*Exit* MUSICIAN *with his fellows*]

CASSIO: Dost thou hear, my honest friend?

CLOWN: No, I hear not your honest friend. I hear you.   20

CASSIO: Prithee keep up thy quillets. There's a poor piece of gold for
thee. If the gentlewoman that attends the general's wife be stirring,
tell her there's one Cassio entreats her a little favor of speech. Wilt
thou do this?

---

1 *content* reward.   4 *Naples* (notorious for its association with venereal disease).
21 *quillets* quips.

CLOWN: She is stirring, sir. If she will stir hither, I shall seem to notify unto her.

CASSIO: Do, good my friend.   [*Exit* CLOWN]

[*Enter* IAGO]

In happy time, Iago.

IAGO: You have not been abed then?

CASSIO: Why, no; the day had broke
Before we parted. I have made bold, Iago,   30
To send in to your wife: my suit to her
Is that she will to virtuous Desdemona
Procure me some access.

IAGO: I'll send her to you presently;
And I'll devise a mean to draw the Moor
Out of the way, that your converse and business
May be more free.

CASSIO: I humbly thank you for't.   [*Exit* IAGO]

                              I never knew
A Florentine more kind and honest.

[*Enter* EMILIA]

EMILIA: Good morrow, good lieutenant. I am sorry
For your displeasure; but all will sure be well.   40
The general and his wife are talking of it,
And she speaks for you stoutly. The Moor replies
That he you hurt is of great fame in Cyprus
And great affinity, and that in wholesome wisdom
He might not but refuse you; but he protests he loves you,
And needs no other suitor but his likings
To take the safest occasion by the front
To bring you in again.

CASSIO: Yet I beseech you,
If you think fit, or that it may be done,
Give me advantage of some brief discourse   50
With Desdemona alone.

27 *In happy time* well met.   38 *Florentine* i.e. even a Florentine (like Cassio; Iago was a Venetian).   44 *affinity* family connections.   47 *occasion* opportunity *front* forelock.

EMILIA: Pray you come in.
I will bestow you where you shall have time
To speak your bosom freely.

CASSIO: I am much bound to you.   [*Exeunt*]

SCENE II

A room in the castle.

[*Enter* OTHELLO, IAGO, *and* GENTLEMEN]

OTHELLO: These letters give, Iago, to the pilot
And by him do my duties to the Senate.
That done, I will be walking on the works;
Repair there to me.

IAGO: Well, my good lord, I'll do't.

OTHELLO: This fortification, gentlemen, shall we see't?

GENTLEMEN: We'll wait upon your lordship.   [*Exeunt*]

SCENE III

The garden of the castle.

[*Enter* DESDEMONA, CASSIO, *and* EMILIA]

DESDEMONA: Be thou assured, good Cassio, I will do
All my abilities in thy behalf.

EMILIA: Good madam, do. I warrant it grieves my husband
As if the cause were his.

DESDEMONA: O, that's an honest fellow. Do not doubt, Cassio,
But I will have my lord and you again
As friendly as you were.

CASSIO: Bounteous madam,
Whatever shall become of Michael Cassio,
He's never anything but your true servant.

DESDEMONA: I know't; I thank you. You do love my lord;   10
You have known him long; and be you well assured

---

53 *your bosom* your inmost thoughts.   3 *works* fortifications.

He shall in strangeness stand no farther off
Than in a politic distance.

CASSIO: Ay, but, lady,
That policy may either last so long,
Or feed upon such nice and waterish diet,
Or breed itself so out of circumstance,
That, I being absent, and my place supplied,
My general will forget my love and service.

DESDEMONA: Do not doubt that; before Emilia here
I give thee warrant of thy place. Assure thee,   20
If I do vow a friendship, I'll perform it
To the last article. My lord shall never rest;
I'll watch him tame and talk him out of patience;
His bed shall seem a school, his board a shrift;
I'll intermingle everything he does
With Cassio's suit. Therefore be merry, Cassio,
For thy solicitor shall rather die
Than give thy cause away.

[*Enter* OTHELLO *and* IAGO *at a distance*]

EMILIA: Madam, here comes my lord.

CASSIO: Madam, I'll take my leave.   30

DESDEMONA: Why, stay, and hear me speak.

CASSIO: Madam, not now: I am very ill at ease,
Unfit for mine own purposes.

DESDEMONA: Well, do your discretion.   [*Exit* CASSIO]

IAGO: Ha! I like not that.

OTHELLO: What dost thou say?

IAGO: Nothing, my lord; or if—I know not what.

OTHELLO: Was not that Cassio parted from my wife?

IAGO: Cassio, my lord? No, sure, I cannot think it,
That he would steal away so guilty-like,
Seeing you coming.

OTHELLO: I do believe 'twas he.   40

12 *strangeness* aloofness. 13 *Than . . . distance* than wise policy requires. 15 *Or . . . diet* or be continued for such slight reasons. 19 *doubt* fear. 23 *watch him tame* keep him awake until he gives in. 24 *shrift* confessional.

DESDEMONA: How now, my lord?
    I have been talking with a suitor here,
    A man that languishes in your displeasure.

OTHELLO: Who is't you mean?

DESDEMONA: Why, your lieutenant, Cassio. Good my lord,
    If I have any grace or power to move you,
    His present reconciliation take;
    For if he be not one that truly loves you,
    That errs in ignorance, and not in cunning,
    I have no judgment in an honest face.   50
    I prithee call him back.

OTHELLO: Went he hence now?

DESDEMONA: Yes, faith; so humbled
    That he hath left part of his grief with me
    To suffer with him. Good love, call him back.

OTHELLO: Not now, sweet Desdemon; some other time.

DESDEMONA: But shall't be shortly?

OTHELLO: The sooner, sweet, for you.

DESDEMONA: Shall't be to-night at supper?

OTHELLO: No, not to-night.

DESDEMONA: To-morrow dinner then?

OTHELLO: I shall not dine at home;
    I meet the captains at the citadel.

DESDEMONA: Why then, to-morrow night, or Tuesday morn,   60
    On Tuesday noon or night, or Wednesday morn.
    I prithee name the time, but let it not
    Exceed three days. I' faith, he's penitent;
    And yet his trespass, in our common reason
    (Save that, they say, the wars must make examples
    Out of their best), is not almost a fault
    T' incur a private check. When shall he come?
    Tell me, Othello. I wonder in my soul
    What you could ask me that I should deny
    Or stand so mamm'ring on. What? Michael Cassio,   70
    That came a-wooing with you, and so many a time,

---

47 *present* immediate.   66 *not almost* hardly.   67 *a private check* even a private reprimand.   70 *mamm'ring on* hesitating about.

When I have spoke of you dispraisingly,
Hath ta'en your part—to have so much to do
To bring him in? By'r Lady, I could do much—

OTHELLO: Prithee no more. Let him come when he will!
I will deny thee nothing.

DESDEMONA: Why, this is not a boon;
'Tis as I should entreat you wear your gloves,
Or feed on nourishing dishes, or keep you warm,
Or sue to you to do a peculiar profit
To your own person. Nay, when I have a suit   80
Wherein I mean to touch your love indeed,
It shall be full of poise and difficult weight,
And fearful to be granted.

OTHELLO: I will deny thee nothing!
Whereon I do beseech thee grant me this,
To leave me but a little to myself.

DESDEMONA: Shall I deny you? No. Farewell, my lord.

OTHELLO: Farewell, my Desdemon: I'll come to thee straight.

DESDEMONA: Emilia, come.—Be as your fancies teach you;
Whate'er you be, I am obedient.   [*Exit with* EMILIA]

OTHELLO: Excellent wretch! Perdition catch my soul   90
But I do love thee! and when I love thee not,
Chaos is come again.

IAGO: My noble lord—

OTHELLO: What dost thou say, Iago?

IAGO: Did Michael Cassio, when you wooed my lady,
Know of your love?

OTHELLO: He did, from first to last. Why dost thou ask?

IAGO: But for a satisfaction of my thought;
No further harm.

OTHELLO: Why of thy thought, Iago?

IAGO: I did not think he had been acquainted with her.

OTHELLO: O, yes, and went between us very oft.   100

90 *wretch* (a term of endearment).

IAGO: Indeed?

OTHELLO: Indeed? Ay, indeed! Discern'st thou aught in that?
    Is he not honest?

IAGO: Honest, my lord?

OTHELLO: Honest. Ay, honest.

IAGO: My lord, for aught I know.

OTHELLO: What dost thou think?

IAGO: Think, my lord?

OTHELLO: Think, my lord?
    By heaven, he echoes me,
    As if there were some monster in his thought
    Too hideous to be shown. Thou dost mean something:
    I heard thee say but now, thou lik'st not that,
    When Cassio left my wife. What didst not like?   110
    And when I told thee he was of my counsel
    In my whole course of wooing, thou cried'st 'Indeed?'
    And didst contract and purse thy brow together,
    As if thou then hadst shut up in thy brain
    Some horrible conceit. If thou dost love me,
    Show me thy thought.

IAGO: My lord, you know I love you.

OTHELLO: I think thou dost;
    And, for I know thou'rt full of love and honesty
    And weigh'st thy words before thou giv'st them breath,
    Therefore these stops of thine fright me the more;   120
    For such things in a false disloyal knave
    Are tricks of custom; but in a man that's just
    They are close dilations, working from the heart
    That passion cannot rule.

IAGO: For Michael Cassio,
    I dare be sworn I think that he is honest.

OTHELLO: I think so too.

IAGO: Men should be what they seem;
    Or those that be not, would they might seem none!

---

    115 *conceit* fancy.   123–24 *close dilations* . . . *rule* secret emotions which well up
in spite of restraint.   127 *seem none* i.e. not pretend to be men when they are really
monsters.

OTHELLO: Certain, men should be what they seem.

IAGO: Why then, I think Cassio's an honest man.

OTHELLO: Nay, yet there's more in this. 130
I prithee speak to me as to thy thinkings,
As thou dost ruminate, and give thy worst of thoughts
The worst of words.

IAGO: Good my lord, pardon me:
Though I am bound to every act of duty,
I am not bound to that all slaves are free to.
Utter my thoughts? Why, say they are vile and false,
As where's that palace whereinto foul things
Sometimes intrude not? Who has a breast so pure
But some uncleanly apprehensions
Keep leets and law days, and in session sit 140
With meditations lawful?

OTHELLO: Thou dost conspire against thy friend, Iago,
If thou but think'st him wronged, and mak'st his ear
A stranger to thy thoughts.

IAGO: I do beseech you—
Though I perchance am vicious in my guess
(As I confess it is my nature's plague
To spy into abuses, and oft my jealousy
Shapes faults that are not), that your wisdom yet
From one that so imperfectly conjects
Would take no notice, nor build yourself a trouble 150
Out of his scattering and unsure observance.
It were not for your quiet nor your good,
Nor for my manhood, honesty, or wisdom,
To let you know my thoughts.

OTHELLO: What dost thou mean?

IAGO: Good name in man and woman, dear my lord,
Is the immediate jewel of their souls.
Who steals my purse steals trash; 'tis something, nothing;
'Twas mine, 'tis his, and has been slave to thousands;
But he that filches from me my good name
Robs me of that which not enriches him 160
And makes me poor indeed.

---

135 *bound . . . free to* bound to tell that which even slaves are allowed to keep
to themselves. 140 *leets and law days* sittings of the courts. 147 *jealousy* suspicion.
149 *conjects* conjectures. 156 *immediate* nearest the heart.

OTHELLO: By heaven, I'll know thy thoughts!

IAGO: You cannot, if my heart were in your hand;
Nor shall not whilst 'tis in my custody.

OTHELLO: Ha!

IAGO: O, beware, my lord, of jealousy!
It is the green-eyed monster, which doth mock
The meat it feeds on. That cuckold lives in bliss
Who, certain of his fate, loves not his wronger;
But O, what damnèd minutes tells he o'er
Who dotes, yet doubts—suspects, yet strongly loves!   170

OTHELLO: O misery!

IAGO: Poor and content is rich, and rich enough;
But riches fineless is as poor as winter
To him that ever fears he shall be poor.
Good God, the souls of all my tribe defend
From jealousy!

OTHELLO: Why, why is this?
Think'st thou I'ld make a life of jealousy,
To follow still the changes of the moon
With fresh suspicions? No! To be once in doubt
Is once to be resolved. Exchange me for a goat   180
When I shall turn the business of my soul
To such exsufflicate and blown surmises,
Matching thy inference. 'Tis not to make me jealous
To say my wife is fair, feeds well, loves company,
Is free of speech, sings, plays, and dances well;
Where virtue is, these are more virtuous.
Nor from mine own weak merits will I draw
The smallest fear or doubt of her revolt,
For she had eyes, and chose me. No, Iago;
I'll see before I doubt; when I doubt, prove;   190
And on the proof there is no more but this—
Away at once with love or jealousy!

IAGO: I am glad of this; for now I shall have reason
To show the love and duty that I bear you
With franker spirit. Therefore, as I am bound,
Receive it from me. I speak not yet of proof.

166 *mock* play with, like a cat with a mouse.   173 *fineless* unlimited.   182 *exsufflicate and blown* spat out and flyblown.   188 *revolt* unfaithfulness.

Look to your wife; observe her well with Cassio;
Wear your eye thus, not jealous nor secure:
I would not have your free and noble nature,
Out of self-bounty, be abused. Look to't.   200
I know our country disposition well:
In Venice they do let God see the pranks
They dare not show their husbands; their best conscience
Is not to leave't undone, but keep't unknown.

OTHELLO: Dost thou say so?

IAGO: She did deceive her father, marrying you;
And when she seemed to shake and fear your looks,
She loved them most.

OTHELLO: And so she did.

IAGO: Why, go to then!
She that, so young, could give out such a seeming
To seel her father's eyes up close as oak—   210
He thought 'twas witchcraft—but I am much to blame.
I humbly do beseech you of your pardon
For too much loving you.

OTHELLO: I am bound to thee for ever.

IAGO: I see this hath a little dashed your spirits.

OTHELLO: Not a jot, not a jot.

IAGO: I' faith, I fear it has.
I hope you will consider what is spoke
Comes from my love. But I do see y' are moved.
I am to pray you not to strain my speech
To grosser issues nor to larger reach
Than to suspicion.   220

OTHELLO: I will not.

IAGO: Should you do so, my lord,
My speech should fall into such vile success
As my thoughts aim not at. Cassio's my worthy friend—
My lord, I see y' are moved.

OTHELLO: No, not much moved:
I do not think but Desdemona's honest.

---

198 *secure* overconfident.   200 *self-bounty* natural goodness.   210 *seel* close   *oak*
oak grain.   219 *To grosser issues* to mean something more monstrous.   222 *vile success*
evil outcome.   225 *honest* chaste.

IAGO: Long live she so! and long live you to think so!

OTHELLO: And yet, how nature erring from itself—

IAGO: Ay, there's the point! as (to be bold with you)
Not to affect many proposèd matches
Of her own clime, complexion, and degree,   230
Whereto we see in all things nature tends—
Foh! one may smell in such a will most rank,
Foul disproportion, thoughts unnatural—
But pardon me—I do not in position
Distinctly speak of her; though I may fear
Her will, recoiling to her better judgment,
May fall to match you with her country forms,
And happily repent.

OTHELLO: Farewell, farewell!
If more thou dost perceive, let me know more.
Set on thy wife to observe. Leave me, Iago.   240

IAGO: My lord, I take my leave.   [*Going*]

OTHELLO: Why did I marry? This honest creature doubtless
Sees and knows more, much more, than he unfolds.

IAGO: [*Returns*]   My lord, I would I might entreat your honor
To scan this thing no further: leave it to time.
Although 'tis fit that Cassio have his place,
For sure he fills it up with great ability,
Yet, if you please to hold him off awhile,
You shall by that perceive him and his means.
Note if your lady strain his entertainment   250
With any strong or vehement importunity;
Much will be seen in that. In the mean time
Let me be thought too busy in my fears
(As worthy cause I have to fear I am)
And hold her free, I do beseech your honor.

OTHELLO: Fear not my government.

IAGO: I once more take my leave.   [*Exit*]

OTHELLO: This fellow's of exceeding honesty,
And knows all qualities, with a learnèd spirit

234 *position* definite assertion.   236 *recoiling* reverting.   237 *fall to match* happen
to compare.   238 *happily* haply, perhaps.   250 *strain his entertainment* urge his recall.   253 *busy* meddlesome.   255 *hold her free* consider her guiltless.   256 *government* self-control.   259 *qualities* natures.   259–60 *learned spirit* Of mind informed
about.

Of human dealings. If I do prove her haggard, 260
Though that her jesses were my dear heartstrings,
I'd whistle her off and let her down the wind
To prey at fortune. Haply, for I am black
And have not those soft parts of conversation
That chamberers have, or for I am declined
Into the vale of years—yet that's not much—
She's gone. I am abused, and my relief
Must be to loathe her. O curse of marriage,
That we can call these delicate creatures ours,
And not their appetites! I had rather be a toad 270
And live upon the vapor of a dungeon
Than keep a corner in the thing I love
For others' uses. Yet 'tis the plague of great ones;
Prerogatived are they less than the base.
'Tis destiny unshunnable, like death.
Even then this forkèd plague is fated to us
When we do quicken. Look where she comes.

[*Enter* DESDEMONA *and* EMILIA]

If she be false, O, then heaven mocks itself!
I'll not believe't.

DESDEMONA: How now, my dear Othello?
    Your dinner, and the generous islanders 280
    By you invited, do attend your presence.

OTHELLO: I am to blame.

DESDEMONA: Why do you speak so faintly?
    Are you not well?

OTHELLO: I have a pain upon my forehead, here.

DESDEMONA: Faith, that's with watching; 'twill away again.
    Let me but bind it hard, within this hour
    It will be well.

OTHELLO: Your napkin is too little;

    260 *haggard* a wild hawk.   261 *jesses* thongs for controlling a hawk.   262–63
whistle . . . fortune turn her out and let her take care of herself.   263 *for* because.
264 *soft . . . conversation* ingratiating manners.   265 *chamberers* courtiers.   273 *great
ones* prominent men.   274 *Prerogatived* privileged.   276 *forkèd plague* i.e. horns of
a cuckold.   277 *do quicken* are born.   280 *generous* noble.   285 *watching* working
late.   287 *napkin* handkerchief.

[*He pushes the handkerchief from him, and it falls unnoticed*]

Let it alone. Come, I'll go in with you.

DESDEMONA: I am very sorry that you are not well.   [*Exit with Othello*]

EMILIA: I am glad I have found this napkin;   290
This was her first remembrance from the Moor.
My wayward husband hath a hundred times
Wooed me to steal it; but she so loves the token
(For he conjured her she should ever keep it)
That she reserves it evermore about her
To kiss and talk to. I'll have the work ta'en out
And give't Iago.
What he will do with it heaven knows, not I;
I nothing but to please his fantasy.

[*Enter* IAGO]

IAGO: How now? What do you here alone?   300

EMILIA: Do not you chide; I have a thing for you.

IAGO: A thing for me? It is a common thing—

EMILIA: Ha?

IAGO: To have a foolish wife.

EMILIA: O, is that all? What will you give me now
For that same handkerchief?

IAGO: What handkerchief?

EMILIA: What handkerchief!
Why, that the Moor first gave to Desdemona;
That which so often you did bid me steal.

IAGO: Hast stol'n it from her?   310

EMILIA: No, faith; she let it drop by negligence,
And to th' advantage, I, being here, took't up.
Look, here it is.

IAGO: A good wench! Give it me.

EMILIA: What will you do with't, that you have been so earnest
To have me filch it?

288 *it* i.e. his forehead.   296 *work ta'en out* pattern copied.   299 *fantasy* whim.

IAGO: Why, what's that to you? [*Snatches it*]

EMILIA: If it be not for some purpose of import,
         Give't me again. Poor lady, she'll run mad
         When she shall lack it.

IAGO: Be not acknown on't; I have use for it.
        Go, leave me.   [*Exit* EMILIA]   320
        I will in Cassio's lodging lose this napkin
        And let him find it. Trifles light as air
        Are to the jealous confirmations strong
        As proofs of holy writ. This may do something.
        The Moor already changes with my poison:
        Dangerous conceits are in their natures poisons,
        Which at the first are scarce found to distaste,
        But with a little act upon the blood
        Burn like the mines of sulphur.

[*Enter* OTHELLO]

                         I did say so.
        Look where he comes! Not poppy nor mandragora,   330
        Nor all the drowsy syrups of the world,
        Shall ever med'cine thee to that sweet sleep
        Which thou owedst yesterday.

OTHELLO: Ha! ha! false to me?

IAGO: Why, how now, general? No more of that!

OTHELLO: Avaunt! be gone! Thou hast set me on the rack.
         I swear 'tis better to be much abused
         Than but to know't a little.

IAGO: How now, my lord?

OTHELLO: What sense had I of her stol'n hours of lust?
         I saw't not, thought it not, it harmed not me;
         I slept the next night well, fed well, was free and merry;   340
         I found not Cassio's kisses on her lips.
         He that is robbed, not wanting what is stol'n,
         Let him not know't, and he's not robbed at all.

IAGO: I am sorry to hear this.

   316 *import* importance.   319 *Be . . . on't* do not acknowledge it.   326 *conceits*
ideas.   330 *mandragora* a narcotic.   340 *free* carefree.   342 *wanting* missing.

OTHELLO: I had been happy if the general camp,
                Pioners and all, had tasted her sweet body,
                So I had nothing known. O, now for ever
                Farewell the tranquil mind! farewell content!
                Farewell the plumèd troop, and the big wars
                That make ambition virtue! O, farewell!   350
                Farewell the neighing steed and the shrill trump,
                The spirit-stirring drum, th' ear-piercing fife,
                The royal banner, and all quality,
                Pride, pomp, and circumstance of glorious war!
                And O you mortal engines whose rude throats
                Th' immortal Jove's dread clamors counterfeit,
                Farewell! Othello's occupation's gone!

IAGO: Is't possible, my lord?

OTHELLO: Villain, be sure thou prove my love a whore!
                Be sure of it; give me the ocular proof;   360
                Or, by the worth of man's eternal soul,
                Thou hadst been better have been born a dog
                Than answer my waked wrath!

IAGO: Is't come to this?

OTHELLO: Make me to see't; or at the least so prove it
                That the probation bear no hinge nor loop
                To hang a doubt on—or woe upon thy life!

IAGO: My noble lord—

OTHELLO: If thou dost slander her and torture me,
                Never pray more; abandon all remorse;
                On horror's head horrors accumulate;   370
                Do deeds to make heaven weep, all earth amazed;
                For nothing canst thou to damnation add
                Greater than that.

IAGO: O grace! O heaven forgive me!
                Are you a man? Have you a soul or sense?—
                God b' wi' you! take mine office. O wretched fool,
                That liv'st to make thine honesty a vice!
                O monstrous world! Take note, take note, O world,
                To be direct and honest is not safe.
                I thank you for this profit; and from hence
                I'll love no friend, sith love breeds such offense.   380

      346 *Pioners* sappers, laborers.   349 *big* stately.   354 *circumstance* pageantry.   355
mortal engines deadly artillery.   356 *counterfeit* imitate.   365 *probation* proof.   379
profit profitable lesson.

OTHELLO: Nay, stay. Thou shouldst be honest.

IAGO: I should be wise; for honesty's a fool
And loses that it works for.

OTHELLO: By the world,
I think my wife be honest, and think she is not;
I think that thou art just, and think thou art not.
I'll have some proof. Her name, that was as fresh
As Dian's visage, is now begrimed and black
As mine own face. If there be cords, or knives,
Poison, or fire, or suffocating streams,
I'll not endure it. Would I were satisfied! 390

IAGO: I see, sir, you are eaten up with passion:
I do repent me that I put it to you.
You would be satisfied?

OTHELLO: Would? Nay, I will.

IAGO: And may; but how? how satisfied, my lord?
Would you, the supervisor, grossly gape on?
Behold her topped?

OTHELLO: Death and damnation! O!

IAGO: It were a tedious difficulty, I think,
To bring them to that prospect. Damn them then,
If ever mortal eyes do see them bolster
More than their own! What then? How then? 400
What shall I say? Where's satisfaction?
It is impossible you should see this,
Were they as prime as goats, as hot as monkeys,
As salt as wolves in pride, and fools as gross
As ignorance made drunk. But yet, I say,
If imputation and strong circumstances
Which lead directly to the door of truth
Will give you satisfaction, you may have't.

OTHELLO: Give me a living reason she's disloyal.

IAGO: I do not like the office. 410
But sith I am entered in this cause so far,
Pricked to't by foolish honesty and love,
I will go on. I lay with Cassio lately,

---

390 *satisfied* completely informed. 395 *supervisor* spectator. 399 *bolster* lie together. 403 *prime* lustful. 404 *salt* lecherous *pride* heat.

And being troubled with a raging tooth,
I could not sleep.
There are a kind of men so loose of soul
That in their sleeps will mutter their affairs.
One of this kind is Cassio.
In sleep I heard him say, 'Sweet Desdemona,
Let us be wary, let us hide our loves!'   420
And then, sir, would he gripe and wring my hand,
Cry 'O sweet creature!' and then kiss me hard,
As if he plucked up kisses by the roots
That grew upon my lips; then laid his leg
Over my thigh, and sighed, and kissed, and then
Cried 'Cursèd fate that gave thee to the Moor!'

OTHELLO: O monstrous! monstrous!

IAGO: Nay, this was but his dream.

OTHELLO: But this denoted a foregone conclusion:
'Tis a shrewd doubt, though it be but a dream.

IAGO: And this may help to thicken other proofs   430
That do demonstrate thinly.

OTHELLO: I'll tear her all to pieces!

IAGO: Nay, but be wise. Yet we see nothing done;
She may be honest yet. Tell me but this—
Have you not sometimes seen a handkerchief
Spotted with strawberries in your wife's hand?

OTHELLO: I gave her such a one; 'twas my first gift.

IAGO: I know not that; but such a handkerchief—
I am sure it was your wife's—did I to-day
See Cassio wipe his beard with.

OTHELLO: If't be that—

IAGO: If it be that, or any that was hers,   440
It speaks against her with the other proofs.

OTHELLO: O, that the slave had forty thousand lives!
One is too poor, too weak for my revenge.
Now do I see 'tis true. Look here, Iago:
All my fond love thus do I blow to heaven.
'Tis gone.

428 *foregone conclusion* previous experience.   429 *a shrewd doubt* cursedly suspicious.

Arise, black vengeance, from the hollow hell!
Yield up, O love, thy crown and hearted throne
To tyrannous hate! Swell, bosom, with thy fraught,
For 'tis of aspics' tongues!

IAGO: Yet be content.   450

OTHELLO: O, blood, blood, blood!

IAGO: Patience, I say. Your mind perhaps may change.

OTHELLO: Never, Iago. Like to the Pontic sea,
Whose icy current and compulsive course
Ne'er feels retiring ebb, but keeps due on
To the Propontic and the Hellespont,
Even so my bloody thoughts, with violent pace,
Shall ne'er look back, ne'er ebb to humble love,
Till that a capable and wide revenge
Swallow them up. [*He kneels*] Now, by yond marble heaven,   460
In the due reverence of a sacred vow
I here engage my words.

IAGO: Do not rise yet.   [*Iago kneels*]
Witness, you ever-burning lights above,
You elements that clip us round about,
Witness that here Iago doth give up
The execution of his wit, hands, heart
To wronged Othello's service! Let him command,
And to obey shall be in me remorse,
What bloody business ever.   [*They rise*]

OTHELLO: I greet thy love,
Not with vain thanks but with acceptance bounteous,   470
And will upon the instant put thee to't.
Within these three days let me hear thee say
That Cassio's not alive.

IAGO: My friend is dead; 'tis done at your request.
But let her live.

OTHELLO: Damn her, lewd minx! O, damn her!
Come, go with me apart. I will withdraw
To furnish me with some swift means of death
For the fair devil. Now art thou my lieutenant.

IAGO: I am your own for ever.   [*Exeunt*]

---

449 *fraught* burden.   450 *aspics* deadly poisonous snakes.   453 *Pontic sea* Black
Sea.   459 *capable* all-embracing.   464 *clip* encompass.   466 *execution* activities   *wit*
mind.   468 *remorse* pity.

SCENE IV

Before the castle.

[*Enter* DESDEMONA, EMILIA, *and* CLOWN]

DESDEMONA: Do you know, sirrah, where Lieutenant Cassio lies?

CLOWN: I dare not say he lies anywhere.

DESDEMONA: Why, man?

CLOWN: He's a soldier, and for me to say a soldier lies is stabbing.

DESDEMONA: Go to. Where lodges he?

CLOWN: To tell you where he lodges is to tell you where I lie.

DESDEMONA: Can anything be made of this?

CLOWN: I know not where he lodges; and for me to devise a lodging, and say he lies here or he lies there, were to lie in mine own throat.

DESDEMONA: Can you enquire him out, and be edified by report?   10

CLOWN: I will catechize the world for him; that is, make questions, and by them answer.

DESDEMONA: Seek him, bid him come hither. Tell him I have moved my lord on his behalf and hope all will be well.

CLOWN: To do this is within the compass of man's wit, and therefore I'll attempt the doing of it.   [*Exit*]

DESDEMONA: Where should I lose that handkerchief, Emilia?

EMILIA: I know not, madam.

DESDEMONA: Believe me, I had rather have lost my purse
Full of crusadoes; and but my noble Moor   20
Is true of mind, and made of no such baseness
As jealous creatures are, it were enough
To put him to ill thinking.

EMILIA: Is he not jealous?

DESDEMONA: Who? he? I think the sun where he was born
Drew all such humors from him.

[*Enter* OTHELLO]

2 *lies* lives, lodges.   20 *crusadoes* Portuguese gold coins.   26 *humors* inclinations.

EMILIA: Look where he comes.

DESDEMONA: I will not leave him now till Cassio
Be called to him.—How is't with you, my lord?

OTHELLO: Well, my good lady. [*Aside*] O, hardness to dissemble!—
How do you, Desdemona?

DESDEMONA: Well, my good lord.

OTHELLO: Give me your hand. This hand is moist, my lady. 30

DESDEMONA: It yet hath felt no age nor known no sorrow.

OTHELLO: This argues fruitfulness and liberal heart.
Hot, hot, and moist. This hand of yours requires
A sequester from liberty, fasting and prayer,
Much castigation, exercise devout;
For here's a young and sweating devil here
That commonly rebels. 'Tis a good hand,
A frank one.

DESDEMONA: You may, indeed, say so;
For 'twas that hand that gave away my heart.

OTHELLO: A liberal hand! The hearts of old gave hands; 40
But our new heraldry is hands, not hearts.

DESDEMONA: I cannot speak of this. Come now, your promise!

OTHELLO: What promise, chuck?

DESDEMONA: I have sent to bid Cassio come speak with you.

OTHELLO: I have a salt and sorry rheum offends me.
Lend me thy handkerchief.

DESDEMONA: Here, my lord.

OTHELLO: That which I gave you.

DESDEMONA: I have it not about me.

OTHELLO: Not?

DESDEMONA: No, faith, my lord.

OTHELLO: That is a fault.
That handkerchief
Did an Egyptian to my mother give. 50

---

34 *sequester* removal.   41 *heraldry* heraldic symbolism.   45 *salt . . . rheum* distressing head-cold.   50 *Egyptian* gypsy.

She was a charmer, and could almost read
The thoughts of people. She told her, while she kept it,
'Twould make her amiable and subdue my father
Entirely to her love; but if she lost it
Or made a gift of it, my father's eye
Should hold her loathly, and his spirits should hunt
After new fancies. She, dying, gave it me,
And bid me, when my fate would have me wive,
To give it her. I did so; and take heed on't;
Make it a darling like your precious eye.   60
To lose't or give't away were such perdition
As nothing else could match.

DESDEMONA: Is't possible?

OTHELLO: 'Tis true. There's magic in the web of it.
A sibyl that had numbered in the world
The sun to course two hundred compasses,
In her prophetic fury sewed the work;
The worms were hallowed that did breed the silk;
And it was dyed in mummy which the skillful
Conserved of maidens' hearts.

DESDEMONA: I' faith? Is't true?

OTHELLO: Most veritable. Therefore look to't well.   70

DESDEMONA: Then would to God that I had never seen't!

OTHELLO: Ha! Wherefore?

DESDEMONA: Why do you speak so startingly and rash?

OTHELLO: Is't lost? Is't gone? Speak, is it out o' th' way?

DESDEMONA: Heaven bless us!

OTHELLO: Say you?

DESDEMONA: It is not lost. But what an if it were?

OTHELLO: How?

DESDEMONA: I say it is not lost.

OTHELLO: Fetch't, let me see't!

---

51 *charmer* sorceress.   53 *amiable* lovable.   61 *perdition* disaster.   65 *compasses*
annual rounds.   68 *mummy* a drug made from mummies.

DESDEMONA: Why, so I can, sir; but I will not now.   80
    This is a trick to put me from my suit:
    Pray you let Cassio be received again.

OTHELLO: Fetch me the handkerchief! My mind misgives.

DESDEMONA: Come, come!
    You'll never meet a more sufficient man.

OTHELLO: The handkerchief!

DESDEMONA: I pray talk me of Cassio.

OTHELLO: The handkerchief!

DESDEMONA: A man that all his time
    Hath founded his good fortunes on your love,
    Shared dangers with you—

OTHELLO: The handkerchief!   90

DESDEMONA: I'faith, you are to blame.

OTHELLO: Zounds! [*Exit*]

EMILIA: Is not this man jealous?

DESDEMONA: I ne'er saw this before.
    Sure there's some wonder in this handkerchief;
    I am most unhappy in the loss of it.

EMILIA: 'Tis not a year or two shows us a man.
    They are all but stomachs, and we all but food;
    They eat us hungerly, and when they are full,
    They belch us.

[*Enter* IAGO *and* CASSIO]

             Look you—Cassio and my husband!   100

IAGO: There is no other way; 'tis she must do't.
    And lo the happiness! Go and importune her.

DESDEMONA: How now, good Cassio? What's the news with you?

CASSIO: Madam, my former suit. I do beseech you
    That by your virtuous means I may again
    Exist, and be a member of his love
    Whom I with all the office of my heart

102 *happiness* good luck.

Entirely honor. I would not be delayed.
If my offense be of such mortal kind
That neither service past, nor present sorrows,   110
Nor purposed merit in futurity,
Can ransom me into his love again,
But to know so must be my benefit.
So shall I clothe me in a forced content,
And shut myself up in some other course,
To fortune's alms.

DESDEMONA: Alas, thrice-gentle Cassio!
My advocation is not now in tune.
My lord is not my lord; nor should I know him,
Were he in favor as in humor altered.
So help me every spirit sanctified   120
As I have spoken for you all my best
And stood within the blank of his displeasure
For my free speech! You must awhile be patient.
What I can do I will; and more I will
Than for myself I dare. Let that suffice you.

IAGO: Is my lord angry?

EMILIA: He went hence but now,
And certainly in strange unquietness.

IAGO: Can he be angry? I have seen the cannon
When it hath blown his ranks into the air
And, like the devil, from his very arm   130
Puffed his own brother—and can he be angry?
Something of moment then. I will go meet him.
There's matter in't indeed if he be angry.

DESDEMONA: I prithee do so.   [*Exit* IAGO]
                     Something sure of state,
Either from Venice or some unhatched practice
Made demonstrable here in Cyprus to him,
Hath puddled his clear spirit; and in such cases
Men's natures wrangle with inferior things,
Though great ones are their object. 'Tis even so;
For let our finger ache, and it endues   140
Our other, healthful members even to that sense

---

115 *shut myself up in* confine myself to.   117 *advocation* advocacy.   119 *favor* appearance.   122 *blank* bull's-eye of the target.   134 *state* public affairs.   135 *unhatched practice* budding plot.   137 *puddled* muddied.   140 *endues* brings.

Of pain. Nay, we must think men are not gods,
Nor of them look for such observancy
As fits the bridal. Beshrew me much, Emilia,
I was, unhandsome warrior as I am,
Arraigning his unkindness with my soul;
But now I find I had suborned the witness,
And he's indicted falsely.

EMILIA: Pray heaven it be state matters, as you think,
And no conception nor no jealous toy   150
Concerning you.

DESDEMONA: Alas the day! I never gave him cause.
EMILIA: But jealous souls will not be answered so;
They are not ever jealous for the cause,
But jealous for they are jealous. 'Tis a monster
Begot upon itself, born on itself.

DESDEMONA: Heaven keep that monster from Othello's mind!

EMILIA: Lady, amen.

DESDEMONA: I will go seek him. Cassio, walk here about:
If I do find him fit, I'll move your suit   160
And seek to effect it to my uttermost.

CASSIO: I humbly thank your ladyship.

[*Exeunt* DESDEMONA *and* EMILIA]

[*Enter* BIANCA]

BIANCA: Save you, friend Cassio!

CASSIO: What make you from home?
How is it with you, my most fair Bianca?
I' faith, sweet love, I was coming to your house.

BIANCA: And I was going to your lodging, Cassio.
What, keep a week away? seven days and nights?
Eightscore eight hours? and lovers' absent hours,
More tedious than the dial eightscore times?
O weary reck'ning!

CASSIO: Pardon me, Bianca: 170
I have this while with leaden thoughts been pressed;

145 *unhandsome warrior* inadequate soldier.   146 *Arraigning . . . soul* indicting
his unkindness before the bar of my soul.   150 *toy* fancy.   169 *dial* clock.

But I shall in a more continuate time
Strike off this score of absence. Sweet Bianca,

[*Gives her* DESDEMONA'S *handkerchief*]

Take me this work out.

BIANCA: O Cassio, whence came this?
This is some token from a newer friend.
To the felt absence now I feel a cause.
Is't come to this? Well, well.

CASSIO: Go to, woman!
Throw your vile guesses in the devil's teeth,
From whence you have them. You are jealous now
That this is from some mistress, some remembrance.   180
No, by my faith, Bianca.

BIANCA: Why, whose is it?

CASSIO: I know not, sweet; I found it in my chamber.
I like the work well; ere it be demanded,
As like enough it will, I'd have it copied.
Take it and do't, and leave me for this time.

BIANCA: Leave you? Wherefore?

CASSIO: I do attend here on the general
And think it no addition, nor my wish,
To have him see me womaned.

BIANCA: Why, I pray you?

CASSIO: Not that I love you not.

BIANCA: But that you do not love me!   190
I pray you bring me on the way a little,
And say if I shall see you soon at night.

CASSIO: 'Tis but a little way that I can bring you,
For I attend here; but I'll see you soon.

BIANCA: 'Tis very good. I must be circumstanced.

[*Exeunt*]

---

172 *continuate* uninterrupted.   174 *Take . . . out* copy this embroidery for me.
195 *circumstanced* governed by circumstances.

ACT IV. SCENE I

Cyprus. Before the castle.

[*Enter* OTHELLO *and* IAGO]

IAGO: Will you think so?

OTHELLO: Think so, Iago?

IAGO: What,
          To kiss in private?

OTHELLO: An unauthorized kiss.

IAGO: Or to be naked with her friend in bed
          An hour or more, not meaning any harm?

OTHELLO: Naked in bed, Iago, and not mean harm?
          It is hypocrisy against the devil.
          They that mean virtuously, and yet do so,
          The devil their virtue tempts, and they tempt heaven.

IAGO: So they do nothing, 'tis a venial slip.
          But if I give my wife a handkerchief—   10

OTHELLO: What then?

IAGO: Why, then 'tis hers, my lord; and being hers,
          She may, I think, bestow't on any man.

OTHELLO: She is protectress of her honor too;
          May she give that?

IAGO: Her honor is an essence that's not seen;
          They have it very oft that have it not.
          But for the handkerchief—

OTHELLO: By heaven, I would most gladly have forgot it!
          Thou said'st—O, it comes o'er my memory   20
          As doth the raven o'er the infected house,
          Boding to all!—he had my handkerchief.

IAGO: Ay, what of that?

OTHELLO: That's not so good now.

IAGO: What
          If I had said I had seen him do you wrong?

6 *hypocrisy . . . devil* i.e. feigned sin instead of feigned virtue.   21 *infected* plague-stricken.

Or heard him say—as knaves be such abroad
Who having, by their own importunate suit,
Or voluntary dotage of some mistress,
Convincèd or supplied them, cannot choose
But they must blab—

OTHELLO: Hath he said anything?

IAGO: He hath, my lord; but be you well assured,   30
No more than he'll unswear.

OTHELLO: What hath he said?

IAGO: Faith, that he did—I know not what he did.

OTHELLO: What? what?

IAGO: Lie—

OTHELLO: With her?

IAGO: With her, on her; what you will.

OTHELLO: Lie with her? lie on her?—We say lie on her when they
belie her.—Lie with her! Zounds, that's fulsome.—Handkerchief—
confessions—handkerchief!—To confess, and be hanged for his
labor—first to be hanged, and then to confess! I tremble at it. Nature would not invest herself in such shadowing passion without
some instruction. It is not words that shakes me thus.—Pish!   40
Noses, ears, and lips? Is't possible?—Confess?—Handkerchief?—
O devil! [Falls in a trance]

IAGO: Work on,
My med'cine, work! Thus credulous fools are caught,
And many worthy and chaste dames even thus,
All guiltless, meet reproach.—What, ho! my lord!
My lord, I say! Othello!

[Enter CASSIO]

                         How now, Cassio?

CASSIO: What's the matter?

IAGO: My lord is fall'n into an epilepsy.
This is his second fit; he had one yesterday.   50

CASSIO: Rub him about the temples.

---

28 Convincèd or supplied overcome or gratified.   38–40 Nature . . . instruction
my natural faculties would not be so overcome by passion without reason.

IAGO: No, forbear.
The lethargy must have his quiet course.
If not, he foams at mouth, and by and by
Breaks out to savage madness. Look, he stirs.
Do you withdraw yourself a little while.
He will recover straight. When he is gone,
I would on great occasion speak with you.   [*Exit* CASSIO]
How is it, general? Have you not hurt your head?

OTHELLO: Dost thou mock me?

IAGO: I mock you? No, by heaven.
Would you would bear your fortune like a man!   60

OTHELLO: A hornèd man's a monster and a beast.

IAGO: There's many a beast then in a populous city,
And many a civil monster.

OTHELLO: Did he confess it?

IAGO: Good sir, be a man.
Think every bearded fellow that's but yoked
May draw with you. There's millions now alive
That nightly lie in those unproper beds
Which they dare swear peculiar: your case is better.
O, 'tis the spite of hell, the fiend's arch-mock,
To lip a wanton in a secure couch,   70
And to suppose her chaste! No, let me know;
And knowing what I am, I know what she shall be.

OTHELLO: O, thou art wise! 'Tis certain.

IAGO: Stand you awhile apart;
Confine yourself but in a patient list.
Whilst you were here, o'erwhelmèd with your grief—
A passion most unsuiting such a man—
Cassio came hither. I shifted him away
And laid good 'scuse upon your ecstasy;
Bade him anon return, and here speak with me;
The which he promised. Do but encave yourself   80
And mark the fleers, the gibes, and notable scorns
That dwell in every region of his face;
For I will make him tell the tale anew—

61 *hornèd man* cuckold.   67 *unproper* not exclusively their own.   68 *peculiar* exclusively their own.   70 *secure* free from fear of rivalry.   74 *in a patient list* within the limits of self-control.   78 *ecstasy* trance.   80 *encave* conceal.

Where, how, how oft, how long ago, and when
He hath, and is again to cope your wife.
I say, but mark his gesture. Marry, patience!
Or I shall say you are all in all in spleen,
And nothing of a man.

OTHELLO: Dost thou hear, Iago?
I will be found most cunning in my patience;
But—dost thou hear?—most bloody.

IAGO: That's not amiss;   90
But yet keep time in all. Will you withdraw?

[OTHELLO *retires*]

Now will I question Cassio of Bianca,
A huswife that by selling her desires
Buys herself bread and clothes. It is a creature
That dotes on Cassio, as 'tis the strumpet's plague
To beguile many and be beguiled by one.
He, when he hears of her, cannot refrain
From the excess of laughter. Here he comes.

[*Enter* CASSIO]

As he shall smile, Othello shall go mad;
And his unbookish jealousy must conster   100
Poor Cassio's smiles, gestures, and light behavior
Quite in the wrong. How do you now, lieutenant?

CASSIO: The worser that you give me the addition
Whose want even kills me.

IAGO: Ply Desdemona well, and you are sure on't.
Now, if this suit lay in Bianca's power,
How quickly should you speed!

CASSIO: Alas, poor caitiff!

OTHELLO: Look how he laughs already!

IAGO: I never knew a woman love man so.

CASSIO: Alas, poor rogue! I think, i' faith, she loves me.   110

OTHELLO: Now he denies it faintly, and laughs it out.

IAGO: Do you hear, Cassio?

---

85 *cope* meet.   87 *all in all in spleen* wholly overcome by your passion.   93 *house-wife* hussy.   100 *unbookish* instructed   *conster* construe interpret.   103 *addition* title.   107 *caitiff* wretch.

OTHELLO: Now he importunes him
    To tell it o'er. Go to! Well said, well said!

IAGO: She gives it out that you shall marry her.
    Do you intend it?

CASSIO: Ha, ha, ha!

OTHELLO: Do you triumph, Roman? Do you triumph?

CASSIO: I marry her? What, a customer? Prithee bear some charity to
    my wit; do not think it so unwholesome. Ha, ha, ha!

OTHELLO: So, so, so, so! They laugh that win!   120

IAGO: Faith, the cry goes that you shall marry her.

CASSIO: Prithee say true.

IAGO: I am a very villain else.

OTHELLO: Have you scored me? Well.

CASSIO: This is the monkey's own giving out. She is persuaded I will
    marry her out of her own love and flattery, not out of my promise.

OTHELLO: Iago beckons me; now he begins the story.

CASSIO: She was here even now; she haunts me in every place. I was
    t' other day talking on the sea bank with certain Venetians, and
    thither comes the bauble, and, by this hand, she falls me thus   130
    about my neck—

OTHELLO: Crying 'O dear Cassio!' as it were. His gesture imports it.

CASSIO: So hangs, and lolls, and weeps upon me; so hales and pulls me!
    Ha, ha, ha!

OTHELLO: Now he tells how she plucked him to my chamber. O, I see
    that nose of yours, but not that dog I shall throw't to.

CASSIO: Well, I must leave her company.

[*Enter* BIANCA]

IAGO: Before me! Look where she comes.

CASSIO: 'Tis such another fitchew! marry, a perfumed one.
    What do you mean by this haunting of me?   140

---

    118 *customer* prostitute.   124 *scored me* settled my account.   127 *beckons* signals.
130 *bauble* plaything.   133 *hales* hauls.   139 *fitchew* polecat (slang for whore).

BIANCA: Let the devil and his dam haunt you! What did you mean by that same handkerchief you gave me even now? I was a fine fool to take it. I must take out the whole work? A likely piece of work that you should find it in your chamber and know not who left it there! This is some minx's token, and I must take out the work? There! Give it your hobby-horse. Wheresoever you had it, I'll take out no work on't.

CASSIO: How now, my sweet Bianca? How now? how now?

OTHELLO: By heaven, that should be my handkerchief!

BIANCA: An you'll come to supper to-night, you may; an you will not,   150
come when you are next prepared for.   [Exit]

IAGO: After her, after her!

CASSIO: Faith, I must; she'll rail i' th' street else.

IAGO: Will you sup there?

CASSIO: Yes, I intend so.

IAGO: Well, I may chance to see you; for I would very fain speak with you.

CASSIO: Prithee come. Will you?

IAGO: Go to! say no more.   [Exit CASSIO]

OTHELLO: [Comes forward]   How shall I murder him, Iago?   160

IAGO: Did you perceive how he laughed at his vice?

OTHELLO: O Iago!

IAGO: And did you see the handkerchief?

OTHELLO: Was that mine?

IAGO: Yours, by this hand! And to see how he prizes the foolish woman your wife! She gave it him, and he hath giv'n it his whore.

OTHELLO: I would have him nine years a-killing!—A fine woman! a fair woman! a sweet woman!

IAGO: Nay, you must forget that.

OTHELLO: Ay, let her rot, and perish, and be damned to-night; for she   170
shall not live. No, my heart is turned to stone; I strike it, and it

146 *hobby-horse* harlot.

hurts my hand. O, the world hath not a sweeter creature! She might lie by an emperor's side and command him tasks.

IAGO: Nay, that's not your way.

OTHELLO: Hang her! I do but say what she is. So delicate with her needle! an admirable musician! O, she will sing the savageness out of a bear! Of so high and plenteous wit and invention—

IAGO: She's the worse for all this.

OTHELLO: O, a thousand thousand times! And then, of so gentle a condition!   180

IAGO: Ay, too gentle.

OTHELLO: Nay, that's certain. But yet the pity of it, Iago! O Iago, the pity of it, Iago!

IAGO: If you are so fond over her iniquity, give her patent to offend; for if it touch not you, it comes near nobody.

OTHELLO: I will chop her into messes! Cuckold me!

IAGO: O, 'tis foul in her.

OTHELLO: With mine officer!

IAGO: That's fouler.

OTHELLO: Get me some poison, Iago, this night. I'll not expostulate   190
with her, lest her body and beauty unprovide my mind again. This night, Iago!

IAGO: Do it not with poison. Strangle her in her bed, even the bed she hath contaminated.

OTHELLO: Good, good! The justice of it pleases. Very good!

IAGO: And for Cassio, let me be his undertaker: you shall hear more by midnight.

OTHELLO: Excellent good!   [A *trumpet*]
                            What trumpet is that same?

IAGO: Something from Venice, sure.

[*Enter* LODOVICO, DESDEMONA, *and* ATTENDANTS]

180 *condition* disposition.   184 *patent* license.   191 *unprovide* unsettle.   196 *be his undertaker* undertake to deal with him.

'Tis Lodovico,
Come from the Duke; and see, your wife is with him.   200

LODOVICO: God save you, worthy general!

OTHELLO: With all my heart, sir.

LODOVICO: The Duke and senators of Venice greet you.   [*Gives him a letter*]

OTHELLO: I kiss the instrument of their pleasures. [*Opens the letter and reads*]

DESDEMONA: And what's the news, good cousin Lodovico?

IAGO: I am very glad to see you, signior.
Welcome to Cyprus.

LODOVICO: I thank you. How does Lieutenant Cassio?

IAGO.   Lives, sir.

DESDEMONA: Cousin, there's fall'n between him and my lord
An unkind breach; but you shall make all well.

OTHELLO: Are you sure of that?   210

DESDEMONA: My lord?

OTHELLO: [*Reads*]   'This fail you not to do, as you will—'

LODOVICO: He did not call; he's busy in the paper.
Is there division 'twixt thy lord and Cassio?

DESDEMONA: A most unhappy one. I would do much
T' atone them, for the love I bear to Cassio.

OTHELLO: Fire and brimstone!

DESDEMONA: My lord?

OTHELLO: Are you wise?

DESDEMONA: What, is he angry?

LODOVICO: May be the letter moved him;
For, as I think, they do command him home,
Deputing Cassio in his government.   220

DESDEMONA: By my troth, I am glad on't.

OTHELLO: Indeed?

216 *atone* reconcile.

DESDEMONA: My lord?

OTHELLO: I am glad to see you mad.

DESDEMONA: Why, sweet Othello—

OTHELLO: Devil!   [*Strikes her*]

DESDEMONA: I have not deserved this.

LODOVICO: My lord, this would not be believed in Venice,
   Though I should swear I saw't. 'Tis very much.
   Make her amends; she weeps.

OTHELLO: O devil, devil!
   If that the earth could teem with woman's tears,
   Each drop she falls would prove a crocodile.
   Out of my sight!

DESDEMONA: I will not stay to offend you.   [*Going*]   230

LODOVICO: Truly, an obedient lady.
   I do beseech your lordship call her back.

OTHELLO: Mistress!

DESDEMONA: My lord?

OTHELLO: What would you with her, sir?

LODOVICO: Who? I, my lord?

OTHELLO: Ay! You did wish that I would make her turn.
   Sir, she can turn, and turn, and yet go on
   And turn again; and she can weep, sir, weep;
   And she's obedient; as you say, obedient,
   Very obedient.—Proceed you in your tears.—
   Concerning this, sir—O well-painted passion!—   240
   I am commanded home.—Get you away;
   I'll send for you anon.—Sir, I obey the mandate
   And will return to Venice.—Hence, avaunt!   [*Exit* DESDEMONA]
   Cassio shall have my place. And, sir, to-night
   I do entreat that we may sup together.
   You are welcome, sir, to Cyprus.—Goats and monkeys!   [*Exit*]

LODOVICO: Is this the noble Moor whom our full Senate
   Call all in all sufficient? Is this the nature
   Whom passion could not shake? whose solid virtue

---

228 *teem* breed.   229 *crocodile* (crocodiles were supposed to shed hypocritical tears
to lure men to destruction).   240 *passion* grief.

The shot of accident nor dart of chance   250
Could neither graze nor pierce?

IAGO: He is much changed.

LODOVICO: Are his wits safe? Is he not light of brain?

IAGO: He's that he is; I may not breathe my censure.
What he might be—if what he might he is not—
I would to heaven he were!

LODOVICO: What, strike his wife?

IAGO: Faith, that was not so well; yet would I knew
That stroke would prove the worst!

LODOVICO: Is it his use?
Or did the letters work upon his blood
And new-create this fault?

IAGO: Alas, alas!
It is not honesty in me to speak   260
What I have seen and known. You shall observe him,
And his own courses will denote him so
That I may save my speech. Do but go after
And mark how he continues.

LODOVICO: I am sorry that I am deceived in him.   [*Exeunt*]

SCENE II

A room in the castle.

[*Enter* OTHELLO *and* EMILIA]

OTHELLO: You have seen nothing then?

EMILIA: Nor ever heard, nor ever did suspect.

OTHELLO: Yes, you have seen Cassio and she together.

EMILIA: But then I saw no harm, and then I heard
Each syllable that breath made up between them.

OTHELLO: What, did they never whisper?

EMILIA: Never, my lord.

OTHELLO: Nor send you out o' th' way?

257 *use* custom.

EMILIA: Never.

OTHELLO: To fetch her fan, her gloves, her mask, nor nothing?

EMILIA: Never, my lord.   10

OTHELLO: That's strange.

EMILIA: I durst, my lord, to wager she is honest,
  Lay down my soul at stake. If you think other,
  Remove your thought; it doth abuse your bosom.
  If any wretch have put this in your head,
  Let heaven requite it with the serpent's curse!
  For if she be not honest, chaste, and true,
  There's no man happy; the purest of their wives
  Is foul as slander.

OTHELLO: Bid her come hither. Go.   [*Exit* EMILIA]   20
  She says enough; yet she's a simple bawd
  That cannot say as much. This is a subtle whore,
  A closet lock and key of villainous secrets;
  And yet she'll kneel and pray; I have seen her do't.

[*Enter* DESDEMONA *and* EMILIA]

DESDEMONA: My lord, what is your will?

OTHELLO: Pray, chuck, come hither.

DESDEMONA: What is your pleasure?

OTHELLO: Let me see your eyes.
  Look in my face.

DESDEMONA: What horrible fancy's this?

OTHELLO: [*To* EMILIA]   Some of your function, mistress.
  Leave procreants alone and shut the door;
  Cough or cry hem if anybody come.
  Your mystery, your mystery! Nay, dispatch!   [*Exit* EMILIA]   30

DESDEMONA: Upon my knees, what doth your speech import?
  I understand a fury in your words,
  But not the words.

OTHELLO: Why, what art thou?

DESDEMONA: Your wife, my lord; your true
  And loyal wife.

  30 *mystery* trade, occupation.

OTHELLO: Come, swear it, damn thyself;
Lest, being like one of heaven, the devils themselves
Should fear to seize thee. Therefore be double-damned—
Swear thou art honest.

DESDEMONA: Heaven doth truly know it.

OTHELLO: Heaven truly knows that thou art false as hell.

DESDEMONA: To whom, my lord? With whom? How am I false?   40

OTHELLO: Ah, Desdemon! away! away! away!

DESDEMONA: Alas the heavy day! Why do you weep?
Am I the motive of these tears, my lord?
If haply you my father do suspect
An instrument of this your calling back,
Lay not your blame on me. If you have lost him,
Why, I have lost him too.

OTHELLO: Had it pleased heaven
To try me with affliction, had they rained
All kinds of sores and shames on my bare head,
Steeped me in poverty to the very lips,   50
Given to captivity me and my utmost hopes,
I should have found in some place of my soul
A drop of patience. But, alas, to make me
A fixèd figure for the time of scorn
To point his slow unmoving finger at!
Yet could I bear that too; well, very well.
But there where I have garnered up my heart,
Where either I must live or bear no life,
The fountain from the which my current runs
Or else dries up—to be discarded thence,   60
Or keep it as a cistern for foul toads
To knot and gender in—turn thy complexion there,
Patience, thou young and rose-lipped cherubin!
Ay, there look grim as hell!

DESDEMONA: I hope my noble lord esteems me honest.

OTHELLO: O, ay; as summer flies are in the shambles,
That quicken even with blowing. O thou weed,
Who art so lovely fair, and smell'st so sweet,
That the sense aches at thee, would thou hadst ne'er been born!

---

36 *being . . . heaven* looking like an angle.   38 *honest* chaste.   45 *An instrument*
to be the cause.   54 *time of scorn* scornful world.   62 *turn thy complexion* there
change thy color a that point.   66 *shambles* slaughterhouse.   67 *quicken* come to life.

DESDEMONA: Alas, what ignorant sin have I committed?   70

OTHELLO: Was this fair paper, this most goodly book,
Made to write 'whore' upon? What committed?
Committed? O thou public commoner!
I should make very forges of my cheeks
That would to cinders burn up modesty,
Did I but speak thy deeds. What committed?
Heaven stops the nose at it, and the moon winks;
The bawdy wind, that kisses all it meets,
Is hushed within the hollow mine of earth
And will not hear it. What committed?   80
Impudent strumpet!

DESDEMONA: By heaven, you do me wrong!

OTHELLO: Are not you a strumpet?

DESDEMONA: No, as I am a Christian!
If to preserve this vessel for my lord
From any other foul unlawful touch
Be not to be a strumpet, I am none.

OTHELLO: What, not a whore?

DESDEMONA: No, as I shall be saved!

OTHELLO: Is't possible?

DESDEMONA: O, heaven forgive us!

OTHELLO: I cry you mercy then.
I took you for that cunning whore of Venice
That married with Othello.—[*Calling*] You, mistress,   90
That have the office opposite to Saint Peter
And keep the gate of hell!

[*Enter* EMILIA]

                    You, you, ay, you!
We have done our course; there's money for your pains:
I pray you turn the key, and keep our counsel.   [*Exit*]

EMILIA: Alas, what does this gentleman conceive?
How do you, madam? How do you, my good lady?

DESDEMONA: Faith, half asleep.

EMILIA: Good madam, what's the matter with my lord?

73 *commoner* harlot.   77 *winks* closes her eyes.   88 *cry you mercy* beg your pardon.

DESDEMONA: With who?

EMILIA: Why, with my lord, madam.   100

DESDEMONA: Who is thy lord?

EMILIA: He that is yours, sweet lady.

DESDEMONA: I have none. Do not talk to me, Emilia.
    I cannot weep; nor answer have I none
    But what should go by water. Prithee to-night
    Lay on my bed my wedding sheets, remember;
    And call thy husband hither.

EMILIA: Here's a change indeed!   [*Exit*]

DESDEMONA: 'Tis meet I should be used so, very meet.
    How have I been behaved, that he might stick
    The small'st opinion on my least misuse?

[*Enter* IAGO *and* EMILIA]

IAGO: What is your pleasure, madam? How is't with you?   110

DESDEMONA: I cannot tell. Those that do teach young babes
    Do it with gentle means and easy tasks:
    He might have chid me so; for, in good faith,
    I am a child to chiding.

IAGO: What is the matter, lady?

EMILIA: Alas, Iago, my lord hath so bewhored her,
    Thrown such despite and heavy terms upon her
    As true hearts cannot bear.

DESDEMONA: Am I that name, Iago?

IAGO: What name, fair lady?

DESDEMONA: Such as she says my lord did say I was.

EMILIA: He called her whore. A beggar in his drink   120
    Could not have laid such terms upon his callet.

IAGO: Why did he so?

DESDEMONA: I do not know; I am sure I am none such.

IAGO: Do not weep, do not weep. Alas the day!

---

109 *small'st opinion* least suspicion   *least misuse* slightest misconduct.   121 *callet*
whore.

EMILIA: Hath she forsook so many noble matches,
      Her father and her country, all her friends,
      To be called whore? Would it not make one weep?

DESDEMONA: It is my wretched fortune.

IAGO: Beshrew him for't!
      How comes this trick upon him?
DESDEMONA: Nay, heaven doth know.

EMILIA: I will be hanged if some eternal villain,   130
      Some busy and insinuating rogue,
      Some cogging, cozening slave, to get some office,
      Have not devised this slander. I'll be hanged else.

IAGO: Fie, there is no such man! It is impossible.

DESDEMONA: If any such there be, heaven pardon him!

EMILIA: A halter pardon him! and hell gnaw his bones!
      Why should he call her whore? Who keeps her company?
      What place? what time? what form? what likelihood?
      The Moor's abused by some most villainous knave,
      Some base notorious knave, some scurvy fellow.   140
      O heaven, that such companions thou'dst unfold,
      And put in every honest hand a whip
      To lash the rascals naked through the world
      Even from the east to th' west!

IAGO: Speak within door.

EMILIA: O, fie upon them! Some such squire he was
      That turned your wit the seamy side without
      And made you to suspect me with the Moor.

IAGO: You are a fool. Go to.

DESDEMONA: O good Iago,
      What shall I do to win my lord again?
      Good friend, go to him; for, by this light of heaven,   150
      I know not how I lost him. Here I kneel:
      If e'er my will did trespass 'gainst his love
      Either in discourse of thought or actual deed,
      Or that mine eyes, mine ears, or any sense

---

  129 *trick* freakish behavior. 132 *cogging, cozening* cheating, defrauding. 141 *companions* rogues *unfold* expose. 144 *within door* with restraint. 153 *discourse* course.

Delighted them in any other form,
Or that I do not yet, and ever did,
And ever will (though he do shake me off
To beggarly divorcement) love him dearly,
Comfort forswear me! Unkindness may do much;
And his unkindness may defeat my life,   160
But never taint my love. I cannot say 'whore.'
It doth abhor me now I speak the word;
To do the act that might th' addition earn
Not the world's mass of vanity could make me.

IAGO: I pray you be content. 'Tis but his humor.
The business of the state does him offense,
And he does chide with you.

DESDEMONA: If 'twere no other—

IAGO: 'Tis but so, I warrant.

[*Trumpets within*]

Hark how these instruments summon you to supper.
The messengers of Venice stay the meat: 170
Go in, and weep not. All things shall be well.

[*Exeunt* DESDEMONA *and* EMILIA]

[*Enter* RODERIGO]

How now, Roderigo?

RODERIGO: I do not find that thou deal'st justly with me.

IAGO: What in the contrary?

RODERIGO: Every day thou daff'st me with some device, Iago, and rather,
as it seems to me now, keep'st from me all conveniency than sup-
pliest me with the least advantage of hope. I will indeed no longer
endure it; nor am I yet persuaded to put up in peace what already
I have foolishly suffered.

IAGO: Will you hear me, Roderigo?   180

RODERIGO: Faith, I have heard too much; for your words and performance are no kin together.

IAGO: You charge me most unjustly.

159 *Comfort forswear* happiness forsake.   160 *defeat* destroy.   175 *thou . . .
device* you put me off with some trick.   176 *conveniency* favorable opportunities.

RODERIGO: With naught but truth. I have wasted myself out of means. The jewels you have had from me to deliver to Desdemona would half have corrupted a votarist. You have told me she hath received them, and returned me expectations and comforts of sudden respect and acquaintance; but I find none.

IAGO: Well, go to; very well.

RODERIGO: Very well! go to! I cannot go to, man; nor 'tis not very 190 well. By this hand, I say 'tis very scurvy, and begin to find myself fopped in it.

IAGO: Very well.

RODERIGO: I tell you 'tis not very well. I will make myself known to Desdemona. If she will return me my jewels, I will give over my suit and repent my unlawful solicitation; if not, assure yourself I will seek satisfaction of you.

IAGO: You have said now.

RODERIGO: Ay, and said nothing but what I protest intendment of doing. 200

IAGO: Why, now I see there's mettle in thee; and even from this instant do build on thee a better opinion than ever before. Give me thy hand, Roderigo. Thou hast taken against me a most just exception; but yet I protest I have dealt most directly in thy affair.

RODERIGO: It hath not appeared.

IAGO: I grant indeed it hath not appeared, and your suspicion is not without wit and judgment. But, Roderigo, if thou hast that in thee indeed which I have greater reason to believe now than ever, I mean purpose, courage, and valor, this night show it. If thou the next night following enjoy not Desdemona, take me from this 210 world with treachery and devise engines for my life.

RODERIGO: Well, what is it? Is it within reason and compass?

IAGO: Sir, there is especial commission come from Venice to depute Cassio in Othello's place.

RODERIGO: Is that true? Why, then Othello and Desdemona return again to Venice.

---

186 *votarist* nun. 187–88 *sudden respect* immediate notice. 192 *fopped* duped. 211 *engines for* plots against.

IAGO: O, no; he goes into Mauritania and takes away with him the fair Desdemona, unless his abode be lingered here by some accident; wherein none can be so determinate as the removing of Cassio.

RODERIGO: How do you mean removing of him? 220

IAGO: Why, by making him uncapable of Othello's place—knocking out his brains.

RODERIGO: And that you would have me to do?

IAGO: Ay, if you dare do yourself a profit and a right. He sups to-night with a harlotry, and thither will I go to him. He knows not yet of his honorable fortune. If you will watch his going thence, which I will fashion to fall out between twelve and one, you may take him at your pleasure. I will be near to second your attempt, and he shall fall between us. Come, stand not amazed at it, but go along with me. I will show you such a necessity in his death that you 230 shall think yourself bound to put it on him. It is now high supper time, and the night grows to waste. About it!

RODERIGO: I will hear further reason for this.

IAGO: And you shall be satisfied. [*Exeunt*]

SCENE III

Another room in the castle.

[*Enter* OTHELLO, LODOVICO, DESDEMONA, EMILIA, *and* ATTENDANTS]

LODOVICO: I do beseech you, sir, trouble yourself no further.

OTHELLO: O, pardon me; 'twill do me good to walk.

LODOVICO: Madam, good night. I humbly thank your ladyship.

DESDEMONA: Your honor is most welcome.

OTHELLO: Will you walk, sir?
O, Desdemona—

DESDEMONA: My lord?

OTHELLO: Get you to bed on th' instant; I will be returned forthwith. Dismiss your attendant there. Look't be done.

DESDEMONA: I will, my lord.

218 *abode . . . here* stay here be extended.   219 *determinate* effective.

[*Exit* OTHELLO, *with* LODOVICO *and* ATTENDANTS]

EMILIA: How goes it now? He looks gentler than he did.   10

DESDEMONA: He says he will return incontinent.
He hath commanded me to go to bed,
And bade me to dismiss you.

EMILIA: Dismiss me?

DESDEMONA: It was his bidding; therefore, good Emilia,
Give me my nightly wearing, and adieu.
We must not now displease him.

EMILIA: I would you had never seen him!

DESDEMONA: So would not I. My love doth so approve him
That even his stubbornness, his checks, his frowns—
Prithee unpin me—have grace and favor in them.   20

EMILIA: I have laid those sheets you bade me on the bed.

DESDEMONA: All's one. Good faith, how foolish are our minds!
If I do die before thee, prithee shroud me
In one of those same sheets.

EMILIA: Come, come! You talk.

DESDEMONA: My mother had a maid called Barbary.
She was in love; and he she loved proved mad
And did forsake her. She had a song of 'Willow';
An old thing 'twas; but it expressed her fortune,
And she died singing it. That song to-night
Will not go from my mind; I have much to do   30
But to go hang my head all at one side
And sing it like poor Barbary. Prithee dispatch.

EMILIA: Shall I go fetch your nightgown?

DESDEMONA: No, unpin me here.
This Lodovico is a proper man.

EMILIA: A very handsome man.

DESDEMONA: He speaks well.

EMILIA: I know a lady in Venice would have walked barefoot to Pales-
tine for a touch of his nether lip.

---

11 *incontinent* at once. 19 *stubbornness* roughness *checks* rebukes. 26 *mad*
wild, faithless. 33 *nightgown* dressing-gown.

DESDEMONA: [*Sings*]
      'The poor soul sat sighing by a sycamore tree,
         Sing all a green willow;   40
      Her hand on her bosom, her head on her knee,
         Sing willow, willow, willow.
      The fresh streams ran by her and murmured her moans;
         Sing willow, willow, willow;
      Her salt tears fell from her, and soft'ned the stones'—
Lay by these.
         'Sing willow, willow, willow'—
Prithee hie thee; he'll come anon.
         'Sing all a green willow must be my garland.
         Let nobody blame him; his scorn I approve'—   50
Nay, that's not next. Hark! who is't that knocks?

EMILIA: It is the wind.

DESDEMONA: [*Sings*]
      'I called my love false love; but what said he then?
         Sing willow, willow, willow:
      If I court moe women, you'll couch with moe men.'
So, get thee gone; good night. Mine eyes do itch.
Doth that bode weeping?

EMILIA: 'Tis neither here nor there.

DESDEMONA: I have heard it said so. O, these men, these men!
Dost thou in conscience think—tell me, Emilia—
That there be women do abuse their husbands   60
In such gross kind?

EMILIA: There be some such, no question.

DESDEMONA: Wouldst thou do such a deed for all the world?

EMILIA: Why, would not you?

DESDEMONA: No, by this heavenly light!

EMILIA: Nor I neither by this heavenly light.
I might do't as well i' th' dark.

DESDEMONA: Wouldst thou do such a deed for all the world?

EMILIA: The world's a huge thing; it is a great price for a small vice.

DESDEMONA: Good troth, I think thou wouldst not.

48 *hie thee* hurry.

EMILIA: By my troth, I think I should; and undo't when I had done it.
Marry, I would not do such a thing for a joint-ring, nor for meas- 70
ures of lawn, nor for gowns, petticoats, nor caps, nor any petty
exhibition; but, for all the whole world—'Ud's pity! who would
not make her husband a cuckold to make him a monarch? I
should venture purgatory for't.

DESDEMONA: Beshrew me if I would do such a wrong
For the whole world.

EMILIA: Why, the wrong is but a wrong i' th' world; and having the
world for your labor, 'tis a wrong in your own world, and you
might quickly make it right.

DESDEMONA: I do not think there is any such woman. 80

EMILIA: Yes, a dozen; and as many to th' vantage as would store the
world they played for.
But I do think it is their husbands' faults
If wives do fall. Say that they slack their duties
And pour our treasures into foreign laps;
Or else break out in peevish jealousies,
Throwing restraint upon us; or say they strike us,
Or scant our former having in despite—
Why, we have galls; and though we have some grace,
Yet have we some revenge. Let husbands know 90
Their wives have sense like them. They see, and smell,
And have their palates both for sweet and sour,
As husbands have. What is it that they do
When they change us for others? Is it sport?
I think it is. And doth affection breed it?
I think it doth. Is't frailty that thus errs?
It is so too. And have not we affections,
Desires for sport, and frailty, as men have?
Then let them use us well; else let them know,
The ills we do, their ills instruct us so. 100

DESDEMONA: Good night, good night. God me such usage send,
Not to pick bad from bad, but by bad mend! [*Exeunt*]

---

70 *joint-ring* ring made in separable halves. 72 *exhibition* gift. 81 *to th' vantage*
besides *store* populate. 86 *peevish* senseless. 88 *having* allowance. 89 *galls* spirits
to resent. 101 *usage* habits.

ACT V. SCENE I

Cyprus. A street.

[*Enter* IAGO *and* RODERIGO]

IAGO: Here, stand behind this bulk; straight will he come.
        Wear thy good rapier bare, and put it home.
        Quick, quick! Fear nothing; I'll be at thy elbow.
        It makes us, or it mars us—think on that,
        And fix most firm thy resolution.

RODERIGO: Be near at hand; I may miscarry in't.

IAGO: Here, at thy hand. Be bold, and take thy stand. [*Stands aside*]

RODERIGO: I have no great devotion to the deed,
        And yet he hath given me satisfying reasons.
        'Tis but a man gone. Forth my sword! He dies!   10

IAGO: I have rubbed this young quat almost to the sense,
        And he grows angry. Now whether he kill Cassio,
        Or Cassio him, or each do kill the other,
        Every way makes my gain. Live Roderigo,
        He calls me to a restitution large
        Of gold and jewels that I bobbed from him
        As gifts to Desdemona.
        It must not be. If Cassio do remain,
        He hath a daily beauty in his life
        That makes me ugly; and besides, the Moor   20
        May unfold me to him; there stand I in much peril.
        No, he must die. Be't so! I hear him coming.

[*Enter* CASSIO]

RODERIGO: I know his gait. 'Tis he. Villain, thou diest! [*Makes a pass at* CASSIO]

CASSIO: That thrust had been mine enemy indeed
        But that my coat is better than thou know'st.
        I will make proof of thine. [*Draws, and wounds* RODERIGO]

RODERIGO: O, I am slain!

[IAGO *darts from concealment behind* CASSIO, *wounds him in the
leg, and exit*]

---

1 *bulk* projecting shopfront.   11 *quat* pimple   *sense* quick.   16 *bobbed* swindled.
25 *coat* under-shirt of mail.

CASSIO: I am maimed for ever. Help, ho! Murder! murder! [*Falls*]

[*Enter* OTHELLO]

OTHELLO: The voice of Cassio. Iago keeps his word.

RODERIGO: O, villain that I am!

OTHELLO: It is even so.

CASSIO: O, help, ho! light! a surgeon!   30

OTHELLO: 'Tis he. O brave Iago, honest and just,
            That hast such noble sense of thy friend's wrong!
            Thou teachest me. Minion, your dear lies dead,
            And your unblest fate hies. Strumpet, I come.
            Forth of my heart those charms, thine eyes, are blotted.
            Thy bed, lust-stained, shall with lust's blood be spotted.   [*Exit*]

[*Enter* LODOVICO *and* GRATIANO]

CASSIO: What, ho? No watch? No passage? Murder! murder!

GRATIANO: 'Tis some mischance. The cry is very direful.

CASSIO: O, help!

LODOVICO: Hark!   40

RODERIGO: O wretched villain!

LODOVICO: Two or three groan. It is a heavy night.
            These may be counterfeits. Let's think't unsafe
            To come in to the cry without more help.

RODERIGO: Nobody come? Then shall I bleed to death.

LODOVICO: Hark!

[*Enter* IAGO, *with a light*]

GRATIANO: Here's one comes in his shirt, with light and weapons.

IAGO: Who's there? Whose noise is this that cries on murder?

LODOVICO: We do not know.

IAGO: Did not you hear a cry?

CASSIO: Here, here! For heaven's sake, help me!

33 *Minion* mistress.   34 *hies* hurries on.   37 *passage* passers-by.   42 *heavy* cloudy,
dark.

IAGO: What's the matter?   50

GRATIANO: This is Othello's ancient, as I take it.

LODOVICO: The same indeed, a very valiant fellow.

IAGO: What are you here that cry so grievously?

CASSIO: Iago? O, I am spoiled, undone by villains!
    Give me some help.

IAGO: O me, lieutenant! What villains have done this?

CASSIO: I think that one of them is hereabout
    And cannot make away.

IAGO: O treacherous villains!
    [*To* LODOVICO *and* GRATIANO] What are you there? Come in, and
    give some help.   60

RODERIGO: O, help me here!

CASSIO: That's one of them.

IAGO: O murd'rous slave! O villain!

    [*Stabs* RODERIGO]

RODERIGO: O damned Iago! O inhuman dog!

IAGO: Kill men i' th' dark?—Where be these bloody thieves?—
    How silent is this town!—Ho! murder! murder!—
    What may you be? Are you of good or evil?

LODOVICO: As you shall prove us, praise us.

IAGO: Signior Lodovico?

LODOVICO: He, sir.

IAGO: I cry you mercy. Here's Cassio hurt by villains.   70

GRATIANO: Cassio?

IAGO: How is it, brother?

CASSIO: My leg is cut in two.

IAGO: Marry, heaven forbid!
    Light, gentlemen. I'll bind it with my shirt.

[*Enter* BIANCA]

BIANCA: What is the matter, ho? Who is't that cried?

IAGO: Who is't that cried?

BIANCA: O my dear Cassio! my sweet Cassio!
O Cassio, Cassio, Cassio!

IAGO: O notable strumpet!—Cassio, may you suspect
Who they should be that thus have mangled you?   80

CASSIO: No.

GRATIANO: I am sorry to find you thus. I have been to seek you.

IAGO: Lend me a garter. So. O for a chair
To bear him easily hence!

BIANCA: Alas, he faints! O Cassio, Cassio, Cassio!

IAGO: Gentlemen all, I do suspect this trash
To be a party in this injury.—
Patience awhile, good Cassio.—Come, come!
Lend me a light. Know we this face or no?
Alas, my friend and my dear countryman   90
Roderigo? No.—Yes, sure.—O heaven, Roderigo!

GRATIANO: What, of Venice?

IAGO: Even he, sir. Did you know him?

GRATIANO: Know him? Ay.

IAGO: Signior Gratiano? I cry you gentle pardon.
These bloody accidents must excuse my manners
That so neglected you.

GRATIANO: I am glad to see you.

IAGO: How do you, Cassio?—O, a chair, a chair!

GRATIANO: Roderigo?

IAGO: He, he, 'tis he! [*A chair brought in*] O, that's well said; the chair.
Some good man bear him carefully from hence.   100
I'll fetch the general's surgeon. [*To* BIANCA] For you, mistress,
Save you your labor.—He that lies slain here, Cassio,
Was my dear friend. What malice was between you?

CASSIO: None in the world; nor do I know the man.

83 *chair* litter.   99 *well said* well done.

IAGO: [*To* BIANCA]   What, look you pale?—O, bear him out o' th' air.

[CASSIO *and* RODERIGO *are borne off*]

Stay you, good gentlemen.—Look you pale, mistress?—
Do you perceive the gastness of her eye?—
Nay, if you stare, we shall hear more anon.
Behold her well; I pray you look upon her.
Do you see, gentlemen? Nay, guiltiness will speak,   110
Though tongues were out of use.

[*Enter* EMILIA]

EMILIA: 'Las, what's the matter? What's the matter, husband?

IAGO: Cassio hath here been set on in the dark
By Roderigo, and fellows that are scaped.
He's almost slain, and Roderigo dead.

EMILIA: Alas, good gentleman! alas, good Cassio!

IAGO: This is the fruit of whoring. Prithee, Emilia,
Go know of Cassio where he supped to-night.
[*To* BIANCA]   What, do you shake at that?

BIANCA: He supped at my house; but I therefore shake not.   120

IAGO: O, did he so? I charge you go with me.

EMILIA: Fie, fie upon thee, strumpet!

BIANCA: I am no strumpet, but of life as honest
As you that thus abuse me.

EMILIA: As I? Foh! fie upon thee!

IAGO: Kind gentlemen, let's go see poor Cassio dressed.
[*To* BIANCA]   Come, mistress, you must tell's another tale.
Emilia, run you to the citadel
And tell my lord and lady what hath happed.   [*Exit* EMILIA]
Will you go on afore?   [*Exeunt all but* IAGO]
                              This is the night
That either makes me or fordoes me quite.   [*Exit*]   130

107 *gastness* terror.   123 *honest* chaste.   130 *fordoes* destroys.

SCENE II

A bedchamber in the castle.

[DESDEMONA *asleep in her bed. Enter* OTHELLO *with a light*]

OTHELLO: It is the cause, it is the cause, my soul.
Let me not name it to you, you chaste stars!
It is the cause. Yet I'll not shed her blood,
Nor scar that whiter skin of hers than snow,
And smooth as monumental alabaster.
Yet she must die, else she'll betray more men.
Put out the light, and then put out the light.
If I quench thee, thou flaming minister,
I can again thy former light restore,
Should I repent me; but once put out thy light,   10
Thou cunning'st pattern of excelling nature,
I know not where is that Promethean heat
That can thy light relume. When I have plucked the rose,
I cannot give it vital growth again;
It needs must wither. I'll smell thee on the tree.

[*He kisses her*]

O balmy breath, that dost almost persuade
Justice to break her sword! One more, one more!
Be thus when thou art dead, and I will kill thee,
And love thee after. One more, and this the last!
So sweet was ne'er so fatal. I must weep,   20
But they are cruel tears. This sorrow's heavenly;
It strikes where it doth love. She wakes.

DESDEMONA: Who's there? Othello?

OTHELLO: Ay, Desdemona.

DESDEMONA: Will you come to bed, my lord?

OTHELLO: Have you prayed to-night, Desdemon?

DESDEMONA: Ay, my lord.

OTHELLO: If you bethink yourself of any crime
Unreconciled as yet to heaven and grace,
Solicit for it straight.

---

1 *cause* cause of justice.   8 *minister* servant.   12 *Promethean heat* divine fire.   13 *relume* relight.

DESDEMONA: Alack, my lord, what may you mean by that?

OTHELLO: Well, do it, and be brief; I will walk by.   30
    I would not kill thy unpreparèd spirit.
    No, heaven forfend! I would not kill thy soul.

DESDEMONA: Talk you of killing?

OTHELLO: Ay, I do.

DESDEMONA: Then heaven
    Have mercy on me!

OTHELLO: Amen, with all my heart!

DESDEMONA: If you say so, I hope you will not kill me.

OTHELLO: Hum!

DESDEMONA: And yet I fear you; for you are fatal then
    When your eyes roll so. Why I should fear I know not,
    Since guiltiness I know not; but yet I feel I fear.

OTHELLO: Think on thy sins.

DESDEMONA: They are loves I bear to you.   40

OTHELLO: Ay, and for that thou diest.

DESDEMONA: That death's unnatural that kills for loving.
    Alas, why gnaw you so your nether lip?
    Some bloody passion shakes your very frame.
    These are portents; but yet I hope, I hope,
    They do not point on me.

OTHELLO: Peace and be still!

DESDEMONA: I will so. What's the matter?

OTHELLO: That handkerchief which I so loved and gave thee
    Thou gav'st to Cassio.

DESDEMONA: No, by my life and soul!
    Send for the man and ask him.

OTHELLO: Sweet soul, take heed,   50
    Take heed of perjury; thou art on thy deathbed.

DESDEMONA: Ay, but not yet to die.

    32 *forfend* forbid.

OTHELLO: Yes, presently.
Therefore confess thee freely of thy sin;
For to deny each article with oath
Cannot remove nor choke the strong conception
That I do groan withal. Thou art to die.

DESDEMONA: Then Lord have mercy on me!

OTHELLO: I say amen.

DESDEMONA: And have you mercy too! I never did
Offend you in my life; never loved Cassio
But with such general warranty of heaven 60
As I might love. I never gave him token.

OTHELLO: By heaven, I saw my handkerchief in's hand!
O perjured woman! thou dost stone my heart,
And mak'st me call what I intend to do
A murder, which I thought a sacrifice.
I saw the handkerchief.

DESDEMONA: He found it then.
I never gave it him. Send for him hither.
Let him confess a truth.

OTHELLO: He hath confessed.

DESDEMONA: What, my lord?

OTHELLO: That he hath used thee.

DESDEMONA: How? unlawfully?

OTHELLO: Ay. 70

DESDEMONA: He will not say so.

OTHELLO: No, his mouth is stopped.
Honest Iago hath ta'en order for't.

DESDEMONA: O, my fear interprets. What, is he dead?

OTHELLO: Had all his hairs been lives, my great revenge
Had stomach for them all.

DESDEMONA: Alas, he is betrayed, and I undone!

OTHELLO: Out, strumpet! Weep'st thou for him to my face?

---

52 *presently* at once.   55 *conception* belief.   59 *Offend* wrong.   63 *stone my heart* turn my heart to stone.   72 *ta'en order* taken measures.

DESDEMONA: O, banish me, my lord, but kill me not!

OTHELLO: Down, strumpet!

DESDEMONA: Kill me to-morrow; let me live to-night!   80

OTHELLO: Nay, an you strive—

DESDEMONA: But half an hour!

OTHELLO: Being done, there is no pause.

DESDEMONA: But while I say one prayer!

OTHELLO: It is too late.

[*Smothers her*]

DESDEMONA: O Lord, Lord, Lord!

[EMILIA *at the door*]

EMILIA: [*Calls within*]   My lord, my lord! What, ho, my lord, my lord!

OTHELLO: What noise is this? Not dead? not yet quite dead?
         I that am cruel am yet merciful;
         I would not have thee linger in thy pain.
         So, so.

EMILIA: [*Within*]   What, ho! my lord, my lord!

OTHELLO: Who's there?   90

EMILIA: [*Within*]   O, good my lord, I would speak a word with you!

OTHELLO: Yet, 'tis Emilia.—By and by.—She's dead.—
         'Tis like she comes to speak of Cassio's death.
         The noise was here. Ha! no more moving?
         Still as the grave.—Shall she come in? Were't good?—
         I think she stirs again. No.—What's best to do?
         If she come in, she'll sure speak to my wife.
         My wife! my wife! what wife? I have no wife.
         O, insupportable! O heavy hour!
         Methinks it should be now a huge eclipse   100
         Of sun and moon, and that th' affrighted globe
         Should yawn at alteration.

EMILIA: [*Within*]   I do beseech you
         That I may speak with you, O good my lord!

102 *yawn* open, as in an earthquake.

OTHELLO: I had forgot thee. O, come in, Emilia.
Soft, by and by.—Let me the curtains draw.—

[*Closes the bed-curtains*]

Where art thou? [*Opens the door*]

[*Enter* EMILIA]

What's the matter with thee now?

EMILIA: O my good lord, yonder's foul murder done!

OTHELLO: What? Now?

EMILIA: But now, my lord.

OTHELLO: It is the very error of the moon.   110
She comes more nearer earth than she was wont
And makes men mad.

EMILIA: Cassio, my lord, hath killed a young Venetian
Called Roderigo.

OTHELLO: Roderigo killed?
And Cassio killed?

EMILIA: No, Cassio is not killed.

OTHELLO: Not Cassio killed? Then murder's out of tune,
And sweet revenge grows harsh.

DESDEMONA: O, falsely, falsely murdered!

EMILIA: O Lord! what cry is that?

OTHELLO: That? What?

EMILIA: Out and alas! that was my lady's voice.   120
Help! help, ho! help! O lady, speak again!
Sweet Desdemona! O sweet mistress, speak!

DESDEMONA: A guiltless death I die.

EMILIA: O, who hath done this deed?

DESDEMONA: Nobody—I myself. Farewell.
Commend me to my kind lord. O, farewell! [*She dies*]

OTHELLO: Why, how should she be murd'red?

110 *error* straying off course.

EMILIA: Alas, who knows?

OTHELLO: You heard her say herself, it was not I.

EMILIA: She said so. I must needs report the truth.

OTHELLO: She's like a liar gone to burning hell!   130
   'Twas I that killed her.

EMILIA: O, the more angel she,
   And you the blacker devil!

OTHELLO: She turned to folly, and she was a whore.

EMILIA: Thou dost belie her, and thou art a devil.

OTHELLO: She was false as water.

EMILIA: Thou art rash as fire to say
   That she was false. O, she was heavenly true!

OTHELLO: Cassio did top her. Ask thy husband else.
   O, I were damned beneath all depth in hell
   But that I did proceed upon just grounds
   To this extremity. Thy husband knew it all.   140

EMILIA: My husband?

OTHELLO: Thy husband.

EMILIA: That she was false to wedlock?

OTHELLO: Ay, with Cassio. Nay, had she been true,
   If heaven would make me such another world
   Of one entire and perfect chrysolite,
   I'ld not have sold her for it.

EMILIA: My husband?

OTHELLO: Ay, 'twas he that told me first.
   An honest man he is, and hates the slime
   That sticks on filthy deeds.

EMILIA: My husband?   150

OTHELLO: What needs this iterance? Woman, I say thy husband.

EMILIA: O mistress, villainy hath made mocks with love!
   My husband say that she was false?

   151 *iterance* repetition.

OTHELLO: He, woman.
I say, thy husband. Dost understand the word?
My friend, thy husband; honest, honest Iago.

EMILIA: If he say so, may his pernicious soul
Rot half a grain a day! he lies to th' heart.
She was too fond of her most filthy bargain.

OTHELLO: Ha!

EMILIA: Do thy worst. 160
This deed of thine is no more worthy heaven
Than thou wast worthy her.

OTHELLO: Peace, you were best.

EMILIA: Thou hast not half the power to do me harm
As I have to be hurt. O gull! O dolt!
As ignorant as dirt! thou hast done a deed—
I care not for thy sword; I'll make thee known,
Though I lost twenty lives. Help! help! O, help!
The Moor hath killed my mistress! Murder! Murder!

[*Enter* MONTANO, GRATIANO, IAGO, *and others*]

MONTANO: What is the matter? How now, general?

EMILIA: O, are you come, Iago? You have done well, 170
That men must lay their murders on your neck.

GRATIANO: What is the matter?

EMILIA: Disprove this villain, if thou be'st a man.
He says thou told'st him that his wife was false.
I know thou didst not; thou'rt not such a villain.
Speak, for my heart is full.

IAGO: I told him what I thought, and told no more
Than what he found himself was apt and true.

EMILIA: But did you ever tell him she was false?

IAGO: I did. 180

EMILIA: You told a lie, an odious damnèd lie!
Upon my soul, a lie! a wicked lie!
She false with Cassio? Did you say with Cassio?

164 *to be hurt* to endure hurt.

IAGO: With Cassio, mistress. Go to, charm your tongue.

EMILIA: I will not charm my tongue; I am bound to speak:
My mistress here lies murdered in her bed—

ALL: O heavens forfend!

EMILIA: And your reports have set the murder on.

OTHELLO: Nay, stare not, masters. It is true indeed.

GRATIANO: 'Tis a strange truth.   190

MONTANO: O monstrous act!

EMILIA: Villainy, villainy, villainy!
I think upon't—I think I smell't!—O villainy!
I thought so then.—I'll kill myself for grief.—
O villainy, villainy!

IAGO: What, are you mad? I charge you get you home.

EMILIA: Good gentlemen, let me have leave to speak.
'Tis proper I obey him, but not now.
Perchance, Iago, I will ne'er go home.

OTHELLO: O! O! O! [Falls on the bed]

EMILIA: Nay, lay thee down and roar!
For thou hast killed the sweetest innocent   200
That e'er did lift up eye.

OTHELLO: O, she was foul! [Rises]
I scarce did know you, uncle. There lies your niece,
Whose breath, indeed, these hands have newly stopped.
I know this act shows horrible and grim.

GRATIANO: Poor Desdemon! I am glad thy father's dead.
Thy match was mortal to him, and pure grief
Shore his old thread in twain. Did he live now,
This sight would make him do a desperate turn;
Yea, curse his better angel from his side,
And fall to reprobation.   210

OTHELLO: 'Tis pitiful; but yet Iago knows
That she with Cassio hath the act of shame
A thousand times committed. Cassio confessed it;
And she did gratify his amorous works

---

184 *charm* cast a spell on. 204 *shows* appears. 208 *turn* act. 210 *reprobation*
rejection by God, damnation. 214 *gratify* reward.

With that recognizance and pledge of love
Which I first gave her. I saw it in his hand.
It was a handkerchief, an antique token
My father gave my mother.

EMILIA: O God! O heavenly God!

IAGO: Zounds, hold your peace!

EMILIA: 'Twill out, 'twill out! I peace?   220
No, I will speak as liberal as the north.
Let heaven and men and devils, let them all,
All, all, cry shame against me, yet I'll speak.

IAGO: Be wise, and get you home.

EMILIA: I will not.

[IAGO *draws and threatens* EMILIA]

GRATIANO: Fie!
Your sword upon a woman?

EMILIA: O thou dull Moor, that handkerchief thou speak'st of
I found by fortune, and did give my husband;
For often with a solemn earnestness—
More than indeed belonged to such a trifle—
He begged of me to steal't.

IAGO: Villainous whore!   230

EMILIA: She give it Cassio? No, alas, I found it,
And I did give't my husband.

IAGO: Filth, thou liest!

EMILIA: By heaven, I do not, I do not, gentlemen.
O murd'rous coxcomb! what should such a fool
Do with so good a wife?

OTHELLO: Are there no stones in heaven
But what serves for the thunder? Precious villain!

[*The* MOOR *runs at* IAGO, *but is disarmed by* MONTANO.
IAGO *kills his wife*]

GRATIANO: The woman falls. Sure he hath killed his wife.

EMILIA: Ay, ay. O, lay me by my mistress' side.   [*Exit* IAGO]

215 *recognizance* token. 221 *liberal as the north* unchecked as the north wind
blows. 235 *stones* bolts like those used for thunderbolts.

GRATIANO: He's gone, but his wife's killed.

MONTANO: 'Tis a notorious villain. Take you this weapon,   240
　　　　Which I have here recovered from the Moor.
　　　　Come, guard the door without. Let him not pass,
　　　　But kill him rather. I'll after that same villain,
　　　　For 'tis a damnèd slave.

　　　　[*Exit* MONTANO, *with all but* OTHELLO *and* EMILIA]

OTHELLO: I am not valiant neither;
　　　　But every puny whipster gets my sword.
　　　　But why should honor outlive honesty?
　　　　Let it go all.

EMILIA: What did thy song bode, lady?
　　　　Hark, canst thou hear me? I will play the swan,
　　　　And die in music. [*Sings*] 'Willow, willow, willow.'
　　　　Moor, she was chaste. She loved thee, cruel Moor: 250
　　　　So come my soul to bliss as I speak true.
　　　　So speaking as I think, I die, I die.   [*She dies*]

OTHELLO: I have another weapon in this chamber;
　　　　It is a sword of Spain, the Isebrook's temper.
　　　　O, here it is.—Uncle, I must come forth.

GRATIANO: [*Within*]   If thou attempt it, it will cost thee dear.
　　　　Thou hast no weapon, and perforce must suffer.

OTHELLO: Look in upon me then and speak with me,
　　　　Or, naked as I am, I will assault thee.

[*Enter* GRATIANO]

GRATIANO: What is the matter?

OTHELLO: Behold, I have a weapon;   260
　　　　A better never did itself sustain
　　　　Upon a soldier's thigh. I have seen the day
　　　　That with this little arm and this good sword
　　　　I have made my way through more impediments
　　　　Than twenty times your stop. But O vain boast!
　　　　Who can control his fate? 'Tis not so now.
　　　　Be not afraid, though you do see me weaponed.
　　　　Here is my journey's end, here is my butt,

　　240 *notorious* notable.   245 *puny whipster* top-whipping boy.   254 *Isebrook's tem-*
per i.e. tempered at Innsbruck, where the finest armorer's steel of the time was made.
259 *naked* disarmed.   265 *stop* power to stop.   268 *butt* limit.

And very seamark of my utmost sail.
Do you go back dismayed? 'Tis a lost fear. 270
Man but a rush against Othello's breast,
And he retires. Where should Othello go?
Now, how dost thou look now? O ill-starred wench!
Pale as thy smock! When we shall meet at compt,
This look of thine will hurl my soul from heaven,
And fiends will snatch at it. Cold, cold, my girl?
Even like thy chastity.
O cursèd, cursèd slave! Whip me, ye devils,
From the possession of this heavenly sight!
Blow me about in winds! roast me in sulphur! 280
Wash me in steep-down gulfs of liquid fire!
O Desdemona, Desdemona! dead!
O! O! O!

[*Enter* LODOVICO, MONTANO, IAGO, *as prisoner, and* OFFICERS;
CASSIO *in a chair*]

LODOVICO: Where is this rash and most unfortunate man?

OTHELLO: That's he that was Othello. Here I am.

LODOVICO: Where is that viper? Bring the villain forth.

OTHELLO: I look down towards his feet—but that's a fable.
If that thou be'st a devil, I cannot kill thee. [*Wounds* IAGO]

LODOVICO: Wrench his sword from him. [OTHELLO *is disarmed*]

IAGO: I bleed, sir, but not killed.

OTHELLO: I am not sorry neither. I'ld have thee live; 290
For in my sense, 'tis happiness to die.

LODOVICO: O thou Othello that wert once so good,
Fall'n in the practice of a damnèd slave,
What shall be said to thee?

OTHELLO: Why, anything:
An honorable murderer, if you will;
For naught did I in hate, but all in honor.

LODOVICO: This wretch hath part confessed his villainy.
Did you and he consent in Cassio's death?

269 *seamark* beacon, destination.   270 *lost* wasted.   271 *Man but a rush* wield
only a reed.   274 *compt* final accounting, Last Judgment.   287 *I . . . feet* i.e. to see
if they are cloven, like the Devil's.   293 *practice* plot.   298 *consent in* agree upon.

OTHELLO: Ay.

CASSIO: Dear general, I never gave you cause.   300

OTHELLO: I do believe it, and I ask your pardon.
    Will you, I pray, demand that demi-devil
    Why he hath thus ensnared my soul and body?

IAGO: Demand me nothing. What you know, you know.
    From this time forth I never will speak word.

LODOVICO: What, not to pray?

GRATIANO: Torments will ope your lips.

OTHELLO: Well, thou dost best.

LODOVICO: Sir, you shall understand what hath befall'n,
    Which, as I think, you know not. Here is a letter
    Found in the pocket of the slain Roderigo;   310
    And here another. The one of them imports
    The death of Cassio to be undertook
    By Roderigo.

OTHELLO: O villain!

CASSIO: Most heathenish and most gross!

LODOVICO: Now here's another discontented paper
    Found in his pocket too; and this, it seems,
    Roderigo meant t' have sent this damnèd villain;
    But that, belike, Iago in the nick
    Came in and satisfied him.

OTHELLO: O thou pernicious caitiff!—
    How came you, Cassio, by that handkerchief   320
    That was my wife's?

CASSIO: I found it in my chamber;
    And he himself confessed but even now
    That there he dropped it for a special purpose
    Which wrought to his desire.

OTHELLO: O fool! fool! fool!

CASSIO: There is besides in Roderigo's letter,
    How he upbraids Iago that he made him

    318 *nick* nick of time.

Brave me upon the watch; whereon it came
That I was cast; and even but now he spake,
After long seeming dead—Iago hurt him,
Iago set him on.   330

LODOVICO: You must forsake this room and go with us.
Your power and your command is taken off,
And Cassio rules in Cyprus. For this slave,
If there be any cunning cruelty
That can torment him much and hold him long,
It shall be his. You shall close prisoner rest
Till that the nature of your fault be known
To the Venetian state. Come, bring away.

OTHELLO: Soft you! a word or two before you go.
I have done the state some service, and they know't.   340
No more of that. I pray you, in your letters,
When you shall these unlucky deeds relate,
Speak of me as I am. Nothing extenuate,
Nor set down aught in malice. Then must you speak
Of one that loved not wisely, but too well;
Of one not easily jealous, but, being wrought,
Perplexed in the extreme; of one whose hand,
Like the base Judean, threw a pearl away
Richer than all his tribe; of one whose subdued eyes,
Albeit unusèd to the melting mood,   350
Drop tears as fast as the Arabian trees
Their med'cinable gum. Set you down this.
And say besides that in Aleppo once,
Where a malignant and a turbaned Turk
Beat a Venetian and traduced the state,
I took by th' throat the circumcisèd dog
And smote him—thus.   [*He stabs himself*]

LODOVICO: O bloody period!

GRATIANO: All that's spoke is marred.

OTHELLO: I kissed thee ere I killed thee. No way but this,
Killing myself, to die upon a kiss.   360

[*He falls upon the bed and dies*]

328 *cast* dismissed.   347 *Perplexed* distracted.   348 *Judean* Judas Iscariot (?)
(quarto reads "Indian").   349 *subdued* i.e. conquered by grief.   358 *period* ending.

CASSIO: This did I fear, but thought he had no weapon;
      For he was great of heart.

LODOVICO: [To IAGO]   O Spartan dog,
      More fell than anguish, hunger, or the sea!
      Look on the tragic loading of this bed.
      This is thy work. The object poisons sight;
      Let it be hid. Gratiano, keep the house,
      And seize upon the fortunes of the Moor,
      For they succeed on you. To you, lord governor,
      Remains the censure of this hellish villain,
      The time, the place, the torture. O, enforce it!   370
      Myself will straight aboard, and to the state
      This heavy act with heavy heart relate.   [Exeunt]

---

363 *fell* cruel.   366 *Let it be hid* i.e. draw the bed curtains.   367 *seize upon* take legal possession of.   369 *censure* judicial sentence.

WILLIAM SHAKESPEARE

❧ *Measure for Measure*

CHARACTERS

Vincentio, *the Duke*
Angelo, *the deputy*
Escalus, *an ancient lord*
Claudio, *a young gentleman*
Lucio, *a fantastic*
Two other like Gentlemen
[Varrius, *a gentleman attending on the Duke*]
Provost
[A Justice]
Thomas ⎱ *two friars*
Peter ⎰
Elbow, *a simple constable*
Froth, *a foolish gentleman*
Clown [Pompey, *tapster to Mistress Overdone*]
Abhorson, *an executioner*
Barnardine, *a dissolute prisoner*
Isabella, *sister to Claudio*
Mariana, *betrothed to Angelo*
Juliet, *beloved of Claudio*
Francisca, *a nun*
Mistress Overdone, *a bawd*
Lords, Officers, Citizens, Boy, and Attendants

THE SCENE *Vienna*

ACT I. SCENE I

An apartment in the Duke's palace.

[*Enter* DUKE, ESCALUS, LORDS, *and* ATTENDANTS]

DUKE: Escalus.

ESCALUS: My lord.

DUKE: Of government the properties to unfold,
Would seem in me t'affect speech and discourse,
Since I am put to know that your own science
Exceeds, in that, the lists of all advice
My strength can give you. Then no more remains
But that, to your sufficiency, as your worth is able,
And let them work. The nature of our people,
Our city's institutions, and the terms   10
For common justice, y'are as pregnant in
As art and practice hath enrichèd any
That we remember. There is our commission,
From which we would not have you warp. Call hither,
I say, bid come before us Angelo.   [*Exit an* ATTENDANT]
What figure of us think you he will bear?
For you must know, we have with special soul
Elected him our absence to supply,
Lent him our terror, dressed him with our love,
And given his deputation all the organs   20
Of our own power. What think you of it?

ESCALUS: If any in Vienna be of worth
To undergo such ample grace and honor,
It is Lord Angelo.

[*Enter* ANGELO]

DUKE: Look where he comes.

ANGELO: Always obedient to your grace's will,
I come to know your pleasure.

DUKE: Angelo,
There is a kind of character in thy life,
That to th' observer doth thy history
Fully unfold. Thyself and thy belongings
Are not thine own so proper, as to waste   30
Thyself upon thy virtues, they on thee.
Heaven doth with us as we with torches do,
Not light them for themselves; for if our virtues
Did not go forth of us, 'twere all alike
As if we had them not. Spirits are not finely touched
But to fine issues, nor Nature never lends
The smallest scruple of her excellence

---

5 *science* knowledge.   6 *lists* limits.   8 (one or more lines probably missing after this line).   14 *warp* swerve.   16 *What . . . bear* i.e. how will he represent me.   20 *deputation* office as deputy   *organs* instruments, authority.   29 *belongings* endowments.   30 *proper* exclusively.

But like a thrifty goddess she determines
Herself the glory of a creditor,
Both thanks and use. But I do bend my speech 40
To one that can my part in him advertise.
Hold therefore, Angelo:
In our remove be thou at full ourself.
Mortality and mercy in Vienna
Live in thy tongue and heart. Old Escalus,
Though first in question, is thy secondary.
Take thy commission.

ANGELO: Now, good my lord,
Let there be some more test made of my mettle
Before so noble and so great a figure
Be stamped upon it.

DUKE: No more evasion. 50
We have with a leavened and preparèd choice
Proceeded to you; therefore take your honors.
Our haste from hence is of so quick condition
That it prefers itself, and leaves unquestioned
Matters of needful value. We shall write to you,
As time and our concernings shall importune,
How it goes with us, and do look to know
What doth befall you here. So fare you well:
To th'hopeful execution do I leave you
Of your commissions.

ANGELO: Yet give leave, my lord, 60
That we may bring you something on the way.

DUKE: My haste may not admit it;
Nor need you, on mine honor, have to do
With any scruple. Your scope is as mine own,
So to enforce or qualify the laws
As to your soul seems good. Give me your hand.
I'll privily away; I love the people,
But do not like to stage me to their eyes;
Though it do well, I do not relish well
Their loud applause and aves vehement, 70
Nor do I think the man of safe discretion
That does affect it. Once more, fare you well.

---

40 *use* interest.   41 *my part . . . advertise* instruct that part of me now vested
in him.   43 *remove* absence.   46 *first in question* the first to be considered.   48 *mettle*
(pun with "metal").   51 *leavened* slowly rising (in the mind).   54 *prefers* presents
unquestioned uninvestigated.   61 *bring . . . way* escort you part of the way.   70
aves salutations.

ANGELO: The heavens give safety to your purposes.

ESCALUS: Lead forth and bring you back in happiness!

DUKE: I thank you; fare you well.   [*Exit*]

ESCALUS: I shall desire you, sir, to give me leave
        To have free speech with you; and it concerns me
        To look into the bottom of my place.
        A power I have, but of what strength and nature
        I am not yet instructed.   80

ANGELO: 'Tis so with me. Let us withdraw together,
        And we may soon our satisfaction have
        Touching that point.

ESCALUS: I'll wait upon your honor.   [*Exeunt*]

SCENE II

A street.

[*Enter* LUCIO *and two other* GENTLEMEN]

LUCIO: If the Duke, with the other dukes, come not to composition
    with the king of Hungary, why then all the dukes fall upon the
    king.

1. GENTLEMAN: Heaven grant us its peace, but not the king of Hun-
    gary's!

2. GENTLEMAN: Amen.

LUCIO: Thou conclud'st like the sanctimonious pirate, that went to sea
    with the Ten Commandments, but scraped one out of the table.

2. GENTLEMAN: "Thou shalt not steal"?

LUCIO: Ay, that he razed.   10

1. GENTLEMAN: Why, 'twas a commandment to command the captain
    and all the rest from their functions; they put forth to steal.
    There's not a soldier of us all that, in the thanksgiving before
    meat, do relish the petition well that prays for peace.

2. GENTLEMAN: I never heard any soldier dislike it.

LUCIO: I believe thee, for I think thou never wast where grace was said.

78 *bottom . . . place* scope of my power. 1 *composition* agreement.

2. GENTLEMAN: No? a dozen times at least.

1. GENTLEMAN: What? In meter?

LUCIO: In any proportion or in any language.

1. GENTLEMAN: I think, or in any religion.   20

LUCIO: Ay, why not? Grace is grace, despite of all controversy: as, for example, thou thyself art a wicked villain, despite of all grace.

2. GENTLEMAN: Well, there went but a pair of shears between us.

LUCIO: I grant: as there may between the lists and the velvet. Thou art the list.

1. GENTLEMAN: And thou the velvet. Thou art good velvet; thou'rt a three-piled piece, I warrant thee. I had as lief be a list of an English kersey as be piled, as thou art piled, for a French velvet. Do I speak feelingly now?

LUCIO: I think thou dost; and indeed with most painful feeling of thy   30
speech. I will, out of thine own confession, learn to begin thy health; but, whilst I live, forget to drink after thee.

1. GENTLEMAN: I think I have done myself wrong, have I not?

2. GENTLEMAN: Yes, that thou hast, whether thou art tainted or free.

[*Enter Bawd* MISTRESS OVERDONE]

LUCIO: Behold, behold, where Madam Mitigation comes!

1. GENTLEMAN: I have purchased as many diseases under her roof as come to—

2. GENTLEMAN: To what, I pray?

LUCIO: Judge.

2. GENTLEMAN: To three thousand dolors a year.   40

1. GENTLEMAN: Ay, and more.

LUCIO: A French crown more.

1. GENTLEMAN: Thou art always figuring diseases in me; but thou art full of error. I am sound.

LUCIO: Nay, not—as one would say—healthy, but so sound as things that are hollow. Thy bones are hollow; impiety has made a feast of thee.

---

23 *there went . . . us* i.e. we are cut from the same cloth.   24 *lists* selvage.   27 *three-piled* with triple nap.   28 *kersey* homespun   *piled* (1) having a nap (2) afflicted with piles.   *French* (syphilis was known as "the French disease").   31–32 *learn . . . after thee* drink a health to you but not drink out of the same cup after you (to avoid infection).   40 *dolors* (pun with "dollars").

1. GENTLEMAN: How now, which of your hips has the most profound sciatica?

MISTRESS OVERDONE: Well, well; there's one yonder arrested and carried   50
to prison was worth five thousand of you all.

2. GENTLEMAN: Who's that, I pray thee?

MISTRESS OVERDONE: Marry, sir, that's Claudio, Signior Claudio.

1. GENTLEMAN: Claudio to prison? 'Tis not so.

MISTRESS OVERDONE: Nay, but I know 'tis so. I saw him arrested, saw him carried away, and, which is more, within these three days his head to be chopped off.

LUCIO: But, after all this fooling, I would not have it so. Art thou sure of this?

MISTRESS OVERDONE: I am too sure of it; and it is for getting Madam   60
Julietta with child.

LUCIO: Believe me, this may be. He promised to meet me two hours since, and he was ever precise in promise-keeping.

2. GENTLEMAN: Besides, you know, it draws something near to the speech we had to such a purpose.

1. GENTLEMAN: But most of all agreeing with the proclamation.

LUCIO: Away; let's go learn the truth of it. [*Exit* LUCIO *with the* GENTLEMEN]

MISTRESS OVERDONE: Thus, what with the war, what with the sweat, what with the gallows, and what with poverty, I am custom-shrunk.

[*Enter* CLOWN POMPEY]

How now? What's the news with you?   70

POMPEY: Yonder man is carried to prison.

MISTRESS OVERDONE: Well, what has he done?

POMPEY: A woman.

MISTRESS OVERDONE: But what's his offense?

POMPEY: Groping for trouts in a peculiar river.

68 *sweat* sweating sickness, plague.   75 *peculiar* private.

MISTRESS OVERDONE: What? Is there a maid with child by him?

POMPEY: No, but there's a woman with maid by him. You have not heard of the proclamation, have you?

MISTRESS OVERDONE: What proclamation, man?

POMPEY: All houses in the suburbs of Vienna must be plucked down. 80

MISTRESS OVERDONE: And what shall become of those in the city?

POMPEY: They shall stand for seed: they had gone down too, but that a wise burgher put in for them.

MISTRESS OVERDONE: But shall all our houses of resort in the suburbs be pulled down?

POMPEY: To the ground, mistress.

MISTRESS OVERDONE: Why, here's a change indeed in the commonwealth; what shall become of me?

POMPEY: Come, fear not you; good counsellors lack no clients. Though you change your place, you need not change your trade; I'll be 90 your tapster still. Courage, there will be pity taken on you; you that have worn your eyes almost out in the service, you will be considered.

MISTRESS OVERDONE: What's to do here, Thomas Tapster? Let's withdraw.

POMPEY: Here comes Signior Claudio, led by the provost to prison; and there's Madam Juliet. [*Exeunt*]

[*Enter* PROVOST, CLAUDIO, JULIET, OFFICERS, LUCIO, *and two* GENTLEMEN]

CLAUDIO: Fellow, why dost thou show me thus to th' world?
Bear me to prison, where I am committed.

PROVOST: I do it not in evil disposition, 100
But from Lord Angelo by special charge.

CLAUDIO: Thus can the demigod Authority
Make us pay down for our offense by weight
The words of heaven; on whom it will, it will;
On whom it will not, so: yet still 'tis just.

---

80 *suburbs* (in London, the area of the brothels).   103 (one or more lines probably missing after this line).   104 *words of heaven* (probably Romans 9:18).

LUCIO: Why, how now, Claudio? Whence comes this restraint?

CLAUDIO: From too much liberty, my Lucio, liberty.
  As surfeit is the father of much fast,
  So every scope by the immoderate use
  Turns to restraint. Our natures do pursue,   110
  Like rats that ravin down their proper bane,
  A thirsty evil, and when we drink we die.

LUCIO: If I could speak so wisely under an arrest, I would send for
  certain of my creditors. And yet, to say the truth, I had as lief
  have the foppery of freedom as the morality of imprisonment.
  What's thy offense, Claudio?

CLAUDIO: What but to speak of would offend again.

LUCIO: What, is't murder?

CLAUDIO: No.

LUCIO: Lechery?   120

CLAUDIO: Call it so.

PROVOST: Away, sir, you must go.

CLAUDIO: One word, good friend. Lucio, a word with you.

LUCIO: A hundred, if they'll do you any good.
  Is lechery so looked after?

CLAUDIO: Thus stands it with me: upon a true contract
  I got possession of Julietta's bed.
  You know the lady, she is fast my wife
  Save that we do the denunciation lack
  Of outward order. This we came not to,   130
  Only for prorogation of a dower
  Remaining in the coffer of her friends,
  From whom we thought it meet to hide our love
  Till time had made them for us. But it chances
  The stealth of our most mutual entertainment
  With character too gross is writ on Juliet.

LUCIO: With child, perhaps?

CLAUDIO: Unhappily, even so.
  And the new deputy now for the Duke—

---

109 *scope* freedom.   111 *ravin . . . bane* gulp down what is poisonous to them.
115 *foppery* foolishness.   129 *denunciation* declaration.   131 *for prorogation* because of
delay.   132 *friends* relatives.

Whether it be the fault and glimpse of newness,
Or whether that the body public be   140
A horse whereon the governor doth ride,
Who, newly in the seat, that it may know
He can command, lets it straight feel the spur;
Whether the tyranny be in his place,
Or in his eminence that fills it up,
I stagger in—but this new governor
Awakes me all the enrollèd penalties
Which have, like unscoured armor, hung by th'wall
So long that nineteen zodiacs have gone round
And none of them been worn; and for a name   150
Now puts the drowsy and neglected act
Freshly on me: 'tis surely for a name.

LUCIO: I warrant it is, and thy head stands so tickle on thy shoulders
that a milkmaid, if she be in love, may sigh it off. Send after the
Duke and appeal to him.

CLAUDIO: I have done so, but he's not to be found.
I prithee, Lucio, do me this kind service:
This day my sister should the cloister enter,
And there receive her approbation.
Acquaint her with the danger of my state;   160
Implore her, in my voice, that she make friends
To the strict deputy; bid herself assay him.
I have great hope in that; for in her youth
There is a prone and speechless dialect,
Such as move men; beside, she hath prosperous art
When she will play with reason and discourse,
And well she can persuade.

LUCIO: I pray she may, as well for the encouragement of the like, which
else would stand under grievous imposition, as for the enjoying of
thy life, who I would be sorry should be thus foolishly lost at a   170
game of tick-tack. I'll to her.

CLAUDIO: I thank you, good friend Lucio.

LUCIO: Within two hours.

CLAUDIO: Come, officer, away.   [*Exeunt*]

146 *stagger in* am uncertain.   147 *enrollèd* written out in full on a parchment roll.
149 *zodiacs* i.e. years.   153 *tickle* unsteady.   159 *approbation* novitiate.   164 *prone*
apt   *dialect* language.

SCENE III

A monastery.

[*Enter* DUKE *and* FRIAR THOMAS]

DUKE: No, holy father, throw away that thought;
    Believe not that the dribbling dart of love
    Can pierce a complete bosom; why I desire thee
    To give me secret harbor hath a purpose
    More grave and wrinkled than the aims and ends
    Of burning youth.

FRIAR: May your grace speak of it?

DUKE: My holy sir, none better knows than you
    How I have ever loved the life removed
    And held in idle price to haunt assemblies
    Where youth and cost witless bravery keeps.   10
    I have delivered to Lord Angelo,
    A man of stricture and firm abstinence,
    My absolute power and place here in Vienna,
    And he supposes me travelled to Poland;
    For so I have strewed it in the common ear,
    And so it is received. Now, pious sir,
    You will demand of me why I do this?

FRIAR: Gladly, my lord.

DUKE: We have strict statutes and most biting laws,
    The needful bits and curbs to headstrong wills,   20
    Which for this fourteen years we have let slip;
    Even like an o'ergrown lion in a cave,
    That goes not out to prey. Now, as fond fathers,
    Having bound up the threatening twigs of birch,
    Only to stick it in their children's sight
    For terror, not to use, in time the rod
    Becomes more mocked than feared; so our decrees,
    Dead to infliction, to themselves are dead,
    And Liberty plucks Justice by the nose;
    The baby beats the nurse, and quite athwart   30
    Goes all decorum.

---

2 *dribbling* missing the mark. 3 *complete* strong, mature. 10 *witless bravery* senseless display. 12 *stricture* strictness. 28 *Dead to infliction* completely unenforced. 29 *Liberty . . . nose* lack of restraint flouts justice. 30 *athwart* awry.

FRIAR: It rested in your grace
To unloose this tied-up justice when you pleased;
And it in you more dreadful would have seemed
Than in Lord Angelo.

DUKE: I do fear, too dreadful;
Sith 'twas my fault to give the people scope,
'Twould be my tyranny to strike and gall them
For what I bid them do: for we bid this be done
When evil deeds have their permissive pass
And not the punishment. Therefore, indeed, my father,
I have on Angelo imposed the office,   40
Who may, in th'ambush of my name, strike home,
And yet my nature never in the sight
To do it slander. And to behold his sway
I will, as 'twere a brother of your order,
Visit both prince and people. Therefore, I prithee,
Supply me with the habit, and instruct me
How I may formally in person bear
Like a true friar. Moe reasons for this action
At our more leisure shall I render you;
Only this one: Lord Angelo is precise,   50
Stands at a guard with envy; scarce confesses
That his blood flows, or that his appetite
Is more to bread than stone. Hence shall we see,
If power change purpose, what our seemers be.   [*Exit with Friar*]

SCENE IV

A nunnery.

[*Enter* ISABELLA *and* FRANCISCA, *a* NUN]

ISABELLA: And have you nuns no farther privileges?

NUN: Are not these large enough?

ISABELLA: Yes, truly. I speak not as desiring more,
But rather wishing a more strict restraint
Upon the sisterhood, the votarists of Saint Clare.

[LUCIO *within*]

---

    41 *in th'ambush* under the cover.   48 *Moe* more.   50 *precise* morally strict.   51
at a guard on defense.

LUCIO: Ho! Peace be in this place.

ISABELLA: Who's that which calls?

NUN: It is a man's voice. Gentle Isabella,
    Turn you the key, and know his business of him.
    You may, I may not; you are yet unsworn.
    When you have vowed, you must not speak with men   10
    But in the presence of the prioress;
    Then, if you speak, you must not show your face,
    Or, if you show your face, you must not speak.
    He calls again; I pray you, answer him.   [*Exit*]

ISABELLA: Peace and prosperity; who is't that calls?

[*Enter* LUCIO]

LUCIO: Hail, virgin, if you be, as those cheek-roses
    Proclaim you are no less. Can you so stead me
    As bring me to the sight of Isabella,
    A novice of this place, and the fair sister
    To her unhappy brother, Claudio?   20

ISABELLA: Why "her unhappy brother"? let me ask,
    The rather for I now must make you know
    I am that Isabella, and his sister.

LUCIO: Gentle and fair, your brother kindly greets you.
    Not to be weary with you, he's in prison.

ISABELLA: Woe me, for what?

LUCIO: For that which, if myself might be his judge,
    He should receive his punishment in thanks.
    He hath got his friend with child.

ISABELLA: Sir, make me not your story.

LUCIO: 'Tis true.   30
    I would not, though 'tis my familiar sin
    With maids to seem the lapwing and to jest,
    Tongue far from heart, play with all virgins so.
    I hold you as a thing enskied and sainted,
    By your renouncement an immortal spirit,
    And to be talked with in sincerity,
    As with a saint.

---

    17 *stead* help.   30 *story* theme for mirth.   32 *lapwing* bird which runs to and fro
to divert attention from its nest.

ISABELLA: You do blaspheme the good in mocking me.

LUCIO: Do not believe it. Fewness and truth, 'tis thus:
Your brother and his lover have embraced;   40
As those that feed grow full, as blossoming time
That from the seedness the bare fallow brings
To teeming foison, even so her plenteous womb
Expresseth his full tilth and husbandry.

ISABELLA: Someone with child by him? My cousin Juliet?

LUCIO: Is she your cousin?

ISABELLA: Adoptedly, as schoolmaids change their names
By vain though apt affection.

LUCIO: She it is.

ISABELLA: O, let him marry her.

LUCIO: This is the point.
The Duke is very strangely gone from hence;   50
Bore many gentlemen—myself being one—
In hand and hope of action; but we do learn
By those that know the very nerves of state,
His givings-out were of an infinite distance
From his true-meant design. Upon his place,
And with full line of his authority,
Governs Lord Angelo, a man whose blood
Is very snow-broth; one who never feels
The wanton stings and motions of the sense,
But doth rebate and blunt his natural edge   60
With profits of the mind, study and fast.
He—to give fear to use and liberty,
Which have for long run by the hideous law,
As mice by lions—hath picked out an act,
Under whose heavy sense your brother's life
Falls into forfeit; he arrests him on it,
And follows close the rigor of the statute
To make him an example. All hope is gone,
Unless you have the grace by your fair prayer
To soften Angelo. And that's my pith of business   70
'Twixt you and your poor brother.

ISABELLA: Doth he so seek his life?

---

39 *Fewness and truth* briefly and truly. 42 *seedness* sowing. 43 *foison* harvest.
51–52 *Bore . . . In hand and hope* deluded . . . with the hope. 62 *use and liberty*
habitual license.

LUCIO: Has censured him
    Already and, as I hear, the provost hath
    A warrant for his execution.

ISABELLA: Alas, what poor ability's in me
    To do him good?

LUCIO: Assay the power you have.

ISABELLA: My power? Alas, I doubt—

LUCIO: Our doubts are traitors
    And make us lose the good we oft might win,
    By fearing to attempt. Go to Lord Angelo
    And let him learn to know, when maidens sue,   80
    Men give like gods; but when they weep and kneel,
    All their petitions are as freely theirs
    As they themselves would owe them.

ISABELLA: I'll see what I can do.

LUCIO: But speedily.

ISABELLA: I will about it straight,
    No longer staying but to give the Mother
    Notice of my affair. I humbly thank you;
    Commend me to my brother; soon at night
    I'll send him certain word of my success.

LUCIO: I take my leave of you.

ISABELLA: Good sir, adieu.   [*Exeunt*]   90

ACT II. SCENE I

A hall in Angelo's house.

[*Enter* ANGELO, ESCALUS, *and* SERVANTS, JUSTICE]

ANGELO: We must not make a scarecrow of the law,
    Setting it up to fear the birds of prey,
    And let it keep one shape, till custom make it
    Their perch and not their terror.

ESCALUS: Ay, but yet
    Let us be keen and rather cut a little,
    Than fall and bruise to death. Alas, this gentleman

---

72 *censured* passed judgment on. 83 *owe* possess. 89 *success* fortune. 6 *fall*
let fall.

Whom I would save had a most noble father.
Let but your honor know,
Whom I believe to be most strait in virtue,
That, in the working of your own affections,   10
Had time cohered with place or place with wishing,
Or that the resolute acting of your blood
Could have attained th'effect of your own purpose,
Whether you had not sometime in your life
Erred in this point which now you censure him,
And pulled the law upon you.

ANGELO: 'Tis one thing to be tempted, Escalus,
Another thing to fall. I not deny,
The jury passing on the prisoner's life
May in the sworn twelve have a thief or two   20
Guiltier than him they try; what's open made to justice,
That justice seizes; what knows the laws
That thieves do pass on thieves? 'Tis very pregnant
The jewel that we find, we stoop and take't
Because we see it; but what we do not see
We tread upon, and never think of it.
You may not so extenuate his offense
For I have had such faults; but rather tell me,
When I that censure him do so offend,
Let mine own judgment pattern out my death   30
And nothing come in partial. Sir, he must die.

[*Enter* PROVOST]

ESCALUS: Be it as your wisdom will.

ANGELO: Where is the provost?

PROVOST: Here, if it like your honor.

ANGELO: See that Claudio
Be executed by nine tomorrow morning;
Bring him his confessor, let him be prepared;
For that's the utmost of his pilgrimage.   [*Exit* PROVOST]

ESCALUS: Well, heaven forgive him, and forgive us all.
Some rise by sin, and some by virtue fall:
Some run from breaks of ice, and answer none,
And some condemnèd for a fault alone.   40

---

10 *affections* passions.   23 *pass on* pass judgment on   *pregnant* natural.   28 *For* because.   31 *partial* in my favor.   39 *answer none* do not have to account for their acts.

[*Enter* ELBOW, FROTH, CLOWN (POMPEY), OFFICERS]

ELBOW: Come, bring them away. If these be good people in a com-
monweal that do nothing but use their abuses in common houses,
I know no law. Bring them away.

ANGELO: How now, sir, what's your name? And what's the matter?

ELBOW: If it please your honor, I am the poor Duke's constable, and
my name is Elbow. I do lean upon justice, sir, and do bring in
here before your good honor two notorious benefactors.

ANGELO: Benefactors? Well, what benefactors are they? Are they not
malefactors?

ELBOW: If it please your honor, I know not well what they are; but   50
precise villains they are, that I am sure of, and void of all profanation in the world that good Christians ought to have.

ESCALUS: This comes off well; here's a wise officer.

ANGELO: Go to: what quality are they of? Elbow is your name? Why
dost thou not speak, Elbow?

POMPEY: He cannot, sir; he's out at elbow.

ANGELO: What are you, sir?

ELBOW: He, sir, a tapster, sir, parcel-bawd; one that serves a bad
woman, whose house, sir, was, as they say, plucked down in the suburbs, and now she professes a hot-house, which I think is a very ill   60
house too.

ESCALUS: How know you that?

ELBOW: My wife, sir, whom I detest before heaven and your honor—

ESCALUS: How? Thy wife?

ELBOW: Ay, sir, whom I thank heaven is an honest woman—

ESCALUS: Dost thou detest her therefore?

ELBOW: I say, sir, I will detest myself also, as well as she, that this
house, if it be not a bawd's house, it is pity of her life, for it is
a naughty house.

ESCALUS: How dost thou know that, constable?   70

58 *parcel-bawd* partly a bawd.   60 *hot-house* bath-house, bagnio.

ELBOW: Marry, sir, by my wife, who, if she had been a woman cardinally given, might have been accused in fornication, adultery, and uncleanliness there.

ESCALUS: By the woman's means?

ELBOW: Ay, sir, by Mistress Overdone's means; but as she spit in his face, so she defied him.

POMPEY: Sir, if it please your honor, this is not so.

ELBOW: Prove it before these varlets here, thou honorable man, prove it.

ESCALUS: Do you hear how he misplaces?

POMPEY: Sir, she came in great with child, and longing—saving your honor's reverence—for stewed prunes. Sir, we had but two in the house, which at that very distant time stood, as it were, in a fruit dish, a dish of some threepence; your honors have seen such dishes; they are not china dishes, but very good dishes— 80

ESCALUS: Go to, go to; no matter for the dish, sir.

POMPEY: No, indeed, sir, not of a pin; you are therein in the right: but to the point. As I say, this Mistress Elbow, being, as I say, with child, and being great-bellied, and longing, as I said, for prunes, and having but two in the dish, as I said, Master Froth here, this very man, having eaten the rest, as I said and, as I say, paying for them very honestly, for, as you know, Master Froth, I could not give you threepence again— 90

FROTH: No, indeed.

POMPEY: Very well: you being then, if you be remembered, cracking the stones of the foresaid prunes—

FROTH: Ay, so I did, indeed.

POMPEY: Why, very well: I telling you then, if you be remembered, that such a one and such a one were past cure of the thing you wot of, unless they kept very good diet, as I told you—

FROTH: All this is true. 100

POMPEY: Why, very well then—

ESCALUS: Come, you are a tedious fool; to the purpose. What was done to Elbow's wife, that he hath cause to complain of? Come me to what was done to her.

71–72 *cardinally* i.e. carnally.

POMPEY: Sir, your honor cannot come to that yet.

ESCALUS: No, sir, nor I mean it not.

POMPEY: Sir, but you shall come to it, by your honor's leave. And I
beseech you look into Master Froth here, sir; a man of fourscore
pound a year, whose father died at Hallowmas. Was't not at
Hallowmas, Master Froth?   110

FROTH: Allhallond-Eve.

POMPEY: Why, very well; I hope here be truths. He, sir, sitting, as I
say, in lower chair, sir—'twas in the Bunch of Grapes, where indeed
you have a delight to sit, have you not?

FROTH: I have so, because it is an open room and good for winter.

POMPEY: Why, very well then; I hope here be truths.

ANGELO: This will last out a night in Russia
When nights are longest there. I'll take my leave,
And leave you to the hearing of the cause,
Hoping you'll find good cause to whip them all.   120

ESCALUS: I think no less. Good morrow to your lordship. [*Exit
ANGELO*]
Now, sir, come on; what was done to Elbow's wife, once more?

POMPEY: Once, sir? There was nothing done to her once.

ELBOW: I beseech you, sir, ask him what this man did to my wife.

POMPEY: I beseech your honor, ask me.

ESCALUS: Well, sir, what did this gentleman to her?

POMPEY: I beseech you, sir, look in this gentleman's face. Good
Master Froth, look upon his honor; 'tis for a good purpose. Doth
your honor mark his face?

ESCALUS: Ay, sir, very well.   130

POMPEY: Nay, I beseech you, mark it well.

ESCALUS: Well, I do so.

POMPEY: Doth your honor see any harm in his face?

ESCALUS: Why, no.

109 *Hallowmas* All Saints' Day, November 1st.   111 *Allhallond-Eve* Hallowe'en,
October 31st.

POMPEY: I'll be supposed upon a book, his face is the worst thing about him. Good, then; if his face be the worst thing about him, how could Master Froth do the constable's wife any harm? I would know that of your honor.

ESCALUS: He's in the right. Constable, what say you to it?

ELBOW: First, an it like you, the house is a respected house; next, 140 this is a respected fellow; and his mistress is a respected woman.

POMPEY: By this hand, sir, his wife is a more respected person than any of us all.

ELBOW: Varlet, thou liest; thou liest, wicked varlet. The time is yet to come that she was ever respected with man, woman, or child.

POMPEY: Sir, she was respected with him before he married with her.

ESCALUS: Which is the wiser here, Justice or Iniquity? Is this true?

ELBOW: O thou caitiff, O thou varlet, O thou wicked Hannibal! I re-spected with her before I was married to her? If ever I was re-spected with her, or she with me, let not your worship think me 150 the poor Duke's officer. Prove this, thou wicked Hannibal, or I'll have my action of battery on thee.

ESCALUS: If he took you a box o'th'ear, you might have your action of slander, too.

ELBOW: Marry, I thank your good worship for it; what is't your wor-ship's pleasure I shall do with this wicked caitiff?

ESCALUS: Truly, officer, because he hath some offenses in him that thou wouldst discover if thou couldst, let him continue in his courses till thou know'st what they are.

ELBOW: Marry, I thank your worship for it. Thou seest, thou wicked 160 varlet, now, what's come upon thee; thou art to continue now, thou varlet, thou art to continue.

ESCALUS: Where were you born, friend?

FROTH: Here in Vienna, sir.

ESCALUS: Are you of fourscore pounds a year?

FROTH: Yes, an't please you, sir.

135 *supposed* i.e. deposed. 147 *Justice or Iniquity* i.e. Elbow or Pompey (com-pared as stock characters in morality plays).

ESCALUS: So. [*To* POMPEY]   What trade are you of, sir?

POMPEY: A tapster, a poor widow's tapster.

ESCALUS: Your mistress' name?

POMPEY: Mistress Overdone.   170

ESCALUS: Hath she had any more than one husband?

POMPEY: Nine, sir; Overdone by the last.

ESCALUS: Nine! Come hither to me, Master Froth. Master Froth, I
would not have you acquainted with tapsters; they will draw you,
Master Froth, and you will hang them. Get you gone, and let me
hear no more of you.

FROTH: I thank your worship. For mine own part, I never come into
any room in a taphouse but I am drawn in.

ESCALUS: Well, no more of it, Master Froth; farewell.   [*Exit* FROTH]
Come you hither to me, master tapster. What's your name, master   180
tapster?

POMPEY: Pompey.

ESCALUS: What else?

POMPEY: Bum, sir.

ESCALUS: Troth, and your bum is the greatest thing about you, so that,
in the beastliest sense, you are Pompey the Great. Pompey, you
are partly a bawd, Pompey, howsoever you color it in being a tapster, are you not? Come, tell me true; it shall be the better for
you.

POMPEY: Truly, sir, I am a poor fellow that would live.   190

ESCALUS: How would you live, Pompey? By being a bawd?
What do you think of the trade, Pompey? Is it a lawful trade?

POMPEY: If the law would allow it, sir.

ESCALUS: But the law will not allow it, Pompey; nor it shall not be
allowed in Vienna.

POMPEY: Does your worship mean to geld and splay all the youth of
the city?

174 *draw you* empty you.   187 *color* camouflage.

ESCALUS: No, Pompey.

POMPEY: Truly, sir, in my poor opinion, they will to't then. If your worship will take order for the drabs and the knaves, you need not   200
to fear the bawds.

ESCALUS: There is pretty orders beginning, I can tell you; it is but heading and hanging.

POMPEY: If you head and hang all that offend that way but for ten year together, you'll be glad to give out a commission for more heads. If this law hold in Vienna ten year, I'll rent the fairest house in it after threepence a bay; if you live to see this come to pass, say Pompey told you so.

ESCALUS: Thank you, good Pompey; and, in requital of your prophecy, hark you: I advise you, let me not find you before me again upon   210
any complaint whatsoever; no, not for dwelling where you do. If I do, Pompey, I shall beat you to your tent, and prove a shrewd Caesar to you. In plain dealing, Pompey, I shall have you whipt; so, for this time, Pompey, fare you well.

POMPEY: I thank your worship for your good counsel;   [*Aside*]   but I shall follow it as the flesh and fortune shall better determine. Whip me! No, no, let carman whip his jade. The valiant heart's not whipt out of his trade.   [*Exit*]

ESCALUS: Come hither to me, Master Elbow; come hither, master constable. How long have you been in this place of constable?   220

ELBOW: Seven year and a half, sir.

ESCALUS: I thought, by the readiness in the office, you had continued in it some time; you say, seven years together?

ELBOW: And a half, sir.

ESCALUS: Alas, it hath been great pains to you; they do you wrong to put you so oft upon't. Are there not men in your ward sufficient to serve it?

ELBOW: Faith, sir, few of any wit in such matters. As they are chosen, they are glad to choose me for them; I do it for some piece of money, and go through with all.   230

202–03 *heading* beheading.   207 *bay* part of a house, viz. that part beneath a single gable.   229 *for them* i.e. as their deputy.

ESCALUS: Look you bring me in the names of some six or seven, the
      most sufficient of your parish.

ELBOW: To your worship's house, sir?

ESCALUS: To my house. Fare you well.   [*Exit* ELBOW]
      What's o'clock, think you?

JUSTICE: Eleven, sir.

ESCALUS: I pray you home to dinner with me.

JUSTICE: I humbly thank you.

ESCALUS: It grieves me for the death of Claudio,
      But there's no remedy.   240

JUSTICE: Lord Angelo is severe.

ESCALUS: It is but needful.
      Mercy is not itself, that oft looks so;
      Pardon is still the nurse of second woe.
      But yet poor Claudio; there is no remedy.
      Come, sir.   [*Exeunt*]

SCENE II

Another room in the same.

[*Enter* PROVOST *and a* SERVANT]

SERVANT: He's hearing of a cause; he will come straight;
      I'll tell him of you.

PROVOST: Pray you, do. [*Exit* SERVANT]   I'll know
      His pleasure; maybe he will relent. Alas,
      He hath but as offended in a dream.
      All sects, all ages smack of this vice—and he
      To die for't!

[*Enter* ANGELO]

ANGELO: Now, what's the matter, provost?

PROVOST: Is it your will Claudio shall die tomorrow?

ANGELO: Did not I tell thee, yea? Hadst thou not order?
      Why dost thou ask again?

      5 *sects* kinds.

PROVOST: Lest I might be too rash.
Under your good correction, I have seen 10
When, after execution, judgment hath
Repented o'er his doom.

ANGELO: Go to; let that be mine.
Do you your office, or give up your place,
And you shall well be spared.

PROVOST: I crave your honor's pardon.
What shall be done, sir, with the groaning Juliet?
She's very near her hour.

ANGELO: Dispose of her
To some more fitter place, and that with speed.

[*Enter* SERVANT]

SERVANT: Here is the sister of the man condemned
Desires access to you.

ANGELO: Hath he a sister?

PROVOST: Ay, my good lord, a very virtuous maid, 20
And to be shortly of a sisterhood,
If not already.

ANGELO: Well, let her be admitted. [*Exit* SERVANT]
See you the fornicatress be removed;
Let her have needful, but not lavish, means;
There shall be order for't.

[*Enter* LUCIO *and* ISABELLA]

PROVOST: 'Save your honor.

ANGELO: Stay a little while. [*To* ISABELLA] Y'are welcome: what's
your will?

ISABELLA: I am a woeful suitor to your honor,
Please but your honor hear me.

ANGELO: Well: what's your suit?

ISABELLA: There is a vice that most I do abhor,
And most desire should meet the blow of justice, 30
For which I would not plead, but that I must,
For which I must not plead, but that I am
At war 'twixt will and will not.

12 *mine* my concern.

ANGELO: Well: the matter?

ISABELLA: I have a brother is condemned to die.
    I do beseech you, let it be his fault,
    And not my brother.

PROVOST: [*Aside*]   Heaven give thee moving graces.

ANGELO: Condemn the fault, and not the actor of it?
    Why, every fault's condemned ere it be done:
    Mine were the very cipher of a function,
    To fine the faults whose fine stands in record,   40
    And let go by the actor.

ISABELLA: O just, but severe law!
    I had a brother then; heaven keep your honor.

LUCIO: [*Aside to* ISABELLA]   Give't not o'er so: to him again, entreat
    him,
    Kneel down before him, hang upon his gown;
    You are too cold. If you should need a pin,
    You could not with more tame a tongue desire it;
    To him, I say.

ISABELLA: Must he needs die?

ANGELO: Maiden, no remedy.

ISABELLA: Yes, I do think that you might pardon him,   50
    And neither heaven nor man grieve at the mercy .

ANGELO: I will not do't.

ISABELLA: But can you if you would?

ANGELO: Look, what I will not, that I cannot do.

ISABELLA: But might you do't, and do the world no wrong,
    If so your heart were touched with that remorse
    As mine is to him?

ANGELO: He's sentenced; 'tis too late.

LUCIO: [*Aside to* ISABELLA]   You are too cold.

ISABELLA: Too late? Why, no: I that do speak a word
    May call it back again. Well, believe this,

    40 *To fine . . . record* i.e. to do what has already been done, condemn faults as
faults.   55 *remorse* pity.

No ceremony that to great ones 'longs, 60
Not the king's crown, nor the deputed sword,
The marshal's truncheon, nor the judge's robe,
Become them with one half so good a grace
As mercy does;
If he had been as you, and you as he,
You would have slipped like him; but he, like you,
Would not have been so stern.

ANGELO: Pray you, be gone.

ISABELLA: I would to heaven I had your potency,
And you were Isabel; should it then be thus?
No, I would tell what 'twere to be a judge, 70
And what a prisoner.

LUCIO: [*Aside to* ISABELLA]   Ay, touch him; there's the vein.

ANGELO: Your brother is a forfeit of the law,
And you but waste your words.

ISABELLA: Alas, alas;
Why, all the souls that were were forfeit once,
And He that might the vantage best have took,
Found out the remedy. How would you be,
If He, which is the top of judgment, should
But judge you as you are? O think on that,
And mercy then will breathe within your lips,
Like man new made.

ANGELO: Be you content, fair maid, 80
It is the law, not I, condemns your brother;
Were he my kinsman, brother, or my son,
It should be thus with him: he must die tomorrow.

ISABELLA: Tomorrow? O, that's sudden; spare him, spare him;
He's not prepared for death. Even for our kitchens
We kill the fowl of season; shall we serve heaven
With less respect than we do minister
To our gross selves? Good, good my lord, bethink you:
Who is it that hath died for this offense?
There's many have committed it.

---

77 *which . . . judgment* who is supreme judge.   86 *of season* in season.

LUCIO: [*Aside to* ISABELLA]   Ay, well said.   90

ANGELO: The law hath not been dead, though it hath slept.
          Those many had not dared to do that evil
          If that the first that did th' edict infringe
          Had answered for his deed. Now 'tis awake,
          Takes note of what is done, and like a prophet
          Looks in a glass that shows what future evils,
          Either new, or by remissness new-conceived,
          And so in progress to be hatched and born,
          Are now to have no successive degrees,
          But, ere they live, to end.

ISABELLA: Yet show some pity.   100

ANGELO: I show it most of all when I show justice,
          For then I pity those I do not know,
          Which a dismissed offense would after gall,
          And do him right that, answering one foul wrong,
          Lives not to act another. Be satisfied;
          Your brother dies tomorrow; be content.

ISABELLA: So you must be the first that gives this sentence,
          And he, that suffers. O, it is excellent
          To have a giant's strength, but it is tyrannous
          To use it like a giant.

LUCIO: [*Aside to* ISABELLA]   That's well said.   110

ISABELLA: Could great men thunder
          As Jove himself does, Jove would ne'er be quiet,
          For every pelting, petty officer
          Would use his heaven for thunder,
          Nothing but thunder. Merciful heaven,
          Thou rather with thy sharp and sulphurous bolt
          Splits the unwedgeable and gnarlèd oak
          Than the soft myrtle; but man, proud man,
          Dressed in a little brief authority,
          Most ignorant of what he's most assured—   120
          His glassy essence—like an angry ape
          Plays such fantastic tricks before high heaven
          As makes the angels weep; who, with our spleens,
          Would all themselves laugh mortal.

---

  96 *glass* crystal.   98 *in progress* in due course.   99 *degrees* stages.   103 *dismissed*
forgiven   *gall* hurt.   104 *do him right* do right by him (Claudio).   113 *pelting* paltry.
121 *glassy* fragile.

LUCIO: [*Aside to* ISABELLA] O, to him, to him, wench; he will relent.
    He's coming, I perceive't.

PROVOST: [*Aside*] Pray heaven she win him.

ISABELLA: We cannot weigh our brother with ourself:
    Great men may jest with saints: 'tis wit in them,
    But in the less foul profanation.

LUCIO: [*Aside to* ISABELLA] Thou'rt i'th'right, girl, more o'that.   130

ISABELLA: That in the captain's but a choleric word,
    Which in the soldier is flat blasphemy.

LUCIO: [*Aside to* ISABELLA] Art avised o'that? More on't.

ANGELO: Why do you put these sayings upon me?

ISABELLA: Because authority, though it err like others,
    Hath yet a kind of medicine in itself
    That skins the vice o'th'top; go to your bosom,
    Knock there, and ask your heart what it doth know
    That's like my brother's fault; if it confess
    A natural guiltiness such as is his,   140
    Let it not sound a thought upon your tongue
    Against my brother's life.

ANGELO: [*Aside*] She speaks, and 'tis
    Such sense that my sense breeds with it.—Fare you well.

ISABELLA: Gentle my lord, turn back.

ANGELO: I will bethink me; come again tomorrow.

ISABELLA: Hark how I'll bribe you; good my lord, turn back.

ANGELO: How! Bribe me?

ISABELLA: Ay, with such gifts that heaven shall share with you.

LUCIO: [*Aside to* ISABELLA] You had marred all else.

ISABELLA: Not with fond sicles of the tested gold,   150
    Or stones whose rates are either rich or poor
    As fancy values them; but with true prayers
    That shall be up at heaven and enter there
    Ere sunrise: prayers from preservèd souls,
    From fasting maids whose minds are dedicate
    To nothing temporal.

133 *avised* informed. 137 *That . . . top* that skims off the upper, and visible,
layer of vice. 150 *sicles* shekels.

ANGELO: Well, come to me tomorrow.

LUCIO: [*Aside to* ISABELLA]   Go to, 'tis well; away.

ISABELLA: Heaven keep your honor safe.

ANGELO: [*Aside*]   Amen.
          For I am that way going to temptation,
          Where prayers cross.

ISABELLA: At what hour tomorrow   160
          Shall I attend your lordship?

ANGELO: At any time 'fore-noon.

ISABELLA: 'Save your honor.   [*Exeunt* ISABELLA, LUCIO, *and* PROVOST]

ANGELO: From thee: even from thy virtue.
          What's this? what's this? is this her fault or mine?
          The tempter, or the tempted, who sins most?
          Ha!
          Not she, nor doth she tempt; but it is I
          That, lying by the violet in the sun,
          Do as the carrion does, not as the flower,
          Corrupt with virtuous season. Can it be
          That modesty may more betray our sense   170
          Than woman's lightness? Having waste ground enough,
          Shall we desire to raze the sanctuary
          And pitch our evils there? O fie, fie, fie!
          What dost thou? or what art thou, Angelo?
          Dost thou desire her foully for those things
          That make her good? O, let her brother live:
          Thieves for their robbery have authority
          When judges steal themselves. What, do I love her,
          That I desire to hear her speak again,
          And feast upon her eyes? what is't I dream on?   180
          O cunning enemy that, to catch a saint,
          With saints dost bait thy hook: most dangerous
          Is that temptation that doth goad us on
          To sin in loving virtue. Never could the strumpet
          With all her double vigor, art and nature,
          Once stir my temper; but this virtuous maid
          Subdues me quite. Ever till now,
          When men were fond, I smiled and wondered how.   [*Exit*]

     160 *cross* are at cross purposes.   169 *Corrupt . . . season* go bad in the season
that matures the flower.   173 *pitch our evils* erect our evil structures.   188 *fond* infatuated.

SCENE III

A prison.

[*Enter* DUKE *disguised as a friar and* PROVOST]

DUKE: Hail to you, provost—so I think you are.

PROVOST: I am the provost. What's your will, good friar?

DUKE: Bound by my charity and my blest order,
I come to visit the afflicted spirits
Here in the prison; do me the common right
To let me see them and to make me know
The nature of their crimes, that I may minister
To them accordingly.

PROVOST: I would do more than that, if more were needful.

[*Enter* JULIET]

Look, here comes one: a gentlewoman of mine,   10
Who, falling in the flaws of her own youth,
Hath blistered her report. She is with child,
And he that got it, sentenced: a young man
More fit to do another such offense
Than die for this.

DUKE: When must he die?

PROVOST: As I do think, tomorrow.
[*To Juliet*] I have provided for you; stay a while
And you shall be conducted.

DUKE: Repent you, fair one, of the sin you carry?

JULIET: I do, and bear the shame most patiently.   20

DUKE: I'll teach you how you shall arraign your conscience
And try your penitence, if it be sound,
Or hollowly put on.

JULIET: I'll gladly learn.

DUKE: Love you the man that wronged you?

JULIET: Yes, as I love the woman that wronged him.

DUKE: So then it seems your most offenseful act
Was mutually committed?

23 *hollowly* falsely.

JULIET: Mutually.

DUKE: Then was your sin of heavier kind than his.

JULIET: I do confess it, and repent it, father.

DUKE: 'Tis meet so, daughter: but lest you do repent   30
        As that the sin hath brought you to this shame,
        Which sorrow is always toward ourselves, not heaven,
        Showing we would not spare heaven as we love it,
        But as we stand in fear—

JULIET: I do repent me as it is an evil,
        And take the shame with joy.

DUKE: There rest.
        Your partner, as I hear, must die tomorrow,
        And I am going with instruction to him.
        Grace go with you, *Benedicite.*   [*Exit*]

JULIET: Must die tomorrow! O injurious love,   40
        That respites me a life whose very comfort
        Is still a dying horror.

PROVOST: 'Tis pity of him.   [*Exeunt*]

SCENE IV

Angelo's house.

[*Enter* ANGELO]

ANGELO: When I would pray and think, I think and pray
        To several subjects: heaven hath my empty words,
        Whilst my invention, hearing not my tongue,
        Anchors on Isabel: heaven in my mouth,
        As if I did but only chew his name,
        And in my heart the strong and swelling evil
        Of my conception. The state, whereon I studied,
        Is like a good thing, being often read,
        Grown sere and tedious; yea, my gravity,
        Wherein, let no man hear me, I take pride,   10
        Could I, with boot, change for an idle plume
        Which the air beats for vain. O place, O form,

---

    38 *instruction* religious counsel.   2 *several* separate.   3 *invention* imagination.   7
conception thought   *The state* i.e. statecraft.   11 *with boot* profitably.

How often dost thou with thy case, thy habit,
Wrench awe from fools, and tie the wiser souls
To thy false seeming! Blood, thou art blood;
Let's write 'good Angel' on the devil's horn,
'Tis not the devil's crest. How now, who's there?

[*Enter* SERVANT]

SERVANT: One Isabel, a sister, desires access to you.

ANGELO: Teach her the way. [*Exit* SERVANT] O heavens, 20
Why does my blood thus muster to my heart,
Making both it unable for itself,
And dispossessing all my other parts
Of necessary fitness?
So play the foolish throngs with one that swounds,
Come all to help him, and so stop the air
By which he should revive; and even so
The general, subject to a well-wished king,
Quit their own part, and in obsequious fondness
Crowd to his presence, where their untaught love
Must needs appear offense.

[*Enter* ISABELLA]

How now, fair maid! 30

ISABELLA: I am come to know your pleasure.

ANGELO: That you might know it, would much better please me
Than to demand what 'tis. Your brother cannot live.

ISABELLA: Even so: heaven keep your honor.

ANGELO: Yet may he live a while; and it may be
As long as you or I: yet he must die.

ISABELLA: Under your sentence?

ANGELO: Yea.

ISABELLA: When, I beseech you? that in his reprieve,
Longer or shorter, he may be so fitted 40
That his soul sicken not.

ANGELO: Ha! fie, these filthy vices! It were as good
To pardon him that hath from nature stol'n

16 *Angel* (Angelo is punning on his own name). 28 *part* places. 39 *reprieve*
delay of execution.

A man already made, as to remit
Their saucy sweetness that do coin heaven's image
In stamps that are forbid: 'tis all as easy
Falsely to take away a life true made,
As to put mettle in restrainèd means
To make a false one.

ISABELLA: 'Tis set down so in heaven, but not in earth.   50

ANGELO: Say you so? then I shall pose you quickly.
          Which had you rather, that the most just law
          Now took your brother's life, or to redeem him
          Give up your body to such sweet uncleanness
          As she that he hath stained?

ISABELLA: Sir, believe this,
          I had rather give my body than my soul.

ANGELO: I talk not of your soul: our compelled sins
          Stand more for number than for accompt.

ISABELLA: How say you?

ANGELO: Nay, I'll not warrant that; for I can speak
          Against the thing I say. Answer to this: 60
          I, now the voice of the recorded law,
          Pronounce a sentence on your brother's life;
          Might there not be a charity in sin
          To save this brother's life?

ISABELLA: Please you to do't,
          I'll take it as a peril to my soul;
          It is no sin at all, but charity.

ANGELO: Pleased you to do't, at peril of your soul,
          Were equal poise of sin and charity.

ISABELLA: That I do beg his life, if it be sin,
          Heaven let me bear it: you granting of my suit,   70
          If that be sin, I'll make it my morn prayer
          To have it added to the faults of mine
          And nothing of your answer.

ANGELO: Nay, but hear me;
          Your sense pursues not mine: either you are ignorant,
          Or seem so craftily; and that's not good.

44 *remit* pardon.   45 *saucy sweetness* wanton enjoyments.   48 *restrainèd* forbidden.
58 *Stand . . . accompt* are recorded but not added up against us.   68 *poise* balance.

ISABELLA: Let me be ignorant, and in nothing good
    But graciously to know I am no better.

ANGELO: Thus wisdom wishes to appear most bright
    When it doth tax itself, as these black masks
    Proclaim an enshield beauty ten times louder   80
    Than beauty could, displayed. But mark me;
    To be receivèd plain, I'll speak more gross:
    Your brother is to die.

ISABELLA: So.

ANGELO: And his offense is so, as it appears,
    Accountant to the law upon that pain.

ISABELLA: True.

ANGELO: Admit no other way to save his life—
    As I subscribe not that, nor any other,
    But in the loss of question—that you, his sister,   90
    Finding yourself desired of such a person
    Whose credit with the judge, or own great place,
    Could fetch your brother from the manacles
    Of the all-binding law; and that there were
    No earthly mean to save him, but that either
    You must lay down the treasures of your body
    To this supposed, or else to let him suffer,
    What would you do?

ISABELLA: As much for my poor brother as myself:
    That is, were I under the terms of death,   100
    Th'impression of keen whips I'ld wear as rubies,
    And strip myself to death as to a bed
    That longing have been sick for, ere I'ld yield
    My body up to shame.

ANGELO: Then must your brother die.

ISABELLA: And 'twere the cheaper way:
    Better it were a brother died at once
    Than that a sister, by redeeming him,
    Should die for ever.

ANGELO: Were not you then as cruel as the sentence
    That you have slandered so?   110

---

79 *tax* accuse.   80 *enshield* screened, hidden.   86 *Accountant* accountable   *pain* penalty.   89 *subscribe* assent to.   90 *But . . . question* except that discussion would flag.   97 *supposed* imaginary person.

ISABELLA: Ignomy in ransom and free pardon
            Are of two houses: lawful mercy
            Is nothing kin to foul redemption.

ANGELO: You seemed of late to make the law a tyrant,
          And rather proved the sliding of your brother
          A merriment than a vice.

ISABELLA: O pardon me, my lord; it oft falls out
            To have what we would have, we speak not what we mean.
            I something do excuse the thing I hate
            For his advantage that I dearly love.   120

ANGELO: We are all frail.

ISABELLA: Else let my brother die,
            If not a fedary, but only he
            Owe and succeed thy weakness.

ANGELO: Nay, women are frail too.

ISABELLA: Ay, as the glasses where they view themselves,
            Which are as easy broke as they make forms.
            Women, help heaven! Men their creation mar
            In profiting by them. Nay, call us ten times frail,
            For we are soft as our complexions are,
            And credulous to false prints.

ANGELO: I think it well: 130
          And from this testimony of your own sex—
          Since I suppose we are made to be no stronger
          Than faults may shake our frames—let me be bold.
          I do arrest your words. Be that you are,
          That is, a woman; if you be more, you're none.
          If you be one, as you are well expressed
          By all external warrants, show it now,
          By putting on the destined livery.

ISABELLA: I have no tongue but one. Gentle my lord,
            Let me entreat you speak the former language.   140

ANGELO: Plainly conceive, I love you.

---

112 *of two houses* i.e. completely different. 116 *merriment* light matter. 122 *fedary* accomplice. 122–23 (meaning uncertain; a line has probably dropped out). 126 *forms* images. 130 *credulous* susceptible. 134 *I . . . words* I take you at your word. 136 *expressed* shown to be. 138 *destined livery* behavior which properly belongs to you.

ISABELLA: My brother did love Juliet,
And you tell me that he shall die for't.

ANGELO: He shall not, Isabel, if you give me love.

ISABELLA: I know your virtue hath a license in't,
Which seems a little fouler than it is,
To pluck on others.

ANGELO: Believe me, on mine honor,
My words express my purpose.

ISABELLA: Ha! little honor to be much believed,
And most pernicious purpose. Seeming, seeming!   150
I will proclaim thee, Angelo, look for't!
Sign me a present pardon for my brother,
Or with an outstretched throat I'll tell the world aloud
What man thou art.

ANGELO: Who will believe thee, Isabel?
My unsoiled name, th' austereness of my life,
My vouch against you, and my place i'th'state,
Will so your accusation overweigh
That you shall stifle in your own report
And smell of calumny. I have begun,
And now I give my sensual race the rein.   160
Fit thy consent to my sharp appetite,
Lay by all nicety and prolixious blushes,
That banish what they sue for: redeem thy brother
By yielding up thy body to my will,
Or else he must not only die the death,
But thy unkindness shall his death draw out
To lingering sufferance. Answer me tomorrow,
Or, by the affection that now guides me most,
I'll prove a tyrant to him. As for you,
Say what you can, my false o'erweighs your true.   [*Exit*]   170

ISABELLA: To whom should I complain? Did I tell this,
Who would believe me? O perilous mouths,
That bear in them one and the selfsame tongue,
Either of condemnation or approof,
Bidding the law make curtsy to their will,

---

147 *pluck* lure. 156 *vouch* testimony. 162 *prolixious* long drawn out. 167 *sufferance* torture. 168 *affection* passion. 174 *approof* approval. 175 *make curtsy to* bow down before.

Hooking both right and wrong to th'appetite,
To follow as it draws. I'll to my brother.
Though he hath fall'n by prompture of the blood,
Yet hath he in him such a mind of honor
That, had he twenty heads to tender down   180
On twenty bloody blocks, he'ld yield them up,
Before his sister should her body stoop
To such abhorred pollution.
Then, Isabel, live chaste, and, brother, die:
More than our brother is our chastity.
I'll tell him yet of Angelo's request,
And fit his mind to death, for his soul's rest.   [*Exit*]

ACT III. SCENE I

The prison.

[*Enter* DUKE *as a friar,* CLAUDIO, *and* PROVOST]

DUKE: So then you hope of pardon from Lord Angelo?

CLAUDIO: The miserable have no other medicine
          But only hope:
          I have hope to live, and am prepared to die.

DUKE: Be absolute for death: either death or life
          Shall thereby be the sweeter. Reason thus with life:
          If I do lose thee, I do lose a thing
          That none but fools would keep; a breath thou art,
          Servile to all the skyey influences
          That dost this habitation where thou keep'st   10
          Hourly afflict; merely, thou art death's fool,
          For him thou labor'st by thy flight to shun,
          And yet run'st toward him still. Thou art not noble,
          For all th'accommodations that thou bear'st
          Are nursed by baseness. Thou'rt by no means valiant,
          For thou dost fear the soft and tender fork
          Of a poor worm; thy best of rest is sleep,
          And that thou oft provok'st, yet grossly fear'st
          Thy death, which is no more. Thou art not thyself,
          For thou exists on many a thousand grains   20
          That issue out of dust. Happy thou art not,
          For what thou hast not, still thou striv'st to get,

---

177 *as* in whatever direction.   9 *skyey influences* influences of the stars.   10 *keep'st*
livest.   14 *accommodations* comforts.

And what thou hast, forget'st. Thou art not certain,
For thy complexion shifts to strange effects,
After the moon. If thou art rich, thou'rt poor,
For, like an ass whose back with ingots bows,
Thou bear'st thy heavy riches but a journey,
And death unloads thee. Friend hast thou none,
For thine own bowels, which do call thee sire,
The mere effusion of thy proper loins,   30
Do curse the gout, serpigo, and the rheum
For ending thee no sooner. Thou hast nor youth nor age,
But as it were an after-dinner's sleep,
Dreaming on both, for all thy blessed youth
Becomes as agèd, and doth beg the alms
Of palsied eld: and when thou art old and rich,
Thou hast neither heat, affection, limb, nor beauty,
To make thy riches pleasant. What's yet in this
That bears the name of life? Yet in this life
Lie hid moe thousand deaths; yet death we fear,   40
That makes these odds all even.

CLAUDIO: I humbly thank you.
To sue to live, I find I seek to die,
And, seeking death, find life: let it come on.

[*Enter* ISABELLA]

ISABELLA: What, ho! Peace here; grace and good company.

PROVOST: Who's there? Come in, the wish deserves a welcome.

DUKE: Dear sir, ere long I'll visit you again.

CLAUDIO: Most holy sir, I thank you.

ISABELLA: My business is a word or two with Claudio.

PROVOST: And very welcome. Look, signior, here's your sister.

DUKE: Provost, a word with you.   50

PROVOST: As many as you please.

DUKE: Bring me to hear them speak, where I may be concealed.

    [DUKE *and* PROVOST *withdraw*]

CLAUDIO: Now, sister, what's the comfort?

---

   23 *certain* constant. 24–25 *thy . . . moon* i.e., your nature is changeable in its desires. 29 *bowels* offspring. 30 *mere* very *proper* own. 31 *serpigo* skin eruption *rheum* catarrh. 36 *eld* old age. 37 *heat, affection, limb* warmth of blood, strength of feeling, vigor of limb.

ISABELLA: Why,
          As all comforts are: most good, most good indeed.
          Lord Angelo, having affairs to heaven,
          Intends you for his swift ambassador,
          Where you shall be an everlasting leiger;
          Therefore your best appointment make with speed;
          Tomorrow you set on.

CLAUDIO: Is there no remedy?   60

ISABELLA: None but such remedy as, to save a head,
          To cleave a heart in twain.

CLAUDIO: But is there any?

ISABELLA: Yes, brother, you may live;
          There is a devilish mercy in the judge,
          If you'll implore it, that will free your life,
          But fetter you till death.

CLAUDIO: Perpetual durance?

ISABELLA: Ay, just—perpetual durance, a restraint,
          Though all the world's vastidity you had,
          To a determined scope.

CLAUDIO: But in what nature?

ISABELLA: In such a one as, you consenting to't,   70
          Would bark your honor from that trunk you bear,
          And leave you naked.

CLAUDIO: Let me know the point.

ISABELLA: O, I do fear thee, Claudio, and I quake,
          Lest thou a feverous life shouldst entertain,
          And six or seven winters more respect
          Than a perpetual honor. Dar'st thou die?
          The sense of death is most in apprehension,
          And the poor beetle that we tread upon
          In corporal sufferance finds a pang as great
          As when a giant dies.

CLAUDIO: Why give you me this shame?   80
          Think you I can a resolution fetch

58 *leiger* resident ambassador. 59 *appointment* preparation. 66 *durance* imprisonment. 68–69 *Though . . . scope* though you had the whole extent of the world set out to move about in. 77 *sense* feeling.

From flow'ry tenderness? If I must die,
I will encounter darkness as a bride,
And hug it in mine arms.

ISABELLA: There spake my brother: there my father's grave
Did utter forth a voice. Yes, thou must die:
Thou art too noble to conserve a life
In base appliances. This outward-sainted deputy,
Whose settled visage and deliberate word
Nips youth i'th'head, and follies doth enew   90
As falcon doth the fowl, is yet a devil:
His filth within being cast, he would appear
A pond as deep as hell.

CLAUDIO: The prenzie Angelo!

ISABELLA: O, 'tis the cunning livery of hell,
The damned'st body to invest and cover
In prenzie guards; dost thou think, Claudio,
If I would yield him my virginity,
Thou mightst be freed!

CLAUDIO: O heavens, it cannot be.

ISABELLA: Yes, he would give't thee, from this rank offense,
So to offend him still. This night's the time   100
That I should do what I abhor to name,
Or else thou diest tomorrow.

CLAUDIO: Thou shalt not do't.

ISABELLA: O, were it but my life,
I'd throw it down for your deliverance
As frankly as a pin.

CLAUDIO: Thanks, dear Isabel.

ISABELLA: Be ready, Claudio, for your death tomorrow.

CLAUDIO: Yes. Has he affections in him,
That thus can make him bite the law by th'nose,
When he would force it? Sure it is no sin,
Or of the deadly seven it is the least.   110

ISABELLA: Which is the least?

88 *appliances* remedies, means.   90 *Nips . . . head* checks youth from above   *enew*
drive down into water.   92 *cast* vomited up.   93, 96 *prenzie* (word of uncertain meaning).   96 *guards* trimmings.   107 *affections* feelings, desires.   108–09 *bite . . . force
it* assail the law when he would enforce it.

CLAUDIO: If it were damnable, he being so wise,
                    Why would he for the momentary trick
                    Be perdurably fined? O Isabel!

ISABELLA: What says my brother?

CLAUDIO: Death is a fearful thing.

ISABELLA: And shamèd life a hateful.

CLAUDIO: Ay, but to die, and go we know not where,
                    To lie in cold obstruction and to rot,
                    This sensible warm motion to become
                    A kneaded clod; and the delighted spirit   1 20
                    To bathe in fiery floods, or to reside
                    In thrilling region of thick-ribbèd ice,
                    To be imprisoned in the viewless winds
                    And blown with restless violence round about
                    The pendent world; or to be worse than worst
                    Of those that lawless and incertain thought
                    Imagine howling, 'tis too horrible.
                    The weariest and most loathèd worldly life
                    That age, ache, penury, and imprisonment
                    Can lay on nature is a paradise   1 30
                    To what we fear of death.

ISABELLA: Alas, alas.

CLAUDIO: Sweet sister, let me live.
                    What sin you do to save a brother's life,
                    Nature dispenses with the deed so far
                    That it becomes a virtue.

ISABELLA: O you beast,
                    O faithless coward, O dishonest wretch!
                    Wilt thou be made a man out of my vice?
                    Is't not a kind of incest, to take life
                    From thine own sister's shame? What should I think?
                    Heaven shield my mother played my father fair,   140
                    For such a warpèd slip of wilderness
                    Ne'er issued from his blood. Take my defiance,
                    Die, perish. Might but my bending down
                    Reprieve thee from thy fate, it should proceed.

---

213 *trick* trifle.   114 *perdurably fined* eternally damned.   118 *obstruction* stagnation.   119 *sensible* sentient   *motion* organism.   120 *delighted* capable of delight.   134
dispenses with grants a dispensation, or permit, for.   141 *wilderness* wildness.

I'll pray a thousand prayers for thy death,
No word to save thee.

CLAUDIO: Nay, hear me, Isabel.

ISABELLA: O, fie, fie, fie!
Thy sin's not accidental, but a trade;
Mercy to thee would prove itself a bawd,
'Tis best that thou diest quickly.   [*Going*]

CLAUDIO: O hear me, Isabella.   150

[DUKE *comes forward*]

DUKE: Vouchsafe a word, young sister, but one word.

ISABELLA: What is your will?

DUKE: Might you dispense with your leisure, I would by and by have some speech with you: the satisfaction I would require is likewise your own benefit.

ISABELLA: I have no superfluous leisure; my stay must be stolen out of other affairs, but I will attend you a while.

DUKE: [*Aside to* CLAUDIO] Son, I have overheard what hath passed between you and your sister. Angelo had never the purpose to corrupt her; only he hath made an assay of her virtue to practice his   160 judgment with the disposition of natures. She, having the truth of honor in her, hath made him that gracious denial which he is most glad to receive. I am confessor to Angelo, and I know this to be true; therefore prepare yourself to death. Do not satisfy your resolution with hopes that are fallible: tomorrow you must die; go to your knees and make ready.

CLAUDIO: Let me ask my sister pardon. I am so out of love with life that I will sue to be rid of it.

DUKE: Hold you there: farewell.   [*Exit* CLAUDIO]

[*Enter* PROVOST]

Provost, a word with you.   170

PROVOST: What's your will, father?

DUKE: That now you are come, you will be gone. Leave me a while with the maid; my mind promises with my habit no loss shall touch her by my company.

---

157 *attend* wait for. 160 *assay* trial. 160–61 *practice . . . natures* test his judgment of character. 173 *with my habit* i.e. as well as my priestly robes.

PROVOST: In good time.   [*Exit*]

DUKE: The hand that hath made you fair hath made you good. The
goodness that is cheap in beauty makes beauty brief in goodness:
but grace, being the soul of your complexion, shall keep the body
of it ever fair. The assault that Angelo hath made to you, fortune
hath conveyed to my understanding; and, but that frailty hath   180
examples for his falling, I should wonder at Angelo. How will you
do to content this substitute, and to save your brother?

ISABELLA: I am now going to resolve him. I had rather my brother die
by the law than my son should be unlawfully born. But O, how
much is the good Duke deceived in Angelo! If ever he return and
I can speak to him, I will open my lips in vain, or discover his government.

DUKE: That shall not be much amiss: yet, as the matter now stands,
he will avoid your accusation; he made trial of you only. Therefore fasten your ear on my advisings: to the love I have in doing 190
good a remedy presents itself. I do make myself believe that you
may most uprighteously do a poor wronged lady a merited benefit, redeem your brother from the angry law, do no stain to your
own gracious person, and much please the absent Duke, if peradventure he shall ever return to have hearing of this business.

ISABELLA: Let me hear you speak farther; I have spirit to do anything
that appears not foul in the truth of my spirit.

DUKE: Virtue is bold, and goodness never fearful. Have you not heard
speak of Mariana, the sister of Frederick, the great soldier who
miscarried at sea?   200

ISABELLA: I have heard of the lady, and good words went with her
name.

DUKE: She should this Angelo have married, was affianced by her oath,
and the nuptial appointed: between which time of the contract
and limit of the solemnity, her brother Frederick was wracked at
sea, having in that perished vessel the dowry of his sister. But
mark how heavily this befell to the poor gentlewoman: there she
lost a noble and renowned brother, in his love toward her ever most
kind and natural; with him the portion and sinew of her fortune,
her marriage dowry; with both, her combinate husband, this well- 210
seeming Angelo.

178 *complexion* character.   183 *resolve* answer.   186–87 *discover his government*
expose his conduct.   205 *limit of the solemnity* date set for the marriage ceremony.
210 *combinate* affianced.

ISABELLA: Can this be so? Did Angelo so leave her?

DUKE: Left her in her tears, and dried not one of them with his comfort; swallowed his vows whole, pretending in her discoveries of dishonor; in few, bestowed her on her own lamentation, which she yet wears for his sake; and he, a marble to her tears, is washed with them, but relents not.

ISABELLA: What a merit were it in death to take this poor maid from the world! What corruption in this life, that it will let this man live! But how out of this can she avail? 220

DUKE: It is a rupture that you may easily heal; and the cure of it not only saves your brother, but keeps you from dishonor in doing it.

ISABELLA: Show me how, good father.

DUKE: This forenamed maid hath yet in her the continuance of her first affection; his unjust unkindness, that in all reason should have quenched her love, hath, like an impediment in the current, made it more violent and unruly. Go you to Angelo, answer his requiring with a plausible obedience, agree with his demands to the point. Only refer yourself to this advantage: first, that your stay with him may not be long, that the time may have all shadow and silence 230 in it, and the place answer to convenience. This being granted in course—and now follows all—we shall advise this wronged maid to stead up your appointment, go in your place. If the encounter acknowledge itself hereafter, it may compel him to her recompense; and here, by this is your brother saved, your honor untainted, the poor Mariana advantaged, and the corrupt deputy scaled. The maid will I frame and make fit for his attempt. If you think well to carry this, as you may, the doubleness of the benefit defends the deceit from reproof. What think you of it?

ISABELLA: The image of it gives me content already, and I trust it will 240 grow to a most prosperous perfection.

DUKE: It lies much in your holding up. Haste you speedily to Angelo; if for this night he entreat you to his bed, give him promise of satisfaction. I will presently to St. Luke's; there at the moated grange resides this dejected Mariana. At that place call upon me, and dispatch with Angelo, that it may be quickly.

ISABELLA: I thank you for this comfort; fare you well, good father.

[*Exit*]

220 *avail* benefit. 233 *stead up your appointment* keep your appointment for you. 237 *scaled* weighed *frame* prepare. 242 *It . . . up* it depends much on your support. 244 *presently* at once.

SCENE II

The street before the prison.

[*Enter* ELBOW, CLOWN (POMPEY), *and* OFFICERS]

ELBOW: Nay, if there be no remedy for it but that you will needs buy
and sell men and women like beasts, we shall have all the world
drink brown and white bastard.

DUKE: O heavens, what stuff is here?

POMPEY: 'Twas never merry world since, of two usuries, the merriest
was put down, and the worser allowed by order of law a furred
gown to keep him warm; and furred with fox and lamb skins too,
to signify that craft, being richer than innocency, stands for the
facing.

ELBOW: Come your way, sir. Bless you, good father friar.   10

DUKE: And you, good brother father. What offense hath this man made
you, sir?

ELBOW: Marry, sir, he hath offended the law; and, sir, we take him to
be a thief too, sir, for we have found upon him, sir, a strange pick-
lock, which we have sent to the deputy.

DUKE: Fie, sirrah, a bawd, a wicked bawd!
The evil that thou causest to be done,
That is thy means to live. Do thou but think
What 'tis to cram a maw or clothe a back
From such a filthy vice; say to thyself,   20
From their abominable and beastly touches
I drink, I eat, array myself, and live.
Canst thou believe thy living is a life,
So stinkingly depending? Go mend, go mend.

POMPEY: Indeed, it does stink in some sort, sir; but yet, sir, I would
prove—

DUKE: Nay, if the devil have given thee proofs for sin,
Thou wilt prove his. Take him to prison, officer.
Correction and instruction must both work
Ere this rude beast will profit.   30

3 *bastard* (pun) a sweet Spanish wine. 8–9 *stands for the facing* supports the
trimming.

ELBOW: He must before the deputy, sir; he has given him warning. The deputy cannot abide a whoremaster; if he be a whoremonger, and comes before him, he were as good go a mile on his errand.

DUKE: That we were all, as some would seem to be,
Free from our faults, as faults from seeming free.

[*Enter* LUCIO]

ELBOW: His neck will come to your waist—a cord, sir.

POMPEY: I spy comfort, I cry bail. Here's a gentleman and a friend of mine.

LUCIO: How now, noble Pompey? What, at the wheels of Caesar? Art thou led in triumph? What, is there none of Pygmalion's images 40 newly made woman to be had now, for putting the hand in the pocket and extracting it clutched? What reply? ha? What say'st thou to this tune, matter and method? Is't not drowned i'th'last rain, ha? What say'st thou, trot? Is the world as it was, man? Which is the way? Is it sad, and few words, or how? The trick of it?

DUKE: Still thus, and thus, still worse.

LUCIO: How doth my dear morsel, thy mistress? Procures she still, ha?

POMPEY: Troth, sir, she hath eaten up all her beef, and she is herself in the tub.

LUCIO: Why, 'tis good. It is the right of it; it must be so. Ever your 50 fresh whore and your powdered bawd; an unshunned consequence, it must be so. Art going to prison, Pompey?

POMPEY: Yes, faith, sir.

LUCIO: Why, 'tis not amiss, Pompey; farewell. Go, say I sent thee thither. For debt, Pompey? or how?

ELBOW: For being a bawd, for being a bawd.

LUCIO: Well, then, imprison him. If imprisonment be the due of a bawd, why, 'tis his right. Bawd is he doubtless, and of antiquity too; bawd-born. Farewell, good Pompey; commend me to the prison, Pompey. You will turn good husband now, Pompey, you 60 will keep the house.

33 *he . . . errand* i.e. he has a hard road ahead. 36 *cord* (worn with the friar's habit). 40 *Pygmalion's images* i.e. prostitutes (in classical myth Pygmalion's work of sculpture came to life in response to his passion for it). 49 *in the tub* taking the cure for veneral disease. 51 *powdered* pickled. 60 *husband* manager *keep the house* stay indoors (pun).

POMPEY: I hope, sir, your good worship will be my bail.

LUCIO: No, indeed will I not, Pompey; it is not the wear. I will pray, Pompey, to increase your bondage: if you take it not patiently, why, your mettle is the more. Adieu, trusty Pompey. 'Bless you, friar.

DUKE: And you.

LUCIO: Does Bridget paint still, Pompey, ha?

ELBOW: Come your ways, sir, come.

POMPEY: You will not bail me then, sir?   70

LUCIO: Then, Pompey, nor now. What news abroad, friar, what news?

ELBOW: Come your ways, sir, come.

LUCIO: Go to kennel, Pompey, go. [*Exeunt* ELBOW, POMPEY, *and* OFFICERS]

What news, friar, of the Duke?

DUKE: I know none. Can you tell me of any?

LUCIO: Some say he is with the emperor of Russia; other some, he is in Rome. But where is he, think you?

DUKE: I know not where; but wheresoever, I wish him well.

LUCIO: It was a mad fantastical trick of him to steal from the state, and usurp the beggary he was never born to. Lord Angelo dukes it well   80 in his absence; he puts transgression to't.

DUKE: He does well in't.

LUCIO: A little more lenity to lechery would do no harm in him. Something too crabbed that way, friar.

DUKE: It is too general a vice, and severity must cure it.

LUCIO: Yes, in good sooth, the vice is of a great kindred; it is well allied, but it is impossible to extirp it quite, friar, till eating and drinking be put down. They say this Angelo was not made by man and woman after this downright way of creation. Is it true, think you?

DUKE: How should he be made then?   90

LUCIO: Some report a sea-maid spawned him; some that he was begot between two stock-fishes. But it is certain that when he makes

63 *wear* fashion.   65 *mettle* impatience (with pun on the metal of shackles).   87 *extirp* eradicate.   92 *stock-fishes* dried cod.

water his urine is congealed ice, that I know to be true. And he is a motion generative, that's infallible.

DUKE: You are pleasant, sir, and speak apace.

LUCIO: Why, what a ruthless thing is this in him, for the rebellion of a cod-piece to take away the life of a man! Would the Duke that is absent have done this? Ere he would have hanged a man for the getting a hundred bastards, he would have paid for the nursing a thousand. He had some feeling of the sport, he knew the service, 100 and that instructed him to mercy.

DUKE: I never heard the absent Duke much detected for women; he was not inclined that way.

LUCIO: O, sir, you are deceived.

DUKE: 'Tis not possible.

LUCIO: Who? Not the Duke? Yes, your beggar of fifty, and his use was to put a ducat in her clack-dish; the Duke had crotchets in him. He would be drunk, too; that let me inform you.

DUKE: You do him wrong, surely.

LUCIO: Sir, I was an inward of his. A shy fellow was the Duke, and I 110 believe I know the cause of his withdrawing.

DUKE: What, I prithee, might be the cause?

LUCIO: No, pardon. 'Tis a secret must be locked within the teeth and the lips. But this I can let you understand, the greater file of the subject held the Duke to be wise.

DUKE: Wise? Why, no question but he was.

LUCIO: A very superficial, ignorant, unweighing fellow.

DUKE: Either this is envy in you, folly, or mistaking. The very stream of his life and the business he hath helmed must, upon a warranted need, give him a better proclamation. Let him be but testimonied 120 in his own bringings-forth, and he shall appear to the envious a scholar, a statesman, and a soldier. Therefore you speak unskillfully; or, if your knowledge be more, it is much darkened in your malice.

---

94 *motion generative* masculine puppet.   102 *detected* open to accusation.   107 *clack-dish* wooden dish.   *crotchets* whims.   110 *inward* intimate.   114–15 *file of the subject* rank and file.   119 *helmed* steered.   119–20 *must . . . proclamation* must, if he should really need it, proclaim that he is better than you allege.   120–21 *testimonied . . . bringings-forth* tested by his own actions.

LUCIO: Sir, I know him, and I love him.

DUKE: Love talks with better knowledge, and knowledge with dearer love.

LUCIO: Come, sir, I know what I know.

DUKE: I can hardly believe that, since you know not what you speak. But if ever the Duke return, as our prayers are he may, let me de-   130 sire you to make your answer before him. If it be honest you have spoke, you have courage to maintain it. I am bound to call upon you; and, I pray you, your name?

LUCIO: Sir, my name is Lucio, well known to the Duke.

DUKE: He shall know you better, sir, if I may live to report you.

LUCIO: I fear you not.

DUKE: O, you hope the Duke will return no more, or you imagine me too unhurtful an opposite, but indeed I can do you little harm; you'll forswear this again.

LUCIO: I'll be hanged first; thou art deceived in me, friar. But no more   140 of this; canst thou tell if Claudio die tomorrow or no?

DUKE: Why should he die, sir?

LUCIO: Why? For filling a bottle with a tun-dish. I would the Duke we talk of were returned again; this ungenitured agent will unpeople the province with continency. Sparrows must not build in his house-eaves because they are lecherous. The Duke yet would have dark deeds darkly answered; he would never bring them to light; would he were returned. Marry, this Claudio is condemned for untrussing. Farewell, good friar; I prethee, pray for me. The Duke, I say to thee again, would eat mutton on Fridays. He's not past it yet, and I say   150 to thee, he would mouth with a beggar, though she smelt brown bread and garlic. Say that I said so; farewell.   [*Exit*]

DUKE: No might nor greatness in mortality
Can censure 'scape; back-wounding calumny
The whitest virtue strikes. What king so strong
Can tie the gall up in the slanderous tongue?
But who comes here?

138 *opposite* opponent.   143 *tun-dish* funnel.   144 *ungenitured* sexless.   148 *untrussing* undressing.   150 *mutton* harlot (pun).

[*Enter* ESCALUS, PROVOST, *and* OFFICERS *with* BAWD (MISTRESS OVER-
DONE)]

ESCALUS: Go, away with her to prison.

MISTRESS OVERDONE: Good my lord, be good to me. Your honor is accounted a merciful man, good my lord.   160

ESCALUS: Double and tremble admonition, and still forfeit in the same
kind! This would make mercy swear, and play the tyrant.

PROVOST: A bawd of eleven years' continuance, may it please your
honor.

MISTRESS OVERDONE: My lord, this is one Lucio's information against
me. Mistress Kate Keepdown was with child by him in the Duke's
time; he promised her marriage. His child is a year and a quarter
old, come Philip and Jacob; I have kept it myself, and see how he
goes about to abuse me.

ESCALUS: That fellow is a fellow of much license; let him be called   170
before us. Away with her to prison; go to, no more words. [*Exeunt*
OFFICERS *with* MISTRESS OVERDONE] Provost, my brother Angelo
will not be altered; Claudio must die tomorrow. Let him be furnished with divines, and have all charitable preparation. If my
brother wrought by my pity, it should not be so with him.

PROVOST: So please you, this friar hath been with him, and advised him
for th' entertainment of death.

ESCALUS: Good even, good father.

DUKE: Bliss and goodness on you!

ESCALUS: Of whence are you?   180

DUKE: Not of this country, though my chance is now
To use it for my time. I am a brother
Of gracious order, late come from the See,
In special business from his Holiness.

ESCALUS: What news abroad i'th'world?

DUKE: None, but that there is so great a fever on goodness that the dissolution of it must cure it. Novelty is only in request, and it is as
dangerous to be aged in any kind of course as it is virtuous to be
constant in any undertaking. There is scarce truth enough alive to

168 *Philip and Jacob* May 1st.   187–89 *it is . . . undertaking* to be constant is as
dangerous as it is virtuous.

make societies secure, but security enough to make fellowships ac-   190
cursed. Much upon this riddle runs the wisdom of the world. This
news is old enough, yet it is every day's news. I pray you, sir, of
what disposition was the Duke?

ESCALUS: One that, above all other strifes, contended especially to know
himself.

DUKE: What pleasure was he given to?

ESCALUS: Rather rejoicing to see another merry, than merry at anything
which professed to make him rejoice: a gentleman of all temperance. But leave we him to his events, with a prayer they may prove
prosperous, and let me desire to know how you find Claudio pre-   200
pared. I am made to understand that you have lent him visitation.

DUKE: He professes to have received no sinister measure from his judge,
but most willingly humbles himself to the determination of justice;
yet had he framed to himself, by the instruction of his frailty, many
deceiving promises of life, which I, by my good leisure, have discredited to him, and now is he resolved to die.

ESCALUS: You have paid the heavens your function, and the prisoner
the very debt of your calling. I have labored for the poor gentleman to the extremest shore of my modesty, but my brother-justice
have I found so severe that he hath forced me to tell him he is   210
indeed Justice.

DUKE: If his own life answer the straitness of his proceeding, it shall
become him well; wherein if he chance to fail, he hath sentenced
himself.

ESCALUS: I am going to visit the prisoner. Fare you well.

DUKE: Peace be with you!   [*Exeunt* ESCALUS *and* PROVOST]
He who the sword of heaven will bear
Should be as holy as severe;
Pattern in himself to know,
Grace to stand, and virtue go;   220
More nor less to others paying
Than by self-offenses weighing.
Shame to him whose cruel striking
Kills for faults of his own liking.
Twice treble shame on Angelo,

190–91 *security . . . accursed* i.e. endorsing bonds has become the curse of friendship.   209 *extremist . . . modesty* furthest limits of propriety.   212 *straitness* strictness.

To weed my vice and let his grow.
O, what may man within him hide,
Though angel on the outward side!
How may likeness made in crimes,
Making practice on the times, 230
To draw with idle spider's strings
Most ponderous and substantial things?
Craft against vice I must apply;
With Angelo tonight shall lie
His old betrothèd, but despisèd:
So disguise shall by th'disguisèd
Pay with falsehood, false exacting,
And perform an old contracting.   [*Exit*]

ACT IV. SCENE I

The moated grange.

[*Enter* MARIANA, *and* BOY *singing*]

SONG: Take, O take those lips away,
      That so sweetly were forsworn;
And those eyes, the break of day,
      Lights that do mislead the morn;
But my kisses bring again, bring again,
Seals of love, but sealed in vain, sealed in vain.

[*Enter* DUKE *disguised as before*]

MARIANA: Break off thy song, and haste thee quick away.
Here comes a man of comfort, whose advice
Hath often stilled my brawling discontent.   [*Exit* BOY]
I cry you mercy, sir, and well could wish 10
You had not found me here so musical.
Let me excuse me, and believe me so,
My mirth it much displeased, but pleased my woe.

DUKE: 'Tis good; though music oft hath such a charm
To make bad good, and good provoke to harm.
I pray you tell me, hath anybody inquired for me here today? Much
upon this time have I promised here to meet.

MARIANA: You have not been inquired after; I have sat here all day.

[*Enter* ISABELLA]

DUKE: I do constantly believe you; the time is come even now. I shall
    crave your forbearance a little; may be I will call upon you anon,   20
    for some advantage to yourself.

MARIANA: I am always bound to you. [*Exit*]

DUKE: Very well met, and welcome.
    What is the news from this good deputy?

ISABELLA: He hath a garden circummured with brick,
    Whose western side is with a vineyard backed;
    And to that vineyard is a planchèd gate,
    That makes his opening with this bigger key.
    This other doth command a little door
    Which from the vineyard to the garden leads.   30
    There have I made my promise,
    Upon the heavy middle of the night,
    To call upon him.

DUKE: But shall you on your knowledge find this way?

ISABELLA: I have ta'en a due and wary note upon't.
    With whispering and most guilty diligence,
    In action all of precept, he did show me
    The way twice o'er.

DUKE: Are there no other tokens
    Between you 'greed concerning her observance?

ISABELLA: No, none, but only a repair i'th'dark,   40
    And that I have possessed him my most stay
    Can be but brief; for I have made him know
    I have a servant comes with me along,
    That stays upon me, whose persuasion is
    I come about my brother.

DUKE: 'Tis well borne up.
    I have not yet made known to Mariana
    A word of this. What ho, within; come forth.

[*Enter* MARIANA]

    I pray you, be acquainted with this maid;
    She comes to do you good.

25 *circummured* walled about.   27 *planchèd* boarded.   28 *makes his opening* may
be opened.   37 *In . . . precept* teaching by demonstration.   39 *observance* prescribed
conduct.   41 *possessed* informed.   44 *stays upon* waits for.

ISABELLA: I do desire the like.

DUKE: Do you persuade yourself that I respect you? 50

MARIANA: Good friar, I know you do, and have found it.

DUKE: Take then this your companion by the hand,
　　Who hath a story ready for your ear.
　　I shall attend your leisure, but make haste;
　　The vaporous night approaches.

MARIANA: Will't please you walk aside? [*Exeunt* MARIANA *and* ISABELLA]

DUKE: O place and greatness, millions of false eyes
　　Are stuck upon thee; volumes of report
　　Run with these false and most contrarious quests
　　Upon thy doings; thousand escapes of wit 60
　　Make thee the father of their idle dream,
　　And rack thee in their fancies.

[*Enter* MARIANA *and* ISABELLA]

　　　　　　　　　　Welcome, how agreed?

ISABELLA: She'll take the enterprise upon her, father,
　　If you advise it.

DUKE: 　　　　　It is not my consent,
　　But my entreaty too.

ISABELLA: 　　　　　Little have you to say
　　When you depart from him but, soft and low,
　　'Remember now my brother.'

MARIANA: 　　　　　Fear me not.

DUKE: Nor, gentle daughter, fear you not at all;
　　He is your husband on a pre-contract;
　　To bring you thus together, 'tis no sin, 70
　　Sith that the justice of your title to him
　　Doth flourish the deceit. Come, let us go;
　　Our corn's to reap, for yet our tilth's to sow. [*Exeunt*]

---

60 *escapes* sallies. 62 *rack thee* twist thee about. 69 *pre-contract* legally binding proposal. 73 *tilth* fallow field.

SCENE II

The prison.

[*Enter* PROVOST *and* CLOWN (POMPEY)]

PROVOST: Come hither, sirrah; can you cut off a man's head?

POMPEY: If the man be a bachelor, sir, I can; but if he be a married
man, he's his wife's head, and I can never cut off a woman's head.

PROVOST: Come, sir, leave me your snatches, and yield me a direct answer. Tomorrow morning are to die Claudio and Barnardine. Here
is in our prison a common executioner, who in his office lacks a
helper; if you will take it on you to assist him, it shall redeem you
from your gyves; if not, you shall have your full time of imprisonment, and your deliverance with an unpitied whipping, for you
have been a notorious bawd.   10

POMPEY: Sir, I have been an unlawful bawd time out of mind, but yet
I will be content to be a lawful hangman. I would be glad to receive some instruction from my fellow partner.

PROVOST: What ho, Abhorson; where's Abhorson there?

[*Enter* ABHORSON]

ABHORSON: Do you call, sir?

PROVOST: Sirrah, here's a fellow will help you tomorrow in your execution. If you think it meet, compound with him by the year, and let
him abide here with you; if not, use him for the present and dismiss him. He cannot plead his estimation with you; he hath been
a bawd.   20

ABHORSON: A bawd, sir? Fie upon him, he will discredit our mystery.

PROVOST: Go to, sir, you weigh equally; a feather will turn the scale.
[*Exit*]

POMPEY: Pray, sir, by your good favor—for surely, sir, a good favor you
have, but that you have a hanging look—do you call, sir, your occupation a mystery?

ABHORSON: Ay, sir, a mystery.

---

4 *snatches* quips.   8 *gyves* fetters.   17 *compound* make an agreement.   19 *estimation* reputation.   21 *mystery* profession.   23 *favor* face (pun).

POMPEY: Painting, sir, I have heard say, is a mystery, and your whores, sir, being members of my occupation, using painting, do prove my occupation a mystery; but what mystery there should be in hanging, if I should be hanged, I cannot imagine. 30

ABHORSON: Sir, it is a mystery.

POMPEY: Proof?

ABHORSON: Every true man's apparel fits your thief. If it be too little for your thief, your true man thinks it big enough. If it be too big for your thief, your thief thinks it little enough; so every true man's apparel fits your thief.

[*Enter* PROVOST]

PROVOST: Are you agreed?

POMPEY: Sir, I will serve him, for I do find that your hangman is a more penitent trade than your bawd; he doth oftener ask forgiveness. 40

PROVOST: You, sirrah, provide your block and your axe tomorrow four o'clock.

ABHORSON: Come on, bawd. I will instruct thee in my trade; follow.

POMPEY: I do desire to learn, sir; and I hope, if you have occasion to use me for your own turn, you shall find me yare. For truly, sir, for your kindness I owe you a good turn.

PROVOST: Call hither Barnardine and Claudio. [*Exeunt* POMPEY *and* ABHORSON]
Th'one has my pity, not a jot the other,
Being a murderer, though he were my brother.

[*Enter* CLAUDIO]

Look, here's the warrant, Claudio, for thy death. 50
'Tis now dead midnight, and by eight tomorrow
Thou must be made immortal. Where's Barnardine?

CLAUDIO: As fast locked up in sleep as guiltless labor
When it lies starkly in the traveller's bones;
He will not wake.

---

33 *true* honest. 39–40 *ask forgiveness* (the executioner always asked forgiveness of the condemned man). 45 *turn* execution (pun). *yare* ready. 54 *starkly* stiffly.

PROVOST: Who can do good on him?
Well, go, prepare yourself. [*Knocking within*] But hark, what noise?
Heaven give your spirits comfort. [*Exit* CLAUDIO] By and by.
I hope it is some pardon or reprieve
For the most gentle Claudio.

[*Enter* DUKE *disguised as before*]

                                   Welcome, father.

DUKE: The best and wholesom'st spirits of the night   60
Envelop you, good provost. Who called here of late?

PROVOST: None since the curfew rung.

DUKE: Not Isabel?

PROVOST: No.

DUKE: They will then, ere't be long.

PROVOST: What comfort is for Claudio?

DUKE: There's some in hope.

PROVOST: It is a bitter deputy.

DUKE: Not so, not so; his life is paralleled
Even with the stroke and line of his great justice.
He doth with holy abstinence subdue
That in himself which he spurs on his power
To qualify in others. Were he mealed with that   70
Which he corrects, then were he tyrannous,
But this being so, he's just. [*Knocking within*] Now are they come.

    [*Exit* PROVOST]

This is a gentle provost; seldom when
The steelèd gaoler is the friend of men. [*Knocking*]
How now, what noise? That spirit's possessed with haste
That wounds th'unsisting postern with these strokes.

[*Enter* PROVOST]

PROVOST: There he must stay until the officer
Arise to let him in; he is called up.

DUKE: Have you no countermand for Claudio yet,
But he must die tomorrow?

    70 *qualify* mitigate   *mealed* stained.   76 *unsisting* unassisting   *postern* small door.

PROVOST: None, sir, none.   80

DUKE: As near the dawning, provost, as it is,
    You shall hear more ere morning.

PROVOST: Happily
    You something know, yet I believe there comes
    No countermand; no such example have we.
    Besides, upon the very siege of justice,
    Lord Angelo hath to the public ear
    Professed the contrary.

[*Enter a* MESSENGER]

DUKE: This is his lordship's man.

PROVOST: And here comes Claudio's pardon.

MESSENGER: My lord hath sent you this note, and by me this further   90
    charge: that you swerve not from the smallest article of it, neither
    in time, matter, or other circumstance. Good morrow; for, as I take
    it, it is almost day.

PROVOST: I shall obey him.   [*Exit* MESSENGER]

DUKE: [*Aside*]   This is his pardon, purchased by such sin
    For which the pardoner himself is in:
    Hence hath offense his quick celerity,
    When it is borne in high authority.
    When vice makes mercy, mercy's so extended
    That for the fault's love is th' offender friended.   100
    Now, sir, what news?

PROVOST: I told you. Lord Angelo, belike thinking me remiss in mine
    office, awakens me with this unwonted putting on—methinks
    strangely, for he hath not used it before.

DUKE: Pray you, let's hear.

PROVOST: [*Reads the letter*]   "Whatsoever you may hear to the contrary,
    let Claudio be executed by four of the clock; and, in the afternoon,
    Barnardine. For my better satisfaction, let me have Claudio's head
    sent me by five. Let this be duly performed, with a thought that
    more depends on it than we must yet deliver. Thus fail not to do   110
    your office, as you will answer it at your peril."

    What say you to this, sir?

DUKE: What is that Barnardine who is to be executed in th'afternoon?

85 *siege* seat.   102 *belike* perhaps.   103 *putting on* urging.

PROVOST: A Bohemian born, but here nursed up and bred; one that is a prisoner nine years old.

DUKE: How came it that the absent Duke had not either delivered him to his liberty or executed him? I have heard it was ever his manner to do so.

PROVOST: His friends still wrought reprieves for him; and, indeed, his fact, till now in the government of Lord Angelo, came not to an   120 undoubtful proof.

DUKE: It is now apparent?

PROVOST: Most manifest, and not denied by himself.

DUKE: Hath he borne himself penitently in prison? How seems he to be touched?

PROVOST: A man that apprehends death no more dreadfully but as a drunken sleep: careless, reckless, and fearless of what's past, present, or to come; insensible of mortality, and desperately mortal.

DUKE: He wants advice.

PROVOST: He will hear none. He hath evermore had the liberty of the   130 prison; give him leave to escape hence, he would not. Drunk many times a day, if not many days entirely drunk. We have very oft awaked him, as if to carry him to execution, and showed him a seeming warrant for it; it hath not moved him at all.

DUKE: More of him anon. There is written in your brow, provost, honesty and constancy; if I read it not truly, my ancient skill beguiles me; but in the boldness of my cunning I will lay myself in hazard. Claudio, whom here you have warrant to execute, is no greater forfeit to the law than Angelo who hath sentenced him. To make you understand this in a manifested effect, I crave but four days'   140 respite, for the which you are to do me both a present and a dangerous courtesy.

PROVOST: Pray, sir, in what?

DUKE: In the delaying death.

PROVOST: Alack, how may I do it, having the hour limited, and an express command, under penalty, to deliver his head in the view of

---

120 *fact* deed, crime.   129 *wants* need.   137 *boldness of my cunning* assurance of my knowledge.   *lay myself in hazard* take a risk.   140 *in a manifested effect* by direct evidence.   145 *limited* determined.

Angelo? I may make my case as Claudio's, to cross this in the smallest.

DUKE: By the vow of mine order I warrant you, if my instructions may be your guide. Let this Barnardine be this morning executed, and 150 his head borne to Angelo.

PROVOST: Angelo hath seen them both, and will discover the favor.

DUKE: O, death's a great disguiser, and you may add to it. Shave the head, and tie the beard; and say it was the desire of the penitent to be so bared before his death; you know the course is common. If anything fall to you upon this, more than thanks and good fortune, by the saint whom I profess, I will plead against it with my life.

PROVOST: Pardon me, good father, it is against my oath.

DUKE: Were you sworn to the Duke or to the deputy? 160

PROVOST: To him, and to his substitutes.

DUKE: You will think you have made no offense, if the Duke avouch the justice of your dealing?

PROVOST: But what likelihood is in that?

DUKE: Not a resemblance, but a certainty; yet since I see you fearful, that neither my coat, integrity, nor persuasion can with ease attempt you, I will go further than I meant, to pluck all fears out of you. Look you, sir; here is the hand and seal of the Duke; you know the character, I doubt not, and the signet is not strange to you. 170

PROVOST: I know them both.

DUKE: The contents of this is the return of the Duke. You shall anon over-read it at your pleasure, where you shall find within these two days he will be here. This is a thing that Angelo knows not, for he this very day receives letters of strange tenor, perchance of the Duke's death, perchance entering into some monastery, but by chance nothing of what is writ. Look, th'unfolding star calls up the shepherd. Put not yourself into amazement how these things should be; all difficulties are but easy when they are known. Call your executioner, and off with Barnardine's head; I will give him 180

152 *discover the favor* recognize the face. 169 *character* handwriting. 177 *th'unfolding star* morning star, signal for leading the sheep from the fold.

a present shrift and advise him for a better place. Yet you are amazed, but this shall absolutely resolve you. Come away; it is almost clear dawn. [*Exit with* PROVOST]

SCENE III

Another room in the same.

[*Enter* CLOWN (POMPEY)]

POMPEY: I am as well acquainted here as I was in our house of profession: one would think it were Mistress Overdone's own house, for here be many of her old customers. First, here's young Master Rash; he's in for a commodity of brown paper and old ginger, nine-score and seventeen pounds, of which he made five marks ready money; marry, then ginger was not much in request, for the old women were all dead. Then is there here one Master Caper, at the suit of Master Threepile the mercer, for some four suits of peach-colored satin, which now peaches him a beggar. Then have we here young Dizzy, and young Master Deepvow,   10 and Master Copperspur, and Master Starve-lackey, the rapier and dagger man, and young Drop-heir that killed lusty Pudding, and Master Forthright the tilter, and brave Master Shoe-tie the great traveller, and wild Half-can that stabbed Pots, and I think forty more, all great doers in our trade, and are now "for the Lord's sake."

[*Enter* ABHORSON]

ABHORSON: Sirrah, bring Barnardine hither.

POMPEY: Master Barnardine, you must rise and be hanged, Master Barnardine.

ABHORSON: What ho, Barnardine!   20

BARNARDINE: [*Within*] A pox o' your throats, who makes that noise there? What are you?

POMPEY: Your friends, sir, the hangman. You must be so good, sir, to rise and be put to death.

---

181 *shrift* absolution after confession. 4 *commodity* goods bought on credit for resale. 5 *marks* (a mark was two-thirds of a pound). 9 *peaches* betrays. 13 *tilter* fighter. 15–16 *for the Lord's sake* (the cry of poor prisoners who begged through the grating of passers-by).

BARNARDINE: [*Within*]   Away, you rogue, away! I am sleepy.

ABHORSON: Tell him he must awake, and that quickly too.

POMPEY: Pray, Master Barnardine, awake till you are executed, and sleep afterwards.

ABHORSON: Go in to him, and fetch him out.

POMPEY: He is coming, sir, he is coming; I hear his straw rustle.   30

[*Enter* BARNARDINE]

ABHORSON: Is the axe upon the block, sirrah?

POMPEY: Very ready, sir.

BARNARDINE: How now, Abhorson, what's the news with you?

ABHORSON: Truly, sir, I would desire you to clap into your prayers: for look you, the warrant's come.

BARNARDINE: You rogue, I have been drinking all night; I am not fitted for't.

POMPEY: O, the better, sir: for he that drinks all night, and is hanged betimes in the morning, may sleep the sounder all the next day.

[*Enter* DUKE *disguised as before*]

ABHORSON: Look you, sir, here comes your ghostly father; do we jest   40
now, think you?

DUKE: Sir, induced by my charity, and hearing how hastily you are to depart, I am come to advise you, comfort you, and pray with you.

BARNARDINE: Friar, not I: I have been drinking hard all night and I will have more time to prepare me, or they shall beat out my brains with billets. I will not consent to die this day, that's certain.

DUKE: O, sir, you must; and therefore I beseech you look forward on the journey you shall go.

BARNARDINE: I swear I will not die today for any man's persuasion.

DUKE: But hear you—   50

BARNARDINE: Not a word; if you have anything to say to me, come to my ward, for thence will not I today.   [*Exit*]

[*Enter* PROVOST]

39 *betimes* early.   46 *billets* cudgels.   52 *ward* cell.

DUKE: Unfit to live or die. O gravel heart!
        After him, fellows: bring him to the block.   [*Exeunt* ABHORSON
        and POMPEY]

PROVOST: Now, sir, how do you find the prisoner?

DUKE: A creature unprepared, unmeet for death,
        And to transport him in the mind he is
        Were damnable.

PROVOST: Here in the prison, father,
        There died this morning of a cruel fever
        One Ragozine, a most notorious pirate,   60
        A man of Claudio's years, his beard and head
        Just of his color. What if we do omit
        This reprobate till he were well inclined,
        And satisfy the deputy with the visage
        Of Ragozine, more like to Claudio?

DUKE: O, 'tis an accident that heaven provides;
        Dispatch it presently; the hour draws on
        Prefixed by Angelo. See this be done,
        And sent according to command, whiles I
        Persuade this rude wretch willingly to die.   70

PROVOST: This shall be done, good father, presently;
        But Barnardine must die this afternoon,
        And how shall we continue Claudio,
        To save me from the danger that might come
        If he were known alive?

DUKE: Let this be done.
        Put them in secret holds, both Barnardine and Claudio.
        Ere twice the sun hath made his journal greeting
        To th'under generation, you shall find
        Your safety manifested.

PROVOST: I am your free dependant.   80

DUKE: Quick, dispatch, and send the head to Angelo.   [*Exit* PROVOST]
        Now will I write letters to Angelo—
        The provost, he shall bear them—whose contents
        Shall witness to him I am near at home,
        And that by great injunctions I am bound
        To enter publicly. Him I'll desire

---

57 *transport* dispatch.   67 *presently* at once.   68 *Prefixed* determined in advance.
76 *holds* cells   77 *journal* daily.   80 *your free dependant* freely at your service.

To meet me at the consecrated fount
A league below the city; and from thence,
By cold gradation and well-balanced form,
We shall proceed with Angelo.   90

[*Enter* PROVOST]

PROVOST: Here is the head; I'll carry it myself.

DUKE: Convenient is it; make a swift return,
For I would commune with you of such things
That want no ear but yours.

PROVOST: I'll make all speed.   [*Exit*]

ISABELLA: [*Within*]   Peace, ho, be here.

DUKE: The tongue of Isabel. She's come to know
If yet her brother's pardon be come hither,
But I will keep her ignorant of her good,
To make her heavenly comforts of despair
When it is least expected.

[*Enter* ISABELLA]

ISABELLA: Ho, by your leave!   100

DUKE: Good morning to you, fair and gracious daughter.

ISABELLA: The better, given me by so holy a man.
Hath yet the deputy sent my brother's pardon?

DUKE: He hath released him, Isabel, from the world;
His head is off and sent to Angelo.

ISABELLA: Nay, but it is not so.

DUKE: It is no other. Show your wisdom, daughter,
In your close patience.

ISABELLA: O, I will to him and pluck out his eyes!

DUKE: You shall not be admitted to his sight.   110

ISABELLA: Unhappy Claudio, wretched Isabel,
Injurious world, most damnèd Angelo!

DUKE: This nor hurts him nor profits you a jot;
Forbear it therefore, give your cause to heaven.
Mark what I say, which you shall find

89 *cold gradation* deliberate steps.   94 *want* need.   108 *close* silent.

By every syllable a faithful verity.
The Duke comes home tomorrow—nay, dry your eyes—
One of our covent, and his confessor,
Gives me this instance; already he hath carried
Notice to Escalus and Angelo,   120
Who do prepare to meet him at the gates,
There to give up their power. If you can, pace your wisdom
In that good path that I would wish it go,
And you shall have your bosom on this wretch,
Grace of the Duke, revenges to your heart,
And general honor.

ISABELLA: I am directed by you.

DUKE: This letter then to Friar Peter give—
'Tis that he sent me of the Duke's return—
Say, by this token, I desire his company
At Mariana's house tonight. Her cause and yours   130
I'll perfect him withal, and he shall bring you
Before the Duke; and to the head of Angelo
Accuse him home and home. For my poor self,
I am combinèd by a sacred vow
And shall be absent. Wend you with this letter;
Command these fretting waters from your eyes
With a light heart; trust not my holy order
If I pervert your course. Who's here?

[*Enter* LUCIO]

LUCIO: Good even. Friar, where's the provost?

DUKE: Not within, sir.   140

LUCIO: O pretty Isabella, I am pale at mine heart to see thine eyes so
red; thou must be patient. I am fain to dine and sup with water
and bran; I dare not for my head fill my belly; one fruitful meal
would set me to't. But they say the Duke will be here tomorrow.
By my troth, Isabel, I loved thy brother; if the old fantastical Duke
of dark corners had been at home, he had lived.   [*Exit* ISABELLA]

DUKE: Sir, the Duke is marvellous little beholding to your reports; but
the best is, he lives not in them.

LUCIO: Friar, thou knowest not the Duke so well as I do; he's a better
woodman than thou tak'st him for.   150

118 *covent* convent.   119 *instance* proof.   124 *bosom* desire.   134 *combinèd*
bound.   150 *woodman* hunter (here of women).

DUKE: Well, you'll answer this one day. Fare ye well.

LUCIO: Nay, tarry, I'll go along with thee; I can tell thee pretty tales of the Duke.

DUKE: You have told me too many of him already, sir, if they be true; if not true, none were enough.

LUCIO: I was once before him for getting a wench with child.

DUKE: Did you such a thing?

LUCIO: Yes, marry, did I; but I was fain to forswear it.
They would else have married me to the rotten medlar.

DUKE: Sir, your company is fairer than honest. Rest you well. 160

LUCIO: By my troth, I'll go with thee to the lane's end. If bawdy talk offend you, we'll have very little of it. Nay, friar, I am a kind of burr; I shall stick. [*Exeunt*]

SCENE IV

Angelo's house.

[*Enter* ANGELO *and* ESCALUS]

ESCALUS: Every letter he hath writ hath disvouched other.

ANGELO: In most uneven and distracted manner. His actions show much like to madness; pray heaven his wisdom be not tainted. And why meet him at the gates, and redeliver our authorities there?

ESCALUS: I guess not.

ANGELO: And why should we proclaim it in an hour before his entering, that if any crave redress of injustice, they should exhibit their petitions in the street?

ESCALUS: He shows his reason for that: to have a dispatch of com- 10 plaints, and to deliver us from devices hereafter, which shall then have no power to stand against us.

ANGELO: Well, I beseech you let it be proclaimed.
Betimes i'th'morn I'll call you at your house;

---

159 *medlar* a pear that rotted as it ripened (here, a prostitute). 11 *devices* contrived complaints. 14 *Betimes* early.

> Give notice to such men of sort and suit
> As are to meet him.

ESCALUS: I shall, sir: fare you well.

ANGELO: Good night.   [*Exit* ESCALUS]
> This deed unshapes me quite, makes me unpregnant
> And dull to all proceedings. A deflowered maid,
> And by an eminent body that enforced   20
> The law against it! But that her tender shame
> Will not proclaim against her maiden loss,
> How might she tongue me? Yet reason dares her no,
> For my authority bears off a credent bulk,
> That no particular scandal once can touch
> But it confounds the breather. He should have lived,
> Save that his riotous youth with dangerous sense
> Might in the times to come have ta'en revenge,
> By so receiving a dishonored life
> With ransom of such shame. Would yet he had lived.   30
> Alack, when once our grace we have forgot,
> Nothing goes right; we would, and we would not.   [*Exit*]

SCENE V

Fields without the town.

[*Enter* DUKE *in his own habit and* FRIAR PETER]

DUKE: These letters at fit time deliver me.
> The provost knows our purpose and our plot;
> The matter being afoot, keep your instruction,
> And hold you ever to our special drift,
> Though sometimes you do blench from this to that,
> As cause doth minister. Go call at Flavius' house,
> And tell him where I stay; give the like notice
> To Valencius, Rowland, and to Crassus,
> And bid them bring the trumpets to the gate,
> But send me Flavius first.

FRIAR PETER: It shall be speeded well.   [*Exit*]   10

[*Enter* VARRIUS]

---

15 *men of sort and suit* courtiers of rank.   24 *bears . . . bulk* keeps away a great
deal otherwise credible.   26 *But it confounds* without confounding.   27 *sense* reason.
4 *drift* aim.   5 *blench* turn aside.

DUKE: I thank thee, Varrius; thou hast made good haste.
Come, we will walk; there's other of our friends
Will greet us here anon, my gentle Varrius.   [*Exeunt*]

SCENE VI

Street near the city gate.

[*Enter* ISABELLA *and* MARIANA]

ISABELLA: To speak so indirectly I am loath;
I would say the truth; but to accuse him so,
That is your part. Yet I am advised to do it,
He says, to veil full purpose.

MARIANA: Be ruled by him.

ISABELLA: Besides, he tells me that if peradventure
He speaks against me on the adverse side,
I should not think it strange, for 'tis a physic
That's bitter to sweet end.

MARIANA: I would Friar Peter—

[*Enter* FRIAR PETER]

ISABELLA: O, peace, the friar is come.

FRIAR PETER: Come, I have found you out a stand most fit,   10
Where you may have such vantage on the Duke
He shall not pass you. Twice have the trumpets sounded.
The generous and gravest citizens
Have hent the gates, and very near upon
The Duke is entering; therefore hence, away.   [*Exeunt*]

ACT V. SCENE I

A public place near the city gate.

[*Enter* DUKE, VARRIUS, LORDS, ANGELO, ESCALUS, LUCIO, PROVOST,
OFFICERS, *and* CITIZENS *at several doors*]

DUKE: My very worthy cousin, fairly met.
Our old and faithful friend, we are glad to see you.

ANGELO, ESCALUS: Happy return be to your royal grace.

13 *generous* well-born.   14 *hent* taken up positions at   *very near upon* almost at
once.   1 *cousin* (a sovereign formally addresses a nobleman as "cousin").

DUKE: Many and hearty thankings to you both;
            We have made inquiry of you, and we hear
            Such goodness of your justice, that our soul
            Cannot but yield you forth to public thanks,
            Forerunning more requital.

ANGELO: You make my bonds still greater.

DUKE: O, your desert speaks loud, and I should wrong it
            To lock it in the wards of covert bosom,   10
            When it deserves with characters of brass
            A forted residence 'gainst the tooth of time
            And razure of oblivion. Give me your hand,
            And let the subject see, to make them know
            That outward courtesies would fain proclaim
            Favors that keep within. Come, Escalus,
            You must walk by us on our other hand;
            And good supporters are you.

[*Enter* FRIAR PETER *and* ISABELLA]

FRIAR PETER: Now is your time. Speak loud and kneel before him.

ISABELLA: Justice, O royal Duke; vail your regard   20
            Upon a wronged—I would fain have said, a maid.
            O worthy prince, dishonor not your eye
            By throwing it on any other object
            Till you have heard me in my true complaint
            And given me justice, justice, justice, justice!

DUKE: Relate your wrongs. In what? By whom? Be brief.
            Here is Lord Angelo shall give you justice;
            Reveal yourself to him.

ISABELLA: O worthy Duke,
            You bid me seek redemption of the devil;
            Hear me yourself; for that which I must speak   30
            Must either punish me, not being believed,
            Or wring redress from you. Hear me, O hear me, here.

ANGELO: My lord, her wits, I fear me, are not firm.
            She hath been a suitor to me for her brother,
            Cut off by course of justice—

8 *more requital* further reward.   10 *lock . . . bosom* confine it in the secret cell of
the heart.   13 *razure* erasure.   16 *keep* dwell.   20 *vail* let fall.

ISABELLA: By course of justice!

ANGELO: And she will speak most bitterly and strange.

ISABELLA: Most strange, but yet most truly, will I speak.
That Angelo's forsworn, is it not strange?
That Angelo's a murderer, is't not strange?
That Angelo is an adulterous thief,   40
A hypocrite, a virgin-violator,
Is it not strange, and strange?

DUKE: Nay, it is ten times strange.

ISABELLA: It is not truer he is Angelo
Than this is all as true as it is strange.
Nay, it is ten times true, for truth is truth
To th'end of reck'ning.

DUKE: Away with her; poor soul,
She speaks this in th'infirmity of sense.

ISABELLA: O prince, I conjure thee, as thou believ'st
There is another comfort than this world,
That thou neglect me not with that opinion   50
That I am touched with madness. Make not impossible
That which but seems unlike. 'Tis not impossible
But one, the wicked'st caitiff on the ground,
May seem as shy, as grave, as just, as absolute
As Angelo; even so may Angelo,
In all his dressings, characts, titles, forms,
Be an arch-villain; believe it, royal prince.
If he be less, he's nothing; but he's more,
Had I more name for badness.

DUKE: By mine honesty,
If she be mad, as I believe no other,   60
Her madness hath the oddest frame of sense,
Such a dependency of thing on thing,
As e'er I heard in madness.

ISABELLA: O gracious Duke,
Harp not on that; nor do not banish reason
For inequality, but let your reason serve
To make the truth appear where it seems hid,
And hide the false seems true.

---

50 *neglect me not with* ignore me not because of.   56 *dressings* ceremonial attire
characts insignia of office.   65 *inequality* injustice.   67 *seems* which seems.

DUKE: Many that are not mad
Have sure more lack of reason; what would you say?   70

ISABELLA: I am the sister of one Claudio,
Condemned upon the act of fornication
To lose his head, condemned by Angelo.
I, in probation of a sisterhood,
Was sent to by my brother, one Lucio
As then the messenger—

LUCIO: That's I, an't like your grace.
I came to her from Claudio, and desired her
To try her gracious fortune with Lord Angelo
For her poor brother's pardon.

ISABELLA: That's he indeed.

DUKE: You were not bid to speak.

LUCIO: No, my good lord,
Nor wished to hold my peace.

DUKE: I wish you now, then;
Pray you, take note of it, and when you have   80
A business for yourself, pray heaven you then
Be perfect.

LUCIO: I warrant your honor.

DUKE: The warrant's for yourself: take heed to't.

ISABELLA: This gentleman told somewhat of my tale—

LUCIO: Right.

DUKE: It may be right, but you are i'the wrong
To speak before your time; proceed.

ISABELLA: I went
To this pernicious caitiff deputy—

DUKE: That's somewhat madly spoken.

ISABELLA: Pardon it,
The phrase is to the matter.   90

DUKE: Mended again. The matter: proceed.

ISABELLA: In brief, to set the needless process by,
How I persuaded, how I prayed, and kneeled,

82 *perfect* well prepared.   90 *matter* purpose.

How he refelled me, and how I replied—
For this was of much length—the vile conclusion
I now begin with grief and shame to utter.
He would not, but by gift of my chaste body
To his concupiscible intemperate lust,
Release my brother; and after much debatement
My sisterly remorse confutes mine honor,   100
And I did yield to him; but the next morn betimes,
His purpose surfeiting, he sends a warrant
For my poor brother's head.

DUKE: This is most likely!

ISABELLA: O, that it were as like as it is true.

DUKE: By heaven, fond wretch, thou know'st not what thou speak'st,
Or else thou art suborned against his honor
In hateful practice. First, his integrity
Stands without blemish; next, it imports no reason
That with such vehemency he should pursue
Faults proper to himself. If he had so offended,   110
He would have weighed thy brother by himself,
And not have cut him off. Someone hath set you on;
Confess the truth, and say by whose advice
Thou cam'st here to complain.

ISABELLA: And is this all?
Then, O you blessèd ministers above,
Keep me in patience, and with ripened time
Unfold the evil which is here wrapt up
In countenance. Heaven shield your grace from woe,
As I thus wronged hence unbelievèd go.

DUKE: I know you'd fain be gone. An officer!   120
To prison with her. Shall we thus permit
A blasting and a scandalous breath to fall
On him so near us? This needs must be a practice;
Who knew of your intent and coming hither?

ISABELLA: One that I would were here, Friar Lodowick.

DUKE: A ghostly father, belike; who knows that Lodowick?

LUCIO: My lord, I know him; 'tis a meddling friar,
I do not like the man. Had he been lay, my lord,

94 *refelled* refuted.   100 *remorse* pity.   107 *practice* conspiracy.   128 *lay* i.e. not a
cleric.

For certain words he spake against your grace
In your retirement I had swinged him soundly.   130

DUKE: Words against me? This' a good friar, belike,
And to set on this wretched woman here
Against our substitute! Let this friar be found.

LUCIO: But yesternight, my lord, she and that friar,
I saw them at the prison; a saucy friar,
A very scurvy fellow.

FRIAR PETER: Blessed be your royal grace,
I have stood by, my lord, and I have heard
Your royal ear abused. First, hath this woman
Most wrongfully accused your substitute,   140
Who is as free from touch or soil with her
As she from one ungot.

DUKE: We did believe no less.
Know you that Friar Lodowick that she speaks of?

FRIAR PETER: I know him for a man divine and holy,
Not scurvy, nor a temporary meddler,
As he's reported by this gentleman;
And, on my trust, a man that never yet
Did, as he vouches, misreport your grace.

LUCIO: My lord, most villainously, believe it.

FRIAR PETER: Well, he in time may come to clear himself,   150
But at this instant he is sick, my lord,
Of a strange fever. Upon his mere request,
Being come to knowledge that there was complaint
Intended 'gainst Lord Angelo, came I hither,
To speak, as from his mouth, what he doth know
Is true and false; and what he with his oath
And all probation will make up full clear,
Whensoever he's convented. First, for this woman,
To justify this worthy nobleman,   160
So vulgarly and personally accused,
Her shall you hear disprovèd to her eyes,
Till she herself confess it.

DUKE: Good friar, let's hear it.

145 *temporary meddler* meddler in temporal affairs.   157 *probation* proof.   158
convented summoned.

[ISABELLA *withdraws, guarded. Enter* MARIANA]

Do you not smile at this, Lord Angelo?
O heaven, the vanity of wretched fools!
Give us some seats. Come, cousin Angelo,
In this I'll be impartial; be you judge
Of your own cause. Is this the witness, friar?
First, let her show her face, and after speak.

MARIANA: Pardon, my lord, I will not show my face   170
Until my husband bid me.

DUKE: What, are you married?

MARIANA: No, my lord.

DUKE: Are you a maid?

MARIANA: No, my lord.

DUKE: A widow, then?

MARIANA: Neither, my lord.

DUKE: Why, you are nothing then; neither maid, widow, nor wife?

LUCIO: My lord, she may be a punk; for many of them are neither maid,
widow, nor wife.   180

DUKE: Silence that fellow. I would he had some cause
To prattle for himself.

LUCIO: Well, my lord.

MARIANA: My lord, I do confess I ne'er was married,
And I confess besides I am no maid;
I have known my husband, yet my husband
Knows not that ever he knew me.

LUCIO: He was drunk, then, my lord; it can be no better.

DUKE: For the benefit of silence, would thou wert so too.

LUCIO: Well, my lord.

DUKE: This is no witness for Lord Angelo.   190

MARIANA: Now I come to't, my lord:
She that accuses him of fornication,
In selfsame manner doth accuse my husband;

179 *punk* harlot.   185 *known* cohabited with.

And charges him, my lord, with such a time
When, I'll depose, I had him in mine arms,
With all th'effect of love.

ANGELO: Charges she moe than me?

MARIANA: Not that I know.

DUKE: No? You say your husband?

MARIANA: Why, just, my lord, and that is Angelo,
Who thinks he knows that he ne'er knew my body,   200
But knows he thinks that he knows Isabel's.

ANGELO: This is a strange abuse; let's see thy face.

MARIANA: My husband bids me; now I will unmask.   [*Unveiling*]
This is that face, thou cruel Angelo,
Which once thou swor'st was worth the looking on;
This is the hand which, with a vowed contract,
Was fast belocked in thine; this is the body
That took away the match from Isabel,
And did supply thee at thy garden-house
In her imagined person.

DUKE: Know you this woman?   210

LUCIO: Carnally, she says.

DUKE: Sirrah, no more!

LUCIO: Enough, my lord.

ANGELO: My lord, I must confess I know this woman,
And five years since there was some speech of marriage
Betwixt myself and her, which was broke off,
Partly for that her promisèd proportions
Came short of composition, but in chief
For that her reputation was disvalued
In levity; since which time of five years
I never spake with her, saw her, nor heard from her,   220
Upon my faith and honor.

MARIANA: Noble prince,
As there comes light from heaven and words from breath,
As there is sense in truth and truth in virtue,

216 *proportions* portion, dowry.   217 *composition* agreement.   218 *disvalued* discredited.   219 *In levity* for lightness.

I am affianced this man's wife as strongly
As words could make up vows; and, my good lord,
But Tuesday night last gone in's garden-house
He knew me as a wife. As this is true,
Let me in safety raise me from my knees
Or else forever be confixèd here
A marble monument.

ANGELO: I did but smile till now;   230
Now, good my lord, give me the scope of justice;
My patience here is touched. I do perceive
These poor informal women are no more
But instruments of some more mightier member
That sets them on. Let me have way, my lord,
To find this practice out.

DUKE: Ay, with my heart,
And punish them to your height of pleasure.
Thou foolish friar, and thou pernicious woman,
Compact with her that's gone, think'st thou thy oaths,
Though they would swear down each particular saint,   240
Were testimonies against his worth and credit
That's sealed in approbation? You, Lord Escalus,
Sit with my cousin; lend him your kind pains
To find out this abuse, whence 'tis derived.
There is another friar that set them on;
Let him be sent for.

FRIAR PETER: Would he were here, my lord, for he indeed
Hath set the women on to this complaint.
Your provost knows the place where he abides
And he may fetch him.

DUKE: Go do it instantly; [*Exit* PROVOST]   250
And you, my noble and well-warranted cousin,
Whom it concerns to hear this matter forth,
Do with your injuries as seems you best,
In any chastisement; I for a while
Will leave you, but stir not you till you have
Well determined upon these slanderers.

ESCALUS: My lord, we'll do it throughly. [*Exit* DUKE]
Signior Lucio, did not you say you knew that Friar
Lodowick to be a dishonest person?

233 *informal* rash, turbulent.   239 *Compact* leagued.

LUCIO: "Cucullus not facit monachum"; honest in nothing but in his   260
clothes, and one that hath spoke most villainous speeches of the
Duke.

ESCALUS: We shall entreat you to abide here till he come and enforce
them against him; we shall find this friar a notable fellow.

LUCIO: As any in Vienna, on my word.

ESCALUS: Call that same Isabel here once again; I would speak with
her. [Exit an ATTENDANT] Pray you, my lord, give me leave to
question; you shall see how I'll handle her.

LUCIO: Not better than he, by her own report.

ESCALUS: Say you?   270

LUCIO: Marry, sir, I think, if you handled her privately, she would
sooner confess; perchance publicly she'll be ashamed.

[Enter DUKE in his friar's habit, PROVOST, ISABELLA, and OFFICERS]

ESCALUS: I will go darkly to work with her.

LUCIO: That's the way, for women are light at midnight.

ESCALUS: Come on, mistress, here's a gentlewoman denies all that you
have said.

LUCIO: My lord, here comes the rascal I spoke of—here with the provost.

ESCALUS: In very good time. Speak not you to him, till we call upon
you.   280

LUCIO: Mum.

ESCALUS: Come, sir, did you set these women on to slander Lord
Angelo? They have confessed you did.

DUKE: 'Tis false.

ESCALUS: How! know you where you are?

DUKE: Respect to your great place; and let the devil
Be sometime honored for his burning throne.
Where is the Duke? 'Tis he should hear me speak.

ESCALUS: The Duke's in us, and we will hear you speak;
Look you speak justly.   290

---

260 *Cucullus non facit monachum* a cowl does not make a monk.   273 *darkly* slyly.
287 *sometime* on occasion.

DUKE: Boldly at least. But O, poor souls,
    Come you to seek the lamb here of the fox?
    Good night to your redress! Is the Duke gone?
    Then is your cause gone too. The Duke's unjust,
    Thus to retort your manifest appeal
    And put your trial in the villain's mouth
    Which here you come to accuse.

LUCIO: This is the rascal; this is he I spoke of.

ESCALUS: Why, thou unreverend and unhallowed friar,
    Is't not enough thou hast suborned these women   300
    To accuse this worthy man but, in foul mouth,
    And in the witness of his proper ear,
    To call him villain? And then to glance from him
    To the Duke himself, to tax him with injustice?
    Take him hence; to the rack with him. We'll touse you
    Joint by joint, but we will know his purpose.
    What, unjust?

DUKE: Be not so hot. The Duke
    Dare no more stretch this finger of mine than he
    Dare rack his own: his subject am I not,
    Nor here provincial. My business in this state   310
    Made me a looker-on here in Vienna,
    Where I have seen corruption boil and bubble
    Till it o'errun the stew. Laws for all faults,
    But faults so countenanced that the strong statutes
    Stand like the forfeits in a barber's shop,
    As much in mock as mark.

ESCALUS: Slander to th'state. Away with him to prison.

ANGELO: What can you vouch against him, Signior Lucio?
    Is this the man that you did tell us of?

LUCIO: 'Tis he, my lord. Come hither, goodman baldpate; do you   320
know me?

DUKE: I remember you, sir, by the sound of your voice. I met you at
the prison in the absence of the Duke.

LUCIO: O, did you so? And do you remember what you said of the
Duke?

    295 *retort* turn back.   302 *proper* very.   305 *touse* tear.   310 *provincial* subject
to the laws of this province, or state.   315 *forfeits* extracted teeth (since barbers acted
as dentists).   316 *mock as mark* jest as earnest.

DUKE: Most notedly, sir.

LUCIO: Do you so, sir? And was the Duke a fleshmonger, a fool, and
a coward, as you then reported him to be?

DUKE: You must, sir, change persons with me, ere you make that my
report. You, indeed, spoke so of him, and much more, much   330
worse.

LUCIO: O thou damnable fellow, did not I pluck thee by the nose for
thy speeches?

DUKE: I protest I love the Duke as I love myself.

ANGELO: Hark how the villain would close now, after his treasonable
abuses.

ESCALUS: Such a fellow is not to be talked withal; away with him to
prison. Where is the provost? Away with him to prison, lay bolts
enough upon him, let him speak no more. Away with those
giglets too, and with the other confederate companion.   340

[*The* PROVOST *lays hands on the* DUKE]

DUKE: Stay, sir, stay a while.

ANGELO: What, resists he? Help him, Lucio.

LUCIO: Come, sir, come, sir, come, sir. Foh, sir, why, you bald-pated,
lying rascal, you must be hooded, must you? Show your knave's
visage, with a pox to you; show your sheep-biting face, and be
hanged an hour. Will't not off?

[*Pulls off the* FRIAR's *hood, and discovers the* DUKE]

DUKE: Thou art the first knave that e'er mad'st a duke.
First, provost, let me bail these gentle three;
[*To* LUCIO]   Sneak not away, sir, for the friar and you
Must have a word anon. Lay hold on him.   350

LUCIO: This may prove worse than hanging.

DUKE: [*To* ESCALUS]   What you have spoke I pardon. Sit you down,
We'll borrow place of him.   [*To* ANGELO]   Sir, by your leave.
Hast thou or word, or wit, or impudence
That yet can do thee office? If thou hast,
Rely upon it till my tale be heard,
And hold no longer out.

    335 *close* come to terms.   337 *withal* with.   338 *bolts* fetters.   340 *giglets* lewd
women.   345 *sheep-biting* currish.   355 *office* service.

ANGELO: O my dread lord,   360
I should be guiltier than my guiltiness
To think I can be undiscernible,
When I perceive your grace, like power divine,
Hath looked upon my passes. Then, good prince,
No longer session hold upon my shame,
But let my trial be mine own confession.
Immediate sentence, then, and sequent death
Is all the grace I beg.

DUKE: Come hither, Mariana.
Say, wast thou ere contracted to this woman?

ANGELO: I was, my lord.

DUKE: Go take her hence, and marry her instantly.
Do you the office, friar; which consummate,
Return him here again. Go with him, provost. [*Exit* ANGELO,   370
with MARIANA, FRIAR PETER, *and* PROVOST]

ESCALUS: My lord, I am more amazed at his dishonor
Than at the strangeness of it.

DUKE: Come hither, Isabel;
Your friar is now your prince. As I was then
Advertising and holy to your business,
Not changing heart with habit, I am still
Attorneyed at your service.

ISABELLA: O, give me pardon,
That I, your vassal, have employed and pained
Your unknown sovereignty.

DUKE: You are pardoned, Isabel;
And now, dear maid, be you as free to us.
Your brother's death, I know, sits at your heart,   380
And you may marvel why I obscured myself,
Laboring to save his life, and would not rather
Make rash remonstrance of my hidden power
Than let him so be lost. O most kind maid,
It was the swift celerity of his death,
Which I did think with slower foot came on,
That brained my purpose; but peace be with him.
That life is better life past fearing death,

---

364 *passes* trespasses.   374 *Advertising* attentive.   376 *Attorneyed* acting as attorney.   383 *remonstrance* demonstration.

Than that which lives to fear. Make it your comfort,
So happy is your brother.

[*Enter* ANGELO, MARIANA, FRIAR PETER, PROVOST]

ISABELLA: I do, my lord.   390

DUKE: For this new-married man approaching here,
           Whose salt imagination yet hath wronged
           Your well-defended honor, you must pardon
           For Mariana's sake. But as he adjudged your brother,
           Being criminal, in double violation
           Of sacred chastity, and of promise-breach,
           Thereon dependent, for your brother's life,
           The very mercy of the law cries out
           Most audible, even from his proper tongue,
           "An Angelo for Claudio, death for death!"   400
           Haste still pays haste, and leisure answers leisure,
           Like doth quit like, and Measure still for Measure.
           Then, Angelo, thy fault's thus manifested,
           Which though thou wouldst deny, denies thee vantage.
           We do condemn thee to the very block
           Where Claudio stooped to death, and with like haste.
           Away with him.

MARIANA: O, my most gracious lord,
           I hope you will not mock me with a husband.

DUKE: It is your husband mocked you with a husband.
           Consenting to the safeguard of your honor,   410
           I thought your marriage fit; else imputation,
           For that he knew you, might reproach your life
           And choke your good to come. For his possessions,
           Although by confiscation they are ours,
           We do instate and widow you with all,
           To buy you a better husband.

MARIANA: O my dear lord,
           I crave no other, nor no better man.

DUKE: Never crave him; we are definitive.

MARIANA: Gentle my liege—

DUKE: You do but lose your labor.
           Away with him to death.   [To LUCIO]   Now, sir, to you.   420

392 *salt* salacious.   398 *mercy* justice (the law's mercy; see II, ii, 100).   404
vantage way of escape.   418 *definitive* determined.

MARIANA: O my good lord! Sweet Isabel, take my part,
Lend me your knees, and, all my life to come,
I'll lend you all my life to do you service.

DUKE: Against all sense you do importune her;
Should she kneel down in mercy of this fact,
Her brother's ghost his pavèd bed would break,
And take her hence in horror.

MARIANA: Isabel,
Sweet Isabel, do yet but kneel by me,
Hold up your hands, say nothing, I'll speak all.
They say best men are moulded out of faults,   430
And, for the most, become much more the better
For being a little bad; so may my husband.
O Isabel, will you not lend a knee?

DUKE: He dies for Claudio's death.

ISABELLA: [*Kneeling*] Most bounteous sir,
Look, if it please you, on this man condemned
As if my brother lived. I partly think
A due sincerity governèd his deeds
Till he did look on me. Since it is so,
Let him not die; my brother had but justice,
In that he did the thing for which he died.   440
For Angelo,
His act did not o'ertake his bad intent,
And must be buried but as an intent
That perished by the way. Thoughts are no subjects,
Intents but merely thoughts.

MARIANA: Merely, my lord.

DUKE: Your suit's unprofitable; stand up, I say.
I have bethought me of another fault.
Provost, how came it Claudio was beheaded
At an unusual hour?

PROVOST: It was commanded so.

DUKE: Had you a special warrant for the deed?   450

PROVOST: No, my good lord, it was by private message.

DUKE: For which I do discharge you of your office;
Give up your keys.

426 *pavèd bed* slab-covered grave.   444 *no subjects* not answerable to authority.

PROVOST: Pardon me, noble lord;
    I thought it was a fault, but knew it not,
    Yet did repent me after more advice;
    For testimony whereof, one in the prison
    That should by private order else have died
    I have reserved alive.

DUKE: What's he?

PROVOST: His name is Barnardine.

DUKE: I would thou hadst done so by Claudio.
    Go, fetch him hither; let me look upon him. [*Exit* PROVOST]   460

ESCALUS: I am sorry, one so learned and so wise
    As you, Lord Angelo, have still appeared,
    Should slip so grossly, both in the heat of blood
    And lack of tempered judgment afterward.

ANGELO: I am sorry that such sorrow I procure,
    And so deep sticks it in my penitent heart
    That I crave death more willingly than mercy;
    'Tis my deserving, and I do entreat it.

[*Enter* BARNARDINE *and* PROVOST, CLAUDIO *muffled,* JULIET]

DUKE: Which is that Barnardine?

PROVOST: This, my lord.

DUKE: There was a friar told me of this man.   470
    Sirrah, thou art said to have a stubborn soul,
    That apprehends no further than this world,
    And squar'st thy life according. Thou'rt condemned;
    But, for those earthly faults, I quit them all,
    And pray thee take this mercy to provide
    For better times to come. Friar, advise him:
    I leave him to your hand. What muffled fellow's that?

PROVOST: This is another prisoner that I saved,
    Who should have died when Claudio lost his head—
    As like almost to Claudio as himself. [*Unmuffles* CLAUDIO]   480

DUKE: [*To* ISABELLA] If he be like your brother, for his sake
    Is he pardoned, and for your lovely sake—

---

454 *knew it not* was not sure. 455 *advice* consideration. 462 *still* always. 473
squar'st regulate. 474 *quit* pardon.

Give me your hand and say you will be mine—
He is my brother too. But fitter time for that.
By this Lord Angelo perceives he's safe;
Methinks I see a quickening in his eye.
Well, Angelo, your evil quits you well.
Look that you love your wife; her worth, worth yours.
I find an apt remission in myself,
And yet here's one in place I cannot pardon.   490
[*To* LUCIO] You, sirrah, that knew me for a fool, a coward,
One all of luxury, an ass, a madman,
Wherein have I so deserved of you,
That you extol me thus?

LUCIO: 'Faith, my lord, I spoke it but according to the trick.
If you will hang me for it, you may; but I had rather it would please
you, I might be whipped.

DUKE: Whipped first, sir, and hanged after.
Proclaim it, provost, round about the city,
If any woman wronged by this lewd fellow—   500
As I have heard him swear himself there's one
Whom he begot with child—let her appear,
And he shall marry her. The nuptial finished,
Let him be whipped and hanged.

LUCIO: I beseech your highness, do not marry me to a whore.
Your highness said even now, I made you a duke; good my lord,
do not recompense me in making me a cuckold.

DUKE: Upon mine honor, thou shalt marry her.
Thy slanders I forgive, and therewithal
Remit thy other forfeits. Take him to prison,   510
And see our pleasure herein executed.

LUCIO: Marrying a punk, my lord, is pressing to death, whipping, and
hanging.

DUKE: Slandering a prince deserves it.   [*Exeunt* OFFICERS *with* LUCIO]
She, Claudio, that you wronged, look you restore.
Joy to you, Mariana; love her, Angelo;
I have confessed her and I know her virtue.
Thanks, good friend Escalus, for thy much goodness;
There's more behind that is more gratulate.

489 *remission* wish to remit, or pardon.   492 *luxury* lust.   495 *trick* fashion.   519
behind in store   *gratulate* gratifying.

Thanks, provost, for thy care and secrecy;   520
We shall employ thee in a worthier place.
Forgive him, Angelo, that brought you home
The head of Ragozine for Claudio's;
Th'offense pardons itself. Dear Isabel,
I have a motion much imports your good,
Whereto if you'll a willing ear incline,
What's mine is yours, and what is yours is mine.
So, bring us to our palace, where we'll show
What's yet behind, that's meet you all should know.   [*Exeunt*]

525 *motion* proposal.

HENRIK IBSEN

❧ *Hedda Gabler*

CHARACTERS

Jörgen Tesman, *a scholar engaged in research in the history of civilisation*
Hedda Tesman, *his wife*
Juliane Tesman, *his aunt*
Mrs. Elvsted
Brack, *a puisne judge*
Ejlert Lövborg
Berte, *the Tesmans' servant*

The action takes place in the TESMANS' *villa on the west side of the town*

ACT I

A *large drawing-room, well furnished, in good taste, and decorated in dark colours. In the back wall there is a wide doorway with its curtains pulled back. This opening leads into a smaller room decorated in the same style as the drawing-room. In the right wall of this outer room is a folding door that leads into the hall. In the opposite wall, left, is a glass door also with curtains pulled back. Through its panes can be seen part of a verandah outside and autumn foliage. In the middle of the stage is an oval table with a cloth on it and chairs round it. Downstage, against the right wall are a large, dark porcelain stove, a high-backed arm-chair, a padded foot-rest and two stools. Up in the right corner are a corner sofa and a little round table. Downstage, left, a little way from the wall, is a sofa. Above the glass door, a piano. On each side of the doorway at the back stands a what-not with terra-cotta and majolica ornaments. Against the back wall of the inner room can be seen a sofa, a table and a chair or two. Over this sofa hangs the portrait of a handsome, elderly man in a general's uniform. Over the table a hanging lamp with a soft, opal glass shade. All round the drawing-room are bouquets of flowers in vases and glasses; others are lying on the tables. The floors in both rooms are covered with thick carpets. Morning light: the sun shines in through the glass doors.*

Translated by Una Ellis-Fermor.

MISS JULIANE TESMAN, *wearing her hat and carrying a parasol, comes in from the hall followed by* BERTE *carrying a bouquet wrapped in paper.* MISS TESMAN *is a comely, sweet-tempered-looking woman of about sixty-five, well but simply dressed in grey outdoor clothes.* BERTE *is a servant getting on in years, with a homely, rather countrified look.*

MISS TESMAN: [*Stops just inside the door, listens and says softly*] Why, I don't believe they're up yet!

BERTE: [*Softly, too*] That's what I said, Miss. Think how late the boat came in last night. And on top of that, my goodness! All the things the young mistress *would* unpack before she'd settle down.

MISS TESMAN: Well, well. Let them have their sleep out, of course. But they must have fresh morning air to breathe when they do come out. [*She goes over to the glass door and throws it wide open*]

BERTE: [*Standing by the table, not knowing what to do with the bouquet in her hand*] Well, upon my word, there just isn't anywhere left for it. I think I'd better put it here, Miss. [*She stands it up on the piano*]

MISS TESMAN: Well now, Berte my dear, you've got a new mistress. Heaven knows it was dreadfully hard for me to part with you!

BERTE: [*Nearly crying*] What do you think it was for *me*, Miss? I just can't tell you. After all these many years I've been with you two ladies.

MISS TESMAN: We must try to be contented, Berte. There's really nothing else to be done. You know, Jörgen must have you in the house with him. He simply *must*. You have been used to looking after him ever since he was a little boy.

BERTE: Yes, Miss. But I keep thinking of her lying there at home. Poor thing! So helpless and all. And that new girl, too! *She'll* never learn to look after a sick person properly. Never!

MISS TESMAN: Oh, I shall manage to train her. And, you know, I shall take over most of it myself. Berte dear, there's no need for you to worry so much about my poor sister.

BERTE: Yes, but there's another thing, Miss. I'm really afraid I'll never manage to suit the young mistress.

MISS TESMAN: Oh, come now! Just at first, perhaps, there may be one or two things . . .

BERTE: Because, of course, she's a fine lady—and that particular!

MISS TESMAN: You can understand that, can't you, with General Gabler's daughter? Think what she was accustomed to in the General's day. Do you remember her riding along the road with her father? In that long black habit? And feathers in her hat?

BERTE: My, yes! I should think I do. But, upon my word, I never thought it would be a match between her and Mr Jörgen. Not in those days.

MISS TESMAN: Nor did I. But that reminds me, Berte, while I think of it— you mustn't call Jörgen 'Mr' any more. You must say 'Doctor'.

BERTE: Yes, the young mistress said something about that, too, as soon as they got in last night. Is it true, then, Miss?

MISS TESMAN: Yes, perfectly true. Just think of it, Berte, they made him a doctor abroad! While he was away this time, you know. I didn't know a single word about it, not till he told me down at the pier.

BERTE: Oh, of course, he can be anything—he can. Clever, like he is. But I never thought he'd take up doctoring, too.

MISS TESMAN: Oh, it's not *that* kind of doctor he is. [*With a nod full of meaning*] Come to that, you may soon be able to call him something else—something even grander.

BERTE: You don't say, Miss! What would that be, Miss?

MISS TESMAN: [*Smiling*] Ah! If you only knew! [*Touched*] God bless us! If poor dear Jochum could look up from his grave and see what his little boy has grown up to be! [*Looking about her*] Oh, but—I say, Berte! Why *have* you done that? Taken all the covers off the furniture?

BERTE: The mistress said I was to. Says she can't do with covers on the chairs.

MISS TESMAN: Are they going to use this room for every day, then?

BERTE: So it seemed, from what the mistress said. The master—the Doctor— he didn't say anything.

[*JÖRGEN TESMAN, humming to himself, comes into the inner room from the right. He is carrying an empty, unfastened suit-case. He is a youngish-looking man of thirty-three, middle-sized, stoutish, with a round, frank, happy face. His hair and beard are fair; he wears glasses. He is comfortably—almost carelessly—dressed, in an indoor suit*]

MISS TESMAN: Good morning, good morning, Jörgen!

TESMAN: [*In the doorway between the rooms*] Aunt Julle! My dear Aunt Julle! [*Goes up and shakes her hand affectionately*] All the way out here so early! Eh?

MISS TESMAN: Well, you can just imagine! I *had* to have a look at you both.

TESMAN: Although you haven't had anything like a proper night's rest!

MISS TESMAN: Oh, that doesn't make a bit of difference to me.

TESMAN: But you did get home from the pier all right? Eh?

MISS TESMAN: Oh yes, quite all right, I'm glad to say. Mr Brack was so very kind and saw me right to my door.

TESMAN: We *were* so sorry we couldn't give you a lift. But you saw how it was yourself. Hedda had so much luggage that she had to have with her.

MISS TESMAN: Yes, she certainly did have a tremendous lot of luggage.

BERTE: [*To* TESMAN]   Shall I go in and ask the mistress if there's anything I could help her with?

TESMAN: No, thanks, Berte, you needn't do that. If she wants you for anything, she says she'll ring.

BERTE: [*To the right*]   Very well.

TESMAN: Oh, but, here—take this suit-case, will you?

BERTE: [*Taking it*]   I'll put it up in the attic. [*Goes out by the hall door*]

TESMAN: Just think, Aunt Julle, I had that whole suit-case crammed full, just with the stuff I'd copied. You wouldn't believe what I've managed to collect, going through the archives. Curious old things that no one really knows about.

MISS TESMAN: Well, well, Jörgen, you certainly haven't wasted your time on your honeymoon.

TESMAN: No, I jolly well haven't! But take your hat off, Aunt Julle. Here, let me unfasten the bow. Eh?

MISS TESMAN: [*While he is doing it*]   Bless me! It's just as though you were still at home with us.

TESMAN: [*Turning and twisting the hat in his hand*]   Why! What a fine, smart hat you've bought yourself!

MISS TESMAN: I got it because of Hedda.

TESMAN: Because of Hedda? Eh?

MISS TESMAN: Yes. So that Hedda shan't be ashamed of me if we go out together.

TESMAN: [*Patting her cheek*]   *Dear* Aunt Julle! You think of absolutely everything. [*Puts the hat on a chair by the table*] Now, look here; let's sit on the sofa and have a little chat till Hedda comes.

[*They sit down. She puts her parasol in the sofa-corner*]

MISS TESMAN: [*Taking both his hands and looking at him*] What a blessing it is to have you again, Jörgen, as large as life! My dear! Poor Jochum's own boy!

TESMAN: So it is for me, Aunt Julle, to see *you* again! You who've been my father and my mother.

MISS TESMAN: Yes, I know you'll always have a corner in your heart for your old aunts.

TESMAN: But I suppose there's no improvement in Aunt Rina, eh?

MISS TESMAN: Well, you know, we can't really expect any improvement in her, poor dear. She just lies there, the same as she has all these years. But I hope the good Lord will let me keep her a little longer. For I shan't know what to do with my life otherwise, Jörgen. Especially now, you know, that I haven't got you to look after any more.

TESMAN: [*Patting her on the back*] Come, come, come!

MISS TESMAN: [*With a sudden change*] But just think, Jörgen, you're a married man! And to think it was you who carried off Hedda Gabler! The lovely Hedda Gabler! To think of it! She, who always had so *many* admirers.

TESMAN: [*Humming a little, with a satisfied smile*] Yes, I expect a certain number of my good friends are going about this town feeling pretty envious. Eh?

MISS TESMAN: And to think that you were able to have such a long honeymoon! Over five months. Nearly six.

TESMAN: Well, for me it's been a kind of research tour as well—with all those old records I had to hunt through. And then, you know, the enormous number of books I had to read.

MISS TESMAN: Yes, that's quite true. [*Dropping her voice a little and speaking confidentially*] But look here, Jörgen, haven't you anything . . . anything, well, *special* to tell me?

TESMAN: About the trip?

MISS TESMAN: Yes.

TESMAN: No, I don't think there's anything else, except what I told you in my letters. About my taking my doctorate down there—well, I told you that yesterday.

MISS TESMAN: Oh, yes, that kind of thing. Yes. But, I mean, haven't you any . . . well, any hopes . . . er . . . ?

TESMAN: Hopes?

MISS TESMAN: Oh, come, Jörgen! After all, I *am* your old aunt!

TESMAN: Well, yes, of course I have hopes. . . .

MISS TESMAN: Ah!

TESMAN: . . . I've the very best hopes of getting a professorship one of these days.

MISS TESMAN: Oh yes, a professorship. Yes.

TESMAN: Or I might say, rather, there's a certainty of my getting it. But, my dear Aunt Julle, you know that yourself perfectly well!

MISS TESMAN: [*With a little laugh*] Yes, of course I do. You're quite right. [*Changing her tone*] But we were talking about your travels. It must have cost a lot of money, Jörgen?

TESMAN: Ye-es. But, you know, that big fellowship took us a good bit of the way.

MISS TESMAN: But I don't see how you can possibly have made that do for two.

TESMAN: Well, no; one could hardly expect that. Eh?

MISS TESMAN: Especially when it's a lady one's travelling with. For that usually comes more expensive—very much more, I've heard.

TESMAN: Well, yes, of course. It does come rather more expensive. But Hedda had to have that trip, Aunt Julle. She really had to. Nothing else would have done.

MISS TESMAN: No, no. Of course it wouldn't. A honeymoon abroad seems quite a matter of course, nowadays. But tell me, now. Have you had a chance yet to have a good look at the house?

TESMAN: You bet I have! I have been wandering round ever since it was light.

MISS TESMAN: And what do you think of it, on the whole?

TESMAN: Splendid! Absolutely splendid! There's only one thing I can't see— what we're going to do with the two empty rooms there between the back sitting-room and Hedda's bedroom.

MISS TESMAN: [*With a little laugh*]   Oh, my dear Jörgen, there may be a use for them—all in good time.

TESMAN: Yes, you're perfectly right, Aunt Julle! Because, by degrees, as I get a bigger library, well—Eh?

MISS TESMAN: Of course, my dear boy. It was the library I was thinking of.

TESMAN: I'm specially glad for Hedda's sake. She often said, before we were engaged, that she'd never care to live anywhere except in Mrs Falk's house.

MISS TESMAN: Yes, just fancy! And then its happening like that—the house being for sale! Just as you had started.

TESMAN: Yes, Aunt Julle, the luck certainly was with us. Eh?

MISS TESMAN: But expensive, my dear Jörgen! It will be expensive for you, all this.

TESMAN: [*Looking at her, a little disheartened*]   Yes, I suppose it will, perhaps.

MISS TESMAN: Goodness, yes!

TESMAN: How much do you think? Roughly. Eh?

MISS TESMAN: Oh, I can't possibly tell till all the bills come in.

TESMAN: But fortunately Mr Brack has arranged the easiest possible terms for me. He wrote and told Hedda so himself.

MISS TESMAN: Well, don't you worry about it, my child. And as for the furniture and carpets, I have given security for them.

TESMAN: Security? You? My dear Aunt Julle, what kind of security could you give?

MISS TESMAN: I have given a mortgage on the annuity.

TESMAN: [*Jumping up*]   What! On yours and Aunt Rina's annuity?

MISS TESMAN: Yes. I didn't know what else to do, you see.

TESMAN: [*Standing in front of her*]   But, Aunt Julle, have you gone crazy? The annuity! The only thing you and Aunt Rina have to live on!

MISS TESMAN: Now, now—don't get so upset about it. The whole thing is just a formality, you know. That's what Mr Brack said, too. For it was he who so kindly arranged it for me. Just a formality, he said.

TESMAN: Yes, that may be so. But all the same . . .

MISS TESMAN: Because you've got your own salary to rely on now. And— goodness me!—suppose we did have to spend a little too—help a little just at first? Why, it would only be a pleasure for us.

TESMAN: Oh, Aunt Julle, you will never be tired of sacrificing yourself for me.

MISS TESMAN: [*Getting up and laying her hands on his shoulders*] Have I any other joy in this world but in smoothing the way for you, my dear boy? You who've had neither father nor mother to turn to. And now we've reached our goal, my dear! Things may have looked black now and again. But, thank goodness, you're through that now, Jörgen.

TESMAN: Yes, it's wonderful, really, how everything has worked out.

MISS TESMAN: Yes, and the people who stood in your way, who would have stopped your getting on, you have them at your feet. They have gone down before you, Jörgen—most of all, the person who was most danger- ous to you. And there he lies now, on the bed he made for himself, the poor misguided creature.

TESMAN: Have you heard anything of Ejlert? Since I went away, I mean?

MISS TESMAN: No, only that he's supposed to have brought out a new book.

TESMAN: *What?* Ejlert Lövborg? Just recently? Eh?

MISS TESMAN: Yes, so they say. I shouldn't think there can be much in it, would you? Now when *your* new book comes out, that will be quite another story, Jörgen. What is it going to be about?

TESMAN: It's going to be about domestic crafts in Brabant in the Middle Ages.

MISS TESMAN: Well, well! To think you can write about a thing like that!

TESMAN: As a matter of fact, the book may take some time yet. I've got to arrange those enormous collections of material first, you know.

MISS TESMAN: Ah yes. Arranging and collecting—that's what you're so good at. You're not dear Jochum's son for nothing.

TESMAN: I'm looking forward immensely to getting down to it. Especially now that I've got a charming house of my own, my own home to work in.

MISS TESMAN: And first and foremost, my dear, now that you've got the wife your heart was set on.

TESMAN: [*Giving her a hug*] Why, of course, Aunt Julle! Hedda! Why, that's the loveliest thing of all! [*Looking towards the centre doorway*] I think she's coming. Eh?

[HEDDA *comes in from the left, through the inner room. She is a woman of twenty-nine. Her face and figure show breeding and distinc-*

tion, *her complexion has an even pallor. Her eyes are steel-grey; cold, clear and calm. Her hair is a beautiful light brown, though not noticeably abundant. The loose-fitting morning costume she is wearing is in good style.*]

MISS TESMAN: [*Going up to* HEDDA] Good morning, Hedda dear! A very good morning to you!

HEDDA: [*Holding out her hand*] Good morning, my dear Miss Tesman. What an early visit! It was kind of you.

MISS TESMAN: [*Seeming a little taken aback*] Well, has the bride slept well in her new home?

HEDDA: Oh yes, thank you. Tolerably.

TESMAN: Tolerably! I like that, Hedda! You were sleeping like a log when I got up.

HEDDA: Fortunately. In any case, one has to get used to anything new, Miss Tesman. By degrees. [*Looking to the left*] Oh! The maid has gone and opened the verandah door! There's a perfect flood of sunlight coming in.

MISS TESMAN: [*Going towards the door*] Well, we'll shut it, then.

HEDDA: Oh no, don't do that, please. [*To* TESMAN] Just draw the blinds, my dear, will you? That gives a softer light.

TESMAN: [*At the door*] Yes, yes. All right. There you are, Hedda. Now you've got shade *and* fresh air.

HEDDA: Yes, we certainly need fresh air in here. All these precious flowers! But—won't you sit down, Miss Tesman?

MISS TESMAN: No, thank you very much. Now I know everything is going on all right here—thank goodness!—I must see about getting home again. Poor dear, she finds the time very long, lying there.

TESMAN: Give her my love and my best wishes, won't you? And tell her I'll come over and see her later on today.

MISS TESMAN: Yes, yes, I certainly will. But that reminds me, Jörgen. [*Feeling in her bag*] I nearly forgot it. I've brought something of yours.

TESMAN: What is it, Aunt Julle, Eh?

MISS TESMAN: [*Bringing out a flat newspaper package and handing it to him*] Look there, my dear boy.

TESMAN: [*Opening it*] Well, I'm blessed! You've kept them for me, Aunt Julle! That really is sweet of her, Hedda, isn't it? Eh?

HEDDA: [*By the what-not on the right*]   Yes, my dear. What is it?

TESMAN: My old morning shoes. My slippers—look!

HEDDA: Oh yes. I remember, you often spoke about them while we were away.

TESMAN: Yes, I missed them dreadfully. [*Going up to her*] Now you shall see them, Hedda.

HEDDA: [*Going over to the stove*]   No, thanks. It really doesn't interest me.

TESMAN: [*Following her*]   Just think, Aunt Rina embroidered them for me in bed, lying ill like that. Oh, you can't imagine how many memories are worked into them!

HEDDA: Not for me, particularly.

MISS TESMAN: Hedda's right about that, Jörgen.

TESMAN: Yes, but I think, now she belongs to the family—

HEDDA: [*Interrupting*]   My dear, we shall never be able to manage with this maid.

MISS TESMAN: Not manage with Berte?

TESMAN: What makes you say that, my dear? Eh?

HEDDA: [*Pointing*]   Look there. She's left her old hat behind her on the chair.

TESMAN: [*Dropping his slippers on the floor in his dismay*]   But, Hedda—

HEDDA: Suppose anyone were to come in and see it?

TESMAN: But—but, Hedda, that is Aunt Julle's hat!

HEDDA: Oh! Is it?

MISS TESMAN: [*Picking up the hat*]   Yes, it's certainly mine. And it isn't old, either, my dear little Hedda.

HEDDA: I really didn't look at it closely, Miss Tesman.

MISS TESMAN: [*Putting on the hat*]   As a matter of fact, it's the first time I've worn it. The very first, it is.

TESMAN: And a beautiful hat it is, too. Really grand!

MISS TESMAN: Oh, it's not all that, my dear Jörgen. [*Looking round her*] Parasol? Ah, here it is. [*Picking it up*] For that's mine, too. [*Under her breath*] Not Berte's.

TESMAN: A new hat and a new parasol! Think of that, Hedda.

HEDDA: Yes, it's very nice. Charming.

TESMAN: Yes, isn't it? Eh? But, Aunt Julle, take a good look at Hedda before you go. See how nice and charming *she* is.

MISS TESMAN: Ah, my dear, there's nothing new in *that*. Hedda has been lovely all her life. [*She nods and goes towards the right*]

TESMAN: [*Following her*] Yes, but have you noticed how plump she's grown, and how well she is? How much she's filled out on our travels?

HEDDA: [*Crossing the room*] Oh, be quiet—!

MISS TESMAN: [*Who has stopped and turned round*] Filled out?

TESMAN: Of course, you can't see it so well, Aunt Julle, now she has that dress on. But I, who have the opportunity of—

HEDDA: [*At the glass door, impatiently*] Oh, you haven't any opportunity!

TESMAN: It must be the mountain air, down there in the Tyrol—

HEDDA: [*Interrupting curtly*] I am exactly the same as I was when I went away.

TESMAN: Yes, so you keep on saying. But you certainly aren't. Don't you think so too, Aunt Julle?

MISS TESMAN: [*Gazing at her with clasped hands*] Hedda is lovely—lovely—lovely! [*She goes up to* HEDDA, *takes her head in both hands, and, bending it down, kisses her hair*] May God bless and take care of our Hedda. For Jörgen's sake.

HEDDA: [*Freeing herself gently*] Oh—let me go.

MISS TESMAN: [*Quietly, but with emotion*] I shall come over and see you two every single day.

TESMAN: Yes, do, *please*, Aunt Julle! Eh?

MISS TESMAN: Good-bye. Good-bye.

[*She goes out by the hall door.* TESMAN *goes with her, leaving the door half open. He can be heard repeating his messages to* AUNT RINA *and thanking her for the shoes. In the meanwhile* HEDDA *crosses the room, raising her arms and clenching her hands, as if in fury. Then she pulls back the curtains from the glass door and stands there looking out. After a moment* TESMAN *comes in again, shutting the door behind him.*]

TESMAN: [*Picking up the slippers from the floor*] What are you looking at, Hedda?

HEDDA: [*Calm and controlled again*] I'm just looking at the leaves. They're so yellow, and so withered.

TESMAN: [*Wrapping up the shoes and putting them on the table*] Well, after all, we're well on in September now.

HEDDA: [*Disturbed again*] Yes, just think. We're already in—in September.

TESMAN: Don't you think Aunt Julle was rather unlike herself, my dear? A little bit—almost formal? Whatever do you think was the matter? Eh?

HEDDA: I hardly know her, you see. Isn't she like that as a rule?

TESMAN: No, not like she was today.

HEDDA: [*Moving away from the glass door*] Do you think she was really upset about that business with the hat?

TESMAN: Oh, not much. Perhaps a little, just at the moment.

HEDDA: But what extraordinary manners! To throw her hat down here in the drawing-room. One doesn't do that kind of thing.

TESMAN: Well, you can be sure Aunt Julle won't do it again.

HEDDA: Anyway, I'll make it all right with her.

TESMAN: That's sweet of you, Hedda dear! If you would!

HEDDA: When you go in to see them presently, you might ask her over here for the evening.

TESMAN: Yes, I certainly will. And there's another thing you could do that would please her enormously.

HEDDA: Oh? What?

TESMAN: If you could bring yourself to speak a little more affectionately to her—as if you were one of the family. For my sake, Hedda? Eh?

HEDDA: No, no. You mustn't ask me to do that. I've told you that once already. I'll try to call her 'Aunt', and that must be enough.

TESMAN: Oh well, all right. Only it seems to me now that you belong to the family—

HEDDA: Well, I really don't know. . . . [*She goes up towards the centre doorway*]

TESMAN: [*After a pause*] Is there anything the matter, Hedda? Eh?

HEDDA: I'm just looking at my old piano. It doesn't go very well with all these other things.

TESMAN: When I get my first salary cheque, we'll see about an exchange.

HEDDA: Oh no, not an exchange. I don't want to get rid of it. We can put it in there, in the back room. And we can have another in its place here. Some time or other, I mean.

TESMAN: [*A little subdued*]   Yes. We can do that, of course.

HEDDA: [*Picking up the bouquet from the piano*]   These flowers weren't here when we came in last night.

TESMAN: Aunt Julle must have brought them for you.

HEDDA: [*Looking into the bouquet*]   A visiting-card. [*Taking it out and reading it*] 'Will call again later on today.' Can you guess who it's from?

TESMAN: No. Who is it? Eh?

HEDDA: It says, 'Mrs Elvsted'.

TESMAN: Really? The wife of the District Magistrate. Miss Rysing that was.

HEDDA: Yes. Exactly. That girl with the tiresome hair, that she was always showing off. An old flame of yours, I've heard.

TESMAN: [*Laughing*]   Oh, it didn't last long! And it was before I knew you, Hedda. But fancy her being in town.

HEDDA: Odd, that she should call on us. I hardly know her, except that we were at school together.

TESMAN: Yes, I haven't seen her either for—heaven knows how long. I wonder she can bear it up there, in that hole of a place. Eh?

HEDDA: [*Thinks a moment and says suddenly*]   Tell me, isn't it somewhere up there that he lives—er—Ejlert Lövborg?

TESMAN: Yes it is. Up in those parts.

[BERTE *comes in at the hall door*]

BERTE: She's here again, ma'am. The lady who came and left the flowers an hour ago. [*Pointing*] The ones you've got in your hand, ma'am.

HEDDA: Oh, is she? Show her in, will you?

[BERTE *opens the door for* MRS ELVSTED *and goes out herself.* MRS ELVSTED *is a slender little thing with pretty, soft features. Her eyes are light blue, large, round and slightly prominent, with a startled, questioning expression. Her hair is remarkably fair, almost silver-gilt, and exceptionally thick and wavy. She is a couple of years younger than* HEDDA.

*She is wearing a dark calling costume, of a good style but not quite of the
latest fashion.]*

HEDDA: [*Going to meet her in a friendly way*]   How are you, my dear Mrs
Elvsted? It's nice to see you once more.

MRS ELVSTED: [*Nervous, and trying to control herself*]   Yes, it's a very long
time since we met.

TESMAN: [*Giving her his hand*]   Or we two either. Eh?

HEDDA: Thank you for your lovely flowers.

MRS ELVSTED: Oh, please! I would have come here at once, yesterday afternoon. But I heard that you were away.

TESMAN: Have you only just come to town? Eh?

MRS ELVSTED: I got here about midday yesterday. I was absolutely in despair
when I heard that you weren't at home.

HEDDA: In despair? But why?

TESMAN: But my dear, dear Mrs Rysing—Mrs Elvsted, I mean—

HEDDA: There isn't anything the matter, is there?

MRS ELVSTED: Yes, there is. And I don't know a living soul to turn to here in
town, except you.

HEDDA: [*Putting the bouquet down on the table*]   Come now, let's sit here
on the sofa.

MRS ELVSTED: No, I feel too worried and restless to sit down.

HEDDA: Oh no, you don't. Come along here. [*She pulls Mrs Elvsted down on
to the sofa and sits beside her*]

TESMAN: Well now, what is it, Mrs Elvsted?

HEDDA: Has anything gone wrong up there, at home?

MRS ELVSTED: Well, it has and it hasn't. Oh, I do so want you not to misunderstand me.

HEDDA: Then the best thing you can do, Mrs Elvsted, is to tell us all about it.

TESMAN: Because that's what you've come for, isn't it? Eh?

MRS ELVSTED: Yes, yes, it is, of course. Well, then, I must explain—if you
don't know already—that Ejlert Lövborg is in town too.

HEDDA: Lövborg is!

TESMAN: Really? So Ejlert Lövborg's come back again! Fancy that, Hedda!

HEDDA: Quite. I heard all right.

MRS ELVSTED: He's been here a week now, already. Think of it! A whole week in this dangerous town. And alone! And all the bad company he could get into here!

HEDDA: But, my dear Mrs Elvsted, why does *he* specially matter to you?

MRS ELVSTED: [*Gives her a frightened glance and says quickly*]   He used to be the children's tutor.

HEDDA: Your children's?

MRS ELVSTED: My husband's. I haven't got any.

HEDDA: Your step-children's, then.

MRS ELVSTED: Yes.

TESMAN: [*Hesitantly*]   Was he . . . er . . . tolerably . . . then . . . I don't quite know how to put it . . . fairly steady in his habits—enough to be given *that* job? Eh?

MRS ELVSTED: For the last two years there hasn't been a word against him.

TESMAN: Really! Think of that, Hedda!

HEDDA: I heard.

MRS ELVSTED: Not the least thing, I assure you. Nothing of any kind. But still now, when I know he's here—in this great city—and with plenty of money in his pockets . . . I'm desperately anxious about him now.

TESMAN: But why didn't he stay up there where he was, then? With you and your husband? Eh?

MRS ELVSTED: Once the book was out he was too restless and excited to stay up there with us.

TESMAN: Oh yes, that reminds me. Aunt Julle said he'd brought out a new book.

MRS ELVSTED: Yes, a big new book on the history of civilisation; a sort of general survey. It's been out a fortnight now. And now that it's gone so well and made such a tremendous stir—

TESMAN: It has, has it? It must be something he had by him from his better days, then.

MRS ELVSTED: From some time ago, you mean?

TESMAN: Exactly.

MRS ELVSTED: No, he wrote the whole thing up at our place. Just lately—within the last year.

TESMAN: That's good news, isn't it, Hedda? Just fancy!

MRS ELVSTED: Yes, indeed. If only it would last.

HEDDA: Have you met him here in town?

MRS ELVSTED: No, not yet. I had a lot of trouble finding his address. But I got it at last, this morning.

HEDDA: [*Looking searchingly at her*]   You know, it seems a little odd of your husband to . . . er . . .

MRS ELVSTED: [*Starting nervously*]   Of my husband? What does?

HEDDA: To send you to town on an errand like this. Not to come in and look after his friend himself.

MRS ELVSTED: Oh, not at all! My husband hasn't time for that. And then there—there was something I had to do.

HEDDA: [*With a slight smile*]   Ah well, that's a different matter.

MRS ELVSTED: [*Getting up quickly, in some distress*]   So I do implore you, Mr Tesman, be good to Ejlert Lövborg if he comes to you! And he's sure to, because you were such good friends in the old days. And besides, you're both working in the same field. On the same subjects, as far as I can make out.

TESMAN: Well anyway, we were at one time.

MRS ELVSTED: Yes. And that's why I do beseech you—you really will keep a watchful eye on him too, won't you, Mr Tesman? You do promise me?

TESMAN: Yes, I'll be only too glad to, Mrs Rysing—

HEDDA: Elvsted.

TESMAN: I really will do what I can for Ejlert. Everything I possibly can. You can be sure of that.

MRS ELVSTED: Oh, you *are* being kind! [*Clasping his hands*] Thank you, again and again. [*Frightened*] Because my husband is so attached to him.

HEDDA: [*Getting up*]   You ought to write to him, my dear. He may not come to see you of his own accord.

TESMAN: Yes, Hedda, that probably would be best. Eh?

HEDDA: And the sooner the better. Now—at once—I think.

MRS ELVSTED: [*Beseechingly*]   Oh yes! If you *would!*

TESMAN: I'll write this very minute. Have you his address, Mrs—Elvsted?

MRS ELVSTED: [*Taking a small slip of paper out of her pocket and handing it to him*]   Here it is.

TESMAN: Good. Good. I'll go in, then. [*Looking round him*] That reminds me—my slippers? Ah, here they are. [*Picks up the parcel and is just going*]

HEDDA: Now write really kindly and affectionately. And a good long letter, too.

TESMAN: Yes, I certainly will.

MRS ELVSTED: But, please, don't say a word about my having asked you to!

TESMAN: Of course not. That goes without saying. Eh?

[*He goes through the inner room to the right.*]

HEDDA: [*Goes up to* MRS ELVSTED *and says softly*]   That's right. Now we've killed two birds with one stone.

MRS ELVSTED: How do you mean?

HEDDA: Didn't you realise I wanted to get rid of him?

MRS ELVSTED: Yes, to write his letter.

HEDDA: And also so that I could talk to you alone.

MRS ELVSTED: [*Confused*]   About this business?

HEDDA: Exactly. About that.

MRS ELVSTED: [*Alarmed*]   But there isn't anything more, Mrs Tesman! Nothing at all!

HEDDA: Oh yes there is, now. There's a lot more. That much I do realise. Come over here, and we'll sit and be cosy and friendly together.

[*She pushes* MRS ELVSTED *into the easy-chair by the stove and sits on one of the stools herself*]

MRS ELVSTED: [*Looking anxiously at her watch*]   But my dear Mrs Tesman, I really meant to go now.

HEDDA: Oh, surely there's no hurry. Now then, suppose you tell me a little about what your home's like.

MRS ELVSTED: But that's the last thing in the world I wanted to talk about!

HEDDA: Not to me, my dear? After all, we were at school together.

MRS ELVSTED: Yes, but you were a class above me. How dreadfully frightened of you I was in those days!

HEDDA: Were you frightened of me?

MRS ELVSTED: Yes. Dreadfully frightened. Because when we met on the stairs you always used to pull my hair.

HEDDA: No, *did* I?

MRS ELVSTED: Yes, and once you said you would burn it off.

HEDDA: Oh, that was only silly talk, you know.

MRS ELVSTED: Yes, but I was so stupid in those days. And since then, anyhow, we have drifted such a long, long way apart. Our circles were so entirely different.

HEDDA: Well, then, we'll see if we can come together again. Now, look here. When we were at school we used to talk like real close friends and call each other by our Christian names.

MRS ELVSTED: Oh no, you're making quite a mistake.

HEDDA: I certainly am *not*. I remember it perfectly well. So we are going to tell each other everything, as we did in the old days. [*Moving nearer with her stool*] There we are! [*Kissing her cheek*] Now you're to talk to me like a real friend and call me 'Hedda'.

MRS ELVSTED: [*Clasping and patting her hands*] All this goodness and kindness—it's not a bit what I'm used to.

HEDDA: There, there, there! And I'm going to treat *you* like a friend, as I did before, and call you my dear Thora.

MRS ELVSTED: My name's Thea.

HEDDA: Yes, of course. Of course. I meant Thea. [*Looking sympathetically at her*] So you're not used to much goodness or kindness, aren't you, Thea? Not in your own home?

MRS ELVSTED: Ah, if I *had* a home! But I haven't one. Never have had. . . .

HEDDA: [*Looking at her a moment*] I rather thought it must be something of that sort.

MRS ELVSTED: [*Gazing helplessly in front of her*] Yes. Yes. Yes.

HEDDA: I can't quite remember now, but wasn't it as housekeeper that you went up there in the beginning—to the District Magistrate's?

MRS ELVSTED: Actually it was to have been as governess. But his wife—his late wife—was an invalid and was ill in bed most of the time. So I had to take charge of the house too.

HEDDA: But then, in the end, you became the mistress of the house.

MRS ELVSTED: [*Drearily*] Yes, I did.

HEDDA: Let me see. . . . About how long ago is it now?

MRS ELVSTED: Since I was married?

HEDDA: Yes.

MRS ELVSTED: It's five years ago now.

HEDDA: Yes, of course. It must be that.

MRS ELVSTED: Ah! Those five years—or rather the last two or three. Oh, if you could only imagine, Mrs Tesman—

HEDDA: [*Giving her a little slap on the hand*] Mrs Tesman! Come, Thea!

MRS ELVSTED: Oh yes; I will try! Yes, Hedda, if you had any idea—if you understood—

HEDDA: [*Casually*] Ejlert Lövborg was up there too for three years or so, I believe?

MRS ELVSTED: [*Looking at her doubtfully*] Ejlert Lövborg? Why yes. He was.

HEDDA: Did you know him already? From the old days in town?

MRS ELVSTED: Hardly at all. Well I mean—by name, of course.

HEDDA: But when you were up there—then, he used to visit you and your husband?

MRS ELVSTED: Yes, he came over to us every day. You see, he was giving the children lessons. Because, in the long run, I couldn't manage it all myself.

HEDDA: No, I should think not. And your husband? I suppose he is often away from home?

MRS ELVSTED: Yes. You see, Mrs—er—you see, Hedda, being District Magistrate he's always having to go out on circuit.

HEDDA: [*Leaning against the arm of the chair*] Thea, my poor little Thea. Now you're going to tell me all about it. Just how things are.

MRS ELVSTED: Very well. You ask me about it, then.

HEDDA: What is your husband really like, Thea? You know what I mean—in everyday life? Is he nice to you?

MRS ELVSTED: [*Evasively*] He's quite sure himself that he does everything for the best.

HEDDA: Only, it seems to me, he must be much too old for you. More than twenty years older, surely?

MRS ELVSTED: [*Irritably*] Yes, there's that too. What with one thing and another, I'm miserable with him. We haven't an idea in common, he and I. Not a thing in the world.

HEDDA: But isn't he fond of you, all the same? I mean, in his own way?

MRS ELVSTED: Oh, I don't know *what* he feels. I think I'm just useful to him. After all, it doesn't cost much to keep me. I'm cheap.

HEDDA: That's silly of you.

MRS ELVSTED: [*Shaking her head*] It can't be any different. Not with him. He isn't really fond of anyone but himself. And perhaps the children— a little.

HEDDA: And of Ejlert Lövborg, Thea.

MRS ELVSTED: [*Looking at her*] Of Ejlert Lövborg? What makes you think that?

HEDDA: But, my dear—it seems to me, when he sends you all the way into town after him. . . . [*Smiling almost imperceptibly*] And besides, you said so yourself to my husband.

MRS ELVSTED: [*With a nervous start*] What? Oh yes, so I did. [*Breaking out, but in a lowered voice*] No. I might as well tell you now as later. It'll all come out, anyway.

HEDDA: But, my dear Thea—

MRS ELVSTED: Well, to be quite frank, my husband had no idea I was coming.

HEDDA: *What!* Didn't your husband know about it?

MRS ELVSTED: No, of course not. And, anyway, he wasn't at home. He was away too. Oh, I couldn't stand it any longer, Hedda! It was simply impossible. I should have been absolutely alone up there in future.

HEDDA: Well? So then?

MRS ELVSTED: So I packed up some of my things, you see—the ones I needed most. Very quietly, of course. And so I left the place.

HEDDA: Just like that? Nothing more?

MRS ELVSTED: No . . . And then I took the train straight in to town.

HEDDA: But, my dear, precious child! How did you dare risk it?

MRS ELVSTED: [*Getting up and moving across the room*]   Well, what on earth could I do?

HEDDA: But what do you think your husband will say when you go back again?

MRS ELVSTED: [*By the table, looking at her*]   Back there, to him?

HEDDA: Yes, of course. What then?

MRS ELVSTED: I'm never going back there to him.

HEDDA: [*Getting up and going nearer to her*]   Then you've left in real earnest, for good and all?

MRS ELVSTED: Yes. There didn't seem to be anything else for me to do.

HEDDA: And then—your doing it quite openly!

MRS ELVSTED: Oh, you can't keep that kind of thing secret, in any case.

HEDDA: But, Thea, what do you think people will say about you?

MRS ELVSTED: Heaven knows, they must say what they like. [*Sitting down on the sofa wearily and sadly*] I have only done what I *had* to do.

HEDDA: [*After a short silence*]   What do you mean to do now? What kind of job are you going to get?

MRS ELVSTED: I don't know yet. I only know that I must live here, where Ejlert Lövborg lives. That is, if I *must* live. . . .

HEDDA: [*Moves a chair from the table, sits beside her and strokes her hands*] Thea, my dear, how did it happen? This—this friendship between you and Ejlert Lövborg?

MRS ELVSTED: Oh, it happened by degrees, somehow. I came to have some kind of power over him.

HEDDA: Indeed? And then?

MRS ELVSTED: He gave up his old habits. Not because I asked him to. I never dared do that. But of course he noticed I didn't like that kind of thing. And so he left off.

HEDDA: [*Masking an involuntary sneer*]   In fact, you've what they call 're-claimed him', you have, little Thea.

MRS ELVSTED: Yes. At least, he says so himself. And he, for his part, has made me into a real human being! Taught me to think . . . and to understand . . . one thing after another.

HEDDA: Perhaps he gave *you* lessons, too, did he?

MRS ELVSTED: No, not exactly lessons. . . . But he used to talk to me about such endless numbers of things. And then came the glorious, happy moment when I began to share his work! When he let me help him.

HEDDA: And you did, did you?

MRS ELVSTED: Yes. When he was writing anything, we always had to work at it together.

HEDDA: I see. Like two good comrades.

MRS ELVSTED: [*Eagerly*] Comrades! Why, Hedda, that's just what he called it! Oh, I ought to feel so perfectly happy. But I can't, though. Because I really don't know whether it will last.

HEDDA: Aren't you surer of him than that?

MRS ELVSTED: [*Drearily*] There's the shadow of a woman standing between Ejlert Lövborg and me.

HEDDA: [*Looking intently at her*] Who can that be?

MRS ELVSTED: I don't know. Someone or other from—from his past. Someone he's never really forgotten.

HEDDA: What has he said . . . about it?

MRS ELVSTED: He only touched on it once—and quite vaguely.

HEDDA: Oh. And what did he say, then?

MRS ELVSTED: He said that when they parted she wanted to shoot him with a pistol.

HEDDA: [*Cold and controlled*] How absurd! People don't do that kind of thing here.

MRS ELVSTED: No. And that's why I thought it must be that red-haired singer that he once—

HEDDA: Yes, that may be.

MRS ELVSTED: Because I remember people used to talk about her carrying loaded firearms.

HEDDA: Oh well, then, it's obviously she.

MRS ELVSTED: [*Wringing her hands*] Yes, but just think, Hedda, now I hear that that singer—she's in town again! Oh, I'm simply desperate!

HEDDA: [*Glancing towards the inner room*] Sh! Here comes my husband.

[*Getting up and whispering*] Thea, all this must be between our two selves.

MRS ELVSTED: [*Springing up*] Why, yes! For heaven's sake!

[JÖRGEN TESMAN, *with a letter in his hand, comes in from the right through the inner room*]

TESMAN: There we are! The letter's finished and ready.

HEDDA: That's good. But I think Mrs Elvsted wants to go now. Wait a minute. I'm going to the garden gate with her.

TESMAN: I say, Hedda, I wonder if Berte could see to this?

HEDDA: [*Taking the letter*] I'll tell her to.

[BERTE *comes in from the hall*]

BERTE: Mr Brack's here and would like to see the master and mistress, please.

HEDDA: Ask Mr Brack if he will please come in. And—look here—put this letter in the post, will you?

BERTE: [*Taking the letter*] Certainly, ma'am.

[*She opens the door for* BRACK *and goes out herself. He is a man of forty-five, square but well built and light in his movements. His face is round-ish, with a fine profile. His hair, still almost black, is short and carefully waved. His eyes are lively and bright. His eyebrows are thick and so is his moustache with its clipped ends. He is dressed in a well-cut outdoor suit— a little too young for his age. He wears an eye-glass, which he now and then lets fall.*]

BRACK: [*Bowing, with his hat in his hand*] May one call so early as this?

HEDDA: One certainly may!

TESMAN: [*Clasping his hand*] You will always be welcome. [*Introducing him*] Mr Brack, Miss Rysing.

HEDDA: Oh!

BRACK: [*Bowing*] A great pleasure.

HEDDA: [*Looking at him and laughing*] It's very nice to have a look at you by daylight, Mr Brack.

BRACK: Any difference, do you think?

HEDDA: Yes; I think a little younger.

BRACK: Thank you—very much.

TESMAN: But what do you say to Hedda? Eh? Doesn't she look well? She's positively—

HEDDA: Oh, do leave me out of it, please. What about thanking Mr Brack for all the trouble he has taken?

BRACK: Oh, no, no. It was only a pleasure.

HEDDA: Yes. You're a good friend. But here's Mrs Elvsted longing to be off. Excuse me a moment; I shall be back again directly.

[*Mutual good-byes.* MRS ELVSTED *and* HEDDA *go out by the hall door*]

BRACK: Well now; is your wife fairly satisfied?

TESMAN: Rather! We can't thank you enough. Of course, I gather there will have to be a little rearranging. And there's a certain amount needed still. We shall have to get a few little things.

BRACK: Is that so? Really?

TESMAN: But you're not to have any trouble over that. Hedda said she would see to what was needed herself. But why don't we sit down? Eh?

BRACK: Thanks. Just for a minute. [*He sits by the table*] There's something I rather wanted to talk to you about, Tesman.

TESMAN: Is there? Ah, I understand! [*Sits down*] I expect it's the serious part of the fun that's coming now. Eh?

BRACK: Oh, there's no great hurry about the financial side. However, I could wish we'd managed things a little more economically.

TESMAN: But that wouldn't have done at all! Think of Hedda, my dear man. You, who know her so well. I couldn't possibly ask her to live in some little suburban house.

BRACK: No. That's just the difficulty.

TESMAN: Besides, luckily it can't be long now before I get my appointment.

BRACK: Well you know, a thing like that can often be a slow business.

TESMAN: Have you heard anything further? Eh?

BRACK: Well, nothing definite—[*Breaking off*] But that reminds me, there's one piece of news I can tell you.

TESMAN: Oh?

BRACK: Your old friend, Ejlert Lövborg, has come back to town.

TESMAN: I know that already.

BRACK: Do you? How did you come to know?

TESMAN: She told us. The lady who went out with Hedda.

BRACK: Oh, I see. What was her name? I didn't quite catch it.

TESMAN: Mrs Elvsted.

BRACK: Oh yes; the District Magistrate's wife. Of course, it's up there he's been living.

TESMAN: And just think! I hear, to my great delight, that he's become perfectly steady again.

BRACK: Yes, so I'm assured.

TESMAN: And that he's brought out a new book. Eh?

BRACK: Oh yes.

TESMAN: And it's made quite an impression, too.

BRACK: It's made quite an extraordinary impression.

TESMAN: Well, now! Isn't that good news? He, with his remarkable gifts— I was terribly afraid he'd gone under for good.

BRACK: Yes. That was the general opinion about him.

TESMAN: But I can't imagine what he'll do now? What on earth can he be going to live on? Eh?

[*During the last words,* HEDDA *has come in by the hall door*]

HEDDA: [*To* BRACK, *laughing, with a touch of contempt*]   My husband's always worrying about what one's going to live on.

TESMAN: Oh but, my dear, we were talking about poor Ejlert Lövborg.

HEDDA: [*Looking quickly at him*]   Oh, were you? [*Sits in the easy-chair by the stove and asks, with a casual manner*] What's wrong with him?

TESMAN: Well, he must have run through that money he inherited long ago. And he can't very well write a new book every year. Eh? So, you see, I really wonder what will become of him.

BRACK: Perhaps I could tell you something about that.

TESMAN: Really?

BRACK: You must remember that he has relatives with a good deal of influence.

TESMAN: Ah, but unfortunately, his relatives have completely washed their hands of him.

BRACK: Once upon a time they called him the hope of the family.

TESMAN: Once upon a time, yes! But he's wrecked all that himself.

HEDDA: Who knows? [*With a slight smile*] After all, they've 'reclaimed' him up at the Elvsteds' place.

BRACK: And then this book that's come out—

TESMAN: Ah well, let's hope to goodness they'll get something or other for him. I've just written to him. Hedda, my dear, I asked him to come out to us this evening.

BRACK: But, my dear fellow, you're coming to my bachelor party this evening. You promised last night at the pier.

HEDDA: Had you forgotten it, my dear?

TESMAN: Yes, by Jove, I had!

BRACK: In any case, you needn't worry. He isn't likely to come.

TESMAN: Why do you think he won't? Eh?

BRACK: [*Hesitating a little. Gets up and rests his hands on the back of the chair*] My dear Tesman—and you too, Mrs Tesman—I can't, in fairness, leave you in ignorance of something that . . . er . . . that—

TESMAN: Something that has to do with Ejlert?

BRACK: That has to do both with you and with him.

TESMAN: But, my dear Brack, tell me what it is!

BRACK: You must be prepared for your appointment not to come so quickly, perhaps, as you wish or expect it to.

TESMAN: [*Jumping up, uneasily*]   Has anything gone wrong? Eh?

BRACK: There may be some competition—perhaps—before the post is filled.

TESMAN: Competition! Fancy that, Hedda!

HEDDA: [*Leaning farther back in the easy-chair*]   Well, well, now!

TESMAN: But with whom? Surely, never with—?

BRACK: Yes. Just so. With Ejlert Lövborg.

TESMAN: [*Clasping his hands*]   No, no! That's absolutely unthinkable! It's simply impossible! Eh?

BRACK: Well . . . That's what we may see, all the same.

TESMAN: But look here, Brack, it would be incredibly inconsiderate to me! [*Gesticulating with his arms*] Because—why, just think!—I'm a married man. We married on our prospects, Hedda and I. Went and got thoroughly in debt, and borrowed money from Aunt Julle too. Why, good Lord, the appointment was as good as promised to me! Eh?

BRACK: Steady, old man! No doubt you'll get the job, all right. But it will be contested first.

HEDDA: [*Motionless in the easy-chair*] Think of that, my dear. It will be almost like a kind of sport.

TESMAN: But, Hedda dearest, how can you take it all so casually?

HEDDA: [*As before*] I'm not doing that at all. I'm quite excited about the result.

BRACK: At any rate, Mrs Tesman, it's as well you should know now how things stand. I mean, before you start making those little purchases I hear you have in mind.

HEDDA: This can't make any difference.

BRACK: Oh, indeed? Then there's no more to be said. Good-bye. [*To* TESMAN] When I go for my afternoon stroll, I'll come in and fetch you.

TESMAN: Oh yes. Yes. I really don't know *what* I'm going to do. . . .

HEDDA: [*Lying back and reaching out her hand*] Good-bye, Mr Brack. And do come again.

BRACK: Many thanks! Good-bye, good-bye.

TESMAN: [*Going to the door with him*] Good-bye, my dear Brack. You must excuse me. . . .

[BRACK *goes out by the hall door*]

TESMAN: [*Crossing the room*] Well, Hedda, one should never venture into the land of romance. Eh?

HEDDA: [*Looking at him and smiling*] Do *you* do that?

TESMAN: Why, my dear, it can't be denied. It *was* romantic to go and get married and set up house, simply and solely on our prospects.

HEDDA: You may be right, there.

TESMAN: Well, we have our charming home, anyhow. Think, Hedda, it's the home we both used to dream of—that we fell in love with, I might almost say. Eh?

HEDDA: [*Getting up slowly and wearily*] It was understood, of course, that we should entertain—keep up some sort of establishment.

TESMAN: Goodness, yes! How I used to look forward to it, seeing you as hostess to a chosen circle of friends! Well, well, well. For the present we two must get along by ourselves, Hedda. Just have Aunt Julle out here every now and then. . . . Oh, my dear, it was to have been so very, very different for you.

HEDDA: Naturally, now I shan't get a man-servant just at first.

TESMAN: No, I'm afraid you can't. There can be no question of keeping a man-servant, you know.

HEDDA: And the saddle-horse that I was going to—

TESMAN: [*Horrified*] Saddle-horse!

HEDDA: I suppose it's no use even thinking of that now.

TESMAN: Good heavens, no! That goes without saying.

HEDDA: [*Crossing the room towards the back*] Well, anyhow, I still have one thing to kill time with.

TESMAN: [*Beaming with pleasure*] Thank heavens for that! But what is it, Hedda? Eh?

HEDDA: [*At the centre doorway, looking at him with lurking contempt*] My pistols, Jörgen.

TESMAN: [*Anxiously*] Your pistols!

HEDDA: [*With cold eyes*] General Gabler's pistols. [*She goes through the inner room and out to the left*]

TESMAN: [*Running to the centre doorway and calling after her*] For goodness' sake! Hedda, darling! Don't touch those dangerous things! For my sake, Hedda! Eh?

ACT II

The room at the TESMAN'S, *as in the First Act, except that the piano has been taken away and a graceful little writing-table with a book case put in its place. A smaller table has been put by the sofa on the left; most of the bouquets are gone, but* MRS ELVSTED'S *stands on the large table in the front of the stage. It is afternoon.*

    HEDDA, *in an afternoon dress, is alone in the room. She is standing by the open glass door, loading a pistol. The fellow to it lies in an open pistol-case on the writing-table.*

HEDDA: [*Looking down the garden and calling*] How do you do again, Mr Brack?

BRACK: [*Is heard from below, at a little distance*] And you, Mrs Tesman?

HEDDA: [*Lifting the pistol and aiming*] I'm going to shoot you, sir!

BRACK: [*Calling from below*] No, no, no! Don't stand there aiming straight at me.

HEDDA: That comes of using the back way in. [*She shoots*]

BRACK: [*Nearer*] Are you quite crazy?

HEDDA: Dear me! I didn't hit you, did I?

BRACK: [*Still outside*] Now stop this nonsense!

HEDDA: Well, come in then.

    [BRACK, *dressed as for an informal party, comes in by the glass door. He is carrying a light overcoat on his arm*]

BRACK: The deuce! Do you still play that game? What are you shooting at?

HEDDA: Oh, I just stand and shoot up into the blue.

BRACK: [*Taking the pistol gently out of her hand*] If you don't mind, my dear lady. [*Looking at it*] Ah, this one. I know it well. [*Looking round him*] Now, where have we got the case? Ah yes, here. [*Puts the pistol away and shuts the case*] Because we're not going to play that game any more today.

HEDDA: Well, what in heaven's name do you expect me to do with myself?

BRACK: Haven't you had any visitors?

HEDDA: [*Shutting the glass door*] Not a soul. I suppose everybody we know is still in the country.

BRACK: And isn't Tesman at home either?

HEDDA: [*At the writing-table, shutting up the pistol-case in the drawer*]   No, the minute he had finished lunch he tore off to his aunts. He didn't expect you so soon.

BRACK: Hm—and I didn't think of that. That was stupid of me.

HEDDA: [*Turning her head and looking at him*]   Why stupid?

BRACK: Because if I had, I should have come here a little—earlier.

HEDDA: [*Crossing the room*]   Well, then you wouldn't have found anyone at all. I was in my room changing after lunch.

BRACK: And there isn't so much as a tiny chink in the door that one could have communicated through?

HEDDA: You've forgotten to arrange anything like that.

BRACK: That was stupid of me, too.

HEDDA: Well, we shall just have to sit down here and wait. My husband won't be home yet awhile.

BRACK: Well, never mind. I'll be patient.

[HEDDA *sits down in the corner of the sofa.* BRACK *lays his coat over the back of the nearest chair and sits down, keeping his hat in his hand. There is a short pause. They look at each other*]

HEDDA: Well?

BRACK: [*In the same tone*]   Well?

HEDDA: It was I who asked first.

BRACK: [*Leaning forward a little*]   Come now, let's have a cosy little gossip all to ourselves—Madam Hedda.

HEDDA: [*Leaning farther back on the sofa*]   Doesn't it feel like a whole eternity since we last talked to each other? Oh, of course, a word or two last night and this morning—but I don't count that.

BRACK: Not like this, between ourselves? Alone together, you mean?

HEDDA: Yes. More or less that.

BRACK: Here was I, every blessed day, wishing to goodness you were home again.

HEDDA: And there was I, the whole time, wishing exactly the same.

BRACK: You? Really, Madam Hedda! And I, thinking you had thoroughly enjoyed yourself on your travels!

HEDDA: You may be sure I did!

BRACK: But Tesman was always saying so in his letters.

HEDDA: Oh, *he* did all right. Rummaging in libraries is the most entrancing occupation he knows. Sitting and copying out old parchments, or whatever they are.

BRACK: [*With a touch of malice*] After all, that is his vocation in life. Partly, at least.

HEDDA: Oh yes, quite; it is. And of course then one can— But as for me! No, my dear sir. I was excruciatingly bored.

BRACK: Do you really mean it? In sober earnest?

HEDDA: Well, you can just imagine it for yourself. To go a whole six months and never meet a soul even remotely connected with our circle. Not a soul to talk to about the things we're interested in.

BRACK: Well, yes. I should feel the lack of that too.

HEDDA: And then, what's the most intolerable thing of all . . .

BRACK: Well?

HEDDA: Everlastingly having to be with . . . with one and the same person. . . .

BRACK: [*Nodding agreement*] Early and late; I know. At every conceivable moment.

HEDDA: What I said was 'everlastingly'.

BRACK: Quite. But with our good friend Tesman, I should have thought one would be able . . .

HEDDA: Jörgen Tesman is—a learned man, you must remember.

BRACK: Admittedly.

HEDDA: And learned men are *not* entertaining as travelling companions. Not in the long run, anyhow.

BRACK: Not even a learned man one is in love with?

HEDDA: Oh! Don't use that sentimental word.

BRACK: [*Slightly taken aback*] Why, what's the matter, Madam Hedda?

HEDDA: [*Half laughing, half annoyed*] Well, you just try it yourself! Listening to someone talking about the history of civilisation, early and late—

BRACK: —Everlastingly—

HEDDA: Yes, exactly! And all this business about domestic crafts in the Middle Ages! That's the most awful part of all.

BRACK: [*Looking searchingly at her*] But, tell me . . . I don't quite see why, in that case . . . er . . .

HEDDA: Why Jörgen and I ever made a match of it, you mean?

BRACK: Well, let's put it that way; yes.

HEDDA: After all, do you think that's extraordinary?

BRACK: Yes—and no, Madam Hedda.

HEDDA: I had simply danced myself out, my dear sir. My time was up. [*With a little start*] Ah, no! I'm not going to say that. Nor think it, either.

BRACK: And, by Jove, you have no reason to!

HEDDA: Oh, reason! [*Watching him rather carefully*] And Jörgen Tesman . . . one must admit that he's a thoroughly good creature.

BRACK: Good and reliable. No question.

HEDDA: And I can't see that there's anything actually ridiculous about him. Do you think there is?

BRACK: Ridiculous? No—o. I wouldn't exactly say that.

HEDDA: Quite so. But, anyway, he's an indefatigable researcher. And it's always possible that he may get somewhere in time, after all.

BRACK: [*Looking at her a little uncertainly*] I thought you believed, like everyone else, that he was going to become a really eminent man.

HEDDA: [*With a weary expression*] Yes, so I did. And since he insisted with might and main on being allowed to support me, I don't know why I shouldn't have accepted the offer.

BRACK: No, no. Looking at it from that point of view. . . .

HEDDA: Anyhow, it was more than my other friends and admirers were prepared to do, my dear sir.

BRACK: [*Laughing*] Well, I can't answer for all the others. But as far as I myself am concerned, you know quite well that I have always preserved a—a certain respect for the marriage-tie. In a general way; in the abstract, at least, Madam Hedda.

HEDDA: [*Jesting*] Ah, but I never had any hopes with regard to you.

BRACK: All I want is to have a pleasant, intimate circle of friends where I can be useful, in one way and another, and can come and go freely like— like a trusted friend.

HEDDA: Of the husband, you mean?

BRACK: [*Leaning forward*] To be quite frank, preferably of the wife. But of the husband, too, in the second place, of course. I assure you that sort of—shall I call it triangular relationship?—is actually a very pleasant thing for everybody concerned.

HEDDA: Yes. Many a time I longed for a third person on that trip. Driving side by side with just one other person . . . !

BRACK: Fortunately the wedding-journey is over now.

HEDDA: [*Shaking her head*] The journey will go on for a long time yet. I have only come to a stopping-place on the way.

BRACK: Why, then one jumps out and walks about a little, Madam Hedda.

HEDDA: I never jump out.

BRACK: Don't you really?

HEDDA: No. Because there is always someone at hand who—

BRACK: [*Laughing*] —Who looks when you leap, you mean?

HEDDA: Precisely.

BRACK: Oh come, you know!

HEDDA: [*With a gesture of disagreement*] I don't care for that. I prefer to remain sitting where I am, alone with the other person.

BRACK: But suppose, now, a third person were to get in and join the other two?

HEDDA: Ah well, that's quite a different matter.

BRACK: A trusted and sympathetic friend—

HEDDA: —Someone who could talk entertainingly about all sorts of interesting things—

BRACK: —And nothing learned about him!

HEDDA: [*With an audible sigh*] Well, that certainly is a relief.

BRACK: [*Hearing the hall door open and glancing towards it*] The triangle is complete.

HEDDA: [*Half aloud*] And so the train goes on.

[JÖRGEN TESMAN, *in a grey outdoor suit and a soft felt hat, comes in from the hall. He has a number of unbound books under his arm and in his pockets*]

TESMAN: [*Going up to the table by the corner sofa*] It was pretty hot carrying that load. [*Putting the books down*] I'm absolutely streaming, Hedda. Why, there you are, come already, Brack. Eh? Berte didn't say anything about it.

BRACK: [*Getting up*] I came up through the garden.

HEDDA: What are those books you've brought?

TESMAN: [*Standing and dipping into them*] They are some new learned publications that I simply had to have.

HEDDA: Learned publications?

BRACK: Ah yes. Learned publications, Mrs Tesman.

[BRACK *and* HEDDA *exchange an understanding smile*]

HEDDA: Do you need any more learned publications?

TESMAN: Why, my dear Hedda, one can never have too many of them. One has to keep up with everything that's written and printed.

HEDDA: Yes, of course one does.

TESMAN: [*Turning over the books*] And look here—I've got hold of Ejlert Lövborg's new book too. [*Holding it out.*] Perhaps you'd like to have a look at it, Hedda. Eh?

HEDDA: No, thank you very much. Or . . . well perhaps later on.

TESMAN: I dipped into it on the way.

BRACK: Well, what do you think of it—as a learned man?

TESMAN: I think it's remarkable—the balance and judgment it has. He never used to write like this before. [*Gathering the books together*] Now, I'll take all this in with me. It'll be a treat to cut the pages! And then I must tidy myself up a little, too. [*To* BRACK] I say, we don't need to start at once? Eh?

BRACK: Goodness no! There's no hurry for some time yet.

TESMAN: Ah well, I'll take my time, then. [*Is going out with the books, but stops in the centre doorway and turns*] Oh, while I think of it, Hedda, Aunt Julle won't be coming out to you this evening.

HEDDA: Won't she? Perhaps it's that business with the hat that's the trouble?

TESMAN: Oh Lord, no! How can you think that of Aunt Julle? No, the thing is Aunt Rina's very ill.

HEDDA: So she always is.

TESMAN: Yes, but today she was particularly bad, poor dear.

HEDDA: Oh, then it's only natural for the other one to stay with her. I must make the best of it.

TESMAN: And you can't imagine, my dear, how glad Aunt Julle was, in spite of that, that you'd got so plump on your holiday.

HEDDA: [*Half audibly, getting up*] Oh! These everlasting aunts!

TESMAN: Eh?

HEDDA: [*Going to the glass door*] Nothing.

TESMAN: Oh, all right.

[*He goes through the inner room and out to the right*]

BRACK: What hat was it you were talking about?

HEDDA: Oh, that was something that happened with Miss Tesman this morning. She had put her hat down there on the chair. [*Looking at him and smiling*] And I pretended I thought it was the servant's.

BRACK: [*Shaking his head*] But my dear Madam Hedda, how could you do that? And to that nice old lady?

HEDDA: [*Nervously, walking across the room*] Well, you know, that kind of thing comes over me—just like that. And then I can't stop myself. [*Throwing herself down in the easy-chair by the stove*] I don't know, myself, how to explain it.

BRACK: [*Behind the easy-chair*] You're not really happy. That's the trouble.

HEDDA: [*Looking straight in front of her*] And I don't know why I should be—happy. Perhaps you can tell me, can you?

BRACK: Well, among other things, because you've got the very home you wished for.

HEDDA: [*Looking up at him and laughing*] Do you believe that fantasy too?

BRACK: Isn't there something in it, though?

HEDDA: Oh yes . . . *Some*thing.

BRACK: Very well?

HEDDA: There's this much in it. Last summer I used Jörgen Tesman to see me home from evening parties.

BRACK: Unfortunately I was going quite another way.

HEDDA: True enough. You certainly were going another way last summer.

BRACK: [*Laughing*]   You ought to be ashamed of yourself, Madam Hedda! Well, but you and Tesman, then?

HEDDA: Why, we came past here one evening. And he, poor creature, was tying himself in knots because he didn't know how to find anything to talk about. And so I felt sorry for the poor, learned man.

BRACK: [*Smiling doubtfully*]   You did, did you? H'm.

HEDDA: Yes. I really did. And so, to help him out of his misery, I just said— quite casually—that I should like to live here, in this villa.

BRACK: No more than that?

HEDDA: Not that evening.

BRACK: But . . . afterwards?

HEDDA: Yes; my thoughtlessness had its consequences, my dear sir.

BRACK: Unfortunately, our thoughtlessness all too often has, Madam Hedda.

HEDDA: Thank you. But, you see, it was through this passion for the villa of the late Mrs Falk that Jörgen Tesman and I found our way to an understanding. *That* led to our engagement and marriage and wedding trip and everything. Well, well. As one makes one's bed one must lie on it, I was just going to say.

BRACK: This is delightful! And all the time, it seems, you weren't interested in the least?

HEDDA: No. Heaven knows, I wasn't.

BRACK: Well, but now? Now that we have made it more or less comfortable for you?

HEDDA: Oh! I seem to smell lavender and dried roses in all the rooms. But perhaps Aunt Julle brought the smell with her.

BRACK: [*Laughing*]   No, I should think it's more likely the late Mrs Falk bequeathed it to you!

HEDDA: It reminds one of the departed, all right. Like one's bouquet, the day after a ball. [*Clasping her hands at the back of her neck, leaning back in her chair and looking at him*] My friend, you can't imagine how horribly bored I'm going to be out here.

BRACK: But won't there be some object or other in life for you to work for, like other people, Madam Hedda?

HEDDA: An object . . . that would have something fascinating about it?

BRACK: Preferably, of course.

HEDDA: Lord knows what kind of an object it could be. I very often wonder —[*Breaking off*] But that's no use either.

BRACK: It might be. Tell me about it.

HEDDA: Whether I could get my husband to go into politics, I was going to say.

BRACK: [*Laughing*] Tesman! Oh, come now! Things like politics aren't a bit—they're not at all his line of country.

HEDDA: No, I quite believe you. But suppose I could get him to, all the same?

BRACK: Well, but what satisfaction would you get out of it? When he isn't made that way? Why do you want to make him do it?

HEDDA: Because I'm bored, I tell you. [*After a pause*] Then you think, do you, it would be absolutely impossible for him to get into the Government?

BRACK: Well you see, my dear Madam Hedda, to do that he'd need to be a fairly rich man in the first place.

HEDDA: [*Getting up impatiently*] Yes. There we have it. It's this middle-class world that I've got into. [*Crossing the stage*] It's that that makes life so wretched! So absolutely ludicrous! Because that's what it *is*.

BRACK: I rather fancy the trouble lies somewhere else.

HEDDA: Where?

BRACK: You have never gone through anything that really roused you.

HEDDA: Nothing serious, you mean?

BRACK: Yes, that's one way of putting it, certainly. But now perhaps that may come.

HEDDA: [*With a jerk of her head*] Oh, you're thinking of all the bother over that wretched professorship. But that's my husband's affair entirely. I'm not wasting so much as a thought on it.

BRACK: No, no. That wasn't what I was thinking of either. But suppose now there comes what, in rather solemn language, is called a serious claim on you, one full of responsibility? [*Smiling*] A new claim, little Madam Hedda.

HEDDA: [*Angrily*] Be quiet! You'll never see anything of the kind.

BRACK: [*Gently*] We'll talk about it in a year's time—at most.

HEDDA: [*Shortly*]　I have no gift for that kind of thing, Mr Brack. Not for things that make claims on me!

BRACK: Why shouldn't you have a gift, like most other women, for the calling that—?

HEDDA: [*Over by the glass door*]　Oh, be quiet, I tell you! It often seems to me that I've only got a gift for one thing in the world.

BRACK: [*Going nearer*]　And what is that, if I may ask?

HEDDA: [*Stands looking out*]　For boring myself to death. Now you know. [*Turning and looking towards the inner room with a laugh*] Ah, just so! Here is our professor.

BRACK: [*Quietly, and with a warning*]　Now then, Madam Hedda!

[JÖRGEN TESMAN, *dressed for the party, carrying his gloves and hat, comes through the inner room from the right*]

TESMAN: Hedda, Ejlert Lövborg hasn't sent to say he isn't coming? Eh?

HEDDA: No.

TESMAN: Ah, you'll see, then. We shall have him along in a little while.

BRACK: Do you really think he'll come?

TESMAN: Yes, I'm almost sure he will. Because that's only a vague rumour, you know—what you told us this morning.

BRACK: Is it?

TESMAN: Yes. At least, Aunt Julle said she didn't for one moment believe he'd stand in my way again. Just think of it!

BRACK: Oh well, then, everything's quite all right.

TESMAN: [*Putting his hat, with his gloves in it, on a chair to the right*] Yes, but I really must wait as long as possible for him, if you don't mind.

BRACK: We've plenty of time for that. No one will turn up at my place before seven, or half past.

TESMAN: Oh well, we can keep Hedda company till then. And see what happens.

HEDDA: [*Putting* BRACK's *overcoat and hat over on the corner sofa*]　And if the worst comes to the worst, Mr Lövborg can stay here with me.

BRACK: [*Trying to take his things himself*]　Please let me, Mrs Tesman! What do you mean by 'the worst'?

HEDDA: If he won't go with you and my husband.

TESMAN: [*Looking at her dubiously*] But, Hedda dear, do you think that would quite do, for him to stay here with you? Eh? Remember, Aunt Julle can't come.

HEDDA: No, but Mrs Elvsted's coming. So the three of us will have tea together.

TESMAN: Oh, that'll be all right, then.

BRACK: [*Smiling*] And perhaps that might be the wisest plan for him too.

HEDDA: Why?

BRACK: Good gracious, my dear lady, you've often enough said hard things about my little bachelor parties. They weren't suitable for any but men of the strongest principles.

HEDDA: But surely Mr Lövborg is a man of strong enough principles now? A converted sinner—

[BERTE *appears at the hall door.*]

BERTE: There's a gentleman, ma'am, who'd like to see you.

HEDDA: Yes, show him in.

TESMAN: [*Quietly*] I'm sure it's he. Just fancy!

[EJLERT LÖVBORG *comes in from the hall. He is slight and thin, the same age as* TESMAN *but looking older and played out. His hair and beard are dark brown, his face is long and pale but with two patches of colour on the cheek-bones. He is dressed in a well-cut black suit, quite new, and is carrying dark gloves and a top-hat. He remains standing near the door and bows abruptly. He seems a little embarrassed*]

TESMAN: [*Crossing to him and shaking his hand*] Well, my dear Ejlert, so at last we meet once more!

EJLERT LÖVBORG: [*Speaking with lowered voice*] Thank you for your letter, Jörgen. [*Approaching* HEDDA] May I shake hands with you too, Mrs Tesman?

HEDDA: [*Taking his hand*] I am glad to see you, Mr Lövborg. [*With a gesture*] I don't know whether you two—

LÖVBORG: [*With a slight bow*] Mr Brack, I think.

BRACK: [*Returning it*] Of course we do. Some years ago—

TESMAN: [*To Lövborg, with his hands on his shoulders*] And now you're to make yourself absolutely at home, Ejlert. Mustn't he, Hedda? For you're going to settle down in town again, I hear. Eh?

LÖVBORG: I am.

TESMAN: Well, that's only natural. Oh, look here, I've got hold of your new book. But I really haven't had the time to read it yet.

LÖVBORG: You may as well save yourself the trouble.

TESMAN: Why may I?

LÖVBORG: Because there isn't much in it.

TESMAN: Well! Fancy your saying that!

BRACK: But it's very highly spoken of, I hear.

LÖVBORG: That's exactly what I wanted. So I wrote a book that everybody could agree with.

BRACK: Very wise.

TESMAN: Yes, but my dear Ejlert—

LÖVBORG: Because now I'm going to try and build myself up a position again. To begin over again.

TESMAN: [A little embarrassed]   I see; that's what it is? Eh?

LÖVBORG: [Smiling, puts down his hat and takes a packet wrapped in paper out of his pocket]   But when this one comes out, Jörgen Tesman, you must read it. For this is my first real book—the first I have put myself into.

TESMAN: Really? And what kind of book is that?

LÖVBORG: It's the continuation.

TESMAN: Continuation? Of what?

LÖVBORG: Of the book.

TESMAN: Of the new one?

LÖVBORG: Of course.

TESMAN: But my dear Ejlert, that one comes down to our own times!

LÖVBORG: It does. And this one deals with the future.

TESMAN: With the future? But, good gracious, we don't know anything about that.

LÖVBORG: No. But there are one or two things to be said about it, all the same. [Opening the package] Here, you see—

TESMAN: But that's not your handwriting?

LÖVBORG: I dictated it. [*Turning over the pages*] It's divided into two sections. The first is about the factors that will control civilisation in the future. And the second part, here [*Turning over the later pages*], this is about the probable direction civilisation will take.

TESMAN: Amazing! It would never occur to me to write about a thing like that.

HEDDA: [*Drumming on the panes of the glass door*] Hm. No . . . it wouldn't.

LÖVBORG: [*Puts the MS. into the envelope and lays the packet on the table*] I brought it with me because I thought of reading you a little of it this evening.

TESMAN: My dear fellow, that was very good of you. But, this evening . . . ? [*He looks across at* BRACK] I don't quite know how it's to be managed.

LÖVBORG: Well, another time then. There's no hurry.

BRACK: I'll explain, Mr Lövborg. There's a little affair at my place tonight. Chiefly for Tesman, you know—

LÖVBORG: [*Looking for his hat*] Ah, then I won't keep you—

BRACK: No, look here; won't you give me the pleasure of joining us?

LÖVBORG: [*Shortly and decidedly*] No, I can't do that. Thank you very much.

BRACK: Oh, nonsense! Please do. We shall be a small, select circle. And, believe me, we shall have quite a 'gay' time, as Mad—Mrs Tesman puts it.

LÖVBORG: I don't doubt it. But all the same—

BRACK: So you could take your manuscript along and read it to Tesman there, at my place. I've got plenty of rooms.

TESMAN: Yes, what about it, Ejlert? You could do that! Eh?

HEDDA: [*Intervening*] But, my dear, if Mr Lövborg really doesn't want to! I'm sure he would much rather stay here and have supper with me.

LÖVBORG: [*Looking at her*] With you, Mrs Tesman?

HEDDA: And with Mrs Elvsted.

LÖVBORG: Oh. [*Casually*] I met her for a moment this morning.

HEDDA: Did you? Yes, she's coming out. So it's almost imperative for you to stay, Mr Lövborg. Otherwise she'll have no one to see her home.

LÖVBORG: That's true. Well, thank you very much, Mrs Tesman; then I'll stay here.

HEDDA: I'll just have a word with the maid.

[*She goes to the hall door and rings.* BERTE *comes in.* HEDDA *talks to her in an undertone and points to the inner room.* BERTE *nods and goes out again*]

TESMAN: [*At the same time, to* EJLERT LÖVBORG]   Look here, Ejlert, is it this new material—about the future—that you're going to lecture on?

LÖVBORG: Yes.

TESMAN: Because I heard at the book-shop that you are going to give a course of lectures here in the autumn.

LÖVBORG: I am. You mustn't think hardly of me for it, Tesman.

TESMAN: Good gracious, no! But—

LÖVBORG: I can quite understand that it must be rather annoying for you.

TESMAN: [*Dispiritedly*]   Oh, I can't expect you to . . . for my sake . . .

LÖVBORG: But I'm waiting till you've got your appointment.

TESMAN: Waiting? Yes, but—but aren't you going to try for it, then? Eh?

LÖVBORG: No. I only want a *succès d'estime*.

TESMAN: But, good Lord! Aunt Julle was right after all, then! Of course that was it, I knew! Hedda! Think of it, my dear! Ejlert Lövborg isn't going to stand in our way at all!

HEDDA: [*Shortly*]   Our way? Please leave me out of it.

[*She goes up towards the inner room where* BERTE *is putting a tray with decanters and glasses on the table.* HEDDA *nods approvingly and comes down again.* BERTE *goes out*]

TESMAN: [*At the same time*]   But what about you, Judge? What do you say to this? Eh?

BRACK: Why, I should say that honour and a *succèss d'estime* . . . they can be very pleasant things—

TESMAN: They certainly can. But all the same—

HEDDA: [*Looking at* TESMAN *with a cold smile*]   You look to me as though you'd been thunderstruck.

TESMAN: Well, something like that. . . . I almost feel . . .

BRACK: As a matter of fact, a thunderstorm has just passed over us, Mrs Tesman.

HEDDA: [*With a gesture towards the inner room*]   Wouldn't you men like to go in and have a glass of cold punch?

BRACK: [*Looking at his watch*]   By way of a stirrup-cup? That wouldn't be a bad idea.

TESMAN: Good, Hedda! Excellent! I feel so light-hearted now, that—

HEDDA: Won't you too, Mr Lövborg?

LÖVBORG: [*With a gesture of refusal*]   No, thank you very much. Not for me.

BRACK: But, good Lord! Cold punch isn't poison, so far as I know.

LÖVBORG: Not for everybody, perhaps.

HEDDA: I'll entertain Mr Lövborg in the meantime.

TESMAN: That's right, Hedda dear. You do that.

[*He and* BRACK *go into the inner room and sit down. During what follows they drink punch, smoke cigarettes and carry on a lively conversation.* EJLERT LÖVBORG *remains standing by the stove.* HEDDA *goes to the writing-table*]

HEDDA: [*Raising her voice a little*]   I'll show you some photographs, if you like. My husband and I made a trip through the Tyrol on our way home.

[*She brings an album and puts it on the table by the sofa, sitting down herself in the farthest corner.* EJLERT LÖVBORG *goes nearer, stands and looks at her. Then he takes a chair and sits down on her left with his back to the inner room*]

HEDDA: [*Opening the album*]   Do you see this mountain range, Mr Lövborg? It's the Ortler Group. My husband has written it underneath. Here it is: 'The Ortler Group at Meran. '

LÖVBORG: [*Who has been looking intently at her, speaking softly and slowly*] Hedda—Gabler.

HEDDA: [*Glancing quickly at him*]   Hush, now!

LÖVBORG: [*Repeating softly*]   Hedda Gabler.

HEDDA: [*Looking at the album*]   Yes, that was my name once upon a time. In the days—when we two knew one another.

LÖVBORG: And in future—for the whole of my life—then, I must break myself of the habit of saying Hedda Gabler?

HEDDA: [*Going on turning over the pages*] Yes, you must. And I think you'd better practise it in good time. The sooner the better, I should say.

LÖVBORG: [*With resentment in his voice*] Hedda Gabler married? And married to—Jörgen Tesman.

HEDDA: Yes. That's what happened.

LÖVBORG: Oh, Hedda, Hedda, how could you throw yourself away like that?

HEDDA: [*Looking sharply at him*] Now! None of that, please.

LÖVBORG: None of what?

[TESMAN *comes in and goes toward the sofa*]

HEDDA: [*Hearing him coming, and speaking indifferently*] And this one, Mr Lövborg, is from the Vale of Ampezzo. Just look at the mountain peaks there. [*Looking affectionately up at* TESMAN] What is it these queer peaks are called, my dear?

TESMAN: Let me see. Oh, those are the Dolomites.

HEDDA: Oh, of course! Those are the Dolomites, Mr Lövborg.

TESMAN: Hedda, dear, I just wanted to ask if we shouldn't bring you a little punch? For you, at any rate. Eh?

HEDDA: Well, yes; thank you. And a few cakes, perhaps.

TESMAN: No cigarettes?

HEDDA: No, thanks.

TESMAN: Right.

[*He goes into the inner room and out to the right.* BRACK *stays sitting in the inner room, with an eye on* HEDDA *and* LÖVBORG *from time to time*]

LÖVBORG: [*In a low voice, as before*] Answer me, now, Hedda my dear. How could you go and do this?

HEDDA: [*Apparently intent on the album*] If you go on saying 'dear' to me, I won't talk to you.

LÖVBORG: Mayn't I even do it when we are alone?

HEDDA: No. You can think it if you like. But you mustn't say it.

LÖVBORG: Ah, I understand. It offends . . . your love for Jörgen Tesman.

HEDDA: [*Glancing at him and smiling*] Love? That's good!

LÖVBORG: Isn't it love, then?

HEDDA: There isn't going to be any kind of disloyalty, anyhow. I won't have that sort of thing.

LÖVBORG: Hedda, answer me just one thing—

HEDDA: Hush!

[TESMAN, *with a tray, comes from the inner room*]

TESMAN: Look at the good things we've got here. [*He puts the tray on the table*]

HEDDA: Why are you bringing it yourself?

TESMAN: [*Filling the glasses*] Why, because I think it's so jolly waiting on you, Hedda.

HEDDA: Oh, but you've filled both glasses now. And Mr Lövborg won't have any.

TESMAN: No, but Mrs Elvsted will be here soon.

HEDDA: Oh, of course; Mrs Elvsted—

TESMAN: Had you forgotten her? Eh?

HEDDA: We've got so absorbed in this. [*Showing him a picture*] Do you remember that little village?

TESMAN: Ah, that's the one below the Brenner Pass! It was there we stayed the night—

HEDDA: —And met all those jolly tourists.

TESMAN: That's it. It was there. Just think, if we could have had *you* with us, Ejlert! Well, well!

[*He goes in again and sits down with* BRACK]

LÖVBORG: Answer me just this one thing, Hedda.

HEDDA: Well?

LÖVBORG: Was there no love in your feeling for me either? Not a touch—not a flicker of love in that either?

HEDDA: I wonder if there actually was? To me it seems as if we were two good comrades. Two real, close friends. [*Smiling*] You, especially, were absolutely frank.

LÖVBORG: It was you who wanted that.

HEDDA: When I look back at it, there really was something fine, something enthralling. There was a kind of courage about it, about this hidden intimacy, this comradeship that not a living soul so much as guessed at.

LÖVBORG: Yes, there was, Hedda! Wasn't there? When I came up to see your father in the afternoons. . . . And the General used to sit right over by the window reading the papers, with his back to us . . .

HEDDA: And we used to sit on the corner sofa.

LÖVBORG: Always with the same illustrated paper in front of us.

HEDDA: Yes, for lack of an album.

LÖVBORG: Yes, Hedda; and when I used to confess to you! Told you things about myself that no one else knew in those days. Sat there and owned up to going about whole days and nights blind drunk. Days and nights on end. Oh, Hedda, what sort of power in you was it—that forced me to confess things like that?

HEDDA: Do you think it was some power in me?

LÖVBORG: Yes, how else can I account for it? And all these—these questions you used to put to me . . . indirectly.

HEDDA: And that you understood so perfectly well.

LÖVBORG: To think you could sit and ask questions like that! Quite frankly.

HEDDA: Indirectly, mind you.

LÖVBORG: Yes, but frankly, all the same. Cross-question me about . . . about all that kind of thing.

HEDDA: And to think that you could answer, Mr Lövborg.

LÖVBORG: Yes, that's just what I can't understand, looking back. But tell me now, Hedda, wasn't it love that was at the bottom of that relationship? Wasn't it, on your side, as though you wanted to purify and absolve me, when I made you my confessor? Wasn't it that?

HEDDA: No, not quite.

LÖVBORG: What made you do it, then?

HEDDA: Do you find it so impossible to understand, that a young girl, when there's an opportunity . . . in secret . . .

LÖVBORG: Well?

HEDDA: That one should want to have a glimpse of a world that . . .

LÖVBORG: That . . . ?

HEDDA: That one isn't allowed to know about?

LÖVBORG: So that was it, then?

HEDDA: That . . . that as well, I rather think.

LÖVBORG: The bond of our common hunger for life. But why couldn't that have gone on, in any case?

HEDDA: That was your own fault.

LÖVBORG: It was you who broke it off.

HEDDA: Yes, when there was imminent danger of our relationship becoming serious. You ought to be ashamed of yourself, Ejlert Lövborg. How could you take advantage of—your unsuspecting comrade!

LÖVBORG: [*Clenching his hands*] Oh, why didn't you make a job of it! Why didn't you shoot me down when you threatened to!

HEDDA: Yes . . . I'm as terrified of scandal as all that.

LÖVBORG: Yes, Hedda; you are a coward at bottom.

HEDDA: An awful coward. [*Changing her tone*] But it was lucky enough for you. And now you have consoled yourself so delightfully up at the Elvsteds'.

LÖVBORG: I know what Thea has told you.

HEDDA: And you have told her something about us two?

LÖVBORG: Not a word. She's too stupid to understand a thing like that.

HEDDA: Stupid?

LÖVBORG: She is stupid about that sort of thing.

HEDDA: And I'm a coward. [*She leans nearer to him, without meeting his eyes, and says more softly*] But now I will confess something to you.

LÖVBORG: [*Eagerly*] Well?

HEDDA: That, my not daring to shoot you down—

LÖVBORG: Yes?

HEDDA: That wasn't my worst piece of cowardice . . . that night.

LÖVBORG: [*Looks at her a moment, understands and whispers passionately*] Ah, Hedda! Hedda Gabler! Now I see a glimpse of the hidden foundation of our comradeship. You and I! Then it *was* your passion for life—

HEDDA: [*Quietly, with a sharp, angry glance*] Take care! Don't assume anything like that.

[*It has begun to get dark. The hall door is opened from outside by* BERTE]

HEDDA: [*Shutting the album with a snap and calling out with a smile*] There you are at last, Thea darling! Come along in!

[MRS ELVSTED *comes in from the hall, dressed for the evening. The door is closed behind her*]

HEDDA: [*On the sofa, stretching her arms towards her*] My precious Thea— you can't think how I've been longing for you to come!

[MRS ELVSTED, *in the meanwhile, exchanges slight greetings with the men in the inner room and then comes across to the table holding her hand out to* HEDDA. EJLERT LÖVBORG *has got up. He and* MRS ELVSTED *greet each other with a silent nod*]

MRS ELVSTED: Oughtn't I to go in and say a word or two to your husband?

HEDDA: Not a bit of it! Let them be. They're going out directly.

MRS ELVSTED: Are they going out?

HEDDA: Yes, they're going to make a night of it.

MRS ELVSTED: [*Quickly, to* LÖVBORG] You're not, are you?

LÖVBORG: No.

HEDDA: Mr Lövborg—is staying here with us.

MRS ELVSTED: [*Takes a chair and is going to sit beside him*] Oh, it *is* nice to be here!

HEDDA: No, no, Thea my child! Not there. You're coming over here, right beside me. I want to be in the middle.

MRS ELVSTED: All right; just as you like. [*She goes round the table and sits on the sofa on* HEDDA's *right.* LÖVBORG *sits down on his chair again*]

LÖVBORG: [*To* HEDDA, *after a little pause*] Isn't she lovely, just to look at?

HEDDA: [*Stroking her hair lightly*] Only to look at?

LÖVBORG: Yes. Because *we* two—she and I—we really *are* comrades. We trust each other absolutely. That's how it is we can sit and talk to each other quite frankly.

HEDDA: Nothing indirect about it, Mr Lövborg?

LÖVBORG: Oh well . . .

MRS ELVSTED: [*Softly, leaning close to* HEDDA] Oh, Hedda, I am so happy! Just think, he says I have inspired him, too!

HEDDA: [*Looking at her with a smile*] He says that, does he?

LÖVBORG: And then she has the courage that leads to action, Mrs Tesman.

MRS ELVSTED: Good gracious! *Me?* Courage?

LÖVBORG: Immense—when her comrade is concerned.

HEDDA: Ah, courage. Yes. If one only had that.

LÖVBORG: What do you mean?

HEDDA: Then perhaps one could even *live* at last. [*Changing her tone suddenly*] But now, Thea, my dear, you must have a nice glass of cold punch.

MRS ELVSTED: No, thank you. I never drink anything like that.

HEDDA: Well you, then, Mr Lövborg.

LÖVBORG: Thank you, I don't either.

MRS ELVSTED: No, he doesn't either.

HEDDA: [*Looking at him steadily*] But suppose I want you to?

LÖVBORG: That wouldn't alter it.

HEDDA: [*Laughing*] So I, poor thing, have no power over you at all?

LÖVBORG: Not where that's concerned.

HEDDA: But, joking apart, I think you ought to, all the same. For your own sake.

MRS ELVSTED: Oh, but, Hedda!

LÖVBORG: How do you mean?

HEDDA: Or, rather, on account of other people.

LÖVBORG: Really?

HEDDA: Otherwise people might easily get the idea that you didn't feel absolutely secure. Not really sure of yourself.

MRS ELVSTED: [*Softly*] Oh no, Hedda!

LÖVBORG: People may think what they like, for the present.

MRS ELVSTED: [*Happily*] Exactly!

HEDDA: I saw it so plainly with Judge Brack just this minute.

LÖVBORG: What did you see?

HEDDA: That contemptuous smile of his when you were afraid to go in there with them.

LÖVBORG: Afraid! Naturally I preferred to stay here and talk to you.

MRS ELVSTED: That was quite understandable, Hedda!

HEDDA: But Judge Brack couldn't be expected to guess that. And I noticed too that he smiled and glanced at my husband when you were afraid to go to this harmless little party with them either.

LÖVBORG: Afraid! Did you say I was afraid?

HEDDA: I don't. But that's how Judge Brack understood it.

LÖVBORG: Let him, then.

HEDDA: So you're not going with them?

LÖVBORG: I am staying here with you and Thea.

MRS ELVSTED: Why, yes, Hedda; of course.

HEDDA: [Smiling and nodding approvingly at LÖVBORG]   There! Quite im- movable. A man of unshakable principles, always. You know, that's what a man should be. [Turning to Mrs Elvsted and patting her] Now, wasn't that what I said, when you came in here this morning in such a state of distraction—

LÖVBORG: [With surprise]   Distraction?

MRS ELVSTED: [In terror]   Hedda! Oh, Hedda!

HEDDA: Now you see for yourself! There's not the slightest need for you to go about in this deadly anxiety—[Breaking off] There! Now we can all three be cheerful.

LÖVBORG: [Who has made a startled gesture]   What on earth is all this, Mrs Tesman?

MRS ELVSTED: Oh heavens, heavens, Hedda! What are you saying? What are you doing?

HEDDA: Keep quiet. That detestable Judge Brack has got his eye on you.

LÖVBORG: So it was deadly anxiety . . . on my behalf.

MRS ELVSTED: [Softly and in misery]   Oh, Hedda! How could you!

LÖVBORG: [Looking intently at her for a moment, his face haggard]   So that was my comrade's absolute faith in me.

MRS ELVSTED: [Beseeching]   Oh, my dear, my dear—you must listen to me before—

LÖVBORG: [Takes one of the filled glasses, lifts it and says softly in a strained *voice*] Your health, Thea! [*He empties his glass, puts it down and takes the other*]

MRS ELVSTED: [*Softly*] Oh, Hedda, Hedda! Did you *want* this to happen?

HEDDA: Want it? I? Are you crazy?

LÖVBORG: And a health to you too, Mrs Tesman. Thank you for the truth. Here's to it. [*He drains his glass and is about to fill it again*]

HEDDA: [*Laying a hand on his arm*] Now, then. No more for the moment. Remember you're going to a party.

MRS ELVSTED: No, no, no!

HEDDA: Hush! They're looking at you.

LÖVBORG: [*Putting down his glass*] Now, Thea, my dear, tell the truth!

MRS ELVSTED: Yes!

LÖVBORG: Did your husband know that you had followed me?

MRS ELVSTED: [*Wringing her hands*] Oh, Hedda! You hear what he's asking me?

LÖVBORG: Was it an understanding between you and him, that you should come to town and spy on me? Perhaps it was he himself who made you do it? Ah yes, no doubt he wanted me in the office again! Or did he miss me at the card-table?

MRS ELVSTED: [*Softly, with a moan*] Oh, Ejlert, Ejlert!

LÖVBORG: [*Seizing a glass and about to fill it*] A health to the old District Magistrate, too!

HEDDA: [*Checking him*] No more now. Remember, you're going out to read your book to my husband.

LÖVBORG: [*Calmly, putting down the glass*] It was stupid of me, Thea, all this. To take it like that, I mean. And don't be angry with me, dear old friend. You shall see, you and the others, that even if I came to grief once, yet . . . Now I'm on my feet again. Thanks to your help, Thea!

MRS ELVSTED: [*Radiant with joy*] Thank heaven!

[BRACK, *in the meantime, has looked at his watch. He and* TESMAN *get up and come into the drawing-room*]

BRACK: [*Getting his hat and overcoat*] Well, Mrs Tesman, our time's up now.

HEDDA: I expect it is.

LÖVBORG: [*Getting up*] Mine too, Mr Brack.

MRS ELVSTED: [*Softly, and imploring*] Oh, Ejlert, don't!

HEDDA: [*Pinching her arm*] They can hear what you're saying.

MRS ELVSTED: [*With a faint cry*] Oh!

LÖVBORG: [*To* BRACK] You were so kind as to ask me to join you.

BRACK: Oh, are you coming, after all?

LÖVBORG: Yes, thank you very much.

BRACK: I'm delighted.

LÖVBORG: [*Putting his parcel in his pocket and speaking to* TESMAN] Because I should like to show you one or two things before I hand it in.

TESMAN: Fancy! That will be jolly. But, Hedda dear, how are you going to get Mrs Elvsted home, eh?

HEDDA: We'll manage that somehow.

LÖVBORG: [*Looking towards the women*] Mrs Elvsted? I'll come back again and fetch her, of course. [*Coming nearer*] Round about ten o'clock, Mrs Tesman? Will that do?

HEDDA: Certainly. That will do beautifully.

TESMAN: Oh well, everything's all right, then. But you mustn't expect *me* as early as that, Hedda.

HEDDA: My dear, stay—as long as ever you like.

MRS ELVSTED: [*In suppressed anxiety*] I shall wait here, then, Mr Lövborg, till you come.

LÖVBORG: [*With his hat in his hand*] All right, Mrs Elvsted.

BRACK: And so the procession starts, gentlemen. I hope we shall have a gay time, as a certain charming lady puts it.

HEDDA: Ah, if only that charming lady could be there, invisible—

BRACK: Why invisible?

HEDDA: So as to hear a little of your gaiety—uncensored, Mr Brack.

BRACK: [*Laughing*] I shouldn't advise the charming lady to try!

TESMAN: [*Laughing, too*] Oh, Hedda, you're simply priceless! Just think!

BRACK: Well, good-bye, good-bye, ladies.

LÖVBORG: [*Taking leave with a bow*] About ten o'clock, then.

[BRACK, LÖVBORG and TESMAN *go out by the hall door. At the same time* BERTE *comes in from the inner room with a lighted lamp, which she puts on the drawing-room table. She goes out again the same way*]

MRS ELVSTED: [*Who has got up and is wandering restlessly about the room*] Hedda, Hedda, where is all this going to end?

HEDDA: Ten o'clock—then he will come. I can see him. With vineleaves in his hair. Flushed and confident.

MRS ELVSTED: Yes, if only it would be like that.

HEDDA: And then, you see, then he'll have got control of himself again. Then he will be a free man for the rest of his days.

MRS ELVSTED: Heavens, yes. If only he would come like that. As you see him.

HEDDA: He'll come like that—'so and no otherwise'. [*Getting up and going nearer*] Go on doubting him as long as you like. I believe in him. And now we'll try . . .

MRS ELVSTED: There's something behind all this, Hedda.

HEDDA: True; there is. I want, for once in my life, to have power over a human being's fate.

MRS ELVSTED: But haven't you got that?

HEDDA: I have not. And never have had.

MRS ELVSTED: Not over your husband's?

HEDDA: That *would* be worth having, wouldn't it? Ah, if you could only realise how poor I am. And here are you, offered such riches! [*Throwing her arms passionately round her*] I think I shall burn your hair off, after all.

MRS ELVSTED: Let go! Let go! I'm frightened of you, Hedda!

BERTE: [*In the doorway between the rooms*] Tea's laid in the dining-room, ma'am.

HEDDA: Good. We're coming.

MRS ELVSTED: No, no, no! I'd rather go home alone. At once!

HEDDA: Nonsense! You must have tea first, you little goose. And then, at ten o'clock, Ejlert Lövborg will come—with vineleaves in his hair.

[*She pulls* MRS ELVSTED, *almost by force, towards the doorway*]

ACT III

The room at the TESMAN'S. *The curtains across the middle doorway are closed and so are those in front of the glass door. The lamp, with its shade on, is burning, turned half-down, on the table. The door of the stove is open and there has been a fire in it, which is now nearly out.*

    MRS ELVSTED, *wrapped up in a large shawl with her feet on a footstool, is close to the stove, lying sunk in the easy-chair. Hedda is lying asleep on the sofa with her clothes on and a rug over her.*

    After a pause, MRS ELVSTED *sits up quickly in her chair and listens intently. Then she sinks back wearily again, crying softly.*

MRS ELVSTED: Not yet! Oh, heavens, heavens! Not yet!

    [BERTE *comes stealing in cautiously by the hall door. She has a letter in her hand*]

MRS ELVSTED: [*Turning and whispering eagerly*] Well? Has anyone come?

BERTE: Yes. A girl's just been with this letter.

MRS ELVSTED: [*Quickly, holding out her hand*] A letter! Give it to me!

BERTE: No, ma'am, it's for the Doctor.

MRS ELVSTED: Oh.

BERTE: It was Miss Tesman's maid who came with it. I'll put it here on the table.

MRS ELVSTED: Yes, do.

BERTE: [*Putting down the letter*] I think I'd better put the lamp out. It's smoking.

MRS ELVSTED: Yes, put it out. It'll very soon be light now.

BERTE: [*Putting it out*] It's quite light, ma'am.

MRS ELVSTED: Why, it's broad daylight! And still not back!

BERTE: Lord bless you, ma'am, I thought this was how it would be.

MRS ELVSTED: You thought so?

BERTE: Yes. When I saw that a certain person had come back to town again, well . . . And when he went off with them . . . One's heard enough about that gentleman before today.

MRS ELVSTED: Don't speak so loud. You'll wake Mrs Tesman.

BERTE: [*Looking towards the sofa and sighing*] Gracious, yes; let her sleep, poor thing. Shall I put a bit more on the fire?

MRS ELVSTED: No, thank you; not for me.

BERTE: Very good. [*She goes out quietly by the hall door*]

HEDDA: [*Waking as the door shuts and looking up*]   What's that?

MRS ELVSTED: It was only the maid.

HEDDA: [*Looking round her*]   In here? Oh yes, I remember now. [*She sits up on the sofa, stretches and rubs her eyes*] What's the time, Thea?

MRS ELVSTED: [*Looking at her watch*]   It's past seven.

HEDDA: What time did my husband come back?

MRS ELVSTED: He isn't back.

HEDDA: He hasn't come home yet?

MRS ELVSTED: [*Getting up*]   No one's come back at all.

HEDDA: And we sat here and kept ourselves awake, waiting up for them till nearly four o'clock!

MRS ELVSTED: [*Wringing her hands*]   And *how* I waited for him!

HEDDA: [*Yawning and speaking with her hand in front of her mouth*]   Ah, well, we might have saved ourselves that trouble.

MRS ELVSTED: Did you get a little sleep afterwards?

HEDDA: Oh yes. I slept quite well, I think. Didn't you?

MRS ELVSTED: Not a wink! I couldn't, Hedda! It was absolutely impossible.

HEDDA: [*Getting up and going across to her*]   There, there, there! There's nothing to worry about. I can see perfectly well what's happened.

MRS ELVSTED: Why, what do you think then? Tell me! Please!

HEDDA: Well, of course they kept things up frightfully late at the Judge's.

MRS ELVSTED: Heavens, yes. They must have done. But, all the same—

HEDDA: And then, you see, my husband didn't like to come home and disturb us by ringing in the middle of the night. [*Laughing*] Perhaps he didn't much care to show himself either—not straight after making a gay night of it.

MRS ELVSTED: But, Hedda dear, where would he have gone?

HEDDA: He's gone up to his aunts', of course, and slept there. They keep his old room ready.

MRS ELVSTED: No, he can't be with them. Because a letter came for him a little while ago from Miss Tesman. There it is.

HEDDA: Really? [*Looking at the address*] Yes. That's certainly from Aunt Julle; it's her handwriting. Well, then, he's stayed on at the Judge's place. And Ejlert Lövborg, he's sitting reading to him—with vineleaves in his hair.

MRS ELVSTED: Oh, Hedda, you're just saying things you don't believe yourself.

HEDDA: You really are a little goose, Thea.

MRS ELVSTED: Well, I suppose I am—worse luck.

HEDDA: And you look simply tired to death.

MRS ELVSTED: Yes, I am tired to death.

HEDDA: Well then, you're going to do as I tell you. You're going into my room and you're going to lie down on the bed for a little while.

MRS ELVSTED: Oh no. I shan't sleep, anyway.

HEDDA: Yes, you *are* to.

MRS ELVSTED: Yes, but surely your husband must be home soon. And then I must find out at once . . .

HEDDA: I'll let you know all right when he comes.

MRS ELVSTED: Well; you promise me, Hedda?

HEDDA: Yes, you can be sure I will. You just go in and go to sleep in the meantime.

MRS ELVSTED: Thank you. I'll try to, then. [*She goes out through the inner room*]

[HEDDA *goes over to the glass door and pulls back the curtains. Broad daylight pours into the room. She takes a small hand-mirror from the writing-table, looks at herself in it and tidies her hair. Then she crosses to the hall door and presses the bell. After a moment* BERTE *comes to the door*]

BERTE: Is there anything you want, ma'am?

HEDDA: Yes, will you make up the fire? I'm simply freezing here.

BERTE: Bless us! I'll have it warm in no time.

[*She rakes the remains of the fire together and puts some wood on*]

BERTE: [*Stopping to listen*] There was a ring at the front door, ma'am.

HEDDA: You go and answer it, then. I'll see to the fire myself.

BERTE: It'll soon burn up. [*She goes out by the hall door*]

[HEDDA *kneels on the footstool and puts some more wood into the* *stove. After a short pause,* JÖRGEN TESMAN *comes in from the hall. He* *looks tired and rather grave. He steals towards the middle doorway on* *tiptoe and is about to slip through the curtains*]

HEDDA: [*At the stove, without looking up*]   Good morning.

TESMAN: [*Turning*]   Hedda! [*Coming towards her*] But what on earth! You up as early as this! Eh?

HEDDA: Yes, I got up very early today.

TESMAN: And I was so certain you were lying asleep still! Just fancy, Hedda!

HEDDA: Don't speak so loudly. Mrs Elvsted is lying down in my room.

TESMAN: Did Mrs Elvsted stay the night here?

HEDDA: Of course. Nobody came to fetch her.

TESMAN: That's true; nobody did.

HEDDA: [*Shutting the door of the stove and getting up*]   Well, did you have a good time at the Judge's?

TESMAN: Have you been worrying about me, eh?

HEDDA: No, that would never occur to me. I was just asking whether you had a good time.

TESMAN: Not bad. It was rather jolly for once. Mostly at the beginning, as far as I was concerned. Because then Ejlert read me some of his book. We got there more than an hour too soon. Just fancy! And Brack had so much to see to. But then Ejlert read to me.

HEDDA: [*Sitting down on the right-hand side of the table*]   Well now, tell me about it.

TESMAN: [*Sitting down on a footstool by the stove*]   My goodness, Hedda! You can't think what a book that's going to be! I should think it's one of the most remarkable things that's ever been written. Just think!

HEDDA: No doubt. That doesn't interest me.

TESMAN: I must admit one thing, Hedda. When he had read it, a perfectly detestable feeling came over me.

HEDDA: Detestable?

TESMAN: There I was *envying* Ejlert for having been able to write a thing like that! Just think, Hedda!

HEDDA: Yes, yes. I am.

TESMAN: And then to know that he, with the gifts he has . . . Yet he's quite irreclaimable. What a tragedy!

HEDDA: You mean, I suppose, that he has more spirit than other people.

TESMAN: Oh no. The point is—there's no moderation in him.

HEDDA: And what happened, then, in the end?

TESMAN: Well, I really think the best way to describe it is an orgy, Hedda.

HEDDA: Did he have vineleaves in his hair?

TESMAN: Vineleaves? No, I didn't notice any. But he made a long, wandering speech in honour of the woman who had inspired him in his work. Well, that was how he put it.

HEDDA: Did he say who she was?

TESMAN: No, he didn't do that. But I can't imagine it could be anybody but Mrs Elvsted. You watch!

HEDDA: Oh, well. . . . Where did you part from him, then?

TESMAN: On the way back. We broke up—the last of us—at the same time. And Brack came along with us to get a breath of fresh air. And so, you see, we agreed to see Ejlert home. Because, to tell the truth, he'd had far more than he could carry.

HEDDA: I can quite imagine that.

TESMAN: But here's the extraordinary part of it, Hedda. Or rather, the sad part of it, I ought to say. I—I'm almost ashamed to tell you, for Ejlert's sake.

HEDDA: Oh, go on! So—?

TESMAN: Well, as we were on the way back, you see, I happened to be a little behind the others. Only for a minute or two. You see?

HEDDA: Yes, yes. But what then?

TESMAN: And then, as I was hurrying to catch them up, what do you think I found by the roadside. Eh?

HEDDA: No, how could I know?

TESMAN: Don't say anything about it to anyone, Hedda. You understand. Promise me, for Ejlert's sake. [*Taking a paper parcel out of his coat pocket*] Just think! I found this.

HEDDA: Isn't that the parcel he had with him yesterday?

TESMAN: It is. It's the whole of that precious, irreplaceable manuscript of his. And that's what he'd gone and lost, without noticing it. Just think, Hedda! Such a sad—

HEDDA: But why didn't you give the packet back to him at once, then?

TESMAN: Well, I didn't dare to. Not in the state he was in.

HEDDA: Didn't you tell any of the others you'd found it, either?

TESMAN: Certainly not. I didn't want to do that for Ejlert's sake, you know.

HEDDA: Then there's no one who knows you've got Ejlert Lövborg's manuscript?

TESMAN: No. And no one must find out, either.

HEDDA: What did you talk to him about afterwards, then?

TESMAN: I didn't get a chance to talk to him again, you see. Because when we got into the streets, he and two or three others got away from us. Just think!

HEDDA: Oh? They must have seen him home, then.

TESMAN: Yes, it looks as if they had. And Brack went off, too.

HEDDA: And where ever have you been since?

TESMAN: Well, I and some of the others went on home with one of the gay lads and had morning coffee at his place. Or night coffee, it would be better to call it. Eh? But as soon as I've had a moment's rest—and when I think Ejlert's slept it off, poor fellow—I must go over to him with this.

HEDDA: [*Holding out her hand for the package*]   No, don't give it up! Not directly, I mean. Let me read it first.

TESMAN: Oh, Hedda, my dear, I couldn't do that. I really couldn't.

HEDDA: You couldn't?

TESMAN: No. You can just imagine how frantic he will be when he wakes up and misses the manuscript. Because he's got no copy of it, you realise! He said so himself.

HEDDA: [*Looking searchingly at him*]   Can't a thing like that be written again, then? Re-written?

TESMAN: No, I don't think that would ever work. It's a matter of inspiration, you know.

HEDDA: Yes, of course. I suppose that's it. [*Casually*] Oh, by the way, there's a letter for you here.

TESMAN: Really?

HEDDA: [*Passing it to him*]   It came early this morning.

TESMAN: Why, it's from Aunt Julle! [*He puts down the paper package on the other footstool, opens the letter, runs through it and jumps up*] Oh, Hedda! She says poor Aunt Rina's dying.

HEDDA: Well, that was to be expected.

TESMAN: And that if I want to see her again I must be quick. I'll run across there at once.

HEDDA: [*Checking a smile*]   Run?

TESMAN: Oh, Hedda dear, if only you could bring yourself to come along, too! Just think!

HEDDA: [*Getting up and dismissing the matter wearily*]   No, no. Don't ask me to do things like that. I don't want to think of illness or death. You mustn't ask me to have anything to do with ugly things.

TESMAN: Oh well, then. [*Bustling about*] My hat? My overcoat? Oh yes; in the hall. Oh, I do so hope I'm not going to be too late, Hedda! Eh?

[BERTE *comes to the hall door*]

BERTE: Judge Brack's outside, asking can he come in?

TESMAN: At this moment! No, I really can't see him now.

HEDDA: But I can. [*To* BERTE] Ask the Judge to come in. [BERTE *goes out*]

HEDDA: [*Quickly, in a whisper*]   The parcel! [*She snatches it from the stool*]

TESMAN: Yes, give it to me!

HEDDA: No, no. I'll keep it for you till you get back.

[*She crosses to the writing-table and puts it in the bookcase.* TESMAN *is in such a hurry that he cannot get his gloves on.* BRACK *comes in from the hall*]

HEDDA: [*Nodding to him*]   Well, you are an early bird.

BRACK: Yes, don't you think so? [*To* TESMAN] Are you going out, too?

TESMAN: Yes, I simply must go and see the Aunts. Just think, the invalid one, she's dying, poor thing.

BRACK: Dear, dear! Is she? Then you certainly mustn't let me keep you. At such a serious moment—

TESMAN: Yes, I really must be off. Good-bye, good-bye! [*He hurries out through the hall door*]

HEDDA: [*Coming nearer to* BRACK] It seems to have been rather more than 'gay' at your place last night, Mr Brack.

BRACK: So much so that I haven't had my clothes off, Madam Hedda.

HEDDA: Not you either?

BRACK: No, as you see. Well, what has Tesman been telling you about the night's adventures?

HEDDA: Oh, just a dull story. That they'd gone and had coffee somewhere.

BRACK: I know all about that coffee-party. Ejlert Lövborg wasn't with them, I think?

HEDDA: No, they'd seen him home before that.

BRACK: Tesman, too?

HEDDA: No; but some of the others, he said.

BRACK: [*Smiling*] Jörgen Tesman really is a simple soul, Madam Hedda.

HEDDA: Heaven knows he is. Is there something behind this, then?

BRACK: Yes. It's no good denying . . .

HEDDA: Well, then, let's sit down, my friend. Then you can tell your story.

[*She sits down on the left of the table, with* BRACK *at the long side, near her*]

HEDDA: Well, now?

BRACK: I had good reasons for keeping track of my guests last night—or rather, of some of my guests.

HEDDA: And I suppose Ejlert Lövborg was one of them.

BRACK: I must admit he was.

HEDDA: Now you are making me really curious.

BRACK: Do you know where he and a few others spent the rest of the night, Madam Hedda?

HEDDA: If it's the sort of thing that can be told, tell me.

BRACK: Oh yes, it can be told all right. Well, they fetched up at an extremely lively party.

HEDDA: Of the 'gay' kind?

BRACK: Of the very gayest.

HEDDA: Go on, please. I want to hear some more.

BRACK: Lövborg had had an invitation beforehand as well. I knew all about that. But he'd refused to go then, because he's turned over a new leaf now—as you know.

HEDDA: Up at the Elvsteds'. Yes. But he went, then, all the same?

BRACK: Yes. You see, Madam Hedda, unfortunately the inspiration took him at my place last night.

HEDDA: Yes, I gather he found inspiration there.

BRACK: Pretty violent inspiration. Anyway, he changed his mind, I imagine. For we men are unfortunately not always so firm in our principles as we ought to be.

HEDDA: Oh, I am sure you are an exception, Mr. Brack. But what about Lövborg?

BRACK: Well, to be brief, the end of it was that he fetched up at Mademoiselle Diana's rooms.

HEDDA: Mademoiselle Diana's?

BRACK: It was Mademoiselle Diana who was giving the party. For a select circle of her lady friends and admirers.

HEDDA: Is she a red-haired woman?

BRACK: Precisely.

HEDDA: Some kind of a—singer?

BRACK: Yes, among other things. And, moreover, a mighty huntress—of men, Madam Hedda. You must have heard her spoken of. Ejlert Lövborg was one of her warmest supporters, in his hey-day.

HEDDA: And how did all this end?

BRACK: On a less friendly note, it would appear. Mademoiselle Diana seems to have changed from a most tender reception to downright violence.

HEDDA: To Lövborg?

BRACK: Yes. He accused her or her friends of having robbed him. He declared his pocket-book had gone. And other things, too. In fact, he seems to have made an appalling scene.

HEDDA: And what was the result?

BRACK: The result was a general fight, in which both the ladies and the gentlemen were involved. Luckily the police arrived in the end.

HEDDA: The police, too?

BRACK: Yes. But it looks like being a costly game for Ejlert Lövborg, the crazy fool.

HEDDA: Really?

BRACK: He appears to have put up a violent resistance, and hit one of the constables on the head and torn his coat to pieces. So he had to go to the police station too.

HEDDA: How do you know all this?

BRACK: From the police themselves.

HEDDA: [*Gazing in front of her*] So that's how it was? Then he had no vineleaves in his hair.

BRACK: Vineleaves, Madam Hedda?

HEDDA: [*Changing her tone*] But tell me, now. What's your real reason for following up Ejlert Lövborg's movements like this?

BRACK: Well, it obviously can't be a matter of complete indifference to me, if it comes out at the trial that he had come straight from my place.

HEDDA: Will there be a trial too, then?

BRACK: Of course. However, that might pass. . . . But, as a friend of the house, I felt bound to give you and Tesman a full account of his night's exploits.

HEDDA: And why, Mr Brack?

BRACK: Well, because I have a shrewd misgiving that he means to use you as a kind of screen.

HEDDA: Why, how can you imagine such a thing?

BRACK: Good Lord, we're not blind, Madam Hedda! You watch. This Mrs Elvsted, she won't be leaving town again in a hurry.

HEDDA: Well, even supposing there is something between them, there must be plenty of other places where they can meet.

BRACK: No other home. Every decent house will be closed again to Ejlert Lövborg from now onwards.

HEDDA: And so ought mine to be, you mean?

BRACK: Yes. I admit it would be extremely unpleasant to me if this man were on a firm footing here. If he were to force his way in, superfluous and an intruder, into—

HEDDA: Into the triangle?

BRACK: Precisely. It would simply amount to my finding myself without a home.

HEDDA: [*Looking at him with a smile*]   Ah yes. The only cock in the yard. That's your idea.

BRACK: [*Nodding slowly and dropping his voice*]   Yes, that is my idea. And I'll fight for that idea with all the means at my command.

HEDDA: [*Her smile dying away*]   You are really a dangerous person, when it comes to the point.

BRACK: Do you think so?

HEDDA: Yes, I am beginning to think so now. I'm heartily thankful you've no hold or power over me—and I hope you never will.

BRACK: [*Laughing equivocally*]   Well, well, Madam Hedda. You may be right there. Who knows what I mightn't prove capable of in that case?

HEDDA: Now look here, Mr Brack. That sounds almost as though you were threatening me.

BRACK: [*Getting up*]   Oh, far from it! The triangle, you see, is best formed and maintained by free consent.

HEDDA: That's what I think, too.

BRACK: Yes. Well, now I've said what I wanted to and I must see about getting home again. Good-bye, Madam Hedda. [*He goes towards the glass door*]

HEDDA: [*Getting up*]   Are you going through the garden?

BRACK: Yes, it's shorter for me.

HEDDA: Yes, and what's more, it's a back way.

BRACK: Quite true. I have nothing against back ways. They can be quite attractive at times.

HEDDA: When someone's practising shooting, do you mean?

BRACK: [*At the door, laughing to her*]   Oh, I don't think people shoot their farmyard cocks.

HEDDA: [*Laughing, too*]   No, not when one has only the one.

[*They nod good-bye to each other, laughing. He goes out. She shuts the door after him.*

HEDDA *stands a moment, serious now, and looks out. Then she goes across and peeps in through the curtains over the middle doorway and then goes to the writing-table, takes the packet out of the bookcase and is just going to look through it when* BERTE'S *voice is heard, speaking loudly, in the hall.* HEDDA *turns and listens, then quickly locks the package in the drawer and puts the key on the inkstand.*

EJLERT LÖVBORG, *with his overcoat on and his hat in his hand, flings open the hall door. He looks disturbed and excited*]

LÖVBORG: [*Speaking towards the hall*] And I tell you I must go in and I will. There now!

[*He shuts the door, turns, sees* HEDDA, *controls himself at once and bows*]

HEDDA: [*At the writing-table*] Well, Mr Lövborg, it's rather late to come and fetch Thea.

LÖVBORG: Or rather early to come and call on you. I apologise.

HEDDA: How do you know that she is still with me?

LÖVBORG: They said at her lodgings that she had been out all night.

HEDDA: [*Going to the centre table*] Did you notice anything about the people, when they said that?

LÖVBORG: [*Looking at her enquiringly*] Notice anything about them?

HEDDA: I mean, did it look as if they were drawing their own conclusions?

LÖVBORG: [*Understanding suddenly*] Oh yes, of course; that's true. I am dragging her down with me. Actually, though, I didn't notice anything. Tesman isn't up yet?

HEDDA: No, I don't think so.

LÖVBORG: When did he get home?

HEDDA: Pretty late.

LÖVBORG: Did he tell you anything?

HEDDA: Yes, I gathered that things had been very merry at Judge Brack's.

LÖVBORG: Nothing more?

HEDDA: No, I don't think so. But anyhow, I was so terribly sleepy—

[MRS ELVSTED *comes in through the curtains in the middle doorway*]

MRS ELVSTED: [*Going towards him*] Oh, Ejlert! At last!

LÖVBORG: Yes, at last. And too late.

MRS ELVSTED: [*Looking anxiously at him*] What is too late?

LÖVBORG: Everything's too late now. It's all up with me.

MRS ELVSTED: No, no! Don't say that!

LÖVBORG: You'll say so yourself when you hear.

MRS ELVSTED: I won't hear anything.

HEDDA: Perhaps you'd rather talk to her alone? If so, I'll go.

LÖVBORG: No, you stay too, please. I beg you to.

MRS ELVSTED: Yes, but I won't hear anything, I tell you.

LÖVBORG: It's not last night's escapades I want to talk about.

MRS ELVSTED: What is it, then?

LÖVBORG: Just this: our ways must part now.

MRS ELVSTED: Part?

HEDDA: [*Involuntarily*]   I knew it!

LÖVBORG: Because I don't need you any more, Thea.

MRS ELVSTED: And you can stand here and say that! Not need me any more!
I can still help you, can't I, as I did before? Surely we are going on working together?

LÖVBORG: I don't propose to work in future.

MRS ELVSTED: [*In despair*]   What shall I do with my life, then?

LÖVBORG: You must try to go on living as though you had never known me.

MRS ELVSTED: But I *can't* do that!

LÖVBORG: Try to, Thea. You must go home again—

MRS ELVSTED: [*Protesting fiercely*]   Never in this life! Where you are, there
will I be too. I won't let myself be driven away like this. I will stay here
and be with you when the book comes out.

HEDDA: [*Half audibly, in suspense*]   Ah, the book, of course!

LÖVBORG: [*Looking at her*]   My book and Thea's. For that is what it is.

MRS ELVSTED: Yes, that's what I feel it is. And that's why I have the right
to be with you when it comes out. I want to see respect and honour
showered on you again. And the joy—I want to share the joy with you.

LÖVBORG: Thea, our book will never come out.

HEDDA: Ah!

MRS ELVSTED: Never come out!

LÖVBORG: *Can't* ever come out.

MRS ELVSTED: [*In agonised foreboding*] Ejlert, what have you done with the manuscript?

HEDDA: [*Looking intently at him*] Yes, the manuscript?

MRS ELVSTED: Where is it?

LÖVBORG: You'd better not ask me, Thea.

MRS ELVSTED: But I want to know. I've a right to know, at once.

LÖVBORG: The manuscript . . . oh well, then . . . I have torn the manuscript into a thousand pieces.

MRS ELVSTED: [*Shrieking*] Oh no, no!

HEDDA: [*Involuntarily*] But that's not—!

LÖVBORG: [*Looking at her*] Not true, you think?

HEDDA: [*Controlling herself*] I suppose it is, of course. If you say so yourself. . . . But it sounded so fantastic.

LÖVBORG: True, all the same.

MRS ELVSTED: [*Wringing her hands*] Oh, heavens, heavens, Hedda! Torn his own work to pieces!

LÖVBORG: I have torn my own life to pieces. So I might as well tear up my life's work, too.

MRS ELVSTED: And you did it last night, then?

LÖVBORG: Yes, I tell you. Into a thousand pieces. And scattered them out in the fjord. Far out. There at least there is clean sea water. Let them drift in it. Drift with the wind and the tides. And, after a time, they will sink. Deeper and deeper. As I shall, Thea.

MRS ELVSTED: Do you know, Ejlert, this, what you have done to the book— all my life, it will seem to me as if you had killed a little child.

LÖVBORG: You are right. It is like murdering a child.

MRS ELVSTED: But how could you? After all, I had a share in the child, too.

HEDDA: [*Scarcely audible*] Ah, the child. . . .

MRS ELVSTED: [*With a gasp*] It's all over, then. Well, well. I'll go now, Hedda.

HEDDA: But you're not going to leave town?

MRS ELVSTED: Oh, I don't know myself what I'm going to do. Everything is dark ahead of me now.

> [*She goes out by the hall door*]

HEDDA: [*Standing and waiting for a moment*]   So you are not going to see her home, Mr Lövborg?

LÖVBORG: I? Through the streets? Suppose people were to see her walking with me?

HEDDA: Of course, I don't know what else happened to you last night. But is it something so absolutely irreparable?

LÖVBORG: It won't stop at last night only. I know that well enough. But, the point is, I don't *want* to live that kind of life. I don't want to start again, any more, now. It is the courage to live, and to challenge life, that she has broken in me.

HEDDA: [*Looking straight before her*]   That pretty little fool has played her part in a human being's fate. [*Looking at him*] Still, how could you treat her so callously, all the same?

LÖVBORG: Oh, don't say it was callous!

HEDDA: To go and destroy what has filled her soul all this long, long time! You don't call that callous?

LÖVBORG: I can tell you the truth, Hedda.

HEDDA: The truth?

LÖVBORG: Promise me first, give me your word, that Thea shall never know what I tell you.

HEDDA: You have my word for it.

LÖVBORG: Good. Then I will tell you that that was not the truth—the story I told you just now.

HEDDA: About the manuscript?

LÖVBORG: Yes. I didn't tear it to pieces. Nor throw it into the fjord, either.

HEDDA: Well, but—where is it, then?

LÖVBORG: I have destroyed it just the same. Utterly and completely, Hedda.

HEDDA: I don't understand all this.

LÖVBORG: Thea said that what I had done was as good as child-murder to her.

HEDDA: Yes. That's what she said.

LÖVBORG: But that—killing his child—is not the worst thing a father can do to it.

HEDDA: *That's* not the worst?

LÖVBORG: No. It was that worst thing that I wanted to save Thea from hearing.

HEDDA: And what is that worst thing, then?

LÖVBORG: Suppose now, Hedda, that a man, along towards morning, say, after a wild, riotous night, came home to his child's mother and said: Look here. I have been here and there, in such-and-such places. And I took the child with me. In such-and-such places. And I lost the child. Lost it completely. The devil knows what hands it's fallen into, who's got it in his clutches.

HEDDA: Oh but, when all's said and done, this—well, this was only a book.

LÖVBORG: Thea's whole soul was in that book.

HEDDA: Yes, I understand that.

LÖVBORG: And so you understand also that there is no future before us, her and me.

HEDDA: And what are you going to do, then?

LÖVBORG: Nothing. Only make an end of the whole business. The sooner the better.

HEDDA: [*A step nearer*] Ejlert Lövborg, listen to me. Could you not see to it that—that it is done beautifully?

LÖVBORG: Beautifully? [*Smiling*] With vineleaves in the hair, as you used to imagine once upon a time—

HEDDA: Ah, not vineleaves. I don't believe in that any more. But beautifully, nevertheless. For once. Good-bye. You must go now, and not come here again.

LÖVBORG: Good-bye, Madam. Remember me to Jörgen Tesman. [*About to go*]

HEDDA: Wait a minute. You shall have a souvenir to take with you.

[*She goes to the writing-table and opens the drawer and the pistol-case. She comes back to* LÖVBORG *again with one of the pistols*]

LÖVBORG: [*Looking at her*] Is *that* the souvenir?

HEDDA: [*Nodding slowly*] Do you recognise it? It was aimed at you once.

LÖVBORG: You should have used it then.

HEDDA: There it is. Use it yourself now.

LÖVBORG: [*Putting the pistol in his breast pocket*]   Thanks.

HEDDA: And beautifully, Ejlert Lövborg. Promise me that.

LÖVBORG: Good-bye, Hedda Gabler. [*He goes out by the hall door*]

[HEDDA *listens a moment at the door. Then she goes across to the writing-table and takes out the manuscript in its package. She glances inside the wrapper, pulls some of the sheets half out and looks at them. Then she goes across and sits down in the easy-chair by the stove with the packet in her lap. After a moment, she opens the stove-door and then the packet*]

HEDDA: [*Throwing some of the leaves into the fire and whispering to herself*] Now I am burning your child, Thea. You, with your curly hair. [*Throwing a few more leaves into the stove*] Your child and Ejlert Lövborg's. [*Throwing in the rest*] I'm burning it—burning your child.

ACT IV

The same rooms at the TESMANS' *house. Evening. The drawing-room is in darkness. The inner room is lighted by the hanging lamp over the table. The curtains are drawn across the glass door.*

HEDDA, *dressed in black, is walking to and fro in the dark room. Then she goes into the inner room and away to the left side. A few chords on the piano are heard. Then she comes back again and into the drawing-room.*

BERTE *comes in from the right through the inner room with a lighted lamp, which she puts on the table in front of the corner sofa in the drawing-room. Her eyes are red with crying and she has black ribbons in her cap. She goes quietly and discreetly out to the right.* HEDDA *goes across to the glass door, draws the curtain aside a little and looks out into the darkness.*

Soon after, MISS TESMAN *comes in from the hall door, dressed in mourning, with a hat and veil.* HEDDA *goes towards her and holds out her hand.*

MISS TESMAN: Yes, Hedda, here I am dressed in mourning. Because now my poor sister's trials are over at last.

HEDDA: I have heard already, as you see. My husband sent a note out to me.

MISS TESMAN: Yes, he promised he would. But I thought all the same, that to Hedda—here, in the house of the living—I ought myself to bring the news of her death.

HEDDA: It was very kind of you.

MISS TESMAN: Ah, Rina should not have died at such a moment. Hedda's home ought not to be sad just now.

HEDDA: [*Changing the subject*]   She died very peacefully, didn't she, Miss Tesman?

MISS TESMAN: Ah, it was such a beautiful, peaceful release! And then she had the unspeakable happiness of seeing Jörgen once more, so that she was really able to say good-bye to him. Perhaps he hasn't come back yet?

HEDDA: No. He wrote that I mustn't expect him just yet. But do sit down.

MISS TESMAN: No, thank you, my dear, precious Hedda. I should like to, but I have so little time. She must be prepared and made ready as well as I can. She shall go into her grave looking beautiful.

HEDDA: Can't I help you with anything?

MISS TESMAN: Oh, don't think of that! Hedda Tesman mustn't do that kind of thing. Nor dwell on the thought, either. Not at such a time. Certainly not.

HEDDA: Ah, thoughts . . . they are not so easily mastered.

MISS TESMAN: [*Going on*]   Well, bless us. That's how things go in this world. At home we shall be sewing for Rina. And there will be sewing to be done here too, I think, soon. But that will be a different kind, thank God!

[JÖRGEN TESMAN *comes in by the hall door*]

HEDDA: Ah, it's a good thing you're back at last.

TESMAN: Are you here, Aunt Julle? With Hedda? Fancy!

MISS TESMAN: I was just going again, dear boy. Well, did you see to all those things you promised to do?

TESMAN: No, I'm really afraid I've forgotten half of them, you know. I must run in and see you again tomorrow. My head is so muddled today. I can't keep my ideas together.

MISS TESMAN: But, my dear Jörgen. You mustn't take it like this.

TESMAN: No? How, then . . . do you think?

MISS TESMAN: You must be glad in your grief. Glad of what has happened. As I am.

TESMAN: Oh yes, yes. You are thinking of Aunt Rina, of course.

HEDDA: It will be lonely for you now, Miss Tesman.

MISS TESMAN: Just at first, yes. But that won't last very long, I hope. Dear Rina's little room won't stand empty, I know.

TESMAN: Really? Who do you want to take it? Eh?

MISS TESMAN: Oh, there is always some poor sick person or other who needs care and attention, unfortunately.

HEDDA: Do you really want to take a burden like that on you again?

MISS TESMAN: Burden! God forgive you, my child. It has never been a burden to me.

HEDDA: But if a strange person is going to come, why—

MISS TESMAN: Oh, one soon makes friends with sick folk. And I sadly need someone to live for—I, too. Well, thank God there may be things here, too, of one sort and another, that an old aunt can lend a hand with.

HEDDA: Oh, don't bother about things here—

TESMAN: Just think how happy we three could be together, if—

HEDDA: If—?

TESMAN: [Uneasily]   Oh, nothing. It'll all come right. Let's hope so. Eh?

MISS TESMAN: Well, well. You two have plenty to talk to each other about, I expect. [Smiling.] And perhaps Hedda has something to tell you too, Jörgen. Good-bye. Now I must go home to Rina. [Turning at the door.] Dear, dear, how strange it is to think of! Now Rina is with me and with our dear Jochum, too.

TESMAN: Yes, to think of it, Aunt Julle! Eh?

[MISS TESMAN goes out by the hall door]

HEDDA: [Her eyes, cold and searching, following TESMAN]   I almost think the death has affected you more than it has her.

TESMAN: Oh, it's not only Aunt Rina's death. It's Ejlert; I'm so worried about him.

HEDDA: [Quickly]   Has anything fresh happened to him?

TESMAN: I meant to have run over to him this afternoon and told him that his manuscript was in safe keeping.

HEDDA: Well, didn't you find him, then?

TESMAN: No, he wasn't at home. But afterwards I met Mrs Elvsted, and she told me he had been here early this morning.

HEDDA: Yes, directly you'd gone.

TESMAN: And he seems to have said that he had torn up the manuscript. Eh?

HEDDA: Yes, he insisted he had.

TESMAN: But, good heavens, he must have been absolutely off his head! And so, of course, you didn't dare give it back to him, Hedda?

HEDDA: No, he didn't take it.

TESMAN: But you told him, all right, that we had it?

HEDDA: No. [*Quickly*] Did you tell Mrs Elvsted we had?

TESMAN: No, I didn't quite like to do that. But you ought to have told him himself. Suppose he goes off in despair and does himself some injury? Let me have the manuscript, Hedda. I will dash over to him with it at once. Where is the parcel?

HEDDA: [*Cold and immovable, leaning against the easy-chair*] I haven't got it any longer.

TESMAN: You haven't got it? What on earth do you mean by that?

HEDDA: I have burnt it. Every scrap of it.

TESMAN: [*With a start of terror*] Burnt it! Burnt Ejlert Lövborg's manuscript!

HEDDA: Don't scream like that. The maid might hear you.

TESMAN: Burnt! But, good God! No, no, no! This is simply impossible!

HEDDA: Well, it's true, all the same.

TESMAN: But do you realise what you have done, Hedda? It's against the law, to treat lost property like that! Think of it! You just ask Judge Brack and he'll tell you.

HEDDA: I shouldn't advise you to talk about it either to the Judge or to anyone else.

TESMAN: But how could you go and do anything so unheard of? How could such an idea come into your head? How could it come over you? Tell me that. Eh?

HEDDA: [*Suppressing a scarcely perceptible smile*] I did it for your sake, Jörgen.

TESMAN: For my sake!

HEDDA: When you came home in the morning and told me that he'd been reading to you—

TESMAN: Yes, yes, what about it?

HEDDA: You admitted then that you envied him his work.

TESMAN: Good heavens, I didn't mean it literally!

HEDDA: All the same, I couldn't bear the thought of someone else throwing you into the shade.

TESMAN: [*In an outburst of mingled doubt and joy*] Hedda! Is it true what you're saying? Yes, but . . . but . . . I've never known you show your affection in this sort of way before.

HEDDA: Oh well, you'd better know, then, that—just at present—[*Breaking off, violently*] No, you can go and ask Aunt Julle. She'll tell you about it.

TESMAN: Ah, I rather think I understand, Hedda! [*Clasping his hands together*] Good heavens! Can it be possible? Eh?

HEDDA: Don't shout so. The maid might hear you.

TESMAN: [*Laughing, beside himself with joy*] The maid! No, you really are priceless, Hedda! 'The maid'! Why, it's only Berte! I'll go out and tell Berte myself.

HEDDA: [*Clenching her hands in desperation*] Oh, it'll be the death of me. It'll be the death of me, all this!

TESMAN: What will, Hedda? Eh?

HEDDA: [*Cold and controlled*] All this grotesque nonsense, Jörgen.

TESMAN: Nonsense! That I'm so delighted? But, all the same . . . perhaps I had better not say anything to Berte.

HEDDA: Oh yes, why not that, too?

TESMAN: No, no, not yet. But Aunt Julle must certainly know about it. And then, too, that you are beginning to call me Jörgen! Think of it! Oh, Aunt Julle *will* be so glad! So glad!

HEDDA: When she hears that I have burnt Ejlert Lövborg's manuscript, for your sake?

TESMAN: No, that reminds me. That business with the manuscript—no one must get to know about that, of course. But that you feel like this towards me, Hedda, Aunt Julle must certainly hear that! Still, my dear, I should like to know myself whether this kind of thing is usual with young wives. Eh?

HEDDA: You'd better ask Aunt Julle about that, too, I think.

TESMAN: Yes, I certainly will some time. [*Looking worried and dubious again*]

But . . . but that manuscript. Oh heavens, it's dreadful to think of poor Ejlert, all the same!

[MRS ELVSTED, *dressed as on her first visit, with her hat and outdoor clothes, comes in by the hall door.*]

MRS ELVSTED: [*Greeting them quickly and speaking in agitation*] Oh, Hedda, dear, I hope you won't mind my coming again?

HEDDA: What's the matter, Thea?

TESMAN: Is it something to do with Ejlert Lövborg again? Eh?

MRS ELVSTED: Yes, I'm so terribly afraid some accident has happened to him.

HEDDA: [*Seizing her by the arm*] Ah—do you think so?

TESMAN: Bless me, whatever makes you think that, Mrs Elvsted?

MRS ELVSTED: Why, because I heard them talking about him at the boarding-house, just as I came in. Oh, there are the most incredible rumours about him in town today!

TESMAN: Yes, do you know, I heard that too. Yet I could swear that he went straight home to bed. Just fancy!

HEDDA: Well, what did they say at the boarding-house?

MRS ELVSTED: I didn't gather anything definite. Either they didn't know very much or . . . They stopped talking when they saw me. And as for asking—I didn't dare do that.

TESMAN: [*Walking about restlessly*] We'll hope—we'll hope you misunderstood them, Mrs Elvsted.

MRS ELVSTED: No, no, I am certain it was he they were talking about. And, as I heard it, they said something about the hospital, or—

TESMAN: The hospital!

HEDDA: No! That can't be true.

MRS ELVSTED: Oh, I was so dreadfully frightened about him. So I went to his lodgings and asked for him there.

HEDDA: Could you bring yourself to do that, Thea?

MRS ELVSTED: Yes, what else was I to do? I didn't feel as if I could bear the uncertainty any longer.

TESMAN: But you didn't find him either, did you? Eh?

MRS ELVSTED: No. And the people didn't know anything about him. They said he hadn't been home since yesterday afternoon.

TESMAN: Yesterday! Fancy their saying that!

MRS ELVSTED: Oh, I think there's only one explanation—something dreadful must have happened to him!

TESMAN: Hedda, my dear, suppose I were to go in and make some enquiries?

HEDDA: No. Don't mix yourself up in this business.

[BRACK, *with his hat in his hand, comes in by the hall door, which* BERTE *opens and shuts after him. He looks grave and bows silently.*]

TESMAN: Oh, it's you, my dear Judge? Eh?

BRACK: Yes, it was imperative for me to see you this evening.

TESMAN: I can see that you have had Aunt Julle's news.

BRACK: Yes, I have heard that, too.

TESMAN: Isn't it sad? Eh?

BRACK: Well, my dear Tesman, it depends how you look at it.

TESMAN: [*Looking doubtfully at him*] Has anything else happened?

BRACK: Yes, something else.

HEDDA: [*In suspense*] Anything sad, Mr Brack?

BRACK: That, too, depends on how you look at it, Mrs Tesman.

MRS ELVSTED: [*Breaking out, involuntarily*] Oh, it's something about Ejlert Lövborg!

BRACK: [*Glancing at her*] What makes you think that, Madam? Do you happen to know anything already?

MRS ELVSTED: [*Confused*] No, no; not at all! But—

TESMAN: But, good heavens, man, tell us!

BRACK: [*Shrugging his shoulders*] Well, I'm sorry to say Ejlert Lövborg has been taken to the hospital. As a matter of fact, he's dying.

MRS ELVSTED: [*Crying out*] My God! My God!

TESMAN: In hospital? And dying?

HEDDA: [*Involuntarily*] So quickly, then!

MRS ELVSTED: [*Wailing*] And we parted in anger, Hedda!

HEDDA: [*Whispering*]   Come now, Thea! *Thea!*

MRS ELVSTED: [*Without taking any notice*]   I must go to him! I must see him alive!

BRACK: It won't be any use, my dear lady. Nobody's allowed to see him.

MRS ELVSTED: Well, at least tell me what's happened to him. What is the matter?

TESMAN: Why, surely he never did it himself! Eh?

HEDDA: I'm sure he *did*.

TESMAN: Hedda, how can you?

BRACK: [*With his eyes fixed steadily on her*]   Unfortunately, you have guessed quite right, Mrs Tesman.

MRS ELVSTED: Oh, how terrible!

TESMAN: So he did it himself! Think of it!

HEDDA: Shot himself!

BRACK: Rightly guessed again, Mrs Tesman.

MRS ELVSTED: [*Trying to control herself*]   When did it happen, Mr Brack?

BRACK: This afternoon. Between three and four.

TESMAN: But, dear, dear—where did he do it, then? Eh?

BRACK: [*A little uncertainly*]   Where? Why, I suppose at his lodgings.

MRS ELVSTED: No, that can't be right. Because I was there between six and seven.

BRACK: Well, somewhere else, then. I don't exactly know; I only know that he was found. . . . He had shot himself in the chest.

MRS ELVSTED: Oh, how dreadful to think of! That he should end like this.

HEDDA: [*To* BRACK]   Was it in the chest?

BRACK: Yes, as I said.

HEDDA: Not in the temple, then?

BRACK: In the chest, Mrs Tesman.

HEDDA: Yes, well . . . the chest is a good place, too.

BRACK: How do you mean, Mrs Tesman?

HEDDA: [*Evasively*]   Oh, nothing—nothing.

TESMAN: And the wound is dangerous, you say? Eh?

BRACK: The wound is absolutely fatal. Most likely it's all over already.

MRS ELVSTED: Yes, yes, I feel sure it is. It is all over! All over! Oh, Hedda!

TESMAN: But tell me, how did you find out all this?

BRACK: [Shortly]   From one of the police. Whom I had occasion to speak to.

HEDDA: [In a ringing voice]   Something done, at last!

TESMAN: [Horrified]   Good heavens! What are you saying, Hedda?

HEDDA: That there is an element of beauty in this.

BRACK: Hm. Mrs Tesman—

TESMAN: Of beauty! Fancy that!

MRS ELVSTED: Oh, Hedda, how can you talk of beauty in a thing like that!

HEDDA: Ejlert Lövborg has balanced his account with himself. He has had the courage to do . . . what had to be done.

MRS ELVSTED: No, don't ever believe that it happened in that way. What he has done was done in a moment of madness.

TESMAN: Done in despair.

HEDDA: It was not. Of that I am certain.

MRS ELVSTED: Yes, it was. In a moment of madness. Just as when he tore up our manuscript.

BRACK: [In surprise]   Manuscript? The book, do you mean? Has he torn that up?

MRS ELVSTED: Yes, he did it last night.

TESMAN: [Whispering softly]   Oh, Hedda, we shall never get clear of this business.

BRACK: Hm. That was odd.

TESMAN: [Walking about the room]   Fancy Ejlert going out of the world like that! And not even leaving behind him the book that would have made his name immortal.

MRS ELVSTED: Oh, if only it could be put together again!

TESMAN: Yes, just think if it could! I don't know what I wouldn't give—

MRS ELVSTED: Perhaps it can, Mr Tesman.

TESMAN: What do you mean?

MRS ELVSTED: [*Looking in her handbag*] Look here. I have kept the loose notes that he used for dictating from.

HEDDA: [*A step nearer*] Ah!

TESMAN: You've kept them, Mrs Elvsted! Eh?

MRS ELVSTED: Yes, I have them here. I took them with me when I came away, and here they've been, lying in my handbag.

TESMAN: Just let me see them!

MRS ELVSTED: [*Passes him a stack of small sheets*] But they're in such a muddle. All mixed up together.

TESMAN: Fancy, if we could get it straight, though! Perhaps if we help each other—

MRS ELVSTED: Oh yes! Let's try, at any rate!

TESMAN: It *shall* be done! It *must!* I will give my life to this.

HEDDA: You, Jörgen? Your life?

TESMAN: Yes. Or, rather, all my spare time. My own stuff must wait for the present. You understand, Hedda? Eh? It's something I owe to Ejlert's memory.

HEDDA: Perhaps it is.

TESMAN: And so, my dear Mrs Elvsted, we will pull ourselves together. Heaven knows, it's no use brooding over what's done. Eh? We must try to make our minds as calm as possible, and—

MRS ELVSTED: Yes, yes, Mr Tesman. I will do the best I can.

TESMAN: Well, come along. We must look over the notes at once. Where shall we sit? Here? No, in there in the back room. Excuse me, my dear Judge. Now come with me, Mrs Elvsted.

MRS ELVSTED: Dear God! If only it could be done!

[TESMAN *and* MRS ELVSTED *go into the inner room. She takes off her hat and overcoat. They both sit down at the table under the hanging lamp and become absorbed in concentrated examination of the papers.* HEDDA *goes across to the stove and sits in the easy-chair. Shortly afterwards* BRACK *goes across to her*]

HEDDA: [*Half-aloud*] Ah, Mr Brack, what a feeling of release it gives one, this business with Ejlert Lövborg.

BRACK: Release, Madam Hedda? Well, it certainly is a release for him—

HEDDA: I mean for me. A feeling of release, in knowing that there really can
be such a thing in the world as free and fearless action. Something ir-
radiated with spontaneous beauty.

BRACK: [*Smiling*]   Hm. My dear Madam Hedda—

HEDDA: Oh yes. I know what you are going to say. Because you're a professional man too, in your way, like . . . Oh well!

BRACK: [*Looking steadily at her*]   Ejlert Lövborg meant more to you than
you are perhaps willing to admit to yourself. Or am I wrong there?

HEDDA: I don't answer that kind of question. I only know that Ejlert Lövborg had the courage to live life in his own way. And now—this great
deed, with all its beauty! That he had the strength and will to break
away from the feast of life . . . and so early.

BRACK: I am very sorry, Madam Hedda, but I must deprive you of your
pretty illusion.

HEDDA: Illusion?

BRACK: Which you would have been deprived of soon, in any case.

HEDDA: And what is it?

BRACK: He did not shoot himself intentionally.

HEDDA: Not intentionally?

BRACK: No. This affair of Ejlert Lövborg did not happen quite as I described
it.

HEDDA: [*In suspense*]   Have you been keeping something back? What is it?

BRACK: For poor Mrs Elvsted's sake I did make one or two slight modifications.

HEDDA: What were they?

BRACK: In the first place, he is actually dead already.

HEDDA: In hospital?

BRACK: Yes, and without regaining consciousness.

HEDDA: What else did you keep back?

BRACK: The fact that the thing didn't happen at his lodgings.

HEDDA: Well, that doesn't really make much difference.

BRACK: It does, rather. For I must tell you Ejlert Lövborg was found shot in —in Mademoiselle Diana's boudoir.

HEDDA: [*Half gets up, but sinks back again*] That's impossible, Mr Brack. He can't have been *there* again today!

BRACK: He was there this afternoon. He came to demand something that, he said, they had taken away from him. Talked wildly about a child, that had been lost—

HEDDA: Ah! So that was why . . .

BRACK: I thought perhaps it might have been his manuscript. But I gather that he destroyed that himself. So it must have been his wallet.

HEDDA: It must have been. And it was there, then, that he was found?

BRACK: Yes, there. With a discharged pistol that had gone off in his breast-pocket. The shot had wounded him fatally.

HEDDA: In the chest—yes.

BRACK: No. It hit him in the stomach.

HEDDA: [*Looking up at him with an expression of disgust*] That too! The ridiculous and the sordid lies like a curse on everything I so much as touch.

BRACK: There is something more, Madam Hedda. Something that can also be classed as 'sordid'.

HEDDA: What is that?

BRACK: The pistol that he had on him—

HEDDA: [*Breathless*] Well! What about it?

BRACK: He must have stolen it.

HEDDA: [*Jumping up*] Stolen! That's not true! That he did not!

BRACK: No other explanation is possible. He *must* have stolen it . . . Hush!

[TESMAN *and* MRS ELVSTED *have got up from the table in the inner room and come into the drawing-room*]

TESMAN: [*With papers in both hands*] Look here, Hedda, it's hardly possible for me to see in there under the hanging lamp. Just think!

HEDDA: Yes, I am.

TESMAN: I wonder if you would mind our sitting at your writing-table for a little while. Eh?

HEDDA: I don't mind. [*Quickly*] Wait a minute! Let me tidy it up first.

TESMAN: Oh, you needn't do that, Hedda. There's plenty of room.

HEDDA: No, no. Just let me tidy it, I tell you. I'll take all this in and put it on the piano for the time being. There!

   [*She has pulled out something covered with music paper from under the bookshelf, puts some more sheets on it and carries it all in to the left in the inner room.* TESMAN *puts the loose papers on the writing-table and moves the lamp there from the corner table. He and* MRS ELVSTED *sit down and settle to work again.* HEDDA *comes back*]

HEDDA: [*Behind* MRS ELVSTED's *chair, ruffling her hair gently*] Well, my precious Thea, how is Ejlert Lövborg's memorial getting on?

MRS ELVSTED: [*Looking up dispiritedly*] Oh dear! It looks as if it's going to be terribly difficult to straighten out.

TESMAN: It *must* be done. There is nothing else for it. And this—getting another man's papers in order—it's just the job for me.

   [HEDDA *goes over to the stove and sits on one of the footstools.* BRACK *stands over her, leaning against the easy-chair*]

HEDDA: [*Whispers*] What was it you said about the pistol?

BRACK: [*Softly*] That he must have stolen it.

HEDDA: Why, precisely, stolen?

BRACK: Because any other explanation ought to be impossible, Madam Hedda.

HEDDA: Really?

BRACK: [*Glancing at her*] Of course, Ejlert Lövborg was here this morning. Wasn't he?

HEDDA: Yes.

BRACK: Were you alone with him?

HEDDA: Yes, for a time.

BRACK: Didn't you go out of the room while he was here?

HEDDA: No.

BRACK: Think it over. Were you never out of it for a moment?

HEDDA: Well, perhaps just for a moment—out in the hall.

BRACK: And where was your pistol-case in the meantime?

HEDDA: I kept that in . . . I had it locked in . . .

BRACK: Well, Madam Hedda?

HEDDA: The case was there on the writing-table.

BRACK: Have you looked since to see whether both pistols are there?

HEDDA: No.

BRACK: Well, there's no need. I saw the pistol Lövborg had on him. And I knew it again at once, from yesterday. And from longer ago too.

HEDDA: Have you got it?

BRACK: No, the police have it.

HEDDA: What will the police do with the pistol?

BRACK: See if they can trace the owner.

HEDDA: Do you think they can find out?

BRACK: [*Bending over her and whispering*] No, Hedda Gabler. Not so long as I keep silence.

HEDDA: [*Looking askance at him*] And if you do *not* keep silence—what then?

BRACK: [*Shrugging his shoulders*] There is always the other way out: the pistol was stolen.

HEDDA: [*Firmly*] Rather death!

BRACK: [*Smiling*] That is the kind of thing one *says*. One doesn't *do* it.

HEDDA: [*Without answering*] And suppose, now, the pistol isn't stolen. And the owner is discovered. Then what happens?

BRACK: Well, Hedda, what happens then is a scandal.

HEDDA: Scandal!

BRACK: Scandal. Yes! The thing you have such a deadly fear of. Of course you will have to appear in court. Both you and Mademoiselle Diana. She will have to explain how the thing happened. Whether it was accident or homicide. . . . Did he try to pull the pistol out of his pocket to threaten her? And is that how it went off? Or did she snatch the pistol out of his hand, shoot him and put it back in his pocket again? She's quite equal to that. She's a hefty young woman, that same Mademoiselle Diana.

HEDDA: But all these repulsive details don't concern me.

BRACK: No. But you will have to answer the question: Why did you give
Ejlert Lövborg the pistol? And what conclusions will people draw from
the fact that you did give it him?

HEDDA: [*Drooping her head*]   That's true. I didn't think of that.

BRACK: Well, fortunately there is no danger, so long as I say nothing.

HEDDA: [*Looking up at him*]   So I am in your power, Mr Brack. From now
on, you have a hold over me.

BRACK: [*Whispering softly*]   My dearest Hedda, believe me I shall not abuse
the position.

HEDDA: In your power, all the same. At the mercy of your will and demands.
And so a slave! A slave! [*Getting up impatiently*] No! That thought I
cannot tolerate. Never!

BRACK: [*Looking at her half mockingly*]   And yet one usually manages to
tolerate the inevitable.

HEDDA: [*Returning his look*]   Yes, possibly. [*She goes across to the writing-
table*]

HEDDA: [*Suppressing an involuntary smile and imitating* TESMAN's *intonation*]
Well, is it getting on all right, Jörgen? Eh?

TESMAN: The Lord only knows, my dear. In any case, there's months of work
here.

HEDDA: [*As before*]   Well, fancy that! [*Letting her hands stray gently
through* MRS ELVSTED's *hair*] Doesn't it feel strange to you, Thea? Here
you are sitting with Jörgen Tesman just as you once sat with Ejlert Lövborg.

MRS ELVSTED: Well, if only I could inspire your husband too—

HEDDA: Oh, that will come all right—in time.

TESMAN: Yes, do you know, Hedda, I really think I am beginning to feel
something of the kind. But you go back and sit down with Judge Brack
again.

HEDDA: Is there nothing here I can help you two with?

TESMAN: Not a thing in the world. [*Turning his head*] Would you be so
kind as to keep Hedda company for the time being, Judge Brack?

BRACK: [*With a glance at* HEDDA]   It will give me the very greatest pleasure.

HEDDA: Thanks. But I'm tired tonight. I will lie down for a little while on
the sofa in there.

TESMAN: Yes do, my dear. Eh?

> [HEDDA *goes into the inner room and draws the curtains after her. There is a short pause. Suddenly she is heard playing a wild dance tune on the piano*]

MRS ELVSTED: [*Jumping up from her chair*] Oh! What is that?

TESMAN: [*Running to the doorway*] But, Hedda, my dearest—don't play dance music this evening. Think of Aunt Rina! And of Ejlert, too!

HEDDA: [*Putting out her head between the hangings*] And of Aunt Julle. And of all the rest of them. I will be quiet in future. [*She pulls the curtains to again after her*]

TESMAN: [*At the writing-table*] It upsets her to see us at this sad task, of course. I tell you what, Mrs Elvsted. You shall move into Aunt Julle's and I'll come over in the evenings. And then we can sit and work there. Eh?

MRS ELVSTED: Yes, perhaps that would be the best plan—

HEDDA: [*In the inner room*] I can hear perfectly well what you are saying. But how am I going to get through the evenings out here?

TESMAN: [*Turning over the papers*] Oh, I'm sure Judge Brack will be kind enough to come out and see you.

BRACK: [*In the easy-chair, calling gaily*] Willingly! Every single evening, Mrs Tesman. We shall have a very pleasant time together here, you and I.

HEDDA: [*Clearly and distinctly*] Yes, that is what you are looking forward to, isn't it, Mr Brack? You, as the only cock in the yard.

> [*A shot is heard within.* TESMAN, MRS ELVSTED, *and* BRACK *jump up.*]

TESMAN: Ah! Now she's playing with the pistols again.

> [*He pulls the curtains aside and runs in. So does* MRS ELVSTED. HEDDA *is lying lifeless, stretched out on the sofa. Confusion and cries.* BERTE *comes in distractedly from the right.*]

TESMAN: [*Shrieking to* BRACK] Shot herself! Shot herself in the temple! Think of it!

BRACK: [*Half-collapsed in the easy-chair*] But, merciful God! One doesn't *do* that kind of thing!

CURTAIN

GEORGE BERNARD SHAW

❧ *Pygmalion*

PREFACE

A Professor of Phonetics

As will be seen later on, Pygmalion needs, not a preface, but a sequel, which I have supplied in its due place.

The English have no respect for their language, and will not teach their children to speak it. They cannot spell it because they have nothing to spell it with but an old foreign alphabet of which only the consonants—and not all of them—have any agreed speech value. Consequently no man can teach himself what it should sound like from reading it; and it is impossible for an Englishman to open his mouth without making some other Englishman despise him. Most European languages are now accessible in black and white to foreigners: English and French are not thus accessible even to Englishmen and Frenchmen. The reformer we need most today is an energetic enthusiast: that is why I have made such a one the hero of a popular play.

There have been heroes of that kind crying in the wilderness for many years past. When I became interested in the subject towards the end of the eighteen-seventies, the illustrious Alexander Melville Bell, the inventor of Visible Speech, had emigrated to Canada, where his son invented the telephone; but Alexander J. Ellis was still a London Patriarch, with an impressive head always covered by a velvet skull cap, for which he would apologize to public meetings in a very courtly manner. He and Tito Pagliardini, another phonetic veteran, were men whom it was impossible to dislike. Henry Sweet, then a young man, lacked their sweetness of character: he was about as conciliatory to conventional mortals as Ibsen or Samuel Butler. His great ability as a phonetician (he was, I think, the best of them all at his job) would have entitled him to high official recognition, and perhaps enabled him to popularize his subject, but for his Satanic contempt for all academic dignitaries and persons in general who thought more of Greek than of phonetics. Once, in the days when the Imperial Institute rose in South Kensington, and Joseph Chamberlain was booming the Empire, I induced the editor of a leading monthly review to commission an article from Sweet on the imperial importance of his subject. When it arrived, it contained nothing but a savagely derisive attack on a professor of language and literature whose chair Sweet regarded as proper to a phonetic expert only. The article, being libellous, had to be returned as impossible; and I had to renounce my dream of dragging its author into the limelight. When I met him afterwards, for the first time for many years, I found to my astonishment that he, who had been a quite tolerably presentable young man, had actually managed by sheer scorn to alter his personal appearance until he had become a sort of walking repudiation of Oxford and all its traditions. It must have been largely in his own despite that he was squeezed into something called a Readership of phonetics there. The future of phonetics rests probably with his pupils, who all swore by him; but nothing could bring the man himself into any sort of compliance with the university to which he nevertheless clung by divine right in an intensely Oxonian way. I daresay his papers, if he has left any, include some satires that may be published without too destructive results fifty years hence. He was, I believe, not in the least an ill-natured man: very much the opposite, I should say; but he would not suffer fools gladly; and to him all scholars who were not rabid phoneticians were fools.

Those who knew him will recognize in my third act the allusion to the Current Shorthand in which he used to write postcards. It may be acquired from a four and sixpenny manual published by the Clarendon Press. The postcards which Mrs Higgins describes are such as I have received from Sweet. I would decipher a sound which a cockney would represent by *zerr*, and a Frenchman by *seu*, and then write demanding with some heat what on earth it meant. Sweet, with boundless contempt for my stupidity, would reply that it not only meant but obviously was the word Result, as no other word containing that sound, and capable of making sense with the context, existed in any language spoken on earth. That less expert mortals should require fuller indications was beyond Sweet's patience. Therefore, though the whole point of his Current Shorthand is that it can express every sound in the language perfectly, vowels as well as consonants, and that your hand has to make no stroke except the easy and current ones with which you write m, n, and u, l, p, and q, scribbling them at whatever angle comes easiest to you, his unfortunate determination to make this remarkable and quite legible script serve also as a shorthand reduced it in his own practice to the most inscrutable of cryptograms. His true objective was the provision of a full, accurate, legible script for our language; but he was led past that by his contempt for the popular Pitman system of shorthand, which he called the Pitfall system. The triumph of Pitman was a triumph of business organization: there was a weekly paper to persuade you to learn Pitman: there were cheap textbooks and exercise books and transcripts of speeches for you to copy, and schools where experienced teachers coached you up to the necessary proficiency. Sweet could not organize his market in that fashion. He might as well have been the Sybil who tore up the leaves of prophecy that nobody would attend to. The four and sixpenny manual, mostly in his lithographed handwriting, that was never vulgarly advertized, may perhaps some day be taken up by a syndicate and pushed upon the public as The Times pushed the Encyclopædia Britannica; but until then it will certainly not prevail against Pitman. I have bought three copies of it during my lifetime; and I am informed by the publishers that its cloistered existence is still a steady and healthy one. I actually learned the system two several times; and yet the shorthand in which I am writing these lines is Pitman's. And the reason is, that my secretary cannot transcribe Sweet, having been perforce taught in the schools of Pitman. In America I could use the commercially organized Gregg shorthand, which has taken a hint from Sweet by making its letters writable (current, Sweet would have called them) instead of having to be geometrically drawn like Pitman's; but all these systems, including Sweet's, are spoilt by making them available for verbatim reporting, in which complete and exact spelling and word division are impossible. A complete and exact phonetic script is neither practicable nor necessary for ordinary use; but if we enlarge our alphabet to the Russian size, and make our spelling as phonetic as Spanish, the advance will be prodigious.

Pygmalion Higgins is not a portrait of Sweet, to whom the adventure of Eliza Doolittle would have been impossible; still, as will be seen, there are touches of Sweet in the play. With Higgins's physique and temperament Sweet might have set the Thames on fire. As it was, he impressed himself professionally on Europe to an extent that made his comparative personal obscurity, and the failure of Oxford to do justice to his eminence, a puzzle to foreign specialists in his subject. I do not blame Oxford, because I think Oxford is quite right in demanding a certain social amenity from its nurslings (heaven knows it is not exorbitant in its requirement!); for although I well know how hard it is for a man of genius with a seriously underrated subject to maintain serene and kindly relations with the men who underrate it, and who keep all the best places for less important subjects which they profess without originality and sometimes without much capacity for them, still, if he overwhelms them with wrath and disdain, he cannot expect them to heap honors on him.

Of the later generations of phoneticians I know little. Among them towered Robert Bridges, to whom perhaps Higgins may owe his Miltonic sympathies, though here again I must disclaim all portraiture. But if the play makes the public aware that there are such people as phoneticians, and that they are among the most important people in England at present, it will serve its turn.

I wish to boast that Pygmalion has been an extremely successful play, both on stage and screen, all over Europe and North America as well as at home. It is so intensely and deliberately didactic, and its subject is esteemed so dry, that I delight in throwing it at the heads of the wiseacres who repeat the parrot cry that art should never be didactic. It goes to prove my contention that great art can never be anything else.

Finally, and for the encouragement of people troubled with accents that cut them off from all high employment, I may add that the change wrought by Professor Higgins in the flower-girl is neither impossible nor uncommon. The modern concierge's daughter who fulfills her ambition by playing the Queen of Spain in Ruy Blas at the Théâtre Français is only one of many thousands of men and women who have sloughed off their native dialects and acquired a new tongue. Our West End shop assistants and domestic servants are bilingual. But the thing has to be done scientifically, or the last state of the aspirant may be worse than the first. An honest slum dialect is more tolerable than the attempts of phonetically untaught persons to imitate the plutocracy. Ambitious flower-girls who read this play must not imagine that they can pass themselves off as fine ladies by untutored imitation. They must learn their alphabet over again, and differently, from a phonetic expert. Imitation will only make them ridiculous.

NOTE FOR TECHNICIANS: A complete representation of the play as printed in this edition is technically possible only on the cinema screen or on stages furnished with exceptionally elaborate machinery. For ordinary theatrical use the scenes separated by rows of asterisks are to be omitted.

In the dialogue an e upside down indicates the indefinite vowel, sometimes called obscure or neutral, for which, though it is one of the commonest sounds in English speech, our wretched alphabet has no letter.

ACT I

London at 11:15 P.M. Torrents of heavy summer rain. Cab whistles blowing frantically in all directions. Pedestrians running for shelter into the portico of St Paul's Church (not Wren's cathedral but Inigo Jones's church in Covent Garden vegetable market), among them a lady and her daughter in evening dress. All are peering out gloomily at the rain, except one man with his back turned to the rest, wholly preoccupied with a notebook in which he is writing.

The church clock strikes the first quarter.

THE DAUGHTER: [In the space between the central pillars, close to the one on her left] I'm getting chilled to the bone. What can Freddy be doing all this time? He's been gone twenty minutes.

THE MOTHER: [On her DAUGHTER's right] Not so long. But he ought to have got us a cab by this.

A BYSTANDER: [On the lady's right] He wont get no cab not until half-past eleven, missus, when they come back after dropping their theatre fares.

THE MOTHER: But we must have a cab. We cant stand here until half-past eleven. It's too bad.

THE BYSTANDER: Well, it aint my fault, missus.

THE DAUGHTER: If Freddy had a bit of gumption, he would have got one at the theatre door.

THE MOTHER: What could he have done, poor boy?

THE DAUGHTER: Other people got cabs. Why couldnt he?

[FREDDY *rushes in out of the rain from the Southampton Street side, and comes between them closing a dripping umbrella. He is a young man of twenty, in evening dress, very wet round the ankles*]

THE DAUGHTER: Well, havnt you got a cab?

FREDDY: Theres not one to be had for love or money.

THE MOTHER: Oh, Freddy, there must be one. You cant have tried.

THE DAUGHTER: It's too tiresome. Do you expect us to go and get one ourselves?

FREDDY: I tell you theyre all engaged. The rain was so sudden: nobody was prepared; and everybody had to take a cab. Ive been to Charing Cross one way and nearly to Ludgate Circus the other; and they were all engaged.

THE MOTHER: Did you try Trafalgar Square?

FREDDY: There wasn't one at Trafalgar Square.

THE DAUGHTER: Did you try?

FREDDY: I tried as far as Charing Cross Station. Did you expect me to walk to Hammersmith?

THE DAUGHTER: You havnt tried at all.

THE MOTHER: You really are very helpless, Freddy. Go again; and dont come back until you have found a cab.

FREDDY: I shall simply get soaked for nothing.

THE DAUGHTER: And what about us? Are we to stay here all night in this draught, with next to nothing on? You selfish pig—

FREDDY: Oh, very well: I'll go, I'll go. [*He opens his umbrella and dashes off Strandwards, but comes into collision with a flower girl who is hurrying in for shelter, knocking her basket out of her hands. A blinding flash of lightning, followed instantly by a rattling peal of thunder, orchestrates the incident*]

THE FLOWER GIRL: Nah then, Freddy: look wh' y' gowin, deah.

FREDDY: Sorry. [*He rushes off*]

THE FLOWER GIRL: [*Picking up her scattered flowers and replacing them in the basket*] Theres menners f' yer! Tə-oo banches o voylets trod into the mad. [*She sits down on the plinth of the column, sorting her flowers, on the lady's right. She is not at all a romantic figure. She is perhaps eighteen, perhaps twenty, hardly older. She wears a little sailor hat of black straw that has long been exposed to the dust and soot of London and has seldom if ever been brushed. Her hair needs washing rather badly: its mousy color can hardly be natural. She wears a shoddy black coat that reaches nearly to her knees and is shaped to her waist. She has a brown skirt with a coarse apron. Her boots are much the worse for wear. She is no doubt as clean as she can afford to be; but compared to the ladies she is very dirty. Her features are no worse than theirs; but their condition leaves something to be desired; and she needs the services of a dentist*]

THE MOTHER: How do you know that my son's name is Freddy, pray?

THE FLOWER GIRL: Ow, eez ya-ooa san, is e? Wal, fewd dan y' da-ooty bawmz a mather should, eed now bettern to spawl a pore gel's flahrzn than ran awy athaht pyin. Will ye-oo py me f'them? [*Here, with apologies, this desperate attempt to represent her dialect without a phonetic alphabet must be abandoned as unintelligible outside London*]

THE DAUGHTER: Do nothing of the sort, mother. The idea!

THE MOTHER: Please allow me, Clara. Have you any pennies?

THE DAUGHTER: No. Ive nothing smaller than sixpence.

THE FLOWER GIRL: [*Hopefully*]   I can give you change for a tanner, kind lady.

THE MOTHER: [*To* CLARA]   Give it to me. [CLARA *parts reluctantly*] Now [*To the* GIRL] This is for your flowers.

THE FLOWER GIRL: Thank you kindly, lady.

THE DAUGHTER: Make her give you the change. These things are only a penny a bunch.

THE MOTHER: Do hold your tongue, Clara. [*To the* GIRL] You can keep the change.

THE FLOWER GIRL: Oh, thank you, lady.

THE MOTHER: Now tell me how you know that young gentleman's name.

THE FLOWER GIRL: I didnt.

THE MOTHER: I heard you call him by it. Dont try to deceive me.

THE FLOWER GIRL: [*Protesting*]   Who's trying to deceive you? I called him Freddy or Charlie same as you might yourself if you was talking to a stranger and wished to be pleasant.

THE DAUGHTER: Sixpence thrown away! Really, mamma, you might have spared Freddy that. [*She retreats in disgust behind the pillar*]

[*An elderly gentleman of the amiable military type rushes into the shelter, and closes a dripping umbrella. He is in the same plight as* FREDDY, *very wet about the ankles. He is in evening dress, with a light overcoat. He takes the place left vacant by the daughter*]

THE GENTLEMAN: Phew!

THE MOTHER: [*To the* GENTLEMAN] Oh, sir, is there any sign of its stopping?

THE GENTLEMAN: I'm afraid not. It started worse than ever about two minutes ago. [*He goes to the plinth beside the flower girl; puts up his foot on it; and stoops to turn down his trouser ends*]

THE MOTHER: Oh dear! [*She retires sadly and joins her daughter*]

THE FLOWER GIRL: [*Taking advantage of the military gentleman's proximity to establish friendly relations with him*] If it's worse, it's a sign it's nearly over. So cheer up, Captain; and buy a flower off a poor girl.

THE GENTLEMAN: I'm sorry. I havnt any change.

THE FLOWER GIRL: I can give you change, Captain.

THE GENTLEMAN: For a sovereign? Ive nothing less.

THE FLOWER GIRL: Garn! Oh do buy a flower off me, Captain. I can change half-a-crown. Take this for tuppence.

THE GENTLEMAN: Now dont be troublesome: theres a good girl. [*Trying his pockets*] I really havnt any change—Stop: heres three hapence, if thats any use to you. [*He retreats to the other pillar*]

THE FLOWER GIRL: [*Disappointed, but thinking three half-pence better than nothing*] Thank you, sir.

THE BYSTANDER: [*To the girl*] You be careful: give him a flower for it. Theres a bloke here behind taking down every blessed word youre saying. [*All turn to the man who is taking notes*]

THE FLOWER GIRL: [*Springing up terrified*] I aint done nothing wrong by speaking to the gentleman. Ive a right to sell flowers if I keep off the kerb. [*Hysterically*] I'm a respectable girl: so help me, I never spoke to him except to ask him to buy a flower off me.

[*General hubbub, mostly sympathetic to the flower girl, but deprecating her excessive sensibility. Cries of* Dont start hollerin. Who's hurting you? Nobody's going to touch you. Whats the good of fussing?

Steady on. Easy easy, etc., *come from the elderly staid spectators, who
pat her comfortingly. Less patient ones bid her shut her head, or ask
her roughly what is wrong with her. A remoter group, not knowing what
the matter is, crowd in and increase the noise with question and answer:*
What's the row? What-she do? Where is he? A tec taking her down.
What! him? Yes: him over there: Took money off the gentleman, etc.]

THE FLOWER GIRL: [*Breaking through them to the* GENTLEMAN, *crying
wildly*] Oh, sir, dont let him charge me. You dunno what it means to
me. Theyll take away my character and drive me on the streets for
speaking to gentlemen. They—

THE NOTE TAKER: [*With quick interest*] Whats a copper's nark?
There! there! there! there! who's hurting you, you silly girl? What do
you take me for?

THE BYSTANDER: It's aw rawt: e's a genleman: look at his bɜ-oots. [*Explaining
to the note taker*] She thought you was a copper's nark, sir.

THE NOTE TAKER: [*With quick interest*] Whats a copper's nark?

THE BYSTANDER: [*Inapt at definition*] It's a—well, it's a copper's nark, as you
might say. What else would you call it? A sort of informer.

THE FLOWER GIRL: [*Still hysterical*] I take my Bible oath I never said a
word—

THE NOTE TAKER: [*Overbearing but good-humored*] Oh, shut up, shut up.
Do I look like a policeman?

THE FLOWER GIRL: [*Far from reassured*] Then what did you take down my
words for? How do I know whether you took me down right? You just
shew me what youve wrote about me. [*The note taker opens his book
and holds it steadily under her nose, though the pressure of the mob
trying to read it over his shoulders would upset a weaker man*] Whats
that? That aint proper writing. I cant read that.

THE NOTE TAKER: I can. [*Reads, reproducing her pronunciation exactly*]
"Cheer ap, Keptin; n' baw ya flahr orf a pore gel."

THE FLOWER GIRL: [*Much distressed*] It's because I called him Captain. I
meant no harm. [*To the* GENTLEMAN] Oh, sir, dont let him lay a charge
agen me for a word like that. You—

THE GENTLEMAN: Charge! I make no charge. [*To the note taker*] Really, sir,
if you are a detective, you need not begin protecting me against molestation by young women until I ask you. Anybody could see that the girl
meant no harm.

THE BYSTANDERS GENERALLY: [*Demonstrating against police espionage*] Course they could. What business is it of yours? You mind your own affairs. He wants promotion, he does. Taking down people's words! Girl never said a word to him. What harm if she did? Nice thing a girl cant shelter from the rain without being insulted, etc., etc., etc. [*She is conducted by the more sympathetic demonstrators back to her plinth, where she resumes her seat and struggles with her emotion*]

THE BYSTANDER: He aint a tec. He's a blooming busybody: thats what he is. I tell you, look at his bə-oots.

THE NOTE TAKER: [*Turning on him genially*] And how are all your people down at Selsey?

THE BYSTANDER: [*Suspiciously*] Who told you my people come from Selsey?

THE NOTE TAKER: Never you mind. They did. [*To the girl*] How do you come to be up so far east? You were born in Lisson Grove.

THE FLOWER GIRL: [*Appalled*] Oh, what harm is there in my leaving Lisson Grove? It wasnt fit for a pig to live in; and I had to pay four-and-six a week. [*In tears*] Oh, boo—hoo—oo—

THE NOTE TAKER: Live where you like; but stop that noise.

THE GENTLEMAN: [*To the girl*] Come, come! he cant touch you: you have a right to live where you please.

A SARCASTIC BYSTANDER: [*Thrusting himself between the note taker and the gentleman*] Park Lane, for instance. I'd like to go into the Housing Question with you, I would.

THE FLOWER GIRL: [*Subsiding into a brooding melancholy over her basket, and talking very low-spiritedly to herself*] I'm a good girl, I am.

THE SARCASTIC BYSTANDER: [*Not attending to her*] Do you know where *I* come from?

THE NOTE TAKER: [*Promptly*] Hoxton.

[*Titterings. Popular interest in the note taker's performance increases*]

THE SARCASTIC ONE: [*Amazed*] Well, who said I didn't? Bly me! you know everything, you do.

THE FLOWER GIRL: [*Still nursing her sense of injury*] Aint no call to meddle with me, he aint.

THE BYSTANDER: [*To her*]   Of course he aint. Dont you stand it from him. [*To the note taker*] See here: what call have you to know about people what never offered to meddle with you?

THE FLOWER GIRL: Let him say what he likes. I dont want to have no truck with him.

THE BYSTANDER: You take us for dirt under your feet, dont you? Catch you taking liberties with a gentleman!

THE SARCASTIC BYSTANDER: Yes: tell him where he come from if you want to go fortune-telling.

THE NOTE TAKER: Cheltenham, Harrow, Cambridge, and India.

THE GENTLEMAN: Quite right.

> [*Great laughter. Reaction in the* NOTE TAKER's *favor. Exclamations of* He knows all about it. Told him proper. Hear him tell the toff where he come from? etc.]

THE GENTLEMAN: May I ask, sir, do you do this for your living at a music hall?

THE NOTE TAKER: I've thought of that. Perhaps I shall some day.

> [*The rain has stopped; and the persons on the outside of the crowd begin to drop off*]

THE FLOWER GIRL: [*Resenting the reaction*]   He's no gentleman, he aint, to interfere with a poor girl.

THE DAUGHTER: [*Out of patience, pushing her way rudely to the front and displacing the gentleman, who politely retires to the other side of the pillar*]   What on earth is Freddy doing? I shall get pneumownia if I stay in this draught any longer.

THE NOTE TAKER: [*To himself, hastily making a note of her pronunciation of "mownia"*]   Earlscourt.

THE DAUGHTER: [*Violently*]   Will you please keep your impertinent remarks to yourself.

THE NOTE TAKER: Did I say that out loud? I didnt mean to. I beg your pardon. Your mother's Epsom, unmistakeably.

THE MOTHER: [*Advancing between the daughter and the* NOTE TAKER]   How very curious! I was brought up in Largelady Park, near Epsom.

THE NOTE TAKER: [*Uproariously amused*]   Ha! ha! What a devil of a name! Excuse me. [*To the* DAUGHTER] You want a cab, do you?

THE DAUGHTER: Dont dare speak to me.

THE MOTHER: Oh please, please, Clara. [*Her daughter repudiates her with an angry shrug and retires haughtily*] We should be so grateful to you, sir, if you found us a cab. [*The* NOTE TAKER *produces a whistle*] Oh, thank you. [*She joins her daughter*]

[*The* NOTE TAKER *blows a piercing blast*]

THE SARCASTIC BYSTANDER: There! I knowed he was a plainclothes copper.

THE BYSTANDER: That aint a police whistle: thats a sporting whistle.

THE FLOWER GIRL: [*Still preoccupied with her wounded feelings*]   He's no right to take away my character. My character is the same to me as any lady's.

THE NOTE TAKER: I dont know whether youve noticed it; but the rain stopped about two minutes ago.

THE BYSTANDER: So it has. Why didn't you say so before? and us losing our time listening to your silliness! [*He walks off towards the Strand*]

THE SARCASTIC BYSTANDER: I can tell where you come from. You come from Anwell. Go back there.

THE NOTE TAKER: [*Helpfully*]   Hanwell.

THE SARCASTIC BYSTANDER: [*Affecting great distinction of speech*]   Thenk you, teacher. Haw haw! So long [*He touches his hat with mock respect and strolls off*]

THE FLOWER GIRL: Frightening people like that! How would he like it himself?

THE MOTHER: It's quite fine now, Clara. We can walk to a motor bus. Come. [*She gathers her skirts above her ankles and hurries off towards the Strand*]

THE DAUGHTER: But the cab—[*Her mother is out of hearing*] Oh, how tiresome! [*She follows angrily*]

[*All the rest have gone except the* NOTE TAKER, THE GENTLEMAN, *and* THE FLOWER GIRL, *who sits arranging her basket, and still pitying herself in murmurs*]

THE FLOWER GIRL: Poor girl! Hard enough for her to live without being worried and chivied.

THE GENTLEMAN: [*Returning to his former place on the* NOTE TAKER's *left*] How do you do it, if I may ask?

THE NOTE TAKER: Simply phonetics. The science of speech. Thats my profession: also my hobby. Happy is the man who can make a living by his hobby! You can spot an Irishman or a Yorkshireman by his brogue. I can place any man within six miles. I can place him within two miles in London. Sometimes within two streets.

THE FLOWER GIRL: Ought to be ashamed of himself, unmanly coward!

THE GENTLEMAN: But is there a living in that?

THE NOTE TAKER: Oh yes. Quite a fat one. This is an age of upstarts. Men begin in Kentish Town with £80 a year, and end in Park Lane with a hundred thousand. They want to drop Kentish Town; but they give themselves away every time they open their mouths. Now I can teach them—

THE FLOWER GIRL: Let him mind his own business and leave a poor girl—

THE NOTE TAKER: [*Explosively*] Woman: cease this detestable boohooing instantly; or else seek the shelter of some other place of worship.

THE FLOWER GIRL: [*With feeble defiance*] Ive a right to be here if I like, same as you.

THE NOTE TAKER: A woman who utters such depressing and disgusting sounds has no right to be anywhere—no right to live. Remember that you are a human being with a soul and the divine gift of articulate speech: that your native language is the language of Shakespear and Milton and The Bible; and dont sit there crooning like a bilious pigeon.

THE FLOWER GIRL: [*Quite overwhelmed, looking up at him in mingled wonder and deprecation without daring to raise her head*] Ah-ah-ah-ow-ow-ow-oo!

THE NOTE TAKER: [*Whipping out his book*] Heavens! what a sound! [*He writes; then holds out the book and reads, reproducing her vowels exactly*] Ah-ah-ah-ow-ow-ow-oo!

THE FLOWER GIRL: [*Tickled by the performance, and laughing in spite of herself*] Garn!

THE NOTE TAKER: You see this creature with her kerbstone English: the English that will keep her in the gutter to the end of her days. Well, sir, in three months I could pass that girl off as a duchess at an ambassador's garden party. I could even get her a place as lady's maid or shop assistant, which requires better English.

THE FLOWER GIRL: What's that you say?

THE NOTE TAKER: Yes, you squashed cabbage leaf, you disgrace to the noble architecture of these columns, you incarnate insult to the English language: I could pass you off as the Queen of Sheba. [*To* THE GENTLEMAN] Can you believe that?

THE GENTLEMAN: Of course I can. I am myself a student of Indian dialects; and—

THE NOTE TAKER: [*Eagerly*]   Are you? Do you know Colonel Pickering, the author of Spoken Sanscrit?

THE GENTLEMAN: I am Colonel Pickering. Who are you?

THE NOTE TAKER: Henry Higgins, author of Higgins's Universal Alphabet.

PICKERING: [*With enthusiasm*]   I came from India to meet you.

HIGGINS: I was going to India to meet you.

PICKERING: Where do you live?

HIGGINS: 27A Wimpole Street. Come and see me tomorrow.

PICKERING: I'm at the Carlton. Come with me now and lets have a jaw over some supper.

HIGGINS: Right you are.

THE FLOWER GIRL: [*To* PICKERING, *as he passes her*]   Buy a flower, kind gentleman. I'm short for my lodging.

PICKERING: I really havnt any change. I'm sorry [*he goes away*]

HIGGINS: [*Shocked at the girl's mendacity*]   Liar. You said you could change half-a-crown.

THE FLOWER GIRL: [*Rising in desperation*]   You ought to be stuffed with nails, you ought. [*Flinging the basket at his feet*] Take the whole blooming basket for sixpence.

[*The church clock strikes the second quarter*]

HIGGINS: [*Hearing in it the voice of God, rebuking him for his Pharisaic want of charity to the poor girl*] A reminder. [*He raises his hat solemnly; then throws a handful of money into the basket and follows* PICKERING]

THE FLOWER GIRL: [*Picking up a half-crown*] Ah-ow-ooh! [*Picking up a couple of florins*] Aaah-ow-ooh! [*Picking up several coins*] Aaaaah-ow-ooh! [*Picking up a half sovereign*] Aaaaaaaaaaaah-ow-ooh!!!

FREDDY: [*Springing out of a taxicab*]   Got one at last. Hallo! [*To the* GIRL]
Where are the two ladies that were here?

THE FLOWER GIRL: They walked to the bus when the rain stopped.

FREDDY: And left me with a cab on my hands! Damnation!

THE FLOWER GIRL: [*With grandeur*]   Never mind, young man. I'm going
home in a taxi. [*She sails off to the cab. The driver puts his hand behind
him and holds the door firmly shut against her. Quite understanding
his mistrust, she shews him her handful of money*] A taxi fare aint no
object to me, Charlie. [*He grins and opens the door*] Here. What about
the basket?

THE TAXIMAN: Give it here. Tuppence extra.

LIZA: No: I dont want nobody to see it. [*She crushes it into the cab and gets
in, continuing the conversation through the window*] Goodbye, Freddy.

FREDDY: [*Dazedly raising his hat*]   Goodbye.

TAXIMAN: Where to?

LIZA: Bucknam Pellis [Buckingham Palace].

TAXIMAN: What d'ye mean—Bucknam Pellis?

LIZA: Dont you know where it is? In the Green Park, where the King
lives. Goodbye, Freddy. Dont let me keep you standing there. Goodbye.

FREDDY: Goodbye. [*He goes*]

TAXIMAN: Here? Whats this about Bucknam Pellis? What business have you
at Bucknam Pellis?

LIZA: Of course I havnt none. But I wasn't going to let him know that. You
drive me home.

TAXIMAN: And wheres home?

LIZA: Angel Court, Drury Lane, next Meiklejohn's oil shop.

TAXIMAN: That sounds more like it, Judy. [*He drives off*]

.   .   .

Let us follow the taxi to the entrance to Angel Court, a narrow little
archway between two shops, one of them Meiklejohn's oil shop. When
it stops there, Eliza gets out, dragging her basket with her.

LIZA: How much?

TAXIMAN: [*Indicating the taximeter*]   Can't you read? A shilling.

LIZA: A shilling for two minutes!!

TAXIMAN: Two minutes or ten: it's all the same.

LIZA: Well, I dont call it right.

TAXIMAN: Ever been in a taxi before?

LIZA: [*With dignity*] Hundreds and thousands of times, young man.

TAXIMAN: [*Laughing at her*] Good for you, Judy. Keep the shilling, darling, with best love from all at home. Good luck! [*He drives off*]

LIZA: [*Humiliated*] Impidence!

[*She picks up the basket and trudges up the alley with it to her lodging: a small room with very old wall paper hanging loose in the damp places. A broken pane in the window is mended with paper. A portrait of a popular actor and a fashion plate of ladies' dresses, all wildly beyond poor Eliza's means, both torn from newspapers, are pinned up on the wall. A birdcage hangs in the window; but its tenant died long ago: it remains as a memorial only.*

These are the only visible luxuries: the rest is the irreducible minimum of poverty's needs: a wretched bed heaped with all sorts of coverings that have any warmth in them, a draped packing case with a basin and jug on it and a little looking glass over it, a chair and table, the refuse of some suburban kitchen, and an American alarum clock on the shelf above the unused fireplace: the whole lighted with a gas lamp with a penny in the slot meter. Rent: four shillings a week]

Here Eliza, chronically weary, but too excited to go to bed, sits, counting her new riches and dreaming and planning what to do with them, until the gas goes out, when she enjoys for the first time the sensation of being able to put in another penny without grudging it. This prodigal mood does not extinguish her gnawing sense of the need for economy sufficiently to prevent her from calculating that she can dream and plan in bed more cheaply and warmly than sitting up without a fire. So she takes off her shawl and skirt and adds them to the miscellaneous bedclothes. Then she kicks off her shoes and gets into bed without any further change.

ACT II

Next day at 11 a.m. Higgins's laboratory in Wimpole Street. It is a room on the first floor, looking on the street, and was meant for the drawing room. The double doors are in the middle of the back wall; and persons entering find in the corner to their right two tall file cabinets at right angles to one another against the walls. In this corner stands a flat writing-table, on which are a phonograph, a laryngoscope, a row of tiny organ pipes with a bellows, a set of lamp chimneys for singing flames with burners attached to a gas plug in the wall by an indiarubber tube, several tuning-forks of different sizes, a life-size image of half a human head, shewing in section the vocal organs, and a box containing a supply of wax cylinders for the phonograph.

Further down the room, on the same side, is a fireplace, with a comfortable leather-covered easy-chair at the side of the hearth nearest the door, and a coal-scuttle. There is a clock on the mantlepiece. Between the fireplace and the phonograph table is a stand for newspapers.

On the other side of the central door, to the left of the visitor, is a cabinet of shallow drawers. On it is a telephone and the telephone directory. The corner beyond, and most of the side wall, is occupied by a grand piano, with the keyboard at the end furthest from the door, and a bench for the players extending the full length of the keyboard. On the piano is a dessert dish heaped with fruit and sweets, mostly chocolates.

The middle of the room is clear. Besides the easy-chair, the piano bench, and two chairs at the phonograph table, there is one stray chair. It stands near the fireplace. On the walls, engravings: mostly Piranesi and mezzotint portraits. No paintings.

Pickering is seated at the table, putting down some cards and a tuning-fork which he has been using. Higgins is standing up near him, closing two or three file drawers which are hanging out. He appears in the morning light as a robust, vital, appetizing sort of man of forty or thereabouts, dressed in a professional-looking black frock-coat with a white linen collar and black silk tie. He is of energetic, scientific type, heartily, even violently interested in everything that can be studied as a scientific subject, and careless about himself and other people, including their feelings. He is, in fact, but for his years and size, rather like a very impetuous baby "taking notice" eagerly and loudly, and requiring almost as much watching to keep him out of unintended mischief. His manner varies from genial bullying when he is in a good humor to stormy petulance when anything goes wrong; but he is so entirely frank and void of malice that he remains likeable even in his least reasonable moments.

HIGGINS: [*As he shuts the last drawer*]   Well, I think thats the whole show.

PICKERING: It's really amazing. I havnt taken half of it in, you know.

HIGGINS: Would you like to go over any of it again?

PICKERING: [*Rising and coming to the fireplace, where he plants himself with his back to the fire*]   No, thank you: not now. I'm quite done up for this morning.

HIGGINS: [*Following him, and standing beside him on his left*]   Tired of listening to sounds?

PICKERING: Yes. It's a fearful strain. I rather fancied myself because I can pronounce twenty-four distinct vowel sounds; but your hundred and thirty beat me. I cant hear a bit of difference between most of them.

HIGGINS: [*Chuckling, and going over to the piano to eat sweets*]   Oh, that comes with practice. You hear no difference at first; but you keep on listening, and presently you find theyre all as different as A from B. [MRS PEARCE *looks in: she is* HIGGINS's *housekeeper*]   Whats the matter?

MRS PEARCE: [*Hesitating, evidently perplexed*]   A young woman asks to see you, sir.

HIGGINS: A young woman! What does she want?

MRS PEARCE: Well, sir, she says youll be glad to see her when you know what she's come about. She's quite a common girl, sir. Very common indeed. I should have sent her away, only I thought perhaps you wanted her to talk into your machines. I hope Ive not done wrong; but really you see such queer people sometimes—youll excuse me, I'm sure, sir—

HIGGINS: Oh, thats all right, Mrs Pearce. Has she an interesting accent?

MRS PEARCE: Oh, something dreadful, sir, really. I dont know how you can take an interest in it.

HIGGINS: [*To* PICKERING]   Lets have her up. Shew her up, Mrs Pearce. [*He rushes across to his working table and picks out a cylinder to use on the phonograph*]

MRS PEARCE: [*Only half resigned to it*]   Very well, sir. It's for you to say. [*She goes downstairs*]

HIGGINS: This is rather a bit of luck. I'll shew you how I make records. We'll set her talking; and I'll take it down first in Bell's Visible Speech; then in broad Romic; and then we'll get her on the phonograph so that you can turn her on as often as you like with the written transcript before you.

MRS PEARCE: [*Returning*]   This is the young woman, sir.

[THE FLOWER GIRL *enters in state. She has a hat with three ostrich feathers, orange, sky-blue, and red. She has a nearly clean apron, and the shoddy coat has been tidied a little. The pathos of this deplorable figure, with its innocent vanity and consequential air, touches* PICKERING, *who has already straightened himself in the presence of* MRS PEARCE. *But as to* HIGGINS, *the only distinction he makes between men and women is that when he is neither bullying nor exclaiming to the heavens against some feather-weight cross, he coaxes women as a child coaxes its nurse when it wants to get anything out of her*]

HIGGINS: [*Brusquely, recognizing her with unconcealed disappointment, and at once, babylike, making an intolerable grievance of it*]   Why, this is the girl I jotted down last night. She's no use: Ive got all the records I want of the Lisson Grove lingo; and I'm not going to waste another cylinder on it. [*To the girl*] Be off with you: I dont want you.

THE FLOWER GIRL: Dont you be so saucy. You aint heard what I come for yet. [*To* MRS PEARCE, *who is waiting at the door for further instructions*] Did you tell him I come in a taxi?

MRS PEARCE: Nonsense girl! what do you think a gentleman like Mr Higgins cares what you came in?

THE FLOWER GIRL: Oh, we are proud! He aint above giving lessons, not him: I heard him say so. Well, I aint come here to ask for any compliment; and if my money's not good enough I can go elsewhere.

HIGGINS: Good enough for what?

THE FLOWER GIRL: Good enough for yə-oo. Now you know, dont you? Ive come to have lessons, I am. And to pay for em tə-oo: make no mistake.

HIGGINS: [*Stupent*]   Well!!!   [*Recovering his breath with a gasp*]   What do you expect me to say to you?

THE FLOWER GIRL: Well, if you was a gentleman, you might ask me to sit down, I think. Dont I tell you I'm bringing you business?

HIGGINS: Pickering: shall we ask this baggage to sit down, or shall we throw her out of the window?

THE FLOWER GIRL: [*Running away in terror to the piano, where she turns at bay*]   Ah-ah-oh-ow-ow-ow-oo! [*Wounded and whimpering*] I wont be called a baggage when Ive offered to pay like any lady.

[*Motionless, the two men stare at her from the other side of the room, amazed*]

PICKERING: [*Gently*] But what is it you want?

THE FLOWER GIRL: I want to be a lady in a flower shop stead of sellin at the corner of Tottenham Court Road. But they wont take me unless I can talk more genteel. He said he could teach me. Well, here I am ready to pay him—not asking any favor—and he treats me zif I was dirt.

MRS PEARCE: How can you be such a foolish ignorant girl as to think you could afford to pay Mr Higgins?

THE FLOWER GIRL: Why shouldnt I? I know what lessons cost as well as you do; and I'm ready to pay.

HIGGINS: How much?

THE FLOWER GIRL: [*Coming back to him, triumphant*] Now youre talking! I thought youd come off it when you saw a chance of getting back a bit of what you chucked at me last night. [*Confidentially*] Youd had a drop in, hadnt you?

HIGGINS: [*Peremptorily*] Sit down.

THE FLOWER GIRL: Oh, if youre going to make a compliment of it—

HIGGINS: [*Thundering at her*] Sit down.

MRS PEARCE: [*Severely*] Sit down, girl. Do as youre told.

THE FLOWER GIRL: Ah-ah-ah-ow-ow-oo! [*She stands, half rebellious, half bewildered.*]

PICKERING: [*Very courteous*] Wont you sit down? [*He places the stray chair near the hearthrug between himself and* HIGGINS]

LIZA: [*Coyly*] Dont mind if I do. [*She sits down.* PICKERING *returns to the hearthrug*]

HIGGINS: Whats your name?

THE FLOWER GIRL: Liza Doolittle.

HIGGINS: [*Declaiming gravely*]
       Eliza, Elizabeth, Betsy and Bess,
       They went to the woods to get a bird's nes':

PICKERING: They found a nest with four eggs in it:

HIGGINS: They took one apiece, and left three in it.

    [*They laugh heartily at their own fun*]

LIZA: Oh, dont be silly.

MRS PEARCE: [*Placing herself behind* ELIZA'S *chair*]   You mustnt speak to the gentleman like that.

LIZA: Well, why wont he speak sensible to me?

HIGGINS: Come back to business. How much do you propose to pay me for the lessons?

LIZA: Oh, I know whats right. A lady friend of mine gets French lessons for eighteenpence an hour from a real French gentleman. Well, you wouldnt have the face to ask me the same for teaching me my own language as you would for French; so I wont give more than a shilling. Take it or leave it.

HIGGINS: [*Walking up and down the room, rattling his keys and his cash in his pockets*]   You know, Pickering, if you consider a shilling, not as a simple shilling, but as a percentage of this girl's income, it works out as fully equivalent to sixty or seventy guineas from a millionaire.

PICKERING: How so?

HIGGINS: Figure it out. A millionaire has about £150 a day. She earns about half-a-crown.

LIZA: [*Haughtily*]   Who told you I only—

HIGGINS: [*Continuing*]   She offers me two-fifths of her day's income for a lesson. Two-fifths of a millionaire's income for a day would be somewhere about £60. It's handsome. By George, it's enormous! it's the biggest offer I ever had.

LIZA: [*Rising, terrified*]   Sixty pounds! What are you talking about? I never offered you sixty pounds. Where would I get—

HIGGINS: Hold your tongue.

LIZA: [*Weeping*]   But I aint got sixty pounds. Oh—

MRS PEARCE: Dont cry, you silly girl. Sit down. Nobody is going to touch your money.

HIGGINS: Somebody is going to touch you, with a broomstick, if you dont stop snivelling. Sit down.

LIZA: [*Obeying slowly*]   Ah-ah-ah-ow-oo-o! One would think you was my father.

HIGGINS: If I decide to teach you, I'll be worse than two fathers to you. Here! [*He offers her his silk handkerchief*]

LIZA: Whats this for?

HIGGINS: To wipe your eyes. To wipe any part of your face that feels moist. Remember: thats your handkerchief; and thats your sleeve. Dont mistake the one for the other if you wish to become a lady in a shop.

[LIZA, *utterly bewildered, stares helplessly at him*]

MRS PEARCE: It's no use talking to her like that, Mr. Higgins: she doesnt understand you. Besides, youre quite wrong: she doesnt do it that way at all. [*She takes the handkerchief*]

LIZA: [*Snatching it*]   Here! You give me that handkerchief. He gev it to me, not to you.

PICKERING: [*Laughing*]   He did. I think it must be regarded as her property, Mrs Pearce.

MRS PEARCE: [*Resigning herself*]   Serve you right, Mr Higgins.

PICKERING: Higgins: I'm interested. What about the ambassador's garden party? I'll say youre the greatest teacher alive if you make that good. I'll bet you all the expenses of the experiment you cant do it. And I'll pay for the lessons.

LIZA: Oh, you are real good. Thank you, Captain.

HIGGINS: [*Tempted, looking at her*]   It's almost irresistible. She's so deliciously low—so horribly dirty—

LIZA: [*Protesting extremely*]   Ah-ah-ah-ah-ow-ow-oo-oo!!!   I aint dirty: I washed my face and hands afore I come, I did.

PICKERING: Youre certainly not going to turn her head with flattery, Higgins.

MRS PEARCE: [*Uneasy*]   Oh, dont say that, sir: theres more ways than one of turning a girl's head; and nobody can do it better than Mr Higgins, though he may not always mean it. I do hope, sir, you wont encourage him to do anything foolish.

HIGGINS: [*Becoming excited as the idea grows on him*]   What is life but a series of inspired follies? The difficulty is to find them to do. Never lose a chance: it doesnt come every day. I shall make a duchess of this draggletailed guttersnipe.

LIZA: [*Strongly deprecating this view of her*]   Ah-ah-ah-ow-ow-oo!

HIGGINS: [*Carried away*]   Yes: in six months—in three if she has a good ear and a quick tongue—I'll take her anywhere and pass her off as anything. We'll start today: now! this moment! Take her away and clean her, Mrs Pearce. Monkey Brand, if it wont come off any other way. Is there a good fire in the kitchen?

MRS PEARCE: [*Protesting*]   Yes; but—

HIGGINS: [*Storming on*]   Take all her clothes off and burn them. Ring up Whitely or somebody for new ones. Wrap her up in brown paper till they come.

LIZA: Youre no gentleman, youre not, to talk of such things. I'm a good girl, I am; and I know what the like of you are, I do.

HIGGINS: We want none of your Lisson Grove prudery here, young woman. Youve got to learn to behave like a duchess. Take her away, Mrs Pearce. If she gives you any trouble, wallop her.

LIZA: [*Springing up and running between* PICKERING *and* MRS PEARCE *for protection*]   No! I'll call the police, I will.

MRS PEARCE: But Ive no place to put her.

HIGGINS: Put her in the dustbin.

LIZA: Ah-ah-ah-ow-ow-oo!

PICKERING: Oh come, Higgins! be reasonable.

MRS PEARCE: [*Resolutely*]   You must be reasonable, Mr Higgins: really you must. You cant walk over everybody like this.

   [HIGGINS, *thus scolded, subsides. The hurricane is succeeded by a zephyr of amiable surprise*]

HIGGINS: [*With professional exquisiteness of modulation*]   I walk over everybody! My dear Mrs Pearce, my dear Pickering, I never had the slightest intention of walking over anyone. All I propose is that we should be kind to this poor girl. We must help her to prepare and fit herself for her new station in life. If I did not express myself clearly it was because I did not wish to hurt her delicacy, or yours.

   [LIZA, *reassured, steals back to her chair*]

MRS PEARCE: [*To* PICKERING]   Well, did you ever hear anything like that, sir?

PICKERING: [*Laughing heartily*]   Never, Mrs Pearce: never.

HIGGINS: [*Patiently*]   Whats the matter?

MRS PEARCE: Well, the matter is, sir, that you cant take a girl up like that as if you were picking up a pebble on the beach.

HIGGINS: Why not?

MRS PEARCE: Why not! But you dont know anything about her. What about her parents? She may be married.

LIZA: Garn!

HIGGINS: There! As the girl very properly says, Garn! Married indeed! Dont you know that a woman of that class looks a worn out drudge of fifty a year after she's married?

LIZA: Whood marry me?

HIGGINS: [*Suddenly resorting to the most thrillingly beautiful low tones in his best elocutionary style*]   By George, Eliza, the streets will be strewn with the bodies of men shooting themselves for your sake before Ive done with you.

MRS PEARCE: Nonsense, sir. You mustnt talk like that to her.

LIZA: [*Rising and squaring herself determinedly*]   I'm going away. He's off his chump, he is. I dont want no balmies teaching me.

HIGGINS: [*Wounded in his tenderest point by her insensibility to his elocution*]   Oh, indeed! I'm mad, am I? Very well, Mrs Pearce: you neednt order the new clothes for her. Throw her out.

LIZA: [*Whimpering*]   Nah-ow. You got no right to touch me.

MRS PEARCE: You see now what comes of being saucy. [*Indicating the door*] This way, please.

LIZA: [*Almost in tears*]   I didnt want no clothes. I wouldnt have taken them. [*She throws away the handkerchief*] I can buy my own clothes.

HIGGINS: [*Deftly retrieving the handkerchief and intercepting her on her reluctant way to the door*]   Youre an ungrateful wicked girl. This is my return for offering to take you out of the gutter and dress you beautifully and make a lady of you.

MRS PEARCE: Stop, Mr. Higgins. I wont allow it. It's you that are wicked. Go home to your parents, girl; and tell them to take better care of you.

LIZA: I aint got no parents. They told me I was big enough to earn my own living and turned me out.

MRS PEARCE: Wheres your mother?

LIZA: I aint got no mother. Her that turned me out was my sixth stepmother. But I done without them. And I'm a good girl, I am.

HIGGINS: Very well, then, what on earth is all this fuss about? The girl doesnt belong to anybody—is no use to anybody but me. [*He goes to*

MRS PEARCE *and begins coaxing*] You can adopt her, Mrs Pearce: I'm sure a daughter would be a great amusement to you. Now dont make any more fuss. Take her downstairs; and—

MRS PEARCE: But whats to become of her? Is she to be paid anything? Do be sensible, sir.

HIGGINS: Oh, pay her whatever is necessary: put it down in the housekeeping book. [*Impatiently*] What on earth will she want with money? She'll have her food and her clothes. She'll only drink if you give her money.

LIZA: [*Turning on him*]   Oh you are a brute. It's a lie: nobody ever saw the sign of liquor on me. [*To* PICKERING] Oh, sir: youre a gentleman: dont let him speak to me like that.

PICKERING: [*In good-humored remonstrance*]   Does it occur to you, Higgins, that the girl has some feelings?

HIGGINS: [*Looking critically at her*]   Oh no, I dont think so. Not any feelings that we need bother about. [*Cheerily*] Have you, Eliza?

LIZA: I got my feelings same as anyone else.

HIGGINS: [*To* PICKERING, *reflectively*]   You see the difficulty?

PICKERING: Eh? What difficulty?

HIGGINS: To get her to talk grammar. The mere pronunciation is easy enough.

LIZA: I dont want to talk grammar. I want to talk like a lady in a flower-shop.

MRS PEARCE: Will you please keep to the point, Mr Higgins. I want to know on what terms the girl is to be here. Is she to have any wages? And what is to become of her when youve finished your teaching? You must look ahead a little.

HIGGINS: [*Impatiently*]   Whats to become of her if I leave her in the gutter? Tell me that, Mrs Pearce.

MRS PEARCE: Thats her own business, not yours, Mr Higgins.

HIGGINS: Well, when Ive done with her, we can throw her back into the gutter; and then it will be her own business again; so thats all right.

LIZA: Oh, youve no feeling heart in you: you dont care for nothing but yourself. [*She rises and takes the floor resolutely*] Here! Ive had enough of this. I'm going. [*Making for the door*] You ought to be ashamed of yourself, you ought.

HIGGINS: [*Snatching a chocolate cream from the piano, his eyes suddenly beginning to twinkle with mischief*]   Have some chocolates, Eliza.

LIZA: [*Halting, tempted*] How do I know what might be in them? Ive heard of girls being drugged by the like of you.

> [HIGGINS *whips out his penknife; cuts a chocolate in two; puts one half into his mouth and bolts it; and offers her the other half*]

HIGGINS: Pledge of good faith, Eliza. I eat one half: you eat the other. [LIZA *opens her mouth to retort: he pops the half chocolate into it*] You shall have boxes of them, barrels of them, every day. You shall live on them. Eh?

LIZA: [*Who has disposed of the chocolate after being nearly choked by it*] I wouldnt have ate it, only I'm too ladylike to take it out of my mouth.

HIGGINS: Listen, Eliza. I think you said you came in a taxi.

LIZA: Well, what if I did? Ive as good a right to take a taxi as anyone else.

HIGGINS: You have, Eliza; and in future you shall have as many taxis as you want. You shall go up and down and round the town in a taxi every day. Think of that, Eliza.

MRS PEARCE: Mr Higgins: youre tempting the girl. It's not right. She should think of the future.

HIGGINS: At her age! Nonsense! Time enough to think of the future when you havnt any future to think of. No, Eliza: do as this lady does: think of other people's futures; but never think of your own. Think of chocolates, and taxis, and gold, and diamonds.

LIZA: No: I dont want no gold and no diamonds. I'm a good girl, I am. [*She sits down again, with an attempt at dignity*]

HIGGINS: You shall remain so, Eliza, under the care of Mrs Pearce. And you shall marry an officer in the Guards, with a beautiful moustache: the son of a marquis, who will disinherit him for marrying you, but will relent when he sees your beauty and goodness—

PICKERING: Excuse me, Higgins; but I really must interfere. Mrs Pearce is quite right. If this girl is to put herself in your hands for six months for an experiment in teaching, she must understand thoroughly what she's doing.

HIGGINS: How can she? She's incapable of understanding anything. Besides, do any of us understand what we are doing? If we did, would we ever do it?

PICKERING: Very clever, Higgins; but not to the present point. [*To* ELIZA] Miss Doolittle—

LIZA: [*Overwhelmed*] Ah-ah-ow-oo!

HIGGINS: There! That's all youll get out of Eliza. Ah-ah-ow-oo! No use explaining. As a military man you ought to know that. Give her her orders:
thats enough for her. Eliza: you are to live here for the next six months,
learning how to speak beautifully, like a lady in a florist's shop. If youre
good and do whatever youre told, you shall sleep in a proper bedroom,
and have lots to eat, and money to buy chocolates and take rides in taxis.
If youre naughty and idle you will sleep in the back kitchen among the
black beetles, and be walloped by Mrs Pearce with a broomstick. At the
end of six months you shall go to Buckingham Palace in a carriage,
beautifully dressed. If the King finds out youre not a lady, you will be
taken by the police to the Tower of London, where your head will be
cut off as a warning to other presumptuous flower girls. If you are not
found out, you shall have a present of seven-and-sixpence to start life
with as a lady in a shop. If you refuse this offer you will be a most
ungrateful wicked girl; and the angels will weep for you. [To PICKERING]
Now are you satisfied, Pickering? [To MRS PEARCE] Can I put it more
plainly and fairly, Mrs Pearce?

MRS PEARCE: [Patiently] I think youd better let me speak to the girl
properly in private. I dont know that I can take charge of her or consent
to the arrangement at all. Of course I know you dont mean her any
harm; but when you get what you call interested in people's accents,
you never think or care what may happen to them or you. Come with
me, Eliza.

HIGGINS: Thats all right. Thank you, Mrs Pearce. Bundle her off to the bathroom.

LIZA: [Rising reluctantly and suspiciously] Youre a great bully, you are. I
wont stay here if I dont like. I wont let nobody wallop me. I never asked
to go to Bucknam Palace, I didnt. I was never in trouble with the police,
not me. I'm a good girl—

MRS PEARCE: Dont answer back, girl. You dont understand the gentleman.
Come with me. [She leads the way to the door, and holds it open for
ELIZA]

LIZA: [As she goes out] Well, what I say is right. I wont go near the King,
not if I'm going to have my head cut off. If I'd known what I was letting
myself in for, I wouldnt have come here. I always been a good girl; and
I never offered to say a word to him; and I dont owe him nothing; and I
dont care; and I wont be put upon; and I have my feelings the same as
anyone else—

   [MRS PEARCE shuts the door; and ELIZA's plaints are no longer audi-
ble]

. . .

Eliza is taken upstairs to the third floor greatly to her surprise; for she expected to be taken down to the scullery. There Mrs Pearce opens a door and takes her into a spare bedroom.

MRS PEARCE: I will have to put you here. This will be your bedroom.

LIZA: O-h, I couldnt sleep here, missus. It's too good for the likes of me. I should be afraid to touch anything. I aint a duchess yet, you know.

MRS PEARCE: You have got to make yourself as clean as the room: then you wont be afraid of it. And you must call me Mrs Pearce, not missus. [*She throws open the door of the dressingroom, now modernized as a bathroom*]

LIZA: Gawd! whats this? Is this where you wash clothes? Funny sort of copper I call it.

MRS PEARCE: It is not a copper. This is where we wash ourselves, Eliza, and where I am going to wash you.

LIZA: You expect me to get into that and wet myself all over! Not me. I should catch my death. I knew a woman did it every Saturday night; and she died of it.

MRS PEARCE: Mr Higgins has the gentlemen's bathroom downstairs; and he has a bath every morning, in cold water.

LIZA: Ugh! He's made of iron, that man.

MRS PEARCE: If you are to sit with him and the Colonel and be taught you will have to do the same. They wont like the smell of you if you dont. But you can have the water as hot as you like. There are two taps: hot and cold.

LIZA: [*Weeping*] I couldnt. I dursnt. It's not natural: it would kill me. Ive never had a bath in my life: not what youd call a proper one.

MRS PEARCE: Well, dont you want to be clean and sweet and decent, like a lady? You know you cant be a nice girl inside if youre a dirty slut outside.

LIZA: Boohoo!!!!

MRS PEARCE: Now stop crying and go back into your room and take off all your clothes. Then wrap yourself in this [*Taking down a gown from its peg and handing it to her*] and come back to me. I will get the bath ready.

LIZA: [*All tears*]   I cant. I wont. I'm not used to it. Ive never took off all my clothes before. It's not right: it's not decent.

MRS PEARCE: Nonsense, child. Dont you take off all your clothes every night when you go to bed?

LIZA: [*Amazed*]   No. Why should I? I should catch my death. Of course I take off my skirt.

MRS PEARCE: Do you mean that you sleep in the underclothes you wear in the daytime?

LIZA: What else have I to sleep in?

MRS PEARCE: You will never do that again as long as you live here. I will get you a proper nightdress.

LIZA: Do you mean change into cold things and lie awake shivering half the night? You want to kill me, you do.

MRS PEARCE: I want to change you from a frowzy slut to a clean respectable girl fit to sit with the gentlemen in the study. Are you going to trust me and do what I tell you or be thrown out and sent back to your flower basket?

LIZA: But you dont know what the cold is to me. You dont know how I dread it.

MRS PEARCE: Your bed wont be cold here: I will put a hot water bottle in it. [*Pushing her into the bedroom*] Off with you and undress.

LIZA: Oh, if only I'd known what a dreadful thing it is to be clean I'd never have come. I didnt know when I was well off. I—[MRS PEARCE *pushes her through the door, but leaves it partly open lest her prisoner should take to flight.*

   MRS PEARCE *puts on a pair of white rubber sleeves, and fills the bath, mixing hot and cold, and testing the result with the bath thermometer. She perfumes it with a handful of bath salts and adds a palmful of mustard. She then takes a formidable looking long handled scrubbing brush and soaps it profusely with a ball of scented soap.*

   ELIZA *comes back with nothing on but the bath gown huddled tightly round her, a piteous spectacle of abject terror*]

MRS PEARCE: Now come along. Take that thing off.

LIZA: Oh I couldnt, Mrs Pearce: I reely couldnt. I never done such a thing.

MRS PEARCE: Nonsense. Here: step in and tell me whether it's hot enough for you.

LIZA: Ah-oo! Ah-oo! It's too hot.

MRS PEARCE: [*Deftly snatching the gown away and throwing* ELIZA *down on her back*] It wont hurt you. [*She sets to work with the scrubbing brush*]

[ELIZA's *screams are heartrending*]

. . .

Meanwhile the Colonel has been having it out with Higgins about Eliza. Pickering has come from the hearth to the chair and seated himself astride of it with his arms on the back to cross-examine him.

PICKERING: Excuse the straight question, Higgins. Are you a man of good character where women are concerned?

HIGGINS: [*Moodily*] Have you ever met a man of good character where women are concerned?

PICKERING: Yes: very frequently.

HIGGINS: [*Dogmatically, lifting himself on his hands to the level of the piano, and sitting on it with a bounce*] Well, I havnt. I find that the moment I let a woman make friends with me, she becomes jealous, exacting, suspicious, and a damned nuisance. I find that the moment I let myself make friends with a woman, I become selfish and tyrannical. Women upset everything. When you let them into your life, you find that the woman is driving at one thing and youre driving at another.

PICKERING: At what, for example?

HIGGINS: [*Coming off the piano restlessly*] Oh, Lord knows! I suppose the woman wants to live her own life; and the man wants to live his; and each tries to drag the other on to the wrong track. One wants to go north and the other south; and the result is that both have to go east, though they both hate the east wind. [*He sits down on the bench at the keyboard*] So here I am, a confirmed old bachelor, and likely to remain so.

PICKERING: [*Rising and standing over him gravely*] Come, Higgins! You know what I mean. If I'm to be in this business I shall feel responsible for that girl. I hope it's understood that no advantage is to be taken of her position.

HIGGINS: What! That thing! Sacred, I assure you. [*Rising to explain*] You see, she'll be a pupil; and teaching would be impossible unless pupils were sacred. Ive taught scores of American millionairesses how to speak English: the best looking women in the world. I'm seasoned. They might as well be blocks of wood. *I* might as well be a block of wood. It's—

[MRS PEARCE *opens the door. She has* ELIZA's *hat in her hand.* PICK-ERING *retires to the easy-chair at the hearth and sits down*]

HIGGINS: [*Eagerly*]   Well, Mrs Pearce: is it all right?

MRS PEARCE: [*At the door*]   I just wish to trouble you with a word, if I may, Mr Higgins.

HIGGINS: Yes, certainly. Come in. [*She comes forward*] Dont burn that, Mrs Pearce. I'll keep it as a curiosity. [*He takes the hat*]

MRS PEARCE: Handle it carefully, sir, please. I had to promise her not to burn it; but I had better put it in the oven for a while.

HIGGINS: [*Putting it down hastily on the piano*]   Oh! thank you. Well, what have you to say to me?

PICKERING: Am I in the way?

MRS PEARCE: Not in the least, sir. Mr Higgins: will you please be very particular what you say before the girl?

HIGGINS: [*Sternly*]   Of course. I'm always particular about what I say. Why do you say this to me?

MRS PEARCE: [*Unmoved*]   No, sir: youre not at all particular when youve mislaid anything or when you get a little impatient. Now it doesnt matter before me: I'm used to it. But you really must not swear before the girl.

HIGGINS: [*Indignantly*]   I swear! [*Most emphatically*] I never swear. I detest the habit. What the devil do you mean?

MRS PEARCE: [*Stolidly*]   Thats what I mean, sir. You swear a great deal too much. I dont mind your damning and blasting, and what the devil and where the devil and who the devil—

HIGGINS: Mrs Pearce: this language from your lips! Really!

MRS PEARCE: [*Not to be put off*]   —but there is a certain word I must ask you not to use. The girl used it herself when she began to enjoy the bath. It begins with the same letter as bath. She knows no better: she learnt it at her mother's knee. But she must not hear it from your lips.

HIGGINS: [*Loftily*]   I cannot charge myself with having ever uttered it, Mrs Pearce. [*She looks at him steadfastly. He adds, hiding an uneasy conscience with a judicial air*] Except perhaps in a moment of extreme and justifiable excitement.

MRS PEARCE: Only this morning, sir, you applied it to your boots, to the butter, and to the brown bread.

HIGGINS: Oh, that! Mere alliteration, Mrs Pearce, natural to a poet.

MRS PEARCE: Well, sir, whatever you choose to call it, I beg you not to let the girl hear you repeat it.

HIGGINS: Oh, very well, very well. Is that all?

MRS PEARCE: No, sir. We shall have to be very particular with this girl as to personal cleanliness.

HIGGINS: Certainly. Quite right. Most important.

MRS PEARCE: I mean not to be slovenly about her dress or untidy in leaving things about.

HIGGINS: [*Going to her solemnly*] Just so. I intended to call your attention to that. [*He passes on to* PICKERING, *who is enjoying the conversation immensely*] It is these little things that matter, Pickering. Take care of the pence and the pounds will take care of themselves is as true of personal habits as of money. [*He comes to anchor on the hearthrug, with the air of a man in an unassailable position*]

MRS PEARCE: Yes, sir. Then might I ask you not to come down to breakfast in your dressing-gown, or at any rate not to use it as a napkin to the extent you do, sir. And if you would be so good as not to eat everything off the same plate, and to remember not to put the porridge saucepan out of your hand on the clean tablecloth, it would be a better example to the girl. You know you nearly choked yourself with a fishbone in a jam only last week.

HIGGINS: [*Routed from the hearthrug and drifting back to the piano*] I may do these things sometimes in absence of mind; but surely I dont do them habitually. [*Angrily*] By the way: my dressing-gown smells most damnably of benzine.

MRS PEARCE: No doubt it does, Mr Higgins. But if you will wipe your fingers—

HIGGINS: [*Yelling*] Oh very well, very well: I'll wipe them in my hair in future.

MRS PEARCE: I hope youre not offended, Mr Higgins.

HIGGINS: [*Shocked at finding himself thought capable of an unamiable sentiment*] Not at all, not at all. Youre quite right, Mrs Pearce: I shall be particularly careful before the girl. Is that all?

MRS PEARCE: No, sir. Might she use some of those Japanese dresses you brought from abroad? I really cant put her back into her old things.

HIGGINS: Certainly. Anything you like. Is that all?

MRS PEARCE: Thank you, sir. Thats all. [*She goes out*]

HIGGINS: You know, Pickering, that woman has the most extraordinary ideas about me. Here I am, a shy, diffident sort of man. Ive never been able to feel really grown-up and tremendous, like other chaps. And yet she's firmly persuaded that I'm an arbitrary overbearing bossing kind of person. I cant account for it.

[MRS PEARCE *returns*]

MRS PEARCE: If you please, sir, the trouble's beginning already. Theres a dustman downstairs, Alfred Doolittle, wants to see you. He says you have his daughter here.

PICKERING: [*Rising*]   Phew! I say!

HIGGINS: [*Promptly*]   Send the blackguard up.

MRS PEARCE: Oh, very well, sir. [*She goes out*]

PICKERING: He may not be a blackguard, Higgins.

HIGGINS: Nonsense. Of course he's a blackguard.

PICKERING: Whether he is or not, I'm afraid we shall have some trouble with him.

HIGGINS: [*Confidently*]   Oh no: I think not. If theres any trouble he shall have it with me, not I with him. And we are sure to get something interesting out of him.

PICKERING: About the girl?

HIGGINS: No. I mean his dialect.

PICKERING: Oh!

MRS PEARCE: [*At the door*]   Doolittle, sir. [*She admits* DOOLITTLE *and retires*]

[ALFRED *is an elderly but vigorous dustman, clad in the costume of his profession, including a hat with a back brim covering his neck and shoulders. He has well marked and rather interesting features, and seems equally free from fear and conscience. He has a remarkably expressive voice, the result of a habit of giving vent to his feelings without reserve. His present pose is that of wounded honor and stern resolution*]

DOOLITTLE: [*At the door, uncertain which of the two gentlemen is his man*] Professor Iggins?

HIGGINS: Here. Good morning. Sit down.

DOOLITTLE: Morning, Governor. [*He sits down magisterially*] I come about a very serious matter, Governor.

HIGGINS: [*To* PICKERING]   Brought up in Hounslow. Mother Welsh, I should think. [DOOLITTLE *opens his mouth, amazed.* HIGGINS *continues*] What do you want, Doolittle?

DOOLITTLE: [*Menacingly*]   I want my daughter: thats what I want. See?

HIGGINS: Of course you do. Youre her father, arnt you? You dont suppose anyone else wants her, do you? I'm glad to see you have some spark of family feeling left. She's upstairs. Take her away at once.

DOOLITTLE: [*Rising, fearfully taken aback*]   What!

HIGGINS: Take her away. Do you suppose I'm going to keep your daughter for you?

DOOLITTLE: [*Remonstrating*]   Now, now, look here, Governor. Is this reasonable? Is it fairity to take advantage of a man like this? The girl belongs to me. You got her. Where do I come in? [*He sits down again*]

HIGGINS: Your daughter had the audacity to come to my house and ask me to teach her how to speak properly so that she could get a place in a flower-shop. This gentleman and my housekeeper have been here all the time. [*Bullying him*] How dare you come here and attempt to blackmail me? You sent her here on purpose.

DOOLITTLE: [*Protesting*]   No, Governor.

HIGGINS: You must have. How else could you possibly know that she is here?

DOOLITTLE: Dont take a man up like that, Governor.

HIGGINS: The police shall take you up. This is a plant—a plot to extort money by threats. I shall telephone for the police. [*He goes resolutely to the telephone and opens the directory*]

DOOLITTLE: Have I asked you for a brass farthing? I leave it to the gentleman here: have I said a word about money?

HIGGINS: [*Throwing the book aside and marching down on* DOOLITTLE *with a poser*]   What else did you come for?

DOOLITTLE: [*Sweetly*]   Well, what would a man come for? Be human, Governor.

HIGGINS: [*Disarmed*]   Alfred: did you put her up to it?

DOOLITTLE: So help me, Governor, I never did. I take my Bible oath I aint seen the girl these two months past.

HIGGINS: Then how did you know she was here?

DOOLITTLE: [*"Most musical, most melancholy"*] I'll tell you, Governor, if youll only let me get a word in. I'm willing to tell you. I'm wanting to tell you. I'm waiting to tell you.

HIGGINS: Pickering: this chap has a certain natural gift of rhetoric. Observe the rhythm of his native woodnotes wild. "I'm willing to tell you: I'm wanting to tell you: I'm waiting to tell you." Sentimental rhetoric! thats the Welsh strain in him. It also accounts for his mendacity and dishonesty.

PICKERING: Oh, please, Higgins: I'm west country myself. [*To* DOOLITTLE] How did you know the girl was here if you didnt send her?

DOOLITTLE: It was like this, Governor. The girl took a boy in the taxi to give him a jaunt. Son of her landlady, he is. He hung about on the chance of her giving him another ride home. Well, she sent him back for her luggage when she heard you was willing for her to stop here. I met the boy at the corner of Long Acre and Endell Street.

HIGGINS: Public house. Yes?

DOOLITTLE: The poor man's club, Governor: why shouldnt I?

PICKERING: Do let him tell his story, Higgins.

DOOLITTLE: He told me what was up. And I ask you, what was my feelings and my duty as a father? I says to the boy, "You bring me the luggage," I says—

PICKERING: Why didnt you go for it yourself?

DOOLITTLE: Landlady wouldnt have trusted me with it, Governor. She's that kind of woman: you know. I had to give the boy a penny afore he trusted me with it, the little swine. I brought it to her just to oblige you like, and make myself agreeable. Thats all.

HIGGINS: How much luggage?

DOOLITTLE: Musical instrument, Governor. A few pictures, a trifle of jewelry, and a bird-cage. She said she didnt want no clothes. What was I to think from that, Governor? I ask you as a parent what was I to think?

HIGGINS: So you came to rescue her from worse than death, eh?

DOOLITTLE: [*Appreciatively: relieved at being so well understood*] Just so, Governor. Thats right.

PICKERING: But why did you bring her luggage if you intended to take her away?

DOOLITTLE: Have I said a word about taking her away? Have I now?

HIGGINS: [*Determinedly*] Youre going to take her away, double quick. [*He crosses to the hearth and rings the bell*]

DOOLITTLE: [*Rising*] No, Governor. Dont say that. I'm not the man to stand in my girl's light. Heres a career opening for her, as you might say; and—

[MRS PEARCE *opens the door and awaits orders*]

HIGGINS: Mrs Pearce: this is Eliza's father. He has come to take her away. Give her to him. [*He goes back to the piano, with an air of washing his hands of the whole affair*]

DOOLITTLE: No. This is a misunderstanding. Listen here—

MRS PEARCE: He cant take her away, Mr Higgins: how can he? You told me to burn her clothes.

DOOLITTLE: Thats right. I cant carry the girl through the streets like a blooming monkey, can I? I put it to you.

HIGGINS: You have put it to me that you want your daughter. Take your daughter. If she has no clothes go out and buy her some.

DOOLITTLE: [*Desperate*] Wheres the clothes she come in? Did I burn them or did your missus here?

MRS PEARCE: I am the housekeeper, if you please. I have sent for some clothes for your girl. When they come you can take her away. You can wait in the kitchen. This way, please.

[DOOLITTLE, *much troubled, accompanies her to the door; then hesitates; finally turns confidentially to* HIGGINS]

DOOLITTLE: Listen here, Governor. You and me is men of the world, aint we?

HIGGINS: Oh! Men of the world, are we? Youd better go, Mrs Pearce.

MRS PEARCE: I think so, indeed, sir. [*She goes, with dignity*]

PICKERING: The floor is yours, Mr Doolittle.

DOOLITTLE: [*To* PICKERING] I thank you, Governor. [*To* HIGGINS, *who takes refuge on the piano bench, a little overwhelmed by the proximity of his visitor; for* DOOLITTLE *has a professional flavour of dust about him*] Well, the truth is, Ive taken a sort of fancy to you, Governor; and if you want the girl, I'm not so set on having her back home again but what I might be open to an arrangement. Regarded in the light of a young woman, she's a fine handsome girl. As a daughter she's not worth her keep; and so I tell you straight. All I ask is my rights as a father; and youre the last man alive to expect me to let her go for nothing; for I can see youre one of the straight sort, Governor. Well, whats a five-pound note to you? and whats Eliza to me? [*He turns to his chair and sits down judicially*]

PICKERING: I think you ought to know, Doolittle, that Mr Higgins's intentions are entirely honorable.

DOOLITTLE: Course they are, Governor. If I thought they wasnt, I'd ask fifty.

HIGGINS: [*Revolted*]   Do you mean to say that you would sell your daughter for £50?

DOOLITTLE: Not in a general way I would; but to oblige a gentleman like you I'd do a good deal, I do assure you.

PICKERING: Have you no morals, man?

DOOLITTLE: [*Unabashed*]   Cant afford them, Governor. Neither could you if you was as poor as me. Not that I mean any harm, you know. But if Liza is going to have a bit out of this, why not me too?

HIGGINS: [*Troubled*]   I dont know what to do, Pickering. There can be no question that as a matter of morals it's a positive crime to give this chap a farthing. And yet I feel a sort of rough justice in his claim.

DOOLITTLE: Thats it, Governor. Thats all I say. A father's heart, as it were.

PICKERING: Well, I know the feeling; but really it seems hardly right—

DOOLITTLE: Dont say that, Governor. Dont look at it that way. What am I, Governors both? I ask you, what am I? I'm one of the undeserving poor: thats what I am. Think of what that means to a man. It means that he's up agen middle class morality all the time. If theres anything going, and I put in for a bit of it, it's always the same story: "Youre undeserving; so you cant have it." But my needs is as great as the most deserving widow's that ever got money out of six different charities in one week for the death of the same husband. I dont need less than a deserving man: I need more. I dont eat less hearty than him; and I drink a lot more. I want a bit of amusement, cause I'm a thinking man. I want cheerfulness and a song and a band when I feel low. Well, they charge me just the same for everything as they charge the deserving. What is middle class morality? Just an excuse for never giving me anything. Therefore, I ask you, as two gentlemen, not to play that game on me. I'm playing straight with you. I aint pretending to be deserving. I'm undeserving; and I mean to go on being undeserving. I like it; and thats the truth. Will you take advantage of a man's nature to do him out of the price of his own daughter what he's brought up and fed and clothed by the sweat of his brow until she's growed big enough to be interesting to you two gentlemen? Is five pounds unreasonable? I put it to you; and I leave it to you.

HIGGINS: [Rising, and going over to PICKERING] Pickering: if we were to take this man in hand for three months, he could choose between a seat in the Cabinet and a popular pulpit in Wales.

PICKERING: What do you say to that, Doolittle?

DOOLITTLE: Not me, Governor, thank you kindly. Ive heard all the preachers and all the prime ministers—for I'm a thinking man and game for politics or religion or social reform same as all the other amusements—and I tell you it's a dog's life any way you look at it. Undeserving poverty is my line. Taking one station in society with another, it's—it's—well, it's the only one that has any ginger in it, to my taste.

HIGGINS: I suppose we must give him a fiver.

PICKERING: He'll make a bad use of it, I'm afraid.

DOOLITTLE: Not me, Governor, so help me I wont. Dont you be afraid that I'll save it and spare it and live idle on it. There wont be a penny of it left by Monday: I'll have to go to work same as if I'd never had it. It wont pauperize me, you bet. Just one good spree for myself and the missus, giving pleasure to ourselves and employment to others, and satisfaction to you to think it's not been throwed away. You couldnt spend it better.

HIGGINS: [Taking out his pocket book and coming between DOOLITTLE and the piano] This is irresistible. Lets give him ten. [He offers two notes to the dustman]

DOOLITTLE: No, Governor. She wouldnt have the heart to spend ten; and perhaps I shouldnt neither. Ten pounds is a lot of money: it makes a man feel prudent like; and then goodbye to happiness. You give me what I ask you, Governor: not a penny more, and not a penny less.

PICKERING: Why dont you marry that missus of yours? I rather draw the line at encouraging that sort of immorality.

DOOLITTLE: Tell her so, Governor: tell her so. I'm willing. It's me that suffers by it. Ive no hold on her. I got to be agreeable to her. I got to give

her presents. I got to buy her clothes something sinful. I'm a slave to
that woman, Governor, just because I'm not her lawful husband. And
she knows it too. Catch her marrying me! Take my advice, Governor:
marry Eliza while she's young and dont know no better. If you dont
youll be sorry for it after. If you do, she'll be sorry for it after; but better her than you, because youre a man, and she's only a woman and dont
know how to be happy anyhow.

HIGGINS: Pickering: if we listen to this man another minute, we shall have
no convictions left. [*To* DOOLITTLE] Five pounds I think you said.

DOOLITTLE: Thank you kindly, Governor.

HIGGINS: Youre sure you wont take ten?

DOOLITTLE: Not now. Another time, Governor.

HIGGINS: [*Handing him a five-pound note*] Here you are.

DOOLITTLE: Thank you, Governor. Good morning. [*He hurries to the door,
anxious to get away with his booty. When he opens it he is confronted
with a dainty and exquisitely clean young Japanese lady in a simple blue
cotton kimono printed cunningly with small white jasmine blossoms.*
MRS PEARCE *is with her. He gets out of her way deferentially and
apologizes*] Beg pardon, miss.

THE JAPANESE LADY: Garn! Dont you know your own daughter?

DOOLITTLE: ⎧*Exclaiming*⎫ Bly me! it's Eliza!
HIGGINS: ⎨ *simul-* ⎬ Whats that? This!
PICKERING: ⎩*taneously*⎭ By Jove!

LIZA: Dont I look silly?

HIGGINS: Silly?

MRS PEARCE: [*At the door*] Now, Mr Higgins, please dont say anything to
make the girl conceited about herself.

HIGGINS: [*Conscientiously*] Oh! Quite right, Mrs Pearce. [*To* ELIZA] Yes:
damned silly.

MRS PEARCE: Please, sir.

HIGGINS: [*Correcting himself*] I mean extremely silly.

LIZA: I should look all right with my hat on. [*She takes up her hat; puts it
on; and walks across the room to the fireplace with a fashionable air*]

HIGGINS: A new fashion, by George! And it ought to look horrible!

DOOLITTLE: [*With fatherly pride*] Well, I never thought she'd clean up
as good looking as that, Governor. She's a credit to me, aint she?

LIZA: I tell you, it's easy to clean up here. Hot and cold water on tap, just as much as you like, there is. Woolly towels, there is; and a towel horse so hot, it burns your fingers. Soft brushes to scrub yourself, and a wooden bowl of soap smelling like primroses. Now I know why ladies is so clean. Washing's a treat for them. Wish they could see what it is for the like of me!

HIGGINS: I'm glad the bathroom met with your approval.

LIZA: It didnt: not all of it; and I dont care who hears me say it. Mrs Pearce knows.

HIGGINS: What was wrong, Mrs Pearce?

MRS PEARCE: [*Blandly*] Oh, nothing, sir. It doesnt matter.

LIZA: I had a good mind to break it. I didnt know which way to look. But I hung a towel over it, I did.

HIGGINS: Over what?

MRS PEARCE: Over the looking-glass, sir.

HIGGINS: Doolittle: you have brought your daughter up too strictly.

DOOLITTLE: Me! I never brought her up at all, except to give her a lick of a strap now and again. Dont put it on me, Governor. She aint accustomed to it, you see: thats all. But she'll soon pick up your free-and-easy ways.

LIZA: I'm a good girl, I am; and I wont pick up no free-and-easy ways.

HIGGINS: Eliza: if you say again that youre a good girl, your father shall take you home.

LIZA: Not him. You dont know my father. All he come here for was to touch you for some money to get drunk on.

DOOLITTLE: Well, what else would I want money for? To put into the plate in church, I suppose. [*She puts out her tongue at him. He is so incensed by this that* PICKERING *presently finds it necessary to step between them*] Dont you give me none of your lip; and dont let me hear you giving this gentleman any of it neither, or youll hear from me about it. See?

HIGGINS: Have you any further advice to give her before you go, Doolittle? Your blessing, for instance.

DOOLITTLE: No, Governor: I aint such a mug as to put up my children to all I know myself. Hard enough to hold them in without that. If you want

Eliza's mind improved, Governor, you do it yourself with a strap. So long, gentlemen. [*He turns to go*]

HIGGINS: [*Impressively*] Stop. Youll come regularly to see your daughter. It's your duty, you know. My brother is a clergyman; and he could help you in your talks with her.

DOOLITTLE: [*Evasively*] Certainly, I'll come, Governor. Not just this week, because I have a job at a distance. But later on you may depend on me. Afternoon, gentlemen. Afternoon, maam. [*He touches his hat to* MRS PEARCE, *who disdains the salutation and goes out. He winks at* HIGGINS, *thinking him probably a fellow-sufferer from* MRS PEARCE's *difficult disposition, and follows her*]

LIZA: Dont you believe the old liar. He'd as soon you set a bulldog on him as a clergyman. You wont see him again in a hurry.

HIGGINS: I dont want to, Eliza. Do you?

LIZA: Not me. I dont want never to see him again, I dont. He's a disgrace to me, he is, collecting dust, instead of working at his trade.

PICKERING: What is his trade, Eliza?

LIZA: Talking money out of other people's pockets into his own. His proper trade's a navvy; and he works at it sometimes too—for exercise—and earns good money at it. Aint you going to call me Miss Doolittle any more?

PICKERING: I beg your pardon, Miss Doolittle. It was a slip of the tongue.

LIZA: Oh, I dont mind; only it sounded so genteel. I should just like to take a taxi to the corner of Tottenham Court Road and get out there and tell it to wait for me, just to put the girls in their place a bit. I wouldnt speak to them, you know.

PICKERING: Better wait til we get you something really fashionable.

HIGGINS: Besides, you shouldnt cut your old friends now that you have risen in the world. Thats what we call snobbery.

LIZA: You dont call the like of them my friends now, I should hope. Theyve took it out of me often enough with their ridicule when they had the chance; and now I mean to get a bit of my own back. But if I'm to have fashionable clothes, I'll wait. I should like to have some. Mrs Pearce says youre going to give me some to wear in bed at night different to what I wear in the daytime; but it do seem a waste of money when you could get something to shew. Besides, I never could fancy changing into cold things on a winter night.

MRS PEARCE: [*Coming back*] Now, Eliza. The new things have come for you to try on.

LIZA: Ah-ow-oo-ooh! [*She rushes out*]

MRS PEARCE: [*Following her*] Oh, dont rush about like that, girl. [*She shuts the door behind her*]

HIGGINS: Pickering: we have taken on a stiff job.

PICKERING: [*With conviction*] Higgins: we have.

.　　.　　.

There seems to be some curiosity as to what Higgins's lessons to Eliza were like. Well, here is a sample: the first one.

Picture Eliza, in her new clothes, and feeling her inside put out of step by a lunch, dinner, and breakfast of a kind to which it is unaccustomed, seated with Higgins and the Colonel in the study, feeling like a hospital out-patient at a first encounter with the doctors.

Higgins, constitutionally unable to sit still, discomposes her still more by striding restlessly about. But for the reassuring presence and quietude of her friend the Colonel she would run for her life, even back to Drury Lane.

HIGGINS: Say your alphabet.

LIZA: I know my alphabet. Do you think I know nothing? I dont need to be taught like a child.

HIGGINS: [*Thundering*] Say your alphabet.

PICKERING: Say it, Miss Doolittle. You will understand presently. Do what he tells you; and let him teach you in his own way.

LIZA: Oh well, if you put it like that—Ahyee, bəyee, cəyee, dəyee—

HIGGINS: [*With the roar of a wounded lion*] Stop. Listen to this, Pickering. This is what we pay for as elementary education. This unfortunate animal has been locked up for nine years in school at our expense to teach her to speak and read the language of Shakespear and Milton. And the result is Ahyee, Bə-yee, Cə-yee, Dəyee. [*To* ELIZA] Say A, B, C, D.

LIZA: [*Almost in tears*] But I'm sayin it. Ahyee, Bəyee, Cəyee—

HIGGINS: Stop. Say a cup of tea.

LIZA: A cappətə-ee.

HIGGINS: Put your tongue forward until it squeezes against the top of your lower teeth. Now say cup.

LIZA: C-c-c—I cant. C-Cup.

PICKERING: Good. Splendid, Miss Doolittle.

HIGGINS: By Jupiter, she's done it the first shot. Pickering: we shall make a duchess of her. [*To* ELIZA] Now do you think you could possibly say tea? Not tə-yee, mind: if you ever say bə-yee cə-yee də-yee again you shall be dragged round the room three times by the hair of your head. [*Fortissimo*] T, T, T, T.

LIZA: [*Weeping*]   I cant hear no difference cep that it sounds more genteel-like when you say it.

HIGGINS: Well, if you can hear that difference, what the devil are you crying for? Pickering: give her a chocolate.

PICKERING: No, no. Never mind crying a little, Miss Doolittle: you are doing very well; and the lessons wont hurt. I promise you I wont let him drag you round the room by your hair.

HIGGINS: Be off with you to Mrs Pearce and tell her about it. Think about it. Try to do it by yourself: and keep your tongue well forward in your mouth instead of trying to roll it up and swallow it. Another lesson at half-past four this afternoon. Away with you.

[ELIZA, *still sobbing, rushes from the room*]

And that is the sort of ordeal poor Eliza has to go through for months before we meet her again on her first appearance in London society of the professional class.

ACT III

It is Mrs Higgins's at-home day. Nobody has yet arrived. Her drawing room, in a flat on Chelsea Embankment, has three windows looking on the river; and the ceiling is not so lofty as it would be in an older house of the same pretension. The windows are open, giving access to a balcony with flowers in pots. If you stand with your face to the windows, you have the fireplace on your left and the door in the right-hand wall close to the corner nearest the windows.

Mrs Higgins was brought up on Morris and Burne Jones; and her room, which is very unlike her son's room in Wimpole Street, is not crowded with furniture and little tables and nicknacks. In the middle of the room there is a big ottoman; and this, with the carpet, the Morris wall-papers, and the Morris chintz window curtains and brocade covers of the ottoman and its cushions, supply all the ornament, and are much too handsome to be hidden by odds and ends of useless things. A few good oil-paintings from the exhibitions in the Grosvenor Gallery thirty years ago (the Burne Jones, not the Whistler side of them) are on the walls. The only landscape is a Cecil Lawson on the scale of a Rubens. There is a portrait of Mrs Higgins as she was when she defied the fashion in her youth in one of the beautiful Rossettian costumes which, when caricatured by people who did not understand, led to the absurdities of popular estheticism in the eighteen-seventies.

In the corner diagonally opposite the door Mrs Higgins, now over sixty and long past taking the trouble to dress out of the fashion, sits writing at an elegantly simple writing-table with a bell button within reach of her hand. There is a Chippendale chair further back in the room between her and the window nearest her side. At the other side of the room, further forward, is an Elizabethan chair roughly carved in the taste of Inigo Jones. On the same side a piano in a decorated case. The corner between the fireplace and the window is occupied by a divan cushioned in Morris chintz.

It is between four and five in the afternoon.

The door is opened violently; and Higgins enters with his hat on.

MRS HIGGINS: [*Dismayed*] Henry! [*Scolding him*] What are you doing here today? It is my at-home day: you promised not to come. [*As he bends to kiss her, she takes his hat off, and presents it to him*]

HIGGINS: Oh bother! [*He throws the hat down on the table*]

MRS HIGGINS: Go home at once.

HIGGINS: [*Kissing her*] I know, mother. I came on purpose.

MRS HIGGINS: But you mustnt. I'm serious, Henry. You offend all my friends: they stop coming whenever they meet you.

HIGGINS: Nonsense! I know I have no small talk; but people dont mind. [*He sits on the settee*]

MRS HIGGINS: Oh! dont they? Small talk indeed! What about your large talk? Really, dear, you mustnt stay.

HIGGINS: I must. Ive a job for you. A phonetic job.

MRS HIGGINS: No use, dear. I'm sorry; but I cant get round your vowels; and though I like to get pretty postcards in your patent shorthand, I always have to read the copies in ordinary writing you so thoughtfully send me.

HIGGINS: Well, this isnt a phonetic job.

MRS HIGGINS: You said it was.

HIGGINS: Not your part of it. Ive picked up a girl.

MRS HIGGINS: Does that mean that some girl has picked you up?

HIGGINS: Not at all. I dont mean a love affair.

MRS HIGGINS: What a pity!

HIGGINS: Why?

MRS HIGGINS: Well, you never fall in love with anyone under forty-five. When will you discover that there are some rather nice-looking young women about?

HIGGINS: Oh, I cant be bothered with young women. My idea of a lovable woman is somebody as like you as possible. I shall never get into the way of seriously liking young women: some habits lie too deep to be changed. [Rising abruptly and walking about, jingling his money and his keys in his trouser pockets] Besides, theyre all idiots.

MRS HIGGINS: Do you know what you would do if you really loved me, Henry?

HIGGINS: Oh bother! What? Marry, I suppose.

MRS HIGGINS: No. Stop fidgeting and take your hands out of your pockets. [With a gesture of despair, he obeys and sits down again] Thats a good boy. Now tell me about the girl.

HIGGINS: She's coming to see you.

MRS HIGGINS: I dont remember asking her.

HIGGINS: You didnt. I asked her. If youd known her you wouldnt have asked her.

MRS HIGGINS: Indeed! Why?

HIGGINS: Well, it's like this. She's a common flower girl. I picked her off the kerbstone.

MRS HIGGINS: And invited her to my at-home!

HIGGINS: [Rising and coming to her to coax her]   Oh, thatll be all right. Ive taught her to speak properly; and she has strict orders as to her behavior. She's to keep to two subjects: the weather and everybody's health—Fine day and How do you do, you know—and not to let herself go on things in general. That will be safe.

MRS HIGGINS: Safe! To talk about our health! about our insides! perhaps about our outsides! How could you be so silly, Henry?

HIGGINS: [*Impatiently*] Well, she must talk about something. [*He controls himself and sits down again*] Oh, she'll be all right: dont you fuss. Pickering is in it with me. Ive a sort of bet on that I'll pass her off as a duchess in six months. I started on her some months ago; and she's getting on like a house on fire. I shall win my bet. She has a quick ear; and she's easier to teach than my middle-class pupils because she's had to learn a complete new language. She talks English almost as you talk French.

MRS HIGGINS: Thats satisfactory, at all events.

HIGGINS: Well, it is and it isnt.

MRS HIGGINS: What does that mean?

HIGGINS: You see, Ive got her pronunciation all right; but you have to consider not only how a girl pronounces, but what she pronounces; and that's where—

[*They are interrupted by the parlormaid, announcing guests*]

THE PARLORMAID: Mrs and Miss Eynsford Hill. [*She withdraws*]

HIGGINS: Oh Lord! [*He rises; snatches his hat from the table; and makes for the door; but before he reaches it his mother introduces him*]

[MRS *and* MISS EYNSFORD HILL *are the mother and daughter who sheltered from the rain in Covent Garden. The mother is well bred, quiet, and has the habitual anxiety of straitened means. The daughter has acquired a gay air of being very much at home in society: the bravado of genteel poverty*]

MRS EYNSFORD HILL: [*To* MRS HIGGINS] How do you do? [*They shake hands*]

MISS EYNSFORD HILL: How d'you do? [*She shakes*]

MRS HIGGINS: [*Introducing*] My son Henry.

MRS EYNSFORD HILL: Your celebrated son! I have so longed to meet you, Professor Higgins.

HIGGINS: [*Glumly, making no movement in her direction*] Delighted. [*He backs against the piano and bows brusquely*]

MISS EYNSFORD HILL: [*Going to him with confident familiarity*] How do you do?

HIGGINS: [*Staring at her*] Ive seen you before somewhere. I havnt the ghost of a notion where; but Ive heard your voice. [*Drearily*] It doesnt matter. Youd better sit down.

MRS HIGGINS: I'm sorry to say that my celebrated son has no manners. You mustnt mind him.

MISS EYNSFORD HILL: [*Gaily*]   I dont. [*She sits in the Elizabethan chair*]

MRS EYNSFORD HILL: [*A little bewildered*]   Not at all. [*She sits on the otto-man between her daughter and* MRS HIGGINS, *who has turned her chair away from the writing-table*]

HIGGINS: Oh, have I been rude? I didnt mean to be.

[*He goes to the central window, through which, with his back to the company, he contemplates the river and the flowers in Battersea Park on the opposite bank as if they were a frozen desert.
The parlor-maid returns, ushering in* PICKERING]

THE PARLORMAID: Colonel Pickering. [*She withdraws*]

PICKERING: How do you do, Mrs Higgins?

MRS HIGGINS: So glad youve come. Do you know Mrs Eynsford Hill—Miss Eynsford Hill? [*Exchange of bows. The Colonel brings the Chippendale chair a little forward between* MRS HILL *and* MRS HIGGINS, *and sits down*]

PICKERING: Has Henry told you what weve come for?

HIGGINS: [*Over his shoulder*]   We were interrupted: damn it!

MRS HIGGINS: Oh Henry, Henry, really!

MRS EYNSFORD HILL: [*Half rising*]   Are we in the way?

MRS HIGGINS: [*Rising and making her sit down again*]   No, no. You couldnt have come more fortunately: we want you to meet a friend of ours.

HIGGINS: [*Turning hopefully*]   Yes, by George! We want two or three peo-ple. Youll do as well as anybody else.

[*The* PARLORMAID *returns, ushering* FREDDY]

THE PARLORMAID: Mr Eynsford Hill.

HIGGINS: [*Almost audibly, past endurance*]   God of Heaven! another of them.

FREDDY: [*Shaking hands with* MRS HIGGINS]   Ahdedo?

MRS HIGGINS: Very good of you to come. [*Introducing*] Colonel Pickering.

FREDDY: [*Bowing*]   Ahdedo?

MRS HIGGINS: I dont think you know my son, Professor Higgins.

FREDDY: [*Going to* HIGGINS]   Ahdedo?

HIGGINS: [*Looking at him much as if he were a pickpocket*] I'll take my oath Ive met you before somewhere. Where was it?

FREDDY: I dont think so.

HIGGINS: [*Resignedly*] It dont matter, anyhow. Sit down.

[*He shakes* FREDDY'S *hand, and almost slings him on to the ottoman with his face to the window; then comes round to the other side of it*]

HIGGINS: Well, here we are, anyhow! [*He sits down on the ottoman next* MRS EYNSFORD HILL, *on her left*] And now, what the devil are we going to talk about until Eliza comes?

MRS HIGGINS: Henry: you are the life and soul of the Royal Society's soirées; but really youre rather trying on more commonplace occasions.

HIGGINS: Am I? Very sorry. [*Beaming suddenly*] I suppose I am, you know. [*Uproariously*] Ha, ha!

MISS EYNSFORD HILL: [*Who considers* HIGGINS *quite eligible matrimonially*] I sympathize. *I* havnt any small talk. If people would only be frank and say what they really think!

HIGGINS: [*Relapsing into gloom*] Lord forbid!

MRS EYNSFORD HILL: [*Taking up her daughter's cue*] But why?

HIGGINS: What they think they ought to think is bad enough, Lord knows; but what they really think would break up the whole show. Do you suppose it would be really agreeable if I were to come out now with what I really think?

MISS EYNSFORD HILL: [*Gaily*] Is it so very cynical?

HIGGINS: Cynical! Who the dickens said it was cynical? I mean it wouldnt be decent.

MRS EYNSFORD HILL: [*Seriously*] Oh! I'm sure you dont mean that, Mr Higgins.

HIGGINS: You see, we're all savages, more or less. We're supposed to be civilized and cultured—to know all about poetry and philosophy and art and science, and so on; but how many of us know even the meanings of these names? [*To* MISS HILL] What do you know of poetry? [*To* MRS HILL] What do you know of science? [*Indicating* FREDDY] What does he know of art or science or anything else? What the devil do you imagine I know of philosophy?

MRS HIGGINS: [*Warningly*] Or of manners, Henry?

THE PARLORMAID: [*Opening the door*] Miss Doolittle. [*She withdraws*]

HIGGINS: [*Rising hastily and running to* MRS HIGGINS] Here she is, mother.

[*He stands on tiptoe and makes signs over his mother's head to* ELIZA *to indicate to her which lady is her hostess.*

ELIZA, *who is exquisitely dressed, produces an impression of such remarkable distinction and beauty as she enters that they all rise, quite fluttered. Guided by* HIGGINS's *signals, she comes to* MRS HIGGINS *with studied grace*]

LIZA: [*Speaking with pedantic correctness of pronunciation and great beauty of tone*] How do you do, Mrs. Higgins? [*She gasps slightly in making sure of the H in* HIGGINS, *but is quite successful*] Mr Higgins told me I might come.

MRS HIGGINS: [*Cordially*] Quite right: I'm very glad indeed to see you.

PICKERING: How do you do, Miss Doolittle?

LIZA: [*Shaking hands with him*] Colonel Pickering, is it not?

MRS EYNSFORD HILL: I feel sure we have met before, Miss Doolittle. I remember your eyes.

LIZA: How do you do? [*She sits down on the ottoman gracefully in the place just left vacant by* HIGGINS]

MRS EYNSFORD HILL: [*Introducing*] My daughter Clara.

LIZA: How do you do?

CLARA: [*Impulsively*] How do you do? [*She sits down on the ottoman beside* ELIZA, *devouring her with her eyes*]

FREDDY: [*Coming to their side of the ottoman*] Ive certainly had the pleasure.

MRS EYNSFORD HILL: [*Introducing*] My son Freddy.

LIZA: How do you do?

[FREDDY *bows and sits down in the Elizabethan chair, infatuated*]

HIGGINS: [*Suddenly*] By George, yes: it all comes back to me! [*They stare at him*] Covent Garden! [*Lamentably*] What a damned thing!

MRS HIGGINS: Henry, please! [*He is about to sit on the edge of the table*] Dont sit on my writing-table: youll break it.

HIGGINS: [*Sulkily*] Sorry.

[*He goes to the divan, stumbling into the fender and over the fire-irons on his way; extricating himself with muttered imprecations; and finishing his disastrous journey by throwing himself so impatiently on the divan that he almost breaks it.* MRS HIGGINS *looks at him, but controls herself and says nothing.*

> *A long and painful pause ensues]*

MRS HIGGINS: [*At last, conversationally*] Will it rain, do you think?

LIZA: The shallow depression in the west of these islands is likely to move slowly in an easterly direction. There are no indications of any great change in the barometrical situation.

FREDDY: Ha! ha! how awfully funny!

LIZA: What is wrong with that, young man? I bet I got it right.

FREDDY: Killing!

MRS EYNSFORD HILL: I'm sure I hope it wont turn cold. Theres so much influenza about. It runs right through our whole family regularly every spring.

LIZA: [*Darkly*] My aunt died of influenza: so they said.

MRS EYNSFORD HILL: [*Clicks her tongue sympathetically*] !!!

LIZA: [*In the same tragic tone*] But it's my belief they done the old woman in.

MRS HIGGINS: [*Puzzled*] Done her in?

LIZA: Y-e-e-e-es, Lord love you! Why should she die of influenza? She come through diphtheria right enough the year before. I saw her with my own eyes. Fairly blue with it, she was. They all thought she was dead; but my father he kept ladling gin down her throat til she came to so sudden that she bit the bowl off the spoon.

MRS EYNSFORD HILL: [*Startled*] Dear me!

LIZA: [*Piling up the indictment*] What call would a woman with that strength in her have to die of influenza? What become of her new straw hat that should have come to me? Somebody pinched it; and what I say is, them as pinched it done her in.

MRS EYNSFORD HILL: What does doing her in mean?

HIGGINS: [*Hastily*] Oh, thats the new small talk. To do a person in means to kill them.

MRS EYNSFORD HILL: [*To* ELIZA, *horrified*] You surely dont believe that your aunt was killed?

LIZA: Do I not! Them she lived with would have killed her for a hat-pin, let alone a hat.

MRS EYNSFORD HILL: But it cant have been right for your father to pour spirits down her throat like that. It might have killed her.

LIZA: Not her. Gin was mother's milk to her. Besides, he'd poured so much down his own throat that he knew the good of it.

MRS EYNSFORD HILL: Do you mean that he drank?

LIZA: Drank! My word! Something chronic.

MRS EYNSFORD HILL: How dreadful for you!

LIZA: Not a bit. It never did him no harm what I could see. But then he did not keep it up regular. [*Cheerfully*] On the burst, as you might say, from time to time. And always more agreeable when he had a drop in. When he was out of work, my mother used to give him fourpence and tell him to go out and not come back until he'd drunk himself cheerful and loving-like. Theres lots of women has to make their husbands drunk to make them fit to live with. [*Now quite at her ease*] You see, it's like this. If a man has a bit of conscience, it always takes him when he's sober; and then it makes him low-spirited. A drop of booze just takes that off and makes him happy. [*To* FREDDY, *who is in convulsions of suppressed laughter*] Here! what are you sniggering at?

FREDDY: The new small talk. You do it so awfully well.

LIZA: If I was doing it proper, what was you laughing at? [*To* HIGGINS] Have I said anything I oughtnt?

MRS HIGGINS: [*Interposing*]   Not at all, Miss Doolittle.

LIZA: Well, thats a mercy, anyhow. [*Expansively*] What I always say is—

HIGGINS: [*Rising and looking at his watch*]   Ahem!

LIZA: [*Looking round at him; taking the hint; and rising*]   Well: I must go. [*They all rise.* FREDDY *goes to the door*] So pleased to have met you. Goodbye. [*She shakes hands with* MRS HIGGINS]

MRS HIGGINS: Goodbye.

LIZA: Goodbye, Colonel Pickering.

PICKERING: Goodbye, Miss Doolittle. [*They shake hands*]

LIZA: [*Nodding to the others*]   Goodbye, all.

FREDDY: [*Opening the door for her*]   Are you walking across the Park, Miss Doolittle? If so—

LIZA: [*With perfectly elegant diction*]   Walk! Not bloody likely. [*Sensation*] I am going in a taxi. [*She goes out*]

[PICKERING *gasps and sits down.* FREDDY *goes out on the balcony to catch another glimpse of* ELIZA]

MRS EYNSFORD HILL: [*Suffering from shock*]   Well, I really cant get used to the new ways.

CLARA: [*Throwing herself discontentedly into the Elizabethan chair*]   Oh, it's all right, mamma, quite right. People will think we never go anywhere or see anybody if you are so old-fashioned.

MRS EYNSFORD HILL: I daresay I am very old-fashioned; but I do hope you wont begin using that expression, Clara. I have got accustomed to hear you talking about men as rotters, and calling everything filthy and beastly; though I do think it horrible and unladylike. But this last is really too much. Dont you think so, Colonel Pickering?

PICKERING: Dont ask me. Ive been away in India for several years; and manners have changed so much that I sometimes dont know whether I'm at a respectable dinnertable or in a ship's forecastle.

CLARA: It's all a matter of habit. Theres no right or wrong in it. Nobody means anything by it. And it's so quaint, and gives such a smart emphasis to things that are not in themselves very witty. I find the new small talk delightful and quite innocent.

MRS EYNSFORD HILL: [*Rising*]   Well, after that, I think it's time for us to go.

[PICKERING *and* HIGGINS *rise*]

CLARA: [*Rising*]   Oh yes: we have three at-homes to go to still. Goodbye, Mrs Higgins. Goodbye, Colonel Pickering. Goodbye, Professor Higgins.

HIGGINS: [*Coming grimly at her from the divan, and accompanying her to the door*]   Goodbye. Be sure you try on that small talk at the three at-homes. Dont be nervous about it. Pitch it in strong.

CLARA: [*All smiles*]   I will. Goodbye. Such nonsense, all this early Victorian prudery!

HIGGINS: [*Tempting her*]   Such damned nonsense!

CLARA: Such bloody nonsense!

MRS EYNSFORD HILL: [*Convulsively*]   Clara!

CLARA: Ha! ha! [*She goes out radiant, conscious of being thoroughly up to date, and is heard descending the stairs in a stream of silvery laughter*]

FREDDY: [*To the heavens at large*]   Well, I ask you— [*He gives it up, and comes to* MRS HIGGINS] Goodbye.

MRS HIGGINS: [*Shaking hands*] Goodbye. Would you like to meet Miss Doolittle again?

FREDDY: [*Eagerly*] Yes, I should, most awfully.

MRS HIGGINS: Well, you know my days.

FREDDY: Yes. Thanks awfully. Goodbye. [*He goes out*]

MRS EYNSFORD HILL: Goodbye, Mr Higgins.

HIGGINS: Goodbye. Goodbye.

MRS EYNSFORD HILL: [*To* PICKERING] It's no use. I shall never be able to bring myself to use that word.

PICKERING: Dont. It's not compulsory, you know. Youll get on quite well without it.

MRS EYNSFORD HILL: Only, Clara is so down on me if I am not positively reeking with the latest slang. Goodbye.

PICKERING: Goodbye. [*They shake hands*]

MRS EYNSFORD HILL: [*To* MRS HIGGINS] You mustnt mind Clara. [PICKERING, *catching from her lowered tone that this is not meant for him to hear, discreetly joins* HIGGINS *at the window*] We're so poor! and she gets so few parties, poor child! She doesnt quite know. [MRS HIGGINS, *seeing that her eyes are moist, takes her hand sympathetically and goes with her to the door*] But the boy is nice. Dont you think so?

MRS HIGGINS: Oh, quite nice. I shall always be delighted to see him.

MRS EYNSFORD HILL: Thank you, dear. Goodbye. [*She goes out*]

HIGGINS: [*Eagerly*] Well? Is Eliza presentable? [*He swoops on his mother and drags her to the ottoman, where she sits down in* ELIZA's *place with her son on her left.*
      PICKERING *returns to his chair on her right*]

MRS HIGGINS: You silly boy, of course she's not presentable. She's a triumph of your art and of her dressmaker's; but if you suppose for a moment that she doesnt give herself away in every sentence she utters, you must be perfectly cracked about her.

PICKERING: But dont you think something might be done? I mean something to eliminate the sanguinary element from her conversation.

MRS HIGGINS: Not as long as she is in Henry's hands.

HIGGINS: [*Aggrieved*] Do you mean that my language is improper?

MRS HIGGINS: No, dearest: it would be quite proper—say on a canal barge; but it would not be proper for her at a garden party.

HIGGINS: [*Deeply injured*] Well I must say—

PICKERING: [*Interrupting him*] Come, Higgins: you must learn to know yourself. I havent heard such language as yours since we used to review the volunteers in Hyde Park twenty years ago.

HIGGINS: [*Sulkily*] Oh, well, if you say so, I suppose I dont always talk like a bishop.

MRS HIGGINS: [*Quieting* HENRY *with a touch*] Colonel Pickering: will you tell me what is the exact state of things in Wimpole Street?

PICKERING: [*Cheerfully: as if this completely changed the subject*] Well, I have come to live there with Henry. We work together at my Indian Dialects; and we think it more convenient—

MRS HIGGINS: Quite so. I know all about that: it's an excellent arrangement. But where does this girl live?

HIGGINS: With us, of course. Where should she live?

MRS HIGGINS: But on what terms? Is she a servant? If not, what is she?

PICKERING: [*Slowly*] I think I know what you mean, Mrs Higgins.

HIGGINS: Well, dash me if *I* do! Ive had to work at the girl every day for months to get her to her present pitch. Besides, she's useful. She knows where my things are, and remembers my appointments and so forth.

MRS HIGGINS: How does your housekeeper get on with her?

HIGGINS: Mrs Pearce? Oh, she's jolly glad to get so much taken off her hands; for before Eliza came, she used to have to find things and remind me of my appointments. But she's got some silly bee in her bonnet about Eliza. She keeps saying "You dont think, sir": doesnt she, Pick?

PICKERING: Yes: thats the formula. "You dont think, sir." Thats the end of every conversation about Eliza.

HIGGINS: As if I ever stop thinking about the girl and her confounded vowels and consonants. I'm worn out, thinking about her, and watching her lips and her teeth and her tongue, not to mention her soul, which is the quaintest of the lot.

MRS HIGGINS: You certainly are a pretty pair of babies, playing with your live doll.

HIGGINS: Playing! The hardest job I ever tackled: make no mistake about that, mother. But you have no idea how frightfully interesting it is to take a human being and change her into a quite different human being by creating a new speech for her. It's filling up the deepest gulf that separates class from class and soul from soul.

PICKERING: [*Drawing his chair closer to* MRS HIGGINS *and bending over to her eagerly*] Yes: it's enormously interesting. I assure you, Mrs Higgins, we take Eliza very seriously. Every week—every day almost—there is some new change. [*Closer again*] We keep records of every stage—dozens of gramophone disks and photographs—

HIGGINS: [*Assailing her at the other ear*] Yes, by George: it's the most absorbing experiment I ever tackled. She regularly fills our lives up: doesnt she, Pick?

PICKERING: We're always talking Eliza.

HIGGINS: Teaching Eliza.

PICKERING: Dressing Eliza.

MRS HIGGINS: What!

HIGGINS: Inventing new Elizas.

HIGGINS: ⎫ [*Speaking* ⎧ You know, she has the most extraordinary quickness
         ⎬ *together*] ⎨ of ear:
PICKERING: ⎭   ⎩ I assure you, my dear Mrs Higgins, that girl

HIGGINS: ⎫   ⎧ just like a parrot. Ive tried her with every
PICKERING: ⎬   ⎨ is a genius. She can play the piano quite beauti-
         ⎭   ⎩ fully.

HIGGINS: ⎫   ⎧ possible sort of sound that a human being can
         ⎬   ⎨ make—
PICKERING: ⎭   ⎩ We have taken her to classical concerts and to music

HIGGINS: ⎫   ⎧ Continental dialects, African dialects, Hottentot
PICKERING: ⎬   ⎨ halls; and it's all the same to her: she plays every-
         ⎭   ⎩ thing

HIGGINS: ⎫   ⎧ clicks, things it took me years to get hold of; and
PICKERING: ⎬   ⎨ she hears right off when she comes home, whether
         ⎭   ⎩ it's

HIGGINS: ⎫   ⎧ she picks them up like a shot, right away, as if she
         ⎬   ⎨ had
PICKERING: ⎭   ⎩ Beethoven and Brahms or Lehar and Lionel Monck-
                   ton;

HIGGINS: ⎫ [*Speaking*⎧ been at it all her life.
PICKERING: ⎬ *together*] ⎨ though six months ago, she'd never as much as
          ⎭   ⎩ touched a piano—

MRS HIGGINS: [*Putting her fingers in her ears, as they are by this time shout-ing one another down with an intolerable noise*] Sh-sh-sh—sh! [*They stop*]

PICKERING: I beg your pardon. [*He draws his chair back apologetically*]

HIGGINS: Sorry. When Pickering starts shouting nobody can get a word in edgeways.

MRS HIGGINS: Be quiet, Henry. Colonel Pickering: dont you realize that when Eliza walked in Wimpole Street, something walked in with her?

PICKERING: Her father did. But Henry soon got rid of him.

MRS HIGGINS: It would have been more to the point if her mother had. But as her mother didnt something else did.

PICKERING: But what?

MRS HIGGINS: [*Unconsciously dating herself by the word*] A problem.

PICKERING: Oh, I see. The problem of how to pass her off as a lady.

HIGGINS: I'll solve that problem. Ive half solved it already.

MRS HIGGINS: No, you two infinitely stupid male creatures: the problem of what is to be done with her afterwards.

HIGGINS: I dont see anything in that. She can go her own way, with all the advantages I have given her.

MRS HIGGINS: The advantages of that poor woman who was here just now! The manners and habits that disqualify a fine lady from earning her own living without giving her a fine lady's income! Is that what you mean?

PICKERING: [*Indulgently, being rather bored*] Oh, that will be all right, Mrs Higgins. [*He rises to go*]

HIGGINS: [*Rising also*] We'll find her some light employment.

PICKERING: She's happy enough. Dont you worry about her. Goodbye. [*He shakes hands as if he were consoling a frightened child, and makes for the door*]

HIGGINS: Anyhow, theres no good bothering now. The thing's done. Good-bye, mother. [*He kisses her, and follows* PICKERING]

PICKERING: [*Turning for a final consolation*]   There are plenty of openings.
We'll do whats right. Goodbye.

HIGGINS: [*To* PICKERING *as they go out together*]   Lets take her to the
Shakespear exhibition at Earls Court.

PICKERING: Yes: lets. Her remarks will be delicious.

HIGGINS: She'll mimic all the people for us when we get home.

PICKERING: Ripping. [*Both are heard laughing as they go downstairs*]

MRS HIGGINS: [*Rises with an impatient bounce, and returns to her work at
the writing-table. She sweeps a litter of disarranged papers out of the
way; snatches a sheet of paper from her stationery case; and tries resolutely to write. At the third time she gives it up; flings down her pen;
grips the table angrily and exclaims*]   Oh, men! men!! men!!!

·   ·   ·

Clearly Eliza will not pass as a duchess yet; and Higgins's bet remains
unwon. But the six months are not yet exhausted and just in time Eliza
does actually pass as a princess. For a glimpse of how she did it imagine
an Embassy in London one summer evening after dark. The hall door has
an awning and a carpet across the sidewalk to the kerb, because a grand
reception is in progress. A small crowd is lined up to see the guests arrive.

A Rolls-Royce car drives up. Pickering in evening dress, with medals
and orders, alights, and hands out Eliza, in opera cloak, evening dress,
diamonds, fan, flowers and all accessories. Higgins follows. The car drives
off; and the three go up the steps and into the house, the door opening
for them as they approach.

Inside the house they find themselves in a spacious hall from which
the grand staircase rises. On the left are the arrangements for the gentlemen's cloaks. The male guests are depositing their hats and wraps there.

On the right is a door leading to the ladies' cloakroom. Ladies are
going in cloaked and coming out in splendor. Pickering whispers to Eliza
and points out the ladies' room. She goes into it. Higgins and Pickering
take off their overcoats and take tickets for them from the attendant.

One of the guests, occupied in the same way, has his back turned.
Having taken his ticket, he turns round and reveals himself as an important looking young man with an astonishingly hairy face. He has an
enormous moustache, flowing out into luxuriant whiskers. Waves of hair
cluster on his brow. His hair is cropped closely at the back, and glows
with oil. Otherwise he is very smart. He wears several worthless orders.
He is evidently a foreigner, guessable as a whiskered Pandour from Hun-

gary; but in spite of the ferocity of his moustache he is amiable and genially voluble.

Recognizing Higgins, he flings his arms wide apart and approaches him enthusiastically.

WHISKERS: Maestro, maestro. [*He embraces* HIGGINS *and kisses him on both cheeks*] You remember me?

HIGGINS: No I dont. Who the devil are you?

WHISKERS: I am your pupil: your first pupil, your best and greatest pupil. I am little Nepommuck, the marvellous boy. I have made your name famous throughout Europe. You teach me phonetic. You cannot forget ME.

HIGGINS: Why dont you shave?

NEPOMMUCK: I have not your imposing appearance, your chin, your brow. Nobody notice me when I shave. Now I am famous: they call me Hairy Faced Dick.

HIGGINS: And what are you doing here among all these swells?

NEPOMMUCK: I am interpreter. I speak 32 languages. I am indispensable at these international parties. You are great cockney specialist: you place a man anywhere in London the moment he open his mouth. I place any man in Europe.

[A FOOTMAN *hurries down the grand staircase and comes to* NEPOM-MUCK]

FOOTMAN: You are wanted upstairs. Her Excellency cannot understand the Greek gentleman.

NEPOMMUCK: Thank you, yes, immediately.

[*The* FOOTMAN *goes and is lost in the crowd*]

NEPOMMUCK: [*To* HIGGINS] This Greek diplomatist pretends he cannot speak nor understand English. He cannot deceive me. He is the son of a Clerkenwell watchmaker. He speaks English so villainously that he dare not utter a word of it without betraying his origin. I help him to pretend; but I make him pay through the nose. I make them all pay. Ha ha! [*He hurries upstairs*]

PICKERING: Is this fellow really an expert? Can he find out Eliza and black-mail her?

HIGGINS: We shall see. If he finds her out I lose my bet.

[ELIZA *comes from the cloakroom and joins them*]

PICKERING: Well, Eliza, now for it. Are you ready?

LIZA: Are you nervous, Colonel?

PICKERING: Frightfully. I feel exactly as I felt before my first battle. It's the first time that frightens.

LIZA: It is not the first time for me, Colonel. I have done this fifty times— hundreds of times—in my little piggery in Angel Court in my day-dreams. I am in a dream now. Promise me not to let Professor Higgins wake me; for if he does I shall forget everything and talk as I used to in Drury Lane.

PICKERING: Not a word, Higgins. [*To* ELIZA] Now, ready?

LIZA: Ready.

PICKERING: Go.

[*They mount the stairs,* HIGGINS *last.* PICKERING *whispers to the footman on the first landing*]

FIRST LANDING FOOTMAN: Miss Doolittle, Colonel Pickering, Professor Higgins.

SECOND LANDING FOOTMAN: Miss Doolittle, Colonel Pickering, Professor Higgins.

[*At the top of the staircase the* AMBASSADOR *and his wife, with* NEPOMMUCK *at her elbow, are receiving*]

HOSTESS: [*Taking* ELIZA's *hand*]   How d'ye do?

HOST: [*Same play*]   How d'ye do? How d'ye do, Pickering?

LIZA: [*With a beautiful gravity that awes her hostess*]   How do you do? [*She passes on to the drawingroom*]

HOSTESS: Is that your adopted daughter, Colonel Pickering? She will make a sensation.

PICKERING: Most kind of you to invite her for me. [*He passes on*]

HOSTESS: [*To* NEPOMMUCK]   Find out all about her.

NEPOMMUCK: [*Bowing*]   Excellency— [*He goes into the crowd*]

HOST: How d'ye do, Higgins? You have a rival here tonight. He introduced himself as your pupil. Is he any good?

HIGGINS: He can learn a language in a fortnight—knows dozens of them. A sure mark of a fool. As a phonetician, no good whatever.

HOSTESS: How d'ye do, Professor?

HIGGINS: How do you do? Fearful bore for you this sort of thing. Forgive my part in it. [*He passes on*]

In the drawingroom and its suite of salons the reception is in full swing. Eliza passes through. She is so intent on her ordeal that she walks like a somnambulist in a desert instead of a débutante in a fashionable crowd. They stop talking to look at her, admiring her dress, her jewels, and her strangely attractive self. Some of the younger ones at the back stand on their chairs to see.

The Host and Hostess come in from the staircase and mingle with their guests. Higgins, gloomy and contemptuous of the whole business, comes into the group where they are chatting.

HOSTESS: Ah, here is Professor Higgins: he will tell us. Tell us all about the wonderful young lady, Professor.

HIGGINS: [*Almost morosely*]   What wonderful young lady?

HOSTESS: You know very well. They tell me there has been nothing like her in London since people stood on their chairs to look at Mrs Langtry.

[NEPOMMUCK *joins the group, full of news*]

HOSTESS: Ah, here you are at last, Nepommuck. Have you found out all about the Doolittle lady?

NEPOMMUCK: I have found out all about her. She is a fraud.

HOSTESS: A fraud! Oh no.

NEPOMMUCK: YES, yes. She cannot deceive me. Her name cannot be Doolittle.

HIGGINS: Why?

NEPOMMUCK: Because Doolittle is an English name. And she is not English.

HOSTESS: Oh, nonsense! She speaks English perfectly.

NEPOMMUCK: Too perfectly. Can you shew me any English woman who speaks English as it should be spoken? Only foreigners who have been taught to speak it speak it well.

HOSTESS: Certainly she terrified me by the way she said How d'ye do. I had a schoolmistress who talked like that; and I was mortally afraid of her. But if she is not English what is she?

NEPOMMUCK: Hungarian.

ALL THE REST: Hungarian!

NEPOMMUCK: Hungarian. And of royal blood. I am Hungarian. My blood is royal.

HIGGINS: Did you speak to her in Hungarian?

NEPOMMUCK: I did. She was very clever. She said "Please speak to me in English: I do not understand French." French! She pretend not to know the difference between Hungarian and French. Impossible: she knows both.

HIGGINS: And the blood royal? How did you find that out?

NEPOMMUCK: Instinct, maestro, instinct. Only the Magyar races can produce that air of the divine right, those resolute eyes. She is a princess.

HOST: What do you say, Professor?

HIGGINS: I say an ordinary London girl out of the gutter and taught to speak by an expert. I place her in Drury Lane.

NEPOMMUCK: Ha ha ha! Oh, maestro, maestro, you are mad on the subject of cockney dialects. The London gutter is the whole world for you.

HIGGINS: [To the HOSTESS]   What does your Excellency say?

HOSTESS: Oh, of course I agree with Nepommuck. She must be a princess at least.

HOST: Not necessarily legitimate, of course. Morganatic perhaps. But that is undoubtedly her class.

HIGGINS: I stick to my opinion.

HOSTESS: Oh, you are incorrigible.

[The group breaks up, leaving HIGGINS isolated. PICKERING joins him]

PICKERING: Where is Eliza? We must keep an eye on her.

[ELIZA joins them]

LIZA: I dont think I can bear much more. The people all stare so at me. An old lady has just told me that I speak exactly like Queen Victoria. I am sorry if I have lost your bet. I have done my best; but nothing can make me the same as these people.

PICKERING: You have not lost it, my dear. You have won it ten times over.

HIGGINS: Let us get out of this. I have had enough of chattering to these fools.

PICKERING: Eliza is tired; and I am hungry. Let us clear out and have supper somewhere.

ACT IV

The Wimpole Street laboratory. Midnight. Nobody in the room. The clock on the mantelpiece strikes twelve. The fire is not alight: it is a summer night.

Presently HIGGINS *and* PICKERING *are heard on the stairs.*

HIGGINS: [*Calling down to* PICKERING] I say, Pick: lock up, will you? I shant be going out again.

PICKERING: Right. Can Mrs. Pearce go to bed? We dont want anything more, do we?

HIGGINS: Lord, no!

[ELIZA *opens the door and is seen on the lighted landing in all the finery in which she has just won* HIGGINS's *bet for him. She comes to the hearth, and switches on the electric lights there. She is tired: her pallor contrasts strongly with her dark eyes and hair; and her expression is almost tragic. She takes off her cloak; puts her fan and gloves on the piano; and sits down on the bench, brooding and silent. Higgins, in evening dress, with overcoat and hat, comes in, carrying a smoking jacket which he has picked up downstairs. He takes off the hat and overcoat; throws them carelessly on the newspaper stand; disposes of his coat in the same way; puts on the smoking jacket; and throws himself wearily into the easy-chair at the hearth.* PICKERING, *similarly attired, comes in. He also takes off his hat and overcoat, and is about to throw them on* HIGGINS's *when he hesitates*]

PICKERING: I say: Mrs Pearce will row if we leave these things lying about in the drawing room.

HIGGINS: Oh, chuck them over the bannisters into the hall. She'll find them there in the morning and put them away all right. She'll think we were drunk.

PICKERING: We are, slightly. Are there any letters?

HIGGINS: I didnt look. [PICKERING *takes the overcoats and hats and goes downstairs.* HIGGINS *begins half singing half yawning an air from La Fanciulla del Golden West. Suddenly he stops and exclaims*] I wonder where the devil my slippers are!

[ELIZA *looks at him darkly; then rises suddenly and leaves the room.* HIGGINS *yawns again, and resumes his song.* PICKERING *returns, with the contents of the letter-box in his hand*]

PICKERING: Only circulars, and this coroneted billet-doux for you. [*He throws the circulars into the fender, and posts himself on the hearth-rug, with his back to the grate*]

HIGGINS: [*Glancing at the billet-doux*]   Money-lender. [*He throws the letter after the circulars.*

> ELIZA *returns with a pair of large down-at-heel slippers. She places them on the carpet before* HIGGINS, *and sits as before without a word*]

HIGGINS: [*Yawning again*]   Oh Lord! What an evening! What a crew! What a silly tomfoolery! [*He raises his shoe to unlace it, and catches sight of the slippers. He stops unlacing and looks at them as if they had appeared there of their own accord*] Oh! theyre there, are they?

PICKERING: [*Stretching himself*]   Well, I feel a bit tired. It's been a long day. The garden party, a dinner party, and the reception! Rather too much of a good thing. But youve won your bet, Higgins. Eliza did the trick, and something to spare, eh?

HIGGINS: [*Fervently*]   Thank God it's over!

> [ELIZA *flinches violently; but they take no notice of her; and she recovers herself and sits stonily as before*]

PICKERING: Were you nervous at the garden party? I was. Eliza didnt seem a bit nervous.

HIGGINS: Oh, she wasnt nervous. I knew she'd be all right. No: it's the strain of putting the job through all these months that has told on me. It was interesting enough at first, while we were at the phonetics; but after that I got deadly sick of it. If I hadnt backed myself to do it I should have chucked the whole thing up two months ago. It was a silly notion: the whole thing has been a bore.

PICKERING: Oh come! the garden party was frightfully exciting. My heart began beating like anything.

HIGGINS: Yes, for the first three minutes. But when I saw we were going to win hands down, I felt like a bear in a cage, hanging about doing nothing. The dinner was worse: sitting gorging there for over an hour, with nobody but a damned fool of a fashionable woman to talk to! I tell you, Pickering, never again for me. No more artificial duchesses. The whole thing has been simple purgatory.

PICKERING: Youve never been broken in properly to the social routine. [*Strolling over to the piano*] I rather enjoy dipping into it occasionally myself: it makes me feel young again. Anyhow, it was a great success: an immense success. I was quite frightened once or twice because Eliza was doing it so well. You see, lots of the real people cant do it at all: theyre such fools that they think style comes by nature to people in their position; and so they never learn. Theres always something professional about doing a thing superlatively well.

HIGGINS: Yes: thats what drives me mad: the silly people dont know their own silly business. [*Rising*] However, it's over and done with; and now I can go to bed at last without dreading tomorrow.

[ELIZA's *beauty becomes murderous*]

PICKERING: I think I shall turn in too. Still, it's been a great occasion: a triumph for you. Goodnight. [*He goes*]

HIGGINS: [*Following him*] Goodnight. [*Over his shoulder, at the door*] Put out the lights, Eliza; and tell Mrs Pearce not to make coffee for me in the morning: I'll take tea. [*He goes out*]

[ELIZA *tries to control herself and feel indifferent as she rises and walks across to the hearth to switch off the lights. By the time she gets there she is on the point of screaming. She sits down in* HIGGINS's *chair and holds on hard to the arms. Finally she gives way and flings herself furiously on the floor, raging*]

HIGGINS: [*In despairing wrath outside*] What the devil have I done with my slippers? [*He appears at the door*]

LIZA: [*Snatching up the slippers, and hurling them at him one after the other with all her force*] There are your slippers. And there. Take your slippers; and may you never have a day's luck with them!

HIGGINS: [*Astounded*] What on earth—! [*He comes to her*] Whats the matter? Get up. [*He pulls her up*] Anything wrong?

LIZA: [*Breathless*] Nothing wrong—with you. Ive won your bet for you, havnt I? Thats enough for you. *I* dont matter, I suppose.

HIGGINS: You won my bet! You! Presumptuous insect! *I* won it. What did you throw those slippers at me for?

LIZA: Because I wanted to smash your face. I'd like to kill you, you selfish brute. Why didnt you leave me where you picked me out of—in the gutter? You thank God it's all over, and that now you can throw me back again there, do you? [*She crisps her fingers frantically*]

HIGGINS: [*Looking at her in cool wonder*] The creature is nervous, after all.

LIZA: [*Gives a suffocated scream of fury, and instinctively darts her nails at his face*] !!

HIGGINS: [*Catching her wrists*] Ah! would you? Claws in, you cat. How dare you shew your temper to me? Sit down and be quiet. [*He throws her roughly into the easy-chair*]

LIZA: [*Crushed by superior strength and weight*] Whats to become of me? Whats to become of me?

HIGGINS: How the devil do I know whats to become of you? What does it matter what becomes of you?

LIZA: You dont care. I know you dont care. You wouldnt care if I was dead. I'm nothing to you—not so much as them slippers.

HIGGINS: [*Thundering*] Those slippers.

LIZA: [*With bitter submission*] Those slippers. I didnt think it made any difference now.

[*A pause.* ELIZA *hopeless and crushed.* HIGGINS *a little uneasy*]

HIGGINS: [*In his loftiest manner*] Why have you begun going on like this? May I ask whether you complain of your treatment here?

LIZA: No.

HIGGINS: Has anybody behaved badly to you? Colonel Pickering? Mrs Pearce? Any of the servants?

LIZA: No.

HIGGINS: I presume you dont pretend that *I* have treated you badly?

LIZA: No.

HIGGINS: I am glad to hear it. [*He moderates his tone*] Perhaps youre tired after the strain of the day. Will you have a glass of champagne? [*He moves towards the door*]

LIZA: No. [*Recollecting her manners*] Thank you.

HIGGINS: [*Good-humored again*] This has been coming on you for some days. I suppose it was natural for you to be anxious about the garden party. But thats all over now. [*He pats her kindly on the shoulder. She writhes*] Theres nothing more to worry about.

LIZA: No. Nothing more for you to worry about. [*She suddenly rises and gets away from him by going to the piano bench, where she sits and hides her face*] Oh God! I wish I was dead.

HIGGINS: [*Staring after her in sincere surprise*] Why? In heaven's name, why? [*Reasonably, going to her*] Listen to me, Eliza. All this irritation is purely subjective.

LIZA: I dont understand. I'm too ignorant.

HIGGINS: It's only imagination. Low spirits and nothing else. Nobody's hurting you. Nothing's wrong. You go to bed like a good girl and sleep it off.
Have a little cry and say your prayers: that will make you comfortable.

LIZA: I heard your prayers. "Thank God it's all over!"

HIGGINS: [*Impatiently*] Well, dont you thank God it's all over? Now you
are free and can do what you like.

LIZA: [*Pulling herself together in desperation*] What am I fit for? What
have you left me fit for? Where am I to go? What am I to do? Whats
to become of me?

HIGGINS: [*Enlightened, but not at all impressed*] Oh, thats whats worrying
you, is it? [*He thrusts his hands into his pockets, and walks about in his
usual manner, rattling the contents of his pockets, as if condescending
to a trivial subject out of pure kindness*] I shouldnt bother about it if I
were you. I should imagine you wont have much difficulty in settling
yourself somewhere or other, though I hadnt quite realized that you were
going away. [*She looks quickly at him: he does not look at her, but ex-
amines the dessert stand on the piano and decides that he will eat an
apple*] You might marry, you know. [*He bites a large piece out of the
apple and munches it noisily*] You see, Eliza, all men are not confirmed
old bachelors like me and the Colonel. Most men are the marrying sort
(poor devils!); and youre not bad-looking: it's quite a pleasure to look
at you sometimes—not now, of course, because youre crying and looking
as ugly as the very devil; but when youre all right and quite yourself,
youre what I should call attractive. That is, to the people in the marrying line, you understand. You go to bed and have a good nice rest; and
then get up and look at yourself in the glass; and you wont feel so cheap.

    [ELIZA *again looks at him, speechless, and does not stir.*
    *The look is quite lost on him: he eats his apple with a dreamy ex-
pression of happiness, as it is quite a good one*]

HIGGINS: [*A genial afterthought occurring to him*] I daresay my mother
could find some chap or other who would do very well.

LIZA: We were above that at the corner of Tottenham Court Road.

HIGGINS: [*Waking up*] What do you mean?

LIZA: I sold flowers. I didnt sell myself. Now youve made a lady of me I'm
not fit to sell anything else. I wish youd left me where you found me.

HIGGINS: [*Slinging the core of the apple decisively into the grate*] Tosh,
Eliza. Dont you insult human relations by dragging all this cant about

buying and selling into it. You neednt marry the fellow if you dont like him.

LIZA: What else am I to do?

HIGGINS: Oh, lots of thing. What about your old idea of a florist's shop? Pickering could set you up in one: he has lots of money. [*Chuckling*] He'll have to pay for all those togs you have been wearing today; and that, with the hire of the jewellery, will make a big hole in two hundred pounds. Why, six months ago you would have thought it the millennium to have a flower shop of your own. Come! youll be all right. I must clear off to bed: I'm devilish sleepy. By the way, I came down for something: I forget what it was.

LIZA: Your slippers.

HIGGINS: Oh yes, of course. You shied them at me. [*He picks them up, and is going out when she rises and speaks to him*]

LIZA: Before you go, sir—

HIGGINS: [*Dropping the slippers in his surprise at her calling him Sir*] Eh?

LIZA: Do my clothes belong to me or to Colonel Pickering?

HIGGINS: [*Coming back into the room as if her question were the very climax of unreason*] What the devil use would they be to Pickering?

LIZA: He might want them for the next girl you pick up to experiment on.

HIGGINS: [*Shocked and hurt*] Is that the way you feel towards us?

LIZA: I dont want to hear anything more about that. All I want to know is whether anything belongs to me. My own clothes were burnt.

HIGGINS: But what does it matter? Why need you start bothering about that in the middle of the night?

LIZA: I want to know what I may take away with me. I dont want to be accused of stealing.

HIGGINS: [*Now deeply wounded*] Stealing! You shouldnt have said that, Eliza. That shews a want of feeling.

LIZA: I'm sorry. I'm only a common ignorant girl; and in my station I have to be careful. There cant be any feelings between the like of you and the like of me. Please will you tell me what belongs to me and what doesnt?

HIGGINS: [*Very sulky*] You may take the whole damned houseful if you like. Except the jewels. Theyre hired. Will that satisfy you? [*He turns on his heel and is about to go in extreme dudgeon*]

LIZA: [*Drinking in his emotion like nectar, and nagging him to provoke a further supply*] Stop, please. [*She takes off her jewels*] Will you take these to your room and keep them safe? I dont want to run the risk of their being missing.

HIGGINS: [*Furious*] Hand them over. [*She puts them into his hands*] If these belonged to me instead of to the jeweller, I'd ram them down your ungrateful throat. [*He perfunctorily thrusts them into his pockets, unconsciously decorating himself with the protruding ends of the chains*]

LIZA: [*Taking a ring off*] This ring isnt the jeweller's: it's the one you bought me in Brighton. I dont want it now. [HIGGINS *dashes the ring violently into the fireplace, and turns on her so threateningly that she crouches over the piano with her hands over her face, and exclaims*] Dont you hit me.

HIGGINS: Hit you! You infamous creature, how dare you accuse me of such a thing? It is you who have hit me. You have wounded me to the heart.

LIZA: [*Thrilling with hidden joy*] I'm glad. Ive got a little of my own back, anyhow.

HIGGINS: [*With dignity, in his finest professional style*] You have caused me to lose my temper: a thing that has hardly ever happened to me before. I prefer to say nothing more tonight. I am going to bed.

LIZA: [*Pertly*] Youd better leave a note for Mrs Pearce about the coffee; for she wont be told by me.

HIGGINS: [*Formally*] Damn Mrs Pearce; and damn the coffee; and damn you; and [*Wildly*] damn my own folly in having lavished my hard-earned knowledge and the treasure of my regard and intimacy on a heartless guttersnipe. [*He goes out with impressive decorum, and spoils it by slamming the door savagely*]

[ELIZA *goes down on her knees on the hearthrug to look for the ring. When she finds it she considers for a moment what to do with it. Finally she flings it down on the dessert stand and goes upstairs in a tearing rage*]

·   ·   ·

The furniture of Eliza's room has been increased by a big wardrobe and a sumptuous dressing-table. She comes in and switches on the electric light. She goes to the wardrobe; opens it; and pulls out a walking dress, a hat, and a pair of shoes, which she throws on the bed. She takes off her evening dress and shoes; then takes a padded hanger from the wardrobe; adjusts it carefully in the evening dress; and hangs it in the wardrobe, which she shuts with a slam. She puts on her walking shoes, her walking dress, and hat. She takes her wrist watch from the dressing-table and fastens it on. She pulls on her gloves; takes her vanity bag; and looks into it to see that her purse is there before hanging it on her wrist. She makes for the door. Every movement expresses her furious resolution.

She takes a last look at herself in the glass.

She suddenly puts out her tongue at herself; then leaves the room, switching off the electric light at the door.

Meanwhile, in the street outside, Freddy Eynsford Hill, lovelorn, is gazing up at the second floor, in which one of the windows is still lighted.

The light goes out.

FREDDY: Goodnight, darling, darling, darling.

[ELIZA *comes out, giving the door a considerable bang behind her*]

LIZA: Whatever are you doing here?

FREDDY: Nothing. I spend most of my nights here. It's the only place where I'm happy. Dont laugh at me, Miss Doolittle.

LIZA: Dont you call me Miss Doolittle, do you hear? Liza's good enough for me. [*She breaks down and grabs him by the shoulders*] Freddy: you dont think I'm a heartless guttersnipe, do you?

FREDDY: Oh no, no, darling: how can you imagine such a thing? You are the loveliest, dearest—

[*He loses all self-control and smothers her with kisses. She, hungry for comfort, responds. They stand there in one another's arms.*
An elderly police constable arrives]

CONSTABLE: [*Scandalized*]   Now then! Now then!! Now then!!!

[*They release one another hastily*]

FREDDY: Sorry, constable. Weve only just become engaged.

[*They run away*]

The constable shakes his head, reflecting on his own courtship and on the vanity of human hopes. He moves off in the opposite direction with slow professional steps.

The flight of the lovers takes them to Cavendish Square. There they halt to consider their next move.

LIZA: [*Out of breath*]   He didnt half give me a fright, that copper. But you answered him proper.

FREDDY: I hope I havent taken you out of your way. Where were you going?

LIZA: To the river.

FREDDY: What for?

LIZA: To make a hole in it.

FREDDY: [*Horrified*]   Eliza, darling. What do you mean? What's the matter?

LIZA: Never mind. It doesnt matter now. There's nobody in the world now but you and me, is there?

FREDDY: Not a soul.

> [*They indulge in another embrace, and are again surprised by a much younger constable*]

SECOND CONSTABLE: Now then, you two! What's this? Where do you think you are? Move along here, double quick.

FREDDY: As you say, sir, double quick.

> They run away again, and are in Hanover Square before they stop for another conference.

FREDDY: I had no idea the police were so devilishly prudish.

LIZA: It's their business to hunt girls off the streets.

FREDDY: We must go somewhere. We cant wander about the streets all night.

LIZA: Cant we? I think it'd be lovely to wander about for ever.

FREDDY: Oh, darling.

> [*They embrace again, oblivious of the arrival of a crawling taxi. It stops*]

TAXIMAN: Can I drive you and the lady anywhere, sir?

> [*They start asunder*]

LIZA: Oh, Freddy, a taxi. The very thing.

FREDDY: But, damn it, Ive no money.

LIZA: I have plenty. The Colonel thinks you should never go out without ten pounds in your pocket. Listen. We'll drive about all night; and in the morning I'll call on old Mrs Higgins and ask her what I ought to do. I'll tell you all about it in the cab. And the police wont touch us there.

FREDDY: Righto! Ripping. [*To the* TAXIMAN] Wimbledon Common. [*They drive off*]

ACT V

MRS HIGGINS's *drawing room. She is at her writing-table as before. The* PARLORMAID *comes in.*

THE PARLORMAID: [*At the door*]   Mr Henry, maam, is downstairs with Colonel Pickering.

MRS HIGGINS: Well, shew them up.

THE PARLORMAID: Theyre using the telephone, maam. Telephoning to the police, I think.

MRS HIGGINS: What!

THE PARLORMAID: [*Coming further in and lowering her voice*]   Mr Henry is in a state, maam. I thought I'd better tell you.

MRS HIGGINS: If you had told me that Mr Henry was not in a state it would have been more surprising. Tell them to come up when theyve finished with the police. I suppose he's lost something.

THE PARLORMAID: Yes, maam. [*Going*]

MRS HIGGINS: Go upstairs and tell Miss Doolittle that Mr Henry and the Colonel are here. Ask her not to come down til I send for her.

THE PARLORMAID: Yes, maam.

[HIGGINS *bursts in. He is, as the* PARLORMAID *has said, in a state*]

HIGGINS: Look here, mother: heres a confounded thing!

MRS HIGGINS: Yes, dear. Good morning. [*He checks his impatience and kisses her, whilst the* PARLORMAID *goes out*] What is it?

HIGGINS: Eliza's bolted.

MRS HIGGINS: [*Calmly continuing her writing*]   You must have frightened her.

HIGGINS: Frightened her! nonsense! She was left last night, as usual, to turn out the lights and all that; and instead of going to bed she changed her clothes and went right off: her bed wasnt slept in. She came in a cab for her things before seven this morning; and that fool Mrs Pearce let her have them without telling me a word about it. What am I to do?

MRS HIGGINS: Do without, I'm afraid, Henry. The girl has a perfect right to leave if she chooses.

HIGGINS: [*Wandering distractedly across the room*]   But I cant find anything. I dont know what appointments Ive got. I'm— [PICKERING *comes in.* MRS HIGGINS *puts down her pen and turns away from the writing-table*]

PICKERING: [*Shaking hands*]   Good morning, Mrs Higgins. Has Henry told you? [*He sits down on the ottoman*]

HIGGINS: What does that ass of an inspector say? Have you offered a reward?

MRS HIGGINS: [*Rising in indignant amazement*]   You dont mean to say you have set the police after Eliza.

HIGGINS: Of course. What are the police for? What else could we do? [*He sits in the Elizabethan chair*]

PICKERING: The inspector made a lot of difficulties. I really think he suspected us of some improper purpose.

MRS HIGGINS: Well, of course he did. What right have you to go to the police and give the girl's name as if she were a thief, or a lost umbrella, or something? Really! [*She sits down again, deeply vexed*]

HIGGINS: But we want to find her.

PICKERING: We cant let her go like this, you know, Mrs Higgins. What were we to do?

MRS HIGGINS: You have no more sense, either of you, than two children. Why—

[*The* PARLORMAID *comes in and breaks off the conversation*]

THE PARLORMAID: Mr Henry: a gentleman wants to see you very particular. He's been sent on from Wimpole Street.

HIGGINS: Oh, bother! I cant see anyone now. Who is it?

THE PARLORMAID: A Mr Doolittle, sir.

PICKERING: Doolittle! Do you mean the dustman?

THE PARLORMAID: Dustman! Oh no, sir: a gentleman.

HIGGINS: [*Springing up excitedly*]   By George, Pick, it's some relative of hers that she's gone to. Somebody we know nothing about. [*To the* PARLORMAID] Send him up, quick.

THE PARLORMAID: Yes, sir. [*She goes*]

HIGGINS: [*Eagerly, going to his mother*]   Genteel relatives! now we shall hear something. [*He sits down in the Chippendale chair*]

MRS HIGGINS: Do you know any of her people?

PICKERING: Only her father: the fellow we told you about.

THE PARLORMAID: [*Announcing*]   Mr Doolittle. [*She withdraws*]

[DOOLITTLE *enters. He is resplendently dressed as for a fashionable wedding, and might, in fact, be the bridegroom. A flower in his button-hole, a dazzling silk hat, and patent leather shoes complete the effect. He is too concerned with the business he has come on to notice* MRS HIGGINS. *He walks straight to* HIGGINS, *and accosts him with vehement reproach*]

DOOLITTLE: [*Indicating his own person*]   See here! Do you see this? You done this.

HIGGINS: Done what, man?

DOOLITTLE: This, I tell you. Look at it. Look at this hat. Look at this coat.

PICKERING: Has Eliza been buying you clothes?

DOOLITTLE: Eliza! not she. Why would she buy me clothes?

MRS HIGGINS: Good morning, Mr Doolittle. Wont you sit down?

DOOLITTLE: [*Taken aback as he becomes conscious that he has forgotten his hostess*]   Asking your pardon, maam. [*He approaches her and shakes her proffered hand*] Thank you. [*He sits down on the ottoman, on* PICKERING's *right*] I am that full of what has happened to me that I cant think of anything else.

HIGGINS: What the dickens has happened to you?

DOOLITTLE: I shouldnt mind if it had only happened to me: anything might happen to anybody and nobody to blame but Providence, as you might say. But this is something that you done to me: yes, you, Enry Iggins.

HIGGINS: Have you found Eliza?

DOOLITTLE: Have you lost her?

HIGGINS: Yes.

DOOLITTLE: You have all the luck, you have. I aint found her; but she'll find me quick enough now after what you done to me.

MRS HIGGINS: But what has my son done to you, Mr Doolittle?

DOOLITTLE: Done to me! Ruined me. Destroyed my happiness. Tied me up and delivered me into the hands of middle class morality.

HIGGINS: [*Rising intolerantly and standing over* DOOLITTLE]   Youre raving. Youre drunk. Youre mad. I gave you five pounds. After that I had two conversations with you, at half-a-crown an hour. Ive never seen you since.

DOOLITTLE: Oh! Drunk am I? Mad am I? Tell me this. Did you or did you not write a letter to an old blighter in America that was giving five millions to found Moral Reform Societies all over the world, and that wanted you to invent a universal language for him?

HIGGINS: What! Ezra D. Wannafeller! He's dead. [*He sits down again carelessly*]

DOOLITTLE: Yes: he's dead; and I'm done for. Now did you or did you not write a letter to him to say that the most original moralist at present in England, to the best of your knowledge, was Alfred Doolittle, a common dustman?

HIGGINS: Oh, after your first visit I remember making some silly joke of the kind.

DOOLITTLE: Ah! you may well call it a silly joke. It put the lid on me right enough. Just give him the chance he wanted to shew that Americans is not like us: that they reckonize and respect merit in every class of life, however humble. Them words is in his blooming will, in which, Henry Higgins, thanks to your silly joking, he leaves me a share in his Pre-digested Cheese Trust worth four thousand a year on condition that I lecture for his Wannafeller Moral Reform World League as often as they ask me up to six times a year.

HIGGINS: The devil he does! Whew! [*Brightening suddenly*] What a lark!

PICKERING: A safe thing for you, Doolittle. They wont ask you twice.

DOOLITTLE: It aint the lecturing I mind. I'll lecture them blue in the face, I will, and not turn a hair. It's making a gentleman of me that I object to. Who asked him to make a gentleman of me? I was happy. I was free. I touched pretty nigh everybody for money when I wanted it, same as I touched you, Enry Iggins. Now I am worrited; tied neck and heels; and everybody touches me for money. It's a fine thing for you, says my solicitor. Is it? says I. You mean it's a good thing for you, I says. When I was a poor man and had a solicitor once when they found a pram in the dust cart, he got me off, and got shut of me and got me shut of him as quick as he could. Same with the doctors: used to shove me out of the hospital before I could hardly stand on my legs, and nothing to pay. Now they finds out that I'm not a healthy man and cant live unless they looks after me twice a day. In the house I'm not let do a hand's turn for myself: somebody else must do it and touch me for it. A year ago I hadnt a relative in the world except two or three that wouldnt speak to me. Now Ive fifty, and not a decent week's wages among the lot of them. I have to live for others and not for myself: thats middle class morality. You talk of losing Eliza. Dont you be anxious: I bet she's on my doorstep by this: she that could support herself easy by selling flowers if I wasnt respectable. And the next one to touch me will be you, Enry Iggins. I'll have to learn to speak middle class language from you, instead of speaking proper English. Thats where youll come in; and I daresay thats what you done it for.

MRS HIGGINS: But, my dear Mr Doolittle, you need not suffer all this if you are really in earnest. Nobody can force you to accept this bequest. You can repudiate it. Isnt that so, Colonel Pickering?

PICKERING: I believe so.

DOOLITTLE: [*Softening his manner in deference to her sex*] Thats the tragedy of it, maam. It's easy to say chuck it; but I havnt the nerve. Which of us has? We're all intimidated. Intimidated, maam: thats what we are. What is there for me if I chuck it but the workhouse in my old age? I have to dye my hair already to keep my job as a dustman. If I was one of the deserving poor, and had put by a bit, I could chuck it; but then why should I, acause the deserving poor might as well be millionaires for all the happiness they ever has. They dont know what happiness is. But I, as one of the undeserving poor, have nothing between me and the pauper's uniform but this here blasted four thousand a year that shoves me into the middle class. (Excuse the expression, maam; youd use it yourself if you had my provocation.) Theyve got you every way you turn: it's a choice between the Skilly of the workhouse and the Char Bydis of the middle class; and I havnt the nerve for the workhouse. Intimidated: thats what I am. Broke. Bought up. Happier men than me will call for my dust, and touch me for their tip; and I'll look on helpless, and envy them. And thats what your son has brought me to. [*He is overcome by emotion*]

MRS HIGGINS: Well, I'm very glad youre not going to do anything foolish, Mr Doolittle. For this solves the problem of Eliza's future. You can provide for her now.

DOOLITTLE: [*With melancholy resignation*] Yes, maam: I'm expected to provide for everyone now, out of four thousand a year.

HIGGINS: [*Jumping up*] Nonsense! he cant provide for her. He shant provide for her. She doesnt belong to him. I paid him five pounds for her.
Doolittle: either youre an honest man or a rogue.

DOOLITTLE: [*Tolerantly*] A little of both, Henry, like the rest of us: a little
of both.

HIGGINS: Well, you took that money for the girl; and you have no right to
take her as well.

MRS HIGGINS: Henry: dont be absurd. If you want to know where Eliza is,
she is upstairs.

HIGGINS: [*Amazed*] Upstairs!!! Then I shall jolly soon fetch her downstairs.
[*He makes resolutely for the door*]

MRS HIGGINS: [*Rising and following him*] Be quiet, Henry. Sit down.

HIGGINS: I—

MRS HIGGINS: Sit down, dear; and listen to me.

HIGGINS: Oh very well, very well, very well. [*He throws himself ungraciously
on the ottoman, with his face towards the windows*] But I think you
might have told us this half an hour ago.

MRS HIGGINS: Eliza came to me this morning. She told me of the brutal way
you two treated her.

HIGGINS: [*Bounding up again*] What!

PICKERING: [*Rising also*] My dear Mrs Higgins, she's been telling you
stories. We didnt treat her brutally. We hardly said a word to her; and
we parted on particularly good terms. [*Turning on* HIGGINS] Higgins: did
you bully her after I went to bed?

HIGGINS: Just the other way about. She threw my slippers in my face. She
behaved in the most outrageous way. I never gave her the slightest
provocation. The slippers came bang into my face the moment I entered
the room—before I had uttered a word. And used perfectly awful language.

PICKERING: [*Astonished*] But why? What did we do to her?

MRS HIGGINS: I think I know pretty well what you did. The girl is naturally
rather affectionate, I think. Isnt she, Mr Doolittle?

DOOLITTLE: Very tender-hearted, maam. Takes after me.

MRS HIGGINS: Just so. She had become attached to you both. She worked very
hard for you, Henry. I dont think you quite realize what anything in

the nature of brain work means to a girl of her class. Well, it seems that when the great day of trial came, and she did this wonderful thing for you without making a single mistake, you two sat there and never said a word to her, but talked together of how glad you were that it was all over and how you had been bored with the whole thing. And then you were surprised because she threw your slippers at you! *I* should have thrown the fire-irons at you.

HIGGINS: We said nothing except that we were tired and wanted to go to bed. Did we, Pick?

PICKERING: [*Shrugging his shoulders*]   That was all.

MRS HIGGINS: [*Ironically*]   Quite sure?

PICKERING: Absolutely. Really, that was all.

MRS HIGGINS: You didnt thank her, or pet her, or admire her, or tell her how splendid she'd been.

HIGGINS: [*Impatiently*]   But she knew all about that. We didnt make speeches to her, if thats what you mean.

PICKERING: [*Conscience stricken*]   Perhaps we were a little inconsiderate. Is she very angry?

MRS HIGGINS: [*Returning to her place at the writing-table*]   Well, I'm afraid she wont go back to Wimpole Street, especially now that Mr Doolittle is able to keep up the position you have thrust on her; but she says she is quite willing to meet you on friendly terms and to let bygones be bygones.

HIGGINS: [*Furious*]   Is she, by George? Ho!

MRS HIGGINS: If you promise to behave yourself, Henry, I'll ask her to come down. If not, go home; for you have taken up quite enough of my time.

HIGGINS: Oh, all right. Very well. Pick: you behave yourself. Let us put on our best Sunday manners for this creature that we picked out of the mud. [*He flings himself sulkily into the Elizabethan chair*]

DOOLITTLE: [*Remonstrating*]   Now, now, Enry Iggins! Have some consideration for my feelings as a middle class man.

MRS HIGGINS: Remember your promise, Henry. [*She presses the bell-button on the writing-table*]   Mr Doolittle: will you be so good as to step out on the balcony for a moment. I dont want Eliza to have the shock of your news until she has made it up with these two gentlemen. Would you mind?

DOOLITTLE: As you wish, lady. Anything to help Henry to keep her off my hands. [*He disappears through the window*]

[*The* PARLORMAID *answers the bell.* PICKERING *sits down in* DOO-LITTLE'S *place*]

MRS HIGGINS: Ask Miss Doolittle to come down, please.

THE PARLORMAID: Yes, maam. [*She goes out*]

MRS HIGGINS: Now, Henry: be good.

HIGGINS: I am behaving myself perfectly.

PICKERING: He is doing his best, Mrs Higgins.

[*A pause.* HIGGINS *throws back his head; stretches out his legs; and begins to whistle*]

MRS HIGGINS: Henry, dearest, you dont look at all nice in that attitude.

HIGGINS: [*Pulling himself together*] I was not trying to look nice, mother.

MRS HIGGINS: It doesnt matter, dear. I only wanted to make you speak.

HIGGINS: Why?

MRS HIGGINS: Because you cant speak and whistle at the same time.

[HIGGINS *groans. Another very trying pause*]

HIGGINS: [*Springing up, out of patience*] Where the devil is that girl? Are we to wait here all day?

[ELIZA *enters, sunny, self-possessed, and giving a staggeringly convincing exhibition of ease of manner. She carries a little workbasket, and is very much at home.* PICKERING *is too much taken aback to rise*]

LIZA: How do you do, Professor Higgins? Are you quite well?

HIGGINS: [*Choking*] Am I— [*He can say no more*]

LIZA: But of course you are: you are never ill. So glad to see you again, Colonel Pickering. [*He rises hastily; and they shake hands*] Quite chilly this morning, isnt it? [*She sits down on his left. He sits beside her*]

HIGGINS: Dont you dare try this game on me. I taught it to you; and it doesnt take me in. Get up and come home; and dont be a fool.

[ELIZA *takes a piece of needlework from her basket, and begins to stitch at it, without taking the least notice of this outburst*]

MRS HIGGINS: Very nicely put, indeed, Henry. No woman could resist such an invitation.

HIGGINS: You let her alone, mother. Let her speak for herself. You will jolly soon see whether she has an idea that I havnt put into her head or a word that I havnt put into her mouth. I tell you I have created this thing out of the squashed cabbage leaves of Covent Garden; and now she pretends to play the fine lady with me.

MRS HIGGINS: [*Placidly*]   Yes, dear; but youll sit down, wont you?

[HIGGINS *sits down again, savagely*]

LIZA: [*To* PICKERING, *taking no apparent notice of* HIGGINS, *and working away deftly*]   Will you drop me altogether now that the experiment is over, Colonel Pickering?

PICKERING: Oh dont. You mustnt think of it as an experiment. It shocks me, somehow.

LIZA: Oh, I'm only a squashed cabbage leaf—

PICKERING: [*Impulsively*]   No.

LIZA: [*Continuing quietly*]   —but I owe so much to you that I should be very unhappy if you forgot me.

PICKERING: It's very kind of you to say so, Miss Doolittle.

LIZA: It's not because you paid for my dresses. I know you are generous to everybody with money. But it was from you that I learnt really nice manners; and that is what makes one a lady, isnt it? You see it was so very difficult for me with the example of Professor Higgins always before me. I was brought up to be just like him, unable to control myself, and using bad language on the slightest provocation. And I should never have known that ladies and gentlemen didnt behave like that if you hadnt been there.

HIGGINS: Well!!

PICKERING: Oh, thats only his way, you know. He doesnt mean it.

LIZA: Oh, I didnt mean it either, when I was a flower girl. It was only my way. But you see I did it; and thats what makes the difference after all.

PICKERING: No doubt. Still, he taught you to speak; and I couldnt have done that, you know.

LIZA: [*Trivially*]   Of course: that is his profession.

HIGGINS: Damnation!

LIZA: [*Continuing*] It was just like learning to dance in the fashionable way: there was nothing more than that in it. But do you know what began my real education?

PICKERING: What?

LIZA: [*Stopping her work for a moment*] Your calling me Miss Doolittle that day when I first came to Wimpole Street. That was the beginning of self-respect for me. [*She resumes her stitching*] And there were a hundred little things you never noticed, because they came naturally to you. Things about standing up and taking off your hat and opening doors—

PICKERING: Oh, that was nothing.

LIZA: Yes: things that shewed you thought and felt about me as if I were something better than a scullery-maid; though of course I know you would have been just the same to a scullery-maid if she had been let into the drawing room. You never took off your boots in the dining room when I was there.

PICKERING: You mustnt mind that. Higgins takes off his boots all over the place.

LIZA: I know. I am not blaming him. It is his way, isnt it? But it made such a difference to me that you didnt do it. You see, really and truly, apart from the things anyone can pick up (the dressing and the proper way of speaking, and so on), the difference between a lady and a flower girl is not how she behaves, but how she's treated. I shall always be a flower girl to Professor Higgins, because he always treats me as a flower girl, and always will; but I know I can be a lady to you, because you always treat me as a lady, and always will.

MRS HIGGINS: Please dont grind your teeth, Henry.

PICKERING: Well, this is really very nice of you, Miss Doolittle.

LIZA: I should like you to call me Eliza, now, if you would.

PICKERING: Thank you. Eliza, of course.

LIZA: And I should like Professor Higgins to call me Miss Doolittle.

HIGGINS: I'll see you damned first.

MRS HIGGINS: Henry! Henry!

PICKERING: [*Laughing*] Why dont you slang back at him? Dont stand it. It would do him a lot of good.

LIZA: I cant. I could have done it once; but now I cant go back to it. You told me, you know, that when a child is brought to a foreign country, it picks up the language in a few weeks, and forgets its own. Well, I am a child in your country. I have forgotten my own language, and can speak nothing but yours. Thats the real break-off with the corner of Tottenham Court Road. Leaving Wimpole Street finishes it.

PICKERING: [*Much alarmed*]   Oh! but youre coming back to Wimpole Street, arnt you? Youll forgive Higgins?

HIGGINS: [*Rising*]   Forgive! Will she, by George! Let her go. Let her find out how she can get on without us. She will relapse into the gutter in three weeks without me at her elbow.

> [DOOLITTLE *appears at the centre window. With a look of dignified reproach at* HIGGINS, *he comes slowly and silently to his daughter, who, with her back to the window, is unconscious of his approach*]

PICKERING: He's incorrigible, Eliza. You wont relapse, will you?

LIZA: No: not now. Never again. I have learnt my lesson. I dont believe I could utter one of the old sounds if I tried. [DOOLITTLE *touches her on the left shoulder. She drops her work, losing her self-possession utterly at the spectacle of her father's splendor*] A-a-a-a-ah-ow-ooh!

HIGGINS: [*With a crow of triumph*]   Aha! Just so. A-a-a-a-ahowooh! A-a-a-a-ahowooh! A-a-a-a-ahowooh! Victory! Victory! [*He throws himself on the divan, folding his arms, and spraddling arrogantly*]

DOOLITTLE: Can you blame the girl? Dont look at me like that, Eliza. It aint my fault. Ive come into some money.

LIZA: You must have touched a millionaire this time, dad.

DOOLITTLE: I have. But I'm dressed something special today. I'm going to St George's, Hanover Square. Your stepmother is going to marry me.

LIZA: [*Angrily*]   Youre going to let yourself down to marry that low common woman!

PICKERING: [*Quietly*]   He ought to, Eliza. [*To* DOOLITTLE] Why has she changed her mind?

DOOLITTLE: [*Sadly*]   Intimidated, Governor. Intimidated. Middle class morality claims its victim. Wont you put on your hat, Liza, and come and see me turned off?

LIZA: If the Colonel says I must, I—I'll [*Almost sobbing*] I'll demean myself. And get insulted for my pains, like enough.

DOOLITTLE: Dont be afraid: she never comes to words with anyone now, poor woman! respectability has broke all the spirit out of her.

PICKERING: [*Squeezing* ELIZA's *elbow gently*] Be kind to them, Eliza. Make the best of it.

LIZA: [*Forcing a little smile for him through her vexation*] Oh well, just to shew theres no ill feeling. I'll be back in a moment. [*She goes out*]

DOOLITTLE: [*Sitting down beside* PICKERING] I feel uncommon nervous about the ceremony, Colonel. I wish youd come and see me through it.

PICKERING: But youve been through it before, man. You were married to Eliza's mother.

DOOLITTLE: Who told you that, Colonel?

PICKERING: Well, nobody told me. But I concluded—naturally—

DOOLITTLE: No: that aint the natural way, Colonel: it's only the middle class way. My way was always the undeserving way. But dont say nothing to Eliza. She dont know: I always had a delicacy about telling her.

PICKERING: Quite right. We'll leave it so, if you dont mind.

DOOLITTLE: And youll come to the church, Colonel, and put me through straight?

PICKERING: With pleasure. As far as a bachelor can.

MRS HIGGINS: May I come, Mr Doolittle? I should be very sorry to miss your wedding.

DOOLITTLE: I should indeed be honored by your condescension, maam; and my poor old woman would take it as a tremenjous compliment. She's been very low, thinking of the happy days that are no more.

MRS HIGGINS: [*Rising*] I'll order the carriage and get ready. [*The men rise, except* HIGGINS] I shant be more than fifteen minutes. [*As she goes to the door* ELIZA *comes in, hatted and buttoning her gloves*] I'm going to the church to see your father married, Eliza. You had better come in the brougham with me. Colonel Pickering can go on with the bridegroom.

[MRS HIGGINS *goes out.* ELIZA *comes to the middle of the room between the centre window and the ottoman.* PICKERING *joins her*]

DOOLITTLE: Bridegroom. What a word! It makes a man realize his position, somehow. [*He takes up his hat and goes towards the door*]

PICKERING: Before I go, Eliza, do forgive Higgins and come back to us.

LIZA: I dont think dad would allow me. Would you, dad?

DOOLITTLE: [*Sad but magnanimous*] They played you off very cunning, Eliza, them two sportsmen. If it had been only one of them, you could have nailed him. But you see, there was two; and one of them chaperoned the other, as you might say. [*To* PICKERING] It was artful of you, Colonel; but I bear no malice: I should have done the same myself. I been the victim of one woman after another all my life, and I dont grudge you two getting the better of Liza. I shant interfere. It's time for us to go, Colonel. So long, Henry. See you in St George's, Eliza. [*He goes out*]

PICKERING: [*Coaxing*] Do stay with us, Eliza. [*He follows* DOOLITTLE]

[ELIZA *goes out on the balcony to avoid being alone with* HIGGINS. *He rises and joins her there. She immediately comes back into the room and makes for the door; but he goes along the balcony and gets his back to the door before she reaches it*]

HIGGINS: Well, Eliza, youve had a bit of your own back, as you call it. Have you had enough? and are you going to be reasonable? Or do you want any more?

LIZA: You want me back only to pick up your slippers and put up with your tempers and fetch and carry for you.

HIGGINS: I havnt said I wanted you back at all.

LIZA: Oh, indeed. Then what are we talking about?

HIGGINS: About you, not about me. If you come back I shall treat you just as I have always treated you. I cant change my nature; and I dont intend to change my manners. My manners are exactly the same as Colonel Pickering's.

LIZA: Thats not true. He treats a flower girl as if she was a duchess.

HIGGINS: And I treat a duchess as if she was a flower girl.

LIZA: I see. [*She turns away composedly, and sits on the ottoman, facing the window*] The same to everybody.

HIGGINS: Just so.

LIZA: Like father.

HIGGINS: [*Grinning, a little taken down*] Without accepting the comparison at all points, Eliza, it's quite true that your father is not a snob, and that he will be quite at home in any station of life to which his eccentric destiny may call him. [*Seriously*] The great secret, Eliza, is not having bad manners or good manners or any other particular sort of manners, but having the same manner for all human souls: in short, behaving as if you were in Heaven, where there are no third-class carriages, and one soul is as good as another.

LIZA: Amen. You are a born preacher.

HIGGINS: [*Irritated*]   The question is not whether I treat you rudely, but whether you ever heard me treat anyone else better.

LIZA: [*With sudden sincerity*]   I dont care how you treat me. I dont mind your swearing at me. I shouldnt mind a black eye: Ive had one before this. But [*standing up and facing him*] I wont be passed over.

HIGGINS: Then get out of my way; for I wont stop for you. You talk about me as if I were a motor bus.

LIZA: So you are a motor bus: all bounce and go, and no consideration for anyone. But I can do without you: dont think I cant.

HIGGINS: I know you can. I told you you could.

LIZA: [*Wounded, getting away from him to the other side of the ottoman with her face to the hearth*]   I know you did, you brute. You wanted to get rid of me.

HIGGINS: Liar.

LIZA: Thank you. [*She sits down with dignity*]

HIGGINS: You never asked yourself, I suppose, whether *I* could do without you.

LIZA: [*Earnestly*]   Dont you try to get round me. Youll have to do without me.

HIGGINS: [*Arrogant*]   I can do without anybody. I have my own soul: my own spark of divine fire. But [*With sudden humility*] I shall miss you, Eliza. [*He sits down near her on the ottoman*] I have learnt something from your idiotic notions: I confess that humbly and gratefully. And I have grown accustomed to your voice and appearance. I like them, rather.

LIZA: Well, you have both of them on your gramophone and in your book of photographs. When you feel lonely without me, you can turn the machine on. It's got no feelings to hurt.

HIGGINS: I cant turn your soul on. Leave me those feelings; and you can take away the voice and the face. They are not you.

LIZA: Oh, you are a devil. You can twist the heart in a girl as easy as some could twist her arms to hurt her. Mrs Pearce warned me. Time and again she has wanted to leave you; and you always got round her at the last minute. And you dont care a bit for her. And you dont care a bit for me.

HIGGINS: I care for life, for humanity; and you are a part of it that has come my way and been built into my house. What more can you or anyone ask?

LIZA: I wont care for anybody that doesnt care for me.

HIGGINS: Commercial principles, Eliza. Like [*Reproducing her Covent Garden pronunciation with professional exactness*] s'yollin voylets [*selling violets*], isnt it?

LIZA: Dont sneer at me. It's mean to sneer at me.

HIGGINS: I have never sneered in my life. Sneering doesnt become either the human face or the human soul. I am expressing my righteous contempt for Commercialism. I dont and wont trade in affection. You call me a brute because you couldnt buy a claim on me by fetching my slippers and finding my spectacles. You were a fool: I think a woman fetching a man's slippers is a disgusting sight: did I ever fetch your slippers? I think a good deal more of you for throwing them in my face. No use slaving for me and then saying you want to be cared for: who cares for a slave? If you come back, come back for the sake of good fellowship; for youll get nothing else. Youve had a thousand times as much out of me as I have out of you; and if you dare to set up your little dog's tricks of fetching and carrying slippers against my creation of a Duchess Eliza, I'll slam the door in your silly face.

LIZA: What did you do it for if you didnt care for me?

HIGGINS: [*Heartily*]   Why, because it was my job.

LIZA: You never thought of the trouble it would make for me.

HIGGINS: Would the world ever have been made if its maker had been afraid of making trouble? Making life means making trouble. Theres only one way of escaping trouble; and thats killing things. Cowards, you notice, are always shrieking to have troublesome people killed.

LIZA: I'm no preacher: I dont notice things like that. I notice that you dont notice me.

HIGGINS: [*Jumping up and walking about intolerantly*]   Eliza: youre an idiot. I waste the treasures of my Miltonic mind by spreading them before you. Once for all, understand that I go my way and do my work without caring twopence what happens to either of us. I am not intimidated, like your father and your stepmother. So you can come back or go to the devil: which you please.

LIZA: What am I to come back for?

HIGGINS: [*Bouncing up on his knees on the ottoman and leaning over it to her*] For the fun of it. Thats why I took you on.

LIZA: [*With averted face*] And you may throw me out tomorrow if I dont do everything you want me to?

HIGGINS: Yes; and you may walk out tomorrow if I dont do everything you want me to.

LIZA: And live with my stepmother?

HIGGINS: Yes, or sell flowers.

LIZA: Oh! if I only could go back to my flower basket! I should be independent of both you and father and all the world! Why did you take my independence from me? Why did I give it up? I'm a slave now, for all my fine clothes.

HIGGINS: Not a bit. I'll adopt you as my daughter and settle money on you if you like. Or would you rather marry Pickering?

LIZA: [*Looking fiercely round at him*] I wouldnt marry you if you asked me; and youre nearer my age than what he is.

HIGGINS: [*Gently*] Than he is: not "than what he is."

LIZA: [*Losing her temper and rising*] I'll talk as I like. Youre not my teacher now.

HIGGINS: [*Reflectively*] I dont suppose Pickering would, though. He's as confirmed an old bachelor as I am.

LIZA: Thats not what I want; and dont you think it. I've always had chaps enough wanting me that way. Freddy Hill writes to me twice and three times a day, sheets and sheets.

HIGGINS: [*Disagreeably surprised*] Damn his impudence! [*He recoils and finds himself sitting on his heels*]

LIZA: He has a right to if he likes, poor lad. And he does love me.

HIGGINS: [*Getting off the ottoman*] You have no right to encourage him.

LIZA: Every girl has a right to be loved.

HIGGINS: What! By fools like that?

LIZA: Freddy's not a fool. And if he's weak and poor and wants me, may be he'd make me happier than my betters that bully me and dont want me.

HIGGINS: Can he make anything of you? Thats the point.

LIZA: Perhaps I could make something of him. But I never thought of us making anything of one another; and you never think of anything else. I only want to be natural.

HIGGINS: In short, you want me to be as infatuated about you as Freddy? Is that it?

LIZA: No I dont. Thats not the sort of feeling I want from you. And dont you be too sure of yourself or of me. I could have been a bad girl if I'd liked. Ive seen more of some things than you, for all your learning. Girls like me can drag gentlemen down to make love to them easy enough. And they wish each other dead the next minute.

HIGGINS: Of course they do. Then what in thunder are we quarrelling about?

LIZA: [Much troubled] I want a little kindness. I know I'm a common ignorant girl, and you a book-learned gentleman; but I'm not dirt under your feet. What I done [Correcting herself] what I did was not for the dresses and the taxis: I did it because we were pleasant together and I come—came—to care for you; not to want you to make love to me, and not forgetting the difference between us, but more friendly like.

HIGGINS: Well, of course. Thats just how I feel. And how Pickering feels. Eliza: youre a fool.

LIZA: Thats not a proper answer to give me. [She sinks on the chair at the writing-table in tears]

HIGGINS: It's all youll get until you stop being a common idiot. If youre going to be a lady, youll have to give up feeling neglected if the men you know dont spend half their time snivelling over you and the other half giving you black eyes. If you cant stand the coldness of my sort of life, and the strain of it, go back to the gutter. Work til youre more a brute than a human being; and then cuddle and squabble and drink til you fall asleep. Oh, it's a fine life, the life of the gutter. It's real: it's warm: it's violent: you can feel it through the thickest skin: you can taste it and smell it without any training or any work. Not like Science and Literature and Classical Music and Philosophy and Art. You find me cold, unfeeling, selfish, dont you? Very well: be off with you to the sort of people you like. Marry some sentimental hog or other with lots of money, and a thick pair of lips to kiss you with and a thick pair of boots to kick you with. If you cant appreciate what youve got, youd better get what you can appreciate.

LIZA: [Desperate] Oh, you are a cruel tyrant. I cant talk to you: you turn everything against me: I'm always in the wrong. But you know very well all the time that youre nothing but a bully. You know I cant go back to the gutter, as you call it, and that I have no real friends in the world but you and the Colonel. You know well I couldnt bear to live with a low common man after you two; and it's wicked and cruel of you to insult me by pretending I could. You think I must go back to Wimpole Street because I have nowhere else to go but father's. But dont you be too sure that you have me under your feet to be trampled on and talked down. I'll marry Freddy, I will, as soon as I'm able to support him.

HIGGINS: [*Thunderstruck*]   Freddy!!! that young fool! That poor devil who couldnt get a job as an errand boy even if he had the guts to try for it! Woman: do you not understand that I have made you a consort for a king?

LIZA: Freddy loves me: that makes him king enough for me. I dont want him to work: he wasnt brought up to it as I was. I'll go and be a teacher.

HIGGINS: Whatll you teach, in heaven's name?

LIZA: What you taught me. I'll teach phonetics.

HIGGINS: Ha! ha! ha!

LIZA: I'll offer myself as an assistant to that hairyfaced Hungarian.

HIGGINS: [*Rising in a fury*]   What! That imposter! that humbug! that toadying ignoramus! Teach him my methods! my discoveries! You take one step in his direction and I'll wring your neck. [*He lays hands on her*] Do you hear?

LIZA: [*Defiantly non-resistant*]   Wring away. What do I care? I knew youd strike me some day. [*He lets her go, stamping with rage at having forgotten himself, and recoils so hastily that he stumbles back into his seat on the ottoman*] Aha! Now I know how to deal with you. What a fool I was not to think of it before! You cant take away the knowledge you gave me. You said I had a finer ear than you. And I can be civil and kind to people, which is more than you can. Aha! [*Purposely dropping her aitches to annoy him*] Thats done you, Enry Iggins, it az. Now I dont care that [*Snapping her fingers*] for your bullying and your big talk. I'll advertize it in the papers that your duchess is only a flower girl that you taught, and that she'll teach anybody to be a duchess just the same in six months for a thousand guineas. Oh, when I think of myself crawling under your feet and being trampled on and called names, when all the time I had only to lift up my finger to be as good as you, I could just kick myself.

HIGGINS: [*Wondering at her*]   You damned impudent slut, you! But it's better than snivelling; better than fetching slippers and finding spectacles, isnt it? [*Rising*] By George, Eliza, I said I'd make a woman of you; and I have. I like you like this.

LIZA: Yes: you turn round and make up to me now that I'm not afraid of you, and can do without you.

HIGGINS: Of course I do, you little fool. Five minutes ago you were like a millstone round my neck. Now youre a tower of strength: a consort battleship. You and I and Pickering will be three old bachelors instead of only two men and a silly girl.

[MRS HIGGINS *returns, dressed for the wedding.* ELIZA *instantly becomes cool and elegant*]

MRS HIGGINS: The carriage is waiting, Eliza. Are you ready?

LIZA: Quite. Is the Professor coming?

MRS HIGGINS: Certainly not. He cant behave himself in church. He makes remarks out loud all the time on the clergyman's pronunciation.

LIZA: Then I shall not see you again, Professor. Goodbye. [*She goes to the door*]

MRS HIGGINS: [*Coming to* HIGGINS]   Goodbye, dear.

HIGGINS: Goodbye, mother. [*He is about to kiss her, when he recollects something*] Oh, by the way, Eliza, order a ham and a Stilton cheese, will you? And buy me a pair of reindeer gloves, number eights, and a tie to match that new suit of mine. You can choose the color. [*His cheerful, careless, vigorous voice shews that he is incorrigible*]

LIZA: [*Disdainfully*]   Number eights are too small for you if you want them lined with lamb's wool. You have three new ties that you have forgotten in the drawer of your washstand. Colonel Pickering prefers double Gloucester to Stilton; and you dont notice the difference. I telephoned Mrs Pearce this morning not to forget the ham. What you are to do without me I cannot imagine. [*She sweeps out*]

MRS HIGGINS: I'm afraid youve spoilt that girl, Henry. I should be uneasy about you and her if she were less fond of Colonel Pickering.

HIGGINS: Pickering! Nonsense: she's going to marry Freddy. Ha ha! Freddy! Freddy! ! Ha ha ha ha ha! ! ! ! ! [*He roars with laughter as the play ends*]

The rest of the story need not be shewn in action, and indeed, would hardly need telling if our imaginations were not so enfeebled by their lazy dependence on the ready-mades and reach-me-downs of the ragshop in which Romance keeps its stock of "happy endings" to misfit all stories. Now, the history of Eliza Doolittle, though called a romance because the transfiguration it records seems exceedingly improbable, is common enough. Such transfigurations have been achieved by hundreds of resolutely ambitious young women since Nell Gwynne set them the example by playing queens and fascinating kings in the theatre in which she began by selling oranges. Nevertheless, people in all directions have assumed, for no other reason than that she became the heroine of a romance, that she must have married the hero of it. This is unbearable, not only because her little drama, if acted on such a thoughtless assumption, must be spoiled, but because the true sequel is patent to anyone with a sense of human nature in general, and of feminine instinct in particular.

Eliza, in telling Higgins she would not marry him if he asked her, was not coquetting: she was announcing a well-considered decision. When a bachelor interests, and dominates, and teaches, and becomes important to a spinster, as Higgins with Eliza, she always, if she has character enough to be capable of it, considers very seriously indeed whether she will play for becoming that bachelor's wife, especially if he is so little interested in marriage that a determined and devoted woman might capture him if she set herself resolutely to do it. Her decision will depend a good deal on whether she is really free to choose; and that, again, will depend on her age and income. If she is at the end of her youth, and has no security for her livelihood, she will marry him because she must marry anybody who will provide for her. But at Eliza's age a good-looking girl does not feel that pressure: she feels free to pick and choose. She is therefore guided by her instinct in the matter. Eliza's instinct tells her not to marry Higgins. It does not tell her to give him up. It is not in the slightest doubt as to his remaining one of the strongest personal interests in her life. It would be very sorely strained if there was another woman likely to supplant her with him. But as she feels sure of him on that last point, she has no doubt at all as to her course, and would not have any, even if the difference of twenty years in age, which seems so great to youth, did not exist between them.

As our own instincts are not appealed to by her conclusion, let us see whether we cannot discover some reason in it. When Higgins excused his indifference to young women on the ground that they had an irresistible rival in his mother, he gave the clue to his inveterate old-bachelordom. The case is uncommon only to the extent that remarkable mothers are uncommon. If an imaginative boy has a sufficiently rich mother who has intelligence, personal grace, dignity of character without harshness, and a cultivated sense of the best art of her time to enable her to make her house beautiful, she sets a standard for him against which very few women can struggle, besides effecting for him a disengagement of his affections, his sense of beauty, and his idealism from his specifically sexual impulses. This makes him a standing puzzle to the huge number of uncultivated people who have been brought up in tasteless homes by commonplace or disagreeable parents, and to whom, consequently, literature, painting, sculpture, music, and affectionate personal relations come as modes of sex if they come at all. The word passion means nothing else to them; and that Higgins could have a passion for phonetics and idealize his mother instead of Eliza, would seem to them absurd and unnatural. Nevertheless, when we look round and see that hardly anyone is too ugly or disagreeable to find a wife or a husband if he or she wants one, whilst many old maids and bachelors are above the average in quality and culture, we cannot help suspecting that the disentanglement of sex from the associations with which it is so commonly confused, a disentanglement which persons of genius achieve by sheer intellectual analysis, is sometimes produced or aided by parental fascination.

Now, though Eliza was incapable of thus explaining to herself Higgins's formidable powers of resistance to the charm that prostrated Freddy at the first glance, she was instinctively aware that she could never obtain a complete grip of him, or come between him and his mother (the first necessity of the married woman). To put it shortly, she knew that for some mysterious reason he had not the makings of a married man in him, according to her conception of a husband as one to whom she would be his nearest and fondest and warmest interest. Even had there been no mother-rival, she would still have refused to accept an interest in herself that was secondary to philosophic interests. Had Mrs Higgins died, there would still have been Milton and the Universal Alphabet. Landor's remark that to those who have the greatest power of loving, love is a secondary affair, would not have recommended Landor to Eliza. Put that along with her resentment of Higgins's domineering superiority, and her mistrust of his coaxing cleverness in getting round her and evading her wrath when he had gone too far with his impetuous bullying, and you will see that Eliza's instinct had good grounds for warning her not to marry her Pygmalion.

And now, whom did Eliza marry? For if Higgins was a predestinate old bachelor, she was most certainly not a predestinate old maid. Well, that can be told very shortly to those who have not guessed it from the indications she has herself given them.

Almost immediately after Eliza is stung into proclaiming her considered determination not to marry Higgins, she mentions the fact that young Mr. Frederick Eynsford Hill is pouring out his love for her daily through the post. Now Freddy is young, practically twenty years younger than Higgins: he is a gentleman (or, as Eliza would qualify him, a toff), and speaks like one. He is nicely dressed, is treated by the Colonel as an equal, loves her unaffectedly, and is not her master, nor ever likely to dominate her in spite of his advantage of social standing. Eliza has no use for the foolish romantic tradition that all women love to be mastered, if not actually bullied and beaten. "When you go to women" says Nietzsche "take your whip with you." Sensible despots have never confined that precaution to women: they have taken their whips with them when they have dealt with men, and been slavishly idealized by the men over whom they have flourished the whip much more than by women. No doubt there are slavish women as well as slavish men; and women, like men, admire those that are stronger than themselves. But to admire a strong person and to live under that strong person's thumb are two different things. The weak may not be admired and hero-worshipped; but they are by no means disliked or shunned; and they never seem to have the least difficulty in marrying people who are too good for them. They may fail in emergencies; but life is not one long emergency: it is mostly a string of situations for which no exceptional strength is needed, and with which even rather weak people can cope if they have a stronger partner to help them out. Accordingly, it is a truth everywhere in evidence that strong people, masculine or feminine, not only do not marry stronger people, but do not shew any preference for them in selecting their friends. When a lion meets another with a louder roar "the first lion thinks the last a bore." The man or woman who feels strong enough for two, seeks for every other quality in a partner than strength.

The converse is also true. Weak people want to marry strong people who do not frighten them too much; and this often leads them to make the mistake we describe metaphorically as "biting off more than they can chew." They want too much for too little; and when the bargain is unreasonable beyond all bearing, the union becomes impossible: it ends in the weaker party being either discarded or borne as a cross, which is worse. People who are not only weak, but silly or obtuse as well, are often in these difficulties.

This being the state of human affairs, what is Eliza fairly sure to do when she is placed between Freddy and Higgins? Will she look forward to a lifetime of fetching Higgins's slippers or to a lifetime of Freddy fetching hers? There can be no doubt about the answer. Unless Freddy is biologically repulsive to her, and Higgins biologically attractive to a degree that overwhelms all her other instincts, she will, if she marries either of them, marry Freddy.

And that is just what Eliza did.

Complications ensued; but they were economic, not romantic. Freddy had no money and no occupation. His mother's jointure, a last relic of the opulence of Largelady Park, had enabled her to struggle along in Earlscourt with an air of gentility, but not to procure any serious secondary education for her children, much less give the boy a profession. A clerkship at thirty shillings a week was beneath Freddy's dignity, and extremely distasteful to him besides. His prospects consisted of a hope that if he kept up appearances somebody would do something for him. The something appeared vaguely to his imagination as a private secretaryship or a sinecure of some sort. To his mother it perhaps appeared as a marriage to some lady of means who could not resist her boy's niceness. Fancy her feelings when he married a flower girl who had become disclassed under extraordinary circumstances which were now notorious!

It is true that Eliza's situation did not seem wholly ineligible. Her father, though formerly a dustman, and now fantastically disclassed, had become extremely popular in the smartest society by a social talent which triumphed over every prejudice and every disadvantage. Rejected by the middle class, which he loathed, he had shot up at once into the highest circles by his wit, his dustmanship (which he carried like a banner), and his Nietzschean transcendence of good and evil. At intimate ducal dinners he sat on the right hand of the Duchess; and in country houses he smoked in the pantry and was made much of by the butler when he was not feeding in the dining room and being consulted by cabinet ministers. But he found it almost as hard to do all this on four thousand a year as Mrs Eynsford Hill to live in Earlscourt on an income so pitiably smaller that I have not the heart to disclose its exact figure. He absolutely refused to add the last straw to his burden by contributing to Eliza's support.

Thus Freddy and Eliza, now Mr and Mrs Eynsford Hill, would have spent a penniless honeymoon but for a wedding present of £500 from the Colonel to Eliza. It lasted a long time because Freddy did not know how to spend money, never having had any to spend, and Eliza, socially trained by a pair of old bachelors, wore her clothes as long as they held together and looked pretty, without the least regard to their being many months out of fashion. Still, £500 will not last two young people for ever; and they both knew, and Eliza felt as well, that they must shift for themselves in the end. She could quarter herself on Wimpole Street because it had come to be her home; but she was quite aware that she ought not to quarter Freddy there, and that it would not be good for his character if she did.

Not that the Wimpole Street bachelors objected. When she consulted them, Higgins declined to be bothered about her housing problem when that solution was so simple. Eliza's desire to have Freddy in the house with her seemed of no more importance than if she had wanted an extra piece of bedroom furniture. Pleas as to Freddy's character, and the moral obligation on him to earn his own living, were lost on Higgins. He denied that Freddy had any character, and declared that if he tried to do any useful work some competent person would have the trouble of undoing it: a procedure involving a net loss to the community, and great unhappiness to Freddy himself, who was obviously intended by Nature for such light work as amusing Eliza, which, Higgins declared, was a much more useful and honorable occupation than working in the city. When Eliza referred again to her project of teaching phonetics, Higgins abated not a jot of his violent opposition to it. He said she was not within ten years of being qualified to meddle with his pet subject; and as it was evident that the Colonel agreed with him, she felt she could not go against them in this grave matter, and that she had no right, without Higgins's consent, to exploit the knowledge he had given her; for his knowledge seemed to her as much his private property as his watch: Eliza was no communist. Besides, she was superstitiously devoted to them both, more entirely and frankly after her marriage than before it.

It was the Colonel who finally solved the problem, which had cost him much perplexed cogitation. He one day asked Eliza, rather shyly, whether she had quite given up her notion of keeping a flower shop. She replied that she had thought of it, but had put it out of her head, because the Colonel had said, that day at Mrs Higgins's, that it would never do. The Colonel confessed that when he said that, he had not quite recovered from the dazzling impression of the day before. They broke the matter to Higgins that evening. The sole comment vouchsafed by him very nearly led to a serious quarrel with Eliza. It was to the effect that she would have in Freddy an ideal errand boy.

Freddy himself was next sounded on the subject. He said he had been thinking of a shop himself; though it had presented itself to his pennilessness as a small place in which Eliza should sell tobacco at one counter whilst he sold newspapers at the opposite one. But he agreed that it would be extraordinarily jolly to go early every morning with Eliza to Covent Garden and buy flowers on the scene of their first meeting: a sentiment which earned him many kisses from his wife. He added that he had always been afraid to propose anything of the sort, because Clara would make an awful row about a step that must damage her matrimonial chances, and his mother could not be expected to like it after clinging for so many years to that step of the social ladder on which retail trade is impossible.

This difficulty was removed by an event highly unexpected by Freddy's mother. Clara, in the course of her incursions into those artistic circles which were the highest within her reach, discovered that her conversational qualifications were expected to include a grounding in the novels of Mr H. G. Wells. She borrowed them in various directions so energetically that she swallowed them all within two months. The result was a conversion of a kind quite common today. A modern Acts of the Apostles would fill fifty whole Bibles if anyone were capable of writing it.

Poor Clara, who appeared to Higgins and his mother as a disagreeable and ridiculous person, and to her own mother as in some inexplicable way a social failure, had never seen herself in either light; for, though to some extent ridiculed and mimicked in West Kensington like everybody else there, she was accepted as a rational and normal—or shall we say inevitable?—sort of human being. At worst they called her The Pusher; but to them no more than to herself had it ever occurred that she was pushing the air, and pushing it in a wrong direction. Still, she was not happy. She was growing desperate. Her one asset, the fact that her mother was what the Epsom greengrocer called a carriage lady, had no exchange value, apparently. It had prevented her from getting educated, because the only education she could have afforded was education with the Earlscourt greengrocer's daughter. It had led her to seek the society of her mother's class; and that class simply would not have her, because she was much poorer than the greengrocer, and, far from being able to afford a maid, could not afford even a housemaid, and had to scrape along at home with an illiberally treated general servant. Under such circumstances nothing could give her an air of being a genuine product of Largelady Park. And yet its tradition made her regard a marriage with anyone within her reach as an unbearable humiliation. Commercial people and professional people in a small way were odious to her. She ran after painters and novelists; but she did not charm them; and her bold attempts to pick up and practise artistic and literary talk irritated them. She was, in short, an utter failure, an ignorant, incompetent, pretentious, unwelcome, penniless, useless little snob; and though she did not admit these disqualifications (for nobody ever faces unpleasant truths of this kind until the possibility of a way out dawns on them) she felt their effects too keenly to be satisfied with her position.

Clara had a startling eyeopener when, on being suddenly wakened to enthusiasm by a girl of her own age who dazzled her and produced in her a gushing desire to take her for a model, and gain her friendship, she discovered that this exquisite apparition had graduated from the gutter in a few months time. It shook her so violently, that when Mr H. G. Wells lifted her on the point of his puissant pen, and placed her at the angle of view from which the life she was leading and the society to which she clung appeared in its true relation to real human needs and worthy social structure, he effected a conversion and a conviction of sin comparable to the most sensational feats of General Booth or Gypsy Smith. Clara's snobbery went bang. Life suddenly began to move with her. Without knowing how or why, she began to make friends and enemies. Some of the acquaintances to whom she had been a tedious or indifferent or ridiculous affliction, dropped her: others became cordial. To her amazement she found that some "quite nice" people were saturated with Wells, and that this accessibility to ideas was the secret of their niceness. People she had thought deeply religious, and had tried to conciliate on that tack with disastrous results, suddenly took an interest in her, and revealed a hostility to conventional religion which she had never conceived possible except among the most desperate characters. They made her read Galsworthy; and Galsworthy exposed the vanity of Largelady Park and finished her. It exasperated her to think that the dungeon in which she had languished for so many unhappy years had been unlocked all the time, and that the impulses she had so carefully struggled with and stifled for the sake of keeping well with society, were precisely those by which alone she could have come into any sort of sincere human contact. In the radiance of these discoveries, and the tumult of their reaction, she made a fool of herself as freely and conspicuously as when she so rashly adopted Eliza's expletive in Mrs Higgins's drawing room; for the new-born Wellsian had to find her bearings almost as ridiculously as a baby; but nobody hates a baby for its ineptitudes, or thinks the worse of it for trying to eat the matches; and Clara lost no friends by her follies. They laughed at her to her face this time; and she had to defend herself and fight it out as best she could.

When Freddy paid a visit to Earlscourt (which he never did when he could possibly help it) to make the desolating announcement that he and his Eliza were thinking of blackening the Largelady scutcheon by opening a shop, he found the little household already convulsed by a prior announcement from Clara that she also was going to work in an old furniture shop in Dover Street, which had been started by a fellow Wellsian. This appointment Clara owed, after all, to her old social accomplishment of Push. She had made up her mind that, cost what it might, she would see Mr Wells in the flesh; and she had achieved her end at a garden party. She had better luck than so rash an enterprise deserved. Mr Wells came up to her expectations. Age had not withered him, nor could custom stale his infinite variety in half an hour. His pleasant neatness and compactness, his small hands and feet, his teeming ready brain, his unaffected accessibility, and a certain fine apprehensiveness which stamped him as susceptible from his topmost hair to his tipmost toe, proved irresistible. Clara talked of nothing else for weeks and weeks afterwards. And as she happened to talk to the lady of the furniture shop, and that lady also desired above all things to know Mr Wells and sell pretty things to him, she offered Clara a job on the chance of achieving that end through her.

And so it came about that Eliza's luck held, and the expected opposition to the flower shop melted away. The shop is in the arcade of a railway station not very far from the Victoria and Albert Museum; and if you live in that neighbourhood you may go there any day and buy a buttonhole from Eliza.

Now here is a last opportunity for romance. Would you not like to be assured that the shop was an immense success, thanks to Eliza's charms and her early business experience in Covent Garden? Alas! the truth is the truth: the shop did not pay for a long time, simply because Eliza and her Freddy did not know how to keep it. True, Eliza had not to begin at the very beginning: she knew the names and prices of the cheaper flowers; and her elation was unbounded when she found that Freddy, like all youths educated at cheap, pretentious, and thoroughly inefficient schools, knew a little Latin. It was very little, but enough to make him appear to her a Porson or Bentley, and to put him at his ease with botanical nomenclature. Unfortunately he knew nothing else; and Eliza, though she could count money up to eighteen shillings or so, and had acquired a certain familiarity with the language of Milton from her struggles to qualify herself for winning Higgins's bet, could not write out a bill without utterly disgracing the establishment. Freddy's power of stating in Latin that Balbus built a wall and that Gaul was divided into three parts did not carry with it the slightest knowledge of accounts or business: Colonel Pickering had to explain to him what a cheque book and a bank account meant. And the pair were by no means easily teachable. Freddy backed up Eliza in her obstinate refusal to believe that they could save money by engaging a bookkeeper with some knowledge of the business. How, they argued, could you possibly save money by going to extra expense when you already could not make both ends meet? But the Colonel, after making the ends meet over and over again, at last gently insisted; and Eliza, humbled to the dust by having to beg from him so often, and stung by the uproarious derision of Higgins, to whom the notion of Freddy succeeding at anything was a joke that never palled, grasped the fact that business, like phonetics, has to be learned.

On the piteous spectacle of the pair spending their evenings in shorthand schools and polytechnic classes, learning bookkeeping and typewriting with incipient junior clerks, male and female, from the elementary schools, let me not dwell. There were even classes at the London School of Economics, and a humble personal appeal to the director of that institution to recommend a course bearing on the flower business. He, being a humorist, explained to them the method of the celebrated Dickensian essay on Chinese Metaphysics by the gentleman who read an article on China and an article on Metaphysics and combined the information. He suggested that they should combine the London School with Kew Gardens. Eliza, to whom the procedure of the Dickensian gentleman seemed perfectly correct (as in fact it was) and not in the least funny (which was only her ignorance), took the advice with entire gravity. But the effort that cost her the deepest humiliation was a request to Higgins, whose pet artistic fancy, next to Milton's verse, was caligraphy, and who himself wrote a most beautiful Italian hand, that he would teach her to write. He declared that she was congenitally incapable of forming a single letter worthy of the least of Milton's words; but she persisted; and again he suddenly threw himself into the task of teaching her with a combination of stormy intensity, concentrated patience, and occasional bursts of interesting disquisition on the beauty and nobility, the august mission and destiny, of human handwriting. Eliza ended by acquiring an extremely uncommercial script which was a positive extension of her personal beauty, and spending three times as much on stationery as anyone else because certain qualities and shapes of paper became indispensable to her. She could not even address an envelope in the usual way because it made the margins all wrong.

Their commercial schooldays were a period of disgrace and despair for the young couple. They seemed to be learning nothing about flower shops. At last they gave it up as hopeless, and shook the dust of the shorthand schools, and the polytechnics, and the London School of Economics from their feet for ever. Besides, the business was in some mysterious way beginning to take care of itself. They had somehow forgotten their objections to employing other people. They came to the conclusion that their own way was the best, and that they had really a remarkable talent for business. The Colonel, who had been compelled for some years to keep a sufficient sum on current account at his bankers to make up their deficits, found that the provision was unnecessary: the young people were prospering. It is true that there was not quite fair play between them and their competitors in trade. Their week-ends in the country cost them nothing, and saved them the price of their Sunday dinners; for the motor car was the Colonel's; and he and Higgins paid the hotel bills. Mr F. Hill, florist and greengrocer (they soon discovered that there was money in asparagus; and asparagus led to other vegetables), had an air which stamped the business as classy; and in private life he was still Frederick Eynsford Hill, Esquire. Not that there was any swank about him: nobody but Eliza knew that he had been christened Frederick Challoner. Eliza herself swanked like anything.

That is all. That is how it has turned out. It is astonishing how much Eliza still manages to meddle in the housekeeping at Wimpole Street in spite of the shop and her own family. And it is notable that though she never nags her husband, and frankly loves the Colonel as if she were his favorite daughter, she has never got out of the habit of nagging Higgins that was established on the fatal night when she won his bet for him. She snaps his head off on the faintest provocation, or on none. He no longer dares to tease her by assuming an abysmal inferiority of Freddy's mind to his own. He storms and bullies and derides; but she stands up to him so ruthlessly that the Colonel has to ask her from time to time to be kinder to Higgins; and it is the only request of his that brings a mulish expression into her face. Nothing but some emergency or calamity great enough to break down all likes and dislikes, and throw them both back on their common humanity—and may they be spared any such trial!—will ever alter this. She knows that Higgins does not need her, just as her father did not need her. The very scrupulousness with which he told her that day that he had become used to having her there, and dependent on her for all sorts of little services, and that he should miss her if she went away (it would never have occurred to Freddy or the Colonel to say anything of the sort) deepens her inner certainty that she is "no more to him than them slippers"; yet she has a sense, too, that his indifference is deeper than the infatuation of commoner souls. She is immensely interested in him. She has even secret mischievous moments in which she wishes she could get him alone, on a desert island, away from all ties and with nobody else in the world to consider, and just drag him off his pedestal and see him making love like any common man. We all have private imaginations of that sort. But when it comes to business, to the life that she really leads as distinguished from the life of dreams and fancies, she likes Freddy and she likes the Colonel; and she does not like Higgins and Mr Doolittle. Galatea never does quite like Pygmalion: his relation to her is too godlike to be altogether agreeable.

Glossary

(Cross references are indicated
by SMALL CAPITALS.)

ABSTRACT: Dealing with generalities and ideas, rather than specific, particular objects that evoke vivid mental images. "Honor," "truth," "love" are abstractions. Abstract and general terms are the reverse of CONCRETE and specific terms.

ACT: A major division of a play. Shakespearean DRAMA is normally divided into five acts; modern drama into three. An act, in turn, is usually divided into scenes, in which there is no shift in place and in which the action is continuous in time. On the modern stage, the end of a scene is signalized by the dropping of the curtain or, in the arena theater (theater-in-the-round), by the lowering of the lights.

ALEXANDRINE: A poetic line, usually called a HEXAMETER, that consists of six feet. See METER.

ALLEGORY: Symbolic narration or description in which people, objects, and events directly correspond to other meanings, usually abstract, that they are intended to dramatize.

ALLITERATION: The repetition of initial consonants or consonant sounds in two or more words of a phrase, sentence, or line of poetry. Repetition of initial vowel sounds is occasionally termed alliteration, but is more properly described as ASSONANCE. See CONSONANCE.

ALLUSION: A reference to a historical, literary, or mythical person or event, often used as part of a simile or metaphor.

AMBIGUITY: In the literary sense, the quality of having two or more legitimate meanings that add new dimensions to the word, phrase, or entire work rather than detracting from it.

ANAGNORISIS: See TRAGEDY.

ANAPEST, ANAPESTIC: A poetic foot consisting of two unaccented syllables followed by an accented syllable. See METER.

ANTAGONIST: The character in a work of fiction opposed to the PROTAGONIST. The conflict between them is the occasion of the plot, gives rise to the action.

ANTISTROPHE: One of the stanzas of a triad in a Pindaric ODE or choric song.

ANTITHESIS: A marked contrast of ideas or grammatical elements emphasized by careful balancing of grammatical structure, as in Pope's "Rape of the Lock": "There hero's wits are kept in ponderous vases,/And beau's in snuff-boxes and tweezer cases./There broken vows and death-bed alms are found,/And lovers' hearts with ends of riband bound."

APOSTROPHE: Direct address to a person or object, whether absent or present.

ASIDE: See SOLILOQUY.

ASSONANCE: The repetition of vowels or vowel sounds in two or more words of a phrase, sentence, or line of poetry. See ALLITERATION, CONSONANCE.

ATMOSPHERE: The TONE or mood of a literary composition, which indicates the attitude of the author toward his material. See SETTING.

BALLAD: A short, simple, narrative poem that ordinarily employs a stanza of four lines, alternately of three and four stressed syllables, with only the second and fourth lines rhyming. The folk ballad is anonymous, altered through the ages by individual singers, with a colloquial style and a narrative heavily dependent on dialogue and refrain. The literary ballad (Auden's "The Quarry," for example) is a more complex form written by a single author to present a particular effect or theme.

BALLADE: A French verse form (for instance, Henley's "Ballade of Dead Actors") with three stanzas of eight lines and a concluding stanza, or "envoy," of four lines. The last line of each stanza is the same; only three rhymes are permitted, and no rhyme word may be repeated. The rhyme scheme is thus *ababbcbc* for the stanzas, and *bcbc* for the envoy.

BLANK VERSE: Unrhymed poetry, ordinarily iambic pentameter, as in Shakespeare's *Othello* and *Measure for Measure*.

CACOPHONY: The use of unpleasant, discordant sounds for particular effects, as in Pope's "Rape of the Lock": "Gums and pomatums shall his flight restrain," "Or alum styptics with contracting power/Shrink his thin essence." See EUPHONY.

CAESURA: A momentary pause within a line of poetry. See RHYTHM.

CATASTROPHE: The DÉNOUEMENT in tragedy, the conclusion of the conflict. See PLOT.

CATHARSIS: Literally, purgation. In Aristotle's *Poetics*, the audience's purging of their emotions (especially pity and fear) by their vicarious participation in the action of tragic drama. In this sense, the members of the audience assuage their own emotional conflicts by psychological projection, loading their emotions on a scapegoat. In another interpretation, however, they

are thought to rid themselves of undue emotion by learning, through observation of the protagonist, how to avoid the destruction he brings upon
himself.

CHARACTER: An actor in a story or drama. Character is also the term used to
designate the personality or moral disposition of the actor. Thus Macbeth
is the main character in Shakespeare's tragedy *Macbeth*; the flaw in his
character is overweening ambition.

CHORUS: A character or group of characters that comment on the action of a
play, often by delivering the PROLOGUE and EPILOGUE, or on the action
of a short story or novel (Marlow, in Conrad's "The Lagoon," may be considered a chorus character). In Greek drama, the chorus was a group of
actors whose songs furnished both summary and comment on the action
at regular intervals in the play. The STROPHE of their choric song was
uttered as they moved ritualistically in one direction, the ANTISTROPHE, as
they moved in the opposite direction, and the EPODE as they stood still.

CLICHÉ: A stereotype; a trite, worn-out phrase or idea to which fresh, active
responses are no longer possible.

CLIMAX: The point of maximum emotional intensity or, in PLOT, the TURN-
ING POINT in the fortunes of the hero.

COINCIDENCE: The accidental coming together of two events, persons, etc.
Coincidental occurrences lack any discernible causal relationship.

COMEDY: A type of drama that may or may not aim primarily to evoke laughter, but nevertheless deals with incongruities and inconsistencies of character, action, or traits and in which the various conflicts are resolved "happily," usually by bringing the incongruous elements into accord with some
accepted norm of conduct or outlook. FARCE is to comedy what MELO-
DRAMA is to TRAGEDY; farce relies on humorous situations rather than on
perception of meaning in human action, and its characters are flat, existing
only to take part in the situations that evoke laughter. SLAPSTICK is a type
of farce that relies for laughter on pratfalls and beatings in the manner
of Punch and Judy. Comedy of manners, on the other hand, relies for
its amusing effects on verbal brilliance, wit.

COMEDY OF MANNERS: See COMEDY.

COMPLICATION: In PLOT, the incident or, usually, series of incidents, that lead
from the point of attack to the climax. See RISING ACTION.

CONCEIT: A type of METAPHOR, either brief or elaborately extended, that
achieves its effects by the ingenuity of the author. The Petrarchan conceit
is an extended metaphor, typically comparing a loved one to a rose, a
garden, a summer's day, etc. The metaphysical conceit may be identified
not only by the startling nature of the comparison, but by its highly intellectual quality. See SIMILE, SYMBOL.

CONCRETE: Giving rise to an immediate sense image of sight, sound, smell,
taste, touch. "Grass," "bang," "velvety," "peppermint" are concrete terms.
See ABSTRACT.

CONFLICT: The struggle between opposing persons or forces in fiction that constitutes the essential element of PLOT. See ANTAGONIST.

CONNOTATION: The full range of suggestions, associations, or overtones—the meaning beyond DENOTATION—that adheres to a word as the result of personal experience or the attitudes of our society.

CONSONANCE: The repetition of consonants or consonant sounds within two or more words in close proximity. Repetition of initial consonant sounds is properly termed ALLITERATION. See ASSONANCE.

COUPLET: Two successive, rhymed, lines of poetry. See HEROIC COUPLET.

COWLEIAN ODE: See ODE.

DACTYL, DACTYLIC: A poetic foot consisting of an accented syllable followed by two unaccented ones. See METER.

DENOTATION: The explicit, literal meaning of a word, the meaning stripped of personal or general emotional overtones. See CONNOTATION.

DÉNOUEMENT: The conclusion of the PLOT, the outcome of the action, along with any explanations necessary to clear up all misunderstandings.

DEUS EX MACHINA: Literally, "god from a machine," referring to the actor brought in by stage machinery to intervene in the action of ancient Greek and Roman plays; from this, any character or event improbably introduced to resolve a situation.

DIALOGUE: The speech between two or more characters in a narrative or drama; written conversation.

DICTION: The choice of words and the manner of their arrangement peculiar to an author.

DIMETER: A poetic line of two feet. See METER.

DRAMATIC IRONY: See IRONY.

DRAMATIC MONOLOGUE: A poem in which a single speaker (who is not the poet) addresses a silent auditor in the hope of achieving a particular purpose and in the process ironically reveals his character and his hidden motives.

ELEGY: A lyric poem of lament and praise for the dead. Since the poet chooses his stanza form as he wishes and since the feeling and style are equally elevated and dignified, only the subject matter differentiates an elegy like Gray's "Elegy: Written in a Country Churchyard" from a homostrophic ODE. The pastoral elegy (Milton's "Lycidas," Arnold's "Thyrsis") involves certain obligatory elements and a traditional organization: the poet and his dead friend are imagined to be shepherds of classical times; and the poet's expression of grief proceeds from a statement of his loss to an invocation to the Muses, the poet-shepherd's memories of his friend, a description of the funeral procession, the strewing of flowers, and a resolution of the grief in the realization that the friend has achieved immortality.

END-STOPPED LINE: A line of poetry in which there is a distinct, punctuated, structural pause or stop at the end of the line. See RHYTHM.

ENJAMBMENT: A RUN-ON LINE of poetry. See RHYTHM.

ENVIRONMENT: In a broad sense, the SETTING in which the action takes place in fiction, including the place and the social and cultural background.

EPIC: A long poetic narrative concerned with the histories of one or more heroic characters engaged in an action of great significance. Certain conventional elements are customarily involved. The epic poem begins at or near the most important action of the narrative (*in medias res*), shifting then to incidents that led up to this climax and to those that follow it; the style is elevated, making use of a formal invocation to the Muses, a specific statement of the theme, long formal similes, genealogies of noble figures, catalogues of ships or troops involved in the action, and numerous references to the gods' participation. The folk epic (*Beowulf*, *The Odyssey*) is concerned simply with great actions in the heroic age, whereas the literary epic (*The Aeneid*, *The Argonautica*, *Paradise Lost*) demonstrates more conscious literary control by a single author rather than growth in an oral tradition. The mock epic ("The Rape of the Lock") is a burlesque form that applies all the traditional epic elements to an action of trivial significance.

EPILOGUE: A concluding statement, added to a play or novel, that gives information or provides comment that properly lies outside the bounds of the work itself. In eighteenth-century plays, it was often written by someone other than the author and delivered after the curtain.

EPISODE: An incident complete in itself, yet part of a larger action. In Greek drama, an episode is the action that takes place between two choruses, roughly comparable to a scene in modern drama.

EPITHET: An adjective used to single out a main characteristic of a person or thing, as in Homer's "ox-eyed Hera" or "cloud-gathering Zeus." A transferred epithet is this kind of modifier applied in an unusual way, as in Milton's "Lycidas" ("blind mouths") or Bridges' "Low Barometer" ("sightless footsteps pad the floor").

EPODE: The third stanza of a triad, different from the other two, in a Pindaric ODE or a choric song.

ESSAY: A relatively brief expository composition dealing with a limited subject.

EUPHONY: Any pattern of agreeable, harmonious sounds. The opposite of CACOPHONY.

EXPOSITION: The portion of the PLOT that introduces the characters, sets the tone, and furnishes whatever information about the situation is necessary to understand the subsequent action.

FALLING ACTION: The portion of the dramatic PLOT that leads from the climax to the dénouement.

FARCE: See COMEDY.

FEMININE ENDING: At the end of a poetic line, a word ending with an unstressed syllable. See RHYME.

FEMININE RHYME: See RHYME.

FIGURATIVE LANGUAGE: Language that conveys meaning by the use of an explicit or implied comparison with something else, as in such figures, or TROPES, as the METAPHOR, SIMILE, or SYMBOL.

FLASHBACK: The insertion of antecedent details after an action has started.

FLAT CHARACTER: A character with one dominant trait that governs his actions and makes those actions consistent. E. M. Forster, who invented the term, divided all characters in fiction into flat and round, identifying flat characters with the "humours" of seventeenth-century drama, with types, or with caricatures. A flat character is simple rather than complex; but simplicity is relative, with caricature at one extreme and an individual with considerably more depth, such as Polonius, in *Hamlet*, at the other. Flat characters far outnumber round in fiction. See ROUND CHARACTERS.

FOLK BALLAD: See BALLAD.

FOLK EPIC: See EPIC.

FOOT: In poetry, the basic metrical unit, a pattern of either two or three stressed and unstressed syllables. See METER.

FORESHADOWING: An intimation of events to come.

FREE VERSE: Poetry that does not use rhyme or regular meter as a means of achieving coherence.

GENERALIZATION: An inclusive statement of an idea in an expository essay that is developed by particulars.

GENRE: A term meaning "kind" or "type," used to label both the broad categories of literature (drama, essay, novel, poetry, short story) and the particular species within each category (dramatic monologue, elegy, ode, sonnet, etc.).

HALF RHYME: See RHYME.

HAMARTIA: See TRAGEDY.

HEPTAMETER: A poetic line of seven feet. See METER.

HERO: The central character in a work of fiction, without regard to his moral traits. See PROTAGONIST.

HEROIC COUPLET: Two successive, rhymed, iambic pentameter poetic lines.

HEXAMETER: A poetic line of six feet, sometimes called an ALEXANDRINE. See METER.

HOMOSTROPHIC ODE: See ODE.

HORATIAN ODE: See ODE.

HUBRIS: See TRAGEDY.

HYPERBOLE: See IRONY.

IAMB, IAMBIC: A poetic foot consisting of an unaccented syllable followed by an accented one. See METER.

IMAGERY: In a general sense, any figure of speech or description that helps the reader imaginatively to see, feel, taste, hear, smell, or to experience the sensation of physical movement; more specifically, FIGURATIVE LANGUAGE.

INCREMENTAL REPETITION: Repetition, with variations that provide new information, of one or more lines of a poem or ballad, as in the first two lines of "Edward, Edward."

INTERNAL RHYME: See RHYME.

INTRIGUE: Plot in the drama, especially a plot that revolves around a situation in which one character is completely unaware of the machinations of another.

INVERSION: An unusual twisting of the normal grammatical order of a sentence so that certain elements may be stressed, as in Shakespeare's Sonnet LXXIII: "That time of year thou mayst in me behold." In the hands of less skillful writers, the device often becomes an awkward affectation, purposeless except as a means of ending with the proper rhyming word.

IRONY: A kind of figurative language involving a relationship between the reality described and the terms used to describe it. At least three main types of irony may be distinguished. Verbal irony is based on an incongruous relationship between the apparent and real meanings of a statement. At one extreme is understatement, in which the speaker means much more than he says; at the other extreme is hyperbole, in which the speaker uses extravagantly exaggerated terms; between these extremes are various degrees of verbal incongruity, often no more than a nuance of tone. Structural irony is a principle of organization rather than a kind of statement. In its simplest form, this type of irony is a sharp contrast of events or situations; more subtly, it may involve only minor shades of difference or the collapse of several scattered events into a single moment, as in Jarrell's "The Death of the Ball Turret Gunner." Dramatic irony refers to a situation in a play or a dramatic monologue in which the audience more fully understands the significance of words or actions than do the characters.

ITALIAN SONNET: See SONNET.

LITERARY BALLAD: See BALLAD.

LITERARY EPIC: See EPIC.

LOCAL COLOR: Setting that depends heavily upon the peculiarities of a particular region for its effect.

LYRIC: Originally "a song" (sung to the accompaniment of a lyre), the term now applies to any expository poem revealing the personal response of the poet. See ELEGY, ODE, SONNET.

MASCULINE ENDING: At the end of a poetic line, a word ending with an accented syllable. See RHYME.

MASCULINE RHYME: See RHYME.

MELODRAMA: See TRAGEDY.

METAPHOR: A figure of speech that conveys meaning by use of an implied comparison, whether in a single word or phrase or in a lengthy parallel (an extended metaphor). See SIMILE, SYMBOL.

METAPHYSICAL CONCEIT: See CONCEIT.

METER: The pattern of stressed and unstressed syllables in poetry, described in terms of the basic unit of the pattern, the FOOT, and the number of units, or feet, in each line. Five major types of poetic foot appear in English poetry: the IAMB, an unaccented syllable followed by an accented one (-′); the TROCHEE, an accented syllable followed by an unaccented one (′-); the DACTYL, an accented syllable followed by two unaccented ones (′--); the ANAPEST, two unaccented syllables followed by one accented one (--′); and the SPONDEE, two accented syllables (′′). The number of feet in a line may vary from one to as many as eight. MONOMETER denotes one foot in a line; DIMETER, two; TRIMETER, three; TETRAMETER, four; PENTAMETER, five; HEXAMETER, six; HEPTAMETER, seven, and OCTAMETER, eight. A line of poetry is thus described as iambic pentameter, trochaic hexameter, etc. For a full explanation and examples, see pp. 28–29.

METONYMY: A figure of speech that describes one thing by reference to another very closely related to it but not, strictly speaking, part of it. See Robert Bridges' description in "Low Barometer" of a thing "whose sightless footsteps pad the floor,/ Whose fearful trespass mounts the stair." Literally, "footsteps" cannot walk and "trespass" cannot climb, but Bridges has used what we hear in place of the feet that make sounds, and the result of an action (trespass) in place of what performs the action.

METRICAL ROMANCE: Any verse narrative of adventure, on a less elevated plane than the events of an EPIC, that is told for its own intrinsic popular interest rather than for its significance as history or mythical truth. Originally, a French form categorized by subject matter (e.g., The Matter of France, Matter of Rome, Matter of Britain).

MOCK EPIC: See EPIC.

MONOMETER: A poetic line of one foot. See METER.

MOTIVATION: The purpose that dominates a character in fiction and gives rise to his actions.

NOVEL: Prose fiction of considerable length showing characters in action, and capable of greater complexity in both character and plot than the short story.

NOVELETTE: A short novel; its scope lies beyond the unity of effect of the short story.

OBJECTIVE: A literary work is regarded as objective when there is little or no intrusion of the author, either by way of self-revelation or interpretation of events. Thus the drama is largely objective, since the dramatist usually presents his characters entirely by speech and action, without comment, and without identifying himself with any of them. In an objective point of view in narrative, the author relies heavily upon dialogue and sense details without entering the mind of any of the characters. See SUBJECTIVE.

OCTAMETER: A poetic line of eight feet. See METER.

OCTAVE: See SONNET.

ODE: A lyric poem characterized by lofty feeling, dignified style, and organization according to one of three patterns. The Pindaric, or regular, ode consists of a series of three-stanza units known as TRIADS. Two of these, the STROPHE and ANTISTROPHE, are identical in number of lines, number of accented syllables in each line, and in rhyme scheme; the third stanza, the EPODE, markedly contrasts in one or more elements to the other stanzas of the triad. The Horatian, or homostrophic, ode has none of these complex variations. The poet chooses the form for one stanza and repeats it throughout the poem. The Cowleian, or irregular, ode, the least rigid of the three forms, consists of any number of stanzas, each different from the others in number of lines, number of accented syllables in each line, and rhyme scheme, as in Wordsworth's "Ode: Intimations of Immortality."

OFF RHYME: See RHYME.

OMNISCIENT: The POINT OF VIEW in fiction in which the author gets inside the mind of any of his characters at will.

ONOMATOPOEIA, ONOMATOPOETIC: The use of words whose sounds duplicate those of the object or action that is described, as when Keats writes that the ocean "*Gluts* twice ten thousand caverns."

OTTAVA RIMA: A stanza of eight iambic pentameter lines rhyming *abababcc*, as in Byron's "Don Juan."

OXYMORON: A type of ANTITHESIS that brings together two sharply contrasting terms in a single phrase, as in Milton's "darkness visible" or "bad eminence." See PARADOX.

PARADOX: A figure of speech that links apparently contradictory terms in a single statement that is, in fact, true. OXYMORON resembles paradox, but whereas the first is a phrase, the second is a predication.

PASTORAL ELEGY: See ELEGY.

PATHETIC FALLACY: John Ruskin's term for the practice of endowing nature with human characteristics, particularly emotions. See CONCEIT, PERSONIFICATION.

PENTAMETER: A poetic line of five feet. See METER.

PERIPETEIA: See TRAGEDY.

PERSONIFICATION: A figure of speech based on the assumption that animals, abstract ideas, or things have human characteristics. In a sense, personification is a kind of metaphor equating an object or an abstraction with a human being.

PETRARCHAN CONCEIT: See CONCEIT.

PETRARCHAN, or ITALIAN, SONNET: See SONNET.

PICARESQUE: A form of fiction that takes its name from the Spanish "*picaro*," or "rogue." The action is linear, episodic, and the protagonist, who lives largely by his wits, is engaged in a series of adventures that are often amusing and always related with realistic detail.

PINDARIC ODE: See ODE.

PLOT: A plan of action in narrative and drama containing a conflict and its resolution. The conflict arises out of circumstances that create an unstable situation for the protagonist and proceeds through a series of related actions until some conclusion has been reached. The divisions of the plot, particularly as they apply to the drama, have been called EXPOSITION, POINT OF ATTACK, RISING ACTION (COMPLICATION), CLIMAX (TURNING POINT), FALLING ACTION, and DÉNOUEMENT (or, especially in tragedy, CATASTROPHE). Plot requires a causal relation between events; when this is lacking, the action is called episodic. For plausibility plot requires MOTIVATION, purpose behind the action of the characters. Plot creates SUSPENSE, the desire to discover how the action will turn out.

PLOT-RIDDEN CHARACTER: A character in fiction who acts in a way that is inconsistent with his capabilities or personality because of the demands of the plot.

POETIC DICTION: The particular choice of words and manner of their arrangement regarded by certain authors as the only language refined enough to be used in poetry.

POINT OF ATTACK: That point in the plot at which the complication begins, the event that disturbs the *status quo*.

POINT OF VIEW: The angle from which a story is told, which may be personal or impersonal. In a narrative the author may choose to relate events as they are seen and experienced by one of the characters, by viewing the action completely from the outside, or by injecting himself into the narrative as the one who sees all, knows all, and tells all.

PROBLEM PLAY: A drama that directs attention to a particular sociological problem, as *Hedda Gabler* does to the problem of woman's proper place in late nineteenth-century society.

PROLOGUE: An introduction to a play, novel, or other literary work.

PROSODY: The study of versification. See METER, RHYME, RHYTHM.

PROTAGONIST: The central character in a work of fiction, the hero. In the ensuing conflict his opponent is called the ANTAGONIST.

PURPLE PASSAGE: A passage of verse or prose that is highly emotional, and so constructed by various stylistic devices that it calls attention to itself out of context.

PYRRHIC: A poetic foot consisting of two unaccented syllables.

QUATRAIN: Four lines of poetry linked as a unit by rhyme, usually in the pattern *abab* or *abba*.

REFRAIN: A phrase or verse regularly repeated in a song or poem.

RHYME: Similarity or identity of sound in two or more words, usually the last words of poetic lines. Masculine rhyme is identity of final, accented syllables of rhyming words, as in "heard," "bird," or "seas," "Hebrides"; feminine rhyme is identity of the last two syllables, the first accented, the second unaccented, as in "replying," "dying," or "hopping," "stopping";

triple rhyme is identity of the last three syllables of rhyming words, as in "intellectual," "hen-pecked you all"; slant rhyme, off rhyme or half rhyme, is an approximation rather than an identity of sounds; internal rhyme is identity of sounds in two words within a single line of poetry.

RHYME ROYAL: A stanza of seven iambic pentameter lines rhyming *ababbcc*.

RHYME SCHEME: The order or pattern of rhymes in a poem, described by designating the first rhyming word and all others that rhyme with it *a*; the first new rhyming word and all others that rhyme with it *b*; the next different rhyming word *c*; and so on. Words that do not rhyme with any others are usually marked *x*. A four-line poem in which the first and third lines and the second and fourth lines rhyme would be described as *abab*.

RHYTHM: In poetry, the pattern of phrasing in a line, stanza, or an entire poem. The term should be clearly distinguished from METER, which describes only the pattern of stressed and unstressed syllables in a line. Rhythm is established by the CAESURA, a momentary pause within a line that may or may not be indicated by punctuation; by the presence or absence of END-STOPPED LINES, in which there is a distinct, punctuated, structural pause or stop at the end of the line; and by RUN-ON LINES (also known as ENJAMBMENT), in which there is no structural division or pause between the end of one line and the beginning of the next. For discussion and examples of rhythm in poetry, see pp. 29–31.

RISING ACTION: The COMPLICATION of action between the point of attack and the climax. See PLOT.

ROMANTIC: In literature, a term often used as the opposite of realistic. Romantic literature is, in general, literature somewhat at a remove from ordinary life, with both setting and action tending toward the ideal rather than the real.

RONDEAU: A French verse form (see Dobson's rondeau, "You Bid Me Try") consisting of thirteen lines with only two rhymes. The first phrase of line 1 reappears as a refrain in lines 9 and 13. The rondel, a variant form, consists of fourteen lines, two rhymes, and uses lines 1 and 2 as a refrain repeated twice in the poem, as lines 7 and 8, and 13 and 14.

ROUND CHARACTER: A character of some complexity, whose actions are not as predictable as those of a FLAT CHARACTER. A round character is shown to have varying, and often contradictory, traits, which are subject to change by circumstances, so that he is capable of growth and development. Since all of this demands time, round characters almost never appear in the shorter forms of fiction.

RUN-ON LINE: A line of poetry that has no structural division or pause at the end of it, but leads directly into the following line. See RHYTHM.

SCENE: In drama, a division of an act, marked usually by the dropping of the curtain on the modern stage. Action in a scene is continuous, with no shift in place. In narrative a scene is an incident in which the action is presented in detail and that, like a scene in drama, is continuous in time and action.

SENTIMENTALITY: Any attempt on the part of an author to make his reader react more emotionally than the content of the work warrants. See pp. 5–7.

SESTET: See SONNET.

SESTINA: A French verse form so incredibly complicated that to follow its requirements and yet write something intelligible is a major *tour de force.* See Kipling's "Sestina of the Tramp Royal." The sestina consists of six six-line stanzas and one final three-line stanza. The stanzas do not rhyme; instead, each ends with the same six words used in an entirely different order in each of the first five stanzas according to a regular progression. The last, three-line, stanza must use as end-words the fifth, third, and first end-words of the first stanza (in that order) and must include in the middle of each of the three lines the other three end-words of stanza one.

SETTING: The specific place, time—all that makes up the physical background in which the action of a narrative or drama takes place. It is the total environment that surrounds the characters in fiction.

SHAKESPEAREAN SONNET: See SONNET.

SIMILE: A figure of speech in which one thing is explicitly compared to another by the use of "like," "as," "so," etc. See METAPHOR, SYMBOL.

SLANT RHYME: See RHYME.

SLAPSTICK: See COMEDY.

SOLILOQUY: A speech delivered by a character in a play when he is alone on stage. It is not an aside delivered to the audience, but it has the effect of permitting the audience to know the character's thoughts. Proper justification or plausibility ordinarily requires that the soliloquy be spoken as a result of great stress, and this in turn would seem to imply conflict within the character.

SONNET: A poem of fourteen lines (usually iambic pentameter), rhyming according to one of two main patterns. The Italian sonnet consists of two four-line units—the octave—followed by a six-line unit—the sestet. The rhyme scheme of the octave is always *abba abba*; the scheme of the sestet may be *cdcdcd, cdecde,* or a similar variation. The organization of the poem usually corresponds to the divisions of octave and sestet, often with the octave posing a question that is answered in the sestet. The Shakespearean sonnet consists of three four-line units, or quatrains, followed by a couplet, the entire poem rhyming *abab cdcd efef gg.* The organization of material in the poem may or may not correspond to these divisions. Among other variations, the poet may choose to combine the first two quatrains into a kind of octave, and the last quatrain and couplet into a sestet, or he may treat each quatrain as a separate unit of meaning and use the couplet as summary and brief comment.

SPENSERIAN STANZA: A stanza of nine lines, the first eight iambic pentameter, the last an ALEXANDRINE (see METER), rhyming *ababbcbcc*.

SPONDEE: A poetic foot consisting of two accented syllables. See METER.

STANZA: Two or more lines of poetry (a single line is properly called a VERSE) unified by meter, rhyme, thought, or all of these. See COUPLET, OTTAVA RIMA, QUATRAIN, RHYME ROYAL, SPENSERIAN STANZA, TERCET, TERZA RIMA.

STOCK CHARACTER: A type character found repeatedly in literature, such as the faithful servant or the overpossessive mother. Stock characters, although exhibiting the conventional traits that make them readily identifiable as characters belonging in the tradition of the genre, are often drawn with highly individual traits as well, so that they become memorable in themselves. Thus Partridge, the servant of Tom Jones, in Fielding's novel *Tom Jones*, belongs to a clearly recognizable type in the picaresque story but is, at the same time, a unique individual.

STREAM OF CONSCIOUSNESS: A literary technique that became popular with James Joyce, in which the author of a narrative portrays the thoughts of a character in an almost objective fashion as they presumably run through his mind, following no order but the pattern of association and recollection and usually without recognizable syntax. Another name for stream of consciousness is "interior monologue."

STREAM OF EXPERIENCE: The POINT OF VIEW in fiction that looks out at the action through the eyes and mind of one of the characters, so that all events are filtered through this one consciousness.

STROPHE: One of the stanzas of a triad in a Pindaric ODE or choric song.

SUBJECTIVE: Literature is normally regarded as subjective when it reflects the attitude and personality of the author. Thus lyrical poetry is subjective in comparison with epic poetry, for it is often highly personal, whereas in the epic the author merely presents characters in action without entering the picture himself. See OBJECTIVE.

SUSPENSE: The uncertainty that comes about because of conflict, the desire to know the outcome of the actions of characters who have aroused our interest.

SYMBOL: In literature, a symbol is a word or phrase, an object or action, that has significance over and beyond what it is itself; this significance suggested by the context. Whether briefly described or developed in great detail, the symbol is a figure of speech making use of an implicit comparison in which the second term is more carefully developed than in METAPHOR. Literary symbols are seldom to be equated exactly with what they suggest; they carry layers of suggestion. See SIMILE.

SYNECDOCHE: A form of metaphor that describes something by reference to one small but important part of it, as in Wordsworth's "London, 1802": "altar, sword, and pen,/ Fireside, the heroic wealth of hall and bower."

TERCET: Three successive, rhymed lines of poetry.

TERZA RIMA: A pattern of three-line stanzas successively linked by rhyme in
the pattern of Shelley's "Ode to the West Wind": *aba bcb cdc*, etc. See
RHYME SCHEME.

TETRAMETER: A poetic line of four feet. See METER.

THEME: The unifying idea underlying a literary work, the thesis.

TONE: The attitude of the author toward his subject, indicated by the diction, rhythm, and other matters of style and structure. The tone of a short
story, for instance, might be serious or playful or foreboding. See ATMOS-
PHERE.

TRAGEDY: A type of drama in which the protagonist engages in conflict with
overwhelming forces within or outside himself, suffers in the conflict, learns
about himself and the forces arrayed against him, and often dies. In Aristotle's commentary on Greek tragedy, *hamartia* is the tragic flaw, weakness,
or mistake; *hubris*, or arrogance and pride, is one common type of tragic
flaw, though not the only one; *peripeteia* is a reversal in which an action
produces a result opposite to that intended; and *anagnorisis* is the recognition both of who a character really is (Oedipus' revelation concerning
his birth) and of the general truths to be learned from his conflict and
suffering. Melodrama, one might add, bears the same relationship to
tragedy as farce or slapstick bear to COMEDY. Melodrama involves the
superficial characteristics of tragedy, the noble versus the villainous characters, the horror and suffering, the conflicts of tremendous proportions, but
it presents these as ends in themselves, not as means of presenting the
insights about man that are integral to tragedy.

TRIAD: A unit, consisting of three stanzas, in a Pindaric ODE or choric song.

TRIMETER: A poetic line of three feet. See METER.

TRIOLET: A French verse form (see Bridges' triolet, "When First We Met")
consisting of eight lines and only two rhymes. Line 1 reappears as line 4
and line 7; line 2 reappears as line 8.

TRIPLE RHYME: See RHYME.

TROCHEE, TROCHAIC: A poetic foot consisting of an accented syllable followed
by an unaccented one. See METER.

TROPE: See FIGURATIVE LANGUAGE.

TURNING POINT: The point in the PLOT that marks a change in the fortunes
of the protagonist and from which, at least in retrospect, the outcome of
the conflict is discernible. In tragedy, it marks the high point in the fortunes of the hero. See CLIMAX.

UNDERSTATEMENT: See IRONY.

UNITIES: The dramatic unities traditionally involve action, time, and place:
coherent action, with a clear beginning, middle, and end (some have therefore suggested that a subplot violates this coherence); a single day; and one
place. Shakespeare, of course, brilliantly violates all of these except the first.

VERSE: A single line of poetry, distinguished from the STANZA.

VILLANELLE: A complex French verse form (see Dowson, "Villanelle of the Poet's Road"), consisting of six stanzas totaling nineteen lines—the first five stanzas being each three lines long and the last, four. Line 1 of the poem must reappear as a refrain in lines 6, 12, and 18; line 2 must reappear as lines 9, 15, and 19. Only two rhymes are permitted.

Biographies

ADDISON, JOSEPH (1672–1719) is best remembered for his brilliant collaboration with Richard Steele. When Addison recognized his Oxford friend in writings attributed to Isaac Bickerstaff, editor of the *Tatler*, he wrote Steele offering contributions. Together they established a second journal, *The Spectator* (1711–1712), offering social comment, literary criticism, coffee-house gossip, and accounts of the fictitious Spectators' Club, of which Roger de Coverley, the ideal country gentleman, is the most notable member. Addison's essays are morally earnest, endeavoring "to enliven morality with wit, and to temper wit with morality."

AIKEN, CONRAD (1889–   ), himself a considerable poet, had much to do with establishing the reputation of Emily Dickinson's poetry, having edited her poems in 1924. Aiken's own writing, particularly his short stories, shows a marked interest in psychoanalysis, an interest begun in *Punch, The Immortal Liar* (1924), followed in the Pulitzer Prize–winning *Selected Poems* (1929), and applied autobiographically in *Ushant* (1950).

ANDERSON, SHERWOOD (1876–1941), ashamed of his father's aimless career, established himself in business, successfully managing a paint factory and later writing for an advertising firm. When he came to view this kind of writing as prostitution of his talents, he turned to prose fiction. The psychological penetration into small town life and the experimental techniques in *Winesburg, Ohio* (1919), first attracted the critics. Although he excels in the short story, he has also written novels, poetry, and his own memoirs.

ARISTOTLE (384–322 B.C.), a Greek philosopher, was the pupil of Plato and teacher of Alexander the Great. Although greatly devoted to Plato, Aristotle could not agree with the mystical idealism of his master's later years and developed his own philosophy. Aristotle's importance to literature lies in his reply to Plato's attack that literature is a poor imitation of truth fashioned by one ignorant of the nature and use of the object described and intent on arousing harmful passions in the reader. His analysis of dramatic poetry, especially in the *Poetics*, has had a marked influence on subsequent literary criticism.

ARNOLD, MATTHEW (1822–1888) turned from writing poetry to writing social and religious criticism after his own poems failed to meet the criteria for excellence he had established. His poems, he believed, were too personal. Good poetry was the product of "high seriousness"; it was ideally "a criticism of life." Arnold therefore devoted himself to prose and the questions facing Victorian England. Doubt and dissatisfactions, he felt, could be overcome by awakening the middle class ("Philistines") from narrow-minded complacency to an awareness of culture, "the best that has been thought and said in the world." Arnold's best poetry is much better than he thought; his social and religious criticism was important to contemporary thought; and the influence of his literary criticism extends to the present day.

AUDEN, WYSTAN HUGH (1907–   ), leader of the poets born too late for participation in World War I, turned from the cries of personal disillusion heard in the poems of his contemporaries to a new concern for social abuses. He directed poetry away from excessive intellectualism to the concerns of every man. Like the poets of the twenties, he looked to the past for understanding; but unlike his predecessors, looked to the future for remedy. Auden has been a poet, critic, editor, and professor at Oxford. A revealing self-portrait appears in his *Letter to Lord Byron* (1936; in *Letter from Iceland*). Auden won a Pulitzer Prize in 1947 for *The Age of Anxiety*.

BACON, FRANCIS (1561–1626) appears to have been an unpleasant person, capable of serving as prosecutor of the man (the Earl of Essex) who had been his benefactor. Yet as an intellectual giant, he necessarily commands respect. In an age used to viewing physical nature as accursed, Bacon fostered a spirit of scientific research. He debunked the use of deductive logic in natural study, replacing it with the inductive method of modern science. *Novum Organum* (1620) sets forth his scientific theories; the *Essays* (1597–1625) express advanced ideas on a multitude of subjects.

BETJEMAN, JOHN (1906–   ), English poet and architectural authority, seems intent on capturing in his verse the atmosphere of a particular place and time. The best of his poetry, a curious combination of wit and seriousness, satire and lyricism, has appeared in *Slick But Not Streamlined* (1947).

BISHOP, JOHN PEALE (1892–1944), although connected with the writers of the Southern Renaissance and concerned with the life and problems peculiar to the South, transcends a strictly regional classification. His broader view results partly from his closeness to his "Yankee" father, partly from an extended residence in Europe. Although a poet and critic of lesser gifts than his friends Edmund Wilson, Allen Tate, and Archibald MacLeish, Bishop clearly deserves the praise he has received from his contemporaries.

BLAKE, WILLIAM (1757–1827), a visionary from the age of four, followed a light unseen by lesser men, and thereby made himself difficult to comprehend. Blake believed in synthesis as a means of understanding God, the perfect unity. Thus, the concept of the cruel, hypocritical world of the *Songs of Experience* (1794) is not a negation of the childlike vision in *Songs of Innocence* (1789), but a necessary complement to it. Technically, Blake worked for greater synthesis among the arts. The texts of his poems, which he engraved, were completed by his own illustrations, etched and colored by hand.

BRADLEY, ANDREW CECIL (1851–1935) reached the pinnacle of his career in 1901 when, after holding numerous positions as lecturer and professor of literature, he was unanimously elected Professor of Poetry at Oxford. Oxford had been the site of his own intellectual growth, providing him escape from a rigidly evangelical home and allowing his subsequent immersion in poetry. His major studies, *A Commentary on Tennyson's "In Memoriam"* (1901) and *Shakespearean Tragedy* (1904), won their author much acclaim as a critic.

BRIDGES, ROBERT (1844–1930) made his greatest contribution to literature by preserving the works of his friend and fellow poet, Gerard Manley Hopkins. He shared Hopkins' interest in the technical problems of poetry, but lacked the other's depth and skill. Bridges was one of the founders of the Society for Pure English and did much to improve the quality and accuracy of printing. His artfully crafted verses, collected in *Poetical Works* (1912), advanced his popularity and won him the position of Poet Laureate the following year.

BROWNING, ROBERT (1812–1889), unlike most of his contemporaries, concerned himself primarily with art rather than the social conditions of Victorian England. He believed a man's involvement in life blinded him to much of it, whereas art granted the perspective by which the familiar gained significance. The dramatic monologue, in which an individual is examined to "find how and why/He differs from his fellows utterly," is Browning's most successful form. *The Ring and the Book* (1868–1869) presents nine such monologues, in which each of the characters reveals a unique view of a single incident—the murder of Pompilia. *Men and Women* (1855) and *Dramatis Personae* (1864) include much of his best work.

BRYANT, WILLIAM CULLEN (1794–1878) was an arresting figure in American politics as well as in American poetry. From the age of fifteen he published critical attacks on the government. As editor of the *New York Review and Athenaeum Magazine* his criticism gained widespread effect. His poetry, if narrow in range and depth, is sincere and dignified, with heavy emphasis—as in *Thanatopsis* (1817)—on nature.

BURNS, ROBERT (1759–1796), often characterized as an "untaught genius," was, although self-educated, extremely well-read. His poetry, which is certainly not rude verse, is quite in keeping with the tradition of Scots poets who wrote in the vernacular. Burns used his verses for personal satires, attacks on the church, and political criticism; his songs, which he least esteemed, have remained his best loved works. Among his longer poems, *The Cotter's Saturday Night* (1786) and *The Holy Fair* are most significant. [Unfortunately, a second myth has been connected with his name; Burns unquestionably possessed a weakness for liquor and the lasses, but to claim he wasted his life in dissipation is insupportable.]

BYRON, GEORGE GORDON, LORD (1788–1824), a man of "abnormal genius and abnormal wickedness," has regrettably been considered "a personality first and a poet afterwards." With the appearance of Cantos I and II of *Childe Harold's Pilgrimage* (1812), Byron's popularity was assured. His excesses turned popularity to notoriety, however, and in 1816 Byron left England forever. With the publication of the third canto (1816), "he swept across Europe the pageant of his bleeding heart." Byron's outstanding talent lay in his ability to record his own emotional growth; this talent was buttressed with the gifts of satire (*English Bards and Scotch Reviewers*, 1809) and humor (*Don Juan*, 1818–1824). His publications abroad include the poetic dramas *Cain* and *Manfred*.

CAMPION, THOMAS (1567–1620), a man of varied interests, studied both law and medicine in his youth. As a legal student he began composing verses and setting them to music. *A Book of Airs*, a volume for which he wrote the lyrics and a great part of the musical settings for lute accompaniment, was the first of three similar volumes. If the variety of rhythms within a single poem seems puzzling, it should be remembered that Campion "chiefly aimed to couple my words and notes lovingly together."

CAMUS, ALBERT (1913–1960) did not leave his native Algiers until 1940, at which time, in the face of German occupation, he founded the secret resistance newspaper, *Combat*. The paper remained a powerful voice even after the liberation, and its editor assumed the leadership of the younger writers. His best novel, *The Stranger* (1942), appeared shortly before *The Myth of Sisyphus* (1942), his analysis of the absurdity in human life. Despite the negativism prevalent in his literary works, Camus took a positive position in support of political integrity and social justice. He won the Nobel Prize for Literature in 1957.

CAPOTE, TRUMAN (1924–   ) spent a difficult childhood in the deep South and turned early to writing. Winning a writing contest while still in grammar school brought him early notoriety, because his entry included recognizable portraiture of the townspeople. The appearance of "Miriam" in 1945 caused a more promising stir: eight publishers bid for his future work. With the publication of his first novel, *Other Voices, Other Rooms* (1948), he found himself a literary celebrity. *In Cold Blood* (1966), a "novel of fact," dealing with the murder of an entire family, is his latest success.

CARROLL, LEWIS (Charles Lutwidge Dodgson [1832–1898]) was a man of double interests. As C. L. Dodgson, he lectured in mathematics at Oxford and wrote treatises on mathematics and logic. As Lewis Carroll, he devoted himself to writing for the children he loved. *Alice in Wonderland* (1865) and *Through the Looking Glass* (1871), his best known children's classics, contain the poetry that proves Carroll an expert at metrical caricature of the moral and didactic poems forced on Victorian children.

CATHER, WILLA (1873–1947) worked as a journalist, a high school teacher, and managing editor of *McClure's*, the leading contemporary "muckraking" magazine; but her youth, spent among immigrant families of Nebraska, bears most importantly on her best work. The significance of the land itself becomes increasingly central to her novels, especially in its effects on the artist, who is generally the outstanding figure in her books. Her best novels include *My Antonia* (1918) and *Death Comes for the Archbishop* (1927). Her first collection of short stories, *The Troll Garden*, appeared in 1905. *Not Under Forty* (1936) contains essays revealing her theory of fiction. She won the Pulitzer Prize in 1922.

CHAUCER, GEOFFREY (1340?–1400). His broad view of English society in the later middle-ages resulted from a life active in both literary and extra-literary affairs. Public and court positions that allowed travel at home and on the Continent, an acquaintance with current folklore, and a knowledge of literature both classic and contemporary equipped Chaucer's sensibilities with the material necessary for presenting a poetic pageant of signal importance, rich in lore and personalities. His *Troilus and Criseyde* is second in importance only to the *Canterbury Tales*.

CHEKHOV, ANTON PAVLOVICH (1860–1904) supported his destitute family and put himself through medical school as a hackwriter. As his creativity developed so did his passion for writing, until he admitted, "medicine is my lawful wife and literature is my mistress." Chekhov peoples his works with representatives of the Russian middle class; he reveals their ordinary, even stagnant, lives with honesty, humor, and sympathy. He was a successful dramatist and novelist, but his command of the short story—his stories have had a most significant influence on modern short-story writers—has marked him as a master of the form.

CLOUGH, ARTHUR HUGH (1819–1861) was probably more important to the development of English thought than to the progress of English poetry. He never lived up to the promise of his first work, *The Bothie of Toberna-Vuolich* (1848), a lengthy pastoral romance that revealed a scholar's love for the farmer's daughter. Clough, as his intellectual lyrics often indicate, was concerned with questions of faith. He is the subject of Matthew Arnold's elegy *Thyrsis* (1867).

COLERIDGE, SAMUEL TAYLOR (1772–1834) turned for poetic subject matter to the supernatural, as his greatest poetry—*The Rime of the Ancient Mariner* (1798), *Kubla Khan* (1816), and *Christabel* (1798)—well illustrates. His finest work was produced for *Lyrical Ballads* (1798), a joint collection through which he and Wordsworth hoped to prepare the way for a new poetry that would speak of and to men directly instead of in the elevated poetic diction of an earlier time. Coleridge's *Biographia Literaria* (1817), one of the truly seminal works in English literary criticism, reaffirmed and expounded the philosophy of the new movement.

CONRAD, JOSEPH (Teodor Jozef Konrad Korzeniowski [1857–1924]), the son of Polish exiles, spent nearly twenty years at sea until disease contracted in the Congo prevented further travel. Theorists claim his career at sea was an escape from the duty of battling Czarist forces in Poland and that the escape settled deep feelings of guilt in him. His own demands for perfection compounded the difficulty of writing in a foreign language. Conrad, the master of the sea story, uses the sea as a means for setting characters in isolation. His concern "has been the ideal value of things, events, and people." Outstanding novels include *The Nigger of the Narcissus* (1898) and *Lord Jim* (1900). He also published numerous short stories; some of the best-known are "The Lagoon," "Heart of Darkness," and "The Secret Sharer."

CRASHAW, RICHARD (1613?–1649), the son of a bitterly anti-Catholic Anglican minister, became a convert to Roman Catholicism in 1645. His religious fervor, which dominated him almost completely, and which led him to seek compatible surroundings in Italy, accounts for a certain lack of restraint that often mars his poetry. His major works are *Steps to the Temple* (1646) and *Carmen Deo Nostro* (1652).

CUMMINGS, EDWARD ESTLIN (1894–1962), while serving in the ambulance corps in France during World War I, was mistakenly imprisoned in a French concentration camp; this experience formed the basis for his novel, *The Enor-mous Room* (1922). After the war Cummings devoted his time primarily to painting, but wrote occasional volumes of poetry as well. In his verse, Cummings assails organized society and often attempts to shock by advocating eccen-tricity. He achieves his effects through his lyricism and more notably through unusual typography. His distortions have been hailed by some critics as adding to the meaning of his work and attacked by others who find his manner merely faddish.

DE LA MARE, WALTER (1873–1956) worked as a clerk for the Anglo-American (Standard) Oil Company until a small civil pension allowed him to devote himself to writing poetry. His first efforts, signed with the pseudonym "Walter Ramal," appeared in *Sketch* and *Cornhill Magazine*. His poetry reveals a pre-occupation with childhood and sometimes, in conjunction with this, a search into the sources of fantasy. His best poetry creates a fantasy world; his lesser efforts allow fantasy to slip back into mere fancy. De la Mare has also written novels, prose fantasies, critical essays, and an anthology of poems for children, *Come Hither* (1923).

DICKINSON, EMILY (1830–1886) allowed very little to be known about her life. As a result, fascinating conjectures may distort or block objective reading of her poetry. She grew up in a strict Calvinist home in Massachusetts; she seems to have had a life "outwardly eventless," and she lived out her last twenty-five years as a recluse. Her "dearest earthly friend," Rev. Charles Wads-worth, was one of her few intellectual companions; he later appears as the "lover" of her poems. Of the more than one thousand lyrics she wrote, two were published during her lifetime. Thus, the ordering of her poetic "letter to the world" remains obscure. Her poetry sparkles with wit and rebellion; her conciseness, intellectual metaphors, and eye-rhymes give her work a distinctly modern tone.

DOBSON, HENRY AUSTIN (1840–1921), a skilled writer of light verse, attained literary stature as a literary historian rather than as a poet; his biographies of eighteenth-century figures, from *Hogarth* (1879) to *Fanny Burney* (1903), and his essays, particularly *Eighteenth Century Vignettes* (1892, 1894, 1896), represent solid scholarship. His poetry bears the various influences of the Pre-Raphaelites, Horatian odes, and French verse-forms. Dobson's work offers finish and charm rather than originality. He helped to popularize French verse-forms and presented a high standard for English light verse. His verse is collected in *Vignettes in Rhyme* (1873), *Proverbs in Porcelain* (1877), and *Old-World Idylls* (1883).

DONNE, JOHN (1573–1631), although bothered by thoughts of his earlier dis-solute years, allowed the prompting of the king, financial straits, and a belief that "all churches are beams of one sun" (Donne had earlier been a Roman Catholic) to convince him to take orders in the English Church (1615). His sermons, which made him famous, powerfully record a single soul's struggle with sin and retribution. For Donne, thinking was a passionate experience, and his poetic images, though intellectual, are fired with emotion. Donne is recognized as the leader of the metaphysicals, whose poetry is characterized by what Dr. Johnson called "metaphysical conceits," a "combination of dissimilar images, or discovery of occult resemblances in things apparently unlike."

DOWSON, ERNEST (1867–1900), a painfully shy young man, found strange comfort in sordid surroundings. The comfort was dearly purchased as Dowson traded health, initially frail, for the escapes proffered by hashish and alcohol. What promise he might have had was finally crushed when the daughter of a restaurant proprietor, the girl to whom he wrote his poetry, married one of her father's waiters. Dowson died at thirty-three, leaving a few slight, but graceful, works behind him.

DRAYTON, MICHAEL (1563–1631) is in some ways the most representative and prolific minor Elizabethan poet. His work, throughout his long and active career, changed with the times, and furnishes a map of the various critical periods through which he lived. Not primarily a court poet, Drayton had little patience with the courtly demands for humility and a dilettante's interest in writing. *Ideas Mirror*, a sonnet sequence published in 1594, contains many of his best-known poems.

EBERHART, RICHARD (1904–   ) has been a teacher, naval officer, manufacturing firm vice-president, professor, and one-time tutor to the son of the king of Siam. Eberhart received the B.A. degree from Dartmouth College and the M.A. from Cambridge University, England. While at Cambridge, he published his first verses in an anthology, *New Signatures* (1932), in which the poems of William Empson, C. Day Lewis, W. H. Auden, and Stephen Spender also appeared. The poets' aim was to enrich the language and style of contemporary poetry. Eberhart's contributions may be described as intellectual, often humorous, demanding the strict attention of his readers.

ELIOT, THOMAS STEARNS (1888–1965) was born in St. Louis and educated at Harvard. He left the United States in 1910 and continued his studies at Oxford while working as a bank clerk. In 1927, he became a British subject. In 1917 he published his first volume of verse, *Prufrock and Other Observations*. His criticism, particularly *The Sacred Wood* (1920), has had a profound effect on modern poetry and critical thought. His poetry traces his progress from desperation to an acceptance of faith within the tradition of the English Church. *The Waste Land* (1922), recording the depth of his despair, represents the height of his poetic power. Eliot won the Nobel Prize in 1948.

FAULKNER, WILLIAM (1897–1963), novelist and sometime poet and short-story writer, created a mythical area in the South with its own particular heritage. Yoknapatawpha County, Mississippi, Faulkner's mythic setting, suggests a lazy surface—the cover for biracial tensions and the clashing interests of decadent and opposing modes of life seething below it (*The Sound and the Fury*, 1929; *As I Lay Dying*, 1930; and *Sartoris*, 1929). His exposures of violence, brutality, and perversion kept many from a serious appraisal of his work. Twice his novels were awarded the Pulitzer Prize. In 1950 he became the fourth American to receive the Nobel Prize for Literature. He summarized his own intention in saying, "the poet's voice need not merely be the record of man, it can be one of the props, the pillars to help him endure and prevail."

FEARING, KENNETH (1902–1961) worked as salesman, free-lance writer, journalist, and finally, teacher of poetry. Thus, he was well acquainted with the ways of life he attacks in his poetry. Fearing paints savage urban portraits and, using the symbols of mass media, mocks the disintegrating values of contemporary middle-class America. His best-known poems offer a colloquial idiom set in free verse. His poems appear in several volumes, among them the *Collected Poems* (1940) and *Afternoon of a Pawnbroker* (1943). Fearing wrote clever mystery novels, as well.

FIELDING, HENRY (1707–1754), in spite of his profession of barrister and his devotion—generally unthanked—to public service, wrote the novels that have led to his being called the "Father of the English Novel." *Tom Jones* (1749) has been praised for the excellence of its plot (the result of Fielding's early experience as a dramatist) and for setting the pattern of the English novel for the next hundred years.

FITZGERALD, FRANCIS SCOTT KEY (1896–1940), chronicler of the Jazz Age, left in his novels, stories, and sketches the record of "a whole race gone hedonistic." His first novel, *This Side of Paradise* (1920), made him a success at twenty-three; the consequence was a lifetime of unsuccessful resistance to the temptations money offered. Ironically, his best work shatters the belief that wealth makes happiness. His reputation as an artist lies in his powerful novel, *The Great Gatsby* (1925), and in a few short stories. His literary reputation was restored in the late 1940's and early 1950's by the efforts of critics and friends, most notably Edmund Wilson, who compiled an autobiography, *The Crack-Up* (1945), from Fitzgerald's unpublished work.

FORSTER, EDWARD MORGAN (1879–   ) found the ideal intellectual atmosphere at Cambridge University, one to which he returned in later life and that appears—depicted almost reverently—in some of his works. The "Bloomsbury Group," a cluster of writers and thinkers including Virginia Woolf and Bertrand Russell, inspired by the philosophy of G. E. Moore and dedicated to the beauty of art and the cultivation of personal relationships, also exerted a strong intellectual influence on young Forster. A *Passage to India* (1924), his master-piece, is both powerful and intellectually demanding. Like all of his best work, it was given years for maturing. Forster has resisted modern prose trends, per-fecting instead a style faintly Victorian but clearly his own. His *Aspects of the Novel* (1927) has become a classic of literary criticism.

FROST, ROBERT (1874–1963), poet of New England, had to seek British pub-lishers to win his first recognition as a poet. Upon returning to the United States, Frost published A *Boy's Will* (1913) and *North of Boston* (1914) in this country and at last won the success earlier denied him. Frost left Dart-mouth and Harvard without a degree from either, yet returned in triumph as poet-in-residence at these and other universities. His best poetry, set in rural New England and dealing with its inhabitants in concisely written dramatic situations, is typically in blank verse: Frost once claimed that writing free verse was like playing tennis with the nets down. He won several Pulitzer Prizes.

FRYE, NORTHROP (1912–   ), Canadian literary critic and Principal and Professor of English at Victoria College, Toronto, received his education at the University of Toronto and at Oxford. His use of contemporary psychology and mythopoetic interpretations of literature, notably in his *Anatomy of Criticism* (1957), have made a tremendous impact on contemporary critical thought. Frye seems to be most inspired by the most difficult of challenges: *Fearful Symmetry* (1947), his interpretation of Blake's poetry, lends new in-sights into a particularly complex poetic vision.

GASCOIGNE, GEORGE (1525?–1577), a transitional figure, sought new forms and functions for literature. His translation of Ariosto's *Supposes* is probably the first English prose comedy; his *Certain Notes of Instruction* is one of the earliest English examples of literary criticism. *The Steel Glass* marks an im-portant development in verse satire, since it avoids the devitalizing narrative elements common to earlier English satire. His poems, collected in A *Hundreth Sundry Flowers*, reflect his interest in the possibilities for expression offered by various verse forms.

GRAVES, ROBERT (1895–   ), shortly after enlisting in the Royal Welsh Fusiliers, began writing poetry protesting the horrors of war. Upon his return to England, he studied at Oxford and taught English for a year at the Uni-versity of Cairo. Since that time, he has lived mainly on the island of Majorca. He is an important literary figure for his scholarly and critical work, particularly *The White Goddess: An Historical Grammar of Poetic Myth* (1948), as well as for his poetry and brilliant historical novels. *Collected Poems* (1955) contains those poems he wishes to preserve; *I, Claudius* (1934) is his most successful novel.

GRAY, THOMAS (1716–1771) wrote little, but that little was finely wrought. Gray lacked incentive and suffered from overly fastidious habits of revision: *Elegy Written in a Country Churchyard*, his finest poem, required six years to write. Gray's reputation was established by this poem, however, and its new subject matter—nature and humble life—affected the course of English poetry. An extremely learned man, Gray turned to history for the subjects of his later poems. Among these, *The Progress of Poesy* (1757) and *The Bard* (1757) are the most outstanding.

HAMILTON, EDITH (1867–1963), a student of the classics since childhood, found much greater stimulation reading Greek and Roman authors directly than in gleaning their stories from the works of others. Her own writing resulted from her desire to convey her enthusiasm and knowledge of the ancients. This writing followed a fruitful life of study and teaching. Her retirement after twenty years as headmistress of the Bryn Mawr School in Baltimore, Maryland, made possible the writing of *The Greek Way* (1930) and other studies.

HARDY, THOMAS (1840–1928), when he could not publish his poetry, turned to writing prose fiction and became one of the greatest English novelists. His popularity was established with *The Return of the Native* (1878); *Tess of the d'Urbervilles* (1891) added to his success despite some adverse comment; *Jude the Obscure* (1896), which Hardy called his most moral book, was so shocking to delicate Victorian sensibilities that one reviewer renamed it "Jude the Obscene." Deeply wounded by this public censure, and its apparent acceptance by his reading audience, Hardy forsook prose fiction and returned to poetry. *Wessex Poems* (1898) and *The Dynasts* (1903–1908) were well received, but scarcely equal to the novels in power or popularity.

HAWTHORNE, NATHANIEL (1804–1864), together with Edgar Allen Poe, helped to distinguish the short story as a typically American genre, yet Hawthorne was also capable of writing splendid longer works, as he demonstrated in such novels as *The Scarlet Letter* (1850) and *The Marble Faun* (1860). Hawthorne was deeply involved in the critical issues of his day and even served for a time as a government consul in Europe. His novels, however, deal primarily with the isolation of New England souls and are permeated with the Puritan gloom of his New England forebears. Hawthorne's intense introspection allowed him to understand his own and others' motives; his characterizations objectify his discoveries.

HEMINGWAY, ERNEST MILLER (1898–1963) first attracted attention when, as one of the American expatriate writers of the Lost Generation (the Paris group dominated by Gertrude Stein), he depicted the desperate lives of the post–World War I generation. He filled his writing with situations from his own life—his youth, his interest in sports, particularly big-game hunting and bull-fighting, and his experiences in World War I and the Spanish Civil War. Pursuits demanding dedication and discipline commanded his admiration. His prose style, which approaches the rhythm of free verse, has won the admiration of critics and a vast public audience. A *Farewell to Arms* (1929) and *For Whom the Bell Tolls* (1940) remain his most remarkable novels, while *The Fifth Column* (1938) contains his best short stories. Hemingway won the Nobel Prize in 1954 for *The Old Man and the Sea*. His Paris memoirs, A *Moveable Feast* (1964), were published posthumously.

HENLEY, WILLIAM ERNEST (1849–1903) lost one leg and was advised to have the other removed. He refused and suffered twenty months in a hospital until he recovered. During this time, he began writing his "hospital verses," which later appeared in *A Book of Verses* (1888). Henley was a critic and the editor of several magazines. While editing the *Magazine of Art*, he defended Whistler and introduced Rodin's sculpture to England. More important, he was the friend and discoverer of eminent authors, notably Thomas Hardy, Rudyard Kipling, George Bernard Shaw, William Butler Yeats, and R. L. Stevenson (who used him as the model for Long John Silver of *Treasure Island*).

HERBERT, GEORGE (1593–1633) characterized his own poetry as a "picture of the many spiritual conflicts which have passed betwixt God and my soul. . . ." Never a cold, ascetic person, Herbert found it hard to relinquish the world, yet ultimately became an Anglican priest and through his poetry gave voice to "the beauty of holiness." His best poetry exhibits a childlike clarity of vision. *The Temple* (1633), his collection of poems, was published shortly after he died.

HERRICK, ROBERT (1591–1674) held as his motto: "to live merrily, and to trust to good verses." His verses kept the purity of classical songs, yet they were made thoroughly English. He avoided the romanticizing and the ingenious conceits of the Elizabethans, as well as the subtleties of Donne and his followers. His verses most resemble those of Ben Jonson, yet exhibit a lighter touch. Of his age, he is second only to Milton in the writing of lyrics; he stands with Shakespeare, Burns, and Jonson as one of the few great English song writers. Unfortunately for him, Herrick's sunny verses (*Hesperides*, 1648) appeared when the Puritans were officiously condemning such efforts as dangerous frivolity.

HOPKINS, GERARD MANLEY (1844–1889) destroyed all the verses he had written when, influenced by John Henry Newman, he became first a convert to Catholicism, then a Jesuit priest. "The Wreck of the Deutschland" (1875), written at the request of a superior when a ship carrying nuns met disaster, marked a new beginning in poetry. His work is difficult, often obscure, but its influence on post–World War I poetry is considerable. He is the master of metrical innovation, yet much of his work is rooted in older English (and Welsh) fashions. Robert Bridges, his friend and fellow poet, is responsible for the preservation of Hopkins' work, because Hopkins would not allow its publication during his lifetime.

HOUSMAN, ALFRED EDWARD (1859–1936), Professor of Latin at University College, London, and later at Cambridge University, pursued classical studies throughout his life. His poetic endeavors were not as sustained; he published *A Shropshire Lad* in 1896 and his *Last Poems* in 1922. His poetry was not immediately successful yet steadily gained stature. Today, his lyrics are ranked with the finest. Underneath their lyricism lies profound pessimism, but a brave pessimism that suggests one properly faces life armed with the knowledge of what it might contain.

HUXLEY, THOMAS HENRY (1825–1895) was a natural scientist who became important to literature through lectures and essays advocating greater freedom of thought. Due to the controversy over evolution raging in Victorian England, his numerous essays on scientific matters became as widely read as popular novels. Huxley's own study led him to confirm the theories expounded by Darwin; his ardent defense of the latter accounts for his title, "Darwin's Bulldog." The honesty and intelligence with which Huxley fought sentimentality and dogma did much to ready English minds for the findings of science. His collected essays were published in 1894.

IBSEN, HENRIK (1826–1906) lived a relatively uneventful life, but his dramas revolutionized the modern stage. Ibsen illuminated the way by which drama might become intellectually important rather than merely entertaining. His problem plays, although attacked by contemporaries as "immoral," stem from the serious purpose of social criticism. He was not hesitant about revealing the stagnation of contemporary home life or the criminal abuses involved in accepted institutions. His dramatic innovations stimulated contemporary stagecraft, discharging from the theater artificiality of diction and situation. Among his most successful and influential plays are *A Doll's House* (1879), *Ghosts* (1881), *The Wild Duck* (1884), and *Hedda Gabler* (1890).

JAMES, HENRY (1843–1916), having migrated back and forth from America to Europe during most of his life (he became a British subject in 1915), shows great concern in his early novels for the relative merits of Europe and America— the former appearing sophisticated but dangerously decadent, the latter, creative but hopelessly untutored. In his later work, James became increasingly interested in form and in psychological presentation. His creative work, as well as his critical statements, documents his literary intention: for James, a great novel "must be based on a profound sense of moral values, and then constructed with a classical unity and economy of means." Some critics credit him with much less: "a ponderously warm manner of saying nothing in infinite sentences." Among his best-known novels are *Daisy Miller* (1879), *Portrait of a Lady* (1881), *Wings of the Dove* (1902), and *The Ambassadors* (1903). He was also a master of the long short-story, or novelette, some of his outstanding successes being *The Turn of the Screw* (1898) and *What Maisie Knew* (1897). His essay on "The Art of Fiction" is an important contribution to literary criticism.

JARRELL, RANDALL (1914–1965) claims "half my poems are about the war, half are not." World War II raised deep questions in Jarrell, who in turn poses the questions in his poetry: What was the individual soldier's role in the war? "But why did I die?" Of his poetic subjects in general, Jarrell maintains, "some of these I enjoy writing about, others I could not help writing about." His poetry has appeared in several volumes, *Losses* (1948) being the most significant. He has also written critical essays, *Poetry and the Age* (1953), and a satiric novel, *Pictures from an Institution* (1954).

JEFFERS, JOHN ROBINSON (1887–   ) found poetry "becoming slight and fantastic, unreal, eccentric. . . . It must reclaim substance and sense, and physical and psychological reality." To accomplish this end, Jeffers writes narrative poetry, drawing his subjects from contemporary life. Jeffers and his wife settled on the then wild beach at Carmel, California, built Tor House and Hawk Tower, his writing sanctuary, of sea cobbles and have lived there ever since. His poetry is flexible, lyric, written in colloquial speech yet fully controlled. Jeffers has also written notable verse dramas. His selected poems were published in 1938.

JOHNSON, SAMUEL (1709–1784), literary dictator of the eighteenth century, probably wielded his greatest power as a conversationalist, and the best introduction to him is James Boswell's biographical record of his talk, *Life of Johnson* (1791). Until he received a pension at fifty-three, Johnson's life had been a struggle against poverty; his struggle against physical infirmity was unending. With incredible industry, he set out to accomplish various literary tasks. His *Dictionary* (1747–1755), a volume of definitions and theories (often delightfully biased), won him esteem; his periodical, *The Rambler* (1750–1752), established his reputation. The two were actually complementary works: what the *Dictionary* defined, *The Rambler* expounded. Johnson utilized almost every literary form to express his ideas, but they were most significantly expressed in conversation with members of his literary club who joined him for coffee at the Turk's Head.

JOYCE, JAMES (1882–1941), literary colossus of the twentieth century, passed the greater part of his life in poverty, his writings misunderstood and rejected. In 1904, Joyce fled Ireland for the Continent, an attempt to dispel the influences of family, church, and homeland. Flight simply proved their powers inescapable. Joyce was entranced by art as pure technique—language, structure, narrative development, and the use of traditional genres—yet his works teem with life, for Joyce, like his fictional counterpart Stephen Dedalus, went "to encounter for the millionth time the reality of experience and to forge in the smithy of my soul the uncreated conscience of my race." His short stories, *Dubliners* (1914), and his novels, *A Portrait of the Artist as a Young Man* (1916), *Ulysses* (1922), and *Finnegan's Wake* (1939), have had a profound effect on modern literature.

KEATS, JOHN (1795–1821) fought poor health and a life of little advantage with keen intelligence and a genius for poetry such as the world has rarely seen. At nineteen, Keats gave up plans to become an apothecary; at twenty-six, he was dead. Knowledge of his consumptive condition prevented his marrying Fanny Brawne, but spurred him to compress a lifetime of poetic development into the few years allotted him. His attempts to capture beauty led him to adopt the technique of synesthesia, producing images that blend one order of sensation with another. His sonnets and odes, his greatest achievements, show his talent for new and intricate metrical texture. Beneath the texture, there is keen observation and acute, tough-minded thought. "Adonais," an elegy on the death of Keats, by Shelley, not only mourns his loss but attacks the critical abuse heaped upon him during his life.

KIPLING, RUDYARD (1865–1936) acquired from his position as subeditor of two Indian newspapers discipline, subjects for stories and poems, and a shrewd idea of what would appeal to the English public. He set himself the task of turning out a story a day while supplying filler verses for his newspaper. The stories were compiled in *Plain Tales from the Hills* (1887) and six other volumes; his verses in *Departmental Ditties* (1886). "Prophet of Imperialism" is a misnomer, for Kipling, though fascinated by the British Empire, was one of its severer critics on occasion. His later short stories, written while he lived in Vermont and then in Sussex, are technically brilliant, varied in subject, and quite unlike the stereotype of "imperial" fiction. Kipling won the Nobel Prize in 1907.

KNOX, BERNARD (1914–   ), an authority on classical studies, received the B.A. from Cambridge University, the Ph.D. from Yale, and an honorary M.A. from Harvard. In 1961, he resigned as Professor of Classics at Yale, where he had been a member of the faculty since 1947, to assume the directorship of the Center for Hellenic Studies in Washington, D.C. He is the author of *Oedipus at Thebes* (1957) and of numerous scholarly articles.

LANDOR, WALTER SAVAGE (1775–1864) combined a scholar's love of classical learning with a revolutionist's temper, energy, and idealism. He was expelled from Rugby for fighting over the proper scansion of a line of Latin poetry and from Oxford for firing a bullet through a neighbor's window. In 1808, he organized an armed expedition to aid Spanish revolutionaries, but turned it into a sightseeing tour when angered by the lukewarm reception his men received. Six years later, he fled England for Italy to avoid prosecution for having beaten an impudent lawyer. His literary reputation rests on several mediocre plays, some excellent Latin verse, *Idyllia Heroica* (1820), and several volumes of fascinating prose dialogues titled *Imaginary Conversations* (1824–1829).

LAWRENCE, DAVID HERBERT (1885–1930), the son of a Nottingham coalminer and a former schoolteacher, reveals his early life in what has been called the most celebrated treatment of the Oedipus theme in modern fiction, *Sons and Lovers* (1913). This novel established Lawrence's reputation. The charges of German sympathies (shortly before World War I, he married a divorcée, Frieda von Richthofen, sister of Baron Manfred von Richthofen, the German military aviator), together with the repudiation of one of his novels, *The Rainbow* (1915), as "filth," drove him out of the country on a search for the ideal society. His frank treatment of sex in *Lady Chatterly's Lover* (1920) forced its private printing and ban from the United States as obscene. Primarily a novelist, Lawrence has also written significant poetry, short stories, and literary criticism. His *Psychoanalysis and the Unconscious* (1921) and *Fantasia of the Unconscious* (1922) prove him a serious student of psychology.

LEWIS, CECIL DAY (1904–   ) was associated with the group of poets, including W. H. Auden, who became prominent in the thirties. Lewis had been a teacher until 1935, when he devoted himself exclusively to literary pursuits— editing, poetry, literary criticism, and classical translations. His poetry is most readily accessible in the *Collected Poems of C. Day Lewis* (1954). He also writes detective fiction under the pseudonym of Nicholas Blake.

LOVELACE, RICHARD (1618–1658) has been judged "both soldier, gentleman, and lover, and a fair pretender to the title of poet." Lovelace, described by one observer as "one of the handsomest men of England . . . an extraordinary handsome man . . . a most beautiful gentleman," won the favor of a great lady at the queen's court and at her request obtained his M.A. from Oxford. A fiery speech in Parliament was rewarded with a six weeks' imprisonment, part of which time he spent composing "To Althea from Prison" (1642). He fought in the king's armies and for the French army in Holland at the time of the English civil war. This occasioned his poetry to Lucasta, some of his loveliest lyrics.

LOWELL, ROBERT (1917–   ) converted to Catholicism as an undergraduate at Kenyon College and became "consciously a Catholic poet," although he retained and exhibits some of the Puritan influences exerted upon him. Lowell's poems have been favorably received since the publication of his initial collection, *Land of Unlikeness* (1944). The subjects for his skillful monologues are drawn from a wide range of interests and experiences. He won the Pulitzer Prize in 1946 for *Lord Weary's Castle*.

LYLY, JOHN (1554?–1606), Elizabethan poet, dramatist, and author of *Euphues* (1578), an early precursor of the novel, spent a lifetime attempting to please the queen, yet never attained the office of Master of the Revels, which he sought from her. *Euphues* is most notable for its overly ornate, overly symmetrical style. Lyly was a popularizer, not an originator. As Gabriel Harvey, a cynical contemporary, said of young Euphues, he "but hatched the eggs his elder friends had laid."

MACLEISH, ARCHIBALD (1892–   ), after serving in World War I, returned to practice law in Boston, but in 1923 took his family to Paris, where he devoted himself to writing. Five years and five volumes later MacLeish returned to the United States, having separated himself from the expatriates on the Continent. Turning his attention to social disturbances, he wrote provocative articles for *Fortune* and served in various government positions. He won the Pulitzer Prize in 1933 with *Conquistador*, a long poem; in 1953 with *Collected Poems*; and in 1959 with *J. B.: A Play in Verse*. He was Librarian of Congress 1939–1944.

MACNEICE, LOUIS (1907–   ) came to prominence in the thirties as one of the left-wing Oxford poets in the Auden circle. In agreement with the group's concern for social betterment, he said: "The poet is both critic and entertainer. . . . The poet at the moment will tend to be moralist rather than aesthete. . . . He is not the loudspeaker of society, but something much more like its still, small voice." MacNeice's most significant poetry is contained in *Collected Poems, 1925–1948* (1949). He has been a critic, teacher, and scriptwriter and producer for the British Broadcasting Corporation.

MANSFIELD, KATHERINE (Kathleen Beauchamp Murray [1888–1923]) could not be contained by her native New Zealand after being exposed to bohemian life in London. On her return to London, she developed stormy but artistically enriching friendships with D. H. Lawrence, Aldous Huxley, Virginia Woolf, and critic John Middleton Murray, whom she later married. With Murray she worked on the publication of various "little magazines," but her most significant work was in the short story, which she endeavored to model along the lines set out by Chekhov, but to which she contributed much that was uniquely her own. Her *Journal* (1927) was published posthumously, as were her collected stories.

MARVELL, ANDREW (1621–1678), while at Cambridge, was converted to Catholicism by the Jesuits but later was reconverted by his father, an Anglican minister. Marvell took no part in the English civil war, entrusting the proper victory to heaven. He wrote his lyrical garden poetry within the confines of New Appleton House in York while serving as tutor there; later, after his appointment as assistant to John Milton, at that time Cromwell's Latin Secretary, he wrote a number of poems in honor of Cromwell. After the Restoration, as a member of Parliament, he began writing satirical poetry that won him a reputation as "the liveliest droll of the age." Most of his poetry was not published till after his death.

MAUPASSANT, HENRI RENÉ ALBERT GUY DE (1850–1893) served a rigid literary apprenticeship under Gustave Flaubert, who taught him and criticized his work for seven years. When at last he published his first story, *Boule de Suif* (1880), the value of such discipline was underscored by general acclaim. During the ten years that followed—until insanity prevented further writing—Maupassant published six novels, numerous travel books, a volume of poetry, and over three hundred short stories. He insisted on *le mot juste*: "whatever . . . we wish to say, there is but one word to express it." For him, a story came only after acute observation: "there is an unexplored side to everything, because we are wont never to use our eyes [except] with the memory of what others before us have thought of the things we see."

MELVILLE, HERMAN (1819–1891) achieved measurable success with his largely autobiographical sea stories *Typee* (1846) and *Omoo* (1847). With the publication of his greatest novels, *Moby Dick* (1851), *Pierre* (1852), and *The Confidence Man* (1857), however, Melville lost his nineteenth-century audience. Friendship with Hawthorne had crystallized Melville's tragic sense of life. He no longer strove simply to entertain, but to convey "visible truth," "the apprehension of the absolute condition of present things as they strike the eye of the man who fears them not, though they do their worst to him." Melville died in obscurity; not until the present century was *Moby Dick* recognized as one of the great novels of the world.

MEREDITH, GEORGE (1828–1909), disgruntled by the lack of public regard for his first collection of poems (1851), waited until his novels, notably *The Ordeal of Richard Feverel* (1859), had established his reputation before bringing out a second collection, which included the sonnet sequence, *Modern Love* (1862). The critical dispute over the value of these sonnets kept him from publishing poems for another twenty years, when his position as one of England's greatest novelists guaranteed respect for his work. *The Egoist* (1879) and *Diana of the Crossways* (1885) are two of his best-known novels. In 1897 he published his now-famous *The Idea of Comedy* and *Uses of the Comic Spirit*.

MILTON, JOHN (1608–1674) showed his outstanding talents early in life as an undergraduate at Cambridge University. After taking an M.A. degree in 1632 he gave up the idea of entering the ministry and devoted the next five years to preparing himself for a vocation as a poet. During that time he wrote "L'Allegro," "Il Penseroso," "Lycidas," and the masque "Comus," the last at the invitation of Henry Lawes, who wrote the music. He entered into public life and controversy by writing numerous pamphlets and treatises, among them *Areopagitica* (1644), on the freedom of the press, and *Tenure of Kings and Magistrates* (1649), which dealt with the execution of Charles I. Appointed Latin Secretary under Cromwell, he served the Commonwealth until he lost his sight. After the Restoration, blind and in seclusion, he returned to poetry, writing his great epic *Paradise Lost* (1667), followed by *Paradise Regained* (1671) and *Samson Agonistes* (1671), a tragedy in verse.

MOORE, MARIANNE (1887–   ), believing that "poetry watches life with attention," has filled her verses with every subject imaginable. Her technique demands strict attention, for it abounds in concise images and understated but recognizable metrical forms. Her wit combines sarcasm and humanity. Miss Moore contributed significantly to *The Dial*, a literary magazine that unfortunately came to an end during the 1930's depression. She won the Pulitzer Prize in 1951 for her *Collected Poems*.

MORRIS, WILLIAM (1834–1896) was a man whose artistic talents were not confined to a single field: architecture, painting, the arts of decoration, and poetry all claimed his attention and skill. Morris had been associated with the Pre-Raphaelite Brotherhood in his youth, and the precisely described, artfully constructed medieval scenes of his poetry reveal their influence. *The Defence of Guenevere and Other Poems* (1858), *The Life and Death of Jason* (1867), and *Sigurd the Volsung* (1876) contain his most significant poetry.

MUIR, EDWIN (1887–1959) led a difficult life from beginning to end. When his family left the preindustrial society of Orkney for city living, tragedy struck, killing four of them. Youthful emotional "conversions," first to religion, later to socialism, failed to support the groping youth. Muir next trusted to the doctrines of Nietzsche; finally, after ridding himself of this influence, marrying, and undergoing psychoanalytic treatment, Muir found himself independently strong. At this time he began his career as a poet. He and his wife supported themselves by translations of German works—notably Kafka's. In 1953, Muir's *Collected Poems* were widely acclaimed.

NEMEROV, HOWARD (1920–   ), after graduating from Harvard in 1941, became an instructor at Hamilton College. He is currently a member of the Bennington College faculty. He has received numerous awards for literature. Among his best work, which includes poetry, fiction, and critical essays, notable titles are *New and Selected Poems* (1960) and *Essays on Poetry and Fiction* (1963).

NEWMAN, JOHN HENRY (1801–1890) took Holy Orders in the Anglican Church in 1824, soon after his graduation from Oxford. His increasing antagonism toward liberal, rationalist tendencies in the church led him to study the early Church Fathers and to take active part in the Oxford Movement, designed to clarify the Catholic tradition inherent in Anglicanism. In 1845, after three years of prayer, fasting, and seclusion, Newman renounced Anglicanism to enter the Roman Catholic Church. *The Idea of a University* (1852), his most notable work, began as a series of lectures delivered when Newman was made rector of a planned Catholic university in Dublin. *Apologia pro Vita Sua* (1864) is the important history of his religious opinions.

O'CONNOR, FLANNERY (1925–1965), after graduating from Women's College of Georgia, worked in the writing program at the State University of Iowa. Her short stories and novels expose the Georgia backwoods society. Her preoccupation with traditional Southern themes and her strong theological bias have come under critical fire as "fashionable" and imitative; defenders find her work stylistically original and indicative of an uncommonly comprehensive theological perspective. Her significant writing includes a novel, *Wise Blood* (1952), and collections of stories, *A Good Man Is Hard to Find* (1955) and *Everything That Rises Must Converge* (1965).

OWEN, WILFRED (1893–1918) enlisted when England entered World War I. He served in France, was wounded and sent home, and returned again to France wearing the Military Cross. He was killed in action one week before the signing of the Armistice. Of poetry he said, in the preface of a book he did not live to see published, "Above all I am not concerned with Poetry. My subject is War, and the pity of War. The Poetry is in the pity."

PATER, WALTER (1839–1894) was appointed a Fellow of Brasenose College, Oxford, soon after taking his degree. A tour of Italy in 1865 and his acquaintance with Théophile Gautier, A. C. Swinburne, and other devotees of "Art for Art's sake" stimulated his enthusiasm for Renaissance studies, turning him from consideration of German and English philosophy to critical investigation of such figures as Da Vinci, Botticelli, and Michelangelo. Although his works are solidly based in scholarship, his chief importance is as a prose stylist. His best work is *Studies in the History of the Renaissance* (1873), *Marius the Epicurean* (a novel, 1885), and *Appreciations* (1889).

POE, EDGAR ALLAN (1809–1849) is a name shrouded with a bizarre legend that has confused critical appraisal. The child of itinerant actors, he was raised by foster parents. He was rejected by his foster father and appears to have spent his youth attempting at once to gain approval and to assert his independence. In any case, his defiance and his excesses cost him numerous jobs, his health, and his self-esteem. His attempts to survive on a writer's income resulted in near starvation for him and for his child bride. Whatever he may have been as a man, as a writer he was a giant: a master in creating moods, he wrote notable poetry and criticism and helped to shape the short story into a distinctly American form.

POPE, ALEXANDER (1688–1744), as a Roman Catholic, was denied entrance to public schools and prevented from having literary patrons; consequently, he read what he pleased and was one of the first authors to earn a sufficient income from published work. Pope suffered from a physical deformity that made him both sensitive and irascible. His literary career included a period of predominantly descriptive and didactic poetry, the *Essay on Criticism* (1711) being most notable; a period of editing and translating (Shakespeare, 1725, and Homer, 1726); and a final period, primarily satiric, in which he trounced scores of enemies in *The Dunciad* (1728–1743).

PORTER, KATHERINE ANNE (1894–   ), the great-great-great granddaughter of Daniel Boone, spent a precocious childhood in Texas where, she claims, she made life uncomfortable for herself and for those around her. When she chose literature as a profession, she was under no illusion that she could support herself by it, but *Flowering Judas* (1930), her first collection of stories, established her reputation as a finished artist in prose fiction. She has remained a fastidious craftsman, writing few stories, but all of high distinction. Her long expected novel, *Ship of Fools*, appeared in 1962.

POUND, EZRA LOOMIS (1885–   ), a native American, wrote his poetry and criticism while an expatriate in England, France, and Italy. A knowledge of many languages, ancient and modern, enriched his own poetry and, by his translating— notably from the Chinese—poems hitherto unavailable to English readers, he enriched the body of English poetry. An important leader in tearing down Victorian literary standards, Pound was also important in finding publishers for new artists, among them Eliot, Frost, and Joyce. Political views expressed in Italy during World War II caused Pound to be tried for treason to the United States. He was judged insane, spent many years in an asylum, and is now again an expatriate.

POWERS, JAMES EARL (1917–   ), an American short-story writer whose works have appeared in *Accent* and *The New Yorker* and several other magazines, has taught at Marquette University and studied in Ireland. He draws heavily on his knowledge of the Roman Catholic Church; his stories generally include church figures and religious questions. Powers is one of the minority of contemporary writers who write with optimism, embracing a movement away from violence and the idea of a menacing society. A writer of considerable talent, his stories have appeared in both the *O. Henry Memorial Award Prize Stories* and *Best American Short Stories*. *Prince of Darkness and Other Stories* (1947) and *The Presence of Grace* (1956) are his first two story collections.

RALEGH, SIR WALTER (1552?–1618) is well-known as a Renaissance gentleman who—at least in fiction (Scott's *Kenilworth*)—threw down his cloak so that the queen might avoid the mud. His part in colonial Virginia is equally familiar. Unfortunately, his role as a literary figure has been obscured by the loss of much of his work, which he disdained to publish. Ralegh's talent lay in revitalizing poetic conventions; the verses known to us are preserved in the miscellanies, *England's Helicon* and *The Phoenix Nest*.

RANSOM, JOHN CROWE (1888–   ) has made his most significant contribution to literature as a critic. When a professor at Vanderbilt University, he was one of the founders of the "little magazine," *The Fugitive*; at Kenyon College, he founded and edited the *Kenyon Review*. His own critical views, especially on the importance of strict textual explication, are set forth in several volumes, notably *The World's Body* (1939) and *The New Criticism* (1941). Ransom's poetry illustrates his own critical credo: the poem results from the inseparable, interdependent relationship of texture and structure, form and idea.

ROBINSON, EDWIN ARLINGTON (1869–1935) wrote poetry that bears the stamp of a New England background. Gardiner, Maine, was the prototype for his Tilbury Town, and its inhabitants were the patterns on which his psychological portraits were modeled. Robinson's use of prose speech-rhythms and ironic contrast gives his poetry its modern tone. Theodore Roosevelt, who had admired Robinson's *The Children of the Night* (1897), procured for him a post in the New York Customs House that allowed him the financial means, critical notice, and time to develop as a poet of real stature. He won several Pulitzer Prizes.

ROETHKE, THEODORE (1908–1963) grew up in Saginaw, Michigan, "in and around a beautiful greenhouse owned by my father and uncle." The greenhouse took on great meaning for Roethke, who found it "the whole of life, a womb, a heaven on earth." Its influence is particularly obvious in *The Lost Son and Other Poems* (1948); he implies a distinct relationship between humans and other living things. Roethke was awarded the Pulitzer Prize in 1953 for *The Waking: Poems, 1933–1953*.

RUSKIN, JOHN (1819–1900) saw fundamental truth in the paintings of the much criticized J. M. W. Turner. A defense of Turner in the first volume of *Modern Painters* (1843) established Ruskin as an art critic but, more significantly, led him to an examination of society as a producer of art. His own moral beliefs led him to the theory that only the good man who was the product of a moral society was capable of great art. *Stones of Venice* (1851–1853) upholds Gothic architecture as proof of the beauty that free men in a God-centered society can create. The ugliness of his own machine-centered century led Ruskin to the social criticism of his later period.

SASSOON, SIEGFRIED (1886–   ), an English poet himself, may have made his most important contribution to literature by encouraging his friend Wilfred Owen to write. Sassoon led a pleasant life—the chief joy of which seems to have been fox-hunting—until the outbreak of World War I. He distinguished himself in the service, but so hated war that he is rumored to have thrown his Military Cross into the sea. His writing includes five volumes of memoirs and eight volumes of poetry that describe the horrors of war and satirize the British upper classes.

SHAKESPEARE, WILLIAM (1564–1616). His glory as a dramatist should not be allowed to obscure his power as a poet. His name has been given to the particular form of sonnet actually developed by Surrey. His sonnet sequence, which stands with those of Spenser and Sidney as the greatest of the age, revolves around two figures—a young man and a "dark lady." Neither figure has actually been identified, although Shakespeare's patron, the Earl of Southampton, is generally considered the young man. The sonnets reiterate the Renaissance concept of ideal friendship, but hardly the concept of an ideal lady. The student of poetry or of Shakespeare will not want to overlook his earlier poems, *Venus and Adonis* and *The Rape of Lucrece*, nor the magnificent poetry of the plays.

SHAW, GEORGE BERNARD (1856–1950), with the knowledge obtained from voracious reading and youthful interests in art and music, was able to support himself as a critic and journalist while pouring his real interest into political and economic theories—Shaw was greatly attracted by both Socialist and Nietzschean ideologies. His political concerns, the social attacks in his dramas, and the Puritanical tenor of his life—seen in his vegetarianism, his hatred of alcohol and tobacco, his stands against vaccination and vivisection, and his

sexual prudery—have all been traced (of course) to his repudiation of his
ne'er-do-well, nearly alcoholic father. His plays are generally satiric, probing at
socially sanctified views. Shaw's solidly based fame as a dramatist was further
expanded by his delightful eccentricities as an individual.

SHELLEY, PERCY BYSSHE (1792–1822) suffered throughout his life when time
and again reality thwarted his attempts to discuss or to carry out his ideals. An
undergraduate pamphlet, *The Necessity of Atheism* (1811), resulted in his
expulsion from Oxford. The misery inflicted on the Irish nation inspired his
Address to the Irish People (1812), but the indifference of the Irish peasantry
soon cooled his ardor for their cause. His mistreatment of his wife (he eloped
with Mary Godwin in 1814) resulted in public ostracism. Apart from his great
lyrics, Shelley's masterpieces are his closet drama, *Prometheus Unbound*
(1822), and his critical *Defense of Poetry* (1821).

SIDNEY, SIR PHILIP (1554–1586), Elizabethan poet, scholar, courtier, diplomat,
and soldier, epitomized the Renaissance gentleman. Incredibly, the multifarious
events of his life were encompassed in only thirty-two years. His major literary
achievements are *The Countess of Pembroke's Arcadia* (1590), a lengthy pastoral romance; *The Defence of Poesie* (1598), the most significant English
literary criticism before Dryden's; and his sonnet sequence, *Astrophel and
Stella* (1591), written to the woman, then wife of Lord Rich, who had once
been his betrothed.

SOPHOCLES (496?–406 B.C.) stands with Aeschylus and Euripides as one of the
three great classical tragedians. Although his life centered around the arts,
Sophocles performed commendable public service, notably as a general at Samos
with Pericles and later in the Peloponnesian War. Sophocles made his first
appearance as a tragic poet at twenty-seven; his talents were immediately applauded. He was the first tragedian to portray noble women characters and
contributed vitally to the development of tragic form. Aeschylus has been
credited as the creator of Greek tragedy, but Sophocles brought it to perfection.

SPENCER, THEODORE (1902–1949) combined the vocations of teacher, scholar,
literary critic, and poet. World War II prevented his accepting the post of
permanent lecturer at Cambridge University (a position to which he was the
first American ever elected). Accepting the Boylston Professorship instead, he
continued his work as a lecturer at Harvard. His scholarship on Elizabethan
drama is considerable, and he was an authority on modern theater, poetry, and
fiction as well. Despite his vast scholarly background, Spencer excels in lyrics of
the most simple kind, perhaps best described as lightly metaphysical.

SPENDER, STEPHEN (1909–   ) stands second to Auden in the circle of left-
wing Oxford poets who gained prominence in the thirties. Before the outbreak
of World War II, Spender traveled on the Continent attending leftist political

meetings; during the war he continued to write poetry and became co-editor of *Horizon*. His poetry, while concerned with the social questions of the times, records (quite unlike Auden's work) a personal search for a political and moral credo. Since the war, Spender has continued writing both poetry and criticism and has become co-editor of the international magazine, *Encounter*.

SPENSER, EDMUND (1552?–1599), generally considered the first major English poet after Chaucer, never achieved the widespread popularity he deserved; but his conscious command of language, meter, and form mark him as a poet of special gifts. *The Faerie Queen* (1589–1596), his most notable work, is an intentionally archaic religious allegory leaning heavily on the language of Chaucer's day. His sonnet sequence, the *Amoretti* (1595), ranks with those of Shakespeare and Sidney as one of the most outstanding sonnet sequences of the English Renaissance.

STEELE, RICHARD (1672–1729), Irish-born English playwright and essayist, ran away from Oxford and, to the horror of an uncle who disinherited him, joined the army. His quick wit made him a favorite at the coffeehouses, and his writing talents soon made him a successful editor. *The Tatler* (1709–1711), his first periodical, provided social comment, literary criticism, and fresh coffee-house gossip for the middle-class readers whose lives it reflects. Steele was joined in this venture and in the subsequent *Spectator* (1711–1712) by Joseph Addison. Together they established and gave form to the literary essay.

STEELE, WILBUR DANIEL (1886–   ) trained himself in painting at Denver University, the Boston Museum of Fine Arts, and the Académie Julian in Paris. He did not even attempt writing until his year in Paris, and only the successful appearance of "White Horse Winter" in *The Atlantic* (1912) convinced him to devote his talents to prose fiction rather than the graphic arts. His choice proved a happy one; his stories and novels have been widely read. In 1921 he was honored by an unprecedented special prize from the O. Henry Memorial Award Committee for the high quality of his fiction. His ventures in drama—including the dramatization of "How Beautiful with Shoes"—have also been successful.

STEINBECK, JOHN (1902–   ) came into contact with the social problems about which he would later write in his native area, the Salinas Valley in California. He witnessed social upheavals that destroyed the relationship between rural people and the land and saw the painful life of the economically depressed classes. These sights fill his best works. *Tortilla Flat* (1935), his first success, describes down-and-out life in Monterey; *The Grapes of Wrath* (1939), for which he won the Pulitzer Prize in 1940, exposes the plight of the migrant worker. His short stories were collected in an edition titled *The Long Valley* (1938). He won the Nobel Prize for Literature in 1962, primarily for the novel *The Winter of Our Discontent*.

STEVENS, WALLACE (1879–1955), an insurance-company executive, wrote most of his poetry after he was fifty. His *Collected Poems* (1954) are concerned with the contrast between reality and appearance. He believed that "the eye's plain version" was ordered—often recomposed—by the mind and that each new understanding added to "the amassing harmony." His critical ideas are contained in *The Necessary Angel* (1951).

STEVENSON, ROBERT LOUIS (1850–1894) spent most of his life resisting disease, fighting conventions, and making the best of his literary talents. He defied his pious parents by flaunting his religious doubts and rejecting the career they had planned for him. His tubercular condition led him to travel for his health and eventually to settle in Samoa. *Treasure Island* (1883), *A Child's Garden of Verses* (1885), and *The Strange Case of Dr. Jekyll and Mr. Hyde* (1886) are his best-known works.

SYMONDS, JOHN ADDINGTON (1840–1893) suffered a breakdown upon completing his work at Magdalen College, Oxford, which impaired his health permanently and caused him to seek more pleasant climates on the Continent. Symonds made prolific contributions to scholarship and his translations—particularly from Italian—are significant. His poetry is technically correct rather than inspired, yet he early recognized the talent of Walt Whitman, whose form is far-removed from Symond's cultivated style.

TENNYSON, ALFRED, LORD (1809–1892), the most representative poet of the Victorian Age, reflects in his work the conflicts current in English life. Left to himself, Tennyson might have remained a retiring aesthete; his circle at Cambridge, however, prodded him into social consciousness. The death of Arthur Henry Hallam (1833), Tennyson's closest friend, inspired his most important single poem, *In Memoriam* (1850), which began as an expression of grief but developed into Tennyson's working out and reconciliation of his ideas concerning faith and immortality, science and evolution. In this and in such major works as *The Princess* (1847), *Maud* (1855), and *Idylls of the King* (1859–1872), Tennyson achieved a popularity rarely accorded a poet during his lifetime. He became Poet Laureate in 1850.

THOMAS, DYLAN (1914–1953) wrote poetry of such force as to demand comment; the critics commented, but with confusion. Some noted his facility with words and the music of his measures; others, influenced by the legends that quickly surrounded his name, found his imagery coarse and labeled his impact temporary. It is now obvious that he was a master poet. His vision includes both the Freudian and the Biblical; his sexual imagery conveys themes of metaphysical consequence; whenever he spoke, he was a conjuror with words. *The Collected Poems of Dylan Thomas* appeared in 1953; *Portrait of the Artist as a Young Dog* (1940) is the autobiography of his youth.

THURBER, JAMES GROVER (1894–1961), American author and cartoonist, distinguished himself from other contemporary humorists by his denial of cynicism and despair. His irony and satiric humor depend on sad melancholy rather than angry barbs. He creates a twentieth-century world of the baffled, whose protagonists invite the reader's sympathetic identification. Thurber's work came to prominence in *The New Yorker*. Notable selections appear in *Is Sex Necessary?* (with E. B. White, 1929) and *The Thurber Carnival* (1945). His autobiography is entitled *My Life and Hard Times* (1933).

UPDIKE, JOHN (1932–   ), upon graduation from Harvard, began publishing poems and short stories in *The New Yorker*. The poems appearing in his first collection, *The Carpentered Hen* (1958), continued in this early glib style. His prose, especially his novel, *Rabbit Run* (1960), has achieved popular success. Technical adroitness has won him critical acclaim. He is regarded by many as one of the most promising young writers of our time.

VAUGHAN, HENRY (1622–1695) was at Oxford studying law and beginning to write verses when the English civil war broke out. He returned to his native Wales to study medicine, but happily continued to write poetry. Vaughan's verse is predominantly religious; his tributes to God are inspired by the beauties he finds in nature. Although uneven, his verse powerfully communicates the ecstasies of his spirit. His poetry appears in *Silex Scintillans* (1650) and a smaller volume, *Thalia Rediviva* (1678).

WALLER, EDMUND (1606–1687) was greatly admired by the poets of the subsequent age for the smoothness and harmony of his verses. His grace and smoothness appear to have served him during his lifetime as well: a panegyric to Cromwell relieved his sentence of banishment (pronounced for his complicity in a Royalist plot), while a welcoming tribute to the restored king set him in the latter's good graces. Today, we esteem Waller's lyricism and his facility with the heroic couplet.

WHITMAN, WALT (1819–1892) is the poet of America and American democracy. He was raised in Brooklyn and Long Island and as a young man was engaged in newspaper work and concerned with politics. A trip to New Orleans (1848) enlarged his conception of America (some biographers also insist that Whitman experienced a transforming love affair in New Orleans). Whitman's attempt, in *Leaves of Grass* (1855), to record the freedom that may be achieved through democracy, love, and religion has been criticized as "formless" and "sensual." Whitman defended himself with: "I am the poet of the Body and I am the poet of the Soul."

WILBUR, RICHARD (1921–   ), a professor at Wesleyan University, received much critical commendation for his first book of poems, *The Beautiful Changes* (1947). Since that time, he has been largely applauded for subsequent collections of poetry and for his translations of Molière's *The Misanthrope* and *Tartuffe*. Wilbur's decisive ideas about poetry include a belief in the strictness of form—"the strength of the genie comes of his being confined in a bottle"—and a clear statement of purpose for poetry—"to make or discover some pattern in the world. [A poem] is a conflict with disorder, not a message from one person to another."

WILLIAMS, WILLIAM CARLOS (1883–   ), a practicing pediatrician, as well as a poet, novelist, and short-story writer, reveals his observations in probing, even clinically realistic, terms. While a medical student, Williams began devoting free moments to writing; his own impetus was intensified by his friendship, during graduate school and later in London, with Ezra Pound. Upon returning to the United States, Williams set up practice in New Jersey. His experiences there have provided the inspiration for *Paterson* (1946–1951), his epic poem, and numerous other works. He won the Pulitzer Prize for Poetry in 1963 for his *Pictures from Brueghel*.

WORDSWORTH, WILLIAM (1770–1850) is commonly regarded as a "Nature poet," but it must be realized that Wordsworth was less concerned with representing nature than with depicting nature's power to inspire the mind and the imagination. Wordsworth's friendship with Coleridge resulted in a mutual quickening of sensibilities; their joint volume, *Lyrical Ballads* (1798), in which simple experiences and "humble and rustic life" are given dignity and meaning, had a profound effect on the poetry of the nineteenth century. *The Prelude* (1850), Wordsworth's long autobiographical poem, sets forth his life and intellectual development in a major work of art.

WYATT, SIR THOMAS (1503?–1542), a well-educated courtier, was an intriguing person, as well as a major poet. Twice in his short life he extricated himself from most severe charges—treason and dalliance with Anne Boleyn. He merits our attention for his own poetry and for introducing Italian literature to England. His sonnets, inspired by those of Petrarch and Serafino dell'Aquila, in turn provided inspiration for Henry Howard, Earl of Surrey; their work, so significant to the English literary awakening, was compiled and popularized by Richard Tottel in his miscellany, *The Book of Songs and Sonnets* (1557).

YEATS, WILLIAM BUTLER (1865–1939) exhibits in his poetry the very different influences of his father, a freethinking painter, and of his mother, a woman steeped in Irish folklore. Yeats's early poems are rich with the supernatural, whereas his later work is more personal, realistic, and intellectual. Yeats believed the poet's role was that of prophet; his own ideas became increasingly hard to follow as he developed a personal mythology, and his symbols, too, became increasingly rarified and complex. When his *Collected Poems* appeared in 1908, he was acknowledged Ireland's foremost poet; in 1923 he won the Nobel Prize for Literature.

Index of Authors and Titles